P9-BZB-897

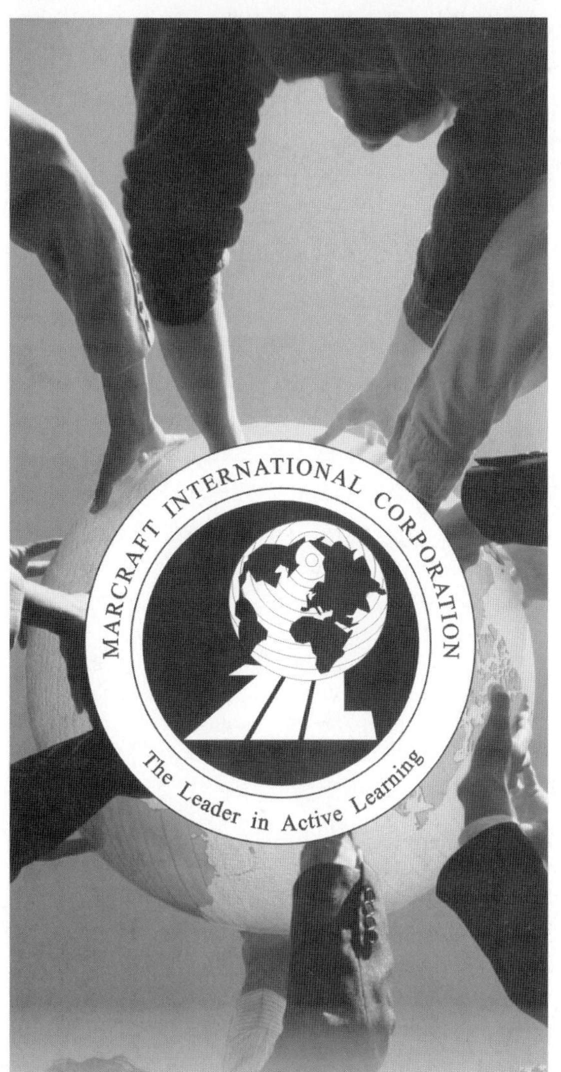

A+ CERTIFICATION: CONCEPTS AND PRACTICE

Editor in Chief: Stephen Helba
Assistant Vice President and Publisher: Charles E. Stewart, Jr.
Production Editor: Alexandrina Benedicto Wolf
Design Coordinator: Robin Chukes
Cover Designer: Michael R. Hall
Cover Art: Bill Leahy
Illustrations: Michael R. Hall and Cathy J. Boulay
Production Manager: Matthew Ottenweller

This book was set in Times New Roman and Arial by Cathy J. Boulay, Marcraft International, Inc. It was printed and bound by R.R. Donnelley & Sons Company. The cover was printed by Phoenix Color Corp.

Pearson Education Ltd., *London*
Pearson Education Australia Pty. Limited, *Sydney*
Pearson Education Singapore, Pte. Ltd.
Pearson Education North Asia Ltd., *Hong Kong*
Pearson Education Canada, Ltd., *Toronto*
Pearson Educacion de Mexico, S.A. de C.V.
Pearson Education–Japan, *Tokyo*
Pearson Education Malaysia, Pte. Ltd.
Pearson Education, *Upper Saddle River, New Jersey*

Earlier editions by Marcraft International Corporation, 2000, 1998, 1997, 1996, 1991, 1988, and 1987.

10 9 8 7 6 5 4 3 2

ISBN 0-13-042393-9

Trademark Acknowledgments

All terms mentioned in this book that are known to be trademarks or service marks are listed below. Marcraft cannot attest to the accuracy of this information. Use of a term in this book should not be regarded as affecting the validity of any trademark or service mark.

IBM®, IBM-PC, PC/XT®, PC-AT, EGA, Micro Channel, OS/2, PS/2, and XGA are registered trademarks of International Business Machines Corporation.

CGA and VGA are trademarks of International Business Machines Corporation.

Microsoft®, MS-DOS®, MS-Windows, Windows 95, Windows 98, and Windows ME are registered trademarks of Microsoft Corporation.

Windows NT and Windows 2000 are a trademark of Microsoft Corporation.

Centronics is a registered trademark of Centronics Data Computer Corporation.

Freon and Mylar are registered trademarks of E.I. du Pont de Nemours and Co., Incorporated.

CompuServe is a registered trademark of CompuServe, Incorporated.

America Online is a registered trademark of America Online, Incorporated.

AMI is a registered trademark of American Megatrends, Incorporated.

Award Bios is a trademark of Award Software, Incorporated.

Panasonic is a registered trademark of Matsushita Communication Industrial Co., Ltd.

Intel, 386, 387, 386SX, 387SX, i486, 486, Pentium, Pentium II, Pentium III, Pentium Pro, and Pentium MMX are trademarks of Intel Corporation.

Cyrix is a registered trademark of the Cyrix Corporation.

NetWare, Novell, and UNIX are a registered trademark of Novell, Incorporated.

Microcom is a registered trademark of Microcom Systems, Incorporated.

Sound Blaster is a trademark of Creative Technology, Ltd.

Hayes is a registered trademark of Hayes Microcomputer Products, Incorporated.

Hewlett-Packard and LaserJet are registered trademarks of Hewlett-Packard Company.

PREFACE

PURPOSE

The author and Marcraft International Corporation have been producing microcomputer architecture and repair courseware since 1988. In those days computer repair functions were typically performed by electronic technicians. That course was very hardware-intensive, using chip-level isolation and repair techniques. Schematic diagrams and electronic test equipment were the order of the day.

Times have changed and so has computer repair. The tasks performed by computer repair technicians have changed considerably since that original course was introduced. Computer hardware has become relatively inexpensive and software has become much more complex. Current computer technicians spend much more time dealing with software-related problems, configuration problems, and compatibility problems than with hardware problems. As a matter of fact, hardware problems in microcomputers are typically solved at the board level now. The time and expense of an IC-level repair quickly goes beyond the value of the board, making it unprofitable to do these kinds of repairs.

Appropriately, Marcraft's original *Microcomputer Systems - Theory & Service* course has changed several times to reflect the evolving nature of the technician's role. This is the seventh edition of the course.

A+ CERTIFICATION

Computing Technology Industry Association (CompTIA) is an organization that establishes certification criteria for service technicians in the computer industry. This organization has created and sponsors the A+ Certification Exam, which is designed to certify technicians in the areas of hardware and software management and repair.

A+ Certification is a two-step process: You must pass a Core Hardware exam and a Microsoft Operating System Technologies exam. The Operating System Technologies exam must be passed within 90 days of the Core Hardware exam. For more information on CompTIA and the A+ exam, visit *http://www.comptia.com*.

The Marcraft/Prentice Hall A+ Certification Concepts and Proactive training guide will provide the knowledge and skills required for you to pass the A+ exam and become a certified computer service technician. A+ certification is recognized nation-wide and is a hiring criterion used by companies such as AT&T, IBM, Lotus, Microsoft, and Digital. Therefore, becoming A + certified will enhance your job opportunities and career advancement potential.

Marcraft has embraced the A+ certification because it sets a standard for excellence that we have been preparing students to achieve from the beginning. Therefore, we are offering this course to prepare students to successfully challenge the A+ examination. We have also retitled the text to reflect this new direction. From its size, one should gather that this course is not simply a cram course for the test. Instead, it is a complete training course designed not only to prepare for the exam, but also to provide the fundamental knowledge base required for you to establish a career in this rapidly changing industry.

The textbook, lab book, and accompanying electronic test-prep materials are intended for anyone interested in pursuing the A+ Certification. It contains all of the pedagogical support materials to be used in a classroom environment, but it can also be used in a self-study mode by experienced technicians to prepare for the exam.

Key Revisions

This edition of the A+ Certification Concepts and Practice guide has been expanded to include information about all of the new (02/01) A+ objectives. It has been streamlined to more closely follow the CompTIA objectives. Much of the basic digital computer information has been removed from the textbook and placed on the accompanying CD in the form of an electronic Reference Shelf. This information can be printed from the CD and used in your classroom. This arrangement provides closer direct linkage between the textbook and the A+ objective material while still providing you with access to this fundamental information.

New information has been added to every chapter as it applies to the new A+ standards. In some cases, material has been trimmed to a level more appropriate for a current A+ Certification text.

The most notable change to the book occurs in two areas: System Boards and Operating System Software. The system board chapter has been updated to include the newest microprocessor and bus information. The original two chapters on operating system software have been expanded into three chapters and moved to the middle of the book. The first operating system chapter deals with OS fundamentals and is titled Operating System Fundamentals. It now includes an extensive discussion of the bootup process, as well as a major section covering DOS troubleshooting. The second operating system-related chapter is devoted to the Microsoft Windows 9x operating systems sold to the general consumer market, including Windows 95, 98, and ME. The Windows material has been expanded significantly from the previous version and includes a substantial amount of Windows 98/ME organizational information. The third operating system-related chapter covers the Windows NT/Windows 2000 operating systems sold primarily to organizations and companies. This information is limited primarily to Windows NT 4.0 Workstation and Windows 2000 Professional systems. Like the Windows 9x chapter, the Windows NT/2000 chapter includes information about navigating, installing, and maintaining these operating systems.

The organization of troubleshooting material has also been revised, expanded, and moved. Because diagnosing and troubleshooting is the highest-order learning level associated with the A+ examination and since these things rely on an understanding of the operation of the parts involved, the troubleshooting material has been expanded and moved to the end of the text. Troubleshooting now comprises two chapters of the text—one for system hardware and the second for operating systems.

Key Features

The pedagogical features of this book were carefully developed to provide readers with key content information, as well as review and testing opportunities. A complete A+ objectives map and Test Tip information boxes are included to help you key in on A+ specific materials.

A+ Core Hardware Exam/Operating System Technologies Exam Coverage

The locations of A+ specific materials are identified with a Test Tip marker in the margin that helps students focus on key content that they will be expected to know for the A+ certification exam. *Appendix A* provides a comprehensive listing of the A+ objectives.

Evaluation and Test Material

An abundance of test materials is available with this course. Each chapter contains a 10-question multiple-choice section and a 15-question section of open-ended review questions. Additional A+ test material can be found on the Interactive CD-ROM that comes with the book. The 10 multiple-choice questions test knowledge of the basic concepts presented in the chapter, while the 15 open-ended review questions are designed to test critical thinking.

Interactive CD-ROM

The *A+ Certification Concepts and Practice* book is accompanied by an additional comprehensive A+ test bank that is sealed on the back cover of the book. This CD testing material was developed to simulate the A+ Certification Exam testing process and materials and to allow students to complete practice tests, determine their weak points, and study more strategically.

The ExamGear test engine included on the accompanying CD provides three styles of testing:

- Study Mode – permits you to review questions and check the answers and references from within the test.
- Test Mode – simulates the actual fixed-length A+ exams.
- Adaptive Mode – permits you to take practice tests in the same adaptive mode that CompTIA eventually converts all of its exams into.

During the question review, the correct answer is presented on the screen along with the reference heading where the material can be found in the text. A single mouse click takes you quickly to the corresponding section of the electronic textbook on the CD.

Pedagogical Features

Over 50 diagrams and screen dumps are included in each chapter to provide constant visual reinforcement of the concepts being discussed.

Each chapter begins with a list of learning objectives that establishes a foundation and systematic preview of the chapter. Each chapter concludes with a chapter summary and a key-point review of its material.

Key terms are presented in bold type throughout the text. A comprehensive glossary of terms appears at the end of the text to provide quick, easy access to key term definitions that appear in each chapter. These terms work in conjunction with the extensive Glossary at the end of the book. Key thoughts in the chapter are presented in special boxes to call special attention to them.

In this edition of the A+ Certification Concepts and Practices book we have moved most of the fundamental "How Things Work" information to the CD-ROM that accompanies the theory manual. You will find a table of contents for the individual subjects on the CD under the Reference Shelf.

The reason for moving this information to the CD is that CompTIA does not require this type of knowledge for their certification. However, this information is important for your students to have a full knowledge of how the elements of the computer do what they do. It provides a base that they can draw on as technology changes throughout their careers. We suggest that you incorporate information from these topics into your presentations as time allows.

The Reference Shelf contains additional information concerning:

1. How Microprocessors Work
2. How DMA Works
3. How Interrupts Work
4. Initiating I/O Transfers
5. Bits, Bytes, And Computer Words
6. Computer Buses
7. How a Parallel Printer Port Works
8. How a Serial Port Works
9. How Keyboards Work
10. How Magnetic Disks Work
11. How Video Displays Work
12. How Printers Work
13. How Modems Work
14. How Multimedia Works
15. How MACs Work
16. The Chips
17. Buses And Support Devices
18. The 8088 Microprocessor
19. Coprocessors
20. Soldering Techniques
21. The Parallel Port
22. Customer Satisfaction
23. Extended Glossary

As you can see from the Reference Shelf topics, we have included sections on the Apple MAC, multimedia, and customer satisfaction that may be of particular interest.

ORGANIZATION

In general, it is not necessary to move through this text in the same order that it is presented. Also, it is not necessary to teach any specific portion of the material to its extreme. Instead, the material can be adjusted to fit the length of your course. As a matter of fact, practicing IT professionals can use the material in the CD test banks to identify the areas where they need to brush up, and then use the text book to study that material directly.

Chapter 1 – *Basic PC Hardware* introduces microcomputer architecture and shows how those basic microcomputer structures come together to form an IBM PC-compatible personal computer system. The chapter charts the evolution of the PC from the days when small keyboard units were connected to a television set up to the powerful PCs available today.

Chapter 2 – *Advanced System Boards* deals with the system boards that form the heart of every microcomputer system. Microprocessors, microprocessor-support systems, and expansion buses are all covered in this chapter. The support systems include timing, DMA, interrupt, common memory structures, and different I/O bus schemes used to connect optional I/O devices to the system. The focus of the system board information in this chapter has shifted away from the ISA standards traditionally employed throughout the industry to the newer ATX standards now being used by most of the industry.

In addition, the chapter covers microprocessors from the Pentium, through the Pentium MMX, Pentium Pro, Pentium II, Pentium III and Pentium 4. The operating characteristics of all these Intel microprocessors are presented in this chapter. Most of the new material in this chapter focuses on the Intel Pentium III models and the Cyrix and AMD Pentium-clone processors.

Chapter 3 – *Standard I/O Systems* begins by examining basic input/output structures used in PCs. The computer's fundamental I/O devices are covered, including the most common ports found in the PC compatible world—the parallel and serial I/O ports. However, there are a host of newer I/O systems being used in PCs these days. A good portion of the new information in this chapter is based on newer I/O bus designs including USB, Firewire, IrDA, and wireless communication specifications.

The chapter concludes by investigating the operation of common input and output devices. In particular, keyboards, CRT monitors, mice, trackballs, joysticks, touch-sensitive screens, and scanners are covered.

Mass storage systems commonly used in microcomputers are presented in **Chapter 4** – *Mass Storage Systems*. These include floppy drives, hard drives, RAID systems, tape drives, and CD-ROM drives. System operation, installation, and configuration are presented for all of the mass storage systems mentioned.

Chapter 5 focuses on one of the hottest area of microcomputer growth: *Data Communications*. This chapter covers both local and wide area networks, along with the equipment and software required to operate them. The LAN material has been modified and expanded to include newer Ethernet specifications, cabling information, and newer networking technologies. Dial-up networking and modems are discussed here along with their application to the Internet.

Printers are covered in **Chapter 6** from the workhorse dot-matrix printer to color ink-jet and high-speed laser printers. Theory, operation, and maintenance information is presented for all three types of printers. Specific troubleshooting information is also provided for each printer type in this chapter.

In previous versions of the A+ exam, CompTIA specified a complete domain for *Portable Computer Systems*. **Chapter 7** focuses on the unique structures associated with this type of computer and how they are installed, configured, and maintained. It also describes the types of problems that are inherent with smaller computer systems.

The software side of the microcomputer system is covered in Chapters 8, 9, and 10. **Chapter 8** – *Operating System Fundamentals* provides a detailed examination of basic operating systems. In particular, it investigates the role of the system's BIOS and the Disk Operating System (DOS) in the operation of the system. The first half of the chapter covers topics associated with the ROM BIOS, including system bootup information, CMOS Setup routines, and Power On Self Test (POST) information.

The second half of the chapter is dedicated to command line operations and uses MS-DOS commands to demonstrate this type of operation. While MS-DOS is no longer covered as an operating system in the A+ exam, this is no reason to believe that it has gone away. For the consumer, DOS has largely passed away. However, the technician must be able of using command line utilities and commands to access and restore defective systems. Topics covered here include DOS disk structures, and drive-level, directory-level, and file-level command line operations.

Chapter 9 – *Windows 9x* is an in-depth study of the Windows 9x operating systems. This chapter looks at installation, startup, structure, and operation of both Windows 95 and Windows 98 operating systems. Materials that apply to both versions are referred to as Windows 9x, while items specific to one version or the other are referred to as Windows 95 or Windows 98. In addition to the installation, configuration, and operation information, the chapter also includes extensive information about handling application programs, printing, and wide and local area networking with Windows 9x.

Chapter 10 – *Windows NT/2000* is an in-depth study of the Windows NT 4.0 and Windows 2000 professional operating systems. This chapter follows the same paths for the Windows NT operating systems that chapter 9 did for the Windows 9x systems. This is only natural since CompTIA lumped all of these operating systems into the same four domains: OS Fundamentals; Installation, Configuration, and Upgrading; Diagnosing and Troubleshooting; and Networking. Information that applies to both versions is referred to as Windows NT/2000, while items specific to one version or the other are referred to as Windows NT or Windows 2000. As with the Windows 9x chapter, this chapter also includes extensive information about handling application programs, printing, and wide and local area networking with Windows NT/2000.

Chapter 11 – *Basic System Troubleshooting* addresses the fundamentals of troubleshooting microprocessor-based equipment. The chapter covers the use of diagnostic software to isolate system hardware problems. It also describes the Field Replaceable Unit (FRU) method of hardware troubleshooting required for most field and bench repair work. The second half of the chapter deals with symptoms and troubleshooting procedures associated with the various hardware components typically associated with PCs. It also provides the first half of a comprehensive computer diagnosing and troubleshooting methodology.

Chapter 12 – *Operating System Troubleshooting* shifts the focus of troubleshooting to the software side of the system. It focuses on the three major categories of operating system-related problems: setup problems, startup problems, and operational problems.

The chapter includes troubleshooting tools available with the different operating system versions and methods of using them. Important HDD support utilities, such as ScanDisk, backup, defragmentation, and anti-virus protection are highlighted here.

This chapter also furnishes the second half of the complete computer troubleshooting methodology. Troubleshooting of application, printer, and networking problems related to operating systems is also covered here.

Chapter 13 discusses important *Preventive Maintenance* procedures and safety considerations. The first section of the chapter investigates topics including cleaning, electrostatic discharges, power line problems, and Universal Power Supplies (UPS) along with other power line conditioning devices.

The chapter features preventive maintenance procedures for various system components. Suggested PM schedules are also presented. This chapter also covers safety issues commonly associated with computer systems. Although not an intrinsically unsafe environment, some areas of a computer system can be harmful if approached unawares.

The Lab Guide

Applying the concepts of the chapter to hands-on exercises is crucial to preparing for a successful career as a computer technician. The Lab Guide provides an excellent hands-on component to emphasize the theoretical materials. There are three types of Procedures included in the labs. First, introductory labs act as introductions to hardware and different types of software. A number of troubleshooting labs allow students to be tested under real problem situations. The instructor can insert software faults, simple hardware faults, or complex hardware faults into the system for the student to track down, isolate, and repair. A number of hardware/software installation labs are included as well. This allows students to install and set up hard drives, CD-ROM drives, modems, network cards, and more.

Teacher Support

An instructor's guide accompanies the course. Answers for all of the end-of-chapter quiz questions are included along with a reference point in the chapter where a particular item is covered. Sample schedules are included as guidelines for possible course implementations. Answers to all lab review questions and fill-in-the-blank steps are provided so that there is an indication of what the expected outcomes should be. Finally, descriptions of the numerous Marcraft software faults, hardware faults, and extended hardware faults are presented, along with suggested faults for particular labs as appropriate.

An electronic copy of the textbook is included on the CD-ROM disk at the back of the lab book. This copy is electronically linked to the A+ Practice Test Bank. This permits the information concerning test questions to be accessed directly and immediately.

Test Taking Tips

The A+ exam is an objective-based timed test. It covers the objectives listed in Appendix C in a multiple-choice format. There are two general methods of preparing for the test. If you are an experienced technician using this material to obtain certification, use the testing features at the end of each chapter and on the accompanying CD to test each area of knowledge. Track your weak areas and spend the most time concentrating on them.

If you are a newcomer to the subject of serious computer repair, plan a systematic study of the materials, reserving the testing functions until each chapter has been completed.

In either case, after completing the study materials use the various testing functions available on the CD to practice taking the test. Use the Study and Exam modes to test yourself by chapter, or on a mixture of questions from all areas of the text. Practice until you are very certain that you are ready. The CD will allow you to immediately refer to the area of the text that covers material that you might miss.

- Answer the questions you know first. You can always go back and work on questions.
- Don't leave any questions unanswered. They will be counted as incorrect.
- There are no trick questions. The most correct answer is in there somewhere.
- Be aware of A+ questions that have more than one correct answer. Questions that have multiple correct answers can be identified by the special formatting applied to the letters of their possible answers. They are enclosed in a square box. When you encounter these questions, make sure to mark every answer that applies.

- Get plenty of hands-on practice before the test, using the time limit set for the test.
- Make certain to prepare for each test category listed above. The key is not to memorize but to understand the topics.
- Take your watch. The A+ exam is a timed test. You will need to keep an eye on the time to make sure that you are getting to the items that you are most sure of.
- Get plenty of rest before taking the test.

ACKNOWLEDGMENTS

I would like to mention some of the people and groups who have been responsible for the success of this book. First I would like to thank Greg Michael, formerly of Howard W. Sams, for getting me involved in writing about microcomputer systems back in the early days of the IBM PC.

This A+ book has really mushroomed into a full-blown group project here at Marcraft. My staff here at Marcraft makes it easy to turn out a good product. Thanks to Paul Haven, Wanda Dawson, Gregory Ter-Oganov, and Caleb Sarka from the Technical Services area for trying things out for me, giving me the latest updates for today's bus speeds and microprocessor ratings, as well as what's hot and not in the Windows OS world. Also, thanks to Mike Hall, Cathy Boulay, Yu-Wen Ho, Evan Samaritano, Tony Tonda, and Stuart Palmer from the Product Development department for their excellent work in getting the text and lab books ready to go and looking good. Without these folks, there would be no timely delivery of the A+ product.

I also want to thank our new associates at Prentice Hall for all they bring to our projects. Charles Stewart, Alex Wolf, Karrie Converse-Jones, Bret Workman, and Matt Ottenweller for their excellent work in getting this book to you.

In addition, I would like to say thanks to Brian Alley of Boston University for his excellent guidance in bringing yet another version of this book up to speed.

As always, I want to thank my wife Robbie for all of her understanding, support, and help with these projects, as well as Robert, Jamaica, and Michael.

TABLE OF CONTENTS

CHAPTER 1 - BASIC PC HARDWARE

CHAPTER 2 - ADVANCED SYSTEM BOARDS

CHAPTER 3 - STANDARD I/O SYSTEMS

CHAPTER 4 - MASS STORAGE SYSTEMS

CHAPTER 5 - DATA COMMUNICATIONS

CHAPTER 6 - PRINTERS

CHAPTER 7 - PORTABLE SYSTEMS

CHAPTER 8 - OPERATING SYSTEM FUNDAMENTALS

CHAPTER 9 - WINDOWS 9X

CHAPTER 10 - WINDOWS NT/2000

CHAPTER 11 - BASIC SYSTEM TROUBLESHOOTING

CHAPTER 12 - OPERATING SYSTEM TROUBLESHOOTING

CHAPTER 13 - PREVENTIVE MAINTENANCE

APPENDIX A

BASIC PC HARDWARE

OBJECTIVES

OBJECTIVES

Upon completion of this chapter and its related lab procedures, you should be able to perform these tasks:

1. Locate the power supply unit, system board, system speaker, disk drive unit, and expansion slots.
2. Discuss the differences between different PC case styles and explain the strong and weak points associated with each.
3. Describe the function of typical PC power supplies.
4. Locate the system's RAM banks and use documentation to determine the amount of RAM installed.
5. Identify different types of RAM modules (DIP, SIPP, SIMM, DIMM).
6. Identify common microprocessor IC package types.
7. Identify a Video/Graphics/Array (VGA) adapter card.
8. Recognize different disk drive types associated with PCs.
9. Describe typical external connections associated with purchase.
10. Define the functions of the computer's Input/Output Units.
11. Explain the three classes of software used with computer systems.
12. Explain the function of the system ROM BIOS.
13. Describe the function and purpose of Disk Operating System.
14. Describe the value of a Graphical User Interface.
15. Describe popular software applications programs.

BASIC PC HARDWARE

INTRODUCTION

Every computer system consists of two parts: hardware devices that perform physical operations and software routines and programs that oversee and guide the actions of the hardware. Hardware consists of those parts of the computer that you can touch. Software is the logical, intangible parts of the computer. For this reason, the CompTIA (Computer Technology Industry Association) has established two distinct parts for their A+ Certification examination. The first part is the Core Hardware portion of the Certification. This makes sense because the hardware platform is the core of any computer system.

The first objective in the first domain of the A+ exam states that the technician should be able to: Identify basic terms, concepts, and functions of computer system modules, including how each module should work during normal operation. To this end, this first chapter is designed to introduce you to personal computer fundamentals.

As with any group or industry, the personal computer world has produced a peculiar vocabulary to describe its products and their functions. As this A+ objective indicates, the computer technician must be able to use that vocabulary to identify personal computer products and to understand how they work and what they do.

This chapter provides an introduction to common personal computer components, which includes a brief discussion of their theories of operation and the basic functions that each component supplies. This information also includes the standards that the industry has developed for these components.

The first portion of the chapter presents a short history of the personal computer. The remainder of the chapter deals with the hardware structures that make up typical PC-compatible computer systems. This serves as a foundation for presenting more advanced theory and troubleshooting materials in the following chapters.

PERSONAL COMPUTER EVOLUTION

In the early years of microcomputer history, the market was dominated by a group of small companies that produced computers intended mainly for playing video games. Serious computer applications were a secondary concern. Companies such as Commodore, Timex/Sinclair, Atari, and Tandy produced eight-bit machines for the emerging industry based on microprocessors from Intel, Motorola, Zilog, and Commodore.

In 1977 Apple Computers produced the Apple I. This was followed by a series of 8-bit microcomputers: the Apple II, Apple IIc, and Apple IIe. These units were single-board computers with built-in keyboards and a discrete monitor. With the IIe unit, Apple installed seven expansion connectors on its main board. They were included to allow the addition of adapter cards. Apple also produced a set of adapter cards that could be used with the IIe to provide additional capabilities. These units were very advanced for their time. In 1981, however, Apple introduced their powerful 16-bit **Macintosh** (**MAC**) system to the market. The features offered by the MAC represented a major shift in computing power. Departing from command-line operations, it offered a graphical operating environment. Using a small input device called a mouse, visual objects were selected from the display monitor to guide the operation of the system. This operating method found an eager audience of non-technical and public school system users.

Macintosh (MAC)

Late in 1981, IBM entered the microcomputer market with the unveiling of their now famous IBM Personal Computer (PC). At the time of its introduction, the IBM PC was a drastic departure from the status quo of the microcomputer world. The original Apple MAC and IBM PC are depicted in Figure 1-1.

IBM PC

APPLE MAC

Figure 1-1: Apple Mac and IBM PC

The IBM PC employed an Intel 8088 16/8-bit microprocessor (it processes data 16 bits at a time internally, but moves it around in 8-bit packages). Relatively speaking, the IBM PC was fast, powerful, flexible, and priced within the range of most individuals. The general public soon became aware of the tremendous possibilities of the personal computer, and the microcomputer quickly advanced from a simple game machine to an office tool with a seemingly endless range of advanced personal and business applications.

Extended Technology (XT)

Advanced Technology PC (PC-AT)

In 1983, IBM added a small hard disk drive to the PC, and introduced its **Extended Technology** (**XT**) version. The success continued when, in 1984, IBM introduced the **Advanced Technology PC** (**PC-AT**). The AT used a true 16-bit microprocessor (it processed 16 bits at a time internally and had a 16-bit external data bus) from Intel, called the 80286. The wider bus increased the speed of the computer's operation, because the 80286 was then able to transfer and process twice as much data as the 8088 could. The IBM PC-AT is depicted in Figure 1-2.

In addition to a more powerful microprocessor, the AT featured a higher capacity hard drive, a half-height floppy drive, and a 101-key keyboard.

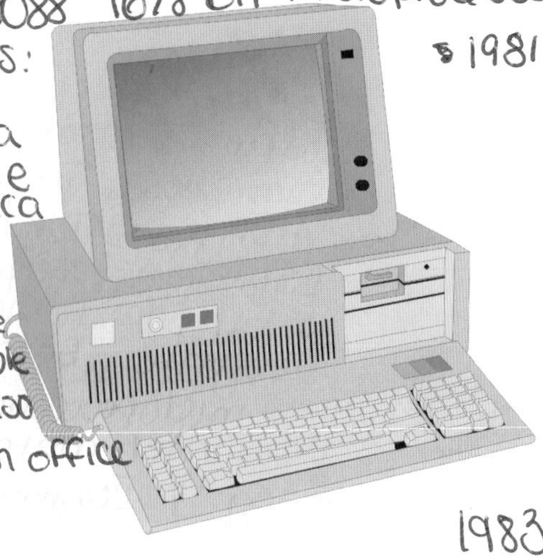

Pseudo Standards

Industry Standard Architecture (ISA)

The tremendous popularity of the original IBM PC-XT and AT systems created a set of **Pseudo Standards** for hardware and software compatibility. The AT architecture was so popular that it became known as the **Industry Standard Architecture** (**ISA**). Even today, the majority of microcomputers are both hardware- and software-compatible with the original AT design.

Figure 1-2: IBM PC-AT

PC Compatibles

PC look-alikes

PC clones

PC-compatibles

Electronic Research and Service Organization (ERSO)

The openness of the PC architecture coupled with an abundance of PC-compatible hardware and software enticed several companies to develop PC-like computers of their own. These computers were referred to as **PC look-alikes**, **PC clones**, or more commonly as **PC-compatibles**. The cloning process was made possible by two events. The government-backed **Electronic Research and Service Organization** (**ERSO**) in Taiwan produced a non-copyright infringing version of the XT BIOS firmware that controlled the operation of the system. Secondly, IBM did not secure exclusive rights to the Microsoft Disk Operating System, which controlled the interaction between the system's hardware and application software.

Since the advent of PC-compatibles, the PC market has been fueled by the introduction of increasingly powerful microprocessors. Intel and other microprocessor manufacturers have introduced several improved microprocessors, such as the 80386, 80486, Pentium, Pentium Pro, Pentium MMX, Pentium II, and Pentium III. All of these processors maintain backward compatibility with the original 8088 design. Intel resorted to using the Pentium name when clone microprocessor manufacturers used the 80x86 nomenclature. Intel dropped the numbering system and adopted the name strategy so that they could copyright it.

Many of the decisions made in designing the original PC-AT still influence the PC-compatible computer today. The AT architecture established industry standards for its:

- expansion bus
- system addressing
- peripheral addressing
- system resource allocations

The majority of all microcomputers today are based on the AT design but incorporate newer microprocessors, expansion buses, and memory management structures. For this reason, every computer technician should possess a thorough understanding of the architecture developed in these systems. As you read through this book, you may notice that the majority of the discussion in it deals with PC-compatible designs. This is due to the fact that they occupy such a large portion of the personal computer market.

THE PC SYSTEM

A typical personal computer (PC) system, shown in Figure 1-3, is modular by design. It is called a system because it includes all of the components required to have a functional computer:

Input devices

Computer

system unit

Output devices

- **Input devices**—keyboard and mouse
- **Computer—system unit**
- **Output devices**—CRT monitor and a character printer

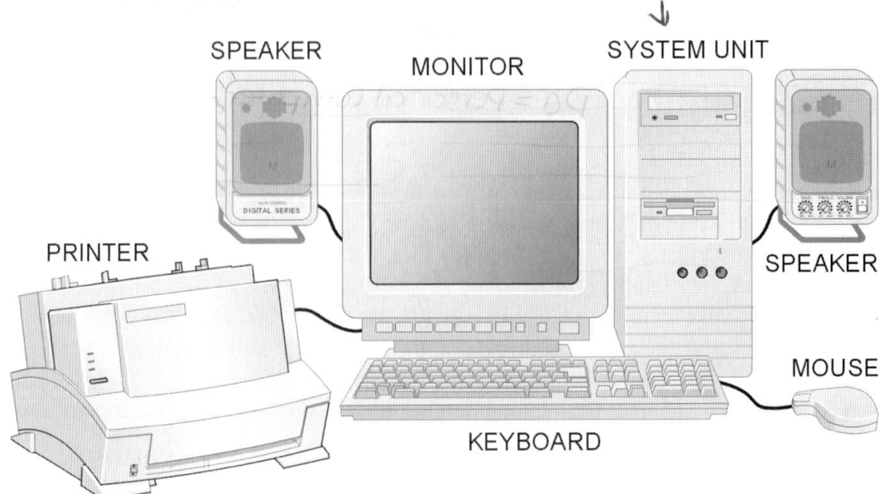

Figure 1-3: Typical Personal Computer System

The system unit is the main portion of the microcomputer system and is the basis of any PC system arrangement.

The components surrounding it vary from system to system, depending on what particular functions the system is supposed to serve.

Cases

The system unit is typically a metal and plastic case that contains the basic parts of the computer system. PCs have been packaged in a number of different case designs. These designs fall into three basic styles: desktops, towers, and portables. Each design offers characteristics that adapt the system for different environments. These characteristics for case design include mounting methods for the printed circuit boards, ventilation characteristics, total drive capacity, footprint (the amount of desk space they take up), and portability.

Desktops

Some of the most familiar PC case styles are the desktop designs illustrated in Figure 1-4. These units are designed to sit horizontally on a desk top (hence the name). The original IBM-PC, XT, and AT designs use this case style. The PC and XT case styles measured 21"w by 17"d by 5-1/2"h, whereas the AT case grew to 23"w by 17"d by 5-1/2"h.

baby AT case

A narrower desktop style, referred to as a **baby AT case**, was developed to take up less desk space than the XT and AT. The reduced footprint was accomplished by using a half-height power supply unit and limiting the number of disk drives. The disk drive cage did not reach down to the floor of the system unit, allowing the system board to slide under the power supply and disk drive cage. The widths of baby AT cases varied from manufacturer to manufacturer.

I/O = input/output

Los "low-profile desktops" redujeron la altura de las PC (unidades). A estas unidades se les colocaba a short bus-extender llamado back plane que permitía montar adapter cards de manera horizontal.

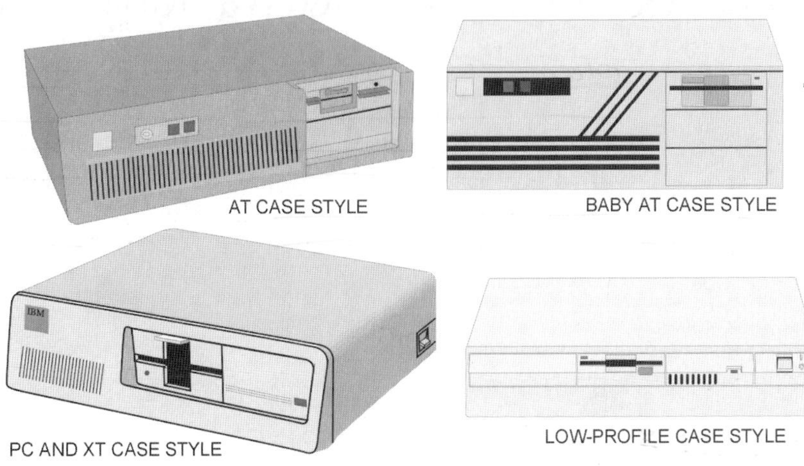

Figure 1-4: Desktop Case Designs

A special variety of desktop cases, referred to as **low-profile desktops**, reduce the vertical height of the unit. A short bus-extender card, called a **back plane**, mounts in an expansion slot and allows option adapter cards to be mounted in the unit horizontally. The case is thus enabled to be shorter. The horizontal mounting of the I/O cards in a low-profile case tends to create heat build-up problems. The heat rising from the system board flows around the I/O cards, adding to the heat they are generating. A standard back plane card is depicted in Figure 1-5. Low-profile power supplies and disk drives are also required to achieve the reduced height.

low-profile desktops

back plane

Pero esta nueva motura produce problemas de sobrecalentamiento. (heat)

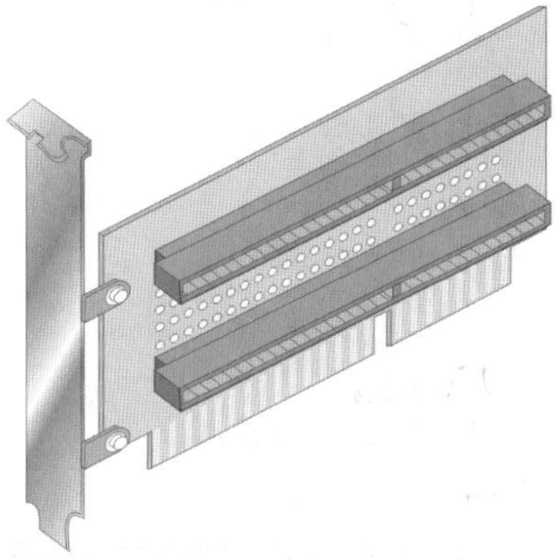

Figure 1-5: Back Plane Card

System **indicator lights** and **control buttons** are built into the front panel. Typical indicator lights include a power light, a hard drive activity light, and a turbo speed indicator light. Control buttons include a power switch, a turbo speed selection switch, and a RESET button. Older system units used an ON/OFF flip switch that extended from the power supply at the right-rear edge of the case. Newer units place the on/off switch on the machine's front panel and use an internal power cable between the switch and the power supply unit. The power supply's external connections are made in the rear of the unit. The system's installed options adapter cards are also accessed through the system's back panel. Figure 1-6 shows typical front panel controls and indicators.

indicator lights

control buttons

- Indicator lights + control buttons son construidos en la parte frontal de la unidad:
- Indicator light include:
1o- power light
2o- hard drive activity light
3o- turbo

Antes on/off eran colocados en la parte tracera de las unidades ahora an sido translados a la parte frontal, y sus conexiones externas en la parte tracera de la unidad.

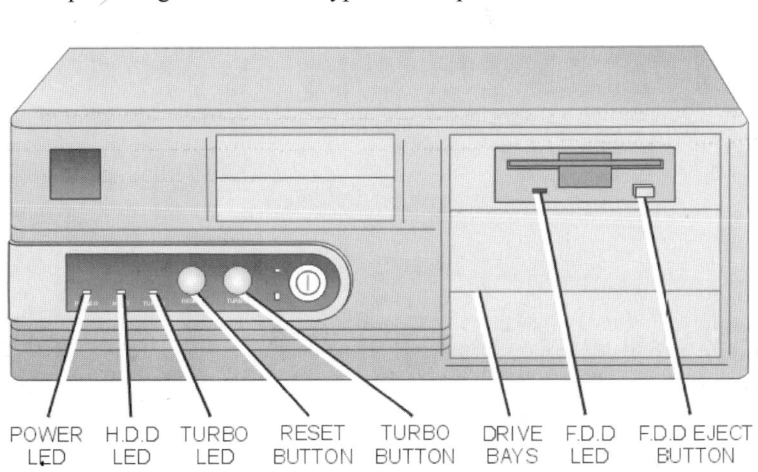

Figure 1-6: Typical Front Panel Controls and Indicators

The cover of the system unit slides (or lifts) off the base, as shown in Figure 1-7. The top of some designs slides forward after screws securing it to the back panel have been removed. In this style of case, the plastic front panel usually slides off with the metal top. In other designs, the top swings up from the rear and slides backwards to clear the case. The tops of these units are secured to the base by screws in the rear of the unit and screws or clips along the sides of the case. The plastic front panel is attached directly to the case.

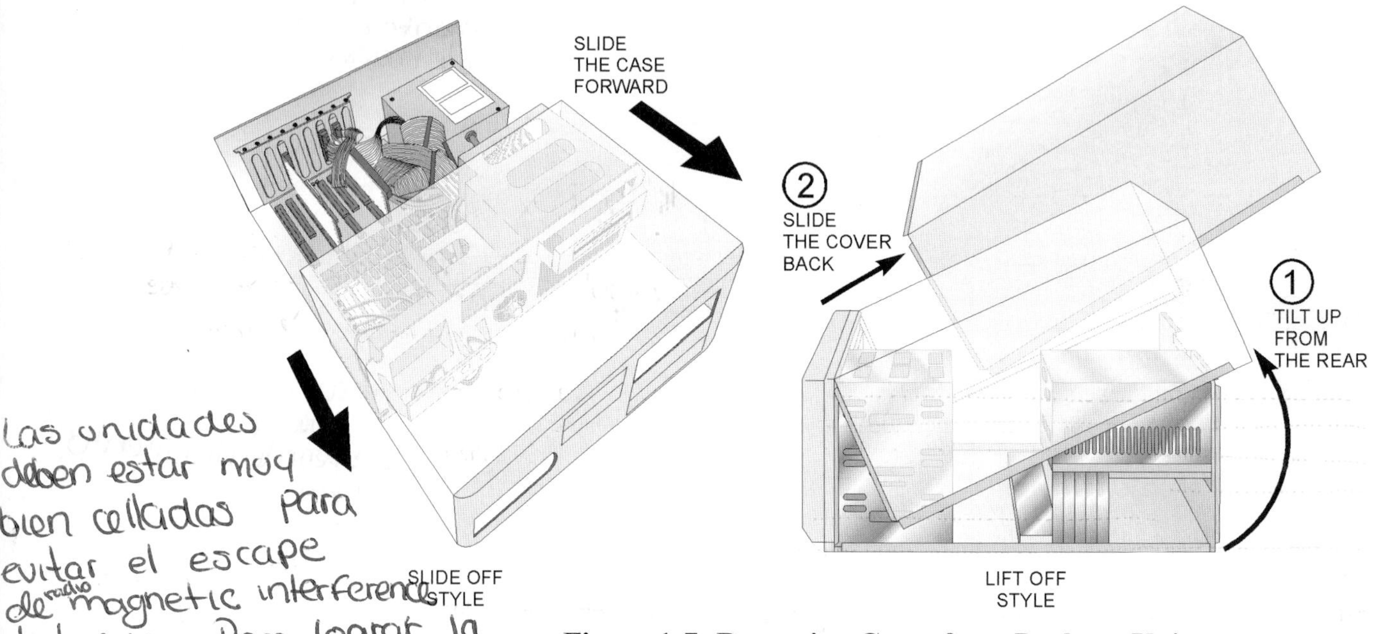

Figure 1-7: Removing Cases from Desktop Units

The fit between the top and the case is very important in achieving FCC certification. A tight fit and electrical conductivity between the case and top are necessary to prevent unwanted radio interference from escaping the interior of the case. The inside face or the plastic front panel is coated with a conductive paint to limit the radio magnetic interference escaping from the case.

IC cooler fans

A fan in the power supply unit pulls in air through slots in the front of the case. The air flows over the system unit's internal components, into the power supply unit, and is exhausted through the back of the case. Heat build-up inside the system unit increases as more internal options are added to the system. To compensate for additional heat, it may be necessary to add additional fans to the case. Special **IC cooler fans** are often added to advanced microprocessors. They are designed to be fitted directly onto the IC and plug into one of the power supply's connectors.

Towers

Tower cases

Tower cases are designed to set vertically on the floor beneath a desk. Some AT users resorted to standing the computers on their sides under the desk to provide more usable workspace on the desktop. This prompted computer makers to develop cases that would naturally fit under the desk. IBM validated the tower design when they introduced their PS/2 models 60 and 80. Different tower case styles are depicted in Figure 1-8.

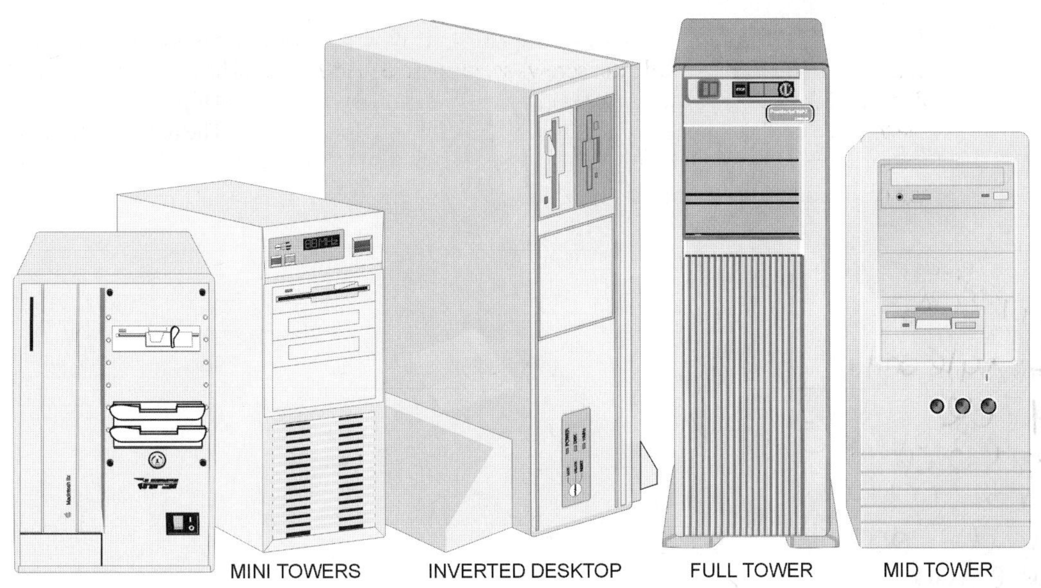

Figure 1-8: Tower Case Designs

Mini towers

Mini towers and mid towers are short towers designed to take up less vertical space. Internally, their design resembles a vertical desktop unit. They are considerably less expensive than the larger towers due to the reduced materials needed to produce them. Unlike their taller relatives, mini towers do not provide abundant space for internal add-ons or disk drives. However, they do possess the shortcomings of the full towers. Mini towers exist more as a function of marketing than as an application solution.

Many easy-access schemes have been developed to allow quick or convenient access to the inside of the system unit. Some towers use removable trays that the system board and I/O cards are plugged into before being slid into the unit. This allows all of the boards to be assembled outside of the system unit. Other tower cases use hinged doors on the side of the case, allowing the system and I/O boards to swing away from the chassis.

The ventilation characteristics of most tower units tend to be poor. The reason is associated with the fact that the I/O cards are mounted horizontally. This permits the heat produced by lower boards to rise past the upper boards, adding to the cooling problem. To compensate for this deficiency, most tower units include a secondary case fan to help increase the airflow and dissipate the heat.

Portables

portable PCs

To free the computer user from the desk, an array of **portable PCs** have been developed. These units package the system unit, input units and output unit into a single, light-weight package that can be carried along with the user.

notebook computer

While early attempts at developing a portable PC produced smaller computers that could be carried by the user, they tended to be heavy and inconvenient to carry, and had short operating times between battery recharges. However, continued advancements in IC and peripheral component designs have provided truly portable, PC-compatible computers. A typical **notebook computer**, such as the one depicted in Figure 1-9, features a video display that is larger than those typically associated with PC-AT machines, hard drives that range into the tens of gigabytes, and CD-ROM/DVD drives. The capabilities of modern portable computers make them the equivalent of desktop or tower units in most respects.

Figure 1-9:
A Typical Portable Computer

Although portable systems operate like desktop and tower PCs, they have characteristics that are considerably different than the other PC designs. Therefore, they are covered in detail in Chapter 7—*Portable Systems*.

The System Unit

The components inside the system unit can be divided into four distinct subunits: a switching power supply, the disk drives, the system board, and the options adapter cards, as illustrated in Figure 1-10.

TEST TIP

Know the names of all the components of a typical PC system and be able to identify them by sight.

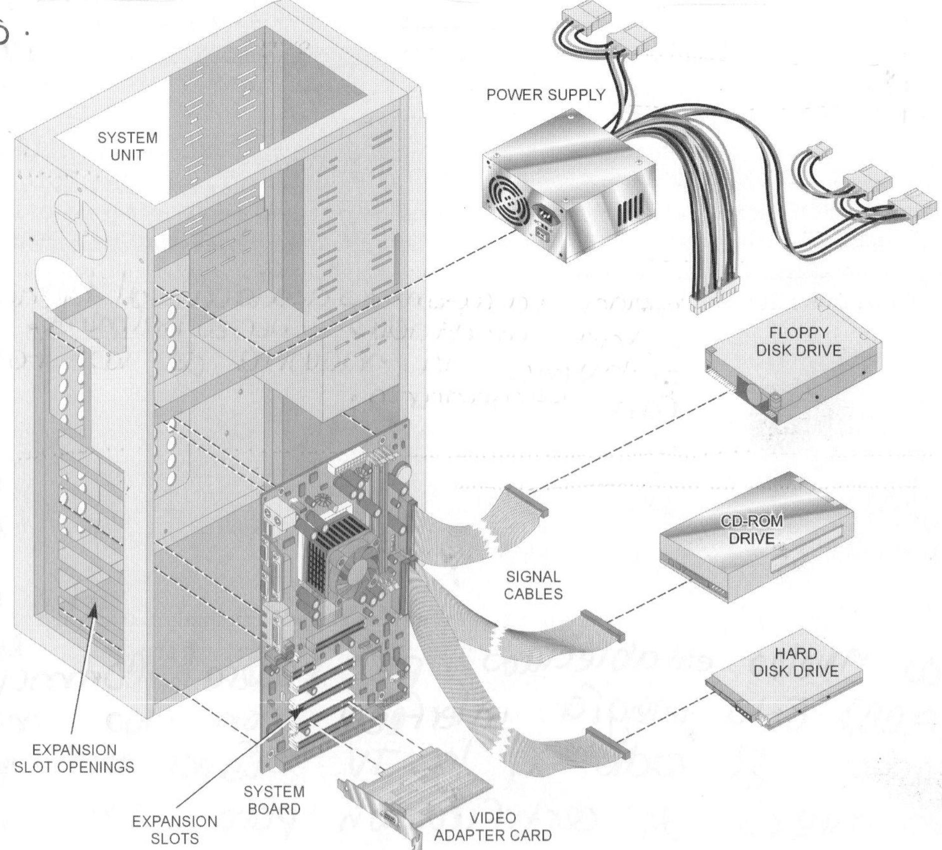

Figure 1-10:
Components Inside the System Unit

A typical system unit contains a single power supply unit that converts commercial power into the various levels required by the different devices in the system. The number and types of disk drives in the system vary according to the application the system is designed for. However, a single floppy disk drive unit, a single hard disk drive unit, and a single CD-ROM drive are typically installed to handle the system's mass storage requirements.

The **system board** is the center of the system. It contains the portions of the system that define its computing power and speed.

system board

motherboards

planar boards

video adapter card

Input/Output (I/O) adapter card

expansion slot connectors

System boards are also referred to as **motherboards**, or **planar boards**. Any number of plug-in options adapter cards may be installed to handle a wide array of PC peripheral equipment. Typical adapter cards installed in a system include a **video adapter card** and some sort of **Input/Output (I/O) adapter card**. Peripheral devices such as printers and mice normally connect to the system through the rear of the system unit. These cards plug into **expansion slot connectors** on the back of the system board. In most desktop cases the keyboard also plugs into the back panel.

In desktop cases, the system board is located in the floor of the unit, toward the left-rear corner. The power supply is located in the right-rear corner. Raised reinforcement rails in the floor of the system unit contain threaded holes and slip-in slots that the system board is anchored to. Small plastic feet are inserted into the system board and are set down in the slots. The system board is secured by sliding its feet into the narrow portion of the slot.

TEST TIP

Memorize the different names the industry uses for system boards.

One or more brass standoffs are inserted into the threaded holes before installing the system board. After the system board has been anchored in place, a small machine screw is inserted through the system board opening and into the brass standoff. This arrangement provides electrical grounding between the system board and the case and helps to reduce **Electromagnetic Field Interference (EFI)** emitted from the board.

Electromagnetic Field Interference (EFI)

Every electrical conductor radiates a field of electromagnetic energy when an electrical current passes through it. Computer systems are made of hundreds of conductors. The intensity of these fields increases as the current is turned on and off. Modern computers turn millions of digital switches in their ICs on and off each second, resulting in a substantial amount of energy radiating from the computer. The levels generated by the components of a typical system can easily surpass maximum-allowable radiation levels set by the **Federal Communications Commission (FCC)**. The fields generated can potentially interfere with reception of radio, television, and other communications signals under the FCC's jurisdiction. Therefore, computer manufacturers design grounding systems and case structures to limit the amount of EFI that can escape from the case. Basically, the FCC has established two certification levels for microcomputer systems:

Federal Communications Commission (FCC)

- Class A, for computers in business environments
- Class B, a stricter level directed at general consumers for the home environment

To be legal, FCC compliance stickers are required on computer units, along with certain information in their documentation. Looking inside a desktop system unit, as depicted in Figure 1-11, the arrangement of its major components can be seen.

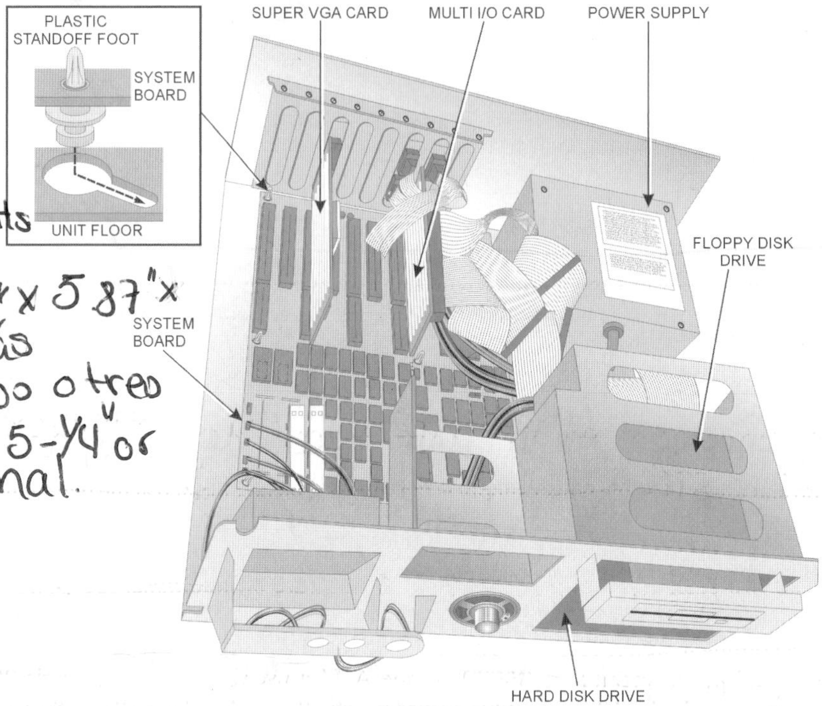

Figure 1-11: Inside a Desktop Unit

full-height drive

half-height drives

The disk drive units are located in bays at the right-front corner of the system. XT-style units provided two side-by-side bays, each capable of handling a **full-height drive** (3.38" by 5.87" by 8") 5-1/4" unit. Newer desktops are designed to hold between three and five half-height 5-1/4" drives. Normally, a fixed drive bay capable of holding two or three **half-height drives** is built into the unit. Additional 5-1/4" or 3-1/2" removable drive bays may also be included. The removable bays are secured to the system unit with machine screws and provide easier access to the system board when removed.

Some cases require that the drive be attached to the case using machine screws, whereas AT-type cases have grooves in the drive bays that use slide-in mounting rails that are attached to the drive. The drives are held in place by the front panel of the slide-on case. The smaller 3-1/2" drives require special mounting brackets that adapt them to the 5-1/4" bays found in many desktop cases.

In tower units, the system board is mounted to the right side-panel of the case. The power supply unit is attached to the back panel. Indicator lights and control buttons are located toward the upper part of the front panel. The drive units are mounted in the disk drive bays located in the upper half of the front panel.

Although there is no real problem mounting hard and floppy drives on their side, as they were in the adapted PC-AT cases, older drives could lose tracking accuracy when mounted this way. Tower cases permit the disk drives to be mounted in a horizontal fashion. They also offer extended drive bay capabilities that make them especially useful in file server applications where many disk, CD-ROM, and tape drives are desired.

Portable computer manufacturers are typically concerned with two main objectives: minimize power consumption and minimize the size of the unit as far as practical. To accomplish the latter objective, the designers create proprietary designs that squeeze internal components into the smallest space possible. The result of these designs is that no two models are alike. Each one has a different, non-standard case and system board design.

Power Supplies

The system's power supply unit provides electrical power for every component inside the system unit, as well as supplying alternating current (ac) to the display monitor.

It converts commercial electrical power received from a 120-Vac, 60-Hz (or 220-Vac, 50-Hz outside the U.S.) outlet into other levels required by the components of the system. In desktop and tower PCs, the power supply is the shiny metal box located at the rear of the system unit.

AT power supplies

ATX power supplies

There are two basic types of power supplies to be aware of, traditional **AT power supplies**—designed to support AT-compatible system boards, and **ATX power supplies**—designed according to newer ATX design specifications. The AT power supply has two 6-pin system board power connectors (P8/P9), while ATX power supplies use a single 20-pin power connector. In the AT-compatible power supply, the cooling fan pulls air through the case from the front and exhausts it out the rear of the power supply unit. Conversely, the ATX design pulls air in through the rear of the power supply unit and blows it directly on the ATX system board.

The desktop/tower power supply produces four (or five) different levels of efficiently regulated dc voltage. These are; +5V, -5V, +12V, and -12V (the ATX design also provides a +3.3V level to the system board). The power supply unit also provides the system's ground. The +5V level is used by the IC devices on the system board and adapter cards. The +3.3V level is used by the microprocessor.

System board power connectors provide the system board and the individual expansion slots with up to 1 ampere of current each. The basic four voltage levels are available for use through the system board's expansion slot connectors.

Several bundles of cable emerge from the power supply to provide power to the components of the system unit and to its peripherals. The power supply delivers power to the system board, and its expansion slots, through the system board power connectors. The ATX system board connector is a 20-pin keyed connector. Figure 1-12 shows the wiring configuration diagram of an ATX system board power connector. Notice that it is keyed so that it cannot be installed incorrectly.

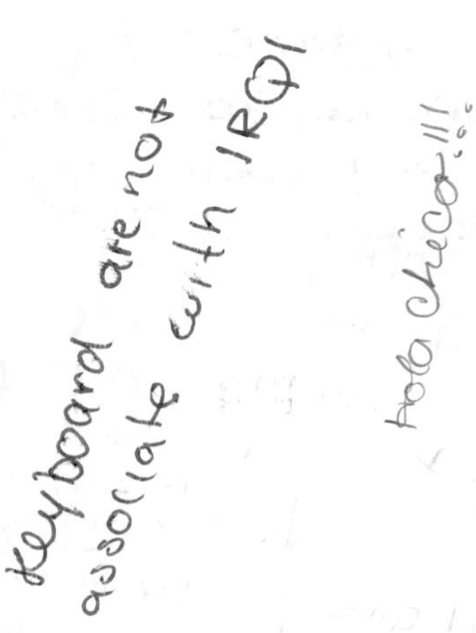

Figure 1-12: The ATX System Board Power Connector

In AT-compatible power supplies, two six-wire bundles are typically marked P8 and P9. The physical construction of these power connectors is significantly different than that of the other bundles. They are designed to be plugged into the system board's P1 and P2 power plugs, respectively, as depicted in Figure 1-13.

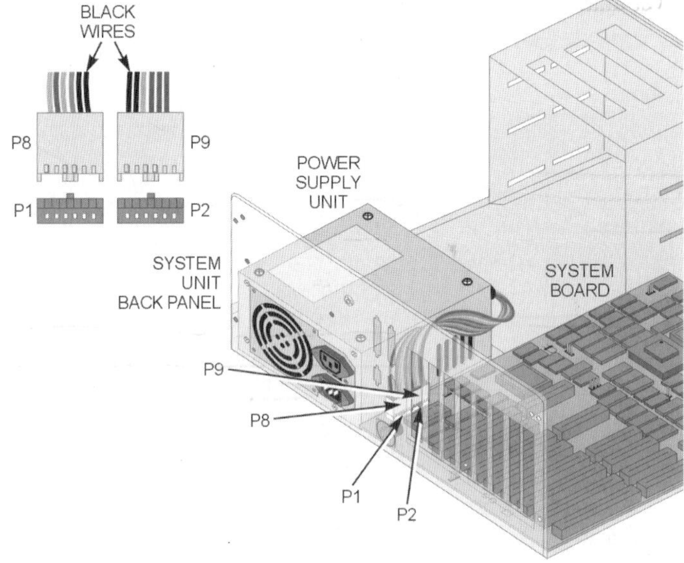

Figure 1-13: P1/P2–P8/P9 Connection

> **WARNING**
>
> **Don't switch the P8/P9 connectors!**—Although they look alike, the voltage levels of each plug are different. Reversing them can cause **severe damage**.

The P8/P9 connectors are normally keyed and numbered. However, their construction and appearance are identical. The voltage levels associated with each plug are different and **severe damage could result** to the computer by reversing them. The power connector labeled P8 should be plugged into the circuit board connector nearest the rear of the unit, while connector P9 should be plugged into the connector next to it. A good rule of thumb to remember when attaching these two connectors to the system board is that the black wires in each bundle should be next to each other.

The other power supply bundles are used to supply power to optional systems, such as the disk and CD-ROM drives. These bundles provide a +5 and +12 Vdc supply, as described in Figure 1-14. The larger connector is carried over from older PC/XT/AT designs, while the smaller connector has gained widespread usage with smaller form factor disk drives. The +5 V supply provides power for electronic components on the optional devices, while the +12V level is used for disk drive motors and other devices that require a higher voltage. As the figure illustrates, these connectors are keyed, so they must be plugged in correctly.

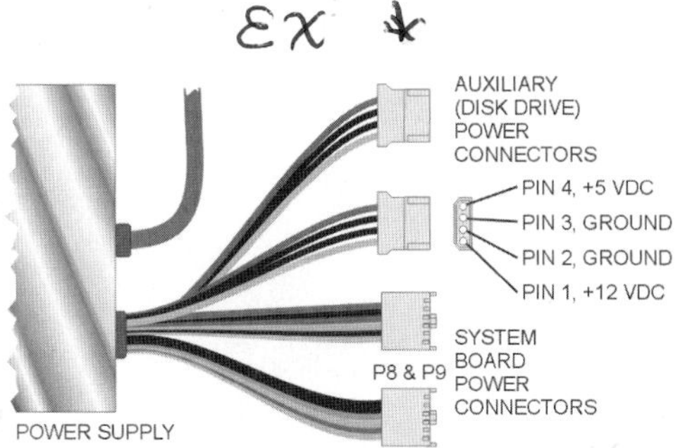

Figure 1-14: Auxiliary Power Connectors

Power may be delivered to the monitor through a special plug in the rear of the AT-style power supply. This permits the monitor to be switched on and off via the system's power switch. In PC and XT units, the power switch was an integral part of the power supply and extended from its right side. In AT and ATX units, the on/off switch is located on the front panel of the system unit and connected to the power supply by a cable. In the ATX design, a special *Soft Switch* line is included that enables the system to shut itself off under control of the system software. This allows power management components of the operating system software to manage the hardware's power usage. This concept is discussed further in the Power Management section later in this chapter. Figure 1-15 illustrates the typical power-supply connections found in a desktop or tower unit.

> **TEST TIP**
>
> Be aware that ATX power supplies can be shut off from the system itself.

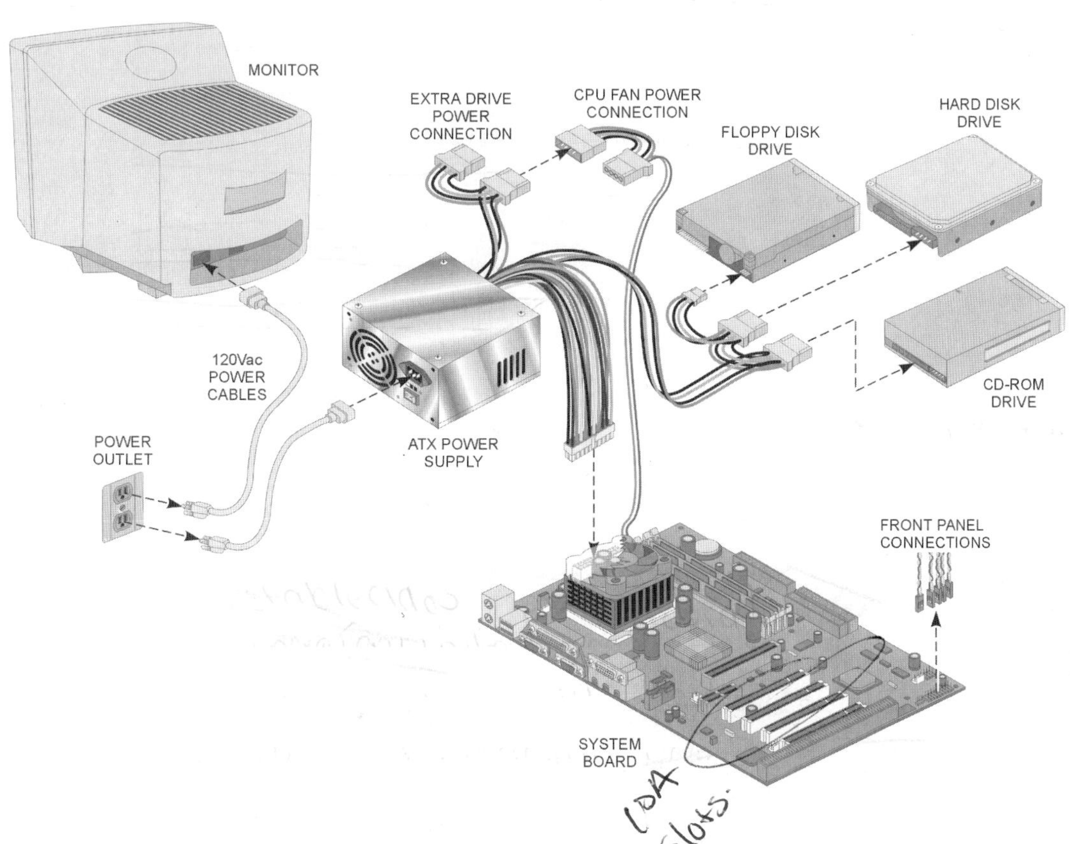

Figure 1-15: System Power Supply Connections

In the United States, a grounded, three-prong power cord provides the ac input voltage to the power supply. The smaller vertical blade in the connector is considered the hot or phase side of the connector. A small slide switch on the back of the unit permits the power supply to be switched over to operate on 220 Vac input voltages found outside the United States. When the switch is set to the 220 position, the voltage supplied to the power supply's monitor outlet will also be 220. In this position, it is usually necessary to exchange the power cord for one that has a plug suited to the country the computer is being used in.

Power supply units come in a variety of shapes and power ratings. The shapes of the various power supplies are determined by the type of case they are designed to work in. The major difference between these two power supply types is in their form factors. The ATX power supply is somewhat smaller in size than the AT-style power supply and their hole patterns are different. Figure 1-16 illustrates the various power supply shapes that have been used with different case types.

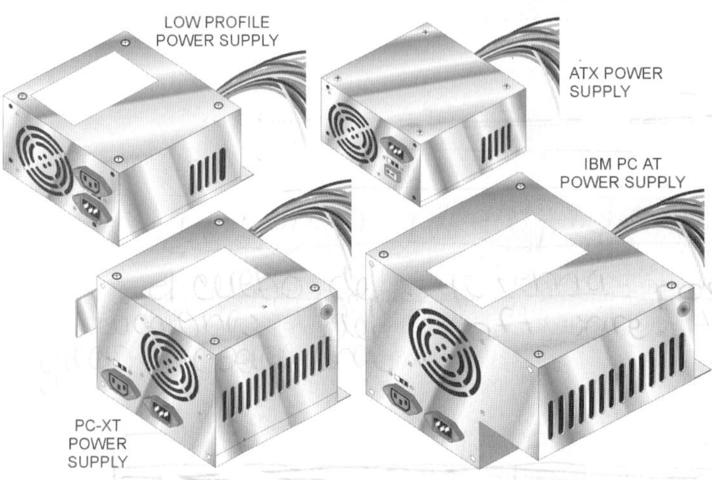

Figure 1-16: Desktop/Tower Power Supplies

Another point that differentiates power supplies is their power (or wattage) rating. Typical power ratings include 150, 200, and 250-watt versions.

> **TEST TIP**
>
> Be aware that power supply's form factor and wattage ratings must be taken into account when ordering a replacement power supply for a system.

Notebooks and other portables use a detachable, rechargeable battery and an external power supply, as illustrated in Figure 1-17 (battery sizes vary between manufacturers). They also employ power-saving circuits and ICs designed to lengthen the battery's useful time. The battery unit contains a recharging regulator circuit that allows the battery to recharge while it is being used with the external power supply. Like other hardware aspects of notebook computers, there are no standards for the power supply units. They use different connector types and possess different voltage and current delivery capabilities. Therefore, a power supply from one notebook will not necessarily work with another.

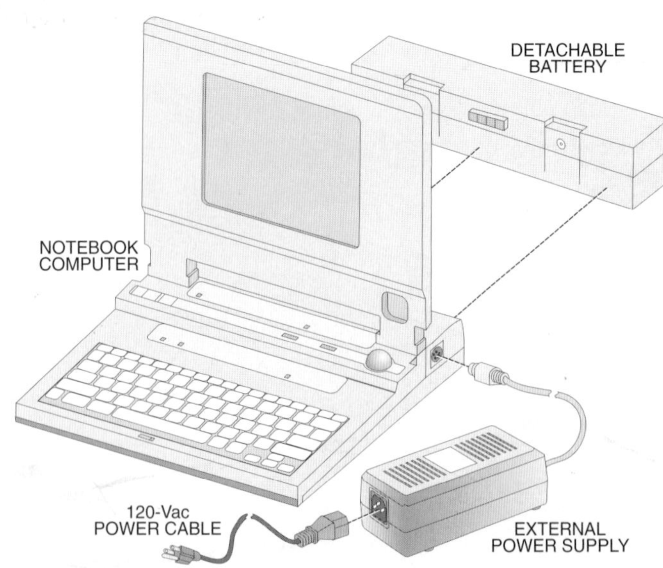

Figure 1-17: Laptop/Notebook Power Supplies

> **TEST TIP**
>
> Be aware that the external power supply used with portable systems basically converts ac voltage into a dc voltage that the system can use to power its internal components and recharge its batteries.

System Boards

The system board is the center of the PC-compatible microcomputer system. It contains the circuitry that determines the computing power and speed of the entire system. In particular, it contains the microprocessor and control devices that form the brains of the system. The major components of interest on a PC system board are the microprocessor, the system's primary **read only (ROM)**, **random access (RAM)**, and **cache memory** sections, expansion slot connectors, and microprocessor support ICs that coordinate the operation of the system. A typical system board layout is depicted in Figure 1-18.

read only (ROM)

random access (RAM)

cache memory

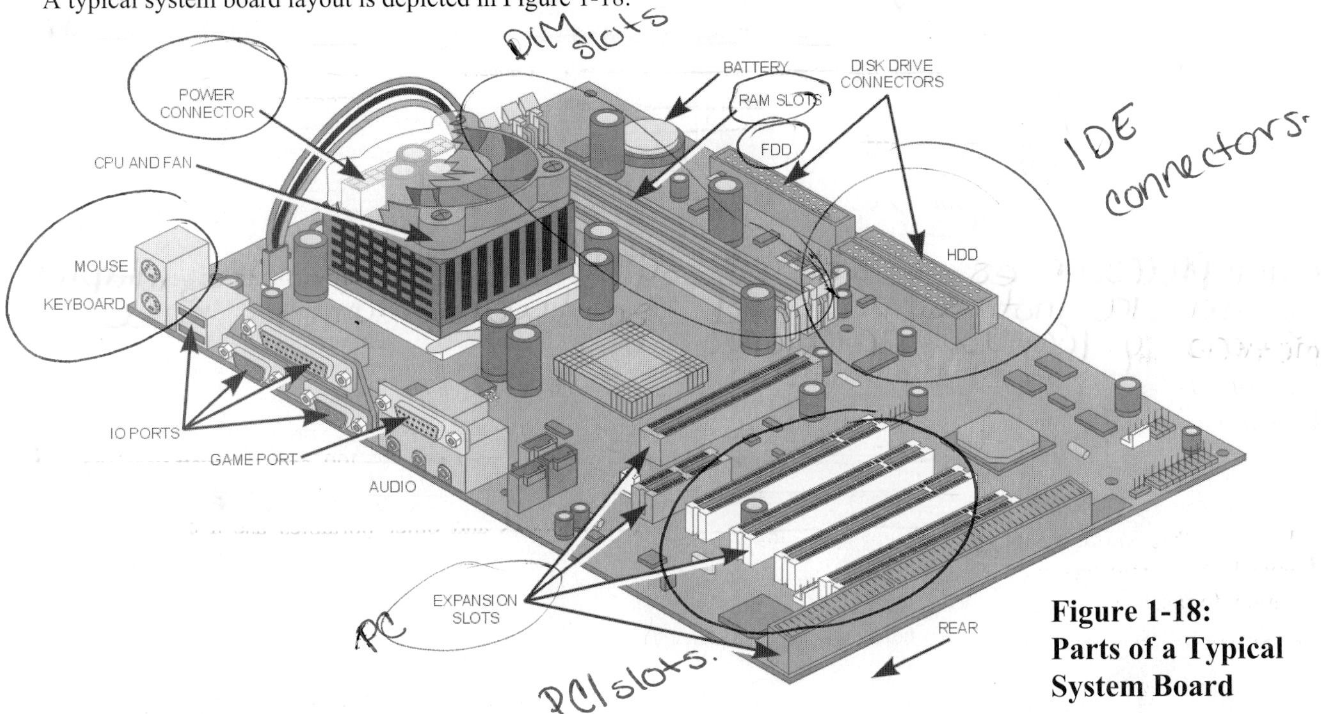

Figure 1-18: Parts of a Typical System Board

TEST TIP

Know the parts of a typical system board and make sure that you can identify these components (and variations of them) from a pictorial or photographic representation.

Major Components

For orientation purposes, the end of the board where the keyboard connector, expansion slots, and power connectors are located is generally referred to as the rear of the board.

As mentioned earlier, the system board receives power from the power supply unit through special power connectors. These connectors are often located along the right-rear corner of the system board so that they are near the power supply unit. They are also keyed so that the power cord cannot be plugged in backward. AT power connectors are typically labeled as P1 and P2 and are always located directly beside each other. However, they are identical and can be reversed. Therefore, AT system board power connectors should always be installed so that the black wires from each connector are together.

The system's keyboard connector is normally located along the back edge of the board as well. In most AT-compatible systems, the keyboard connector is a round, five-pin DIN connector. ATX systems place a standard block of input/output connections along the back edge of the system board. This block contains connectors for the ATX keyboard and mouse.

input/output (I/O)

memory systems

expansion slots

The system board communicates with various optional **input/output (I/O)** and **memory systems** through adapter boards that plug into its **expansion slots**. These connectors are normally located along the left-rear portion of the system board so that the external devices they serve can access them through the rear case openings.

Microprocessors

The microprocessor is the major component of any system board. It can be thought of as the "brains" of the computer system, because it reads, interprets, and executes software instructions, and also carries out arithmetic and logical operations for the system.

REFERENCE SHELF

For more in-depth information about how microprocessor systems actually work, refer to the Electronic Reference Shelf located on the CD that accompanies this book.

The original PC and PC-XT computers were based on the 8-bit 8088 microprocessor from Intel. This microprocessor featured an 8-bit data bus and a 20-bit address bus. Its 20-bit address bus established the size of the PC's memory map at 1 MB.

The IBM PC-AT system employed a 16-bit 80286 microprocessor. The 80286 remained compatible with the 8088 microprocessor used in the earlier PC and XT systems, while offering increased processing power and speed. The 80286 would run the same software that the 8088 did, but it would run it much faster.

multiuser

multitasking

The 80286 was much more than a fast 8088 microprocessor, however. Unlike the 8088, the 80286 microprocessor was designed to support **multiuser** and **multitasking** operations. In these types of operations, the computer appears to work on several tasks, or to serve several users, simultaneously. Of course, the microprocessor cannot actually work on more than one item at a time; the appearance of simultaneous operations is created by storing the parameters of one task, leaving the task, loading up the state of another task, and beginning operation on it.

real mode

virtual-protected mode

The 80286's internal register set was identical to the register set of the 8088. However, it possessed an extended instruction set and a 24-bit address bus. The address bus enabled it to directly access up to 16 MB of physical memory, and the extended instruction set provided two distinctly different addressing modes: **real mode** and **virtual-protected mode**.

In real-mode operation, the microprocessor emulates an 8088/86 microprocessor, and can directly access only the first 1 MB of RAM addresses in segments of 64 KB. It can also only work on one task at a time. In this mode, the microprocessor produces addresses on its first 20 address pins only.

If software increments the 80286's addresses past 0FFFFFh in this mode, the address will just roll over to 000000h and the four highest address bits will not be activated. This is the mode that Intel microprocessors default to on startup and reset.

protected mode

In **protected mode**, the microprocessor's upper address bits are enabled, and it can access physical memory addresses above the 1 MB limit (up to 16 MB for the 80286). If software increments the microprocessor's addresses past 0FFFFFh in protected mode, the address will increment to 100000h.

virtual memory

Protected mode can also be used to perform **virtual memory** operations. Virtual memory is RAM that doesn't physically exist. In these operations, the system treats an area of disk space as an extension of RAM memory. It uses this designated area to shift data from RAM memory to the disk (and vice versa) as required. This method enables the system to simulate large areas of RAM.

Since the days of the original AT design, Intel has introduced several different microprocessors for the PC market. These include devices such as the 80386DX and SX, the 80486DX and SX, the Pentium (80586), the Pentium Pro (80686), and Pentium II. Intel used the SX notation to define reduced-function versions of exiting microprocessors (that is, the 80486SX was a version of the 80486DX that had some functionality removed). SX devices were normally created to produce price variations that kept the Intel product competitive with other devices.

Pentium

Other IC manufacturers produce work-alike versions of the Intel processors that are referred to as clones. In response to clone microprocessor manufactures using the 80x86 nomenclature, Intel dropped their 80x86 numbering system after the 80486 and adopted the **Pentium** name so that they could copyright it.

All these microprocessors are backward compatible with the 8088—that is, programs written specifically for the 8088 can be executed by any of the other processors.

Microprocessor Packages

Microprocessors have been produced in a number of different IC package styles depending on their vintage and manufacturer.

Dual In-line (DIP)

The 8088 and 8086 microprocessors were housed in a 40-pin **Dual In-line (DIP)**–style package. It was used on the original IBM PC and PC-XT units. It featured a 20-bit address bus, an 8-bit data bus, and a 16-bit internal word size. The 20-bit address bus allowed it to access 1 MB of address space. The mismatch between its internal word size and external data bus size required multiplexed, two-transfer operations with external system devices. Another more expensive version, called the 8086, featured a full 16-bit external data bus.

Although some XTs used 8086-based system boards, the vast majority of PCs, XTs, and clones used the 8088. Later XT versions employed a Turbo Speed function that allowed faster versions of the 8088 (8088-10 and 8088-12) to be used in systems that maintained speed compatibility with the 4.77MHz PC bus expansion slot.

Ceramic Leadless Chip Carrier (CLCC)

Plastic Leaded Chip Carrier (PLCC)

Pin Grid Array (PGA)

The 80286 was manufactured in a variety of 68-pin IC types including a **Ceramic Leadless Chip Carrier (CLCC)**, a **Plastic Leaded Chip Carrier (PLCC)**, and a **Pin Grid Array (PGA)** package. CLCC devices are designed to set inside sockets. Contacts along the side and bottom of the device make connection with spring-loaded contacts embedded in the socket. PLCC ICs have small pins that gull-wing out from the sides of the chip and are soldered to the top of a PC board. PGA packages employ metal pins that protrude from the bottom of the chip. These pins are pressed into a corresponding flat socket that has been mounted on the PC board.

The 80286 processors were used in the IBM PC-AT and its compatibles. It featured a 24-bit address bus, a 16-bit data bus, and a 16-bit internal word size. The 24-bit address bus allowed it to directly access up to 16 MB of address space, even though DOS could only handle the 1 MB that it had been designed to handle with the 8088 systems. The full 16-bit internal and external word size gave it a 4X speed increase over 8088 systems running at the same clock speed. 80286s were produced in various speed ratings.

The 80386DX continued the evolution of the AT architecture and was produced in a 132-pin PGA package. A reduced-function 80386SX version was also produced in a 100-pin surface-mount IC package. These microprocessors were mainly used in AT clone systems. The DX version provided a 32-bit address bus, a 32-bit data bus, and a 32-bit internal word size. The 32-bit address bus provided up to 4 GB of memory addressing. The SX version featured a reduced 24-bit address bus and a 16-bit data bus. Both versions were produced in a variety of operating speeds and included advanced addressing modes.

The 80486DX and first-generation Pentium microprocessors returned to 168-pin and 273-pin PGA packages. Figure 1-19 depicts these microprocessor packages. The 80486 featured a 32-bit address bus, a 32-bit external data bus, and a 64-bit internal word size. The Pentium also features a 32-bit address bus. However, both the internal and external word size are 64-bits. Both units include on-board math coprocessors for intense numerical operations and special built-in memory areas, called cache memory, for high-speed data access to selected data. Like the 80386, these microprocessors are typically used in advanced AT clone computers.

Advanced Pentium processors use a variety of package and pin configurations that are discussed in Chapter 2—*Advanced System Boards*.

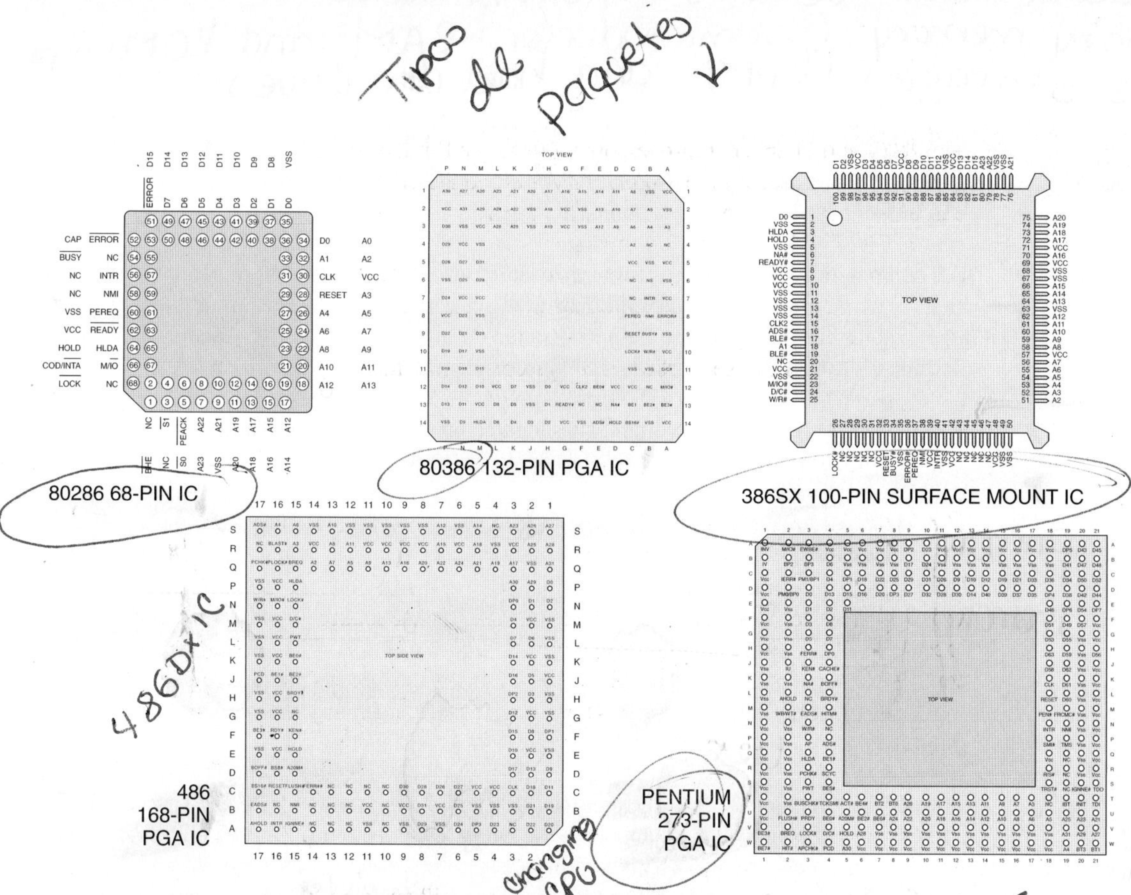

Figure 1-19: Microprocessor Packages

PC manufacturers mount microprocessors in **sockets** so that they can be replaced easily. This allows a failed microprocessor to simply be exchanged with a working unit. More often though, the microprocessor is replaced with an improved version to upgrade the speed or performance of the system.

sockets

The notches and dots on the various ICs are important keys when replacing a microprocessor. They specify the location of the IC's number 1 pin. This pin must be lined up with the **pin-1 notch** of the socket for proper insertion. In older systems, the microprocessors had to be forcibly removed from the socket using an IC extractor tool. As the typical microprocessor's pin count increased, special **Zero Insertion Force (ZIF)** sockets were implemented that allowed the microprocessor to be set in the socket without force and then clamped in place. An arm-activated clamping mechanism in the socket shifts to the side, locking the pins in place. All of the microprocessors discussed here are covered in greater detail in Chapter 6, along with their significant variations.

pin-1 notch

Zero Insertion Force (ZIF)

For mathematically intensive operations, some programs may shift portions of the work to special **high-speed math coprocessors**, if they are present in the system. These devices are specialized microprocessors that work in parallel with the main microprocessor and extend its instruction set to speed up math and logic operations. They basically add large register sets to the microprocessor, along with additional arithmetic processing instructions. The 8088, 80286, 80386SX/DX, and 80486SX microprocessors used external coprocessors. The 80486DX and Pentium processors have built-in coprocessors that are an integral part of the IC design.

high-speed math coprocessors

The writing on the package is also significant. It contains the number that identifies the type of device in the package and normally includes a speed rating for the device.

Memory Units

primary memory

mass storage

All computers need a place to temporarily store information while other pieces of information are being processed. In digital computers, information storage is normally conducted at two different levels: **primary memory** (made up of semiconductor RAM and ROM chips) and **mass storage** (usually involving floppy and hard disk drives).

Most of the system's primary memory is located on the system board and typically exists in two or three forms:

Read Only Memory (ROM)

Random Access Memory (RAM)

Cache memory

- **Read Only Memory (ROM)**—which contains the computer's permanent startup programs
- **Random Access Memory (RAM)**—which is quick enough to operate directly with the microprocessor and can be read from and written to as often as desired
- **Cache memory**—which a fast RAM system uses to hold information that the microprocessor is likely to use

TEST TIP

Be aware of which memory types are volatile and what this means.

ROM devices store information permanently and are used to hold programs and data that do not change. RAM devices only retain the information stored in them as long as electrical power is applied to the IC. Any interruption of power will cause the contents of the memory to vanish. This is referred to as **volatile** memory. ROM, on the other hand, is **nonvolatile**.

volatile

nonvolatile

Basic Input/Output System (BIOS)

Every system board contains one or two ROM ICs that hold the system's **Basic Input/Output System (BIOS)** program. The BIOS program contains the basic instructions for communications between the microprocessor and the various input and output devices in the system. Until recently, this information was stored permanently inside the ROM chips and could only be changed by replacing the chips.

flash ROM

downloaded

Advancements in EEPRROM technology have produced **flash ROM** devices that enable new BIOS information to be written (**downloaded**) into the ROM to update it. This can be done from an update disk, or it can be downloaded from another computer. Unlike RAM ICs, the contents of the flash ROM remain after the power has been removed from the chip. In either case, the upgraded BIOS must be compatible with the system board it is being used with and should be the latest version available.

firmware

The information in the BIOS represents all of the intelligence the computer has until it can load more information from another source, such as a hard or floppy disk. Taken together, the BIOS software (programming) and hardware (the ROM chip) are referred to as **firmware**. These ICs can be located anywhere on the system board and are usually easy to recognize due to their size and immediate proximity to each other.

Dual In-line Pin (DIP)

In older PC designs—XT and AT—the system's RAM memory was composed of banks of discrete RAM ICs in **Dual In-line Pin (DIP)** sockets. Most of these system boards arranged nine pieces of 1 by 256 kb DRAM chips in the first two banks (0 and 1) and nine pieces of 1 by 64 kb chips in banks two and three. The two banks of 256k chips provided a total of 512 kB of storage (the ninth chip of each bank supplied a parity bit for error checking). The two banks of 64 kB chips extended the RAM memory capacity out to the full 640 kB. As with the 256 kB chips, the ninth bit was for parity.

Some system boards used two 4-by-256 kb chips with a 1-by-256 kb chip to create each of the first two banks. In any event, the system would typically run with one bank installed, two banks installed, or all of the banks installed. Bank 0 had to be filled first, followed by bank 1, and then all four.

Intermediate clone designs placed groups of RAM ICs on small 30-pin daughter boards that plugged into the system board vertically. This mounting method required less horizontal board space. These RAM modules had pins along one side of the board and were referred to as **Single In-line Pin (SIP)** modules.

Single In-line Pin (SIP)

Further refinements of the RAM module produced snap-in **Single In-line Memory Modules (SIMMs)** and **Dual In-line Memory Modules (DIMMs)**. Like the SIP, the SIMM and DIMM units mount vertically on the system board. However, instead of using a pin and socket arrangement, both use special snap-in sockets that support the module firmly. SIMMs and DIMMs are also keyed, so they cannot be plugged in backwards. SIMMs are available in 30- and 72-pin versions, whereas DIMMs are larger 168-pin boards.

Single In-line Memory Modules (SIMMs)

Dual In-line Memory Modules (DIMMs)

SIMM and DIMM sockets are quite distinctive in that they are normally arranged side by side. However, they can be located anywhere on the system board. SIMMs typically come in 8- or 32- bit data storage configurations. The 8-bit modules must be arranged in **banks** to match the data bus size of the system's microprocessor. In order to work effectively with a 32-bit microprocessor, a bank of four 8-bit SIMMs would need to be used. Conversely, a single 32-bit SIMM could do the same job.

banks

DIMMs, on the other hand, typically come in 32- and 64-bit widths to service more powerful microprocessors. Like the SIMMs, they must be arranged properly to fit the size of the system data bus. In both cases, the modules can be accessed in smaller 8- and 16-bit segments. SIMMs and DIMMs also come in 9-, 36-, and 72-bit versions that include parity checking bits for each byte of storage.

PCs are usually sold with less than their full RAM capacity. This enables users to purchase less expensive computers to fit their individual needs and yet retain the option to install more RAM if future applications call for it. SIMM and DIMM sizes are typically specified in an a-by-b format. For example, a 2-by-32 SIMM specification indicates that it is a dual, non-parity, 32-bit (4-byte) device. In this scheme, the capacity is derived by multiplying the two numbers and then dividing by eight (or nine for parity chips). DIP, SIP, SIMM, and DIMM modules are depicted in Figure 1-20.

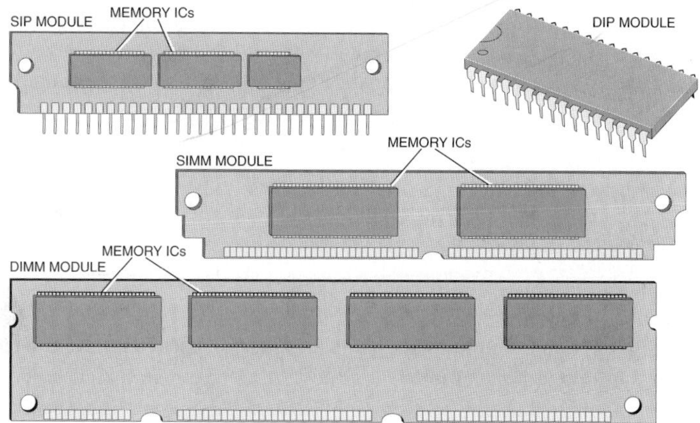

Figure 1-20: DIP, SIP, SIMM, and DIMM Memory Modules

Chipsets

Microprocessor manufacturers and third-party IC makers produce microprocessor-support chipsets that provide auxiliary services for each type of microprocessor.

integrated circuit (IC)

small-scale integration (SSI)

chip

medium-scale integration (MSI)

large-scale integration (LSI)

very large-scale integration (VLSI)

application-specific integrated circuits (ASICs)

The first digital computers were giants that took up entire rooms and required several technicians and engineers to operate. They were constructed with vacuum tubes and their computing power was very limited by comparison to modern computers. However, the advent of **integrated circuit** (**IC**) technology in 1964 launched a new era in compact electronic packaging. The much smaller, low-power transistor replaced the vacuum tube and the size of the computer began to shrink.

The first ICs were relatively small devices that performed simple digital logic. These basic digital devices still exist and occupy a class of ICs referred to as **small-scale integration** (**SSI**) devices. SSI devices range up to 100 transistors per **chip**. As manufacturers improved techniques for creating ICs, the number of transistors on a chip grew and complex digital circuits were fabricated together. These devices are categorized as **medium-scale integration** (**MSI**) devices. MSI devices range between 100 and 3,000 circuit elements. Eventually, **large-scale integration** (**LSI**) and **very large-scale integration** (**VLSI**) devices were produced. LSI devices contain between 3,000 and 100,000 electronic components, and VLSI devices exceed 100,000 elements.

IC technology today allows millions of circuit elements to be constructed on a single small piece of silicon. Some VLSI devices contain complete computer modules.

These devices are commonly referred to as **application-specific integrated circuits** (**ASICs**). By connecting a few ASIC devices together on a printed circuit board, computers that once inhabited an entire room have shrunk to fit on the top of an ordinary work desk, and now, into the palm of the hand. Figure 1-21 shows various integrated circuit package types.

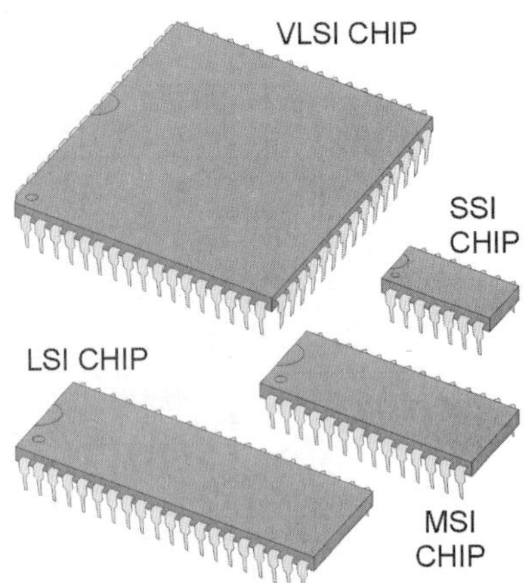

Figure 1-21: Integrated Circuit Packages

For the IC manufacturer, PC compatibility means designing chipsets that use the same basic memory map that was employed in the IBM PC-AT (that is, the chipset's programmable registers, RAM, ROM, and other addresses had to be identical to those of the AT). Therefore, instructions and data in the program would be interpreted, processed, and distributed the same way in both systems. In doing so, the supporting chipset was decreased from eight major ICs and dozens of SSI devices to two or three VLSI chips and a handful of SSI devices.

In some highly integrated system boards, the only ICs that remain are the microprocessor, one or two ROM BIOS chips, a single chipset IC, and the system's memory modules.

Connectors and Jumpers

switches

jumper blocks

BERG connectors

System boards possess a number of jumpers and connectors that you must be aware of. PC-compatible system boards include **switches** and **jumper blocks** (called **BERG connectors** after the BERG connector company that developed them) to select operating options such as processor speed, installed RAM size, and so forth. You may be required to alter these settings if you change a component or install a new module in the system.

Figure 1-22 illustrates the operation of typical configuration jumpers and switches. A metal clip in the cap of the jumper creates an electrical short between the pins it is installed across. When the cap is removed, the electrical connection is also removed and an electrically open condition is created.

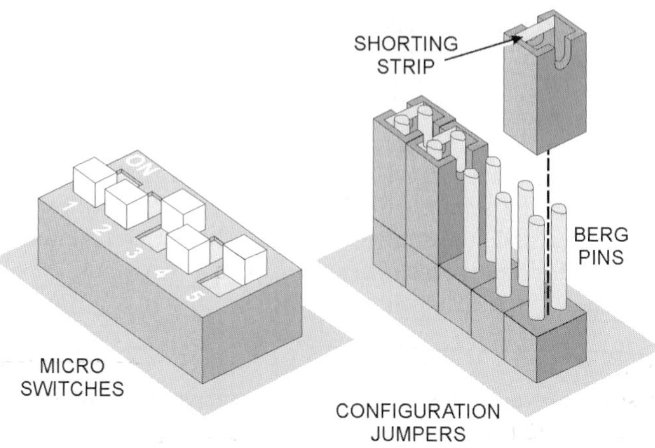

Figure 1-22: Jumpers and Configuration Switches

System boards and I/O cards may use **micro switches** for configuration purposes. These micro switches are normally integrated into a DIP package, as illustrated in the figure. The switches may use a rocker or slide switch mechanism to create the short or open condition. The switches are typically numbered sequentially and marked for on/off positioning. Since the switches are so small, they may simply be marked with an On or Off, or with a 1 or 0.

micro switches

It is usually necessary to consult the PC board's installation guide to locate and properly set configuration jumpers and switches. The installation guide typically provides the locations of all the board's configuration jumpers and switches. It also defines the possible configuration settings, along with corresponding switch or jumper positions.

The system board is connected to the front panel's indicators and controls by BERG connectors. Over time, these connection points have become fairly standard between cases. The normal connections are the **power LED**, **turbo LED**, **turbo switch**, **keylock switch**, **reset switch**, and **system speaker**. A typical front panel connector layout is described in Figure 1-23. It will be necessary to access these points when the system board is replaced or upgraded. Additional system board connectors that would have to be dealt with include the keyboard and power supply connectors.

power LED
turbo LED
turbo switch
keylock switch
reset switch
system speaker

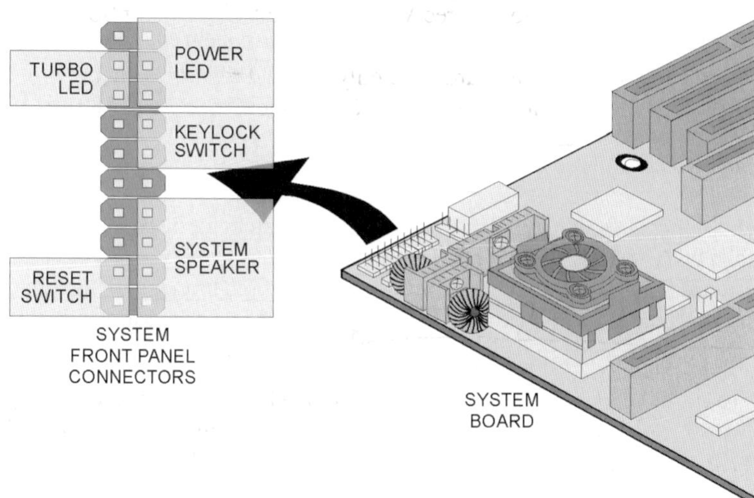

Figure 1-23: Typical System Board Connection Points

Configuration Settings

configuration settings

Each time the system is turned on, or reset, the BIOS program checks the system's **configuration settings** to determine what types of optional devices may be included in the system.

CMOS RAM

Depending on the model of the computer, the configuration information may be read from hardware jumper or switch settings, from battery-powered RAM, or, in some cases, a combination of jumper and software settings. The PC, PC-XT, and their clones used hardware switches for configuration purposes. The original PC-AT featured a battery-powered RAM area that held some of the system's advanced configuration information. This configuration storage area became known as **CMOS RAM**.

Real Time Clock (RTC)

Clone IC manufacturers quickly integrated the advanced software configuration function to their chipsets along with the system's **Real Time Clock (RTC)** function. The RTC function keeps track of time and date information for the system. Clone system board designers added a rechargeable, Ni-Cad battery to their system boards to maintain the information when the system was turned off.

In newer systems, there are no rechargeable Ni-Cad batteries for the CMOS storage. Instead, the CMOS storage area and RTC functions have been integrated with a 10-year, non-replaceable lithium cell in an independent RTC module.

Since these configuration settings are the system's primary method of getting information about what options are installed, they must be set to accurately reflect the actual options being used with the system. If not, an error will occur. You should always suspect configuration problems if a machine fails to operate immediately after a new component has been installed. The CMOS configuration values can be accessed for change by pressing the CTRL and DEL keys (or some other key combination) simultaneously during the bootup procedure.

Plug-and-Play (PnP)

Plug-and-Play—Newer PCs possess the ability to automatically reconfigure themselves for new options that are installed. This feature is referred to as **Plug-and-Play (PnP)** capability.

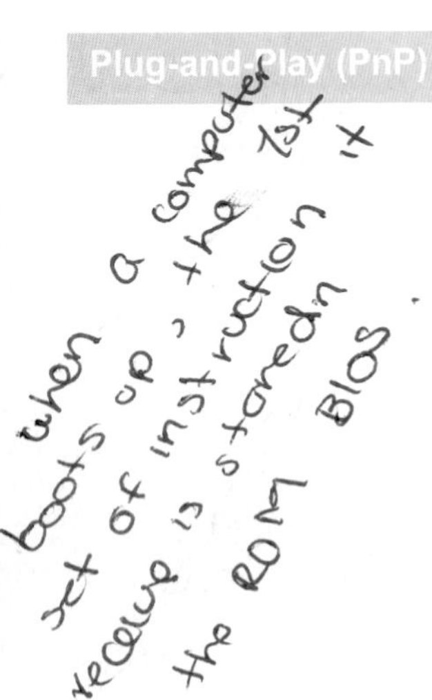

In 1994, Microsoft and Intel teamed up to produce a set of system specifications that would enable options added to the system to automatically be configured for operation. Under this scenario, the user is not involved in setting hardware jumpers or CMOS entries. To accomplish this, the system's BIOS, expansion slots, and adapter cards are designed in a manner so that they can be reconfigured automatically by the system software.

During the startup process, the PnP BIOS examines the system for installed devices. Devices designed for Plug-and-Play compatibility can tell the BIOS what types of devices they are and how to communicate with them. This information is stored in an area of the CMOS memory so that the system can work with the device. Plug-and-Play information will be scattered throughout the remainder of the text as it applies to the topic being covered.

Expansion Slots

It would be very expensive to design and build a computer that fits every conceivable user application. With this in mind, computer designers include standardized connectors that enable users to configure the system to their particular computing needs.

Most PCs use standardized expansion slot connectors that enable various types of peripheral devices to be attached to the system. Optional input/output devices, or their interface adapter boards, are plugged into these slots to connect the devices to the system's address, data, and control buses.

The system board communicates with various optional input/output (I/O) and **memory systems** through adapter boards that plug into its **expansion slots**. These connectors are normally located along the left-rear portion of the system board so that the external devices they serve can access them through openings at the rear of the case.

memory systems

expansion slots

PC-bus

AT-bus

Extended ISA (EISA)

Video Electronics Standards Association (VESA)

Peripheral Component Interconnect (PCI)

Industry Standard Architecture (ISA)

Several different types of expansion slots are in use today. A particular system board may contain only one type of slot, or it may have a few of each type of expansion slot. Be aware that adapter cards are compatible with particular types of slots, so it is important to know which type of slot is being used. The major expansion slot types are:

- 8-bit **PC-bus**
- 16-bit **AT-bus**, or **Industry Standard Architecture (ISA)** bus
- 32-bit **Extended ISA (EISA)** and Micro Channel Architecture (MCA) buses
- **Video Electronics Standards Association (VESA)** and **Peripheral Component Interconnect (PCI)** local buses

These expansion slots are depicted in Figure 1-24 and are discussed in more detail in Chapter 2—*Advanced System Boards*.

The PC-bus slot is the most famous example of an 8-bit expansion slot, while the AT-bus, or ISA bus, slot is the consummate 16-bit expansion bus. The 32-bit expansion buses include the MCA, EISA, VESA, and PCI buses.

The PC bus was included in the original PC, PC-XT, and XT clone computers. The expansion bus in the IBM PC-AT and its clones became the de facto Industry Standard Architecture for 16-bit computers. The EISA bus was used in 80386 and 80486-based AT clone computers. The MCA bus was featured in some models of IBM's Personal System 2 (PS/2) line of computers.

The 32-bit VESA and PCI buses are typical included on 80486- and Pentium-based computers along with traditional ISA slots.

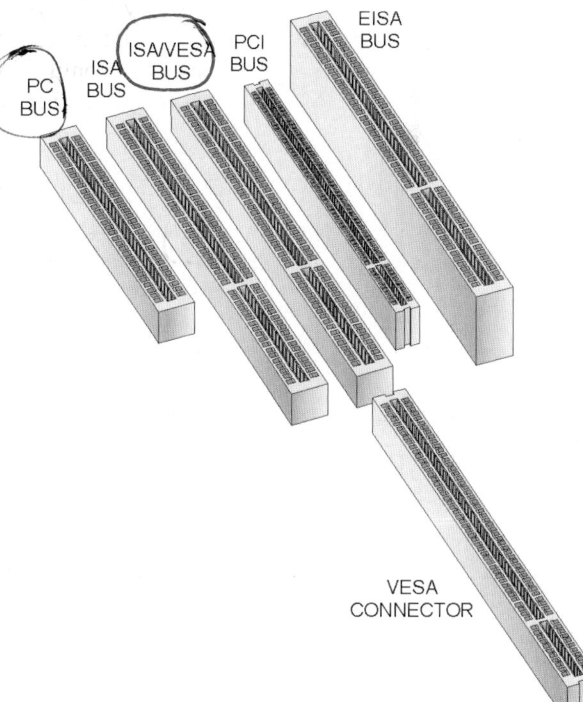

Figure 1-24: Expansion Slot Connectors

Adapter Cards

The openness of the IBM PC XT and AT architectures, coupled with their overwhelming popularity, led companies to develop a wide assortment of expansion devices for them. Most of these devices communicate with the basic system through **adapter cards** that plug into the expansion slots of the computer's main board, as illustrated in Figure 1-25. They typically contain the interfacing and controller circuitry for the peripheral. However, in some cases the entire peripheral may be included on the adapter card.

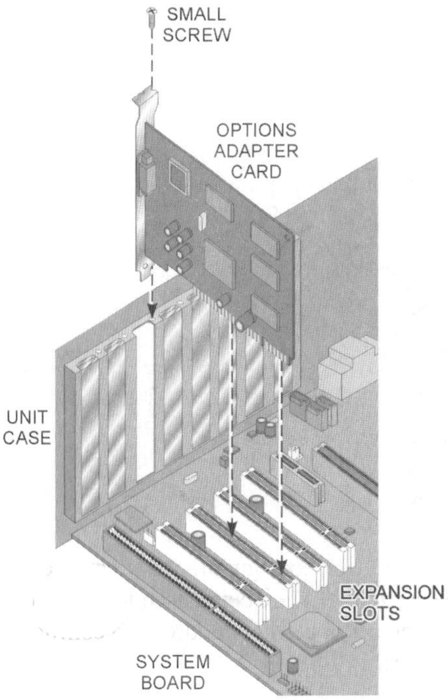

adapter cards

Figure 1-25: Plugging in a Typical Adapter Card

This expansion approach enables a wide variety of peripheral devices to be added to the basic system to modify it for particular applications. For example, adapter cards allow less expensive devices to be used with an introductory system and yet still allow high-end, high-performance peripherals to be used with the same system for advanced applications.

There are three important characteristics associated with any adapter card:

- function
- expansion slot connector style
- size

Many companies have developed expansion cards and devices for different types of computer applications. These include I/O controllers, disk drive controllers, video controllers, modems, and proprietary input/output devices, such as scanners.

The adapter cards in the original IBM PC were 13.2"l x 4.2"h. The PC normally came with a disk drive adapter card and a video card. These units were referred to as **full-size adapter cards**. They were so long that plastic guide rails were present at the front of the system unit to keep them from flexing due to system heating. A smaller (6.0"l x 4.2"h) printer adapter card was also made available for the PC. This size card is referred to as a **half-size card**. When the AT appeared the I/O cards became more powerful and taller (13.2"l x 4.8"h).

full-size adapter cards

half-size card

The AT cards became the standard against which later I/O cards have been measured. Like system boards, adapter cards have developed into smaller, more powerful units. Most current adapter cards are **2/3-size cards**, half-size cards, or smaller cards. In addition, the height of the cards has been significantly reduced. Many adapters are only half the height, or less, of the original AT cards. Therefore, they are referred to as **half-height cards**.

2/3-size cards

half-height cards

The only real requirements for adapter cards now are that they fit securely in the expansion slot, cover the slot opening in the rear of the system unit, and provide standard connectors for the types of devices they serve. Various adapter card designs are depicted in Figure 1-26. In this example, all of the cards employ an ISA edge connector. The same I/O functions and card sizes can be used to create cards for all of the other expansion connector types.

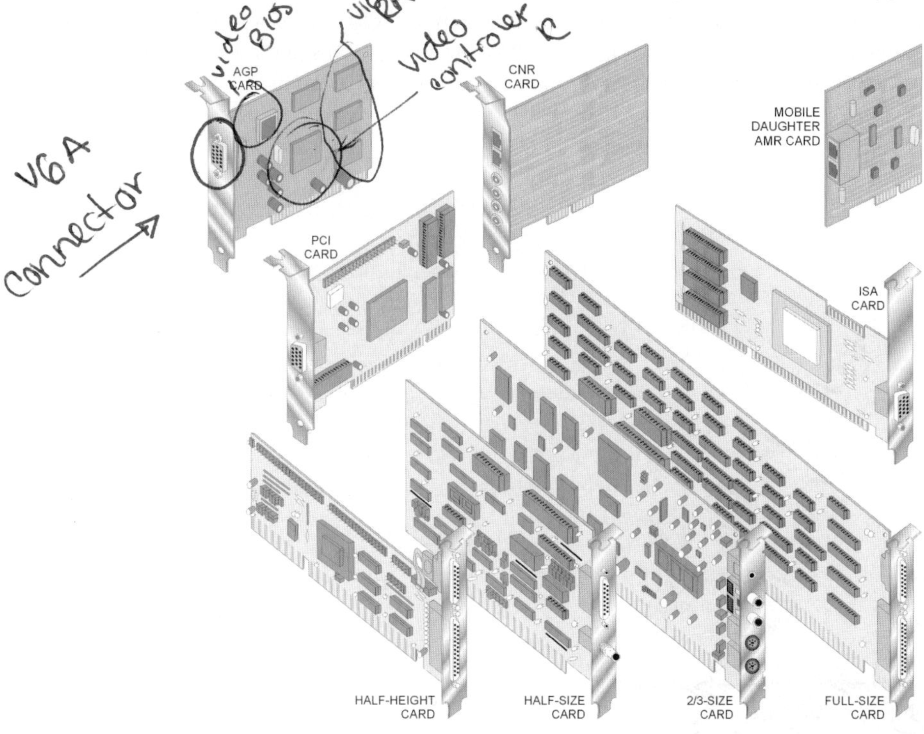

Figure 1-26: Adapter Card Designs

Most early adapter cards employed hardware jumpers, or configuration switches, that enabled them to be configured specifically for the system they were being used in. The user had to set up the card for operation and solve any interrupt or memory addressing conflicts that occurred. Such cards are referred to as **legacy cards**.

legacy cards

In newer PnP systems, adapter cards have the ability to identify themselves to the system during the startup process, along with supplying information about what type of device they are, how they are configured, and what resources they need access to. In addition, these cards must be able to be reconfigured by the system software if a conflict is detected between it and another system device.

Prior to the Pentium-based system boards, two types of options adapter cards were traditionally supplied as standard equipment in most desktop and tower PC systems. These were a **video adapter card** and a **multi-I/O adapter card**. However, in Pentium units, the MI/O functions have been built into the system board. Similarly, both the video and I/O functions are an integral part of the system board in portable systems.

video adapter card

multi-I/O Adapter card

Video Adapter Cards

The video adapter card provides the interface between the system board and the display monitor.

Monochrome Display Adapter (MDA)

Color Graphic Adapter (CGA)

Video Graphic Array (VGA)

The original IBM PCs and XTs offered two types of display adapters, a **Monochrome** (single color) **Display Adapter** (**MDA**) and a **Color Graphic Adapter** (**CGA**). Both of these units also included the system's first parallel printer port connector.

These initial units have been followed by a number of improved and enhanced video adapters and monitors. The most common type of video adapter card currently in use is the **Video Graphic Array** (**VGA**) card, like the one depicted in Figure 1-27. The system uses it to control video output operations.

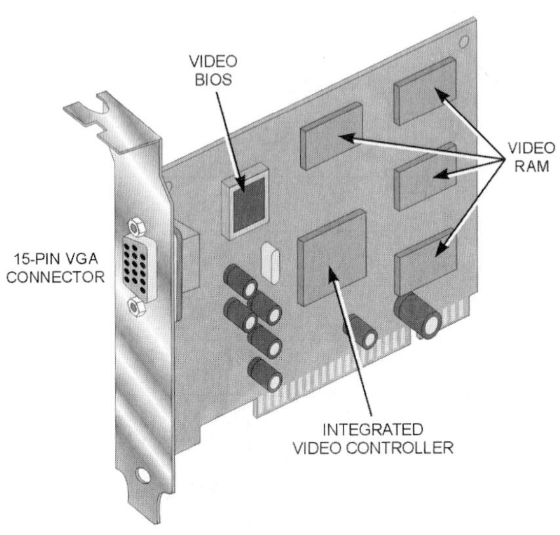

**Figure 1-27:
A Typical VGA Card**

Integrated Video Controller

Unlike most other computer components, the VGA video standard uses analog signals and circuitry rather than digital signals. The main component of most video adapter cards is an ASIC device called the **Integrated Video Controller**. It is a microprocessor-like chip that oversees the operation of the entire adapter. It is capable of accessing RAM and ROM memory units on the card. The video RAM chips hold the information that is to be displayed on the screen. Their size determines the card's video and color capacities.

Super VGA

In addition to offering vastly improved color production capabilities, VGA provided superior resolution capabilities. Standard VGA resolution is defined as 720 x 400 pixels using 16 colors in text mode, and 640 x 480 pixels using 16 on-screen colors in graphics mode. However, improved-resolution VGA systems, referred to as **Super VGA**s, are now commonly available in formats of 1024 x 768 with 256 colors, 1024 x 768 with 16 colors, and 800 x 600 with 256 colors. The SVGA definition continues to expand, with video controller capabilities ranging up to 1280 x 1024 (with reduced color capabilities) currently available in the market.

Extended Graphics Array

XGA

IBM produced its own **Extended Graphics Array** standard, called the **XGA**. This standard was capable of both 800 x 600 and 1024 x 768 resolutions, but added a 132-column, 400-scan line resolution. Unfortunately, IBM based the original XGA on interlaced monitors, and therefore never received a large following.

The maximum resolution/color capabilities of a particular VGA adapter are ultimately dependent on the amount of on-board memory the adapter had installed. The standard 640 x 480 display format, using 16 colors, requires nearly 256 KB of video memory to operate (640x480x4/8=153,600 bytes). With 512 KB of video memory installed, the resolution can be improved to 1024 x 768, but only 16 colors are possible (1024x768x4/8=393,216 bytes). To achieve full 1024 x 768 resolution with 256 colors, the video memory has to be expanded to a full 1 MB (1024x768x8/8=786,432 bytes). Access to this memory is very flexible.

Standard VGA monitors employ a 31.5 kHz horizontal scanning rate, while Super VGA monitors use frequencies between 35 and 48 kHz for their horizontal sync, depending on the **vertical refresh rate** of the adapter card. Standard VGA monitors repaint the screen (vertical refresh) at a frequency of 60 or 70 Hz, while Super VGA vertical scanning occurs at frequencies of 56, 60, and 72 Hz. A summary of the different video standards is presented in Table 1-1.

vertical refresh rate

Table 1-1: Video Standards

STANDARD	MODE	RESOLUTION (HXV PIXELS)	A/N DISPLAY	A/N CHARACTER	REFRESH RATE	HORIZONTAL SWEEP RATE	BUFFER ADDRESS
MDA (Monochrome Display Adapter)	Alphanumeric (A/N)	720 x 348 720 x 348	80 x 25	7 x 9 in 9 x 14	50/60	(Non-interlaced	B0000–B7FFF B0000–B7FFF B0000–BFFFF
CGA (Color Graphics Adapter)	(A/N) Low-resolution Medium-resoluti on High-resolution (APA) All Points Addressable graphics	640 x 200 160 x 100 320 x 200 640 x 200	80 x 25	7 x 7 in 8 x 8	60	15 KHz	B8000–BBFFF
HGA (Hercules Graphics Adapter)	A/N Diag/Half/Full Graphics	720 x 348	80 x 25	7 x 9 in 9 x 14	50	18.1 KHz	B0000–BFFFF
EGA (Extended Graphics Adapter)	A/N Graphics	640 x 350 640 x 350	80 x 25 80 x 43	7 x 9 in 8 x 14	60 Hz	22.1 KHz	0A0000
VGA (Video Graphics Array Adapter)	Text Graphics	720 x 400 640 x 480	80 x 25 80 x 43	9 x 16	60 or 70 Hz	31.5 KHz	0A0000–0BFFFF
Super VGA (SVGA)	Text Graphics	1280 x 1024 1024 x 768 800 x 600	80 x 25 80 x 43	9 x 16	50, 60, or 72	35-48 KHz	0A0000–0BFFFF
XGA	Text Graphics	1024 x 768 800 x 600	132 x 25	9 x 16 8 x 16	44/70	35.5 KHz	0A0000–0BFFFF

The adapter also has a **video BIOS ROM** that is similar to the ROM BIOS on the system board. This BIOS acts as an extension of the system BIOS and is located between address C0000h and C7FFFh. It is used to store firmware routines that are specific only to video functions. This example supports 27 distinct modes of operation, as described in Table 1-2. These modes include various character-box sizes and resolution selections. It also includes two different methods of storing screen data in the video memory. The first method is the **A/N (Alphanumeric) mode**, which is used for text operations. The second method is an **All Points Addressable (APA)** mode, which is normally used for graphics applications.

video BIOS ROM

A/N (Alphanumeric) mode

All Points Addressable (APA) mode

Table 1-2: Video BIOS Mode Table

MODE (HEX)	T/G	COLOR	BOX SIZE	ALPHA SIZE	SCREEN SIZE	BUFFER START	PG	HSYNE (KHz)	VSYNE (Hz)	CRYSTAL (MHz)	RAM (kB)
0,1	A/N	16	8 x 8	40 x 25	320 x 200	B8000	8	31.5	70	25.175	256
2,3	A/N	16	8 x 8	80 x 25	640 x 200	B8000	8	31.5	70	25.175	256
0*,1*	A/N	16	8 x 14	40 x 25	320 x 350	B8000	8	31.5	70	25.175	256
2*,3*	A/N	16	8 x 14	80 x 25	640 x 350	B8000	8	31.5	70	25.175	256
0+,1+	A/N	16	9 x 16	40 x 25	360 x 400	B8000	8	31.5	70	28.322	256
2+,3+	A/N	16	9 x 16	80 x 25	720 x 400	B8000	8	31.5	70	38.322	256
4,5	APA	4	8 x 8	40 x 25	320 x 200	B8000	1	31.5	70	25.175	256
6	APA	2	8 x 8	80 x 25	640 x 200	B8000	1	31.5	70	25.175	256
7	A/N	-	9 x 14	80 x 25	720 x 350	B0000	8	31.5	70	28.322	256
7+	A/N	-	9 x 16	80 x 25	720 x 400	B0000	8	31.5	70	28.322	256
D	APA	16	8 x 8	40 x 25	320 x 200	A0000	8	31.5	70	25.175	256
E	APA	16	8 x 8	80 x 25	640 x 200	A0000	4	31.5	70	25.175	256
F	APA	-	8 x 14	80 x 25	640 x 350	A0000	2	31.5	70	25.175	256
10	APA	16	8 x 14	80 x 25	640 x 350	A0000	2	31.5	70	25.175	256
11	APA	2	8 x 16	80 x 30	640 x 480	A0000	1	31.5	60	25.175	256
12	APA	16	8 x 16	80 x 30	640 x 480	A0000	1	31.5	60	25.175	256
13	APA	256	8 x 8	40 x 25	320 x 200	A0000	1	31.5	70	25.175	256
18	A/N	16	9 x 16	80 x 30	720 x 480	B8000	1	31.5	60	28.322	256
19	A/N	16	9 x 8	80 x 43	720 x 473	B8000	1	31.5	70	28.322	256
1A	A/N	16	9 x 8	80 x 60	720 x 480	B8000	1	31.5	60	28.322	256
1B	A/N	16	9 x 16	132 x 25	1188 x 350	B8000	1	31.2	70	40.0	256
1C	A/N	16	9 x 16	132 x 30	1188 x 480	B8000	1	31.2	60	40.0	256
1D	A/N	16	9 x 8	132 x 43	1188 x 473	B8000	1	31.2	70	40.0	256
1E	A/N	16	9 x 8	132 x 60	1188 x 480	B8000	1	31.2	60	40.0	256
1F	APA	16	8 x 8	100 x 75	800 x 600	A0000	1	31.5	57	36	256
1F V	APA	16	8 x 8	100 x 75	800 x 600	A0000	1	48.0	70	50.35	256
20	APA	16	8 x 16	120 x 45	960 x 720	A0000	1	31.5	43 / 43	44.9	512

DAC (Digital-to-Analog Converter)

The video controller also contains the video **DAC** (**Digital-to-Analog Converter**) that converts digital data in the controller into the analog signal used to drive the display. The video output connector is a three-row DB-15 female connector used with analog VGA displays.

Other Adapter Cards

Floppy-Disk Drive Controller (FDC)

Hard-Disk Drive Controller/Interface (HDC)

game port

parallel printer port

serial ports

In pre-Pentium systems, an adapter card referred to as a Multi I/O (MI/O) adapter card, was a standard part of the system. These cards integrated common AT-compatible I/O functions into a single options adapter card to provide an array of interfaces for the system. Most MI/O cards combine a **Floppy-Disk Drive Controller** (**FDC**), an IDE **Hard-Disk Drive Controller/Interface** (**HDC**), a **game port**, a **parallel printer port**, and two **serial ports** all on one board. Prior to VLSI technology, the circuitry involved in each of these functions required a separate adapter card. However, the MI/O adapter combines the circuitry for all of these functions into a single ASIC device. Figure 1-28 depicts a typical MI/O adapter showing a sample of its connectors and configuration jumpers.

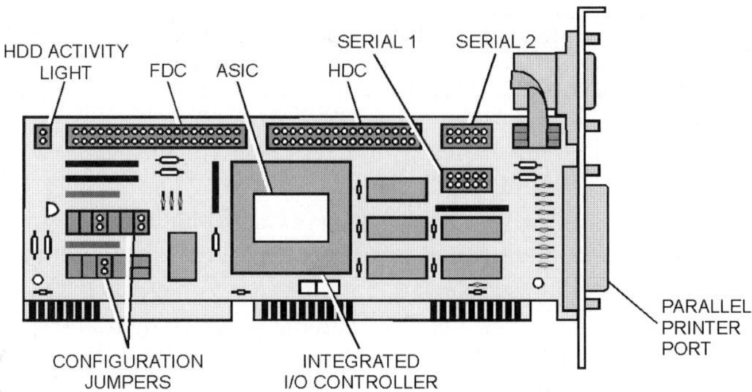

Figure 1-28: A Typical MI/O Adapter

In a Pentium class computer most of the support for standard I/O port connections has been moved to the system board and the MI/O functions have been integrated into the system board's chipset. Therefore the MI/O card has disappeared as a standard item. However, there are still occasions, such as upgrading disk drives in older machines and substituting for defective ports and controllers on newer boards, where it makes sense to install an I/O card in an expansion slot.

While the Multi I/O card has largely disappeared and the video display adapter card is typically the only adapter card required in the system, many other input/output functions can be added to the system through adapter cards. Some of the most popular I/O cards in modern Pentium systems include:

Modem cards

Local Area Network cards

Sound cards

- **Modem cards** - used to carry out data communications through telephone lines.
- **Local Area Network cards** - used to connect the local system to a group of other computers so they can share data and resources.
- **Sound cards** - used to provide high-quality audio output to the computer system.

Figure 1-29 shows samples of these cards and their connections. While they represent the most options added to computer systems, there are many other I/O devices that can be plugged into expansion slots to enhance the operation of the system.

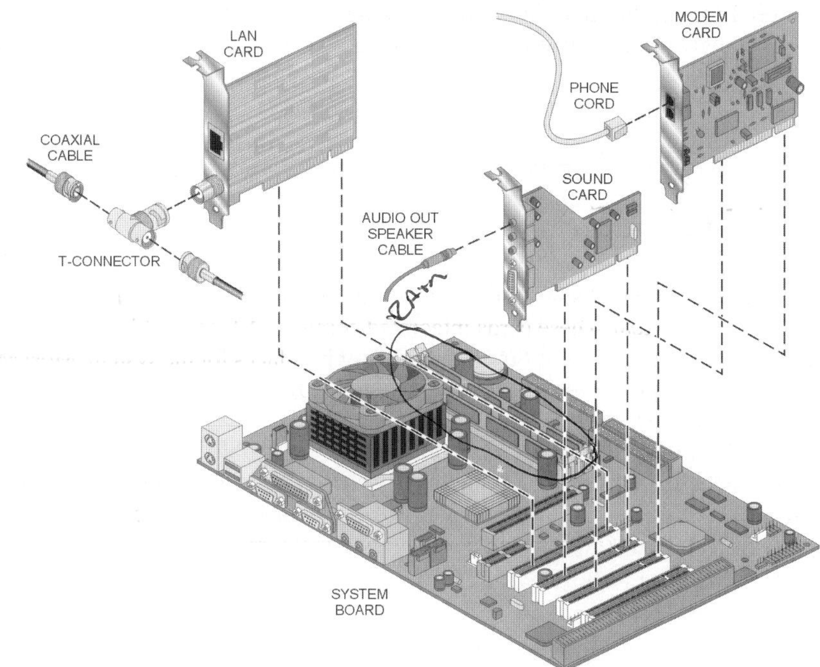

Figure 1-29: Typical I/O Cards

The System Speaker

The system's primary audio output device is a 2.25-inch, 8-ohm, ½-watt speaker, similar to the one depicted in Figure 1-30. This unit can be located behind the vertical vents in the front panel or under the power supply unit in a small plastic retainer. The system uses the speaker to prompt the user during certain events and to indicate certain errors in the system, such as video display failures, which can't be displayed on the screen. The user can also control the operation of the speaker through software. Its output frequency range extends through the complete audio range and, with proper programming, can be used to create arcade sounds and music.

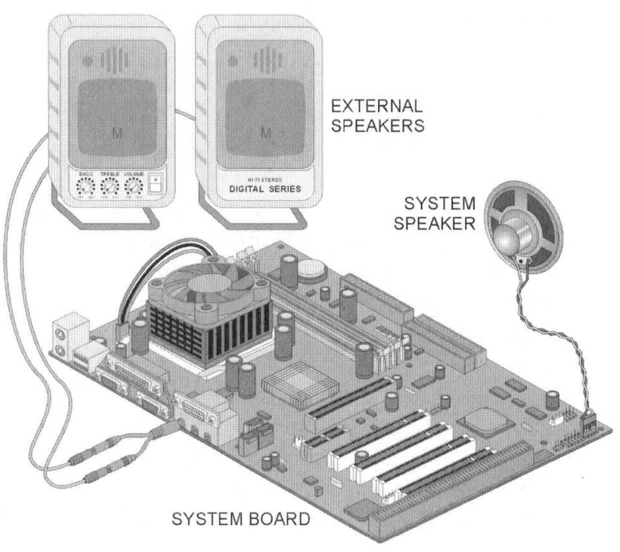

Figure 1-30: System Speaker

Storage Devices

Programs and data disappear from the system's RAM when the computer is turned off. In addition, IC RAM devices tend to be too expensive to construct large memories that can hold multiple programs and large amounts of data. Therefore, storage systems that can be used for long-term data storage are desirable as a second level of memory.

With this in mind, a number of secondary memory technologies have been developed to extend the computer's memory capabilities and store data on a more permanent basis. These systems tend to be too slow to be used directly with the computer's microprocessor. The secondary memory unit holds the information and transfers it in batches to the computer's faster internal memory when requested.

> From the beginning, most secondary memory systems have involved storing binary information in the form of magnetic charges on moving magnetic surfaces. However, optical storage methods such as CD-ROM and DVD have quickly moved to rival magnetic storage for popularity.

Magnetic storage has remained popular due to three factors:

- Low cost-per-bit of storage
- Intrinsically non-volatile nature
- It has successfully evolved upward in capacity

The major magnetic storage media are floppy disks, hard disks, and tape.

tracks

In magnetic disk systems, information is stored as magnetized spots arranged in concentric circles around the disk. These circles are referred to as **tracks** and are numbered, beginning with 0, from the outside edge inward. The number of tracks may range from 40 up to 2048, depending on the type of disk and drive being used.

cylinder

In hard disk drives, multiple disks are stacked together on a common spindle. The corresponding tracks of each surface are logically arranged to form a **cylinder** (i.e., all of the track-0 tracks are taken together to form cylinder-0).

sectors

Since the tracks at the outer edge of the disk are longer than those at its center, each track is divided into an equal number of equal-sized blocks called **sectors.** This arrangement is used so that the logic circuitry for processing data going to, or coming from the disk can be as simple as possible. The number of sectors on a track may range from 8 to more than 60, depending on the disk and drive type, and the operating system software used to format it.

As an example, a typical IBM floppy disk will have 40 or 80 tracks per surface, with each track divided into 8, 9, or 18 sectors each. In a PC-compatible system each sector holds 512 bytes of data. The organizational structure of a typical magnetic disk is illustrated in Figure 1-31.

TEST TIP

Be able to describe the organization of PC-compatible disks (i.e., sectors, tracks, cylinders) and recognize examples of them associated with different disk types.

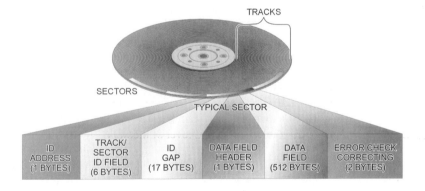

TRACKS

SECTORS

TYPICAL SECTOR

ID ADDRESS (1 BYTES)	TRACK/ SECTOR ID FIELD (6 BYTES)	ID GAP (17 BYTES)	DATA FIELD HEADER (1 BYTES)	DATA FIELD (512 BYTES)	ERROR CHECK CORRECTING (2 BYTES)

Figure 1-31: The Organizational Structure of a Magnetic Disk

For more in-depth information about how magnetic disk systems work, refer to the Electronic Reference Shelf located on the CD that accompanies this book.

REFERENCE SHELF

Multiple tracks

serpentine

In magnetic tape systems, data is stored in sequential tracks along the length of the tape, as depicted in Figure 1-32. Each track is divided into equal-sized blocks. The blocks are separated by small gaps of unrecorded space. **Multiple tracks** can be recorded across the width of the tape. Using multiple read/write heads, the tracks can be read simultaneously as the tape moves forward. The tracks can also be read in a **serpentine** manner, using a single read/write head.

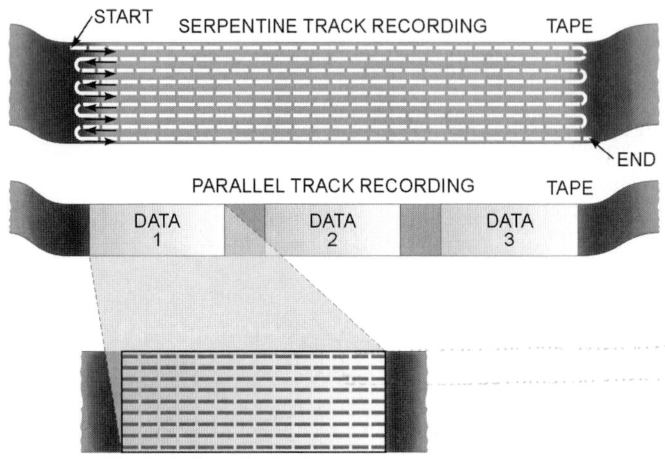

Figure 1-32: Formats for Storing Data on Magnetic Tape

While it is possible to directly access any of the sectors on a magnetic disk, the sections on the tape can only be accessed in a linear order. To access the information in block 32 of the tape, the previous 31 blocks must pass through the drive.

Tape generally represents a cheaper storage option, but its inherent slowness, due to its sequential nature, makes it less desirable than rotating magnetic disks. The disks offer much quicker access to large blocks of data, at a cost that is still affordable to most users.

Disk Drives

floppy disk drive (FDD)

hard disk drive (HDD)

CD-ROM drive

The system unit normally comes from the manufacturer with a **floppy disk drive** (**FDD**), a **hard disk drive** (**HDD**), and a **CD-ROM drive** installed, as illustrated in Figure 1-33.

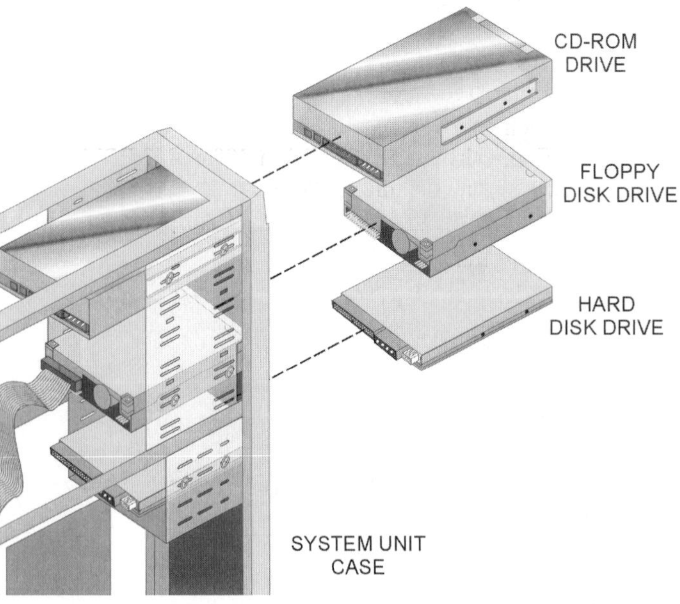

Figure 1-33: The Disk Drives of a Typical System

The system's disk-drive capacity is not usually limited to the standard units installed. In most cases, the system cabinet is designed to hold additional disk drive units. These units can be an additional FDD, HDD, or CD-ROM unit, or a combination of these devices. Although three FDD units could physically be installed in most systems, the typical floppy-drive controller supports only two drives.

One or more HDD units can be installed in the system unit, along with the floppy drive(s). The system should normally be set up to recognize a single hard disk unit in the system as the **C: drive**. However, a single, physical hard disk drive can be partitioned into two or more volumes that the system recognizes as **logical drives** C:, D:, and so on.

C: drive

logical drives

Floppy Drives

The most widely used data storage systems in personal computers are floppy disk drive units. These units store information in the form of tiny, magnetized spots on small flexible diskettes that can be removed from the drive unit. Once the information has been written on the diskette, it will remain there until the disk is magnetically erased or written over. The information remains on the diskette even if it is removed from the disk drive or if power is removed from the system. Whenever the information is required by the system, it can be obtained by inserting the disk back into the drive and causing the software to read it from the disk.

The floppy disks are relatively inexpensive and are easy to transport and store. In addition, they can easily be removed and replaced if they become full. Figure 1-34 depicts the major components of a typical floppy disk drive unit.

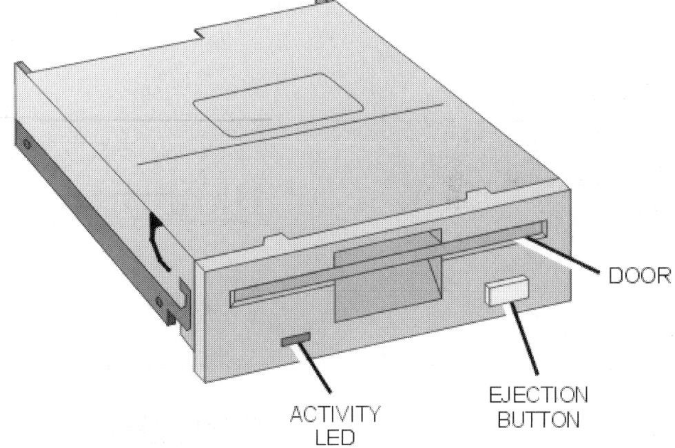

Figure 1-34: The Floppy Disk Drive System

The standard floppy disk drive for 8088-based machines was the 5.25-inch, full-height and half-height drive. These drives used diskettes capable of storing 368,640 bytes (referred to as 360 KB of information. The term **half-height** was used to describe drive units that were half as tall as the **full-height** drive units used with the original IBM PC. Smaller 3.5-inch half-height drives, capable of storing 720 KB (737,280 bytes) of information, were also used with 8088-based computers.

The PC AT and its compatibles originally used high-density, 5.25-inch drives that could hold over 1,200,000 bytes (1.2 MB) of information. In newer machines, high-density, 3.5-inch floppy drives capable of holding 1.44 MB (1,474,560 bytes) are the norm.

half-height

full-height

The typical floppy disk, depicted in Figure 1-35, is a flexible, 3.5-inch diameter mylar disk that has been coated with a ferromagnetic material. It is encased in a protective, hard plastic envelope that contains a low-friction liner which removes dust and contaminants from the disk as it turns within the envelope. Typical floppy drives turn the disk at 300 or 360 RPM and the drive's R/W heads ride directly on the disk surface. Information is written to or read from the disk as it spins inside the envelope. The small LED on the front of the disk drive unit lights up whenever either of these operations is in progress.

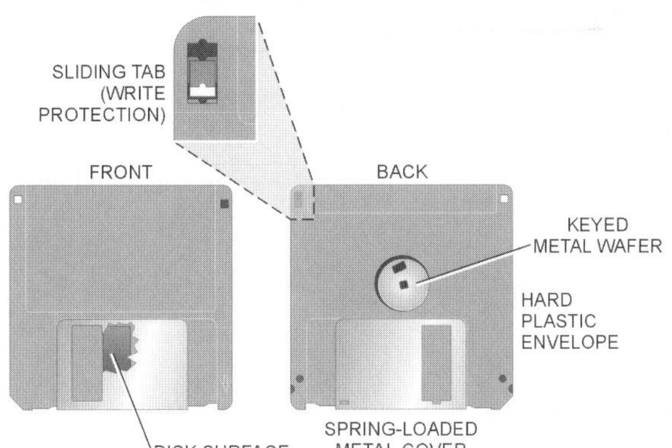

Figure 1-35: Floppy Disks

The drive's read/write heads access the disk surface through a spring-loaded metal cover, which the drive unit moves out of the way. The drive spindle turns the disk by engaging a keyed metal wafer attached to the lower side of the disk. A small, sliding tab in the left-front corner of the envelope performs a write-protect function for the disk. If the tab covers the opening, the disk may be written to. If, however, the opening is clear, the disk is said to be "Write Protected," and the drive will not write information on the disk.

Current PC systems use a type of floppy disk referred to as Double-Sided, High-Density (DS-HD). This means that the disk can be used on both sides, and that advanced magnetic recording techniques may be used to effectively double or triple the storage capacity previously available using older recording techniques. These diskettes can hold 1.44 MB of information using the MS-DOS operating system.

This type of floppy disk drive can also operate with an older type of floppy disk that is referred to as a Double-Sided, Double-Density (DS-DD) diskette. This notation indicates that the disks are constructed so that they can be used on both sides, and that they can support recording techniques that double the storage capacity available with older recording techniques.

Hard Drives

The system's data storage potential is extended considerably by high-speed, high-capacity hard disk drive units like the one shown in Figure 1-36. These units store much more information than floppy disks do. Modern hard drives typically have storage capacities ranging up to several gigabytes. Hard drives also differ from floppy disk units in that they use rigid disks that are permanently sealed in the drive unit (non-removable).

Figure 1-36: Inside a Hard Disk Drive

The disks are aluminum platters coated with a nickel-cobalt or ferromagnetic material. Two or more platters are usually mounted on a common spindle, with spacers between them, to allow data to be recorded on both sides of each disk. The drive's read/write mechanism is sealed inside a dust-free compartment along with the disks.

Modern hard disk drives come in sizes of 5.25-, 3.5-, and 2.5-inch diameters. Of these sizes, the 3.5-inch version is by far the most popular due to their association with personal and business desktop computers. Although popular for many years, 5.25-inch hard drives are quickly disappearing from the marketplace. Conversely, the popularity of the 2.5-inch drives is growing with the rising popularity of laptop and notebook-size computers. Hard drives ranging into gigabytes of storage are available for these machines.

The hard disk drives normally used with personal computers typically contain between 1 and 5 disks that are permanently mounted inside a sealed enclosure, along with the **Read/Write (R/W)** head mechanisms. There is one R/W head for each disk surface. The platters are typically turned at a speed of 5400 RPM. This high rotational speed creates a thin cushion of air around the disk surface that causes the R/W heads to fly just above the disk.

Read/Write (R/W)

The major differences between floppy and hard disk drives are storage capacity, data transfer rates, and cost.

Another difference to note is the fact that hard disk drives tend to be more delicate than floppy drives. Therefore, they require some special handling considerations to prevent both damage to the unit and a loss of data. The disks in the HDD are not removable as floppy disks are. Therefore, it is possible to fill up a hard disk drive. When this occurs, it will be necessary to delete information from the unit to make room for new information to be stored.

Conversely, floppy disks are prone to damage due to mishandling, static, temperature, etc. In addition, they are easy to misplace and they provide limited storage of application software.

CD-ROM Drives

Soon after the **Compact Disc (CD)**—the term "disc" is used in place of disk to denote the fact that it is an optical disc instead of a magnetic disk—became popular for storing audio signals on optical material, the benefits of storing computer information in this manner became apparent. The typical CD can hold upwards of 600 MB of programs and data on a single, inexpensive, removable media. Originally, the information had to be placed on the CD by a disc manufacturer. Therefore, early discs used to hold digital data for computers were referred to as **CD-ROMs**. The ROM designation refers to the fact that most of the original discs and drives were read-only in nature. While newer optical technologies have produced low-cost drives and discs that can be written and erased multiple times, the CD-ROM title is still commonly associated with this type of device. Figure 1-37 shows the components generally associated with a CD-ROM drive system.

CD-ROMs

Data is written on a CD digitally on a light-sensitive material by a powerful, highly-focused laser beam.

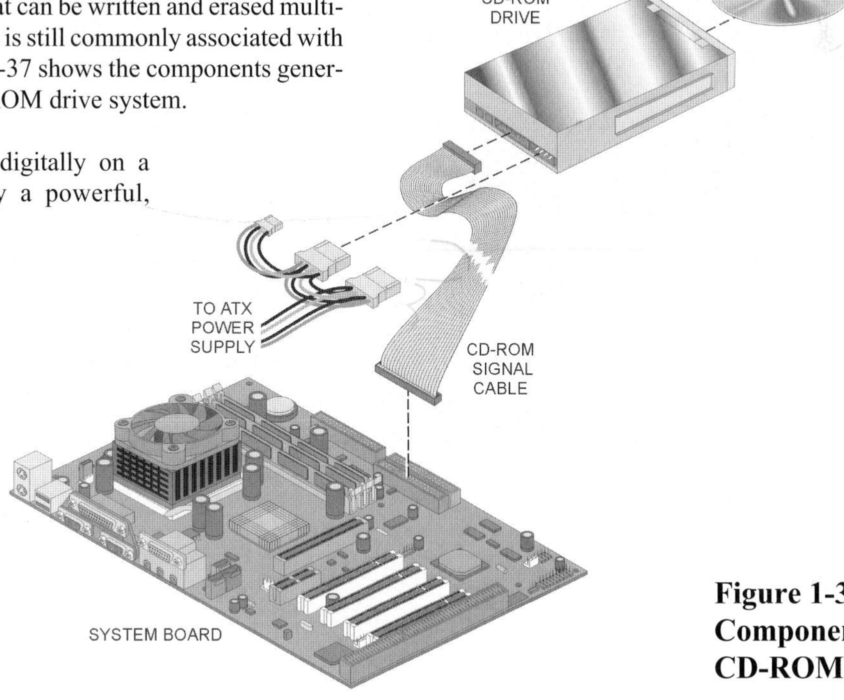

Figure 1-37: Components of a CD-ROM System

pits

lands

The writing laser is pulsed with the modulated data to be stored on the disc. When the laser is pulsed, a microscopic blister is burned into the optical material, causing it to reflect light differently from the material around it. The blistered areas are referred to as **pits**, while the areas between them are called **lands**. Figure 1-38 illustrates the writing of data on the optical disc.

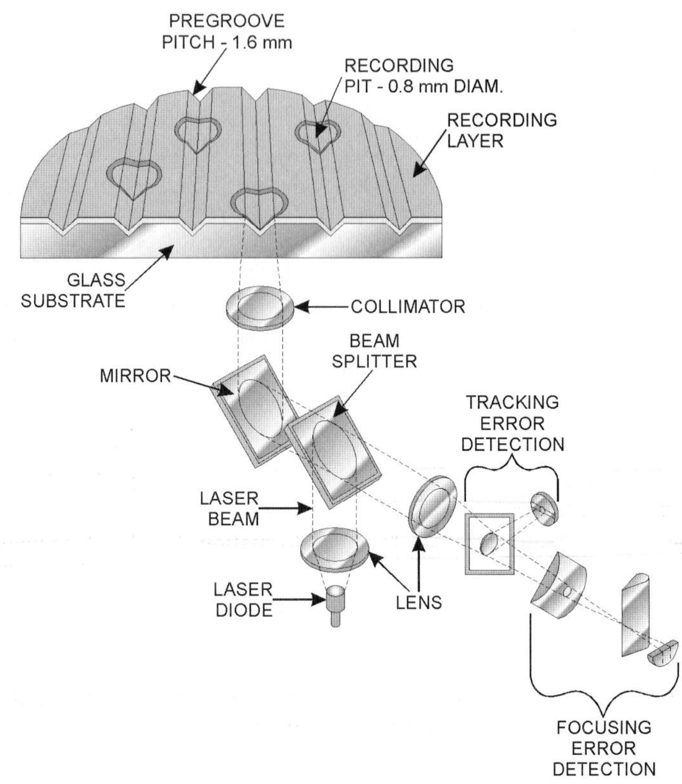

Figure 1-38: Writing on a CD-ROM Drive

The recorded data is read from the disc by scanning it with a lower-power, continuous laser beam. The laser diode emits the highly-focused, narrow beam that is reflected back from the disc. The reflected beam passes through a prism, and is bent 90 degrees, where it is picked up by the diode detector and converted into an electrical signal. Only the light reflected from a land on the disc is picked up by the detector. Light that strikes a pit is scattered and is not detected. The lower power level used for reading the disc ensures that the optical material is not affected during the read operation. With an audio CD, the digital data retrieved from the disk is passed through a digital-to-analog converter (DAC) to reproduce the audio sound wave. However, this is not required for digital computer systems, since the information is already in a form acceptable to the computer. Therefore, CD players designed for use in computer systems are referred to as **CD-ROM drives**, to differentiate them from audio CD players. Otherwise, the mechanics of operation are very similar between the two devices.

CD-ROM drives

single-speed (1x) drives

double-speed (2X) drives

triple-speed (3X) drives

CD-ROM drives that operate at the speed of a conventional audio CD player are called **single-speed (1x) drives**. Advanced drives that spin twice, and three times, as fast as the typical CD player are referred to as **double-speed (2X) drives**, **triple-speed (3X) drives**, and so forth. Single-speed drives transfer data at a rate of 150 KB per second. Double-speed drive transfers occur at 300 KB per second, and so on. Most manufacturers are now focusing on 24X and 32X drives.

CD-ROM drives are capable of playing audio CDs. However, a CD player will not be able to produce any output from the CD-ROM disc. CDs are classified by a color-coding system that corresponds to their intended use. CDs that contain digital data intended for use in a computer are referred to as **Yellow Book** CDs. **Red Book** CDs refer to those formatted to contain digital music. **Orange Book** refers to the standard for CDs that are used in WORM drives. **Green Book** CDs are used with interactive CD systems, and **Blue Book** CDs are those associated with laser disc systems.

Yellow Book
Red Book
Orange Book
Green Book
Blue Book

Tape Drives

Tape drive units are another popular type of information storage system. These systems can store large amounts of data on small **tape cartridges**, similar to the one depicted in Figure 1-39.

Tape drive units
tape cartridges

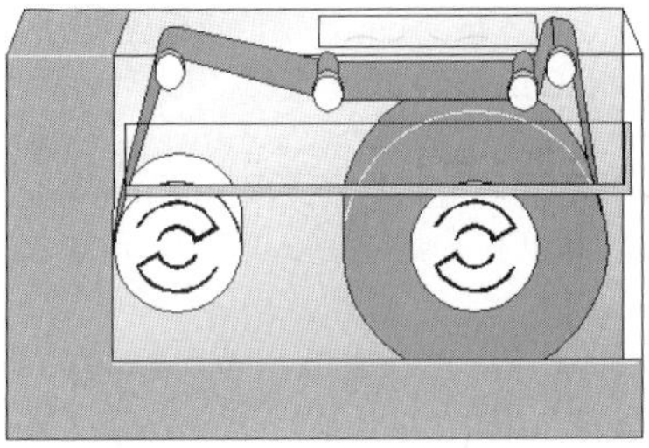

Figure 1-39: A Tape Cartridge

Tapes tend to be more economic that other magnetic media when storing large amounts of data. However, access to information stored on tape tends to be very slow. This is caused by the fact that, unlike disks, tape operates in a linear fashion. The tape transport must run all of the tape past the drive's R/W heads to access data that is physically stored at the end of the tape.

Therefore, tape drives are generally used to store large amounts of information that will not need to be accessed often, or quickly. Such applications include making **backup copies** of programs and data. This type of data security is a necessity with records such as business transactions, payroll, artwork, etc.

backup copies

Data backup has easily become the most widely used tape application. With the large amounts of information that can be stored on a hard disk drive, a disk crash is a very serious problem. If the drive crashes, all of the information stored on the disk can be destroyed. This can easily add up to billions of pieces of information. Therefore, an inexpensive method of storing data away from the hard drive is desirable.

Peripherals

Peripherals are devices and systems that are added to the basic system to extend its capabilities. These devices and systems can be divided into three general categories: **input systems**, **output systems**, and **memory systems**.

Peripherals
input systems
output systems
memory systems

keyboard

CRT monitor

mouse

character printer

The standard peripherals associated with PCs are the alphanumeric **keyboard** and the **CRT monitor**. With the rapid growth of GUI-oriented software, the **mouse** has become a common input peripheral as well. The next most common peripheral is the **character printer**. These peripherals are used to produce hard-copy output on paper.

Many other types of peripheral equipment are routinely added to the basic system. Most peripheral devices interact with the basic system through adapter cards that plug into the system board's expansion slots. The peripheral devices connect to the adapter cards through expansion slot openings in back of the system unit. As long as there are open expansion slots, or other standard I/O connectors, it is possible to add compatible devices to the system.

External Connections and Devices

Video Graphics Array (VGA)

As we have already mentioned, the standard peripherals used with PCs are keyboards, CRT monitors, and mice. Figure 1-40 depicts a sample system with these devices. Most PCs use detachable keyboards that are connected to the system by a coiled cable. This cable may plug into a 5-pin DIN or 6-pin mini-DIN connector located on the rear of the system board. The connector is normally keyed so that it cannot be misaligned. The most widely used display device for current PCs is the **Video Graphics Array** (**VGA**) color monitor. The monitor's signal cable connects to a 15-pin D-shell connector at the back of the system unit. A mouse can be connected to a PC by attaching it to a 9-pin D-shell or 6-pin mini-DIN connector at the rear of the system.

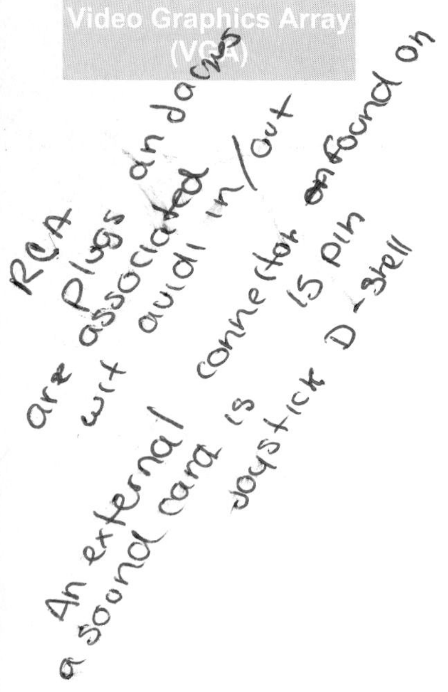

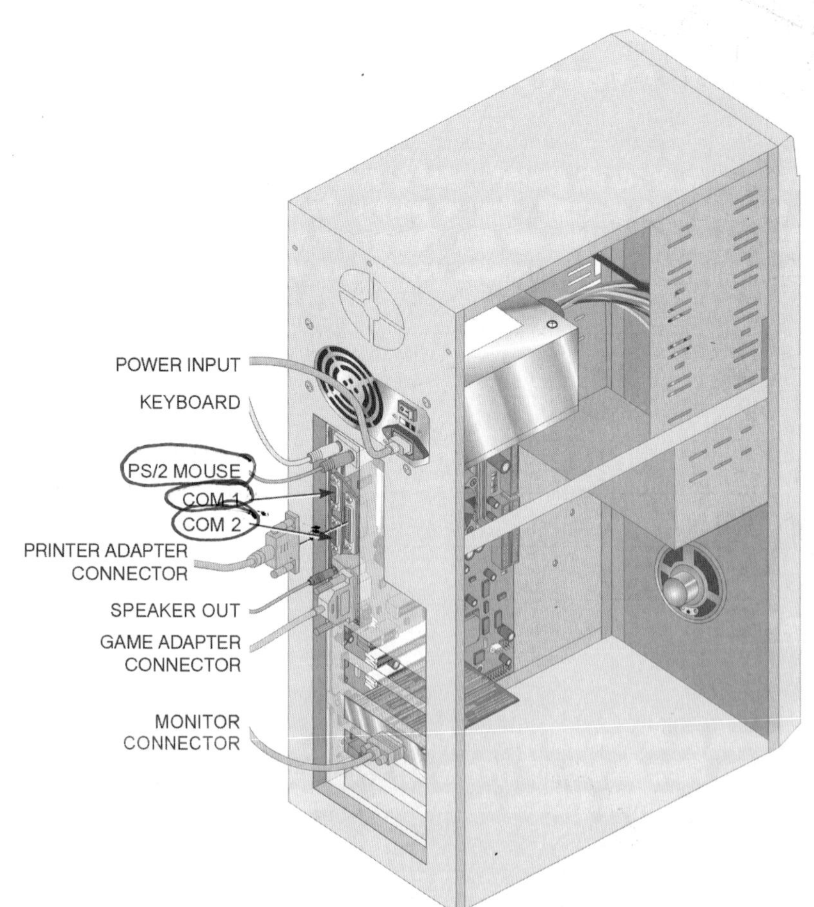

Figure 1-40: Typical PC Peripherals

As you can see, most peripheral devices interact with the basic system through adapter cards that plug into the system board's expansion slots. The peripheral devices connect to the adapter cards through expansion slot openings in back of the system unit. As long as there are open expansion slots, or other standard I/O connectors, it is possible to add compatible devices to the system. Figure 1-41 illustrates external connections for a basic AT-style system configuration.

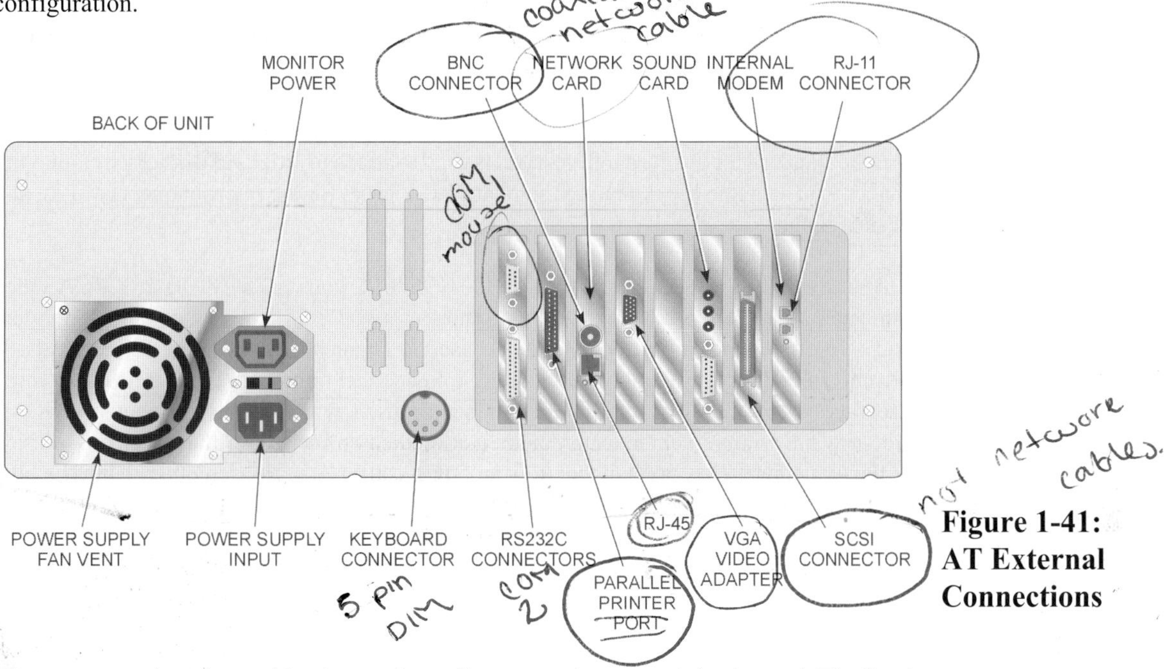

Figure 1-41: AT External Connections

The power supply unit provides three points of interest at the system's back panel. The first is the female power receptacle, which may be used to provide power to IBM PC-compatible monitors. Next to the monitor power receptacle is the power supply's input connector. The detachable power cord plugs into this socket. Beside the power connector is the power supply's fan vent. In a small opening near the power supply openings is the circular, five-pin DIN connector for connecting a keyboard to the system.

Across the remainder of the back panel are eight expansion-slot openings. Typical interface connections found in a basic system include two RS-232C connectors, a parallel printer port connector, and a game adapter connector. In this illustration, the game-port connector is located above the parallel-port connector. On other systems, the locations of the various connectors may vary. The last connector on the back panel is the video adapter's monitor connector. This example features a VGA-compatible, three-row, 15-pin RGB color-output port connector.

Figure 1-42 illustrates typical connectors found on the back of an ATX-style system.

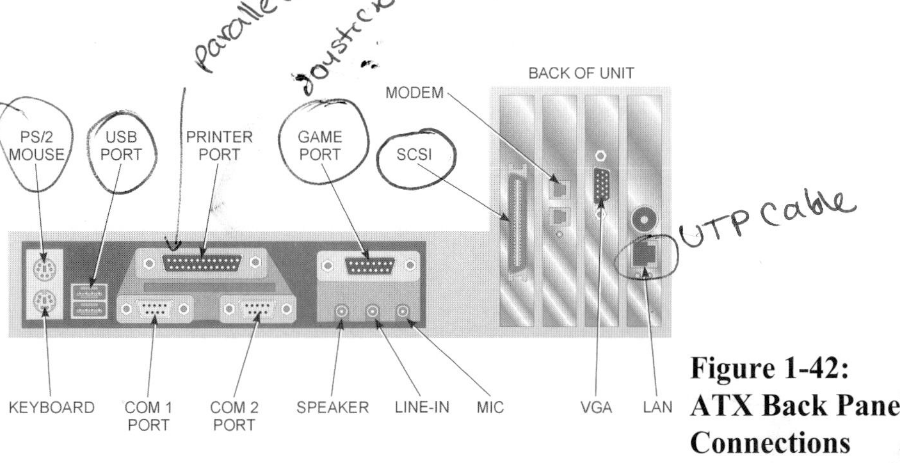

Figure 1-42: ATX Back Panel Connections

On the ATX back panel, many of the system board-related I/O functions have been grouped into a standardized block of connections as illustrated. The panel features two six-pin PS/2 mini-DIN connectors. The lower connector is for the keyboard, while the upper connector is intended for use with a PS/2 serial mouse. Because these connectors are physically identical, it is relatively easy to confuse them. Just to the right of the keyboard and mouse ports are two USB connectors for attaching USB devices to the system. The master I/O block contains two DB-9M COMM port connectors for use with serial devices and a DB-25F parallel-port connector for SPP, EPP, and ECP parallel devices. This board also features a game port and built-in audio connections. The DB-15F connector is the standard for the PC game port and is used to attach joysticks and other game-playing devices to. The audio block features standard RCA jacks for the microphone, audio-in, and speaker connections.

TEST TIP

Be aware that the mouse connector type is an important consideration in selecting a mouse for use.

Network Interface Card (NIC)

Unshielded Twisted Pair (UTP)

British Naval Connector (BNC)

In the expansion slots to the right of the ATX I/O block, you will see a DB-15F VGA video connector, a 50-pin Centronics SCSI bus connector, two RJ-11 jacks for an internal modem (one is for the phone line while the other is used to attach a traditional telephone handset), and an RJ-45/BNC combination for making LAN connections with the system's **Network Interface Card (NIC)**. The DB-15F connector used with VGA video devices uses a three-row pin arrangement to differentiate it from the two-row DB-15F connector specified for the game port. This prevents them from being confused with each other. With the NIC card, the RJ-45 jack is used with **Unshielded Twisted Pair (UTP)** LAN cabling, while the **British Naval Connector (BNC)** is provided for coaxial cable connections. Network cabling is discussed in more detail in Chapter 5—*Data Communications.*

Keyboards

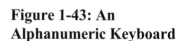

The keyboard type most widely used with desktop and tower units is a detachable, low-profile 101/102-key model depicted in Figure 1-43. These units are designed to provide the user with a high degree of mobility and functionality. The key tops are slightly concave to provide a comfortable feel to the typist. In addition, the key makes a noticeable tap when it bottoms out during a keystroke.

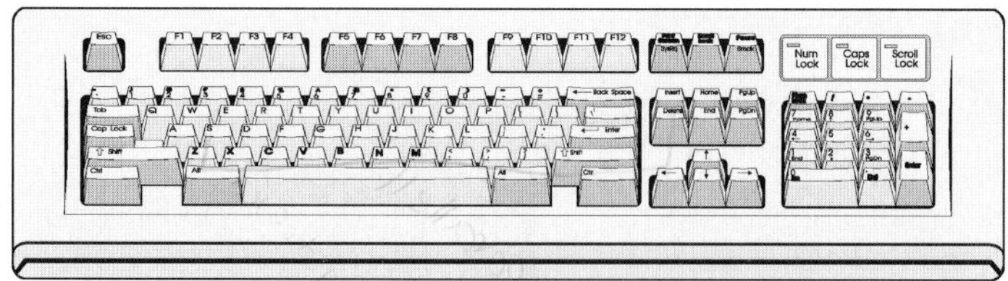

Figure 1-43: An Alphanumeric Keyboard

AT-style detachable keyboards use a round, 0.5", 5-pin DIN connector to plug into the PC's system board. The connection is most often made through a round opening in the rear of the system unit's case. In some case designs, a front-mounted 5-pin plug-in is included. The front-mounted connector is routed to the system board through an extension cable.

With the IBM PS/2 line, a smaller (0.25"), 6-pin mini-DIN connector was adopted. This connector type has been adopted in the ATX specification for both the mouse and keyboard. Other PC-compatibles use a modular, 6-pin AMP connector to interface the keyboard to the system. Figure 1-44 shows the various connection schemes used with detachable keyboards.

TEST TIP

Be aware that plugging non-hot swappable devices like the keyboard into the system while it is turned on can damage parts of the system.

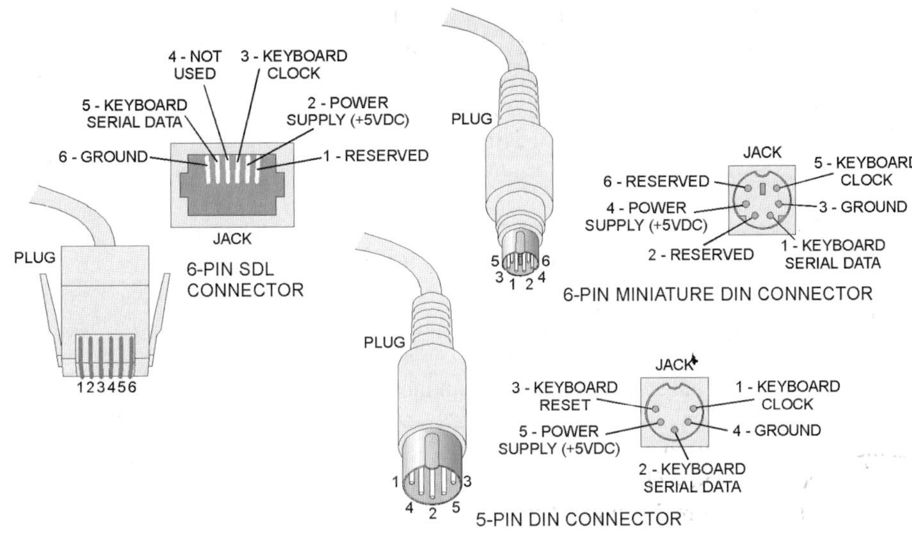

Figure 1-44: Connection Schemes for Detachable Keyboards

Video Displays

Desktop and tower units normally use a color **Cathode-Ray Tube** (**CRT**) display monitor, similar to the one shown in Figure 1-45, as standard video output equipment. The PC, PC/XT, and PC-AT often used monochrome (single-color) monitors. They could also use color monitors by simply adding a color video adapter card and monitor. The **color CRT monitor** is sometimes referred to as an **RGB monitor**, since the three primary colors that make a color CRT are red, green, and blue.

Cathode-Ray Tube (CRT)

color CRT monitor

RGB monitor

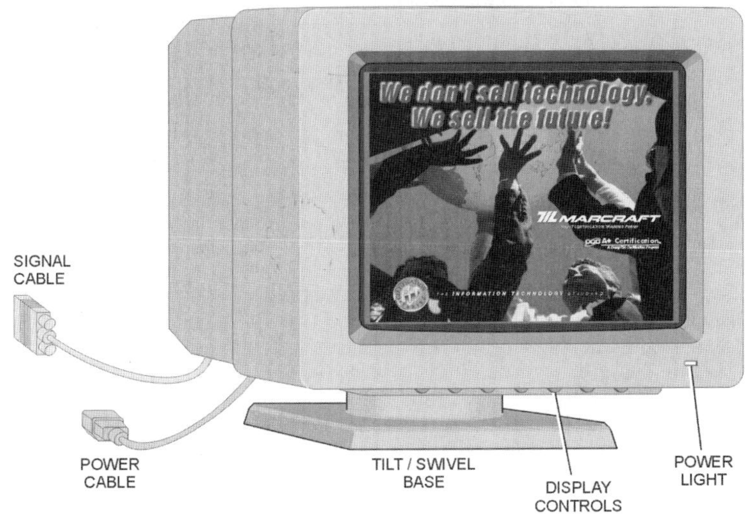

Figure 1-45: The CRT Display Monitor

In an AT-compatible system, the monitor can be plugged either into a commercial power receptacle, or into the special receptacle provided by the power supply at the rear of the unit. This option depends on the type of power cable provided by the manufacturer. There is a special adapter cable available to match a standard 120 Vac plug to this power supply receptacle. ATX-style power supplies do not provide a pass-through power connection for the monitor. The monitor's **signal cable** (connected to the video adapter card) permits the monitor to be positioned away from the system unit if desired.

signal cable

The display's normal external controls are brightness and contrast. These controls are located in different positions on the monitor depending on its manufacturer. There is also a power on/off switch on the monitor. Its location varies from model to model as well. If the monitor receives power through the system unit's power supply, the monitor's power switch can be set to On and the monitor will turn on and off along with the system.

Other Peripherals

Mice, joysticks, trackballs, and touch pads belong to a category of input devices called **pointing devices**. They are all small, handheld input devices that enable the user to interact with the system by moving a cursor or some other screen image around the display screen, and to choose options from an onscreen menu, instead of typing commands from a keyboard. Because pointing devices make it easier to interact with the computer than other types of input devices, they are, therefore, friendlier to the user.

pointing devices

The most widely used pointing device is the mouse. Mice are handheld devices that produce input data by being moved across a surface, such as a desktop. The mouse has become a standard input device for most systems because of the popularity of GUI-based software.

The **trackball mouse** detects positional changes through the movement of a rolling trackball that it rides on. As the mouse moves across a surface, the mouse circuitry detects the movement of the trackball and creates pulses that the system converts into positional information.

trackball mouse

Mice may have one, two, or three buttons that can be pressed in different combinations to interact with software running in the system. When the cursor has been positioned onscreen, one or more of the mouse buttons can be "clicked" to execute an operation or select a variable from the screen. Specialized graphics software enables the user to operate the mouse as a drawing instrument.

A newer mouse design, referred to as **wheel mice**, includes a small thumb wheel built into the top of the mouse between the buttons. This wheel enables the user to efficiently scroll up and down the video screen without using scroll bars or arrows.

wheel mice

Some scrolling functions, such as click-and-drag text highlighting in a word processor, can be awkward when the text extends off the bottom of the screen. In faster computers, the automatic scroll functions in some software packages will take off at the bottom of the screen and scroll several pages before stopping. The wheel in the mouse is designed to control this type of action. Additional software drivers must be installed to handle the additional wheel functions for the mouse.

Joysticks

gimbal

Joysticks are very popular input devices used primarily with computer video games. However, they can also provide a convenient computer/human interface for a number of other applications. These peripherals are X-Y positioning devices with a **gimbal** (handle) that can be moved forward, backward, left, right, or at any angular combination of these basic directions to move a cursor or other screen element across a video display. Buttons on the joystick can be used in the same manner as buttons on a mouse. Joysticks are normally connected to a two-row, 15-pin female D-shell game-port connector on the back panel of the computer.

Touch pads

Touch pads (or touch panels) are pointing devices that supply X-Y positioning for cursors and other screen elements. The touch pad typically replaces the mouse in the system. The user controls the screen element by moving a finger across the pad surface. Clicking and double-clicking functions associated with mice can be accomplished by tapping a finger on the pad. Touch pads come as an integral part of many portable computers. However, they can be obtained as add-on devices that plug into standard serial ports.

Character printers

Character printers are widely used peripheral devices. Most printers communicate with the system through a parallel interface. Parallel printers are connected to the 25-pin female D-shell connector at the rear of the system. However, many printers use serial interfacing so that they can be located further from the computer. Serial interface versions normally plug into a 9-pin or 25-pin male D-shell connector. Most often, the serial printer is connected to the 25-pin connector that has been set up as the system's second serial port. The first serial port is typically set up with the 9-pin connector and handles the mouse connection.

Newer printers may supply either a standard parallel connection , a standard serial port connection interface, or both, as well as newer Universal Serial Bus or direct network connections. These interfaces are covered in greater detail in Chapter 6—*Printers*. Common PC peripheral connections are depicted in Figure 1-46.

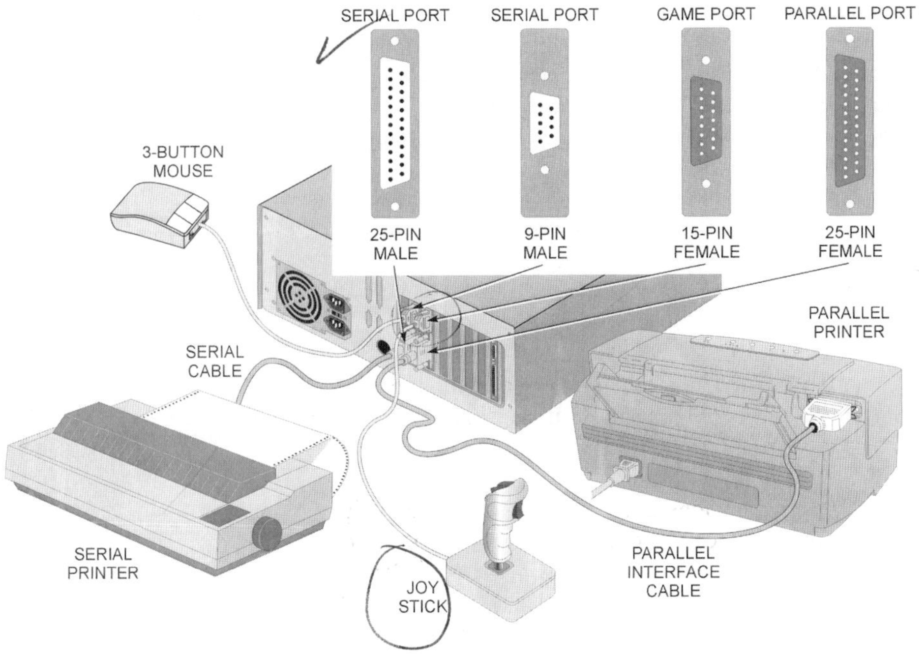

Figure 1-46: Typical Peripheral Connectors

SOFTWARE

software

Once the system's components are connected together and their power connectors have been plugged into a receptacle, the system is ready for operation. However, there is one thing still missing—the **software**. Without good software to oversee its operation, the most sophisticated computer hardware is worthless.

There are actually three general classes of software that can be discussed:

system software

applications software

games

learning software

- **system software**
- **applications software**
- **games** and **learning software**

The bulk of the software discussed in this book falls into the system software category. This is due to the fact that this type of software requires more technical skills to manipulate and, therefore, most often involves the service person.

System Software

Basic Input/Output System (BIOS)

Disk Operating System (DOS)

ROM BIOS

The system software category consists of special programs used by the system itself to control the computer's operation. Two classic examples of this type of software are the system's **Basic Input/Output System (BIOS)** program and the **Disk Operating System (DOS)**. These programs, described in Figure 1-47, control the operation of the other classes of software. The BIOS is located in a ROM IC device on the system board. Therefore, it is commonly referred to as **ROM BIOS**. The DOS software is normally located on a magnetic disk.

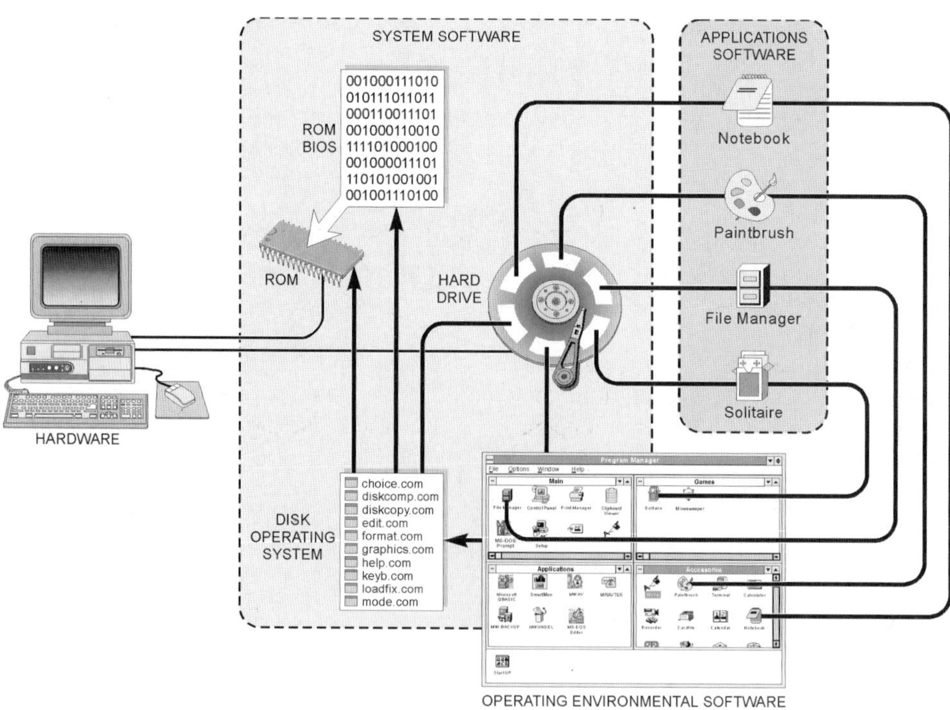

Figure 1-47: System Software

Basic Input/Output Systems

When a PC is turned on, the entire system is reset to a predetermined starting condition. From this state it begins carrying out software instructions from its BIOS program. This small program is permanently stored in the ROM memory ICs located on the system board. The information stored in these chips represents all the inherent intelligence that the system has to begin with.

compatibility

A system's BIOS program is one of the keys to its **compatibility**. For example, to be IBM PC-compatible, the computer's BIOS must perform the same basic functions that the IBM PC's BIOS does. However, since the IBM BIOS software is copyrighted, the compatible's software must accomplish the same results that the original did, but it must do it in some different way.

POST (Power-On Self-Tests)

During the execution of the BIOS firmware routines, three major sets of operations are performed. First, the BIOS performs a series of diagnostic tests on the system, called **POST** or **Power-On Self-Tests**, to verify that it is operating correctly. If any of the system's basic components are malfunctioning, the tests will cause an error message or code to be displayed on the monitor screen, and/or an audio code to be output through the system's speaker.

initialization

The BIOS program also places starting values in the system's various programmable devices. These intelligent devices regulate the operation of different portions of the computer's hardware. This process is called **initialization**. As an example, when the system is first started, the BIOS moves the starting address and mode information into the DMA controller. Likewise, the locations of the computer's interrupt handler programs are written into the interrupt controller. This process is repeated for several of the microprocessor's support devices so that they have the information they need to begin operation.

Master Boot Record

Finally, the BIOS checks the system for a special program that it can use to load other programs into RAM. This program is called the **Master Boot Record** (**MBR**). The boot record program contains information that allows the system to load a much more powerful control program, called the Disk Operating System, into RAM memory. Once the operating system has been loaded into the computer's memory, the BIOS gives it control over the system. From this point, the operating system will oversee the operation of the system.

booting up

cold boot

Reset

warm boot

This operation of transferring control of the system from the BIOS to the operating system is referred to as **booting up** the system. If the computer is started from the OFF condition, the process is referred to as a **cold boot**. If the system is restarted from the ON condition, the process is called a **Reset**, or a **warm boot**.

The bootup process may take several seconds to perform depending on the configuration of the system. If a warm boot is performed, or if the POST has been disabled, the amount of time required for the system to get into operation is decreased. The three components of the bootup process are illustrated in Figures 1-48, 1-49, and 1-50.

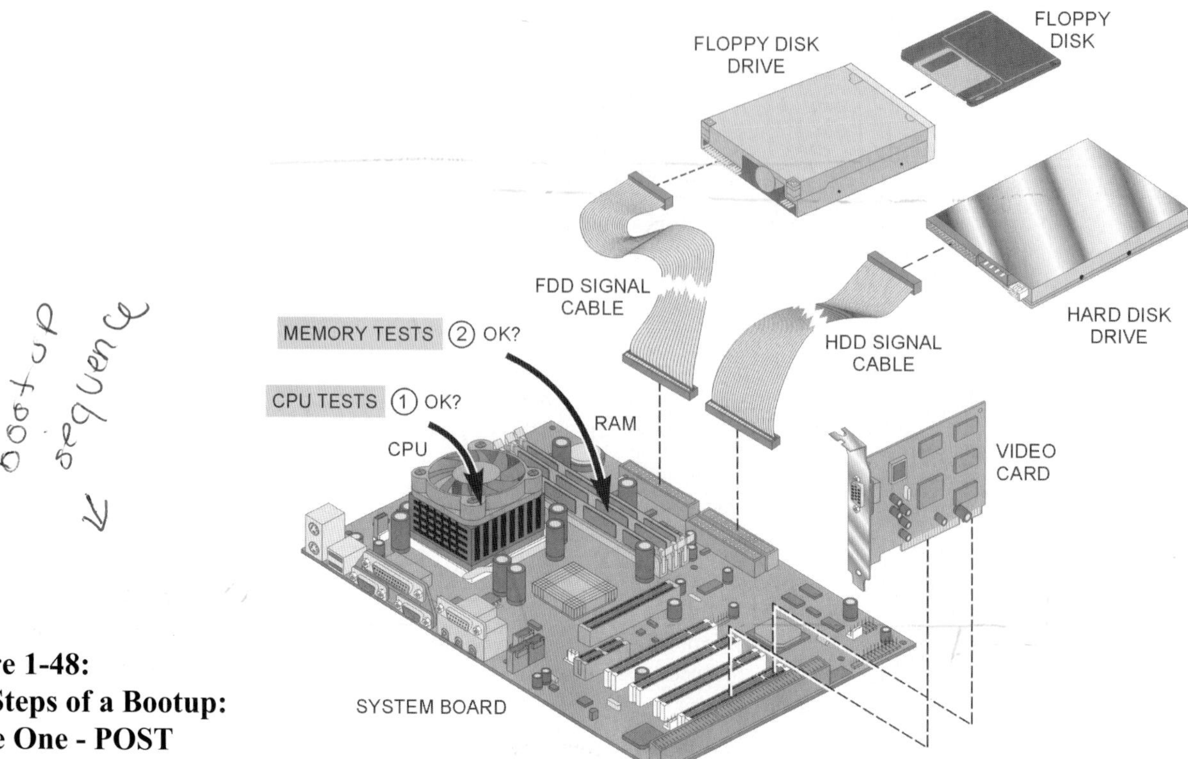

Figure 1-48: The Steps of a Bootup: Phase One - POST

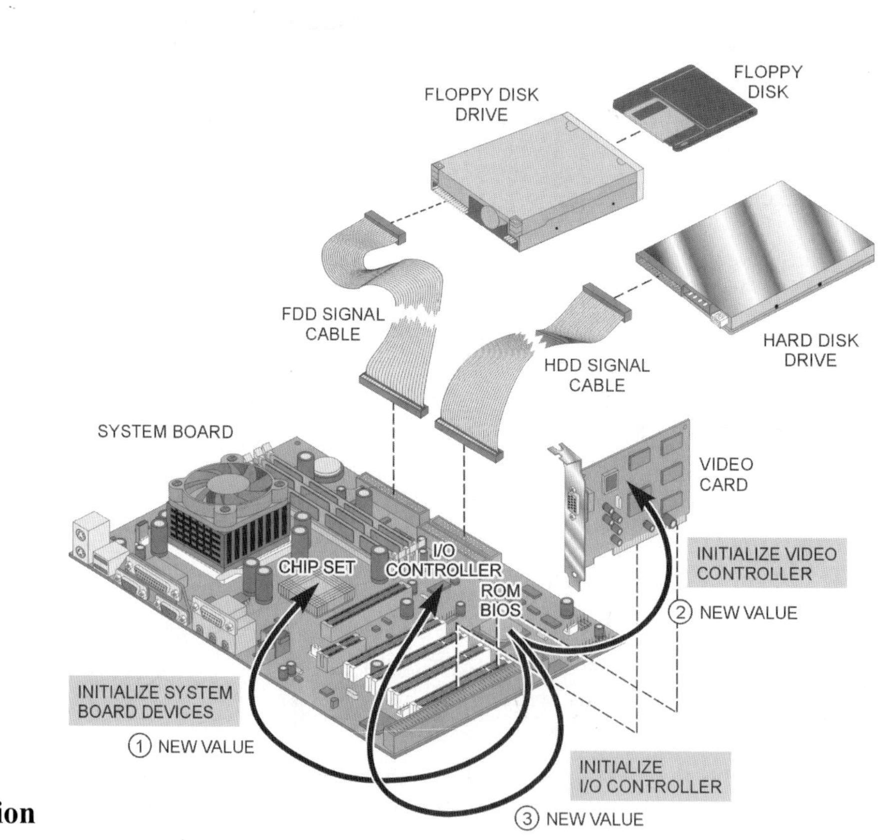

Figure 1-49: The Steps of a Bootup: Phase Two - Initialization

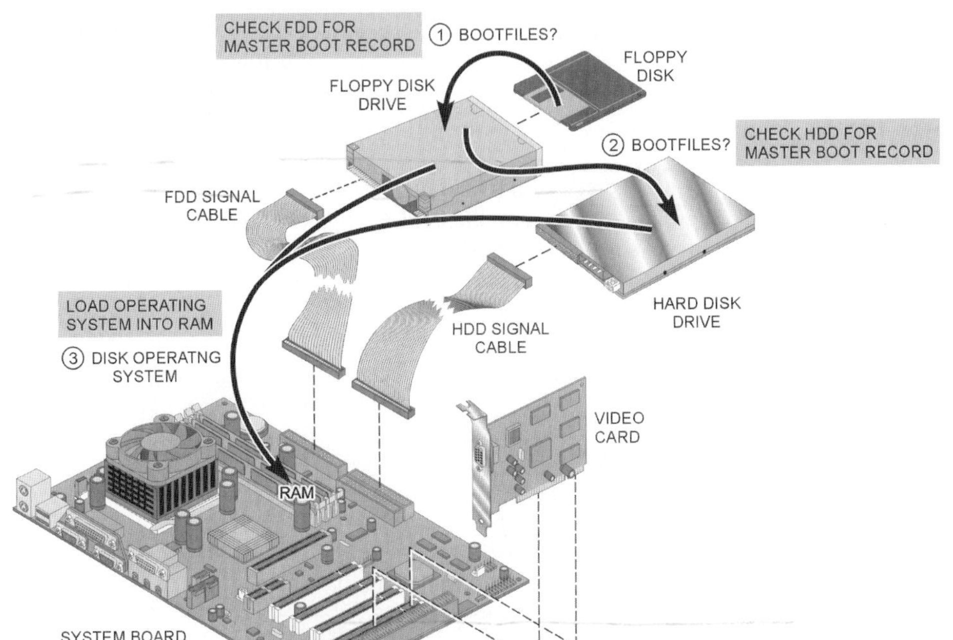

Figure 1-50: The Steps of a Bootup: Phase Three - Bootup

In the first phase of the operation, the BIOS tests the microprocessor (1) and the system's RAM memory (2). In the second phase, it furnishes starting information to the system's microprocessor support devices (1), video adapter card (2), and disk drive adapter card (3). Finally, the BIOS searches through the system in a predetermined sequence for a master boot record to turn over control of the computer to. In this case, it checks the floppy disk drive first (1) and the hard disk drive second (2). If a boot record is found in either location, the BIOS will move it onto the computer's RAM memory and turn over control to it (3).

CMOS Setup

CMOS RAM

CMOS Setup utility

During the initialization process, PCs check a battery-powered storage area on the system board called the **CMOS RAM** to determine what types of options were installed in the system. During bootup, the BIOS permits users to have access to this configuration information through its **CMOS Setup utility**.

When the computer is set up for the first time, or when new options are added to the system, it is necessary to run the CMOS Configuration Setup utility. The values input through the utility are stored in the system's CMOS Configuration registers. These registers are examined each time the system is booted up to tell the computer what types of devices are installed. Early in the startup process, the BIOS places a prompt on the display to tell the user that the CMOS Setup utility can be accessed by pressing a special key, or a given key combination. Typical keys and key combinations include: the DEL key, the ESC key, the F2 function key, the CTRL and ESC keys, and the CTRL-ALT-ESC key combination.

The keys, or key combinations, used to access the setup menus vary from one BIOS manufacturer to another. If the proper keys are not pressed within a predetermined amount of time, the BIOS program will continue with the bootup process. However, if the keys are pressed during this time interval, the bootup routine will be put on hold and the program will display a "CMOS Setup Selection" screen.

Every chipset variation has a specific BIOS designed for it. Therefore, there are functions specific to the design of system boards using that chipset. The example screen in the figure serves as the main menu for entering and exiting the CMOS Setup utility and for moving between its configuration pages.

A typical Configuration Setup screen is shown in Figure 1-51. Through this screen, the user enters the desired configuration values into the CMOS registers. The cursor on the screen can be moved from item to item using the keyboard's cursor control keys.

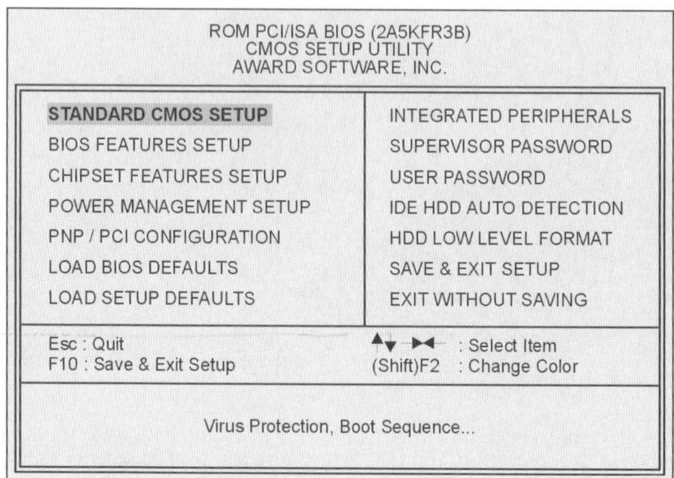

Figure 1-51: A CMOS Setup Selection Screen

Plug-and-Play

Plug-and-Play (PnP)

In most newer PCs, the BIOS, peripheral devices, and operating system employ **Plug-and-Play (PnP)** technology that enables the system to automatically determine what hardware devices are actually installed in the system and to allocate system resources to the devices to configure and manage them. This removes some of the responsibility for system configuration from the user or the technician. All three of the system components just mentioned must be PnP-compliant before automatic configuration can be carried out.

Extended System Configuration Data (ESCD)

Basically, the PnP device communicates with the BIOS during the initialization phase of the startup to tell the system what type of device it is, where it is located in the system, and what its resource needs are. This information is stored on the device in the form of firmware. The BIOS stores the PnP information it collects from the devices in a special section of the CMOS RAM known as the **Extended System Configuration Data (ESCD)** area. This information is stored in the same manner as standard BIOS settings are stored. The BIOS and operating system both access the ESCD area each time the system is restarted to see if any information has changed. This enables the BIOS and operating system to work together in sorting out the needs of the installed devices and assigning them needed system resources. Figure 1-52 illustrates the basic PnP process.

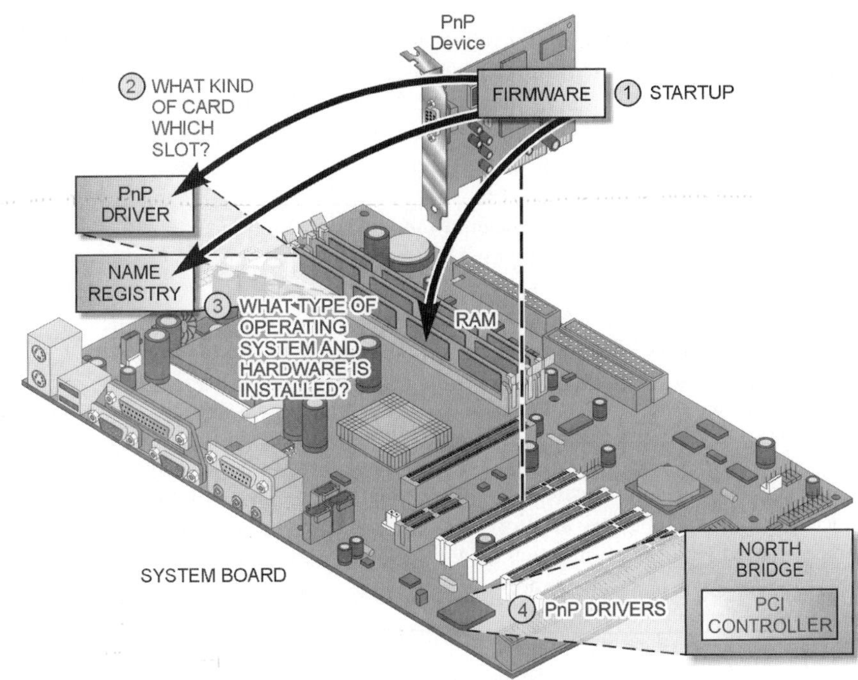

Figure 1-52: Plug-and-Play Operations

If no changes have occurred in the contents of the ESCD since the last bootup occurred, the BIOS will detect this and skip that portion of the boot process. When a PnP operating system checks the ESCD to see if any hardware changes have occurred, it will react accordingly and record any changes it finds in the hardware portion of its Registry. On some occasions, the system's PnP logic may not be able to resolve all of its resource needs and a configuration error will occur. In these cases, the technician, or the user, will have to manually resolve the configuration problem. The BIOS and operating system typically provide interfaces to the hardware configuration information so that users can manually override the system's Plug-and-Play resource assignments.

Operating Systems

Every portion of the system must be controlled and coordinated so that the millions of operations that occur every second are carried out correctly and on time. In addition, it is the job of the operating system to make the complexity of the personal computer as invisible as possible to the user.

Operating systems

Operating systems are programs designed to control the operation of a computer system. As a group, they are easily some of the most complex programs devised.

Likewise, the operating system acts as an intermediary between nearly as complex software applications, and the hardware they run on. Finally, the operating system accepts commands from the computer user, and carries them out to perform some desired operation.

Disk Operating System (DOS)

A **Disk Operating System** (**DOS**) is a collection of programs used to control overall computer operation in a disk-based system. These programs work in the background to allow the user of the computer to input characters from the keyboard, to define a file structure for storing records, or to output data to a monitor or printer. The disk operating system is responsible for finding and organizing your data and applications on the disk.

The disk operating system can be divided into three distinct sections:

boot files

file management files

utility files

- **boot files** - take over control of the system from the ROM BIOS during startup
- **file management files** - enable the system to manage information within itself
- **utility files** - permit the user to manage system resources, troubleshoot the system, and configure the system

The operating system acts as a bridge between the application programs and the computer, as described in Figure 1-53. These application programs allow the user to create files of data pertaining to certain applications such as word processing, remote data communications, business processing, and user programming languages.

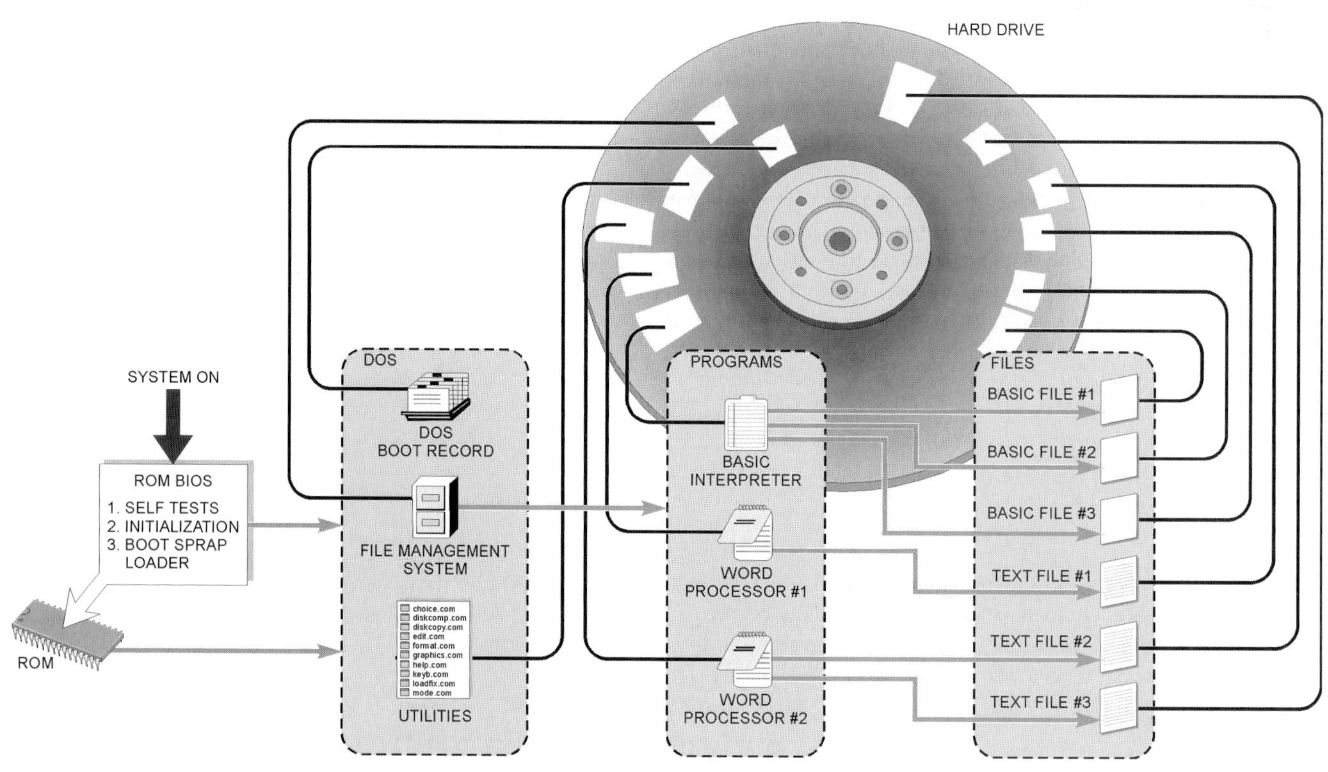

Figure 1-53: The Position of DOS in the Computer System

Graphical User Interfaces

Another form of operating environment, referred to as a **Graphical User Interface (GUI)**, has gained widespread popularity in recent years. GUIs, like the Windows desktop depicted in Figure 1-54, employ a graphics display to represent procedures and programs that can be executed by the computer. These programs routinely use small pictures, called **icons**, to represent different programs. The advantage of using a GUI is that the user doesn't have to remember complicated commands to execute a program.

Graphical User Interface (GUI)

icons

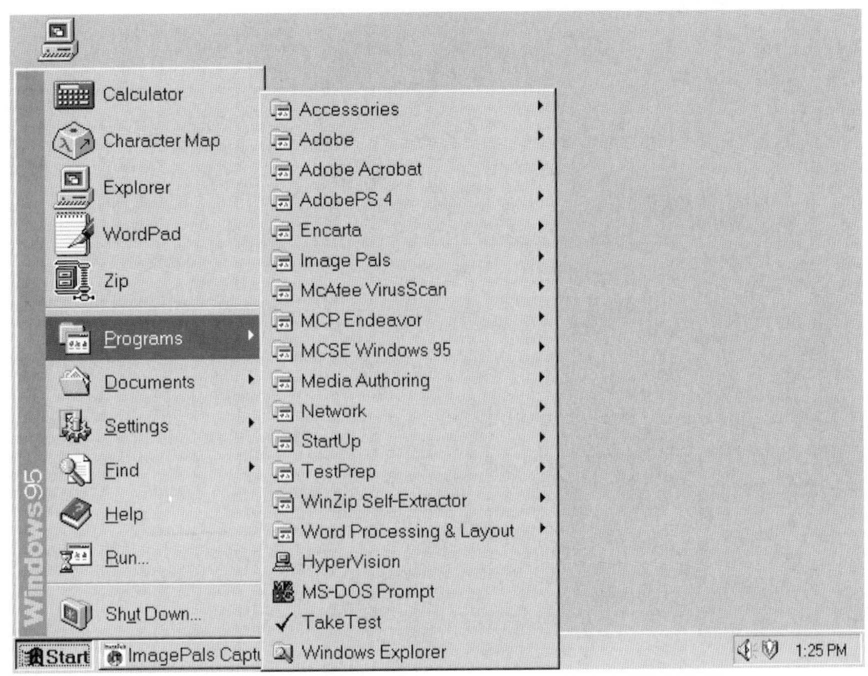

Figure 1-54: A Graphical User Interface Screen

APPLICATION SOFTWARE

The second major software category is application software. This category consists of programs that perform specialized tasks, such as word processing, accounting, and so forth. This category of software exists in two formats:

- Commercially available, user-oriented packages that may be purchased and used directly
- Programming language packages that developers can use to create user-oriented programs

Application software packages operate as extensions of the operating system. Depending on the type of operating system being used, an application program may directly control some system resources, such as printers and modems, while the operating system lends fundamental support in the background. In more advanced systems, the operating system supplies common input, output, and disk management functions for all the applications in the system.

Commercial Application Packages

The openness of the personal computer market has generated a wide variety of different applications programs designed for use with them. Even a short discussion of all the software types available for the PC would take up more space than we can afford. However, a small group of these programs make up the vast majority of the software sold in this category. These programs are:

- Word processors
- Spreadsheets
- Graphic design packages
- Personal productivity tools
- Database Management Systems (DBMS)

Word processors

Word processors are specialized software packages that can be used to create and edit alphanumeric texts, such as letters, memos, contracts, and other documents. These packages convert the computer into a super typewriter. Unlike typewriters, word processors enable the user to edit, check, and correct any errors before the document is committed to paper. Many word processors offer extended functions such as spelling checkers, as well as on-line dictionary and thesaurus functions that aid the writer in preparing the document. A typical word processor working page is depicted in Figure 1-55.

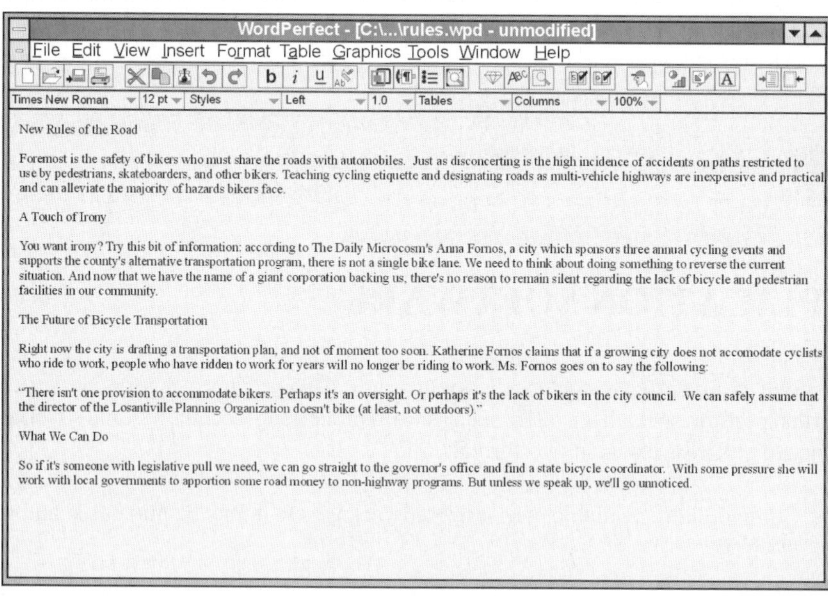

Figure 1-55: Typical Word Processor

Spreadsheets

Spreadsheets are specialized financial worksheets that enable the user to prepare and manipulate numerical information in a comparative format. Paper spreadsheets were used by business people for many years before the personal computer came along. Spreadsheets are used to track business information such as budgets, cash flow, and earnings. Because the information in these documents is updated and corrected often, working on paper was always a problem. With electronic spreadsheets, like the one illustrated in Figure 1-56, this work is much quicker to perform and less fatiguing. This software is probably most responsible for the growth of personal computers into serious work machines.

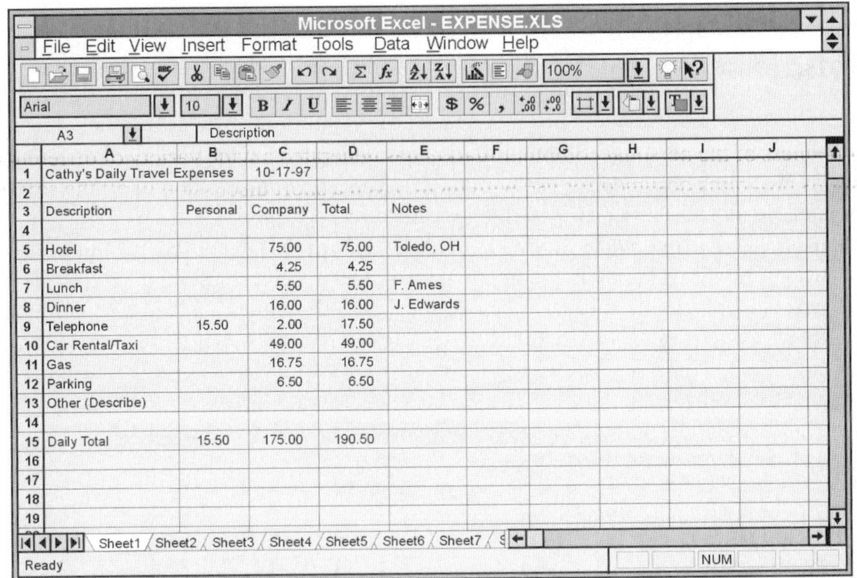

Figure 1-56: Typical Spreadsheet Program

Database management systems

databases

Database management systems (or simply **databases**) are programs that enable the user to store and track vast amounts of related information about different subjects. Databases can be thought of as electronic boxes of note cards. You can keep on these electronic note cards several pieces of information related to a given subject.

For example, you might keep information on a note card for each of your relatives. The card might contain their phone numbers, addresses, and birthdays. The database enables you to sort through the information in different ways. With a database program it would be no problem to sort out all of the relatives that have a birthday in a given month. A typical database working page is shown in Figure 1-57.

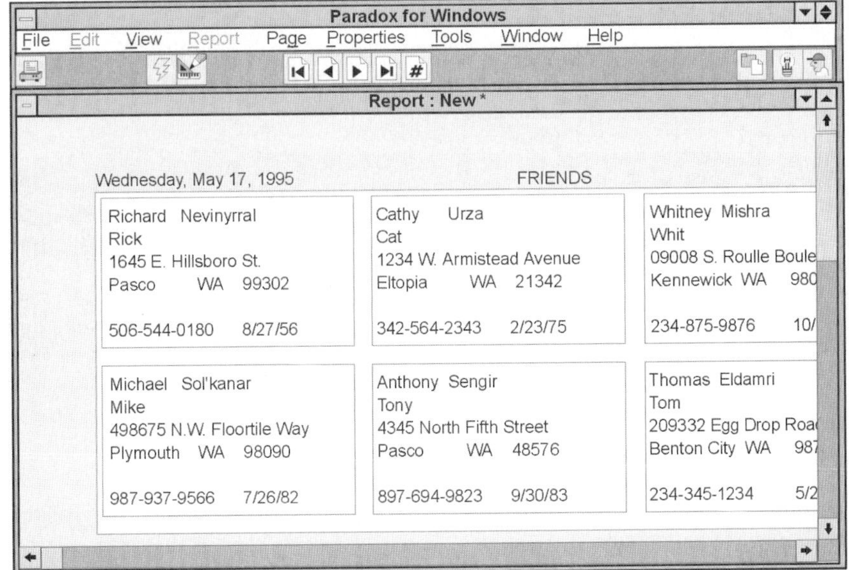

Figure 1-57: Typical Database Program

Graphics programs

bit-mapped images

vector images

pixel

Graphics programs enable the user to create non-alphanumeric output from the computer. Simple graphics programs are used to create charts and graphs that represent data. More complex programs can be used to create artistic output in the form of lines, shapes, and images. Typically, graphic design programs produce graphics in two formats: as **bit-mapped images** and as **vector images**. With bit-mapped graphics, every dot (**pixel**) in the image is defined in memory. Vector images are defined as a starting point and a set of mathematical formulas in memory. Because vector images exist only as a set of mathematical models, their size can be scaled up or down easily without major distortions. Vector images can also be rotated easily, allowing three-dimensional work to take place on these images. On the other hand, bit-mapped graphics are tightly specified collections of spots across and down the screen. These types of images would be difficult to scale or rotate without distortion. A typical graphics package is depicted in Figure 1-58.

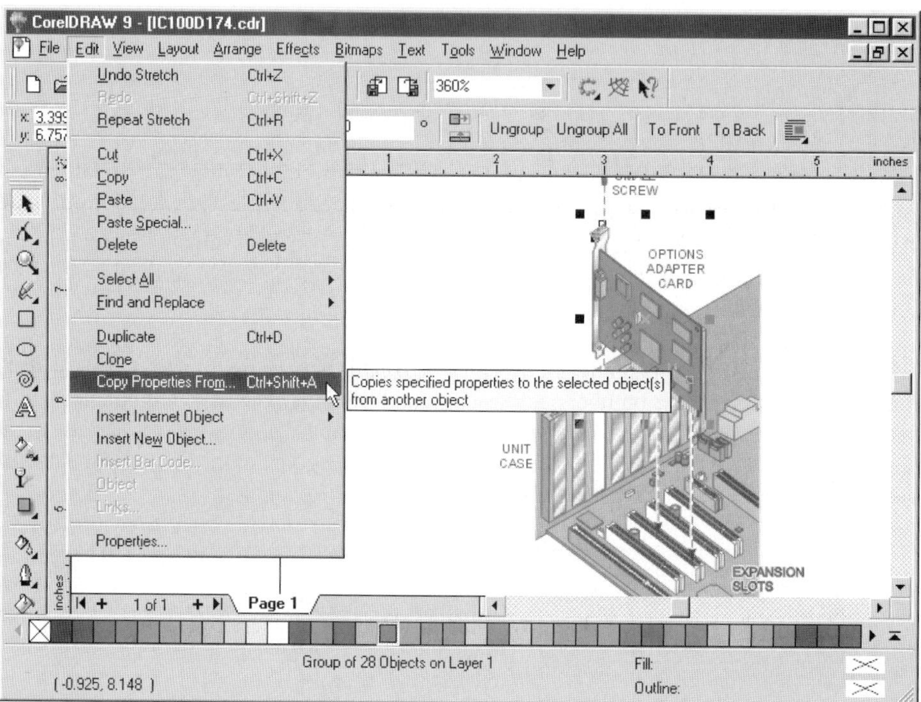

Figure 1-58: Typical Graphics Design Program

Personal productivity programs

desktop organizers

Personal productivity programs, also referred to as **desktop organizers**, encompass a variety of programs that simulate tools found on typical business desks. They normally include items such as telephone directories, calculators, note pads, and calendar programs. Of course, many other types of applications software is available for use with the PC. A meaningful discussion of all these software types is well beyond the scope of this book and certainly goes well beyond the scope of preparing for A+ testing.

Programming Packages

Because the only language that computers understand is their own machine language, and most humans don't relate well to machine languages, you'll need a piece of system software to convert whatever language you're programming into the machine's language. These conversion packages exist in two forms: **interpreters** and **compilers**. The distinction between the two is in how and when they convert the user language into machine language. Interpreters convert the program as it is being **run** (executed). Compilers convert the entire user-language program into machine code before it is executed. Typically, compiled-language programs execute much faster than those written in interpretive languages. In addition, compiled languages typically provide the user with a much higher level of direct control over the computer's operation.

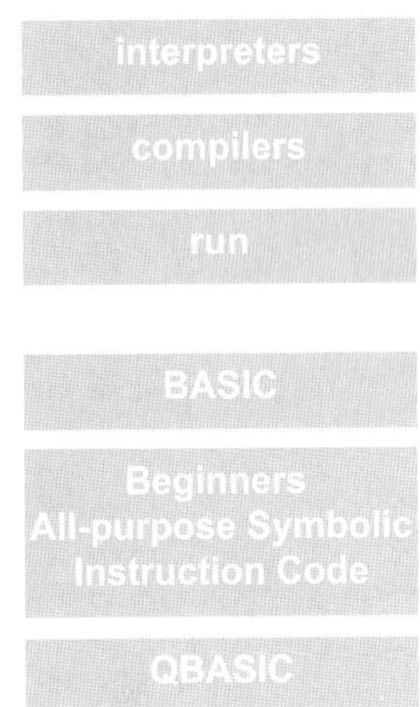

In contrast, interpreted languages are usually slower, and less powerful, but their programs tend to be easier to write and use than those of compiled languages.

BASIC is probably the best known example of an interpreted *high-level* programming language. The term **BASIC** stands for **Beginners All-purpose Symbolic Instruction Code**, while "high-level" refers to the fact that the language uses commands that are English-like. This all contributes to making BASIC a popular user language, which almost anyone can learn to use (see Figure 1-59 for an example of a **QBASIC** program).

```
File  Edit  View  Search  Run  Debug  Options                          Help
                        CONTPROG.BAS
MOVEPROARM:
  CLS
  PRINT "Move the Pro-Arm"
  PRINT
  GOSUB GETVALS
  Outstr$ = "M" + Outstr$
  PRINT "The following move command has been sent to the Pro-Arm."
  PRINT Outstr$
  LPRINT Outstr$
IF Saving$ = "YES" GOTO SAVEMOVE
  GOSUB PAUSEPROGRAM
  RETURN
SAVEMOVE:
  PRINT #1, "LPRINT "; CHR$(34); Outstr$; CHR$(34)
  PRINT "The Move Command was saved to file"
  GOSUB PAUSEPROGRAM
  RETURN

GETVALS:
  INPUT "Enter the number of steps for the base axis move: ", BaseAxis
  INPUT "Enter the number of steps for the shoulder axis move: ", Shoulder
  INPUT "Enter the number of steps for the elbow axis move: ", Elbow
  INPUT "Enter the number of steps for the wrist roll axis move: ",Wristroll
  INPUT "Enter the number of steps for the wrist pitch axis move: ", Wristpitch
  INPUT "Enter the number of steps for the gripper axis move: ", Gripper
  Outstr$ = RTRIM$(LTRIM$(STR$(BaseAxis)))
  Outstr$ = Outstr$ + "," + RTRIM$(LTRIM$(STR$(Shoulder)))
  Outstr$ = Outstr$ + "," + RTRIM$(LTRIM$(STR$(Elbow)))
  Outstr$ = Outstr$ + "," + RTRIM$(LTRIM$(STR$(Wristroll)))
  Outstr$ = Outstr$ + "," + RTRIM$(LTRIM$(STR$(Wristpitch)))
  Outstr$ = Outstr$ + "," + RTRIM$(LTRIM$(STR$(Gripper)))
  RETURN
                        Immediate
<Shift+F1=Help> <F6=Windows> <F2=Subs> <F5=Run> <F8=Step>        N 00001:001
```

Figure 1-59: QBASIC Program

An example of a compiled language is FORTRAN. FORTRAN is one of the oldest user languages still in use today and is primarily used in engineering and scientific applications. Many of FORTRAN's attributes resemble those you'll find in BASIC. This is due to the fact that most versions of BASIC are modified derivatives of FORTRAN.

There are also commercially available BASIC compiler programs that enable you to take BASIC programs, written with an interpreter, and compile them so that they will run faster. Other compiled language packages that run on almost any PC include COBOL (a business applications language), LISP (an artificial intelligence applications language), and the popular user languages C+, FORTH, and PASCAL.

Assembly language

assembler

mnemonics

Another alternative in programming exists for your computer—that is, to write programs in **Assembly language** (one step away from machine language) and run them through an **assembler** program. Assembly language is a human-readable form of machine language that uses short, symbolic instruction words, called **mnemonics**, to tell the computer what to do. Each line of an Assembly language program corresponds directly to one line of machine code. Writing programs in Assembly language enables the programmer to precisely control every aspect of the computer's operation during the execution of the program. This makes Assembly language the most powerful programming language you can use. To its detriment, Assembly language is complex, and requires the programmer to be extremely familiar with the internal operation of the system using the program.

A number of steps are required to create an Assembly-language program:

assembler program

linking program

1. You must create the program using an alphanumeric text editor.
2. The text file must be run through an **assembler program**, to convert the Assembly language into machine code.
3. Finally, the machine code must be run through a **linking program**, which puts the assembled machine code into the proper format to work with the operating system. In this final form, the program can be executed from DOS.

DEBUG

For short and simple Assembly language programs, a DOS utility called **DEBUG** can be used to enter and run machine language and limited Assembly-language programs, without going through the various assembly steps. A sample DEBUG program is shown in Figure 1-60.

```
c:\>debug
-r

AX=0000  BX=0000  CX=0000  DX=0000  SP=FFEE  BP=0000  SI=0000  DI=0000
DS=20AB  ES=20AB  SS=20AB  IP=0100  NU  UP  EI  PL  NZ  NA  PO  NC
20AB:100  0F     DB    0F

-d

20AB:0100 0F 00 B9 A8  FFF3 AE 47-61 03 IF 8B C3 48 12 B1   .......Ga.........H..
20AB:0110 04 8B C6 F7 0A 0A D0 D3-48 DA 2B D0 34 00 9A 20   ..........H.+.4.......
20AB:0120 00 DB D2 D3 E0 03 F0 8E-DA 8B C7 16 C2 B6 01 16   ........................
20AB:0130 C0 16 F8 8E C2 AC 8A D0-00 00 4E AD 8B C8 46 8A   ................N...F.
20AB:0140 C2 24 FE 3C B0 75 05 AC-F3 AA A0 0A EB 06 3C B2   ..$.<.U.............>.
20AB:0150 75 6D 6D 13 A8 01 50 14-74 B1 BE 32 01 8D 8B 1E   umm....P.+.2.......
20AB:0160 8E FC 12 A8 33 D2 29 E3-13 8B C2 03 C3 69 02 00   ......3.).......i.......
20AB:0170 0B F8 83 FF FF 74 11 26-01 1D E2 F3 81 00 94 FA   .......+.&.............
```

Figure 1-60: DEBUG Program

Visual Basic

Microsoft introduced a radically different programming environment when it delivered **Visual Basic**. Unlike the previous BASIC language versions, Visual Basic is a graphical programming tool that allows programmers to develop Windows applications on an artistic rather than a command-line basis. The programmer draws graphic elements and places them on the screen as desired. This tool is so powerful that it is used to produce large blocks of major applications, as well as finished Windows products. The finished product can be converted into an executable file using a Visual Basic utility. The only major drawback of Visual Basic is that major applications written in it tend to run slowly, because it is an interpreted language.

Games and Educational Packages

Games and learning programs are among the leading titles in retail software sales. The games market has exploded as PC speeds have increased, and as output graphics have improved. However, on the technical side, there is generally not much call for repair associated with games software. Most games work with well-developed pointing devices, such as trackballs and joysticks, as the primary input devices. Although the housing designs of these products can be quite amazing, they tend to be simple and well-proven devices, requiring relatively little maintenance. Likewise, the software tends to be pretty straightforward from a user's point of view. It simply gets installed and runs.

Computer-Aided Instruction (CAI)

Computer-Based Instruction (CBI)

Computer-Aided Instruction (**CAI**) and **Computer-Based Instruction** (**CBI**) have become accepted means of delivering instructional materials. In CAI operations, the computer assists a human instructor in delivering information and tracking student responses. In CBI operations, the computer becomes the primary delivery vehicle for instructional materials.

As these teaching systems proliferate, more complex input, output, and processing devices are added to the system. A basic teaching system requires a minimum of a sound card, a fast hard drive, a CD-ROM drive, and a high-resolution video card. Beyond this, CAI and CBI systems may employ such wide-ranging peripherals as large LCD display panels, VGA-compatible overhead projectors, intelligent white boards, wireless mice and touch-sensitive screens as input devices, full-motion video capture cards, and a host of other multimedia related equipment.

Version Numbers

version numbers

All types of software are referred to by **version numbers**. When a programmer releases a software program for sale, a version number is assigned to it, such as Windows 3.11 or MS-DOS 6.22. The version number distinguishes the new release from prior releases of that same software. The larger the version number, the more recent the program. When new features or capabilities are added to a program, it is given a new version number. Therefore, referring to a software package by its version number indicates its capabilities and operation. The number to the left of the decimal point is the major revision number, which usually changes when new features are added. The number(s) to the right of the decimal are minor revision numbers, which usually change when corrections are made to the program.

CHAPTER SUMMARY

This chapter has covered the fundamental hardware structures and components associated with PC-compatible personal computer systems. It has presented a mini-course on the basic organization and operation of the personal computer.

You should be able to identify the major components of a typical personal computer system and describe the function of each component. Finally, you should be able to describe the different levels of system software associated with a personal computer.

At this point, review the objectives listed at the beginning of the chapter to be certain that you understand and can perform each item listed there.

KEY POINTS REVIEW

This chapter has covered the fundamental hardware structures and components associated with PC-compatible personal computer systems. Review the following key points before moving into the Review and Exam Questions sections to make sure you are comfortable with each point. Afterward, answer the Review Questions that follow to verify your knowledge of the information.

- The tremendous popularity of the original IBM PC-XT and AT systems created a set of Pseudo Standards for hardware and software compatibility. The AT architecture became so popular that it has become the Industry Standard Architecture (ISA). The majority of microcomputers are both hardware- and software-compatible with the original AT design.
- The system unit is the main portion of the microcomputer system and is the basis of any PC system arrangement.
- The system board is the center of the system. It contains the portions of the system that define its computing power and speed.
- Notebook computer designers work constantly to decrease the size and power consumption of the computer's components.
- The drawback of portable computers from a service point of view is that conventions and compatibility disappear. Therefore, interchangeability of parts with other machines or makers goes by the wayside.
- The system's power supply unit provides electrical power for every component inside the system unit, as well as supplying ac power to the video display monitor.
- The system board communicates with various optional Input/Output (I/O) and memory systems through adapter boards that plug into its expansion slots. These connectors are normally located along the left-rear portion of the system board so that the external devices they serve can access them through openings at the rear of the case.
- The microprocessor is the major component of any system board. It executes software instructions, and carries out arithmetic operations for the system.
- Microprocessor manufacturers always produce microprocessor-support chipsets that provide auxiliary services for the microprocessor.

- Each time the system is turned on, or reset, the BIOS program checks the system's Configuration Settings to determine what types of optional devices are included in the system.
- Newer microcomputers possess the capability to automatically reconfigure themselves for new options that are installed. This feature is referred to as plug-and-play (PnP) capability.
- The local bus connects special peripherals to the system board (and the microprocessor) through a proprietary expansion slot connector and allows the peripheral to operate at speeds close to the speed of the microprocessor.
- The video adapter card provides the interface between the system board and the display monitor.
- The system unit normally comes from the manufacturer with both a floppy disk drive unit and a hard disk drive unit installed.

REVIEW QUESTIONS

The following questions test your knowledge of the material presented in this chapter.

1. What are the major differences between AT and ATX power supplies (name three)?
2. List the four subunits typically found inside the system unit. p 10
3. How can you avoid confusion between the DB-15M connectors for VGA and game port connections?
4. List three types of memory typically found on modern system boards. p 22
5. Describe how data is stored on a magnetic disk.
6. List the devices normally found outside the system unit. p 42 *
7. How are legacy cards different from PnP cards and how do they affect the system?
8. When connecting an AT power supply to a system board what precaution should be taken? p. 14
9. What do the terms SIMM and DIMM stand for and what kind of devices are they?
10. Describe the two input devices that are commonly included in a PC purchase.

11. Name a major drawback of tower cases.
12. How is upgrading a system with a Flash ROM BIOS different than upgrading a system with a standard ROM BIOS?
13. What is ESCD and how does it affect the operation of the system?
14. What is the data storage capacity of a typical CD-ROM?
15. List the three major sets of operations performed by the BIOS during startup.

EXAM QUESTIONS

1. What type of IC is the brain of the PC system?
   a. The ROM BIOS
   b. The ASIC device
   c. The memory controller
   d. The microprocessor
2. Name one weak feature of tower cases.
   a. Weak framework due to its vertical height.
   b. Air flow through tower cases is generally not good.
   c. High EFI radiation.
   d. Requires excessive desk space in an office environment.
3. Where is the system's BIOS program located?
   a. ROM ICs located on the system board
   b. In the CMOS chip
   c. In the keyboard encoder
   d. In the microprocessor's L2 cache
4. How many floppy drives can a typical FDC controller handle? How are these drives identified to the system?
   a. The normal FDC controller can control two floppy disk drives that the system will see as drives A: and B:.
   b. The normal FDC controller can control four floppy disk drives that the system will see as drives A:, B:, C:, and D:.
   c. The normal FDC controller can control one floppy disk drive that the system will see as drive A:.
   d. The normal FDC controller can control two floppy disk drives that the system will see as drives A: and an assigned drive name.
5. Where is the MI/O function normally found in an ATX Pentium system?
   a. On the multi I/O card
   b. On the system board
   c. On the video card
   d. On the SCSI adapter card

6. In a PC-compatible system, ________.
   a. the BIOS must perform the same functions as the BIOS in an IBM PC
   b. the operating system must perform the same functions as the OS in an IBM PC
   c. the system must use the same ICs that the IBM PC used
   d. the system must use an IBM BIOS
7. Starting the computer from the power off condition is known as ________.
   a. warm boot
   b. cold boot
   c. initialization
   d. reset
8. Which of the following is not part of the bootup process?
   a. POST tests
   b. initialization
   c. bootstrap operation
   d. executing utility files
9. The process of placing the starting values in a system's programmable devices is known as ______.
   a. POSTing
   b. initializing
   c. booting
   d. resetting
10. The Master Boot Record is normally found in ________.
   a. the BIOS
   b. the hard disk drive
   c. RAM memory
   d. the disk-drive adapter card

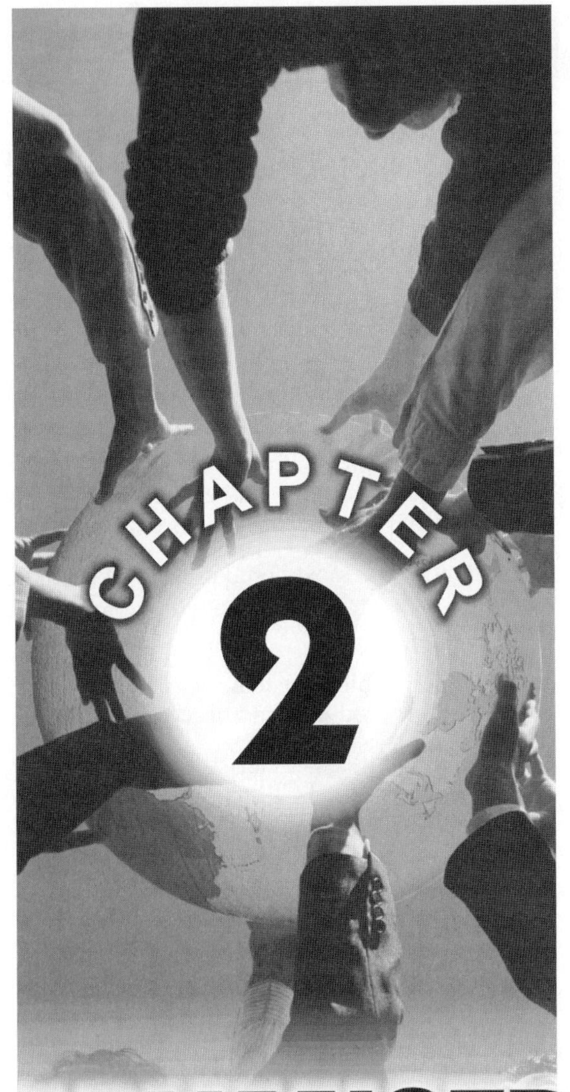

ADVANCED SYSTEM BOARDS

OBJECTIVES

OBJECTIVES

Upon completion of this chapter and its related lab procedures, you will be prepared to:

1. Name popular Pentium class microprocessors and describe their basic characteristics, such as speeds, voltages, form-factors, and cache capabilities.
2. Differentiate between the characteristics of various types of RAM used in a PC system, including the different types of dynamic and static RAM.
3. Discuss typical memory organization schemes used with different system board types and given a specific memory arrangement identify the types of devices employed.
4. Identify the most popular types of motherboards, their components, and their architecture including, ATX as well as full and baby AT designs.
5. Identify typical system board components, including COMM ports, memory modules, and processor sockets.
6. Describe the characteristics of different expansion bus architectures, including ISA, PCI, AGP, USB, VESA, and PC Card specifications.
7. Discuss basic compatibility guidelines for different types of disk drive interfaces used with Pentium system boards, including the various types of IDE and SCSI devices.
8. State the purpose of CMOS RAM, what it typically contains, and how to change its basic parameters.

CHAPTER 2

ADVANCED SYSTEM BOARDS

INTRODUCTION

The system board contains the components that form the basis of the computer system. Even though the system board's physical structure has changed over time, its logical structure has remained relatively constant. Since the original PC, the system board has contained the microprocessor, its support devices, the system's primary memory units, and the expansion-slot connectors. Figure 2-1 depicts a typical system board layout.

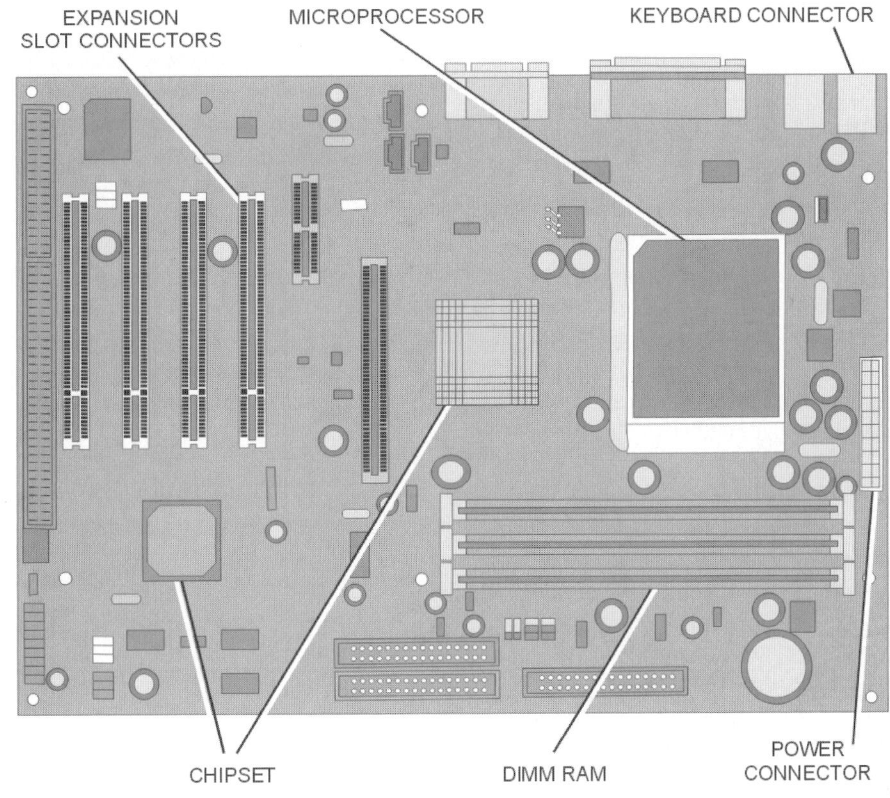

Figure 2-1: A Typical System Board Layout

SYSTEM BOARD EVOLUTION

System boards fundamentally change for four reasons: new industry form-factors, new microprocessor designs, new expansion-slot types, and reduced chip counts. Reduced chip counts are typically the result of improved microprocessor support chipsets.

System Board Form Factors

form factor

It should be evident that all system boards are not alike. The term **form factor** is used to refer to the physical size and shape of a device. However, in the case of system boards, it also refers to their case style and power supply compatibility, as well as their I/O connection placement schemes. These factors come into play when assembling a new system from components, as well as in repair and upgrade situations where the system board is being replaced.

ATX System Boards

ATX form factor

The newest system board designation is the **ATX form factor** developed by Intel for Pentium-based systems. This specification is an evolution of the older baby AT form factor that moves the standard I/O functions to the system board.

> **NOTE**
>
> **The Changing Face of System Boards**—Chipset-based system boards and I/O cards tend to change often as IC manufacturers continue to integrate higher levels of circuitry into their devices.

The **ATX specification** basically rotates the baby AT form factor by 90 degrees, relocates the power supply connection, and moves the microprocessor and memory modules away from the expansion slots.

ATX specification

Figure 2-2 depicts a Pentium-based, ATX system board that directly supports the FDD, HDD, serial, and parallel ports. The board is 12" (305mm) wide and 9.6" (244mm) long. A revised, mini-ATX specification allows for 11.2"-by-8.2" system boards. The hole patterns for the ATX and mini-ATX system boards require a case that can accommodate the new boards. Although ATX shares most of its mounting-hole pattern with the baby-AT specification, it does not match exactly.

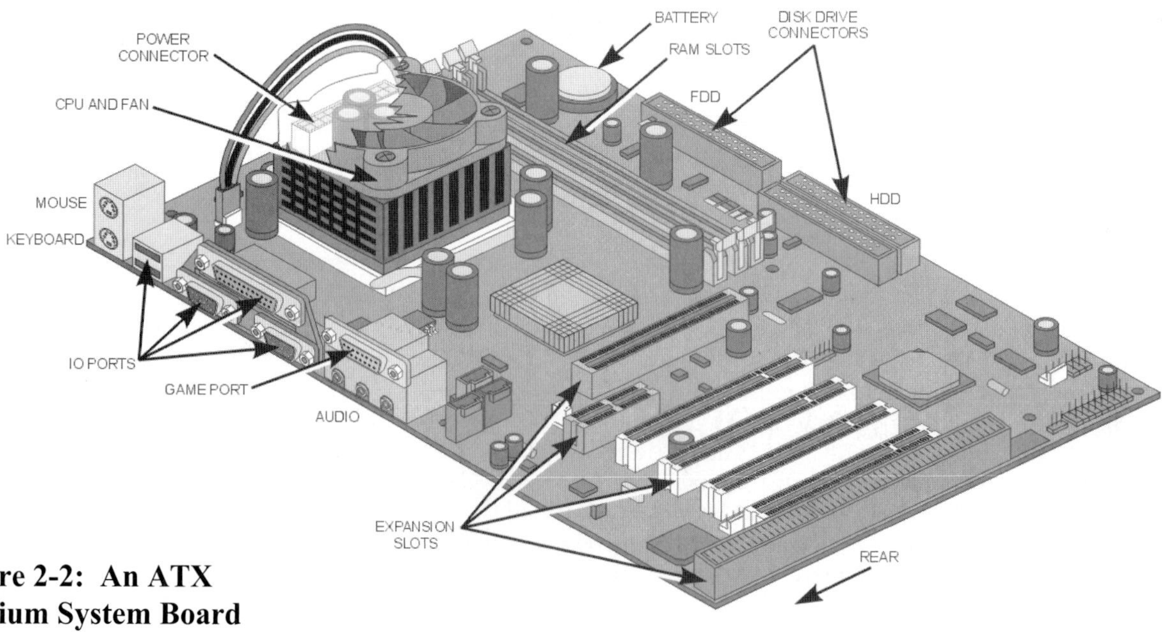

Figure 2-2: An ATX Pentium System Board

The power supply orientation enables a single fan to be used to cool the system. This provides reduced cost, reduced system noise, and improved reliability. The relocated microprocessor and memory modules allow full-length cards to be used in the expansion slots while providing easy upgrading of the microprocessor, RAM, and I/O cards.

The fully implemented ATX format also contains specifications for the power supply and I/O connector placements. In particular, the ATX specification for the power supply connection calls for a single, 20-pin power cord between the system board and the power supply unit rather than the typical P8/P9 cabling.

As illustrated in Figure 2-3, the new cable adds a +3.3V (DC) supply to the traditional +/– 12V (DC) and +/– 5 V (DC) supplies. A software-activated power switch can also be implemented through the ATX power connector specification. The PS-ON and 5VSB (5V Standby) signals can be controlled by the operating system to perform automatic system shut downs.

> **TEST TIP**
>
> Know which type of system board can use a software power-off switch.

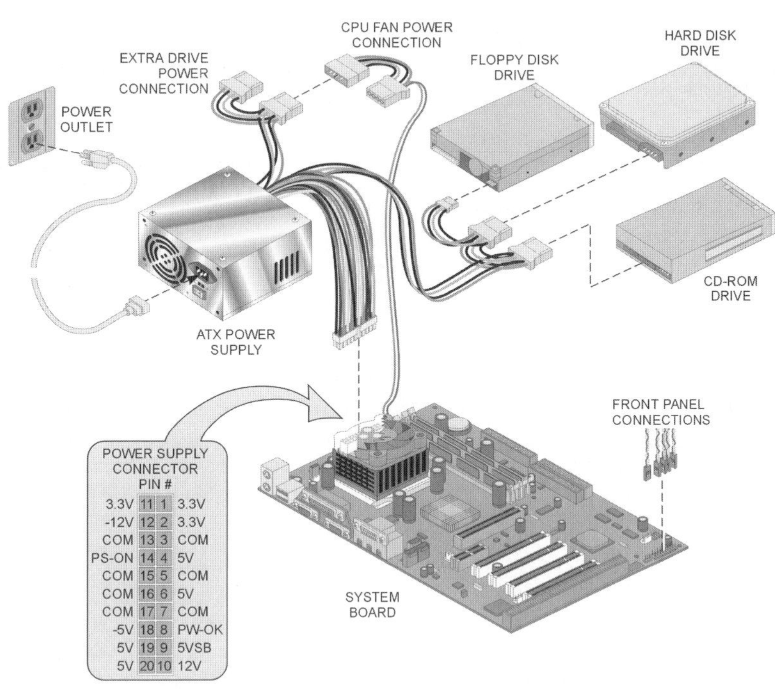

Figure 2-3: An ATX Power Supply Connector

AT System Boards

The forerunner of the ATX system board was a derivative of the Industry Standard Architecture system board developed for the IBM PC-AT. The original **PC-AT system board** measured 30.5 x 33 centimeters.

As the AT design became the de facto industry standard, printed-circuit-board manufacturers began to combine portions of the AT design into larger IC devices to reduce the size of their system boards. These chipset-based system boards were quickly reduced to match the original **PC** and **PC-XT system boards** (22 x 33cm). This permitted the new 80286 boards to be installed in the smaller XT-style cases. This particular system board size, depicted in Figure 2-4, is referred to as a **baby AT system board**.

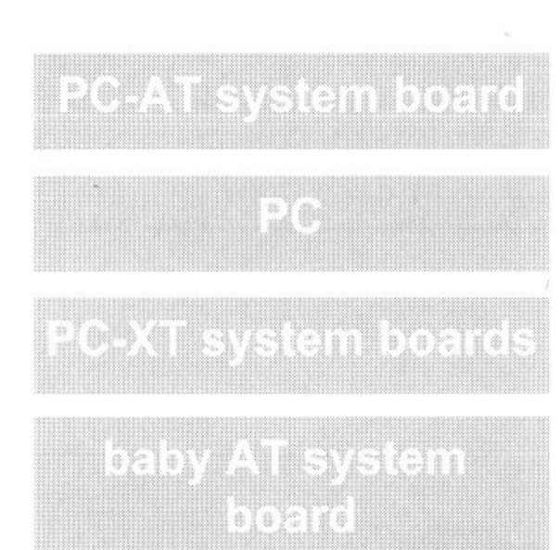

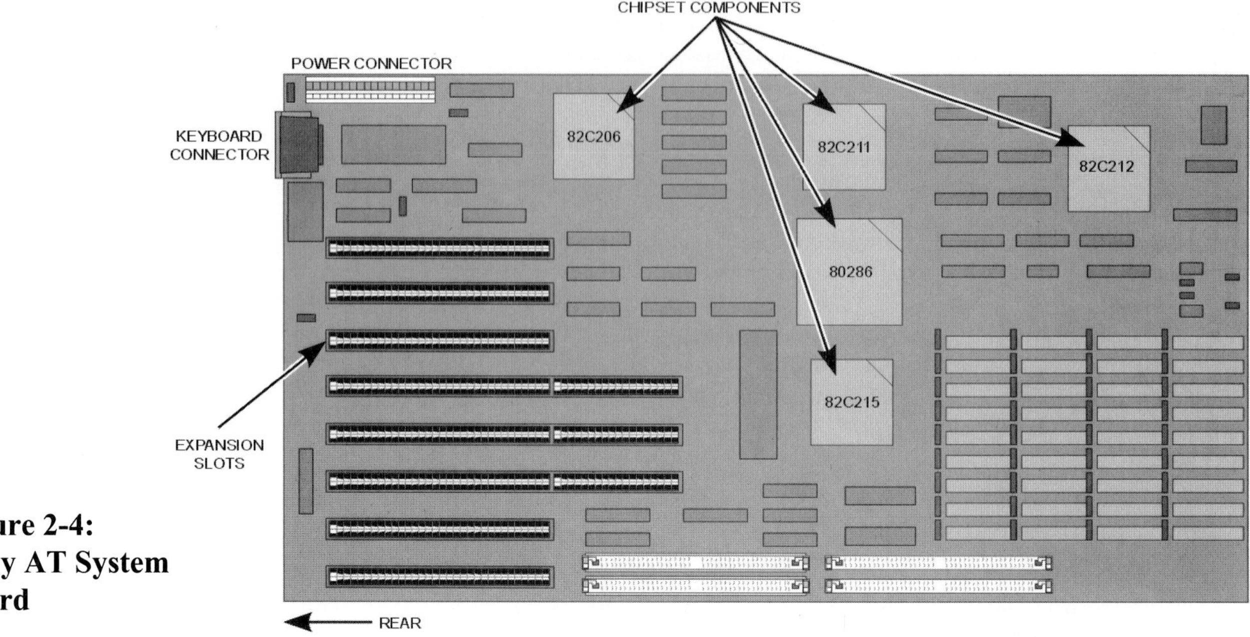

Figure 2-4: Baby AT System Board

System Board Compatibility

Obviously, the first consideration when installing or replacing a system board is whether it will physically fit and work with the other system components. In both of these situations, the following basic compatibility issues must be dealt with:

- The system board's form factor
- The case style
- The power supply connection type

System boards of different types have different mounting-hole patterns. Obviously the hole patterns of the replacement system board must match that of the case. If not, the replacement board cannot be installed or grounded properly.

Standard PC, PC-XT, and baby AT system boards share the same mounting hole patterns and can be exchanged with each other. However, the original PC-AT and ATX system boards have different hole pattern specifications. Most case manufacturers provide a variety of hole patterns in their designs to permit as many system board form factors as possible to be used with their cases.

Some clone system boards do not observe standard sizes (only compatible standoff spacing). If the case has a power supply that mounts in the floor of the unit, there may not be enough open width in the case to accommodate an extra-wide system board. The same can be said for a full-height disk drive bay. If the disk drive bay reaches from the floor of the case to its top, there will be no room for a wide system board to fit under it.

In addition to the mounting hole alignment issue, the case openings for expansion slots and port connections must be compatible with those of the system board. Various types of keyboard connectors have been used in different types of systems. Figure 1-44 (in Chapter 1) demonstrated the most common connectors used with PC keyboards: 6-pin mini DINs, 5-pin DINs, and RJ-11 plugs and jacks. PC-XT- and AT-compatible systems have historically used the 5-pin DIN connector. However, the 6-pin mini DIN is used with ATX systems. All three types of connectors have been used in non-compliant clone systems. If this is not taken into account when selecting a replacement board, additional expense may be incurred through the need to purchase an additional keyboard with the proper connector type.

Likewise, expansion-slot placement may vary somewhat between different form factors. The bad alignment created by this situation can make it difficult to install I/O cards in some systems. Similarly, I/O connectors mounted directly on the backs of some system boards may not line up with any openings in other case styles.

TEST TIP

Remember which system board types use a 5-pin DIN connector.

Expansion Slot Considerations

The types of adapter cards used in the system are another issue when replacing a system board. Make sure the new board has enough of the correct types of expansion slots to handle all the I/O cards that must be reinstalled. There is some upward compatibility between PC-bus, ISA, EISA, and VESA cards. Some PC-bus cards can be installed in ISA, EISA, and VESA slots—most cannot, however, because of a small skirt on the bottom of the card that conflicts with the ISA extension portion of the slot. Both the EISA and VESA slots can accommodate ISA cards. Be aware that these relationships are not backward compatible. MCA and PCI are not compatible with the other bus types.

Some **low-profile (LTX)** cases are designed to be used with backplanes. In these units, the I/O cards are mounted horizontally on a backplane card that extends from an expansion slot on the motherboard. This arrangement produces a very low-profile desktop case style. The expansion slots in the back panel of the cases are horizontal as well. Therefore, standard system-board/adapter-card arrangements will not fit.

low-profile (LTX)

Power Supply Considerations

Power supply size, orientation, and connectors present another compatibility consideration. For example, an AT power supply cannot be installed in an ATX case. Because the AT bolt pattern is different than the ATX bolt pattern, it cannot be properly secured and grounded in the ATX case. Also, the single power connector from the ATX power supply will not connect to an AT system board's dual (P8/P9) power connector. Finally, ATX fans blow air into the case from the rear; AT power supplies pull it through the case from the front.

FRU Components

If system board FRU components, such as the microprocessor and/or RAM devices, are to be moved from the original system board to a replacement, they must be compatible with the new system board in terms of both physical characteristics and operating speed. Devices to be exchanged between system boards must physically fit in the sockets of the new board and be fast enough to work with the new system.

In the case of DRAM devices, a 30-pin SIMM from an older system cannot physically be used in a newer 72-pin SIMM slot. Even if the SIMM, or a 168-pin DIMM from the original board can be transferred, it must still have a sufficient speed rating to work in the new system. The same is true for cache memory upgrades. When moving a microprocessor to a new board, it must be socket compatible, voltage compatible, and speed compatible with the new board.

Major Components

The original IBM PC used a 6-chip chipset to support the 8088 microprocessor. These devices included the following intelligent support devices:

- An 8284 Clock Generator
- An 8288 Bus Controller
- An 8255 Parallel Peripheral Interface (PCI)
- An 8259 Programmable Interrupt Controller (PIC)
- An 8237 DMA Controller (DMAC)
- An 8253 Programmable Interval Timer (PIT)
- An 8042 Intelligent Keyboard Controller

The clock generator and bus controller ICs assisted the microprocessor with system clock and control bus functions. The PCI chip handled system configuration and on-board addressing functions for the system's intelligent devices.

The interrupt controller provided the system with eight channels of programmable interrupt capabilities. The 8237 DMA Controller provided four channels of high-speed DMA data transfer service for the system. The 8253 was used to produce three programmable timer channel outputs to drive the system's time-of-day clock, DRAM refresh signal, and system speaker output signal. The PC/XT interrupt and DMA Controller functions are described in Figure 2-5.

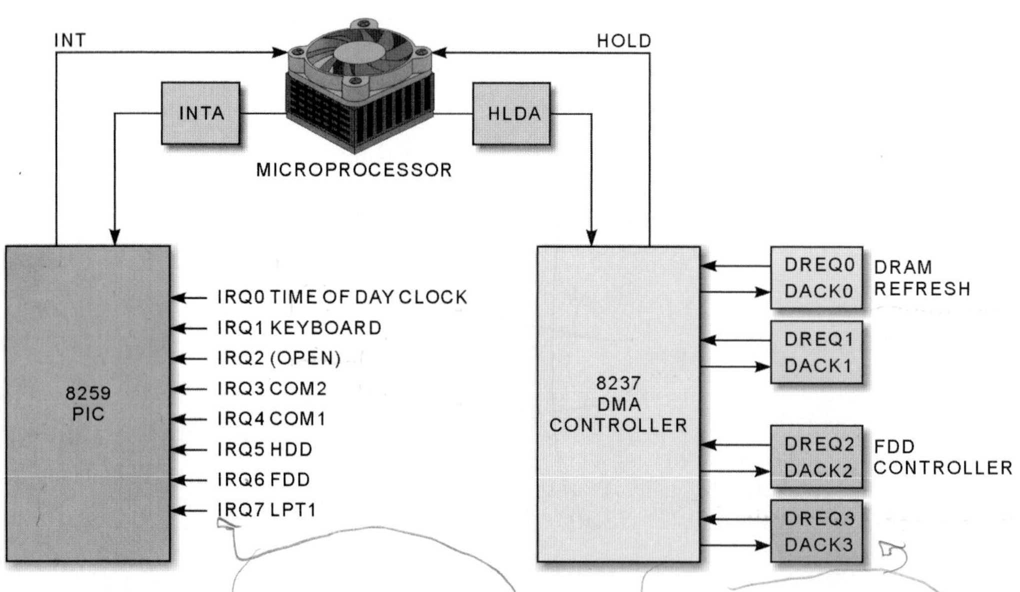

Figure 2-5: PC/XT Interrupt and DMA Controller Functions

When the IBM PC-AT came to the market, it brought an upgraded chipset that expanded the capabilities of the system. IBM improved the basic 8284 and 8288 devices by upgrading them to 82284 and 82288 versions. Likewise, the keyboard controller and the three-channel timer/counter were updated in the AT.

The AT's interrupt and DMA channel capabilities were both doubled by cascading two of each device together. Actually, the usable channel counts only rose to 15 and 7 respectively. In each case, one IC is the master device and the other is the slave device. One channel of each master device was used to accept input from the slave device. Therefore, that channel was not available for use by the system.

As an example, the output of the secondary interrupt controller is cascaded through the IRQ2 input of the master controller. In this way, the system sees all of the devices attached to the secondary controller as IRQ2. A priority resolver sorts out which interrupt from the slave controller is causing the interrupt. The PC-AT interrupt and DMA controller functions, described in Figure 2-6, still form the basis for all PC-compatible architectures.

> **TEST TIP**
>
> Remember how many total IRQ and DMA channels are involved in the PC/XT and PC-AT systems.

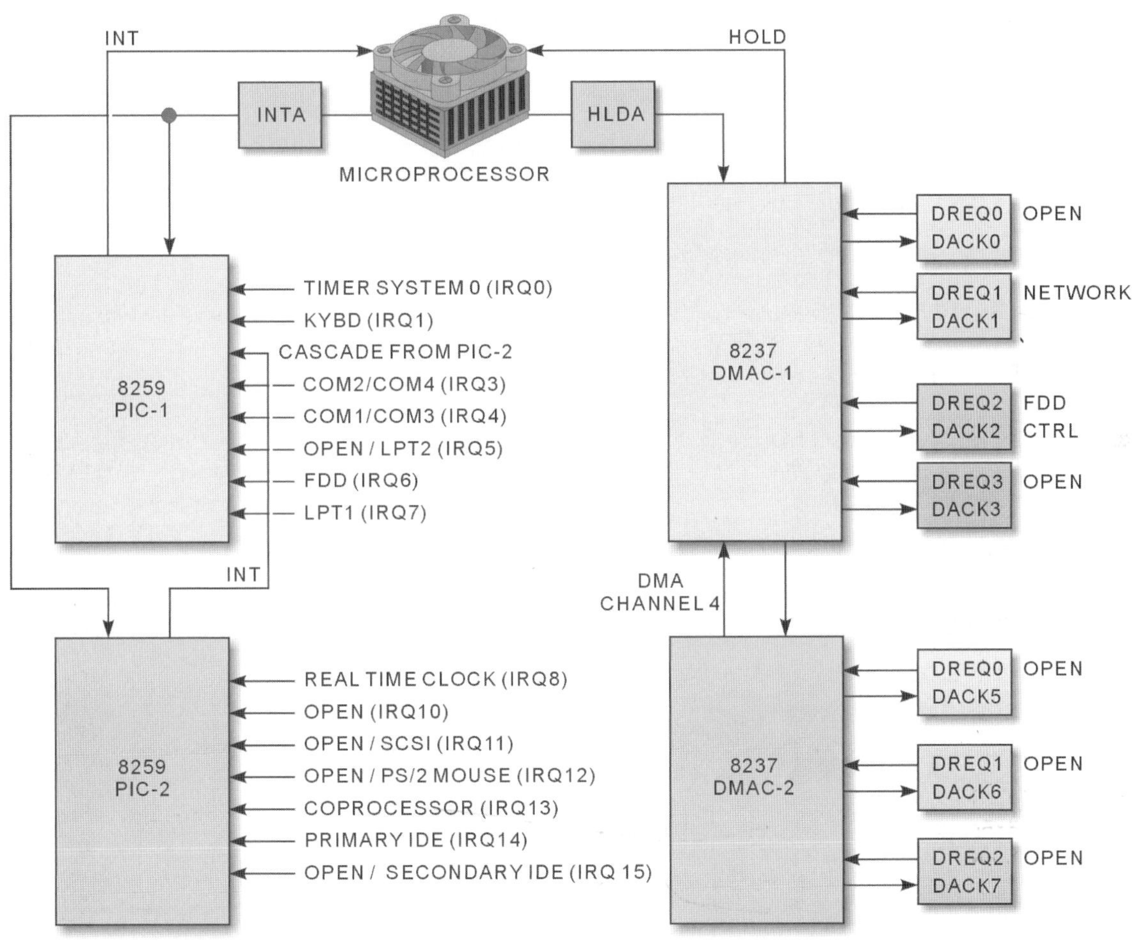

Figure 2-6: PC-AT Interrupt and DMA Controller Functions

TEST TIP

Know the standard assignment for each IRQ channel in an ISA-compatible PC system.

Since the second interrupt controller is cascaded through the first controller, the system sees the priority of the IRQ lines as described in Table 2-1. The table also indicates the usage of each IRQ line.

Table 2-1: IRQ's Priorities

AT PRIORITY	USE
IRQ0	System Board
IRQ1	System Board
IRQ2	System Board
IRQ8	System Board
IRQ9	I/O
IRQ10	I/O
IRQ11	I/O
IRQ12	I/O - System Board
IRQ13	System Board
IRQ14	I/O
IRQ15	I/O
IRQ3	I/O
IRQ4	I/O
IRQ5	I/O
IRQ6	I/O
IRQ7	I/O

TEST TIP

Remember which IRQ channel is used by the system's real-time clock (RTC).

Chipsets

chipset

IC manufacturers produce **chipset** packages that system board designers can use to support different microprocessors and standardized functions. While microprocessors have always had supporting chipsets supplied by their manufacturers, third-party chipsets began to appear when the AT architecture became the pseudo-standard for PC-compatible computers. Since then, IC manufacturers have tended to create chipsets for any complex circuitry that becomes a standard.

The original system board chipsets combined the major PC- and AT-compatible structures into larger integrated circuits. In particular, many IC makers produced single ICs that perform the AT interrupt, DMA, timer/counter, and real-time clock functions. These ICs also contained the address decoding and timing circuitry to support those functions.

Because chipset-based system boards require much fewer small- and medium-sized discrete devices to produce, printed-circuit-board manufacturers have been able to design much smaller PC boards.

As VLSI technology improves, IC manufacturers continue to integrate higher levels of circuitry into their chips. All the functions of the four-chip chipset system board of Figure 2-4 are duplicated using the two-chip chipset depicted in Figure 2-7. The high level of circuit concentration in this chipset allows the size of the system board to be reduced even further. It is approximately half the length of a standard baby AT system board; therefore, this size system board is referred to as a **half-size system board**.

half-size system board

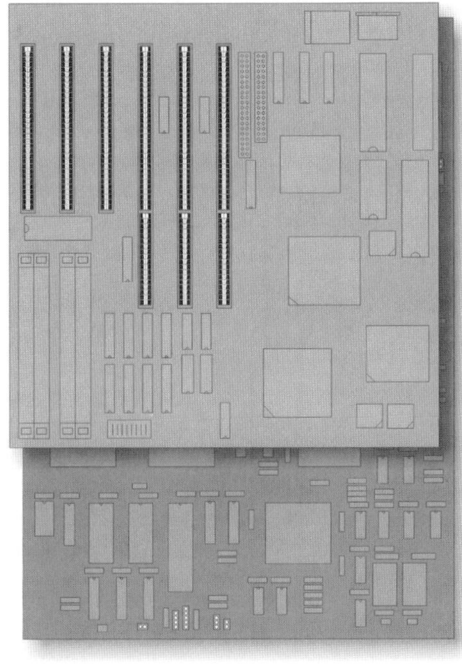

Figure 2-7: A Half-Size System Board

By combining larger blocks of circuitry into fewer ICs, a price reduction spiral is created. Fewer ICs on the board leads to reduced manufacturing costs to produce the board. The material cost of the board is decreased due to its smaller physical size. The component cost is decreased because it is cheaper to buy a few VLSI chips than several SSI or MSI devices. Finally, the assembly cost is less because only a few items must be mounted on the board.

Reduced board costs create lower computer prices, which in turn creates greater consumer demand for the computers. Increased demand for the computers, and therefore the chipsets, acts to further push down the prices of all the computer components.

It is normal to consider the ROM BIOS as an integral part of any chipset model because it is designed to support the register structure of a particular chipset. Therefore, replacing a ROM BIOS chip on a system board is not as simple as placing another ROM BIOS IC in the socket. The replacement BIOS must be correct for the chipset being used on the system board.

Pentium Chipsets

Several IC manufacturers have developed chipsets to support the Pentium processor and its clones. Most of these designs feature a three-chip chipset that supports a combination PCI/ISA bus architecture. Figure 2-8 depicts a generic chipset arrangement for this type of system board.

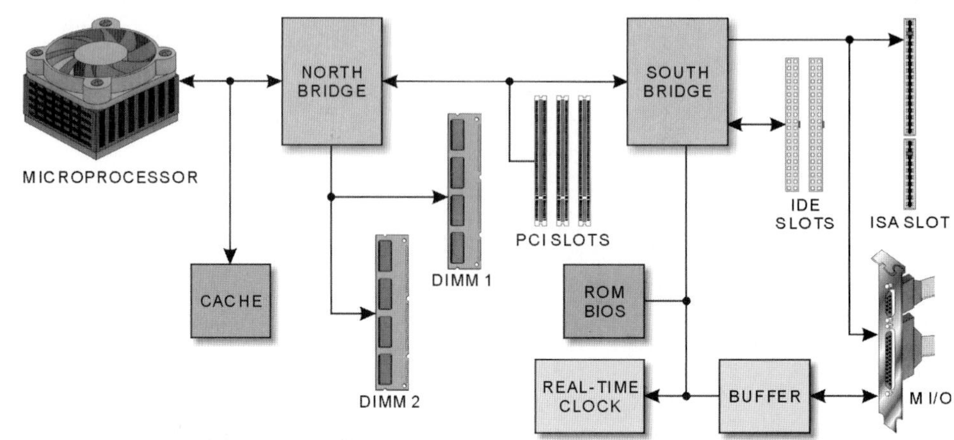

Figure 2-8: Typical Pentium Chipset

North Bridge

South Bridge

The typical Pentium chipset consists of a Memory Controller (called the **North Bridge**), a PCI-to-ISA Host Bridge (referred to as the **South Bridge**), and an Enhanced I/O Controller. The Memory Controller provides the interface between the system's microprocessor, its various memory sections, and the PCI bus. In turn, the Host Bridge provides the interface between the PCI bus, the IDE bus, and the ISA bus. The Enhanced I/O Controller chip interfaces the standard PC peripherals (LPT, COM, and FDD interfaces) to the ISA bus.

This typical chipset arrangement may vary for a couple of reasons. The first reason is to include a specialized function, such as an AGP or USB interface. The second reason is to accommodate changes in bus specifications.

System Bus Speeds

Microprocessor and chipset manufacturers are continually developing products to speed up the operation of the system. One method of doing this is to speed up the movement of data across the system's data buses. Looking at the arrangement shown in Figure 2-8, you should note that the buses operating directly with the microprocessor and North Bridge are running at one speed, while the PCI bus is running at a different speed, and the ISA/MIO devices are running at still another speed. The chipset devices are responsible for coordinating the movement of signals and data between these different buses.

The buses between the microprocessor and the North Bridge are referred to as the **front side buses** (**FSB**), while the PCI and ISA buses are referred to as the **back side buses** (**BSB**). Historically, the Pentium processors have operated at many speeds between 50 MHz and 1.1 GHz. At the same time the front side buses have been operating at 66 MHz, 100 MHz, and 133 MHz. Likewise, the PCI bus has operated at standard speeds of 33 MHz, 44 MHz, and 66 MHz. While the speeds of these buses have been improved, the speed of operation for the ISA bus has remained constant at 8 MHz.

front side buses (FSB)

back side buses (BSB)

Using an example of a current Pentium system board, the processor may run at 1.1 GHz internally, while the front side bus runs at 133 MHz, the PCI bus runs at 44.3 MHz, the IDE bus runs at 100 MHz, and the ISA bus runs at 8 MHz.

TEST TIP

Know which processors can be used with which system board bus speeds.

Expansion Slots

The system's expansion slots provide the connecting point for most of its I/O devices. Interface cards communicate with the system through the extended microprocessor buses in these slots.

As mentioned in Chapter 1—*Basic PC Hardware*, expansion slots basically come in three formats: 8-bit, 16-bit, and 32-bit data buses. The PC-bus slot is the most famous example of an 8-bit expansion slot, while the ISA slot is the consummate 16-bit expansion bus. The 32-bit expansion buses include the MCA bus, the EISA bus, the VESA bus, and the PCI bus. Let's cover the 8-bit expansion slots first.

8-Bit Slots

The 8-bit expansion slots in the original PC, PC-XT, and their compatibles became the **de facto** industry connection standard for 8-bit systems. It was dubbed the **PC-bus standard**.

de facto

PC-bus standard

The PC-bus expansion slot connector, illustrated in Figure 2-9, featured an 8-bit, bi-directional data bus and 20 address lines for the I/O channel. It also provided six interrupt channels, control signals for memory and I/O read or write operations, clock and timing signals, and three channels of DMA control lines. In addition, the bus offered memory refresh timing signals, and an I/O channel check line for peripheral problems, as well as power and ground lines for the adapters that plug into the bus.

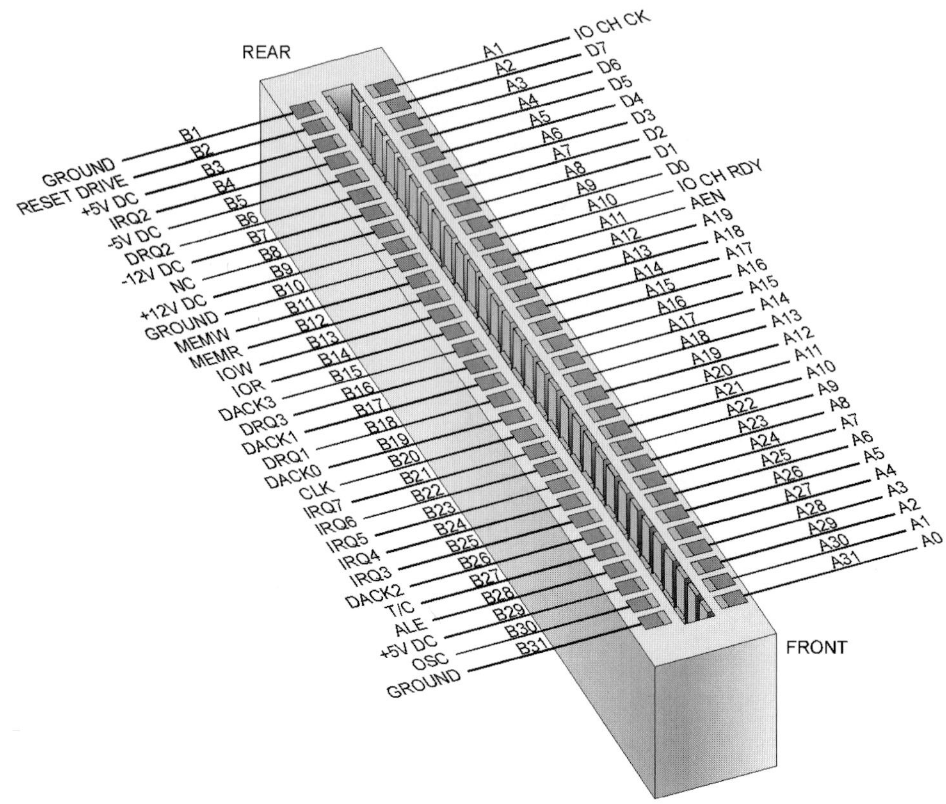

Figure 2-9: An 8-bit PC-Bus Expansion Slot

16-Bit Slots

AT bus

Industry Standard Architecture (ISA)

The overwhelming popularity of the IBM PC-AT established it as the 16-bit standard to which all other PC-compatible equipment is compared. Originally, this bus was called the **AT bus**. However, its widespread acceptance earned it the **Industry Standard Architecture (ISA)** title it now carries. As a matter of fact, the ISA slot is the most common expansion slot used with microcomputers. Even in units that have newer, faster 32-bit expansion slots, it is not uncommon to find one or more ISA slots.

This bus specification originally appeared on the 16-bit, 80286-based PC-AT system board. Its 16-bit data bus improved the performance of the system by enabling twice as much data to pass through the slot at a time. It also made transfers with 16-bit microprocessors a single-step operation. While the ISA bus ran at microprocessor-compatible speeds up to 10 or 12 MHz, incompatibility with slower I/O cards caused manufacturers to settle for running the bus at 8 or 8.33 MHz in newer designs.

TEST TIP

Remember that the ISA bus features a 16-bit data bus and runs at 8 or 8.33 MHz.

Figure 2-10 shows an ISA-compatible expansion slot connector. These expansion slots actually exist in two parts: the slightly altered, 62-pin I/O connector, similar to the standard PC-bus connector, and a 36-pin auxiliary connector.

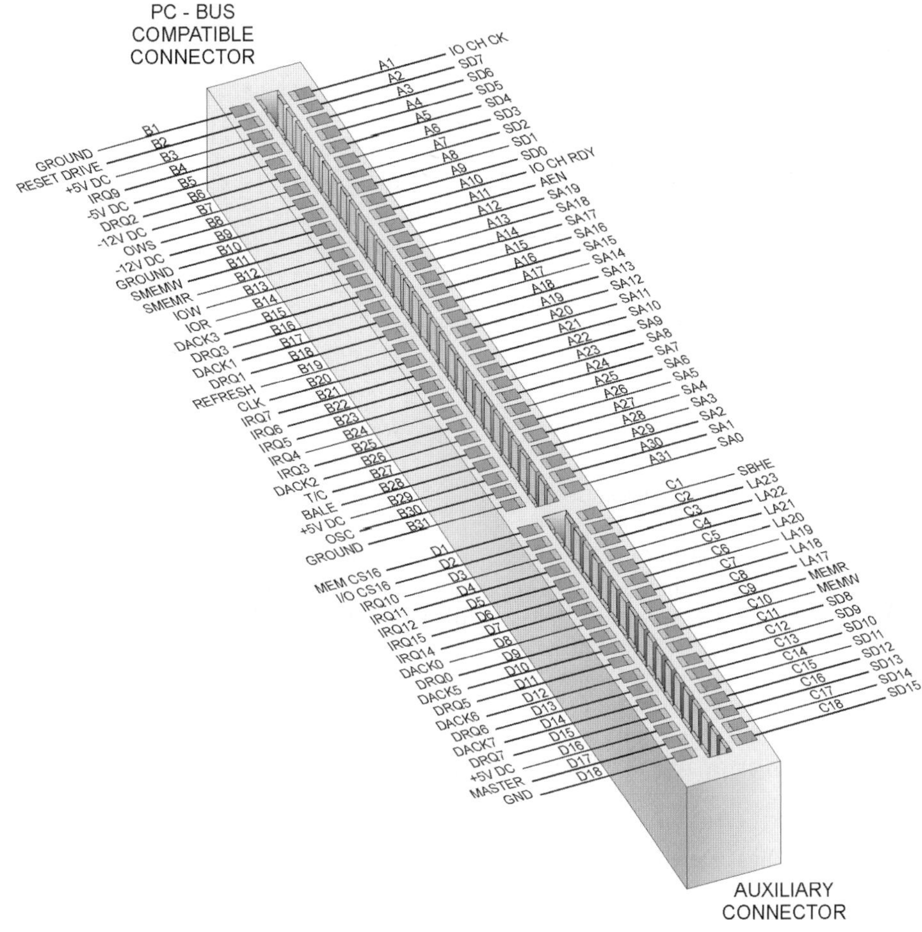

Figure 2-10: A 16-bit ISA Expansion Slot

It provides twice as many interrupt and DMA channels as the PC bus specification. This made it possible to connect more peripheral devices to ISA systems. In order to maintain compatibility with older adapter cards, the transfer speed for the ISA bus was limited to the same speed as that of the older PC bus.

32-Bit Architectures

As 32-bit microprocessors gained popularity, the shortcomings and restrictions of the 16-bit ISA bus became noticeable. Obviously, the ISA bus could not support the full, 32-bit capabilities of microprocessors such as the 80386DX, the 80486DX, and the Pentium. In addition, the physical organization of the signal lines in the ISA bus produced unacceptable levels of **Radio Frequency Interference** (**RFI**) as the bus speed increased. These factors caused designers to search for a new bus system to take advantage of the 32-bit bus and the faster operation of the processors.

Radio Frequency Interference (RFI)

Extended Industry Standard Architecture (EISA)

Micro Channel Architecture (MCA)

Two legitimate 32-bit bus standards were developed to meet these challenges. These were the **Extended Industry Standard Architecture** (**EISA**) bus, which, as its name implies, was an extension of the existing ISA standard bus, and an IBM-sponsored proprietary bus standard called **Micro Channel Architecture** (**MCA**).

Although both 32-bit designs were revolutionary and competed for the market, both have passed from the scene. In both cases, market demand did not support these designs and they were eventually replaced by other more acceptable standards.

Local Bus Designs

local buses

In order to speed up the operation of their systems, system board manufacturers began to add proprietary bus designs to their board to increase the speed and bandwidth for transfers between the microprocessor and a few selected peripherals. This was accomplished by creating special **local buses** between the devices that would enable the peripherals to operate at speeds close to that of the microprocessor.

When these designs began to appear, the peripherals that could be used in them were typically only available from the original system board manufacturer. The industry soon realized the benefits of such designs and the need for "standards." Currently, most Pentium system boards include a combination of ISA, AGP, and PCI expansion slots.

Initally, the **VL bus** offered the advantages of higher performance and lower costs than similar boards with PCI buses. In addition, the VL bus was typically implemented in such a way that 16-bit ISA cards could still use the traditional part of the expansion slot. However, improvements in the PCI standard have made it the bus of choice for most Pentium system boards.

Both local bus specifications include slot addressing capabilities and reserve memory space to allow for plug-and-play reconfiguration of each device installed in the system. Unfortunately, system boards that use these expansion slots normally have a few ISA-compatible slots also. This feature can seriously disrupt the plug-and-play concept since no identification or reconfiguration capabilities were designed into the ISA bus specification.

Due to industry moves away from anything related to ISA cards, the PCI bus has become the dominant force in system board designs. Each generation of PCI designs has provided fewer and fewer ISA buses. Current designs may include a single ISA connector for compatibility purposes or none at all.

TEST TIP

Remember which expansion slot types are most prevalent on a modern system board.

PCI Local Bus

The Peripheral Component Interconnect (PCI) local bus was developed jointly by IBM, Intel, DEC, NCR, and Compaq. Its design incorporates three elements: a low-cost, high-performance local bus, an automatic configuration of installed expansion cards (plug-and-play), and the ability to expand with the introduction of new microprocessors and peripherals. The data transfer performance of the PCI local bus is 132 MBps using a 32-bit bus and 264 MBps using a 64-bit bus. This is accomplished even though the bus has a maximum clock frequency of 33 MHz.

The PCI peripheral device has 256 bytes of on-board memory to hold information as to what type of device it is. The peripheral device can be classified as a controller for a mass-storage device, a network interface, a display, or other hardware. The configuration space also contains control, status, and latency timer values. The latency timer register on the device determines the length of time that the device can control the bus for bus mastering operations.

Figure 2-11 illustrates the structure of a system based on PCI local bus chipset components.

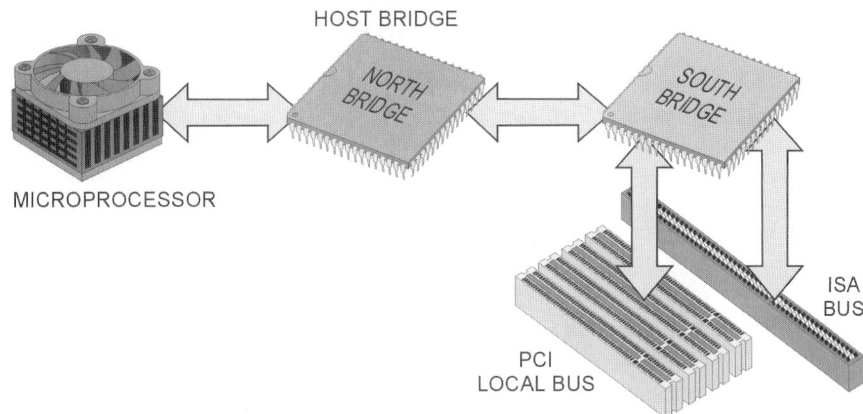

Figure 2-11: PCI Bus Structure

The main component in the PCI-based system is the PCI bus controller, called the **host bridge**. This device monitors the microprocessor's address bus to determine whether addresses are intended for devices on the system board, in a PCI slot, or in one of the system board's other expansion slots.

host bridge

In PC-compatible systems, the PCI bus normally co-exists with an ISA bus. The PCI portion of the bus structure functions as a **mezzanine bus** between the ISA bus and the microprocessor's main bus system. The figure also depicts a **PCI-to-ISA bridge** that allows ISA adapters to be used in the PCI system. Other bridge devices can also accommodate either EISA or MCA adapters.

mezzanine bus

PCI-to-ISA bridge

The host bridge routes 32-bit PCI data directly to the PCI expansion slots through the local bus. These transfers occur at speeds compatible with the microprocessor. However, it must route non-PCI data to the PCI-to-ISA bridge that converts it into a format compatible with the ISA expansion slot. In the case of ISA slots, the data is converted from the 32-bit to the 16-bit ISA format. These transfers occur at typical ISA bus speeds.

Figure 2-12 shows the pin-out of a PCI connector. The PCI bus specification uses multiplexed address and data lines to conserve the pins of the basic 124-pin PCI connector. Within this connector are signals for control, interrupt, cache support, error reporting, and arbitration.

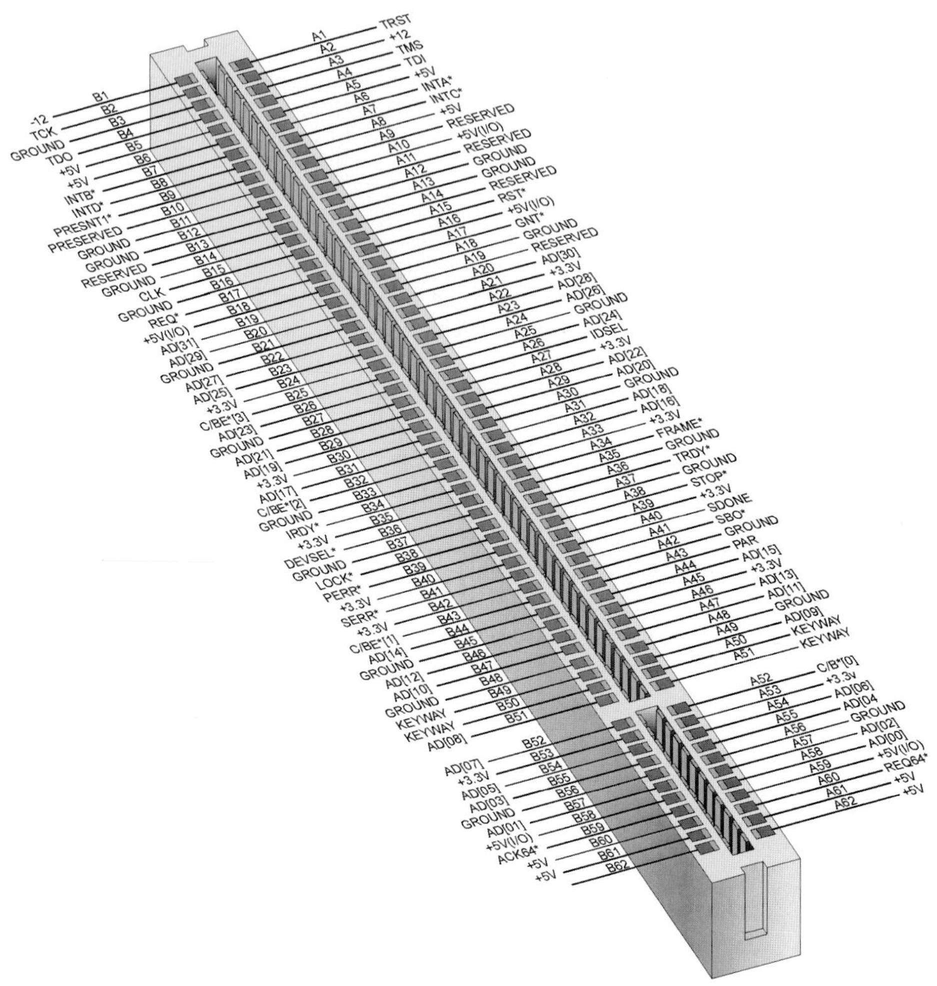

Figure 2-12: PCI Slot Pin-out

The PCI bus uses 32-bit address and data buses (AD0–AD31). However, its specification also defines 64-bit multiplexed address and data buses for use with 64-bit processors such as the Pentium. Its clock (CLK) line was originally defined for a maximum frequency of 33 MHz and a 132 MB/second transfer rate, but it can be used with microprocessors operating at higher clock frequencies (66 MHz under the PCI 2.1 specification).

Request (REQ)

Grant (GNT)

The **Request** (**REQ**) and **Grant** (**GNT**) lines provide arbitration conventions for bus-mastering operations. The arbitration logic is contained in the host bridge. To allow for faster access, a bus master can request use of the bus while the current bus cycle is in progress. When the current bus cycle ends, the master can immediately begin to transfer data, assuming the request has been granted.

PCI Configuration

detection phase

The PCI standard is part of the plug-and-play hardware standard. As such, the system's BIOS and system software must support the PCI standard. Although the PCI function is self-configuring, many of its settings can be viewed and altered through the CMOS Setup utility. Figure 2-13 depicts the PCI PnP configuration information from a typical BIOS.

ROM PCI/ISA BIOS (P155TVP4)
PNP AND PCI SETUP
AWARD SOFTWARE, INC.

Slot 1 (Right) IRQ	: Auto	DMA 1 Used By ISA	: No/ICU
Slot 2 IRQ	: Auto	DMA 3 Used By ISA	: No/ICU
Slot 3 IRQ	: Auto	DMA 5 Used By ISA	: No/ICU
Slot 4 IRQ	: Auto		
PCI Latency Timer	: 32 PCI Clock	ISA MEM Block BASE	: No/ICU
		NCR SCSI BIOS	: Auto
IRQ 3 Used By ISA	: No/ICU	USB Function	: Disabled
IRQ 4 Used By ISA	: No/ICU		
IRQ 5 Used By ISA	: No/ICU		
IRQ 6 Used By ISA	: No/ICU		
IRQ 7 Used By ISA	: No/ICU		
IRQ 8 Used By ISA	: No/ICU		
IRQ 9 Used By ISA	: No/ICU		
IRQ 10 Used By ISA	: No/ICU		
IRQ 11 Used By ISA	: No/ICU		
IRQ 12 Used By ISA	: No/ICU		
IRQ 13 Used By ISA	: No/ICU	ESC : Quit ↑↓←→	: Select Item
IRQ 14 Used By ISA	: No/ICU	F1 : Help PU/PD/+/-	: Modify
IRQ 15 Used By ISA	: No/ICU	F5 : Old Values (Shift) F2	: Color
		F6 : Load BIOS Defaults	
		F7 : Load Setup Defaults	

Figure 2-13: PCI Configuration Settings

During a portion of the bootup known as the **detection phase**, the PnP-compatible BIOS checks the system for devices installed in the expansion slots to see what types they are, how they are configured, and which slots they are in. For PnP-compatible I/O cards, this information is held in a ROM device on the adapter card.

The BIOS reads the information from all of the cards and then assigns each adapter a **handle** (logical name) in the **PnP registry**. It then stores the configuration information for the various adapters in the registry as well. This process is described in Figure 2-14. Next, the BIOS checks the adapter information against the system's basic configuration for **resource conflicts**. After evaluating the requirements of the cards and the system's resources, the PnP routine assigns system resources to the cards as required.

handle

PnP registry

resource conflicts

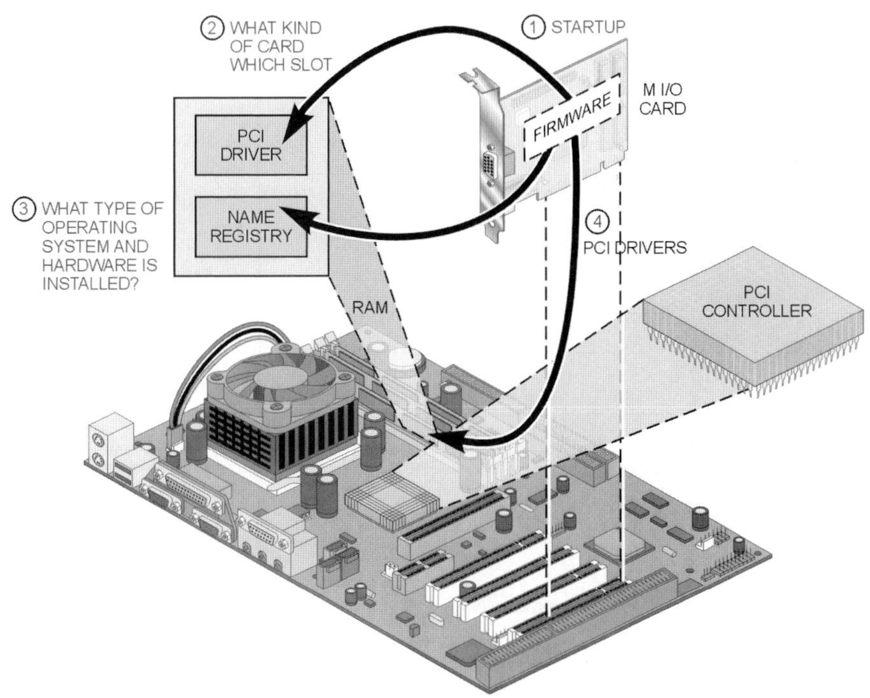

Figure 2-14: PCI Information Acquisition

TEST TIP

Know which system resources the PnP system must assign first and why.

Since the PnP process has no method for reconfiguring legacy devices during the resource assignment phase, it begins by assigning resources, such as IRQ assignments, to legacy devices before servicing the system's PnP devices.

TEST TIP

Know the process the PnP system employs to allocate resources to a new device in an existing system.

Likewise, if the BIOS detects the presence of a new device during the detection phase, it disables the resource settings for its existing cards, checks to see what resources are required and available, and then reallocates the system's resources as necessary.

Depending on the CMOS settings available with a particular PCI chipset, the startup procedure may be set up to configure and activate all of the PnP devices at startup. With other chipsets, it may also be possible to check all cards, but only enable those actually needed for startup. Some CMOS routines may contain several user-definable PCI configuration settings. Typically, these settings should be left in default positions. The rare occasion for changing a PCI setting occurs when directed to do so by a product's installation guide.

Systems may theoretically contain an unlimited number of PCI slots. However, a maximum of four slots are normally included on a system board due to signal loading considerations. The PCI bus includes four internal interrupt lines (INTa through INTd, or INT1 through INT4) that allow each PCI slot to activate up to four different interrupts. PCI interrupts should not be confused with the system's IRQ channels, although they can be associated with them if required by a particular device. In these cases, IRQ9 and IRQ10 are typically used.

VESA Local Bus

VESA

VL bus

The **VESA** local bus was developed by the Video Electronics Standards Association. This local bus specification, also referred to as the **VL bus**, was originally developed to provide a local bus connection to a video adapter. However, its functionality has since been defined for use with other adapter types, such as drive controllers and network interfaces.

Figure 2-15 illustrates the flow of information through the VL bus-based computer. It also indicates data transfer priority levels.

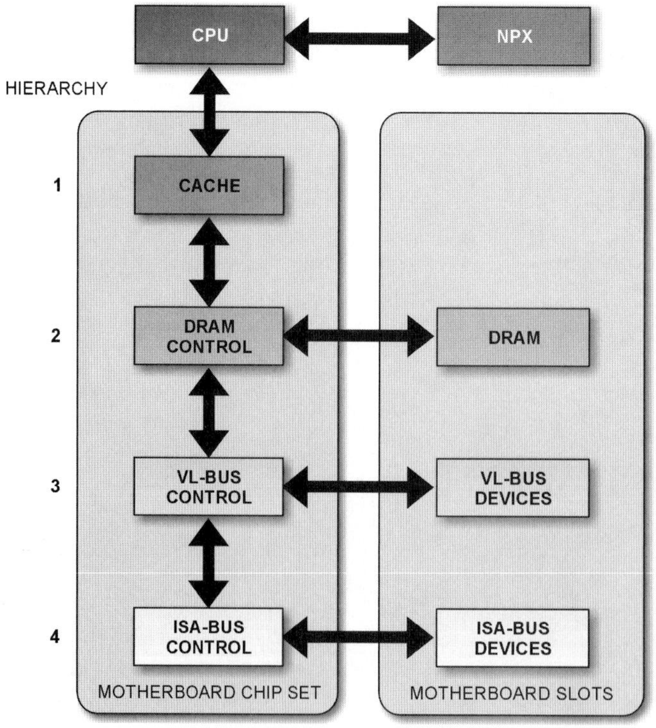

Figure 2-15: VL Bus Block Diagram

Like the PCI bus, the VL-bus controller monitors the microprocessor's bus to determine what type of operation is being performed, and where the address is located in the system.

The highest level of activity occurs between the microprocessor and the system's cache memory unit. The second level of priority exists between the microprocessor and the system's DRAM memory unit. The third priority level is between the microprocessor and the VL-bus controller. The final priority level exists between the VL-bus controller and the non-VESA bus controller.

VL-bus data is passed to the VESA slots on the local bus in 32-bit format at VL-bus speeds. The VL-bus controller passes non-VESA data to the ISA bus controller to be applied to the ISA expansion slots. These transfers are carried out in 16-bit ISA format, at ISA-compatible speeds.

local bus controller

local bus master

local bus target

The VL bus also defines the operation of devices connected to the bus, and classifies them as either **local bus controller**, **local bus master**, or **local bus target**. The local bus controller arbitrates requests for use of the bus between the microprocessor and local bus masters. A local bus master is any device, such as a SCSI controller, that is capable of initiating data transfers on the VL bus. A local bus target is any device capable of only answering requests for a data transfer. The data transfer can be either a read or a write operation. The VESA connector is depicted in Figure 2-16.

The VL bus defines a local bus that was originally designed for use with 80386 or 80486 microprocessors. It can operate at up to 66 MHz if the VL-bus device is built directly on the system board. However, if the VL-bus devices are installed into an expansion slot, the maximum frequency allowed is 50 MHz.

Newer revisions of the VESA bus standard multiplex the address and data buses to provide 64-bit buses for use with the Pentium, and future generation microprocessors. These revisions allow for a 32-bit adapter to operate in a 64-bit slot, or vice versa.

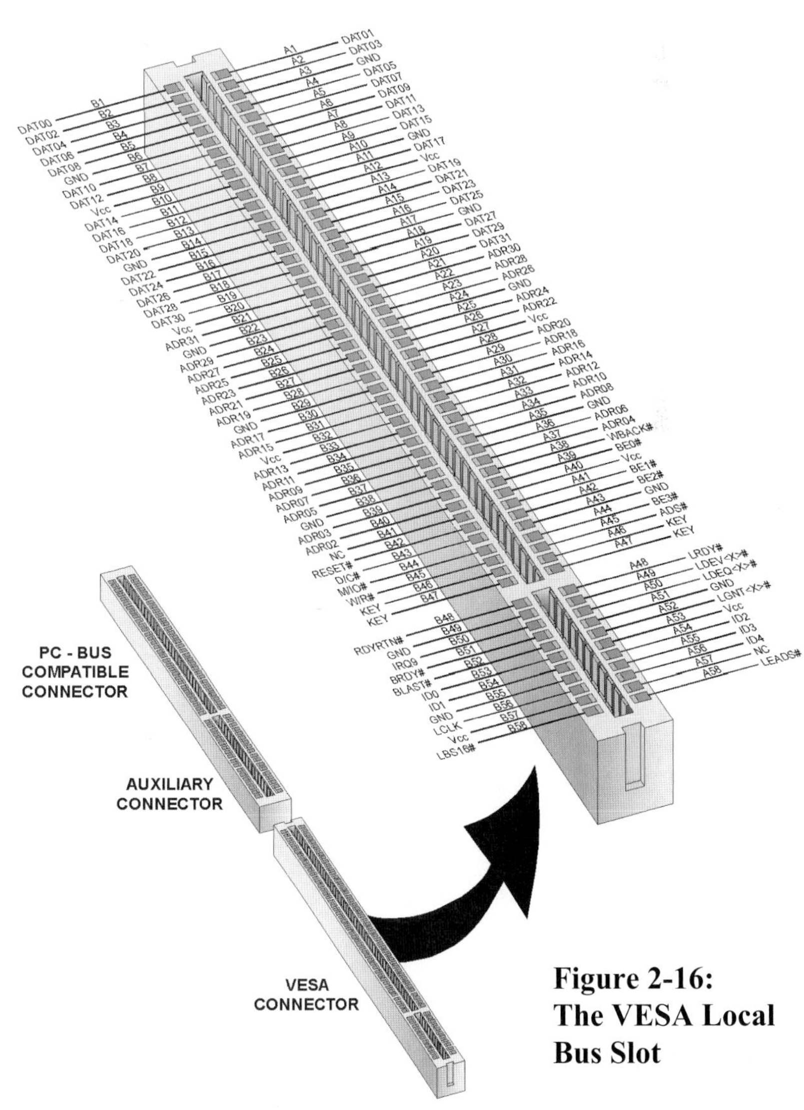

Figure 2-16: The VESA Local Bus Slot

AGP Slots

Accelerated Graphics Port (AGP)

Newer Pentium systems include an advanced **Accelerated Graphics Port** (**AGP**) interface for video graphics. The AGP interface is a variation of the PCI bus design that has been modified to handle the intense data throughput associated with 3 dimensional graphics.

TEST TIP

Know what type of device is plugged into an AGP slot.

The AGP specification was introduced by Intel to provide a 32-bit video channel that runs at 66 MHz in basic 1X video mode. The standard also supports two high-speed modes that include a 2X (5.33 MBps) and a 4X (1.07 GBps) mode.

The AGP standard provides for a direct channel between the AGP graphic controller and the system's main memory, instead of using the expansion buses for video data. This removes the video data traffic from the PCI buses. The speed provided by this direct link permits video data to be stored in system RAM instead of in special video memory.

Figure 2-17 shows the standard AGP slot connector used with desktop system boards. The system board typically supports a single slot that is supported by a Pentium/AGP-compliant chipset. System boards designed for portable systems and single-board systems may incorporate the AGP function directly into the board without using a slot connector.

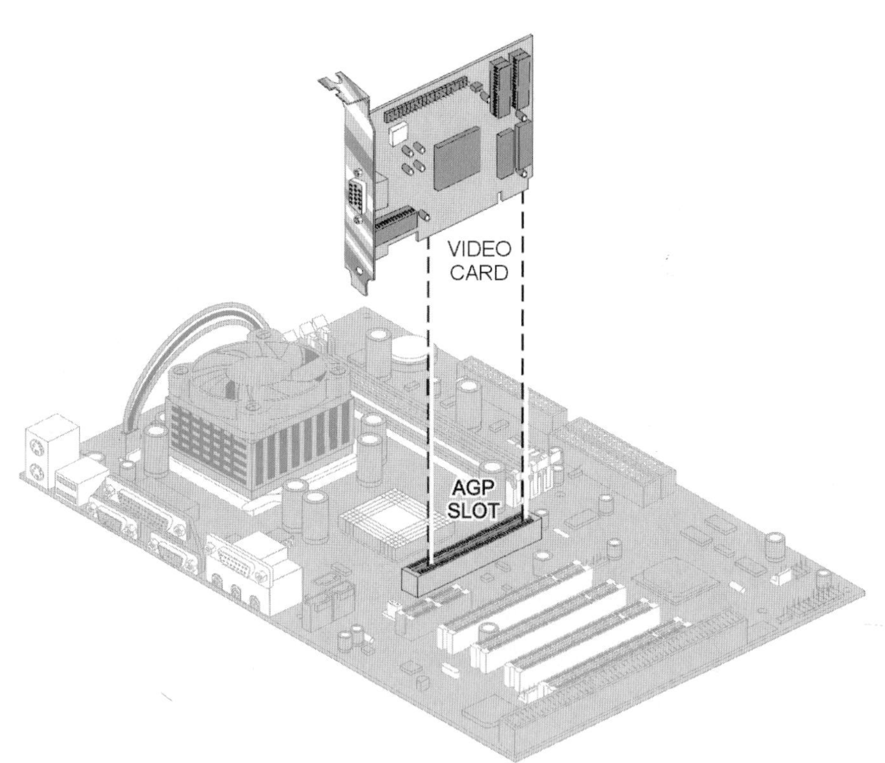

Figure 2-17: An AGP Slot

Audio Modem Risers

Intel has developed a new audio/modem standard for system board designs. This standard includes an expansion slot connection, called the **Audio/Modem Riser (AMR)**, and a companion expansion card format, known as the **Mobile Daughter Card (MDC)**. These components are depicted in Figure 2-18.

Audio/Modem Riser (AMR)

Mobile Daughter Card (MDC)

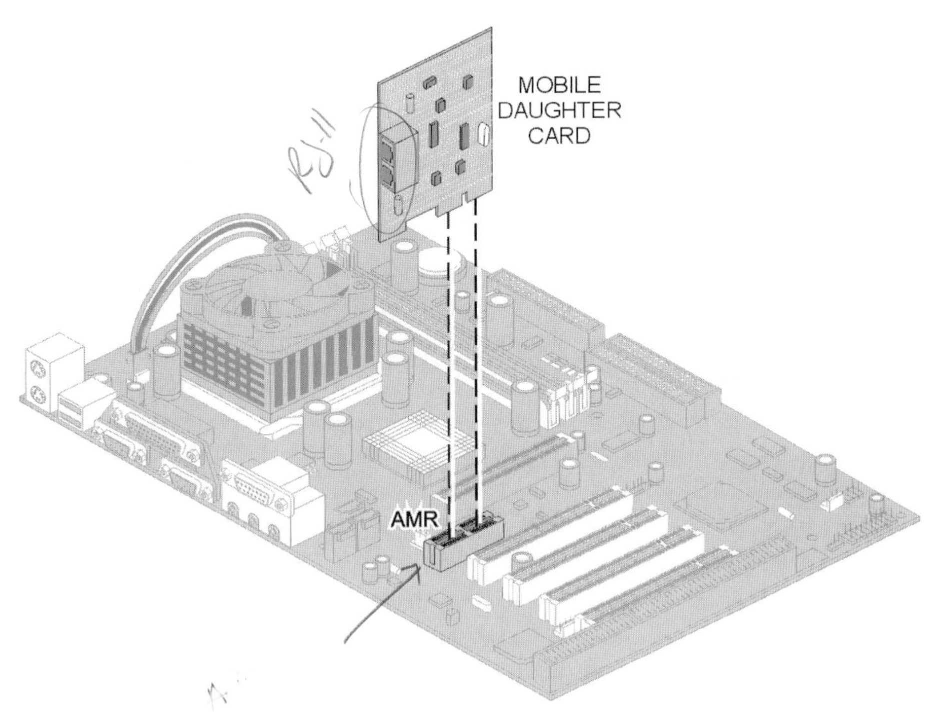

Figure 2-18: Audio/Modem Riser Components

The design specification separates the analog and digital functions of audio (sound card) and modem devices. The analog portion of the function is placed on the MDC riser card while the digital functions are maintained on the system board. This permits the system board to be certified without passing through the extended FCC and international telecom certification process attached with modem certifications. Only the MDC needs to pass the FCC certification process.

The contents of the MDC basically consist of an analog audio **coder/decoder (codec)** or a modem circuit. The digital functions performed by the system board are a function of software instead of a hardware device such as a UART. The system microprocessor basically performs the UART functions under the control of the audio or modem software. This relationship makes the AMR device much less expensive, but places additional overhead on the operation of the microprocessor.

coder/decoder (codec)

AMR slots are already being replaced in Pentium systems by a new design called the **Communications and Networking Riser (CNR)** card, depicted in Figure 2-19. This specification improves on the AMR specification by including support for advanced V.90 analog modems, multi-channel audio, telephone-based dial-up networking, and USB devices, as well as 10/100 Ethernet-based LAN adapters.

Communications and Networking Riser (CNR)

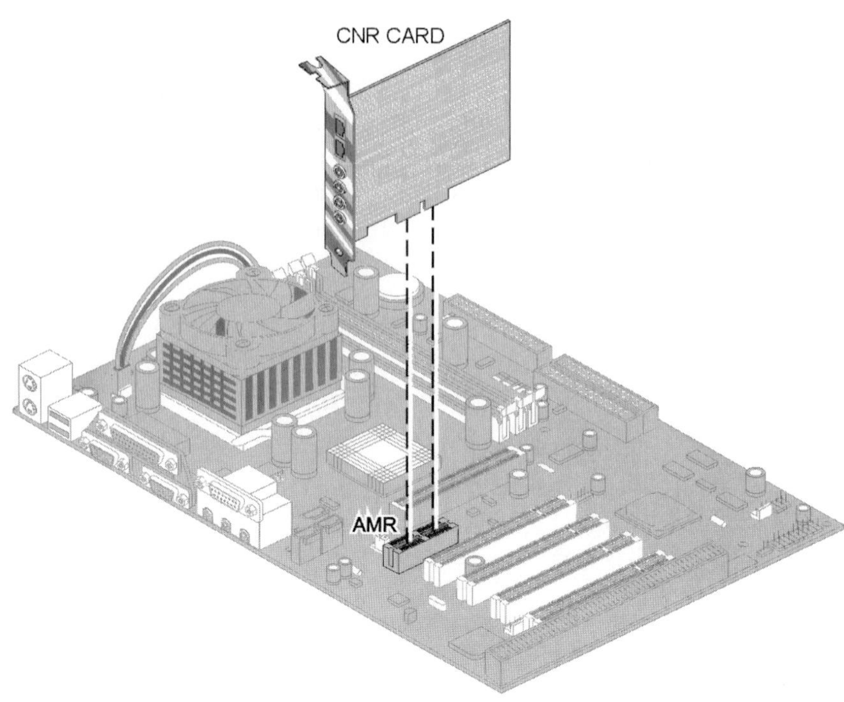

Figure 2-19: Communications and Networking Riser Card

PCMCIA Slots

As more and more desktop users began to adopt laptop and notebook computers for travel, they demanded that additional peripheral systems be included. With the limited space associated with portables, it became clear that a new method for installing options would need to be developed. At first, laptop and notebook manufacturers included proprietary expansion connectors for adding such devices as fax/modems, additional memory, and additional storage devices.

Personal Computer Memory Card International Association's (PCMCIA)

PC Card

In 1989, the **Personal Computer Memory Card International Association's (PCMCIA)** bus standard was introduced using a 68-pin JEIDA connector. A small form-factor expansion-card format, referred to as the **PC Card** format, was also adopted for use. This format was derived from earlier laptop/notebook memory card designs. The design of the bus specification enables the PC Card interface to be used for a wide variety of peripheral devices.

The PCMCIA slot connector is typically recessed in the portable's case. The credit card-sized PC cards slide into bays in the side of the case. They are normally pushed through a spring-loaded door on the side of the case and slide along guide rails molded into the sides of the bay. When fully inserted, the sockets built into the end of the cards engage the pins of the recessed connector. Peripheral devices are attached to the exposed end of the card through a small PC-Card connector, as illustrated in Figure 2-20.

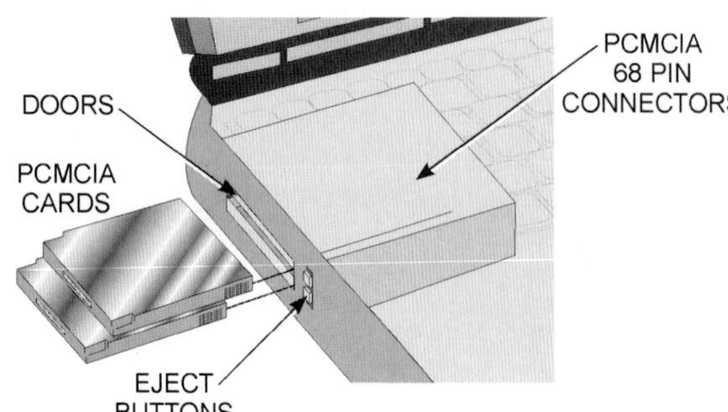

Figure 2-20: PCMCIA Connections

Since PC Cards are primarily used with portable computer systems, they are discussed in detail in Chapter 7—*Portable Systems*.

Table 2-2 compares the capabilities of the various bus types commonly found in personal computers. It is quite apparent that the data transfer rates possible with each new version increase dramatically. The reason this is significant is that the expansion bus is a speed-limiting factor for many of the system's operations. Every peripheral access made through the expansion slots requires the entire computer to slow down to the operating speed of the bus.

Table 2-2: Expansion Bus Specifications

BUS TYPE	TRANSFER RATE	DATA BITS	ADDRESS BITS	DMA CHANNELS	INT CHANNELS
PC	1 MBps	8	20	4	6
ISA	8 MBps	16	24	8	11
EISA	32 MBps	32	32	8	11
MCA	20–40 MBps	32	32	None	11
VESA	150/275 MBps	32/64	32	None	1
PCI 2	132/264 MBps	32/64	32	None	3
PCI 2.1	264/528 MBps	32/64	32	None	3
AGP	266/533/1,070 MBps	32	32	None	3

I/O Connections

Pre-Pentium computers typically employed a Multi I/O (MI/O) adapter card to provide standardized AT-compatible I/O connections. However, the chipsets used to construct Pentium-based system boards move these I/O functions to the system board by including the ports' interfaces and controllers in the chipset.

Pentium AT Ports

The typical Pentium chipset integrates the circuitry for all the traditional MI/O functions, except the game port, into one or two VLSI chips. Figure 2-21 illustrates a sample arrangement for the AT-style Pentium system board's standard I/O connectors (ports).

The Pentium chipset normally provides a single, programmable parallel printer port, which allows a wide range of printers and other parallel devices to be connected to the system. Parallel I/O devices plug into a DB-25F connector located on an expansion-slot cover. This port is connected to the system board at the 26-pin BERG pin block PRT1.

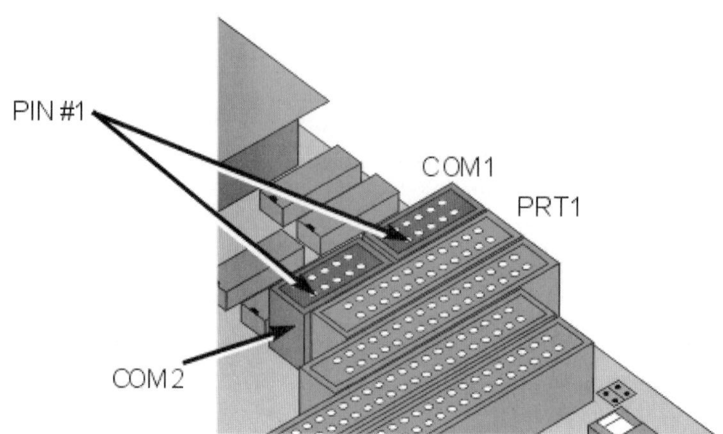

Figure 2-21: Pentium System Board I/O Connections

The last of the system board's I/O adapter functions are the RS-232C serial/asynchronous interface-port connections COM1 and COM2. These ports support serial communications for serial I/O devices, such as mice and modems. A ribbon cable connects the system board's COM1 connector to a DB-9M connector located on one of the unit's slot covers. This serial port is typically the system's first serial port and is normally the mouse connector.

Another ribbon cable connects the system board's COM2 connection to a DB-25F connector on one of the expansion-slot covers. This connector serves as the second logical serial port.

Separate hardware jumpers on the system board are typically used to configure the interrupt levels for the first and second serial ports (COM1 and COM2). Care should be taken when setting these jumpers because the two serial ports cannot share the same COM-port designation. Figure 2-22 illustrates the proper connection of the serial-port ribbon cables to the AT-style system board.

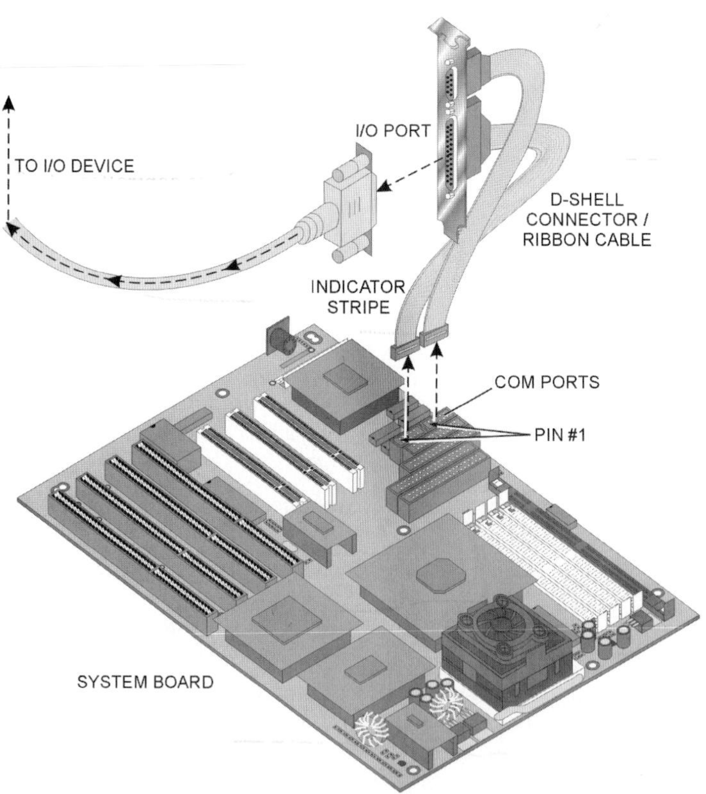

Figure 2-22: AT-Style Serial-Port Connections

Pentium ATX Ports

On ATX-compliant system boards, the MI/O port connections have been moved to a vertical stack form factor located at the rear of the board. Figure 2-23 depicts the standard arrangement of the I/O port connections in an ATX system.

The ATX specification employs two 6-pin mini-DIN connectors for the mouse and keyboard. Of course, the fact that both connections use the same type of connector can lead to problems if they are reversed. The standard also provides for two USB port connections, a DB-25F D-shell parallel printer port connector, two RS-232 serial COM ports implemented in a pair of DB-9M D-shell connectors, a DB-15F D-shell game port, and an RCA audio port. Unlike the AT-style integrated I/O connections, these port connections require no system board connecting cables that can become defective.

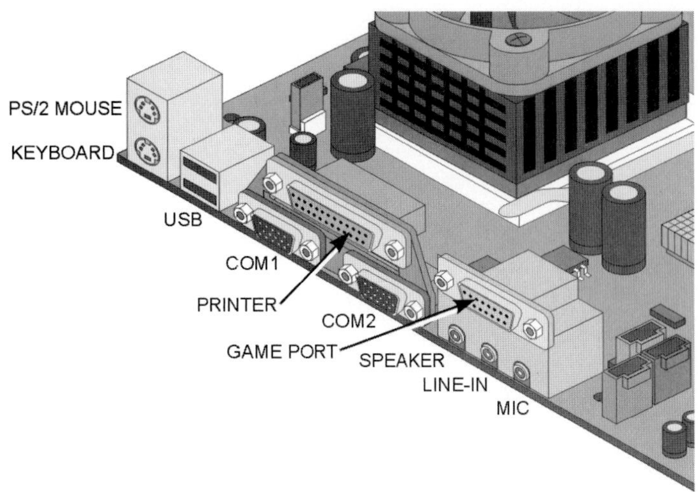

Figure 2-23: Pentium System Board I/O Connections

TEST TIP

Be aware that the use of the 6-pin mini DIN in ATX systems can cause confusion between the keyboard and PS/2 mouse connection.

On-Board Disk Drive Connections

Along with the I/O port connections, Pentium system boards moved the hard- and floppy-disk drive controller functions and interface connections to the system board, as illustrated in Figure 2-24. As is the case with most Pentium-based system boards, this example provides the system's IDE host adapter and floppy-disk drive controller interface connections.

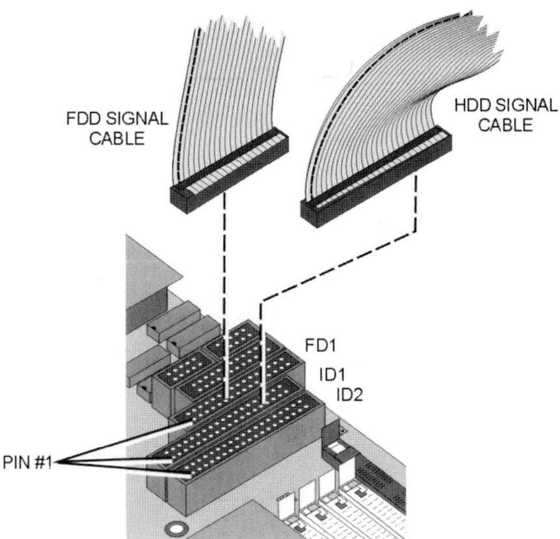

Figure 2-24: Pentium Board Disk Drive Connections

The FDC portion of the chipset can control two floppy disk drives whose signal cable connects to the system board at the 34-pin BERG block (labeled FD1 in Figure 2-24). As with any disk-drive connections, caution must be taken when connecting the floppy disk drive signal cable to the system board; pin 1 of the connector must line up with the signal cable's indicator stripe.

The IDE host adapter portion of the chipset is normally capable of controlling up to four hard disk, or CD-ROM, drives. These adapters furnish two complete IDE channels: IDE1 and IDE2. Each channel can handle one master and one slave device. The hard drives and CD-ROM drives are connected to the system board's IDE connectors by 40-conductor ribbon cables at connectors ID1 or ID2.

The primary partition of the drive attached to the ID1 connector will be designated as a logical C: drive. If a second drive is attached to ID1 as a slave, its primary partition will be designated as a logical D: drive. If there is an additional partition on the first drive, it will be designated as the E: drive. The hierarchy of assigning logical drive designations in the IDE interface calls for primary partitions to be assigned sequentially from ID1 master, ID1 slave, ID2 master, to ID2 slave. This is followed by assigning extended partitions for each drive in the same order.

The hard drives are connected in much the same manner as the floppy drives. The first hard drive is connected to the end of the cable farthest away from the ID1 or ID2 connector. Observe the same cable orientation that was used for connecting the floppy disk drives when connecting the cable to the FD1 connector for the hard drives. Figure 2-25 provides an example of the alignment of the FDD and HDD cables on the system board.

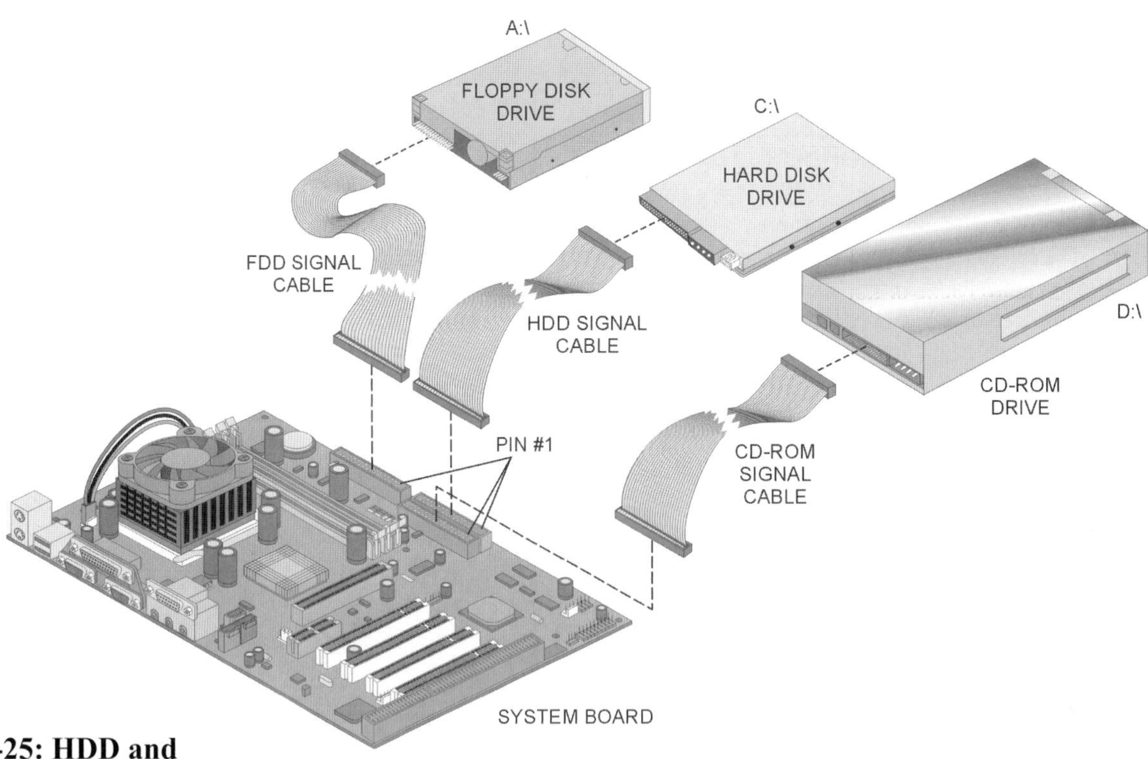

Figure 2-25: HDD and FDD System Board Connections

There are also two versions of the IDE interface, the original IDE specification and a newer, Enhanced IDE, or EIDE standard. The EIDE interface has been redefined to allow faster transfer rates, as well as the handling of more storage capacity. It can also be used to control drive units such as a tape or CD-ROM. The EIDE interface is often described as an **ATAPI (AT Attachment Packet Interface), or a Fast ATA (Fast AT Attachment**) interface.

ATAPI (AT Attachment Packet Interface)

Fast ATA (Fast AT Attachment)

These operating modes must be configured correctly through the system's CMOS Setup utility. These settings are discussed under the Chipset Features Screen heading later in this chapter.

There is no industry-accepted equivalent for on-board SCSI adapters. Although a few such system board designs are available, they are not standard boards and have probably been created to fill the specific needs of a particular application. Therefore, SCSI devices require that a SCSI host adapter card be installed in most systems. SCSI host adapters are typically available for use with ISA, EISA, and PCI bus interfaces.

TEST TIP

Be aware of the types of expansion slots that SCSI cards are typically available for.

MICROPROCESSORS

The A+ Core objective 4.1 states that the test taker should be able to distinguish between the popular CPU chips in terms of their basic characteristics. Popular CPU chips include:

- Intel, AMD, and Cyrix

Characteristics include:

- Physical size
- Voltage
- Speeds
- On-board cache or not
- Sockets/ SEC (Single Edge Contact) Cartridge
- Number of pins

INTEL PROCESSORS

When IBM was designing the first PC, it chose the Intel 8088 microprocessor and its supporting chipset as the standard CPU for its design. This was a natural decision since one of IBM's major competitors (Apple) was using the Motorola microprocessor for its designs. The choice to use the Intel microprocessor still impacts the design of PC-compatible systems. As a matter of fact, the microprocessors used in the vast majority of all PC-compatible microcomputers include the Intel 8088/86, 80286, 80386, 80486, and Pentium (80586 and 80686) devices.

The popularity of the original PCs, PC-XTs, and PC-ATs (and the software developed for them) has caused limitations to be built into the newer microprocessors to maintain compatibility with the microprocessors used in these systems. The popularity of these processors has been so high that it has produced a microprocessor clone market that designs processors to mimic the Intel design.

For the most part, the previous generations of microprocessors have disappeared from the marketplace, leaving the Pentium as the only processor type that needs to be discussed in detail. Therefore, the microprocessor material that follows builds on the earlier Intel models described in Chapter 1—*Basic PC Hardware*. We will first look at the Intel Pentium microprocessors that have set the trends in PC design and then explore the clone versions of these processors to see how they are different.

The Pentium Processor

Pentium processor

80x86

The **Pentium processor** succeeded the 80486 microprocessor, and maintained compatibility with the other **80x86** microprocessors. When Intel introduced the Pentium, it discontinued the 80x86 naming convention it had previously used for its microprocessors. This was done so that Intel could copyright the name (numbers cannot be copyrighted) and prevent clone microprocessor manufacturers from using the same convention. Therefore, the 80586 became the Pentium.

Quad Word (Qword)

The Pentium is a 32/64-bit microprocessor contained in a Ceramic Pin Grid Array package. The internal architecture of the Pentium is shown in Figure 2-26. The registers for the microprocessor and floating-point sections of the Pentium are identical to those of the 80486. It has a 64-bit data bus that allows it to handle **Quad Word** (or **Qword**) data transfers. The Pentium also contains two separate 8-kB caches, compared to only one in the 80486. One of the caches is used for instructions or code, and the other is used for data. The internal architecture of the Pentium resembles an 80486 in expanded form. The floating-point section operates up to five times faster than that of the FPU in the 80486.

superscalar

pipelining

stages

U-pipe

V-pipe

The Pentium is referred to as a **superscalar** microprocessor because its architecture allows multiple instructions to be executed simultaneously. This is achieved by a **pipelining** process. Pipelining is a technique that uses multiple **stages** to speed up instruction execution. Each stage in the pipeline performs a part of the overall instruction execution, with all operations being completed at one stage before moving on to another stage. This technique allows streamlined circuitry to perform a specific function at each stage of the pipeline, thereby improving execution time. When an instruction moves from one stage to the next, a new instruction moves into the vacated stage. The Pentium contains two separate pipelines that can operate simultaneously. The first is called the **U-pipe** and the second the **V-pipe**.

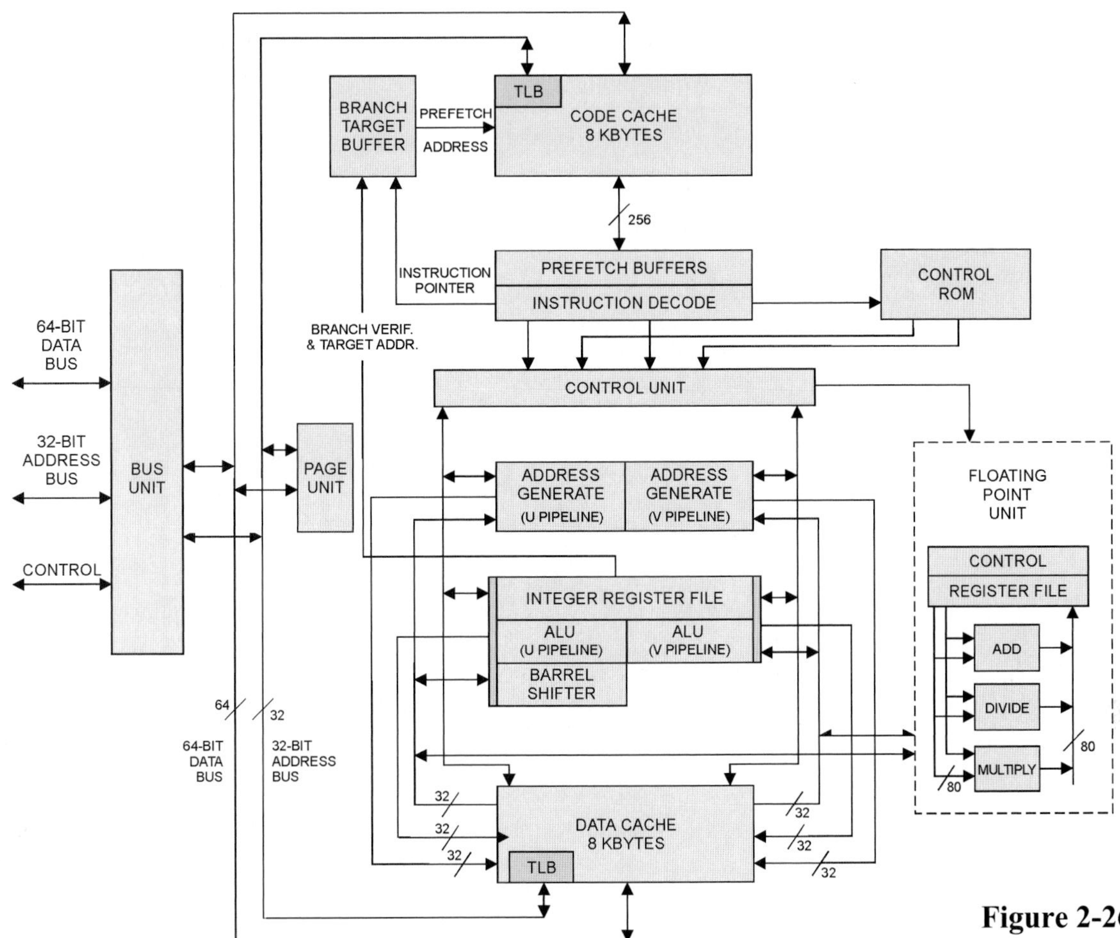

Figure 2-26: Inside the Pentium Microprocessor

The original Pentium processor architecture has appeared in three generations. The first-generation design, code named the P5, came in a 273-pin PGA package and operated at 60 or 66 MHz speeds. It used a single +5 Vdc operating voltage, which caused it to consume a large amount of power and generate a large amount of heat. The Pentium processor generated so much heat during normal operation that an additional **CPU cooling fan** was usually required.

CPU cooling fan

The second-generation Pentiums, referred to as **P54Cs**, came in a 296-pin **Staggered Pin Grid Array (SPGA)** package and operated at 75, 90, 100, 120, 133, 150, and 166 MHz in different versions. For these devices, Intel reduced the power supply voltage level to +3.3 Vdc to consume less power and provide faster operating speeds. Reducing the power supply level in effect moves the processor's high and low logic levels closer together, requiring less time to switch back and forth between them. The SPGA packaging made the second-generation of Pentium devices incompatible with the first-generation system boards.

P54Cs

Staggered Pin Grid Array (SPGA)

The second-generation devices also employed internal clock multipliers to increase performance. In this scenario, the system's buses run at the same speed as the clock signal introduced to the microprocessor. However, the internal clock multiplier causes the microprocessor to operate internally at some multiple of the external clock speed (i.e., a Pentium operating from a 50 MHz external clock and a 2x internal multiplier is actually running internally at 100 MHz).

Basically, all Pentium microprocessors use 50, 60, or 66 MHz external clock frequencies to generate their internal operating frequencies. The value of the internal multiplier is controlled by external hardware jumper settings on the system board.

P55Cs

Pentium MMX (Multimedia Extension)

The third-generation Pentiums, referred to as the **P55Cs**, use a 296-pin SPGA arrangement. This package adheres to the 321-pin Socket-7 specification designed by Intel. The P55C has been produced in versions that operate at 150, 166, 180, 200, and 233 MHz. This generation of Pentium devices operate at voltages below the +3.3 level established in the second generation of devices. The P55C is known as the **Pentium MMX (Multimedia Extension)** processor and is described in greater detail later in this chapter. A pin-out for the first-generation Pentium is shown in Figure 2-27.

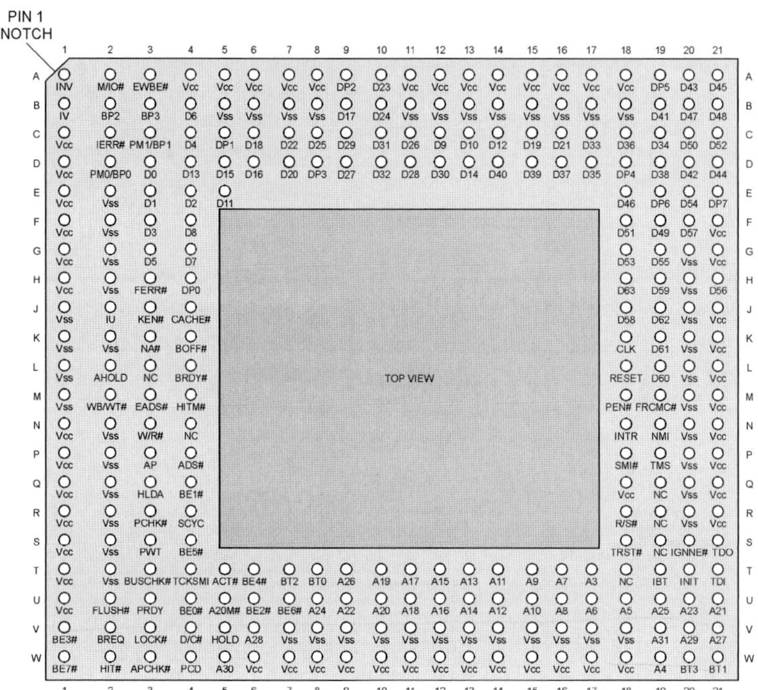

Figure 2-27: The Pins of the Pentium Microprocessor

Advanced Pentium Architectures

Intel has continued to advance its Pentium line of microprocessors by introducing additional specifications including the Pentium MMX, Pentium Pro, Pentium II, and Pentium III processors.

At the same time, Intel's competitors have developed clone designs that equal or surpass the capabilities of the Intel versions. The following sections will look at the advancements Intel has produced and then focus on the clone processors that compete with them.

Pentium MMX

In the **Pentium MMX** processor, the multimedia and communications processing capabilities of the original Pentium device were extended by the addition of 57 multimedia-specific instructions to the instruction set.

Intel also increased the on-board L1 cache size to 32 kB. The cache has been divided into two separate 16 kB caches: the instruction cache and the data cache. The typical L2 cache used with the MMX was 256 kB or 512 kB.

The MMX added an additional multimedia-specific stage to the integer pipeline. This integrated stage handled MMX and integer instructions quickly. Improved branching prediction circuitry was also implemented to offer higher prediction accuracy and, thereby, provide higher processing speeds. The four Prefetch buffers in the MMX could hold up to four successive streams of code. The four write buffers were shared between the two pipelines to improve the memory write performance of the MMX.

The Pentium MMX processor was available in 166, 200, and 233-MHz versions and used a 321-pin, SPGA Socket-7 format. It required two separate operating voltages. One source was used to drive the Pentium processor core, while the other was used to power the processor's I/O pins. The pin-out of the Pentium MMX is shown in Figure 2-28.

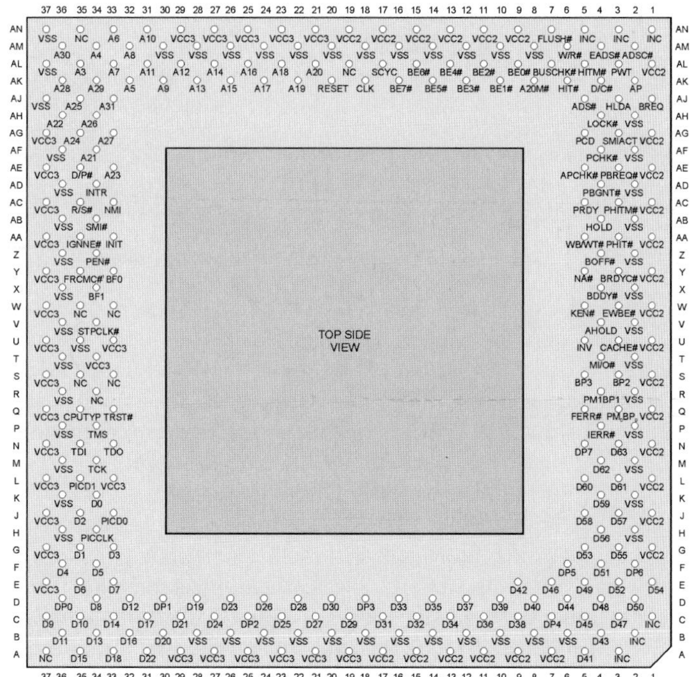

Figure 2-28: The Pins of the Pentium MMX Microprocessor

Compare Figures 2-27 and 2-28. Notice the staggered pin arrangement of the MMX device compared to the uniform row and column arrangement of the original Pentium devices. Also, notice the new signals added to the Pentium architecture for later versions. Some of these additional signals were used to implement the VRM and internal clock multiplier functions for the advanced Pentiums.

Pentium Pro

Pentium Pro

Intel departed from simply increasing the speed of its Pentium processor line by introducing the **Pentium Pro** processor. While compatible with all of the previous software written for the Intel processor line, the Pentium Pro is optimized to run 32-bit software.

processor core

However, it did not remain pin-compatible with the previous Pentium processors. Instead, Intel adopted a 2.46" x 2.66", 387-pin PGA configuration to house a Pentium Pro **processor core**, and an on-board 256 kB (or 512 kB) L2 cache. The L2 cache complements the 16 kB L1 cache in the Pentium core. This arrangement is illustrated in Figure 2-29. Notice that while they are on the same PGA device, the two components are not integrated into the same IC. The unit is covered by a gold-plated, copper/tungsten heat spreader.

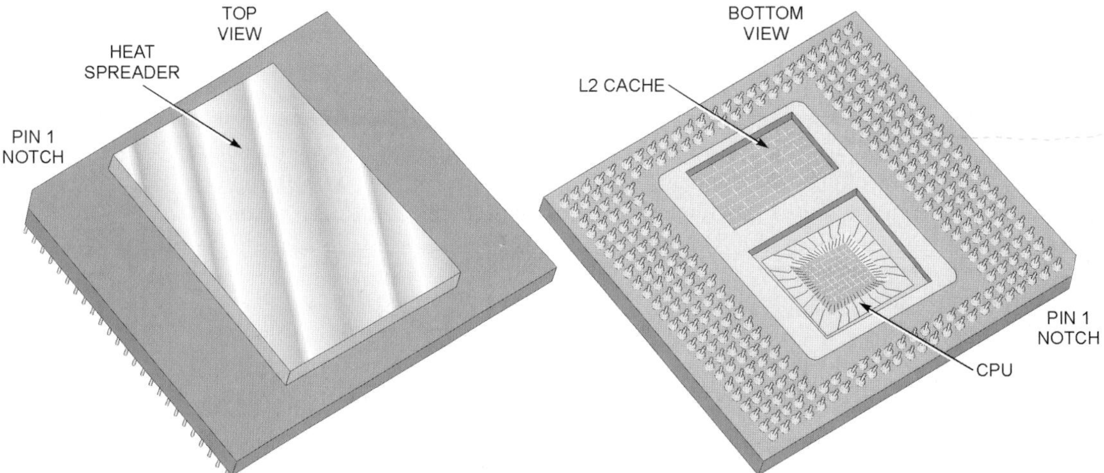

Figure 2-29: The Pentium Pro Microprocessor

The L2 on-board cache stores the most frequently used data not found in the processor's internal L1 cache, as close to the processor core as it can be without being integrated directly into the IC. A high-bandwidth cache bus connects the processor and cache unit together. The bus (0.5 inches in length) allows the processor and external cache to communicate at a rate of 1.2 GB/second.

The Pentium Pro is designed in a manner so that it can be used in typical, single-microprocessor applications or in multiple-processor environments, such as high-speed, high-volume file servers and workstations. Several dual-processor system boards have been designed for twin Pentium Pro processors. These boards, like the one shown in Figure 2-30, are created with two Pentium Pro sockets so that they can operate with either a single processor, or with dual processors. When dual processors are installed, logic circuitry in the Pentium Pro's core manages the requests for access to the system's memory and 64-bit buses.

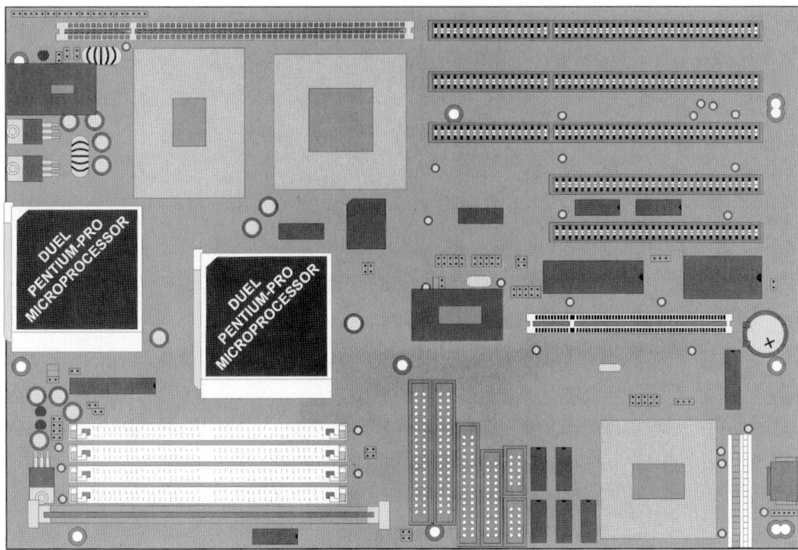

Figure 2-30: A Dual-Processor System Board

Pentium II

Pentium II

Single Edge Contact (SEC) cartridge

retention mechanism

Intel radically changed the form factor of the Pentium processors by housing the **Pentium II** processor in a new, **Single Edge Contact (SEC) cartridge**, depicted in Figure 2-31. This cartridge uses a special **retention mechanism** built into the system board to hold the device in place. The new proprietary socket design is referred to as the **Slot 1** specification and is designed to allow the microprocessor to eventually operate at bus speeds in excess of 300 MHz. This is the upper operating frequency limit for pin grid sockets.

TEST TIP

Remember which components Intel included in the SEC cartridge.

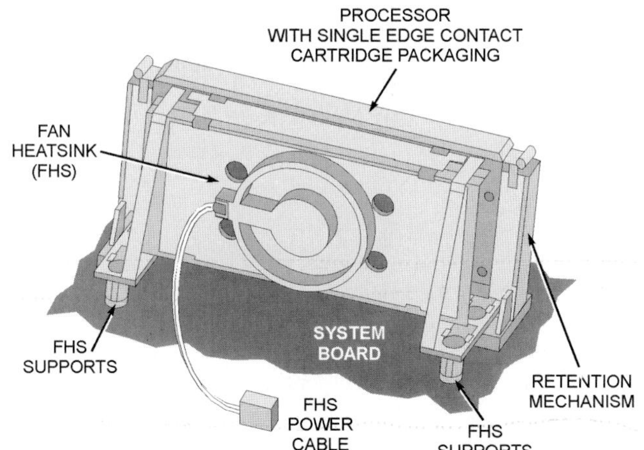

Figure 2-31: The Pentium II Cartridge

Slot 1

Fan Heat Sink (FHS)

Tag RAM

L2 Burst SRAM

The cartridge also requires a special **Fan Heat Sink** (**FHS**) module and fan. Like the SEC cartridge, the FHS module requires special support mechanisms to hold it in place. The fan draws power from a special power connector on the system board, or from one of the system's optional power connectors.

Inside the cartridge, there is a substrate material on which the processor and related components are mounted. The components consist of the Pentium II processor core, a **Tag RAM**, and an **L2 Burst SRAM**. Tag RAM is used to track the attributes (read, modified, etc.) of data stored in the cache memory.

Pentium II—The Pentium II includes all of the multimedia enhancements from the MMX processor, as well as retaining the power of the Pentium Pro's dynamic execution and 512 kB L2 cache features. The L1 cache is increased to 32 kB, while the L2 cache operates with a half-speed bus.

Figure 2-32 depicts the contents of the Pentium II cartridge.

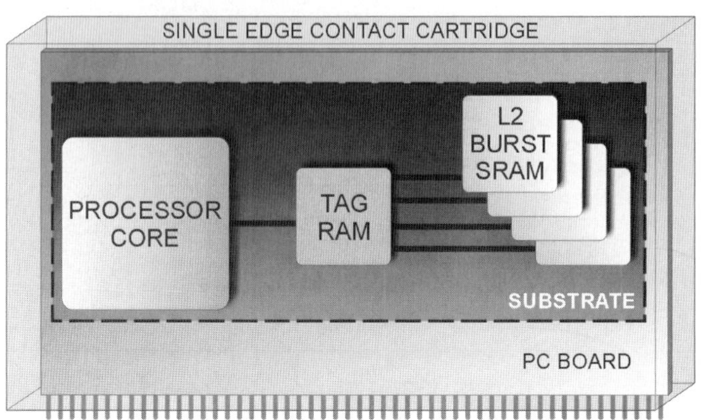

Figure 2-32: Inside the Pentium II Cartridge

A second cartridge type, called the Single Edged Processor Package (SEPP), has been developed for use with the Slot 1 design. In this design, the boxed processor is not completely covered by the plastic housing as it is in the SECC design. Instead, the SEPP circuit board is accessible from the back side.

Application Programming Interface (API)

The operation of Pentium Pro and Pentium II processors can be modified by uploading processor update information into BIOS that have **Application Programming Interface (API)** capabilities built into them. The microprocessor manufacturer places update information on its web site that can be downloaded onto a floppy disk by customers. The user transfers the update information from the update diskette to the system's BIOS via the API. If the updated data is relevant (as indicated by checking its processor stepping code), the API writes the updated microcode into the BIOS. This information will, in turn, be loaded into the processor each time the system is booted.

Pentium III

Pentium III

Intel followed the Pentium II processor with a new Slot 1-compatible design it called the **Pentium III**. The original Pentium III processor (code-named Katmai) was designed around the Pentium II core, but increased the L2 cache size to 512 KB. It also increased the speed of the processor to 600 MHz including a 100 MHz front-side bus speed.

TEST TIP

Be able to state the difference between Pentium II and Pentium III processors.

Intel followed the Pentium III design with a less expensive version that it named the Pentium **Celeron**. Unlike the original Pentium III, the Celeron version featured a 66 MHz bus speed and only 128 KB of L2 cache. Initially, the **Celeron Mendocino** was packaged in the SECC cartridge.

Celeron

Celeron Mendocino

Later versions of the Pentium III and Celeron processors were developed for the Intel **Socket 370** specification. This design returned to a 370-pin, ZIF socket/SPGA package arrangement, depicted in Figure 2-33.

Socket 370

The first pin grid array versions of the Pentium III and Celeron processors conformed to a standard called the **Plastic Pin Grid Array (PPGA)** 370 specification. Intel repackaged its processors into a PGA package to fit this specification. The PPGA design was introduced to produce inexpensive, moderate performance Pentium systems. The design topped out at 533 MHz with a 66 MHz bus speed.

Figure 2-33: Socket 370/Celeron

Intel upgraded the Socket 370 specification by introducing a variation called the **Flip Chip Pin Grid Array (FC-PGA)** 370 design. Intel made small modifications to the wiring of the socket to accommodate the Pentium III processor design. In addition, they employed a new 0.18 micron IC manufacturing technology to produce faster processor speeds (up to 1.12 GHz) and front-side bus speeds (100 MHz and 133 MHz). However, the new design only provides 256 KB of L2 cache.

Plastic Pin Grid Array (PPGA)

Flip Chip Pin Grid Array (FC-PGA)

Pentium III and Celeron processors designed with the 0.18 micron technology are referred to as **Coppermine** and **Coppermine 128** processors, respectively (the L2 cache in the Coppermine 128 is only 128 KB). Future Coppermine versions should employ 0.13 micron IC technology to achieve 1.4 GHz operating speeds.

Coppermine

Coppermine 128

Intel has also introduced an edge-connector-based **Slot 2** specification that extends the Slot 1, boxed-processor scheme to a 330-contact design. For the Slot 2 design, Intel has produced 3 special versions of the Pentium III that they have named the Pentium Xeon. Each version features a different level of L2 cache (512 KB, 1 MB, 2 MB). The Xeon designs were produced to fill different, high-end server needs.

Slot 2

Pentium 4

Late in 2000, Intel released their newest Pentium version called the *Williamette 423*, or **Pentium 4** microprocessor. It employs a modified Socket 370 PGA design that uses 423 pins and boasts operating speeds above 1.3 GHz. The system bus has been increased from 64 to 128 bits and will operate at 400 MHz. Advanced plans for the Pentium 4 call for an improved 479-pin version (*Williamette 479*) to be released in 2001.

Pentium 4

In reality, the Pentium 4 is not a continuation of the Pentium design. It is actually a new design (IA-32 NetBurst architecture) based on .18 micron construction technology. In addition to the new front side bus size, the Pentium 4 features new WPNI (Williamette Processor New Instructions) instructions in its instruction set. The L1 cache size has been reduced from 16 KB in the Pentium III to 8 KB for the Pentium 4. The L2 cache is 256 KB and can handle transfers on every clock cycle.

The operating voltage level for the Pentium 4 core is 1.7 volts. To dissipate the 55 watts of power (heat) that the microprocessor generates at 1.5 GHz, the case incorporates a metal cap. In addition, firm contact between the microprocessor's case and the heat sink feature built into the Pentium 4 system board must be maintained.

Table 2-3 summarizes the characteristics of the Intel Pentium microprocessors.

Table 2-3: Characteristics of the Intel Pentium Microprocessors

TYPE	ADDRESS BUSWIDTH	SPACE	INTERNAL CLOCK SPEED (MHz)	DATA BUSWIDTH	MATH CO-PROCESSOR
Pentium	32	4 GB	50 - 100	64	Onboard
Pentium MMX	32	4 GB	166 - 233	64	Onboard
Pentium Pro	36	4 GB x 4	150 - 200	64	Onboard
Pentium II	36	64 GB	233 - 450	64	Onboard
Pentium III	36	64 GB	450 - 1 GHz	64	Onboard
Celeron	36	64 GB	266 - 766	64	Onboard
Pentium 4	36	64 GB	1.4 - 1.5 GHz	128	Onboard

Pentium Clones

clone microprocessor

As mentioned earlier in this chapter, Intel abandoned the 80x86 nomenclature in favor of names that could be copyrighted in an effort to distance themselves from the **clone microprocessor** manufacturers. When this occurred, the other manufacturers largely followed the 80x86 path, but eventually moved toward alternative numbering schemes as well.

AMD Processors

Advanced Micro Devices (AMD)

Advanced Micro Devices (AMD) offers several clone microprocessors: the 5x86 (X5), the 5x86 (K5), the K6, the K6PLUS-3D, and K7 microprocessors. The X5 offers operational and pin compatibility with the DX4. Its performance is equal to that of the Pentium and MMX processors. The K5 processor is compatible with the Pentium, and the K6 is compatible with the MMX. Both the K5 and K6 models are Socket-7 compatible, enabling them to be used in conventional Pentium and Pentium MMX system-board designs (with some small modifications). The K6 employs an extended 64 kB L1 cache that doubles the internal cache size of the Pentium II.

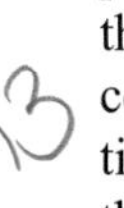

The K6PLUS-3D is operationally and performance compatible with the Pentium Pro, and the K7 is operationally and performance compatible with the Pentium II. However, neither of these units has a pin-out compatibility with another processor.

NextGen produced three processors that can perform at the same level as the P5 (Nx586) and P54C (Nx686) Pentium devices. These devices use proprietary pin-outs, however, so they are not compatible with other processors. Although the performance levels compete with the Pentium, the devices offer compatibility with 80386/87 operation only. Eventually, NextGen was purchased by AMD and its designs were incorporated in the K6 design.

AMD continues to produce clone versions of Pentium processors. In some cases, the functions and performance of the AMD devices go beyond the Intel design they are cloning. Two notable AMD clone processors are the Athlon and the Duron.

Athlon

Slot A

The **Athlon** is a Pentium III clone processor. It is available in a Slot 1 cartridge clone, called the Slot-A specification. Figure 2-34 depicts the cartridge version of the Athlon processor with a **Slot A** connector.

The Athlon is also available in a proprietary SPGA Socket-A design that mimics the Intel Socket 370 specification. The **Socket-A** specification employs a 462-pin ZIF socket and is only supported by two available chipsets.

Three versions of the Athlon processor have been introduced so far. The first version was the K7 version that ran between 500 MHz and 700 MHz, provided a 128 kB L1 cache and a 512 kB L2 cache, and employed a 100 MHz system bus.

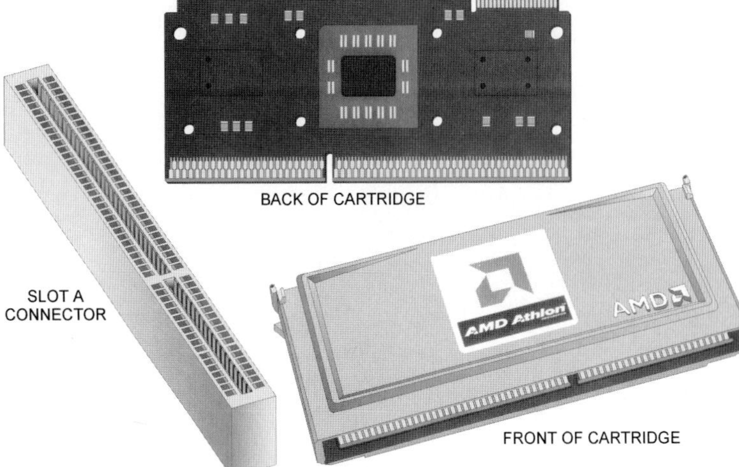

Figure 2-34: Slot A/Athlon Version

Subsequent Athlon versions have included the K75 and Thunderbird versions. Both versions are constructed using the 0.18 micron manufacturing technology. The K75 processors ran between 750 MHz and 1 GHz. Like the K7 version, it provided a 128 kB L1 cache and a 512 kB L2 cache, and employed a 100 MHz system bus. The Thunderbird version ran between 750 MHz and 1.2 GHz, provided a 128 kB L1 cache and a 256 kB L2 cache, and employed a 133 MHz system bus.

Socket-A

Duron

The **Duron** processor is a Celeron clone processor that conforms to the AMD Socket-A specification. The Duron features processor speeds between 600 MHz and 800 MHz. It includes a 128 kB L1 cache and a 64 kB L2 cache. Like the newer Celerons, the Duron is constructed using 0.18 micron IC manufacturing technology.

Cyrix Processors

Cyrix

Cyrix uses an Mx numbering system in addition to the 5x/6x86 numbers. The M5/M6/M7 devices are compatible with their Intel counterparts in performance, compatibility, and pin-out. The 5x86 device is compatible with the 80486DX4 in performance, compatibility, and pin-out. The M1 (6x86) and M2 (6x86MX) processors are compatible with the Intel P54C and P55C units in performance and pin-out. The M1 unit is operationally compatible with the 80486DX4, and the M2 processor is operationally compatible with the Pentium MMX and Pentium Pro processors.

The 6x86 design uses a 16 KB dual-ported cache for instructions and data and a 256-byte instruction cache. The 6x86MX version includes a 64 kB L1 cache that competes with the K6 AMD design.

Cyrix III

Joshua Processor

Samuel

Like AMD, Cyrix has continued to develop clones of the various Pentium products. These clones include the Socket 370-compatible Celeron clone processor called the **Cyrix III** (originally called the **Joshua Processor**). The Cyrix III, shown in Figure 2-35, can be used in system boards designed for Celeron processors. However, the system's BIOS will need to be upgraded to work with the Cyrix clock multipliers. The latest version of the processor (the **Samuel** version) runs at 533 MHz but supports a very fast 133 MHz front-side bus. It also possesses a large (128 kB) L1 cache but has no support for an L2 cache.

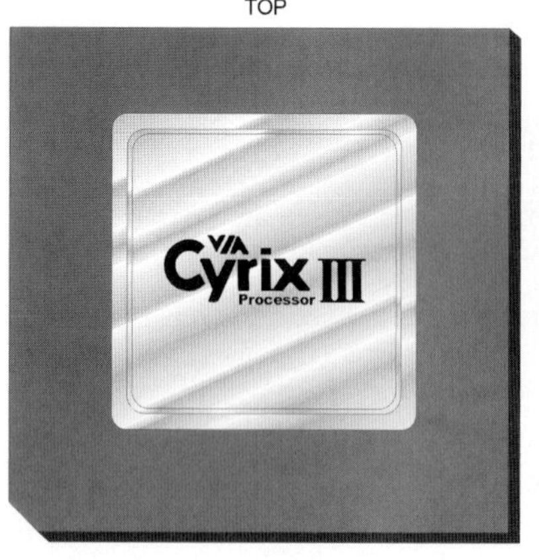

Figure 2-35: Cyrix III Processor

Properly installing both the AMD and Cyrix devices require that their power-supply levels and clock multipliers be set correctly. These settings are discussed in the "Configuring Microprocessors" section in this chapter.

Table 2-4 shows the relationship among the various numbering systems. In addition to the 80x86 numbering system, Intel used a Px identification up to the Pentium II. The Pentium II is identified as the Klamath processor. Subsequent improved versions have been dubbed: Deschutes, Covington, Mendocino, Katmai, Willamette, Flagstaff (P7), Merced, and Tahoe.

Table 2-4: Clone Processors

INTEL	CYRIX	AMD	NEXTGEN
Pentium (P5/P54C)	M1 (6X86)	-K5(5X86)	NX586/686
Pentium MMX (P55C)	M2 (6X86MX)	-K6	
Pentium Pro (P6)	MXi	-K6PLUS-3D	
Pentium II	M3	-K7	
Pentium III	N/A	K75/Thunderbird	
Pentium Celeron	Cyrix III	Duron	

Socket Specifications

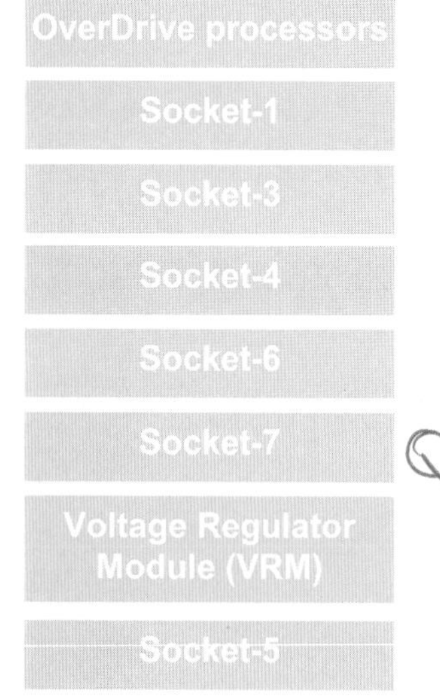

In addition to the clone processors, Intel has developed a line of upgrade microprocessors for their original units. These are referred to as **OverDrive processors**. The OverDrive unit may simply be the same type of microprocessor running at a higher clock speed, or it may be an advanced architecture microprocessor designed to operate from the same socket/pin configuration as the original. To accommodate this option, Intel has created specifications for eight socket designs, designated Socket-1 through Socket-8.

The specifications for **Socket-1** through **Socket-3** were developed for 80486SX, 80486DX, and 80486 OverDrive versions that use different pin numbers and power supply requirements. Likewise, **Socket-4** through **Socket-6** deal with various Pentium and OverDrive units that use different speeds and power supply requirements. The **Socket-7** design works with the fastest Pentium units and includes provision for a **Voltage Regulator Module (VRM)** to allow various power settings to be implemented through the socket. The **Socket-7** specification corresponds to the second generation of Pentium devices that employ SPGA packaging. It is compatible with the **Socket-5**, straight-row PGA specification that the first-generation Pentium processors employed. Finally, the **Socket-8** specification is specific to the Pentium Pro processor.

Although the Intel Slot 1 design was originally developed for the Pentium II, it also serves its Celeron and Pentium III processor designs. Like Socket 7, the Slot 1 specification provides for variable processor core voltages (2.8 to 3.3) that permit faster operation and reduced power consumption. In addition, some suppliers have created daughter boards containing the Pentium Pro processor that can be plugged into the Slot 1 connector. This combination Socket 8/Slot 1 device is referred to as a slotket processor.

Slot 2

SECC-2

Xeon

The **Slot 2** specification from Intel expands the Slot 1 SECC technology to a 330-contact cartridge (**SECC-2**) used with the Intel **Xeon** processor.

AMD produced a reversed version of the Slot 1 specification for its Athlon processor by turning the contacts of the Slot 1 design around. They titled the new design Slot A. While serving the same ends as the Slot 1 design, the Slot A and Slot 1 microprocessor cartridges are not compatible.

In a departure from its proprietary Slot connector development, Intel introduced a new ZIF socket standard, called Socket 370, for use with its Celeron processor. There are actually two versions of the Socket 370 specification. The first is the PPGA 370 variation intended for use with the Plastic Pin Grid Array (PPGA) version of the Celeron CPUs. The other is the Flip Chip Pin Grid Array (FC-PGA) version.

The term Flip Chip is used to describe a group of microprocessors that have provisions for attaching a heat sink directly to the microprocessor die. The processors in this category include the Cyrix III, Celeron, and Pentium III. Although the PPGA and FC-PGA processors will both plug into the 370 socket, that does not mean they will work in system boards designed for the other specification.

Likewise, AMD produced a 462-pin ZIF socket specification for the PGA versions of its Athlon and Duron processors. No other processors have been designed for this specification and only two chipsets have been produced to support it.

Table 2-5 summarizes the attributes of the various industry socket and slot specifications.

Table 2-5: Intel Socket Specifications

NUMBER	PINS	VOLTAGES	MICROPROCESSORS
Socket 1	169 PGA	5	80486 SX/DXx, DX4 Overdrive
Socket 2	238 PGA	5	80486 SX/DXx, Pentium Overdrive
Socket 3	237 PGA	5/3.3	80486 SX/DXx, Pent Overdrive
Socket 4	237 PGA	5	Pentium 60/66, 60/66 Overdrive
Socket 5	320 SPGA	3.3	Pentium 75-133, Pent Overdrive
Socket 6	235 PGA	3.3	Never Implemented
Socket 7	321 SPGA	VRM (2.5v-3.6v)	Pentium 75-200, Pent Overdrive
Socket 8	387 SPGA	VRM (2.2v-3.5v)	Pentium Pro
Slot 1	242 SECC/SEPP	VRM (1.5v-2.5v)	Celeron, Pentium II, Pentium III
Slot 2	330 SECC-2	VRM (1.5v-2.5v)	Xeon
Super Socket 7	321 SPGA	VRM (2.0v-3.5v)	AMD K6-2, K6-2+, K6-III, K6-III+, Pentium MMX, Pentium Pro
Socket 370	370 SPGA	VRM (1.1v-2.5v)	Cyrix III, Celeron, Pentium III
Slot A	242 Slot A	VRM (1.2v-2.2v)	AMD Athlon
Socket A	462 SPGA	VRM (12v-2.2v)	AMD Athlon, Duron

TEST TIP

Know which processors can be used with Slot 1 and Socket 370 connections. Also know which processors can be used in Slot A.

Clock Speeds, Power Supplies, and Fans

It should be apparent that there are three compatibility issues to consider when dealing with clone processors. These are performance, operation, and pin-out compatibility. In addition to these three issues, it is important to be aware of the power supply requirements for the various types of microprocessors.

The Socket-7 specification includes pins that enable the system board to be configured for microprocessors using different operating speeds. It also allows two speed settings to be established for the microprocessor—one speed for its internal core operations, and a second speed for its external bus transfers. In the Pentium processor, the two speeds are tied together by an internal clock multiplier. Advanced Pentium designs have additional pins that work with the Socket-7 specification to determine the operating speed of the microprocessor.

passive heat sinks

active heat sinks

Beginning with the Pentium MMX, Intel adopted dual voltage supply levels for the overall IC and for its core. Common Intel voltage supplies are +5/+5 for older units, and +3.3/+3.3, +3.3/+2.8, +3.3/+1.8 for newer units. Clone processors may use compatible voltages (especially if they are pin compatible), or may use completely different voltage levels.

Common voltages for clone microprocessors include: +5, +3.3, +2.5, and +2.2. The additional voltage levels are typically generated by special regulator circuits on the system board. In each case, the system board's user's guide should be consulted any time the microprocessor is being replaced or upgraded.

The Pentium processor requires the presence of a heat-sinking device and a microprocessor fan unit for cooling purposes. These devices come in many forms including simple **passive heat sinks** and fan-cooled **active heat sinks**. Both types of cooling systems are illustrated in Figure 2-36.

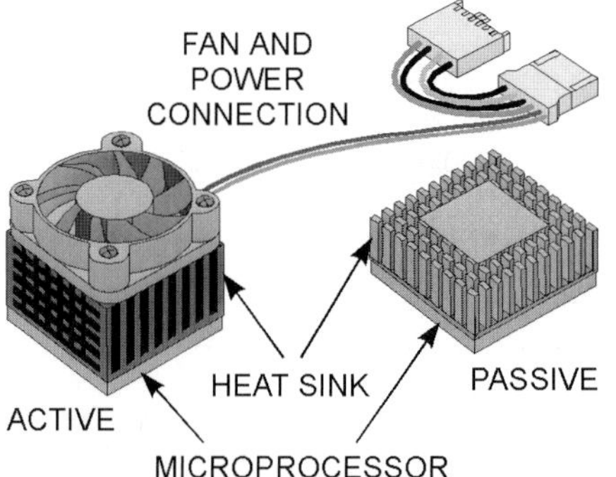

Figure 2-36: Microprocessor Cooling Systems

Passive heat sinks are metal slabs with fins that can be clipped onto the microprocessor, or glued on the top of the processor with a heat transmitting adhesive. The fins increase the surface area of the heat sink allowing it to dissipate heat more rapidly. Active heat sinks include a fan unit to move air across the heat sink. The fan moves the heat away from the heat sink and the microprocessor more rapidly.

ATX-style systems use a power supply that employs a reverse flow fan that blows cool air from the back of the unit onto the microprocessor. Of course, for this to work properly, the system board must adhere to the ATX form factor and place the microprocessor in the correct position on the system board. Theoretically, this design eliminates the need for special microprocessor cooling fans.

Configuring Microprocessors

Most Pentium system boards are designed so that they support a number of different microprocessor types and operating speeds. Table 2-6 gives an example of the types of processors that are known to operate with a particular Socket-7 system board design. This example supports Pentium and Pentium clone processors from AMD, Cyrix, IBM, and Intel. Two hardware jumpers, labeled J10 and J13, are used to identify the processor type to the system board.

Table 2-6: Configuring a Socket-7 Microprocessor

	"♦" are the CPUs with Heat Pipe Solution					JP15	JP14	JP13	JP22		JP10
						CORE/BUS		CPU	(BUS) Freq.		CPU
	CPU Model	Freq.	Freq.	Voltage	Ratio	Ratio		Type	1,2	3,4	Type
	AMD-SSA/5-75 ABR	75MHz	50MHz	3.52V	1.5x	Open	Open	Open	Short	Short	1,2
	AMD-K5-PR90ABQ	90MHz	60MHz	3.52V	1.5x	Open	Open	Open	Short	Open	1,2
	AMD-K5-PR100ABR	100MHz	50MHz	3.52V	2x	Open	Short	Open	Short	Short	1,2
♦	AMD-K5-PR133ABQ	133MHz	66MHz	3.52V	2x	Open	Short	Open	Open	Short	1,2
♦	AMD-K5-PR166ABR	166MHz	66MHz	3.52V	2.5x	Short	Short	Open	Open	Short	1,2
♦	AMD-K6-166ALR(1) •	166MHz	66MHz	2.9/3.3	2.5x	Short	Short	Open	Open	Short	1,2
♦	AMD-K6-200ALR(1) •	200MHz	66MHz	2.9/3.3	3x	Short	Open	Open	Open	Short	1,2
♦	IBM26 6x86-2V2100GB	100MHz	50MHz	3.3V	2x	Short	Short	Short	Short	Short	2,3
♦	Cyrix 6x86-P150+	120MHz	60MHz	3.52V	2x	Open	Short	Short	Short	Open	2,3
	Cyrix 6x86L-P150+(1)	120MHz	60MHz	2.8/3.3	2x	Open	Short	Short	Short	Open	2,3
♦	Cyrix 6x86-P166+	133MHz	66MHz	3.52V	2x	Open	Short	Short	Open	Short	2,3
♦	Cyrix 6x86 MX-PR166(1)•	133MHz	66MHz	2.9/3.3	2x	Open	Short	Open	Open	Short	2,3
♦	Cyrix 6x86 MX-PR200(1)•	166MHz	66MHz	2.9/3.3	2.5x	Short	Short	Open	Open	Short	2,3
	Intel Pentium	100MHz	50MHz	3.3V	2x	Open	Short	Open	Short	Short	1,2
	Intel Pentium	120MHz	60MHz	3.3V	2x	Open	Short	Open	Short	Open	1,2
	Intel Pentium	133MHz	66MHz	3.3V	2x	Open	Short	Open	Open	Short	1,2
♦	Intel Pentium	166MHz	66MHz	3.3V	2.5x	Short	Short	Open	Open	Short	1,2
♦	Intel Pentium	200MHz	66MHz	3.3V	3x	Short	Open	Open	Open	Short	1,2
♦	Intel Pentium-MMX	166MHz	66MHz	3.3V	2.5x	Short	Short	Open	Open	Short	1,2
♦	Intel Pentium-MMX(1)	200MHz	66MHz	2.8/3.3	3x	Short	Open	Open	Open	Short	1,2
♦	Intel Pentium-MMX(1) •	233MHz	66MHz	2.8/3.3	3.5x	Open	Open	Open	Open	Short	1,2

(1) Dual Supply (split rail) Devices
(2) OMD 11 only supports 50 MHz, 60 MHz and 66 MHz CLK Rate
(3) CPUs with "•" remark will be supported in "L" Ver BIOS

As we mentioned earlier, the original Pentium processors ran on 50, 60, or 66 MHz external clocks and used internal clock multiplier circuits to operate the microprocessor core at a much faster pace. Newer Pentium versions employ 100, 133, and 200 MHz microprocessor/front side bus clocks. Table 2-7 lists the various Pentium class microprocessors along with their associated microprocessor bus speeds.

Table 2-7: Pentium Clock Speeds

PROCESSOR SPEED	MICROPROCESSOR/FRONT SIDE BUS CLOCK
Pentium 75, 100	50 MHz
Pentium 90, 120, 150	60 MHz
Pentium 100, 133, 166, 200	66 MHz
Pentium MMX 166, 200, 233	66 MHz
Pentium Pro	66 MHz
Celeron	66 MHz
Pentium II/233, 333	66 MHz
Pentium II/333, 450	100 MHz
Pentium III	100 MHz
Pentium IIIB/IIIEB	133 MHz
Pentium 4	400 MHz
K6-2	66 MHz
K6-III	100 MHz
Duron	200 MHz
Athlon	200, 266 MHz

In the table, the B notation used with the Pentium III indicates that it is a 133 MHz bus version of the microprocessor. Likewise, the EB notation indicates that the device is a Coppermine Pentium version using a 133 MHz front side bus.

core-to-bus speed ratio

bus frequency

Another pair of jumpers, labeled J14 and J15, are used to establish the **core-to-bus speed ratio** for the selected processor type. For example, both jumpers must be installed (shorted) to establish the Intel Pentium's 166 MHz, 2.5x internal clock multiplier. This setting is necessary to convert the system board's 66 MHz clock signal into a 166 MHz internal operating signal. These jumpers work in conjunction with the **bus frequency** setting determined by jumper J22. If pins 1/2 and 3/4 are shorted, the bus frequency is set at 50 MHz. If pins 3/4 are open, the frequency is shifted to 60 MHz. Finally, if pins 1 and 2 are open and 3 and 4 are shorted, the bus frequency is set at 66 MHz.

Socket 7 systems use a Voltage Regulator Module (VRM) to supply special voltage levels for the microprocessor. The module may be designed as a plug-in module so that it can be replaced easily in case of component failure. This is a somewhat common occurrence with voltage regulator devices. It also allows the system board to be upgraded when a new Pentium device is developed that requires a different voltage level, or a different voltage pairing.

core voltage

Typically a hardware jumper, identified as J23 in this example, is used to establish the processor's **core voltage** level, as described in Table 2-8. The default value for the example's core voltage is 3.3v. The group of jumpers labeled J9 are set to select between single and dual processor voltage levels. If pins 1/2 and 3/4 are shorted together, with pins 5/6 and 7/8 open, a single power supply voltage will be produced. Conversely, opening pins 1/2 and 3/4, while pins 5/6 and 7/8 are shorted, will establish a dual voltage situation for those microprocessors that require it.

Table 2-8: Microprocessor Core Voltage Levels

JP23 CPU VCORE Voltage Selector					
VOUT	1-2	3-4	5-6	7-8	
2.2V	Open	Short	Open	Open	
2.6V	Open	Short	Short	Open	
2.7V	Short	Short	Short	Open	
2.8V	Open	Open	Open	Short	
2.9V	Short	Open	Open	Short	
3.2V	Open	Open	Short	Short	
3.3V	Short	Open	Short	Short	* default
3.5V	Short	Short	Short	Short	

JP9 CPU 3V Selector					
Power	1-2	3-4	5-6	7-8	
Single	Short	Short	Open	Open	* default
Dual	Open	Open	Short	Short	

It should be obvious that these variables must be configured correctly for the type of microprocessor actually installed in the system. If the core voltage level is set too high, then the microprocessor will probably overheat slowly, or burn out, depending on the amount of over-voltage applied. Conversely, if the voltage level is configured too low for the installed processor, then the system will most likely refuse to start.

Likewise, setting the speed selection jumpers incorrectly can cause the system to think that a different processor is installed in the system. As an example, setting the Core/Bus Ratio (JP15/14), CPU Type (JP13), and Bus Frequency (JP22) jumpers in Table 2-7 to Short/Short/Open/Open/Short, would cause the system's BIOS to believe that an AMD K5 – 166 processor were installed. If an AMD K6 – 200 processor were actually installed, the system would still think of it, and report it, as a K5 – 166 processor.

TEST TIP

Be aware of how the system determines what type of microprocessor is installed and what its capabilities are.

RANDOM ACCESS MEMORY

The A+ Core objective 4.2 states that the test taker should be able to identify the categories of RAM (Random Access Memory) terminology, their locations, and physical characteristics. Terminology includes:

- EDO RAM (Extended Data Output RAM)
- DRAM (Dynamic Random Access Memory)
- SRAM (Static RAM)
- VRAM (Video RAM)
- WRAM (Windows Accelerator Card RAM)

Locations and physical characteristics:

- Memory bank
- Memory chips (8-bit, 16-bit, and 32-bit)
- SIMMs (Single In-line Memory Modules)
- DIMMs (Dual In-line Memory Modules)
- Parity chips versus non-parity chips

Memory Systems

As mentioned in Chapter 1—*Basic PC Hardware*, there are normally three types of semiconductor memory found on a typical system board. These include the system's ROM BIOS ICs, the system's RAM memory, and the second-level cache memory unit.

A typical PC system board uses one, or two, 256 kB/128 kB *x* 8 ROM chips to hold the system's BIOS firmware. The system's memory map reserves memory locations from F0000h to FFFFFh. These chips contain the firmware routines to handle startup of the system, the change-over to disk-based operations, video and printer output functions, as well as the Power-On Self-Test.

Static RAM (SRAM)

Dynamic RAM (DRAM)

There are basically two types of semiconductor RAM, **Static RAM (SRAM)** and **Dynamic RAM (DRAM)**, used on system boards. Although they both perform the same types of functions, the methods they use are completely different. Static RAM stores bits in such a manner that they will remain as long as power to the chip is not interrupted. Dynamic RAM requires periodic refreshing to maintain data, even if electrical power is applied to the chip.

Dynamic RAM stores data bits on rows and columns of IC capacitors. Capacitors lose their charge over time. This is the reason that dynamic RAM devices require data refreshing operations. Static RAM uses IC transistors to store data and maintain it as long as power is supplied to the chip. Its transistor structure makes SRAM memory much faster than ordinary DRAM. However, it can only store about 25% as much data in a given size as a DRAM device. Therefore, it tends to be more expensive to create large memories with SRAM.

Whether the RAM is made up of static or dynamic RAM devices, all RAM systems have the disadvantage of being volatile. This means that any data stored in RAM will be lost if power to the computer is disrupted for any reason. On the other hand, both types of RAM have the advantage of being fast, with the ability to be written to and read from with equal ease.

Generally, static RAM is used in smaller memory systems, such as cache and video memories, where the added cost of refresh circuitry would increase the cost-per-bit of storage. Cache memory is a special memory structure that works directly with the microprocessor, while video memory is a specialized area that holds information to be displayed on the screen. On the other hand, DRAM is used in larger memory systems, such as the system's main memory, where the extra cost of refresh circuitry is distributed over a greater number of bits and is offset by the reduced operating cost associated with DRAM chips.

Advanced DRAM

Both types of RAM are brought together to create an improved DRAM, referred to as **Enhanced DRAM (EDRAM)**. By integrating an SRAM component into a DRAM device, a performance improvement of 40% can be gained. An independent write path allows the system to input new data without affecting the operation of the rest of the chip. These devices are used primarily in L2 cache memories.

Enhanced DRAM (EDRAM)

Another modified DRAM type, referred to as **Synchronous DRAM (SDRAM)**, employs special internal registers and clock signals to organize data requests from memory. Unlike asynchronous memory modules, SDRAM devices operate in synchronicity with the system clock. Once an initial Read or Write access has been performed on the memory device, additional accesses can be conducted in a high-speed burst mode that operates at 1 access per clock cycle. This enables the microprocessor to perform other tasks while the data is being organized. Special internal configurations also speed up the operation of the SDRAM memory. The SDRAM device employs internal interleaving that permits one side of the memory to be accessed while the other half is completing an operation. Because there are two versions of SDRAM (2-clock and 4-clock) you must make certain that the SDRAM type you are using is supported by the system board's chipset.

Synchronous DRAM (SDRAM)

Advanced SDRAM

Advanced versions of SDRAM include:

- **SDR-SDRAM** – *Single Data Rate SDRAM*. This version of SDRAM transfers data on one edge of the system clock signal.

SDR-SDRAM

- **SGRAM** – *Synchronous Graphics RAM*. This type of SDRAM is designed to handle high-performance graphics operations. It features dual-bank operations that permit two memory pages to be open at the same time.

SGRAM

- **ESDRAM** – Enhanced SDRAM. This advanced form of SDRAM employs small cache buffers to provide high data access rates. This type of SDRAM is used in L2 cache applications.

ESDRAM

- **VCM-SDRAM** – *Virtual Channel Memory SDRAM*. This memory design has on-board cache buffers to improve multiple access times and to provide I/O transfers on each clock cycle. VCM SDRAM requires a special chipset to support it.

VCM-SDRAM

- **DDR-SDRAM** – *Double Data Rate SDRAM*. A form of SDR-SDRAM which can transfer data on both the leading and falling edges of each clock cycle. This capability doubles the data transfer rate of traditional SDR-DRAM. It is available in a number of standard formats including SODIMMs for portables.

DDR-SDRAM

- **EDDR-SDRAM** – *Enhanced DDR SDRAM*. An advanced form of DDR SRAM that employs on-board cache registers to deliver improved performance.

EDDR-SDRAM

Table 2-9 summarizes the characteristics and usage of various types of SDRAM.

Table 2-9: SRAM Types

	Configuration	Voltage	Density	Frequency (MHz)	Package
RDRAM RIMM	32 x 16 32 x 18 64 x 16 64 x 18 128 x 16	2.5V	64 MB 72 MB 96 MB 108 MB 128 MB 144 MB	300, 356, 400	184-pin RIMMs
DDR SRAM DIMMs (Unbuffered)	16 x 64 32 x 64	2.5V	128 MB 256 MB	200, 266	184-pin DIMMs
DDR SRAM DIMMs (Registered)	32 x 72	2.5V	256 MB	200, 266	184-pin DIMMs
SDRAM AIMM	1 x 32	3.3V	4 MB	166	66-pin AIMM
100-Pin DIMMs	1 x 32 2 x 32	3.3V	4 MB 8 MB	100, 125	100-pin DIMMs
	2 x 32	3.3V	8 MB	125	100-pin DIMM
	4 x 32 8 x 32	3.3V	16 MB 32 MB	100, 125	100-pin DIMMs
	16 x 32	3.3V	64 MB	100, 125	100-pin DIMM
	16 x 32 32 x 32	3.3V	64 MB 128 MB	100, 125	100-pin DIMMs
144-Pin SODIMMs	4 x 64	3.3V	32 MB	100, 125, 133	144-pin SODIMM
	8 x 64	3.3V	64 MB	66, 100	144-pin SODIMM
	8 x 64	3.3V	64 MB	100, 133	144-pin SODIMM
	16 x 64	3.3V	128 MB	66, 100	144-pin SODIMM
	32 x 64	3.3V	256 MB	100, 133	144-pin SODIMM
168-Pin DIMMs	4 x 64 8 x 64 16 x 64	3.3V	32 MB 64 MB 128 MB	66,100, 133	168-pin SDRAM DIMMs
	8 x 64 16 x 64	3.3V	64 MB 128 MB	66,100, 133	168-pin DIMMs
	16 x 64 32 x 64	3.3V	128 MB 256 MB	100, 133	168-pin DIMMs
	4 x 72 8 x 72 16 x 72	3.3V	32 MB 64 MB 128 MB	66,100, 133	168-pin DIMMs
	8 x 72 16 x 72	3.3V	64 MB 128 MB	66,100, 133	168-pin DIMMs
	8 x 72 16 x 72	3.3V	64 MB 128 MB	100, 133	168-pin DIMMs
	16 x 72 32 x 72	3.3V	128 MB 256 MB	100, 133	168-pin DIMM
	16 x 72 32 x 72 64 x 72	3.3V	128 MB 256 MB 512 MB	100, 133	168-pin DIMM
	32 x 72 64 x 72	3.3V	256 MB 512 MB	100, 133	168-pin DIMMs
	64 x 72	3.3V	512 MB	100, 133	168-pin DIMMs
	64 x 72 128 x 72	3.3V	512 MB 1 GB	100, 133	168-pin DIMMs

	Configuration	Voltage	Density	Frequency (MHz)	Package
DRAM SIMMs	1 x 32 2 x 32	5V	4 MB 8 MB	50 (EDO only), 60	72-pin SIMM
	4 x 32 8 x 32	5V	16 MB 32 MB	50 (EDO only), 60	72-pin SIMM
	4 x 36 8 x 36	5V	16 MB 32 MB	60	72-pin SIMMs
	4 x 36 8 x 36	5V	16 MB 32 MB	50, 60	72-pin SIMMs
	Configuration	**Voltage**	**Density**	**Speed (ns)**	**Package**
EDO/FPM DRAM DIMMs/SODIMMs	1 x 32 2 x 32	3.3V	4 MB 8 MB	50 (EDO only), 60	100-pin DIMM
	1 x 32 2 x 32 4 x 32	3.3V	4 MB 8 MB 16 MB	50, 60	100-pin DIMMs
	4 x 32 8 x 32	3.3V	16 MB 32 MB	50, 60	72-pin SODIMMs
	4 x 32 8 x 32	3.3V	16 MB 32 MB	50, 60	144-pin SODIMMs
	4 x 64 8 x 64	3.3V	32 MB 64 MB	50, 60	168-pin DIMMs
	4 x 64 8 x 64	3.3V	32 MB 64 MB	50, 60	168-pin DIMMs
	8 x 64 16 x 64 32 x 64	3.3V	64 MB 128 MB 256 MB	50, 60	168-pin DIMMs
	4 x 72	3.3V	32 MB	50, 60	168-pin DIMMs
	4 x 72	3.3V	32 MB	50, 60	168-pin DIMMs
	8 x 72 16 x 72 32 x 72	3.3V	64 MB 128 MB 256 MB	50, 60	168-pin DIMMs
	8 x 72 16 x 72 32 x 72	3.3V	64 MB 128 MB 256 MB	50, 60	168-pin DIMMs

Table 2-9: SRAM Types (continued)

Extended data out (EDO) memory increases the speed at which RAM operations are conducted by cutting out the 10-nanosecond wait time normally required between issuing memory addresses. This is accomplished by not disabling the data bus pins between bus cycles. EDO is an advanced type of fast page-mode DRAM, also referred to as hyper page-mode DRAM. The advantage of EDO DRAM is encountered when multiple sequential memory accesses are performed. By not turning off the data pin, each successive access after the first access is accomplished in two clock cycles rather than three.

Extended data out (EDO)

TEST TIP

Know the difference between EDO and fast page-mode DRAM.

Special memory devices have also been designed to optimize video memory-related activities. Among these are **Video RAM (VRAM)** and **Windows RAM (WRAM)**. In typical DRAM devices, access to the data stored inside is shared between the system microprocessor and the video controller. The microprocessor accesses the RAM to update the data in it and to keep it refreshed. The video controller moves data out of the memory to become screen information. Normally, both devices must access the data through the same data bus. VRAM employs a special dual-port access system to speed up video operations. WRAM, a special version of VRAM, is optimized to transfer blocks of data at a time. This allows it to operate at speeds of up to 150% of typical VRAM and costs up to 20% less.

Video RAM (VRAM)

Windows RAM (WRAM)

TEST TIP

Remember what type of application VRAM and WRAM are used in.

Rambus DRAM (RDRAM)

Direct Rambus DRAM (DRDRAM)

Rambus Inline Memory Module (RIMM)

heat spreader

A company named Rambus has designed a proprietary DRAM memory technology that promises very high data delivery speeds. The technology has been given a variety of different names that include **Rambus DRAM (RDRAM)**, **Direct Rambus DRAM (DRDRAM)**, and **Rambus Inline Memory Module (RIMM)**. The RIMM reference applies to a special 184-pin memory module that is designed to hold the Rambus devices. Figure 2-37 shows that RIMMs look similar to DIMMS. However, their high-speed transfer modes generate considerably more heat than normal DIMMs. Therefore, RIMM modules include an aluminum heat shield, referred to as a **heat spreader**, to protect the chips from overheating.

The Rambus technology employs a special, internal 16-bit data channel that operates in conjunction with a 400 MHz clock. The 16-bit channel permits the device to operate at much higher speeds than more conventional 64-bit buses. While Intel had expressed some interest in exploring the technology for its future system board designs, the fact that it is a proprietary standard may hinder its acceptance in the market.

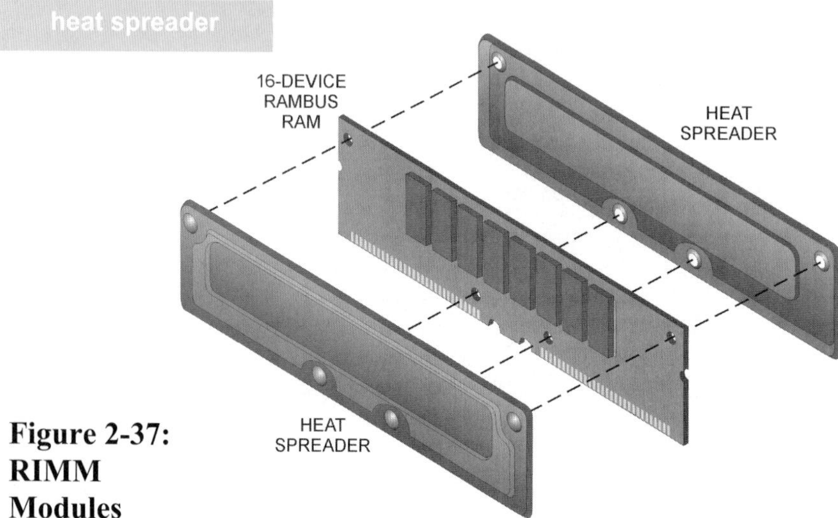

Figure 2-37: RIMM Modules

RIMMs look similar to DIMMs, but have a different pin count. RIMMs transfer data in 16-bit chunks. The faster access and transfer speed generates more heat.

SRAM

Like DRAM, SRAM is available in a number of different types. Many of the memory organization techniques described for DRAM are also implemented in SRAM.

Asynchronous SRAM

Synchronous SRAM

Pipeline SRAM

Burst-mode SRAM

- **Asynchronous SRAM** is standard SRAM and delivers data from the memory to the microprocessor and returns it to the cache in one clock cycle.
- **Synchronous SRAM** uses special clock signals and buffer storage to deliver data to the CPU in one clock cycle after the first cycle. The first address is stored and used to retrieve the data while the next address is on its way to the cache.
- **Pipeline SRAM** uses three clock cycles to fetch the first data and then accesses addresses within the selected page on each clock cycle.
- **Burst-mode SRAM** loads a number of consecutive data locations from the cache, over several clock cycles, based on a single address from the microprocessor.

In digital electronics terms, a *buffer* is a holding area for data shared by devices that operate at different speeds or have different priorities. These devices permit a memory module to operate without the delays that other devices impose. Some types of SDRAM memory modules contain buffer registers directly on the module. The buffer registers hold and retransmit the data signals through the memory chips.

The holding aspect permits the module to coordinate transfers with the outside system. The retransmission factor lowers the signal drain on the host system and enables the memory module to hold more memory chips. Registered and unbuffered memory modules cannot be mixed. The design of the chipset's memory controller dictates which types of memory the computer can use.

Memory Overhead

It has already been mentioned that DRAM devices, commonly used for the system's RAM, require periodic refreshing of their data. Some **refreshing** is performed simply by regular reading and writing of the memory by the system. However, additional circuitry must be used to ensure that every bit in the memory is refreshed within the allotted time frame. In addition to the circuitry, the reading and writing times used for refreshing must be taken into account when designing the system.

refreshing

Another design factor associated with RAM is data **error detection**. A single, incorrect bit can shut down the entire system instantly. With bits constantly moving in and out of RAM, it is crucial that all of the bits be transferred correctly. The most popular form of error detection in PC compatibles is **parity checking**. In this methodology, an extra bit is added to each word in RAM and checked each time it is used. Like refreshing, parity checking requires additional circuitry and memory overhead to operate.

error detection

parity checking

DRAM Refresh

Dynamic RAM devices require that data stored in them be **refreshed**, or rewritten, periodically to keep it from fading away. As a matter of fact, each bit in the DRAM must be refreshed at least once every two milliseconds or the data will dissipate. Since it can't be assumed that each bit in the memory will be accessed during the normal operation of the system (within the time frame allotted), the need to constantly refresh the data in the DRAM requires special circuitry to perform this function.

refreshed

The extra circuitry and inconvenience associated with refreshing may initially make DRAM memory seem like a distant second choice behind static RAM. However, due to the simplicity of DRAM's internal structure, the bit-storage capacity of a DRAM chip is much greater than that of a similar static RAM chip, and it offers a much lower rate of power consumption. Both of these factors contribute to making DRAM memory the economical choice in certain RAM memory systems—even in light of the extra circuitry necessary for refreshing.

Parity Checking

Parity checking is a simple self-test used to detect RAM read-back errors. When a data byte is being stored in memory, the occurrences of logic "1s" in the byte are added together by the parity generator/checker chip. This chip produces a parity bit that is added to, and stored along with, the data byte. Therefore, the data byte becomes a 9-bit word. Whenever the data word is read back from the memory, the parity bit is reapplied to the parity generator and recalculated.

TEST TIP

Know that parity is a method of checking stored data for errors by adding an additional bit to it when it is read from memory.

even parity

odd parity

The recalculated parity value is then compared to the original parity value stored in memory. If the values do not match, a parity-error condition occurs and an error message is generated. Traditionally, there are two approaches to generating parity bits; the parity bit may be generated so that the total number of 1-bits equals an even number (**even parity**), or an odd number (**odd parity**).

To enable parity checking, an additional 9th bit is added to each byte stored in DRAM. On older systems, an extra memory chip was included with each bank of DRAM. In newer units, the extra storage is built into the SIMM and DIMM modules. Whether a particular system employs parity check or not depends on its chipset. Many newer chipsets have moved away from using parity checking altogether. In these cases, SIMMs and DIMMs with parity capability can be used, but the parity function will not function. In Pentium systems, the system board's user's guide, or the BIOS' Extended CMOS Setup screen should be consulted to determine whether parity is supported. If so, the parity function can be enabled through this screen.

The system's parity generator/checker circuitry consisted of discrete 74LS280 ICs in the original PC, PC-XT, PC-AT, and 80386-based compatibles. Figure 2-38 illustrates how the system's RAM and parity checking circuit work together.

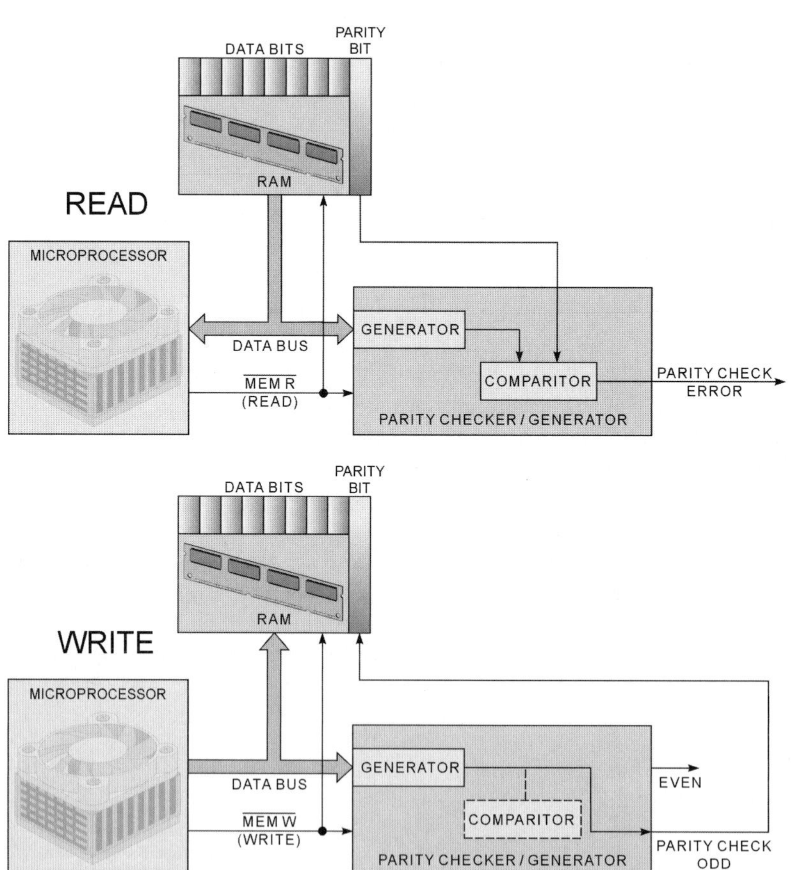

Figure 2-38: How Parity Checking Works

Non-Maskable Interrupt (NMI)

When a parity error occurs, a **Non-Maskable Interrupt (NMI)** signal is co-generated in the system, causing the BIOS to execute its NMI handler routine. This routine will normally place a parity error message on the screen, along with an option to shut down the system, or continue.

TEST TIP

Be aware of the types of problems that can create an NMI error and what the consequences of these errors are.

Advanced Memory Structures

As the operating speeds of microcomputers have continued to increase, it has become increasingly necessary to develop new memory strategies to keep pace with the other parts of the system. Some of these methods, such as developing faster DRAM chips, or including wait states in the memory-access cycles, are very fundamental in nature. However, these methods do not allow the entire system to operate at its full potential. Other, more elaborate memory management schemes have been employed on faster computers to maximize their overall performance.

Cache Memory

caching

One method of increasing the memory-access speed of a computer is called **caching**. This memory management method assumes that most memory accesses are made within a limited block of addresses. Therefore, if the contents of these addresses are relocated into a special section of high-speed SRAM, then the microprocessor could access these locations without requiring any wait states.

Cache memory is normally small to keep the cost of the system as low as possible. However, it is also very fast, even in comparison to fast DRAM devices.

hit

miss

Cache memory operations require a great deal of intelligent circuitry to operate and monitor the cache effectively. The cache controller circuitry must monitor the microprocessor's memory-access instructions to determine if the specified data is stored in the cache. If the information is in the cache, the control circuitry can present it to the microprocessor without incurring any wait states. This is referred to as a **hit**. If the information is not located in the cache, the access is passed on to the system's RAM and it is declared a **miss**.

The primary objective of the cache memory's control system is to maximize the ratio of hits to total accesses (hit rate), so that the majority of memory accesses are performed without wait states. One way to do this is to make the cache memory area as large as possible (thus raising the possibility of the desired information being in the cache). However, the relative cost, energy consumption, and physical size of SRAM devices work against this technique. Practical sizes for cache memories run between 16 kB–512 kB.

Write-Thru Cache

Write-Back Cache

There are two basic methods of writing updated information into the cache. The first is to write data into the cache and the main memory at the same time. This is referred to as **Write-Thru Cache**. This method tends to be slow since the microprocessor has to wait for the slow DRAM access to be completed. The second method is known as **Write-Back Cache**. A write-back cache holds the data in the cache until the system has a *quiet* time and then writes it into the main memory.

L1 cache

L2 cache

The Intel 80486 and Pentium microprocessors have a built-in first-level cache that can be used for both instructions and data. The internal cache is divided into four 2 kB blocks containing 128 sets of 16-byte lines each. Control of the internal cache is handled directly by the microprocessor. The first-level cache is also known as an **L1 cache**. However, many system boards extend the caching capability of the microprocessor by adding an external, second-level 256 kB/512 kB memory cache. Like the L1 cache, the second-level cache may also be referred to as an **L2 cache**. An external L2 cache memory system is depicted in Figure 2-39.

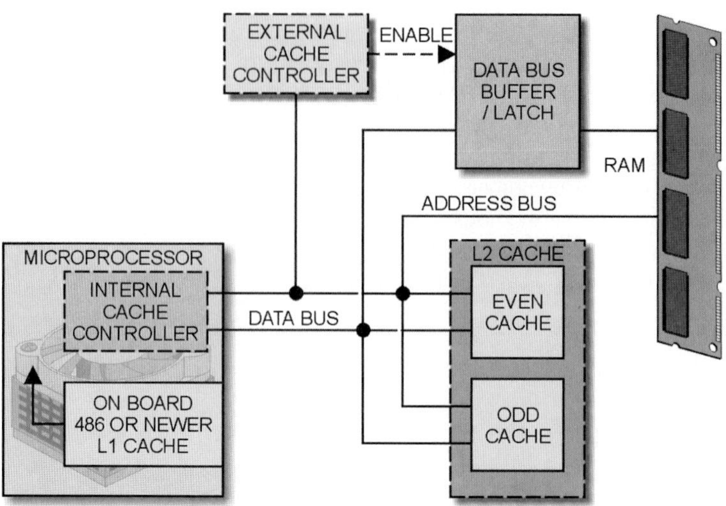

Figure 2-39: An External Cache

Memory Paging and Interleaving

There are also other commonly used methods of organizing RAM memory so that it can be accessed more efficiently. Typically, memory accesses occur in two fashions, instruction fetches (which are generally sequential) and operand accesses (which tend to be random). **Paging** and **interleaving** memory schemes are designed to take advantage of the sequential nature of instruction fetches from memory.

Paging

interleaving

page-mode RAM

static-column RAM

pages

Row Address Strobe (RAS)

fast page mode RAM

Column Address Strobe (CAS)

The basic idea of page-mode DRAM operations is illustrated in Figure 2-40. Special memory devices called **page-mode** (or **static-column**) **RAM** are required for memory paging structures. In these memory devices, data is organized into groups of rows and columns called **pages**. Once a ROW access is made in the device, it is possible to access other column addresses within the same row without pre-charging its **Row Address Strobe** (**RAS**) line. This feature produces access times that are half that of normal DRAM memories. **Fast page mode RAM** is a quicker version of page-mode RAM having improved **Column Address Strobe** (**CAS**) access speed.

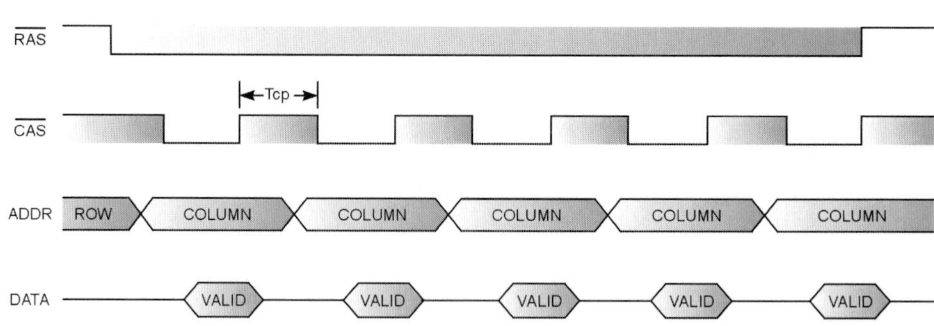

Figure 2-40: Page-Mode DRAM Operation

The operating principle behind memory interleaving is shown in Figure 2-41. Typical interleaving schemes divide the memory into two banks of RAM with one bank storing even addresses and the other storing odd addresses.

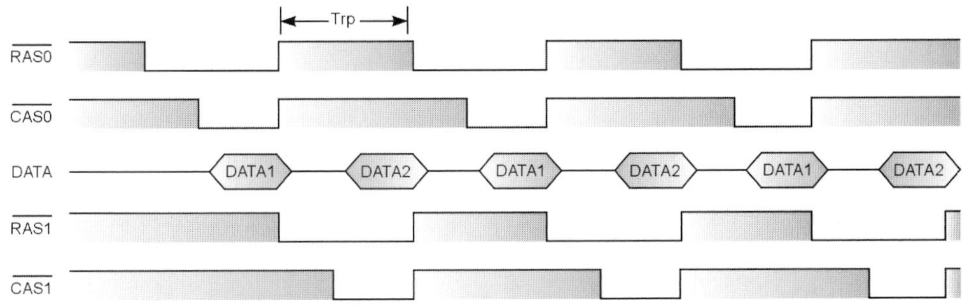

Figure 2-41: Memory Interleaving

pre-charge

The RAS signals of the two banks overlap so that the time required to **pre-charge** one bank's RAS line is used for the active RAS time of the other bank. Therefore, there should never be a pre-charge time for either bank, as long as the accesses continue to be sequential. If a non-sequential access occurs, a miss is encountered and a wait state must be inserted in the timing. If the memory is organized into two banks, the operation is referred to as two-way interleaving. It is also common to organize the memory into four equal-sized banks. This organization effectively doubles the average 0-wait state hit space in the memory.

SIMMs, DIMMs, and Banks

Older PC, PC-XT, and PC-AT system boards employed banks of discrete RAM ICs in Dual In-line Pin (DIP) sockets. Most of these system boards arranged nine pieces of 1 x 256 kb DRAM chips in the first two banks (0 and 1) and nine pieces of 1 x 64 kb chips in banks 2 and 3. The two banks of 256 kb chips provided a total of 512 kB of storage (the ninth chip of each bank supplied a parity bit for error checking).

The two banks of 64 kb chips extended the RAM memory capacity out to the full 640 kB. As with the 256 kb chips, the ninth bit was for parity.

Some system boards used two 4 x 256 kb chips with a 1 x 256 kb chip to create each of the first two banks. In any event, the system would typically run with one bank installed, two banks installed, or all of the banks installed. Bank 0 had to be filled first, followed by bank 1, and then all four.

Early AT-clone system boards moved the system's RAM to 30-pin Single In-line Pin (SIP) modules, while further refinements produced snap-in Single In-line Memory Modules (SIMMs) and Dual In-line Memory Modules (DIMMs). Like the SIP, the SIMM and DIMM units mount vertically on the system board. However, instead of using a pin and socket arrangement, both use special snap-in sockets that support the module firmly. SIMMs and DIMMs are also keyed, so that they cannot be plugged in backwards. SIMMs are available in 30-pin and 72-pin versions, while DIMMs are larger 168-pin boards.

TEST TIP

Know how many pins are used in SIMMs and DIMMS.

SIMM and DIMM sockets are quite distinctive in that they are normally arranged side by side. However, they can be located anywhere on the system board. SIMMs typically come in 8-bit or 32-bit bit data storage configurations. The 8-bit modules must be arranged in banks to match the data bus size of the system's microprocessor. In order to work effectively with a 32-bit microprocessor, a bank of four 8-bit SIMMs would need to be used. Conversely, a single 32-bit SIMM could do the same job.

> **TEST TIP**
>
> Remember that it takes two 32-bit SIMM modules to make a bank for a 64-bit processor such as the Pentium.

DIMMs, on the other hand, typically come in 32-bit and 64-bit widths to service more powerful microprocessors. Like the SIMMs, they must be arranged properly to fit the size of the system data bus. In both cases, the modules can be accessed in smaller 8- and 16-bit segments. SIMMs and DIMMs also come in 9, 36, and 72-bit versions that include parity checking bits for each byte of storage (i.e., a 36-bit SIMM provides 32 data bits and 4 parity bits—one for each byte of data).

PCs are typically sold with less than their full RAM capacity. This allows users to purchase a less expensive computer to fit their individual needs and yet retain the option to install more RAM if future applications call for it. SIMM and DIMM sizes are typically specified in an a-by-b format. For example, a 2x32 SIMM specification indicates that it is a dual, non-parity, 32-bit (4-byte) device. In this scheme, the capacity is derived by multiplying the two numbers and then dividing by eight (or nine for parity chips). Figure 2-42 depicts typical upgrade strategies using SIMM and DIMM modules to increase the memory capabilities of a system board.

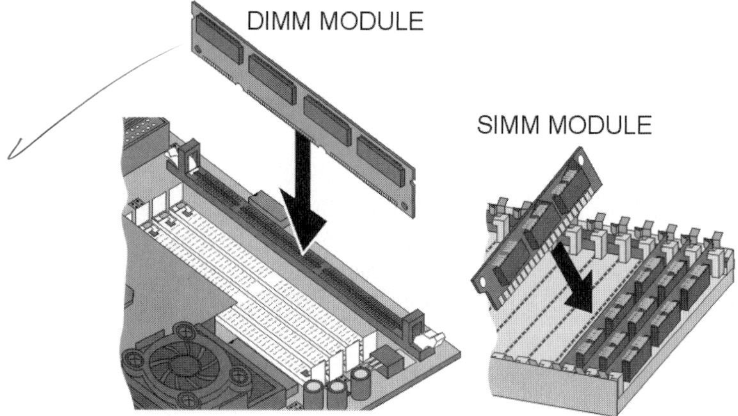

Figure 2-42: Plugging in SIMM and DIMM Memory Modules

Small Outline DIMM (SO DIMM)

A special form factor DIMM, called the **Small Outline DIMM** (**SO DIMM**) has been developed for use in notebook computers. The basic difference between SO DIMMs and regular DIMMs is that the SO DIMM is significantly smaller than the standard DIMM so that it takes up less space in notebook computers. Figure 2-43 depicts a 72-pin and a 144-pin SO DIMM. The 72-pin SO DIMM has a 32-bit data bus while the 144-pin version is 64 bits wide.

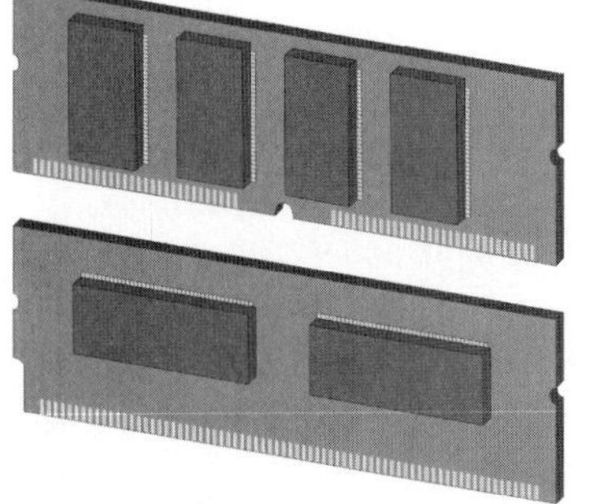

Figure 2-43: Small Outline DIMMs

Another important factor to consider when dealing with RAM is its speed. Manufacturers mark RAM devices with speed information. DRAM modules are marked with a numbering system that indicates the number of clock cycles required for the initial Read operation, followed by information about the number of reads and cycles required to move a burst of data. As an example, a fast page-mode DRAM marked as 6-3-3-3 requires 6 cycles for the initial read and 3 cycles for each of three successive reads. This will move an entire 4-byte block of data. EDO and FPM can operate with bus speeds up to 66 MHz.

SDRAM devices are marked a little different. Since they are designed to run synchronously with the system clock and use no wait states, a marking of 3:3:3 at 100 MHz on an SDRAM module specifies that:

- The CAS signal setup time is 3 bus cycles.
- The RAS to CAS change over time is 3 cycles.
- The RAS signal setup time is 3 clock cycles.

The bus speed is specified in MHz. These memory modules have been produced in the following specifications so far:

- PC66 (66 MHz or 15 nanoseconds)
- PC83 (83 MHz or 12 nanoseconds)
- PC100 (100 MHz or 10 nanoseconds)
- PC133 (133 MHz or 8 nanoseconds)
- PC150 (150 MHz or 4.5 nanoseconds)
- PC166 (166 MHz or 4 nanoseconds)

The PC66 and PC83 specifications were the first versions produced using this system. However, they never really gained widespread acceptance. On the other hand, the PC100 and PC133 versions did gain acceptance and are widely available today. The PC150 and PC166 versions are also common.

Continued advancements in memory module design have made the MHz and CAS setup time ratings obsolete. Onboard buffering and advanced access strategies have made these measurements inconsequential. Instead, memory performance is being measured by total data **throughput** (also referred to as **bandwidth**) and is being measured in terms of gigabytes per second (GBps). As an example, some of the new standard specifications include:

throughput

bandwidth

- PC1600 (1.6 GBps/200 MHz/2:2:2)
- PC2100 (2.1 GBps/266 MHz/2:3:3)
- PC2600 (2.6 GBps/333 MHz/3:3:3)
- PC3200 (3.2 GBps/400 MHz/3:3:3)

The system board's documentation will provide information about the types of devices it can use and their speed ratings. It is important to install RAM that is compatible with the bus speed the system is running. Normally, installing RAM that is rated faster than the bus speed will not cause problems. However, installing slower RAM, or mixing RAM speed ratings in a system will cause the system to not start or to periodically lock up.

TEST TIP

Be aware of the consequences of mixing RAM with different speed ratings within a system.

CMOS RAM

The A+ Core objective 4.4 states that the test taker should be able to identify the purpose of CMOS (Complementary Metal-Oxide Semiconductor), what it contains, and how to change its basic parameters. Examples include:

- printer parallel port - Uni., bi-directional, disable/enable, ECP, EPP
- COM/serial port- memory address, interrupt request, disable
- hard drive - size and drive type
- floppy drive - enable/disable drive or boot, speed, density
- boot sequence
- memory - parity, non-parity
- date/time
- passwords

CMOS Setup Utilities

BIOS Features Setup

Chipset Features Setup

During the POST process, the BIOS Setup routines can be entered by pressing the DEL key. In other BIOS types, the CTRL/ALT/ESC key combination can also be used to access the Setup utilities. The CMOS Setup utility's Main Menu screen, similar to the one depicted in Figure 2-44, appears whenever the CMOS Setup utility is engaged. This menu allows the user to select setup functions and exit choices. The most used entries include the Standard CMOS Setup, **BIOS Features Setup**, and **Chipset Features Setup** options. Selecting these, or any of the other Main Menu options, will lead into a corresponding submenu.

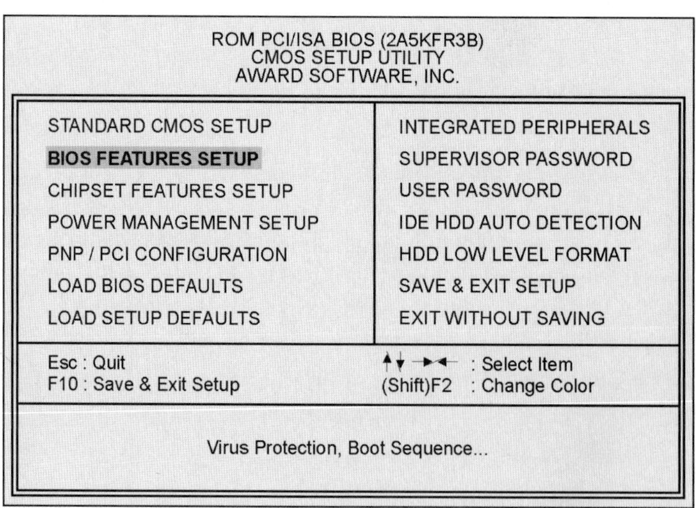

Figure 2-44: CMOS Main Menu Screen

Other typical menu items include **Power Management**, **PnP/PCI Configuration**, **Integrated Peripherals Control**, and **Password Maintenance Services**. A given CMOS Setup utility may contain the same options as those listed in the sample, options that perform the same functions under a different name, or it may not contain some options at all. This example also offers two IDE HDD-related utilities, two options for starting with default system values, and two exit options.

Power Management

PnP/PCI Configuration

Integrated Peripherals Control

Password Maintenance Services

WARNING

Set values with caution—The settings in these menus allow the system to be configured and optimized for specific functions and devices. The default values are generally recommended for normal operation. Since incorrect Setup values can cause the system to fail, you should only change Setup values that really need to be changed. If changes are made that disable the system, pressing the Insert key on reset will override the settings and start the system with default values.

The Standard CMOS Setup Screens

Standard CMOS Setup screens from various manufacturers are depicted in Figure 2-45. They all provide the same basic information. They can be used to set the system clock/calendar, establish disk drive parameters and video display type, and specify which types of errors will halt the system during the POST.

Standard CMOS Setup

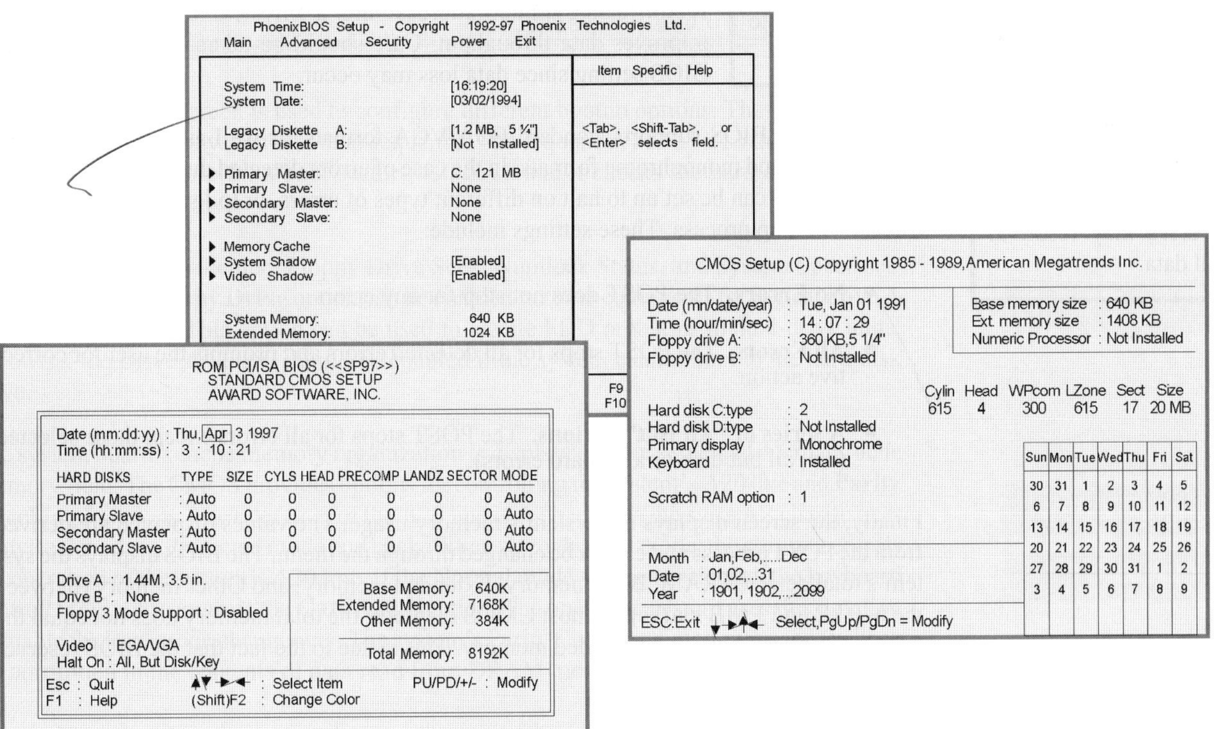

Figure 2-45: Standard CMOS Setup Screens

Auto mode

TEST TIP

Know which portion of the BIOS is responsible for implementing the PnP process.

This CMOS utility can automatically configure all PnP devices if the **Auto mode** is enabled. Under this condition, the system's IRQ and DMA assignment fields disappear as the BIOS assigns them to installed devices. When the configuration process is performed manually, each resource can be assigned as either a legacy device or a PnP/PCI device. The legacy device is one that is compatible with the original ISA slot and requires specific resource settings. The PnP/PCI device must be compliant with the Plug-and-Play specification.

PCI IRQ Map-to

With this chipset, the system board's IDE channels are coordinated with the operation of the PCI bus. The **PCI IRQ Map-to** function lets the user establish the PCI IRQ mapping for the system. Because the PCI interface in the sample chipset has two channels, it requires two interrupt services. The Primary and Secondary IDE interrupt fields default to values appropriate for two PCI IDE channels. The primary channel has a lower interrupt number than the secondary channel. Normally, ISA interrupts reserved for IDE channels are IRQ-14 for the primary channel and IRQ-15 for the secondary channel.

The secondary IDE channel can be deactivated through the PCI IDE Second Channel option. This setting is usually disabled so that an add-on IDE host adapter card can be added to the system. Only the secondary on-board IDE channel is disabled by this setting. The type of action required to trigger the interrupt can also be established in this screen. The PCI IRQ Activated by option is normally set to Level unless a device that requires an ISA-compatible, edge-triggered interrupt is added to the system.

The Integrated Peripherals Setup Functions

Integrated Peripherals

In most Pentium-based systems, the standard I/O functions of the Multi I/O card have been integrated into the system board. In these systems, the BIOS' **Integrated Peripherals** screen, depicted in Figure 2-49, provides configuration and enabling settings for the system board's IDE drive connections, floppy-disk drive controller, on-board UARTs, and on-board parallel port.

ROM PCI/ISA BIOS (2A5KFR3B)
INTEGRATED PERIPHERALS SETUP
AWARD SOFTWARE, INC.

On-Chip IDE Controller	: Enabled	Parallel Port Mode	: Normal
The 2nd channel IDE	: Enabled		
IDE Primary Master PIO	: Auto		
IDE Primary Slave PIO	: Auto		
IDE Secondary Master PIO	: Auto		
IDE Secondary Slave PIO	: Auto		
IDE Primary Master FIFO	: Enabled		
IDE Primary Slave FIFO	: Disabled		
IDE Secondary Master FIFO	: Disabled		
IDE Secondary Slave FIFO	: Disabled		
IDE HDD Block Mode	: Enabled		
Onboard FDC Controller	: Enabled		
Onboard UART 1	: Auto		
UART 1 Operation mode	: Standard		
		ESC : Quit	↑↓→←: Select Item
Onboard UART 2	: Auto	F1 : Help	PU/PD/+/- : Modify
UART 2 Operation mode	: Standard	F5 : Old Values	(Shift)F2 : Color
		F6 : Load BIOS Defaults	
Onboard Parallel Port	: 378/IRQ7	F7 : Load Setup Defaults	

Figure 2-49: Integrated Peripherals Screen

The Integrated Peripherals screen is used to enable the on-board IDE controller. As mentioned earlier, the second IDE channel can be enabled or disabled independently of the first channel, provided that the controller has been enabled. Any of the four possible devices attached to the interface can be configured for Master or Slave operation.

Data Integrity

Error Checking and Correcting (ECC)

Special DRAM paging operations can be enabled in the Chipset Features screen. When this option is disabled, the chip set's memory controller closes the DRAM page after each access. When enabled, it holds the page open until the next access occurs. DRAM refresh period and **Data Integrity** functions are also established here. This particular chipset features both parity-error checking and **Error Checking and Correcting** (**ECC**) error handling modes.

Access to the system buses is controlled through the Chipset Features screen as well. The sample chipset uses internal buffers to control the flow of information between the system's different buses. The ISA Line Buffer, Primary Frame Buffer, and VGA Frame Buffer are manipulated by the chipset for speed matching purposes. When the **Passive Release** option is enabled, the system's microprocessor can access the DRAM during passive release periods. If not, only a PCI bus master can access the local memory.

> **TEST TIP**
>
> Be aware that parity checking only detects data errors while ECC can detect and correct data errors.

Passive Release

Other options allow bytes on the data bus to be merged. Merge options include: Linear Merge, Word Merge, and Byte Merge. The chipset's memory controller checks the system's address bus enable lines to determine if items on the data bus can be used as a single unit.

Finally, the Chipset Features screen supports three fast write modes. These are the Fast Back-to-Back Write, PCI Write Burst, and M1 Linear Burst modes. When enabled, these modes allow the system to conduct consecutive PCI Write cycles in fast or burst fashions.

The sample BIOS features Plug-and-Play (PnP) capability that makes adding options to the system more automatic. PCI devices feature PnP operation. They are questioned by the system during bootup, or when they are plugged into the system, to determine what their system resource requirements are. These requirements are compared to a listing of devices already in the system and necessary system resources such as IRQ and DMA channels are allocated for them.

The PnP/PCI Configuration Screen

The BIOS holds information about the system's resource allocations and supplies it to the operating system as required. Figure 2-48 shows the PCI Configuration screen from the sample CMOS Setup utility. The operating system must be PnP-compatible in order to achieve the full benefits of the PnP BIOS. In most newer PCs, the standard operating system is Windows 95/98, which is PnP compliant.

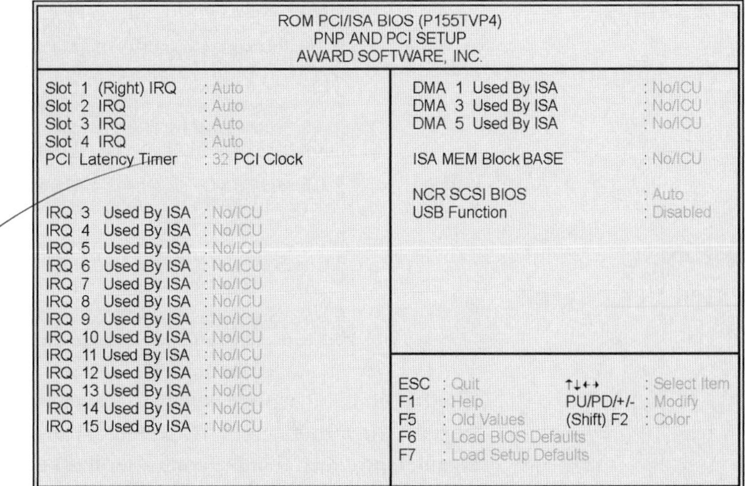

Figure 2-48: PnP/PCI Configuration Options Screen

Auto mode

TEST TIP

Know which portion of the BIOS is responsible for implementing the PnP process.

This CMOS utility can automatically configure all PnP devices if the **Auto mode** is enabled. Under this condition, the system's IRQ and DMA assignment fields disappear as the BIOS assigns them to installed devices. When the configuration process is performed manually, each resource can be assigned as either a legacy device or a PnP/PCI device. The legacy device is one that is compatible with the original ISA slot and requires specific resource settings. The PnP/PCI device must be compliant with the Plug-and-Play specification.

PCI IRQ Map-to

With this chipset, the system board's IDE channels are coordinated with the operation of the PCI bus. The **PCI IRQ Map-to** function lets the user establish the PCI IRQ mapping for the system. Because the PCI interface in the sample chipset has two channels, it requires two interrupt services. The Primary and Secondary IDE interrupt fields default to values appropriate for two PCI IDE channels. The primary channel has a lower interrupt number than the secondary channel. Normally, ISA interrupts reserved for IDE channels are IRQ-14 for the primary channel and IRQ-15 for the secondary channel.

The secondary IDE channel can be deactivated through the PCI IDE Second Channel option. This setting is usually disabled so that an add-on IDE host adapter card can be added to the system. Only the secondary on-board IDE channel is disabled by this setting. The type of action required to trigger the interrupt can also be established in this screen. The PCI IRQ Activated by option is normally set to Level unless a device that requires an ISA-compatible, edge-triggered interrupt is added to the system.

The Integrated Peripherals Setup Functions

Integrated Peripherals

In most Pentium-based systems, the standard I/O functions of the Multi I/O card have been integrated into the system board. In these systems, the BIOS' **Integrated Peripherals** screen, depicted in Figure 2-49, provides configuration and enabling settings for the system board's IDE drive connections, floppy-disk drive controller, on-board UARTs, and on-board parallel port.

ROM PCI/ISA BIOS (2A5KFR3B)
INTEGRATED PERIPHERALS SETUP
AWARD SOFTWARE, INC.

On-Chip IDE Controller	: Enabled	Parallel Port Mode	: Normal
The 2nd channel IDE	: Enabled		
IDE Primary Master PIO	: Auto		
IDE Primary Slave PIO	: Auto		
IDE Secondary Master PIO	: Auto		
IDE Secondary Slave PIO	: Auto		
IDE Primary Master FIFO	: Enabled		
IDE Primary Slave FIFO	: Disabled		
IDE Secondary Master FIFO	: Disabled		
IDE Secondary Slave FIFO	: Disabled		
IDE HDD Block Mode	: Enabled		
Onboard FDC Controller	: Enabled		
Onboard UART 1	: Auto		
UART 1 Operation mode	: Standard		
		ESC : Quit	↑↓→←: Select Item
Onboard UART 2	: Auto	F1 : Help	PU/PD/+/- : Modify
UART 2 Operation mode	: Standard	F5 : Old Values	(Shift)F2 : Color
		F6 : Load BIOS Defaults	
Onboard Parallel Port	: 378/IRQ7	F7 : Load Setup Defaults	

Figure 2-49: Integrated Peripherals Screen

The Integrated Peripherals screen is used to enable the on-board IDE controller. As mentioned earlier, the second IDE channel can be enabled or disabled independently of the first channel, provided that the controller has been enabled. Any of the four possible devices attached to the interface can be configured for Master or Slave operation.

Typematic Action

Typematic Rate

Typematic Delay

The operation of the keyboard can be modified from this screen. **Typematic Action** refers to the keyboard's ability to reproduce characters when a key is held down for a period of time. This action is governed by two parameters set in the BIOS Features screen—Typematic Rate and Typematic Delay. **Typematic Rate** refers to the rate at which characters will be repeated when the key is held down, while **Typematic Delay** defines the amount of time between the initial pressing of the key and when the repeating action begins. Typematic action is normally enabled and values of six characters/second and 250 milliseconds are typical for these settings.

Shadow

The system's **Shadow** feature is controlled through the BIOS Features screen. Shadowing can be used to copy various system firmware routines into high memory. This allows the system to read firmware from a 16-bit or 32-bit data bus instead of the normal 8-bit PC-compatible X-bus. This technique speeds up firmware read operations but reduces the high memory space available for loading device drivers. Shadowing should be enabled for individual sections of memory as needed.

The Chipset Features Screen

The Chipset Features screen, depicted in Figure 2-47, contains advanced setting information that system designers and service personnel use to optimize the chipset.

ROM PCI/ISA BIOS (2A5KFR3B)
CHIPSET FEATURES SETUP
AWARD SOFTWARE, INC.

Auto Configuration	: Enabled	Word Merge	: Enabled
AT Bus Clock	: CLK2/4	Byte Merge	: Disabled
Asysc. SRAM Write WS	: X-3-3-3	Fast Back-to-Back	: Disabled
Asysc. SRAM Read WS	: X-3-3-3	PCI Write Burst	: Enabled
EDO Read WS	: X-3-3-3	SDRAM Access Timing	: Normal
Page Mode Read WS	: X-3-3-3	SDRAM CAS Latency	: 3
DRAM Write WS	: X-2-2-2	TAG [10-8] Config	: Default
CPU to DRAM Page Mode	: Disabled		
DRAM Refresh Period	: 60 us		
DRAM Data Integrity Mode	: Parity		
Pipelined Function	: Disabled		
16 Bit ISA I/O Command WS	: 2 Wait		
16 Bit ISA Mem Command WS	: 2 Wait		
Local Memory 15-16M	: Enabled		
Passive Release	: Enabled		
ISA Line Buffer	: Enabled	ESC : Quit	↑↓→←: Select Item
Delay Transaction	: Enabled	F1 : Help	PU/PD/+/- : Modify
Primary Frame Buffer	: 2 MB	F5 : Old Values	(Shift)F2 : Color
VGA Frame Buffer	: Enabled	F6 : Load BIOS Defaults	
Linear Merge	: Enabled	F7 : Load Setup Defaults	

Figure 2-47: Chipset Features Screen

Auto Configuration

The **Auto Configuration** option selects predetermined optimal values for the chipset to start with. When this feature is enabled, many of the screen's fields are not available to the user. When this setting is disabled, the chipset's setup parameters are obtained from the system's CMOS RAM. Many of the system's memory configuration parameters are established in this screen.

These parameters include Wait State timing for Asynchronous SRAM read and writes, as well as EDO and Page-Mode RAM reads. Wait state settings for slower ISA I/O and memory devices can also be configured in this screen (16-bit ISA Memory and I/O Command WS options). The Local Memory 15-16M option sets up mapping in the chipset to shift slower ISA device memory into faster local bus memory to increase system performance.

The BIOS Features Setup Screen

The BIOS Features Setup screen, shown in Figure 2-46, provides access to options that extend the standard ISA BIOS functions. This BIOS example includes a built-in Virus Warning utility that produces a warning message whenever a program tries to write to the boot sector of an HDD partition table. This function should be enabled for normal operations. However, it should be turned off when conducting an upgrade to the operating system. The built-in virus warning utility checks the drive's boot sector for changes. The changes that the new operating system will attempt to make to the boot sector will be interpreted as a virus and the utility will act to prevent the upgrade from occurring. If a warning message is displayed under normal circumstances, a full-feature antivirus utility should be run on the system.

Virus Warning

TEST TIP

Be aware that you should turn off any BIOS antivirus protection settings when changing operating systems.

```
ROM PCI/ISA BIOS (2A5KFR3B)
STANDARD CMOS SETUP
AWARD SOFTWARE, INC.

Virus Warning               : Disabled   Video    BIOS Shadow : Enabled
CPU Internal Cache          : Enabled    C8000-CBFFF Shadow   : Disabled
External Cache              : Enabled    CC000-CFFF  Shadow   : Disabled
Quick Power On Self Test    : Disabled   D0000-D3FFF Shadow   : Disabled
Boot Sequence               : A,C, SCSI  D4000-D7FFF Shadow   : Disabled
Swap Floppy Drive           : Disabled   D8000-DBFFF Shadow   : Disabled
Boot Up Floppy Seek         : Enabled    DC000-DFFFF Shadow   : Disabled
Boot Up Numlock Status      : On
Boot Up System Speed        : High
Gate A20 Option             : Fast
Memory Parity Check         : Disabled
Typematic Rate Setting      : Disabled
Typematic Rate (Chars/Sec)  : 6
Typematic Delay (Msec)      : 250
Security Option             : Setup      ESC : Quit         ↑↓→←: Select Item
PCI/VGA Palette Snoop       : Disabled   F1  : Help         PU/PD/+/- : Modify
OS Select For DRAM > 64M    : Non-OS2    F5  : Old Values   (Shift)F2  Color
                                         F6  : Load BIOS  Defaults
                                         F7  : Load Setup Defaults
```

Figure 2-46: BIOS Features Setup Screen

The Features Setup screen is used to configure different bootup options. These options include establishing the system's bootup sequence. The sequence can be set so that the system checks the floppy drive for a boot sector first, or so that it checks the hard drive without checking the floppy drive.

Other bootup options include: Floppy Drive Seek, Numlock Status, and System Speed settings. The **Swap Floppy Drive** option can be enabled to route commands for logical drive A to physical drive B. This option can be used to isolate FDD problems in dual-drive units. Likewise, the Drive A option should be enabled if the system cannot boot to the hard disk drive.

Swap Floppy Drive

The system board's cache memory organization is displayed in the screen's External Cache Memory field. The CMOS provides options for controlling the system's A20 line and **Parity Checking** functions. The operation of the A20 line is connected to the system's change over from Real mode to Protected mode and back. When set to the Fast mode, the chipset controls the operation of the system's A20 line. If the Normal mode setting is selected, the keyboard controller circuitry controls the **Gate A20** function. The operating system uses this function to enable the Real mode changeover. The system's Parity Checking function is used to check for corruption in the contents of data read from DRAM memory.

Parity Checking

Gate A20

Other typical menu items include **Power Management**, **PnP/PCI Configuration**, **Integrated Peripherals Control**, and **Password Maintenance Services**. A given CMOS Setup utility may contain the same options as those listed in the sample, options that perform the same functions under a different name, or it may not contain some options at all. This example also offers two IDE HDD-related utilities, two options for starting with default system values, and two exit options.

Power Management

PnP/PCI Configuration

Integrated Peripherals Control

Password Maintenance Services

> **WARNING**
>
> **Set values with caution**—The settings in these menus allow the system to be configured and optimized for specific functions and devices. The default values are generally recommended for normal operation. Since incorrect Setup values can cause the system to fail, you should only change Setup values that really need to be changed. If changes are made that disable the system, pressing the Insert key on reset will override the settings and start the system with default values.

The Standard CMOS Setup Screens

Standard CMOS Setup screens from various manufacturers are depicted in Figure 2-45. They all provide the same basic information. They can be used to set the system clock/calendar, establish disk drive parameters and video display type, and specify which types of errors will halt the system during the POST.

Standard CMOS Setup

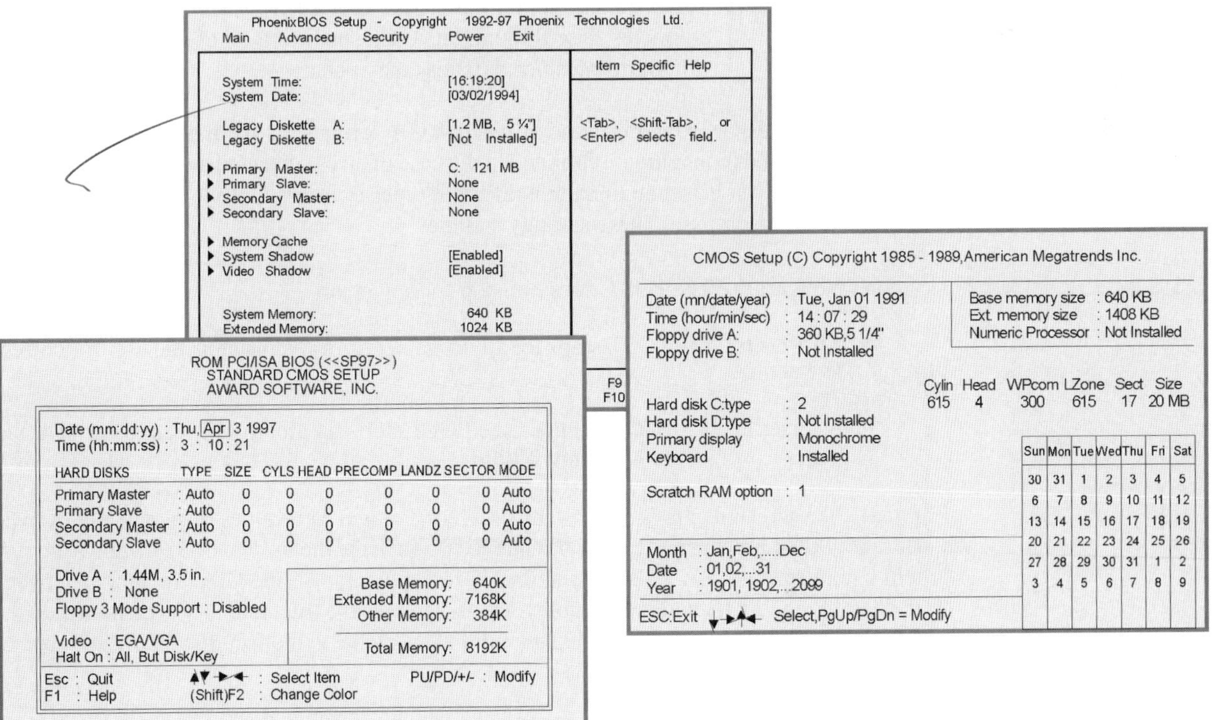

Figure 2-45: Standard CMOS Setup Screens

The BIOS uses military time settings (i.e., 13:00:00 = 1 PM). The PgUp and PgDn keys are used to change the setting after it has been selected using the arrow keys. This BIOS version supports Daylight Savings time by adding an hour when daylight saving time begins and subtracts it when standard time returns.

Current BIOS typically support 360 kB, 720 kB, 1.2 MB, 1.44 MB, and 2.88 MB floppy drive formats. The other area in this screen that may require some effort to set up is the HDD parameters section. All BIOS come with a list of hard drive types that they can support directly. However, they also provide a position for user-definable drive settings. Historically, this has been referred to as the "Type 47" entry, but this entry may be located at any number in the list.

Auto Detect

Newer BIOS possess **Auto Detect** options to detect the type of hard drives installed in the system and automatically load their parameters into CMOS. Systems with Enhanced IDE capabilities support up to four IDE drives. However, the CMOS does not typically display information about CD-ROM drives, or SCSI devices.

translation modes

Cyl/Hds/Sec (CHS)

Logical Block Addressing (LBA)

When the AUTO Detect selection is chosen, the BIOS attempts to detect IDE devices in the system during the POST process, and determine the specifications and Optimum Operating mode for those devices. The drive specifications can also be selected from a built-in list of drive parameters, or they can be entered directly using the User option at the end of the list.

Four **translation modes** can be selected for each drive type; Auto, Normal, Large, and LBA. In Auto mode, the BIOS determines the best operating mode for the drive. In Normal mode, the BIOS will support a maximum **Cyl/Hds/Sec** (**CHS**) setting of 1024/16/63. For larger drives (above 1024 cylinders), the Large and LBA modes are used. The Large option can be used with large drives that do not support **Logical Block Addressing** (**LBA**) techniques. For those drives that do, the LBA mode should be selected. In this mode, the IDE controller converts the sector/head/cylinder address into a physical block address that improves data throughput. Care should be taken when chaning this BIOS setting since data loss may occur.

TEST TIP

Know that the LBA mode for SCSI and IDE disk drives must be enabled in the CMOS to support hard drive sizes over 528 MB.

TEST TIP

Be aware that changing the translation mode setting for an existing drive may result in loss of all data.

Similarly, this BIOS supports standard EGA/VGA formats, as well as older 40- and 80-column CGA and monochrome formats. In the case of errors detected during the POST process, the BIOS can be set up to halt on different types of errors, or to ignore them and continue the bootup process. These settings include:

- **No Errors.** The POST does not stop for any errors.
- **All Errors.** The POST stops for all detected errors and prompts the user for corrective action.
- **A series of "All But" options.** The POST stops for all errors except those selected (i.e., all but disk or keyboard errors).

Finally, the screen displays the system's memory usage. The values displayed are derived from the POST process and cannot be changed through the menu. The BIOS displays the system's total detected RAM, Base memory, Extended memory, and Other memory (between the 640 kB and 1 MB marks). In most CMOS displays, the total memory does not equal the summation of the base and extended memory. This is due to the fact that the BIOS reserves 384 kB for shadowing purposes.

Programmed Input/Output (PIO)

First In/First Out (FIFO) buffering

Each IDE device can also be enabled for **Programmed Input/Output** (**PIO**) modes and **First In/First Out (FIFO) buffering**. The PIO field allows the user to select any of four PIO modes (0-4) for each device. The PIO mode determines how fast data will be transferred between the drive and the system. The performance level of the device typically increases with each higher mode value.

In Mode-0, the transfer rate is set at 3.3 MB/second with a 600 nanosecond (ns) cycle time. Mode-1 steps up to 5.2 MB/s with a 3.3ns cycle time. Mode-2 improves to 8.3 MB/s using a 240ns cycle time. Most faster drives support PIO Modes-3 and -4 through the ATA-2 specification. These modes use 11.1 MB/s with a 180ns cycle time and 16.6 MB/s using a 120ns cycle time respectively. These modes require that the IDE port be located on a local bus, such as a PCI bus.

If the Auto mode option is selected, the system will determine which mode is best suited for each device. If FIFO operation is selected, the system establishes special FIFO buffers for each device to speed up data flow between the device and the system.

The IDE HDD Block mode selection should be set to Enabled for most new hard drives. This setting, also referred to as Large Block Transfer, Multiple Command, and Multiple-Sector Read/Write mode, supports LBA disk drive operations so that partitions larger than 528 MB can be used on the drive.

TEST TIP

Remember that ECP and EPP modes for the parallel port must be enabled through the CMOS Setup utility.

The other MI/O functions supported through the CMOS utility include: enabling the FDD controller, selecting the logical COM port addressing and operating modes for the system's two built-in UARTs, and selecting logical addressing and operating modes for the parallel port.

Standard Parallel Port (SPP)

Extended Parallel Port (EPP)

Extended Capabilities Port (ECP)

The UARTs can be configured to support half-duplex or full-duplex transmission modes through an infrared port, provided the system board is equipped with one. This allows wireless communications with serial peripheral devices over short distances.

The parallel printer port can be configured for normal PC-AT compatible **Standard Parallel Port** (**SPP**) operation, for extended bidirectional operation (**Extended Parallel Port - EPP**), for fast, buffered bidirectional operation (**Extended Capabilities Port - ECP**), or for combined ECP+EPP operation. The normal setting should be selected unless both the port hardware and driver software support EPP and/or ECP operation.

Power Management Functions

Power Management

Doze mode

Standby mode

Suspend mode

The **Power Management** fields allow the user to select from three power saving modes: **Doze**, **Standby**, and **Suspend**. These are green PC-compatible power saving modes that cause the system to step down from maximum power usage. The Doze setting causes the microprocessor clock to slow down after a defined period of inactivity. The Standby mode causes the hard drive and video to shut down after a period of inactivity. Finally, everything in the system except the microprocessor shuts down in Suspend mode. Certain system events, such as IRQ and DRQ activities, cause the system to wake up from these modes and resume normal operation.

Password Setting

The **Password Setting** options, depicted in Figure 2-50, permit the user to enter and modify password settings. Password protection can be established for the system, so that a password must be entered each time the system boots up or when the Setup utility is entered, or it can simply be set up so that it is only required to access the Setup utility.

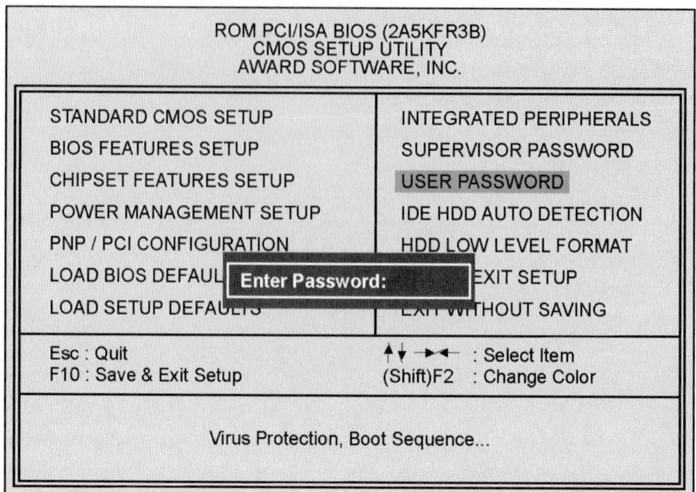

Figure 2-50: Password Setting Options

ADDING AND REMOVING FRU MODULES

The A+ Core objective 1.2 states that the test taker should be able to identify basic procedures for adding and removing field replaceable modules. As this A+ objective points out, every technician should be aware of typical personal computer components that can be exchanged in the field. They should be able to install, connect, and configure these components to upgrade or repair an existing system. The following sections of this chapter present standard procedures for installing and removing typical field replaceable units in a microcomputer system.

System Boards

System boards are generally removed for one of two possible reasons. Either the system board has failed, and needs to be replaced, or the user wants to install a new system board with better features. In either case, it will be necessary to remove the current system board and replace it. The removal procedure can be defined in five steps, as described in the following Hands-On Activity:

Hands-On Activity

1. Remove all external I/O systems.
2. Remove the system unit's outer cover.
3. Remove the option adapter cards.
4. Remove the cables from the system board.
5. Remove the system board.

To replace a system board, it is necessary to disconnect several cables from the old system board and reconnect them to the new system board. The easiest method of handling this is to use tape (preferably masking tape) to mark the wires and their connection points (on the new system board) before removing any wires from the old system board.

Removing External I/O Systems

Unplug all power cords from the commercial outlet. Remove all peripherals from the system unit. Disconnect the mouse, keyboard, and monitor signal cable from the rear of the unit. Finally, disconnect the monitor power cable from the system (or the outlet). Figure 2-51 illustrates the system unit's back panel connections.

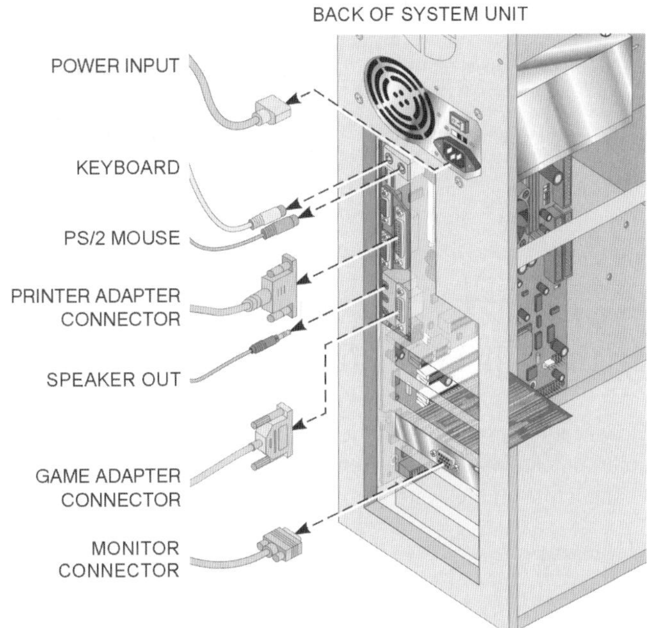

Figure 2-51: System Unit Back Panel Connections

Removing the System Unit's Outer Cover

Unplug the 120 Vac power cord from the system unit. Determine which type of case you are working on. If the case is a desktop model, does the cover slide off the chassis in a forward direction, bringing the front panel with it, or does it raise off the chassis from the rear? If the back lip of the outer cover folds over the edge of the back panel, then the lid raises up from the back, after the retaining screws are removed. If the retaining screws go through the back panel without passing through the lip, then the outer cover will slide forward after the retaining screws have been removed.

Determine the number of screws that hold the outer cover to the chassis. Do not confuse the power supply retaining screws with those holding the back panel. The power supply unit requires four screws. Check for screws along the lower edges of the outer cover that would hold it to the sides of the chassis. Remove the screws that hold the cover to the chassis. Store the screws properly.

Remove the system unit's outer cover, as illustrated in Figure 2-52, and set it aside. Slide the case forward. Tilt the case upward from the front and remove it from the unit. Or, lift the back edge of the outer cover to approximately 45 degrees, and then slide it toward the rear of the chassis.

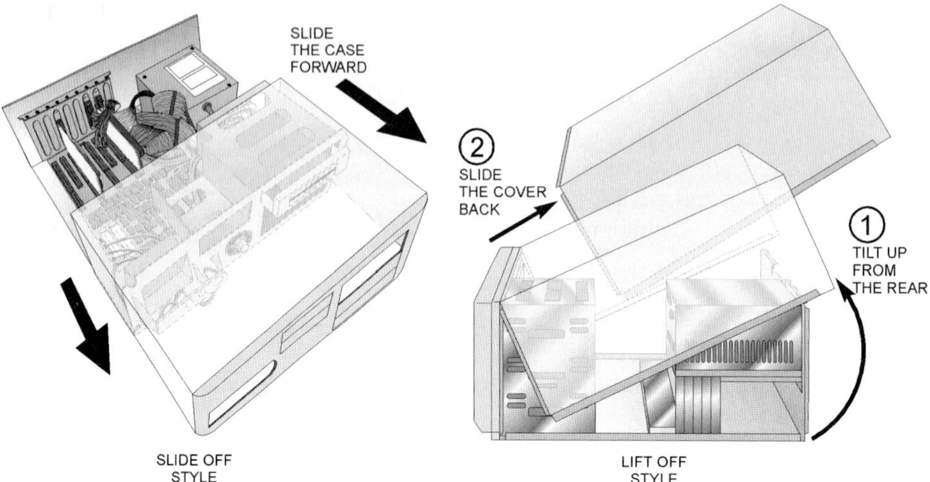

Figure 2-52: Removing the Case

Removing the Option Adapter Cards

There are a wide variety of peripheral devices used with PC-compatible systems. Many of these devices communicate with the main system through options adapter cards that fit into expansion slot connectors on the system board.

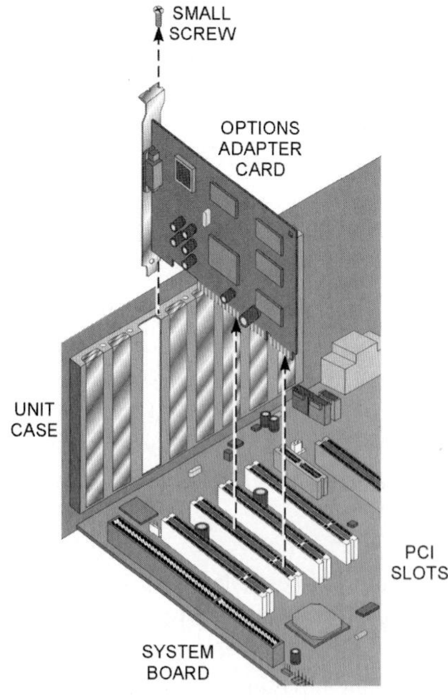

Figure 2-53: Removing Adapter Cards

Remove the retaining screws that secure the options adapter cards to the system unit's back panel. Remove the adapter cards from the expansion slots. It is a good practice to place adapter cards back into the same slots they were removed from, if possible. Store the screws properly. Refer to Figure 2-53 to perform this procedure.

If the system employs an MI/O card, disconnect the floppy drive signal cable (smaller signal cable) and the hard drive signal cable (larger signal cable) from the card. Also disconnect any I/O port connections from the card before removing it from the expansion slot.

Removing the Cables from the System Board

The system board provides an operator interface through a set of front panel indicator lights and switches. These indicators and switches connect to the system board by BERG connectors, as depicted in Figure 2-54.

The front panel connectors must be removed in order to exchange the system board for a new one. Since it is quite easy to get these connections reversed, make sure that you mark them for identification purposes before removing them from their connection points. Record the color and function of each connection. Trace each wire back to its front panel connection to determine what its purpose is. This will ensure that they are reinstalled correctly after the exchange is completed.

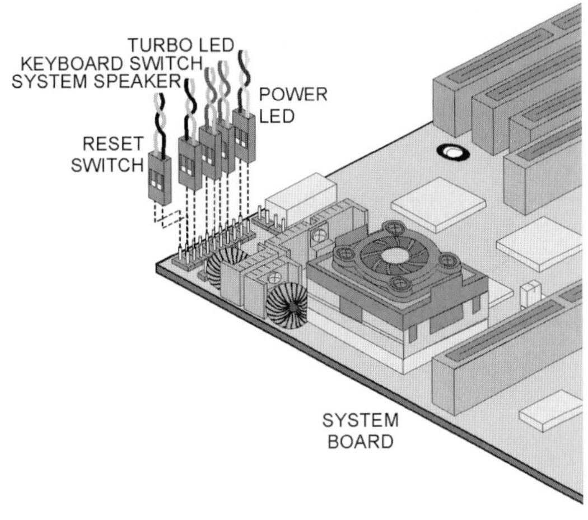

Figure 2-54: Front Panel Connections

Disconnect the power supply connections from the system board as well.

Removing the System Board

Verify the positions of all jumper and switch settings on the old system board. Record these settings and verify their meanings before removing the board from the system. This may require the use of the board's user's manual, if available. Remove the grounding screw (or screws) that secure the system board to the chassis. Store the screws properly.

In a desktop unit, slide the system board toward the left (as you face the front of the unit) to free its plastic feet from the slots in the floor of the system unit. Tilt the left edge of the board up, and then lift it straight up and out of the system unit, as illustrated in Figure 2-55.

In a tower unit, slide the system board toward the bottom of the system unit to free its plastic feet from the slots in the side panel. Tilt the bottom edge of the board away from the unit and pull it straight out of the chassis, as shown in Figure 2-56.

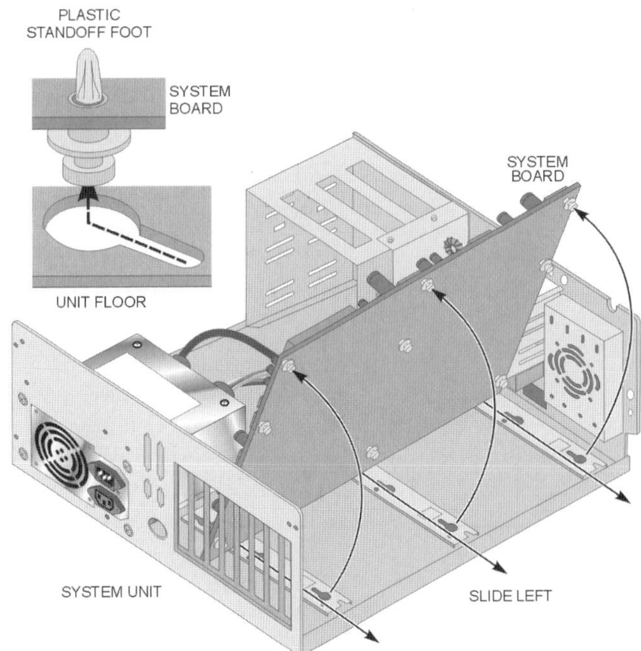

Figure 2-55: Removing the System Board from a Desktop Case

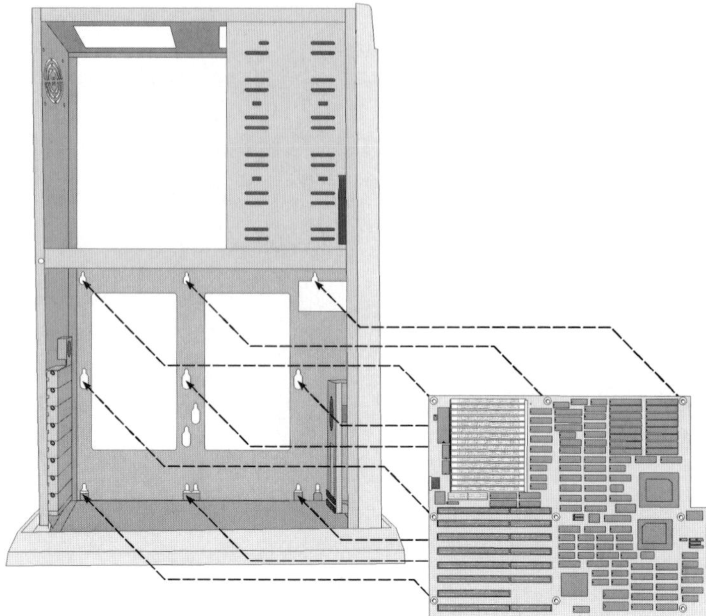

Figure 2-56: Removing the System Board from a Tower Case

System Board Devices

There are a few serviceable devices on the system board. These include:

- the microprocessor
- the system RAM modules
- specialized support ICs

Like the system board itself, there are really only two possible reasons for replacing any of these devices: to replace a failed unit or to upgrade the unit.

Microprocessors

sockets

PC manufacturers mount microprocessors in **sockets** so that they can be replaced easily. This enables a failed microprocessor to simply be exchanged with a working unit. More often though, the microprocessor is replaced with an improved version to upgrade the speed or performance of the system.

pin-1 notch

The notches and dots on the various ICs are important keys when replacing a microprocessor. They specify the location of the IC's number 1 pin. This pin must be lined up with the **pin-1 notch** of the socket for proper insertion. In older systems, the microprocessors had to be forcibly removed from the socket using an IC extractor tool. As the typical microprocessor's pin count increased, special Zero Insertion Force (ZIF) sockets were designed that allowed the microprocessor to be set in the socket without force and then be clamped in place. An arm-activated clamping mechanism in the socket shifts to the side, locking the pins in place. A ZIF socket and microprocessor arrangement is depicted in Figure 2-57.

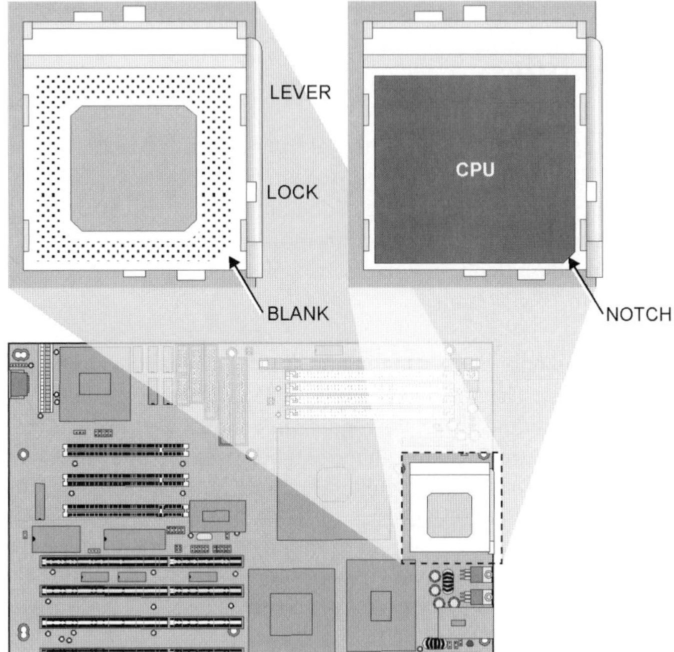

Figure 2-57: A Microprocessor and ZIF Socket

To release the microprocessor from the socket, the lever arm beside the socket must be pressed down and away from the socket. When it comes free from the socket, the arm raises up to release the pressure on the microprocessor's pins.

A notch and dot in one corner of the CPU marks the position of the processor's #1 pin. The dot and notch should be located at the free end of the socket's locking lever for proper installation. Both the CPU and the socket have one corner that does not have a pin (or pin hole) in it. This feature prevents the CPU from being inserted into the socket incorrectly.

Pentium processors generate a considerable amount of heat during normal operation. To prevent this heat from reaching a destructive level for the device, all Pentiums require that a CPU cooling fan and heat sink unit be installed on the microprocessor. These units are available in glue-on and snap-on models. A special heat-conducting grease is typically used with snap-on heat sinks to provide good thermal transfer between the microprocessor and the heat sink. Power for the fans is normally obtained from one of the system's options power connectors, or from a special jumper block on the system board. These items must be installed before operating the microprocessor.

Pentium microprocessors come in a number of speed ratings and many use a dual processor voltage arrangement. In addition, the processor unit may be a Pentium clone unit manufactured by someone other than Intel. The microprocessor's supply voltage is controlled by a **Voltage Regulator Module (VRM)** on the system board. Jumpers on the system board are used to establish the proper +3V and **CPU Core voltage** settings for the particular type of microprocessor being installed in the system.

Voltage Regulator Module (VRM)

CPU Core voltage

All Pentium processors operate from one of three external clock frequencies—50 MHz, 60 MHz, or 66 MHz. Their advertised speed ratings are derived from internal clock multiplier circuitry. System board jumpers are also used to establish the external/internal clock ratio for the microprocessor, as well as its external bus frequency.

Memory Modules

Single In-line Memory Module (SIMM)

Dual In-line Memory Module (DIMM)

Modern system boards typically provide rows of **Single In-line Memory Module (SIMM)** sockets and a single, **Dual In-line Memory Module (DIMM)** socket. These sockets accept small, piggy-back memory modules that can contain various combinations of DRAM devices. Both SIMMs and DIMMs use edge connectors that snap into a retainer on the system board. The SIMMs used on Pentium boards are typically 72-pin SIMMs while the DIMM socket accepts 168-pin DIMM units.

bank-0

bank-1

The SIMM modules can only be inserted in one direction because of a plastic safety tab at one end of the SIMM slot. The notched end of the SIMM module must be inserted into this end. To install a SIMM module, insert the module into the slot at a 45-degree angle, making sure that all of the contacts are aligned with the slot. Rock the module into a vertical position so that it snaps into place and the plastic guides go through the SIMM's mounting holes. The metal clip should lock into place. To release the SIMM module, gently push the metal clips outward and rotate the module out of the slot. The DIMM module simply slides vertically into the socket and is locked in place by a tab at each end. These processes are illustrated in Figure 2-58.

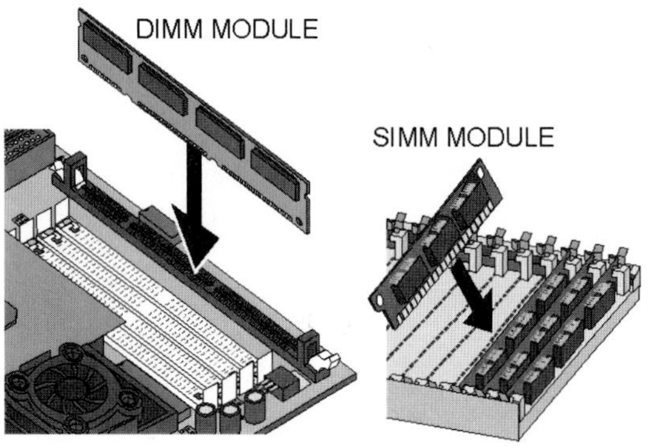

Figure 2-58: Installing SIMM and DIMM Modules

On most Pentium system boards, the SIMM sockets are organized so that slots 1 and 2 make up **bank-0**, while slots 2 and 3 form **bank-1**. Each bank can be filled with single-sided (32-bit) SIMMs, or double-sided (64-bit) SIMMs. The system can be operated with only bank-0 full. It will also operate with both banks full. However, it cannot be operated with a portion of any banks filled (a bank in use must be full).

SYSTEM UPGRADING AND OPTIMIZING

The A+ Core hardware objective 1.8 states that the test taker should be able to identify concepts and procedures relating to BIOS. It also states that the test taker should be able to identify hardware methods of system optimization and when to use them.

The modular design of the PC-compatible system enables portions of the system to be upgraded as new, or better, components become available, or as the system's application changes. As this A+ objective points out, computer technicians must be capable of upgrading the system's BIOS as part of a system upgrade. Technicians should also be able to optimize PC hardware to obtain the best performance possible for a given system configuration. The following sections cover upgradeable components found in common PC systems, including information about when and how to upgrade them.

System Board Upgrading

There are typically five serviceable components on the system board. These include:

- the microprocessor
- the RAM modules
- the CMOS backup battery
- the ROM BIOS IC(s)
- the cache memory

Of the five items listed, three—the microprocessor, the RAM modules, and the cache memory—can be exchanged to increase the performance of the system. These devices are normally mounted in sockets to make replacing or upgrading them an easy task.

Electrostatic Discharge (ESD)

Great care should be taken when exchanging these parts to avoid damage to the ICs from **Electrostatic Discharge** (**ESD**). ESD prevention is covered in detail in Chapter 13—*Preventive Maintenance*. In addition, care should be taken during the extraction and replacement of the ICs to avoid misalignment and bent pins. Make sure to correctly align the IC's pin #1 with the socket's pin #1 position. In the case of microprocessors that plug into standard sockets, the force required to insert them may overstress the system board if not properly supported.

As stated earlier in this chapter, microprocessor manufacturers have devised upgrade versions for virtually every type of microprocessor in the market. It is also common for clone microprocessors to be pin-for-pin compatible with older Intel socket designs. This strategy allows the end user to realize a speed increase by upgrading, along with an increase in processing power.

Flashed

Upgrading the processor is a fairly easy operation after gaining access to the system board. Simply remove the microprocessor from its socket and replace it with the upgrade. The physical upgrade should also be accompanied by a logical upgrade. When the microprocessor is upgraded, the BIOS should also be **Flashed** with the latest compatibility firmware. If the BIOS does not possess the flash option and does not support the new microprocessor, a new BIOS chip that does support it must be obtained. If not, the entire system board will typically need to be upgraded. Two items must be observed when changing the microprocessor:

- make sure the replacement microprocessor is hardware compatible with the original, or that the system board will support the new microprocessor type
- make certain to properly orient the new processor in the socket so that its pin #1 matches the socket's pin #1

Upgrading system board memory is also a fairly simple process. Having more RAM on board allows the system to access more data from extended or expanded memory, without having to access the disk drive. This speeds up system operation considerably. Normally, upgrading memory simply amounts to installing new memory modules in vacant SIMM or DIMM slots. If the slots are already populated, it will be necessary to remove them to install faster, or higher-capacity modules.

TEST TIP

Know what precautions to take before upgrading the system's BIOS.

Consult the system board user's guide to determine what speed the memory devices must be rated for. You should be aware that RAM and other memory devices are rated in access time instead of clock speed. Therefore, a 70-nanosecond (ns) RAM device is faster than an 80-nanosecond device. The guide should also be checked for any memory configuration settings that must be made to accept the new memory capacity.

If the system has socketed cache memory, some additional performance can be gained by optimizing the cache. Upgrading the cache on these system boards normally only requires that additional cache ICs be installed in vacant sockets. If the sockets are full but the system's cache size is less than maximum, it will be necessary to remove the existing cache chips and replace them with faster, higher-capacity devices. Make sure to observe the pin #1 alignment as well as check the system board's user's guide for any configuration jumper changes.

Before upgrading the system board's FRU units, check the cost of the proposed component upgrade against the cost of upgrading the system board itself. In many cases, the RAM from the original board can be used on a newer, faster model that should include a more advanced microprocessor. Before finalizing the choice to install a new system board, however, make sure that the current adapters, software, and peripherals will function properly with the updated board. If not, the cost of upgrading may be unexpectedly higher than simply replacing an FRU component.

CHAPTER SUMMARY

The chapter picked up where the general system board discussion from Chapter 1 left off. The opening sections featured an expanded discussion of motherboards (components and architecture) roughly equivalent with CompTIA's Core Hardware objective 4.3. This section was used to start the chapter because it permitted the discussion of all the system board objectives to flow better. After completing this section, you should be able to describe the major architectural differences between system board types.

After completing the discussion of motherboard fundamentals, the chapter keyed in on its main component—the microprocessor. You should be able to describe the basic characteristics of popular microprocessors after examining this section.

Following the microprocessors section, the chapter moved into an extended discussion of system memory structures. This section should enable you to describe the different categories of RAM and identify their normal system-board locations and physical characteristics.

Leaving memory structures, the chapter next explored CMOS Setup utilities in detail. After completing this section, you should be able to describe the purpose of CMOS RAM, discuss what a typical CMOS utility contains, and explain how to change basic parameters.

The chapter concluded with a discussion of adding and removing various FRU modules.

At this point, review the objectives listed at the beginning of the chapter to be certain that you understand and can perform each item listed there.

KEY POINTS REVIEW

This chapter has examined the major components that make up typical PC-compatible system boards. These items include microprocessors, memory types, microprocessor support systems, and expansion buses. Review the following key points before moving into the Review and Exam Questions sections to make sure you are comfortable with each point. Afterward, answer the Review Questions that follow to verify your knowledge of the information.

- The system board is the main component of any personal computer system.
- System boards fundamentally change for three reasons: new microprocessors, new expansion-slot types, and reduced chip counts. Reduced chip counts are typically the result of improved microprocessor support chipsets. Chipsets combine PC- and AT-compatible structures into larger integrated circuits.
- Since chipset-based system boards require much fewer SSI, MSI, and LSI devices to produce, printed-circuit-board manufacturers have been able to design much smaller boards.
- Chipset-based system boards and I/O cards tend to change often as IC manufacturers continue to integrate higher levels of circuitry into their devices.

- The system's expansion slots provide the connecting point for most of its I/O devices. Interface cards communicate with the system through the extended microprocessor buses in these slots.
- In order to speed up the operation of their systems, system board manufacturers began to add proprietary bus designs to their board to increase the speed and bandwidth for transfers between the microprocessor and a few selected peripherals. This was accomplished by creating special local buses between the devices that would enable the peripherals to operate at speeds close to that of the microprocessor.
- The main component in the PCI-based system is the PCI bus controller, called the host bridge. This device monitors the microprocessor's address bus to determine whether addresses are intended for devices on the system board, in a PCI slot, or in one of the system board's other expansion slots.
- Like the PCI bus, the VL-bus controller monitors the microprocessor's bus to determine what type of operation is being performed, and where the address is located in the system.
- A new serial interface scheme, called the Universal Serial Bus (USB), has been developed to provide a fast, flexible method of attaching up to 127 peripheral devices to the computer. The USB provides a connection format designed to replace the system's traditional serial and parallel port connections.
- The microprocessors used in the vast majority of all PC-compatible microcomputers include: the 8088/86, the 80286, the 80386, the 80486, and the Pentium (80586 and 80686) devices.
- The Pentium is a 32/64-bit microprocessor contained in a Ceramic Pin Grid Array package. The registers for the microprocessor and floating-point sections of the Pentium are identical to those of the 80486. It has a 64-bit data bus that allows it to handle Quad Word (or Qword) data transfers. The Pentium also contains two separate 8-kB caches, compared to only one in the 80486. One of the caches is used for instructions or code, and the other is used for data. The internal architecture of the Pentium resembles an 80486 in expanded form. The floating-point section operates up to five times faster than that of the FPU in the 80486.

- In the Pentium MMX processor, the multimedia and communications processing capabilities of the original Pentium device are extended by the addition of 57 multimedia-specific instructions to the instruction set.

- Intel departed from simply increasing the speed of its Pentium processor line by introducing the Pentium Pro processor. While compatible with all of the previous software written for the Intel processor line, the Pentium Pro is optimized to run 32-bit software.

- The Pentium II includes all of the multimedia enhancements from the MMX processor, as well as retaining the power of the Pentium Pro's dynamic execution and 512 kB L2 cache features. The L1 cache is increased to 32 kB, while the L2 cache operates with a half-speed bus.

- There are normally three types of semiconductor memory found on a typical system board. These include the system's ROM BIOS ICs, the system's RAM memory, and the second-level cache memory unit.

- The microprocessor, the RAM modules, and the cache memory can be exchanged to increase the performance of the system. These devices are normally mounted in sockets to make replacing or upgrading them an easy task.

- One method of increasing the memory-access speed of a computer is called caching. This memory management method assumes that most memory accesses are made within a limited block of addresses. Therefore, if the contents of these addresses are relocated into a special section of high-speed SRAM, then the microprocessor could access these locations without requiring any wait states.

- There are also other commonly used methods of organizing RAM memory so that it can be accessed more efficiently. Typically, memory accesses occur in two fashions: instruction fetches (which are generally sequential) and operand accesses (which tend to be random). Paging and interleaving memory schemes are designed to take advantage of the sequential nature of instruction fetches from memory.

REVIEW QUESTIONS

The following questions test your knowledge of the material presented in this chapter.

1. Referring to the sample core-to-bus ratio configurations listed in Table 2-7, what is the fastest Pentium device that can be installed in the sample system?
2. Refer to the example system board settings in the chapter and describe the jumper arrangements that would have to be in place to install an AMD K6-200ALR(1) microprocessor in the sample system.
3. Where are the basic I/O functions located in a typical Pentium system?
4. What system board device does Plug-and-Play apply to?
5. Why do Pentium system boards employ VRMs?
6. How many hardware interrupt channels are available in an AT-compatible system?

7. Which interrupts are used with PC-compatible parallel ports?
8. What function does IRQ 2 serve in an AT-compatible system?
9. Which IRQ channel services the FDD in PC-compatible systems?
10. Can a Pentium MMX processor be used to upgrade a system board that has a Pentium 66 installed?
11. Can an AMD K6 processor be used to upgrade a system board that has a Pentium 75 installed?
12. To install an Intel Pentium 166 in the sample system board from this chapter, operating with an external clock frequency of 66 MHz, what conditions must be established at JP14 and JP15?
13. How are local buses different than other expansion buses?
14. Can a Pentium MMX processor be used to upgrade a Pentium 100 system?
15. Name two advantages of using chipsets to design circuit boards.

EXAM QUESTIONS

1. Which 32-bit bus can accept cards from PC and ISA buses?
   a. The ISA bus
   b. The EISA bus
   c. The MCA bus
   d. The PCI bus
2. How many hardware interrupt channels are there in a PC- or XT-compatible system?
   a. Sixteen
   b. Two
   c. Four
   d. Eight
3. What clock frequency should be applied to an Intel Pentium 166 microprocessor with a 2.5x multiplier setting?
   a. 50 MHz
   b. 60 MHz
   c. 66 MHz
   d. 166 MHz
4. Where can interrupt request #1 be found in a PC-compatible system?
   a. At the keyboard's encoder chip
   b. At the system board's keyboard controller chip
   c. At the system's DRAM Refresh controller chip
   d. At the system's FDD controller chip

5. Which expansion bus type will not accept an ISA card?
   a. A VESA bus slot
   b. An EISA bus slot
   c. An ISA slot
   d. A PCI slot
6. What function does IRQ-0 play in a PC-compatible system?
   a. It drives the system's DRAM Refresh signal.
   b. It drives the system's time-of-day clock.
   c. It drives the system's FDD interrupt.
   d. It drives the system's keyboard interrupt.
7. How many DMA channels are included in a PC- or XT-compatible system?
   a. Eight
   b. Sixteen
   c. One
   d. Four
8. What function does DMA channel 2 serve in a PC-compatible system?
   a. It provides the system's HDD DMA channel.
   b. It provides the system's Keyboard DMA channel.
   c. It provides the system's FDD DMA channel.
   d. It provides the system's Video DMA channel.
9. Which function is not typically found in a standard CMOS Setup screen?
   a. Date
   b. Floppy Drive A:
   c. Hard disk D: type:
   d. Virus Warning
10. Select the microprocessor type that would be used in a Socket 370 system board.
    a. Xeon
    b. Pentium III
    c. Athlon
    d. Pentium MMX

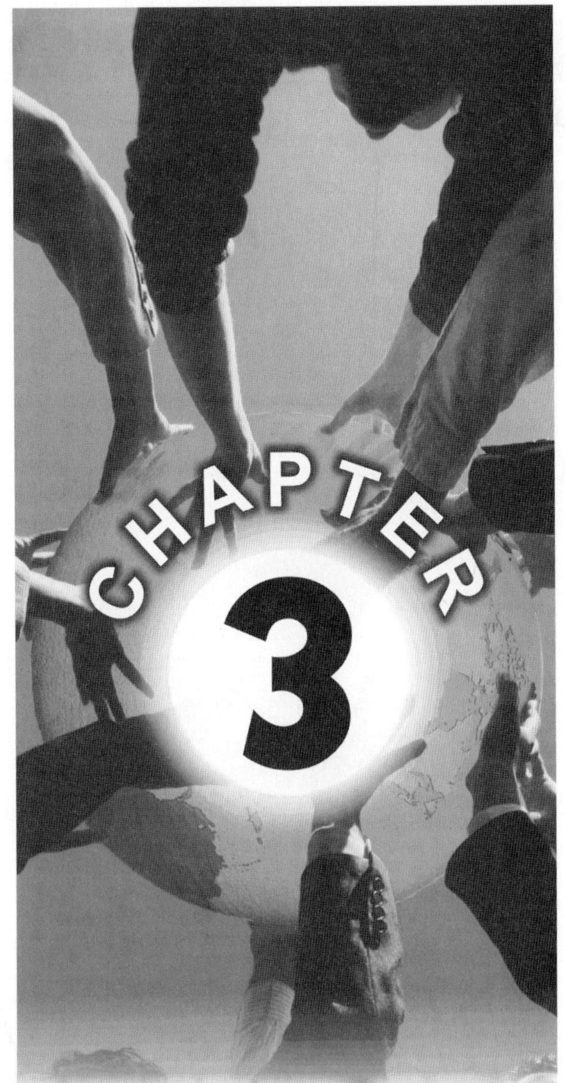

STANDARD I/O SYSTEMS

OBJECTIVES

OBJECTIVES

Upon completion of this chapter and its related lab procedures, you should be able to:

1. Define the overall function of the computer's input/output units.
2. Describe differences between parallel and serial ports.
3. Identify the various port connectors used in PC-compatible systems.
4. Describe the differences between synchronous and asynchronous transmissions, stating advantages and disadvantages for both.
5. Describe the need for parallel/serial conversions.
6. Explain the operation of an RS-232C serial communication port and define its signal lines.
7. Describe the operation of the Universal Serial Bus (USB).
8. List the events that occur when a key is depressed on the keyboard.
9. Describe the operation of the PC's keyboard.
10. Explain the operation of a mouse and a trackball.
11. Describe the operation of a game port used with joysticks and game paddles.
12. Describe the operation of hand-held and flat-bed scanners.
13. Describe the physical aspects of a cathode-ray tube.
14. Explain how a single dot can be positioned anywhere on the face of the CRT, using raster scanning.
15. Describe how color displays are created on the screen.
16. Define the terms pixel and PEL.
17. Describe the function of a shadow mask in a CRT monitor.
18. State the characteristics of the VGA video standard, including the type of physical connector specified for this video standard.
19. Identify standard PC-compatible resource allocations.
20. Differentiate between the operating characteristics of IEEE-1394 and USB ports.

CHAPTER 3

STANDARD I/O SYSTEMS

INTRODUCTION

Although the circuitry on the system board forms the nucleus of the personal computer system, it cannot stand alone. The computer must be able to acquire data from the outside world. In most applications, it must also be able to deliver results of operations it performs to the outside world in a useful format. Many different systems have been developed for both inputting and outputting data.

In a PC-compatible system, there are more than 65,000 input and output addresses available. Part of the previous chapter described how the system treats its on-board intelligent devices as I/O devices. This chapter examines peripheral I/O in detail. The first portion covers the standard I/O port assignments and configurations in PC systems. The second half of the chapter deals with typical I/O devices associated with PC systems.

SYSTEM RESOURCES

The A+ Core Hardware objective 1.3 states that the test taker should be able to identify available IRQs, DMAs, and I/O addresses with procedures for configuring them for device installation. Examples include the following:

- Standard IRQ settings
- Modems
- Floppy drives
- Hard drives
- USB ports
- Infrared ports

An IBM-compatible PC system is a very flexible tool because it can be configured to perform so many tasks. By selecting appropriate hardware and software options, the same basic system can be customized to be an inventory management business machine, a multimedia development system, or a simple game machine. As this A+ objective indicates, the computer technician must be able to determine what system resources are required for the component, what resources are available in the system, and how they may be allocated in order to successfully install hardware components in a PC. The following sections describe various standard I/O methods and peripheral connection schemes used to attach options to a PC system. However, installing and configuring floppy and hard disk drives is covered in the following chapter.

Input/Output

In addition to the millions of possible memory locations in a PC, there are typically thousands of addresses set aside for input and output devices in a system. In order for any device to operate with the system's microprocessor, it must have an address (or group of addresses) where the system can find it.

Referring to the computer system depicted in Figure 3-1, it can be seen that external input and output devices connect to the computer's bus systems through interfacing circuits. The job of the interfacing circuits is to make the peripherals compatible with the system. In the PC, standard interface circuits are provided by the system board's chipset or by an adapter card. The interface's physical connector is typically presented to the world on the system unit's back panel. In an ATX system, all of the standard PC interfaces are provided by the system board. The physical connectors for these ports (with the exception of the hard and floppy disk drives) are grouped into a block of I/O connectors at the back of the system board.

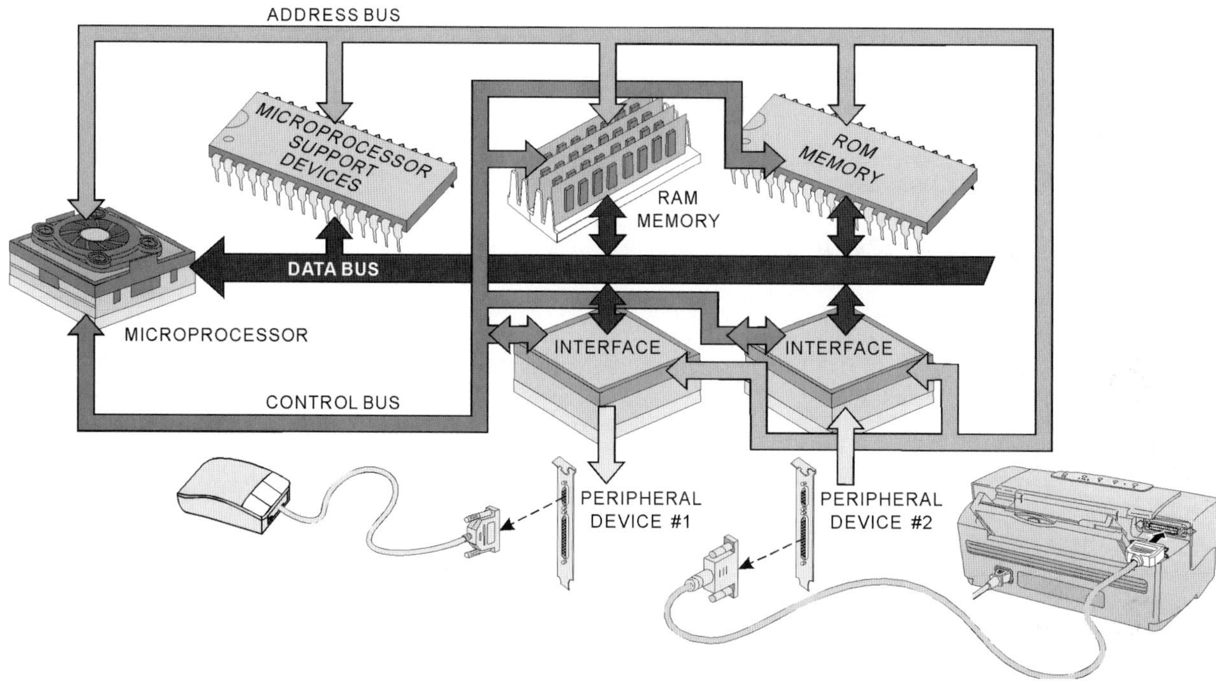

Figure 3-1: Basic Input/Output Organization

When discussing the standard PC I/O ports, it is common to differentiate between traditional standard ports that include:

- Keyboard port
- Centronic parallel ports
- RS-232C serial ports
- Game ports

And newer standard ports that include:

- PS/2 mouse and keyboard ports
- USB ports
- Firewire ports
- Infrared ports
- Improved parallel ports

Interface circuits—Interface **circuits** are necessary because the characteristics of most peripherals differ greatly from those of the basic computer. Most interface circuits in the PC-compatible world have been integrated into application-specific ICs.

Interface circuits

circuits

The microcomputer is a completely solid-state, digital electronic device that uses parallel words of a given length and adheres to basic digital logic levels. However, computer peripherals generally tend to be more mechanical and analog in nature. Conversely, humans are analog in nature.

The computer's input and output units enable it to communicate with the outside world. The input units contain all of the circuitry necessary to accept data and programs from peripheral input devices such as keyboards, light pens, mice, joysticks, etc., and convert the information into a form that is usable by the microprocessor. The input unit may be used to enter programs and data into the memory unit before execution, or it may be used to enter data directly into the microprocessor during execution.

The output units contain all of the circuitry necessary to transform data from the computer's language into a form that is more convenient for the outside world. Most often that is in the form of alphanumeric characters, which are convenient for humans to use. Common output devices include video display monitors, audio speakers, and character printers. Figure 3-2 depicts several common I/O devices associated with personal computers.

Some computer peripherals do double duty as both input and output units. These devices are collectively referred to as I/O devices and include secondary storage devices such as hard disk drives, floppy disk drives and magnetic tape drives, as well as modems and sound cards. In these devices, the form that data takes is not for the convenience of human beings, but the form most suitable to carry out the function of the device.

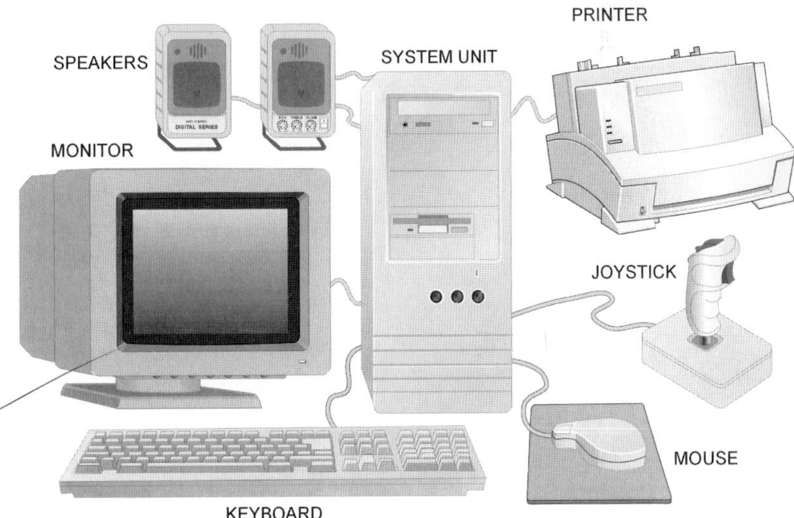

Figure 3-2: Common I/O Devices Used with PCs

Moving Data

parallel mode

serial mode

The most frequent operation performed in a computer is the movement of information from one location to another. This information is moved in the form of words. Basically, there are two modes in which the words can be transferred. These modes are **parallel mode**, where an entire word is transferred from location A to location B by a set of parallel conductors at one instant, and **serial mode**, where the bits of the word are transmitted along a single conductor, one bit at a time. Serial transfers require more time to accomplish than parallel transfers since a clock cycle must be used for each bit transferred.

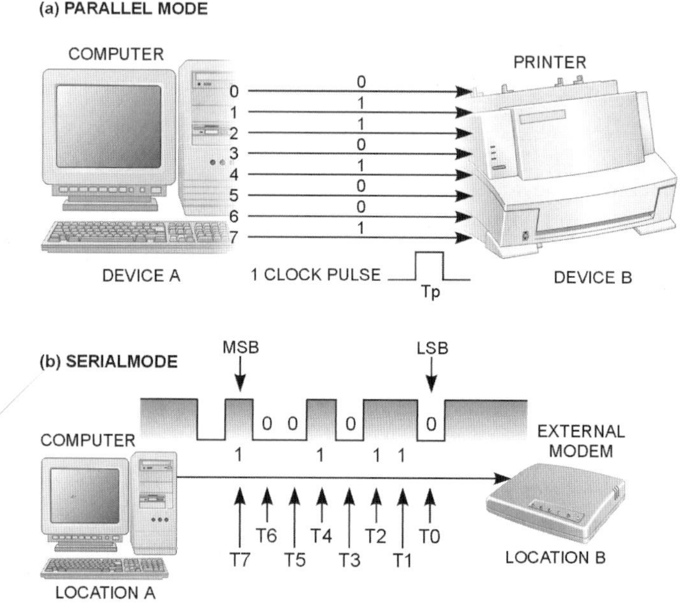

Figure 3-3: Parallel and Serial Data Transfers

A parallel transfer requires only one clock pulse. Examples of both parallel and serial transfers are depicted in Figure 3-3. Since speed is normally of the utmost importance in computer operations, all data movements within the computer are conducted in parallel, as shown in (a). But when information is being transferred between the computer and its peripherals (or another computer), conditions may dictate that the transfer be carried out in Serial mode, as shown in (b).

Peripherals may use parallel or serial transmission modes between themselves and the system board. Parallel buses are generally used for high-speed devices, such as disk drives and some printers. Conversely, serial transmission is used with remotely located devices or with devices whose operation is more compatible with serial data flow, such as monitors, modems, certain input devices, and some printers.

Initiating I/O Transfers

During a program's execution, the microprocessor constantly Reads from or Writes to memory locations. The program may also call on the microprocessor to Read from or Write to one of the system's I/O devices. Regardless of how the peripheral is connected to the system (serial or parallel), one of four methods may be used to initiate data transfer between the system and the peripheral. These four methods are listed as follows:

Polling

Programmed I/O

Interrupt-driven I/O

DMA

- **Polling** is where the microprocessor examines the status of the peripheral under program control.
- **Programmed I/O** is where the microprocessor alerts the designated peripheral by applying its address to the system's address bus.
- **Interrupt-driven I/O** is where the peripheral alerts the microprocessor that it's ready to transfer data.
- **DMA** is where the intelligent peripheral assumes control of the system's buses to conduct direct transfers with primary memory.

Polling and Programmed I/O

Both polling and programmed I/O represent software approaches to data transfer while interrupt-driven and DMA transfers are basically hardware approaches.

In the polling method, the software periodically checks with the system's I/O devices to determine if any device is ready to conduct a data transfer. If so, it will begin reading or writing data to the corresponding I/O port. The polling method is advantageous in that it is easy to implement and reconfigure since the program controls the entire sequence of events during the transfer. However, polling is often inconvenient since the microprocessor must be totally involved in the polling routine and cannot perform other functions.

The programmed I/O method calls for the microprocessor to alert the desired peripheral of an I/O operation by issuing its address to the address bus. The peripheral can delay the transfer by asserting its Busy line. If the microprocessor receives a Busy signal from the peripheral, it continues to perform other tasks, but periodically checks the device until the Busy signal is replaced by a Ready signal.

In order to establish an orderly flow of data during the transfer, a number of **handshakes** may occur between the peripheral and the system. This prevents the microprocessor from sending or requesting data at a faster rate than the peripheral can handle. In both methods, the main system resource that is used is the microprocessor's time.

handshakes

Interrupts

In the course of normal operations, the various I/O devices attached to a PC, such as the keyboard and disk drives, require servicing from the system's microprocessor. Although I/O devices may be treated like memory locations, there is one big difference between the two; I/O devices generally have the capability to interrupt the microprocessor while it is executing a program. The I/O device does this by issuing an **Interrupt Request (IRQ)** input signal to the microprocessor. Each device in a PC-compatible system that is capable of interrupting the microprocessor must be assigned its own unique IRQ number. The system uses this number to identify which device is in need of service.

Interrupt Request (IRQ)

If the microprocessor is responding to INT signals and a peripheral device issues an interrupt request on an IRQ line, the microprocessor will finish executing its current instruction and issue an **Interrupt Acknowledge (INTA)** signal on the control bus. The microprocessor suspends its normal operation and stores the contents of its internal registers in a special storage area referred to as the stack.

Interrupt Acknowledge (INTA)

The interrupting device responds by sending the starting address of a special program called the **interrupt service routine** to the microprocessor. The microprocessor uses the interrupt service routine to service the interrupting device. After it finishes servicing the interrupting device, the contents of the stack are restored to their original locations, and the microprocessor returns to the original program at the point where the interrupt occurred. If two interrupt signals occur at the same instant, the interrupt that has the highest priority will be serviced first.

interrupt service routine

Maskable Interrupts (MI)

Non-Maskable Interrupts (NMI)

Two varieties of interrupts are used in microcomputers:

- **Maskable Interrupts (MI)**—which the computer can ignore under certain conditions.
- **Non-Maskable Interrupts (NMI)**—which it must always respond to.

A programmable interrupt controller, and its relationship to the system's microprocessor, is illustrated in Figure 3-4. The interrupt controller chip accepts prioritized IRQ signals from up to eight peripheral devices on IRQ lines 0 through 7. When one of the peripherals desires to communicate with the microprocessor, it sends an IRQ to the interrupt controller. The controller responds by sending an INT signal to the microprocessor. If two interrupt requests are received at the same instance, the interrupt controller accepts the one that has the higher priority and acts on it first. The priority order is highest for the device connected to the IRQ-0 line and descends in order, with the IRQ-7 input given the lowest priority.

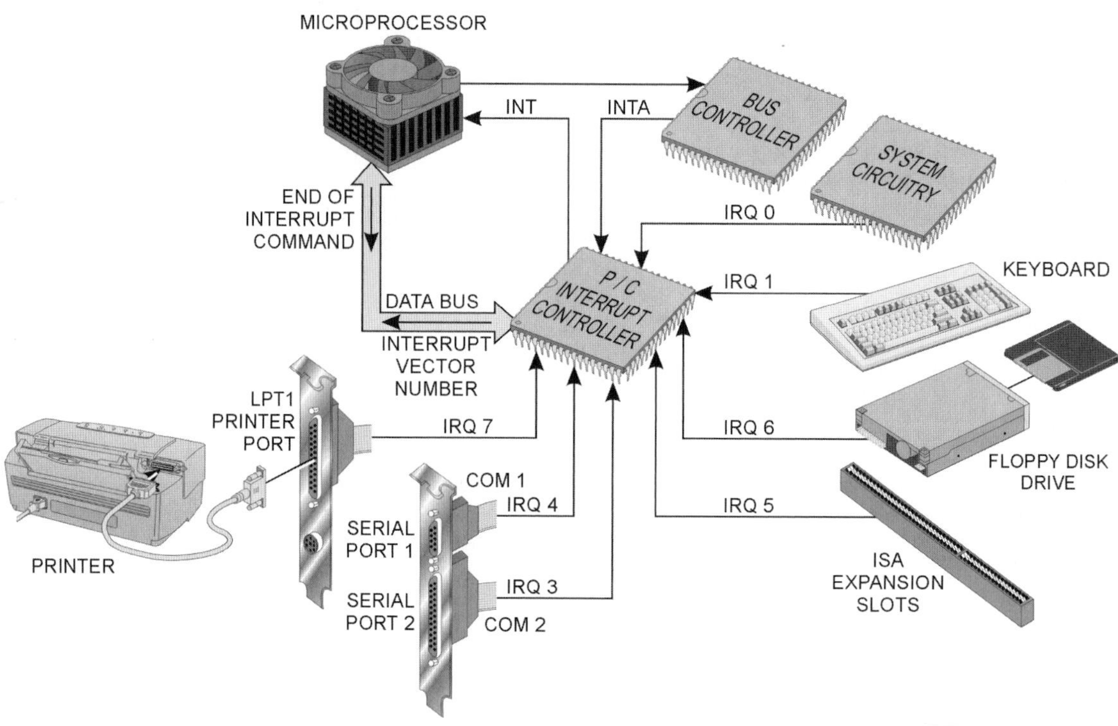

Figure 3-4: A Programmable Interrupt Controller Operation

INTC1

INTC2

In AT-compatible systems, the IRQ capabilities of the system are doubled by providing two 8-line interrupt controllers (**INTC1** and **INTC2**), each of which is equivalent to the original 8259 PIC used in the original PC. These interrupt controllers are internally cascaded together to provide the 16 interrupt channels necessary for AT-compatibility.

Of the 16 interrupt channels (IRQ0 through IRQ15) available, several are generally used inside the PC. Therefore, they do not have external IRQ pins. The other thirteen IRQ inputs are available to the system for user-definable interrupt functions. Each IRQ input is assigned a priority level. IRQ0 is the highest and IRQ15 is the lowest. The internally connected channels are:

Channel 0 (IRQ0) Timer/Counter interrupt

Channel 1 (IRQ1) Keyboard buffer full

Channel 2 (IRQ2) Cascaded to INTC2

Channel 8 (IRQ8) Real-Time Clock interrupt

Channel 9 (IRQ9) Cascade between INTC1 and INTC2

Channel 13 (IRQ13) Math Coprocessor interrupt

Table 3-1 shows the designations for the various interrupt levels in the system.

Table 3-1: System Interrupt Levels

INTERRUPT	DESCRIPTION	INTERRUPT	DESCRIPTION
NMI	I/O CHANNEL CHECK OR PARITY CHECK ERROR		
INTC1		INTC2	
IRQ0	TIMER/COUNTER ALARM	IRQ8	REAL-TIME CLOCK
IRQ1	KEYBOARD BUFFER FULL	IRQ9	CASCADE TO INTC1
IRQ2	CASCADE FROM INTC2	IR110	SPARE
IRQ3	SERIAL PORT 2	IRQ11	SPARE
IRQ4	SERIAL PORT 1	IRQ12	SPARE PS/2 MOUSE
IRQ5	PARALLEL PORT 2	IRQ13	COPROCESSOR
IRQ6	FDD CONTROLLER	IRQ14	PRIMARY IDE CTRL
IRQ7	PARALLEL PORT 1	IRQ15	SECONDARY IDE CTRL

IO Channel Check (IOCHCK)

Parity Check (PCK)

There are two system board-based conditions that will cause a Non-Maskable Interrupt (NMI) signal to be sent to the microprocessor. The first condition occurs when an active **IO Channel Check** (**IOCHCK**) input is received from an options adapter card located in one of the board's expansion slots. The other event that will cause an NMI signal to be generated is the occurrence of a **Parity Check** (**PCK**) **Error** in the DRAM memory.

TEST TIP

Memorize the system resources available in an ISA-compatible system and what their typical assignments are.

Direct Memory Access

Direct Memory Access (DMA)

Another difference between memory and some intelligent, high-speed I/O devices is that the I/O devices may have the ability to perform Read and Write data transfers on their own. This type of operation is called **Direct Memory Access** (**DMA**). DMA generally involves a high-speed I/O device taking over the system's buses to perform Read and Write operations with the primary memory, without the intervention of the system microprocessor.

DMA Request (DREQ)

DMA controller

HOLD

Buses Available (BA)

Hold Acknowledge (HLDA)

DMA Acknowledge (DACK)

When the peripheral device has data ready to be transferred, it sends a **DMA Request (DREQ)** signal to a special IC device called a **DMA controller**, which in turn, sends a **HOLD** input signal to the microprocessor. The microprocessor finishes executing the instruction it is currently working on and places its address and data pins in a floating state, effectively disconnecting the microprocessor from the buses. At this time, the microprocessor issues a **Buses Available** (**BA**) or **Hold Acknowledge** (**HLDA**) signal to the DMA controller. The DMA controller, in turn, issues a **DMA Acknowledge** (**DACK**) to the peripheral and the necessary R/W and enable signals for the data transfer to begin. The key to DMA operations is that the DMA controller has been designed specifically to transfer data bytes faster than the microprocessor can.

The PC-compatible DMA subsystem provides an AT-compatible PC with four channels for 8-bit DMA transfers (DMA1) and three channels (DMA2) for 16-bit DMA transfers. The DMA1 channels are used to carry out DMA transfers between 8-bit options adapters and 8- or 16-bit memory locations. These 8-bit transfers are conducted in 64 kB blocks and can be performed throughout the system's address space. The DMA2 channels (channels 5, 6, and 7) are used only with 16-bit devices and can only transfer words in 128 kB blocks. The first 16-bit DMA channel (DMA channel 4) is used internally to cascade the two DMA controllers together. Table 3-2 describes the system's DMA channel designations.

Table 3-2: System's DMA Channel Designations

CHANNEL	FUNCTION	CONTROLLER	PAGE REGISTER ADDRESS
CH0	SPARE	1	0087
CH1	SDLC (NETWORK)	1	0083
CH2	FDD CONTROLLER	1	0082
CH3	SPARE	1	0081
CH4	CASCADE TO CNTR 1	2	
CH5	SPARE	2	008B
CH6	SPARE	2	0089
CH7	SPARE	2	008A

On-Board I/O

on-board I/O

When dealing with a PC-compatible, there are two forms of I/O to contend with. These include the system board's **on-board I/O**, and peripheral devices that interact with the system through its expansion slots.

In a PC-compatible system, certain I/O addresses are associated with intelligent devices on the system board, such as the interrupt and DMA controllers, timer counter channels, and keyboard controller. Other system I/O ports and their interfaces are located on optional plug-in cards. These easily installed options give the system a high degree of flexibility in adapting to a wide variety of peripheral devices.

Most of the I/O functions associated with PC-compatible systems have become so standardized that IC manufacturers produce them in single-chip ASIC formats. Figure 3-5 illustrates an ASIC for standard, AT-compatible system board functions.

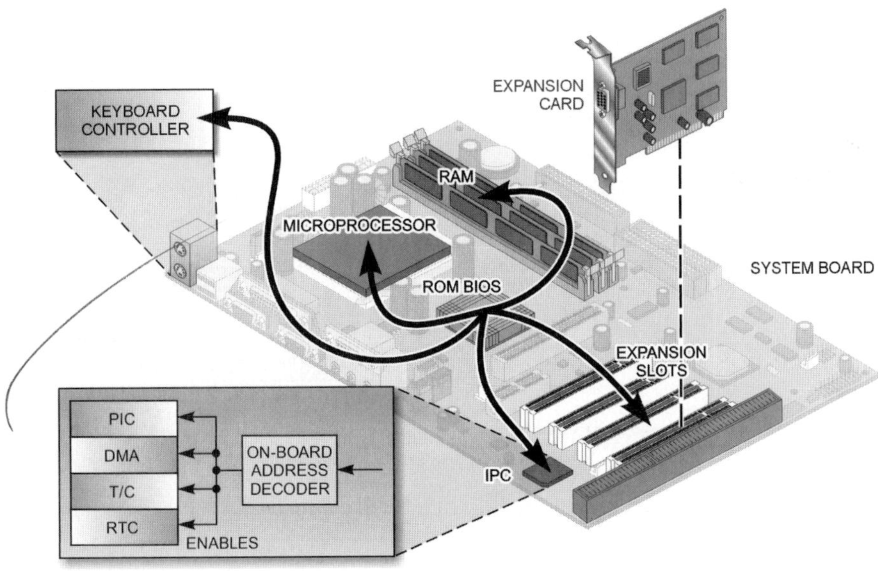

Figure 3-5: On-Board I/O

There are certain I/O connections that have become standards associated with PC-compatibles. These include the system's parallel printer ports, RS-232 serial ports, and the game port. Figure 3-6 depicts an M/IO ASIC for standard peripheral control.

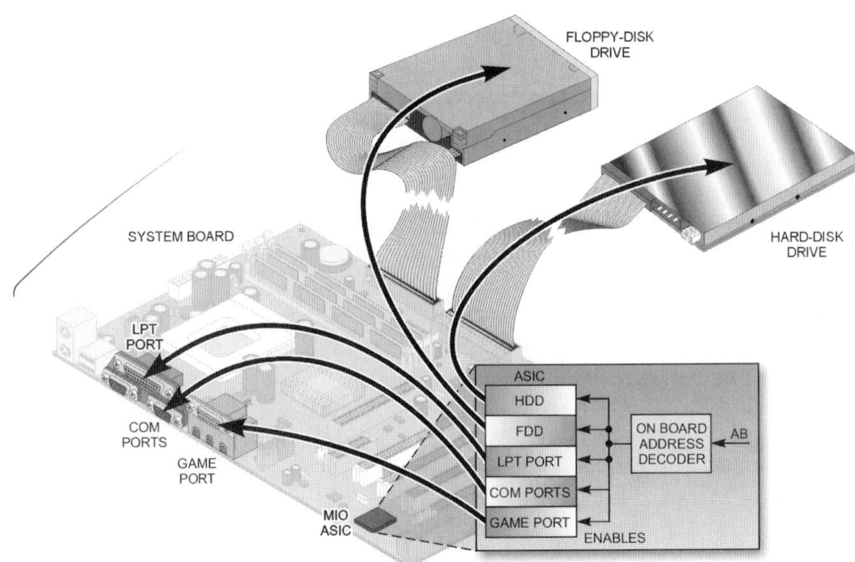

Figure 3-6: System I/O Methods

In both cases, the I/O controllers integrated into the ASIC are responsible for matching signal levels and protocols between the system and the I/O device.

The system treats its on-board intelligent devices as I/O addresses. The on-board address decoder, similar to the one displayed in Figure 3-7, converts addresses from the address bus into enabling bits for the system's intelligent devices. These addresses are included in the overall I/O addressing map of the system.

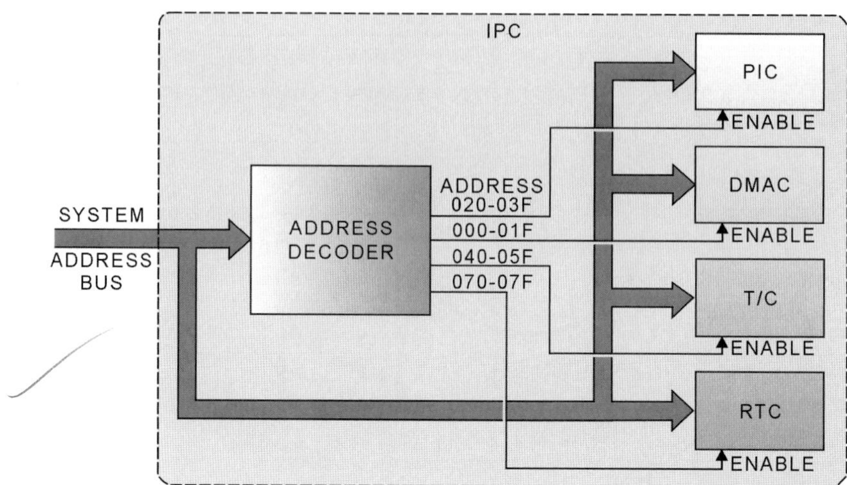

Figure 3-7: On-Board Address Decoding

Hexadecimal Addresses

Addresses in PC systems are always referred to by their hexadecimal value. The reason for this is that digital computers are built on components that only work with two logic levels: On/Off, High/Low, 1/0. This corresponds directly to the base-2 or binary numbering system. In the binary system, each piece of information represents a binary digit, or bit.

hexadecimal (hex)

The power of the digital computer lies in how it groups bits of information into words. The basic word length in PCs is the 8-bit word called a byte. Some computers can handle data as 16-, 32-, and 64-bit words. With the byte as the basic data unit it is easier for humans to speak of computer numbers in the base-16 or **hexadecimal (hex)** numbering system. In this system, groups of 4 bits can be represented directly by a single hex character (i.e., 1001 base2 = 09 base16). For human representation, the values in the numbering system run from 0 to 9 and then from A through F, as illustrated in Table 3-3.

Table 3-3: Decimal, Binary, and Hexadecimal Numbers

DECIMAL (10)	BINARY (2)	HEXADECIMAL (16)
0	0000	0
1	0001	1
2	0010	2
3	0011	3
4	0100	4
5	0101	5
6	0110	6
7	0111	7
8	1000	8
9	1001	9
10	1010	A
11	1011	B
12	1100	C
13	1101	D
14	1110	E
15	1111	F
16	10000	10

While this may seem a little inconvenient for those of you not familiar with binary and hexadecimal systems, it is much easier to convey the number 3F8h to someone than it is 001111111000. The real difficulty of reconciling a hexadecimal value comes when you try to convert binary or hexadecimal values to the decimal (base 10) number system you are familiar with.

REFERENCE SHELF

For more in-depth information about computer-related numbering systems, refer to the Electronic Reference Shelf located on the CD that accompanies this book.

The various I/O port addresses listed in Table 3-4 are used by standard I/O adapters in the PC-compatible system. Notice that these addresses are the same as those stated for the system's Interrupt Vectors given in Table 3-5. This method of addressing is referred to as redundant addressing. Figure 3-8 illustrates how a system address is routed through the system to an I/O port location.

Table 3-4: I/O Port Addresses

HEX ADDRESS	DEVICE	USAGE
000–01F	DMA Controller (IPC)	System
020–03F	Interrupt Controller (IPC)	System
040–05F	Timer/Counter (IPC)	System
060–06F	Keyboard Controller	System
070–07F	Real-Time Clock, NMI Mask (IPC)	System
080–09F	DMA Page Register (IPC)	System
0A0–0BF	Interrupt Controller (IPC)	System
0F0	Clear Math Coprocessor Busy	System
0F1	Reset Math Coprocessor	System
0F8–0FF	Math Coprocessor	System
1F0–1F8	Hard-Disk Controller	I/O
200–207	Game Port	I/O
278–27F	Parallel Printer Port #2	I/O
2F8–2FF	Serial Port #2	I/O
378–37F	Parallel Printer Port #1	I/O
3B0–3BF	MGA/first Printer Port	I/O
3D0–3DF	CGA	I/O
3F0–3F7	FDD Controller	I/O
3F8–3FF	Serial Port #1	I/O
FF80-FF9F	USB Controller	I/O

TEST TIP

Memorize the I/O port addresses for the first and second IDE controllers.

Table 3-5: System Memory Map

ADDRESS	FUNCTION
0–3FF	Interrupt Vectors
400–47F	ROM-BIOS RAM
480–5FF	BASIC and Special System Function RAM
600–9FFFF	Program Memory
0A0000–0AFFFF	VGA/EGA Display Memory
0B0000–0B0FFF	Monochrome Display Adapter Memory
0B8000–0BFFFF	Color Graphics Adapter Memory
0C0000–0C7FFF	VGA/SVGA BIOS
0C8000-0CBFFF	EIDE/SCSI ROM (also older HDD Types)
0D0000–0D7FFF	Spare ROM
0D0000–0DFFFF	LAN Adapter ROM
0E0000–0E7FFF	Spare ROM
0E8000–0EFFFF	Spare ROM
0F0000–0EFFFF	Spare ROM
0F4000–0EFFFF	Spare ROM
0F8000–0EFFFF	Spare ROM
0FC000–0FDFFF	ROM BIOS
0FE000–0FFFFF	ROM BIOS

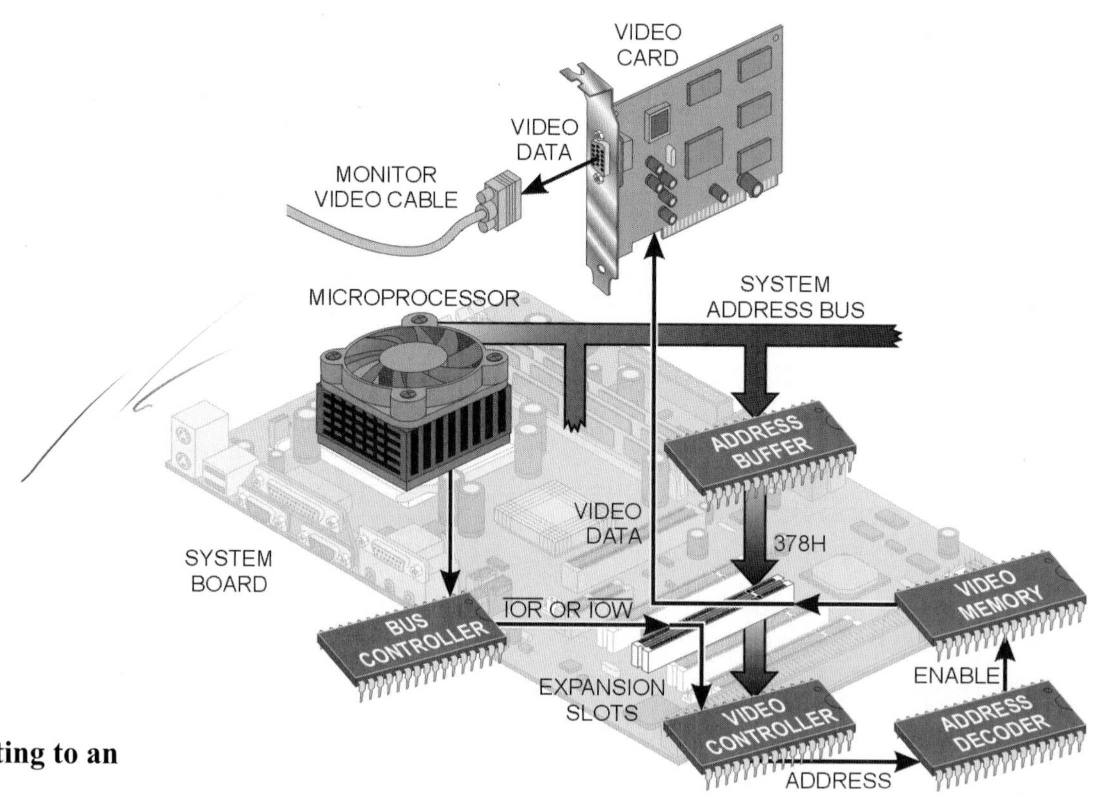

Figure 3-8: Address Routing to an I/O Port

PERIPHERALS AND PORTS

The A+ Core Hardware objective 1.4 states that the test taker should be able to identify common peripheral ports, associated cables, and their connectors. Examples include:

- Cable types
- Cable orientation
- Serial versus parallel
- Pin connections

Examples of connector types include:

- DB-9
- DB-25
- RJ-11
- BNC
- RJ-45
- PS2/Mini-DIN

As mentioned earlier, a wide variety of peripheral devices can be added to a PC-compatible system. Most of these devices are designed to employ some type of PC-compatible I/O connection method. As this A+ objective indicates, the computer technician must be able to recognize what type of port the device requires, locate standard I/O port connections, and determine what type of cabling is required to successfully connect the port and the device, in order to successfully add peripheral devices to a PC system. The following sections of the chapter describe standardized I/O ports and connections found in a PC-compatible system.

Standard I/O Ports

Although many different methods have been developed to connect devices to the PC-compatible system, there are three ports that have been standard since the original PCs were introduced. These are:

- the IBM versions of the **Centronics parallel port**
- the **RS-232C serial port**
- the **IBM game port**

Centronics parallel port

RS-232C serial port

IBM game port

Typical connectors found on the PC's back panel are described in Figure 3-9.

TEST TIP

Memorize the appearance, type, and pin configuration of the standard PC port connectors (i.e., parallel ports use 25-pin female D-shell connectors).

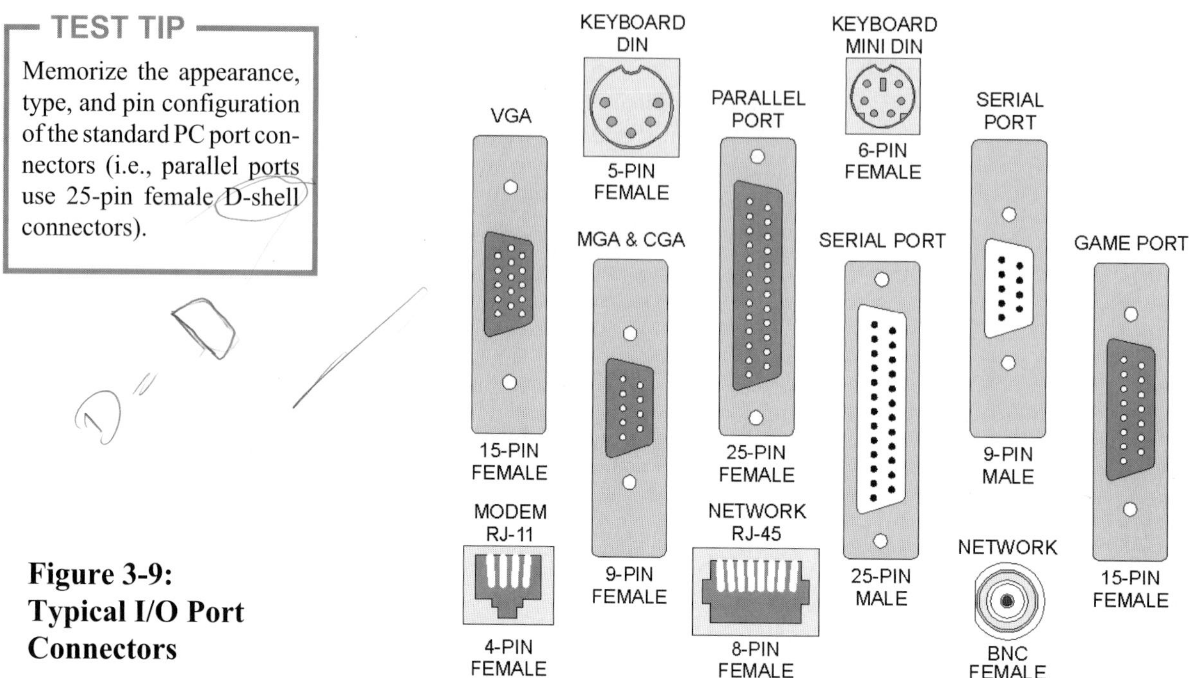

Figure 3-9: Typical I/O Port Connectors

Parallel Ports

Parallel ports

Parallel ports have been a staple of the PC system since the original PCs were introduced. They have traditionally been the most widely used port for connecting printers to the computer.

In many instances, parallel ports are referred to as parallel printer ports. Due to the parallel port's ability to quickly transfer bytes of data in parallel mode, it has been adopted to interface a number of other peripheral devices to the computer. These devices include X-Y plotters, fast computer-to-computer transfer systems, high-speed, high volume, removable disk backup systems, and optical scanners.

The Centronics Standard

Figure 3-10 shows a typical parallel printer connection, using the IBM version of the Centronics standard. This interface enables the computer to pass information to the printer, 8 bits at a time, across the 8 data lines. The other lines in the connection carry control signals (handshaking signals) back and forth between the computer and the printer.

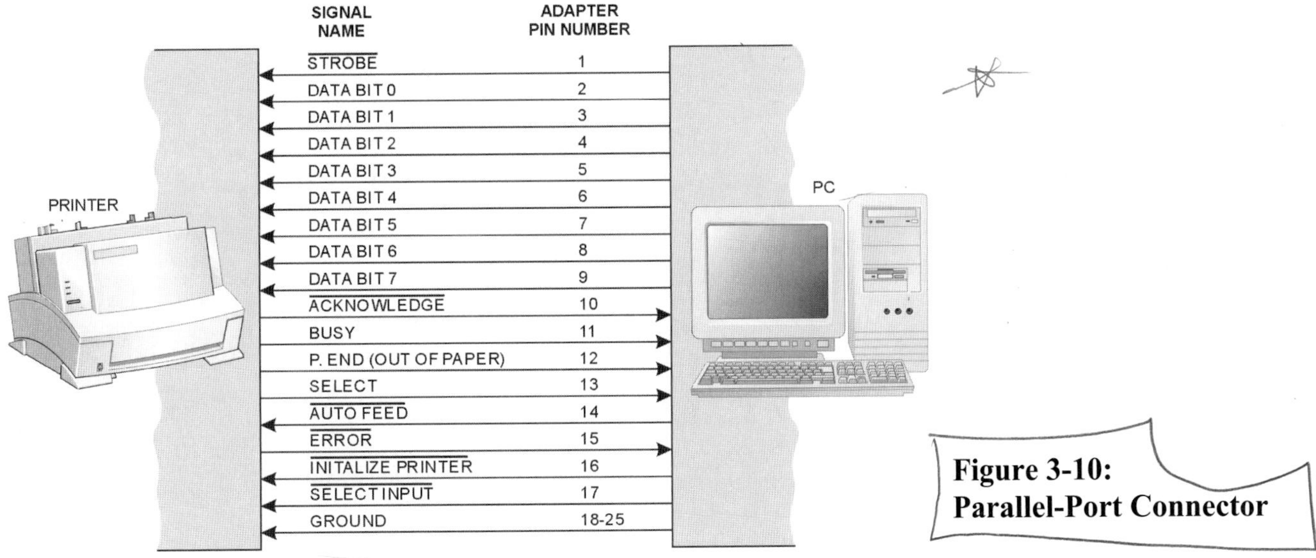

Figure 3-10: Parallel-Port Connector

The original Centronics interface employed a 36-pin D-shell connector on the adapter and a 36-pin Centronics connector on the printer end. The IBM version of the interface, which became known as the **Standard Parallel Port (SPP)** specification for printers, reduced the pin count to 25 at the computer end of the connection.

Standard Parallel Port (SPP)

The PC-compatible parallel port interface offers 8-bit parallel data words and nine I/O control lines at a 25-pin, female D-shell connector at the rear of the system unit. The printer port connector may be provided through the I/O block of an ATX system board, mounted directly on the back plate of an I/O card, or its interface circuitry may be connected, via a ribbon cable, to the 25-pin D-shell connector on the unit's back panel.

data strobe

busy

Acknowledge (ACK)

Select (SLCT)

Paper End (PE)

Auto Feed (AUTO-FD)

Error

Initialize Printer (INIT)

Select Input (SLCT-IN)

Under the SPP specification, the computer uses the **data strobe** line to signal the printer that it has a character available on the data lines. The printer reads the character from the data lines into its buffer, to be printed at the printer's convenience. If for some reason, the printer cannot accept the character from the data lines, such as being out of paper or its buffer being full, the printer sends a busy signal to the computer on the **busy** line, telling the computer not to send any more data.

After the peripheral device has read the data word from the Data lines, it pulses the **Acknowledge (ACK)** line to tell the computer it is ready to accept another data word, as long as the Busy line is not asserted. The printer also uses the **Select (SLCT)** line to let the computer know that data can be sent to it. In the event that the SLCT signal is not present, the computer can't send the printer any data.

In addition to the lines discussed above, the Centronics standard calls for additional printer-related control lines, which include **Paper End (PE)**, **Auto Feed (AUTO-FD)**, **Error, Initialize Printer (INIT)**, and **Select Input (SLCT-IN)**. Not all printers use the complete standard and all of its control lines. In many instances, only a few of the lines are used and non-standard pin numbers and connector types may be employed.

TTL (Transistor-Transistor Logic)

Electromagnetic Field Interference (EFI)

When the port is used in SPP mode, All the printer port's signals are transmitted between the adapter card and the printer at standard **TTL (Transistor-Transistor Logic)** levels. This means that the signals can deteriorate quickly with long lengths of cable. The cable length used for the parallel printer should be kept to less than 10 feet. If longer lengths are needed, the cable should have a low-capacitance value. The cable should also be shielded, to minimize **Electromagnetic Field Interference (EFI)** peripherals.

TEST TIP

Know the recommended length of a standard parallel printer cable.

LPT Handles

Microsoft operating systems keep track of the system's installed printer ports by assigning them the logical device names (handles) LPT1, LPT2, and LPT3. Whenever the system is booted up, DOS searches the hardware for parallel ports installed at hex addresses 3BCh, 378h, and 278h consecutively.

If a printer port is found at 3BCh, then DOS assigns it the title of LPT1. If, however, no printer port is found at 3BCh, but there is one at 378h, then DOS will assign LPT1 to the latter address. Likewise, a system that has printer ports at physical addresses 378h and 278h would have LPT1 assigned at 378h, and LPT2 at location 278h.

The address of the printer port can normally be changed to respond as LPT1, LPT2, or LPT3, depending on the setting of address selection jumpers. The printer port can also be disabled completely through these jumper settings.

TEST TIP

Memorize the system resources that the PC typically assigns to parallel ports.

The interrupt level of the printer port may be set at a number of different levels by changing its configuration jumpers, or CMOS enabling setting. Normal interrupt settings for printer ports in a PC-compatible system are IRQ5 or IRQ7. IRQ7 is normally assigned to the LPT1 printer port, while IRQ5 typically serves the LPT2 port, if installed.

Although the data pins of the parallel printer port are defined as output pins, the figure illustrates that they are actually bi-directional. However, some less-expensive ports may not have the electronics built into them to handle the input function. This is not important for most printer operations, so many users won't notice.

Enhanced Parallel Port (EPP)

Extended Capabilities Port (ECP)

However, the newer **Enhanced Parallel Port** (**EPP**) and **Extended Capabilities Port** (**ECP**) an be converted between *uni-directional* and *bi-directional* operation through the CMOS Setup screen. If a bi-directional port is being used to support an I/O device, such as a local area network adapter, or a high-capacity storage device, then this feature would need to be checked at both a hardware and software level.

TEST TIP

As you study the I/O ports in this chapter, be aware of which ports provide bi-directional, half-duplex and full-duplex operation.

Enhanced Parallel Port Operations

When EPP mode is selected in the port's configuration register, the standard and bi-directional modes are enabled. The functions of the port's pins are redefined under the EPP specification. Table 3-6 provides the EPP pin definitions.

When the EPP mode is enabled, the port can operate either as a standard, bi-directional parallel port, or as a bi-directional EPP port. The software controlling the port will specify which type of operation is required. If no EPP read, write, or address cycle is being executed, the port and its control signals function as an SPP port. When the software calls for an EPP read, write, or address cycle, however, all the port's registers are enabled and the signal lines take on the functions defined by the selected EPP standard.

Table 3-6: EPP Pin Definitions

HOST CONNECTOR	PIN NO.	STANDARD	EPP	ECP
1	77	Strobe	Write	Strobe
2-9	71-68, 66-63	Data <0:7>	Data <0:7>	Data <0:7>
10	62	Ack	Intr	Ack
11	61	Busy	Wait	Busy, PeriphAck
12	60	PE	Not Used	PError nAckReverse
13	59	Select	Not Used	Select
14	76	Autofd	DSTRB	AutoFd HostAck
15	75	Error	Not Used	Fault PeriphRequest
16	74	Init	Not Used	Init ReverseRqst
17	73	Selectin	Astrb	Selectin

ECP Mode

The ECP mode provides a number of advantages over the SPP and EPP modes. The ECP mode employs DMA operations to offer higher performance than either of the other two modes. As with the EPP mode, the pins of the interface are redefined when ECP mode is selected in the system's BIOS. Table 3-7 lists the ECP definitions for the port's pins.

Table 3-7: ECP Pin Definitions

EPP SIGNAL	EPP NAME	TYPE	EPP DESCRIPTION
WRITEJ	WriteJ	O	This signal is active low. It denotes a write operation.
PD<0:7>	Address/ Data	I/O	Bi-directional EPP byte-wide address and data bus.
INTR	Interrupt	I	This signal is active high and positive edge triggered. (Pass through with no inversion. Same as SPP.)
WAIT	WaitJ	I	This signal is active low. It is driven inactive as a positive acknowledgement from the device that the transfer of data is completed. It is driven active as an indication that the device is ready for the next transfer.
DATASTB	DATA StrobeJ	O	This signal is active low. It is used to denote data read or write operation.
RESET	ResetJ	O	This signal is active low. When driven active, the EPP device is reset to its initial operational mode.
ADDRSTB	Address StrobeJ	O	This signal is active low. It is used to denote address read or write operation.
PE	Paper End	I	Same as SPP mode.
SLCT	Printer Select Status	I	Same as SPP mode.
ERRJ	Error	I	Same as SPP mode.
PDIR	Parallel Port Direction	O	This output shows the direction of the data transfer on the parallel ports bus. A low means an output/write condition and a high means an input/read condition. This signal is normally low (output/write) unless PCD of the control register is set or if an EPP read cycle is in progress.

Note 1: SPP and EPP can use 1 common register.
Note 2: WriteJ is the only EPP output that can be overridden by SPP control port during an EPP cycle. For correct EPP read cycles, PCD is required to be a low.

In ECP mode, the parallel port operates in forward (host-to-peripheral) and reverse (peripheral-to-host) directions. It employs interlocked handshaking for reliable, half-duplex transfers through the port. The capabilities of the ECP port enable it to be used in peer-to-peer applications.

The ECP port is compatible with the standard LPT port and is used in the same manner when no ECP read or write operations are called for. However, it also supports high-throughput DMA operations for both forward- and reverse-direction transfers.

Prior to ECP operation, the system examines the peripheral device attached to the port to determine that it can perform ECP operations. This operation is carried out in SPP mode. Afterward, the system initializes the port's registers for operation. In particular, it sets a direction bit in the port controller to enable the ECP drivers and sets the port's mode to ECP.

The host computer may switch the direction of the port's operation by changing the mode value in the controller and then negotiating for the forward/reverse channel setting. Afterward, the mode is set back to ECP. During normal operation, commands and data may be passed through the port.

TEST TIP

Remember that the ECP specification employs DMA operations to provide the highest data throughput for a parallel port.

ECP transfers may be conducted in DMA or programmed I/O modes. DMA transfers use standard PC DMA services. To use this method, the host must set the port direction and program its DMA controller with the desired byte count and memory-address information.

Serial Ports

As the distance between the computer and a peripheral reaches a certain point (10 feet), it becomes less practical to send data as parallel words. An alternative method of sending data is to break the parallel words into their individual bits, and transmit them, one at a time, in a serial bit stream over a single conductor.

communication (COM) ports

In this manner, the number of conductors connecting the computer and the peripheral is reduced from eight or more data lines, and any number of control lines, to one (or two) communications lines, a ground line, and maybe a few control lines. Therefore, when a peripheral device must be located at some distance from the computer the cost of connecting equipment is reduced by using serial communication techniques. In the PC, serial communications have traditionally been conducted using one of its standard RS-232 **communication (COM) ports**.

Serial Transmission Modes

The biggest problem encountered when sending data serially is keeping the transmitted data-bit timing synchronized between the two devices.

Two methods are used to provide the proper timing for serial transfers: the data bits may be sent **synchronously** (in conjunction with a synchronizing clock pulse), or **asynchronously** (without an accompanying clock pulse).

synchronously

asynchronously

When data is transmitted synchronously, the bits of a word, or character, are synchronized by a common clock signal, which is applied to both the transmitting and receiving shift registers. The two registers are initialized before data transmission begins, when the transmitting circuitry sends a predefined bit pattern, which the receiver recognizes as the initialization command. After this, receiving circuitry processes the incoming bit stream by counting clock pulses, and dividing the bit stream into words of a predetermined length. If the receiver misses a bit for any reason, all the words that follow will be processed erroneously. Figure 3-11 depicts a simplified synchronous transmission scheme.

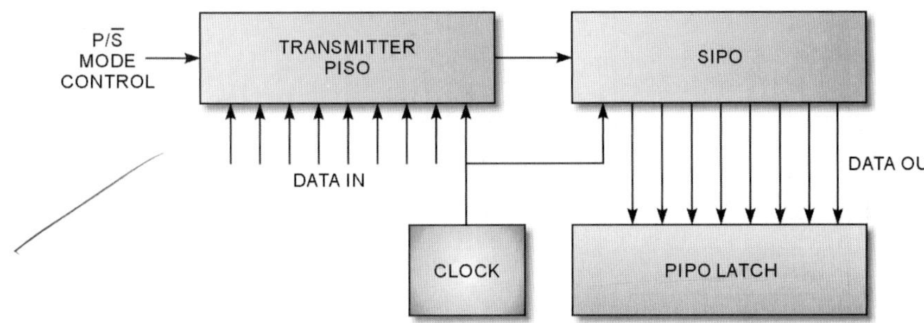

Figure 3-11: Synchronous Transmission

When data is transferred asynchronously, the receiving system is not synchronized with the sending system. In asynchronous communications, the transmission is dependent on the ability of two separate clocks, running at the same frequency, to remain synchronized for a short period of time. The transmitted material is sent character by character (usually ASCII), with the beginning and end of each character framed by character Start and Stop bits. Between these bits, the bits of the character are sent at a constant rate, but the time interval between characters may be irregular, as illustrated in Figure 3-12.

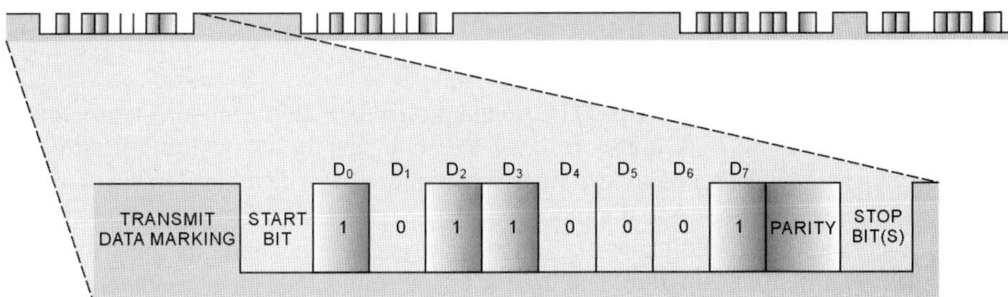

Figure 3-12: Asynchronous Transmission

Over a given period of time, synchronous communications are much faster than asynchronous methods. This is due to the extra number of bits required to send each character asynchronously. PC serial ports and analog modems use asynchronous communications methods, while digital modems and local area network adapters use synchronous methods.

Serial Interface ICs

Asynchronous Communication Interface Adapters (ACIAs)

Universal Asynchronous Receiver/Transmitters (UARTs)

USARTs (Universal Synchronous/ Asynchronous Receiver/ Transmitters)

Like the single-chip parallel ports, IC manufacturers have developed a number of single-chip devices that perform all of the functions necessary for serial transfers to occur. These serial port IC's are referred to as **Asynchronous Communication Interface Adapters** (**ACIAs**), or as **Universal Asynchronous Receiver/Transmitters** (**UARTs**). Synchronous devices are usually called **USARTs** (**Universal Synchronous/Asynchronous Receiver/Transmitters**).

Not only do these devices provide the parallel-to-serial and serial-to-parallel conversions required for serial data communications, but they also handle the parallel interface requirements for the computer's internal buses, and all the control functions associated with the transmission.

The original serial adapters featured 8250 UARTs with programmable baud rates from 50 to 9600 baud, a fully programmable interrupt system, and variable character lengths (5, 6, 7, or 8-bit characters). In addition, the adapter added and removed start, stop, and parity bits, had false start-bit detection, line-break detection and generation, and possessed built-in diagnostics capabilities. As modems became faster and faster, upgraded UARTs were included, or integrated, to keep up.

Notable advanced UART versions include the 16450 and 16550. The 16450 was the 16-bit improvement of the 8250, while the 16550 was a high-performance UART, with an on-board 16-byte buffer. The buffer allows the UART to store, or transmit, a string of data without interrupting the system's microprocessor to handle them. This provides the 16550 with an impressive speed advantage over previous UARTs. These advanced UARTs allow serial ports to reach data transmission rates of up to 115 Kbps. While some features have changed between these UARTs, and while they are sometimes integrated directly into an integrated I/O chip, they must still adhere to the basic 8250 structure to remain PC-compatible.

Serial Interface Connections

Electronic Industry Association (EIA)

RS-232C

Because of the popularity of asynchronous serial data transmissions and the number of devices that use them, such as printers and modems, standardized bit-serial signals and connection schemes have been developed to simplify the connecting of serial devices to computers. The most popular of these serial interface standards is the **Electronic Industry Association** (**EIA**) RS-232C interface standard.

Basically, the IBM version of the **RS-232C** standard calls for a 25-pin, male D-type connector, as depicted in Figure 3-13. It also designates certain pins for data transmission and receiving, along with a number of control lines. The standard was developed to cover a wide variety of peripheral devices, and therefore, not all the lines are used in any given application. Normally, only nine of the pins are active for a given application. The other lines are used for secondary, or backup, lines and grounds. Different device manufacturers may use various combinations of the RS-232C lines, even for peripherals of the same type.

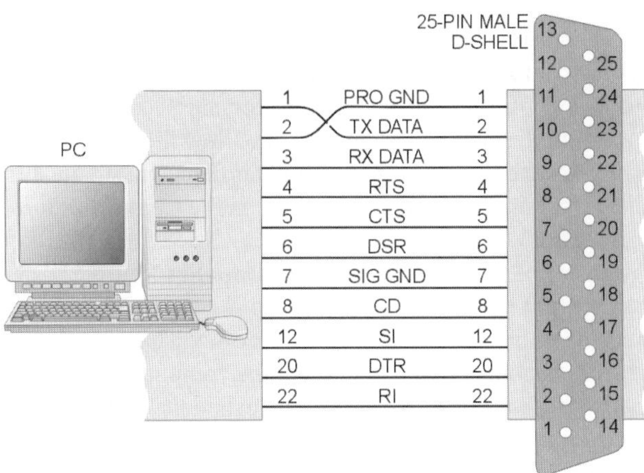

Figure 3-13: RS-232C Connector

In addition to defining the type of connector to be used, and the use of its individual pins, the RS-232 standard also establishes acceptable voltage levels for the signals on its pins. These levels are generally converted to and from standard digital logic levels. These levels can produce a maximum baud rate of 20,000 baud over distances less than 50 feet.

> **TEST TIP**
>
> Know the maximum recommended length of an RS-232 cable.

Advanced Serial Standards

With the advent of the mouse as a common input device, a 9-pin, male D-shell version of the RS-232 serial port became common. This version is commonly used as the COM1 serial port for the mouse, in Windows-based systems. Figure 3-14 depicts the 9-pin version of the interface being used to connect a serial printer.

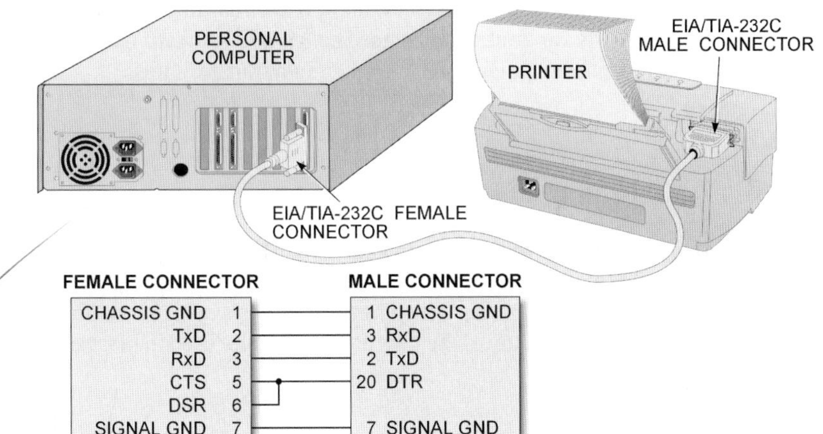

Figure 3-14: RS-232C 9-Pin Serial Printer Connection

The exchanging of pins 2 and 3 between the two devices forms the basis of the null modem. Since the device in the figure is a serial printer, pins 5 and 6 of the DTE equipment are tied to the DTR pin of the DCE equipment.

Transmit Data (TXD)

Receive Data (RXD)

The character bit stream is transmitted to the printer on the line designated as the **Transmit Data** line (**TXD**) at the computer connector and **Receive Data** line (**RXD**) at the printer connector. A reciprocal line (TXD at the printer connector and RXD at the computer connector) is also used in the printer interface. Since data does not flow from the printer to the computer, this line basically informs the computer that a printer is connected to the interface, turned on, and ready to receive data (much like the Select line in the Centronics interface standard).

Data Set Ready (DSR)

Data Terminal Ready (DTR)

Clear To Send (CTS)

Ready To Send (RTS)

The flow of data to the printer is moderated by the **Data Set Ready** (**DSR**) line at the computer connector, and **Data Terminal Ready** (**DTR**) line at the printer connector. The printer uses this line in much the same manner as the Busy line of the Centronics interface. When the buffer is full, the printer signals on this line to tell the computer to not send any more data. More complex serial interfacing may include a line called the **Clear To Send** (**CTS**) line at the computer connector and the **Ready To Send** (**RTS**) line at the printer connector, and its reciprocal line, where the identifications are reversed.

transmission errors

At the printer's end of the cable, another UART receives the serial bit stream, removes the start and stop bits, checks the parity bit for **transmission errors**, and reassembles the character data into parallel form.

Because the movement of data is asynchronous using the UART, an agreement must be established between the computer's UART and the printer's UART, concerning the speed at which characters will be sent. The baud rate of the UART is generally set by software. On the other hand, the printer's baud rate is usually designated by a set of DIP switches in the printer. Common baud rates used with serial printers are 300, 1200, 2400, and 9600 **bits per second** (**bps**). One of the most common problems associated with getting a serial interface to work, is mismatched baud rate.

bits per second (bps)

RS-422

RS-423

Since the adoption of the RS-232C standard, the EIA has also adopted two more improved serial standards, the **RS-422** and **RS-423**, which are enhancements of the RS-232C standard. The RS-422 uses twisted-pair transmission lines, and differential line signals to provide a high degree of noise immunity for transmitted data. The RS-423 standard uses coaxial cable to provide extended transmission distances and higher data transfer rates.

Serial Cables

Figure 3-15 illustrates the basic 25-pin to 25-pin variation of the RS-232 serial cable. In this example, the connection depicted is a straight-through cabling scheme associated with PCs and PC XTs. Even though the information in Figure 3-13 shows a designation for nearly every pin in the RS-232 connection, many of the pins are not actually used in most serial cables.

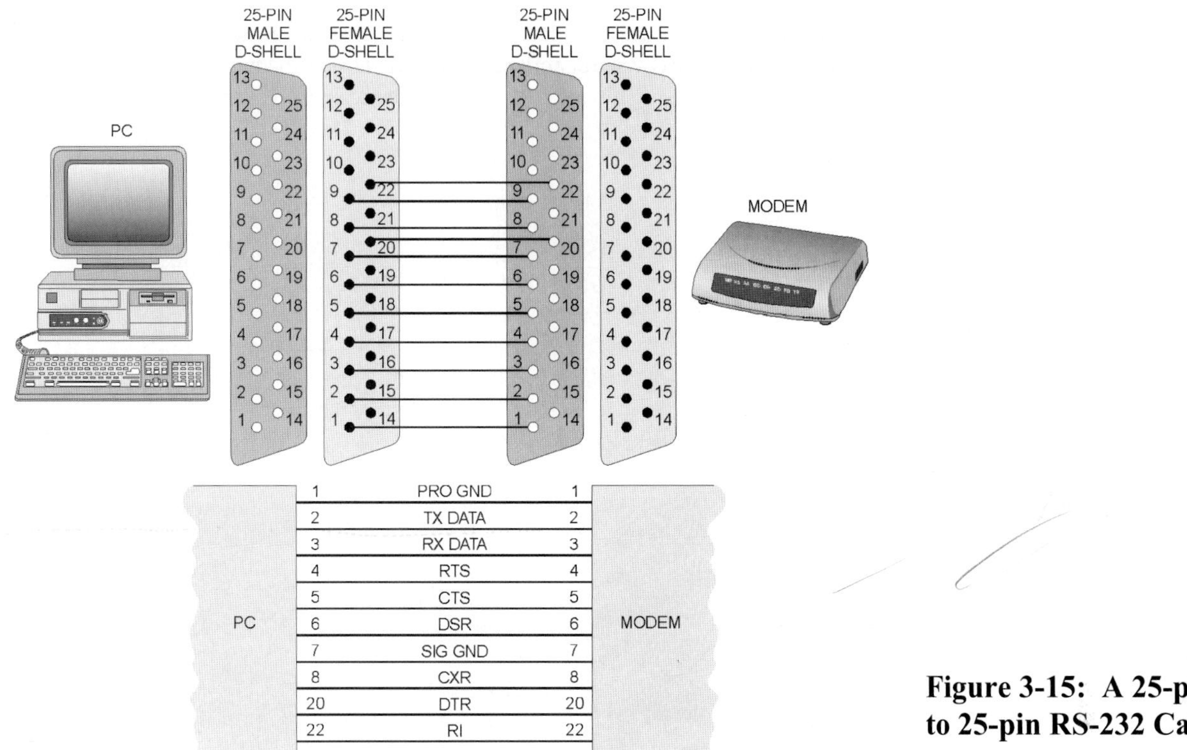

PC				MODEM
	1	PRO GND	1	
	2	TX DATA	2	
	3	RX DATA	3	
	4	RTS	4	
	5	CTS	5	
	6	DSR	6	
	7	SIG GND	7	
	8	CXR	8	
	20	DTR	20	
	22	RI	22	

Figure 3-15: A 25-pin to 25-pin RS-232 Cable

Since the advent of the PC AT, the system's first serial port has typically been implemented in a 9-pin D-shell male connector on the DTE. Figure 3-16 depicts a typical 9-pin to 25-pin connection scheme. Notice the crossover wiring technique employed for the TXD/RXD lines displayed in this example. This type of connection became popular with the 9-pin PC AT serial port.

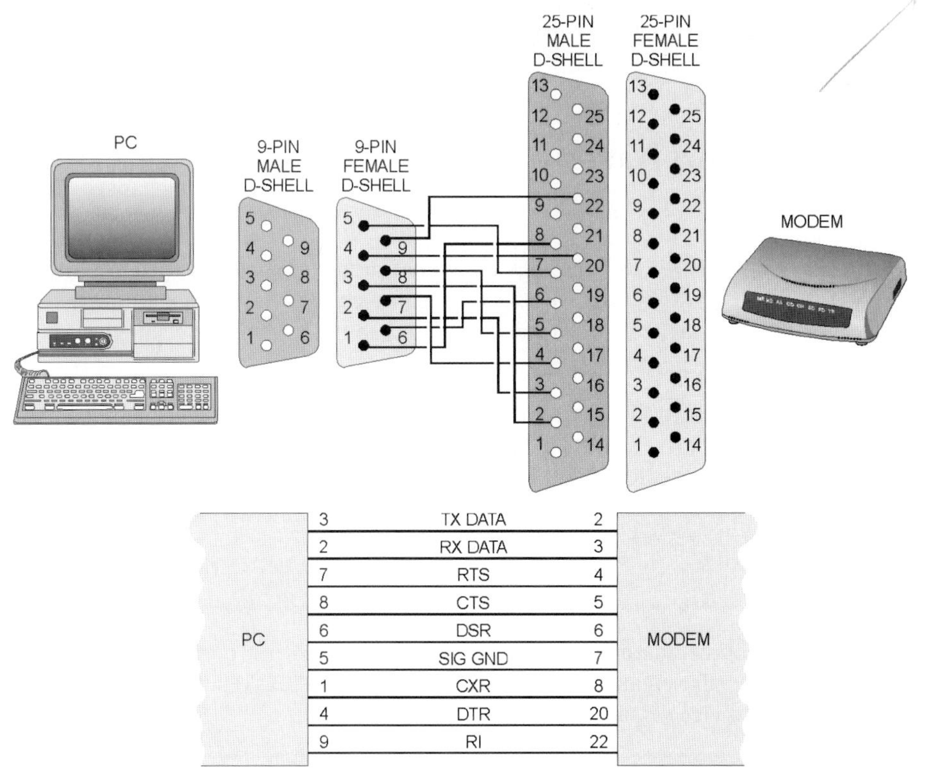

PC				MODEM
	3	TX DATA	2	
	2	RX DATA	3	
	7	RTS	4	
	8	CTS	5	
	6	DSR	6	
	5	SIG GND	7	
	1	CXR	8	
	4	DTR	20	
	9	RI	22	

Figure 3-16: A 9-pin to 25-pin RS-232 Cable

In cases where the serial ports are located close enough to each other, a null modem connection can be implemented. A null modem connection allows the two serial ports to communicate directly without using modems. A typical null modem connection scheme is illustrated in Figure 3-17.

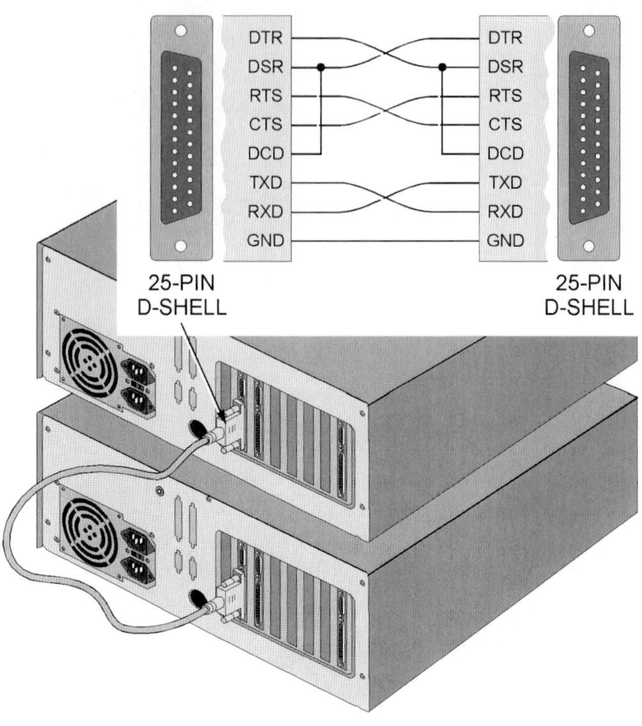

Figure 3-17: A Null Modem Cable

In any event, it should be apparent from the previous figures that all serial cables are not created equal. Incorrect serial cabling can be a major problem when attaching third-party communication equipment to the computer. Read the modem's user's manual carefully to make certain the correct pins are being connected together.

DOS Serial Port Names

COM1

COM2

COM3

COM4

As with parallel ports, DOS assigns COM port designations to the system's serial ports during bootup. COM port designations are normally **COM1** and **COM2** in most systems, but they can be extended to **COM3** and **COM4** in advanced systems.

Either RS-232 port may be designated as COM1, COM2, COM3, or COM4, as long as both ports are not assigned to the same COM port number. In most PCs, COM1 is assigned as port address hex 3F8h and use IRQ channel 4. The COM2 port is typically assigned port address hex 2F8h and IRQ3. Likewise, COM3 uses IRQ4 and is assigned an I/O address of 3E8h, while COM4 usually resides at 2E8 and uses IRQ3.

TEST TIP

Know the system addresses and other resources that a PC-compatible system uses for serial ports. It may be easy to remember that IBM set up these standards so that the odd-numbered COM ports use the even-numbered IRQ channel, and vice versa.

Game Ports

game control adapter

The **game control adapter** enables two joysticks to be used with the system. The adapter converts resistive input values into relative joystick positions, in much the same manner as described in the previous section. This adapter can also function as a general-purpose I/O converter, featuring four analog and four digital input points.

fire buttons

The input to the game port is generally a pair of resistive joysticks. Joysticks are defined as having two variable resistances, each of which should be variable between 0 and 100 k-ohms. Joysticks may have one or two normally-open **fire buttons**. The order of fire buttons should correspond with that of the resistive elements (A and B or A, B, C, and D). The wiring structure for the two-row, 15-pin D-shell female connector is shown in Figure 3-18.

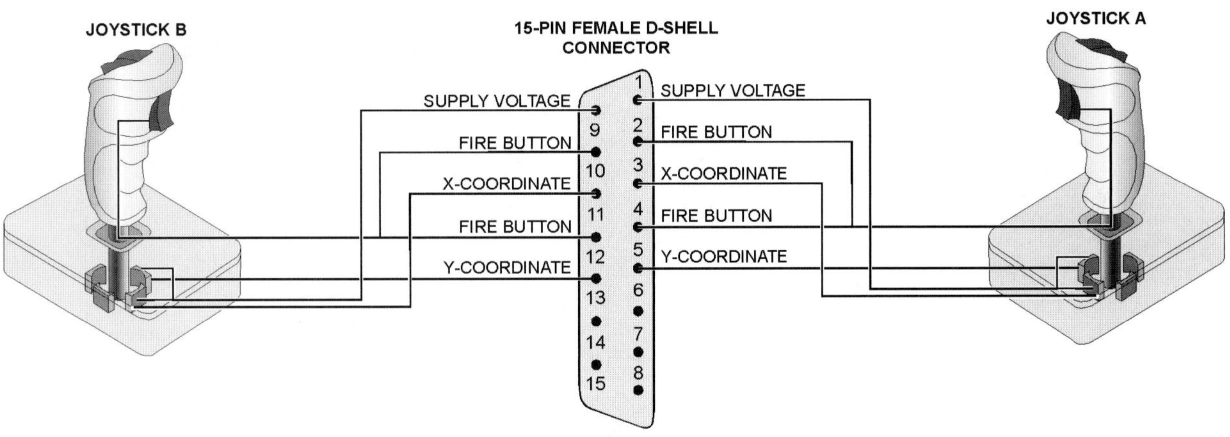

Figure 3-18: Game-Port Connections

Universal Serial Bus

Universal Serial Bus (USB)

A new serial interface scheme, called the **Universal Serial Bus (USB)**, has been developed to provide a fast, flexible method of attaching up to 127 peripheral devices to the computer. The USB provides a connection format designed to replace the system's traditional serial- and parallel-port connections.

USB peripherals can be daisy-chained, or networked together using connection hubs that enable the bus to branch out through additional port connections. A practical USB desktop connection scheme is presented in Figure 3-19.

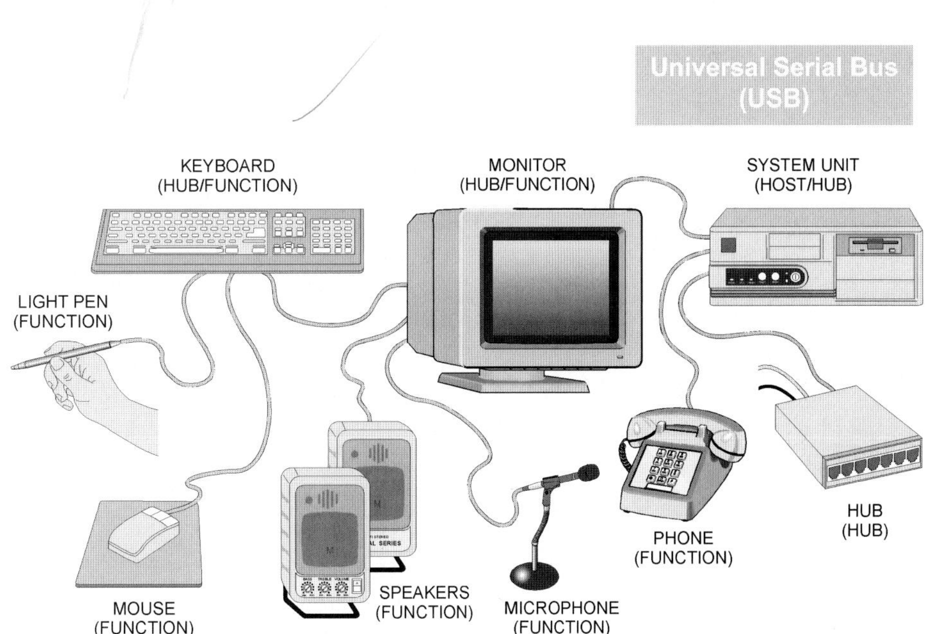

Figure 3-19: A 9-pin to 25-pin RS-232 Cable

In this example, some of the peripheral devices are simply devices, while others serve as both devices and connection hubs. The system provides a USB host connection that serves as the main USB connection.

USB devices can be added to or removed from the system while it is powered up and fully operational. This is referred to as hot-swapping or hot plugging the device. The Plug-and-Play capabilities of the system will detect the presence (or absence) of the device and configure it for operation.

USB Cabling and Connectors

USB transfers are conducted over a four-wire cable, as illustrated in Figure 3-20. The signal travels over a pair of twisted wires (D+ and D–) in a 90-ohm cable. The differential signal and twisted-pair wiring provide minimum signal deterioration over distances and high noise immunity.

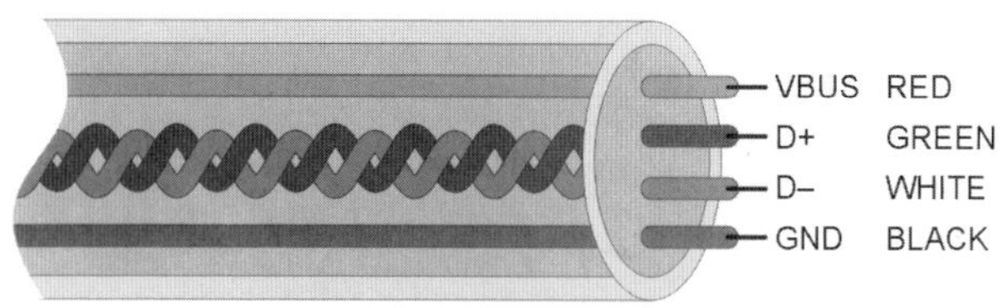

Figure 3-20: The USB Cable

A Vbus and Ground (GND) wire are also present. The Vbus is the +5V (DC) power cord. The interface provides power to the peripheral attached to it. The root hub provides power directly from the host system to those devices directly connected to it. Hubs also supply power to the devices connected to them. Even though the interface supplies power to the USB devices, they are permitted to have their own power sources if necessary.

In these instances, the device must be designed specifically to avoid interference with the bus' power-distribution scheme. The USB host's power-management software can apply power to devices when needed and suspend power to them when not required.

The USB specification defines two types of plugs: series-A and series-B. Series-A connectors are used for devices where the USB cable connection is permanently attached to devices at one end. Examples of these devices include keyboards, mice, and hubs. Conversely, the series-B plugs and jacks are designed for devices that require detachable cabling (printers, scanners, and modems, for example). Both are four-contact plugs and sockets embedded in plastic connectors, as shown in Figure 3-21. The sockets can be implemented in vertical, right-angle, and panel-mount variations. The icon used to represent a USB connector is depicted by the centers of the A and B "plug connectors".

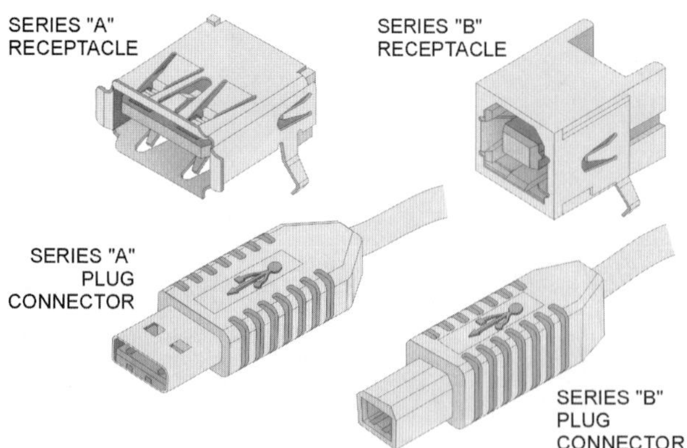

Figure 3-21: USB Connectors

The connectors for both series are keyed so that they cannot be plugged in backward. All hubs and functions possess a single, permanently attached cable with a series B connector at its end. The connectors are designed so that the A- and B-series connections cannot be interchanged.

USB Architecture

When USB devices are daisy-chained together, the resulting connection architecture forms a tiered-star configuration, like the one depicted in Figure 3-22.

TEST TIP

Memorize the number of devices that can be attached to a USB port.

The USB system is composed of a USB host and USB devices. The devices category consists of hubs and nodes. In any system, there is one USB host. This unit contains the interface that provides the USB host controller. The controller is actually a combination of USB hardware, firmware, and software.

Hubs are devices that provide additional connection points for other USB devices. A special hub, called the **root hub**, is an integral part of the host system and provides one or more attachment points for USB devices.

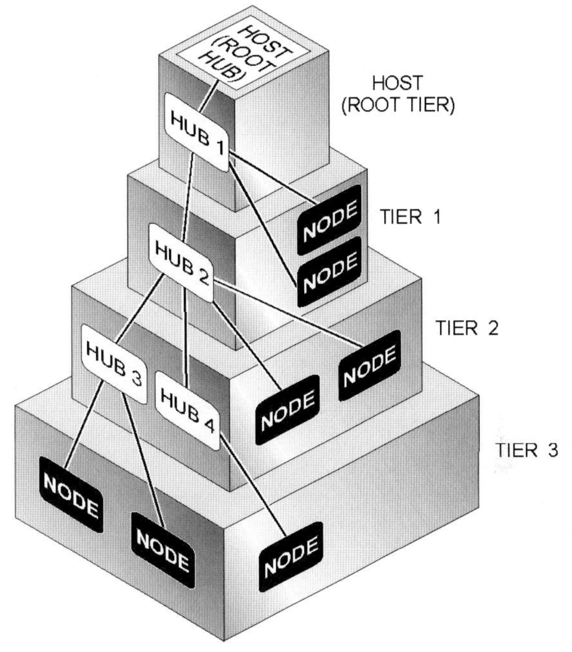

Figure 3-22: Universal Serial Bus Architecture

Many of the newer AT and ATX system boards feature built in USB host ports. In the AT-style boards, the port is furnished as part of a BERG pin connection, as illustrated in Figure 3-23. The ports are converted to standard connectors through an additional back panel cable set that mounts in an open back panel slot. On the other hand, ATX boards feature a pair of USB port connectors as part of the ATX port connection block as illustrated in the figure. There are also PCI card-mounted USB ports that can be added to the system to enable even more USB devices to be attached to the system. These host ports function as the system's root hub.

root hub

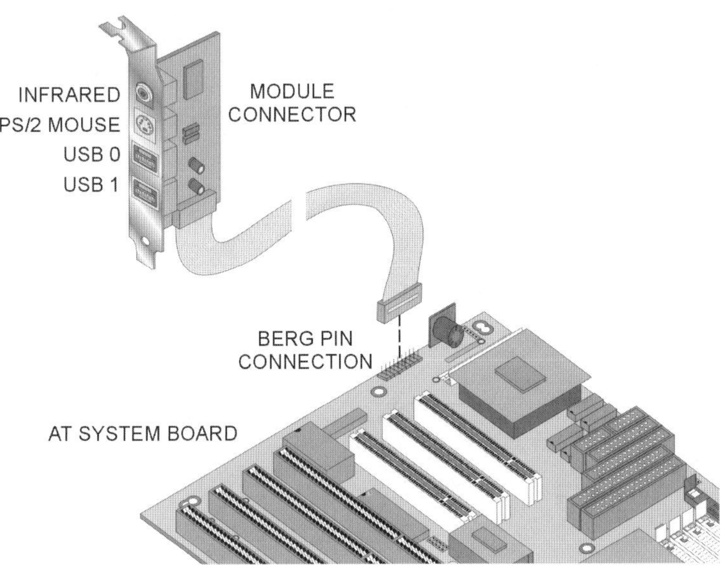

Figure 3-23: Implementing USB Ports

In the case of built-in USB ports, the operation of the port connections is controlled by settings in the system board's CMOS Setup Utility. In most cases, it will be necessary to access the CMOS Setup Utility's PCI Configuration Screen and enable the USB function and assign the ports IRQ channels to use. If no USB device is being used with the system, the IRQ allocation should be set to "NA" to free up the IRQ line for use by other devices.

It is evident that some of the components of the system serve as both a function and as a hub (that is, the keyboard and monitor). In these devices, the package holds the components of the function, as well as providing an embedded hub that other functions can be connected to. These devices are referred to as compound devices.

Full speed

Low speed

Although the tiered architecture described in Figure 3-22 approaches the complexity and capabilities of the LAN architectures covered in Chapter 5—*Data Communications*, the overhead for managing the port is much easier to implement. As mentioned earlier, USB devices can be added to or removed from the system while it is fully operational. In reality, this means that the USB organizational structure is modified any time a device is added to or removed from the system.

TEST TIP

Know the length limits for Full- and Low-speed USB devices. It should help you to remember that the low-speed distance is actually shorter than the high-speed length.

USB devices are rated as **Full-speed** and **Low-speed** devices based on their communication capabilities. The length limit for a cable serving a Full-speed device is 16 feet - 5 inches (5 meters). Likewise, the length limit for cables used between Low-speed devices is 9 feet 10 inches (3 meters).

USB Data Transfers

data packets

endpoint device

host controller

endpoint number

not acknowledge (NACK)

token packet

start-of-frame (SOF)

data packet

handshake packet

Unlike traditional serial interfaces that transmit framed characters one at a time, data moves across the USB in the form of **data packets**. Packet sizes vary with the type of transmission being carried out. However, they are typically 8, 16, 32, or 64 bytes in length. All transmissions require that two or three packets of information be exchanged between the host, the source location, and the destination location.

All data transfers are conducted between the host and an **endpoint device**. The flow of data can occur in either direction. USB transactions begin when the **host controller** sends a token packet that contains information about the type of transaction to take place, the direction of the transmission, the address of the designated USB device, and an **endpoint number**. If the device is the source of the transaction, it either places a data packet on the bus, or informs the host that it has no data to send. If the host is the source, it just places the data packet on the bus.

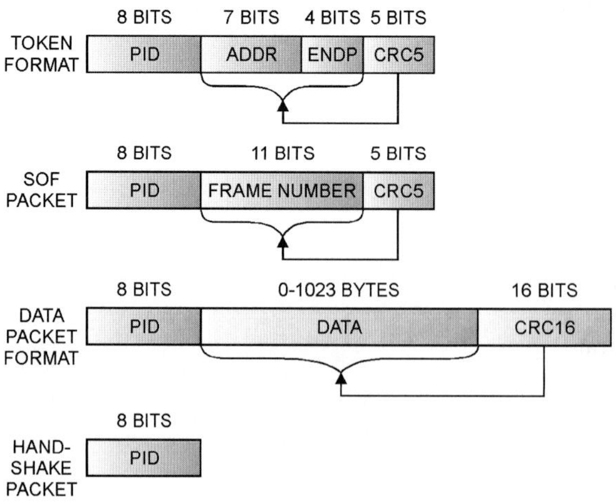

Figure 3-24: USB Packet Formats

In either case, the destination returns a handshake packet if the transfer was successful. If an error is detected in the transfer, a **not acknowledge (NACK)** packet is generated. Figure 3-24 demonstrates the USB's four packet formats: **token packet**, the **start-of-frame (SOF)** packet, the **data packet**, and the **handshake packet**.

Each type of packet begins with an 8-bit **packet ID (PID)** section. The SOF packet adds an 11-bit frame-number section and a 5-bit **Cyclic Redundancy Check (CRC)** error-checking code section. In the data packet, a variable-length data section replaces the frame-number section, and the CRC frame is enlarged to 16 bits. The data section can range up to 1023 bytes in length. The handshake packet just consists of a PID byte.

packet ID (PID)

Cyclic Redundancy Check (CRC)

The USB management software dynamically tracks what devices are attached to the bus and where they are. This process of identifying and numbering bus devices is known as **bus enumerating**. The USB specification allows **hot-swap** peripheral connection that does not require the system to be shut down. The system automatically detects peripherals and configures the proper driver. Instead of just detecting and charting devices at startup in a PnP style, the USB continuously monitors the bus and updates the list whenever a device is added to or removed from it.

bus enumerating

hot-swap

The USB specification allows for the following four types of transfers to be conducted:

- **Control transfers** are used by the system to configure devices at startup or time of connection. Other software can use control transfers to perform other device-specific operations.
- **Bulk data transfers** are used to service devices that can handle large batches of data (scanners and printers, for example). Bulk transfers are typically made up of large bursts of sequential data. The system arranges for bulk transfers to be conducted when the bus has plenty of capacity to carry out the transfer.
- **Interrupt transfers** are small, spontaneous transfers from a device that are used to announce events, provide input coordinate information, or transfer characters.
- **Isochronous transfers** involve large streams of data. This format is used to move continuous, real-time data streams such as voice or video. Data delivery rates are predetermined and correspond to the sampling rate of the device.

Control transfers

Bulk data transfers

Interrupt transfers

Isochronous transfers

TEST TIP

Be aware of the USB high-speed data streaming mode.

Firewire

While the USB specification was being refined for the computer industry, a similar serial interface bus was being developed for the consumer products market. Apple Computers and Texas Instruments worked together with the **IEEE (Institute of Electrical and Electronic Engineers)** to produce the **Firewire** (or **IEEE-1394**) specification. The new bus offers a very fast option for connecting consumer electronics devices, such as camcorders and DVDs, to the computer system.

IEEE (Institute of Electrical and Electronic Engineers)

Firewire

IEEE-1394

The Firewire bus is similar to USB in that devices can be daisy-chained to the computer using a single connector and host adapter. It requires a single IRQ channel, an I/O address range, and a single DMA channel to operate. Firewire is also capable of using the high-speed Isochronous transfer mode described for USB to support data transfer rates up to 400 Mbps. This actually makes the Firewire bus superior to the USB bus. Its high-speed capabilities make Firewire well suited for handling components, such as video and audio devices, which require real-time, high-speed data transfer rates.

TEST TIP

Be aware that the Firewire bus is faster than the USB bus.

A single IEEE-1394 connection can be used to connect up to 63 devices to a single port. However, up to 1023 Firewire buses can be interconnected. PCs most commonly use a PCI expansion card to provide the Firewire interface. While AV equipment typically employ 4-pin 1394 connectors, computers normally use a 6-pin connector, with a 4-pin to 6-pin converter. The maximum segment length for an IEEE1394 connection is 4.5m (14 ft.). Figure 3-25 depicts the Firewire connector and plug most commonly used with PCs.

TEST TIP

Remember how many devices can be attached to a single IEEE-1394 port.

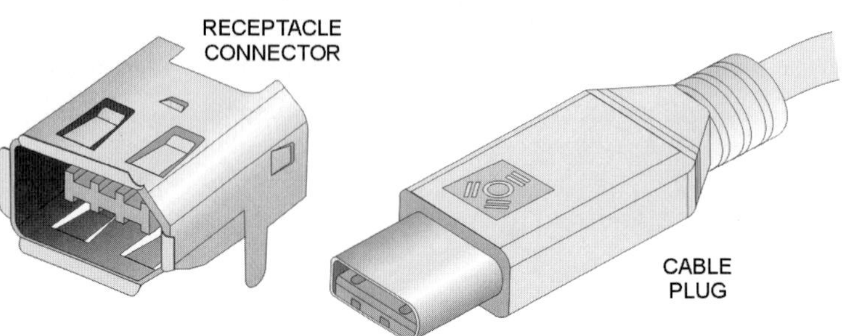

Figure 3-25: Firewire Plug and Connector

The IEEE-1394 cable is composed of two twisted-pair conductors similar to those used in the local area networks described later in the chapter. Like USB, it supports both PnP and hot-swapping of components. It also provides power to the peripheral devices through one pair of the twisted conductors in the interface cable.

Firewire operates in peer-to-peer mode and is supported in both the Windows 9x and Windows NT/2000 operating systems. Both operating systems support advanced Firewire operations by including support for three critical 1394-related specifications: OHCI, IEC61883, and SBP-2. The Open Host Controller Interface (OHCI) standard defines the way Firewire interfaces to a PC. The IEC 61883 standard defines the details for controlling specific audio-video devices over the IEEE-1394 bus. The Serial Bus Protocol - 2 (SBP-2) specification defines standard ways of encapsulating device commands over 1394 and is essential for DVD players, printers, scanners, and other devices. The Home AV interoperability (HAVi) standard is another layer of protocols for the Firewire specification. This standard is directed at making Firewire devices plug-and-play capable in networks where no PC host is present.

A proposed version of the IEEE-1394 standard (titled P1394b) provides an additional electrical signaling method that permits data transmission speeds of 800 Mbps and greater. The new version of the standard also supports new transport media including glass and plastic optical fiber, as well as Category 5 copper cable. With the new media come extended distances, e.g., 100 meters over Cat5 cabling.

Infrared Ports

Infrared Data Association (IrDA)

The **Infrared Data Association** (**IrDA**) has produced a wireless peripheral connection standard based on infrared light technology, similar to that used in consumer remote control devices. Many system board designs include an IrDA-compliant port standard to provide wireless communications with devices such as character printers, Personal Digital Assistants, and notebook computers. Figure 3-26 illustrates an IrDA-connected printer. The same technology has been employed to carry out transfers between computer communications devices such as modems and Local Area Network cards.

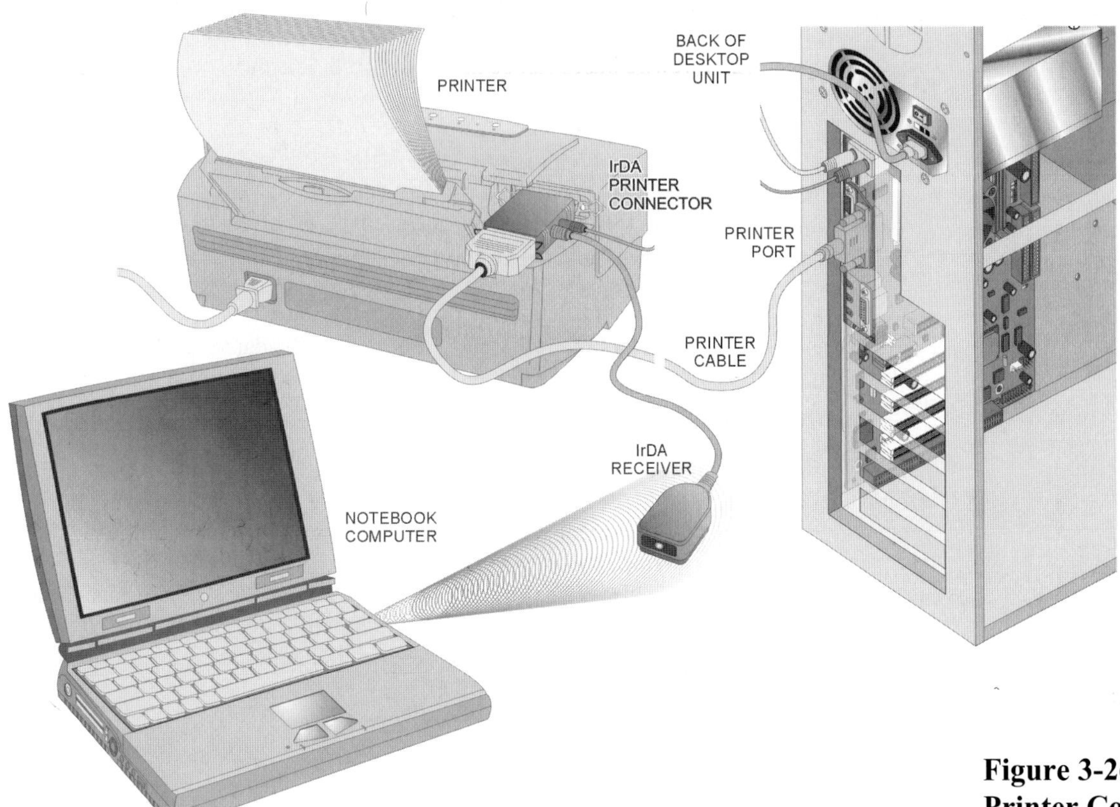

Figure 3-26: An IrDA Printer Connection

The IrDA standard specifies four protocols that are used with different types of devices:

- *IrLPT*—used with character printers to provide a wireless interface between the computer and the printer.
- *IrDA-SIR*—the standard infrared protocol used to provide a standard serial port interface with transfer rates ranging up to 115 Kbps.
- *IrDA-FIR*—The fast infrared protocol used to provide a high-speed serial port interface with transfer rates ranging up to 4 Mbps.
- *IrTran-P*—used to provide a digital image transfer standard for communications with digital image capture devices.

These protocols specify communication ranges up to 2 meters (6 feet) but most specifications usually state 1 meter as the maximum range. All IrDA transfers are carried out in half-duplex mode and must have a clear line of sight between the transmitter and receiver. The receiver must be situated within 15 degrees of center with the line of transmission.

TEST TIP

Remember that the IrLPT port is a new, high-speed printer interface that can be used to print from a wide array of computing devices.

The Windows operating system supports the use of infrared devices. The properties of installed IrDA devices can be viewed through its Device Manager. Likewise, connections to another IrDA computer can be established through the Windows Network Dialup Connections applet. By installing a **Point-to-Point Protocol (PPP)** or an **IrDA LAN protocol** through this applet, you can conduct wireless communications with other computers without a modem or network card.

Point-to-Point Protocol (PPP)

IrDA LAN protocol

Typical Peripherals

input systems

output systems

memory systems

Peripherals are devices and systems that are added to the basic system to extend its capabilities. These devices and systems can be divided into three general categories: **input systems**, **output systems**, and **memory systems**.

Most peripheral devices interact with the basic system through adapter cards that plug into the system board's expansion slots. The peripheral devices connect to the adapter cards through expansion slot openings in the back of the system unit.

keyboard

CRT monitor

mouse

character printer

The standard peripherals associated with personal computers are the **keyboard** and the **CRT monitor**. With the rapid growth of GUI-oriented software, the **mouse** has become a common input peripheral as well. The next most common peripheral is the **character printer**. These peripherals are used to produce hard copy output on paper. Many other types of peripheral equipment are routinely added to the basic system. As long as there are open expansion slots, or other standard I/O connectors, it is possible to add compatible devices to the system. Figure 3-27 illustrates external connections for a basic system configuration.

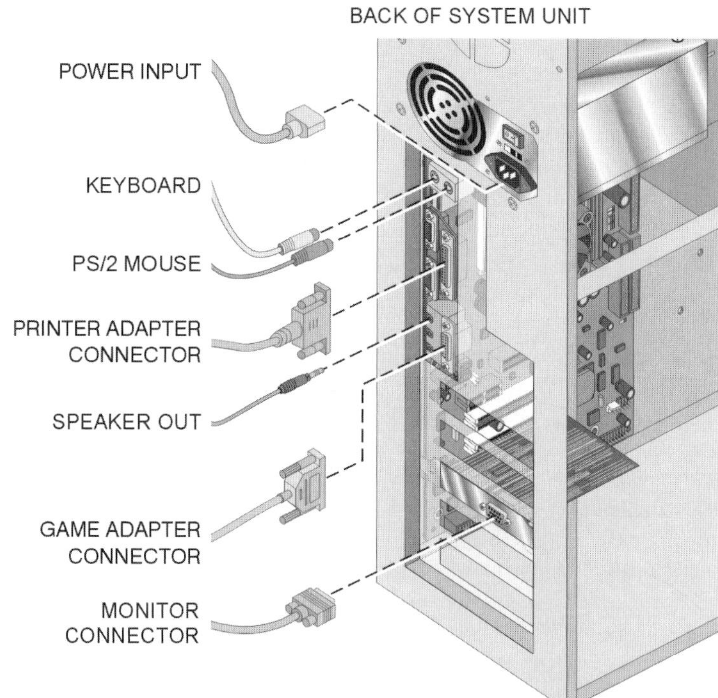

Figure 3-27: External Connections

Input Devices

Input devices convert physical quantities into electronic signals that can be manipulated by interface units. The input devices typically used with microcomputers convert human physical activity into electronic impulses that can be processed by the computer. The chief devices of this type are keyboards, joysticks, mice, trackballs and touch pads. These devices are illustrated in Figure 3-28. Other types of input devices convert physical quantities (such as temperature, pressure, and motion) into signals that can be processed. These devices are normally found in industrial control applications.

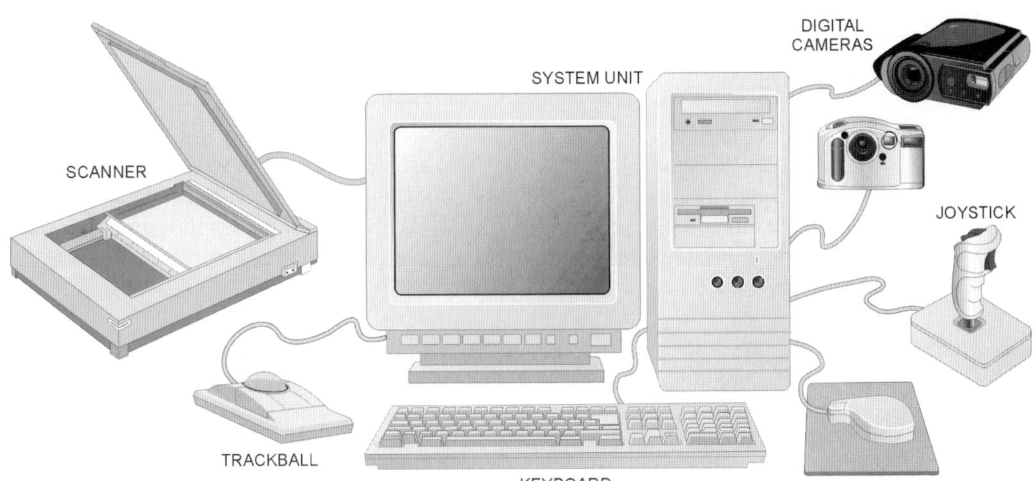

Figure 3-28: Typical Input Devices

Keyboards

The alphanumeric keyboard is the most widely used input device for microcomputers. It provides a simple, finger-operated method of entering numbers, letters, symbols, and special control characters into the computer. Modern computer keyboards are adaptations of earlier typewriter-like keyboards used with teletypewriters. In addition to the alphabetic and numeric keys found on conventional typewriters, the computer keyboard may also contain any number of special function and command keys to extend its basic operation and provide special-purpose entry functions.

The pattern in which keyboards are arranged and constructed has traditionally sparked some debate among users. Everyone seems to have a favorite key pattern that they prefer in a keyboard. Obviously, an individual who is trained to touch-type on a standard QWERTY typewriter keyboard would prefer that the computer keyboard be laid out in the same manner. The contour of the key top, the amount of pressure, and the length of the stroke that must be applied to the key to actuate it are also important ergonomic considerations in keyboard design. Some keyboards offer a defined click at the bottom of the keystroke to identify a complete entry. Others offer shorter key strokes with a soft bottom and no feedback click.

Keyboard design is part form and part function. Although the QWERTY keyboard remains the standard for key arrangement, a second key pattern, known as the DVORAK keyboard, has gained some notoriety. This keyboard layout, depicted in Figure 3-29, attempts to arrange the keyboard characters in a more logical pattern that should lead to faster operation. Its basic premise is that the new key placement should lead to alternate hand usage.

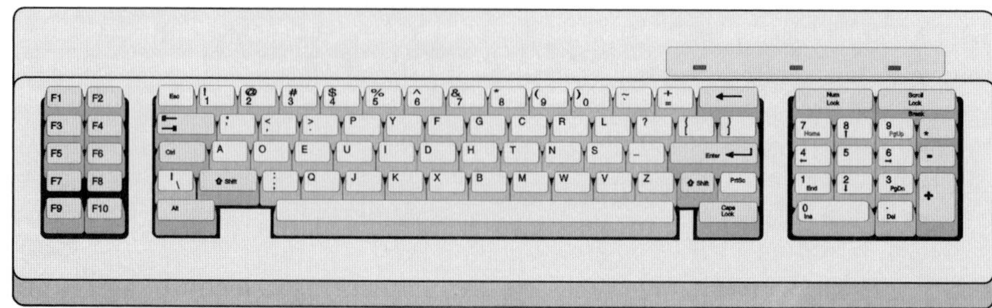

Figure 3-29: DVORAK Keyboard

Although the layout is quite old, (devised in 1936) and does offer some speed advantages, the DVORAK keyboard has gained only minimal acceptance by users. However, the programmability of PC-compatible keyboards make DVORAK conversion easy if desired. The only physical action required to implement a DVORAK layout involves repositioning the keyboard's keycaps.

Still other designs have been adapted to make using the keyboard more comfortable for the user. Some units include a special cushion along the front edge to provide support for the wrists. Another innovative design divides the keyboard in half and angles each side back slightly, as illustrated in Figure 3-30. This ergonomic design is supposed to offer a more natural angle for the human hands than straight-across designs.

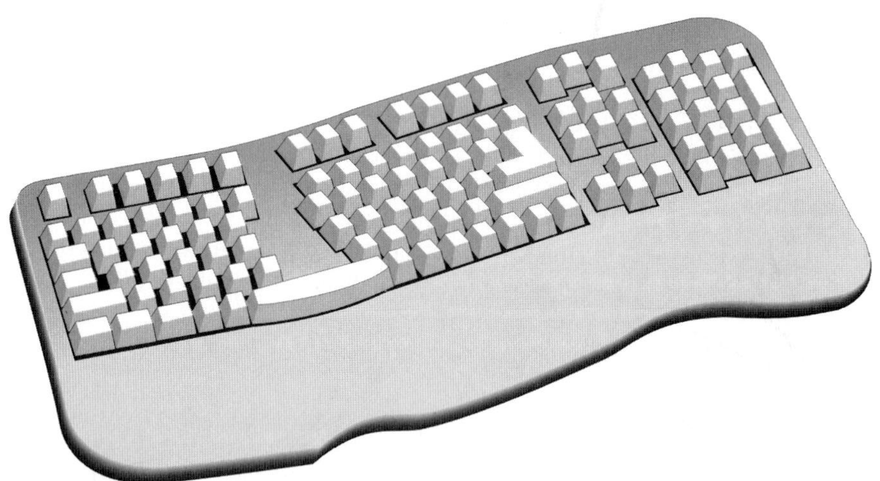

Figure 3-30: Ergonomic Keyboard Design

Inside, a keyboard is basically an X-Y matrix arrangement of switch elements, as shown in Figure 3-31. To produce meaningful data from a key depression, the keyboard must be capable of detecting and identifying the depressed key and then encoding the key closure into a form the computer can use.

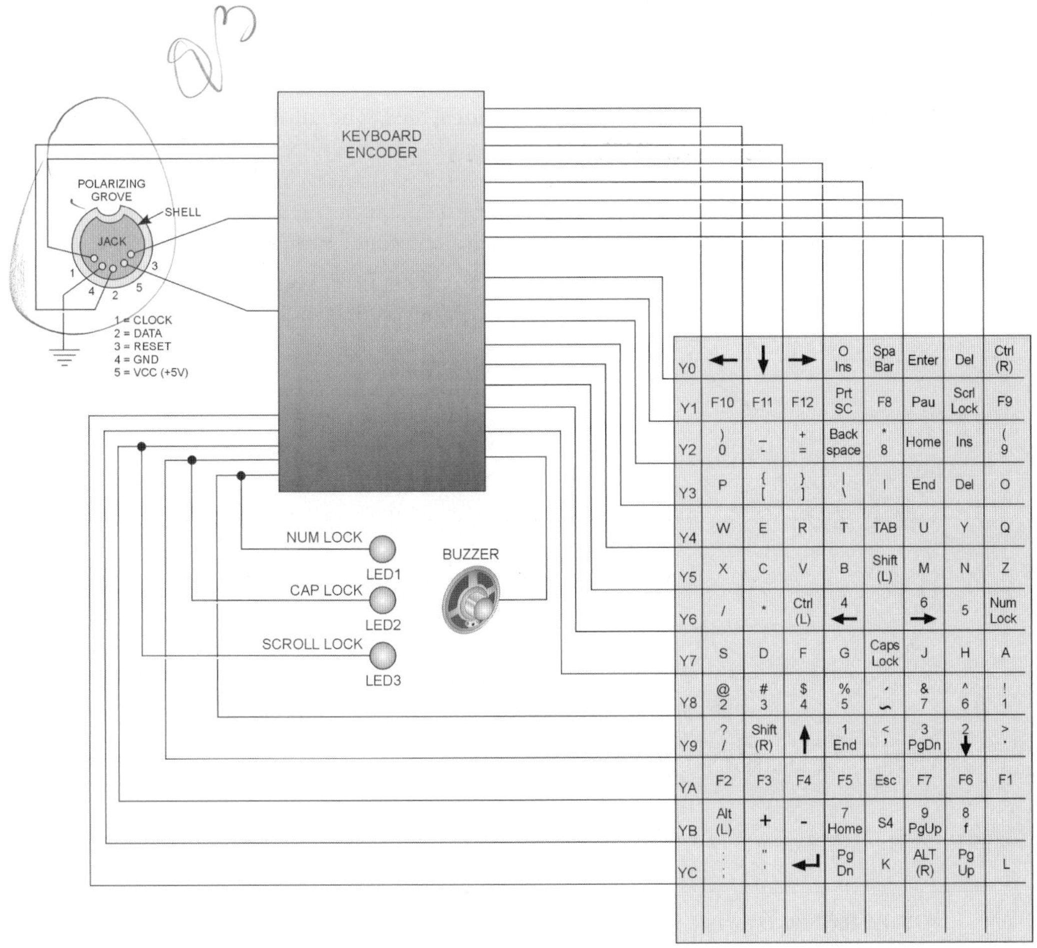

Figure 3-31: 101-Key Keyboard

The 101 keys of the sample keyboard depicted in the figure are arranged in a matrix of 13 Strobe lines and 8 Sense lines. Computer keyboards employ a dedicated microprocessor, called a **keyboard encoder**, to scan the keyboard matrix and send an interrupt request signal to the system when a key closure occurs. The keyboard encoder scans the lines of the matrix sequentially at a scan rate much faster than it is humanly possible to close one of the key switches and release it. A typical encoder scans the entire keyboard within 3 to 5 milliseconds.

keyboard encoder

Several types of switches are used to perform the keying function for the keyboard. Older designs use simple mechanical switches that function similar to a light switch found in a residential home. Newer non-contact electronic switches have gained wide acceptance in computer keyboards. This is due to their low cost, high performance, and longevity of operation. These designs are based on non-contact capacitive and magnetic-core switching techniques.

When a switch closure shorts a particular row to a particular column, an active signal appears at one of the keyboard encoder's sense inputs. When the active logic level is detected, the keyboard encoder pauses for a few milliseconds to enable the switch closure to settle out. Afterward, the keyboard encoder stores the closure in its buffer and continues scanning until all the rows have been scanned.

Each time the keyboard encoder receives a valid key closure from the matrix, it generates two serially coded characters: a scan code that corresponds to the key closure, and a break code that is generated when the key closure is broken. The encoder notifies the system unit that it is ready to transmit a scan code by sending it a start bit. The encoder then begins transmitting the codes to the system unit.

keyboard controller

On most AT and ATX-compatible system boards, the keyboard-interfacing function is handled by an intelligent **keyboard controller** built into the system board chipset. When the keyboard controller receives serial data from the keyboard, it checks the parity of the data, converts it into a scan code and generates a keyboard interrupt request (IRQ1) to the system. The keyboard encoder transmits the codes to the keyboard controller through the cable, as illustrated in Figure 3-32. The keyboard controller releases the code to the system's keyboard interrupt handler routine.

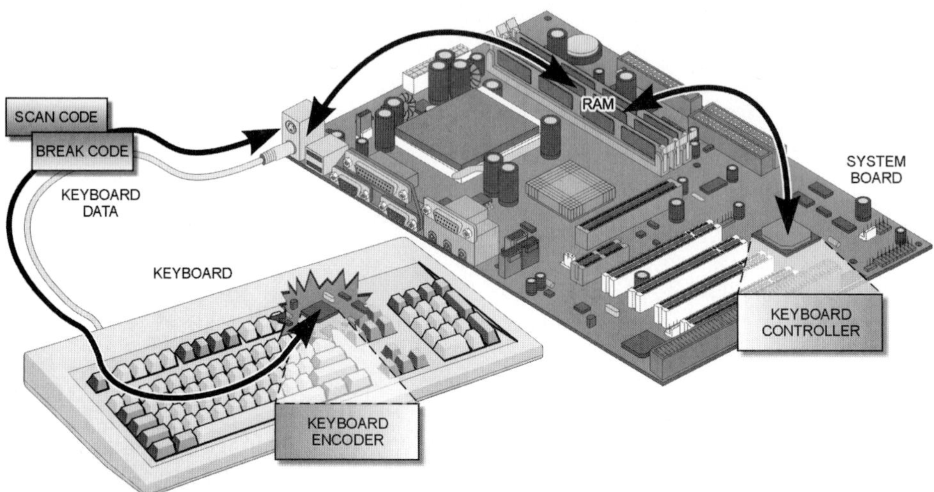

Figure 3-32: Moving Keyboard Data

Finally, the routine sends the ASCII character code to the program that called for it. The program delivers the code to the activated output device (monitor, modem, or printer). Sending a character to a display device through the CPU is called an echo and may be suppressed by programming so that the character is not displayed.

Pointing Devices

pointing devices

Mice, joysticks, trackballs, and touch pads belong to a category of input devices called **pointing devices**. They are all small, hand held input devices that allow the user to interact with the system by moving a cursor, or some other screen image around the display screen, to choose options from an on-screen menu, instead of typing commands from a keyboard. Since pointing devices make it easier to interact with the computer than other types of input devices, they are, therefore, friendlier to the user.

The most widely used pointing device is the mouse. A mouse is a hand held device that produces input data by being moved across a surface, such as a desktop. The mouse has become a standard input device for most systems due to the popularity of GUI-based software.

The most common mouse type is the trackball mouse, depicted in Figure 3-33. The trackball mouse detects positional changes through the movement of a rolling trackball that it rides on. As the mouse is moved across a surface, its circuitry detects the movement of the trackball, and creates pulses that the system converts into positional information.

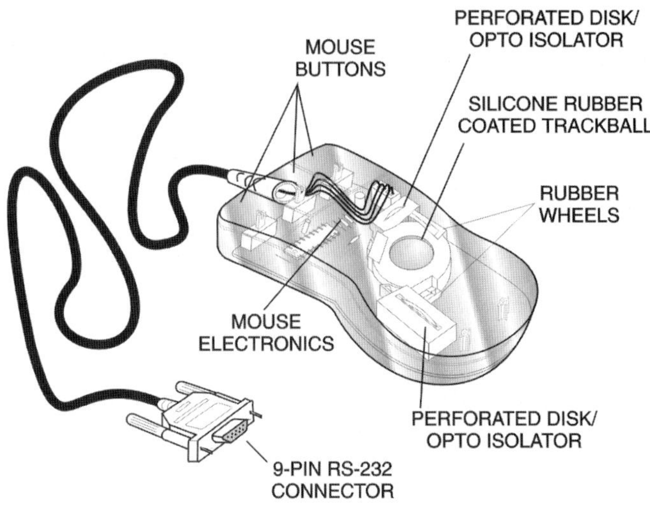

Figure 3-33: Typical Trackball Mouse

The movement of the mouse causes the trackball to roll. Inside the mouse, the trackball drives two small wheels that are attached to the shafts of two potentiometers (one X and one Y). As the trackball rolls, the wheels turn and the resistance of the potentiometers varies proportionally. The varying resistance is converted to an analog signal that undergoes an analog to digital conversion process, by which it is changed into a digital input that represents movement of the mouse. The trackball mice use opto-coupling techniques to generate a string of digital pulses when the ball is moved. These devices are referred to as opto-mechanical mice. The trackball turns two perforated wheels by friction. Light from light emitting diodes shines through holes in the wheels (which are not attached to potentiometers) as the mouse moves. The light pulses are detected by a photoconductive device that converts them into digital voltage pulses. The pulses are applied to counters that tabulate the distance (both X and Y) that the mouse moves.

optical mouse

Another popular type of mouse is the **optical mouse**. The optical mouse requires a special pad, which is divided into a number of X and Y coordinates by horizontal and vertical lines on the surface of the pad. The mouse detects motion by emitting an infrared light stream, which is disturbed when the mouse crosses one of the lines on the pad. Both trackball and optical mice have similar appearances, although they may differ in the number of buttons on their top.

trackball

In some applications, such as notebook computers, it is desirable to have a pointing device that does not require a surface to be moved across. The **trackball** can be thought of as an inverted mouse that enables the user to directly manipulate it. Trackballs, such as the one depicted in Figure 3-34, may be separate units that sit on a desk or clip to the side of the computer, and connect to one of the system's serial ports. In many laptop and notebook computers, trackballs are frequently built directly into the system housing and are connected directly to its I/O circuitry. As with mice, trackballs may come with one to three buttons.

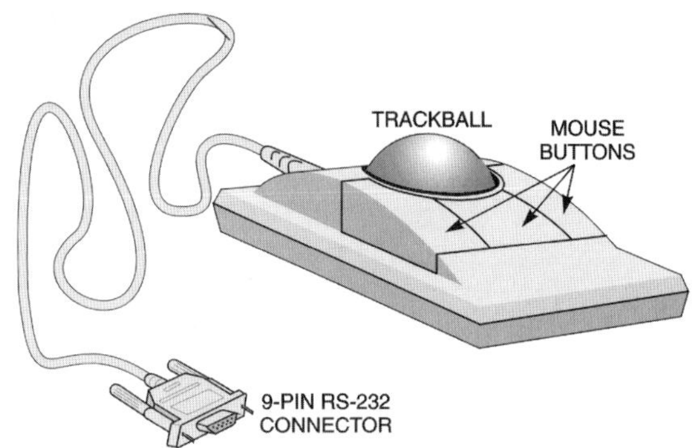

Figure 3-34: Trackball Unit

There are two major types of joysticks that can be used with PC-compatible systems: analog and digital joysticks.

gimbal

The analog version employs two resistive potentiometer elements, one for the X-direction and one for the Y-direction. Both potentiometers are mechanically connected to the movable **gimbal** that causes the resistance elements to produce variable levels of output signal when the gimbal is moved along the X-axis, Y-axis, or at some angle between them (this varies both the X and Y voltages). The computer's game port interface uses these analog signals to produce digital X-Y coordinate information for the system. When this type of joystick is used to position a screen image, the position of the image on the screen corresponds to the X-Y position of the gimbal.

A somewhat simpler design is used in the construction of digital joysticks. The gimbal is used to mechanically open and close different combinations of an internal, four-switch arrangement, as depicted in Figure 3-35. The joystick produces a single-byte output, which encodes the gimbal's movement in any of eight possible directions. Unlike analog joysticks, the position of the controlled image on the screen does not correspond to the X-Y position of the gimbal. Instead, the gimbal position only produces the direction of movement for the screen image. When the gimbal is returned to its neutral position, the screen image simply stops where it is.

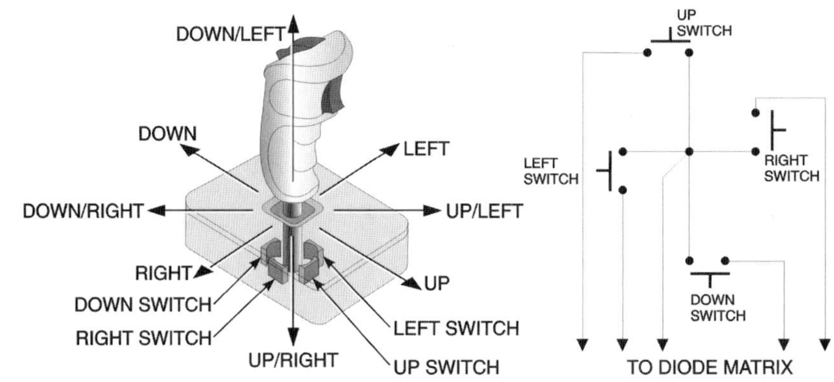

Figure 3-35: A Digital Joystick

Touch Pads

Hewlett-Packard introduced the first touch-screen monitor in 1983. These screens divide the display into rows and columns that correspond to x and y coordinates onscreen. This technology has been adapted to notebook computers in the form of touch pad pointing devices, like the one illustrated in Figure 3-36. This pointing device normally takes the place of the mouse as the pointing device in the system. The user controls the screen cursor by moving a finger across the pad surface. Small buttons are included near the pad to duplicate the action of the mouse buttons. With some touch pads, single- and double-clicking can be simulated by tapping a finger on the pad.

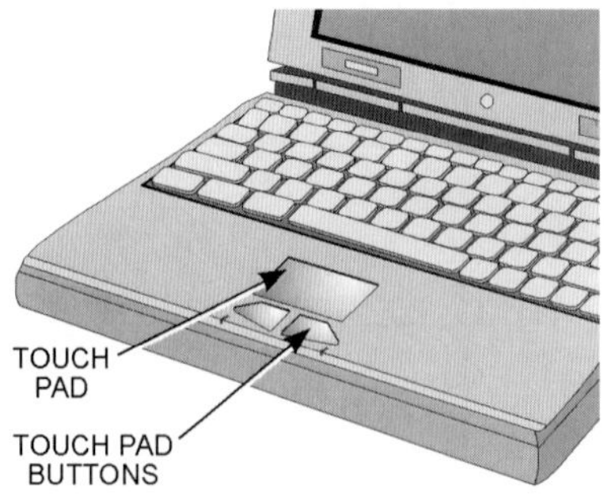

Figure 3-36: A Touch Pad

The touch pad contains a grid of electric conductors that organize it in a row and column format, as described in Figure 3-37. When the user presses the touch pad, the protective layer over the grid flexes and causes the capacitance between the two grids within the pad to change. This produces a signal change that is detected by the touch pad controller at one x-grid line and one y-grid line. The controller converts the signal generated between the two strips into an approximate x/y position on the video display.

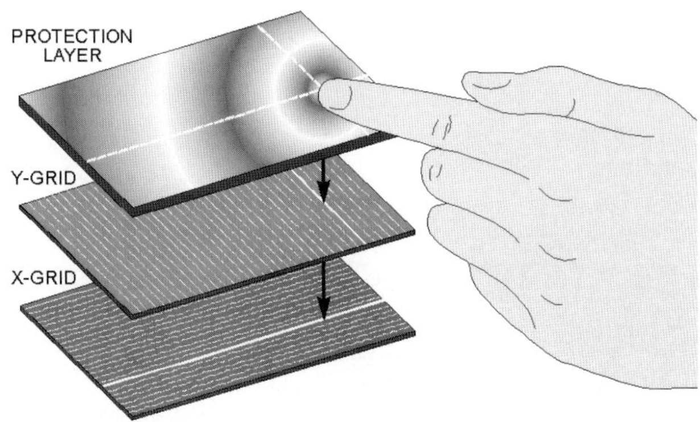

Figure 3-37: Inside a Touch Pad

The human fingertip is broad and does not normally provide a fine enough pointing device to select precise points onscreen. Therefore, accurately locating a small item onscreen may be difficult due to the relative size of the fingertip. The touch pad software designers have created drivers that take this possibility into account and compensate for it.

Touch pads are available as built-in units in some portables; others are designed as add-ons to existing units. These units clip onto the body of the computer, or set on a desktop, and plug into the PS/2 mouse port or into one of the system's serial ports, just as a mouse or trackball does.

Scanners

Scanners convert pictures, line art, photographs, and text into electronic signals that can be processed by software packages such as desktop publishers and graphic design programs.

Scanners

These programs, in turn, can display the image on the video display or can print it out on a graphics printer.

Scanners basically come in two types: **handheld scanners** and **flatbed scanners**. Handheld scanners tend to be less expensive than flatbed scanners due to less-complex mechanics. However, handheld scanners also tend to produce lower-quality images than flatbed scanners. These types normally require two passes to scan an entire page-sized image, but flatbed scanners can pick up the complete image in one pass. The handheld scanner can be used to scan images from large documents or from irregular surfaces, but they depend on the steadiness of the user for their accuracy.

handheld scanners

flatbed scanners

Scanners may also be classified by the types of images they can reproduce. Some scanners can differentiate only between different levels of light and dark. These scanners are called **grayscale scanners**. **Color scanners**, on the other hand, include additional hardware that helps them distinguish among different colors.

grayscale scanners

Color scanners

Handheld Scanners

The handheld scanner depicted in Figure 3-38 operates by being pulled across an image. The user begins the scanning process by pressing the Scan button and then moving the scanner body across the image. An LED in the scanner projects light on the image as the scanner moves. As the light passes over darker and lighter areas of the page, varying levels of light are reflected back to a focusing lens.

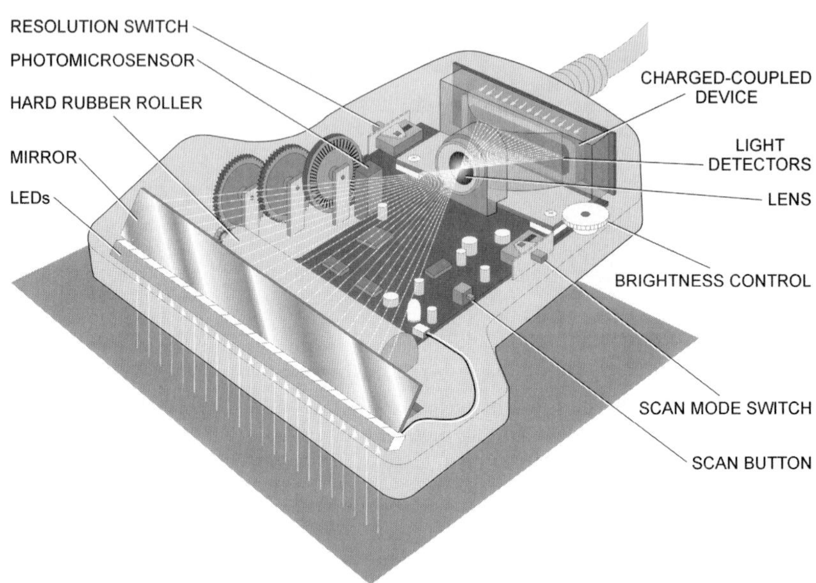

Figure 3-38: Inside a Handheld Scanner

charge-coupled device (CCD)

The lens focuses the reflected light stream onto a **charge-coupled device (CCD)**, which converts the intensity of the light into a proportional voltage signal. The CCD is the same type of device used in the lens of a typical handheld video recorder. The voltage level produced corresponds to black, gray, and white light levels.

The color of the light source used in the scanner also affects how the human eye perceives the output. When scans of color material are made, the color of the scanning light used may not produce brightness levels compatible with how the human eye perceives it. This is true in both color and grayscale output. The two most common scanner light source colors are red and green. The green light produces output that looks much closer to the way the eye perceives it than the red light can. For line art and text scans, the color of the light source is not important.

As the scanner moves across the surface, a wide rubber roller turns a series of gears, which in turn rotate a perforated disk. A light shines through the slots in the disk as it turns and strikes an optical sensor on the other side of the disk. This arrangement produces pulses as the spokes interrupt the light stream. The pulses are used to coordinate the transmission of the digitized image values with the movement of the scanner. Each time a line of image data is transmitted to the adapter card, the scanner's buffer is cleared and it begins gathering a new line of image data. Figure 3-39 illustrates how the scanner's mechanical parts are used to coordinate the process of gathering and transmitting images.

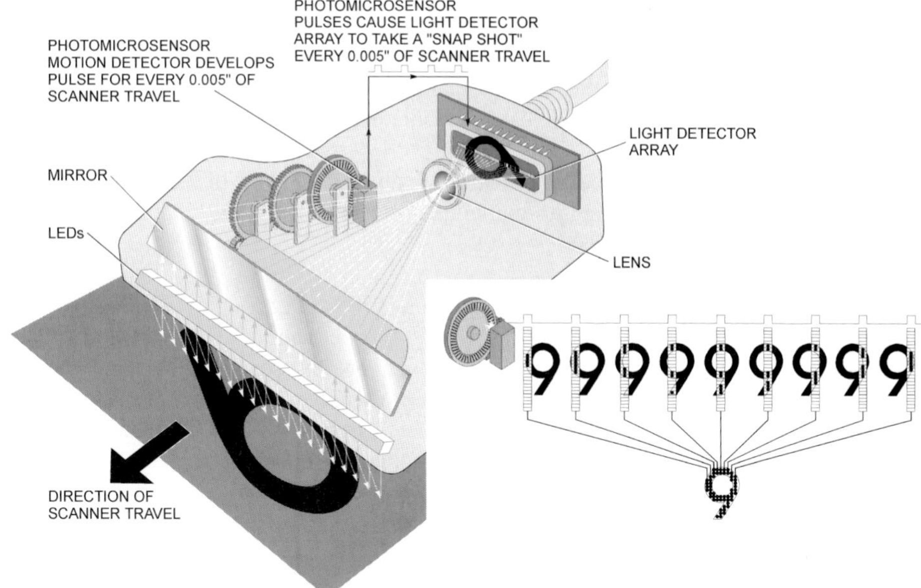

Figure 3-39: The Scanner's Mechanical Structure

The software included with most scanners provides the user with at least a limited capability to manipulate the image after it has been scanned. Because of the limited width of most hand scanners, the software also provides for integrating two consecutive scans to form a complete picture.

Older hand scanners provided scanning resolutions up to 300 **dots per inch (dpi)**. Common scanning resolutions are 600 dpi and 1,200 dpi. Newer color hand scanners can produce 24-bit, high-resolution (3,200 dpi) image editing with 16 million colors.

dots per inch (dpi)

Flatbed Scanners

Flatbed scanners differ from handheld units in a couple of areas. First, the scanner body remains stationary in a flatbed scanner as a scan head moves past the paper. Figure 3-40 describes this process. The paper is placed face down on the scanner's glass window. The light source from the scanning mechanism is projected up through the glass and onto the paper. The lighter areas of the page reflect more light than the darker areas do.

A precision positioning motor moves the scan head below the paper. As the head moves, light reflected from the paper is captured and channeled through a series of mirrors. The mirrors pivot to continually focus the reflected light on a light-sensitive diode. The diode converts the reflected light intensity into a corresponding digital value.

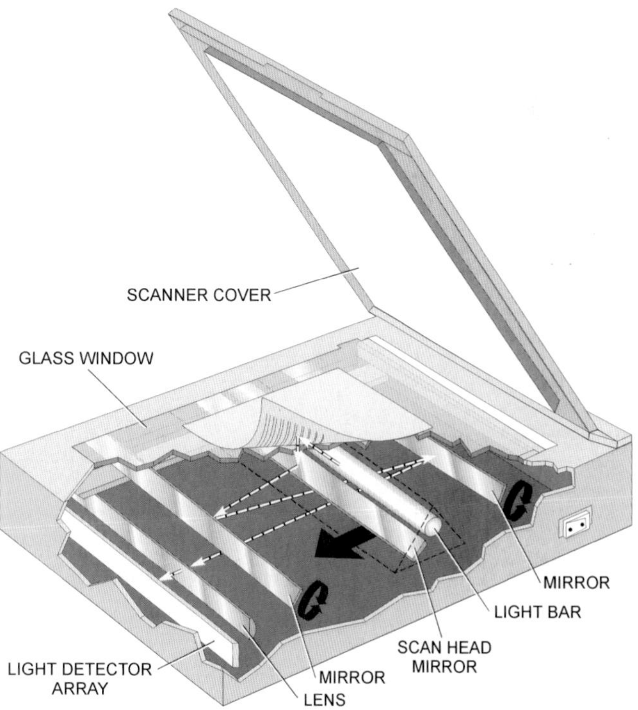

Figure 3-40: A Flatbed Scanner

A normal scanner resolution is 300 dots (or pixels) per inch. Newer flatbed scanners can achieve resolutions up to 4,800 dpi. At these resolutions, each dot corresponds to about 1/90,000 of an inch. The higher the selected scanning resolution, the slower the computer and printer operate, because of the increased amount of data that must be processed.

The digitized information is routed to the scanner adapter card in one of the PC's expansion slots. In main memory, the graphic information is stored in a format that can be manipulated by graphic design software.

Grayscale scanners can differentiate between varying levels of gray on the page. This capability is stated in shades. A good-quality grayscale scanner can differentiate between 256 levels of gray. Color scanners, on the other hand, use three passes to scan an image. Each scan passes the light through a different color filter to separate the colors from each other. The red, blue, and green filters create three different electronic images that can be integrated to form a complete picture. For intermediate colors, varying levels of the three colors are blended to create the desired shade. Figure 3-41 illustrates this concept.

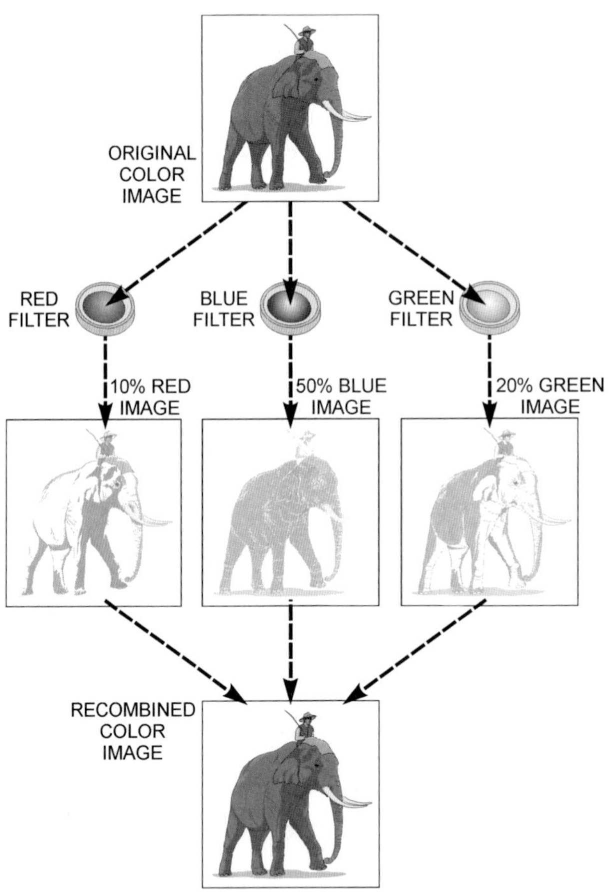

Figure 3-41: Color Filters

As with the handheld scanners, many flatbed scanners use a proprietary adapter card and cable to communicate with the system. However, a number of SCSI-interfaced scanners are available. One of the most common problems with installing scanners involves finding a vacant expansion slot for the adapter card. This is particularly true with Pentium boards that use a mixture of ISA and local bus slots. To overcome this problem, scanners are now being produced that operate through the system's parallel printer port. In these units, the printer plugs into the scanner, which, in turn, connects to the port. In older PC and XT units the limited number of available interrupt request lines often became a problem.

Output Devices

Common output devices are depicted in Figure 3-42. The most widely used output device for personal computers is the **Cathode-Ray Tube (CRT)** video display monitor. The most widely used display device for current PCs is the **Video Graphics Array (VGA)** color monitor. The monitor's signal cable connects to a 15-pin D-shell connector at the back of the system unit. After the monitor, the next most often added output device is the character printer. These peripherals are used to produce hard copy output on paper. They convert text and graphical data from the computer into print on a page.

Cathode-Ray Tube (CRT)

Video Graphics Array (VGA)

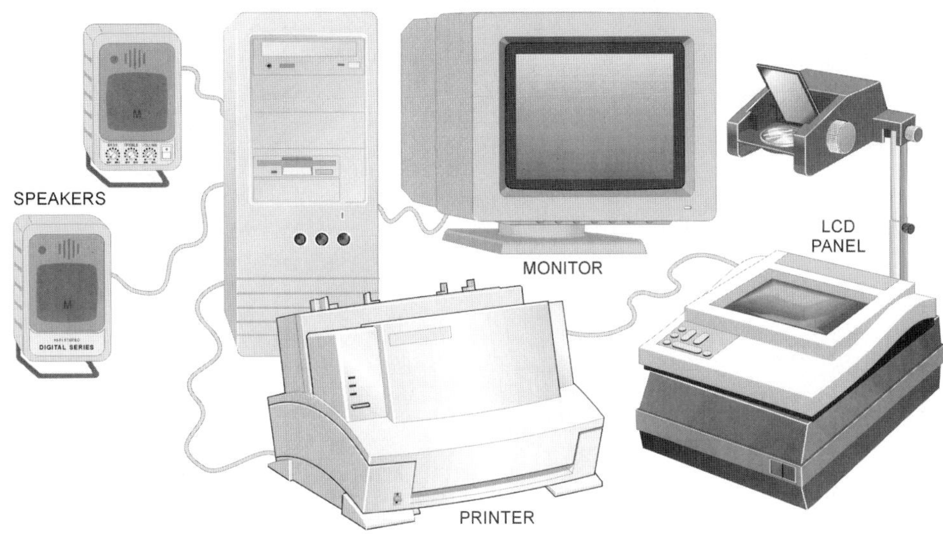

Figure 3-42: Typical Output Devices

Video Displays

The video monitor has long been one of the most popular methods of displaying computer data. At the heart of the monitor is the cathode ray tube (CRT), familiar to us from the television receivers we have in our homes. As a matter of fact, the early personal computers used televisions as video units. The basic difference between the television and a monitor is that no radio-frequency demodulation electronics are used in the video monitor.

As an output device, the monitor can be used to display alphanumeric characters and graphic images. Two possible methods are used to create these displays: the raster scan method and the X-Y, or vector scan, method. All television sets ,and most video displays, are of the raster scan type, so this is the type on which this text focuses. An oscilloscope display is a prime example of vector scanning.

Desktop and tower computers normally employ a color CRT display monitor, similar to the one shown in Figure 3-43, as standard video output equipment. The PC and PC/XT and PC-AT often used monochrome (single-color) monitors. They could also use color monitors by simply adding a color video adapter card and monitor. The color CRT monitor is sometimes referred to as an RGB monitor, since the three primary colors that make a color CRT are red, green, and blue.

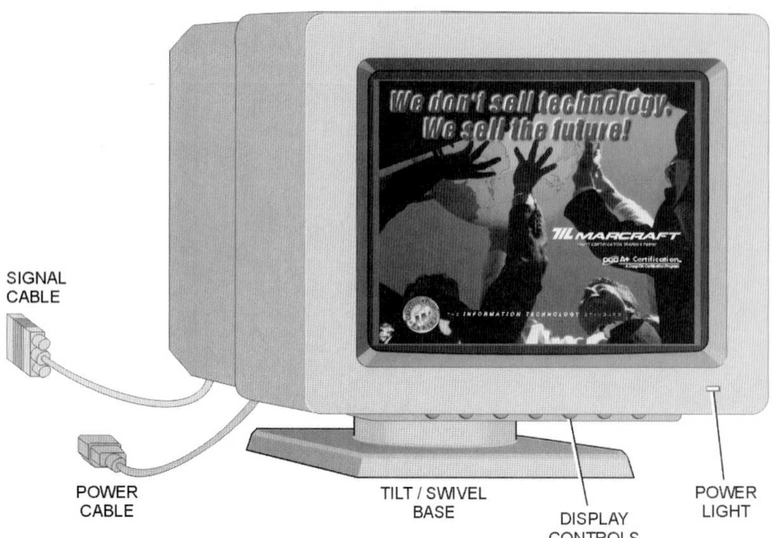

Figure 3-43: The CRT Display Monitor

The popularity of portable computers has created a large market for lightweight display devices. The main devices used in this market are the Liquid Crystal Display (LCD) displays. These devices do not use a CRT tube or its supporting circuitry, so the weight associated with the CRT and its high-voltage components is not present. The flat-panel nature of these devices also works well in the portable computer due to its reduced size. LCDs are covered in detail in Chapter 7—*Portable Systems*.

Basic CRT Display Operations

electron gun

A CRT is an evacuated glass tube with an **electron gun** in its neck, and a fluorescent coated surface opposite the electron gun. A typical CRT is depicted in Figure 3-44. When activated, the electron gun emits a stream of electrons that strike the fluorescent coating on the inside of the screen, causing an illuminated dot to be produced.

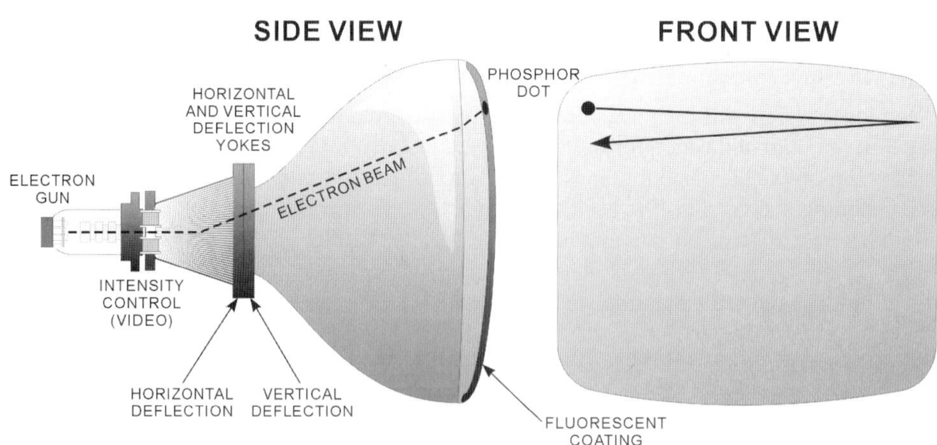

Figure 3-44: A Cathode Ray Tube

The sweeping electron beam begins at the upper left-hand corner of the screen, and moves across its face to the upper right-hand corner, leaving a line across the screen. This is called a **raster line**. Upon reaching the right side of the screen, the trace is blanked out, and the electron beam is repositioned to the left side of the screen, one line below from the first trace in an operation called the **horizontal retrace**. At this point, the horizontal sweep begins producing the second display line on the screen. The scanning continues until the horizontal sweep reaches the bottom of the screen, as shown in Figure 3-45. At that point, the electron beam is blanked again and returned to the upper-left corner of the screen in a move referred to as the **vertical retrace**, completing one **field**.

raster line

horizontal retrace

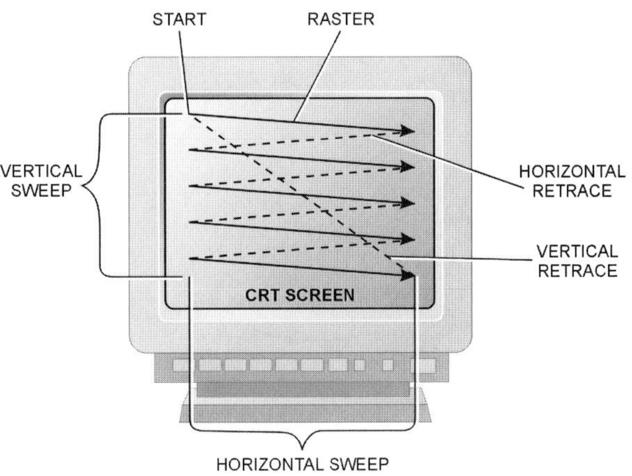

Figure 3-45: Raster Scan Video

vertical retrace

field

persistence

As the beam moves across the screen, it leaves an illuminated trace, which requires a given amount of time to dissipate. The amount of time depends on the characteristics of the fluorescent coating and is referred to as **persistence**. Video information is introduced to the picture by varying the voltage applied to the electron gun as it scans the screen. The human eye perceives only the picture due to the blanking of the retrace lines, and the frequency at which the entire process is performed.

Cathode-Ray Tube Controller (CRTC)

The video adapter's **Cathode-Ray Tube Controller** (**CRTC**) circuitry develops the video signals, and the horizontal (HSYNC) and vertical (VSYNC) synchronization signals for the CRT. Typically, a horizontal sweep requires about 63 microseconds to complete, while a complete field requires approximately 1/60 of a second, or 1/30 of a second per frame.

National Television Standards Committee (NTSC)

interlaced scanning

non-interlaced scanning

The **National Television Standards Committee** (**NTSC**) specifies 525 lines per frame, composed of two fields of 262.5 lines, for television pictures. The two fields, one containing the even-numbered lines, and the other containing the odd-numbered lines, are interlaced to produce smooth, flicker-less images. This method of creating display images is referred to as **interlaced scanning**, and is primarily used with television. Most computer monitors use **Non-Interlaced Scanning** methods.

In text mode operations, the most common monitor arrangement calls for 25 lines of text, with 80 characters per line. This requires that the top row of up to 80 character blocks be serialized during the first horizontal trace of the CRT. Afterwards, the second line of 80 character blocks is serialized for the second horizontal trace. This serialization is repeated until all the horizontal traces have been made.

flicker

screen memory

After a line, or a page, of text has been displayed on the screen, it must be rewritten periodically to prevent it from fading away. In order for the rewrite to be performed fast enough to avoid display **flicker**, the contents of the display are stored in a special memory, called the **screen memory**. This memory is typically located on the video adapter card. However, some newer systems use sections of the system's on-board memory for the video screen memory function. In our example of 25 lines of text at 80 characters per line, the memory must be able to hold at least 2000 bytes of screen data for a single display.

The 80 x 25 format listed above is for alphanumeric text mode. When the adapter is in text mode, it will typically require at least two bytes of screen memory for each character position on the screen. The first byte is for the ASCII code of the character itself while the second byte is used to specify the screen attributes of the character and its cell. Under this scenario, the screen memory must be capable of holding at least 4000 bytes. The attribute byte specifies how the character is to be displayed. Common attributes include underlining, blinking, and the color of a text character for the color displays.

Color Monitors

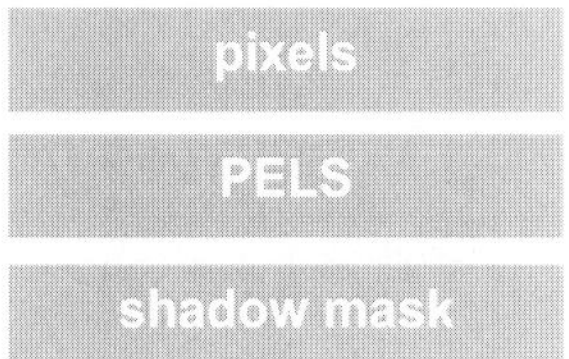

The monitor we have been discussing so far is referred to as a monochrome monitor, because it is capable of displaying only shades of a single phosphor color. A color monitor, on the other hand, employs a combination of three, color phosphors, red, blue, and green, arranged in adjacent trios of dots or bars, called **pixels** or **PELS**. By using a different electron gun for each element of the trio, the individual elements can be made to glow at different levels to produce almost any color desired. The electron guns scan the front of a screen in unison, in the same fashion as described earlier for a monochrome CRT. Color CRTs add a metal grid in front of the phosphor coating called a **shadow mask**. It ensures that an electron gun assigned to one color doesn't strike a dot of another color. The basic construction of a color CRT is shown in Figure 3-46.

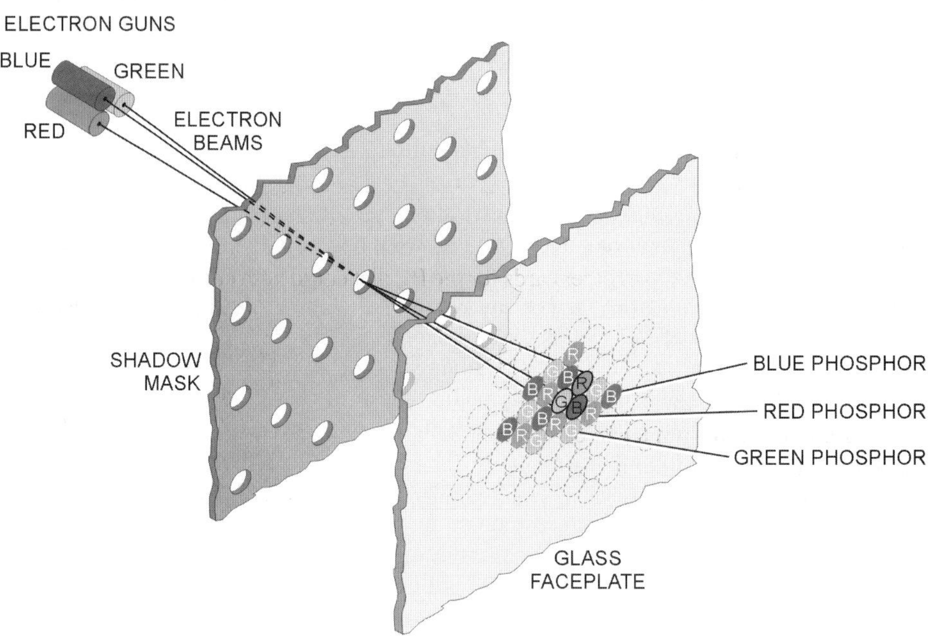

Figure 3-46: A Color CRT Construction

Screen Resolution

The quality of the image produced on the screen is a function of two factors, the speed at which the image is retraced on the screen, and the number of pixels on the screen. The more pixels on a given screen size, the higher the image quality. This quantity is called resolution, and is often expressed in an X-by-Y format. Using this format, the quality of the image is still determined by how big the viewing area is (i.e., an 800 x 600 resolution on a 14-inch monitor will produce much better quality than the same number of pixels spread across a 27-inch monitor).

Resolution

dot pitch

Resolution can be expressed as a function of how close pixels can be grouped together on the screen. This form of resolution is expressed in terms of **dot pitch**. A monitor with a .28 dot pitch has pixels that are located .28mm apart. In monochrome monitors, dot pitch is measured from center to center of each pixel. In a color monitor, the pitch is measured from the center of one dot trio to the center of the next trio.

TEST TIP

Be able to explain the definition of dot pitch.

For more in-depth information about how monitors work, refer to the Electronic Reference Shelf located on the CD that accompanies this book.

REFERENCE SHELF

Sound Cards

The sound-producing capabilities of early PCs were practically non-existent. They included a single, small speaker that was used to produce beep-coded error messages. Even though programs could be written to produce a wide array of sounds from this speaker, the quality of the sound was never any better than the limitations imposed by its small size. This led various companies to design audio digitizer cards for the PC that could both convert sound into digital quantities that the computer could manipulate and play back digitized sound produced by the computer. These cards are referred to as **sound cards**.

sound cards

A typical audio digitizer system is depicted in Figure 3-47. A microphone converts sound waves from the air into an encoded analog electrical signal. The analog signal is applied to the audio input of the sound card. On the card, the signal is applied to an A/D converter circuit, which changes the signal into corresponding digital values, as described in Figure 3-48.

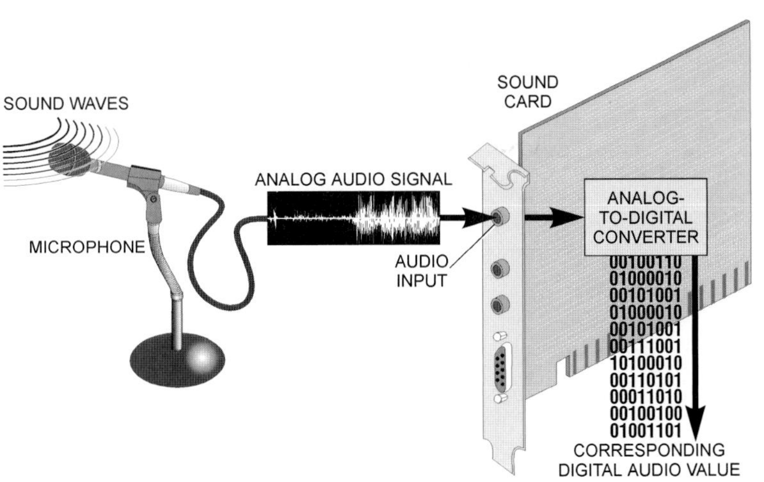

Figure 3-47: A Typical Audio Digitizer System

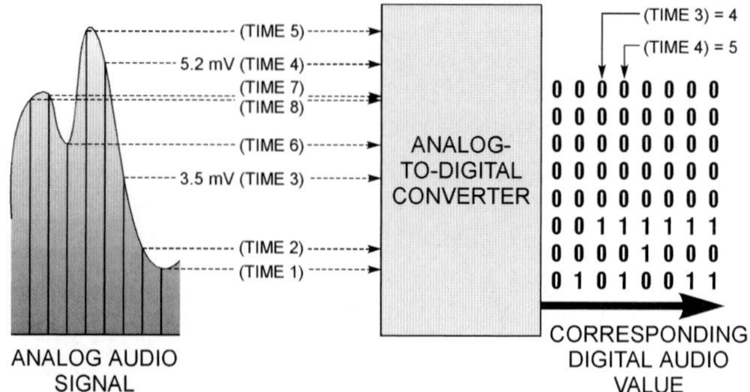

Figure 3-48: Converting Signal Changes to Digital Values

The sound card takes samples of the analog waveform at predetermined intervals, and converts them into corresponding digital values. Therefore, the digital values approximate the instantaneous values of the sound wave.

fidelity

resolution

The **fidelity** (the measure of how closely the original sound can be reproduced) of the digital samples is dependent on two factors: the accuracy of the samples taken, and the rate at which the samples are taken. The accuracy of the sample is determined by the **resolution** capabilities of the A/D converter. Resolution is the capability to differentiate between values. If the value of the analog waveform is 15.55 microvolts at a given point, how closely can that value be approximated with a digital value?

Resolution of an A/D converter is determined by the number of digital output bits it can produce. For example, an 8-bit A/D converter can represent up to 256 (2^8) different values. On the other hand, a 16-bit A/D converter can represent up to 65,536 (2^{16}) different amplitudes. The more often the samples are taken, the more accurately the original waveform can be reproduced.

Playback of the digitized audio signal is accomplished by applying the digital signals to a D/A converter at the same rate the samples were taken. When the audio files are called for, the sound card's software driver sends commands to the audio output controller on the sound card. The digitized samples are applied to the audio output IC, and converted back into the analog signal.

The analog signal is applied to an audio preamplifier that boosts the power of the signal, and sends it to an RCA, or mini jack. This signal is still too weak to drive conventional speakers. However, it can be applied to an additional amplifier, or to a set of speakers that have an additional amplifier built into them.

A CD-quality audio signal requires a minimum of 16-bit samples, taken at approximately 44 kHz. If you calculate the disk space required to store all of the 16-bit samples collected in one minute of audio at this rate, the major consideration factor associated with using digitized audio becomes clear (16 x 44,000 x 60 x 8 = 5.28 MB). If you want stereo sound, this will double to a whopping 10.56 MB. Therefore, CD-quality audio is not commonly used in multimedia productions. The audio sampling rate used in multimedia titles is generally determined by the producer. Another alternative is to limit the digitized audio used in a product to short clips.

INSTALLING AND CONFIGURING PERIPHERAL DEVICES

The A+ Core Hardware objective 1.7 states that the test taker should be able to identify proper procedures for installing and configuring peripheral devices. Topics include:

- Monitor/video card
- Modem
- Storage devices

While the A+ objective mentions three different types of peripherals that technicians must know how to install, there are many different devices that can be installed in a PC system. In this text, we have decided to cover the installation of these devices along with the other information about them. The procedures for installing storage devices are presented in Chapter 4—*Mass Storage Systems*. Likewise, modems are covered in Chapter 5—*Data Communications*. Therefore, the installation processes involved in these devices are covered in those chapters.

Video/Monitor Systems

The video display system is one of the easiest systems to add to the computer. The components associated with the video display are depicted in Figure 3-49. The video adapter card typically plugs into one of the system's expansion slots. The monitor's signal cable plugs into the video adapter card. The monitor's power cable may be plugged into a commercial wall outlet, or it may be attached to the special power outlet provided by an AT-class power supply unit. Using this outlet enables the monitor to be turned on and off along with the system unit.

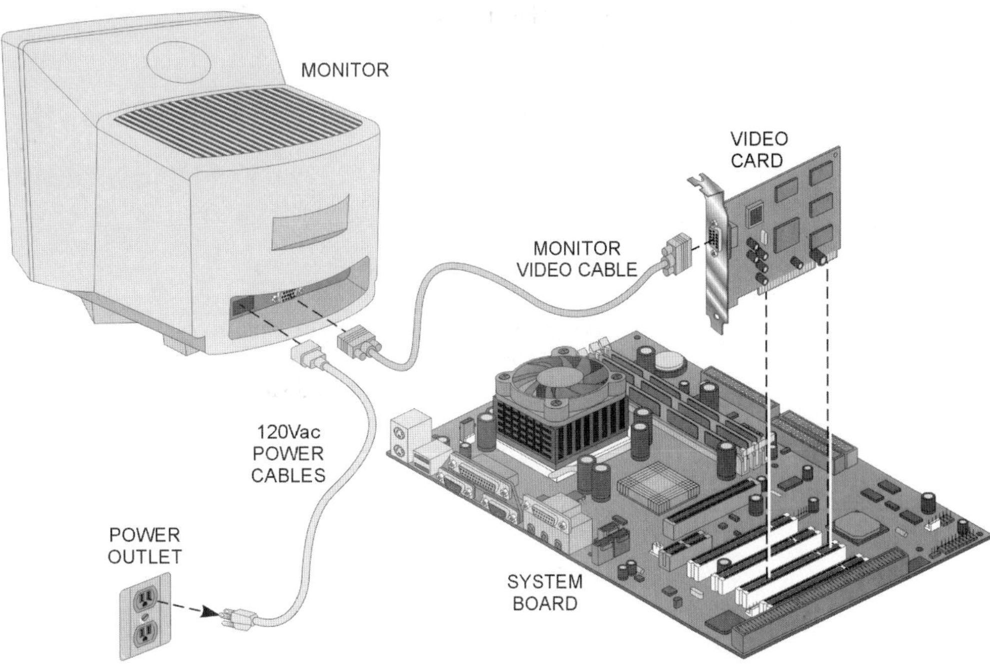

Figure 3-49: Video System Components

After the video card has been installed and the monitor has been connected to the video card and plugged into the power outlet, it will be necessary to install the correct drivers for the video card. The Windows 9x operating systems should detect the video card, start the system with basic VGA video drivers, and ask you if you want to install the manufacturer's video drivers. The Windows 2000 operating system is even more proactive. It will detect the new video card, tell you that it has found the new card, and then automatically load its video drivers. The only time that you should need to be directly involved with the system's video drivers is when PnP fails or the video card is not recognized by the operating system.

Installing Other Peripherals

The typical PC features built-in logic and physical connection support for the standard PC peripherals. The system board provides the controllers and connectors for the system's hard- and floppy disk drives. It also furnishes the standard keyboard (and possibly the mouse) connection. As we have seen, newer systems provide industry standard parallel- and serial-port connections, and may supply a game port connector.

In addition to installing hard drives and peripheral devices that connect to standard I/O ports, technicians must be able to successfully install and configure peripheral devices (or systems) that connect to the system in other ways—such as through the system's expansion slots. The steps for installing these types of peripherals and systems are generally very similar from device to device:

1. Remove the system unit's cover and take out an expansion slot cover.
2. Check the adapter card's user's manual for any manual configuration information and set the card up as required.
3. Insert the card into the empty expansion slot.
4. Connect any necessary cabling to the adapter card.
5. Connect any external power supply connections to the peripheral device.
6. Start the machine. The Windows operating system should detect the new device if it is PnP-compatible. If not, you will need to load drivers for the device from its installation media (disk or CD).
7. Shut down the system, turn it off, and reinstall the system unit's outer cover.

This process can be used to install diverse I/O devices such as modems and LAN adapters, as well as scanners and other devices that use options adapter cards in expansion slots. However, for many devices, the advent of newer hot-swap I/O buses, such as USB and Firewire, has reduced this process to simply connecting the device to the bus.

CHAPTER SUMMARY

The first half of this chapter has examined standard I/O port assignments in a PC-compatible system. At this point, you should be able to identify the type of port being used from a description of its structure. In addition, you should be able to use the troubleshooting information provided for each port type to isolate and correct typical port problems in a PC-compatible system.

The second half of the chapter dealt with common I/O devices used with PCs. You should be able to describe the operation of each type of input and output device. You should also be able to list the types of devices that are normally associated with each I/O port type. As with the I/O ports in the first half of the chapter, you should be able to use the troubleshooting information provided for each input device to isolate and correct problems typically associated with that device.

At this point, review the objectives listed at the beginning of the chapter to be certain that you understand and can perform each item listed there.

KEY POINTS REVIEW

The first half of this chapter examined standard I/O port assignments in a PC-compatible system. The second half of the chapter dealt with common input/output devices used with purchase. Review the following key points before moving into the Review and Exam Questions sections to make sure you are comfortable with each point. Afterward, answer the Review Questions that follow to verify your knowledge of the information.

- In addition to the millions of possible memory locations in a PC, there are typically thousands of addresses set aside for input and output devices in a system. In order for any device to operate with the system's microprocessor, it must have an address (or group of addresses) where the system can find it.

- Interface circuits are necessary because the characteristics of most peripherals differ greatly from those of the basic computer. Most interface circuits in the PC-compatible world have been integrated into application-specific ICs.

- When dealing with a PC-compatible, there are two forms of I/O to contend with. These include the system board's on-board I/O, and peripheral devices that interact with the system through its expansion slots.

- Parallel ports have been a staple of the PC system since the original PCs were introduced. They are most widely used to connect printers to the computer.

- A typical parallel printer connection, using the IBM version of the Centronics standard, allows the computer to pass information to the printer, 8 bits at a time, across the 8 data lines. The other lines in the connection carry control signals (handshaking signals) back and forth between the computer and the printer.

- Microsoft operating systems keep track of the system's installed printer ports by assigning them the logical device names (handles) LPT1, LPT2, and LPT3. Whenever the system is booted up, DOS searches the hardware for parallel ports installed at hex addresses 3BCh, 378h, and 278h consecutively.

- Although the data pins of the parallel printer port are defined as output pins, the figure illustrates that they are actually bi-directional. However, some less-expensive ports may not have the electronics built into them to handle the input function. This is not important for most printer operations, so many users won't notice.

- As the distance between the computer and a peripheral reaches a certain point (10 feet), it becomes less practical to send data as parallel words. An alternative method of sending data is to break the parallel words into their individual bits, and transmit them, one at a time, in a serial bit stream over a single conductor.

- Two methods are used to provide the proper timing for serial transfers: The data bits may be sent synchronously (in conjunction with a synchronizing clock pulse), or asynchronously (without an accompanying clock pulse).

- As with parallel ports, DOS assigns COM port designations to the system's serial ports during bootup. COM port designations are normally COM1 and COM2 in most systems, but they can be extended to COM3 and COM4 in advanced systems.

- Peripherals are devices and systems that are added to the basic system to extend its capabilities. These devices and systems can be divided into three general categories: input systems, output systems, and memory systems.

REVIEW QUESTIONS

The following questions test your knowledge of the material presented in this chapter.

1. What is the maximum recommended length of a standard parallel printer cable?
2. Describe the standard system resources allocated to the LPT1 port in a PC.
3. Describe the standard system resources allocated to the COM1 serial port in a PC.
4. Describe the types of connectors on the back of a PC that a serial mouse might plug into (describe 2).
5. What type of I/O device is normally found at location 3F8?
6. What is the function of a shadow mask in a CRT display?
7. Define the term dot-pitch as it applies to monitors.
8. Which IRQ is normally used for a modem attached to the system's COM2 port?
9. How many USB devices can be attached to a USB root hub?
10. What is the maximum recommended distance for an IrDA link?

11. State the maximum segment lengths for low and high speed USB connections.
12. Describe the mechanical operation of an opto-mechanical mouse.
13. What advantage does a trackball have over a mouse? In what type of application is this useful?
14. In an ATX system, which back panel connections are likely to get confused?
15. Where is the EPP mode enabled in an ATX system?

EXAM QUESTIONS

1. What type of integrated circuits are normally found in a PC-compatible keyboard?
   a. The keyboard buffer IC
   b. The keyboard encoder IC
   c. The keyboard output port IC
   d. The keyboard controller IC
2. Identify the maximum recommended length of an RS-232C serial cable.
   a. 10 ft
   b. 25 ft
   c. 50 ft
   d. 100 ft
3. What type of connector is normally found on PC-compatible keyboards?
   a. A 6-pin mini-DIN connector
   b. A 5-pin DIN connector
   c. An RJ-11 connector
   d. An RJ-45 connector
4. What portion of the system board is dedicated to the operation of the keyboard?
   a. The keyboard encoder IC
   b. The keyboard buffer IC
   c. The keyboard controller IC
   d. The keyboard output port IC
5. Which port type employs DMA transfers for high speed operation?
   a. SPP
   b. EPP
   c. ECP
   d. IrDA

6. What is the standard PC address given to a second parallel printer port?
   a. 378
   b. 3F8
   c. 278
   d. OFF
7. What type of device is normally associated with a 15-pin, male D-shell connector?
   a. A mouse
   b. A trackball
   c. A keypad
   d. A joystick
8. What type of device is a mouse?
   a. An I/O device
   b. An output device
   c. A pointing device
   d. A cursor-positioning device
9. Which DMA channel is used in a standard PC?
   a. 6 for the FDD
   b. 2 for the FDD
   c. 3 for the EPP
   d. 1 for the keyboard
10. Choose the event that will cause an NMI error to occur.
    a. Adapter card error
    b. Hard drive failure
    c. Power failure
    d. User error

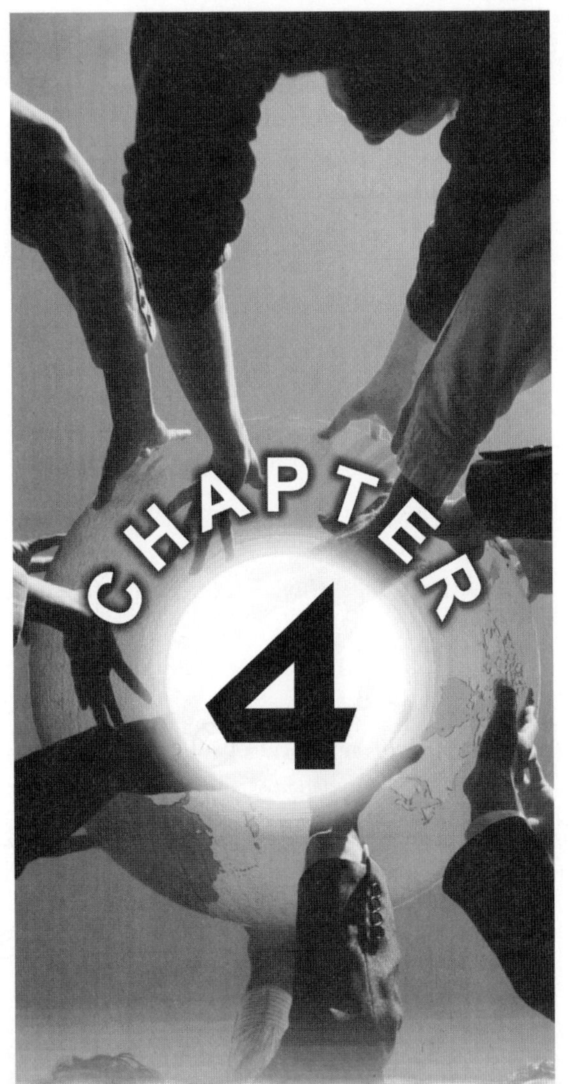

MASS STORAGE SYSTEMS

OBJECTIVES

OBJECTIVES

Upon completion of this chapter and its related Lab Procedures, you should be able to:

1. Differentiate between different types of hard- and floppy-disk drive types.
2. State reasons for the popularity of magnetic disks as computer data storage systems.
3. Describe the format or organization of a typical hard or floppy disk.
4. Identify the major physical blocks of the disk drive unit.
5. Explain why the DOS software is so important to the operation of a disk drive.
6. Differentiate between common connecting cables (i.e., SCSI, IDE, FDD).
7. Discuss the different RAID advisory levels and apply them to given applications.
8. Install IDE and EIDE devices, including setting Master/Slave/Single designations.
9. Install and configure single and complex SCSI device chains.
10. Establish proper addressing and termination for SCSI devices to avoid conflicts and problems.
11. Describe the operation of a Writable CD drive.
12. Differentiate between different types of CDs.
13. Install and configure a CD-ROM drive for operation.

CHAPTER 4

MASS STORAGE SYSTEMS

INTRODUCTION

Nearly every microcomputer includes some type of mass information storage system that allows it to store data or programs for an extended period of time. Unlike primary memory devices, which are fast and have a relatively low storage capacity, mass storage systems are usually slower, and possess much larger storage potential. These systems are an acceptable alternative to the IC RAM and ROM devices used on system and video cards. Like the ROM devices, these systems must be able to hold information even when the computer is turned off. On the other hand, they are like RAM devices in that their information can be updated and changed often.

The most widely used mass storage systems have typically involved covering some medium with a magnetic coating. However, optical storage technologies such as compact discs and DVDs, have made great inroads into the digital data storage market.

STORAGE DEVICES

The problem with electronic devices is that programs and data disappear from the system's memory when the device is turned off, or loses power. In addition, the costs associated with IC RAM devices tend to be too expensive to construct large memories that can hold multiple programs and large amounts of data. Therefore, storage systems that can be used for long-term data storage are desirable as a second level of memory.

With this in mind, a number of secondary memory technologies have been developed to extend the computer's memory capabilities and store data on a more permanent basis. These systems tend to be too slow to be used directly with the computer's microprocessor. The secondary memory unit holds the information and transfers it in batches to the computer's faster internal memory when requested.

Magnetic Storage

From the early days of digital computers, most secondary memory systems have involved storing binary information in the form of magnetic charges on moving magnetic surfaces.

These include flexible Mylar diskettes (called floppy disks), rigid aluminum hard disks, and various widths of flexible Mylar tape, as illustrated in Figure 4-1. The information to be stored on the medium is converted into electromagnetic pulses, which in turn are used to create tiny positive and negative magnetized spots on the magnetic surface. To retrieve, or read, the information back from the surface, the storage system needs only to detect the spots and decode them. The stored information can be changed at any time by remagnetizing the surface with the new information.

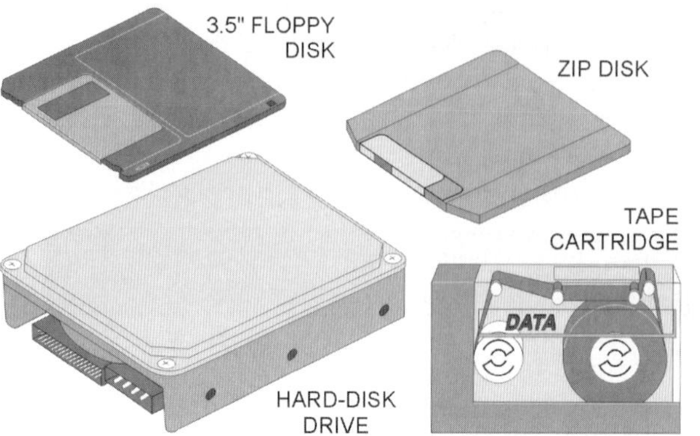

Figure 4-1: Typical Magnetic Storage Systems

Magnetic Disk Drives

tracks

sectors

Magnetic disks resemble grooveless phonograph records, and fall into two general categories: high-speed hard disks, and slower flexible diskettes. Data bits are recorded serially in concentric circles, called **tracks**, around the disk. Since the tracks toward the outer edge of the disk are longer than the inner tracks, all tracks are divided into an equal number of equal-size data blocks called **sectors**. Therefore, each block of data has an address, which is the combination of its track number and its sector number. Since each sector can be accessed for a read or write operation as fast as any other sector on the disk, disk memories are classified as Direct Access Memory.

cylinder

The tracks of the disk are numbered, beginning with 00, from the outer edge of the disk, inward. Each side of the disk may hold 80 or more tracks, depending on the type of disk and the drive being used. When disks are stacked, such as in a hard disk drive, all of the tracks having the same number are referred to collectively as a **cylinder**. The number of sectors on each track runs between 8 and 50, also depending on the disk and drive type.

soft sectoring

In floppy and hard disk systems, track and sector address information is contained in a track/sector identification code recorded on the disk. This method of address specification is known as **soft sectoring**, because the sector information is written in software. Figure 4-2 depicts a typical soft-sectored track and sector arrangement. PC-compatible systems use soft-sectored disks.

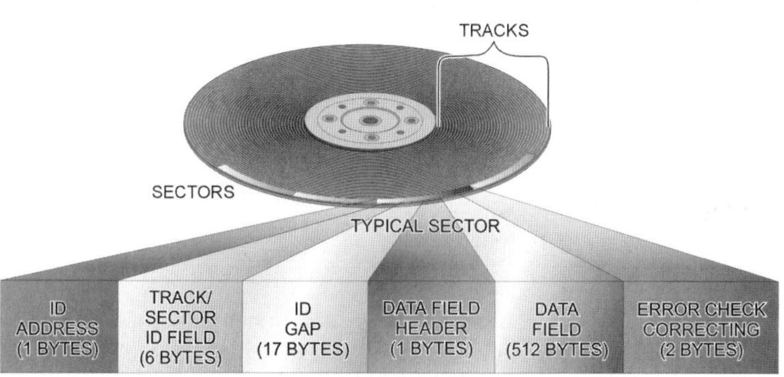

Figure 4-2: Disk Tracks and Sectors

Each sector is separated from the previous and following sectors by a small gap of unrecorded space. A typical sector contains 256 (2^8) or 512 (2^9) bytes, but on some systems this value may range as low as 128 (2^7) or as high as 1024 (2^{10}) bytes per sector. The most common sector size in the IBM-compatible/Microsoft world is 512 bytes. Within these confines, the sector is segmented, beginning with an ID field header, which tells the controlling circuitry that an ID area containing the physical address information is approaching. A small data field header precedes the actual data field. The data field is followed by a postamble, containing error-checking and correcting codes for the data recorded in the sector.

TEST TIP

Remember the standard sector size of a sector in an IBM compatible system.

In their original conditions, hard disks and soft-sectored diskettes, as well as magnetic tapes, are blank. The system must prepare them to hold data. The system's disk-drive control circuitry accomplishes this by writing track/sector identification and gap locations on the disk, in a process known as **formatting**. This leads to some confusion when disk storage capacity is specified. Capacity may be stated for either formatted or unformatted conditions. Obviously, the capacity of an unformatted disk is greater, because no gap or ID information has been added to the disk.

formatting

Reading and Writing on Magnetic Surfaces

Data is read from, or written to, the disk one sector at a time. In order to perform a read or write operation, the address of the particular track and sector to be accessed is applied to a stepper motor, which moves a **Read/Write (R/W) head** over the desired track. As the desired sector passes beneath the R/W head, the data transfer occurs. Information read from, or to be written to, the disk is usually held in a dedicated part of the computer's RAM memory. The system then accesses the data from this memory location at microprocessor-compatible speeds.

Read/Write (R/W) head

The R/W head consists of a coil of wire wrapped around a soft iron core, as depicted in Figure 4-3. A small air gap in the core rides above the magnetic coating on the disk's surface. Data is written on the disk by applying pulses to the coil, which produces magnetic lines of flux in the soft iron core. At the air gap, the lines of flux dip down into the disk's magnetic coating, due to its low reluctance (compared to the air). This, in turn, causes the magnetic domains in the recording surface to align themselves in a direction dictated by the direction of current flow in the coil. The magnetic domains of the surface can assume one of three possible states depending on the direction of current flow through the R/W head:

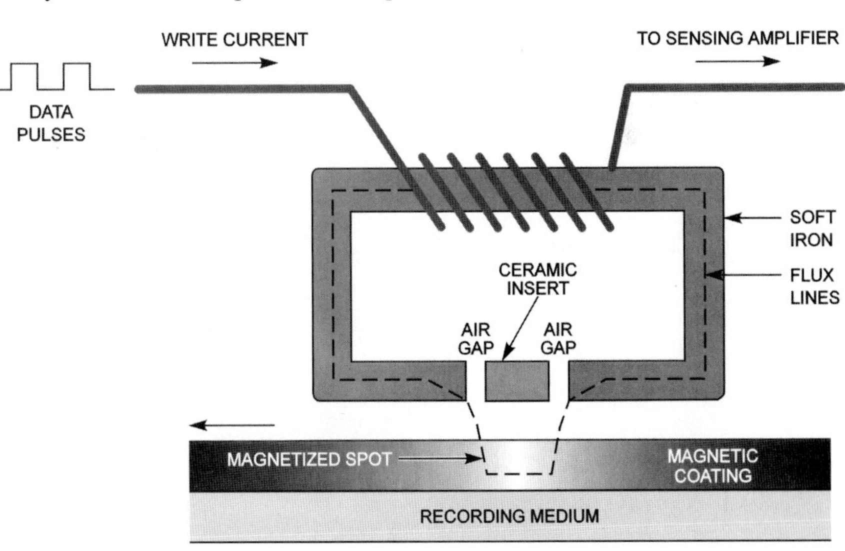

Figure 4-3: A Typical R/W Head

- Unmagnetized (randomly arranged domains)
- Magnetized in a positive direction
- Magnetized in a negative direction

Data is read from the disk in a reversal of this process. As the magnetized spots on the surface pass by the R/W head, changes in magnetic polarity of the spots induce lines of flux into the R/W head's core. This, in turn, induces a small voltage in the R/W head that is sensed and amplified to the proper digital logic levels by the drive's Read circuitry.

Contact vs. Non-Contact Recording

Depending on the nature of the magnetic medium being read from or written to, the R/W head may ride directly on the medium's surface (contact recording), or it may "fly" slightly above it on a thin cushion of air created by the moving surface (non-contact recording). Hard disks, whether fixed or removable, must use flying heads, whereas flexible media (tapes and diskettes) generally use contact recording.

Head-to-Disk Interference (HDI)

head crash

Hard disks use non-contact heads that fly over the medium. The extremely high speed of the medium, and the thin and fragile nature of its magnetic oxide coating, makes almost any contact between the R/W head and the disk surface a cause of considerable damage to both the head and the disk. Such contact is known as **Head-to-Disk Interference (HDI)**, or simply as a **head crash**. Recent advances, such as smaller and lighter R/W heads, and ever-harder damage-resistant disk surfaces, have lowered the possibilities of damaging crashes somewhat. Because the medium is dimensionally stable, and spins at a high rate of speed, the data density associated with hard disks is relatively high.

The flying R/W heads glide over the disks at a height of approximately 50 microinches. This may seem like an unimportant measurement until you consider the size of a common dust particle or a human hair.

This relationship is illustrated in Figure 4-4. If the R/W head should strike one of these contaminants as the disk spins at high speed, the head would be lifted into the air and then crash into the disk surface, damaging the R/W head and/or the disk surface. To avoid this, hard disks are encased in sealed protective housings. It is important to realize that at no time should the disk housing be opened to the atmosphere. Repairs to hard disk drives are performed in special repair facilities having ultra-clean rooms. In these rooms, even particles the size of those described in the figure have been removed from the air.

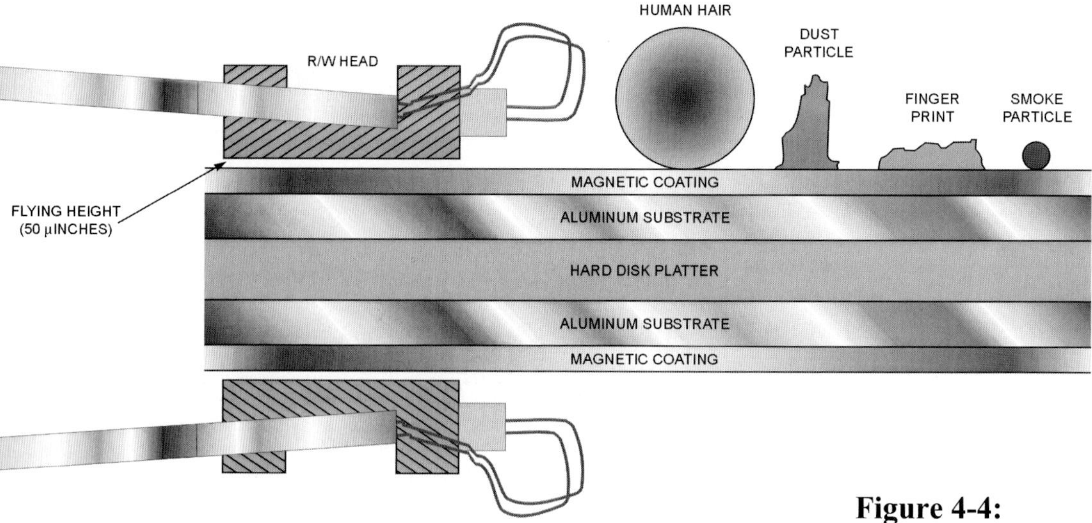

Figure 4-4: Flying R/W Heads

Flexible media such as floppy disks and tape expand and shrink with temperature and humidity variations. This causes the data tracks on the media to migrate in terms of track-location accuracy of the R/W head. To compensate for such shifting, the R/W heads ride directly on the media's surface, the track density is kept low, and the heads are made more complex to create special zones in the track construction, which compensate for some of the misalignment due to shifting.

DISK DRIVE OPERATIONS

The basic organization of both hard and floppy disk drives is similar in many respects. Both have drive spindles, which are actuated by precision synchronous motors, and a set of movable R/W heads that are positioned by a digital stepper motor, or voice coil. In addition, both systems have intelligent control circuitry to position the R/W head and to facilitate the transfer of information between the disk and the computer's memory. Figure 4-5 depicts the major components of a typical disk drive system.

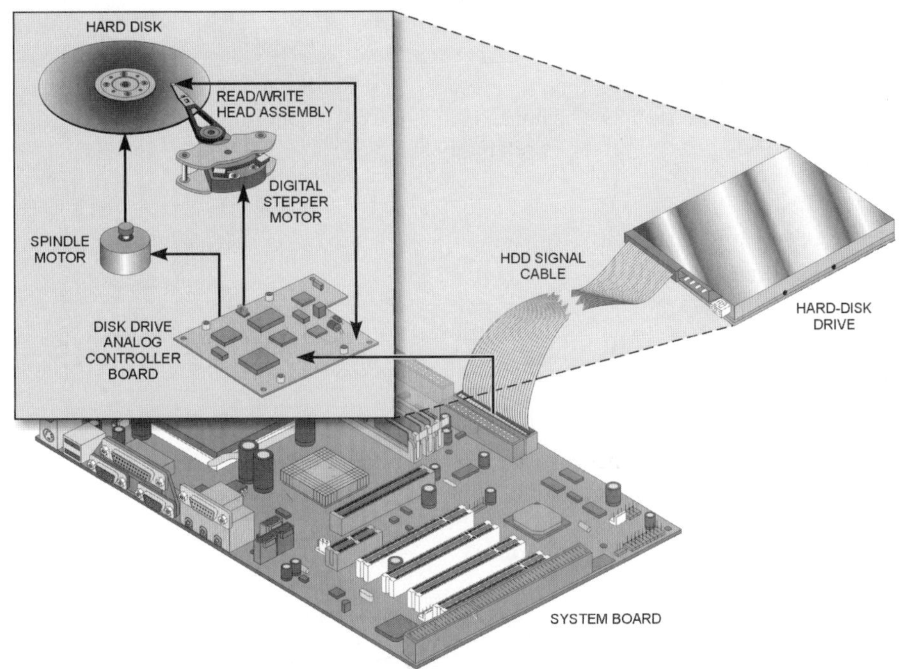

Figure 4-5: Disk Drive Components

The heart of the disk drive's circuitry is the **disk-drive controller**. The controller is responsible for providing the necessary interfacing between the disk drive and the computer's I/O channel. It does this by decoding the computer's instructions to the disk drive, and generating the control signals that the disk drive must have to carry out the instruction. The controller must also convert back and forth between the parallel data format of the computer's bus, and the serial format of the disk drive.

disk-drive controller

In addition, the controller must accurately position the R/W heads, direct the read and write operations, check and correct data received from the processor, generate error-correction codes for outbound data, and mark the location of defective sectors on the disk, closing them to use. After all of these responsibilities, the disk controller must also provide addressing for the tracks and sectors on the disk, and control the transfer of information to and from the internal memory.

Initialization

To transfer a file from the system to the disk (a Write operation), the operating system sends the disk-drive controller a Write command, along with parameters required to carry out the operation. It also specifies the track and sector number where writing will begin. It obtains this information by referring to the disk's file system table (FAT) and locating the address of the next available sector. Figure 4-6 illustrates the type of information used to initialize a disk drive for operation.

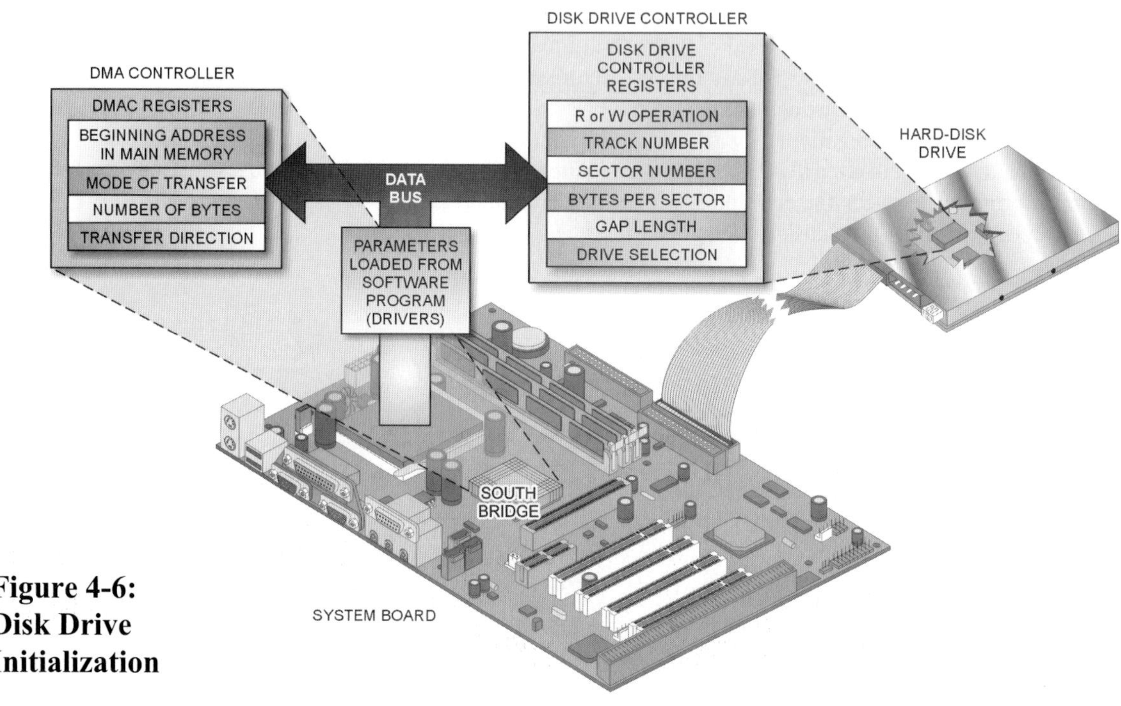

Figure 4-6: Disk Drive Initialization

Track-Seek Operations

track-seek

To position the drive's R/W heads over the desired track, the controller must conduct a **track-seek** operation. In this operation, the controller enables the drive and produces a burst of step pulses to position the R/W head over the proper track. The controller accomplishes this by keeping a record of the current track location of the drive's R/W heads.

direction

step

When the controller receives a Read or Write command from the system, it compares the current location information to the track number specified by the command. The controller decides which direction the head must be moved, issues a direction signal to the drive on its **direction** line, and begins producing step pulses on its **step** line. Each step pulse causes the drive unit to move the R/W heads over one track, in the direction specified by the direction signal. When the value of the present location matches the track number that was specified for the Read or Write operation, the step-pulses stop and the R/W heads settle over the desired track. The positioning of the R/W heads is illustrated in Figure 4-7.

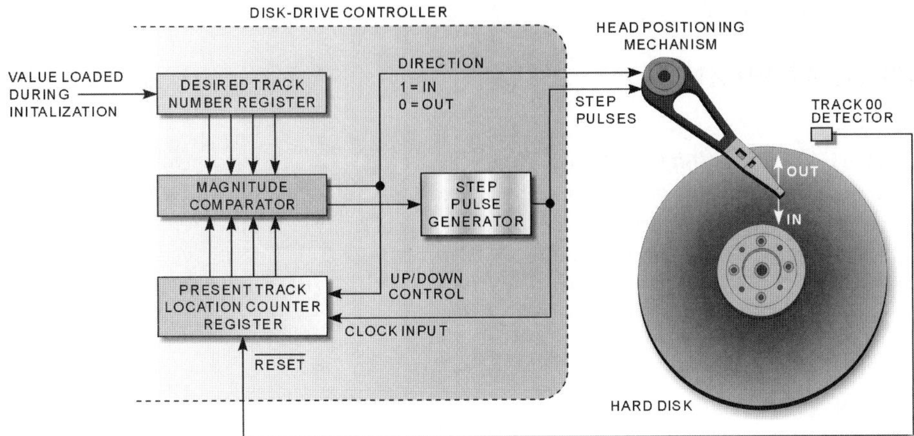

Figure 4-7: A Track-Seek Operation

Write Operations

Write command

When the system wants to send data to the disk drive for storage, it sends a **Write command** to the drive. But first, it performs a lookup operation on the drive's FAT to determine where to store the data. It then performs a track-seek operation to position the R/W heads over the designated track. When the head is over the track, the controller begins looking for the proper sector by reading the sector headers as they pass by. Once the sector is found, the controller changes from Read to Write operation and data serialization/transfer begins.

The drive controller requests a byte of data (DREQ) from the DMA controller, which places the byte on the data bus, and also sends a DACK signal to the disk controller. The disk controller obtains the byte from the data bus, encodes it into the proper form, and applies it to the R/W head, as illustrated in Figure 4-8.

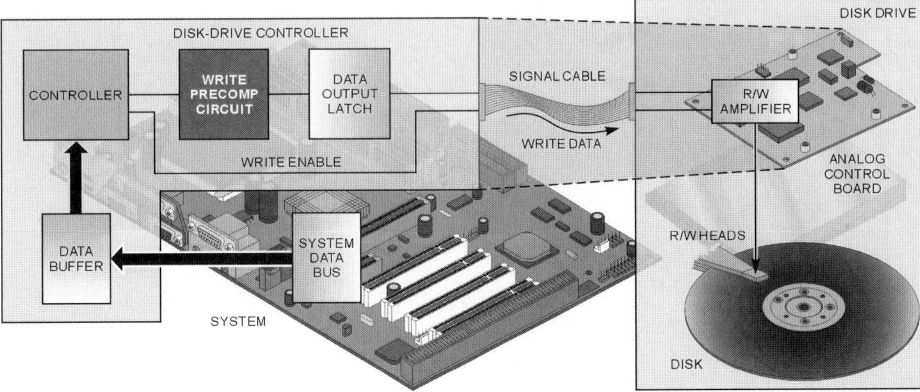

Figure 4-8: Data Transfers

If the data from the computer requires more than one sector to be written, as it usually does, these logically related sectors may not be located sequentially on the disk. When data is transferred a block at a time, some time will be required to process each sector of data. In order to give the drive time to process the information, logically sequential sectors are **interleaved** (separated) by a fixed number of other sectors. This way, the motion of the disk is moving the second sector into position to be written (or read), while the drive is processing the previous sector of information. A common interleaving factor is 8 sectors between logically related sectors on a floppy drive, a factor of 3 on older hard disk systems, and a factor of 1 on newer systems.

interleaved

Read Operations

Read operation

When a **Read operation** is performed, the operating system examines the disk's directory to get the starting track/sector address of the data to be read. This address is loaded into the disk controller and a track-seek operation is performed. The R/W heads are stepped to the desired track and the designated head is enabled. After a few milliseconds delay to permit the R/W head to settle precisely over the track, the operating system gives the disk controller the command to Read the desired sector. The controller begins reading the sector ID headers, looking for the assigned sector.

When the sector is identified, the preamble is read and the controller synchronizes its operation with the incoming bit stream from the disk drive. At the beginning of the sector's data field, a *data start marker* coordinates the first bit of the first data byte with the controller's operation. At this point, the controller begins dividing the incoming bit stream into bytes for transmission to the system. The transfer may continue over multiple sectors or tracks until an *end-of-file marker* is encountered, indicating that the entire file has been transferred.

Figure 4-9 depicts the process of a typical disk drive Read operation.

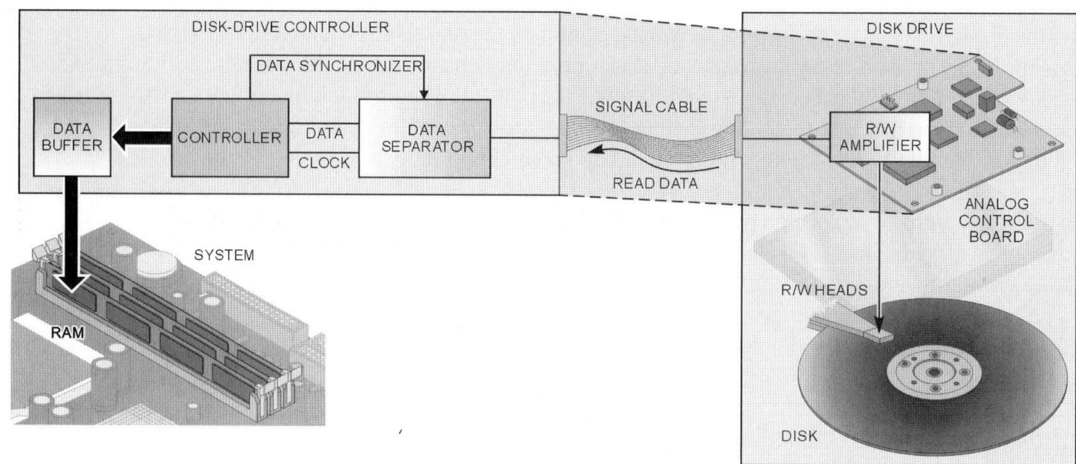

Figure 4-9: The Read Operation

FLOPPY DISK DRIVES

The discussion of general disk drive operations applies to both hard and floppy drives alike. However, the physical construction and operation of the drives are quite different. The FDD is an exposed unit, with an opening in the front to allow the floppy disk to be inserted and removed. In addition, the R/W heads are open to the atmosphere, and ride directly on the surface of the diskette. Modern 3-1/2" floppy disk drives have ejection buttons that kick the disk out of the drive when they are pushed. Table 4-1 provides a comparison of the two different formats used with 3-1/2" floppy drives.

Table 4-1: FDD Disk Parameters

DIAMETER	DENSITY	CAPACITY	TRACK	SECTORS
3 ½"	DD	720 kB	80	9
3 ½"	HD	1.44 MB	80	18

Data moves back and forth between the system's RAM memory and the floppy disk surface. Along the way, it passes from the system RAM, to the **Floppy-Disk Controller (FDC)**, through the floppy drive signal cable, and into the floppy drive's analog control board. The analog control board converts the data into signals that can be applied to the drive's Read/Write heads, which in turn produce the magnetic spots on the disk surface.

Floppy-Disk Controller (FDC)

In the original PCs and XTs, the FDC circuitry was located on an FDD controller card. In AT-compatible systems, it migrated onto a Multi I/O card along with parallel, serial, game and HDD control ports. With ATX systems, all of this circuitry has been integrated into the system board.

The circuitry on the floppy drive unit is usually distributed between two printed circuit boards: the analog control board and the drive's spindle motor control board.

Under direction of the operating system, the FDC divides the 3-1/2" floppy disk into 80 tracks per side, with nine or eighteen 512-byte sectors per track. This provides the system with 737,280 (720 KB) or 1,474,560 (1.44 MB) total bytes of storage on each disk. Table 4-2 lists the operating specifications for a typical 3-1/2" floppy disk drive unit.

Table 4-2: FDD Drive Specifications

DRIVE UNIT PART	DSSD	DSHD
Track	80	80
Heads	2	2
Sectors per Track	9	18
Bytes per Sector	512	512
Formatted Capacity	720 kB	1.44 MB
Unformatted Capacity	1 MB	2 MB
Rotational Speed (RPM)	300	300
Recording Density (bits/inch)	8717	17,432
Tracks per Inch	135	135
Transfer Rate Unformatted (Kbps)	250	500

The FDC also supplies interface signals that permit it to be connected to microprocessor systems with or without DMA capabilities. In most systems, however, the FDC operates in conjunction with the system's DMA controller, and is assigned to the DRQ2 and DACK2 lines. In operation, the FDC presents a DRQ2 request for every byte of data to be transferred. In addition, the disk-drive controller is assigned to the IRQ6 line. The FDC generates an interrupt signal each time it receives a Read, Write, or Format command from the system unit. An interrupt will also be generated when the controller receives a Ready signal from one of the disk drive units.

Floppy Drive Cables

Pin #1 indicator stripe

A single ribbon cable is used to connect the floppy drive to the system board's FDD adapter connector. Generally, the cable has two 34-pin, two-row BERG headers along its length. The other end of the cable terminates in a 34-pin, two-row BERG header. A small, colored stripe normally runs along one edge of the cable, as illustrated in Figure 4-10. This is the **Pin #1 indicator stripe** that marks the side of the cable, which should be aligned with the #1 pin of the FDD connector and the disk drive's signal connector. The location of this pin is normally marked on the drive's printed-circuit board.

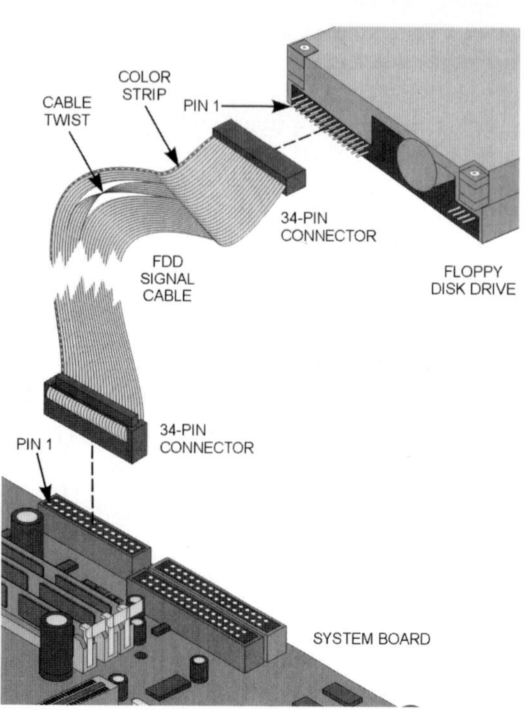

Figure 4-10: The FDD Signal Cable

The floppy disk drive connected to the 34-pin header at the end of the cable will be assigned the drive A designation by the system. A floppy drive connected to the edge connector in the middle of the cable will be designated as the B drive. A small twist of wires between the A and B connectors reroutes key lines that determine which drive is which.

The 34-pin interface connection enables the FDC to manage two floppy disk drive units. Figure 4-11 depicts the connections between the disk drive adapter and the disk drives. The directions of signal flow between the drives and the adapter are indicated by the arrow-tips.

DISK DRIVE ⟷ MULTI I/O

SIGNAL NAME	ADAPTER PIN NUMBER
GROUND (ODD NUMBERS)	1-33
DENSITY SELECT	2
UNUSED	4, 6
INDEX	8
MOTOR ENABLE A	10
DRIVE SELECT B	12
DRIVE SELECT A	14
MOTOR ENABLE B	16
DIRECTION	18
STEP	20
WRITE DATA	22
WRITE ENABLE	24
TRACK 0	26
WRITE PROTECT	28
READ DATA	30
SELECT HEAD 1	32
DISK CHANGE	34

Figure 4-11: FDD Cable Signal Definitions

HARD DISK DRIVES

Whereas early PCs did not rely on hard drives, nearly every modern PC has at least one of them installed. After the original PC, the hard drive became standard equipment. The XT featured a 10 MB MFM unit. Modern systems feature drives that typically have storage capacities well into the gigabyte (GB) range. Logically, the hard drive is organized as a stack of disks similar to a floppy disk. Each surface is divided into tracks, which are, in turn, divided into sectors. Each disk possesses a matching set of tracks on the top and bottom of the disk. The disks are stacked on top of each other and the R/W heads move in and out between them. Since there are matching tracks on the top and bottom of each disk in the stack, the HDD controller organizes them into cylinders. For example, cylinder 1 of a four-platter HDD would consist of track 1 of each disk surface. The cylinder concept is described in Figure 4-12.

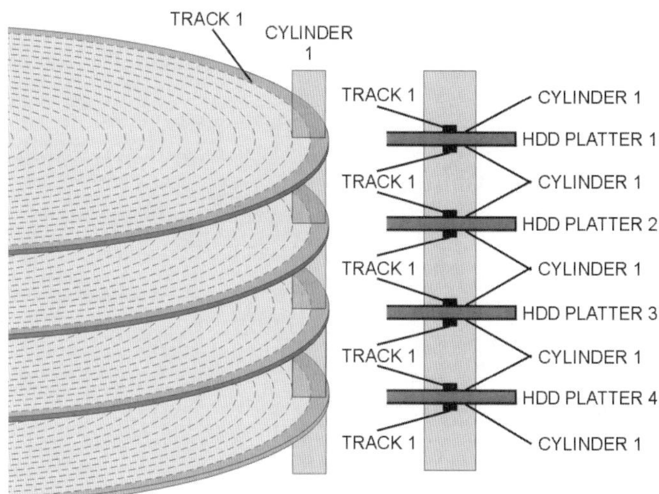

Figure 4-12: HDD Cylinders

The physical make-up of a hard disk system is depicted in Figure 4-13. It involves a controller (either on an I/O card, or built into the system board), one or more signal cables, a power cable, and a disk drive unit. In some cases, floppy- and hard-disk drive signal cables may look similar. However, there are some slight differences in their construction that prevent them from being compatible. Therefore, great caution must be used when installing these cables. Many skilled technicians have encountered problems by not paying attention to which type of cable they were installing with a particular type of drive.

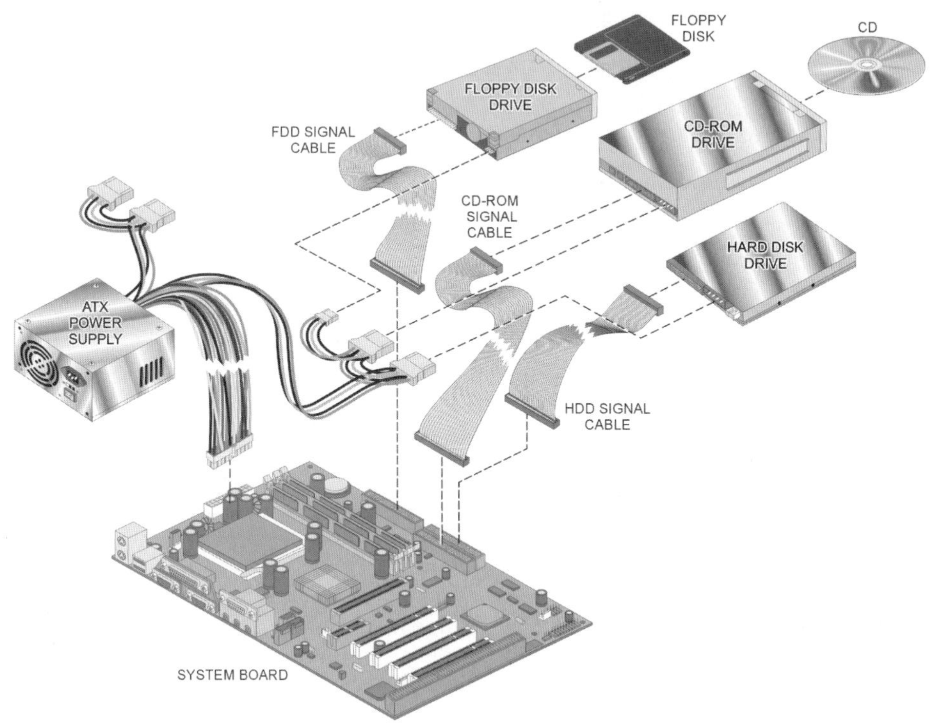

Figure 4-13: Components of the HDD System

The system's CMOS Setup holds the HDD configuration settings. As with other configuration settings, these must be set correctly for the installed drive. Typical HDD information required for the CMOS setup includes its capacity, number of cylinders, number of R/W heads, number of sectors/track, amount of pre-compensation, and the track number to be used as the landing zone for the R/W heads when the drive is shut down. In Pentium-class systems, the PnP BIOS and operating system work with the newer system-level drives to **auto-detect** the drive and supply its configuration information to the CMOS Setup utility. Otherwise, this information must be obtained from the drive manufacturer, or a third-party maintenance. Table 4-3 shows typical HDD format information associated with a particular BIOS. Systems using other BIOS may have different values. Most BIOS tables also provide a user-definable HDD entry, where the values can be entered manually into the CMOS settings.

auto-detect

Table 4-3: Typical HDD Format Values

Type	Cylinders	Heads	Write-Precompensate	Capacity
1	306	4	128	11
2	615	4	300	21
3	615	6	300	32
4	940	8	512	65
5	940	6	512	49
6	615	4	65535	21
7	462	8	256	32
8	733	5	65535	32
9	900	15	65535	118
10	820	3	65535	21
11	855	5	65535	37
12	855	7	65535	52
13	306	8	128	21
14	733	7	65535	45
15	*	*	*	*
16	612	4	*	21
17	977	5	300	43
18	977	7	65535	60
19	1024	7	512	62
20	733	5	300	32
21	733	7	300	45
22	733	5	300	32
23	306	4	*	11
24	925	7	*	56
25	925	9	65535	72
26	754	7	754	46
27	754	11	65535	72
28	699	7	256	43
29	823	10	65535	72
30	918	7	918	56
31	1024	11	65535	98
32	1024	15	65535	134
33	1024	5	1024	45
34	612	2	128	11
35	1024	9	65535	80
36	1024	8	512	71
37	615	8	128	43
38	987	3	987	26
39	987	7	987	60
40	820	6	820	43
41	977	5	977	43
42	981	5	981	43
43	830	7	512	51
44	830	10	65535	72
45	917	15	65535	120
46	1224	15	65535	160
User	16383	16	0	8456

The other important hard disk drive specifications to consider are access time, seek time, data transfer rate, and storage capacity. These quantities designate how much data the drive can hold, how fast it can get to a specific part of the data, and how fast it can move it to the system.

Hard Drive Preparation

Unlike floppy drives, which basically come in four accepted formats, hard disk drives are created in a wide variety of storage capacities. When the drive is created, its surface is electronically blank. To prepare the disk for use by the system, three levels of preparation must take place. These are, in order, the **low-level format**, the **partition**, and the **high-level format**.

low-level format

partition

high-level format

A low-level format is very similar to a land developer sectioning off a field for a new housing development. The process begins with surveying the property, and placing markers for key structures such as roads, water lines, and electrical service. The low-level format routine is similar in that it marks off the disk into cylinders and sectors, and defines their placement on the disk. **System-level drive** types, such as IDE and SCSI drives, come with the low-level format already performed. Therefore, they do not require any low-level formatting from the user.

System-level drive

Attempts to perform low-level formats on IDE and SCSI drives may result in damage to the drive. This is not physical damage, but the loss of pre-recorded bad track and sector information that would occur during a low-level format. The drive also contains alignment information used to control the R/W heads for proper alignment over the tracks. This alignment information would also be lost during a low-level format. If this occurs, it will normally be necessary that the drive be sent to the manufacturer to restore this information to the disk.

Logical and Physical Drives

Before a high-level format can be performed, the drive must be partitioned. The disk management capabilities of the oldest versions of MS-DOS (2.x, 3.x) imposed a limit on the size of a drive at 32 MB. However, as HDD technology steadily increased, the capacities of the physical drives eventually passed this limit. Fortunately, operating systems can partition, or divide, large physical drives into multiple logical drives. Each logical drive is identified by a different drive letter (such as C, D, E, and so on).

logical drives

Figure 4-14 illustrates the concept of creating multiple **logical drives** on a single physical hard drive. This is normally done for purposes of organization and increased access speeds. However, drives may also be partitioned to enable multiple operating systems to exist on the same physical drive.

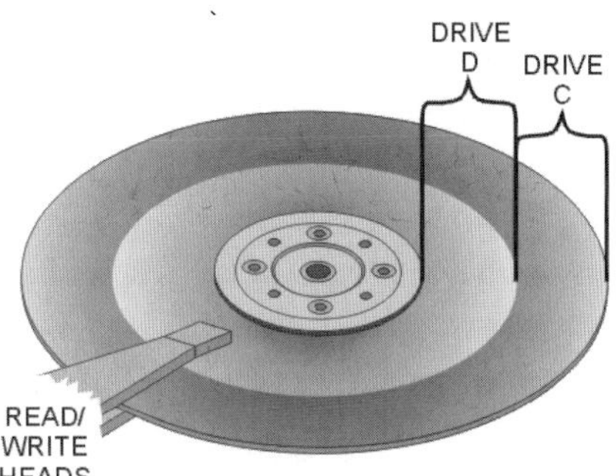

Figure 4-14: Partitions on an HDD

Basically, DOS provides for two partitions on an HDD unit. The first partition, or the primary partition, must exist as drive C. The system files must be located in this partition, and the partition must be set to **Active** for the system to boot up from the drive. The active partition is the logical drive that the system will boot to. After the primary partition has been established and properly configured, an additional partition, referred to as an extended partition, is also permitted. However, the extended partition may be subdivided into 23 logical drives (the letters of the alphabet minus a, b, and c). The extended partition cannot be deleted if logical drives have been defined within it.

Active

On a partitioned drive, only one logical drive can be active at a time. When the system checks the MBR of the physical disk during the boot process, it also checks to see which partition on the disk has been marked as active and then boots to the partition boot record located in that logical drive. This arrangement enables a single physical disk to hold different operating systems that the system can boot to.

In local and wide area networks, the concept of logical drives is carried a step further. A particular hard disk drive may be a logical drive in a large system of drives along a peer-to-peer network. On the other hand, a very large centralized drive may be used to create several logical drives for a server/client type of network. Local area networks are covered in detail in Chapter 5—*Data Communications*.

FDISK

The partitioning program for MS-DOS and Windows 9x is named **FDISK**. The FDISK utility in MS-DOS version 4.0 raised the maximum size of a logical drive to 128 MB, and version 5.0 raised it to 528 MB. The FDISK utility in Windows 9x provided upgraded support for very large hard drives. The original version of Windows 95 set a size limit for logical drives at 2 GB. The FDISK version in the upgraded OSR2 version of Windows 95 extended the maximum partition size to 8 GB.

Disk Administrator

Disk Management

In Windows NT and Windows 2000 the partitioning process is performed through the **Disk Administrator** and **Disk Management** utilities respectively. These utilities perform the same basic functions as the FDISK utility; however, they can also provide many additional functions associated with enterprise computing systems. When activated, they will show you the basic layout of the system's disks, including:

- The size of each disk
- The size and file system type used in each logical drive
- The size and location of any unformatted (free) space on the drive

The Disk Administrator and Disk Management utilities can be used to create both traditional primary and extended partitions as FAT or NTFS. They can also be used to create four types of volumes:

- Volume sets
- Striped sets
- Mirrored sets
- Striped sets with parity

These types of volumes are used in the RAID systems described later in this chapter.

When newer operating system versions provided for partitions larger than 528 MB, another limiting factor for the size of disk partitions was encountered—the BIOS. The standard BIOS featured a 504 MB capacity limit. To overcome this, newer BIOS include an enhanced mode that employs **Logical Block Addressing (LBA)** techniques to utilize the larger partition sizes available through newer operating systems. This technique—known as **Enhanced Cylinder, Heads, Sectors (ECHS)**—effectively increases the number of R/W heads the system can recognize from 16 to 256. The parameters of 1,024 cylinders, 63 sectors/track, and 512 bytes/sector remains unchanged.

Logical Block Addressing (LBA)

Enhanced Cylinder, Heads, Sectors (ECHS)

The high-level format procedure is performed by the operating system and creates logical structures on the disk that tell the system what files are on the disk and where they can be found. In MS-DOS and Windows 9x systems, the format process creates a blank **File Allocation Table (FAT)** and **root directory** structure on the disk. In the case of Windows NT and Windows 2000 systems, the format operation may produce FATs and root directories, or it may produce more flexible **Master File Table (MFT)** structures. Chapter 8 provides more detailed information about the organization of disks, including FATs, MFTs, and directory structures.

File Allocation Table (FAT)

root directory

Master File Table (MFT)

HDD Interfaces

Four hard disk drive interfaces have commonly been associated with microcomputers. These include two device-level interfaces and two system-level interfaces. The device-level interfaces are the **ST-506/412** and **Enhanced Small Device Interface (ESDI)**. These types of drives typically used a controller card that contains the system-level interface for the drive. These drive types required the user to perform all three levels of drive preparation. These types of drives have been replaced with more efficient, easier to manage drives that employ system-level interfaces.

ST-506/412

Enhanced Small Device Interface (ESDI)

The system-level interfaces, **Integrated Drive Electronics (IDE)** and **Small Computer System Interface (SCSI)**, place most of the controller circuitry on the drive itself. Therefore, the system sees the entire HDD system as an attachment to its bus systems. These units come with the low-level format already in place.

Integrated Drive Electronics (IDE)

Small Computer System Interface (SCSI)

Since both the SCSI and IDE interfaces are system-level interfaces, most of their controller circuitry is actually located on the drives. In pre-Pentium systems, the SCSI and IDE drives employed host adapter cards that plugged into the system board's expansion slots. In the Pentium environment, the IDE host adapter function has been integrated into the system board. The IDE interface connectors are located on the system board.

SCSI systems continue to use **host adapter cards** as their interface connectors. The host adapter provides a BERG pin connector for the system's internal SCSI ribbon cable. However, there are many versions of the SCSI standard and several types of SCSI connecting cables.

host adapter cards

There are also two versions of the IDE interface, the original IDE specification and a newer, Enhanced IDE, or EIDE standard. The EIDE interface has been redefined to allow faster transfer rates, as well as the handling of more storage capacity. It can also be used to control drive units such as a tape or CD-ROM. The EIDE interface is often described as an **ATAPI (AT Attachment Packet Interface)**, or a **Fast ATA (Fast AT Attachment)** interface. These standards are described in the Installing and Configuring Disk Drives section, presented later in this chapter.

ATAPI (AT Attachment Packet Interface)

Fast ATA (Fast AT Attachment)

RAID Systems

drive array

As applications pushed storage capacity requirements past available drive sizes, it became logical to combine several drives together to hold all of the data produced. In a desktop unit, this can be as simple as adding an additional physical drive to the system. Wide area and local area networks connect computers together, so that their resources (including disk drives) can be shared. If you extend this idea of sharing disk drives to include several different drive units operating under a single controller, you have a **drive array**. A drive array is depicted in Figure 4-15.

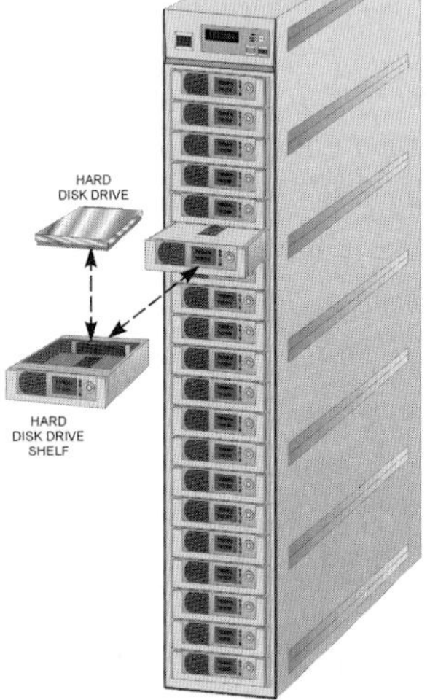

Figure 4-15: A Drive Array Stack

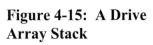

Drive arrays have evolved in response to storage requirements for local area networks. They are particularly useful in client/server networks, where the data for the network tends to be centrally located, and shared by all of the users around the network.

In the cases of multiple drives within a unit, and drives scattered around a network, all of the drives assume a different letter designation. In a drive array, the stack of drives can be made to appear as a single, large hard drive. The drives are operated in parallel so that they can deliver data to the controller in a parallel format. If the controller is simultaneously handling 8 bits of data from 8 drives, the system will see the speed of the transfer as being 8 times faster. This technique of using the drives in a parallel array is referred to as a striped drive array.

mirrored drive array

It is also possible to simply use a small drive array as a data backup system. This is referred to as a **mirrored drive array**, in which the drives are each supplied with the same data. In the event that the data from one drive is corrupted, or one of the drives fails, the data is still safe. Both types of arrays are created through a blend of connection hardware and control software.

Redundant Arrays of Inexpensive Disks (RAID)

RAID Advisory Board

The most common drive arrays are **RAID** systems. RAID is an acronym for **Redundant Arrays of Inexpensive Disks**. Later usage of the term RAID exchanges the word Independent for Inexpensive. Five levels of RAID technology specifications are given by the **RAID Advisory Board**.

RAID 0

RAID 1

The RAID Advisory Board designated the classic striped array described above as RAID level-0 (**RAID 0** - *Striped Disk Array without Fault Tolerance*). Likewise, the mirrored drive array described above is labeled RAID 1.

RAID 1 (*Mirroring and Duplexing*) is a redundancy scheme that uses two equal-sized drives, where both drives hold the same information. Each drive serves as a backup for the other. Figure 4-16 illustrates the operation of a mirrored array used in a RAID 1 application.

Duplicate information is stored on both drives. When a file is retrieved from the array, the controller reads alternate sectors from each drive. This effectively reduces the data read time by half.

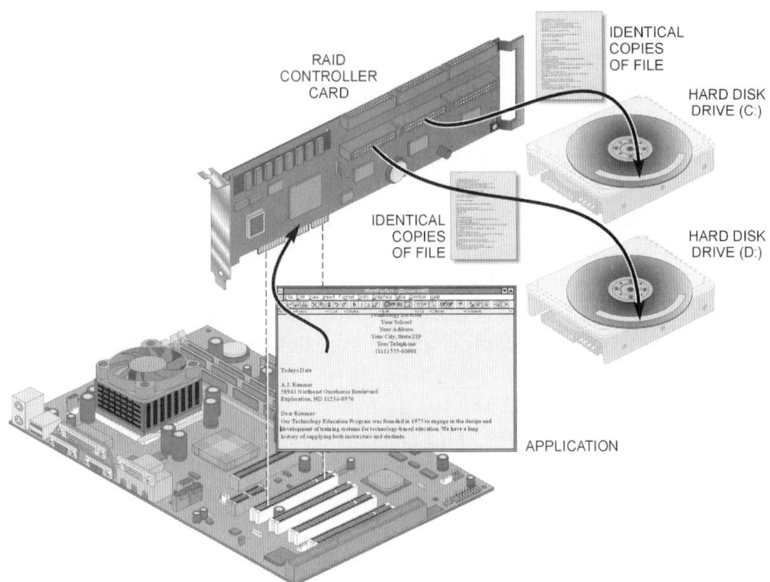

Figure 4-16: Operation of a Mirrored Array

RAID 2

The **RAID 2** (*Data Striping with Error Recovery*) strategy interleaves data on parallel drives, as described in Figure 4-17. Bits or blocks of data are interleaved across the disks in the array. The speed afforded by collecting data from the disks in a parallel format is the biggest feature of the system. In large arrays, complete bytes, words, or double words can be written to, and read from, the array simultaneously.

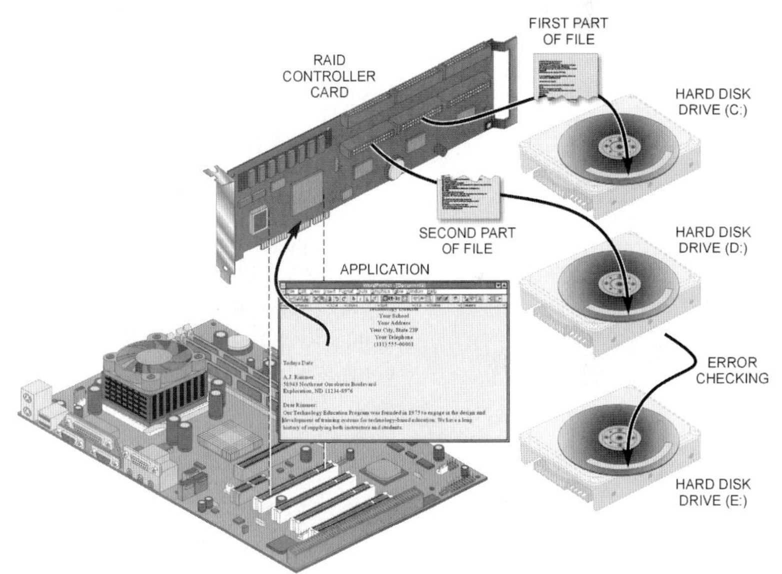

Figure 4-17: Interleaved Data on Parallel Drives

The RAID 2 specification uses multiple disks for **error-detection and correction functions**. Depending on the error-detection and correction algorithms used, large portions of the array are used for non-data storage overhead. Of course, the reliability of the data being delivered to the system is excellent, and there is no need for time-consuming corrective read operations when an error is detected. Arrays dealing with large systems may use between 3 and 7 drives for error-correction purposes. Because of the high hardware overhead, RAID 2 systems are not normally used with microcomputer systems.

error-detection and correction functions

When the array is used in this manner, a complex **error-detection and correction algorithm** is normally employed. The controller contains circuitry based on the algorithm that detects, locates, and corrects the error without re-transmitting any data. This is a very quick and efficient method of error-detection and correction.

error-detection and correction algorithm

In Figure 4-17, the data block being sent to the array is broken apart, and distributed to the drives in the array. The data word already has a parity bit added to it. The controller generates parity for the block, and stores it on the error-detection drive. When the controller reads the data back from the array, it regenerates the error-check character, and compares it to the one written on the error-check drive. By comparing the error-check character to the rewritten one, the controller can detect the error in the data field, and determine which bit within the field is incorrect. With this information in hand, the controller can simply correct that bit as it is being processed.

RAID 3

In a **RAID 3** (Parallel Transfer with Parity Striping) arrangement, the drives of the array operate in parallel like a RAID 2 system. However, only parity checking is used for error-detection and correction, requiring only one additional drive. If an error occurs, the controller reads the array again to verify the error. This is a time-consuming, low-efficiency method of error correction.

RAID 4

A **RAID 4** (*Independent Data Disks with Shared Parity Disk*) controller interleaves sectors across the drives in the array. This creates the appearance of one, very large drive. The RAID 4 format is generally used for smaller drive arrays, but can be used for larger arrays as well. Only one parity-checking drive is allotted for error control. The information on the parity drive is updated after reading the data drives. This creates an extra write activity for each data read operation performed.

RAID 5

The **RAID 5** scheme (*Independent Data Disks with Distributed Parity Blocks*) alters the RAID 4 specification by allowing the parity function to rotate through the different drives. Under this system, error-checking and correction is the function of all the drives. If a single drive fails, the system is capable of regenerating its data from the parity information on the other drives. RAID 5 is usually the most popular RAID system, since it can be used on small arrays, and it has a high level of error recovery built in.

RAID 6

A variation of RAID 5 that implements two independent error-correcting schemes (Independent Data Disks with two Independent Distributed Parity Schemes) has been devised and labeled **RAID 6**. This format is relatively expensive, but it provides extremely high fault tolerance level for critical applications. This RAID level requires at least two additional drives to operate.

RAID 10

The **RAID 10** (*Very High Reliability/High Performance RAID*) specification combines mirroring and striping to produce a high-performance, high-reliability backup system. This arrangement combines RAID 1 striped array segments with mirroring to provide increased performance to a RAID 1 installation.

RAID 53

A variation of RAID 3, referred to as **RAID 53** (High I/O Rates and Data Transfer Performance RAID), combines RAID 0 striped arrays with RAID 3 parallel segments. The outcome is a high-performance RAID 3 system.

CD-ROM

Compact Disc (CD)

Soon after the **Compact Disc (CD)** became popular for storing audio signals on optical material, the benefits of storing computer information in this manner became apparent. With a CD, data is written digitally on a light-sensitive material by a powerful, highly focused laser beam.

pits

lands

The writing laser is pulsed with the modulated data to be stored on the disc. When the laser is pulsed, a microscopic blister is burned into the optical material, causing it to reflect light differently from the material around it. The blistered areas are referred to as **pits**, while the areas between them are called **lands**. Figure 4-18 illustrates the writing of data on the optical disc.

The recorded data is read from the disc by scanning it with a lower-power, continuous laser beam. The laser diode emits the highly focused, narrow beam that is reflected back from the disc. The reflected beam passes through a prism, and is bent 90 degrees, where it is picked up by the diode detector and converted into an electrical signal. Only the light reflected from the lands is picked up by the detector. Light that strikes a pit is scattered and is not detected. The lower power level used for reading the disc ensures that the optical material is not affected during the read operation. With an audio CD, the digital data retrieved from the disc is passed through a digital-to-analog converter to reproduce the audio sound wave. However, this is not required for digital computer systems, since the information is already in a form acceptable to the computer. Therefore, CD players designed for use in computer systems are referred to as **CD-ROM drives**, to differentiate them from audio CD players. Otherwise, the mechanics of operation are very similar between the two devices. The ROM designation refers to the fact that the original drives were basically Read-Only.

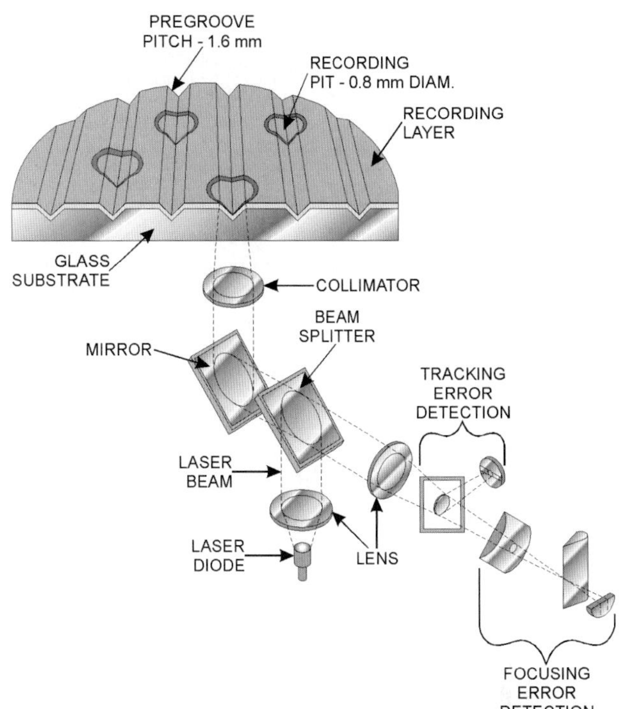

Figure 4-18: Writing on a CD-ROM Drive

CD-ROM drives

CD-ROM Discs

A typical CD-ROM disc is 4.7 inches in diameter, and consists of three major parts:

- acrylic substrate
- aluminized, mirror-finished data surface
- lacquer coating

The scanning laser beam comes up through the disc, strikes the aluminized data surface, and is reflected back. Since there is no physical contact between the reading mechanism and the disc, the disc never wears out. This is one of the main advantages of the CD system. The blisters on the data surface are typically just under 1 micrometer in length, and the tracks are 1.6 micrometers apart. The data is encoded by the length and spacing of the blisters, and the lands between them. This concept is illustrated in Figure 4-19.

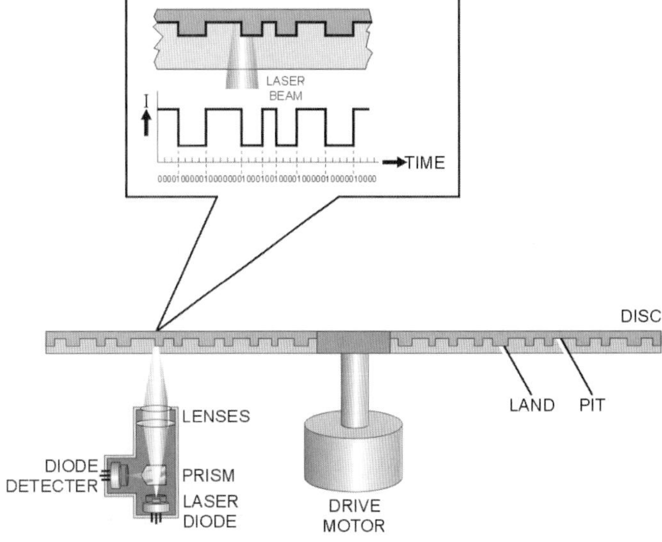

Figure 4-19: Encoding Data on a CD-ROM

spiral track

The information on a compact disc is stored in one continuous **spiral track**, unlike floppy disks, where the data is stored in multiple, concentric tracks. The compact disc storage format still divides the data into separate sectors. However, the sectors of a CD-ROM disc are physically the same size. The disc spins counter-clockwise, and it slows down as the laser diode emitter/detector unit approaches the outside of the disc.

It begins spinning at approximately 500 RPM at the inner edge of the disc and slows down to about 200 RPM at the outer edge of the disc.

The spindle motor controls the speed of the disc, so that the track is always passing the laser at between 3.95 and 4.6 feet per second. Therefore, CD-ROM drives must have a variable-speed spindle motor, and cannot just be turned on and off like a floppy drive's spindle motor. The variable speed of the drive allows the disc to contain more sectors, thereby giving it a much larger storage capacity. In fact, the average storage capacity of a CD-ROM disc is about 680 MB.

CD-ROM Drives

single-speed (1x) drives

double-speed (2X) drives

triple-speed (3X) drives

Yellow Book

Red Book

Orange Book

Green Book

Blue Book

CD-ROM drives that operate at the speed of a conventional audio CD player are called **single-speed (1x) drives**. Advanced drives that spin twice, and three times, as fast as the typical CD player are referred to as **double-speed (2X) drives**, **triple-speed (3X) drives**, and so forth. Single-speed drives transfer data at a rate of 150 kB per second. Double-speed drive transfers occur at 300 KB per second, and so on. Most manufacturers are now focusing on 50X and 52X drives.

CD-ROM drives are capable of playing audio CDs. However, a CD player will not be able to produce any output from the CD-ROM disc. CDs are classified by a color-coding system that corresponds to their intended use. CDs that contain digital data intended for use in a computer are referred to as **Yellow Book** CDs. **Red Book** CDs refer to those formatted to contain digital music. **Orange Book** refers to the standard for CDs that are used in WORM drives. **Green Book** CDs are used with interactive CD systems, and **Blue Book** CDs are those associated with laser disc systems.

CD Writers

Write Once, Read Many (WORM) drive

Another type of CD drive is a **Write Once, Read Many (WORM) drive**. As the acronym implies, these drives allow users to write information to the disc once, and then retrieve this information as you would with a CD-ROM drive. Once information is stored on a WORM drive, the data cannot be changed or deleted.

CD Writer

CD-Recordable (CD-R)

CD-RW disc

CD Writer technology has developed to the point where it is inexpensive enough to be added to CD-ROM drives used in typical PC systems. CD Writers record data on blank **CD-Recordable (CD-R)** discs. A CD-R is a *Write Once, Read Many* media that is generally available in 120 mm and 80 mm sizes. The drives are constructed using a typical 5.25" half-height drive form factor. This form factor is convenient in that it fits into a typical PC drive bay. The CD-R technology has continued to evolve into a recordable, ReWritable compact disc, called a **CD-RW disc**. These discs can be recorded, erased and rewritten just like a floppy disk.

The physical construction of the CD-R disc is considerably different than that of the CD-ROM disc. The workable disc is constructed as described in Figure 4-20. The CD-R disc is created by coating a transparent polycarbonate substrate with an opaque polymer dye. The dye is covered with a thin layer of gold and topped with a protective lacquer layer and a label. The CD-R writing mechanism is not as strong as that of a commercial CD-ROM duplicator. Instead of burning pits into the substrate of the disc, the CD writer uses a lower-power laser to discolor the dye material.

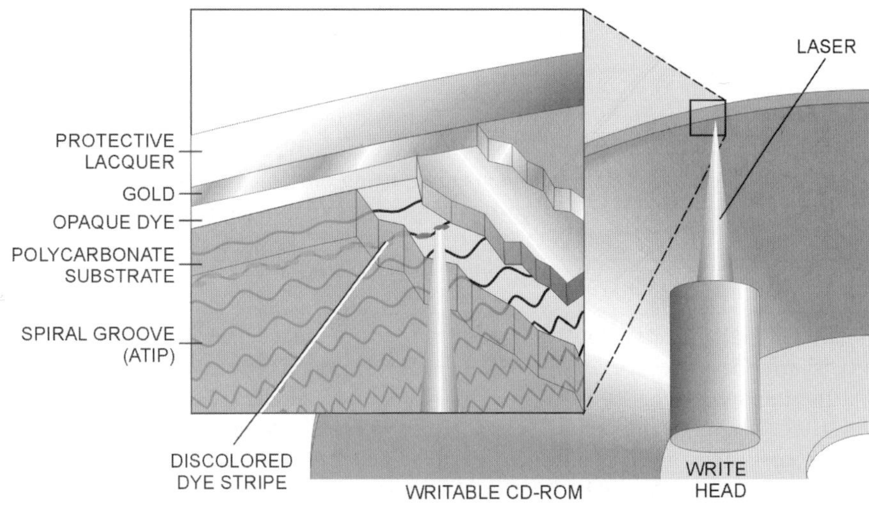

Figure 4-20: Writable CD-R Disc

The CD-R disc format is identical to that of a CD-ROM and information written on it can be read by a typical CD-ROM drive. The spiral track formation and sectoring are the same as those used with CD-ROM discs. In addition, the CD writer can produce recordings in the standard CD book formats (i.e., Red, Yellow, Orange, and Green).

During the write operation, the CD Writer uses a medium-intensity laser to write the data on the thermally sensitive media. The laser light is applied to the bottom side of the disc. It passes through the substrate to the reflective layer and is reflected back through the substrate. The light continues through the drive's optics system until it reaches the laser detector.

When the polymer is exposed to the light of the writing laser, it heats up and becomes transparent. This exposes the reflective gold layer beneath the polymer. During readback, the reflective layer reflects more light than the polymer material does. The transitions between lighter and darker areas of the disc are used to encode the data.

CD writers are typically able to write to the CD-R at either 4x or 8x CD speeds. These settings have nothing to do with playback speeds. CD-RW drives are specified in a Record x Write-once x Rewrite speed format (i.e., a 32 x 8 x 4 CD-RW can read at 32x, write at 8x, and rewrite at 4x speeds).

Digital Versatile Discs

Newer compact disc technologies have produced a high capacity disc, called a **digital versatile disc**, **digital video disc**, or **DVD** for short. These discs have capacities that range between 4.7 GB and 17 GB of data. Transfer rates associated with DVD drives range between 600 KBps and 1.3 MBps.

digital versatile disc

digital video disc (DVD)

Like CDs, DVDs are available in DVD-ROM (write-once) and DVD-RAM (rewritable), formats. There are also *DVD-Audio* and *DVD-video* specifications that can store up to 75 songs or an entire full-length movie. The DVD-Video standard employs the MPEG-2 compression standard to compress and decompress video data on the disc.

REFERENCE SHELF

For more information about MPEG, video data compression, and multimedia refer to the *How Multimedia Works* section of the electronic Reference Shelf on the CD that accompanies this book.

The drives used for DVD are backward compatible with old CD-ROM discs and newer DVD drives can be used to read CD-R and CD-RW discs. Currently, there are two standards in the rewritable DVD field – the DVD-RAM standard being presented by the DVD consortium and the DVD-RW standard developed by a group of manufacturers that include Philips, Sony and Hewlett Packard. The DVD-RAM format supports 2.6 GB of storage per disc, the DVD-RW standard supports 3.0 GB per disc.

Physically, the DVD drive looks and operates in the same manner as the traditional CD-ROM drive described earlier in this chapter. Newer manufacturing methods for the discs permit the minimum length of the *pits* and *lands* to be smaller. Therefore, they can be squeezed closer together on the disc. DVD drives also employ higher resolution lasers to decrease the *track pitch* (distance between adjacent tracks). Together, these two factors create the high data densities offered by DVD.

CD-ROM Interfaces

With as many speed choices as there are, there are also several choices of architectures for CD-ROM drives. The choices include:

- SCSI interfaces
- USB interfaces
- proprietary interfaces
- IDE/EIDE interfaces
- IEEE-1394 interfaces

An internal SCSI CD-ROM drive must be capable of connecting to the type of SCSI cable being used. The SCSI interface that employs a Centronics-type connector is the most widely used method for connecting external CD-ROM drives to systems.

Controllers for proprietary interfaces are often included with the drive, or with a sound card. To gain full advantage of a CD-ROM, it's essential to also have a sound card. Many sound cards include a CD-ROM drive interface, or controller. However, these controllers may not be IDE- or SCSI-compatible. They often contain proprietary interfaces that work with only a few CD-ROM models.

Software drivers are required to operate a CD-ROM drive from DOS, or Windows 3.x. Normally, the drivers come packaged with the drive if an IDE interface is being used. Conversely, the drivers are included with the interface card when a SCSI interface is employed.

Tape Drives

Tape drive units are another popular type of information storage system. These systems can store large amounts of data on small **tape cartridges**, similar to the one depicted in Figure 4-21.

Tape drive units

tape cartridges

Tapes tend to be more economic than other magnetic media, when storing large amounts of data. However, access to information stored on tape tends to be very slow. This is caused by the fact that, unlike magnetic disks, tape operates in a linear fashion. The tape transport must run all of the tape past the drive's R/W heads to access data that is physically stored at the end of the tape.

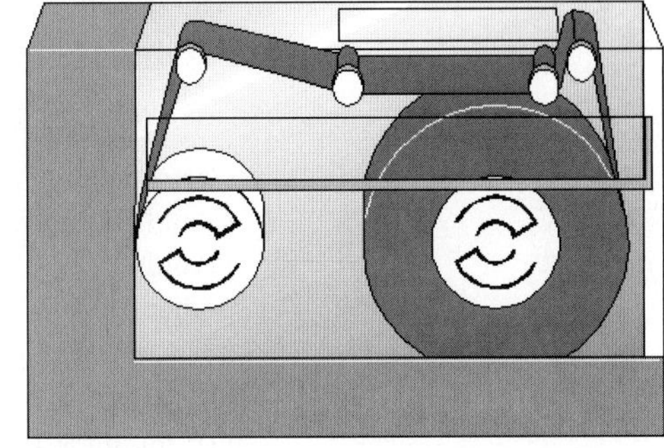

Figure 4-21: A Tape Cartridge

Therefore, tape drives are generally used to store large amounts of information that will not need to be accessed often or quickly. Such information includes **backup copies** of programs and data. This type of data security is a necessity with records such as business transactions, payroll, artwork, etc.

backup copies

Data backup has easily become the most widely used tape application. With the large amounts of information that can be stored on a hard disk drive, a disk crash is a very serious problem. If the drive crashes, all of the information stored on the disk can be destroyed. This can easily add up to billions of pieces of information. Therefore, an inexpensive method of storing data away from the hard drive is desirable.

Tape Standards

As more users employed tape as a backup media, standards for tape systems were formed. The most widely-used tape standard is the **Quarter Inch Cartridge (QIC)** standard. This standard calls for a tape cartridge like the one depicted in Figure 4-22. Its physical dimensions are 6"x 4"x 5/8". The cartridge has a head access door in the front that swings open when it is inserted in the drive unit.

Quarter Inch Cartridge (QIC)

Unlike audio cassette tapes, cartridge tapes are not driven by capstans that extend through their tape spools. Instead, they employ a belt drive system that loops through the cartridge and turns both spools synchronously. The belt is driven by a rubber drive wheel, which in turn is driven by the capstan. This design provides smoother, more precise operation than the audio cassette is capable of.

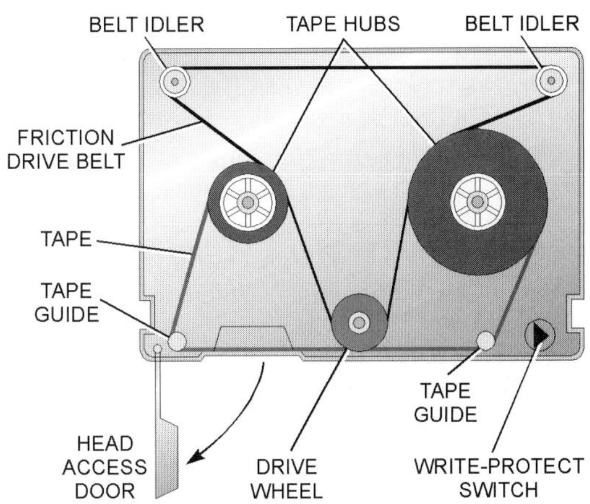

Figure 4-22: A 1/4" Tape Cartridge

The R/W heads magnetize the tape as it passes by, in much the same manner as described for other magnetic storage media. The data is placed on the tape serially as it moves past the head. The tape is organized into sectors of data, separated by inter-gap blocks. The data can be applied in parallel tracks (using multiple R/W heads) in a continuous stream of data (streaming tape systems), or in a serpentine manner, where the data is applied to the tape in one direction for odd tracks, and in the other direction for even tracks.

Magnetic tape must be formatted before use, just like a magnetic disk. In the formatting process, the controller marks the tape off into sectors. In addition, it establishes a file allocation table in its header, similar to that of a floppy or hard disk. The header also contains a bad-sector table to prevent defective areas of the tape from being used. Some of the tape is devoted to the error-detection and correction information that must be used with tape systems.

Cartridge tapes formerly were referred to as DC-6000 style tapes. Their model numbers would normally include a reference to their tape capacity as the last digits (i.e., DC-6200 would be a 200 MB tape). As the cartridge tape industry matured, manufacturers came together to establish standards for tape formats and labeling. In the process, the DC-6000 number has been replaced in discussions about capacity and format.

For the most part, a series of QIC numbers have been used to describe different tape cartridges. Table 4-4 provides a sample list of QIC standard numbers.

Table 4-4: QIC Standard Numbers

SPECIFICATION	TRACKS	CAPACITY	CARTRIDGE
QIC-02	9	60 MB	DC-3000
QIC-24	9	60 MB	DC-6000
QIC-40	20	40 MB	DC-2000
QIC-80	32	80 MB	DC-2000
QIC-100	12 / 24	100 MB	DC-2000
QIC-150	18	250 MB	DC-6000
QIC-1000	30	1.0 GB	DC-6000
QIC-1350	30	1.35 GB	DC-6000
QIC-2100	30	2.1 GB	DC-6000

minicartridge

A **minicartridge** version of the quarter-inch tape cartridge, with dimensions of 3-1/4"x 2-1/2"x 5/8", has been developed to provide a more compact form factor to fit in 3-1/2" drive bays. The internal operation of the cartridge has remained the same, but the amount of tape inside has been reduced. The reduced amount of tape in the cartridge is offset by the use of more advanced data-encoding schemes that store more data on less tape. Minicartridges are referred to as DC-2000 style cartridges. Like the DC-6000 tapes, the DC-2000 model numbers will normally include a reference to their tape capacity as the last digits.

A number of QIC tape standards have developed over time. The original QIC standard was QIC-40. This standard called for a unit that could be connected to a floppy disk drive interface so that it acted like a large drive B:. It specified a 20-track format, with each track consisting of 68 segments, having 29 sectors of 1024 bytes each. This format provided 40 MB of data storage. The specification treated the tape's sectors like the sectors of a floppy disk in that they were organized into files.

An updated QIC-80 specification was developed to replace the QIC-40 standard. Advanced R/W head designs enable the QIC-80 to place 32 tracks on the tape instead of 20. Coupled together with improved data-per-inch storage capabilities, the total capacity of the cartridge was boosted to 80 MB. The QIC-80 systems included data compression software that could effectively double the capacity of the drive from its stated value.

The QIC-80 standard has been superseded by the QIC-500M format, which allows for up to 500 MB of data to be stored on the cartridge. Newer standards for tape drives continue to emerge. Specifications that depart from the floppy disk drive interface and use the IDE or SCSI interfaces are producing data storage potentials into the multiple gigabyte range.

Digital Audio Tape (DAT)

Digital Linear Tape (DLT)

Newer digital tape standards have appeared in the personal computer market as the need to back up larger blocks of data has increased. The most noteworthy of these is the **Digital Audio Tape** (**DAT**) and the **Digital Linear Tape** (**DLT**) formats.

The DAT format borrows helical scan techniques from video tape recording to recording large blocks of information in a small length of tape. The system uses a dual, read-after-write recording head to place data on the tape at angles. The first write head records data on the tape in stripes that run at an angle to the motion of the tape. The angled recording acts to minimize the linear space required for the data. The follow-after read head reads the data back to verify that it has been recorded correctly.

The second Write head records additional data over the stripes of the first data. The second data is written at an angle to the first data, using an opposite polarity encoding method. The second Read head follows behind and verifies that the second data has been recorded accurately.

Digital Data Storage (DDS)

DAT tapes can store up to 24 GB of compressed data, depending on the data format used. There are three **Digital Data Storage** (**DDS**) formats in use:

- DDS-1 - 2 GB Uncompressed/4 GB Compressed
- DDS-2 - 4 GB Uncompressed/8 GB Compressed
- DDS-3 - 12 GB Uncompressed/24 GB Compressed

DLT tape drives provide reliable, high-speed, high-capacity tape backup functions. DLT drives use multiple parallel tracks and high-speed data streaming techniques to provide fast backup operations with capacities in excess of 70 GB.

INSTALLING STORAGE DEVICES

For installation purposes, storage devices fall into one of two categories: internal and external. Internal devices are typically mounted in the system unit's drive bays. External devices normally connect to options adapter cards installed in the system board's expansion slots. Whereas internal devices typically derive their power from the system unit's power supply, external storage devices tend to employ separate, external power supply units.

Most internal storage devices conform to traditional disk drive form factors. Therefore, the hardware installation procedures for most storage devices are the same.

universal mounting kit

To install a storage device in a disk drive bay, disconnect the system's power cord from the back of the unit. Slide the device into one of the system unit's open drive bays, and install 2 screws on each side to secure the unit to the disk drive cage. If the unit is a 3-1/2" drive, and it is being installed into a 5-1/4" drive bay, you will need to fit the drive with a **universal mounting kit**. These kits attach to the drive and extend its form factor, so that it fits correctly in the 5-1/4" half-height space.

Connect the device's signal cable to the proper interface header on the system board (or on an I/O card). Then connect the signal cable to the storage device. Use caution when connecting the disk drives to the adapter. Make certain that the Pin #1 indicator stripe on the cable aligns with the Pin #1 position of the connectors on both the storage device and its controller. Proper connection of a signal cable is depicted in Figure 4-23. Finally, connect one of the power supply's optional power connectors to the storage device.

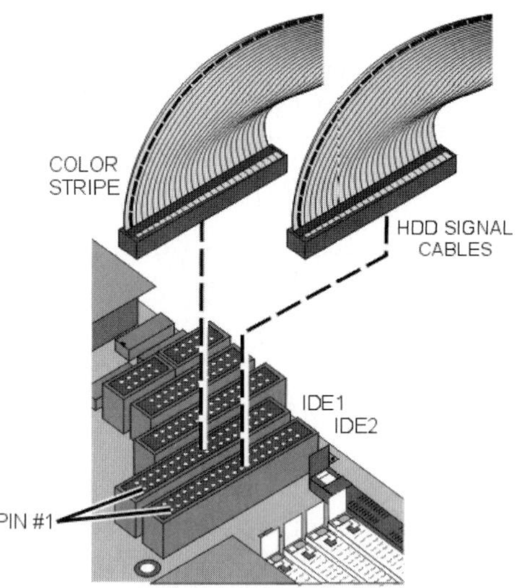

Figure 4-23: Connecting a Drive's Signal Cable

FDD Installation

The FDD installation procedure follows the sample procedure described earlier. Simply slide the FDD into one of the system unit's open drive bays, install 2 screws on each side to secure the drive to the system unit, and connect the signal and power cables to the drive. Figure 4-24 illustrates the steps required to install the floppy drive.

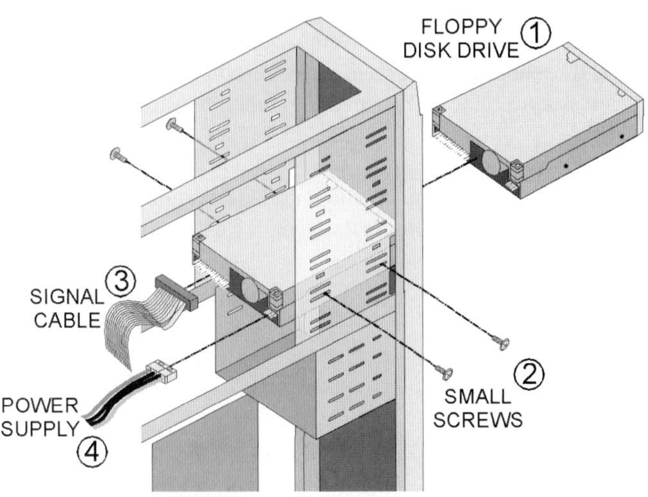

Figure 4-24: Installing a Floppy Disk Drive

The PC-compatible FDD unit uses a 34-pin signal cable. The FDD signal cable is designed to accommodate two FDD units, as illustrated in Figure 4-25. If the drive is the only floppy in the system, or intended to operate as the A: drive, connect it to the connector at the end of the cable. If it is being installed as a B: drive, attach it to the connector toward the center of the cable. On older floppy drives, the cable connected to an edge connector on the drive's printed-circuit board. With newer units, the connection is made to a BERG connector.

> **TEST TIP**
>
> Know what makes a floppy drive an A: or B: drive in a PC system.

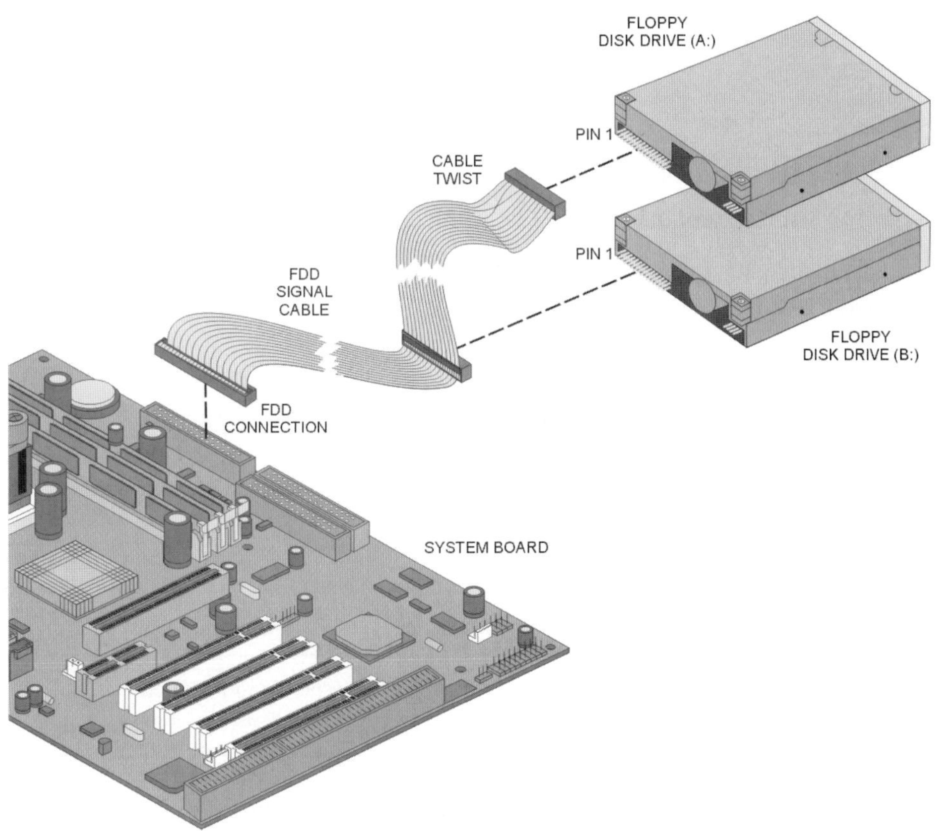

Figure 4-25: Connecting Floppy Drives

On Pentium and other types of all-in-one system boards, check the system board's installation guide for an FDD enabling jumper and make certain that it is set correctly for the FDD installed. In newer systems, the FDD enabling function should be set in the Advanced CMOS Setup screen.

Reinstall the system unit's power cord and boot up the computer. As the system boots, move into the CMOS Setup utility and configure the CMOS for the type of FDD being installed.

HDD Installation

The HDD hardware installation process is the similar to that of other storage devices, as illustrated in Figure 4-26. However, the configuration and preparation of a typical hard disk drive is more involved than that of a floppy drive. It is a good idea to confirm the IDE drive's Master/Slave/Single, or the SCSI drive's ID configuration setting before installing the unit in the drive bay. If a replacement hard drive is being installed for repair or upgrading purposes, the data on the original drive should be backed up to some other media before replacing it (if possible).

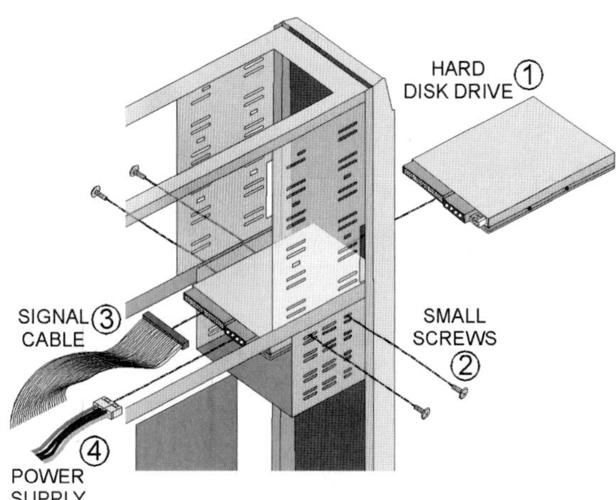

Figure 4-26: Securing the Drive Unit

After completing the hardware installation process, the drive will need to be configured and formatted. Unlike floppy drives, which basically come in four accepted formats, hard disk drives are created in a wide variety of storage capacities. When the disk is created its surface is electronically blank. With system-level drive types, the manufacturer performs the low-level formatting process. To prepare the disk for use by the system, four levels of preparation must take place. The order of these steps is as follows:

Preparing a Hard Drive for Use by the System

1. Set up the CMOS configuration for the drive
2. Low-level format the drive
3. Partition the drive
4. High-level format the drive

auto-detection

The system's CMOS Setup holds the hard drive's configuration settings. As with other I/O devices, these settings must be set correctly for the type of drive being installed. Newer BIOS versions possess **auto-detection** capabilities that enable them to find and identify the drives in the system. However, if the BIOS does not support auto-detection, it will be necessary to move into the CMOS Setup utility and identify the drive type being installed.

The *Hard Disk C: Type* entry is typically located in the CMOS Setup utility's main screen. Simply move to the entry and scroll through the HDD selections until an entry is found that matches the type of you are installing. In some cases, such as with SCSI drives, it will be necessary for the CMOS configuration entry be set to None Installed before the drive will operate correctly. Store this parameter in the CMOS configuration file by following the directions given on the menu screen.

A **low-level format** routine marks off the disk into cylinders and sectors and defines their placement on the disk. System-level interface devices, such as IDE and SCSI drives, come with automatic low-level formatting routines already performed. Therefore, no low-level formatting needs to be performed on these drives before they can be partitioned and high-level formatted. Low-level formatting will not produce physical damage, but it may cause the loss of pre-recorded bad track and sector information, as well as loss of alignment information used to control the R/W heads for proper alignment over the tracks. If this occurs, it will normally be necessary to send the drive to the manufacturer to restore this information to the disk.

low-level format

Installing CD-ROM Drives

Before installing an internal CD-ROM drive, confirm its Master/Slave/Single, or SCSI ID configuration setting. Afterwards, install the CD-ROM unit in one of the drive bays, connect the power and signal cables, and load the CD-ROM driver software. (Due to their widespread use with portable systems, the procedure for installing external CD-ROM drives is presented in Chapter 7—*Portable Systems*.)

Figure 4-27 illustrates the installation of an internal CD-ROM drive. If the interface type is different than that of the HDD, it will be necessary to install a controller card in an expansion slot. Finally, refer to the owner's manual regarding any necessary jumper or switch settings.

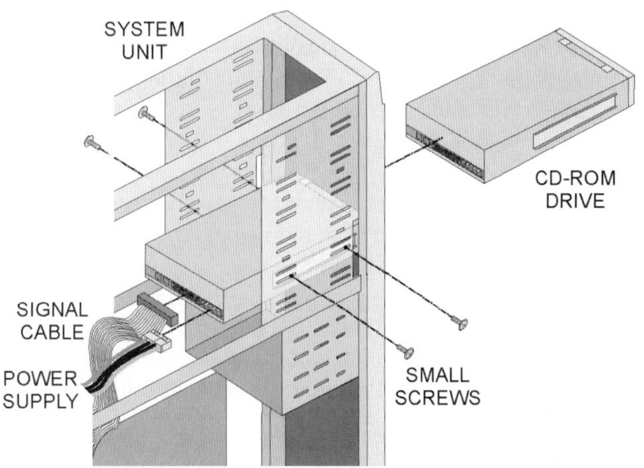

Figure 4-27: Installing an Internal CD-ROM Drive

To connect the drive to the system, hook up the CD-ROM drive to the HDD signal cable, observing proper orientation. Connect the audio cable to the drive and to the sound card's **CD Input** connection (if a sound card is installed).

CD Input

Configuring CD-ROM Drives

As previously indicated, the CD-ROM drive must be properly configured for the system it is being installed in. In an IDE system, the Master/Slave setting must be confirmed. In a SCSI system, the ID setting must be correct. In a SCSI system, the only requirement is that a valid ID setting is configured. In an IDE system, however, some thought may be required as to how to configure the drive.

In a single HDD system, the CD-ROM drive is normally set up as the Slave drive on the primary interface. However, in a two HDD system, the CD-ROM drive would most likely be configured as the Master or Single drive on the secondary interface. If the system also contains a sound card with a built-in IDE interface, it should be disabled to prevent it from interfering with the primary or secondary interfaces.

After the hardware has been installed, it will be necessary to install its software drivers. Consult the owner's manual for instructions on software installation. Typically, all that is required is to insert the OEM driver disk into the floppy drive, and follow the manufacturer's directions for installing the drivers. If the drive fails to operate at this point, reboot the system using single-step verification and check the information on the various boot screens for error messages associated with the CD-ROM drive.

Microsoft CD Extension (MSCDEX)

driver signature

You should check the system to determine whether it has AUTOEXEC.BAT and CONFIG.SYS files. If so, these files should be examined for updated information. In particular, check for the presence of the **Microsoft CD Extension** (**MSCDEX**) driver. This driver was used to provide access to the system's CD-ROM drives under older Microsoft operating system versions. It must be loaded from the CONFIG.SYS file using a DEVICE= or DEVICEHIGH command. This driver assigns the logical drive letters to all CD-ROM drives in the system along with a unique **driver signature** (name). The signature is used to differentiate one CD-ROM drive from another in the system.

TEST TIP

Remember what type of device the MSCDEX file is used with and where it should be located.

CDFS (CD-ROM File System)

In Windows 95, an advanced CD-ROM driver called **CDFS** (**CD-ROM File System**) was implemented to provide protected-mode operation of the drive. Windows 9x retains the MSCDEX files for real-mode operation. If Windows 9x detects that the CDFS has taken over control of the CD-ROM on its initial bootup, it will REM any MSCDEX lines in the AUTOEXEC.BAT file.

The performance of a Windows 9x system can be enhanced by establishing a supplemental CD-ROM cache. This cache enables the system to store pages of information cached from the CD in RAM memory, and as we already know, RAM access is always faster than accessing any other computer structure. The supplemental cache is established through the Control Panel's System icon as follows:

1. Under the System icon, click the Performance tab and select the File System button.
2. Set the Supplemental Cache Size slider to the desired cache size.
3. Set the Optimize Access Pattern for setting to the Quad-speed or higher option (unless you have an old single- or double-speed drive). This will establish a 1238 KB supplemental cache (provided the system's RAM size is larger than 12 MB).
4. Click the OK button and restart the system to create the cache.

INSTALLING AND CONFIGURING DISK DRIVES

The A+ Core objective 1.5 states that the test taker should be able to identify proper procedures for installing and configuring IDE/EIDE devices. Examples include:

- Master/slave
- Devices per channel

The A+ Core objective 1.6 states that the test taker should be able to identify proper procedures for installing and configuring SCSI devices. Topics include:

- Address/termination conflicts
- Cabling
- Types (standard, wide, fast, ultra-wide)
- Internal versus external
- Switch and jumper settings

Hard disk drives are the mainstays of mass data storage in PC-compatible systems. In modern PC systems, IDE and SCSI drives are most commonly used. Therefore, the computer technician must be able to successfully install and configure both IDE and SCSI drives, as well as other devices that employ IDE and SCSI interfaces. The following sections of the chapter cover the characteristics of these two interfaces, including standard variations and common connector types associated with each.

Integrated Drive Electronics Interface

AT Attachment (ATA)

The Integrated Drive Electronics (IDE) interface, also referred to as an **AT Attachment (ATA)** interface, is a system-level interface designed to connect disk drive units to the system. The IDE interface places most of the controller electronics on the drive unit. Therefore, data travels in parallel between the computer and the drive unit. The controller circuitry on the drive handles all of the parallel-to-serial and serial-to-parallel conversions. This permits the interface to be independent of the host computer design.

An IDE drive stores low-level formatting information on itself. This information is placed on the drive by its manufacturer, and is used by the controller for alignment and sector sizing of the drive. The IDE controller extracts the raw data (format and actual data information) coming from the R/W heads and converts it into signal that can be applied to the computer's buses.

host adapter

The IDE interface uses a single 40-pin cable to connect the hard drives to the adapter card or system board. Its signal cable arrangement is depicted in Figure 4-28. In a system-level interface, the I/O card that plugs into the expansion slot is called a **host adapter** instead of a controller card. It should be apparent from the figure that the IDE host adapter is quite simple, since most of the interface signals originate directly from the system's extended bus lines.

PIN DESCRIPTION

Pin	Description	Pin	Description
1	Reset	2	Ground
3	Data 7	4	Data 8
5	Data 6	6	Data 9
7	Data 5	8	Data 10
9	Data 4	10	Data 11
11	Data 3	12	Data 12
13	Data 2	14	Data 13
15	Data 1	16	Data 14
17	Data 0	18	Data 15
19	Ground	20	Unused
21	Unused	22	Ground
23	$\overline{IOW}$	24	Ground
25	$\overline{IOR}$	26	Ground
27	IOCHRDY	28	Bale
29	Unused	30	Ground
31	IRQ14	32	$\overline{IOCS16}$
33	A1	34	PDAIG
35	A0	36	A2
37	$\overline{HDCS0}$	38	$\overline{HDCS1}$
39	$\overline{SLV ACT}$	40	Ground

CONNECTOR ENDS

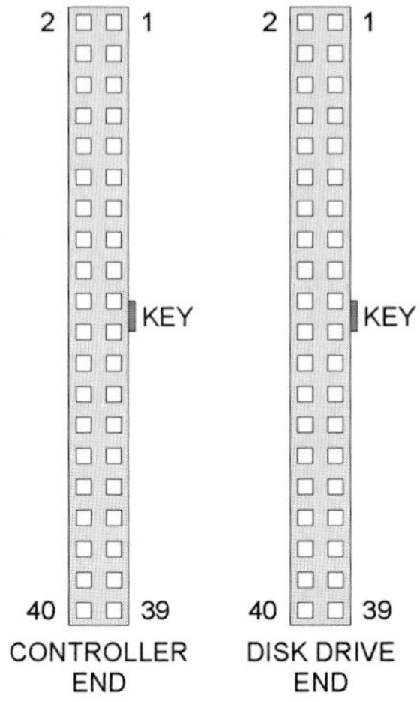

Figure 4-28: The IDE Signal Cable

Configuring IDE Drives

single -drive

master

slave

The host adapter basically serves three functions. These include providing the select signals to differentiate between a **single-drive** system, or the **master** and **slave** drives. It also provides the 3 least significant address bits (A0-A2), and the interface Reset signal. The HDCS0 signal is used to enable the master drive, and the HDCS1 signal is used to enable the slave drive. The relationships between the host adapter, the system buses, and the IDE interfaces are described in Figure 4-29.

> **TEST TIP**
>
> Remember the three configurations that can be set on an IDE drive.

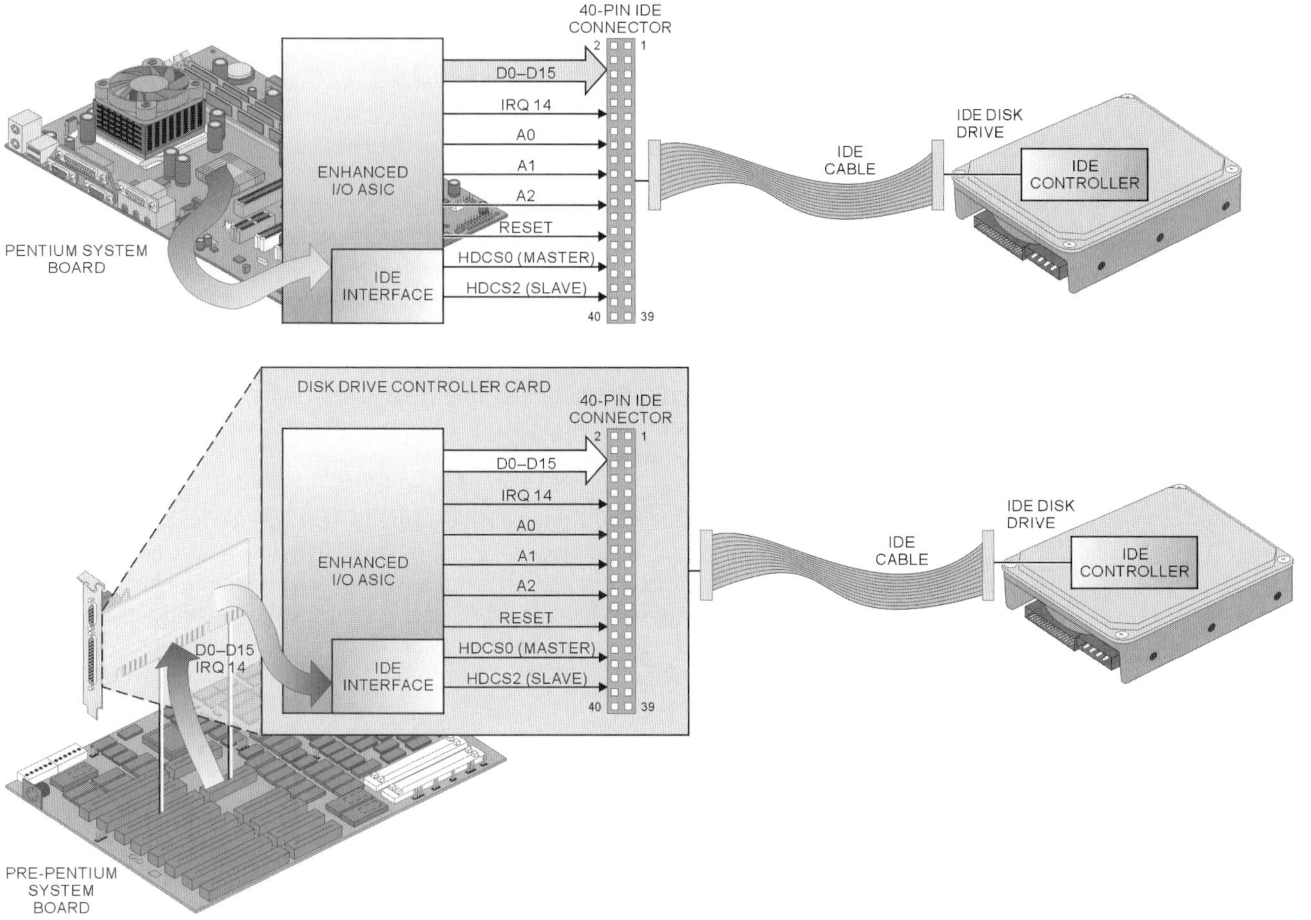

Figure 4-29: The Host Adapter, System Buses, and IDE Interface

Most IDE drives come from the manufacturer configured for operation as a single drive, or as the master drive in a multi-drive system. In order to install the drive as a second, or slave, drive, it is usually necessary to install, remove, or to move a jumper block, as illustrated in Figure 4-30. Some hosts disable the interface's Cable Select pin for slave drives. With these types of hosts, it is necessary to install a jumper for the Cable Select option on the drive. Consult the system's user's manuals to see if it supports this function.

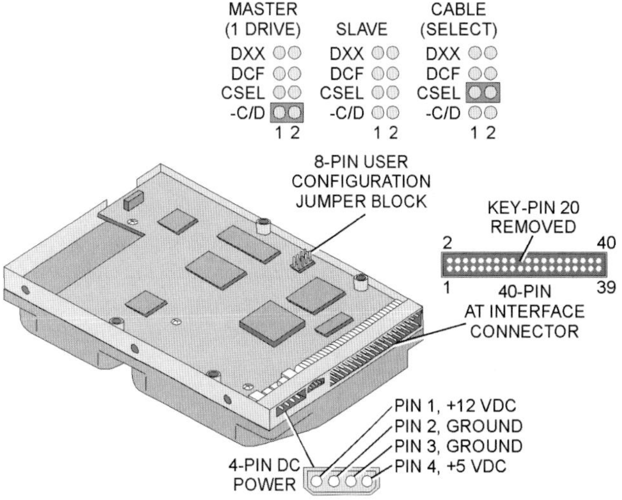

Figure 4-30: IDE Master/Slave Settings

In the MS-DOS system, the primary partitions of multiple IDE hard drives are assigned the first logical drive identifiers. If an IDE drive is partitioned into two logical drives, the system will identify them as drives C: and D:. If a second IDE drive is added as a slave drive with two additional logical drives, MS-DOS will reassign the partitions on the first drive to be logical drives C: and E:, while the partitions on the slave drive will be D: and F:.

Advanced EIDE Specifications

As mentioned earlier in this chapter, there are a variety of IDE-related specifications. The initial IDE standard was the IDE/ATA specification. IDE and ATA are the same standard. It supported a maximum throughout of 8.3 MBps through the 40-pin IDE signal cable.

Enhanced IDE (EIDE)

ATA-2

AT Attachment Packet Interface (ATAPI)

Updated IDE specifications have been developed to enable more than two drives to exist on the interface. This new IDE specification is called **Enhanced IDE** (**EIDE**), or the **ATA-2** interface. The new standard actually includes the ATA-2/EIDE/ATAPI specifications (the ATAPI standard is a derivative of the ATA-2 standard). The **AT Attachment Packet Interface** (**ATAPI**) specification provides improved IDE drivers for use with CD-ROM drives and new data transfer methods. This specification provides maximum throughput of 16.7 MBps through the 40-pin IDE signal cable.

Programmed I/O (PIO)

The ATA standards provide for different **Programmed I/O** (**PIO**) modes that offer higher performance capabilities, as illustrated in Table 4-5. Most IDE devices are now capable of operating in modes 3 or 4. However, the IDE port must be attached to the PCI bus to use these modes. Some system boards only place the IDE1 connection on this bus, while the IDE2 connection is a function of the ISA bus. In these cases, devices installed on the IDE2 connector will only be capable of mode 2 operation.

Table 4-5: ATA PIO Modes

PIO MODE	TRANSFER	ATA VERSION
0	3.3 MB/sec	ATA-1
1	5.2 MB/sec	ATA-1
2	8.3 MB/sec	ATA-1
3	11.1 MB/sec	ATA-2
4	16.6 MB/sec	ATA-2
4	33.3 MB/sec	ATA-3/Ultra DMA 33
4	66.6 MB/sec	ATA-4/Ultra DMA 66
4	100 MB/sec	ATA 100

Ultra DMA (UDMA)

An additional development of the ATA standard has provided the ATA-3/Ultra ATA 33 specification that boosts throughput between the IDE device and the system to 33.3 MBps. This standard still employs the 40-pin IDE signal cable. It relies on the system to support the 33.3 MBps burst mode transfer operation through the **Ultra DMA** (**UDMA**) protocol.

Newer IDE enhancements called ATA-4/Ultra ATA 66 and Ultra ATA 100 provide even higher data throughput by doubling the number of conductors in the IDE signal cable. The IDE connector has remained compatible with the 40-pin IDE connection, but each pin has been provided with its own ground conductor in the cable. The Ultra ATA 66 specification provides 66 MBps while the Ultra ATA 100 connection provides 100 MBps.

TEST TIP

Remember how the Ultra ATA 66 interface cable can be identified.

Both Ultra ATA versions support 33.3 MBps data rates when used with a standard 40-pin/40-conductor IDE signal cable. Therefore, Ultra ATA 66 and 100 devices can still be used with systems that don't support the new IDE standards.

These operating modes must be configured correctly through the system's CMOS Setup utility. These settings are discussed under the Chipset Features Setup Functions heading as described in Chapter 2.

TEST TIP

Remember that IDE bus driver support is built into the BIOS of system boards that have integrated IDE host adapters.

Small Computer System Interface

Small Computer System Interface (SCSI)

scuzzy

SCSI host adapter

The **Small Computer System Interface** (**SCSI**), often referred to as the "**scuzzy**" standard, like the IDE concept, provides a true system-level interface for the drive. Nearly all of the drive's controller electronics are located on the peripheral device. As with the IDE host adapter, the duties of the **SCSI host adapter** are reduced to mostly physical connection functions, along with some signal compatibility handling.

Using this arrangement, data arrives at the system interface in a form that is already usable by the host computer. This can be seen through the SCSI interface description in Figure 4-31. Note that the original SCSI interface described in the figure only makes provisions for 8-bit parallel data transfers.

PIN DESCRIPTION

Pin	Description	Pin	Description
1	Ground	2	Data 0
3	Ground	4	Data 1
5	Ground	6	Data 2
7	Ground	8	Data 3
9	Ground	10	Data 4
11	Ground	12	Data 5
13	Ground	14	Data 6
15	Ground	16	Data 7
17	Ground	18	Data Parity (Odd)
19	Ground	20	Ground
21	Ground	22	Ground
23	Ground	24	Ground
25	No Connection	26	No Connection
27	Ground	28	Ground
29	Ground	30	Ground
31	Ground	32	Attention
33	Ground	34	Ground
35	Ground	36	Busy
37	Ground	38	ACK
39	Ground	40	Reset
41	Ground	42	Message
43	Ground	44	Select
45	Ground	46	C/D
47	Ground	48	Request
49	Ground	50	I/O

CONNECTOR ENDS

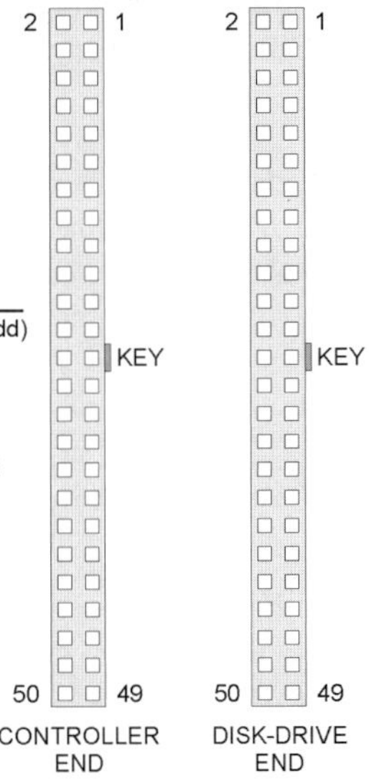

2 1 KEY 50 49
CONTROLLER END

2 1 KEY 50 49
DISK-DRIVE END

Figure 4-31: The SCSI Interface Connection

The SCSI interface can be used to connect diverse types of peripherals to the system. As an example, a SCSI chain could connect a controller to a hard drive, a CD-ROM drive, a high-speed tape drive, a scanner, and a printer. Additional SCSI devices are added to the system by daisy-chaining them together: The input of the second device is attached to the SCSI output of the first device, and so forth.

SCSI Cables and Connectors

The SCSI standard has been implemented using a number of cable types. In PC-compatible systems, the SCSI interface uses a 50-pin signal cable arrangement. Internally, the cable is a 50-pin flat ribbon cable. However, 50-pin shielded cables, with Centronics-like connectors, are used for external SCSI connections. The 50-pin SCSI connections are referred to as **A-cables**.

A-cables

Advanced SCSI specifications have created additional cabling specifications. A 50-conductor alternative cable using 50-pin D-shell connectors has been added to the A-cable specification for SCSI-2 devices. A second cable type, referred to as **B-cable**, was added to the SCSI-2 specification to provide 16- and 32-bit parallel data transfers. However, this arrangement employed multiple connectors at each end of the cable and never received widespread acceptance in the market. A revised 68-pin **P-cable** format, using D-shell connectors, was introduced to support 16-bit transfers in the SCSI-3 specification. A 68-pin **Q-cable** version was also adopted in SCSI for 32-bit transfers. The P and Q cables must be used in parallel to conduct 32-bit transfers.

B-cable

P-cable

Q-cable

For some PS/2 models, IBM used a special 60-pin Centronics-like connector for their SCSI connections. The version of the SCSI interface used in the Apple Macintosh employs a variation of the standard that features a proprietary miniature 25-pin D-shell connector.

These cabling variations create a hardware incompatibility between different SCSI devices. Likewise, there are SCSI devices that just will not work with each other due to software incompatibilities.

In addition, SCSI devices may be classified as internal or as external devices. An internal SCSI device has no power supply of its own and, therefore, must be connected to one of the system's options power connectors. On the other hand, external SCSI devices come with built-in or plug-in power supplies that need to be connected to a commercial ac outlet. Therefore, when choosing a SCSI device, always inquire about compatibility between it and any other SCSI devices installed in the system.

Figure 4-32 depicts a 25-pin D-shell, a 50-pin Centronics, and a 68-pin Centronics-type SCSI connectors used for external connections. Inside the computer, the SCSI specification uses 50-pin and 68-pin ribbon cables with BERG pin connectors.

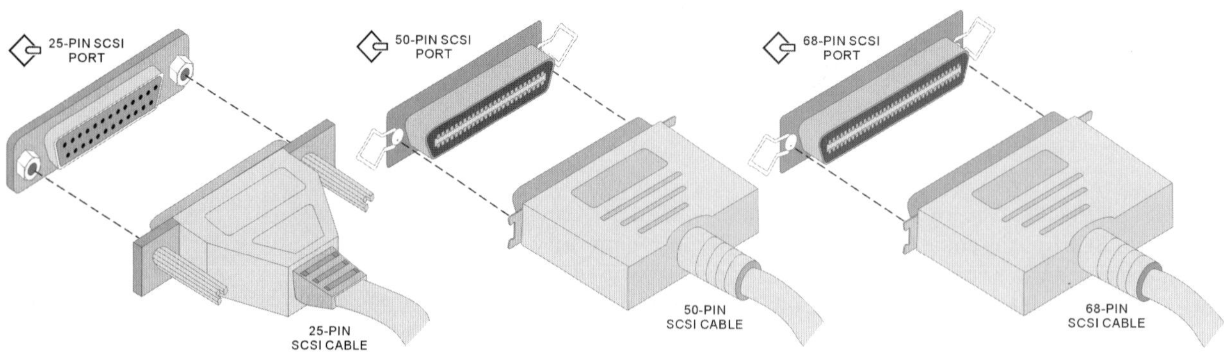

Figure 4-32: SCSI Connectors

SCSI Addressing

SCSI-In

SCSI-Out

The SCSI specification allows up to eight SCSI devices to be connected together. The SCSI port can be daisy-chained to allow up to six external peripherals to be connected to the system. To connect multiple SCSI devices to a SCSI host, all of the devices, except the last one, must have two SCSI connectors. One for **SCSI-In**, and one for **SCSI-Out**. Which connector is which does not matter. However, if the device only has one SCSI connector, it must be connected to the end of the chain.

TEST TIP

Remember how many devices can be daisy chained on a standard SCSI interface, and which ID numbers are assumed automatically.

It is possible to use multiple SCSI host adapters within a single system to increase the number of devices that can be used. The system's first SCSI controller can handle up to 7 devices, while the additional SCSI controller can boost the system to support up to 14 SCSI devices.

SCSI ID numbers

SCSI-7

SCSI-0

Each SCSI device in a chain must have a unique ID number assigned to it. Even though there are a total of eight possible **SCSI ID numbers** for each controller, only six are available for use with external devices. The SCSI specification refers to the SCSI controller as **SCSI-7** (by default), and then classifies the first internal hard drive as **SCSI-0**. If two devices are set to the same ID number, one or both of them will appear invisible to the system.

TEST TIP

Be aware of how SCSI ID priorities are set.

With older SCSI devices, address settings were established through jumpers on the host adapter card. Each device had a SCSI number selection switch, or a set of configuration jumpers for establishing its ID number. Figure 4-33 illustrates a three-jumper configuration block that can be used to establish the SCSI ID number. In the figure, an open jumper pair can be counted as a binary 0 while a shorted pair represents a binary 1. With a three-pair jumper block, it is possible to represent the numbers 0 through 7. In PnP systems, the BIOS will configure the device addresses using information obtained directly from the SCSI host adapter during the bootup process.

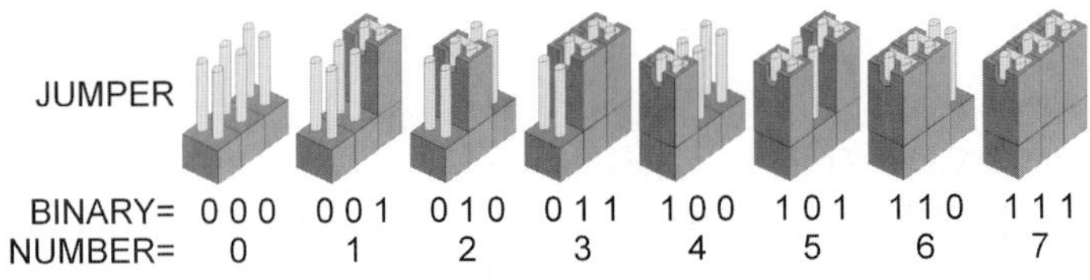

Figure 4-33: Configuring a SCSI ID Number

Unlike other HDD types, SCSI hard drives are not configured as part of the system's CMOS Setup function. This is due to the fact that DOS and Windows 3.x never included support for SCSI devices. Therefore, SCSI drivers must be loaded during bootup before the system can communicate with the drive. However, Windows 9x and Windows 2000 do offer SCSI support. SCSI drives also require no low-level formatting. Therefore, the second thing you do when installing a SCSI drive is to partition it.

SCSI Termination

terminated

The SCSI daisy chain must be **terminated** with a resistor network pack at both ends. Single-connector SCSI devices are normally terminated internally. If not, a SCSI terminator cable (containing a built-in resistor pack) must be installed at the end of the chain. SCSI termination is a major cause of SCSI-related problems. Poor terminations cause a variety of different system problems including:

- failed system startups
- hard drive crashes
- random system failures

SCSI Specifications

TEST TIP

Memorize the permissible lengths stated for SCSI cables and chains.

The maximum recommended length for a complete standard SCSI chain is 20 feet (6 m). However, unless the cables are heavily shielded, they become susceptible to data corruption caused by induced noise. Therefore, a maximum single SCSI segment of less than 3 feet (1 m) is recommended. Don't forget the length of the internal cabling when dealing with SCSI cable distances. You can realistically count on about three feet of internal cable, so reduce the maximum total length of the chain to about 15 feet (4.5 m).

Wide SCSI-2

An updated SCSI specification was developed by the ANSI committee to double the number of data lines in the standard interface. It also adds balanced, dual-line drivers that allow much faster data transfer speeds to be used. This implementation is referred to as **Wide SCSI-2**. The specification expands the SCSI specification into a 16/32-bit bus standard and increased the cable and connector specification to 68 pins.

Fast SCSI-2

An additional improvement increased the synchronous data transfer option for the interface from 5 Mbps to 10 Mbps. This implementation became known as **Fast SCSI-2**. Under this system, the system and the I/O device conduct non-data message, command, and status operations in 8-bit asynchronous mode. After agreeing on a larger, or faster, file-transfer format, they conduct transfers using an agreed-upon word size and transmission mode. The increased speed of the Fast SCSI specification reduced the maximum length of the SCSI chain to about 10 feet. Fast SCSI-2 connections use 50-pin connectors.

Wide Fast SCSI-2

A third version brought together both improvements and became known as **Wide Fast SCSI-2**. This version of the standard doubles the bus size to 16 bits and employs the faster transfer methods to provide a maximum bus speed of 20 MBps supporting a chain of up to 15 additional devices.

Ultra SCSI

A newer update, referred to as **Ultra SCSI**, makes provisions for a special high-speed serial transfer mode and special communications media, such as fiber-optic cabling. This update has been combined with both wide and fast revisions to produce:

- ULTRA SCSI
- ULTRA2 SCSI
- WIDE ULTRA SCSI
- WIDE ULTRA2 SCSI
- WIDE ULTRA3 SCSI

The addition of the wide specification doubles the bus width and number of devices that can be serviced by the interface. Likewise, the Ultra designation indicates a speed increase due to improved technology. Combining the two technologies will yield a 4X increase in data throughput (i.e., Wide Ultra SCSI= 40 MBps compared to Ultra SCSI = 20 MBps and Wide and Fast SCSI = 10 MBps).

The latest SCSI specification, referred to as Ultra 320 SCSI, boosts the maximum bus speed to 320 MBps, using a 16-bit bus and supporting up to 15 external devices. The Ultra 320 SCSI connection employs a special 80-pin **Single Connector Attachment (SCA)** connector.

Single Connector Attachment (SCA)

TEST TIP

Know the number of devices that can be attached to an IDE, EIDE, and standard SCSI interfaces.

The increased speed capabilities of the SCSI interfaces make them attractive for intensive applications such as large file servers for networks, and multimedia video stations. However, the EIDE interface is generally more widely used due to its lower cost and nearly equal performance. Table 4-6 contrasts the specifications of the SCSI and IDE interfaces.

Table 4-6: SCSI/IDE Specifications

INTERFACE	BUS SIZE	# DEVICES	ASYNC. SPEED	SYNC. SPEED
IDE (ATA-1)	16 bits	2	4 MB/s	3.3/5.2/8.3 MB/s
EIDE (ATA-2)	16 bits	4	4 MB/s	11/16 MB/s
SCSI (SCSI-1)	8 bits	7	2 MB/s	5 MB/s
WIDE SCSI (SCSI-2)	8/16 bits	15	2 MB/s	5 MB/s
FAST SCSI (SCSI-2)	8/16 bits	7	2 MB/s	5/10 MB/s
WIDE FAST SCSI (SCSI-2)	8/16 bits	15	2 MB/s	10/20 MB/s
ULTRA SCSI	8 bits	7	2 MB/s	10/20 MB/s
ULTRA WIDE SCSI (SCSI-3)	16 bits	15	2 MB/s	10/20/40 MB/s
ULTRA2 SCSI	8 bits	7	2 MB/s	10/20/40 MB/s
WIDE ULTRA2 SCSI	16 bits	15	2 MB/s	10/20/40/80 MB/s
WIDE ULTRA3 SCSI	16 bits	15	2 MB/s	10/20/40/160 MB/s
ULTRA320 SCSI	16 bits	15	2 MB/s	10/20/40/320 MB/s

Peripheral Storage Devices

External storage devices normally connect to options adapter cards installed in the system board's expansion slots. They also tend to employ separate, external power supply units.

Several newer storage technologies, such as removable hard drive media, have been designed to take advantage of the enhanced parallel port specifications of modern systems. These devices can be connected directly into the system's parallel port, or can be connected to the system through another device that is connected to the port. The device's installation software is used to configure it for use in the system.

Installing External Storage Devices

The general procedure for installing external storage devices is:

1. Configure the device for operation.

   a. Refer to the device's user's manual regarding any IRQ and COM jumper or switch settings.
   b. Record the card's default IRQ and COM settings.
   c. Set the device's configuration jumpers to operate at the default setting.

2. Install the device's adapter card (if necessary).

   a. Turn the system off.
   b. Remove the cover from system unit.
   c. Locate a compatible empty expansion slot.
   d. Remove the expansion slot cover from the rear of the system unit.
   e. Install the adapter card in the expansion slot.
   f. Reinstall the screw to secure the card to the back panel of the system unit.

3. Make the device's external connections.

   a. Connect the device's signal cable to the appropriate connector at the rear of the system.
   b. Connect the opposite end of the cable to the device.
   c. Verify that the power switch or power supply is turned off.
   d. Connect the power supply to the external storage unit.

4. Configure the device's software.

   a. Turn the system on.
   b. Check the CMOS Setup to ensure that the port setting is correct.
   c. Run the device's installation routine.

DISK DRIVE UPGRADING AND OPTIMIZING

The A+ Core Hardware objective 1.8 states that the test taker should be able to identify hardware methods of upgrading system performance, procedures for replacing basic subsystem components, unique components and when to use them. One of the components listed under this objective is the hard drive unit. CD-ROM drives are also good candidates for periodic upgrading.

As with other modules in the PC, the hard disk and CD-ROM drives can be upgraded as new, or better, components become available, or as the system's application changes. As this A+ objective points out, computer technicians must be capable of upgrading the various components of the system—including its disk drives. The technician should also be able to optimize the operation of the drive to obtain the best performance possible for a given system configuration.

HDD Upgrading

One of the key components in keeping the system up to date is the hard disk drive. Software manufacturers continue to produce larger and larger programs. In addition, the types of programs found on the typical PC are expanding. Many newer programs place high demands on the hard drive to feed information, such as large graphics files or digitized voice and video, to the system for processing.

Invariably, the system will begin to produce error messages that say that the hard drive is full. The first line of action is to use software disk utilities to optimize the organization of the drive. These utilities, such as **CHKDSK**, **SCANDISK**, and **DEFRAG**, are covered in detail in Chapter 12—*Operating System Troubleshooting*. The second step is to remove unnecessary programs and files from the hard drive. Programs and information that are rarely, or never, used should be moved to an archival media, such as removable disks or tape.

CHKDSK

SCANDISK

DEFRAG

In any event, there may come a time when it is necessary to determine whether the hard drive needs to be replaced in order to optimize the performance of the system. One guideline suggests that the drive should be replaced if the percentage of unused disk space drops below 20%.

Another reason to consider upgrading the HDD involves its ability to deliver information to the system. If the system is constantly waiting for information from the hard drive, replacing it should be considered as an option. Not all system slow-downs are connected to the HDD, but many are. Remember that the HDD is the mechanical part of the memory system, whereas everything else is electronic.

As with the storage space issue, HDD speed can be optimized through software configurations, such as a disk cache. However, once it has been optimized in this manner, any further speed increases must be accomplished by upgrading the hardware.

When considering an HDD upgrade, determine what the real system needs are for the hard drive. Multimedia-intensive applications can place heavy performance demands on the hard disk drive to operate correctly. Moving large image, audio, and video files into RAM on demand requires high performance from the drive. Critical HDD specifications associated with disk drive performance include:

- **Access Time**—The average time, expressed in milliseconds, required to position the drive's R/W heads over a specified track/cylinder and reach a specified sector on the track.
- **Track-Seek Time**—The amount of time required for the drive's R/W heads to move between cylinders and settle over a particular track following the seek command being issued by the system.
- **Data Transfer Rate**—The speed, expressed in megabytes per second (MBps), at which data is transferred between the system and the drive.

Access Time

Track-Seek Time

Data Transfer Rate

These factors should be checked thoroughly when upgrading an HDD unit for speed-critical applications. In contemporary systems, the choice of hard drives for high-performance applications alternates back and forth between IDE/EIDE drives and SCSI drives. The EIDE drives are competitive and relatively easy to install, whereas the high-end SCSI specifications offer additional performance, but require additional setup effort and an additional host adapter card. Refer to Table 4-2 for comparisons of SCSI and IDE specifications.

Before upgrading the HDD unit, make certain that the existing drive is providing all of the performance that it can. Check for SMARTDRV or VCACHE arrangements at the software configuration level and optimize them if possible. Also, determine how much performance increase can be gained through other upgrading efforts before changing out the hard drive.

If the drive is being upgraded substantially, such as from a 500 MB IDE drive to a 1.4 GB EIDE drive, check the capabilities of the system's ROM BIOS. If the BIOS does not support LBA or ECHS enhancements, the drive capacity of even the largest hard drive will be limited to 528 MB.

TEST TIP

Be aware that the BIOS may be a size-limiting factor in disk drive partition sizes.

Finally, determine how much longer the unit in question is likely to be used before being replaced. If the decision to upgrade the HDD stands, ultimately, the best advice is to get the biggest, fastest hard drive possible. Don't forget to look at the fact that a different I/O bus architecture may add to the performance increase.

CHAPTER SUMMARY

The first section of the chapter explained the fundamentals of recording and reading data with magnetic media.

This introductory information was followed by an extensive explanation of general disk drive operations.

The third section dealt with installation and operation of disk drive systems.

The final sections of the chapter covered other magnetic storage devices and strategies commonly used with personal computer systems.

At this point, review the objectives listed at the beginning of the chapter to be certain that you understand and can perform each item listed there.

KEY POINTS REVIEW

This chapter has explored the use of magnetic media to provide long-term, high-volume data storage for personal computer systems. Review the following key points before moving into the Review and Exam Questions sections to make sure you are comfortable with each point. Afterward, answer the Review Questions that follow to verify your knowledge of the information.

- From the beginning, most secondary memory systems have involved storing binary information in the form of magnetic charges on moving magnetic surfaces.
- The system unit normally comes from the manufacturer with a floppy disk drive (FDD), a hard disk drive (HDD), and a CD-ROM drive installed.
- The most common drive arrays are RAID systems. RAID is an acronym for Redundant Arrays of Independent (Inexpensive) Disks. Five levels of RAID technology specifications are given by the RAID Advisory Board.
- Soon after the Compact Disc (CD) became popular for storing audio signals on optical material, the benefits of storing computer information in this manner became apparent. With a CD, data is written digitally on a light-sensitive material by a powerful, highly focused laser beam.
- The information on a compact disc is stored in one continuous spiral track, unlike floppy disks, where the data is stored in multiple, concentric tracks. The compact disc storage format still divides the data into separate sectors. However, the sectors of a CD-ROM disc are physically the same size. The disc spins counterclockwise, and it slows down as the laser diode emitter/detector unit approaches the outside of the disc.
- Another type of CD drive is a Write Once, Read Many (WORM) drive. As the acronym implies, these drives allow users to write information to the disc once, and then retrieve this information as you would with a CD-ROM drive. With WORM drives, once information is stored on a disc, the data cannot be changed or deleted.
- Tape drive units are another popular type of information storage system. These systems can store large amounts of data on small tape cartridges.
- Tape drives are generally used to store large amounts of information that will not need to be accessed often, or quickly. Such information includes backup copies of programs and data. This type of data security is a necessity with records such as business transactions, payroll, artwork, etc.
- Before a high-level format can be performed, the drive must be partitioned. The disk management capabilities of the oldest versions of MS-DOS (2.x, 3.x) imposed a limit on the size of a drive at 32 MB. However, as HDD technology steadily increased, the capacities of the physical drives eventually passed this limit. Fortunately, operating systems can partition, or divide, large physical drives into multiple logical drives. Each logical drive is identified by a different drive letter (such as C, D, E, and so on).
- The high-level format procedure is performed by the operating system. This format routine creates a blank File Allocation Table (FAT) and root directory on the disk.
- In Windows 95, an advanced CD-ROM driver called CDFS (CD-ROM File System) was implemented to provide protected-mode operation of the drive. Windows 95 retains the MSCDEX files for real-mode operation. If Windows 95 detects that the CDFS has taken over control of the CD-ROM on its initial bootup, it will REM the MSCDEX lines in the AUTOEXEC.BAT file.

REVIEW QUESTIONS

The following questions test your knowledge of the material presented in this chapter.

1. What is the table that tracks files and directories on an NTFS drive called?
2. Which interrupt request channel is normally used with floppy disk drives in a PC-compatible system?
3. Name the tool that is used to perform partitioning in an NTFS system like Windows 2000.
4. How can the A: and B: floppy drives be differentiated by looking into the system unit?
5. What action should be taken if a "Disk Boot Failure" message is displayed on the monitor screen?
6. List the HDD-related hardware components tested by the chapter's HDD troubleshooting procedure, in the order they are checked.
7. List the non-hardware items checked by the HDD troubleshooting procedure, in the order they are checked.
8. What protected-mode driver did the Windows operating system use to replace the real-mode MSCDEX driver?
9. Describe how data is stored on a magnetic disk.
10. List the steps involved in installing a hard disk drive in a desktop system.
11. Describe the differences between the two types of drive array applications.
12. How and why is a cartridge tape different than a standard audio cassette tape?
13. What is formatting as it applies to a disk?
14. What is the major procedural difference between installing a floppy drive and a hard drive?
15. What is the main function of the high-level format?

EXAM QUESTIONS

1. The maximum size of a disk partition using Windows 98 is ______.
   a. 500 MB
   b. 2 GB
   c. 100 MB
   d. 2 TB
2. What action should always be taken before upgrading a hard disk drive?
   a. Use the DOS VER command to determine what version of DOS is currently in use.
   b. Use the FDISK command to locate any lost cluster chains on the original drive.
   c. The contents of the installed drive should be backed up to some other media.
   d. Save the values of the installed drive's CMOS setup values for use with the new drive.
3. Head-to-Disk Interference (HDI) is also referred to as _________.
   a. a head crash
   b. R/W head bounce
   c. interleaving
   d. data compression
4. Identify the function that you would not employ on a SCSI drive when installing it.
   a. Low level format it
   b. Partition it
   c. Format it
   d. Install the operating system on it
5. What precaution should always be taken before reformatting a hard disk drive?
   a. Use the DOS VER command to determine what version of DOS is currently in use.
   b. Use the FDISK command to locate any lost cluster chains.
   c. Use the Defrag utility to remove any fragmentation from the drive before formatting.
   d. Use an anti-virus utility to remove any viruses from the drive before formatting.
6. The _____ partition is the partition that the system will boot to.
   a. Active
   b. Primary
   c. System
   d. Extended
7. A group of logically related disk sectors is called _____.
   a. a FAT entry
   b. a cluster
   c. a byte-sync
   d. a bit-sync

8. What is the main purpose of a RAID 1 drive array?
   a. To act as an error-checking and correction method
   b. To create the appearance of one very large drive
   c. To act as a redundant data-backup method
   d. To act as a high-speed retrieval system
9. What function does the FDISK utility perform?
   a. It removes lost allocation units from the drive.
   b. It creates partitions on the physical disk.
   c. It provides the low-level format for the drive.
   d. It provides the high-level format for the drive.
10. Which IDE interface version employs an 80-wire, 40-pin cable?
   a. IDE
   b. ATA-2
   c. ATA-66
   d. EIDE

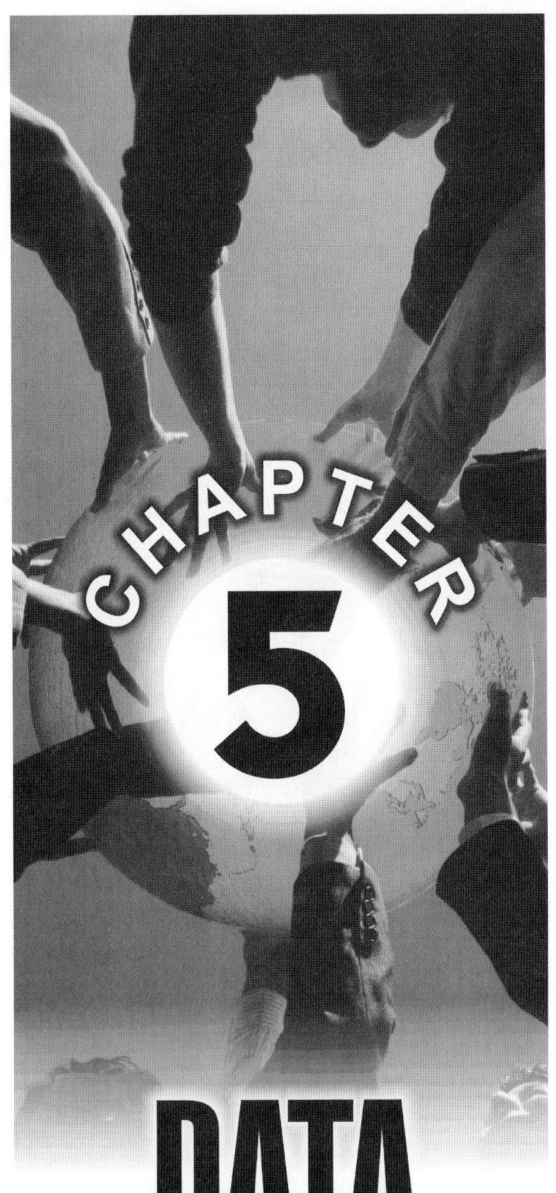

DATA COMMUNICATIONS

OBJECTIVES

OBJECTIVES

Upon completion of this chapter and its related lab procedures, you should be able to perform these tasks:

1. Define the term modem.
2. Define the term baud.
3. Compare hardware- and software-oriented (code control) protocols.
4. Describe the operation and hardware of an Ethernet LAN system.
5. Differentiate among typical LAN topologies.
6. Differentiate among different types of network media (10BASE-2, 10BASE-5, and so on).
7. Define the term wide area network (WAN).
8. Describe the function of routers, hubs, and bridges in network systems.
9. Discuss basic concepts relating to Internet access (i.e., dial-up, ISP connections, browsers).
10. Discuss ISDN, DSL and cable modem connections.
11. Describe FTP operations.
12. Discuss common Internet concepts and terminology (such as email).
13. Discuss the purpose and use of on Internet browser.

CHAPTER 5

DATA COMMUNICATIONS

INTRODUCTION

The most explosive area of personal computer use is in the realm of data communications. Increasingly, personal computers are being connected to one another. Data communications can be as simple as connecting two units together so they can talk to each other. This can be accomplished by wiring their serial, or parallel, ports together when they are in close physical proximity to each other (up to a few feet). Communicating over longer distances requires additional hardware in the form of a modem, or a network card, and software, in the form of drivers and protocols.

When more than two computers are linked together so they can share information, a network is formed. Networks in a relatively confined geographical area are called Local Area Networks (LANs), while networks distributed over wider geographical areas are referred to as Wide Area Networks (WANs).

BASIC NETWORKING CONCEPTS

The A+ Core Hardware objective 6.1 states that the test taker should be able to identify basic networking concepts, including how a network works and the ramifications of repairs on the network. Content may include the following:

- Installing and configuring network cards
- Network access
- Full-duplex, half-duplex
- Cabling (twisted pair, coaxial, fiber optic)
- Ways to network a PC
- Physical network topologies
- Increasing bandwidth
- Loss of data
- Network slowdown
- Infrared
- Hardware protocols
- Network interface cards

Within a very short time span, the use of local area networks has grown immensely. They have become such an integral part of commercial computer systems, that, as the A+ objective points out, the PC technician must understand how they function. The following sections will present basic local area networking concepts and practices.

LOCAL AREA NETWORKS

Local area networks (LANs)

Local area networks (LANs) are systems designed to connect computers together in relatively close proximity. These connections enable users attached to the network to share resources such as printers and modems. LAN connections also enable users to communicate with each other and share data among their computers.

topology

protocol

When discussing LANs, there are two basic topics to consider: the LAN's **topology** (hardware connection method) and its **protocol** (communication control method). In concept, a minimum of three stations must be connected to have a true LAN. If only two units are connected, point-to-point communications software and a simple null modem could be employed.

LAN Topologies

Network topologies are physical connection/configuration strategies. LAN topologies fall into four types of configurations:

Bus

Ring

Star

Mesh

bus topology

nodes

stations

- **Bus**
- **Ring**
- **Star**
- **Mesh**

Figure 5-1 illustrates all four topologies. In the **bus topology**, the **nodes**, or **stations**, of the network connect to a central communication link. Each node has a unique address along the bus that differentiates it from the other users on the network. Information can be placed on the bus by any node. The information must contain network address information about the node, or nodes, that the information is intended for. Other nodes along the bus will ignore the information.

TEST TIP

Be able to recognize network topologies from this type of drawing.

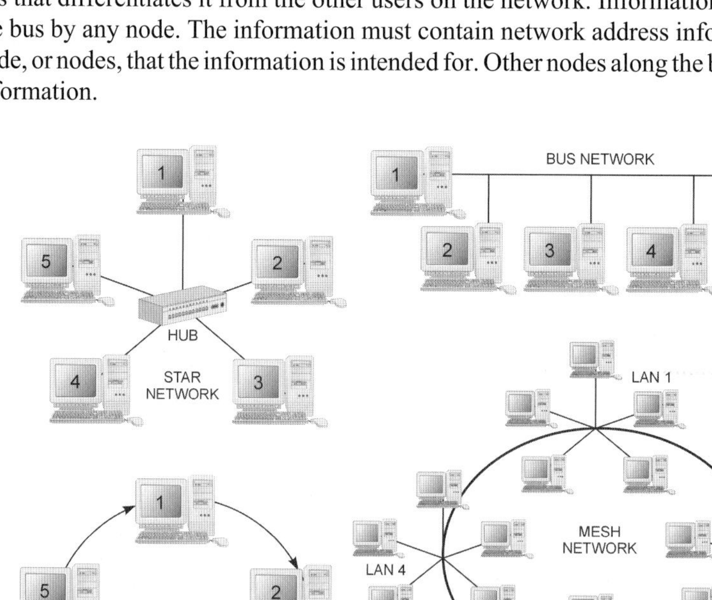

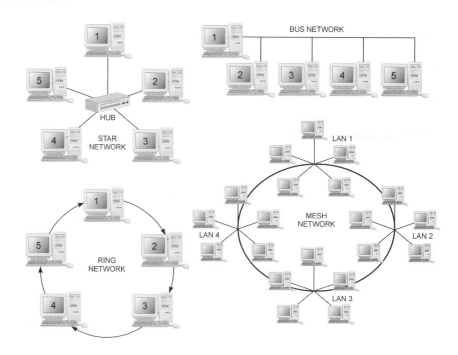

Figure 5-1: Star, Bus, Ring, and Mesh Configurations

In a ring network configuration, the communication bus is formed into a closed loop. Each node inspects the information on the LAN as it passes by. A repeater, built into each ring LAN card, regenerates every message not directed to it and sends it to the next appointed node. The originating node eventually receives the message back and removes it from the ring.

Ring topologies

Ring topologies tend to offer very high data transfer rates but require additional management overhead. The additional management is required for dependability. If a node in a ring network fails, the entire network fails. To overcome this, ring designers have developed rings with primary and secondary data paths as depicted in Figure 5-2. If a break occurs in a primary link, the network controller can reroute the data onto the secondary link to avoid the break.

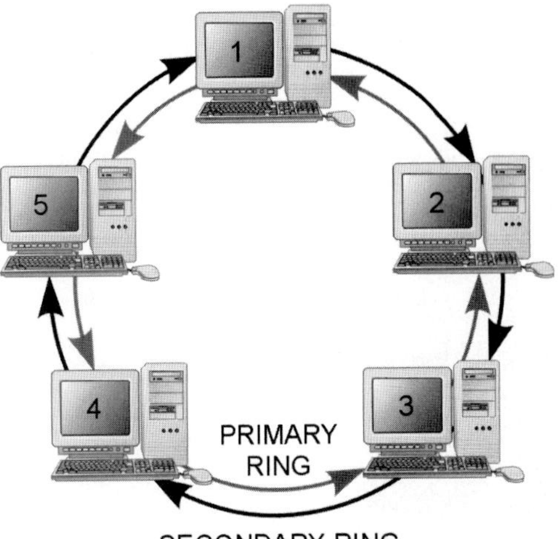

Figure 5-2: Primary/Secondary Ring Topologies

In a **star topology**, the logical layout of the network resembles the branches of a tree. All the nodes are connected in branches that eventually lead back to a central unit. Nodes communicate with each other through the central unit. The central station coordinates the network's activity by polling the nodes, one by one, to determine whether they have any information to transfer. If so, the central station gives that node a predetermined slice of time to transmit. If the message is longer than the time allotted, the transmissions are chopped into small packets of information that are transmitted over several polling cycles.

star topology

mesh design

The **mesh design** offers the most basic network connection scheme. In this design, each node has a direct physical connection to all the other nodes in the network. While the overhead for connecting a mesh network topology together in a LAN environment is prohibitive, this topology is employed in two very large network environments—the public telephone system and the Internet.

Logical Topologies

physical topologies

hubs

routers

logical topology

It would be easy to visualize the connections of the **physical topologies** just described if the nodes simply connected to each other. However, this is typically not the case in newer LAN arrangements. This is due to the fact that most LAN installations employ connection devices, such as **hubs** and **routers**, which alter the appearance of the actual connection scheme. Therefore, the **logical topology** will not match the appearance of the physical topology. The particulars of the connection scheme are hidden inside the connecting device. As an illustration, Figure 5-3 shows a typical network connection scheme using a router. The physical topology appears as a star. However, the internal wiring of the connecting router provides a logical bus topology.

It is not uncommon for a logical ring or mesh topology to be implemented in a physical star topology.

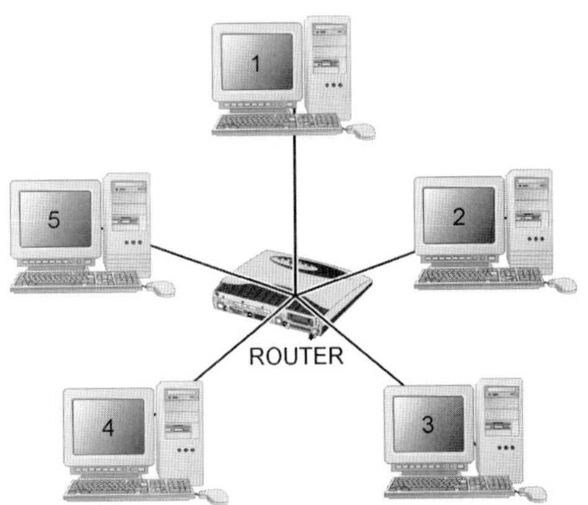

Figure 5-3: Logical Topologies

Network Control Strategies

When you begin to connect computers to other computers and devices so that they can share resources and data, the issue of how and who will control the network comes up very quickly. In some applications, such as developing a book like this one, it is good for the author, artists, and pagination people to be able to share access to text and graphics files, as well as access to devices such as printers. However, in a business network, companies must have control over who can have access to sensitive information and company resources, as well as when and how much.

Control of a network can be implemented in two ways:

peer-to-peer network

client/server network

file server

(1) As a **peer-to-peer network** in which each computer is attached to the network in a ring or bus fashion and is equal to the other units on the network.

(2) As a **client/server network** where dependent workstations, referred to as clients, operate in conjunction with a dedicated master computer (**file server**).

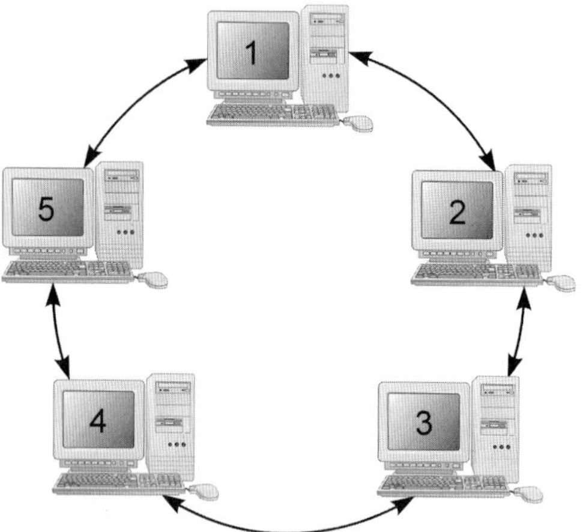

Figure 5-4: A Peer-to-Peer Network

Figure 5-4 illustrates a typical peer-to-peer network arrangement. In this arrangement, the users connected to the network can share access to different network resources, such as hard drives and printers. However, control of the local unit is fairly autonomous. The nodes in this type of network configuration usually contain local hard drives and printers that the local computer has control of. These resources can be shared at the discretion of the individual user. A common definition of a peer-to-peer network is one in which all of the nodes can act as both clients and servers of the other nodes under different conditions.

Figure 5-5 depicts a typical client/server LAN configuration. In this type of LAN, control tends to be very centralized. The server typically holds the programs and data for its client computers. It also provides security and network policy enforcement.

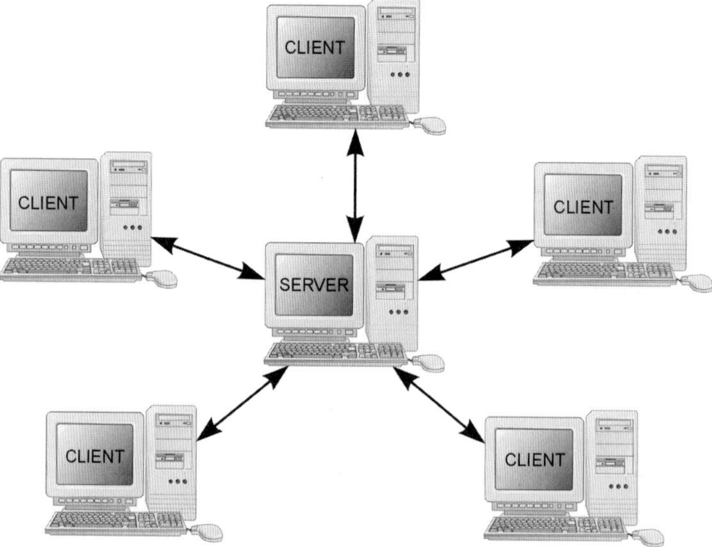

Figure 5-5: A Client/Server Network

In some cases, the client units do not even include a local hard drive or floppy drive unit. The bootup process is performed through an onboard BIOS, and no data is stored at the client machine. This type of client is referred to as a diskless **workstation**.

workstation

The major advantages of the client/server networking arrangement include:

- Centralized administration
- Data and resource security

TEST TIP

Know the characteristic differences between peer-to-peer and client/server networks.

Network Cabling

Basically four media are used to transmit data between computers. These media include:

- Copper cabling
- Fiber optic cabling
- Infrared light
- Wireless radio frequency (RF) signals

Under the heading of copper cabling, there are basically two categories to consider twisted-pair cabling and coaxial cabling. Twisted pair cabling consists of two or more pairs of wires twisted together to provide noise reduction. The twist in the wires cause induced noise signals to tend to cancel each other out. In this type of cabling, the number of twists in each foot of wire indicates its relative noise immunity level.

When discussing twisted-pair cabling with data networks, there are two basic types to consider: **Unshielded Twisted Pair (UTP)** and **Shielded Twisted Pair (STP)**. UTP networking cable contains four pairs of individually insulated wires as illustrated in Figure 5-6. STP cable is similar with the exception that it contains an additional foil shield that surrounds the four-pair wire bundle. The shield provides extended protection from induced electrical noise and cross talk by supplying a grounded path to carry the induced electrical signals away from the conductors in the cable.

Unshielded Twisted Pair (UTP)

Shielded Twisted Pair (STP)

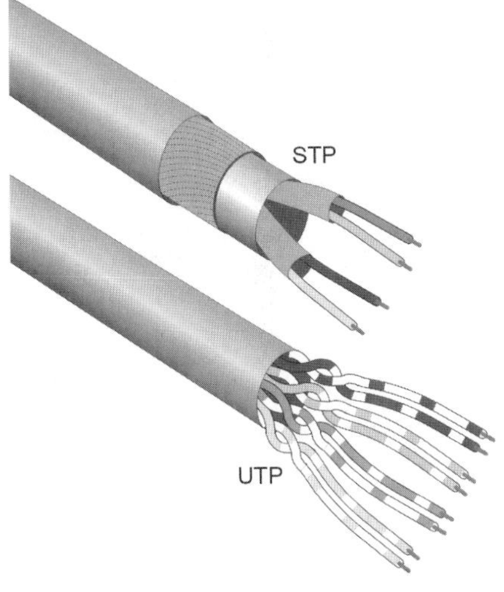

Figure 5-6: UTP and STP Cabling

Telecommunications Industry Association (TIA)

EIA/TIA UTP wiring category (CAT) ratings

Cat3

Cat5

UTP Cable

UTP cable specifications have been established jointly by two groups: the Electronic Industry Association and the **Telecommunications Industry Association (TIA)**. They have categorized different grades of cable along with connector, distance, and installation specifications to produce the **EIA/TIA UTP wiring category (CAT) ratings** for the industry (i.e., **Cat3** and **Cat5** cabling). Table 5-1 lists the industry's various Cat cable ratings that apply to UTP data communications cabling. Cat5 cabling is currently the most widely used specification for data communication wiring.

Table 5-1: UTP Cable Category Ratings

CATEGORY	MAXIMUM BANDWIDTH	WIRING TYPES	APPLICATIONS
3	16 MHz	100Ω UTP Rated Category 3	10 Mbps Ethernet 4 Mbps Token Ring
4	20 MHz	100Ω UTP Rated Category 4	10 Mbps Ethernet 16 Mbps Token Ring
5	100 MHz	100Ω UTP Rated Category 5	100 Mbps TPDDI 155 Mbps ATM
5E	160 MHz	100Ω UTP Rated Category 5E	1.2 Gbps 1000BASE-T High-Speed ATM
6 Proposed	200-250 MHz	100Ω UTP Rated Category 6	1.2 Gbps 1000BASE-T High-Speed ATM and beyond
7 Proposed	600-862 MHz	100Ω UTP Rated Category 7	1.2 Gbps 1000BASE-T High-Speed ATM and beyond

TEST TIP

Know what type of cabling is involved in the Cat5 cable rating.

The connector and color-coded connection schemes specified for 4-pair, Cat5 UTP network cabling is illustrated in Figure 5-7. UTP cabling is terminated in an 8-pin RJ-45 plug. The color code for attaching the connector to the cable is also provided in the figure.

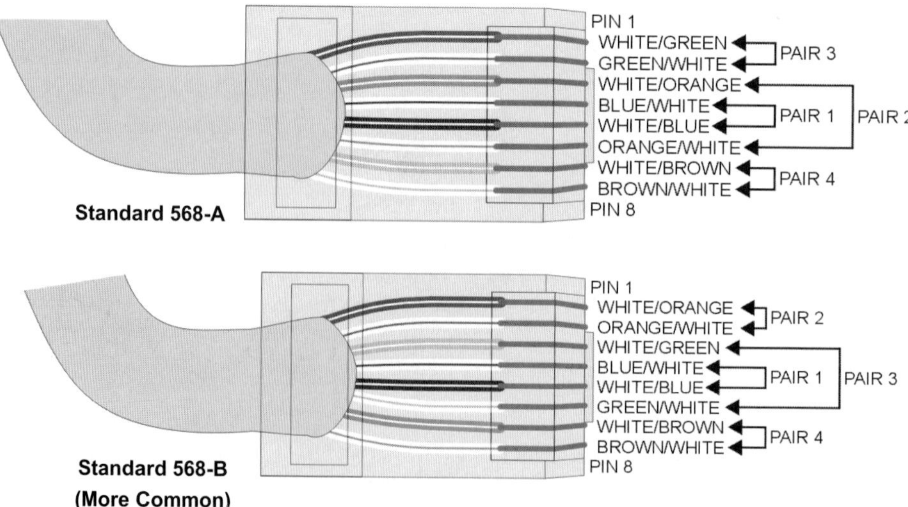

Figure 5-7: UTP Cable Connections

Coaxial Cable

Coaxial cable is familiar to most people as the conductor that carries cable TV into their homes. Coax has a single copper conductor in its center, and a protective braided copper shield around it, as illustrated in Figure 5-8.

Coaxial cable

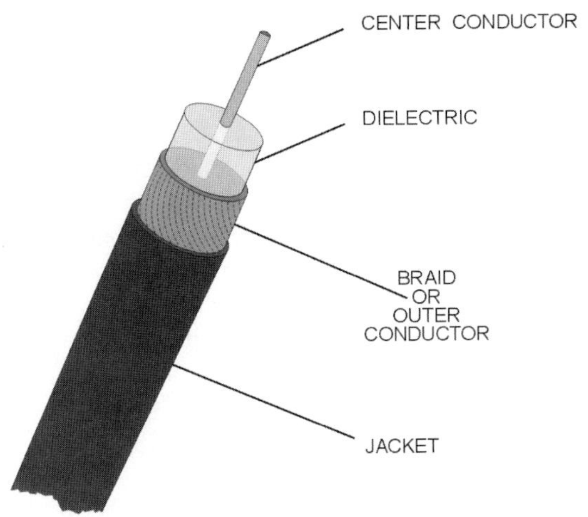

Figure 5-8: Coaxial Cable

Fiber-Optic Cable

Fiber-optic cable is plastic or glass cable designed to carry voice or digital data in the form of light pulses. The signals are introduced into the cable by a laser diode and bounce along its interior until they reaches the end of the cable, as illustrated in Figure 5-9. At the end, a light detecting circuit receives the light signals and converts them back into usable information. This type of cabling offers potential signaling rates in excess of 200,000 Mbps. However, current access protocols still limit fiber-optic LAN speeds to 100 Mbps.

Fiber-optic cable

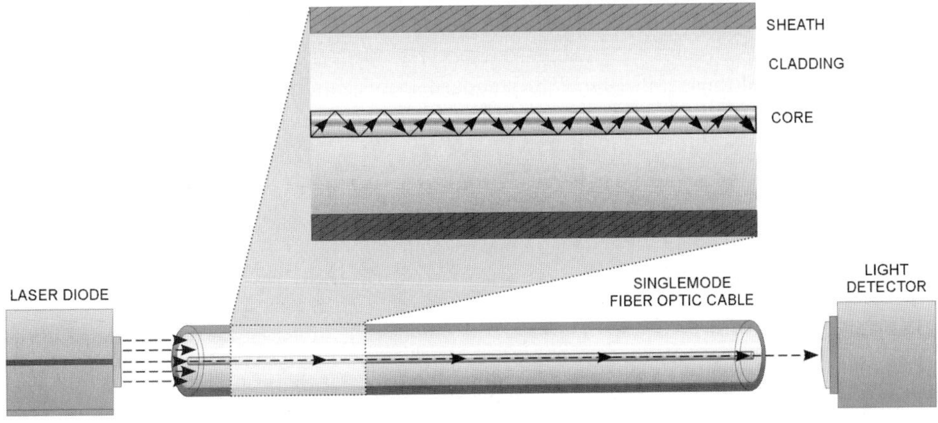

Figure 5-9: Transmitting Over Fiber-Optic Cable

Because light moving through a fiber-optic cable does not attenuate (lose energy) as quickly as electrical signals moving along a copper conductor, segment lengths between transmitters and receivers can be much longer with fiber-optic cabling. In some fiber-optic applications, the maximum cable length can range up to 2 kilometers.

Fiber-optic cable also provides a much more secure data transmission medium than copper cable because it cannot be tapped without physically breaking the conductor. Basically, light introduced into the cable at one end does not leave the cable except through the other end. In addition, it electrically isolates the transmitter and receiver so that no signal level matching normally needs to be performed between the two ends.

Straight Tip (ST) connector

SC connector

Getting the light out of the cable without significant attenuation is the key to making fiber-optic connections. The end of the cable must be perfectly aligned with the receiver and be free from scratches, film, or dust that would distort or filter the light.

Figure 5-10: Fiber-Optic Cable Connectors

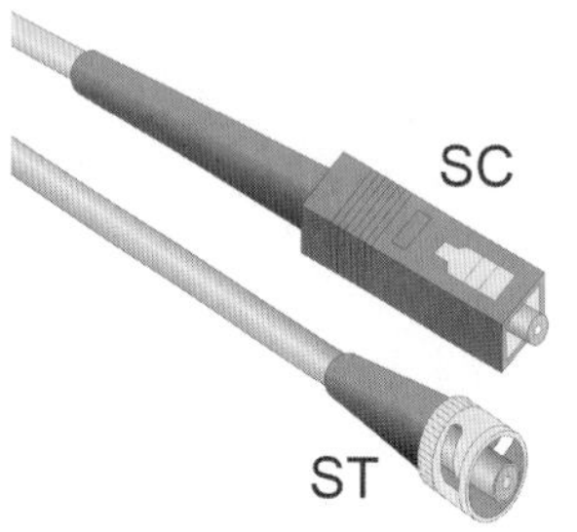

Figure 5-10 depicts two types of fiber-optic connectors. The connector on the top is a **SC connector** while the one on the bottom is an **Straight Tip (ST) connector**. The SC connector is the dominant connector for fiber-optic Ethernet networks. In both cases, the connectors are designed so that they correctly align the end of the cable with the receiver.

Network Access Protocols

protocol

In a network, some method must be used to determine which node has use of the network's communications paths, and for how long it can have it. The network's **protocol** handles these functions, and it is necessary to prevent more than one user from accessing the bus at any given time.

If two sets of data are placed on the network at the same time, a data collision occurs and data is lost. Basically, there are two de-facto networking protocols in use: Ethernet and Token Ring.

Ethernet

Ethernet

International Electrical and Electronic Association (IEEE)

IEEE-802.3 Ethernet protocol

carrier sense multiple access with collision detection (CSMA/CD)

Xerox developed Ethernet in 1976. The standard specification for **Ethernet** has been published by the **International Electrical and Electronic Association (IEEE)** as the **IEEE-802.3 Ethernet protocol**. Its methodology for control is referred to as **carrier sense multiple access with collision detection (CSMA/CD)**. Using this protocol, a node that wants to transfer data over the network first listens to the LAN to determine whether it is in use. If the LAN is not in use, the node begins transmitting its data. If the network is busy, the node waits for the LAN to clear for a predetermined time, and then takes control of the LAN.

If two nodes are waiting to use the LAN, they will periodically attempt to access the LAN at the same time. When this happens, a data collision occurs, and the data from both nodes is rendered useless. The receiver portion of the Ethernet controller monitors the transmission to detect collisions.

When it senses the data bits overlapping, it halts the transmission, as does the other node. The transmitting controller generates an abort pattern code that is transmitted to all the nodes on the LAN, telling them that a collision has occurred. This alerts any nodes that might be waiting to access the LAN that there is a problem.

The receiving node (or nodes) dump any data that it might have received before the collision occurred. Other nodes waiting to send data generate a random timing number and go into a holding pattern. The timing number is a waiting time that the node sits out before it tries to transmit. Because the number is randomly generated, the odds against two of the nodes trying to transmit again at the same time are very low.

The first node to time out listens to the LAN to determine whether any activity is still occurring. Because it almost always finds a clear LAN, it begins transmitting. If two of the nodes do time out at the same time, another collision happens and the abort pattern/number generation/time-out sequence begins again. Eventually, one of the nodes will gain clear access to the network and successfully transmit its data.

Limitations of Ethernet—The Ethernet strategy allows for up to 1,024 users to share the LAN. From the description of its collision-recovery technique, however, it should be clear that with more users on an Ethernet LAN, more collisions are likely to occur, and the average time to complete an actual data transfer will be longer.

Limitations of Ethernet

The Ethernet Frame

Under the Ethernet standard, information is collected into a package called a **frame**. Figure 5-11 depicts a typical Ethernet frame. The frame carries the following six sections of information:

frame

- A preamble
- A destination address
- An originating address
- A type field
- The data field
- The frame check error-detection and correction information

8 BYTES	6 BYTES	6 BYTES	2 BYTES	0 TO 1500 BYTES	4 BYTES
PREAMBLE	DESTINATION ADDRESS	ORIGINATING ADDRESS	TYPE FIELD	DATA	FRAME CHECK SEQUENCE

Figure 5-11: A Typical Ethernet Frame

This organizational structure is very similar to that of a sector on a hard disk. The preamble synchronizes the receiver's operation to that of the transmitter. This action also tells the other nodes that a transmission is under way. The Ethernet preamble is a 64-bit string, made up of alternating 1s and 0s, ending in two consecutive 1s.

individual node address

address of a grouping of nodes

broadcast code

The destination address field is 6 bytes long, and is used to define one of three address locations. This number can represent the **individual node address** of the intended receiver, the **address of a grouping of nodes** around the LAN, or it can be a **broadcast code** that allows the node to send a message to everyone on the LAN.

The originating address field contains the identification address for the transmitting node. The type field is a 2-byte field that identifies the user protocol of the frame.

The data field is a variable-length field that contains the actual information. Because it is sent in a synchronous mode, the data field can be as long as necessary. The Ethernet standard does not allow for data fields less than 46 bytes, however, or longer than 1,500 bytes.

The frame-check block contains an error-detection and correction word. Like parity and other error-detection schemes, the receiver regenerates the error code from the received data (actually the data, the address bytes, and the type field), and compares it to the received code. If a mismatch occurs, an error signal is generated from the LAN card to the system.

Ethernet Specifications

Ethernet is classified as a bus topology. The original Ethernet scheme was classified as a 10 Mbps transmission protocol. The maximum length specified for Ethernet is 1.55 miles (2.5 km), with a maximum segment length between nodes of 500 meters. This type of LAN is referred to as a 10BASE-5 LAN by the IEEE organization.

baseband

broadband

10BASE-xx

The XXBaseYY IEEE nomenclature designates that the maximum data rate across the LAN is 10 Mbps, that it is a **baseband** LAN (verses **broadband**), and that its maximum segment length is 500 meters. One exception to this method is the 10BASE-2 implementation. The maximum segment length for this specification is 185 meters (almost 200).

TEST TIP

Be aware that the **10BASE-xx** system roughly uses the xx value to represent the distance (in meters) that a network segment can be (the notable exception is the 185 meter BASE-2 value—its almost 200 meters).

Unshielded Twisted Pair (UTP)

10BASE-T

100BASE-T

100BASE-TX

Fast Ethernet

100BASE-FX

Newer Ethernet implementations are producing LAN speeds of up to 100 Mbps using **Unshielded Twisted Pair** (**UTP**) copper cabling. For these networks, the IEEE adopted **10BASE-T**, **100BASE-T**, and **100BASE-TX** designations, indicating that they operate on twisted-pair cabling and depend on its specifications for the maximum segment length. The 100BASE designation is referred to as **Fast Ethernet**. The TX version of the Fast Ethernet specification employs two pairs of twisted cable to conduct high-speed, full-duplex transmissions. The cables used with the TX version can be Cat5 UTP or STP. There is also a **100BASE-FX** Fast Ethernet designation that indicates the network in using fiber optic cabling. This specification is described later in this chapter.

Network cards capable of supporting both transmission rates are classified as 10/100 Ethernet cards. The recommended maximum length of a 10/100BASE-T segment is 100 meters.

TEST TIP

Know what type of cable 10BASE-T and 100BASE-T use.

Ethernet Connections

Ethernet connections can be made through 50 ohm, coaxial cable (10BASE-5), thinnet coaxial cable (10BASE-2), or UTP cabling (10BASE-T).

The UTP specifications are based on telephone cable, and is normally used to connect a small number of PCs together. The twisted pairing of the cables uses magnetic-field principles to minimize induced noise in the lines. The original UTP LAN specification had a transmission rate that was stated as 1 Mbps. Using UTP cable, a LAN containing up to 64 nodes can be constructed with the maximum distance between nodes set at 250 meters. Figure 5-12 depicts typical coaxial and UTP connections.

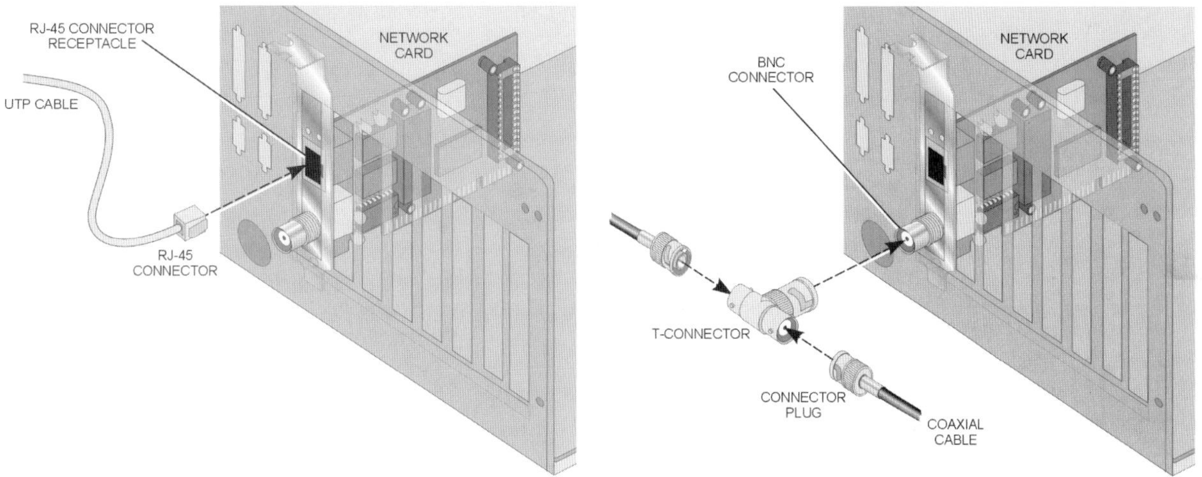

Figure 5-12: Typical Coax and UTP Connections

The original 10BASE-5 connection scheme required that special transceiver units be clamped to the cable. A pin in the transceiver pierced the cable to establish electrical contact with its conductor. An additional length of cable, called the drop cable, was then connected between the LAN adapter card and the transceiver. The 10BASE-2 Ethernet LAN uses thinner, industry-standard RG-58 coaxial cable, and has a maximum segment length of 185 meters.

Coaxial cables are attached to equipment through BNCs (British Naval Connectors). In a 10BASE-2 LAN, the node's LAN adapter card is usually connected directly to the LAN cabling, using a T-connector for peer-to-peer networks, or a BNC connector in a client/server LANs.

UTP LAN connections are made through modular RJ-45 registered jacks and plugs. RJ-45 connectors are very similar in appearance to the RJ-11 connectors used with telephones and modems. However, the RJ-45 connectors are considerably larger than the RJ-11 connectors. Some Ethernet adapters include 15-pin sockets that enable special systems, such as fiber-optic cabling, to be interfaced to them. Other cards provide specialized ST connectors for fiber-optic connections.

concentrators

UTP systems normally employ **concentrators**, or hubs, like the one in Figure 5-13, for connection purposes. Both coaxial connection methods require that a terminating resistor be installed at each end of the transmission line. Ethernet systems use 52-ohm terminators.

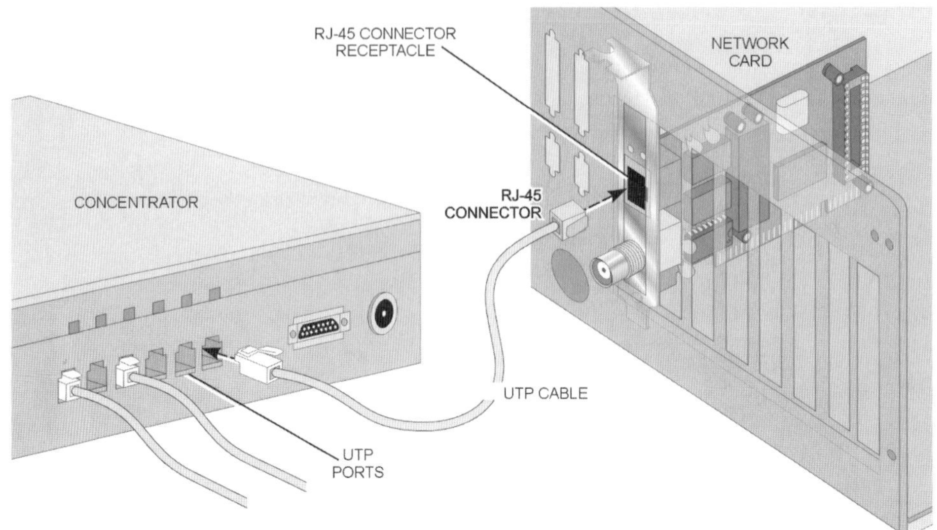

Figure 5-13: UTP Between a Computer and a Concentrator

Table 5-2 summarizes the different Ethernet specifications. Other CSMA/CD-based protocols exist in the market. Some are actually Ethernet compatible. However, these systems may, or may not, achieve the performance levels of a true Ethernet system. Some may actually perform better.

Table 5-2: Ethernet Specifications

CLASSIFICATION	CONDUCTOR	MAX. SEGMENT LENGTH	NODES	MAX. LENGTH	TRANS. RATE
10BASE-2	RG-58	185m	30/1024	250m	10 Mbps
10BASE-5	RG-8	500m	100/1024	2.5km	10 Mbps
10BASE-T	UTP/STP	100m/200m	2/1024	2.5km	10 Mbps
100BASE-T	UTP	100m	2/1024	2.5km	100 Mbps
100BASE-FX	FO	412m	1024	5km	100 Mbps

TEST TIP

Know the types of connectors and physical cable types used with each network type.

100VG (Voice Grade) AnyLAN

demand priority

A completely different 100 Mbps standard has been developed jointly by Hewlett Packard and AT&T. This standard is referred to as the **100VG (Voice Grade) AnyLAN**. The 100VG AnyLAN runs on UTP cabling. It simultaneously employs four pairs of cable strands for transfers. Instead of using CSMA/CD for collision avoidance, the 100VG AnyLAN employs an access protocol called **demand priority**. This scenario requires that the network nodes request and be granted permission before they can send data across the LAN. The overwhelming popularity of the Fast Ethernet specification has caused 100VG AnyLAN to nearly disappear from the market.

Token Ring

token-passing LAN protocol

Token Ring

In 1985, IBM developed a **token-passing LAN protocol** called the **Token Ring**. As its name implies, Token Ring is a token-passing protocol operating on a ring topology. The token is a small frame that all nodes can recognize instantly. This access protocol standard specification is referred to as the IEEE-802.5 Token Ring Protocol.

In a token-passing system, contention for use of the LAN between different nodes is handled by passing an electronic enabling code, called a token, from node to node. Only the node possessing the token can have control of the LAN. Figure 5-14 illustrates this concept.

The token is passed from node to node along the LAN. Each node is allowed to hold the token a prescribed amount of time. After sending its message, or after its time runs out, the node must transfer the token to the next node. If the next node has no message, it just passes the token along to the next designated node. Nodes do not have to be in numeric sequence; their sequences are programmed in the network management software. All nodes listen to the LAN during the token-passing time.

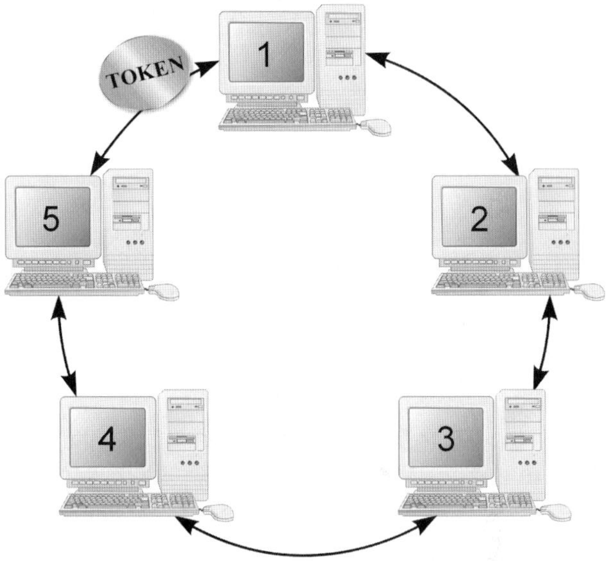

Figure 5-14: A Token-passing Scheme

In a token-passing network, new or removed nodes must be added to, or deleted from, the rotational list in the network-management software. If not, the LAN will never grant access to the new nodes. Token Ring management software and cards are built so that each device attached to the LAN is interrogated when the LAN is started up. In this way, the rotational file is verified each time that the network is started.

New nodes that start up after the LAN has been initialized transmit a reconfiguration burst that can be heard by all the nodes. This burst grabs the attention of all the installed nodes, and erases their token destination addresses. Each node goes into a wait state determined by its station number. The node with the highest station number times out first and tries to access the LAN.

The highest-numbered node is responsible for starting the token-passing action, after a new unit is added to the LAN. This is accomplished by broadcasting a signal to all nodes telling them what it believes is the lowest numbered node in the LAN, and asking whether it will accept the token. If no response is given, the node moves to the next known address in the LAN management software's roster and repeats the request. This action continues until an enabled node responds. At this point, the token is passed to the new node and the forwarding address is stored in the LAN manager's list. Each successive node goes through the same process until all the nodes have been accessed.

The node passing the token must always monitor the LAN. This is done to prevent the loss of the token during its passage. If the node remains inactive for a predetermined amount of time, the transmitting node must reclaim the token and search for the next active node to pass it to. In this case, the transmitting node just increments its next-node address by one, and then attempts to make contact with a node at that address. If not, it will increment the count by one again, and retry, until it reaches an enabled node. This new node number is stored in the transmitting node and will be the pass-to number for that node, until the system is shut down or reconfigured.

When the ring is idle, the token just passes counterclockwise, from station to station. A station can transmit information on the ring any time that it receives the token. This is accomplished by turning the token packet into the start of a data packet, and adding its data to it.

At the intended receiver, the packet is copied into a buffer memory, serially, where it is stored. The receiver also places the packet back on the ring so that the transmitter can get it back. Upon doing so, the transmitter reconstructs the token and places it back on the ring. Figure 5-15 depicts this concept.

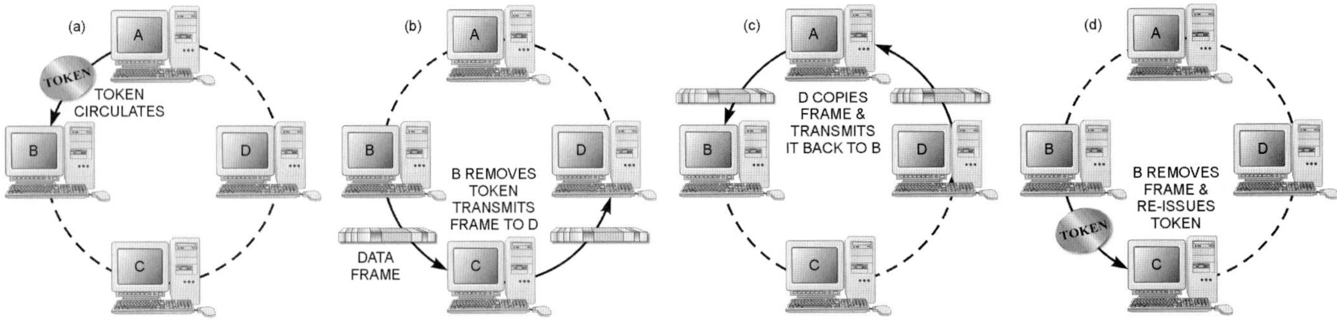

Figure 5-15: Token Ring Concept

trunk cable

concentrators

Shielded Twisted Pair (STP)

The Token Ring cabling is a two-pair, shielded twisted-pair cable. The main cable is called the **trunk cable**, and the individual drops are referred to as the interface cables. The cables are grouped together by hardware units called **concentrators**. Internally, the concentrator's ports are connected into a ring configuration. In this manner, the concentrator can be placed in a convenient area, and have nodes positioned where they are needed. Some Token Ring adapters provide nine pin connectors for **Shielded Twisted Pair** (**STP**) cables as well.

The data-transfer rate stated for Token Ring systems is 4 to 16 Mbps. Token-passing is less efficient than other protocols when the load on the network is light. It evenly divides the network's usage among nodes, however, when traffic is heavy. It can also be extremely vulnerable to node crashes when a node has the token. LAN adapter cards are typically designed to monitor the LAN for such occurrences so that they can be corrected without shutting down the entire network.

Token Ring (802.5)

The IEEE specifications for both Ethernet (802.3) and **Token Ring** (**802.5**) make provisions for a high-speed, full-duplexing mode (two-way simultaneous communication). This mode is normally encountered in large networks that have multiple servers. Its primary use is to perform backup functions between the large system servers where lots of data must be moved through the network. In full-duplex mode, the standard Ethernet transfer rate of 10 Mbps is boosted to 20 Mbps; the Token Ring rate is raised to 32 Mbps. This mode is rarely encountered on desktop client units. These units tend to operate in half-duplex mode (two-way communication, but in only one direction at a time).

TEST TIP

Be aware that Ethernet and Token Ring networks have full duplex capabilities.

Fiber-Optic LANs

As indicated earlier in this chapter, **fiber-optic cabling** offers the prospect of very high performance links for LAN implementation. It can handle much higher data-transfer rates than copper conductors, and can use longer distances between stations before signal deterioration becomes a problem. In addition, fiber-optic cable offers a high degree of security for data communications: Because it does not radiate EMI signal information that can be detected outside the conductor, it does not tap easily, and it shows a decided signal loss when it is tapped into.

fiber-optic cabling

Fiber Ethernet Standards

The IEEE organization has created several fiber optic variations of the Ethernet protocol. They classify these variations under the **IEEE-803** standard. These standards are referenced as the 10/100BASE-F specification. Variations of this standard include:

IEEE-803

10/100BASE-F

- **10BASE-FP**. This specification is used for passive star networks running at 10 Mbps. It employs a special hub that uses mirrors to channel the light signals to the desired node.

10BASE-FP

- **10BASE-FL**. This specification is used between devices on the network. It operates in full-duplex mode and runs at 10 Mbps. Cable lengths under this specification can range up to 2 kilometers.

10BASE-FL

- **100BASE-FX**. This protocol is identical to the 10BASE-FL specification with the exception that it runs at 100 Mbps. This particular version of the specification is referred to as *Fast Ethernet* since it can easily run at the 100 Mbps rate.

100BASE-FX

The FDDI Ring Standard

There is a Token Ring-like network standard that has been developed around fiber-optic cabling. This standard is the **Fiber Distributed Data Interface** (**FDDI**) specification. The FDDI network was designed to work almost exactly like a Token Ring network, with the exception that it works on two counterrotating rings of fiber-optic cable, as illustrated in Figure 5-16. All other differences in the two specifications are associated with their speed differences.

Fiber Distributed Data Interface (FDDI)

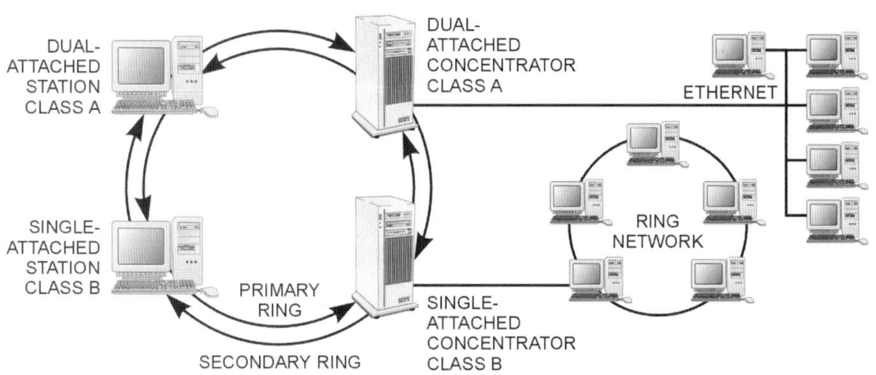

Figure 5-16: An FDDI Network

FDDI employs token-passing access control and provides data-transfer rates of 100 Mbps. Using the second ring, FDDI can easily handle multiple frames of data moving across the network at any given time. Of course, the dual ring implementation provides additional network dependability since it can shift over to a single ring operation if the network controller senses that a break has occurred in one of the rings.

Infrared LANs

IrDA

The **IrDA** infrared transmission specification makes provisions for multiple IrDA devices to be attached to a computer so that it can have multiple, simultaneous links to multiple IrDA devices. Figure 5-17 shows how IrDA links can be used to share computers and devices through a normal Ethernet hub. In these scenarios, the IrDA link provides the high-speed transmission media between the Ethernet devices.

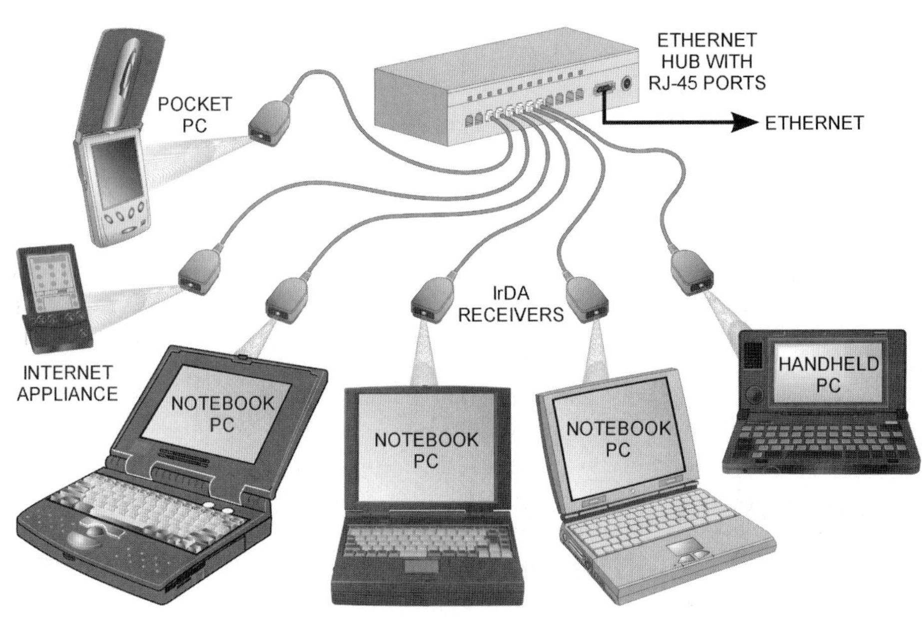

Figure 5-17: IrDA Networking

Wireless LANs

Wireless Local Area Networking (WLAN or LAWN)

Recently, there have been a variety of **Wireless Local Area Networking (WLAN** or **LAWN)** specification introduced into the market. These networks connect computer nodes together using high-frequency radio waves. The IEEE organization has presented a specification titled IEEE-802.11 to describe its wireless networking standard.

spread spectrum

Frequency Hopping Spread Spectrum (FHSS)

Direct Sequence Spread Spectrum (DSSS)

Time Division Multiplexing (TDM)

The wireless networking community is working with two **spread spectrum** technologies as the basis of their transmission method. In spread spectrum transmissions, the frequency of the radio signal hops in a random, defined sequence that is known to the receiving device. These technologies are referred to as **Frequency Hopping Spread Spectrum** (**FHSS**) and **Direct Sequence Spread Spectrum** (**DSSS**). The FHSS method spreads the signal across the time spectrum using **Time Division Multiplexing** (**TDM**) techniques. The DSSS method combines the data with a faster carrier signal according to a predetermined frequency spreading ratio for transmission.

Time Division Multiple Access (TDMA)

CDMA (Code Division Multiple Access)

Time Division Multiple Access (**TDMA**) technology employs TDM to divide a radio carrier signal into time-slices, called **cells**, and then funneling data from different sources into the cells. This technique enables a single frequency signal to serve a number of different customers simultaneously. A similar technology known as **CDMA** (**Code Division Multiple Access**) does not assign users a specific frequency. Instead, it spreads the user's data across a range of frequencies in a random digital sequence.

Bluetooth

convergence

Another interesting wireless networking specification is known as **Bluetooth**. This specification was originally put forth by a consortium made up of Ericsson, IBM, Intel, Nokia, and Toshiba as a short range, wireless radio technology designed to coordinate communications between network devices and the Internet. The meshing together of personal computers, cell phones, web devices, LAN devices, and other intelligent devices in a common forum is referred to as **convergence**. The bluetooth specification is intended to promote convergence of these systems.

access point

A typical wireless LAN, depicted in Figure 5-18, consists of wireless LAN adapter cards with an RF antenna. The WLAN adapter cards in the various systems of the LAN communicate with each other and a host system through an **access point** device. Current wireless LANs operate in the range of 1 Mbps transfer rates. Wireless LAN adapters are typically available in the form of PCI and PCMCIA cards.

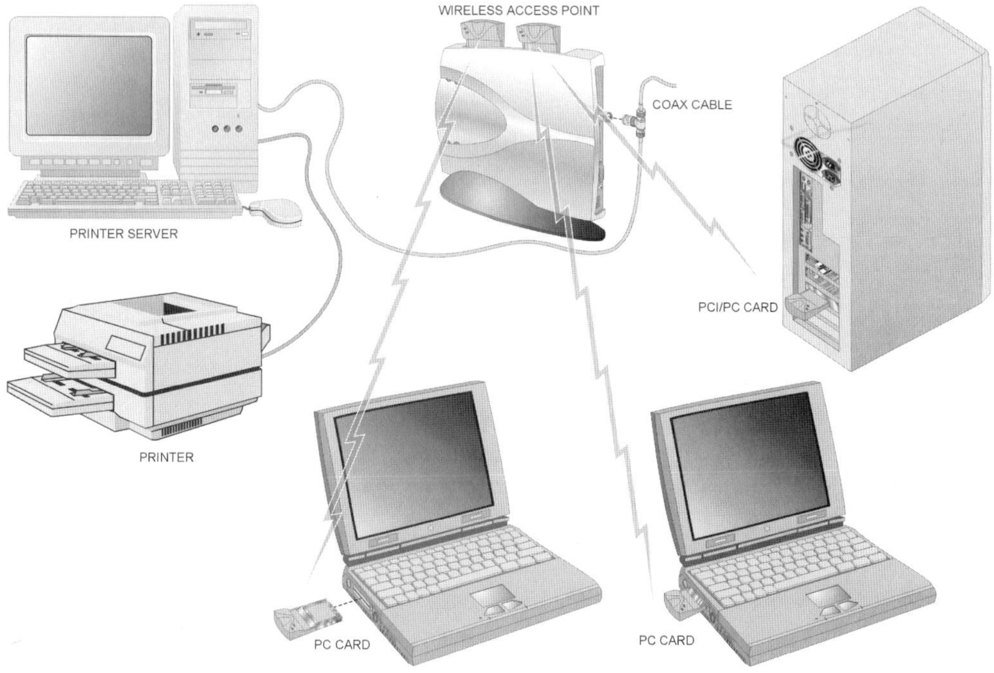

Figure 5-18: A Wireless LAN

INSTALLING AND CONFIGURING LANS

A portion of the A+ Core Hardware objective 6.1 states that the test taker should be able to identify procedures for swapping and configuring network interface cards.

Because PC technicians are typically responsible for maintaining the portion of the network that attaches to the computer, they must be able to install, configure, and service the network adapter card and cable. The following sections deal with installing and configuring LAN cards.

LAN Adapter Cards

Network Adapter Card (NIC)

network interface card (NIC)

In a LAN, each computer on the network requires a **network adapter card** (also referred to as a **Network Interface Card** or **NIC**) and every unit has to be connected to the network by some type of cabling. These cables are typically either twisted-pair wires, thick or thin coaxial cable, or fiber-optic cable.

LAN adapter cards must have connectors that are compatible with the type of LAN cabling being used. Many Ethernet LAN cards come with both an RJ-45 and a BNC connector, so the cards can be used in any type of Ethernet configuration.

Figure 5-19 depicts a typical LAN card. In addition to its LAN connectors, the LAN card may have a number of configuration jumpers that must be set up.

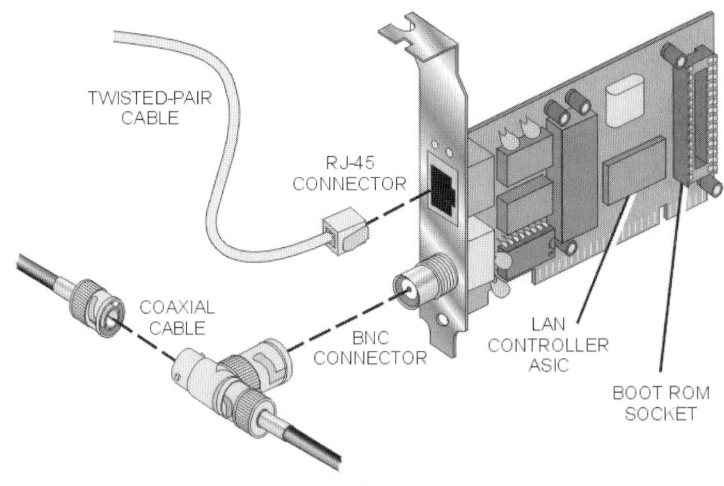

Figure 5-19: A Typical LAN Card

> **WARNING**
>
> **Use the user guide**—Although some cards may have jumper instructions printed directly on themselves, the card's user manual is normally required to configure it for operation. Great care should be taken with the user manual, because its loss might render the card useless. At the very least, the manufacturer would have to be contacted to get a replacement.

Another item that can be found on many LAN cards is a vacant ROM socket. This socket is included so that it can be used to install a **bootup ROM** that will enable the unit to be used as a diskless workstation. One or more activity lights may also be included on the card's back plate. These lights can play a very important part in diagnosing problems with the LAN connection. Check the card's user manual for definitions of its activity lights.

bootup ROM

Each adapter must have an adapter driver program loaded in its host computer to handle communications between the system and the adapter. These are the Ethernet and Token Ring drivers loaded to control specific types of LAN adapter cards.

In addition to the adapter drivers, the network computer must have a network protocol driver loaded. This program may be referred to as the **transport protocol**, or just as the protocol. It operates between the adapter and the initial layer of network software to package and un-package data for the LAN. In many cases, the computer may have several different protocol drivers loaded so that the unit can communicate with computers that use other types of protocols.

transport protocol

Typical protocol drivers include the **Internetworking Packet Exchange/Sequential Packet Exchange (IPX/SPX)** model produced by Novell, and the standard **Transmission Control Protocol/Internet Protocol (TCP/IP)** developed by the U.S. military for its **ARPA** network. Figure 5-20 illustrates the various LAN drivers necessary to transmit, or receive, data on a network.

Internetworking Packet Exchange/ Sequential Packet Exchange (IPX/SPX)

Transmission Control Protocol/Internet Protocol (TCP/IP)

ARPA

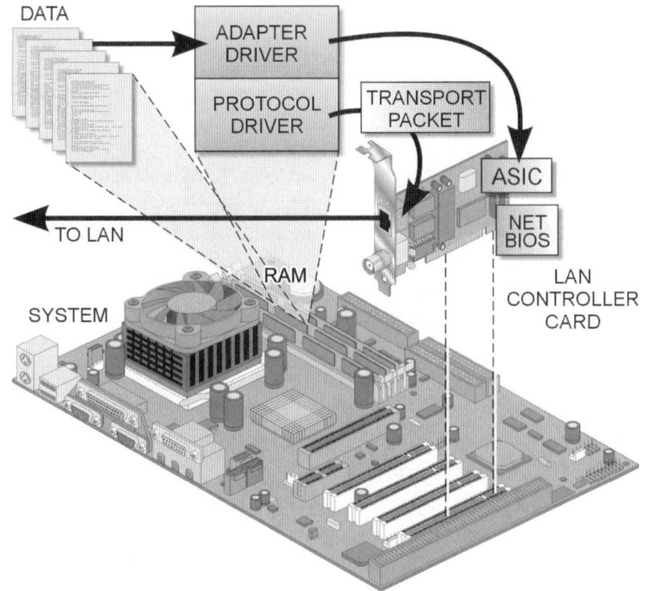

Figure 5-20: Various LAN Drivers

Installing LANs

Installing a LAN card in a PC follows the basic steps of installing most peripheral cards. Check the system for currently installed drivers and system settings. Consult the LAN card's installation guide for default settings information, and compare them to those of the devices already installed in the system. If there are no apparent conflicts between the default settings and those already used by the system, place the adapter card in a vacant expansion slot and secure it to the system unit's back plate.

Connect the LAN card to the network as directed by the manufacturer's installation guide, and load the proper software drivers for the installed adapter (see Table 5-3). Figure 5-21 illustrates connecting the computer to the LAN, using UTP or coaxial cable. If UTP cable is being used, the line drop to the computer would come from a concentrator like the one depicted.

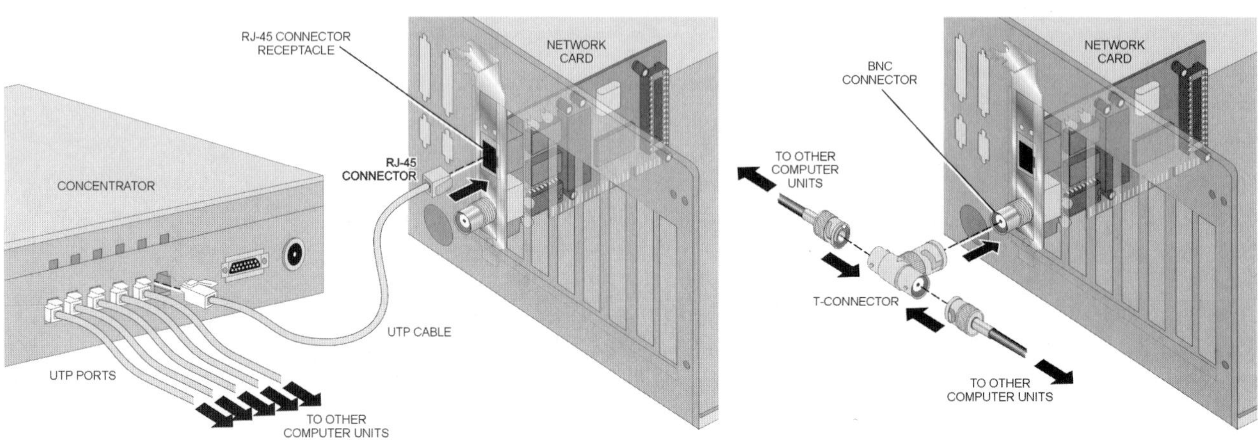

Figure 5-21: Connecting the Computer to the LAN

The following three important pieces of information are required to configure the LAN adapter card for use:

I/O port address

base memory address

- The interrupt request (IRQ) setting the adapter will use to communicate with the system.
- The **I/O port address** the adapter will use to exchange information with the system.
- The **base memory address** that the adapter will use as a starting point in memory for DMA transfers.

Some adapters may require that a DMA channel be defined.

Table 5-3: LAN Card Configuration Settings

I/O ADDRESS OPTIONS	INTERRUPT REQUEST CHANNELS	EXTENDED MEMORY ADDRESSING
240h	IRQ2	C000h
280h	IRQ3	C400h
2C0h	IRQ4	C800h
320h	IRQ10	CC00h
340h	IRQ11	D000h
360h	IRQ12	D400h
	IRQ15	DC00h

Typical configuration settings for the network card's IRQ, I/O port address, and base memory are as follows:

IRQ=5
Port Address=300h
Base Memory=D8000h

If a configuration conflict appears, reset the conflicting settings so that they do not share the same value. Which component's configuration gets changed is determined by examining the options for changing the cards involved in the conflict. A sound card may have many more IRQ options available than a given network card. In that case, it would be easier to change sound card settings than network card settings.

TEST TIP

Know the system resources normally required by network adapter cards.

Networking with Novell NetWare

In a client/server system, such as a **Novell NetWare** or Windows NT/2000 system, the technician's main responsibility is to get the local station to boot up to the network's login prompt. At this point, the network administrator, or network engineer, becomes responsible for directing the troubleshooting process.

Novell NetWare

In a Novell system, check the root directory of the workstation for the NETBIOS and IPX.COM files. Check the AUTOEXEC.BAT file on the local drive for command lines to run the NETBIOS, load the IPX file, and load the ODI (or NETx) files.

Network Basic Input/Output System (NetBIOS)

Internetworking Packet Exchange (IPX)

Open Datalink Interface (ODI)

The NETBIOS file is an emulation of IBM's **Network Basic Input/Output System** (**NetBIOS**), and represents the basic interface between the operating system and the LAN hardware. This function is implemented through ROM ICs, located on the network card. The **Internetworking Packet Exchange** (**IPX**) file passes commands across the network to the file server. The NETBIOS and IPX protocols must be bound together in order to navigate the Novell network from a computer using a Windows operating system. This is accomplished by enabling the NETBIOS bindings in the IPX protocol Properties in the Network Properties window.

The **Open Datalink Interface** (**ODI**) file is the network shell that communicates between the adapter and the system's applications. Older versions of NetWare used a shell program called NETx. These files should be referenced in the AUTOEXEC.BAT or NET.BAT files.

TEST TIP

Be aware of the elements that are required to navigate through a Novell network from a computer running a Microsoft operating system.

DIAL-UP NETWORKING

The world's largest communications network is the public telephone system. When computers use this network to communicate with each other it is referred to as **Dial-Up Networking** (**DUP**). Computers connect to the phone system through devices, called modems, and communicate with each other using audio tone signals. In order to use the telephone system, the modem must duplicate the dialing characteristics of a telephone and be able to communicate within the frequencies that occur within the audible hearing range of human beings (after all, this is the range that telephone lines are set up to accommodate).

Dial-Up Networking (DUP)

Modems

If the peripheral is located at some distance from the computer (greater than 100 ft), they cannot be connected together by simply getting a longer cable. As the connecting cable gets longer, its natural resistance and distributive capacitance tend to distort digital signals until they are no longer digital.

modem

In order to overcome this signal deterioration, a device called a **modem** (short for modulator/demodulator) is used to convert the parallel, digital signals of the computer, into serial, analog signals, that are better suited for transmission over wire. A modem allows a computer to communicate with other computers through the telephone lines, as depicted in Figure 5-22.

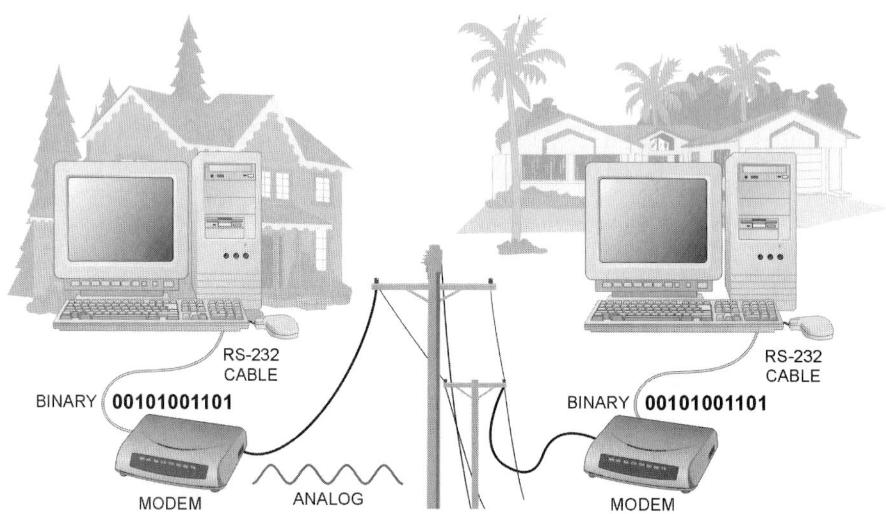

Figure 5-22: Modem Communications

In its simplest form, a modem consists of two major blocks, a modulator and a demodulator. The modulator is a transmitter that converts the parallel/digital computer data into a serial/analog format for transmission. The demodulator is the receiver that accepts the serial/analog transmission format and converts it into a parallel/digital format usable by the computer, or peripheral.

simplex mode

half-duplex mode

full-duplex mode

When a modem is used to send signals in only one direction, it is operating in **simplex mode**. Modems capable of both transmitting and receiving data are divided into two groups, based on their mode of operation. In **half-duplex mode**, modems exchange data, but only in one direction at a time, as illustrated in Figure 5-23. Multiplexing the send and receive signal frequencies will allow both modems to send and receive data simultaneously. This mode of operation is known as **full-duplex mode**.

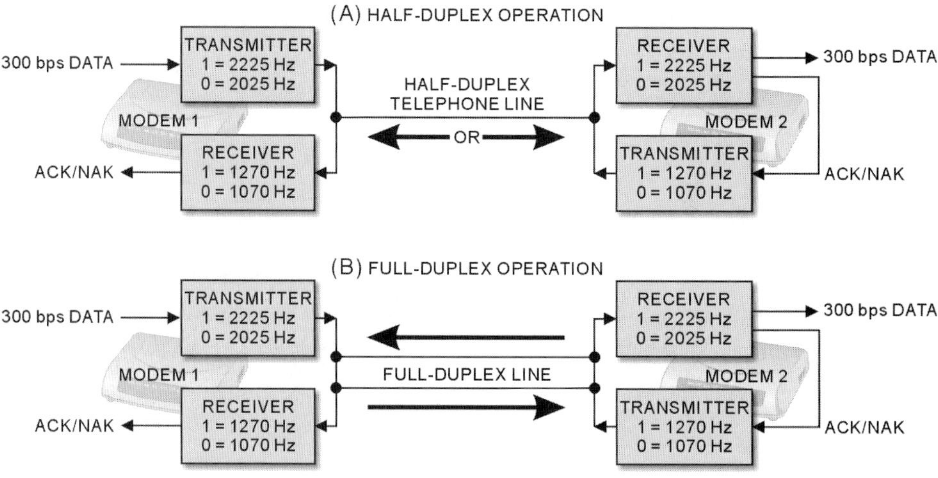

Figure 5-23: Half-Duplex and Full-Duplex Communications

As the distance between terminals increases, it soon becomes impractical to use dedicated cabling to carry data. Fortunately, there is already a very extensive communications network in existence—the public telephone network. Unfortunately, the phone lines were designed to carry analog voice signals instead of digital data. The design of the public phone system limits the frequency at which data may be transmitted over these lines.

TEST TIP

Be able to state the difference between simplex, half-duplex, and full-duplex transmissions and as you move through the text, be able to identify which communications systems use each type.

A modem can be either an internal or an external device, as illustrated in Figure 5-24. An **internal modem** is installed in one of the computer's expansion slots, and has its own interfacing circuitry. The **external modem** is usually a box that resides outside the system unit and is connected to one of the computer's serial ports by an RS-232 serial cable. These units depend on the interfacing circuitry of the computer's serial ports. Most PC-compatible computers contain two serial-port connections. External modems also require a separate power source.

internal modem

external modem

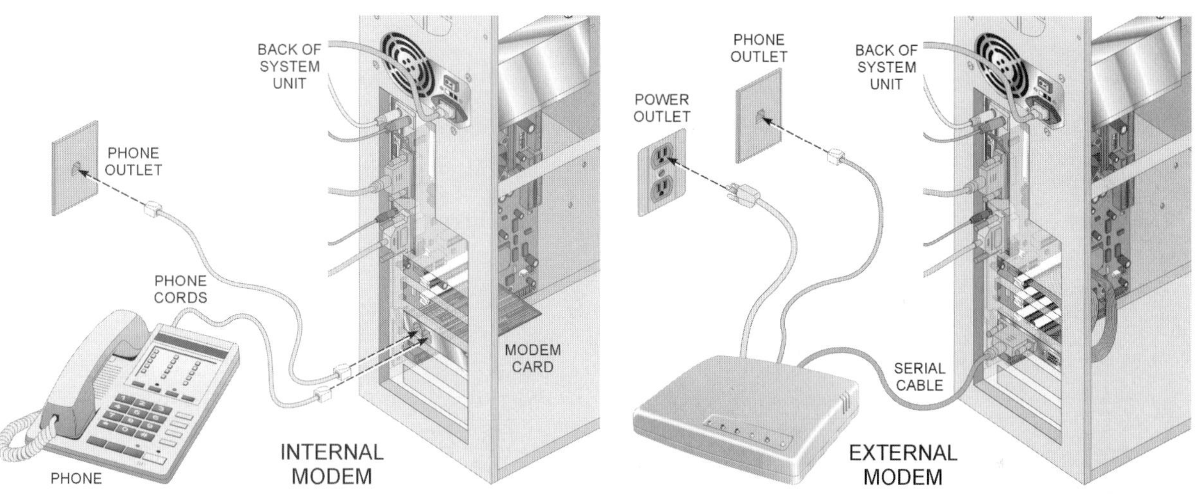

Figure 5-24: Internal and External Modems

In both cases, the modem typically connects to the telephone line through a standard 4-pin RJ-11 telephone jack. The RJ designation stands for **Registered Jack**. A second RJ-11 jack in the modem allows an additional telephone to be connected to the line for voice usage. A still smaller 4-pin RJ-12 connector is used to connect the telephone handset to the telephone base. Be aware that an RJ-14 jack looks exactly like the RJ-11, but that it defines two lines to accommodate advanced telephone features such as Caller ID and Call Waiting.

Registered Jack

How Modems Work

The standard telephone system accommodates a range of frequencies between 300 and 3300 Hz, or a **bandwidth** of 3000 Hz. This is quite adequate to transmit voice, but severely distorts digital data. In order to use the audio characteristics of the phone lines to their best advantage, the modem encodes the digital 1s and 0s into analog signals within this bandwidth.

bandwidth

baud rate

Modems are generally classified by their **baud rate**. Baud rate is used to describe the number of signal changes that occur per second during the transfer of data. Since signal changes are the quantity that is actually being limited by the telephone lines, the baud rate is the determining factor. Most modems encode data into different transmission formats, so that a number of data bits can be represented by a single signal change. In this way, the bit rate can be high, while the baud rate is still low. Common bit rates for telecommunications include 2400, 9600, 14400, 28800, and 33600 bits per second. To complete a successful connection at maximum speed, the other party involved must have a compatible modem capable of using the same baud rate.

local command state

on-line state

To understand the operation of the modem, it is important to understand that it must function in two different modes—the **local command state** and the **on-line state**. Between these two states, there are basically three functions that the modem carries out:

- Dialing
- Data exchange (the call)
- Answering

Figure 5-25 describes the Dial/Answer/Disconnect cycles of a typical modem.

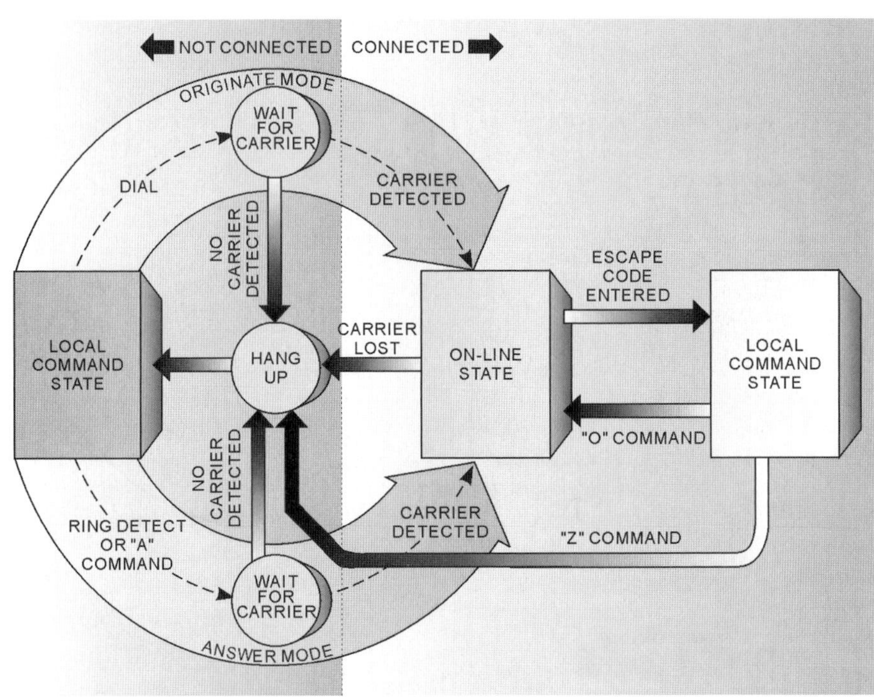

Figure 5-25: AutoDial/AutoAnswer Modem Cycle

off-line

In the local command state, the modem is **off-line** and communicates with the host system to receive and process commands. In the on-line state, the modem facilitates the transfer of data between the host computer and a remote computer or device.

originate mode

ring signal

answer mode

There are two events that can cause the modem to shift from the off-line state to the on-line condition. The system can prompt the modem to go on-line and dial out to another unit. To accomplish this, the host computer places the modem in **originate mode**. The second event involves the modem receiving a **ring signal** from a remote device. In this situation, the host system shifts the modem into **answer mode**.

The modem will automatically shift from the on-line state to the local command state whenever the carrier signal from the incoming line is not detected within a given amount of time, or if it is lost after the connection has been made. An embedded code in the transmitted data can also be used to shift the modem into the local command state.

Dialing

In order to place a call using the modem, the same series of events must occur as for placing a voice telephone call. When the handset is removed from its cradle, a switch inside the telephone closes, connecting the phone to the line. At this point, the phone is off-hook, but it is not yet on-line. When the modem's relay closes, and the dial tone is detected, the modem notifies the host computer that it is connected to the line.

To place a call, the communication software places the modem in originate mode. In this mode, most modems can automatically place calls by issuing the digital tones equivalent of the desired phone number. The number may come from the keyboard, or it may be one which has previously been entered into memory. Some auto-dial modems are capable of producing both pulse and touch-tone dialing equivalents.

Answering

When a call comes in, the ring voltage is detected by the modem if it is turned on. If so, the modem notifies the host computer that a call is coming in, and, depending on its configuration, will answer the call after some preset number of rings. If the receiving computer informs the modem that it is ready to communicate, the modem goes off-hook, and begins the handshaking routine.

The Conversation

After the line connection has been established, a **handshaking sequence** occurs between the modems and their computers. The originating modem signals its computer that the receiving modem is on-line. This is followed by a signal from the remote modem indicating that its computer is ready to transmit and receive data. The originating modem responds by issuing its own carrier tone frequency, which the answering modem must detect in order to notify its computer that the originating modem is on line and ready for data. If both tones have been received successfully, the greetings and handshakes are completed, and the transfer of information begins.

handshaking sequence

While the modem is in the on-line state, no commands can be given to it from the keyboard. However, the local command state can be re-entered while still maintaining the connection by using an escape-code sequence.

For more in-depth information about how modems actually work, refer to the Electronic Reference Shelf on the CD that accompanies this book.

REFERENCE SHELF

INSTALLING AND CONFIGURING MODEMS

A portion of the A+ Core Hardware objective 1.7 states that the test taker should be able to identify proper procedures for installing and configuring peripheral devices. Topics include:

- Monitor/video card
- Modem
- Storage devices

In addition to installing hard drives and peripheral devices that connect to standard I/O ports, technicians must be able to successfully install and configure peripheral devices (or systems) that connect to the system in other ways, such as through the system's expansion slots. The following sections of the chapter deal with installing the system's video output components, internal and external modems, and alternative data storage systems.

The procedures for installing video display systems and storage devices have been covered in previous chapters. The steps for installing a modem vary somewhat depending on whether it is an internal or external device. The steps of both procedures are covered in the following sections.

Installing an Internal Modem

Use the following steps to install an internal modem.

Hands-On Activity

Installing an Internal Modem

1. Prepare the system for installation

   a. Turn the system OFF.
   b. Remove the cover from system unit.
   c. Locate a compatible empty expansion slot.
   d. Remove the expansion slot cover from the rear of the system unit.

2. Configure the modem's IRQ and COM settings

   a. Refer to the modem user's manual regarding any IRQ and COM jumper or switch settings.
   b. Record the card's default IRQ and COM settings.
   c. Set the modem's configuration jumpers to operate the modem as COM 2.

3. Install the modem card in the system

   a. Install the modem card in the expansion slot.
   b. Reinstall the screw to secure the modem card to the back panel of the system unit.

c. Connect the phone line to the appropriate connector on the modem, as shown in Figure 5-26.
d. Connect the other end of the phone line to the commercial phone jack.

4. Disable any competing COM ports

   a. Disable COM2 on the MI/O adapter.

5. Finish the hardware installation

   a. Replace the system unit cover.

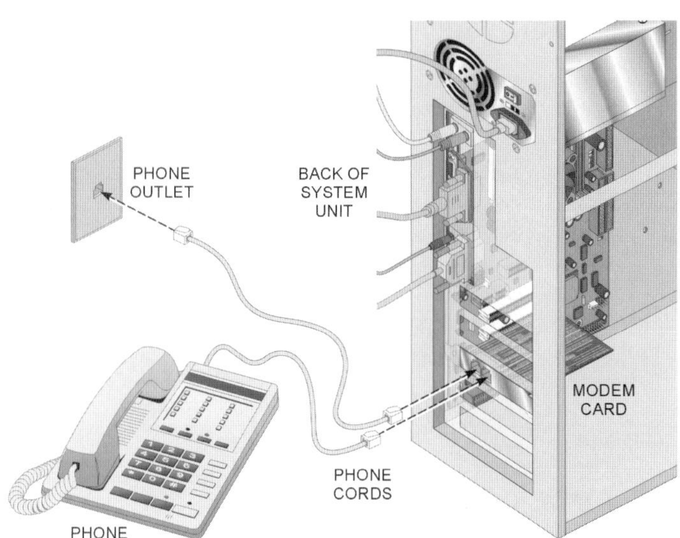

Figure 5-26: Installing an Internal Modem

It is necessary to disable the COM2 port because the system looks to see how many COM ports are available when it boots up. Even if there is no device connected to a COM port, the computer knows the port is there. By disabling this setting, possible interrupt conflict problems are avoided. In addition, some communication software will assign a COM port to an empty serial port. By disabling the port, software that assigns empty COM ports will not see the port at all and, therefore, no conflict will occur.

Installing an External Modem

Use the following steps to install an internal modem.

Hands-On Activity

Installing an External Modem

1. Make the modem connections

   a. Connect the serial cable to the 25-pin serial port at the rear of the system.
   b. Connect the opposite end of the cable to the RS-232 connector of the external modem unit.
   c. Connect the phone line to the appropriate connector on the modem.

d. Connect the other end of the phone line to the phone system jack.
e. Optionally, connect the phone to the appropriate connector on the modem.
f. Verify that the power switch or power supply is turned off.
g. Connect the power supply to the external modem unit.
h. Verify this connection arrangement in Figure 5-27.

2. Enable the system's internal support circuitry

   a. Remove the cover from system unit.
   b. Enable COM2 on the MI/O adapter.
   c. Replace the system unit cover.

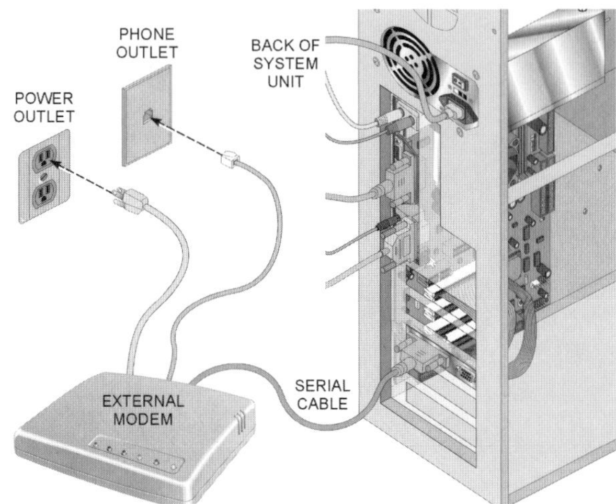

Figure 5-27: Installing an External Modem

Modem Configuration

The parameters for control of the modem, or its supporting COM port, must be established in software. The character frame must be established along with the port's baud rate and flow control information. The method of controlling the flow of information between the two devices must be agreed to by both devices for the transfer to be successful.

Examine the communications software being used to drive the modem to determine which elements need to be configured using the following steps.

Hands-On Activity

Configuring the Modem

1. Install and configure the communications software package

   a. Locate the modem's communication software.
   b. Locate the software documentation.
   c. Locate the installation instructions inside the manual.
   d. Follow the instructions in the manual and on the screen to install the software.
   e. Configure the software to match the system's hardware settings.

2. Set up Windows COM ports and character frame information

   a. Establish the baud rate, character frame, and flow control information in the Windows Control Panel.
   b. Set up the IRQ, COM port, and base address settings in the Control Panel for the COM port the modem is using.

Communication Software

All modems require software to control the communication session. This software is typically included with the purchase of the modem and must be configured to operate in the system the modem will be used in. At the fundamental instruction level, most modem software employs a set of commands known as the **Hayes-Compatible Command Set**.

Hayes-Compatible Command Set

This set of commands is named after the Hayes Microcomputer Products company that first defined them. The command set is based on a group of instructions that begin with a pair of attention characters, followed by command words. Because the attention characters are an integral part of every Hayes command, the command set is often referred to as the AT command set.

command mode

communications mode

guard period

In the Hayes command structure, the operation of the modem shifts back and forth between a **command mode** and a **communications mode**. In the command mode, the modem exchanges commands and status information with the host system's microprocessor. In communications mode, the modem facilitates sending and receiving data between the local system and a remote system. A short **guard period** between communications mode and command mode enables the system to switch smoothly without interrupting a data transmission.

AT Command Set

attention characters (AT)

AT command set

The Hayes command set is based on a group of instructions that begin with a pair of **attention characters** (**AT**), followed by command words. Because the attention characters are an integral part of every Hayes command, the command set is often referred to as the **AT command set**.

Hayes-compatible AT commands are entered at the command line using an ATXn format. The Xn nomenclature identifies the type of command being given (X) and the particular function to be used (n). Except for ATA, ATDn, and ATZn commands, the AT sequence may be followed by any number of commands. The ATA command forces the modem to immediately pick up the phone line (even if it does not ring). The Dn commands are dialing instructions, while the Zn commands reset the modem by loading new default initialization information into it. Table 5-4 provides a summary of the Hayes-compatible AT command set. Most modem user's manuals contain a complete listing of the AT Command Set.

Table 5-4: AT Command Set Summary

COMMAND		FUNCTION
A/		Re-execute command.
A		Go off-hook and attempt to answer a call.
B0		Select V.22 connection at 1200 bps.
B1	*	Select Bell 212A connection at 1200 bps.
C1	*	Return OK message.
Dn		Dial modifier (see Dial Modifier).
E0		Turn off command echo.
E1		Turn on command echo.
F0		Select auto-detect mode (equivalent to N1).
F1	*	Select V.21 of Bell 103.
F2		Reserved.
F3		Select V.23 line modulation.
F4		Select V.22 or Bell 212A 1200 bps line speed.
F5		Select V.22bis 7200 line modulation.
F6		Select V.32bis or V.32 4800 line modulation.
F7		Select V.32bis 7200 line modulation.
F8		Select V.32bis or V.32 9600 modulation.
F9		Select V.32bis 12000 line modulation.
F10		Select V.32bis 14400 line modulation.
H0		Initiate a hang-up sequence.
H1		If on-hook, go off-hook and enter command mode.
I0		Report product code.
I1		Report computed checksum.
I2		Report OK.
I3		Report firmware revision, model, and interface type.
I4		Report response.
I5		Report the country code parameter.
I6		Report modem data pump model and code revision.
L0		Set low speaker volume.
L1		Set low speaker volume.
L2	*	Set medium speaker volume.
L3		Set high speaker volume.
M0		Turn off speaker.
M1	*	Turn speaker on during handshaking, and turn speaker off while receiving carrier.
M2		Turn speaker on during handshaking and while receiving carrie.r
M3		Turn speaker off during dialing and receiving carrier, and turn speaker on during answering.
N0		Turn off Automode detection.
N1	*	Turn on Automode detection.
O0		Go online.
O1		Go online and initiate a retrain sequence.
P		Force pulse dialing.
Q0	*	Allow result codes to PC.
Q1		Inhibit result codes to PC.
Sn		Select S-Register as default.
Sn?		Return the value of S-Register n.
=v		Set default S-Register to value v.
?		Return the value of default S-Register.
T		Force DTMF dialing.
V0		Report short form (terse) result codes.
V1	*	Report long form (verbose) result codes.
W0	*	Report PC speed in EC mode.
W1		Report line speed, EC protocol, and PC speed.
W2		Report modem speed in EC mode.
X0		Report basic progress result codes, OK, CONNECT, RING, NO CARRIER (also for busy, if enabled, and dial tone not detected), NO ANSWER, and ERROR.
X1		Report basic call progress result codes and connection speeds such as OK, CONNECT, RING, NO CARRIER (also for busy, in enabled, and dial tone not detected), NO ANSWER, CONNECT XXXX, and ERROR.
X2		Report basic call progress result codes and connection speeds such as OK, CONNECT, RING, NO CARRIER (also for busy, in enabled, and dial tone not detected), NO ANSWER, CONNECT XXXX, and ERROR.
X3		Report basic call progress result codes and connection rate such as OK, CONNECT, RING, NO CARRIER, NO ANSWER, CONNECT XXXX, BUSY, and ERROR.

* Default

After a command has been entered at the command line, the modem attempts to execute the command and then returns a result code to the screen. Table 5-5 describes the command result codes.

Table 5-5: AT Command Result Codes

RESULT	CODE	DESCRIPTION
0	OK	The OK code is returned by the modem to acknowledge execution of a command line.
1	CONNECT	The modem sends this result code when line speed is 300 bps.
2	RING	The modem sends this result code when incoming ringing is detected on the line.
3	NO CARRIER	The carrier is not detected within the time limit, or the carrier is lost.
4	ERROR	The modem could not process the command line (entry error).
5	CONNECT 1200	The modem detected a carrier at 1200 bps.
6	NO DIAL TONE	The modem could not detect a dial tone when dialing.
7	BUSY	The modem detected a busy signal.
8	NO ANSWER	The modem never detected silence (@ command only).
9	CONNECT 0600	The modem sends this result code when line speed is 7200 bps.
10	CONNECT 2400	The modem detected a carrier at 2400 bps.
11	CONNECT 4800	Connection is established at 4800 bps.
12	CONNECT 9600	Connection is established at 9600 bps.
13	CONNECT 7200	The modem sends this result code when the line speed is 7200 bps.
14	CONNECT 12000	Connection is established at 12000 bps.
15	CONNECT 14400	Connection is established at 14400 bps.
17	CONNECT 38400	Connection is established at 38400 bps.
18	CONNECT 57600	Connection is established at 57600 bps.
22	CONNECT 75TX/1200RX	The modem sends this result code when establishing a V.23 Originate.
23	CONNECT 1200TX/75RX	The modem sends this result code when establishing a V.23 answer.
24	DELAYED	The modem returns this result code when a call fails to connect and is considered delayed.
32	BLACKLISTED	The modem returns this result code when a f/call fails to connect and is considered blacklisted.
40	CARRIER 300	The carrier is detected at 300 bps.
44	CARRIER 1200/75	The modem sends this result code when V.23 backward channel carrier is detected.
45	CARRIER 75/1200	The modem sends this result code when V.23 forward channel carrier is detected.
46	CARRIER 1200	The carrier is detected at 1200 bps.
47	CARRIER 2400	The carrier is detected at 2400 bps.
48	CARRIER 4800	The modem sends this result code when either the high or low channel carrier in V.22bis modem has been detected.
49	CARRIER 7200	The carrier is detected at 7200 bps.
50	CARRIER 9600	The carrier is detected at 9600 bps.
51	CARRIER 12000	The carrier is detected at 12000 bps.
52	CARRIER 14400	The carrier is detected at 14400 bps.
66	COMPRESSION: CLASS 5	MNP Class 5 is active CLASS 5.
67	COMPRESSION: V.42bis	COMPRESSION: V.42bis is active V.42bis.
69	COMPRESSION: NONE	No data compression signals NONE.
70	PROTOCOL: NONE	No error correction is enabled.
77	PROTOCOL: LAPM	V.42 LAP-M error correction is enabled.
80	PROTOCOL: ALT	MNP Class 4 error correction is enabled.

Specialized fax and voice software programs also are included, if the modem has these capabilities. Most communication software packages include an electronic phonebook to hold frequently dialed numbers. Other features include the use of a variety of different software protocols. Common protocols included at this level include Xmodem, Ymodem, and Zmodem. Both the originating and answering modems must agree on the same protocol, baud rate, and data length for the session to succeed.

To communicate with other computers, some information about how the communication will proceed is needed. In particular, it is necessary to match the protocol of the remote unit, as well as its parity, character framing, and baud rate settings. With older modems, this may involve a telephone call to the other computer user. In the case of online services, the information comes with the introductory package the user receives when joining the service.

HyperTerminal

TelNet

The Windows program contains an application called **HyperTerminal** that can be used to control the operation of the system's modem with **TelNet** services. HyperTerminal is capable of operating with several different modem configurations. This flexibility enables it to conduct transfers with a wide variety of other computer systems on the Internet, such as Unix and Linux, without worrying about operating system differences. Using HyperTerminal with TelNet to access other locations is much quicker than browsing web sites with a graphical browser. The HyperTerminal New Connections window, shown in Figure 5-28 provides the options for configuring the communications settings. This program can be accessed through the *Start/Programs/Accessories/Communications* path in Windows 98.

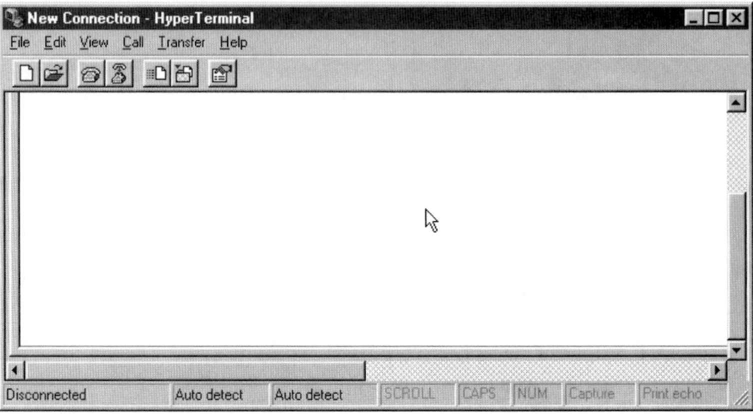

Figure 5-28: HyperTerminal

Using the AT Command Set

ATZ

At the command line, type **ATZ** to reset the modem and enter the Command mode using the Hayes-compatible command set. You should receive a 0, or OK response, if the command was processed.

communications software

If no result code is returned to the screen, check the modem's configuration and setup again for conflicts. Also, check the Speed setting of the **communications software** to make sure it is compatible with that of the modem. On the other hand, a returned OK code indicates that the modem and the computer are communicating properly.

You can use other AT-compatible commands to check the modem at the DOS level. The ATL2 command sets the modem's output volume to medium, to make sure that it is not set too low to be heard. If the modem dials, but cannot connect to a remote station, check the modem's Speed and DTR settings. Change the DTR setting by entering AT&Dn. When

n = 0 - The modem ignores the DTR line.

n = 1 - The modem goes to async command state when the DTR line goes off.

n = 2 - A DTR off condition switches the modem to the off-hook state and back into the Command mode.

n = 3 - When the DTR line switches to off the modem gets initialized.

The modem's User Guide should contain the complete AT command set. Some of the commands and features listed may not work with your particular modem.

If the modem connects, but cannot communicate, check the character-framing parameter of the receiving modem, and set the local modem to match. Also, match the terminal emulation of the local unit to that of the remote unit. ANSI terminal emulation is the most common. Finally, match the file transfer protocol to the other modem.

A number of things can occur to prevent the modem from going into the online state. An intelligent modem waits a specified length of time, after pickup, before it starts dialing. This wait allows the phone system time to apply a dial tone to the line. After the number has been dialed, the modem waits for the ringback from the telephone company. (This is what you hear when you are making a call.)

When the ringing stops, indicating that the call has gone through, the modem waits a specified length of time for an answer tone (carrier) from the receiving modem. If the carrier is not detected within the allotted time, the originating modem begins automatic disconnect procedures. If a busy signal is detected, the originating modem also hangs up, or refers to a second number.

During the data transfer, both modems monitor the signal level of the carrier to prevent the transfer of false data, due to signal deterioration. If the carrier signal strength drops below some predetermined threshold level, or is lost for a given length of time, one or both modems initiate automatic disconnect procedures.

Use the ATDT*70 command to disable call waiting, if the transmission is frequently garbled. The +++ command will interrupt any activity the modem is engaged in, and bring it to the Command mode.

TEST TIP

Be familiar with the basic Hayes AT communication codes.

Protocols

In order to maintain an orderly flow of information between the computer and the modem, and between the modem and another modem, a **protocol**, or set of rules governing the transfer of information, must be in place. All of the participants in the "conversation" must use the same protocols to communicate.

protocol

There are two distinct classes of protocols in widespread use with modems today. These include:

- **Hardware-oriented protocols**
- **Control-code-oriented protocols**

Hardware-oriented protocols

Control-code-oriented protocols

Hardware-Oriented Protocols

Hardware-oriented protocols are tied to the use of particular interface pins to control data flow. As far as stand-alone modems are concerned, the most basic hardware standard is the RS-232C serial interface standard. But within the realm of the RS-232 standard a proliferation of communication methods exists.

The RS-232C standard begins by identifying communication equipment using two categories:

Data Terminal Equipment (DTE)

Data Communication Equipment (DCE)

- **Data Terminal Equipment (DTE)**, usually a computer
- **Data Communication Equipment (DCE)**, usually a modem

The term DTE is applied to any equipment whose main purpose is to process data. On the other hand, any communication equipment that changes data during transmission is referred to as DCE. Figure 5-29 illustrates a typical DTE/DCE relationship.

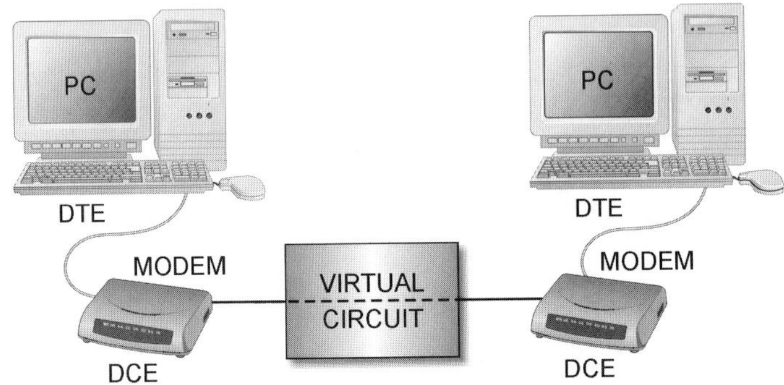

Figure 5-29: The DTE/DCE Relationship

Transmit Data (TXD)

Receive Data (RXD)

In its most basic form, the RS-232C interface makes provision for a full-duplex operating mode through its **Transmit Data (TXD)** and **Receive Data (RXD)** pins. Normally, data passes from the DTE to the DCE on the TXD line, and from the DCE to the DTE on the RXD line, although these two pins may sometimes be reversed.

Data Terminal Ready

Request To Send

The two most common forms of hardware protocols are DTR and RTS, named after the interface's **Data Terminal Ready** and **Request To Send** pins. These lines are toggled On and Off to control when to send, and not send, data. The DTE uses the RTS pin to inform the DCE that it is ready to send Data.

Clear to Send (CTS)

Data Set Ready (DSR)

Data Carrier Detect (CD)

The DCE uses a trio of reciprocal lines, **Clear to Send (CTS)**, **Data Set Ready (DSR)**, and **Data Carrier Detect (CD)** to signal the Data Terminal Equipment. It uses the CTS line to inform the DTE that it is ready to accept data. The modem uses the DSR line to notify the DTE that it is connected to the phone line.

Speed Indicator (SI)

Ring Indicator (RI)

The RS-232C standard also designates a number of other lines that can be used for specialized functions. The **Speed Indicator (SI)** line is used by the DCE to indicate whether the modem is in low- or high-speed mode. The DCE may also use the **Ring Indicator (RI)** line to indicate that ring-in voltage is being received. The complete RS-232C interface specification, and its variations, is described in the Serial Port section of Chapter 3—*Standard I/O Systems.*

Control-Code-Oriented Protocols

Most data-flow control is performed using the control-code class of protocols. In this class of protocols, three types are in widespread use:

- X-ON/X-OFF
- ACK/NAK
- ETX/ACK

In these protocols, control codes are sent across the data lines to control data flow, as opposed to using separate control lines.

X-ON/X-OFF

The **X-ON/X-OFF** protocol, where X represents two special control characters, is a relatively simple concept used to regulate data flow. This control is necessary to prevent buffer memories from over-filling. When data overflows the buffer, the result is usually an error code. The X-ON/X-OFF protocol uses special control characters to start, and stop, data flow.

ACK/NAK

ETX/ACK

The **ACK/NAK** and **ETX/ACK** protocols are considered to be high-level protocols because they require special interface programs called device drivers to be installed. In both cases, these protocols use special control characters, and escape code sequences, to provide functions such as data transmission integrity, flow control, requests for retransmission, and so forth.

Block Check Character (BCC)

The ACK/NAK protocol derives its title from the ASCII control characters for ACKnowledge, and Not ACKnowledge. It uses these characters to provide a means of error correction for transmitted data. Basically, the ACK/NAK protocol expects a block of data to be preceded by a Start-Of-Text (STX) character, and to be followed by both an End-Of-Text (ETX) character and an error-checking code, as depicted in Figure 5-30. At the receiving end, the **Block Check Character (BCC)** is checked for errors. Depending on the outcome of the check, either an ACK signal, indicating a successful transmission, or a NAK signal, indicating an error has occurred will be returned. If a NAK signal is returned, the transmitting device responds by retransmitting the entire block.

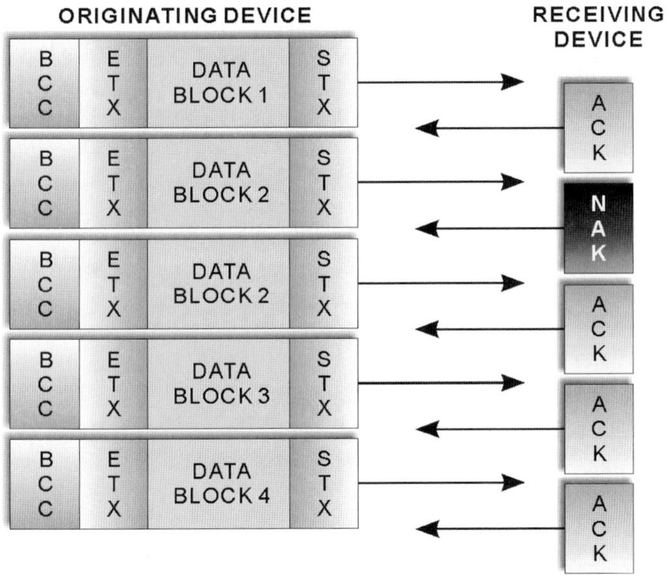

Figure 5-30: ACK/NAK Transmission

The ETX/ACK protocol is somewhat simpler than ACK/NAK, in that no character check is performed. If the receiving device does not return an ACK signal within a predetermined length of time, the sending device assumes an error, or malfunction, has occurred, and re-transmits the character block.

Error-Correcting Protocols

Several error-correcting file transfer protocols have been developed for modem communications packages. Some of the more common protocols include:

TEST TIP

Know the fundamental difference between parity error checking and error-checking and correcting protocols.

- Xmodem
- Ymodem
- Zmodem
- Kermit

checksum

Cyclic Redundancy Checks (CRCs)

These protocols use extensive error detection schemes to maintain the validity of the data as it's being transmitted. Error-detecting and correcting protocols generate more exotic error detection algorithms, such as **checksum** and **Cyclic Redundancy Checks (CRCs)**, to identify, locate, and possibly correct data errors.

Compression Protocols

compression

Advanced communication protocols use data **compression** techniques to reduce the volume of data that must be transmitted. Each protocol involves a mathematical algorithm that reads the data, and converts it into encoded words. The modem at the receiving end must use the same algorithm to decode the words and restore them to their original form.

Comite Consultatif International Telegraphique et Telephonique (CCITT)

Microcom Networking Protocol

Some modem compression standards reach ratios as high as 4 to 1. The major standards for modem data compression have come from a company named Microcom, and the **Comite Consultatif International Telegraphique et Telephonique (CCITT)** worldwide standards organization. The **Microcom Networking Protocol** level7 (MNP7) standard can produce 3:1 compression ratios, while the CCITT V.42bis standard reaches 4:1.

The CCITT standards are identified by a v.xx nomenclature. The original CCITT standard was the v.22 protocol that established transfers at 1200 bps using 600 baud. The v.22bis standard followed providing 2400 bps transfers at 600 baud. The v.32 protocol increased the bps rate to 4800 and 9600.

The CCITT standards also include an error correction protocol and a data compression protocol. The v.42 standard is the error correction protocol while v.42bis protocol is the CCITT equivalent of the MNP5 and MNP7 protocols. Both protocols run as modules along with the v.32 and v.32bis protocols to provide additional transmission speed.

The MNP Microcom standards began with protocols MNP2 through MNP4. These standards dealt with error correction protocols. The MNP5 and MNP 7 standards followed as the first data compression protocols. The MNP10 standard introduced the first Adverse Channel Enhancement protocol. This type of protocol is designed to provide maximum performance for modems used in typically poor connection applications, such as cellular phones. It features multiple connection attempts and automatically adjusted transmission rates. Like the advanced CCITT protocols, the MNP 10 protocol module runs along with a V.42 protocol to maximize the data transmission rate. Newer CCITT and MNP protocols provide modems with 56 Kbps transmission capabilities.

During a special training period conducted at lower speeds, the modem tests the integrity of the transmission medium. The modem then negotiates with the remote modem to determine the maximum transfer rate for the existing line conditions.

Character Framing

character-type

character-framing

Within a particular protocol there are a number of parameters that must be agreed upon before an efficient exchange of information can occur. The most significant of these parameters are **character-type** and **character-framing**. Basically, character-type refers to the character set, or alphabet, understood by the devices. Depending on the systems, the character set may be an 8-bit, ASCII line code; a 7-bit, ASCII code (with an error-checking bit); or an EBCDIC code.

Character-framing refers to the total number of the bits used to transmit a character. This includes the length of the coded character, and the number and type of overhead bits required to send the character. A common character-framing scheme calls for a start bit, seven data bits, an odd-parity bit, and a stop bit, as depicted in Figure 5-31. An additional bit is often added to the frame for error-checking purposes.

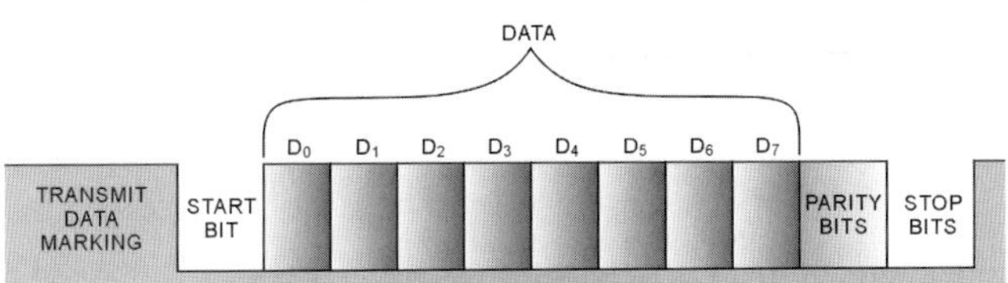

Figure 5-31: Asynchronous Character Format

Although this is a typical character-framing technique, it is not universal throughout the industry. The problem here is one of device comprehension. The local unit may be using a 10-bit character frame consisting of a start bit, seven data bits, an odd-parity bit, and a stop bit. However, if the remote system is using something besides 7-bit, odd-parity ASCII with one stop bit, the response from it would be unintelligible as anything written in English. The composition of the character frame must be the same at both the sending and receiving ends of the transmission.

INTERNET CONCEPTS

The A+ Operating System Technologies objective 4.2 states that the test taker should be able to "identify concepts and capabilities relating to the Internet and basic procedures for setting up a system for Internet access."

The tremendous popularity of the Internet, and its heavy concentration on PC platforms, requires that the PC technician understand how the Internet is organized and how the PC relates to it. The successful technician must be able to establish and maintain Internet connections for customers using the major operating systems and dial-up networking software. The remainder of this chapter focuses on wide area networking/Internet concepts.

WIDE AREA NETWORKS

Wide Area Network (WAN)

A **Wide Area Network (WAN)** is very similar in concept to a widely distributed client/server LAN. In a wide area network, computers are typically separated by distances.

Bulletin Board Service (BBS)

A typical WAN is a local city- or countywide network, like the one in Figure 5-32. This network links network members together through a **Bulletin Board Service (BBS)**. Users can access the bulletin board's server with a simple telephone call.

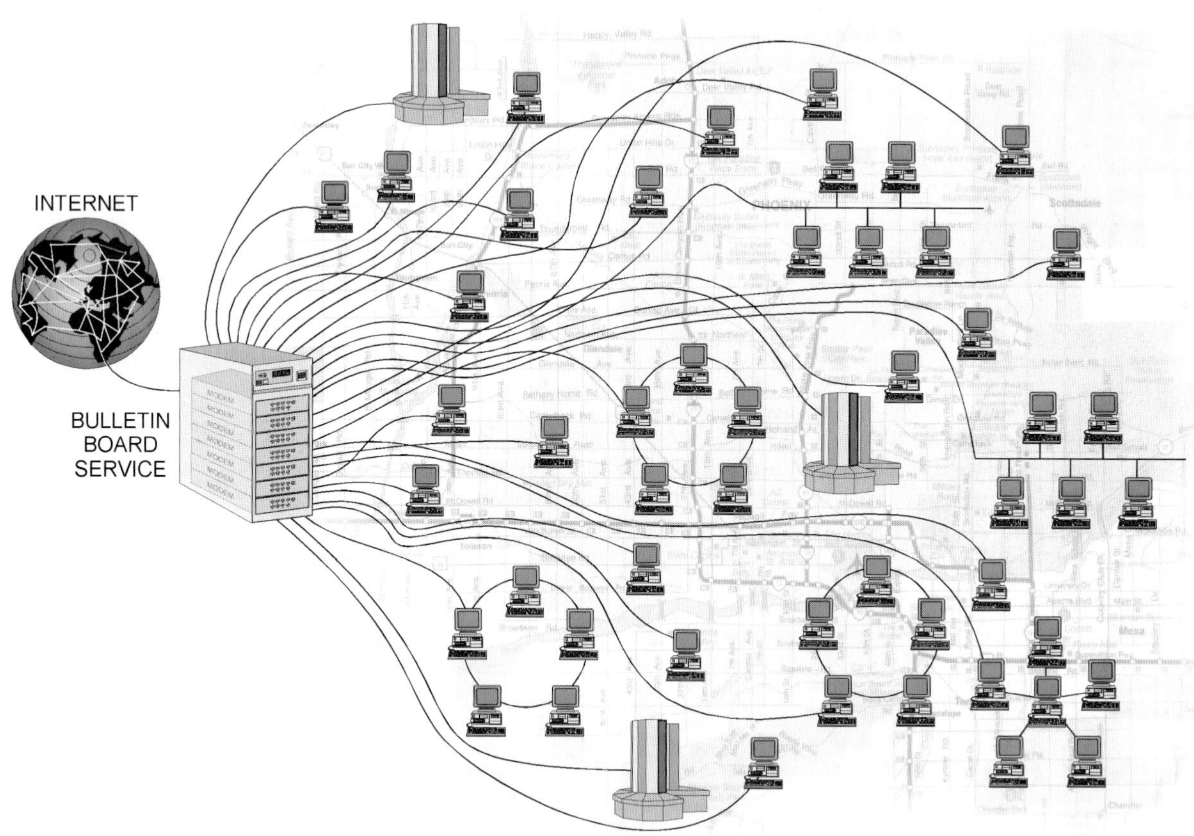

Figure 5-32: County-Wide Network

links

WANs are connected by several different types of communication systems. These communication paths are referred to as **links**. Most users connect to the network via standard telephone lines, using dial-up modems. Dial-up connections are generally the slowest way to connect to a network, but they are inexpensive to establish and use.

Other users, who require quicker data transfers, contract with the telephone company to use special, high-speed **Integrated Service Digital Network** (**ISDN**) lines. These types of links require a **digital modem** to conduct data transfers. Because the modem is digital, no analog conversion is required.

Integrated Service Digital Network (ISDN)

digital modem

Users who require very high volumes lease dedicated **T1** and **T3 lines** from the telephone company. These applications generally serve businesses that put several of their computers or networks on-line. Once the information is transmitted, it may be carried over many types of communications links on its way to its destination. These interconnecting links can include fiber-optic cables, satellite up and down links, UHF, and microwave transmission systems. Figure 5-33 illustrates different ways to access WANs.

T1 and T3 Lines

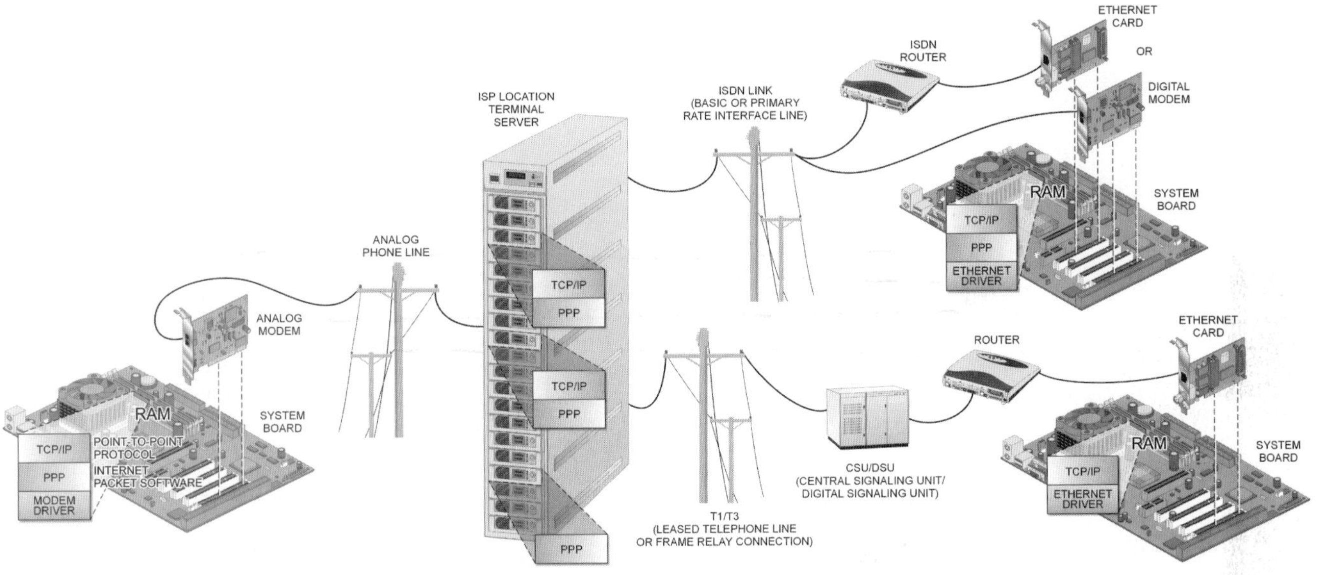

Figure 5-33: Methods of Accessing Wide Area Networks

In some areas, high-speed intermediate-sized networks, referred to as **Metropolitan Area Networks** (**MANs**), are popping up. These networks typically cover areas up to 30 miles (50 kilometers) in diameter and are operated to provide access to regional resources. They are like LANs in speed and operation, but use special high-speed connections and protocols to increase the geographic span of the network, like a WAN.

Metropolitan Area Networks (MANs)

The Internet

Internet

backbone

National Science Foundation (NSF)

The most famous WAN is the **Internet**. The Internet is actually a network of networks, working together. The main communication path for the Internet is a series of networks, established by the U.S. government, to link supercomputers together at key research sites.

This pathway is referred to as the **backbone**, and is affiliated with the **National Science Foundation** (**NSF**). Since the original backbone was established, the Internet has expanded around the world, and offers access to computer users in every part of the globe.

TCP/IP

Transmission Control Protocol/Internet Protocol (TCP/IP)

network packets

header fields

IP header

TCP header

The language of the Internet is **Transmission Control Protocol/Internet Protocol (TCP/IP)** for short. No matter what type of computer platform or software is being used, the information must move across the Internet in this format. This protocol calls for data to be grouped together in bundles called **network packets**.

The U.S. Department of Defense originally developed the TCP/IP protocol as a hacker-resistant, secure protocol for transmitting data on a network. It is considered to be one of the most secure of the network protocols. Because it was developed by the U.S. government, no one actually owns the TCP/IP protocol it was adopted as the transmission standard for the Internet.

The TCP/IP packet is designed primarily to allow for message fragmentation and reassembly. It exists through two **header fields**, the **IP header** and the **TCP header**, followed by the data field, as illustrated in Figure 5-34.

TEST TIP — Know what TCP/IP is and what it does.

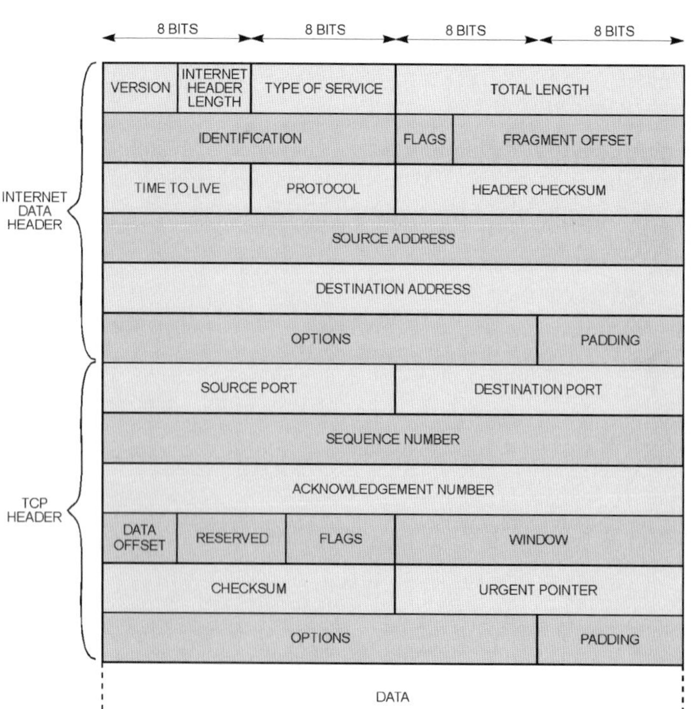

Figure 5-34: TCP/IP Packet

The TCP/IP protocol was so widely accepted by the Internet community that virtually every network operating system supports it, including Apple, MS-DOS/Windows, Unix, Linux, OS/2 and even networked printers. It can also be used on any topology (i.e., Ethernet, Token Ring, etc.). Therefore, all of these computer types can exchange data across a network using the TCP/IP protocol.

TEST TIP

Know the advantages of using the TCP/IP protocol.

In the Windows operating systems, the TCP/IP settings are established through the *Start/Settings/ControlPanel/Network/TCP-IP adapter/Properties*. In this location, you can click on the IP Address tab to establish the method of obtaining an IP address (i.e., automatically from a DHCP Server, or manually, by specifying a static IP address). If you choose the option to Specify an IP address, you will need to enter the IP address and Subnet Mask settings.

TEST TIP

Be able to describe the pathway that should be used to manually establish IP address and Subnet Mask settings.

Internet Service Providers

Internet Service Providers (ISPs)

Connecting all of the users and individual networks together are **Internet Service Providers (ISPs)**. ISPs are companies that provide the technical gateway to the Internet. These companies own blocks of access addresses that they assign to their customers to give to give the customer an identity on the network.

Service that most ISPs deliver to their customers include:

- Internet identity through IP Addresses
- Email services through POP3 and SMTP servers
- Internet News Service through USENET archive servers
- Internet routing through DNS servers

TEST TIP

Be aware of common services that ISPs provide their Internet customers.

All of these services are described in greater detail later in this chapter.

IP Addresses

Internet Protocol addresses

IP addresses

The blocks of Internet access addresses that ISPs provide to their customers are called **Internet Protocol addresses**, or **IP addresses**. The IP address makes each site a valid member of the Internet. This is how individual users are identified to receive file transfers, email, and file requests.

dotted decimal notation

IP addresses exist in the numeric format of XXX.YYY.ZZZ.AAA. Each address consists of four 8-bit fields separated by dots (.). This format of specifying addresses is referred to as **dotted decimal notation**. The decimal numbers are derived from the binary address that the hardware understands. For example, a binary network address of:

10000111.10001011.01001001.00110110 (binary)

corresponds to:

135.139.073.054 (decimal)

Each IP address consists of two parts: the network address and the host address. The network address identifies the entire network; the host address identifies an intelligent member within the network (router, a server, or a workstation).

Three classes of standard IP addresses are supported for LANs: Class A, Class B, and Class C. These addresses occur in four-octet fields like the example.

Class A addresses

- **Class A addresses** Are reserved for large networks and use the last 24 bits (the last three octets or fields) of the address for the host address. The first octet always begins with a 0, followed by a 7-bit number. Therefore, valid Class A addresses range between 001.x.x.x and 126.x.x.x. This allows a Class A network to support 126 different networks with nearly 17 million hosts (nodes) per network.

NOTE

The 127.x.x.x address range is a special block of addresses reserved for testing network systems. The U.S. government owns some of these addresses for testing the Internet backbone. The 127.0.0.1 address is reserved for testing the bus on the local system.

Class B addresses

- **Class B addresses** are assigned to medium-sized networks. The first two octets can range between 128.x.x.x and 191.254.0.0. The last two octets contain the host addresses. This enables Class B networks to include up to 16,384 different networks with approximately 65,534 hosts per network.

Class C addresses

- **Class C addresses** are normally used with smaller LANs. In a Class C address, only the last octet is used for host addresses. The first three octets can range between 192.x.x.x and 223.254.254.0. Therefore, the Class C address can support approximately 2 million networks with 254 hosts each.

subnets

intranets

router

firewall

Within this context, sections of the network can be grouped together into **subnets** that share a range of IP addresses. These groups are referred to as **intranets**. (Actually, a true intranet requires that the segment have a protective gateway to act as an entry and exit point for the segment.) In most cases, the gateway is a device called a **router**. A router is an intelligent device that receives data and directs it toward a designated IP address.

Some networks employ a **firewall** as a gateway to the outside. A firewall is a combination of hardware and software components that provide a protective barrier between networks with different security levels. The firewall is configured by an administrator to only pass only data to and from designated IP addresses and TCP/IP ports.

One reason for creating subnets is to isolate one segment of the network from all the others. Suppose, for example, that a large organization has 1,000 computers, all of which are connected to the network. Without segmentation, data from all 1,000 units would run through every other network node. The effect of this would be that everyone else in the network would have access to all the data on the network, and the operation of the network would be slowed considerably by the uncontrolled traffic.

Another reason to use subnets is to efficiently use IP addresses. Because the IP addressing scheme is defined as a 32-bit code, there are only a certain number of possible addresses. Although 126 networks with 17 million customers may seem like a lot, in the scheme of a worldwide network system, that's not a lot of addresses. In this worldwide context, IP addresses are purchased from a governing body (the Network Information Center, or NIC). Therefore, there are only so many to go around. No more Class A addresses can be obtained. They have all been accounted for. Likewise, Class B and Class C addresses are becoming scarce due to the popularity of the Internet.

A third reason for subnetting is to utilize a single IP address across physically divided locations, such as remotely located areas of a campus. By subnetting a Class C address, half of the 253 possible addresses can be allocated to one campus location, and the other half can be allocated to hosts at the second location. In this manner, both locations can operate using a single Class C address.

Suppose, for example, that a school has two physically separated campuses and that they have purchased a single Class C address. If one campus has 60 hosts and the other has 100 hosts, you need to divide the Class C's 256 possible addresses between the two campuses (by subnetting them), or purchase another Class C address for the second campus. In the process, 156 addresses are wasted at each location.

Subnets are created by masking off (hiding) the network address portion of the IP address on the units within the subnet. This, in effect, limits the mobility of the data to those nodes within the subnet, because they can reconcile only addresses from within their masked range.

Internet Domains

The IP addresses of all the computers attached to the Internet are tracked using a listing system called the **Domain Name Service (DNS)**. This system evolved as a way to organize the members of the Internet into a hierarchical management structure.

Domain Name Service (DNS)

The DNS structure consists of various levels of computer groups called **domains**. Each computer on the Internet is assigned a **domain name**, such as *mic-inc.com* The mic-inc is the user friendly domain name assigned to the Marcraft site.

domains

domain name

In the example, the .com notation at the end of the address is a top level domain that defines the type of organization, or country of origin associated with the address. In this case, the .COM designation identifies the user as a commercial site. The following list identifies the Internet's top level domain codes:

* .com = Commercial Businesses
* .edu = Educational Institutions
* .gov = Government Agencies
* .int = International Organizations
* .mil = Military Establishments
* .net = Networking Organizations
* .org = Non-profit organizations

Fully Qualified Domain Names (FQDN)

On the Internet, domain names are specified in terms of their **Fully Qualified Domain Names (FQDN)**. An FQDN is a human-readable address that describes the location of the site on the Internet. It contains the host name, the domain name and the top-level domain name. For example, the name www.oneworld.owt.com is an FQDN.

host name

The letters www represent the **host name**. The host name specifies the name of the computer that provides services and handles requests for specific Internet addresses. In this case, the host is the world wide web. Other types of hosts include ftp and http sites.

The .owt extension indicates that the organization is a domain listed under the top level domain heading. Likewise, the .oneworld entry is a subdomain of the .owt domain. It is very likely one of multiple networks supported by the .owt domain.

At each domain level, the members of the domain are responsible for tracking the addresses of the domains on the next-lower level. The lower domain is then responsible for tracking the addresses of domains, or end users, on the next level below it.

static IP addressing

dynamic IP addressing

Point-to-Point Protocol (PPP)

UNIX

Serial Line Internet Protocol (SLIP)

America On-Line (AOL)

Compuserve

In addition to its domain name tracking function, the DNS system resolves (links) individual domain names of computers to their current IP address listings. Some IP addresses are permanently assigned to a particular domain name so that whenever the domain name is issued on the Internet it always accesses the same IP address. This is referred to as **static IP addressing**. However, most ISPs use a **dynamic IP addressing** scheme for allocating IP addresses.

If an ISP wanted to service 10,000 customers within its service area using static IP addressing, it would need to purchase and maintain 10,000 IP addresses. However, because most Internet customers are not on line all of the time, their IPs are not always in use. This allows the ISP to purchase a reasonable number of IP addresses that it can hold in a bank and dynamically assign to its users as they log on to their service. When the user logs out, the IP address returns to the bank for other users.

The Internet software communicates with the service provider by embedding the TCP/IP information in a **Point-to-Point Protocol (PPP)** shell for transmission through the modem in analog format. The communications equipment, at the service provider's site, converts the signal back to the digital TCP/IP format. Older units running the **UNIX** operating system used a connection protocol called **Serial Line Internet Protocol (SLIP)** for dial-up services.

Some service providers, such as **America On-Line (AOL)** and **Compuserve**, have become very well known. However, there are thousands of lesser known, dedicated Internet access provider companies offering services around the world. Figure 5-35 illustrates the service provider's position in the Internet scheme, and shows the various connection methods used to access the net.

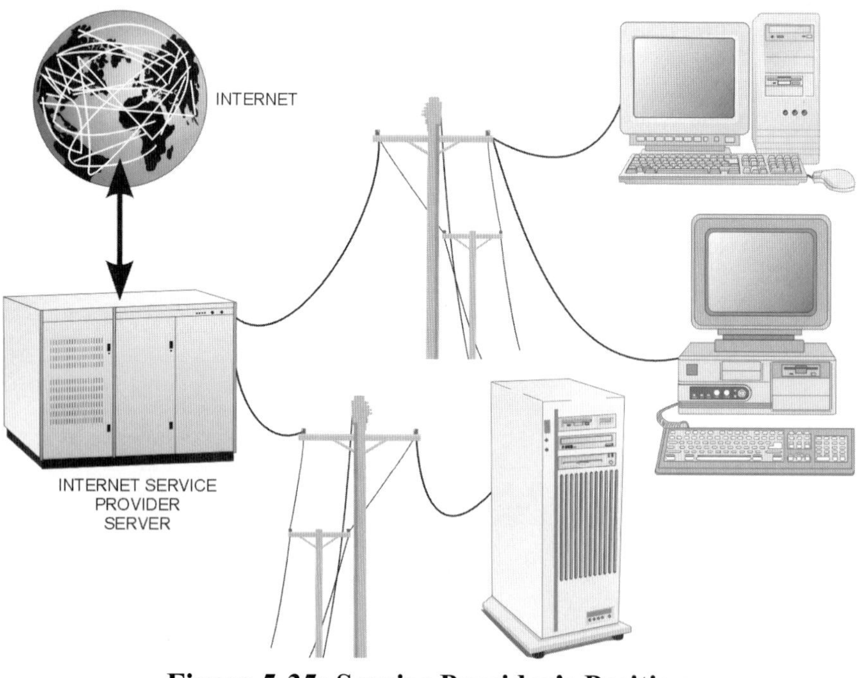

INTERNET

INTERNET SERVICE PROVIDER SERVER

Figure 5-35: Service Provider's Position

When you connect to a service provider, you are connecting to its computer system, which, in turn, is connected to the Internet through devices called **routers**. A router is a device that intercepts network transmissions and determines for which part of the Internet they are intended. It then determines what the best routing scheme is for delivering the message to its intended address. The routing schedule is devised based on the known available links through the Internet and the amount of traffic detected on various segments. The router then transfers the message to a **Network Access Point** (**NAP**).

routers

Network Access Point (NAP)

Dynamic Host Configuration Protocol

The **Dynamic Host Configuration Protocol** (**DHCP**) is an Internet protocol that can be used to automatically assign IP addresses to devices on a network using TCP/IP. Using DHCP simplifies network administration because software, rather than an administrator, assigns and keeps track of IP addresses. For this reason, many ISPs use the dynamic IP addressing function of DHCP to provide access to their dial-up users. The protocol automatically delivers IP addresses, subnet mask and default router configuration parameters, and other configuration information to the devices on the network.

Dynamic Host Configuration Protocol (DHCP)

The dynamic addressing portion of the protocol also means that computers can be added to a network without manually assigning them unique IP addresses. As a matter of fact, the devices can be issued a different IP address each time they connect to the network. In some networks, the device's IP address can even change while it is still connected. DHCP also supports a mix of static and dynamic IP addresses.

DHCP is an open standard, developed by the **Internet Engineering Task Force** (**IETF**). It is a client-server arrangement where a DHCP client contacts a DHCP server to obtain its configuration parameters. The DHCP server dynamically configures the clients with parameters appropriate to the current network structure.

Internet Engineering Task Force (IETF)

The most important configuration parameter carried by DHCP is the IP address. A computer must be initially assigned a specific IP address that is appropriate to the network to which the computer is attached, and that is not assigned to any other computer on that network. If a computer moves to a new network, it must be assigned a new IP address for that new network. DHCP can be used to manage these assignments automatically. The DHCP client support is built into Windows 9x, Windows NT 4.0 Workstation, and Windows 2000 Professional. Windows NT 4 and Windows 2000 Server versions include both client and server support for DHCP. These operating systems and DHCP are covered in greater detail in Chapters 9 and 10.

Internet Transmissions

The TCP/IP protocol divides the transmission into packets of information, suitable for retransmission across the Internet. Along the way, the information passes through different networks that are organized at different levels. Depending on the routing scheme, the packets may move through the Internet using different routes to get to the intended address. At the destination, however, the packets are reassembled into the original transmission.

This concept is illustrated in Figure 5-36.

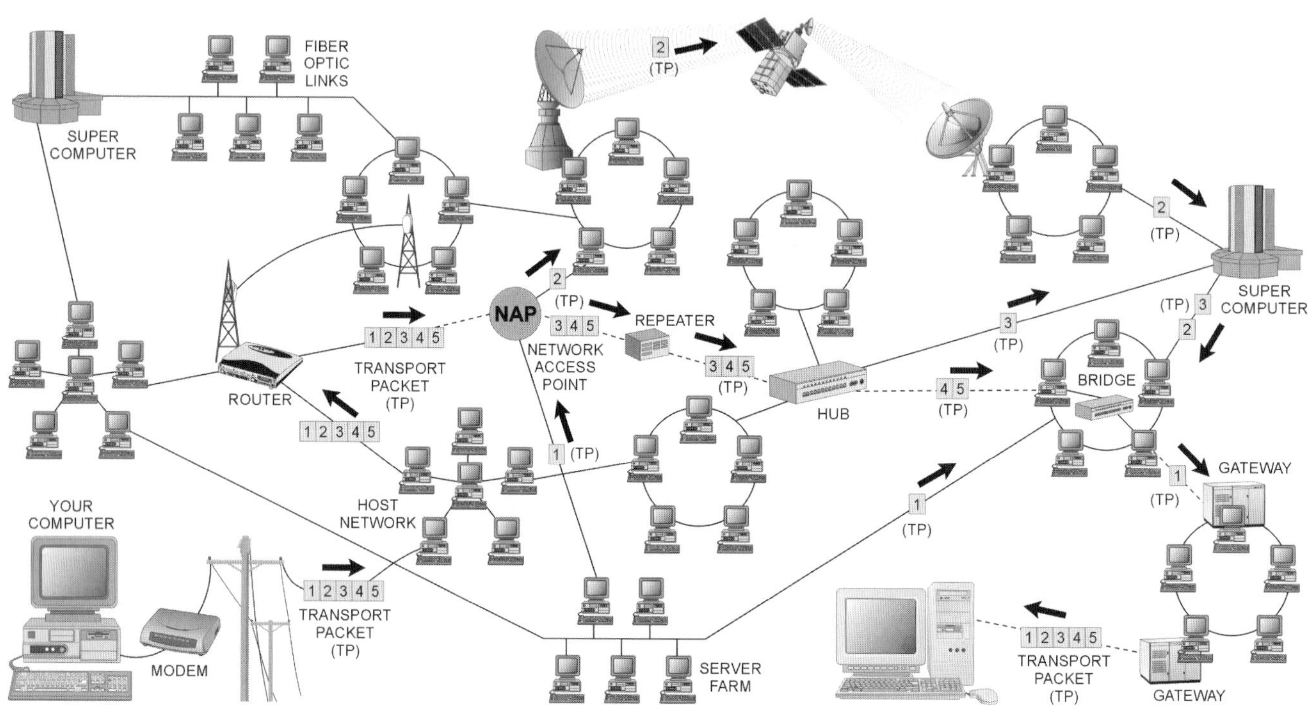

Figure 5-36: Packets Moving Through the Internet

As a message moves from the originating address to its destination, it may pass through LANs, mid-level networks, routers, repeaters, hubs, bridges, and gateways. A mid-level network is simply another network that does not require an Internet connection to carry out communications.

Bridges

gateway

A router receives messages, amplifies them, and retransmits them to keep the messages from deteriorating as they travel. Hubs are used to link networks together, so that nodes within them can communicate with each other. **Bridges** connect networks together, so that data can pass through them as it moves from one network to the next. A special type of bridge, called a **gateway**, translates a message as it passes through, so that it can be used by different types of networks—Apple networks and PC networks.

ISDN

As discussed earlier in the chapter, ISDN service offers high-speed access to the public telephone system. However, ISDN service requires digital modems (also referred to as **Terminal Adapters**, or **TAs**). Not only does the end user require a digital modem, the telephone company's switch gear equipment must be updated to handle digital switching. This fact has slowed implementation of ISDN services until recently.

Terminal Adapters (TAs)

Basic Rate Interface (BRI)

Primary Rate Interface (PRI)

Broadband ISDN (BISDN)

Three levels of ISDN service are available: **Basic Rate Interface** (**BRI**) services, **Primary Rate Interface** (**PRI**) services, and **Broadband ISDN** (**BISDN**) services.

BRI services are designed to provide residential users with basic digital service through the existing telephone system. The cost of this service is relatively low, although it is more expensive than regular analog service. BRI service is not available in all areas of the country, but it is expanding rapidly.

network terminator

Typical residential telephone wiring consists of a four-wire cable. Up to seven devices can be connected to these wires. Under the BRI specification, the telephone company delivers three information channels to the residence over a two-wire cable. The two-wire system is expanded into the four-wire system at the residence through a **network terminator**. The ISDN organization structure is depicted in Figure 5-37.

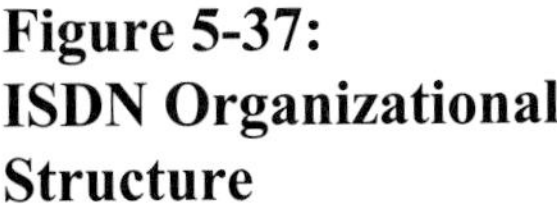

Figure 5-37: ISDN Organizational Structure

The BRI information channels exist as a pair of 64 Kbps channels and a 16 Kbps control channel. The two 64 Kbps channels, called **bearer** or **B channels**, can be used to transmit and receive voice and data information. The 16 Kbps **D channel** is used to implement advanced control features such as call waiting, call forwarding, Caller ID, and others. The D channel also can be used to conduct packet-transfer operations.

bearer

B channels

D channel

PRI services are more elaborate ISDN services that support the very high data rates needed for live video transmissions. This is accomplished using the telephone company's existing wiring and advanced ISDN devices. The operating cost of PRI service is considerably more expensive than BRI services. The higher costs of PRI tend to limit its usage to larger businesses.

The fastest, most expensive ISDN service is broadband ISDN. This level of service provides extremely high transfer rates (up to 622 Mbps) over coaxial or fiber-optic cabling. Advanced transmission protocols are also used to implement broadband ISDN.

Digital modems are available in both internal and external formats. In the case of external devices, the analog link between the computer and the modem requires a D-to-A and A-to-D conversion processes at the computer's serial port and then again at the modem. Of course, with an internal digital modem these conversion processes are not required.

Digital Subscriber Lines

Digital Subscriber Lines (DSL)

The telephone companies have begun to offer a new high bandwidth connection service to home and business customers in the form of **Digital Subscriber Lines** (**DSL**). This technology provides high-speed communication links by using the existing telephone lines to generate bandwidths ranging up to 9Mb/s or more. However, distance limitations and line quality conditions can reduce the actual throughput that can be achieved with these connections.

xDSL

Asynchronous DSL (ADSL)

Synchronous DSL (SDSL)

High-data-rate DSL (HDSL)

Symmetric DSL (SDSL)

POTS (Plain Old Telephone System)

The term **xDSL** is used to refer to all types of DSL collectively. There are two main categories of DSL – **Asynchronous DSL** (**ADSL**) and **Synchronous DSL** (**SDSL**). Two other types of xDSL technologies that have some promise are **High-data-rate DSL** (**HDSL**) and **Symmetric DSL** (**SDSL**). SDSL is refereed to as *symmetric* because it supports the same data rates for upstream and downstream traffic. Conversely, ADSL (also known as *rate-adaptive* DSL) supports different data transfer rates when receiving data (referred to as the *downstream* rate) and transmitting data (known as the *upstream* rate). SDSL supports data transfer rates up to 3 Mbps in both directions while ADSL data transfer rates of from 1.5 to 9 Mbps downstream and from 16 to 640 Kbps upstream. Both forms of DSL require special modems that employ sophisticated modulation schemes to pack data onto telephone wires. However, you should be aware that access speeds may also vary from provider to provider, even if they are using the same central office to provide service.

xDSL is similar to the ISDN arrangements just discussed in that they both operate over existing copper **POTS** (**Plain Old Telephone System**) telephone lines. Also, they both require short geographical cable runs (less than 20,000 feet) to the nearest central telephone office. However, as we've just stated, xDSL services offer much higher transfer speeds. In doing so, the xDSL technologies use a much greater range of frequencies on the telephone lines than the traditional voice services do. In addition, DSL technologies use the telephone lines as a constant connection so users can have access to the Internet and e-mail on a 24/7 basis. There is no need to connect with an ISP each time you want to go on-line.

Cable Modems

Another competitor in the high-speed Internet connection market is the local cable television companies. These companies act as ISPs and provide Internet access through their existing **broadband** cable television networks. To accomplish this, the cable companies offer special **cable modems** that attach the computer to the existing cable TV network connection in the home. Potential transmission rate estimates for cable modem access range up to 30 Mbps from the service provider to the customer.

broadband

cable modems

You should remember from earlier in the chapter that local area networks employ baseband signaling techniques that don't modulate the data onto a carrier signal. However, broadband techniques do employ carrier signals to place the data on. These carriers can be spread across the entire frequency spectrum of the transmission media to allow many transmissions to be conducted simultaneously on different carriers. However, cable networks are traditionally broadcast oriented, meaning that each subscriber in an area receives the same signals as all other subscribers in that area. Therefore, cable networks require two communication paths, one for downstream and one for upstream transmissions. This is accomplished by allocating additional frequency bands in the existing system.

File Transfer Protocol

A special application, called the **File Transfer Protocol (FTP)**, is used to upload and download information to, and from, the net.

File Transfer Protocol (FTP)

FTP is a client/server type of software application. The server version runs on the host computer, while the client version runs on the user's station. To access an FTP site, the user must move into an FTP application, and enter the address of the site to be accessed. After the physical connection has been made, the user must log on to the FTP site by supplying an account number and password. When the host receives a valid password, a communication path opens between the host and the user site, and an **FTP session** begins.

FTP session

Archie Servers

Around the world, thousands of FTP host sites contain millions of pages of information that can be downloaded free of charge. However, most FTP sites are used for file transfers of things like driver updates and large file transfers that are too large for email operations. Special servers, called **Archie Servers** (archival servers), contain listings to assist users in locating specific topics stored at FTP sites around the world.

TEST TIP

Memorize the different file types associated with Internet operations and know what their functions are.

Email

One of the most widely-used functions of WANs is the **electronic mail (email)** feature. This feature enables Internet users to send and receive electronic messages to each other over the Internet.

electronic mail (email)

mailing list

As with the regular postal service, email is sent to an address, from an address. However, with email, you can send the same message to several addresses at the same time using a **mailing list**.

email mailer

attached

Several email programs are available to provide this function. Email is normally written as ASCII text files. These files can be created using an ordinary word processing package. An **email mailer** program is then used to drop the text file into an electronic mailbox. Email messages also can have graphics, audio, and files from other applications **attached** to them. However, the intended user must have the same application packages that were originally used to create the files to run them or conversion or translation add-ins for the email application that may allow the user to view or open the files.

On the Internet, the message is distributed into packets, as with any other TCP/IP file. At the receiving end, the email message is reassembled and stored in the recipient's mailbox. When the designated user boots up on the system, the email program delivers the message, and notifies the user that it has arrived. The user can activate the email reader portion of the program to view the information.

Outlook Express

POP3

Simple Mail Transfer Protocol (SMTP)

The default email reader supported by the Windows 9x **Outlook Express** applet, is the **POP3** standard. Likewise, it includes a standard **Simple Mail Transfer Protocol (SMTP)** email utility for out-going email. These utilities must be accessed through the Tools option of the Outlook Express applet. From the Tools option on the Outlook Express menu bar, select the Accounts entry, highlight an account name, and click the Properties tab. Finally, click the Servers tab to access the email account configuration, as depicted in Figure 5-38.

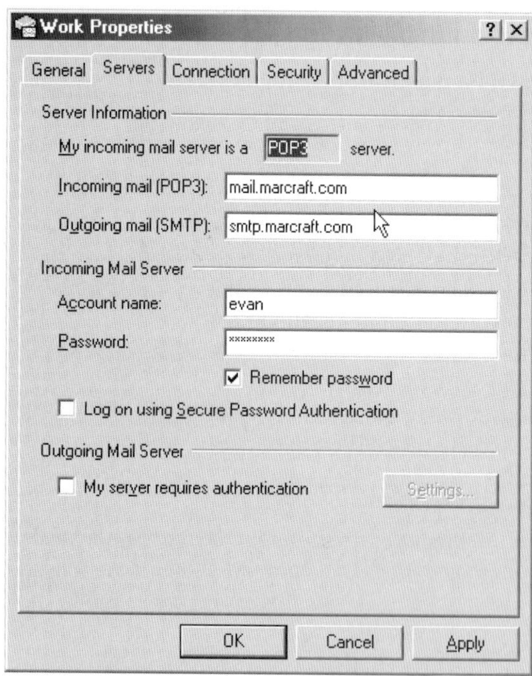

Figure 5-38: Email Account Configurations

When setting up an email account, you must supply the following configuration information:

- Account name
- Password
- POP3 Server address
- SMTP Server address

The order that this information is entered into the email client software varies from program to program. However, you will basically be prompted to enter a account name and password of your choice, followed by POP3 and SMTP Server addresses provided by the network administrator or the ISP.

The World Wide Web

The **World Wide Web (WWW)** is a menu system that ties together Internet resources from around the world. These resources are scattered across computer systems everywhere. **Web servers** inventory the web's resources and store address pointers, referred to as links, to them.

World Wide Web (WWW)

Web servers

These links are used to create **hypermedia** documents that can contain information from computer sites around the world. Inside a hypermedia document, the links permit the user to move around the document in a non-linear manner. For example, in an on-line encyclopedia, the user can move around the encyclopedia to review all of the entries concerning a single topic, without reading through every entry looking for them. The contents of the document can be mixed as well. A hypermedia document may contain text, graphics, and animation, as well as audio and video sequences.

hypermedia

Each web site has a unique address called its **Universal Resource Locator** (**URL**). URLs have a format that is similar to a DOS command line. To access a web site, the user must place the desired URL on the network. Each URL begins with the letters **http://**. These letters stand for **Hypertext Transfer Protocol**, and identify the address as a web site. The rest of the address is the name of the site being accessed (i.e., http://www.mic-inc.com is the homepage of Marcraft, located on a server at One World Telecommunications). Each web site begins with a **home page**. The home page is the menu of the available contents of the site.

Universal Resource Locator (URL)

http://

Hypertext Transfer Protocol

home page

Web Browsers

As the Internet network has grown, service providers have continued to provide more user-friendly software for exploring the World Wide Web. These software packages are called browsers, and are based on **hypertext links**.

hypertext links

Browsers use hypertext links to interconnect the various computing sites in a way that resembles a spider's web. Hence the name web.

Browsers are to the Internet what Windows is to operating environments. Graphical browsers such as **Netscape Navigator** and **Microsoft Internet Explorer** enable users to move around the Internet and make selections from graphically designed pages and menus, instead of operating from a command line. The original Internet operating environment was a command-line program called UNIX. Fortunately, the UNIX structure and many of its commands were the basis used to create MS-DOS. Therefore, users who are DOS literate do not require extensive training to begin using UNIX. With the advent of a variety of browsers, however, it is unlikely that most users will become involved with UNIX.

Netscape Navigator

Microsoft Internet Explorer

The **National Center for Supercomputing Applications** introduced the first graphical browser in 1993. This program was known as Mosaic. As its name implies, Mosaic allowed graphical pages to be created using a mixture of text, graphics, audio, and video files. It translated the **Hypertext Markup Language** (**HTML**) files that were used to create the web, and that ultimately link the various types of files together.

National Center for Supercomputing Applications

Hypertext Markup Language (HTML)

TEST TIP

Be aware of different file types used with the Internet.

Mosaic was quickly followed by the Netscape Navigator and the Microsoft Internet Explorer browsers. Figure 5-39 depicts the home page (presentation screen) for the Netscape Navigator from Netscape Communications Corporation.

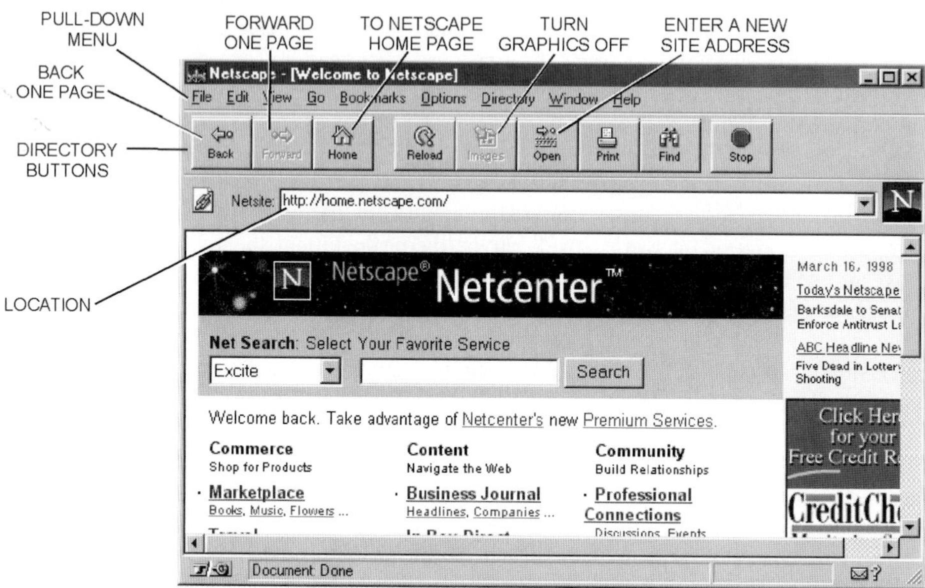

Figure 5-39: Netscape Navigator Home Page

search engines

Figure 5-40 illustrates the Microsoft Internet Explorer. Its features are similar to those of the Netscape Navigator. Both provide a graphical interface for viewing web pages. Links to **search engines** are useful for finding information on the Internet. Both have links to built-in email facilities, and to their respective creator's home pages.

TEST TIP

Memorize the Internet-related abbreviations and acronyms.

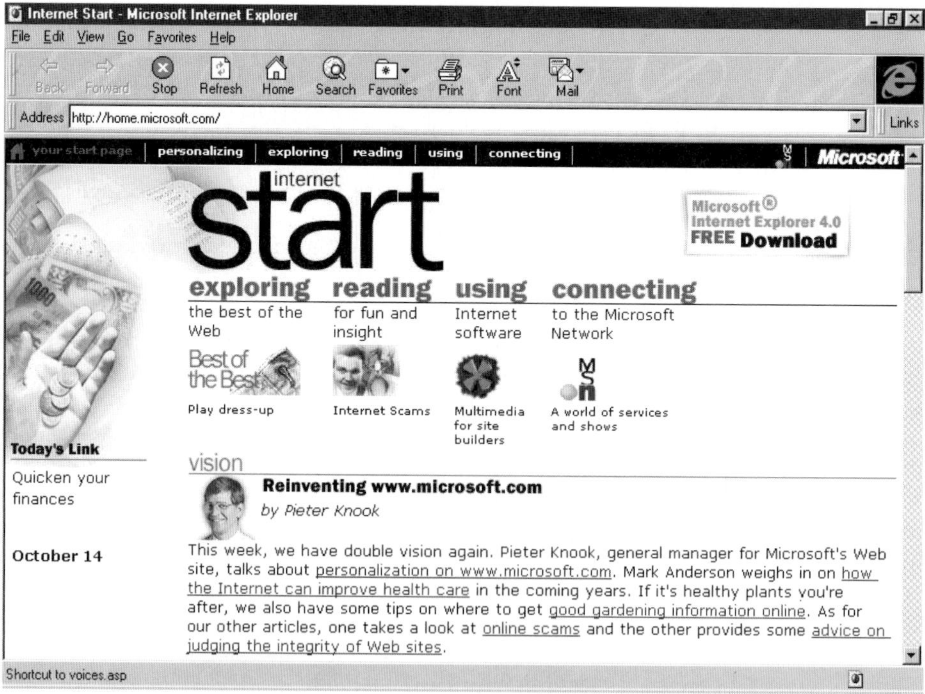

Figure 5-40: Internet Explorer Home Page

In the Netscape navigator, searches look at Netscape-recommended sites, while the Explorer first checks out Microsoft sites. Operating either browser in Windows versions before Windows 95 requires an external **Windows socket** program to be loaded before running the browser. With Windows 95, the socket was integrated directly into the operating environment.

Windows socket

Several software packages allow users to generate their own web pages. Programs such as word processors and desktop publishers have included provisions for creating and saving HTML files, called **applets**, that can be used as home pages. Internet browsers, such as Netscape and Internet Explorer, include facilities for generating home page documents. **Scripting languages**, such as **Java**, also are used to create HTML applets.

applets

Scripting languages

Java

CHAPTER SUMMARY

This chapter has investigated the two major areas of data communications associated with personal computer systems—Local Area Networks and Wide Area Networks. The chapter opens with a short section on basic networking concepts.

The first major section of the chapter dealt at LANs. In this portion of the chapter, the major local area network topologies were described. These included Ethernet, Token Ring, and fiber-optic LANs. Major topics covered in this section included basic LAN installation and operation, as well as LAN troubleshooting procedures.

The second major section of the chapter covered dial-up networking. In particular, it dealt with basic modem installation and operation. Modems are the most widely used data communication devices today. This material works very well with the I/O port information delivered in Chapter 3. As a matter of fact, both sections should be covered when troubleshooting serial communications problems. The steps for troubleshooting modem problems were presented in this section of the chapter.

Dial-up networking is the basis of wide area networking, which invariably leads to the Internet. The final sections of the chapter moved quickly into subjects surrounding the Internet. These subjects included File Transfer Protocol (ftp), e-mail, the World Wide Web, and browsers. As with all the other major sections of this text, a troubleshooting section occurred at the end of the section to cap it off.

At this point, review the objectives listed at the beginning of the chapter to be certain that you understand each point and that you can perform each task listed there. Afterward, answer the Review questions that follow to verify your knowledge of the information.

KEY POINTS REVIEW

This chapter has investigated the two major areas of data communications associated with personal computer systems: LANs and WANs. Review the following key points before moving into the Review and Exam Questions sections to make sure you are comfortable with each point. Afterward, answer the Review Questions that follow to verify your knowledge of the information.

- Local Area Networks (LANs) are systems designed to connect computers together in a relatively close proximity. These connections allow users attached to the net to share resources such as printers and modems. LAN connections also allow users to communicate with each other, and share data between their computers.

- Control of the network can be implemented in two ways: as peer-to-peer networks, in which each computer is equal to the other units on the network), or as client/server networks, in which dependent workstations (referred to as clients) operate in conjunction with a dedicated master computer (server).

- In a network, some method must be used to determine which node has use of the network's communications paths, and for how long it can have it. The network's protocol handles these functions, and it is necessary to prevent more than one user from accessing the bus at any given time.

- The Ethernet strategy allows up to 1024 users to share the LAN. However, from the description of its collision-recovery technique, it should be clear that with more users on an Ethernet LAN, more collisions are likely to occur, and the average time to complete an actual data transfer will be longer.

- Ethernet is classified as a bus topology. The original Ethernet scheme was classified as a 10 Mbps transmission protocol. The maximum length specified for Ethernet is 1.55 miles (2.5 km), with a maximum segment length between nodes of 500 meters. This type of LAN is referred to as a 10BASE-5 LAN by the IEEE organization.

- In 1985, IBM developed a token-passing LAN protocol called the Token Ring. As its name implies, Token Ring is a token-passing protocol operating on a ring topology. The token is a small frame that all nodes can recognize instantly.

- In a LAN, each computer on the net requires a network adapter card (also referred to as a NIC), and every unit is connected to the network by some type of cabling. These cables are typically either twisted-pair wires, thick or thin coaxial cable, or fiber optic cable.

- Generally, the most difficult aspect of connecting peripheral equipment to a computer is obtaining the proper interfacing, and cabling.

- In its simplest form, a modem consists of two major blocks, a modulator and a demodulator. The modulator is a transmitter that converts the parallel/digital computer data into a serial/analog format for transmission. The demodulator is the receiver that accepts the serial/analog transmission format and converts it into a parallel/digital format usable by the computer, or peripheral.

- The standard telephone system accommodates a range of frequencies between 300 and 3300 Hz, or a bandwidth of 3000 Hz. This is quite adequate to transmit voice, but severely distorts digital data. In order to use the audio characteristics of the phone lines to their best advantage, the modem encodes the digital 1s and 0s into analog signals within this bandwidth.

- All modems require software to control the communication session. This software is typically included with the purchase of the modem and must be configured to operate in the system the modem will be used in. At the fundamental instruction level, most modem software employs a set of commands known as the Hayes-Compatible Command Set.

- In order to maintain an orderly flow of information between the computer and the modem, and between the modem and another modem, a protocol, or set of rules governing the transfer of information, must be in place. All of the participants in the "conversation" must use the same protocols to communicate.

- A wide area network is very similar in concept to a widely distributed client/server LAN. In a wide area network, computers are typically separated by distances that must be serviced via modems instead of network cards.

- The most famous wide area network is the Internet. The Internet is actually a network of networks working together. The main communication path for the Internet is a series of networks, established by the U.S. government, to link supercomputers together at key research sites.

- Connecting all of the users and individual networks together are Internet Service Providers (ISPs). ISPs are companies that provide the technical gateway to the Internet. These companies own blocks of access addresses that they assign to their customers to give them an identity on the network.

- The IP addresses of all the computers attached to the Internet are tracked using a listing system called the Domain Name Service (DNS). This system evolved as a method of organizing the members of the Internet into a hierarchical management structure.

- The TCP/IP protocol divides the transmission into packets of information, suitable for retransmission across the Internet. Along the way, the information passes through different networks that are organized at different levels. Depending on the routing scheme, the packets may move through the Internet using different routes to get to the intended address. At the destination, however, the packets are reassembled into the original transmission.

- ISDN service offers high-speed access to the public telephone system. However, ISDN service requires digital modems (also referred to as Terminal Adapters (TAs)). Not only does the end user require a digital modem, the telephone company's switch gear equipment must be updated to handle digital switching. This fact has slowed implementation of ISDN services until recently.

- A special application, called the File Transfer Protocol (FTP), is used to upload and download information to, and from, the net.

- One of the most widely-used functions of wide area networks is the electronic mail (email) feature. This feature allows net users to send, and receive, electronic messages to and from each other over the net.

- The World Wide Web (WWW) is a menu system that ties together Internet resources from around the world. These resources are scattered across computer systems everywhere. Web servers inventory the web's resources and store address pointers, referred to as links, to them.

- As the Internet network has grown, service providers have continued to provide more user-friendly software for exploring the world wide web. These software packages are called browsers and are based on hypertext links.

REVIEW QUESTIONS

The following questions test your knowledge of the material presented in this chapter.

1. What is the primary difference between a client/server type of network and a peer-to-peer network?
2. Describe the three important configuration settings associated with a network adapter card.

3. What element determines the active unit in a Token Ring network?
4. What is TCP/IP, and what does it mean?
5. How does a Token Ring network keep a single unit from dominating the network after it receives the token? What is this called?

6. Which item is usually considered the key to setting the configuration of a LAN card properly?
7. What is the likely function of a vacant socket on a LAN card?
8. Describe the function of the World Wide Web.
9. What is the purpose of a router in a network?
10. What function does a browser perform?
11. Describe the function of the DNS.
12. Define the acronym URL and describe what it is used for.
13. Describe the functions of an Internet Service Provider.
14. What file format is used to send files on the Internet?
15. NIC stands for ______.

EXAM QUESTIONS

1. To which type of communications products do Hayes-compatible commands pertain?
   a. Hubs
   b. Network adapter cards
   c. Routers
   d. Modems
2. What type of topology is Ethernet?
   a. A token-passing topology
   b. A star topology
   c. A ring topology
   d. A bus topology
3. State the maximum segment length of a 10BASE-2 Ethernet network.
   a. 100 feet
   b. 185 meters
   c. 185 feet
   d. 100 meters
4. What does the designation 100BASE-T tell you about a network?
   a. Its maximum cable segment length is 100 ft and it uses BNC T connectors.
   b. Its maximum data rate is 100 Mbps and it uses UTP cabling.
   c. Its maximum data rate is 100 MHz and it uses BNC T connectors.
   d. Its maximum cable segment length is 100 ft and it uses UTP cabling.
5. In a client/ server network, ___________.
   a. at least one unit is reserved just to serve the other units
   b. at least one unit depends on the other units for its information
   c. each unit has its own information and can serve as either client or server
   d. each unit handles some information for the network
6. An RJ-45 connector is most commonly used with ________.
   a. disk drive units
   b. fiber-optic cabling
   c. coaxial cabling
   d. unshielded twisted-pair cabling
7. Which type of network lets its clients transmit data only when they have a turn?
   a. Ethernet
   b. Token Ring
   c. Peer-to-peer
   d. Fiber-optic
8. The maximum segment length of a 10BASE-5 network connection is ______.
   a. 15 meters
   b. 185 meters
   c. 500 meters
   d. 1000 meters

9. Which file type is not associated with the Internet?
   a. HTML
   b. FTP
   c. X.400
   d. POP3
10. In order to connect to the Internet, a computer must be able to use the protocol _______.
   a. MAU
   b. NIC
   c. PPP
   d. TCP/IP

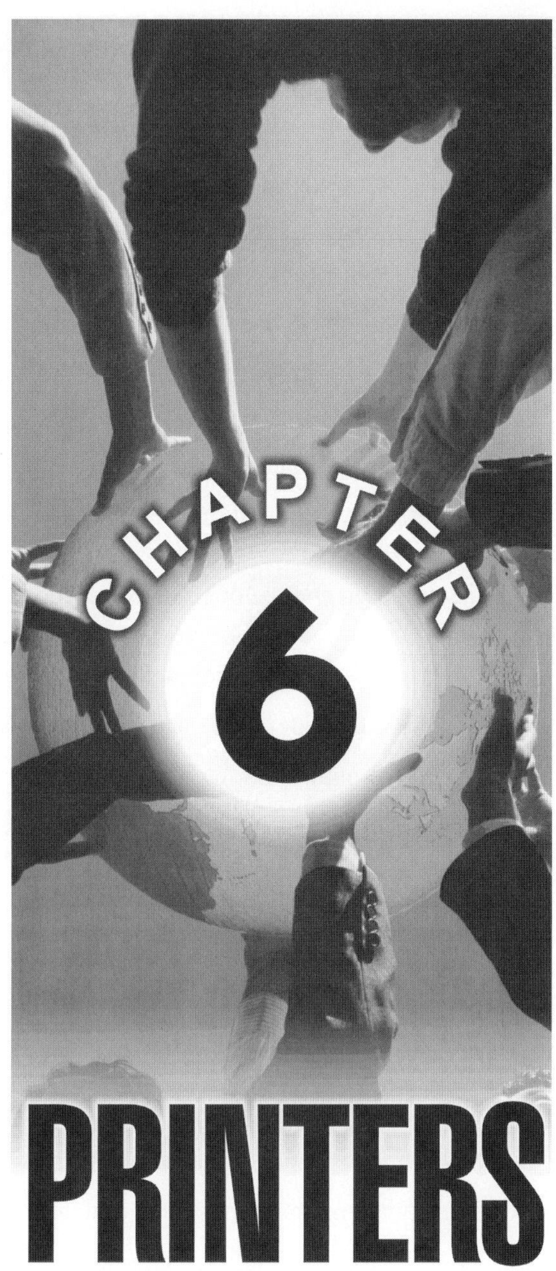

CHAPTER 6

PRINTERS

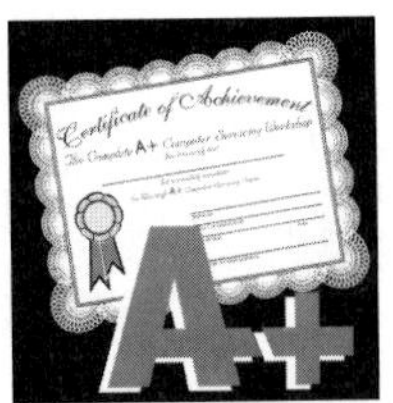
OBJECTIVES

OBJECTIVES

Upon completion of this chapter and its related lab procedures, you should be able to perform the following tasks:

1. Describe the various methods currently used to place computer print on paper.
2. Discuss characteristics of dot-matrix characters.
3. Discuss the types of paper handling common to different printer technologies.
4. Install and configure a printer.
5. List special considerations that must be observed when installing or repairing serial printers.
6. Identify a given type of cable connection between the printer and the computer.
7. Discuss data flow-control methods as they apply to serial printers.
8. Identify the major components of a dot-matrix printer.
9. Describe troubleshooting techniques associated with dot-matrix printers.
10. Relate symptoms to associated components in a dot-matrix printer.
11. Describe general alignment procedures for printhead mechanisms.
12. Describe the operation of a typical ink-jet printer.
13. Identify the major components of an ink-jet printer.
14. Describe troubleshooting techniques associated with ink-jet printers.
15. Relate symptoms to associated components in an ink-jet printer.
16. Describe the process for applying print to a page in a laser printer.
17. Identify the major components of a laser printer.
18. Describe troubleshooting techniques associated with laser printers.
19. Relate symptoms to associated components in a laser printer.

CHAPTER 6

PRINTERS

INTRODUCTION

There are many instances where a permanent copy of a computer's output may be desired. The leading hard-copy output device is the **character printer** (that is, letters, numbers, and graphic images). This definition distinguishes the character printer from the other hard copy output device referred to as **X-Y plotters**. Plotters are typically used to create complex graphics and drawings.

character printer

X-Y plotters

Character printers are the second most common output peripheral used with PCs (behind the video display). As this A+ objective indicates, computer technicians must understand how the different types of printers operate, what their typical components are, and what printer components can be serviced in the field.

As computer systems and their applications have diversified, a wide variety of printer systems have developed to fill the particular printing needs created by the marketplace. These developments have yielded faster and higher quality printing capabilities than ever before. In addition, these printers are now much less expensive than they have ever been before.

PRINTER FUNDAMENTALS

The A+ Core Hardware objective 5.1 states that the test taker should be able to "identify basic concepts, printer operations, and printer components."

The opening sections of this chapter introduce basic printer-related terminology as well as the operation and organization of the most common printer types. These printer types include:

- Laser
- Ink-jet
- Dot-matrix

Along with the diversity of printer systems have come various methods of classifying printers. Printers may be classified in a number of ways:

- Their method of placing characters on a page (**impact** or **non-impact**)
- Their speed of printing (**low speed** and **high speed**)

impact

non-impact

low speed

high speed

letter quality

near-letter quality

draft quality

fully-formed

dot-matrix

- The quality of the characters they produce (**letter quality**, **near-letter quality**, or **draft quality**)
- Or, how they form the character on the page (**fully-formed** or **dot-matrix**)

Printing Methods

The first method of differentiating printers is by how they deliver ink to the page. Impact printers produce the character by causing the print mechanism, or its ink ribbon, to impact the page. Conversely, non-impact printers deliver ink to the page without the print mechanism making contact with the page.

Impact Printers

impact printers

Impact printers place characters on the page by causing a hammer device to strike an inked ribbon. The ribbon, in turn, strikes the printing surface (paper).

The print mechanism may have the image of the character carved on its face, or it may be made up of a group of small print wires, arranged in a matrix pattern. In this case, the print mechanism is used to create the character on the page by printing a pattern of dots resembling it.

FULLY-FORMED

DOT-MATRIX

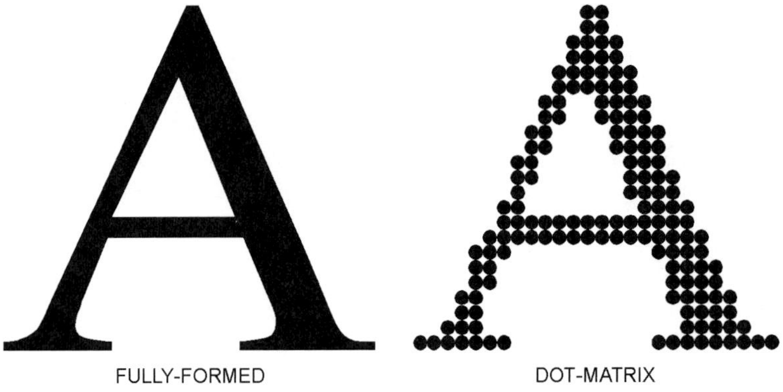

Figure 6-1: Fully Formed and Dot-matrix Characters

Generally, the quality, and therefore, the readability of a fully-formed character is better than that of a dot-matrix character. However, dot-matrix printers tend to be less expensive than their fully-formed character counterparts. In either case, the majority of the printers in use today are of the impact variety. Figure 6-1 depicts both fully-formed and dot-matrix type characters.

Non-Impact Printers

heat-sensitive

chemically-reactive paper

ink-jet printers

Several non-impact methods of printing are used in computer printers. Older, non-impact printers relied on special **heat-sensitive** or **chemically-reactive paper** to form characters on the page. Newer methods of non-impact printing use ink droplets, squirted from a jet-nozzle device (**ink-jet printers**), or a combination of laser/xerographic print technologies (laser printers) to place characters on a page. Currently, the most popular non-impact printers use ink-jet or laser technologies to deliver ink to the page.

In general, non-impact printers are less mechanical than impact counterparts. Therefore, they tend to be more dependable. Also, to their advantage, non-impact printers tend to be very quiet, and faster than comparable impact printers. The major disadvantage of non-impact printers is their inability to produce **carbon copies**.

carbon copies

Character Types

Basically, there are two methods of creating characters on a page. One method places a character on the page that is fully shaped, and fully filled-in. This type of character is called a fully-formed character. The other method involves placing dots on the page in strategic patterns to fool the eye into seeing a character. This type of character is referred to as a dot-matrix character.

A fully-formed impact print mechanism is depicted in Figure 6-2. The quality of **fully-formed characters** is excellent. However, creative choices in print fonts and sizes tend to be somewhat limited. To change the size or shape of a character, the print mechanism would need to be replaced. Conversely, the flexibility of using dots to create characters allows them to be altered as the document is being created. The quality of dot-matrix characters runs from extremely poor to extremely good, depending on the print mechanism.

fully-formed characters

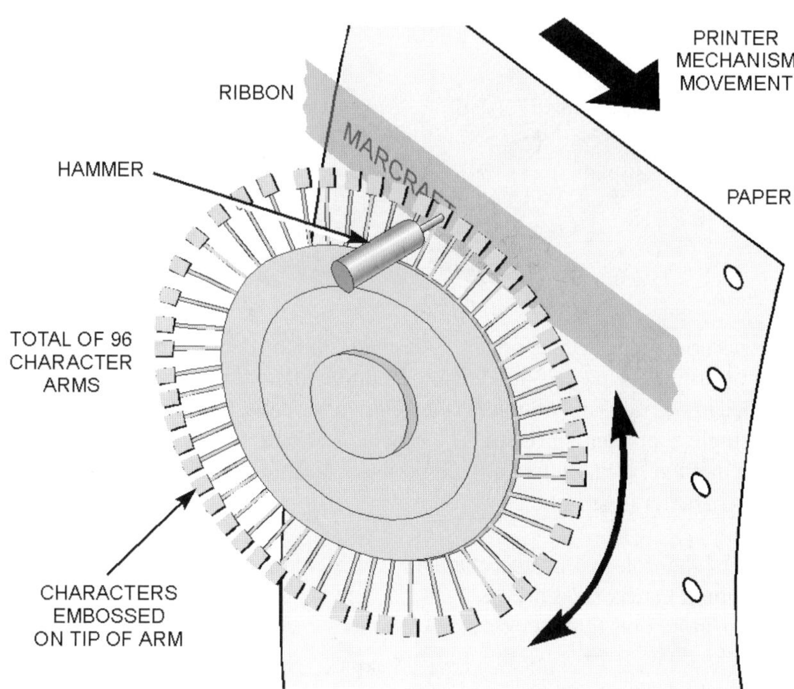

Figure 6-2: A Fully Formed Character Mechanism

Dot-matrix characters are not fully-formed characters. Instead, dot-matrix characters are produced by printing a dot pattern representing the character, as illustrated in Figure 6-3. The reader's eye fills in the gaps between the dots. Today's dot-matrix printers offer good speed and high-quality characters that approach those created by good typewriters, and nearly limitless printing flexibility.

Dot-matrix characters

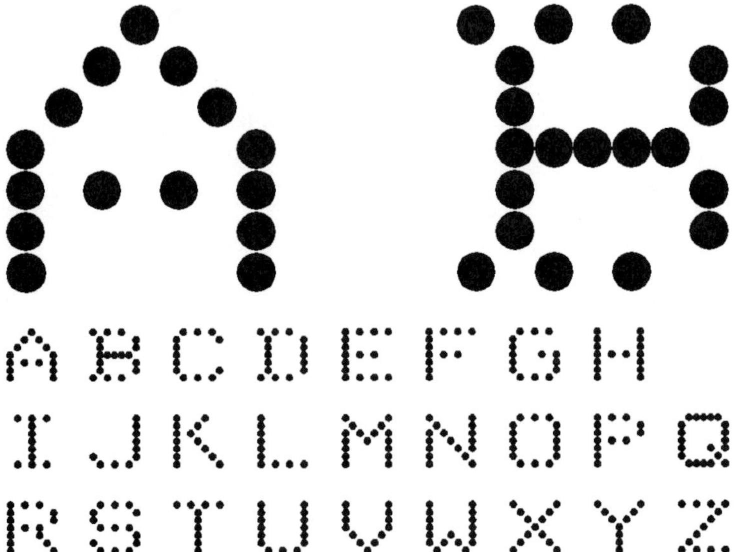

Figure 6-3: Dot-matrix Characters

TEST TIP

Remember the number of print wires in typical dot-matrix printheads.

Basically, the printhead in a dot-matrix printer is a vertical column of print wires that are controlled by electromagnets, as depicted in Figure 6-4. Dots are created on the paper by energizing selected electromagnets, which extend the desired print wires from the printhead. The print wires impact an ink ribbon, which impacts the paper. It's important to note that the entire character is not printed in a single instant of time. A typical printhead may contain 9, 18, or 24 print wires. The number of print wires used in the printhead is a major determining factor when discussing a printer's character quality.

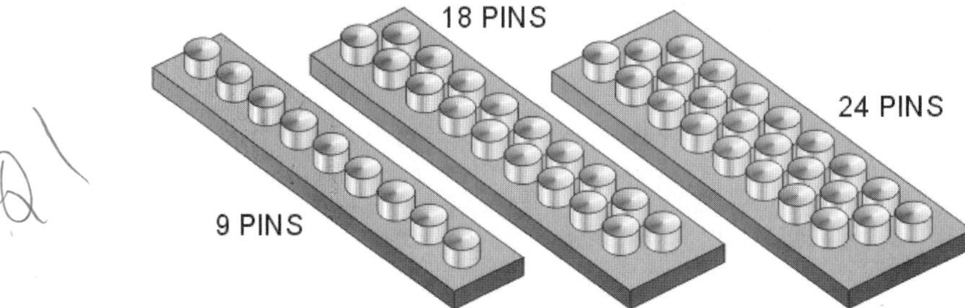

Figure 6-4: Dot-matrix Printer Pinheads

character cells

pitch

The matrix portion of this printer's name is derived from the manner in which the page is subdivided for printing. The page is divided into a number of horizontal rows, or text lines. Each row is divided into groups of columns, called **character cells**. Character cells define the area in which a single character is printed. The size of the character cell is expressed in terms of **pitch**, or the number of characters printed per inch. Within the print cell, the matrix dimensions of the character are defined.

The density of the dots within the character cell determines the quality of the character printed. Common matrix sizes are 5 x 7, 24 x 9, and 36 x 18, to mention only a few of those available. The more dots that the printhead produces within the character cell, the better the character looks. This is because the dots are closer together, making the character more fully-formed and easier to read.

Fonts

The term **font** refers to variations in the size and style of characters. With true fully-formed characters, there is typically only one font available without changing the physical printing element. With all other printing methods, however, it is possible to include a wide variety of font types and sizes.

font

There are three common methods of generating character fonts. These are as bit-mapped, or raster-scanned fonts, as vector-based fonts, and as TrueType outline fonts.

Bit-mapped fonts

normal

bold

italic

point

Vector-based fonts

Bit-mapped fonts store dot patterns for all of the possible size and style variations of the characters in the set. Since a complete set of dots must be stored for each character and size that may be needed, this type of font tends to take up large amounts of memory. For this reason, the number of character sizes offered by bit mapped fonts is typically limited. Font styles refer to the characteristics of the font, such as **normal**, **bold**, and **italic** styles. Font size refers to the physical measurement of the character. Type is measured in increments of 1/72 of an inch. Each increment is referred to as a **point**. Common text sizes are 10-point and 12-point type.

Vector-based fonts store the outlines of the character styles and sizes as sets of starting points and mathematical formulas. Each character is composed of a set of reference points and connecting lines between them. When a particular character is needed, the character generator sets the starting point for the character in the print cell and generates its outline from the formula. These types of fonts can be scaled up and down to achieve various sizes.

TEST TIP

Be aware of the benefits and drawbacks of bitmapped characters.

The vector-based approach requires much less storage space to store a character set and all of its variations than would be necessary for an equivalent bit-mapped character set. In addition, vector-based fonts can be scaled and rotated while bit-mapped fonts typically cannot. Conversely, bit-mapped characters can be printed out directly and quickly, while vector-based characters must be generated when called for.

TEST TIP

Know which font types are generated by establishing starting points and then calculating mathematical formulas.

TrueType fonts

TrueType fonts are a newer type of outline fonts that are commonly used with Microsoft Windows. These fonts are stored as a set of points and outlines that are used to generate a set of bit maps. Special algorithms adjust the bit maps so that they look best at the specified resolution. Once the bitmaps have been created, Windows stores them in a RAM cache that it creates. In this manner, the font is only generated once when it is first selected. Afterwards, the fonts are simply called out of memory, thus speeding up the process of delivering them to the printer. Each TrueType character set requires an **.FOT** and a **.TTF** file to create all of its sizes and resolutions.

.FOT

.TTF

Print Quality

Letter Quality (LQ)

Correspondence Quality (CQ)

Near-Letter Quality (NLQ)

utility

draft mode

The last criterion for comparing printers is the quality of the characters they produce. This is largely a function of how the characters are produced on the page. Printers using techniques that produce fully-formed characters are described as **Letter Quality** (**LQ**) printers. All elements of the character appear to be fully connected when printed. On the other hand, those using techniques that produce characters by forming a dot pattern are simply referred to as matrix printers. Upon close inspection of a character, one can see the dot patterns. The characters produced on some matrix printers are difficult to distinguish from those of fully-formed characters. These printers have been labeled **Correspondence Quality** (**CQ**), or **Near-Letter Quality** (**NLQ**) printers. Often, dot-matrix printers will have two printing modes, one being standard dot-matrix (sometimes called **utility** or **draft mode**), and the other a Near-Letter Quality mode.

Printer Mechanics

By the very nature of their operation, printers tend to be extremely mechanical peripherals. During the printing operation, the print mechanism must be properly positioned over each character cell in sequence.

printhead carriage

Loss of synchronization in impact printers can lead to paper jams, tearing, smudged characters, and/or print-head damage. Non-impact printers may produce totally illegible characters if synchronization is lost. The positioning action may be produced by moving the paper under a stationary printhead assembly, or by holding the paper stationary and stepping the printhead carriage across the page. In the latter operation, the **printhead carriage** rides on rods extending across the front of the page, as shown in Figure 6-5.

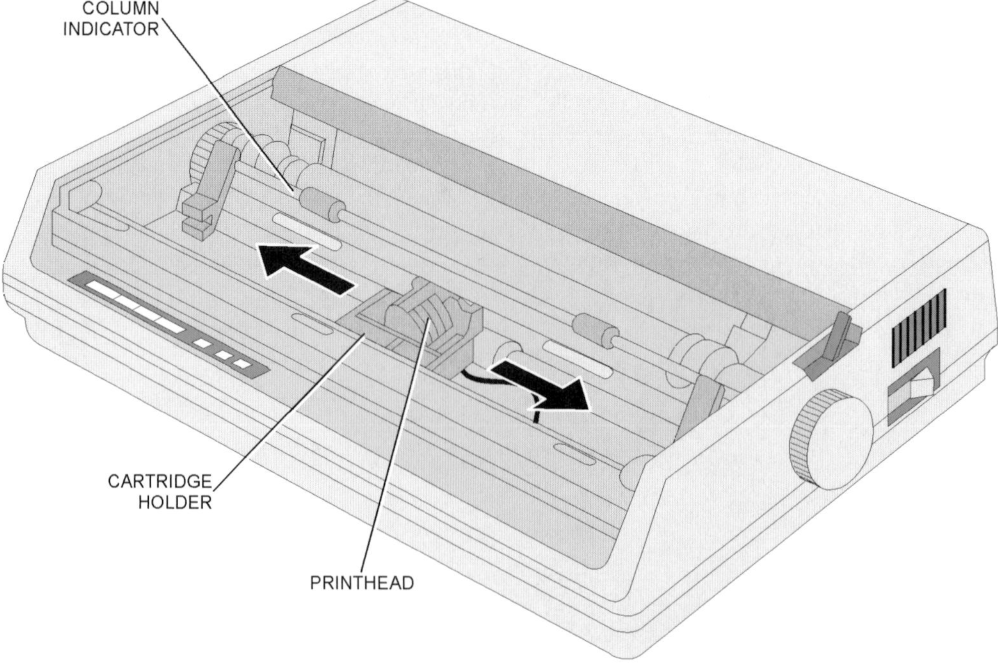

Figure 6-5: The Printhead Carriage

Depending upon the type of print mechanism used, the carriage may be stepped across the page at a rate of one character cell at a time (fully-formed characters), or in sub-character-cell steps (dot-matrix characters). Printing may occur in only one direction (unidirectional), or in both directions (bi-directional). In bi-directional printers, the second line of characters is stored in the printer's buffer memory and printed in the opposite direction, saving the time that would normally be used to return the carriage to the start of the second line.

The printhead carriage assembly is stepped across the page by a **carriage motor/timing belt** arrangement. With many printer models, the number of character columns across the page is selectable, producing variable characters spacing (expressed in **characters per inch**, or **cpi**), which must be controlled by the carriage position motor. Dot-matrix printers may also incorporate variable dot-densities (expressed as **dot-pitches**). Dot-pitch is also a function of the carriage motor control circuitry. Obviously, this discussion excludes continuous-stream, ink-jet printers, in which printing is done by electromagnetic deflection of the ink drops, and laser printers, in which the beam is reflected by a revolving mirror.

carriage motor/timing belt

characters per inch (cpi)

dot-pitches

Paper Handling

In addition to positioning the print mechanism for printing, all printer types must feed paper through the print area. The type of **paper handling mechanism** in a printer is somewhat dependent on the type of form intended to be used with the printer, and its speed.

paper handling mechanism

Paper forms fall into two general categories, **continuous forms**, which come in folded stacks and have holes along their edges, and **single-sheet forms**, such as common typing paper.

continuous forms

single-sheet forms

There are two common methods of moving paper through the printer:

- **Friction-feed**—uses friction to hold the paper against the printer's **platen**. The paper advances through the printer as the platen turns.
- **Pin-feed**—pulls the paper through the printer by a set of pins that fit into the holes along the edge of the form, as shown in Figure 6-6. The pins may be an integral part of the platen, or mounted on a separate, motor-driven **tractor**.

Friction-feed

platen

Pin-feed

tractor

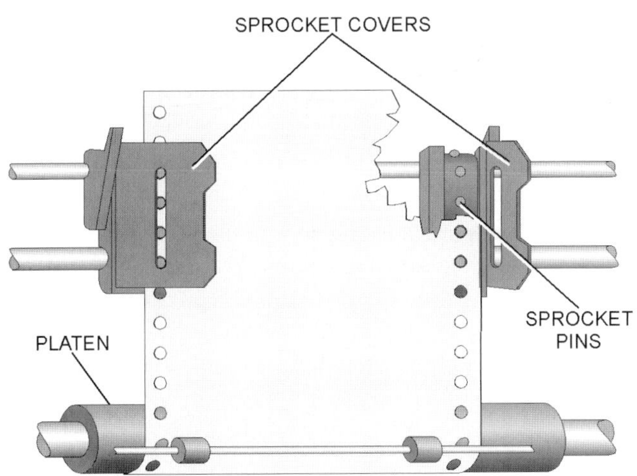

Figure 6-6: A Pin-Feed Tractor Mechanism

Tractor feeds

Friction-feed is normally associated with single sheet printers. The sheet feeding system can be manual or automatic. Platen pin-feed and pin tractors are usually employed with continuous and multi-layer forms. These mechanisms can control paper slippage and misalignment created by the extra weight imposed by continuous forms. Platen pin-feed units can only handle one width of paper while tractors can be adjusted to handle various paper widths. **Tractor feeds** are used with very heavy forms, such as multiple-part continuous forms, and are most commonly found on dot-matrix printers. Most ink-jet and laser printers use single sheet feeder systems.

> **TEST TIP**
>
> Know the major purpose of a tractor-feed mechanism and where it is most commonly used.

The gear trains involved in the paper handling function can be treated as an FRU item in some printers. While it is possible to replace the gears, or gear packs, in dot-matrix and ink-jet printers (if they can be obtained from the manufacturer as separate items), it is not usually economical to do so. Laser printers, on the other hand, are normally expensive enough to warrant replacing the gear trains and clutch assemblies that handle the paper movement through the printer.

Printer Controls

Although printers vary considerably from type to type, and model to model, there are some elements that are common to all printers. These elements are depicted in Figure 6-7.

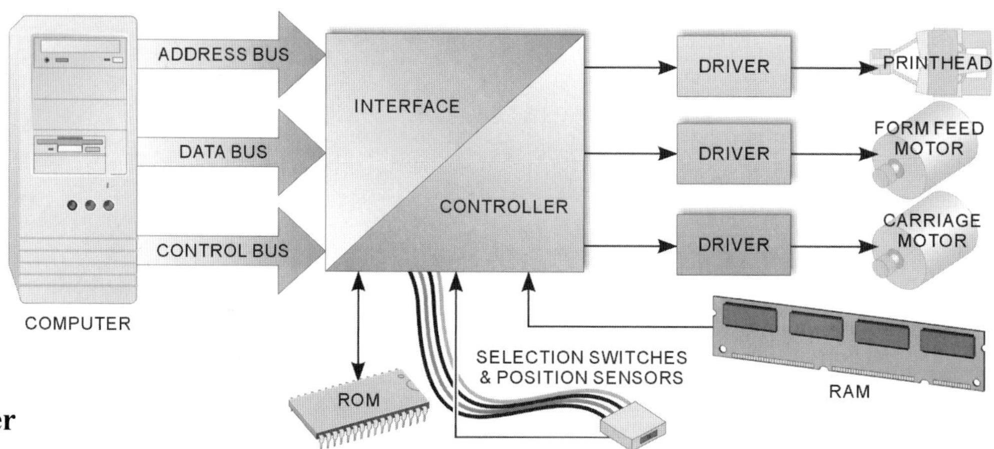

Figure 6-7: Common Printer Components

interface/controller

Like most other peripherals, the heart of a character printer is its **interface/controller** circuitry. The interface circuitry accepts data and instructions from the computer's bus systems, and provides the necessary interfacing (serial or parallel) between the computer and the printer's control circuitry.

This includes decoding the computer's instructions to the printer, converting signal logic levels between the two, and passing data to the printer's controller.

Parallel-port connections are most efficient when the printer is located in close proximity to the computer. If the printer must be located remotely, the serial interface becomes more appropriate. Many manufacturers offer both connections as standard equipment. Others offer the serial connection as an option. More is said about these two interfaces later in this section. A third less common method of connecting printers to computers uses the SCSI interface as the connection port. As with other SCSI devices, the printer must be set up as a unique SCSI device and observe proper connection and termination procedures.

The controller section receives the data and control signals from the interface section, and produces all of the signals necessary to select, or generate, the proper character to be printed. It also advances the print mechanism to the next print position, and feeds the paper at the proper times. In addition, the controller generates status and control signals that tell the computer what is happening in the printer.

Due to the complexity of most character printers, a dedicated **microcontroller** is commonly used to oversee the operation of the printer. The presence of the on-board microprocessor provides greater flexibility, and additional options, for the printer.

microcontroller

Along with the dedicated processor, the printer normally contains on-board memory in the form of RAM, ROM, or both. A speed mismatch exists between the computer and the printer, since the computer is normally capable of generating characters at a much higher rate than the printer can print them. In order to minimize this speed differential, printers typically carry **on-board RAM** memory buffers to hold characters coming from the computer. In this way, the transfer of data between the computer and the printer occurs at a rate that is compatible with the computer's operating speed. The printer obtains its character information from the on-board buffer.

on-board RAM

on-board ROM

character generators

printer initialization programs

downloadable type fonts

variable print modes

Printer FRU modules

In addition to character print information, the host computer can also store printer instructions in the buffer for use by the dedicated processor. The printer may also contain **on-board ROM** in the form of **character generators**, or **printer initialization programs** for start-up. Some printers contain EPROM, instead of ROM, to provide a greater variety of options for the printer, such as **downloadable type fonts** and **variable print modes**.

Printer FRU modules—In some printers, the microcontroller, RAM chips or modules, and ROM/EPROM devices may be treated as FRU components.

Many laser printers come with a preset amount of RAM on board, but allow the memory to be upgraded if needed. Many high-speed laser printers require additional RAM to be installed to handle printing of complex documents, such as desktop-published documents containing large **Encapsulated Post Script (EPS)** graphics files. Similarly, ROM and EPROM devices that contain BIOS or character sets are often socketed so that they can be replaced or upgraded easily.

Encapsulated Post Script (EPS)

As with the gears and gear trains discussed earlier in the chapter, the replaceability of these units depends on the ability to source them from a supplier. In most cases, the question is not "Can the device be exchanged?", but whether it makes economical sense to do so. For a given printer type and model, the manufacturer's service center can provide information about the availability of replacement parts.

Basically, the controller must produce signals to drive the print mechanism, the paper feed motor, the carriage motor, and possibly optional devices, such as single-sheet feeders and add-on tractors. Most of these functions are actually performed by precision stepper motors.

There are usually hardware driver circuits between the motors and the controller to provide current levels high enough to activate the motors.

home-position sensor

end-of-paper sensor

carriage position sensor

On/Off Line

Form Feed (FF)

Line Feed (LF)

operator control panel

The controller also gathers information from the printer through a variety of sensing devices. These include position sensing switches and user-operated, front-panel-mounted, mode-control switches. Some of the more common sensing switches include the **home-position sensor**, **end-of-paper sensor**, and the **carriage position sensor**. The controller also responds to manual input command switches, such as **On/Off Line**, **Form Feed (FF)**, and **Line Feed (LF)**.

The sensors and switches can be treated as FRUs in many printers. This is particularly true with more expensive laser printers. In most printers, the entire **operator control panel** can be exchanged for another unit. This effectively changes all of the user-operated input switches at one time.

Dot-Matrix Printers

The stalwarts of microcomputer printing have been the dot-matrix impact printers.

power supply board

main control board

printhead assembly

ribbon cartridge

paper feed motor

printhead positioning motor

The components of a typical dot-matrix printer are depicted in Figure 6-8. They consist of a **power supply board**, a **main control board**, a **printhead assembly**, a **ribbon cartridge**, a **paper feed motor** (along with its mechanical drive gears), and a **printhead positioning motor** and mechanisms.

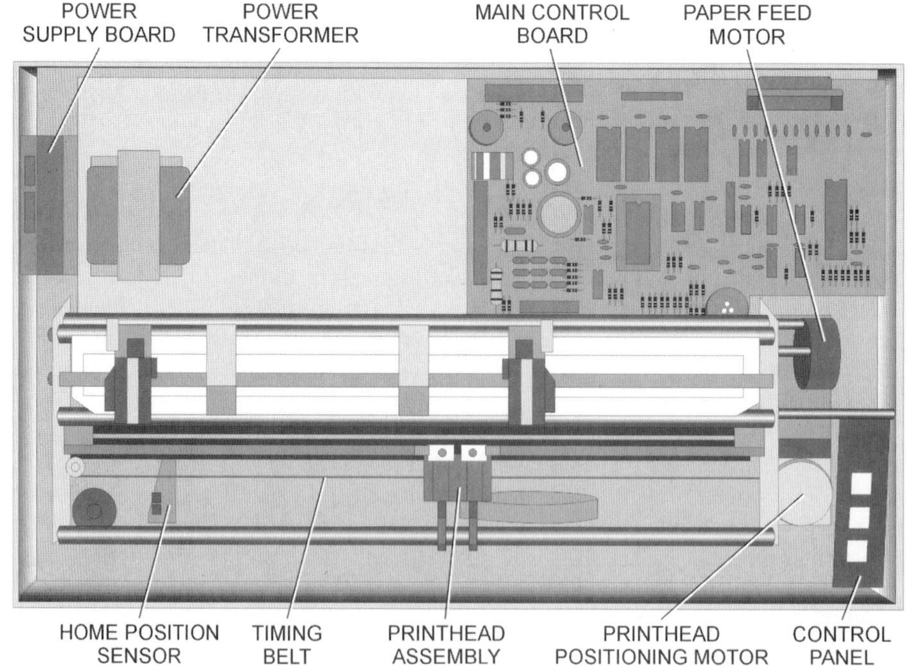

Figure 6-8: Parts of a Dot-matrix Printer

The Power Supply

The power supply board is called on to provide various voltages to power the electronics on the control board. It also drives both the printhead positioning and paper feed motors, and energizes the wires of the printhead so that they will strike the ribbon as directed by the control board.

The Main Control Board

The control board is typically divided into four functional sections, as described in Figure 6-9. These functional blocks include:

- the interface circuitry
- the character generation circuitry
- the printer controller circuitry
- its motor control circuitry

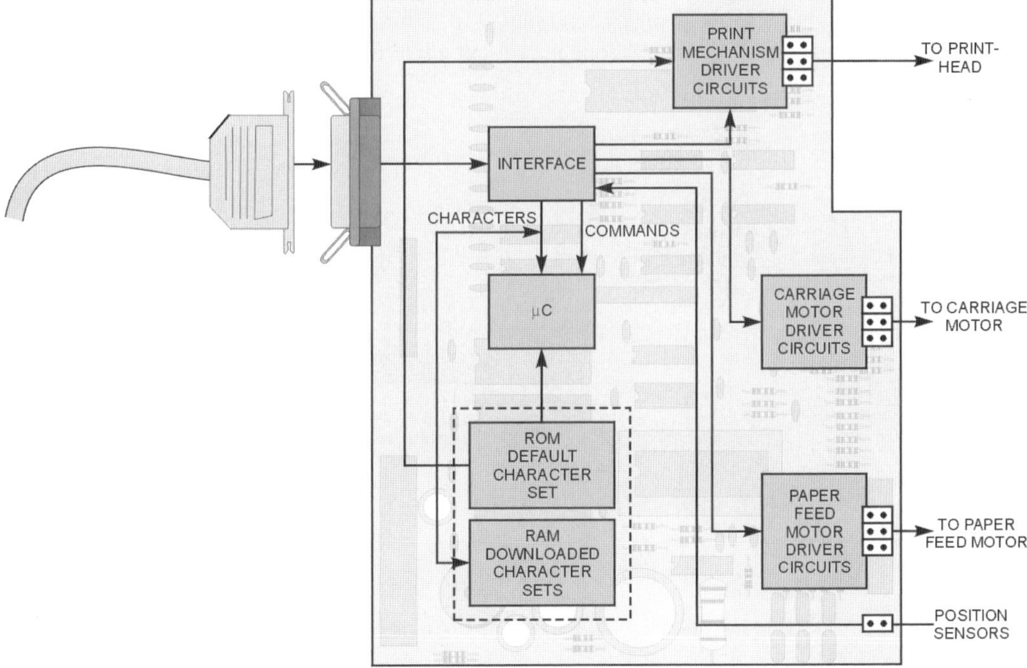

Figure 6-9: Logical Parts of the Control Board

The control board contains the logic circuitry required to convert the signals, received from the computer's adapter card, into character patterns, as well as to generate the proper control signals to position the printhead properly on the page, fire the correct combination of printhead wires to create the character, and to advance the paper properly. The on-board microcontroller, character generators, RAM, and ROM are found on the control board.

The status of the printer's operation is monitored by the control board through a number of sensors. These sensors typically include:

- Paper Out
- Printhead Position
- Home Position (for the printhead carriage)

Input from the printer's operator panel is also routed to the control board. Operator panel information includes:

- On-line
- Form Feed
- Line Feed
- Power/Paper Out

The control panel may contain a number of other buttons, and indicator lights, whose functions are specific to that particular printer. Always consult the printer's user's manual for information about the control panel buttons and indicators.

Centronics parallel port

The printer's interface may contain circuitry to handle serial data, parallel data, or a combination of the two interface types. At the printer end of a **Centronics parallel port**, a 36-pin connector, like the one depicted in Figure 6-10, is used. Of course, the computer end of the cable should have a DB-25M connector to plug into the system's DB-25F LPT port.

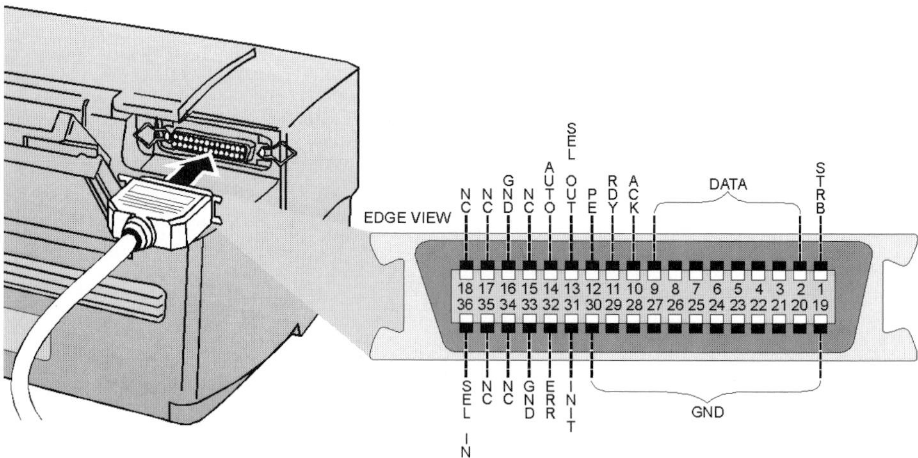

Figure 6-10: A Parallel Connection at the Printer

TEST TIP

Remember the types of connectors used at both the computer and the printer ends of a parallel printer cable.

Dot-matrix printers process bit patterns in much the same way that CRT controllers do. The dot patterns are accessed from a character generator ROM. In addition to the standard ASCII character set, many printers feature preprogrammed sets of block-graphics characters that can be used to create non-text images on a page. Most manufacturers use EPROM (erasable-programmable ROM) character generators instead of the older ROM type. This allows their units to accept downloadable fonts from software.

Roman Gothic

Where used with a high-quality printhead, a variety of type faces, such as **Roman Gothic**, Italic, and foreign language characters can be loaded into the programmable character generator from software. In addition, it is possible for the user to create his own character sets, type faces, and graphic symbols. Some manufacturers even offer standard bar-code graphics software sets for their machines.

Printhead Mechanisms

printhead

The **printhead** is a collection of print wires set in an electromagnetic head unit. The printhead assembly is made up of a permanent magnet, a group of electromagnets, and a housing. In the printhead, the permanent magnet keeps the wires pulled in until electromagnets are energized, causing them to move forward.

printhead carriage assembly

timing belt

The printhead is mounted in the **printhead carriage assembly**. The carriage assembly rides on a bar that passes along the front of the platen. The printhead carriage assembly is attached to the printhead positioning motor by a **timing belt**.

printhead positioning motor

The **printhead positioning motor** is responsible for moving the printhead mechanism across the page, and stopping it in just the right places to print. The printhead rides back and forth across the printer on a pair of carriage rods. A timing belt runs between the printhead assembly and the printhead positioning motor, and converts the rotation of the motor into the linear movement of the printhead assembly. The printhead must stop each time the print wires strike the paper. If this timing is off, the characters will be smeared on the page, and the paper may be damaged. The motor steps a predetermined number of steps to create a character within a character cell. Figure 6-11 illustrates a dot-matrix printhead delivering print to a page.

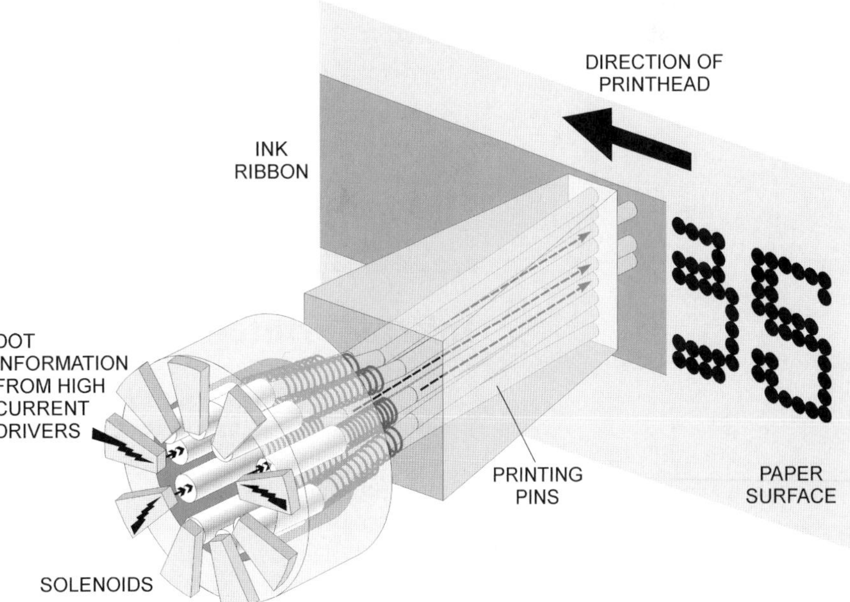

Figure 6-11: Dot-matrix Printhead

Paper Handling

paper feed motor

gear train

platen assembly

friction-feed paper handling

tractor assembly

The **paper feed motor**, and **gear train**, move the paper through the printer. This can be accomplished by driving the **platen assembly**. The platen can be used in two different ways to move the paper through the printer. After the paper has been wrapped halfway around the platen, a set of rollers are used to pin the paper to the platen as it turns. This is **friction-feed paper handling**. As described earlier, the platen may have small pins that can drag the paper through the printer as the platen turns. In either case, the paper feed motor drives the platen to move the paper.

The feed motor's gear train can also be used to drive the extended gear train of a **tractor assembly** when it is installed. The gears of the feed motor mesh with those of the tractor, causing it to pull, or push, the paper through the printer. To use a tractor, the friction-feed feature of the platen must be released. Otherwise, the tractor and the platen may not turn at the same rate, and the paper will rip, or jam. The installation of a tractor assembly is illustrated in Figure 6-12.

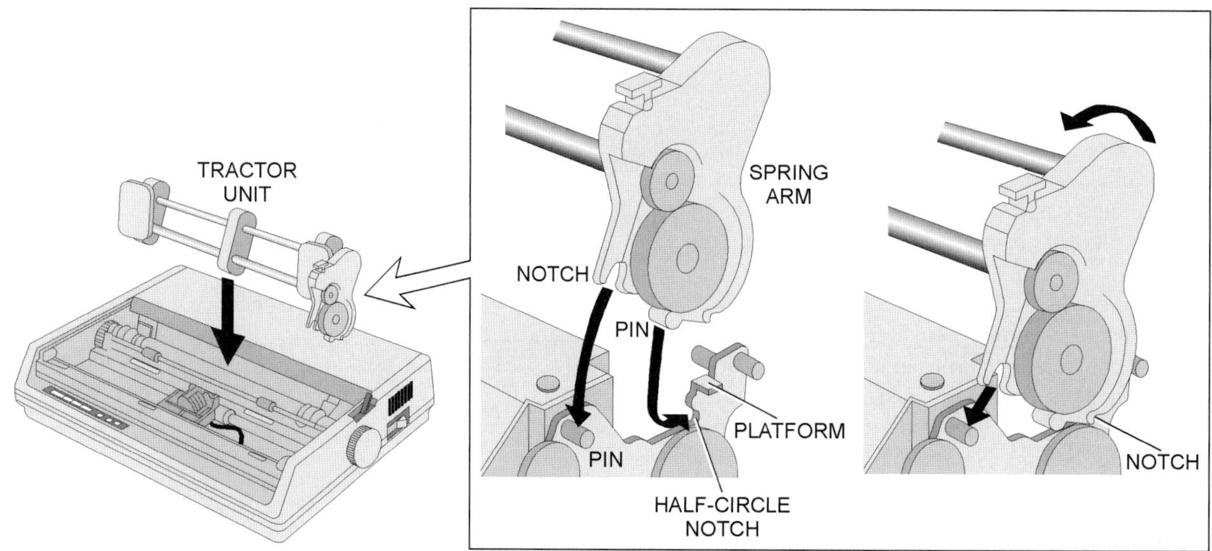

Figure 6-12: Installing a Tractor Assembly

Ink-Jet Printers

Ink-jet printers produce characters by squirting a precisely controlled stream of ink drops onto the paper, as described in Figure 6-13. The drops must be controlled very precisely in terms of their aerodynamics, size, and shape, or the drop placement on the page becomes inexact, and the print quality falters.

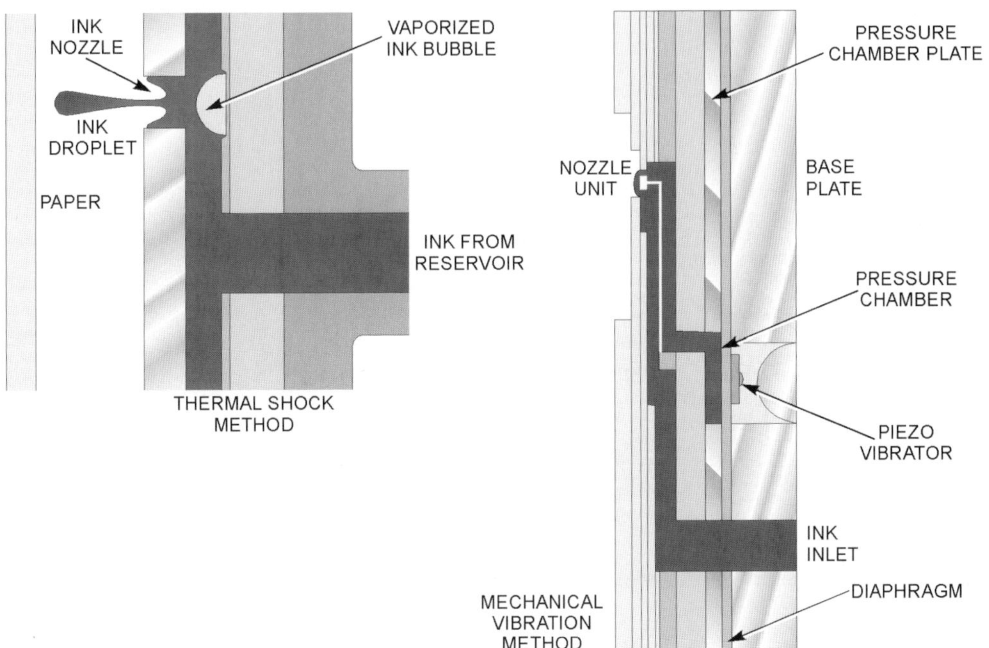

Figure 6-13: Ink-jet Printers

The drops are formed by one of two methods:

thermal shock

mechanical vibration

- **thermal shock**—heats the ink in a capillary tube, just behind the nozzle. This increases the pressure of the ink in the tube and causes it to explode through the opening.
- **mechanical vibration**—uses vibrations from a piezoelectric crystal to force ink through a nozzle.

TEST TIP

Be able to identify the printer type that produces print by squirting ink at the page. Also, remember the techniques used to form the ink drops.

The ink jet nozzle is designed to provide the proper shape and trajectory for the ink drops so that they can be directed precisely toward the page. The nozzles are also designed so that the surface tension of the ink keeps it from running out of the nozzle uncontrollably.

interrupted-stream

drop-on-demand

continuous-stream

There are two methods used by ink-jet printers to deliver the drops to the page: the **interrupted-stream (drop-on-demand)** method and the **continuous-stream** method. The drop-on-demand system forms characters on the page in much the same manner as a dot-matrix printer does. As the printhead mechanism moves across the character cells of the page, the controller causes a drop to be sprayed, only where necessary, to form the dot pattern of a character. Drop-on-demand printing is illustrated in Figure 6-14.

Continuous-stream systems, like the one described in Figure 6-15, produce characters that more closely resemble fully-formed characters. In these systems, the printhead does not travel across the page. Instead, the drops are given a negative charge in an ion chamber and are passed through a set of deflection plates, similar to the electron beam in a CRT tube. The plates deflect the drops to their proper placement on the page, while unused drops are deflected off the page, into an ink recirculation system.

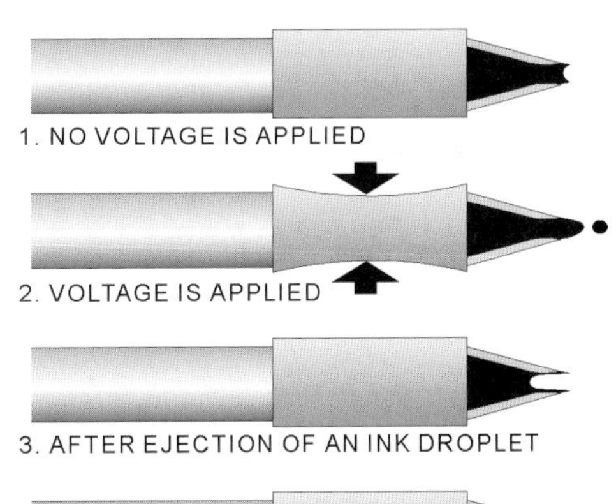

Figure 6-14: Drop-on-Demand Printing

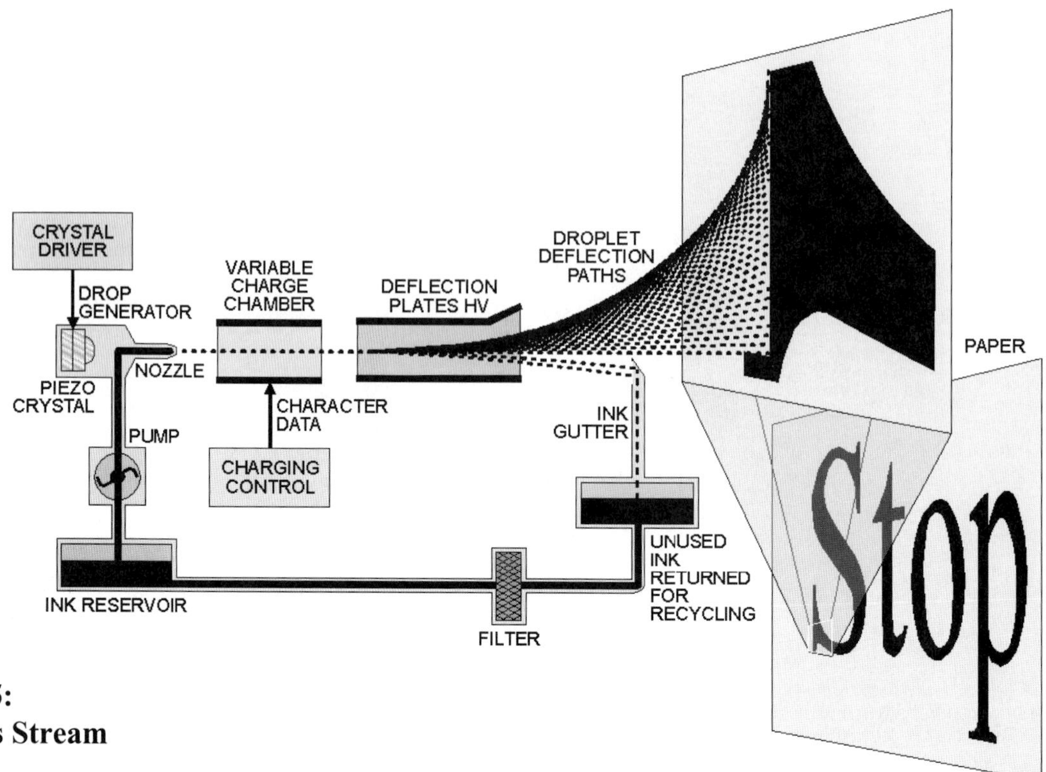

Figure 6-15: Continuous Stream Printing

While capable of delivering very high quality characters at high speeds, continuous-stream systems tend to be expensive, and therefore are not normally found in printers for the consumer market. Instead, they are reserved for high-volume commercial printing applications. The ink-jet printers in the general consumer market use drop-on-demand techniques to deliver ink to the page.

Some ink-jet printers incorporate multiple jets to permit color printing. Four basic colors may be mixed to create a palette of colors by firing the ink jets in different combinations.

Ink-Jet Printer Components

Aside from the printing mechanism, the components of a typical ink-jet printer are very similar to those of a dot-matrix printer. Its primary components are:

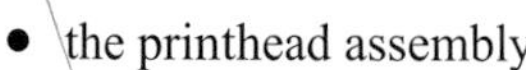

- the printhead assembly
- the power board
- the control board
- the printhead positioning motor and timing belt
- the paper feed motor and gear train
- the printer's sensors

These components are described in Figure 6-16.

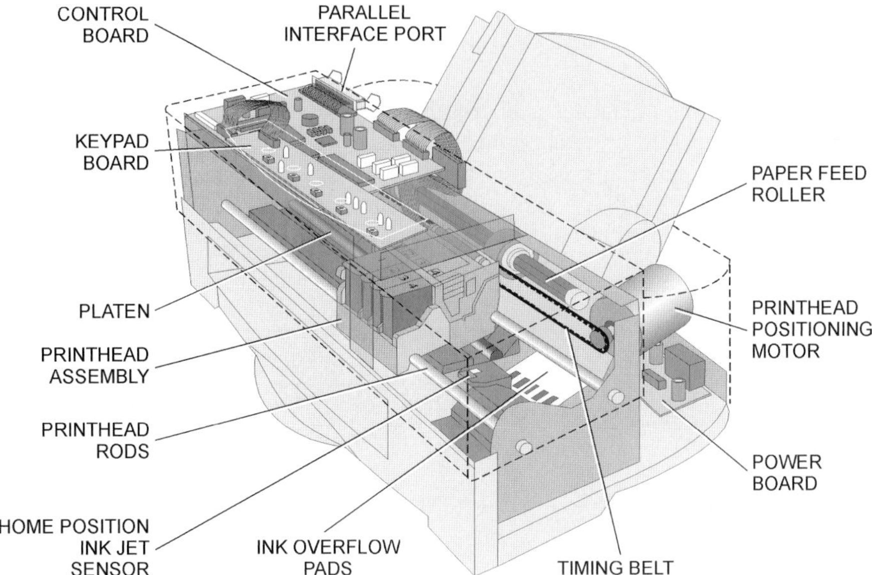

Figure 6-16: Ink-jet Printer Components

The Printhead Assembly

The ink cartridge snaps into the printhead assembly that rides in front of the platen on a rail or rod. The printhead assembly is positioned by a timing belt that runs between it and the positioning motor. A flexible cable carries ink-jet firing information between the control board and the printhead. This cable folds out of the way as the printhead assembly moves across the printer.

Paper Handling

The paper feed motor turns a gear train that ultimately drives the platen, as depicted in Figure 6-17. The paper is friction-fed through the printer, between the platen and the pressure rollers. Almost all ink-jet printers used with microcomputer systems are single-sheet, friction-feed systems. The control board, power supply board, and sensors perform the same functions in an ink-jet printer that they did in the dot-matrix printer.

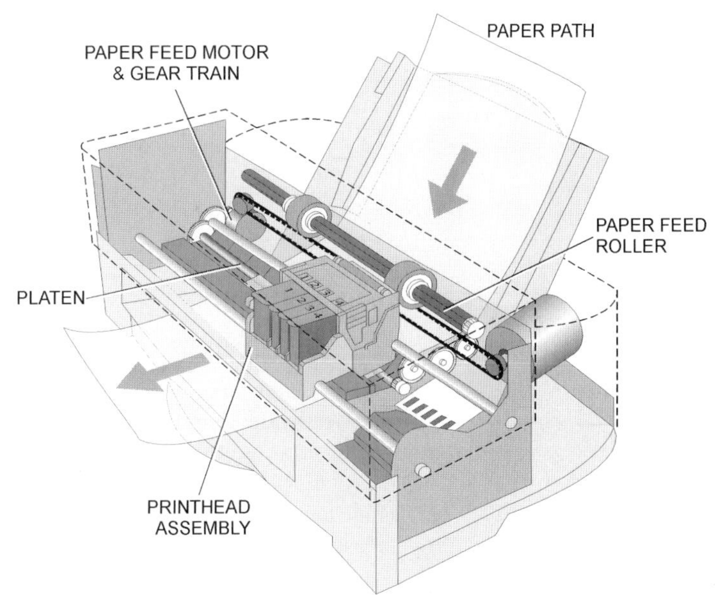

Figure 6-17: Ink-jet Paper Handling

laser printer

Laser Printers

The **laser printer** modulates a highly focused laser beam to produce CRT-like raster-scan images on a rotating drum, as depicted in Figure 6-18.

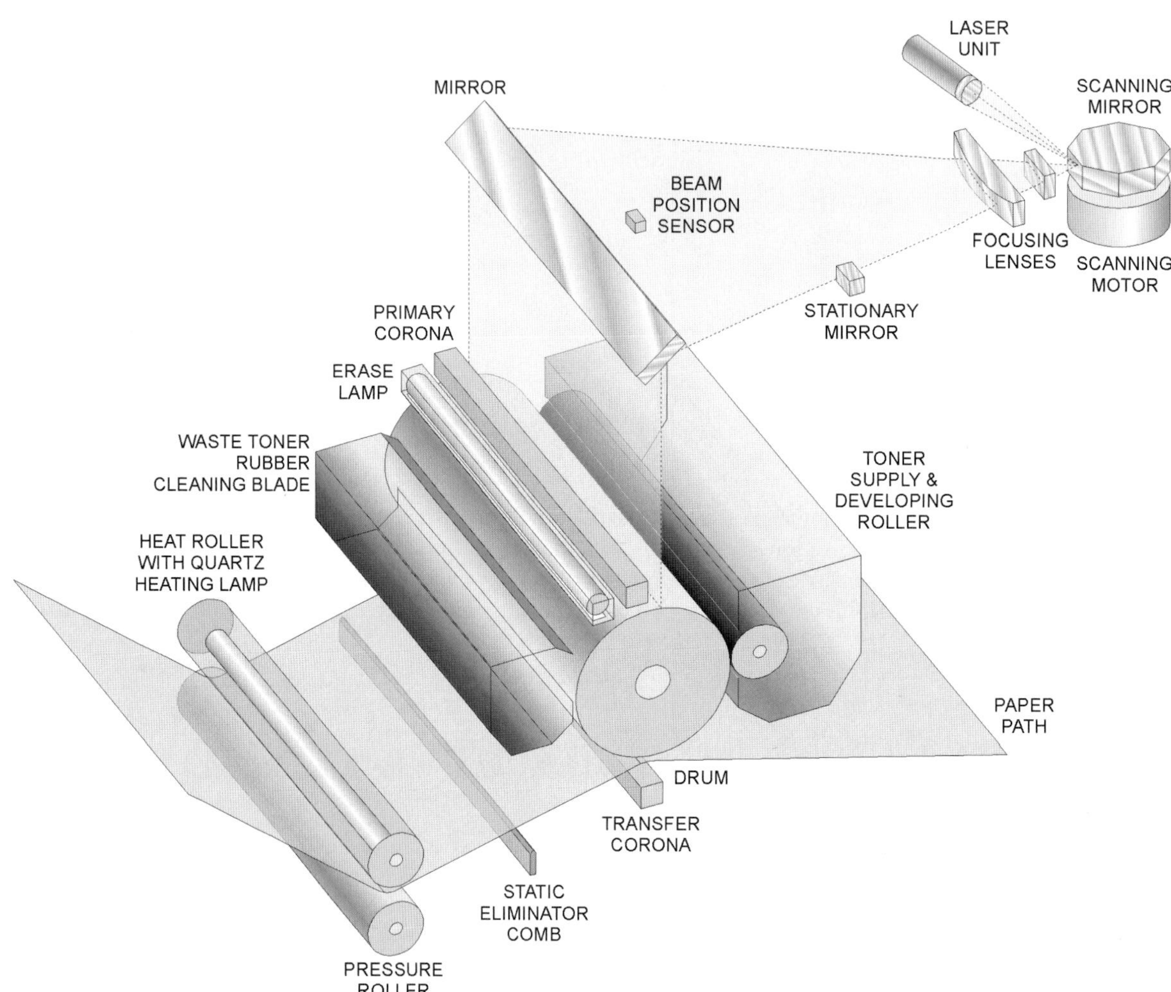

Figure 6-18: A Typical Laser Printer

drum

negative electrical charge

positive electrical charge

toner material

The **drum** is coated with a photosensitive plastic, which is given a **negative electrical charge** over its surface. The modulated laser beam creates spots on the rotating drum. The spots written by the laser take on a **positive electrical charge**. A negatively-charged **toner material** is attracted to the positively-charged, written areas of the drum. The paper is fed past the rotating drum and the toner is transferred to the paper. A pair of compression rollers and a high temperature lamp fuse the toner to the paper. Thus, the image, written on the drum by the laser, is transferred to the paper.

The laser beam scans the drum so rapidly that it is not practical to do the scanning mechanically. Instead, the beam is bounced off a rotating, **polygonal** (many-sided) **mirror**. The faces of the mirror cause the reflected beam to scan across the face of the drum as the mirror revolves. Using the highest dot densities available, these printers produce characters that rival typeset text. Larger laser printers produce characters at a rate of 20,000 lines per minute. Laser printers intended for the personal computer market generate 6 to 45 pages per minute.

polygonal mirror

Laser Printer Components

From manufacturer to manufacturer, and model to model, the exact arrangement and combinations of components may vary in laser printers. However, the order of operations is always the same. The six stages of operation in a laser printer include:

- Cleaning
- Conditioning
- Writing
- Developing
- Transferring
- Fusing

TEST TIP

Memorize the stages of a typical laser printer.

To accomplish these objectives, all laser printers possess the following logical blocks:

- Power supply
- Control board
- Laser writing unit
- Drum unit
- Fusing assembly
- Paper feed motor and gear train
- System's sensors
- Control panel board

The blocks of the typical laser printer are illustrated in Figure 6-19.

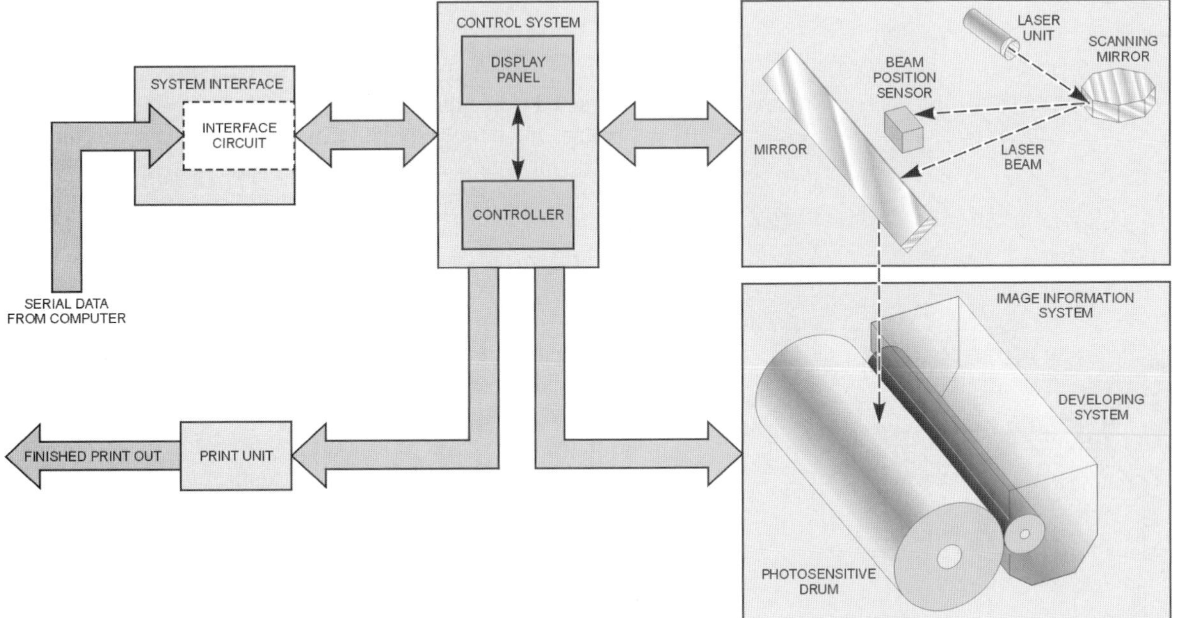

Figure 6-19: Block Diagram of a Laser Printer

ac power

high-voltage dc supply

static charges

dc operating voltages

The laser printer power supply unit is the most complex found in any type of printer. It must deliver **ac power** to the fuser unit. This unit requires power for its fusing heaters and image erase lamps. The power supply also delivers a **high-voltage dc supply** (+1000 Vdc) to the toner transfer mechanisms in the drum area. The high voltages are used to create the **static charges** required to move toner from one component to another (i.e., from the drum to the paper). Finally, the power supply unit must deliver **dc operating voltages** to the scanning and paper handling motors, as well as the digital electronic circuitry on the control board.

The control board contains all of the circuitry required to operate the printer and control its many parts. It receives control signals from the computer, and formats the data to be printed. The control board also monitors the conditions within the printer, and responds to input from the its various sensors.

registration

When data is received from the host computer, the control board generates all of the enabling signals to place the information on the page as directed. The character information is converted into a serial bit stream, which can be applied to the scanning laser. The photosensitive drum rotates as the laser beam is scanned across it. The laser creates a copy of the image on the photosensitive drum in the form of a relatively positive-charged drawing. This operation is referred to as **registration**.

Laser Printing Operations

primary corona wire

conditions

Before the laser writes on the drum, a set of erase lamps shine on the drum to remove any residual traces of the previous image. This leaves the complete drum with a neutral electrical charge. A high voltage, applied to the **primary corona wire**, creates a highly charged negative field that **conditions** the drum to be written on by applying a uniform negative charge (–1000 V) to it.

toner powder

developer roller

restricting blade

As the drum is written on by the laser, it turns through the **toner powder**, which is attracted to the more positively charged image on the drum.

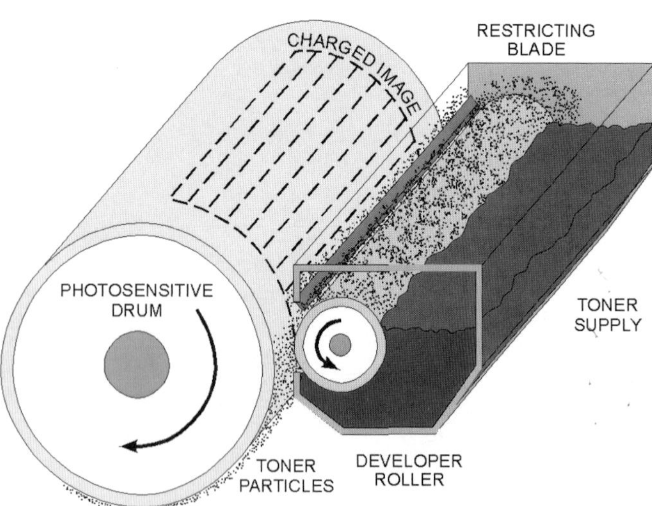

Figure 6-20: The Developer Roller

Toner is a very fine powder, bonded to iron particles that are attracted to the charges written on the drum. The **developer roller**, in the toner cartridge, turns as the drum turns, and expels a measured amount of toner past a **restricting blade,** as illustrated in Figure 6-20. A regulating ac voltage assists the toner in leaving the cartridge, but also pulls back some excess toner from the drum. Excess toner is recycled within the toner cartridge so that it can be used again.

Great care should be taken when installing a new drum unit. Exposing the drum to light for more than a few minutes may damage it. The drum should never be touched, as this too can ruin its surface. Keep the unit away from dust and dirt, as well as away from humidity and high-temperature areas.

TEST TIP

Know that you should never expose the drum of a laser printer to sunlight, or any other strong light source.

The **transfer corona wire (transfer roller)** is responsible for transferring the toner from the drum to the paper. The toner is transferred to the paper because of the highly positive charge the transfer corona wire applies to the paper. The positive charge attracts the more negative toner particles away from the drum, and onto the page. A special, static-eliminator comb acts to prevent the positively-charged paper from sticking to the negatively-charged drum.

transfer corona wire

transfer roller

TEST TIP

Know the functions of the two corona wires in a laser printer.

After the image has been transferred to the paper, a pair of **compression roller** in the **fusing unit** act to press the toner particles into the paper, while they melt them to it. The top compression roller, known as the **fusing roller**, is heated by a quartz lamp. This roller melts the toner to the paper as it exits the unit, while the lower roller applies pressure to the paper. A cleaning pad removes excess particles, and applies a silicon lubricant to the roller to prevent toner from sticking to the Teflon-coated fusing roller. A demonstration of the complete transfer process is given in Figure 6-21.

fusing unit

compression rollers

fusing roller

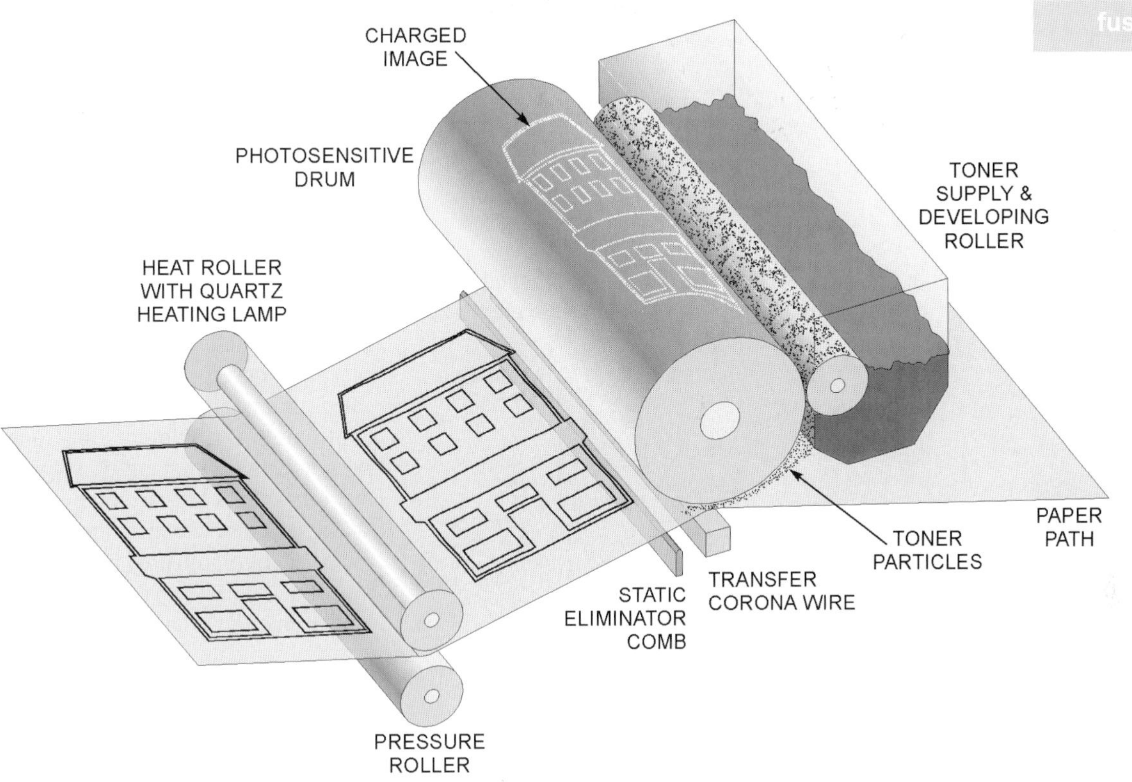

Figure 6-21: The Transfer Process

Component Variations

In Hewlett Packard printers, the main portion of the printing system is contained in the **electrophotographic cartridge**. This cartridge contains the **toner supply**, the **corona wire**, the **drum assembly**, and the **developing roller**. The HP configuration is depicted in Figure 6-22.

electrophotographic cartridge

toner supply

corona wire

drum assembly

developing roller

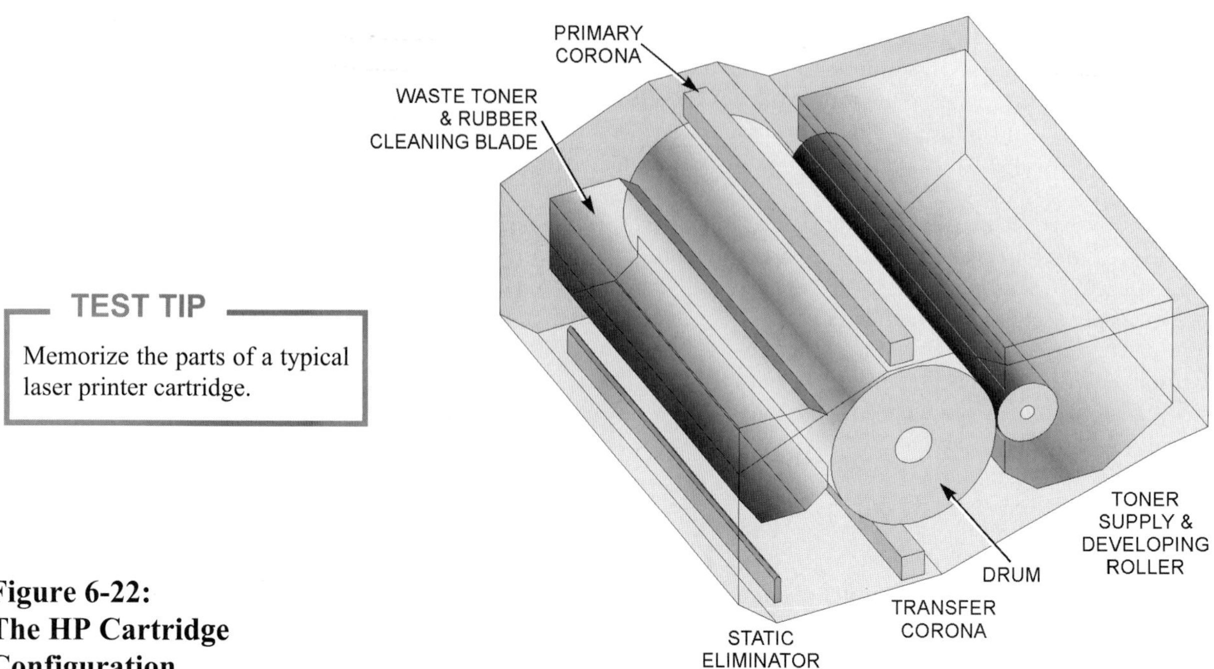

TEST TIP

Memorize the parts of a typical laser printer cartridge.

Figure 6-22: The HP Cartridge Configuration

developer unit

toner cartridge

drum unit

fuser unit

cleaning pad

In other laser printers, like the one depicted in Figure 6-23, the basic components are combined so that the printer consists of a **developer unit**, a **toner cartridge**, a **drum unit**, a **fuser unit**, and a **cleaning pad**. In this case, the developer unit and toner cartridge are separate units. With this configuration, changing the toner does not involve changing some of the other wear-prone components. While it is less expensive to change toner, attention must be paid to how much the other units are wearing. Notice that the photosensitive drum is also a separate component.

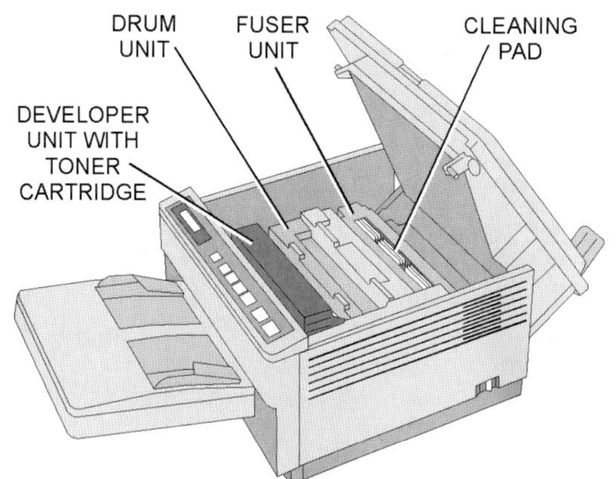

Figure 6-23: Basic Components of a Laser Printer

Paper Handling

paper transport mechanics

Laser printers are very mechanical in nature. The paper handling motor and the gear train assembly perform a tremendous number of operations to process a single sheet of paper. The **paper transport mechanics** must pick up a page from the paper tray, and move it into the printer's registration area. After the drum has been written with the image, the paper handling mechanism moves the paper into registration. A roller system moves the page past the drum, and into the fusing unit. When the page exits through the fusing rollers, the printer senses that the page has exited, and resets itself to wait for another page to print.

In addition to the motor and gear train, the printer uses a number of sensors and solenoid-actuated clutches to control the paper movement. It uses solenoids to engage and disengage different gear sets, and clutches, at appropriate times during the printing process.

Laser printer sensors

Laser printer sensors—A typical laser printer has sensors to determine what paper trays are installed, what size paper is in them, and whether the tray is empty. It also uses sensors to track the movement of the paper through each stage of the printer. This allows the controller to know where the page is at all times, and sequence the activities of the solenoids and clutches properly.

Figure 6-24 gives a summary of the sensors found in a typical laser printer.

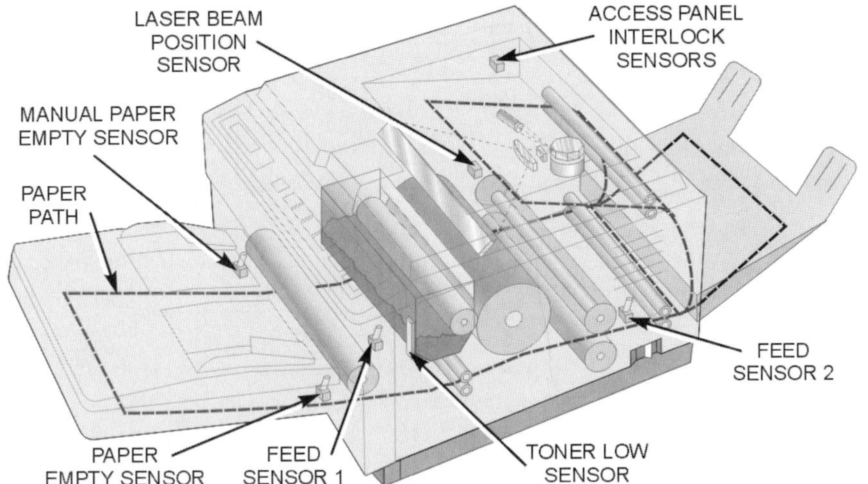

Figure 6-24: Sensor Summary

If the page does not show up at the next sensor at the appropriate time, the printer will know that a paper jam has occurred, and will create an error message that indicates the area of the printer where it is. When a paper jam occurs, it will be necessary to remove the paper from the inside of the printer, and reset the print operation. Gaining access to the area of the printer where the jam is usually requires direction from the printer's user's manual. The printer should always be allowed to cool, and should always be turned off before reaching inside the unit.

interlock switch

Another set of sensor switches monitor the printer's access doors to protect personnel from potentially dangerous conditions inside the printer. The **interlock switch** blocks the laser beam as a vision-protection measure. Likewise, the high-voltage supplies to various printer components are also shut down. To observe the operation of the printer, it will be necessary to locate, and bypass, these interlocks. However, you should always be aware that these interlocks are present for protection, and great care should be taken when working with them defeated.

thermal sensor

Still other sensors are used to monitor the temperatures within different sections of the printer. A **thermal sensor** in the fusing unit monitors the temperature of the unit. This information is applied to the control circuitry so that it can control the fuser temperature between 140°C and 230°C. If the temperature of the fuser is not controlled correctly, it may cause severe damage to the printer, as well as present a potential fire hazard.

thermal fuse

TEST TIP

Remember the purpose of the thermal fuse in laser printers.

beam detector sensor

A **thermal fuse** protects the fuser assembly from overheating and damaging the printer. The thermal fuse should normally snap back after the temperature condition is cleared. If the switch is open under cool conditions, it will need to be replaced. This is normally an indication that the thermal sensor has failed, or that the fuser assembly has been installed improperly.

When the laser beam is turned on, a **beam detector sensor** in the writing unit alerts the control circuitry that the writing process has begun. This signal synchronizes the beginning of the laser-modulating data with the beginning of the scan line.

Paper Specifications

Paper weight

weight

One reason for faint printing is that the paper thickness lever is set to the wrong position for the weight of paper being used.

Paper weight—Paper is specified in terms of its **weight** per 500 sheets at 22" *x* 17" (i.e., 500 sheets of 22" *x* 17", 21-pound bond paper weighs 21 pounds).

TEST TIP

Know how paper weight is specified and how many sheets are involved.

The thickness setting will also cause smudged characters when the paper is too thick for the actual setting. In this case, adjust the thickness lever one or two notches away from the paper.

PRINTER CONNECTIONS AND CONFIGURATIONS

The A+ Core Hardware objective 5.3 states that the test taker should be able to identify the types of printer connections and configurations.

- Parallel
- Serial
- Network

Printers used with personal computers are available in many types and use various connection schemes. As this A+ objective points out, the computer technician must be able to connect a brand-x printer to a brand-y computer and configure it for operation.

The connection method between the printer and the computer will affect many of the troubleshooting steps necessary to isolate printing problems. Likewise, connecting a printer to a network will affect how the technician approaches its configuration and troubleshooting.

The following sections of this chapter concentrate on the various printer connection methods commonly found in personal computer environments.

Printer Installation

Generally speaking, one of the least difficult I/O devices to add to a microcomputer system is a parallel printer. This is largely due to the fact that, from the beginning of the PC era, a parallel printer has been one of the most standard pieces of equipment to add to the system.

This standardization has led to fairly direct installation procedures for most printers. Obtain an IBM Centronics printer cable, plug it into the appropriate LPT port on the back of the computer, connect the Centronic-compatible end to the printer, plug the power cord into the printer, load a device driver to configure the software for the correct printer, and print.

IEEE 1284

One note of caution concerning parallel printer cables. The IEEE has established specifications for bi-directional parallel printer cables (**IEEE 1284**). These cables affect the operation of EPP and ECP parallel devices. Refer to the Enhanced Parallel Port Operations section of Chapter 3 – *Standard I/O Systems*, for additional information about these ports. Using an older, non-compliant unidirectional cable with a bi-directional parallel device will prevent the device from communicating properly with the system and may prevent it from operating.

Printer Not Ready

print spooler

Some failures will produce error messages, such as "**Printer Not Ready**," while others will simply leave the data in the computer's **print spooler**. The symptom normally associated with this condition is that the parallel device simply refuses to operate. If an ECP or EPP device successfully runs a self test, but will not communicate with the host system, check the Advanced BIOS Setup screens to make certain that bi-directional printing has been enabled for the parallel port. If so, check the printer cable by substituting a known, 1284-compliant cable for it.

Setting up serial printers—Serial printers are slightly more difficult to set up, since the communication definition must be configured between the computer and the printer. The serial port will need to be configured for speed, parity type, character frame, and protocol.

Regardless of the type of printer being installed, the steps for adding a printer to a system are basically the same. Connect the printer to the correct I/O port at the computer system. Make sure the port is enabled. Set up the appropriate printer drivers. Configure the port's communication parameters, if a serial printer is being installed. Install the paper. Run the printer's self-test, and then print a document. These steps are summarized in Figure 6-25.

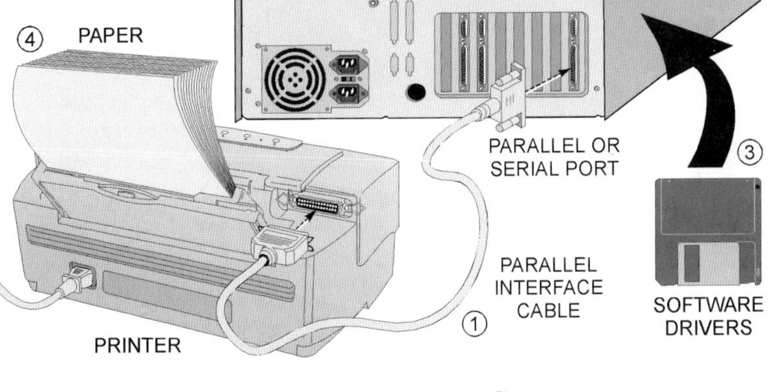
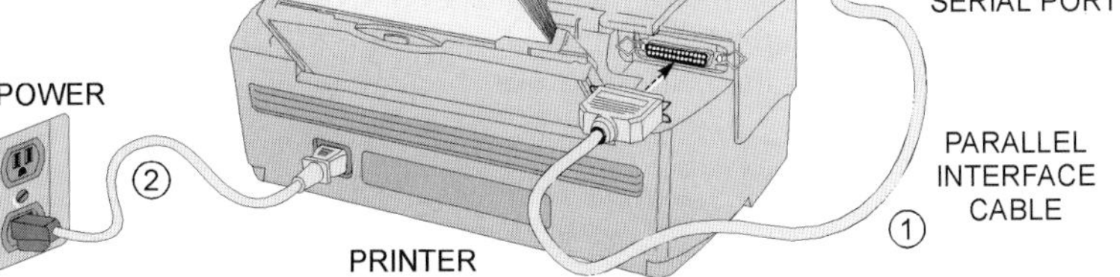

Figure 6-25: Printer Installation Steps

Printer Drivers

Like mice, printers require device driver programs to oversee their operation.

For example, a software developer who is writing a word processing program will not have any way of knowing what type of printers will be used.

printer drivers

Although most printers use the same codes for alphanumeric data, they may use widely different control codes, and special feature codes to produce special text, and to govern the printer's operation. Therefore, software producers often develop the Core Hardware of a program, and then offer a disk full of **printer drivers** to translate between the software package and different standard printers.

The user normally selects the driver program needed to operate the system through a configuration program that comes with the software. This function is usually performed the first time the software is loaded into the system. Figure 6-26 illustrates the functional position of a printer driver in the system.

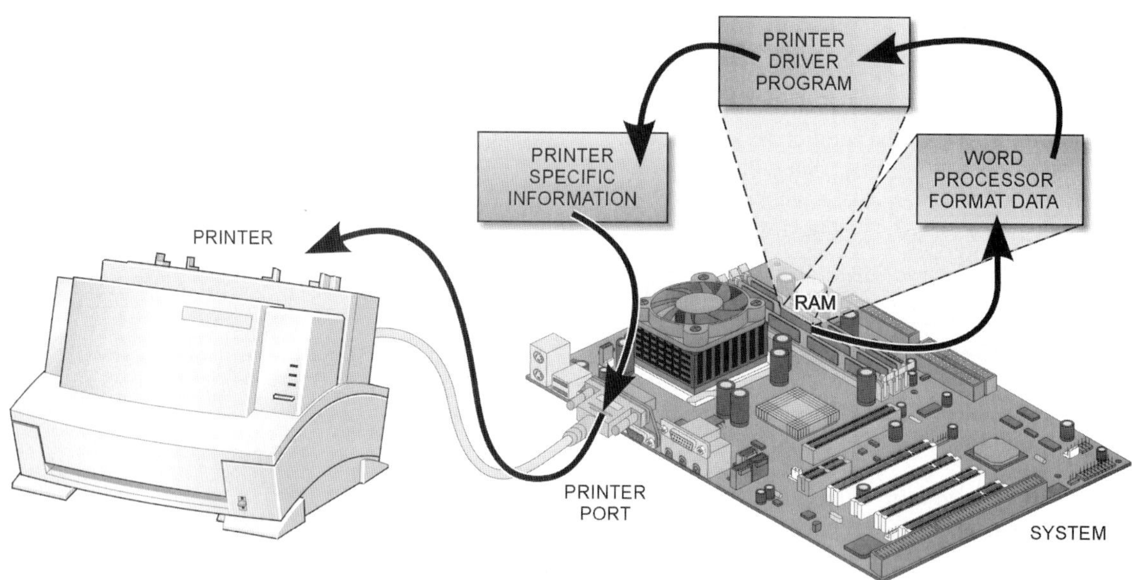

Figure 6-26: Printer Driver Position

Driver programs may be supplied by the software developer as part of the package, or by the hardware developer. It is often in the best interests of a hardware developer to offer drivers that make the hardware compatible with popular pieces of application software. Conversely, if a software developer is introducing a new piece of software, they often offer drivers that make the software compatible with as many hardware variants as possible.

Serial Printer Considerations

Data Terminal Ready

In some applications, it is simply impossible to locate the printer close enough to the host computer to use the parallel connection. In these cases, serially interfaced printers come into play. Printers using a serial interface connection add an extra level of complexity to the system. Unlike the parallel printer interface that basically plugs and plays on most systems, serial interface connections require additional hardware and software configuration steps. Serial printer problems basically fall into three categories:

- Cabling problems
- Configuration problems
- Printer problems

Cabling Problems

Not all serial cables are created equal. In the PC world, RS-232 serial cables can take on several configurations. First of all, they may use either 9-pin or 25-pin D-shell connectors. The cable for a particular serial connection will need to have the correct type of connector at each end. Likewise, the connection scheme inside the cable can vary from printer to printer. Normally, the Transmit Data line (TXD - pin 2) from the computer is connected to the Receive Data line (RXD - pin 3) of the printer. Also, the Data Set Ready (DSR - pin 6) is typically connected to the printer's **Data Terminal Ready** (DTR - pin 20) pin. These connections are used as one method to control the flow of information between the system and the printer. If the printer's character buffer becomes full, it will signal the computer to hold up sending characters by deactivating this line.

Different or additional pin interconnections can be required for other printer models. The actual implementation of the RS-232 connection is solely up to the printer manufacturer. Figure 6-27 depicts typical connection schemes for both 9-pin and 25-pin connections to a typical printer. The connection scheme for a given serial printer model is normally provided in its user's manual.

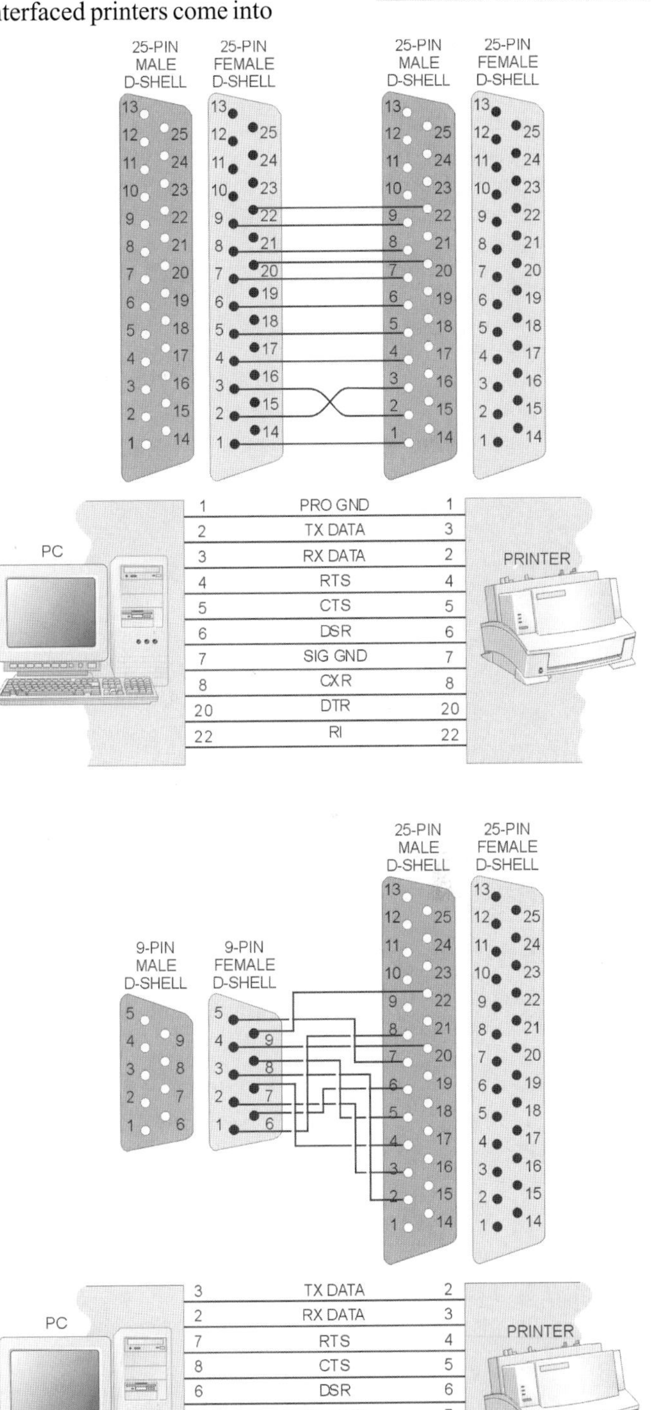

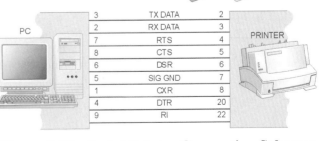

Figure 6-27: Serial Printer Connection Schemes

TEST TIP

Remember the types of connectors used at both the computer and the printer end of an RS-232 serial printer cable.

TEST TIP

Know the recommended maximum length of a standard parallel printer cable and an RS-232 cable.

The other limiting factor for printer cables, both serial and parallel, is length. While cables purchased from reputable suppliers are typically correct in length and contain all of the shielding and connections required, cheaper cables and home-made cables often lack in one of these areas or the other. The recommended signal cable lengths associated with parallel and serial printers are:

- Standard Parallel Printers: 0 – 10 ft. (3 meters), although some equipment manufacturers specify 6 ft (1.8 meters) maximums for their cables. You should believe these recommendations when you see them.
- RS-232 Serial Printers: 10 – 50 ft (15.25 meters). However, some references use 100 ft. as the acceptable length of an RS-232C serial cable. Serial connections are tricky enough without problems generated by the cable being too long. Make the cable as short as possible.

Configuration Problems

After the correct connector and cabling scheme has been implemented, the printer configuration must be established at both the computer and the printer. The information in both locations must match in order for communications to go on. On the system side of the serial-port connection, the software printer driver must be set up to match the setting of the printer's receiving section.

First, the driver must be directed toward the correct serial port. In a Windows-based system, this is typically COM2. Secondly, the selected serial port must be configured for the proper character framing. The number of start, stop, data, and parity bits must be set to match what the printer is expecting to receive. These values are often established through hardware configuration switches located on the printer.

Flow control

software handshaking

hardware handshaking

The printer driver must also be set up to correctly handle the flow of data between the system and the printer. Incorrect flow control settings can result in slow response, lost characters, or continuous errors and retries. **Flow control** can be established through **software** or **hardware handshaking**. In a hardware handshaking mode, the printer tells the port that it is not prepared to receive data by deactivating a control line, such as the DTR line. Conversely, in a software handshaking environment, control codes are sent back and forth between the printer and the computer to enable and disable data flow.

Software data flow control—Two popular methods of implementing software flow control are *Xon/Xoff* and *ETX/ACK*. In the Xon/Xoff method, special ASCII control characters are exchanged between the printer and the computer to turn the data flow on and off. In an ETX/ACK protocol, ASCII characters for *End-of-Text (ETX)* and *ACKnowledge (ACK)* are used to control the movement of data from the port to the printer.

Basically, the computer attaches the ETX character to the end of a data transmission. When the printer receives the ETX character, it checks the incoming data, and when ready, returns an ACK character to the port. This notifies the system that the printer is capable of receiving additional characters. This concept is illustrated in Figure 6-28. In any event, the devices at both ends of the interface connection must be set to use the same flow control method.

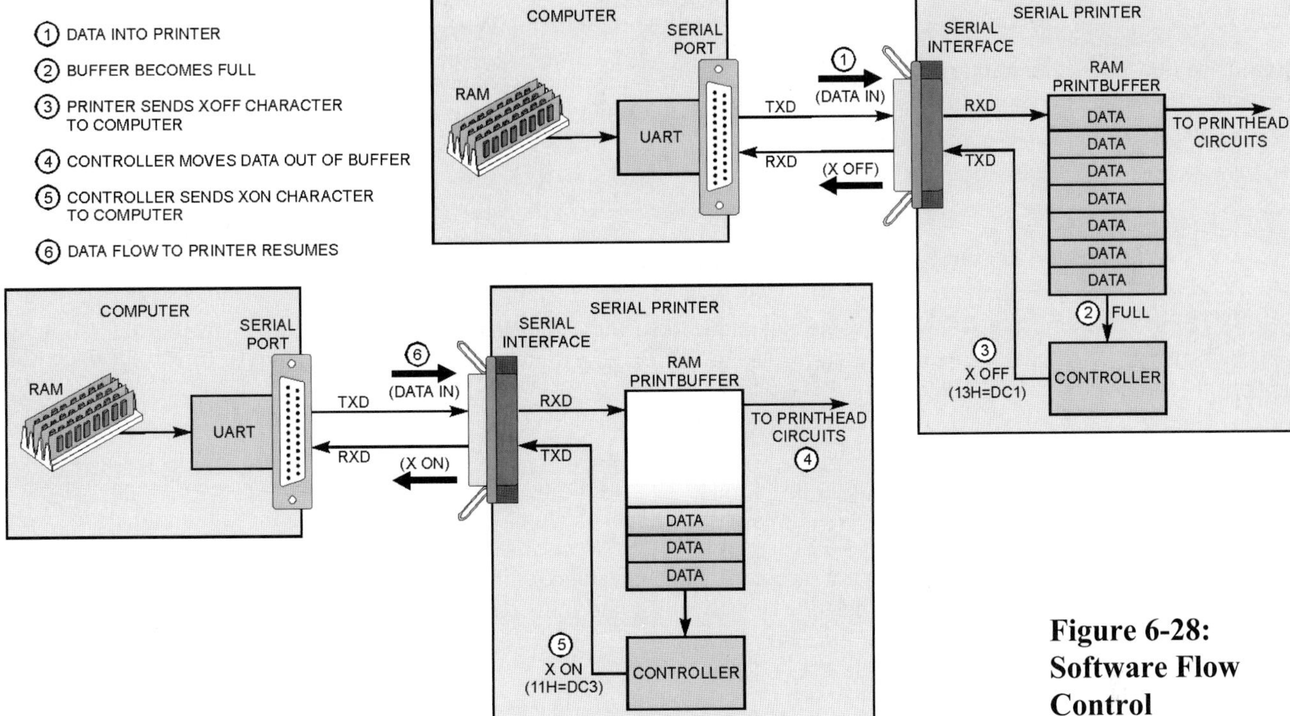

Figure 6-28: Software Flow Control

Serial communications standards and procedures were covered in the "Character Framing" section of Chapter 5—*Data Communications*. Consult that section for more information about character framing, error detection and correction methods, and serial transmission protocols.

Serial Printer Problems

Problems associated with serial printers differ from those of parallel printers only in the area of the serial interface configuration. As mentioned in the preceding section, "Configuration Problems," the protocol, character framing, and baud rate of the printer must match those of the system's interface. After ensuring that the interface settings match, and that the interface is working, the steps of troubleshooting a serial printer are identical to those given for parallel interfaced printers. Therefore, the only steps that need to be added to the Troubleshooting sections later in this chapter are those needed to validate the operation of the serial interface.

Networked Printers

If a printer is installed in a computer system that is part of a network, it is possible for any other computer on the network to send work to the printer. Historically, the **local computer** is attached to the printer through one of the normal printing interfaces (i.e., parallel, serial or USB) and it is also connected to the other **remote computers** through its network connection. In addition to the signal cable, the local computer's operating system must be configured to permit the remote stations on the network to print through it to its printer. This relationship is known as **print sharing**.

local computer

remote computers

print sharing

network-ready printers

network printers

Newer printers, referred to as **network-ready printers**, or simply as **network printers**, come with built-in network interfacing that enables them to be connected directly into the local area network. Most network printers contain an integrated network controller and Ethernet LAN adapter that enables it to work on the LAN without a supporting host computer.

print server port

Other printers may be connected directly to the local area network through a device called a **print server port**. This device resembles a network hub in appearance and can be used to connect up to three printers directly into the network.

While some older network printers used coaxial cable connections, newer network printers feature RJ-45 jacks for connection to twisted-pair Ethernet networks.

TEST TIP

Know how to determine whether a printer is networked or not.

It is relatively easy to determine whether a printer is networked by the presence of a coaxial or a twisted-pair network signal cable connected directly to the printer. The presence of the RJ-45 jacks on the back of the printer also indicate that the printer is network capable, even if it is not being used in that manner. These cables are covered in the section titled "Network Cabling" in Chapter 5—*Data Communications*. In Windows, you can determine that a printer is networked by the appearance of its icon in the Printers folder. The icon will graphically illustrate the network connection. You can also check the Details tab of the printer in the its Windows Properties page.

TEST TIP

Know how to identify the presence of a network-ready printer.

While parallel printers are easy to set up and check, and serial printers require a little more effort to set up, networked printers add another set of variables to the configuration and troubleshooting processes. To avoid dealing directly with the complexity of the network, it is normal to handle printer configuration and troubleshooting at the local level first. Once the operation of the local computer/printer interface has been established, or verified, the network portion of the system can be examined. The "Network Troubleshooting Basics" section of Chapter 11 deals with typical network troubleshooting procedures, while Windows-related network printing problems are covered extensively in the "Troubleshooting Local Area Networks" section of Chapter 12.

SERVICING PRINTERS

The A+ Core Hardware objective 5.2 states that the test taker should be able to identify care and service techniques and common problems with primary printer types. Examples include:

- Feed and output
- Errors
- Paper jam
- Print quality
- Safety precautions
- Preventive maintenance

Printers are connected to personal computers and they break down. Therefore, the computer technician should be familiar with common printer problems and be able to demonstrate current service techniques. The following sections of this chapter deal with typical problems encountered with dot-matrix, ink-jet, and laser printers. They also include troubleshooting methods associated with each type of printer.

Troubleshooting Dot-Matrix Printers

The classical first step in determining the cause of any printer problem is to determine which part of the printer-related system is at fault — the **host computer**, the **signal cable**, or the **printer**.

host computer

signal cable

printer

built-in self-test

Nearly every printer is equipped with a **built-in self-test**. The easiest way to determine whether the printer is at fault is to run its self-test. Consult the printer's user's manual for instructions in running its self-test. Some printers are capable of producing audible tones to indicate the nature of an internal problem. Refer to the printer's user's manual for the definitions of the coded beep tones, if they are available.

If the printer runs the self-test, and prints clean pages, then most of the printer has been eliminated as a possible cause of problems. The problem could be in the computer, the cabling, or the interface portion of the printer. However, if the printer fails the self-test, it will be necessary to diagnose the printer's problem. The following section presents typical problems encountered in dot-matrix printers.

The following are symptoms for dot-matrix printer problems:

- No lights or noise from printer
- Light or uneven print being produced
- Printhead moving, but not printing
- Dots missing from characters
- Printhead printing, but does not move
- Paper will not advance

TEST TIP

Know what it means if the printer produces a satisfactory self-test printout but will not print from the computer.

Dot-Matrix Printer Configuration Checks

The presence of on-board microcontrollers allows modern printers to be very flexible. Like other peripheral devices, printers can be configured to operate in different modes. Operating configuration information can be stored in CMOS RAM on the control board. Some configuration settings may be made through DIP switches mounted inside the printer. These switches are read by the printer's microcontroller at startup.

In the case of dot-matrix printers, the configuration settings are normally entered into the printer through the buttons of its control panel. Typical dot-matrix configuration information includes:

- Printer mode
- Perforation Skip (for continuous forms)
- Automatic Line Feed at the bottom of the page

- Paper Handling type
- ASCII Character Codes (7-bit or 8-bit)
- Basic Character Sets

Other quantities that can be set up include:

- Print Font
- Character Pitch
- Form Length

Most dot-matrix printers contain two or three on-board fonts (character styles), that can be selected through the printer's configuration routines. Typical fonts included in dot-matrix printers are:

- Draft
- Courier
- Prestige
- Bold prestige

character pitch

In many dot-matrix printer models, it is also possible to download other fonts from the computer. The **character pitch** refers to the number of characters printed per inch. Common pitch settings include 10, 11, 12, and 14 characters per inch. Consult the printer's user's guide to find the definitions of such settings.

Dot-Matrix Printer Hardware Checks

To perform work inside the printer, it will be necessary to disassemble its case. Begin by removing any add-on pieces, such as dust covers and paper feeders. Next, remove the paper advancement knob located on the right side of most dot-matrix printers. Turn the printer over, and remove the screws that hold the two halves of the case together. These screws are sometimes hidden beneath rubber feet and compliance stickers. Finally, it may be necessary to disconnect the printer's front panel connections from the main board to complete the separation of the two case halves. This procedure is shown in Figure 6-29.

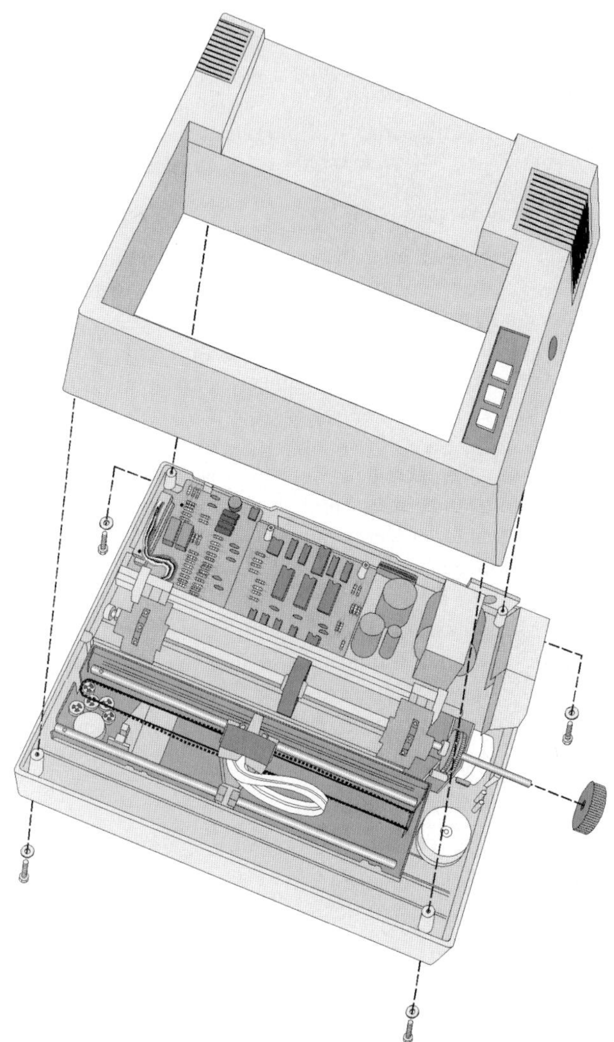

Figure 6-29: Disassembling the Printer

Dot-Matrix Printer Power Supply Problems

If the printer will not function, and displays no lights, no sounds, and no actions, the power supply is generally involved. Troubleshoot printer power supply problems in the same manner as you would a computer power supply. As a matter of fact, the power supply troubleshooting routine is the same.

Check the on-line light. If the printer is off-line, no print action will occur. A missing, or improperly installed, ribbon cartridge will also prevent the unit from printing. Install the ribbon correctly. Check the power outlet to make certain that it is live. Plug a lamp, or other device, in the outlet to verify that it is operative. Check to see that the power cord is plugged in securely to the printer and the socket. Make sure the power switch is on.

If everything is plugged in and in the on position, but still not working, turn OFF the power, and unplug the printer from the outlet. Remove the top of the printer's case, and find the power supply board. Check the power supply's fuse to make sure that it is good. If the fuse is blown, replace it with a fuse of the same type and rating. Do not replace a blown fuse with a conductor, or a slow-blow fuse. To do so could lead to more extensive damage to the printer, and possibly unsafe conditions.

Also, check the power supply and control boards, as well as the paper feed and printhead positioning motors for burnt components, or signs of defect. Fuses usually do not blow, unless another component fails. The other possible cause of excessive current occurs when a motor (or its gear train) binds, and cannot move. Check the drive mechanisms and motors for signs of binding. If the gear train, or positioning mechanisms will not move, they may need to be adjusted before replacing the fuse.

If none of the printer sections work when everything is connected and power is applied, it will be necessary to exchange the power supply board for a new unit. Unlike the computer's power supply, the typical printer power supply is not enclosed in a protective housing and, therefore, presents a shock hazard anytime it is exposed.

To exchange the power supply board, disconnect the power cable from the printer. Disconnect, and mark, the cabling from the control board, and any other components directly connected to the power supply. Remove any screws, or clips, that secure the power supply board to the case. Lift the board out of the cabinet. Install the new board, and reconnect the various wire bundles to it.

Ribbon Cartridges

ribbon cartridge

The single item in a dot-matrix printer that requires the most attention is the **ribbon cartridge**. It is considered a consumable part of the printer and must be changed often. The ink ribbon is stored in a controlled wad inside the cartridge, and moves across the face of the platen, as depicted in Figure 6-30. A take-up wheel draws new ribbon out of the wad as it is used. As the ribbon wears out, the printing will become faint and uneven. When the print becomes noticeably faint, the cartridge should be replaced. Most dot-matrix printers use a snap-in ribbon cartridge.

TEST TIP

Know what the most likely cause of uneven or faded print with a dot-matrix printer is and how to correct it.

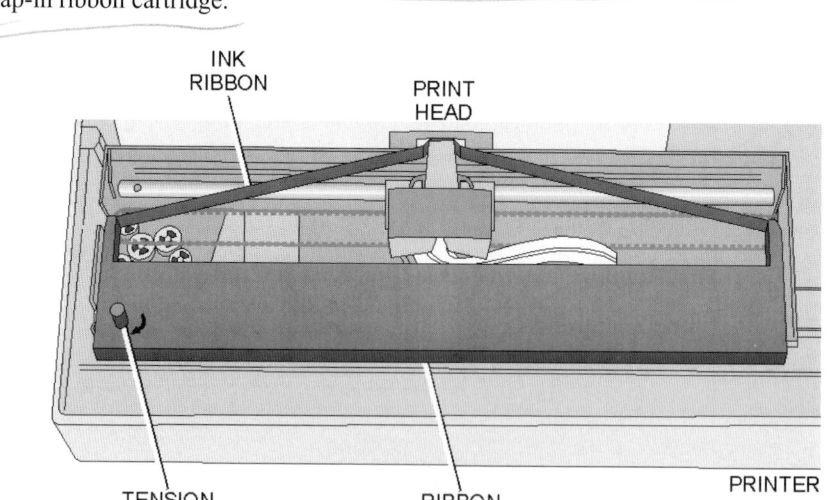

Figure 6-30: The Printer Cartridge

To replace a typical ribbon cartridge, move the printhead carriage assembly to the center of the printer. Remove the old cartridge by freeing it from its clips, or holders, and then lifting it out of the printer.

Tighten the ribbon tension by advancing the tension knob on the cartridge, in a counter-clockwise direction, until the ribbon is taut. Snap the cartridge into place, making certain that the ribbon slides between the printhead and the ribbon mask. Slide the printhead assembly back and forth on the rod to check for proper ribbon movement.

Printhead Not Printing

head gap lever

If the printhead is moving, but not printing, begin by checking the printer's **head gap lever** to make sure that the printhead is not too far back from the paper. If the printhead does not operate, components involved include:

- the printhead
- the flexible signal cable between the control board and the printhead
- the control board
- possibly the power supply board

Run the printer's self-test to see if the printhead will print from the on-board test. Check the flexible signal cable to make sure it is firmly plugged into the control board, and that it is not damaged or worn through. If none of the print wires are being energized, then the first step should be to exchange the control board for a known good one of the same type. If the new control board does not correct the problem, replace the printhead. A power supply problem could also cause the printhead to not print.

A related problem occurs when one, or more, of the print wires does not fire. If this is the case, check the printhead for physical damage. Also check the flexible signal cable for a broken conductor. If the control board is delivering any of the other print wire signals, the problem is most likely associated with the printhead mechanism. Replace the printhead as a first step. If the problem continues after replacing the printhead, however, exchange the control board for a new one.

If the tops of characters are missing, the printhead is misaligned with the platen. It may need to be reseated in the printhead carriage, or the carriage assembly may need to be adjusted to the proper height and angle.

TEST TIP

Know what causes tops of characters to be missing from dot-matrix characters and how to correct the problem.

head locking lever

To exchange the printhead assembly, make sure that the printhead assembly is cool enough to be handled. These units can get hot enough to cause a serious burn. Unplug the printhead assembly from the control board. Slide the printhead assembly to the center of the printer, and rotate the **head locking lever** to release the printhead from the assembly. Remove the printhead by lifting it straight up. Install the new printhead by following the disassembly procedure in reverse. Adjust the new printhead for proper printing. In some printers, the printheads are held in the printhead assembly with screws. To remove the printhead from these units it will be necessary to remove the screws so that the printhead can be exchanged. Refer to the printers documentation for directions concerning exchanging the printhead mechanism.

TEST TIP

Remember that the printhead of dot-matrix printers generate a great deal of heat and can be a burn hazard when working on these units.

ribbon mask

If the output of the printer gets lighter as it moves from left to right across the page, it may become necessary to adjust the printhead mechanism to obtain proper printing. This procedure is illustrated in Figure 6-31. To print correctly, the printhead should be approximately 0.6 mm from the platen when the head position lever is in the center position. Move the printhead to the center of the printer. Adjusting this setting requires that the nut at the left end of the rear carriage shaft be loosened. Using a feeler gauge, set the distance between the platen and printhead (not the **ribbon mask**). Tighten the nut, and check the spacing between the printhead and platen at both ends of the printhead travel.

TEST TIP

Know the most likely cause of print which fades from one side of the page to the other.

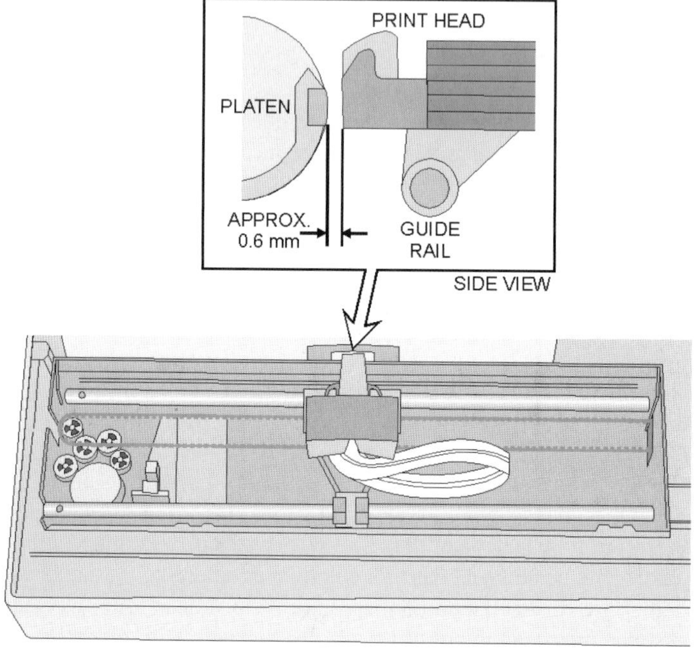

Figure 6-31: Adjusting the Printhead Spacing

Finally, check the distance between the platen and the ribbon mask. This spacing should be 0.3 mm. If not, loosen the screws that hold the ribbon mask to the printhead assembly, and adjust the gap with feeler gauges. There should also be a 0.1 mm spacing between the printhead and the ribbon mask. After setting the various gaps, run the printer's self-test to check for print quality.

Printhead Not Moving

home position

timing sensors

If the printhead is printing but not moving across the page, a single block of print will be generated on the page. When this type of problem occurs, the related components include the printhead positioning motor, the timing belt, the **home position** and **timing sensors**, the control board, and possibly the power supply board.

With the power off, manually move the printhead to the center of the printer. Turn the printer on to see if the printhead seeks the home position at the far left side of the printer. If it moves to the left side of the printer, and does not shut off, or does not return to the center of the printer, then the home position sensor is malfunctioning and should be replaced. If the printhead moves on startup, and will not move during normal printing, the control board should be replaced. In the event that the printhead assembly will not move at any time, the printhead positioning motor should be replaced. If the print is skewed from left to right as it moves down the page, the printer's bi-directional mode settings may be faulty, or the home-position/end-of-line sensors may be defective.

Testing the timing sensor would require test equipment, in the form of a logic probe or an oscilloscope, to look for pulses produced as the printhead is manually moved across the printer.

Figure 6-32 depicts the components associated with the printhead's timing belt. Replacing the timing belt requires that it be removed from the printhead assembly. In many cases, the belt is secured to the printhead assembly with adhesive cement. This will require that the adhesive seal be cut with a single-edged razor blade, or a hobby knife.

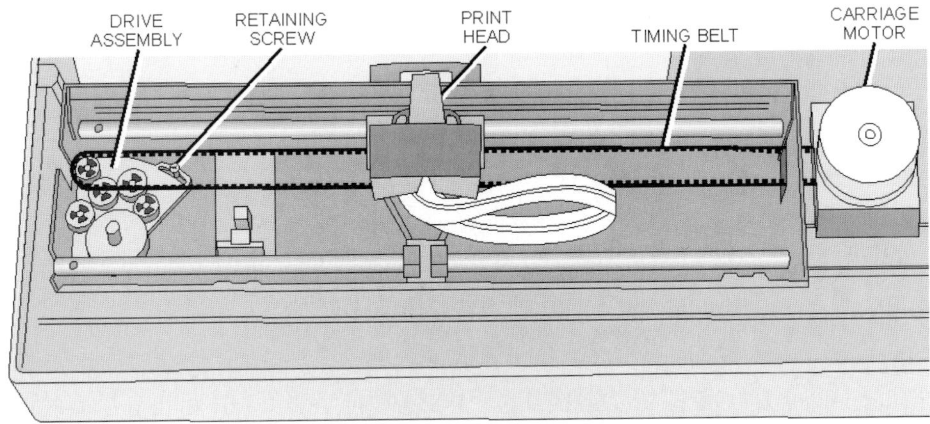

Figure 6-32: Printhead Timing

After the seal has been broken, it should be possible to shove the belt out of the clips that secure it to the printhead assembly. Next, remove the belt from the drive pulley assembly at the positioning motor. It may be necessary to remove the positioning motor from the case to gain access to the pulley.

To reinstall the timing belt, apply a small drop of adhesive to the belt, and reattach it to the printhead assembly. Wrap the belt around the positioning motor's drive pulley, and reinstall the motor. Following this, it will be necessary to adjust the tension on the belt. To set the tension on the belt, loosen the adjustment screw on the belt-tension adjustment plate. Tighten the timing belt until it will not move more than 1/4" when the printhead is at either end of the carriage shaft and the belt is pressed inward. Tighten the retaining screw to lock the tension plate in place. Run the printer's self-test, and check the distance between the characters. If the character spacing is not uniform, replace the belt and perform the check again.

Paper Not Advancing

When the paper does not advance, the output will normally be one line of dark blocks across the page. Examine the printer's **paper feed selector lever** to make sure that it is set properly for the type of paper feed selected (i.e., friction feed, pin feed, or tractor feed). If the paper feed is set correctly, the printer is on-line, and the paper will not move, it will be necessary to troubleshoot the paper handling motor and gear train. Check the motor and gear train by setting the printer to the Off-Line mode, and holding down the Form Feed (FF) button.

paper feed selector lever

If the feed motor and gear train work from this point, the problem must exist on the **control board**, with the **interface cable**, the **printer's configuration**, or in the **computer system**. If the motor and/or gear train does not respond, unplug the paper feed motor cable, and check the resistance of the motor windings. If the windings are open, replace the paper feed motor.

control board

interface cable

printer's configuration

computer system

To replace the paper feed motor and/or gear train, remove the screws that hold the paper feed motor to the frame of the printer. Create a wiring diagram that describes the routing of the feed motor's wiring harness. Disconnect the wiring harness from the control board.

Prepare a drawing that outlines the arrangement of the gear train (if multiple gears are used). Remove the gears from the shafts, taking care not to lose any washers, or springs, that may be located behind the gears. After reinstalling the gears, and new motor, adjust the motor and gear relationships to minimize the **gear lash**, so that they do not bind or lock up. Use the printer's self-test to check the operation of the motor and gears.

gear lash

Troubleshooting Ink-Jet Printers

host computer

signal cable

printer

As with the dot-matrix printer, the first step in determining the cause of an ink-jet printer problem is to determine which part of the printer system is at fault—the **host computer**, the **signal cable**, or the **printer**.

Ink-jet printers are equipped with built-in self-tests. The easiest way to determine if the printer is at fault is to run its self-tests. Consult the printer's user's manual for instructions in running its self-tests.

computer

cabling

interface

If the printer runs the self-tests, and prints clean pages, then most of the printer has been eliminated as a possible cause of problems. The problem could be in the **computer**, the **cabling**, or the **interface** portion of the printer. However, if the printer fails the self-tests, it will be necessary to diagnose the printer problem. The following section presents typical problems encountered in ink-jet printers.

The following are symptoms of ink-jet printer problems:

- No lights or noise from printer
- Light or uneven print being produced
- Printhead moving, but not printing, or printing erratically
- Lines on the page
- Printhead printing, but does not move
- Paper will not advance

Ink-Jet Printer Configuration Checks

The presence of the printer's on-board microcontroller allows modern printers to be very flexible. Like other peripheral devices, printers can be configured to operate in different modes. Operating configuration information can be stored in RAM, on the control board.

In the case of ink-jet printers, the configuration settings are normally entered into the printer through software. Typical configuration information includes:

- **Page Orientation (landscape or portrait)**
- **Paper Size**
- **Collation**
- **Print Quality**

Page Orientation

Paper Size

Collation

Print Quality

Landscape printing

Portrait printing

Landscape printing is specified when the width of the page is greater than the length of the page. **Portrait printing** is specified when the length of the page is greater than the width. In an ink-jet printer, the quality of the printout is specified in the number of dots per inch (dpi) produced. Typical ink-jet resolutions run from 180 *x* 180 dpi to 720 *x* 720 dpi. Ink-jet printers have the capability to download additional fonts from the host computer.

TEST TIP

Be aware that print density can be adjusted through software in an ink-jet printer.

You can also configure the basic appearance of color and **grayscale** images produced by the ink-jet printer. A color ink-jet printer uses four ink colors to produce color images. These are **Cyan**, **Magenta**, **Yellow**, and **Black** (referred to as **CMYK color**). To create other colors, the printer prints a predetermined percentage of the basic colors in close proximity to each other.

grayscale

Cyan

Magenta

Yellow

Black

CMYK color

halftone color

brightness

contrast

saturation

The different percentages determine what the new color will be. The eye does not differentiate the space between them, and perceives only the combined color. This is referred to as **halftone color**. Typical color configurations include setting up the **brightness**, the **contrast**, and the **saturation** settings of images.

Ink-Jet Printer Hardware Checks

To perform work on the printer's hardware, it will be necessary to disassemble the printer's case. Begin by removing all of the add-on pieces, such as dust covers and paper feeders. Remove the screws that hold the outer panels of the case to the printer frame. Removing the access panels of a typical ink-jet printer is shown in Figure 6-33. The retaining screws are sometimes hidden beneath rubber feet and compliance stickers. Finally, it may be necessary to disconnect the printer's front panel connections from the control board to complete the disassembly of the case.

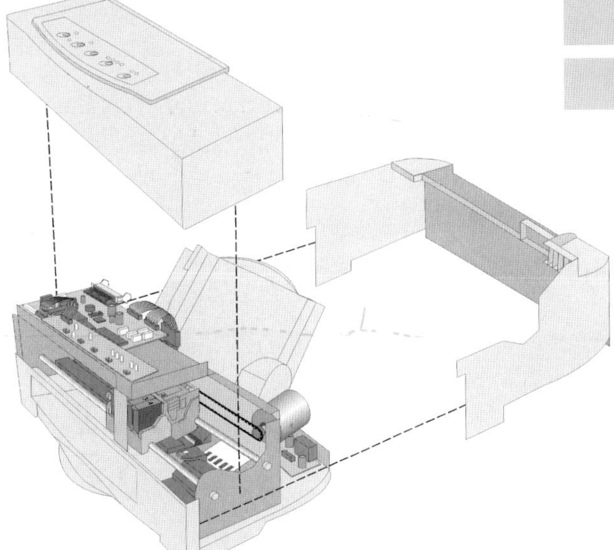

Figure 6-33: Printer Case

Power Supply Problems

If the printer will not function, and displays no lights, no sounds and no actions, the power supply is generally involved. Check the on-line light. If the printer is off-line, no print action will occur. A missing, or improperly installed, ink cartridge will prevent the unit from printing. Install the ink cartridge correctly. Check the power outlet to make certain that it is live. Plug a lamp, or other device, in the outlet to verify that it is operative. Check to see that the power cord is plugged in securely to the printer and the socket. Make sure the power switch is ON.

If the unit is plugged in and turned ON, but still not working, turn it off and unplug it. Remove the top of the printer's case, and locate the power supply board. Check the power supply's fuse to make sure that it is good. If the fuse is blown, replace it with a fuse of the same type and rating. Do not replace a blown fuse with a conductor, or a slow-blow fuse. To do so could lead to more extensive damage to the printer, and possible unsafe conditions.

Also, check the power supply and control boards, as well as the paper feed and printhead positioning motors, for burnt components or signs of defect. Fuses usually do not blow unless another component fails. Another possible cause of over-current occurs when a motor (or its gear train) binds, and cannot move. Check the drive mechanisms and motors for signs of binding. If the gear train, or positioning mechanisms, will not move, they may need to be adjusted, or replaced, before replacing the fuse.

If none of the printer sections work, everything is connected, and power is applied, it will be necessary to exchange the power supply board for a new unit. Unlike the computer's power supply, the typical power supply in a printer is not enclosed in a protective housing and therefore, presents a shock hazard any time it is exposed.

To exchange the power supply board, disconnect the power cable from the printer. Disconnect, and mark, the cabling from the control board, and any other components directly connected to the power supply. Remove any screws, or clips, that secure the power supply board to the case. Lift the board out of the cabinet. Install the new board, and reconnect the various wire bundles to it.

Ink Cartridges

ink cartridge

The single item in an ink-jet printer that requires the most attention is the **ink cartridge** (or cartridges). As the ink cartridge empties, the printing will eventually become faint and uneven, and the resolution of the print on the page will diminish.

The density of the printout from an ink-jet printer can be adjusted through its printing software. However, when the print becomes noticeably faint, or the resolution becomes unacceptable, the cartridge will need to be replaced. Most ink-jet printers use a self-contained, snap-in ink cartridge, like the one in Figure 6-34. Some models have combined ink cartridges that replace all three colors and the black ink at the same time. Other models use individual cartridges for each color. In this way, only the colors that are running low are replaced.

The ink cartridges can be popped out of the printhead assembly to inspect its ink jets. If any, or all, of the jets is clogged, it is normally possible to clear them by gently wiping the face of the cartridge with a swab. A gentle squeeze of the ink reservoir can also help to unblock a clogged jet. Using solvents to clear blockages in the jets can dilute the ink, and allow it to flow uncontrollably through the jet.

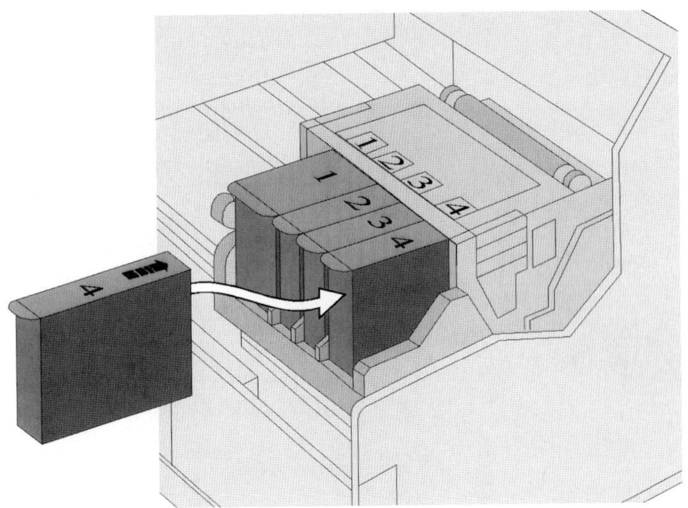

Figure 6-34: Self-Contained, Snap-in Ink Cartridge

To replace a typical ink cartridge, move the printhead carriage assembly to the center of the printer. Remove the old cartridge by freeing it from its clips, or holders, and lifting it out of the printer.

After replacing the ink cartridge, you should cycle the printer on so that it will go through its normal warm up procedures. During these procedures, the printer does a thorough cleaning of the ink jet nozzles and gets the ink flowing correctly from the nozzles. Afterward, print a test page to verify the output of the new ink cartridge.

Printhead Not Printing

If the printhead is moving, but not printing, begin by checking the ink supply in the print cartridge. The reservoir does not have to be completely empty to fail. Replace the cartridge(s) that appear(s) to be low. Some or all of the jets may be clogged. This is particularly common if the printer has not been used for a while. If there are cleaning instructions in the user's manual, clean the jets and attempt to print from the self-test.

If the printer will not print from the self-test, the components involved include:

- the printhead
- the flexible signal cable (between the control board and the printhead)
- the control board
- possibly the power supply board

Check the flexible signal cable to make sure it is firmly plugged into the control board, and that it is not damaged or worn through. If none of the ink jets are firing, the first step should be to exchange the ink cartridges for new ones. If a single ink jet is not firing, replace the cartridge that is not working.

Next, use the ohmmeter function of a multimeter to check the continuity of the conductors in the flexible wiring harness that supplies the printhead assembly. If one of the conductors is broken, a single jet will normally be disabled. However, if the broken conductor is a ground, or common connection, all of the jets should be disabled. Exchange the control board for a known good one of the same type. If the new control board does not correct the problem, replace the printhead. A power supply problem could also cause the printhead to not print.

If a single jet is not functioning, the output will appear as a white line on the page. If one of the jets is activated all of the time, then black or colored lines will be produced on the page. Use the following steps to isolate the cause of these problems—replace the print cartridge; check the flexible cabling for continuity and for short circuits between adjacent conductors; exchange the control board for a known good one; and finally, check the power supply.

Printhead Not Moving

home position sensor

If the printhead is printing, but not moving across the page, a single block of print will normally be generated on the page. When this type of problem occurs, the related components include the printhead positioning motor, the timing belt, the **home position sensor**, the control board, and possibly the power supply. These components are depicted in Figure 6-35.

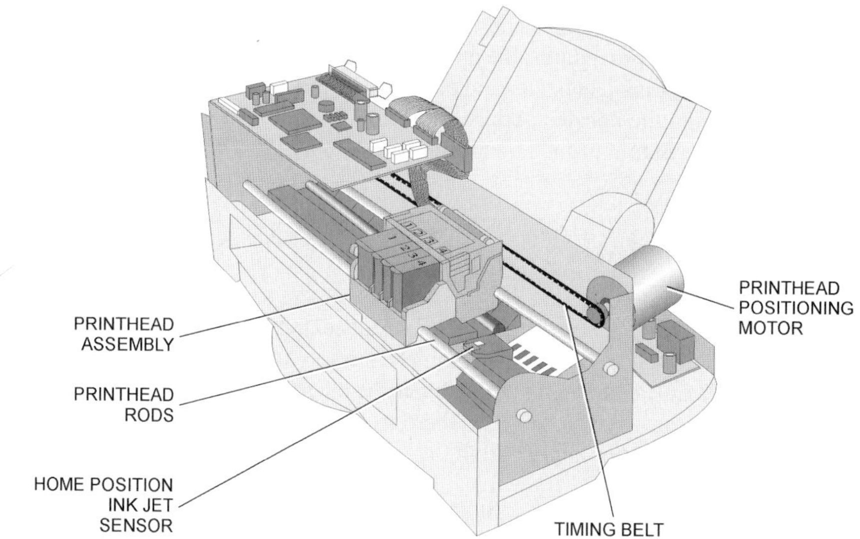

Figure 6-35: Printhead Positioning Components

With the power off, manually move the printhead to the center of the printer. Turn the printer on to see if the printhead seeks the home position at the far end of the printer. If the printhead moves to the end of the printer, and does not shut off, or does not return to the center of the printer, then the home position sensor is malfunctioning and should be replaced. If the printhead moves on startup, and will not move during normal printing, the control board should be replaced. In the event that the printhead assembly will not move at any time, check to see if the printer is in **Maintenance mode**. In this mode, the printer typically keeps the printhead assembly in the home position. If no mode problems are present, the printhead positioning motor should be replaced.

Maintenance mode

If characters are unevenly spaced across the page, the timing sensor may be failing. To test the timing sensor would require test equipment, in the form of a logic probe or an oscilloscope to look for pulses produced as the printhead is manually moved across the printer.

Replacing the timing belt requires that the belt be removed from the printhead assembly. In many cases, the belt will be secured to the printhead assembly with adhesive cement. This will require that the adhesive seal be cut with a single-edged razor blade, or a hobby knife. After the seal has been broken, it should be possible to shove the belt out of the clips that secure it to the printhead assembly. Next, remove the belt from the drive pulley assembly at the positioning motor. It may be necessary to remove the positioning motor from the case to gain access to the pulley.

Paper Not Advancing

When the paper does not advance, the output will normally be a thick, dark line across the page. Check the control panel to see that the printer is on-line. If the printer is on-line, and the paper will not move, it will be necessary to troubleshoot the paper handling motor, and gear train. Check the motor, and gear train, by setting the printer to the off-line mode and holding down the Form Feed button.

If the feed motor and gear train work from this point on, the problem must exist on the control board, the **interface cable**, the printer configuration, or the computer system. If the motor and/or gear train does not respond, unplug the paper feed motor cable, and check the resistance of the motor windings. If the windings are open, replace the paper feed motor.

interface cable

To replace the paper feed motor and/or gear train, remove the screws that hold the paper feed motor to the frame of the printer. Create a wiring diagram that describes the routing of the feed motor's wiring harness. Disconnect the wiring harness from the control board.

Draw an outline of the gear train arrangement (if multiple gears are used). Remove the gears from their shafts, taking care not to lose any washers or springs that may be located behind the gears. After reinstalling the gears, and new motor, adjust the motor and gear relationships to minimize the gear lash, so that they do not bind or lock up. Use the printer's self-test to check the operation of the motor and gears.

If the printer's paper thickness selector is set improperly, or the rollers in its paper feed system becomes worn, the paper can slip as it moves through the printer and cause wavy graphics to be produced. Check the printer's paper thickness settings. If they are correct and the print output is disfigured, you will need to replace the paper feed rollers.

> **TEST TIP**
>
> Know what types of problems can cause disfigured print in an ink-jet printer.

Troubleshooting Laser Printers

Many of the problems encountered in laser printers are similar to those found in other printer types. For example, notice that most of the symptoms listed in the following section relate to the printer **not printing**, or **not printing correctly**, and **not moving paper** through the printer.

not printing

not printing correctly

not moving paper

Due to the extreme complexity of the laser printer's paper handling system, **paper jams** are a common problem. This problem tends to increase in frequency as the printer's components wear from use. Basically, paper jams occur in all three main sections of the printer. These sections are:

paper jams

- the **pickup area**
- the **registration area**
- the **fusing area**

pickup area

registration area

fusing area

If the rubber separation pad in the pickup area is worn excessively, more than one sheet of paper may be drawn into the printer causing it to jam.

> **TEST TIP**
>
> Memorize places where paper jams are likely to occur in a laser printer.

duplexers

collators

If additional paper handling features, such as **duplexers** (for double-sided copying) and **collators** (for sorting) are added to the printer, they will contribute to the possibility of jams as they wear. Paper problems can also cause jams to occur. Using paper that is too heavy or too thick can result in jams, as can overloading paper trays. Similarly, using the wrong type of paper can defeat the separation pad and allow multiple pages to be drawn into the printer. In this case, the multiple sheets may move through the printer together, or they may result in a jam. Using coated paper stock can be hazardous since the coating may melt or catch fire.

TEST TIP

Remember that paper jams in a laser printer can be caused by incorrect paper settings.

WARNING

Laser printer dangers—Unlike other printer types, the laser printer tends to have several high-voltage and high-temperature hazards inside it. To get the laser printer into a position where you can observe its operation, it will be necessary to defeat some interlock sensors. This action will place you in potential contact with the high-voltage, high-temperature areas mentioned above. Take great care when working inside the laser printer.

TEST TIP

Be aware that laser printers can be a source of electrocution, eye damage (from the laser), and burns (from the fuser assembly).

The following are symptoms of laser printer problems:

- Printer dead: power on, but no printing
- The print on the page is light, or washed out
- A blank page is produced
- Stains, or black dust, on paper
- Vertical lines on paper
- The printer will not load paper
- Paper jams in printer
- A paper jam has been cleared, and the unit still indicates a jam is present

Laser Printer Configuration Checks

configure the computer

configure the printer

configure the software

Like other complex peripheral equipment, laser printers must be configured for the desired operational characteristics. The printer is an extension of the computer system and, therefore, must be part of the overall configuration. In order to make the system function as a unit, **configure the computer**, **configure the printer**,and **configure the software**. Review and record the computer's configuration information for use in setting up the printer and software. Configure the printer with the parameters that you want it to use, record these settings, and then set up the software to match. Consult the printer's user's manual for configuration information specific to setting up that particular printer.

Laser Printer Hardware Checks

Variations in the hardware organization of different laser printers makes it impossible to write a general troubleshooting routine that can be applied to all of them without being specific to one model. The following troubleshooting discussions are general, and will require that the user do some interpretation to apply them to a specific laser printer.

Fortunately, laser printer hardware has become highly modularized, as shown in Figures 6-22 and 6-23. This allows entire sections of hardware to be checked by changing a single module. Unfortunately, the mechanical gear train and sensor systems are not usually parts included in the modules. Therefore, their operation will need to be checked individually.

Printer Is Dead or Partially Disabled

As usual, when the printer appears to be dead, the power supply is suspected. Again, as usual, the power supply can affect the operation of basically every section of the printer. In the laser printer, this is particularly complicated, since there are three types of power being delivered to the various printer components.

If the printer does not start up, check all of the normal, power supply-related check points (i.e., **power cord**, **power outlet**, **internal fuses**, etc.). If the printer's fans and lights are working, other components that are associated with a defective power supply include:

power cord
power outlet
internal fuses

- Main motor and gear train
- High-voltage corona wires
- Drum assembly
- Fusing rollers

There are four basic reasons why the main motor may not run, when the printer is supposed to print. These include:

- the portion of the power supply that supplies the motor is defective
- the control circuitry is not sending the enabling signals to turn the motor on
- the motor is dead
- the gear train is bound up, and will not let the motor turn

In the latter case, there should be sounds from the fan running, and lights on the control panel. Isolate the failure, and troubleshoot the components involved in that section.

If the high-voltage portion of the power supply that serves the corona wires and drum sections is defective, the image delivered to the page will be affected. If the high-voltage section of the power supply fails, then the transfers of toner to the drum, and then to the paper, cannot occur. The contrast control will not be operational either.

In cases of partial failure, the image produced will have a washed-out appearance. Replace the high-voltage section of the power supply and/or the drum unit. If a separate corona wire is used, let the printer cool off sufficiently, and replace the wire. Never reach into the high-voltage, high-temperature corona area while power is applied to the printer. Also, avoid placing conductive instruments in this area.

Missing Beam

laser/scanning module

If the dc portion of the power supply fails, the laser beam will not be produced, creating a **Missing Beam** error message. The components involved in this error are the **laser/scanning module**, the control board, and the dc portion of the power supply. Replace the L/S module, the dc portion of the power supply, and the main control board.

When the heating element or lamp in the fusing area does not receive adequate ac power from the power supply, the toner will not affix to the page as it should. This condition will result in smudged output.

If the printer remains in a constant state of starting up, this is equivalent to the computer not passing the POST test portion of the bootup process. If the printer starts up to an off-line condition, there is likely a problem between the printer and the host computer's interface. Disconnect the interface cable, and check to see if the printer starts up to a ready state. If so, then the problem is in the host computer, its interface, its configuration, or its signal cable. Troubleshoot the system in this direction.

If the printer still does not start up, note the error message produced, and check the sections of the printer related to that message. Check to see if the printer is connected to the system through a print-sharing device. If so, connect the printer directly to the system and try it. It is not a good practice to use laser printers with these types of devices.

A better arrangement is to install, or simply use an LPT2 port to attach an additional printer to the system. Beyond two printers, it would be better to network the printers to the system.

Print on Page Is Missing or Bad

Many of the problems encountered in laser printers are associated with missing, or defective print on the page. Normal print delivery problems fall into eight categories. These include:

- Black pages
- White (blank) pages
- Faint print
- Random specks on the page
- Faulty print at regular intervals on the page
- White lines along the page
- Print missing from some portion of the page
- Smudged print

A **black page** indicates that toner has been attracted to the entire page. This condition could be caused by a failure of the **primary corona**, the laser scanning module, or the main control board. If the laser is in a continuous on condition, the entire drum will attract toner. Likewise, if the primary corona is defective, then the uniform negative charge will not be developed on the drum to repel toner. Replace the primary corona and/or drum assembly. If the problem continues, replace the laser scanning module, and the main control board.

black page

primary corona

On the other end of the spectrum, a **white page** indicates that no information is being written on the drum. This condition basically involves the laser scanning module, the control board, and the power supply. Another white page fault occurs when the corona wire becomes broken, contaminated, or corroded, so that the attracting charge between the drum and paper is severely reduced.

white page

TEST TIP

Know what types if problems produce blank pages from a laser printer.

Specks and **stains** on the page may be caused by a worn-out cleaning pad, or a defective corona wire. If the cleaning pad is worn, it will not remove excess toner from the page during the fusing process. If the corona wire's grid does not regulate the charge level on the drum, dark spots will appear in the print. To correct these situations, replace the corona assembly by exchanging the toner cartridge or drum unit. Also, replace the cleaning pad in the fusing unit. If the page still contains specks after changing the cartridge, run several pages through the printer to clear excess toner that may have collected in the printer.

Specks

stains

White lines along the length of the page are generally caused by poorly distributed toner. Try removing the toner cartridge and gently shaking it to redistribute the toner in the cartridge. Other causes of white lines include damaged or weakened corona wires. Check and clean the corona wires, if accessible, or replace the module containing the corona wires.

White lines

Faint print in a laser printer can be caused by a number of different things. If the contrast control is set too low, or the toner level in the cartridge is low, empty, or poorly distributed, print quality can appear washed-out. Correcting these symptoms is fairly easy; adjust the contrast control, remove the toner cartridge, inspect it, shake it gently (if it is a sealed unit), and retry it. If the print does not improve, try replacing the toner cartridge. Other causes of faint print include a weakened corona wire, or a weakened high-voltage power supply that drives it. Replace the unit that contains the corona wire. Replace the high-voltage power supply. Make sure that latent voltages have been drained off the high-voltage power supply before working with it.

Faint print

Faults in the print that occur at regular intervals along the page are normally caused by mechanical problems. When roller and transport mechanisms begin to wear in the printer, bad registration and print appear in cyclic form. This can be attributed to the dimensions of cyclic components such as the drum, the developing roller in the toner cartridge, or the fusing rollers. Examine the various mechanical components for wear or defects.

Missing print is normally attributed to a bad or misaligned laser scanning module. If this module is not correctly installed, then it will not be able to deliver lines of print to the correct areas of the page. Likewise, if the scanning mirror has a defect, or is dirty, portions of the print will not be scanned on the drum. Another cause of missing print involves the toner cartridge, and low or poorly distributed toner. If the toner does not come out of the cartridge uniformly, areas of missing print can be created. A damaged or worn drum can also be a cause of repeated missing print. If areas of the drum do not hold the charge properly, toner will not transfer to it, or the page, correctly.

Missing print

Smudged print is normally a sign of a failure in the fusing section. If the fusing roller's temperature, or pressure, is not sufficient to bond the toner to the page, the print will smudge when touched. Examine the fuser unit, the power supply, and the *fusing roller's heating unit*.

Smudged print

Paper Will Not Feed or Is Jammed

paper trays

If the paper will not feed at all, then the place to begin checking is the paper tray area. The **paper trays** have a complex set of sensors, and pickup mechanisms, that must all be functioning properly to begin the paper handling. Due to the complexity of the paper pickup operation, jams are most likely to occur in this area. Check each paper tray to make sure that there is paper in it, and that it has the correct size of paper in it. Each tray in a laser printer has a set of tabs that contact sensor switches to tell the control circuitry that the tray is installed, and what size paper is in it. A mechanical arm and photodetector are used to sense the presence of paper in the tray. If these switches are set incorrectly, the printer could print a page that was sized incorrectly for the actual paper size. The various paper tray sensors are illustrated in Figure 6-36.

TEST TIP

Be aware of the consequences of incorrectly setting the paper tray switches in a laser printer.

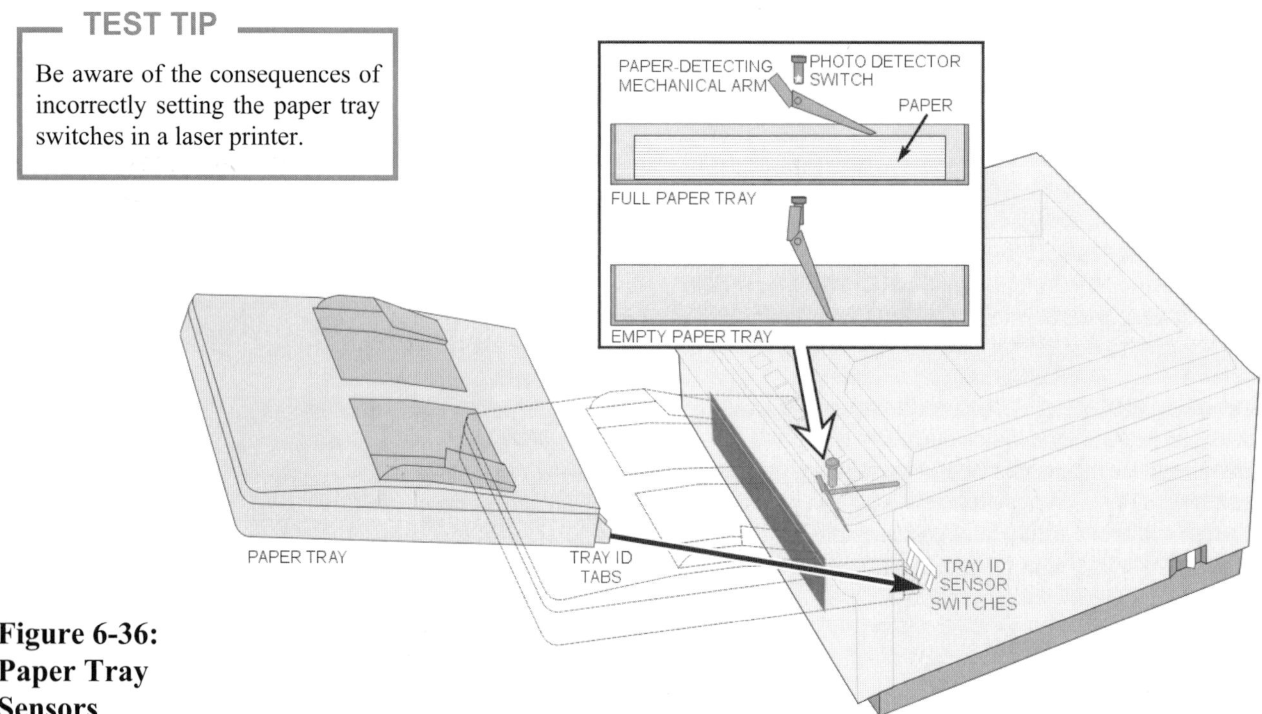

Figure 6-36: Paper Tray Sensors

Paper-Out error

pickup roller

If the printer's display panel indicates a **Paper-Out error** message, locate and actuate the paper detector by hand (lift it up). While holding the paper sensor, check the sensor switches by pressing each one individually. If the Paper Out message does not go out when any of the individual switches is pressed, replace that switch. If none of the switches show good, replace the paper sensor and arm. Also, check the spring-loaded plate in the bottom of the tray to make sure that it is forcing paper up to the **pickup roller** when the tray is installed in the printer.

The paper pickup roller must pull the top sheet of paper off the paper stack in the tray. The controller actuates a solenoid that engages the pickup roller's gear train. The pickup roller moves the paper into position against the registration rollers. If the printer's display panel shows a jam in the pickup area, check to make sure that the paper tray is functional, and then begin troubleshooting the pickup roller and main gear train. If none of the gear train is moving, then the main motor and controller board need to be checked. The power supply board may also be a cause of the problem.

If the paper feeds into the printer, but jams after the process has begun, troubleshoot the particular section of the printer where the jam is occurring — **pickup**, registration, fusing area, and **output devices** (collators and duplexers). This information is generally presented by the laser printer's display panel. Figure 6-37 describes the paper path through a typical laser printer.

pickup

output devices

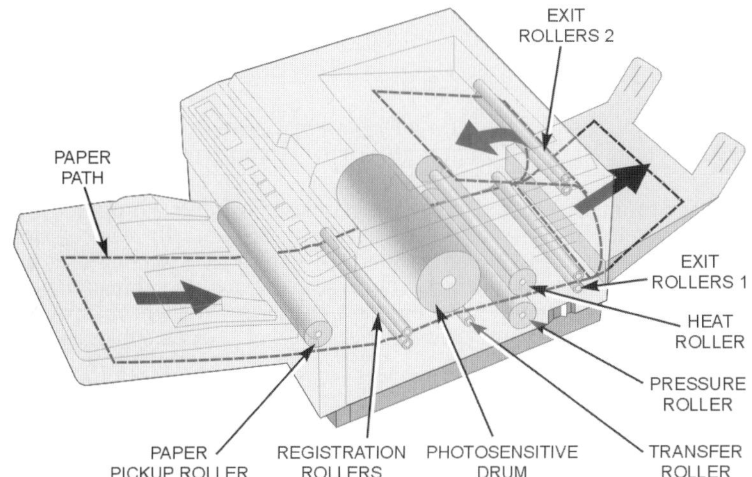

Figure 6-37: The Paper Path

In each stage, you will need to check the action of the gear train in the area. Also, inspect the various rollers in that stage for wear or damage. If the motor and gear train operate, but no action occurs in the pickup roller or registration rollers, check the solenoid and clutches for these units.

Another cause for jams is the presence of some obstruction in the paper path. Check for pieces of paper that have torn loose and lodged in the printer's paper path. In most laser printers, mechanical components are part of a replaceable module (i.e., the drum unit, the developing unit, or the fusing unit). If the motor and all the exposed gears are working, replace these units one at a time.

Many times, a paper-jam error will remain even after the paper has been removed from the laser printer. This is typically caused by an interlock error. Simply opening the printer's main access door should clear the error.

CHAPTER SUMMARY

The focus of this chapter has been printers. The opening section of the chapter presented an introduction to the different types of printers and provided a fundamental course in general printer structure and organization.

Following the general discussions of dot-matrix, ink-jet and laser printer operations, the chapter focused on common types of printer connections and configurations. The largest portion of the chapter presented troubleshooting procedures for each type of printer. Each procedure was divided into logical areas associated with typical printer symptoms.

The final section of the chapter featured preventive maintenance procedures that apply to the different printer types.

KEY POINTS REVIEW

The focus of this chapter has been printers. Review the following key points before moving into the Review and Exam Questions sections to make sure you are comfortable with each point. Afterward, answer the Review Questions that follow to verify your knowledge of the information.

- Impact printers place characters on the page by causing a hammer device to strike an inked ribbon. The ribbon, in turn, strikes the printing surface (paper).

- Several non-impact methods of printing are used in computer printers. Older, non-impact printers relied on special heat-sensitive, or chemically reactive paper, to form characters on the page. Newer methods of non-impact printing use ink droplets, squirted from a jet-nozzle device (ink-jet printers), or a combination of laser/xerographic print technologies (laser printers), to place characters on a page. Currently, the most popular non-impact printers use ink-jet or laser technologies to deliver ink to the page.

- Basically, there are two methods of creating characters on a page. One method places a character on the page that is fully shaped, and fully filled-in. This type of character is called a fully-formed character. The other method involves placing dots on the page in strategic patterns to fool the eye into seeing a character. This type of character is referred to as a dot-matrix character.

- The term font refers to variations in the size and style of characters. With true fully-formed characters, there is typically only one font available without changing the physical printing element. However, with all other printing methods, it is possible to include a wide variety of font types and sizes.

- By the very nature of their operation, printers tend to be extremely mechanical peripherals. During the printing operation, the print mechanism must be properly positioned over each character cell in sequence.

- In addition to positioning the print mechanism for printing, all printer types must feed paper through the print area. The type of paper handling mechanism in a printer is somewhat dependent on the type of form intended to be used with the printer and its speed.

- Like most other peripherals, the heart of a character printer is its interface/controller circuitry. The interface circuitry accepts data and instructions from the computer's bus systems, and provides the necessary interfacing (serial or parallel) between the computer and the printer's control circuitry.

- In some printers, the microcontroller, RAM chips or modules, and ROM/EPROM devices may be treated as FRU components.

- The components of a typical dot-matrix printer are depicted in Figure 6-8. They consist of a power supply board, a main control board, a printhead assembly, a ribbon cartridge, a paper feed motor (along with its mechanical drive gears), and a printhead positioning motor and mechanisms.

- The printhead is a collection of print wires set in an electromagnetic head unit. The printhead assembly is made up of a permanent magnet, a group of electromagnets, and a housing. In the printhead, the permanent magnet keeps the wires pulled in until electromagnets are energized, causing them to move forward.

- Ink-jet printers produce characters by squirting a precisely controlled stream of ink drops onto the paper. The drops must be controlled very precisely in terms of their aerodynamics, size, and shape, or the drop placement on the page becomes inexact, and the print quality falters.

- The laser printer modulates a highly focused laser beam to produce CRT-like raster-scan images on a rotating drum.
- As the drum is written on by the laser, it turns through the toner powder, which is attracted to the charged image on the drum.
- A typical laser printer will have sensors to determine what paper trays are installed, what size paper is in them, and whether the tray is empty. It will also use sensors to track the movement of the paper through each stage of the printer. This allows the controller to know where the page is at all times, and sequence the activities of the solenoids and clutches properly.
- Paper is specified in terms of its weight per 500 sheets at 22" x 17" (i.e., 500 sheets of 22" x 17", 21-pound bond paper weighs 21 pounds).
- Generally speaking, one of the least difficult I/O devices to add to a microcomputer system is a parallel printer. This is largely due to the fact that, from the beginning of the PC era, a parallel printer has been one of the most standard pieces of equipment to add to the system.
- Serial printers are slightly more difficult to set up, since the communication definition must be configured between the computer and the printer. The serial port will need to be configured for speed, parity type, character frame, and protocol.
- Like mice, printers require device driver programs to oversee their operation.
- Not all serial cables are created equal. In the PC world, RS-232 serial cables can take on several configurations. First of all, they may use either 9-pin or 25-pin D-shell connectors. The cable for a particular serial connection will need to have the correct type of connector at each end. Likewise, the connection scheme inside the cable can vary from printer to printer. Normally, the Transmit Data line (TXD - pin 2) from the computer is connected to the Receive Data line (RXD - pin 3) of the printer. Also, the Data Set Ready (DSR - pin 6) is typically connected to the printer's Data Terminal Ready (DTR - pin 20) pin. These connections are used as one method to control the flow of information between the system and the printer. If the printer's character buffer becomes full, it will signal the computer to hold up sending characters by deactivating this line.
- Two popular methods of implementing software flow control are Xon/Xoff and ETX/ACK. In the Xon/Xoff method, special ASCII control characters are exchanged between the printer and the computer to turn the data flow on and off. In an ETX/ACK protocol, ASCII characters for End-of-Text (ETX) and ACKnowledge (ACK) are used to control the movement of data from the port to the printer.
- The classical first step in determining the cause of any printer problem is to determine which part of the printer-related system is at fault—the host computer, the signal cable, or the printer.
- As with the dot-matrix printer, the first step in determining the cause of an ink-jet printer problem is to determine which part of the printer system is at fault—the host computer, the signal cable, or the printer.
- You can also configure the basic appearance of color and grayscale images produced by the ink-jet printer. A color ink-jet printer uses four ink colors to produce color images. These are Cyan, Magenta, Yellow, and Black (referred to as CMYK color). To create other colors, the printer prints a predetermined percentage of the basic colors in close proximity to each other.
- The single item in an ink-jet printer that requires the most attention is the ink cartridge (or cartridges). As the ink cartridge empties, the printing will eventually become faint and uneven, and the resolution of the print on the page will diminish.

- Many of the problems encountered in laser printers are similar to those found in other printer types. For example, notice that most of the symptoms listed in the following section relate to the printer not printing, or not printing correctly, and not moving paper through the printer.

- Unlike other printer types, the laser printer tends to have several high-voltage and high-temperature hazards inside it. To get the laser printer into a position where you can observe its operation, it will be necessary to defeat some interlock sensors. This action will place you in potential contact with the high-voltage, high-temperature areas mentioned above. Take great care when working inside the laser printer.

REVIEW QUESTIONS

The following questions test your knowledge of the material presented in this chapter.

1. Referring to the Hardware Checks sections of the Troubleshooting procedures for all three printer types, describe three general types of problems common to all printers and the additional types of problems that dot-matrix and ink-jet printers have.
2. What common transmission parameters must be set up for a serial printer interface?
3. Describe the purpose for using pin-feed mechanisms to move paper through the printer.
4. Describe the reason for using tractor-feed paper handling.
5. If the resolution of an ink-jet printer becomes unacceptable, what action should be taken?
6. Describe the function of the fuser assembly in a laser printer.

7. Describe the function of the primary corona (conditioning roller) in a laser printer.
8. If a laser printer continues to show a paper jam problem after the paper has been cleared, what type of problem is indicated, and what action should be taken?

9. List the three primary areas where paper jams occur in a laser printer, as well as any other areas where jams are likely to occur.
10. Describe two methods used by ink-jet printers to put ink on the page.

11. Does a successful self-test indicate that the printer is not the cause of the problem? List the parts of the system that can still be problem causes if the self-test runs successfully.
12. How does a dot-matrix printer actually deliver ink to a page?

13. What functions does the printer's controller typically perform?
14. List four things that can be damaging to the photosensitive surface of the laser printer's drum.
15. List the basic components of an ink-jet printer.

EXAM QUESTIONS

1. List three common pin configurations for dot-matrix printers.
   a. 10, 20, and 30 pins
   b. 5, 10, and 15 pins
   c. 9, 18, and 24 pins
   d. 3, 6, and 9 pins
2. Name the four basic components of a Hewlett Packard laser printer cartridge.
   a. Laser, toner supply, drum, and fuser
   b. Toner supply, corona wire, drum assembly, and developing roller
   c. Laser, toner supply, corona wire, and drum
   d. Toner supply, corona wire, drum assembly, and fuser
3. What is the purpose of the primary corona wire in a laser printer?
   a. It cleans the paper as it enters the printer.
   b. It conditions the drum for printing.
   c. It transfers toner from the drum to the paper.
   d. It fuses the toner to the paper.
4. What is the first action that should be taken, if the print generated by a dot-matrix printer becomes faded or uneven?
   a. Change the ribbon cartridge.
   b. Add ink.
   c. Adjust the print carriage.
   d. Add toner.
5. What is the first action that should be taken if the print generated by a laser printer becomes faded or uneven?
   a. Adjust the contrast control.
   b. Change the ink cartridge.
   c. Check the toner cartridge.
   d. Adjust the print mechanism.
6. What type of electrical charge must be placed on the corona wire to transfer toner from the drum to the paper?
   a. Negative
   b. None
   c. Neutral
   d. Positive
7. List the six stages of a typical laser printer.
   a. Pick up, registration, transfer, printing, fusing, and finishing
   b. Pick up, conditioning, transfer, developing, fusing, and finishing
   c. Cleaning, conditioning, writing, developing, transferring, and fusing
   d. Cleaning, registration, writing, transferring, fusing, and finishing

8. List the fundamental parts of a dot-matrix printer.
   a. Power supply, microprocessor, tractor feed motor, printhead mechanism, and printhead positioning motor
   b. Power supply, interface board, paper feed motor, printhead mechanism, printhead positioning motor, and sensors
   c. Interface board, ink cartridge, printhead mechanism, printhead positioning motor, sensors
   d. Controller, paper feed motor, ribbon cartridge, and printhead positioning motor
9. What type of ink delivery system is normally found in ink-jet printers built for the personal computers?
   a. Drop-on-demand ink delivery
   b. Continuous stream ink delivery
   c. Impact ink delivery
   d. Compact spray ink delivery
10. Describe what the specification for 60-pound bond paper means.
   a. 100 22"x 17" sheets weigh 60 pounds
   b. 500 8.5"x 11" sheets weigh 60 pounds
   c. 100 11"x 17" sheets weigh 60 pounds
   d. 500 22"x 17" sheets weigh 60 pounds

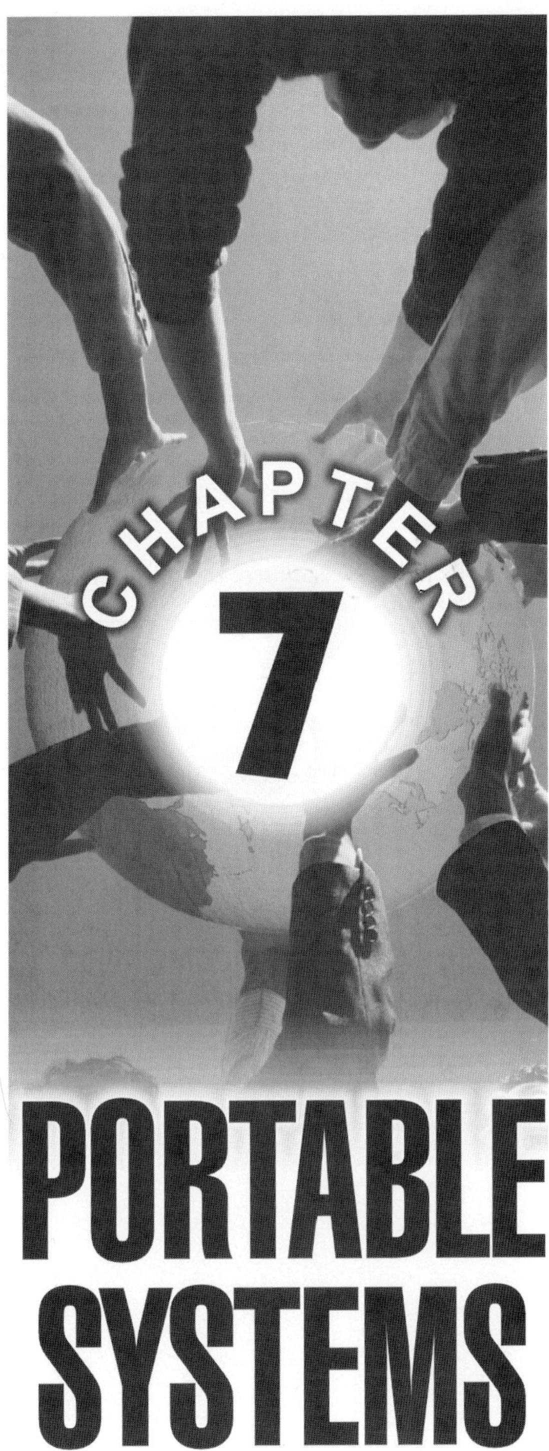

PORTABLE SYSTEMS

OBJECTIVES

OBJECTIVES

Upon completion of this chapter and its related lab procedures you will be able to perform the following tasks:

1. Identify the unique components of portable systems and their unique problems.
2. Describe basic procedures for adding and removing FRU modules associated with portable systems.
3. Identify proper procedures for identifying installing peripheral devices commonly used with portable systems.
4. Describe the applications that the three types of PCMCIA cards can be used to perform.
5. Discuss and recognize the different PCMCIA devices currently available.

CHAPTER 7

PORTABLE SYSTEMS

INTRODUCTION

Portable computers represent a large and growing portion of the personal computer market. Therefore, the computer technician must be aware of how they vary from traditional desktop units and how their service requirements are different from the norm.

Several of the topics in the A+ Core Hardware objective 1.0 – Installation, Configuration and Upgrading, refer to portable computers.

Examples of these topics include:

- LCDs (portables)
- AC adapters
- DC controllers
- PC cards
- Infrared devices
- Batteries
- Hard drives
- Pointing devices
- PDA (Personal Digital Assistants)
- Docking stations
- Port replicators
- Type I, II, III PC cards
- Memory

portable PCs

luggables

PORTABLE COMPUTER TYPES

The original portables were called **luggables**. Although they were smaller than desktop computers they were not truly convenient to transport. The first portables included small, built-in CRT displays and detachable keyboards. Their batteries and CRT equipment made them extremely bulky and heavy to carry. Therefore, they never really had a major impact on the PC market. However, they set the stage for the development of future portable computer systems. Examples of different portable computer designs are shown in Figure 7-1.

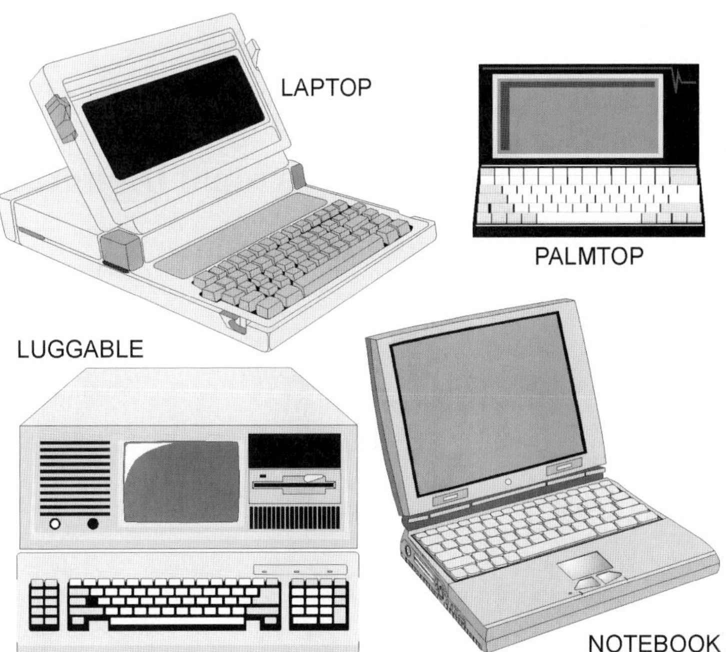

Figure 7-1: Portable Computers

laptops

With advancements in battery design and the advent of usable, large-screen, flat-panel displays, the first truly portable PCs, referred to as **laptops**, were introduced. These units featured all-in-one, AT-compatible PC boards. The system board included the I/O and video controller functions. Laptops featured built-in keyboards and hinged LCD display panels that flipped up from the case for use. They also used an external power supply and a removable, rechargeable battery.

The battery life of typical laptops was minimal and their size was still large enough to be inconvenient at times. However, the inclusion of LCD viewing screens and external power supply/battery arrangements made them useful enough to spawn a healthy portable computer market. Even though these units could weigh in excess of seven pounds, the user could easily take work from the office to the home, or to a hotel room while traveling. They could also get work done at traditionally non-productive times, such as on long automobile or airplane rides. An occasional game of computerized cards or golf was always at hand as well.

notebook computers

Continued advancements in integrated circuitry and peripheral technology allowed the PC's circuitry to be reduced. This allowed portable sizes to be reduced further so that they could achieve sizes of 8.75"d *x* 11"w *x* 2.25"h and smaller. Portables in this size range are referred to as **notebook computers**. The weight of a typical notebook dropped down to 5 or 6 pounds.

sub-notebook PCs

palmtop PCs

Even smaller **sub-notebook PCs** have been created by moving the disk drives outside of the case and reducing the size of the display screen. These units tend to be slightly thinner than traditional notebooks and weigh in the neighborhood of 3 to 4 pounds. Very small sub-notebooks, referred to as **palmtop PCs**, were produced for a short time in the pre-Windows days. These units limited everything as far as possible to reach sizes of 7"w *x* 4"d *x* 1"h and weights of 1 to 2 pounds. Sub-notebooks have decreased in popularity as notebooks have continued to decrease in weight and cost.

The palmtop market has diminished due to the difficulty of running Windows on such small displays. Human ergonomics also come into play when dealing with smaller notebooks. The smaller display screens become difficult to see and keyboards become more difficult to use as the size of the keys decreases.

Personal Digital Assistants

ergonomics

The palmtop market was diminished for some time because of the difficulty of running Windows on such small displays. Human **ergonomics** also come into play when dealing with smaller notebooks. The smaller display screens become difficult to see and keyboards become more difficult to use as the size of the keys decreases.

Personal Digital Assistants (PDAs)

However, the market was revived by the introduction of palm tops known as **Personal Digital Assistants** (**PDAs**). Figure 7-2 depicts a typical PDA. These handheld devices use a special stylus, referred to as a pen, to input data and selections instead of a keyboard or mouse. Basically the PDA is an electronic time management system that may also include computer applications such as word processors, spreadsheets, and databases.

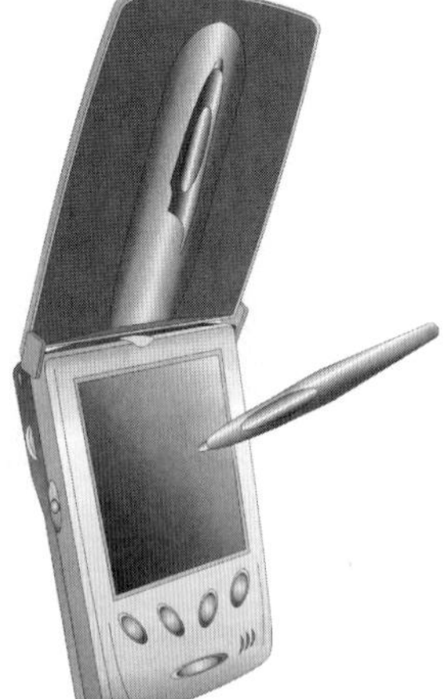

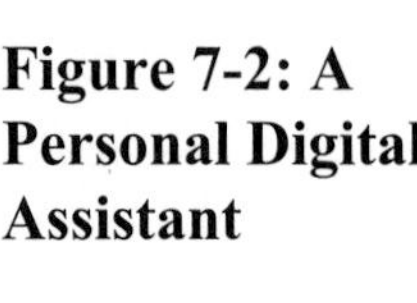

Figure 7-2: A Personal Digital Assistant

The PDA's display is a touch-screen **Liquid Crystal Display** (**LCD**) that works in conjunction with a graphical user interface running on top of a specialized operating system. Some PDAs employ a highly-modified, embedded (on a chip) version of the Microsoft Windows operating system, called **Windows CE**, as their operating system. These systems are particularly well suited for exchanging and synchronizing information with larger Windows-based systems.

Liquid Crystal Display (LCD)

Windows CE

Two items have made PDAs popular: their size and their ability to communicate with the user's desktop computer system. Early PDAs exchanged information with the full-sized computer through serial port connections. Newer models communicate with the user's desktop computer through high-speed USB ports, infrared communications links, or docking stations.

Portable Drawbacks

Portable drawbacks—From a service point of view, the greatest drawback of portable computers is that conventions and compatibility disappear.

The continued minimization of the system comes at a cost. Most notably, the number of I/O ports, memory, and disk drive expansion capabilities are limited. In addition, there is no chance to use common, full-sized options adapter cards that are inexpensive and easy to find.

One of the biggest problems for portable computers is heat buildup inside the case. Since conventional power supplies (and their fans) are not included in portable units, separate fans must be designed into portables to carry the heat out of the unit. The closeness of the portable's components and the small amount of free air space inside their cases also adds to heat-related design problems.

The internal PC boards of the portable computer are designed to fit around the nuances of the portable case and its components, rather than to match a standard design with standard spacing and connections. Therefore, interchangeability of parts with other machines or makers goes by the wayside. The only source of most portable computer parts, with the exception of PC cards and disk drive units, is the original manufacturer. Even the battery case may be proprietary. If the battery dies, you must hope that the original maker has a supply of that particular model.

Access to the notebook's internal components is normally challenging. Each case design has different methods for assembly and disassembly of the unit. Even the simplest upgrade task can be difficult with a notebook computer. Although adding RAM and options to desktop and tower units is a relatively easy and straightforward process, the same tasks in notebook computers can be difficult.

In some notebooks, it is necessary to disassemble the two halves of the case and remove the keyboard in order to add RAM modules to the system. In other portables, the hinged display unit must be removed to disassemble the unit. Once inside the notebook you may find several of the components are hidden behind other units. Figure 7-3 demonstrates a relatively simple disassembly process for a notebook unit.

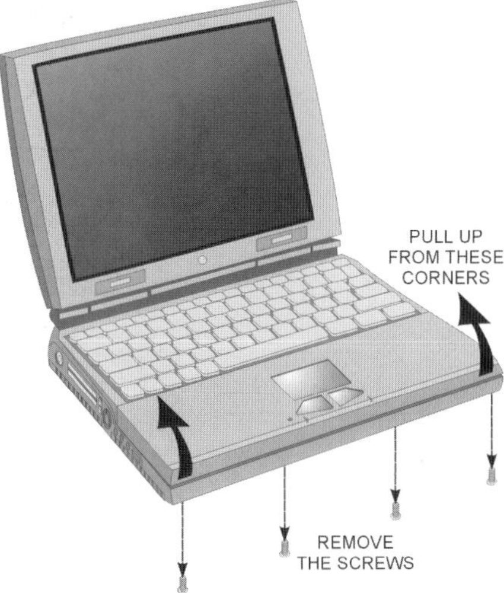

Figure 7-3: Disassembling a Notebook Computer

In this example, a panel in front of the keyboard can be removed to gain access to the notebook's internal user-serviceable components. Four screws along the front edge of the unit's lower body must be removed. Afterward, the LCD panel is opened and the front panel of the notebook's chassis is pulled up and away to expose a portion of the unit's interior.

To overcome the shortfalls of miniaturization, a wide variety of specialty items aimed at the portable computer market have emerged. Items such as small 2-1/2 inch hard disk drives have been developed especially for use in portable computers. Other such items include small internal and external modems, special network adapters that plug into parallel printer ports, docking stations (or ports), special carrying cases and briefcases, detachable key pads, clip-on or built-in trackballs, and touch-sensitive mouse pads.

In addition, a sequence of special credit card-like adapter cards has been designed expressly for use with portable computers. These adapters are standardized through the Personal Computer Memory Card International Association (PCMCIA) and are commonly referred to as PC cards. The different types of PCMCIA cards are covered in greater detail later in this chapter.

Inside Portables

Portable computers have two ideal characteristics: They are compact and lightweight. Portable computer designers work constantly to decrease the size and power consumption of all the computer's components. Special low-power-consumption ICs and disk drives have been developed to extend their battery life.

Likewise, their cases have been designed to be as small as possible while providing as many standard features as possible. Figure 7-4 shows the inside of a typical portable computer.

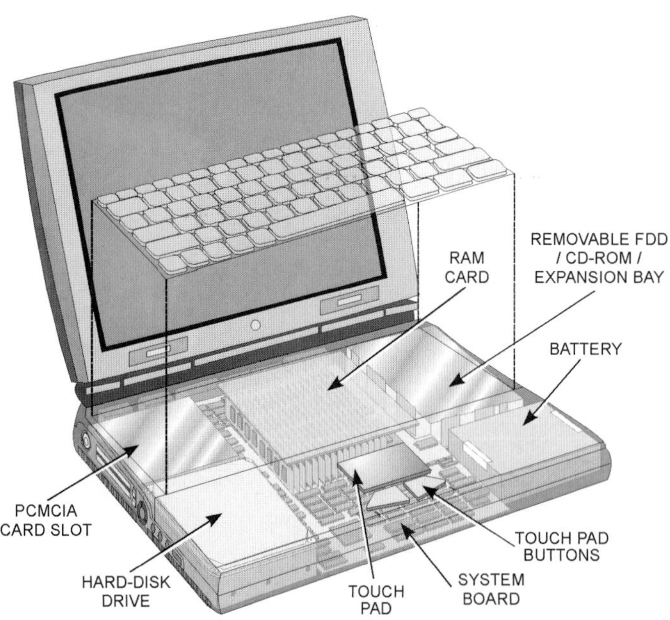

Figure 7-4: Inside a Portable Computer

Notice how the components are interconnected by the design. The system board is designed so that it wraps around other components whose form factors cannot be altered—such as the disk drive units. The components also tend to be layered in portable designs. Disk drives cover portions of the system board, while the keyboard unit covers nearly everything. The internal battery may slide into a cutout area of the system board, or more likely, it may be located beneath the system board.

System Boards

A typical notebook system board is depicted in Figure 7-5. The first thing you should notice about it is its unusual shape. As noted earlier, system boards for portable computers are not designed to fit a standardized form factor. Instead they are designed to fit around all of the components that must be installed in the system. Therefore, system boards used in portable computers tend to be proprietary to the model they are designed for. Mounting hole positions are determined by where they will best suit the placement of the other system components.

The second item to notice is that none of the "standard" expansion slots, or adapter cards are present on the portable's system board. These system board designs typically include the standard MI/O and video circuitry as an integral part of the board. They also provide the physical connections for the unit's parallel and serial I/O ports, as well as on-board connectors for the disk drives, display unit, and keyboard units.

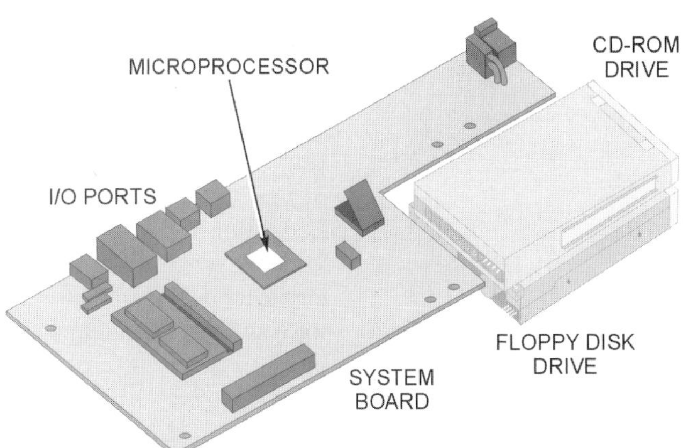

Figure 7-5: Typical Notebook System Board

The computer's external I/O connections, such as serial- and parallel-port connectors, are arranged on the system board so that they align with the corresponding openings in the portable case. It would be highly unlikely that a system board from another portable would match these openings. On the maintenance side, a blown parallel-port circuit would require that the entire system board be replaced in order to correct the problem. In a desktop unit, a simple I/O card could be installed in an expansion slot to overcome such a situation.

The I/O ports included in most notebook computers consist of a single parallel port, a single serial port, an external VGA monitor connector, an external keyboard connector, and a docking port expansion bus. Some models can be found with a second serial-port connector, but they are not common.

Figure 7-6 shows the port connections associated with most portable systems. This example places the connectors on the back of the unit, just as they would be in a typical desktop. Other units may place some of these connectors on each side of the unit instead. High-end portables may include an array of other connectors, such as external microphone and speaker jacks. Some connectors may be hidden behind hinged doors for protection. These doors normally snap closed.

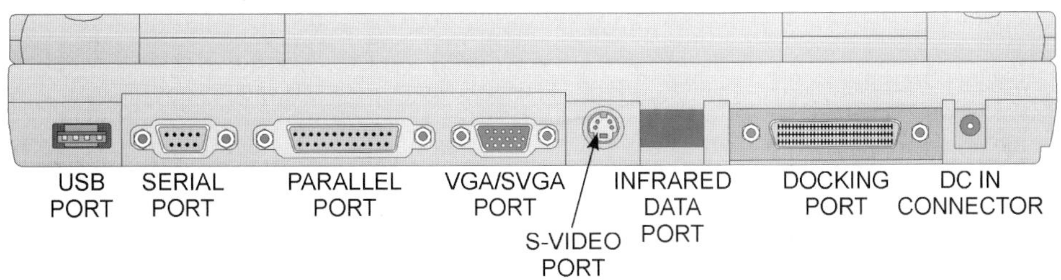

Figure 7-6: Notebook Backpanel Connections

Microprocessors

The portable computer market is so large that it even influences the microprocessor and IC manufacturers. They produce special low-power-consumption microprocessors and chipsets just for portable computer systems. These power-saving IC devices are typically identified by an "SL" designation (i.e., 80486SLC).

mobile Pentium processors

In Chapter 2—*Advanced System Boards*, it was pointed out that Pentium microprocessors produce large amounts of heat, even by desktop standards. Most of the portables currently in the market are based on Pentium devices. To minimize the heat buildup condition, Intel has produced a complete line of **mobile Pentium processors** for use in portable systems. Mobile devices differ from standard microprocessor devices in terms of both their internal construction and their external packaging. In mobile microprocessors, both design aspects have been optimized to provide minimum size and power consumption, as well as maximum heat reduction.

Voltage Reduction Technology

Tape Carrier Package (TCP)

Figure 7-7 depicts a mobile Pentium MMX processor. It is constructed using Intel's **Voltage Reduction Technology,** which enables the processor to run at lower core voltages (1.8 - 2.0 Vdc) and, thereby, consume less energy, and generate less heat. The package style created for the mobile Pentium is referred to as a **Tape Carrier Package** (**TCP**). The microprocessor chip is embedded in a polyimide film (tape) that has been laminated with a copper foil. The leads of the IC are etched into the foil and attached to the processor.

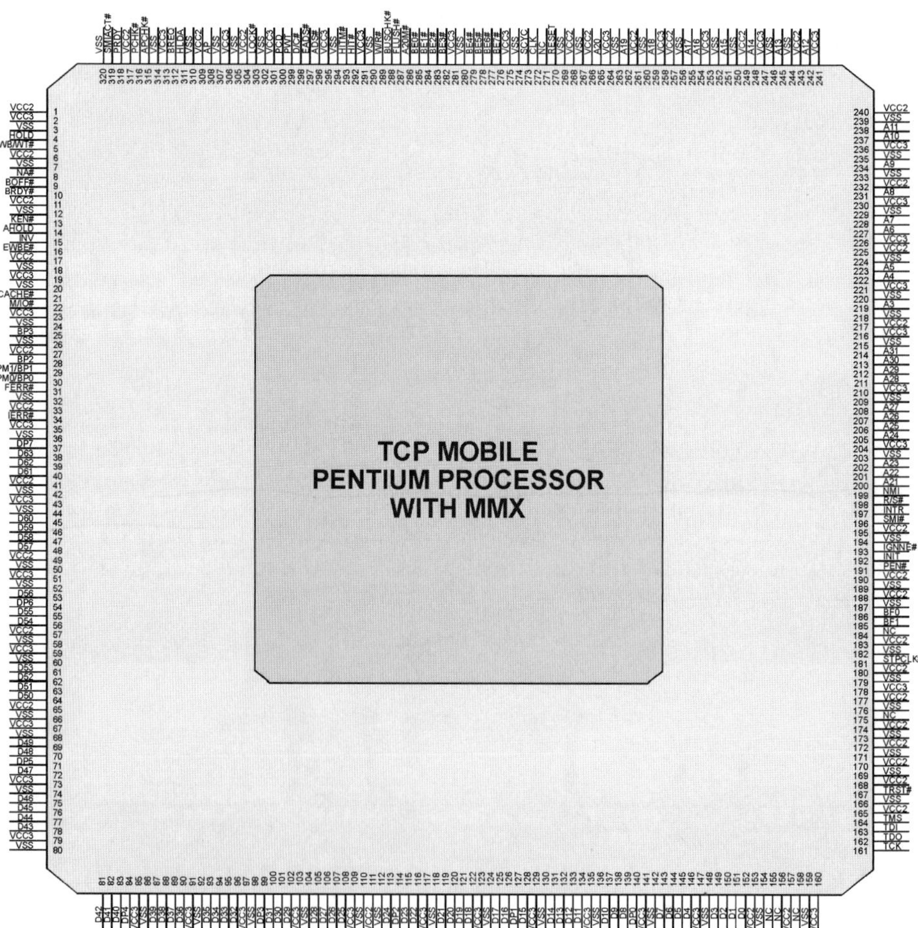

Figure 7-7:
The Mobile Pentium

The tape package arrangement makes the mobile package much smaller and lighter than the PGA and SPGA packages used with the standard Pentium devices. It also mounts directly to the PC board instead of plugging into a bulky heavy socket. A special insertion machine cuts the strip of microprocessors into individual, 24mm units as it is soldered to the system board. The system board furnishes a heat sink area beneath the processor that helps to dissipate heat. A layer of thermal conductive paste is applied to this connection prior to the soldering process to increase the heat transfer away from the processor. This design enables the full-featured Pentium processor to run at competitive speeds without additional heat sinks and fan modules. The cross section of the complete mobile Pentium attachment is depicted in Figure 7-8.

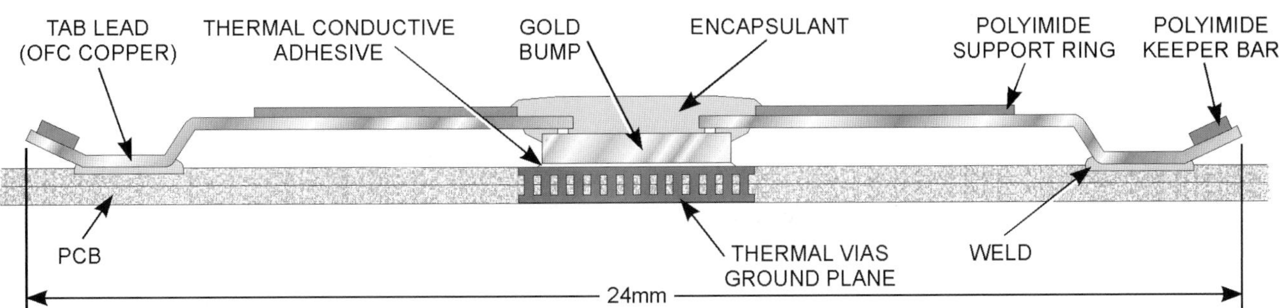

Figure 7-8: The Mobile Pentium Installation

The attachment of the mobile microprocessor to a system board makes the arrangement permanent for all practical purposes. To allow for microprocessor upgrading, portable system boards often employ mobile processors mounted on plug-in daughter boards, or modules. Intel has produced two Pentium plug-in variations. It supplies mobile Pentiums on a 4"x2.5"x0.3" **mobile module**, referred to as an **MMO**. This module is attached to the system board via screws and plugs into it through a 280-pin connector. The other Intel module is a mini-cartridge for the Pentium II.

mobile module (MMO)

Memory

In compact computers, memory and memory expansion hardware standards don't exist. Some designs use standard SIMM or DIMM modules for RAM, while others use proprietary memory modules. Still other designs rely on memory card modules for additional RAM. The key to upgrading or replacing RAM in a portable can be found in its user's guide. Only memory modules recommended by the portable manufacturer should be installed, and only in the configurations suggested.

Drives

Smaller 2.5" form factor hard drives, low-profile 3.5" floppy drives, and combination FDD/CD-ROM drives have been developed to address the portable computer market's need for compact devices. Older portables included one FDD and one HDD as standard equipment. Newer models tend to include a CD-ROM drive and an HDD as standard internal units. Figure 7-9 shows the placement of drives in a high-end notebook unit that includes one of each drive type.

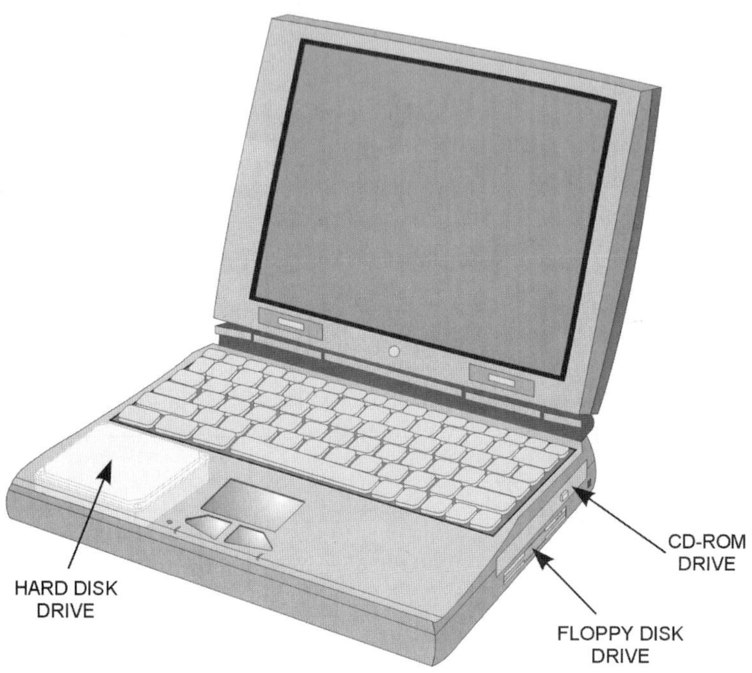

Figure 7-9: Portable Disk Drives

Newer portable models include swappable drive bays that allow the combination of internal drives in the unit to be changed as dictated by the work being performed. In some units, a disk drive that is not needed for a particular task may be removed and replaced by an extra battery.

There are basically three considerations that should be observed when replacing disk drives in a portable. These are its physical size and layout, its power consumption, and whether the BIOS supports it.

BASIC I/O

Personal computer users are creatures of habit as much as anyone else. Therefore, as they moved toward portable computers, they wanted the types of features they had come to expect from their larger desktops and towers. These features typically include an alphanumeric keyboard, a video display, and a pointing device.

Portable Display Types

Notebook and laptop computers use non-CRT displays, such as **Liquid Crystal Display (LCD)** and **gas-plasma panels**. These display systems are well suited to the portability needs of portable computers. They are much lighter and more compact than CRT monitors and require much less electrical energy to operate. Both types of display units can be operated from batteries.

Liquid Crystal Display (LCD)

gas-plasma panels

Portable computers continue to gain popularity due to their ability to travel with the user. This has been made possible by the development of different flat-panel display technologies. Early attempts at developing portable microcomputers used small CRTs that minimized the size of the unit. However, these units quickly gained the label of luggables, due to their weight. The high-voltage circuitry required to operate a CRT device is heavy by nature, and could be reduced only slightly.

> **TEST TIP**
>
> Know that notebook display panels are powered by low-voltage DC power sources such as a battery or converter.

Liquid Crystal Displays

> **Liquid Crystal Displays**—The most common flat-panel displays used with portable PC's are Liquid Crystal Displays. They are relatively thin, flat, and lightweight, and require very little power to operate. In addition to reduced weight and improved portability, these displays offer better reliability and longer life than CRT units.

The LCD, illustrated in Figure 7-10, is constructed by placing **thermotropic** liquid crystal material between two sheets of glass. A set of electrodes is attached to each sheet of glass. Horizontal (row) electrodes are attached to one glass plate, while vertical (column) electrodes are fitted to the other plate. These electrodes are transparent and let light pass through. A **picture element**, or **pixel**, is created in the liquid crystal material at each spot where a row and a column electrode intersect. A special plate called a **polarizer** is added to the outside of each glass plate. There is one polarizer on the front, and one on the back of the display.

thermotropic

picture element

pixel

polarizer

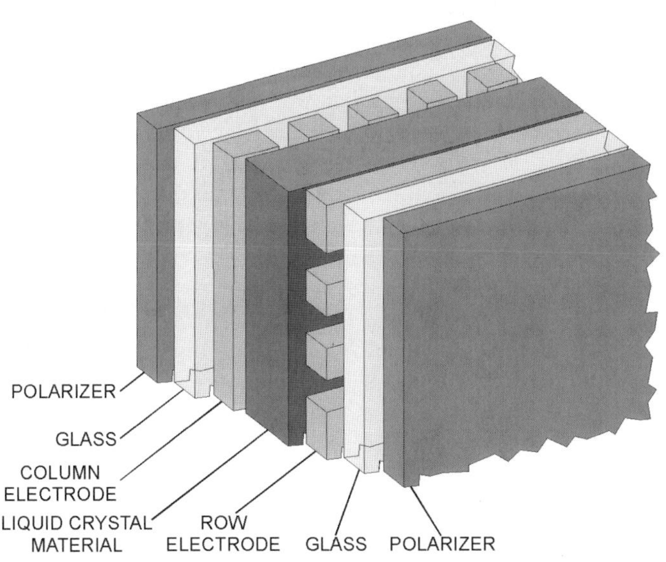

Figure 7-10: LCD Construction

The display is designed so that when the pixel is off, the molecules of the liquid crystal twist from one edge of the material to the other, as depicted in Figure 7-11. The spiral effect created by the twist polarizes light, and prevents it from passing through the display. When an electric field is created between a row and column electrode, the molecules move, lining up perpendicular to the front of the display. This allows light to pass through the display, producing a single dot on the screen.

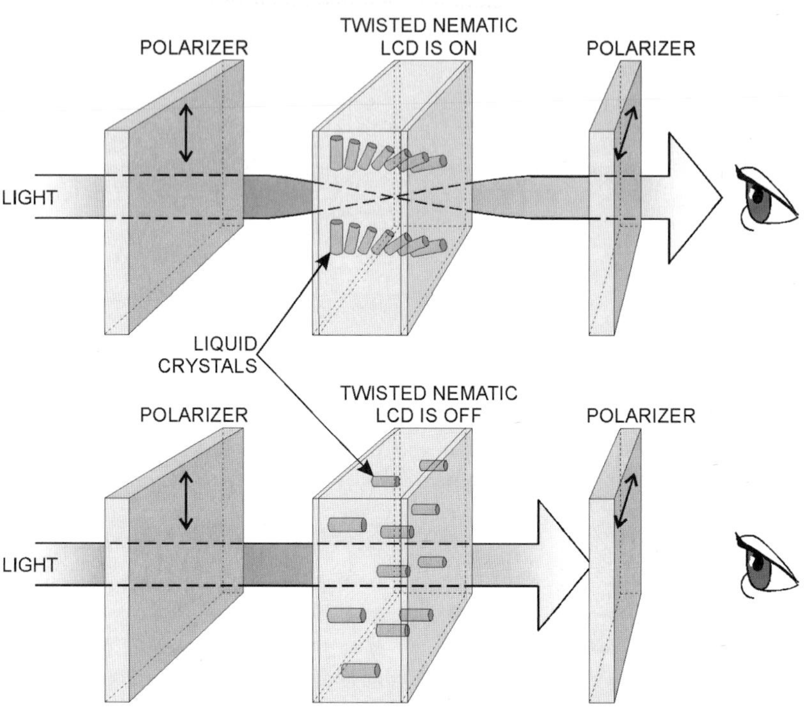

Figure 7-11: LCD Operation

back lighting

Depending on the orientation of the polarizers, the energized pixels can be made to look like a dark spot on a light screen, or a light dot on a dark screen. In most notebook computers, the display is lit from behind the panel. This is referred to as **back lighting**. Some units are constructed so that the display can be removed from the body of the computer, and used with an overhead projector to display computer output on a wall or large screen.

dual scan

passive matrix

Color Super-Twist Nematic (CSTN)

Double-layer Super-Twist Nematic (DSTN)

Because no current passes through the display to light the pixels, the power consumption of LCD displays is very low. The screen is scanned using IC multiplexers and drivers to activate the panel's row and column electrodes. The scanning circuitry addresses each row sequentially, column by column. Although the column electrode is activated for a short portion of each horizontal scan, the pixels appear to be continuously lit because the scanning rate is very high. The electrodes can be controlled (turned on and off) using standard TTL voltage levels. This translates into less control circuitry required to operate the panel. LCDs using this type of construction are referred to as **dual scan**, or **passive matrix** displays. Advanced passive matrix technologies are referred to as **Color Super-Twist Nematic (CSTN)** and **Double-layer Super-Twist Nematic (DSTN)** displays.

An improved LCD approach is similar in design to the passive matrix designs, except that it adds a transistor at each of the matrix' row-column junctions to improve switching times. This technology produces an LCD display type referred to as an **active matrix display**. In these displays, a small current is sent to the transistor through the row-column lines. The energized transistor conducts a larger current, which, in turn, is used to activate the pixel seen on the screen. The active matrix is produced by using **Thin Film Transistor** (**TFT**) arrays to create between one and four transistors for each pixel on a flexible, transparent film. TFT displays tend to be brighter and sharper than dual scan displays. However, they also tend to require more power to operate and to be more expensive.

active matrix display

Thin Film Transistor (TFT)

Color LCD displays are created by adding a three-color filter to the panel. Each pixel in the display corresponds to a red, blue, or green dot on the filter. Activating a pixel behind a blue dot on the filter will produce a blue dot on the screen. Like color CRT displays, the dot color on the screen of the color LCD panel is established by controlling the **relative intensities** of a three-dot (RGB) pixel cluster.

relative intensities

The construction of LCD displays prevents them from providing multiple resolution options like an adapter-driven CRT display can. The resolution of the LCD display is dictated by the construction of the LCD panel.

The life and usefulness of the portable's LCD panel can be extended through proper care and handling. The screen should be cleaned periodically with a glass cleaner and a soft, lint-free cloth. Spray the cleaner on the cloth and then wipe the screen. Never spray the cleaner directly on the screen. Also, avoid scratching the surface of the screen. It is relatively easy to damage the front polarizer of the display. Take care to remove any liquid droplets from the screen since they can cause permanent staining. After cleaning, allow 30 minutes for complete drying.

The screen should be shielded from bright sun light and heat sources. Moving the computer from a cooler location to a hot location can cause damaging moisture to condense inside the housing (including the display). It should also be kept away from ultraviolet light sources and extremely cold temperatures. The liquid crystals can freeze in extremely cold weather. A freeze/thaw cycle may damage the display and cause it to be unusable.

Gas-plasma Displays

The **gas-plasma display** is similar to the LCD panel in physical size and operation. It is a gas-filled, sealed glass enclosure. The type of gas used is most typically neon, or a mixture of neon and argon. The enclosure has small wire electrodes arranged in a row-column matrix like the LCD panel. Where the electrodes intersect, a pixel is created. When one row and one column are energized, the gas around that intersection will discharge, giving off light and producing one dot on the screen. The voltage required for this discharge is usually less than 200 volts. The rows and columns are multiplexed and scanned to produce one full screen of information. The relatively high power consumption of the gas-plasma display is one of the major drawbacks that has caused them to be less desirable than the LCD display in notebook computer designs. The other drawback of the gas-plasma display is that it is a monochrome (one color) display. The inability of the gas-plasma display to compete with high-quality color LCD displays has also placed them at a great disadvantage.

gas-plasma display

Keyboards

> The most widely used notebook keyboard is the 84-key version. The keys are slightly smaller and shorter than those found in full-size keyboards. A number of keys or key functions may be combined or deleted from a notebook keyboard.

A typical notebook keyboard is illustrated in Figure 7-12.

Figure 7-12: 84-Key Notebook Keyboard

Fn

Since portable keyboards tend to be more compact than the detachable models used with desktop units, many of its keys are typically given dual or triple functions. The portable keyboard normally contains an **Fn** function key. This key activates special functions in the portable, such as display brightness and contrast. Other common Fn functions include Suspend mode activation and LCD/external-CRT device selection.

Win keys

application key

Newer keyboard models may also include left and right Windows keys (**Win keys**), and an **application key,** as identified in Figure 7-13. The WIN keys are located next to the ALT keys and provide specialized Windows functions, as described in Table 7-1. Similarly, the application key is located near the right WIN key, or the CTRL key, and provides context-sensitive help for most applications.

Figure 7-13: Win and Application Keys

KEY STROKE	ACTION
WIN/E	Start Windows Explorer
WIN/F	Start Find files or folders
Ctrl/WIN/F	Find the computer
WIN/M	Minimize All
Shift/WIN/M	Undo Minimize All
WIN/R	Display Run dialog box
WIN/F1	Start Help
WIN/Tab	Move through Taskbar objects
WIN/Break	Show System Properties dialog box

Table 7-1: Win Key Definitions

Most portables offer standard connectors to enable full-size keyboards and VGA monitors to be plugged in, as shown in Figure 7-14. The VGA connector is usually the standard 15-pin D-shell type, while the external keyboard connector is generally the 6-pin mini-DIN (PS/2) type. When an external keyboard is plugged in, the built-in keyboard is disabled. The portable's software may allow both displays to remain active while the external monitor is connected.

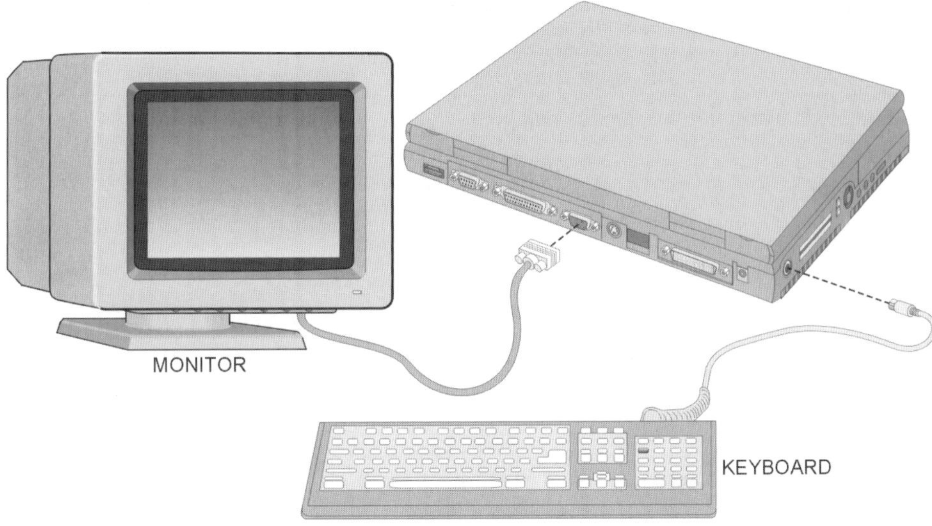

Figure 7-14: Attaching Standard I/O Devices

Trackballs

trackball

In some applications, such as notebook computers, it is desirable to have a pointing device that does not require a surface to be moved across. The **trackball** can be thought of as an inverted mouse that allows the user to directly manipulate it. Trackballs, like the one depicted in Figure 7-15, may be separate units that set on a desk, or clip to the side of the computer, and connect to one of the system's serial ports. In many laptop and notebook computers, trackballs are frequently built directly into the system housing and connected directly to its I/O circuitry. Like mice, trackballs may come with one to three buttons.

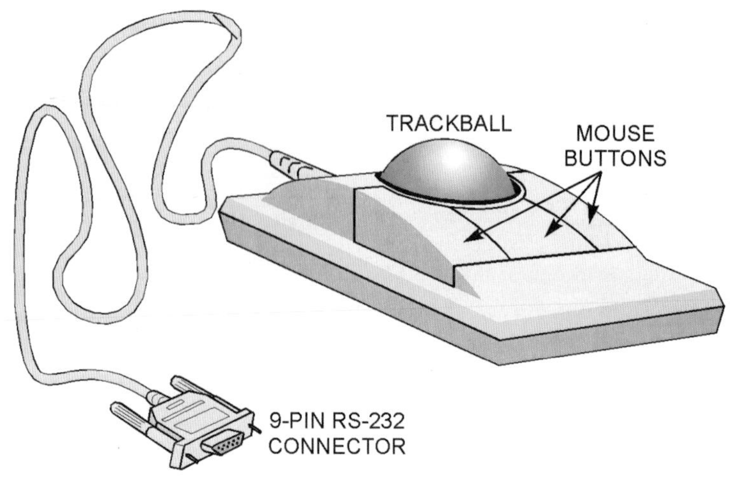

Figure 7-15: A Trackball Unit

Touch Pads

touch screen monitor

touch pad

Hewlett-Packard introduced the first **touch screen monitor** in 1983. These screens divide the display into rows and columns that correspond to X and Y coordinates on the screen. This technology has been adapted to notebook computers in the form of **touch pad** pointing devices, like the one illustrated in Figure 7-16. This pointing device normally takes the place of the mouse as the pointing device in the system. The user controls the screen cursor by moving a finger across the pad surface. Small buttons are included near the pad to duplicate the action of the mouse buttons. With some touch pads, single and double button clicking can be simulated by tapping a finger on the pad.

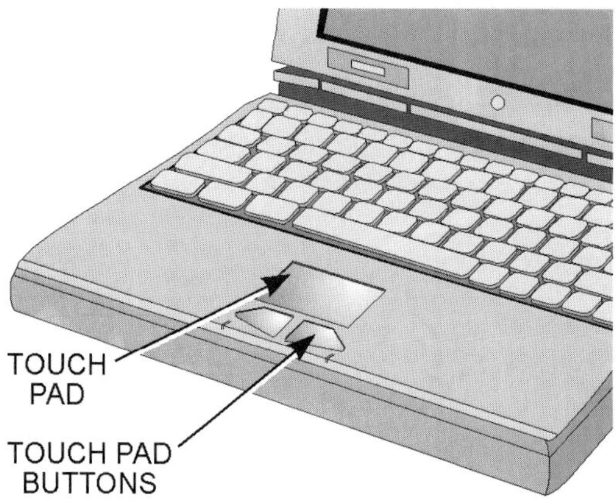

Figure 7-16: A Touch Pad

The touch pad contains a gridwork of electric conductors that organize it in a row and column format, as described in Figure 7-17. When the user presses the touch pad, the protective layer over the grid flexes and causes the capacitance between the two grids within the pad to change. This produces a signal change that is detected by the touch pad controller at one X-grid line and one Y-grid line. The controller converts the signal generated between the two strips into an approximate X/Y position on the video display.

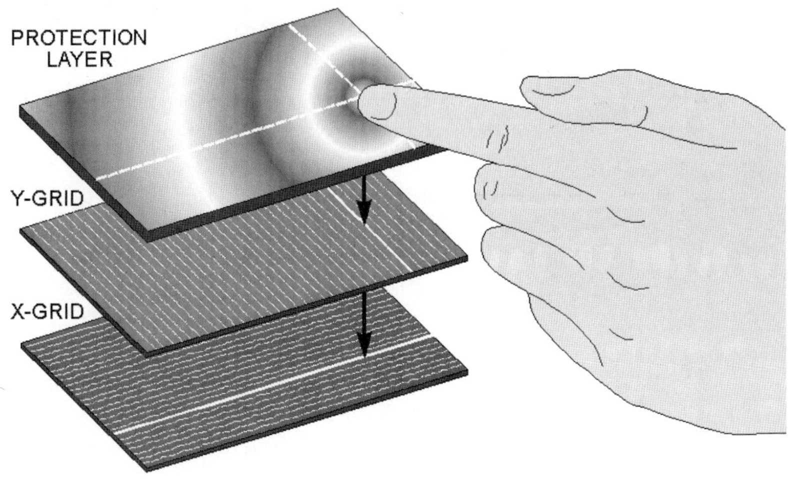

Figure 7-17: Inside a Touch Pad

The human fingertip is broad and does not normally provide a fine enough pointing device to select precise points on the screen. Therefore, accurately locating a small item on the screen may be difficult due to the relative size of the fingertip. The touch pad software designers have created drivers that take this possibility into account and compensate for it.

Touch pads are available as built-in units in some portables, while others are designed as add-ons to existing units. These units clip onto the body of the computer, or set on a desk top, and plug into one of the system's serial ports, just as a mouse or trackball does.

When troubleshooting touch pad problems, there are really only three components to consider. These are the touch sensitive pad, the I/O port the pad is attached to, and its driver software. Review the user's manual for the pad to check its software setup for possible configuration problems. Examine the I/O port connection and configuration to make sure it is properly set up to support the pad. If the pad is an add-on unit, check the port specification to make sure that it is compatible with the touch pad unit. Reinstall the touch pad driver software, carefully reviewing each step. Check for the presence of diagnostic routines in the touch pad's software. Check the I/O port settings.

As with the portable's LCD panel, the life and usefulness of a touch pad can be extended through proper care and handling. The panel should be cleaned periodically with mild soap and water and a soft, lint-free cloth. Rinse the residue from the pad by wiping it with a cloth dampened in clear water. Never pour or spray liquids directly on the computer or the touch pad. After cleaning, allow 30 minutes for complete drying.

Like the other portable components, the touch pad should be shielded from bright sunlight and heat sources, as well as extremely cold temperatures. Never use sharp or pointed objects to tap the pad as these items may damage the surface of the pad.

EXTENDED I/O

As more and more desktop users began to use laptop and notebook computers, they demanded that additional peripheral systems be included. With the limited space inside these units, it became clear that a new method for installing options would need to be developed.

At first, laptop and notebook manufacturers included proprietary expansion connections for adding such devices as fax/modems, additional memory, and additional storage devices. Of course, these devices tended to be expensive since they were proprietary to a single vendor. In addition, they were not useful as the user upgraded to newer or more powerful units.

PC Cards (PCMCIA)

PCMCIA bus

PC Card standard

In 1989, the **PCMCIA bus** standard was introduced primarily to accommodate the notebook and sub-notebook computer markets. A small form-factor expansion-card format, referred to as the **PC Card standard**, was also adopted for use. This format was derived from earlier proprietary laptop/notebook memory card designs. It is based on the 68-pin JEIDA connector, depicted in Figure 7-18.

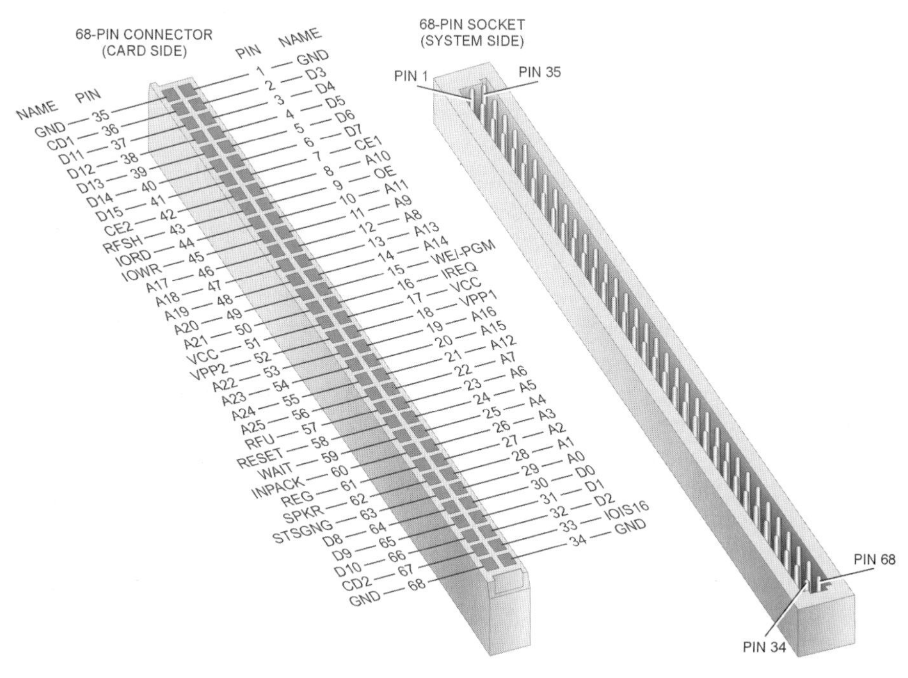

Figure 7-18: PCMCIA Connector Standard

The definitions of the PCMCIA connector's 68 pins are listed in Table 7-2.

hot insertion

The interface is designed so that cards can be inserted into the unit while it is turned on (**hot insertion**). Although the PC Card connection scheme was never intended to be used with a full-sized unit, its design is compatible with all the other bus types. As a matter of fact, PC Card adapters are available for use in desktop and tower units. These slots are often designed so that they can be mounted in a standard disk drive bay of a desktop case.

socket services

execute-in-place mode

The PC Card standard defines a methodology for software programmers to write standard drivers for PC Card devices. The standard is referred to as **socket services** and provides for a software head to identify the type of card being used, its capabilities, and its requirements. Although the card's software driver can be executed directly on the card (instead of moving it into RAM for execution), the system's PC Card enablers must be loaded before the card can be activated. This is referred to as **execute-in-place mode**. In addition, PC cards can use the same file allocation system used by floppy and hard disk drives. This also makes it easier for programmers to write code for PCMCIA devices.

PIN	NAME	DESCRIPTION	PIN	NAME	DESCRIPTION
1	GND	Ground	35	GND	Ground
2	D3	Data bit 3	36	CD1	Card detect 1
3	D4	Data bit 4	37	D11	Data bit 11
4	D5	Data bit 5	38	D12	Data bit 12
5	D6	Data bit 6	39	D13	Data bit 13
6	D7	Data bit 7	40	D14	Data bit 14
7	CE1	Card enable 1	41	D15	Data bit 15
8	A10	Address bit 10	42	CE2	Card enable 2
9	OE	Output enable	43	RFSH	Refresh input
10	A11	Address bit 11	44	IORD	I/O read strobe
11	A9	Address bit 9	45	IOWR	I/O write strobe
12	A8	Address bit 8	46	A17	Address bit 17
13	A13	Address bit 13	47	A18	Address bit 18
14	A14	Address bit 14	48	A19	Address bit 19
15	WE/-PGM	Write enable	49	A20	Address bit 20
16	IREQ	Interrupt request	50	A21	Address bit 21
17	VCC	Card power	51	VCC	Card power
18	VPP1	Programming supply voltage 1	52	VPP2	Programming supply voltage 2
19	A16	Address bit 16	53	A22	Address bit 22
20	A15	Address bit 15	54	A23	Address bit 23
21	A12	Address bit 12	55	A24	Address bit 24
22	A7	Address bit 7	56	A25	Address bit 25
23	A6	Address bit 6	57	RFU	Reserved
24	A5	Address bit 5	58	RESET	Card reset
25	A4	Address bit 5	59	WAIT	Extend bus cycle
26	A3	Address bit 3	60	INPACK	Input port acknowledge
27	A2	Address bit 2	61	REG	Register and I/O select enable
28	A1	Address bit 1	62	SPKR	Digital audio waveform
29	A0	Address bit 0	63	STSGNG	Card status changed
30	D0	Data bit 0	64	D8	Data bit 8
31	D1	Data bit 1	65	D9	Data bit 9
32	D2	Data bit 2	66	D10	Data bit 10
33	IOIS16	IO port is 16 bits	67	CD2	Card detect 2
34	GND	Ground	68	GND	Ground

Table 7-2: 68-Pin Connector Definitions

PC Card Types

Three types of PCMCIA adapters currently exist. The **PCMCIA Type I** cards, introduced in 1990, are 3.3 mm thick and work as memory expansion units. In 1991, the **PCMCIA Type II** cards were introduced. They are 5 mm thick and support virtually any traditional expansion function, except removable hard drive units. Type II slots are backwardly compatible so that Type I cards will work in them. Currently, **PCMCIA Type III** cards are being produced. These cards are 10.5 mm thick and are intended primarily for use with removable hard drives. Both Type I and Type II cards can be used in a Type III slot.

PCMCIA Type I

PCMCIA Type II

PCMCIA Type III

All three card types adhere to a form factor of 2.12"w *x* 3.37"l and use a 68-pin, slide-in socket arrangement. They can be used with 8-bit or 16-bit data bus machines and operate on +5V or +3.3V supplies. The design of the cards allows them to be installed in the computer while it is turned on and running. Figure 7-19 shows the three types of PCMCIA cards.

TEST TIP

Memorize the physical sizes of the three card standards. Also, know what applications each type of card is capable of.

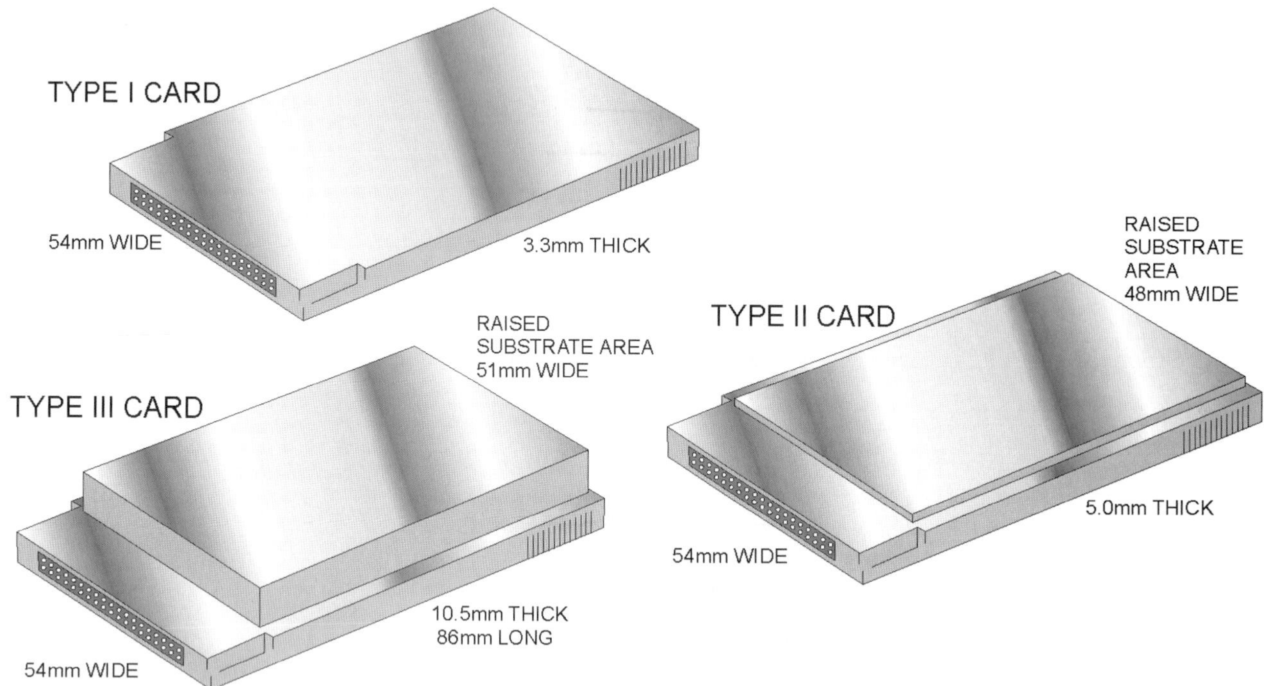

Figure 7-19: PCMCIA Cards

PC Card versions of most adapter types are available in the market place. Even PC Card hard drives (with disks the size of a quarter) can be found. Other common PC Card adapters include fax/modems, SCSI adapters, network adapters, and IDE host adapters. The PCMCIA standard allows up to 255 adapters, each capable of working with up to 16 cards. If a system implemented the standard to its extreme, it could, theoretically, work with over 4,000 PC cards installed. Most portable designs only include two PC Card slots.

Networking

When the portable computer returns to the office, there is usually a gap between what is on the portable and what is on the desktop machine. One alternative is to use a docking station to allow the notebook to function as both a portable and as a desktop system. This concept is explored later in this chapter. The other alternative is to make the portable computer network-ready so that it can plug into the network in the office.

There are PC Card network adapters that can be used with a network socket device to enable the portable to be connected into the office network. The socket device has internal circuitry that prevents the open net connection from adversely affecting the network when the portable is removed. Some network adapters use the system's parallel port and a pocket LAN adapter to connect portables to the network. The LAN adapter actually works between the network, the computer, and its printer, as shown in Figure 7-20.

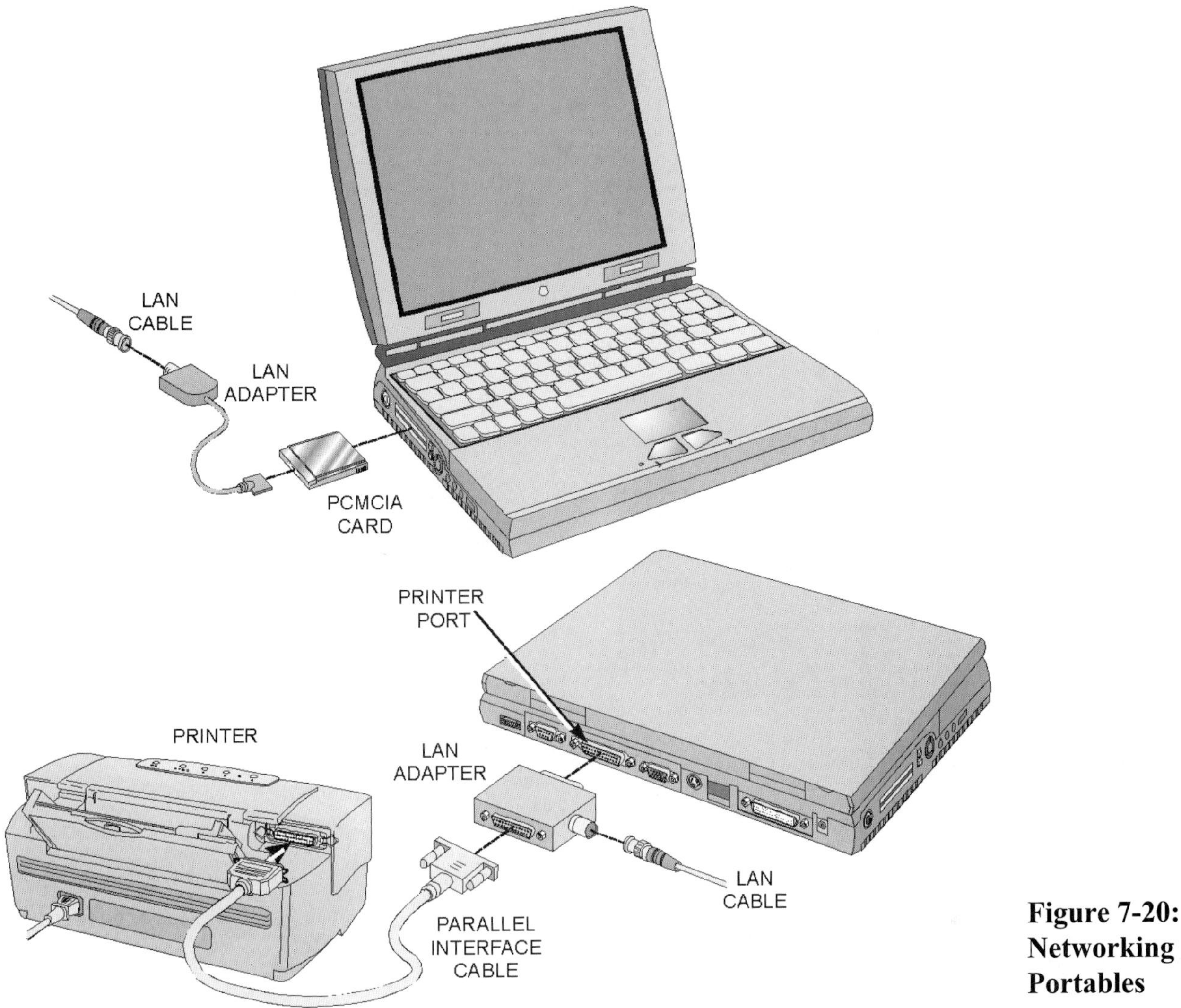

Figure 7-20: Networking Portables

EXTERNAL DEVICES

The basic portable should contain all of the devices that the user needs to do work while away from the office. However, there are always additional items that users have become accustomed to using with their computers. For this reason, portable computers typically offer a full range of I/O port types.

Power Supplies

Notebooks and other portables use a detachable, rechargeable battery and an external power supply, as illustrated in Figure 7-21 (battery sizes will vary from manufacturer to manufacturer). They also employ power-saving circuits and ICs designed to lengthen the battery's useful time. The battery unit contains a recharging regulator circuit that allows the battery to recharge while it is being used with the external power supply. Like other hardware aspects of notebook computers, there are no standards for their power supply units. They use different connector types and possess different voltage and current delivery capabilities. Therefore, a power supply from one notebook will not necessarily work with another portable model.

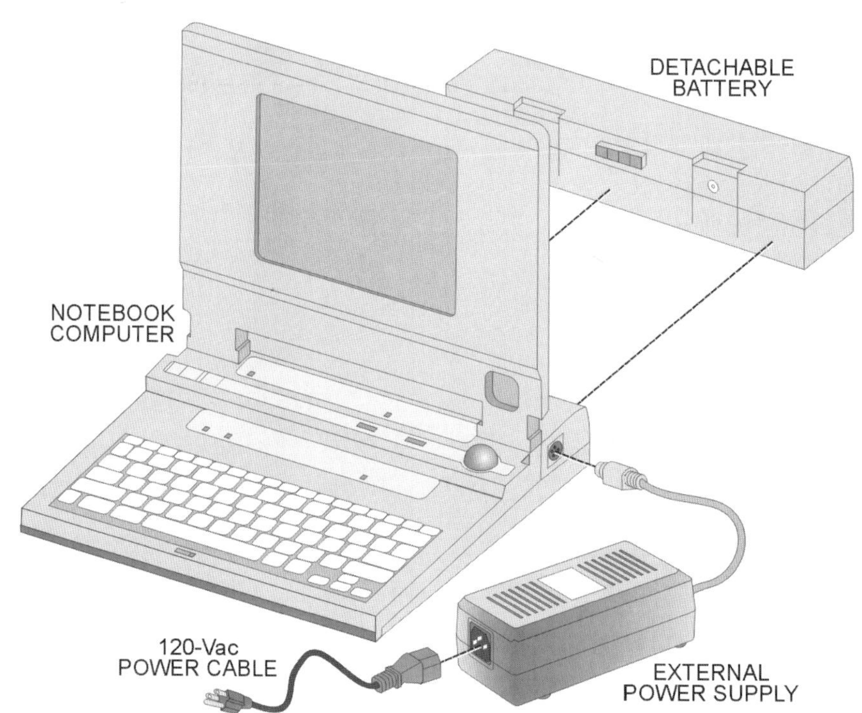

Figure 7-21: Laptop/Notebook Power Supplies

Since the premise of portable computers is mobility, it can be assumed that they should be able to run without being plugged into an ac outlet. The question for most portables is how long will it run without being plugged in. This is the point where portable designs lead the industry. They continuously push forward in three design areas:

- better battery design
- better power-consumption devices
- better power management

Batteries

To be honest, the desktop world doesn't really pay much attention to power conservation issues. Conversely, portable computer designers must deal with the fact that they are really tied to a battery. Older portable designs included the battery as an external, detachable device, as depicted in the previous figure. These units normally contained rows of **Nickel Cadmium (Ni-Cad)** batteries wired together to provide the specified voltage and current capabilities for the portable. The housing was constructed to both hold the Ni-Cads and to attach to the portable case.

Nickel Cadmium (Ni-Cad)

Typical Ni-Cad batteries offer operating times approaching two hours in some models. As with other devices that rely on Ni-Cads, computer battery packs constructed with this type of battery suffer from the charge/discharge cycle "memory effect" problem associated with Ni-Cads. A full recharge for some Ni-Cad packs could take up to 24 hours to complete. For these reasons, Ni-Cad battery packs have all but disappeared from the portable computer market.

Newer portable designs have switched to **Nickel Metal-Hydride (NiMH)**, **Lithium-Ion (Li-ion)**, or **Lithium-Ion Polymer** batteries. These batteries are housed in a plastic case that can be installed inside the portable's case, as illustrated in Figure 7-22. These types of batteries typically provide up to 2 or 3 hours of operation. It is best to run the battery until the system produces a low battery warning message, indicator, or chime.

Nickel Metal-Hydride (NiMH)

Lithium-Ion (Li-ion)

Lithium-Ion Polymer

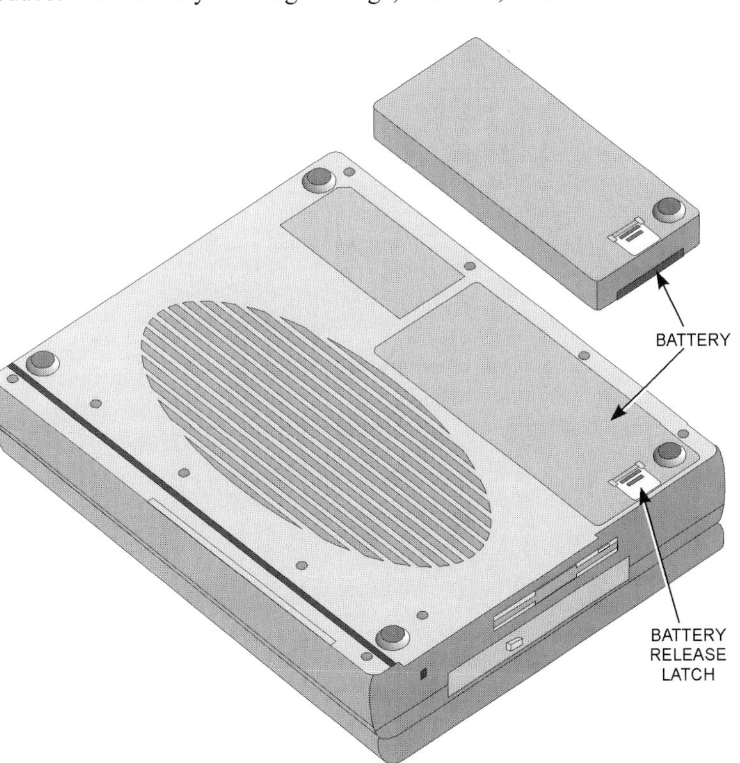

Figure 7-22: Removing Battery Packs

It should take about 2 to 3 hours to fully recharge the typical Ni-MH battery pack and about 4 to 5 hours for a Li-ion pack. The battery packs should always be fully recharged before using. When the ac adapter is used, a trickle charge is applied to the battery pack to keep it in a fully charged condition. The ac adapter should be used whenever possible to conserve the battery.

Power Consumption

standby mode

suspend mode

As mentioned earlier, power consumption consideration has been built into most devices intended for use with portable computers. Many of the Pentium chips sets provide a **standby mode** that turns off selected components, such as the hard drive and display, until a system event, such as a keyboard entry or a mouse movement, occurs. An additional power-saving condition called **suspend mode** places the system in a shut down condition except for its memory units.

hibernate mode

An additional power-saving mode, known as **hibernate mode**, writes the contents of RAM memory to a hard drive file and completely shuts the system down. When the system is restarted, the feature reads the hibernate file back into memory and normal operation is restarted at the place it left off.

Power Management

Each sector of the portable computer market has worked to reduce power consumption levels, including software suppliers. Advanced operating systems include power management features that monitor the system's operation and turn off some higher-power-consumption items when they are not in use (Standby mode), and will switch the system into a low-power-consumption **sleep mode** (Suspend mode) if inactivity continues.

sleep mode

Advanced Power Management (APM)

green mode

These modes are defined by a Microsoft/IBM standard called the **Advanced Power Management (APM)** standard. The hardware producers refer to this condition as a **green mode**. The standard is actually implemented through the cooperation of the system's chipset devices and the operating system. Control of the APM system is provided through the BIOS' CMOS Setup utility, as described in Chapter 2—*Advanced System Boards*.

Most newer portable computers possess a number of automatic power-saving features to maximize battery life. Some can be controlled through the Power menu of the Advanced CMOS Setup utility. If the Hard Disk Timeout value is set to 3 minutes, the Standby Timeout to 5 minutes, and the Auto Suspend value to 10 minutes, the following activities will occur:

1. The hard disk will spin down after 3 minutes of inactivity.
2. After 2 additional minutes of inactivity, the system will enter the standby mode.
3. After 10 additional inactive minutes, the system will store the hibernation file on the hard drive and enter suspend mode.

The suspend mode can also be entered by pressing a key combination for those times when the user must step away from the computer for a few minutes, but does not want to shut down. The POWER.EXE command must be loaded in a Device= line of the CONFIG.SYS file for APM to work properly under DOS 6.x or Windows 3.x. This command is not needed to run APM in Windows 9x.

When the system suspends operation, the following events take place:

- The video screen is turned off.
- The CPU, DMA, clocks, and math coprocessor are powered down.
- All controllable peripheral devices are shut down.

The amount of time the unit can remain in suspend mode is determined by the remaining amount of battery power. For this reason, data should be saved to the hard drive before voluntarily going to suspend mode. Pressing the computer's power button will return the system to its previous operational point.

External Drive Units

The first laptops and notebooks incorporated the traditional single floppy drive and single hard drive concept that was typical in most desktop units. However, as CD-ROM drives and discs became the norm for new operating systems and software packages, a dilemma was created. There is simply not enough room in most notebook computers for three normal-size drive units. Even with reduced size drives, the size limitations of most portables require that one of the three major drives be external.

External FDDs

Typically, the first item to be left out of a new notebook design is the internal floppy drive. So much of the latest software is distributed on CD-ROM that those drives now have preference in newer designs. Even so, there are still so many applications that use floppies that an external FDD is almost always an add-on option for a new notebook. There are still large volumes of software available on floppies, and so many users have cherished data stored on floppies that an additional unit usually makes sense.

The external floppy comes as a complete unit with an external housing and a signal cable. As with other external devices, it requires an independent power source, such as an ac adapter pack. The external floppy drive's signal cable generally connects to a special FDD connector, such as the one shown in Figure 7-23.

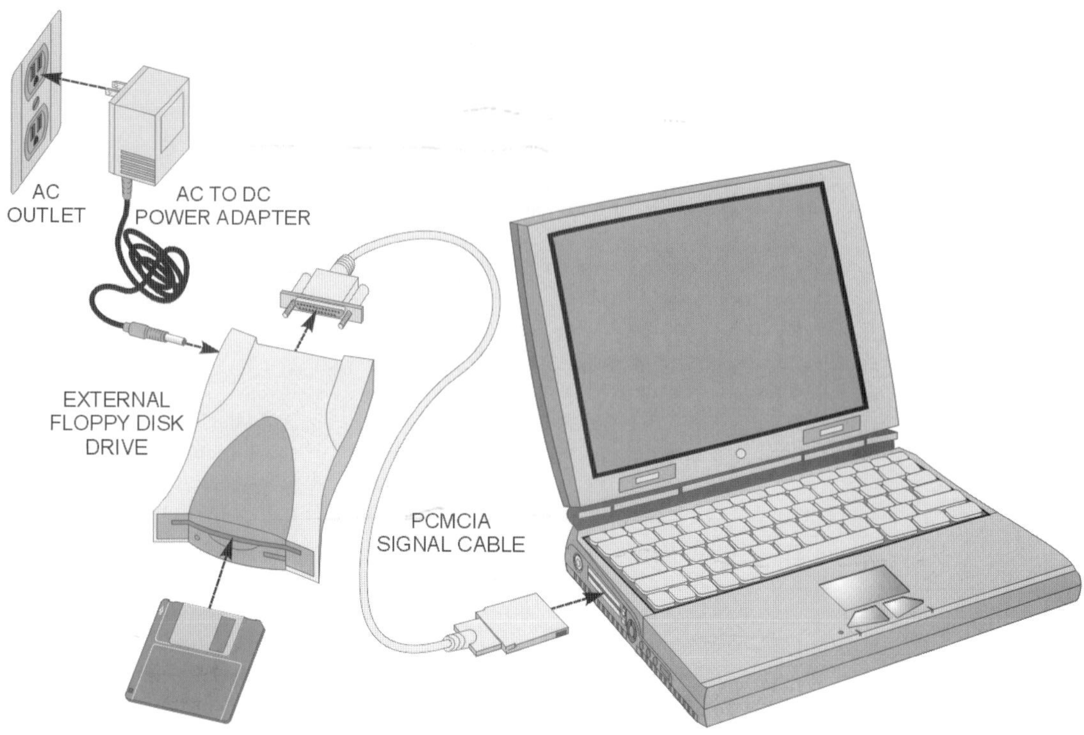

Figure 7-23: An External Floppy Drive

External CD-ROM Drives

Prior to the CD-ROM drive becoming an accepted part of the notebook PC, some manufacturers produced external CD-ROM drives for use with these machines. They are still available as add-ons to all types of PCs. External CD-ROM drives typically connect to a SCSI host adapter, or to an enhanced parallel port. The latter connection requires a fully functional, bi-directional parallel port, and a special software device driver.

Figure 7-24 illustrates the installation of an external SCSI CD-ROM drive. Since the drive is external, connecting the CD-ROM unit to the system usually involves simply connecting a couple of cables together. First, connect the CD-ROM's power supply to the external drive unit. Before making this connection, verify that the power switch, or power supply, is turned off. Connect the signal cable to the computer. Finally, connect the opposite end of the cable to the external CD-ROM unit. Complete the installation by installing the CD-ROM driver software on the system's hard disk drive.

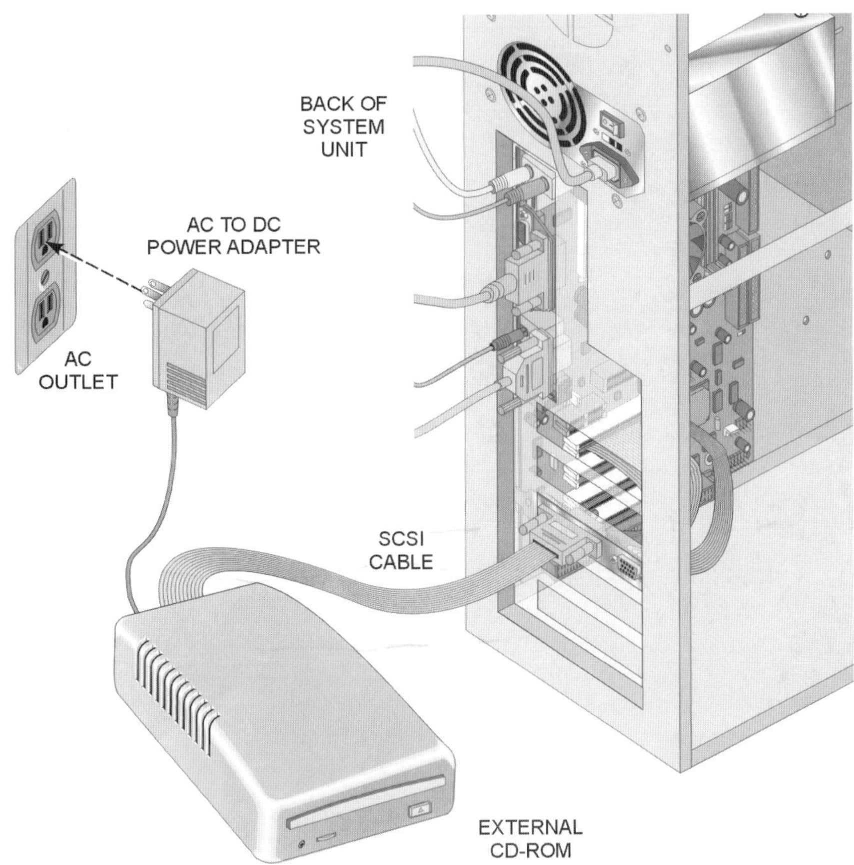

Figure 7-24: Installing an External CD-ROM Drive

Docking Stations

A **docking station,** or **docking port,** is a specialized structure that allows the notebook unit to be inserted into it. Once the notebook is inside, the docking port extends its expansion bus so that it can be used with a collection of desktop devices, such as an ac power source, a full-sized keyboard and CRT monitor, as well as modems, mice, and standard PC port connectors. A typical docking station is depicted in Figure 7-25.

docking station

docking port

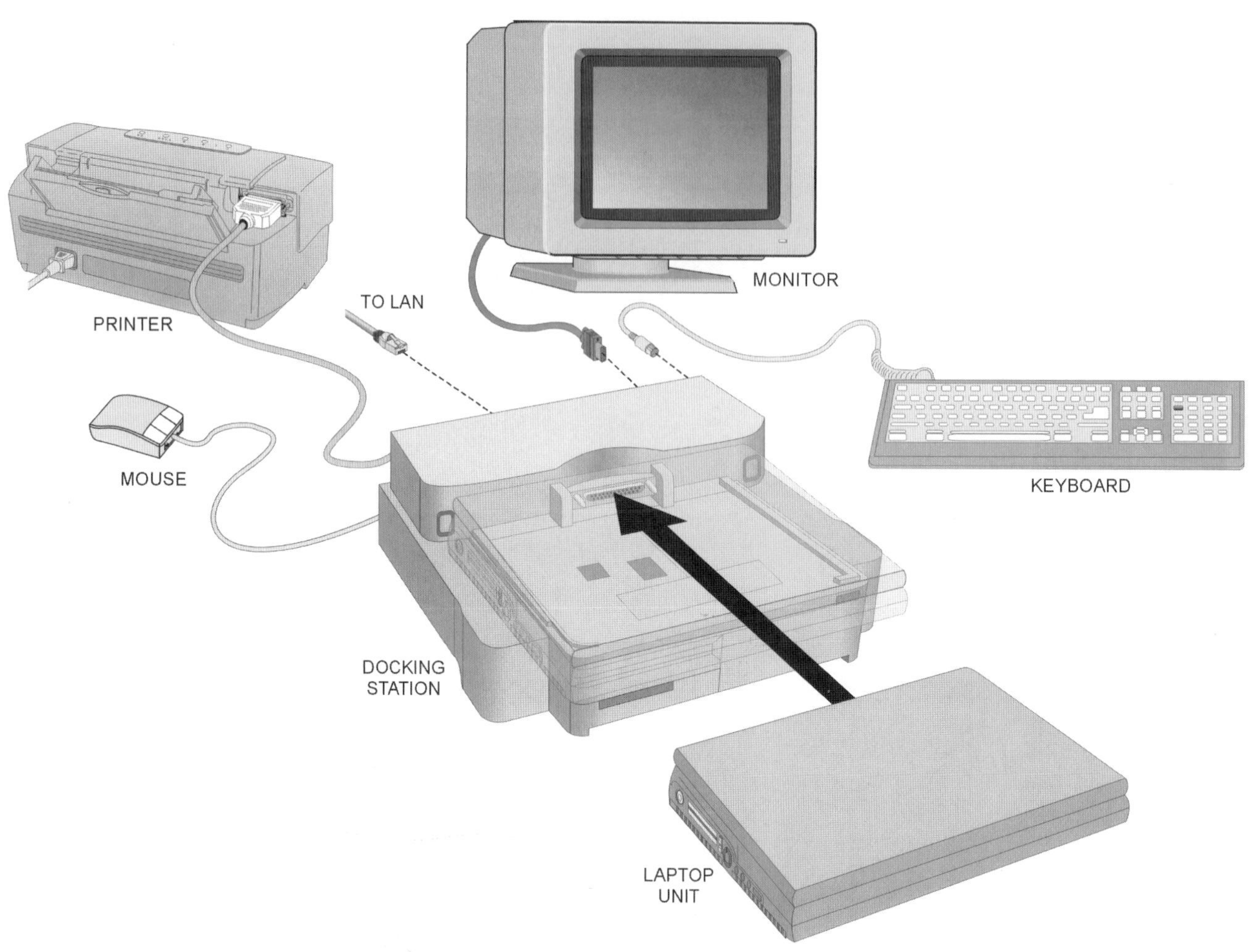

Figure 7-25: A Docking Station

The notebook and the docking station communicate with each other through a special docking port connector in the rear of the notebook. When the notebook is inserted into the docking station, the extension bus in the docking station plugs into the expansion connector in the notebook. Most docking stations provide standard PC expansion slots so that non-notebook peripheral devices, such as network adapters and sound cards, can be used with the system.

When the notebook is in the docking station, its normal I/O devices (keyboard, display, and pointing device) are disabled and the docking station's peripherals take over.

For the most part, docking stations are proprietary to the portable they were designed to work with. The docking port connection in the docking station must correctly align with the connector in the notebook. The notebook unit must also fit correctly within the docking station opening. Since there are no standards for these systems, the chances of two different manufacturers locating the connectors in the same places and/or designing the same case outline are very remote.

CHAPTER SUMMARY

This chapter has dealt expressly with aspects of the portable computer systems. It has documented how portable units differ from conventional personal computer units. After completing the chapter, you should be able to identify the components of portable systems and describe how they differ from typical desktop components. You should also be able to identify their unique problems.

At this point, review the objectives listed at the beginning of the chapter to be certain that you understand and can perform each item listed there.

KEY POINTS REVIEW

The focus of this chapter has been portable computer systems. Review the following key points before moving into the Review and Exam Questions sections to make sure you are comfortable with each point. Afterward, answer the Review Questions that follow to verify your knowledge of the information.

- Continued advancements in IC and peripheral technology allowed the PC's circuitry to be reduced. This allowed portable sizes to be reduced further so that they could achieve sizes of 8.75"d *x* 11"w *x* 2.25"h and smaller. Portables in this size range are referred to asnotebook computers. The weight of a typical notebook dropped down to 5 or 6 pounds.

- However, the market was revived by the introduction of palm tops known as Personal Digital Assistants (PDAs). These handheld devices use a special stylus, referred to as a pen, to input data and selections instead of a keyboard or mouse. Basically the PDA is an electronic time management system that may also include computer applications such as word processors, spreadsheets, and databases.

- The drawback of portable computers from a service point of view is that conventions and compatibility disappear. Therefore, interchangeability of parts with other machines or makers goes by the wayside.

- One of the biggest problems for portable computers is heat buildup inside the case. Since conventional power supplies (and their fans) are not included in portable units, separate fans must be designed into portables to carry the heat out of the unit. The closeness of the portable's components and the small amount of free air space inside their cases also adds to heat-related design problems.

- There are two ideals characteristics for portable computers: compact and light weight. Portable computer designers work constantly to decrease the size and power consumption of all the computer's components. Special low-power consumption ICs and disk drives have been developed to extend their battery life.

- The I/O ports included in most notebook computers consist of a single parallel port, a single serial port, an external VGA monitor connector, an external keyboard connector, and a docking port expansion bus. Some models can be found with a second serial port connector, but they are not common.

- In compact computers, memory and memory expansion hardware standards don't exist. Some designs use standard SIMM or DIMM modules for RAM, while others use proprietary memory modules. Still other designs rely on memory card modules for additional RAM. The key to upgrading or replacing RAM in a portable can be found in its user's guide. Only memory modules recommended by the portable manufacturer should be installed, and only in the configurations suggested.

- The most common flat-panel displays used with portable PC's are Liquid Crystal Displays (LCDs). They are relatively thin, flat, and lightweight, and require very little power to operate. In addition to reduced weight and improved portability, these displays offer better reliability and longer life than CRT units.

- The most widely used notebook keyboard is the 84-key version. The keys are slightly smaller and shorter than those found in full size keyboards. A number of keys or key functions may be combined or deleted from a notebook keyboard.

- Three types of PCMCIA adapters currently exist. The PCMCIA Type I cards, introduced in 1990, are 3.3 mm thick and work as memory expansion units. In 1991, the PCMCIA Type II cards were introduced. They are 5 mm thick and support virtually any traditional expansion function, except removable hard drive units. Type II slots are backwardly compatible so that Type I cards will work in them. Currently, PCMCIA Type III cards are being produced. These cards are 10.5 mm thick and are intended primarily for use with removable hard drives. Both Type I and Type II cards can be used in a Type III slot.

- Notebook computer designers work constantly to decrease the size and power consumption of all the computer's components.

- The PCMCIA bus was developed to accommodate the space conscious notebook and sub-notebook computer market.

REVIEW QUESTIONS

The following questions test your knowledge of the material presented in this chapter.

1. How are mobile processors optimized for use in portable units?
2. List three considerations that must be taken into account when replacing disk drives in a portable.
3. What is the purpose of a docking station?
4. List three power management modes and describe how they are different.
5. What is the purpose of the Fn key on a portable computer keyboard?
6. How are notebook and laptop computers different?
7. Where is the network adapter normally located in a portable computer?
8. Describe the major maintenance problem associated with notebook computers.

9. How are active and passive matrix LCD displays different?
10. What type of device is a touch pad?
11. Describe two typical connection methods for adding an external CD-ROM drive to a portable system.
12. Which type of LCD panel uses less power than the others?
13. Describe two methods of connecting a portable computer to a network.
14. Which type of LCD panel creates sharper images?
15. What type of RAM modules are typically used in a portable PC?

EXAM QUESTIONS

1. What form factor does a notebook computer's system board conform to?
   a. AT
   b. Baby AT
   c. ATX
   d. none
2. A Type I PCMCIA card is __________ thick.
   a. 3.3 mm
   b. 5.0 mm
   c. 7.5 mm
   d. 10.5 mm
3. A Type II PCMCIA card is _______ thick.
   a. 3.3 mm
   b. 5.0 mm
   c. 7.5 mm
   d. 10.5 mm
4. A Type III PCMCIA card is _______ thick.
   a. 3.3 mm
   b. 5.0 mm
   c. 7.5 mm
   d. 10.5 mm

5. Where would you normally expect to encounter a PCMCIA card?
   a. In an ISA expansion slot
   b. In a serial port
   c. In a notebook computer
   d. In an MCA expansion slot

6. Which of the following functions can be served by a Type I PCMCIA card?
   a. Memory expansion functions
   b. Serial port functions
   c. Parallel port functions
   d. Game port functions

7. Which of the following functions cannot be performed with a Type II PCMCIA card?
   a. Memory expansion functions
   b. Removable hard drive functions
   c. Serial port functions
   d. Parallel port functions

8. Select the battery technology that would not likely be used in a newer notebook computer.
   a. Nickel Metal Hydroxide
   b. Lithium Ion
   c. Nickel Cadmium
   d. Lithium Ion Polymer

9. What tool is required to upgrade memory in a typical portable computer?
   a. A soldering iron
   b. The user's guide
   c. Schematic diagrams
   d. A RAM extractor

10. Which function can be performed by a Type III PCMCIA card but not by Type I or Type II cards?
    a. Removable HDD functions
    b. Memory expansion functions
    c. Serial port functions
    d. Parallel port functions

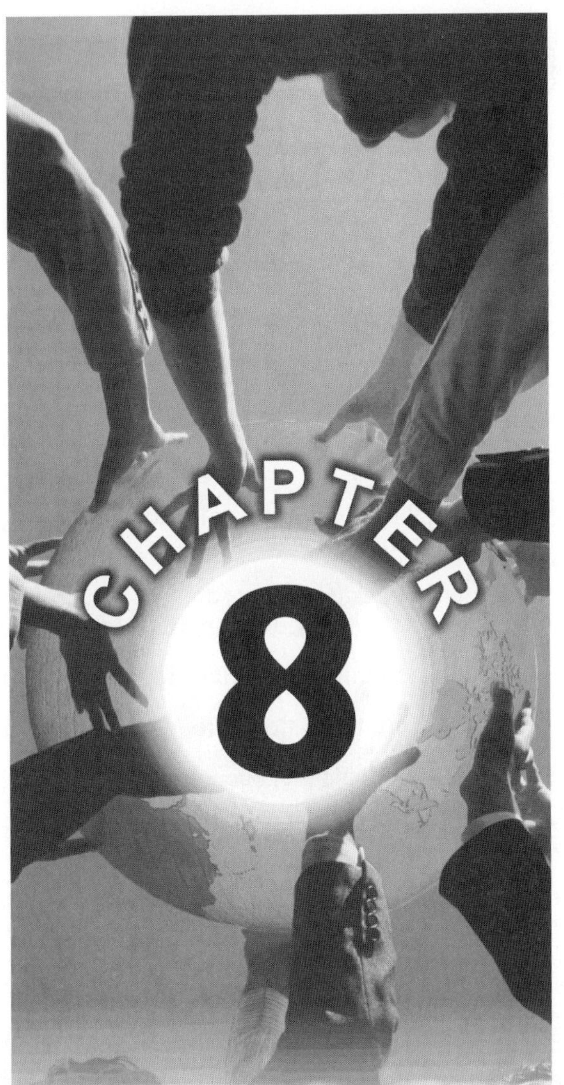

OPERATING SYSTEM FUNDAMENTALS

OBJECTIVES

OBJECTIVES

Upon completion of this chapter and its related lab procedures you will be able to perform the following tasks:

1. Describe the basic functions of an operating system.
2. Differentiate between single-process and multiple-process systems.
3. Differentiate between multiuser, multitasking, and multiprocessor operations.
4. Identify MS-DOS operating system functions, structure, and major system files.
5. Describe procedures for locating, accessing, and retrieving information in an MS-DOS system.
6. Identify basic concepts and procedures for creating and managing files and directories in an MS-DOS system.
7. Define multiuser, multitasking, and multiprocessor operations.
8. Configure the system through the CMOS Setup utilities.
9. List the events that occur during the bootup process.
10. Describe the function and purpose of DOS.
11. Explain the basic organization of a DOS disk.
12. Describe the operation of the DOS command line.
13. Identify and use disk-related DOS commands.
14. Create, delete, and navigate through various directories.
15. Discuss naming conventions as they apply to various types of files.
16. Find, copy, rename, delete, and move files.
17. Manipulate file attributes in a DOS system.
18. Describe the methods used to bypass and correct inoperable DOS startup sequences.
19. Describe the sequence of events associated with the DOS configuration during bootup.
20. Describe the different types of DOS memory.
21. Use the AUTOEXEC.BAT and CONFIG.SYS files to optimize system performance.
22. Load driver software for any devices added to the system.
23. List the standard DOS device drivers.

CHAPTER 8

OPERATING SYSTEM FUNDAMENTALS

INTRODUCTION

The general responsibilities of an operating system were presented in Chapter 1. This chapter will build on that description by presenting concepts that are fundamental to all operating systems.

Every portion of the computer system must be controlled and coordinated so that the millions of operations that occur every second are carried out correctly and on time. In addition, it is the job of the operating system to make the complexity of the personal computer as invisible as possible to the user.

Operating systems are programs designed to control the operation of a computer system. As a group, they are easily some of the most complex programs devised. Likewise, the operating system acts as an intermediary between software applications nearly as complex, and the hardware they run on. Finally, the operating system accepts commands from the computer user, and carries them out to perform some desired operation.

OPERATING SYSTEM BASICS

There are literally thousands of different operating systems in use with microcomputers. The complexity of each operating system typically depends on the complexity of the application the microcomputer is designed to fill.

The operating system for a fuel mixture controller in an automobile is relatively simple, while an operating system for a multiuser computer system that controls many terminals is relatively complex.

The complete operating system for the fuel controller could be stored in a single small ROM device. It would likely take control of the unit as soon as power is applied, reset the system, and test it. During normal operation, the operating system monitors the sensor inputs for accelerator setting, humidity, etc. and adjusts the air/fuel mixing valves according to predetermined values stored in ROM. The fuel mixture controller is depicted in Figure 8-1.

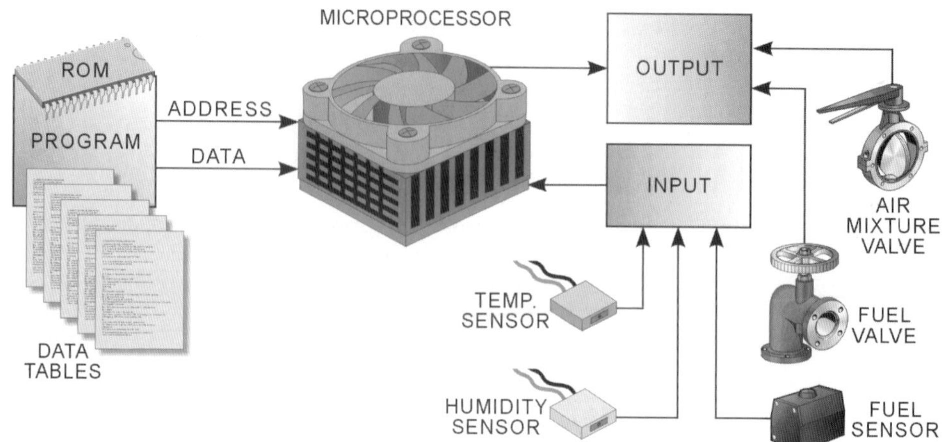

Figure 8-1: A Simple Fuel/Air Mixture Controller

In the large, multiple-user system, the operating system is likely to be stored on disk and have sections loaded into RAM when needed. As illustrated in Figure 8-2, this type of operating system must control several pieces of hardware, manage files created and used by various users, provide security for each user's information, and manage communications between different stations. The operating system would also be responsible for presenting each station with a user interface that can accept commands and data from the user. This interface can be a command line interpreter or a Graphical User Interface (GUI).

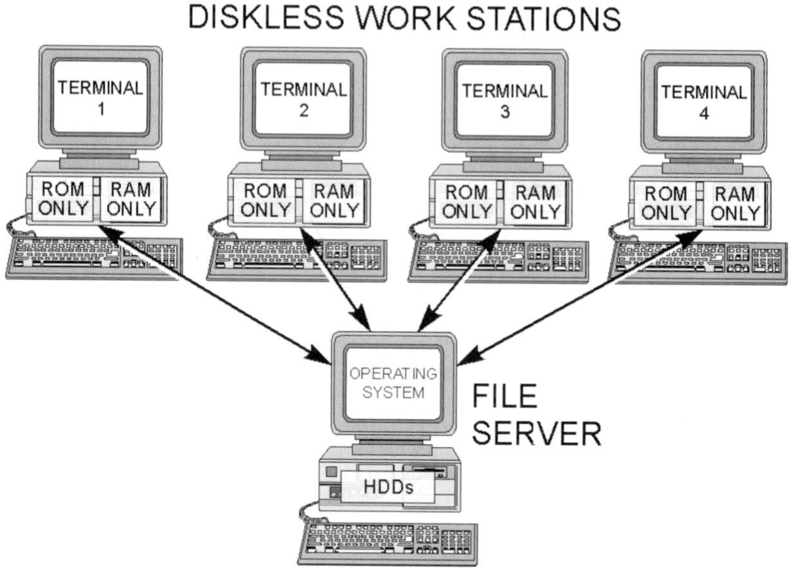

Figure 8-2: A Multiuser System

kernel

Complex operating systems typically contain several millions of lines of computer instructions. Due to this complexity, large operating systems are typically written in modules that handle the various responsibilities assigned to the system. The operating system for the fuel mixture controller is most likely a single module. However, the operating system for the multiple-user system would likely consist of a core module, called the **kernel**, a task manager, a scheduler, a local file manager, and a host of other special-purpose manager modules.

There are two basic types of operating systems:

single-process systems

multiple-process systems

- **single-process systems**
- **multiple-process systems**

batch mode

interactive mode

In a single-process system, the operating system works with a single task only. These operating systems can operate in **batch mode** or **interactive mode**. In batch mode, the operating system runs one program until it is finished. In interactive mode, the operation of the program can be modified by input from external sources, such as sensors, or a user interface device.

tasks

threads

In multiple-process systems, the operating system is designed so that it can appear to work on several **tasks** simultaneously. A task is a portion of a program under execution. Computer programs are made up of several tasks that may work alone or as a unit. Tasks, in turn, can be made up of several **threads** that can be worked on separately. A thread is a section of programming that can be time sliced by the operating system to run at the same time that other threads are being executed.

The multiple-process system breaks the tasks associated with a process into various threads for execution. Typically, one thread may handle video output, another would handle mouse input, and another output from the printer.

multiuser

multitasking

multiprocessor

Multiple process operations can be organized in three different ways:

- **multiuser**
- **multitasking**
- **multiprocessor**

These three types of operating systems are described in Figure 8-3.

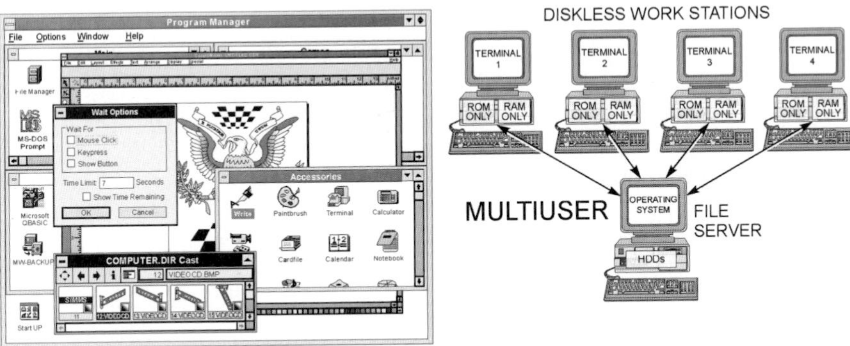

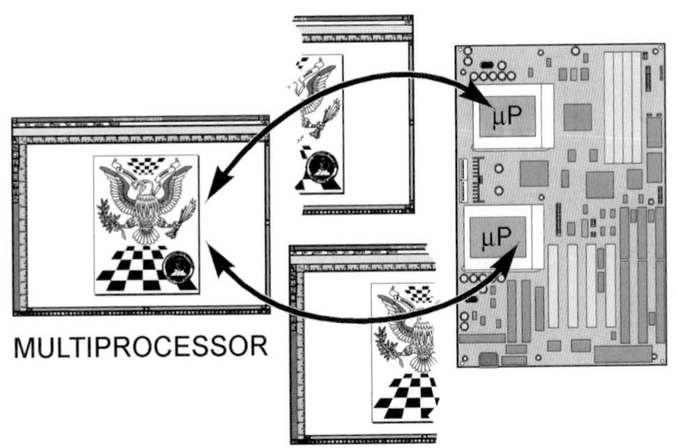

Figure 8-3: Multiple-Process Operating Systems

In multiuser and multitasking operations, the appearance of simultaneous operation is accomplished by switching between different tasks in a predetermined order. The multiuser system switches between different users at multiple locations, while multitasking systems switch between different applications at a single location.

In both cases, the information concerning the first task must be stored and information about the new task loaded each time a task switch occurs. The operating system's scheduler module is responsible for overseeing the switching function.

In a multiprocessor operating system, tasks are divided between multiple microprocessors. This type of operation is referred to as **parallel processing**.

parallel processing

bootstrapping

bootstrap loader

While simple microcomputers store the entire operating system in ROM, most microcomputers use a **bootstrapping** process to load the operating system into RAM. Bootstrapping describes an arrangement where the operating system is loaded into memory by a smaller program called the **bootstrap loader**. The operating system can be loaded from a ROM chip, a floppy disk, a hard disk drive, or from another computer. The term bootstrap refers to the system pulling itself up by its own bootstraps, since, in loading the more-powerful operating system files from the disk, it has increased its on-board intelligence considerably. In personal computers, the bootstrap operation is one of the functions of the ROM BIOS.

BOOTING THE SYSTEM

MS-DOS

The bootstrap process is primarily used in disk drive-based systems to load an operating system that can control such a system. **MS-DOS** is a disk operating system for IBM PC-compatible computers. In its day, it was easily the most popular operating system in the world. It is also the basis from which Windows 9x derives its underlying organization.

As with any other operating system, its function is to oversee operation of the system by providing support for executing programs, controlling I/O devices, handling errors, and providing the user interface. MS-DOS is a disk-based, single-user, single-task operating system.

These qualities make MS-DOS one of the easiest disk operating systems to understand. The remainder of the chapter will use the MS-DOS system to describe basic operating system architecture and operation.

The Boot Process

PC system boards use one or two IC chips to hold the system's BIOS firmware. The system's memory map reserves memory locations from E0000h to FFFFFh for the system board BIOS routines. These chips contain the programs that handle startup of the system, the changeover to disk-based operations, video and printer output functions, and a Power-On Self-Test (POST).

POST Tests and Initialization

The **POST test** is actually a series of tests that are performed each time the system is turned on. The different tests check the operation of the microprocessor, the keyboard, the video display, the floppy and hard disk drive units, as well as both the RAM and ROM memory units.

POST test

When the system board is reset, or when power is removed from it, the system will begin generating clock pulses when power is restored. This action applies a Reset pulse to the microprocessor, causing it to clear most of its registers to 0. However, it sets the **Instruction Pointer (IP) register** to 0FFF0h and the CS register to F0000h. The first instruction is taken from location FFFF0h. Notice that this address is located in the ROM BIOS program. This is not coincidental. When the system is started up, the microprocessor must begin taking instructions from this ROM location to initialize the system for operation.

Instruction Pointer (IP) register

Initial POST Checks

The first instruction that the microprocessor executes causes it to jump to the POST test, where it performs standard tests such as the ROM BIOS **checksum** test (that verifies that the BIOS program is accurate), the system's various **DRAM tests** (that verify the bits of the memory), as well as testing the system's CMOS RAM (to make certain that its contents have not changed due to a battery failure). During the memory tests, the POST displays a running memory count to show that it is testing and verifying the individual memory locations.

checksum

DRAM tests

Sequentially, the system's interrupts are disabled, the bits of the microprocessor's flag register are set, and a Read/Write test is performed on each of its internal registers. The test program simply Writes a predetermined bit pattern into each register and then Reads it back to verify the register's operation. After verifying the operation of the microprocessor's registers, the BIOS program begins testing and initializing the rest of the system. It moves forward by inspecting the ROM BIOS chip itself. It does this by performing a check sum test of certain locations on the chip, and comparing the answer with a known value stored in another location.

A check sum test involves adding the values stored in the key locations together. The result is a rounded-off sum of the values. When the checksum test is performed, the sum of the locations is recalculated and compared to the stored value. If they match, no error is assumed to have occurred. If they do not, an error condition exists and an **error message** or **beep code** is produced.

error message

beep code

At this point, the program checks to see whether the system is being started from an off condition, or being reset from some other state. When the system is started from an off condition, a cold boot is being performed. However, simultaneously pressing the CTRL, ALT, and DEL keys while the system is in operation will generate a reset signal in the system and cause it to perform a shortened bootup routine. This operation is referred to as a warm boot, and allows the system to be shut down and restarted without turning it off. This function also allows the computer's operation to be switched to another operating system.

If power was applied to the system prior to the occurrence of the RESET signal, some of the POST's memory tests are skipped.

If a cold boot is indicated, the program tests the first 16 kB of RAM memory by writing five different bit patterns into the memory and reading them back to establish the validity of each location. The BIOS startup steps are illustrated in Figure 8-4.

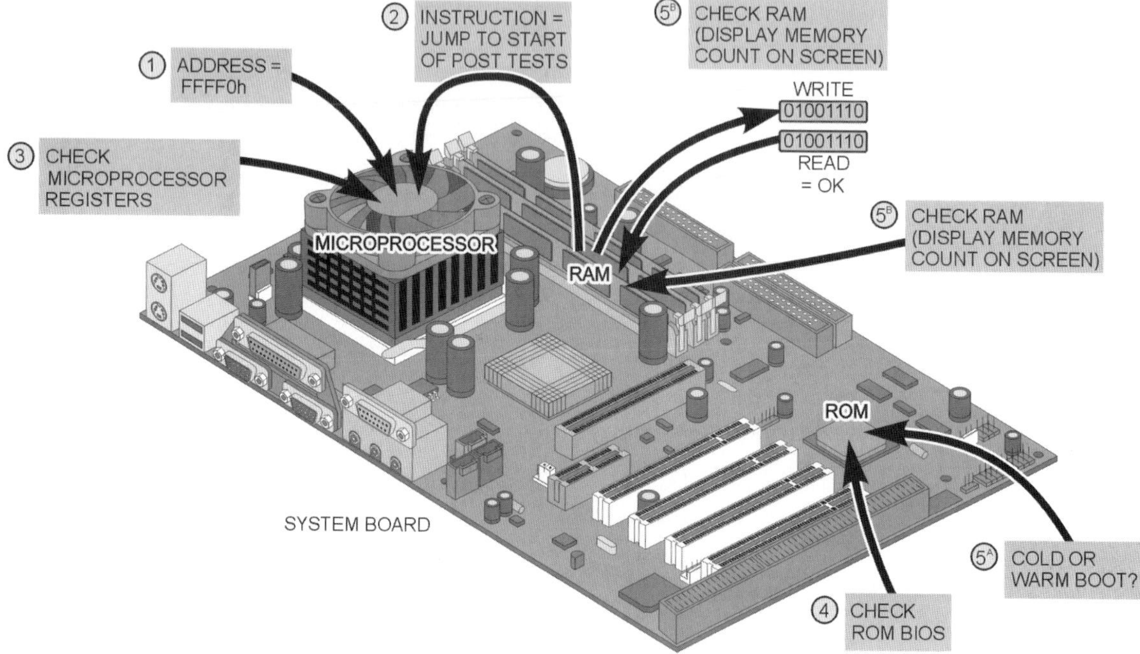

Figure 8-4: The Startup Sequence

System Initialization

initializes

If the first 16 kB of RAM successfully passes all five of the bit-pattern tests, the BIOS routine **initializes** the system's intelligent devices. During this part of the program, startup values stored in the ROM chip are moved into the system's programmable devices to make them functional.

The BIOS loads starting information into all of the system's standard AT-compatible components, such as the interrupt, DMA, keyboard, and video controllers, as well as its timer/counter circuits. The program checks the DMA controller by performing a R/W test on each of its internal registers, and then initializes them with start-up values.

The program continues by setting up the system's interrupt controller. This includes moving the system's interrupt vectors into address locations 00000h through 003FFh. In addition, a R/W test is performed on each of the interrupt controller's internal registers. The routine then causes the controller to mask (disable) all of its interrupt inputs, and tests each one to assure that no interrupts occur.

The programming of the interrupt controller is significant because most of the events in a PC-compatible system are interrupt driven. Its operation affects the operation of the computer in every phase from this point forward. Every peripheral or software routine that needs to get special services from the system makes use of the interrupt controller.

Following the initialization of the interrupt controller, the program checks the output of the system's timer/counter channels. It does this by counting pulses from the counters for a given period of time to verify that the proper frequencies are being produced.

If the timer/counter frequencies are correct, the routine initializes and starts the video controller. The program obtains information about the type of display (monochrome, color, or both) being used with the system by reading configuration information from registers in the system's CMOS RAM. Once this has been established, the program conducts R/W tests on the video adapter's RAM memory.

If the video adapter passes all of these tests, the program causes a cursor symbol to be displayed on the monitor. The steps of the initialization process are described in Figure 8-5.

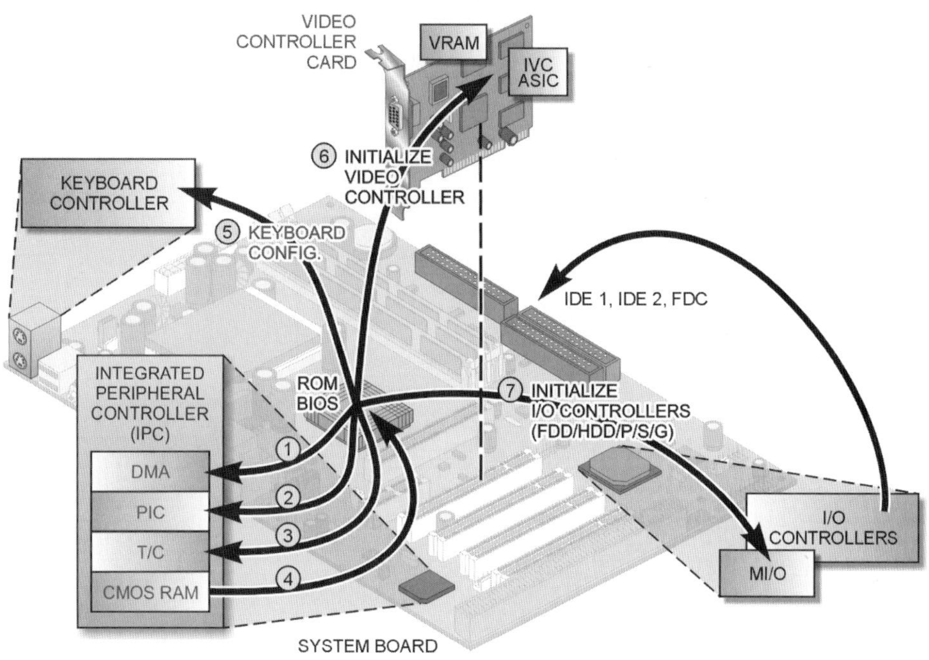

Figure 8-5: System Initialization

Additional POST Checks

Once the display adapter has been checked, the BIOS routine resumes testing the system's on-board memory. First, R/W testing is performed on all the additional RAM on the system board (beyond the first 16 kB). In addition, the BIOS executes the system's built-in setup program to configure its Day/Time setting, its hard disk and floppy disk drive types, and the amount of memory actually available to the system.

Following the final memory test, the remaining I/O devices and adapters are tested. The program begins by enabling the keyboard circuitry and checking for a scan code from the keyboard. No scan code indicates that no key has been depressed. The program then proceeds to test the system's parallel printer and RS-232C serial ports. In each case, the test consists of performing R/W tests on each of the port's registers, storing the addresses of functional ports (some ports may not be installed or in use), and storing time limitations for each port's operation. The steps of the POST process are described in Figure 8-6.

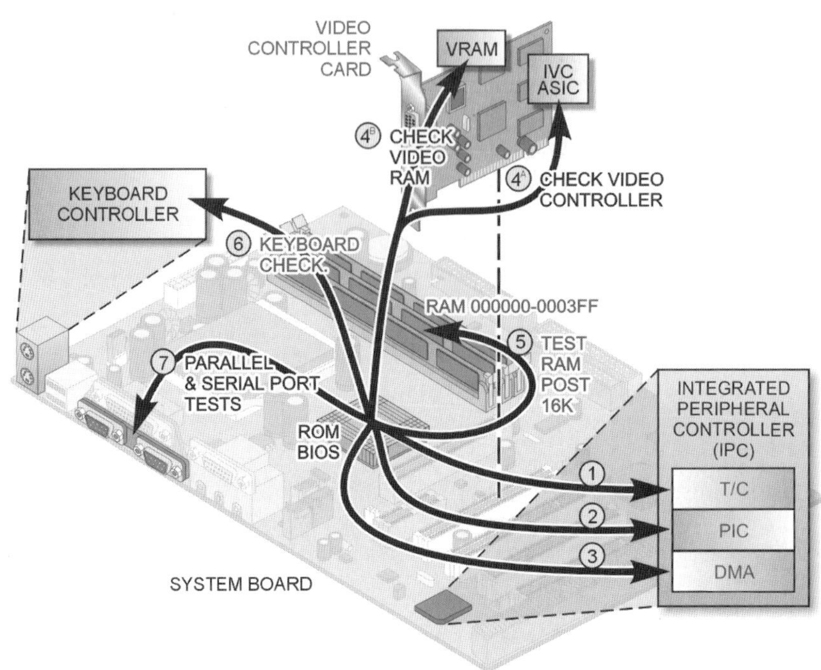

Figure 8-6: Completion of the POST Test

BIOS Extensions

BIOS extension

After the initialization and POST tests are completed, the BIOS checks the area of memory between C0000h and DFFFFh for **BIOS extension** programs.

IBM system designers created this memory area so that new or non-standard BIOS routines could be added to the basic BIOS structure. These extended firmware routines match software commands from the system to the hardware they support. Therefore, the software running on the system does not have to be directly compatible with the hardware.

C8000h

C8800h

BIOS extensions are created in 512-byte blocks that must begin at a 2 kB marker (i.e., **C8000h**, C8200h, C8400h, **C8800h**, etc.), as illustrated in Figure 8-7. A single extension can occupy multiple blocks, but it can only start at one of the markers. When the main BIOS encounters the special two-byte extension code at one of the 2 kB markers, it tests the block of code and then turns control over to the extension.

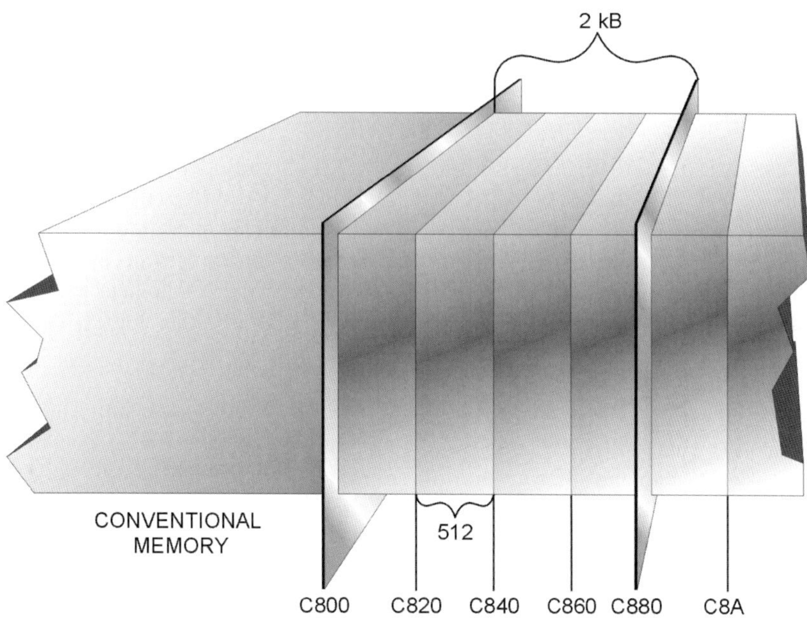

Figure 8-7: BIOS Extension Blocks

Upon completion of the extension code, control is passed back to the main BIOS, which then checks for an extension marker at the next 2 kB marker.

Although the extension addresses are memory addresses, the extension code may be located anywhere in the system. In particular, BIOS extensions are often located on expansion cards. The system simply accesses them through the expansion bus.

Video BIOS

Advanced video cards contain **Video BIOS** code, either in a ROM IC, or built directly into the video controller ASIC. The IBM EGA and VGA standards allow for on-board ROM that uses addresses between C0000h and C7FFFh.

Likewise, different types of HDD controller cards contain a BIOS extension IC. The HDD controllers in old XT units had BIOS extensions that used the address space between C8000h and C9FFFh. Some current HDD controllers, such as ESDI and SCSI adapters, reserve memory blocks between C8000h and CBFFFh.

Initial Program Load (IPL)

Another type of device that commonly uses the C000h-D000h blocks are network adapter cards. These cards allow the computer to be connected to other computers in the local area. The BIOS extension code on a network card may contain an **Initial Program Load (IPL)** routine that will cause the local computer to load up and operate from the operating system of a remote computer.

The system can accommodate as many extensions as will mathematically fit within the allotted memory area. However, two extension programs cannot be located in the same range of addresses. With this in mind, peripheral manufacturers typically include some method of switching the starting addresses of their BIOS extensions so that they can be set to various markers.

Plug-and-Play

Plug-and-Play (PnP)

In the case of **Plug-and-Play** (**PnP**) systems, the BIOS and operating system must also communicate with the adapter cards located in the expansion slots to determine what their characteristics are. Even in a system using a PnP-compliant operating system, such as Windows 9x, the BIOS must be PnP compatible as well before the system can recognize and manipulate system resources. When the system is turned on, the PnP devices involved in the bootup process become active in their default configuration. Other logical devices, not required for bootup, start up in an inactive mode.

software handle (name)

resource conflicts

Before starting the bootup sequence, the PnP BIOS checks the devices installed in the expansion slots to see what types they are, how they are configured, and which slots they are in. It then assigns each adapter a **software handle** (**name**) and stores their names and configuration information in a RAM table. Next, the BIOS checks the adapter information against the system's basic configuration for **resource conflicts**. If no conflicts are detected, all the devices required for bootup are activated.

The devices not required for bootup may be configured and activated by the BIOS, or they may simply be configured and left in an inactive state. In either event, the operating system is left with the task of activating the remaining intelligent devices and resolving any resource conflicts that the BIOS detected and could not resolve. If the PnP option is not working for a particular device, or the operating system cannot resolve the remaining resource conflicts, then it will be necessary to use the manufacturer's setup instructions to perform manual configurations.

CMOS Setup Utilities

As we've already indicated, prior to completing the bootup process, PCs check a battery-powered storage area called the CMOS RAM to determine what types of options are installed in the system.

When the computer is set up for the first time, or when new options are added to the system, it is necessary to run the CMOS configuration setup utility. The values input through the setup utility are stored in the system's CMOS RAM configuration registers. These registers are examined each time the system is booted up to tell the computer what types of devices are installed.

While performing its normal tests and bootup functions, the BIOS program displays an active RAM memory count as it is being tested. Immediately following the RAM test count, the BIOS program places a prompt on the display to tell the user that the CMOS setup utility can be accessed by pressing a special key or a key combination. Typical keys and key combinations include the DELETE key, the ESC key, the F2 function key, the CTRL and ESC keys, and the CTRL-ALT-ESC key combination.

The keys or key combinations used to access the setup menus vary from one BIOS manufacturer to another. If the proper keys are not pressed within a predetermined amount of time, the BIOS program will continue with the bootup process. If the keys are pressed during this time, however, the bootup routine will be put on hold and the program will display a "CMOS Setup" screen, similar to the one depicted in Figure 8-8.

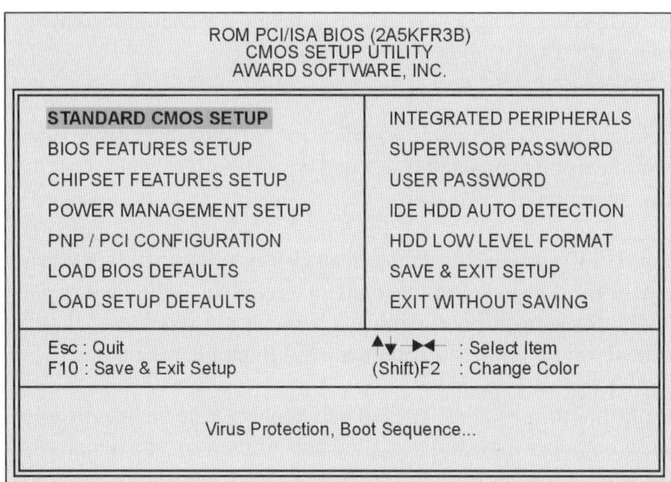

Figure 8-8: A CMOS Setup Selection Screen

Every chipset variation has a specific BIOS designed for it. Therefore, there are functions specific to the design of system boards using that chipset. The example screen in the figure serves as the main menu for entering and exiting the CMOS setup utility and for moving between its configuration pages.

A typical Configuration Setup screen is shown in Figure 8-9. Through this screen, the user enters the desired configuration values into the CMOS registers. The cursor on the screen can be moved from item to item using the keyboard's cursor control keys.

ROM PCI/ISA BIOS (2A5KFDAA)
STANDARD CMOS SETUP
AWARD SOFTWARE, INC.

Date (mm:dd:yy) : Thu, Apr 3 2001
Time (hh:mm:ss) : 3 : 10 : 21

HARD DISKS	TYPE	SIZE	CYLS	HEAD	PRECOMP	LANDZ	SECTOR	MODE
Primary Master	: Auto	0	0	0	0	0	0	Auto
Primary Slave	: Auto	0	0	0	0	0	0	Auto
Secondary Master	: Auto	0	0	0	0	0	0	Auto
Secondary Slave	: Auto	0	0	0	0	0	0	Auto

Drive A : 1.44M, 3.5 in.
Drive B : None
Floppy 3 Mode Support : Disabled

Video : EGA/VGA
Halt On : All Errors

Base Memory: 640K
Extended Memory: 160048K
Other Memory: 384K

Total Memory: 131072K

Esc : Quit
F1 : Help
: Select Item
(Shift)F2 : Change Color
PU/PD/+/- : Modify

Figure 8-9: The CMOS Configuration Setup Screen

When the cursor is positioned on top of a desired option, the PgUp and PgDn cursor keys can be used to change its value. When all the proper options have been configured, pressing the Esc key will cause the routine to exit the setup screen, update any changes made, and resume the bootup process.

BIOS Error Codes

If a hardware error or setup mismatch is encountered, the BIOS will issue an error code, either in message form on the display screen, or in beep-coded form throughout the system's speaker.

Figure 8-10 defines the AMI BIOS program's error messages and beep codes. Likewise, the Award BIOS produces display and beep-coded error messages when a bootup or configuration problem is encountered.

In Plug-and-Play (PnP) systems, the BIOS must also communicate with the adapter cards located in the expansion slots to determine their characteristics. When the system is turned on, the PnP devices involved in the bootup process become active in their default configurations. Other logical devices not required for bootup start in an inactive mode.

Before starting the bootup sequence, the PnP BIOS checks the devices installed in the expansion slots to see what types they are, how they are configured, and which slots they are in. It then assigns each adapter a software handle (name) and stores their names and configuration information in a RAM table. Next, the BIOS checks the adapter information against the system's basic configuration for resource conflicts. If no conflicts are detected, all the devices required for bootup are activated.

The devices not required for bootup may be configured and activated by the BIOS, or may simply be configured and left in an inactive state. Either way, the operating system activates the remaining intelligent devices and resolves any resource conflicts that the BIOS detected and could not resolve. If the PnP option is not working for a particular device, or if the operating system cannot resolve the remaining resource conflicts, then it is necessary to use the manufacturer's setup instructions to perform a manual configuration.

NUMBER OF BEEPS	PROBLEM INDICATED
1	DRAM refresh failure
2	RAM failure (base 640 kB)
3	System timer failure
5	Microprocessor failure
6	Keyboard controller failure
7	Virtual Mode Exception failure
9	ROM BIOS checksum failure
1 long, 2 short	Video controller failure
1 long, 3 short	Conventional and Extended test failure
1 long, 8 short	Display test failure

Figure 8-10: Beep Code Messages

SYSTEM HALTED ERRORS

CMOS INOPERATIONAL - Failure of CMOS shutdown register test
8042 GATE A20 ERROR - Error getting into protected mode
INVALID SWITCH MEMORY FAILURE - Real/Protected mode changeover error.
DMA ERROR - DMA controller failed page register test
DMA #1 ERROR - DMA device # 1 failure
DMA #2 ERROR - DMA device # 2 failure

NON-FATAL ERRORS - WITH SETUP OPTION

CMOS BATTERY LOW - Failure of CMOS battery or CMOS checksum test
CMOS SYSTEM OPTION NOT SET - Failure of CMOS battery or CMOS checksum test
CMOS CHECKSUM FAILURE - CMOS battery low or CMOS checksum test failure
CMOS DISPLAY MISMATCH - Failure of display type verification
CMOS MEMORY SIZE MISMATCH - System Configuration and Setup failure
CMOS TIMER AND DATE NOT SET - System Configuration and Setup failure in timer circuitry

NON-FATAL ERRORS - WITHOUT SETUP OPTION

CH-X TIMER ERROR - Channel X (2, 1, or 0) TIMER failure
KEYBOARD ERROR - Keyboard test failure
KB/INTERFACE ERROR - Keyboard test failure
DISPLAY SWITCH SETTING NOT PROPER - Failure to verify display type
KEYBOARD IS LOCKED - Unlock it
FDD CONTROLLER ERROR - Failure to verify floppy disk setup by System Configuration file
HDD CONTROLLER FAILURE - Failure to verify hard disk setup by System Configuration file
C:DRIVE ERROR - Hard disk setup failure
D:DRIVE ERROR - Hard disk setup failure

Figure 8-10 (continued): Visual Display Error Messages

MS-DOS Bootup

If the option to enter the Setup routine is bypassed, or if the routine has been exited, the BIOS will begin the process of booting up to the operating system. A simple single-operating-system, single-disk bootup process is described in Figure 8-11. As you can see, it is a multiple-access operation that uses two different bootstrap routines to locate and load two different boot records.

Starting the Boot-Up Process—The **bootup** process starts when the BIOS begins looking through the system for a **Master Boot Record** (**MBR**). This record can reside on drive A: or C:, or at any other location.

bootup

Master Boot Record (MBR)

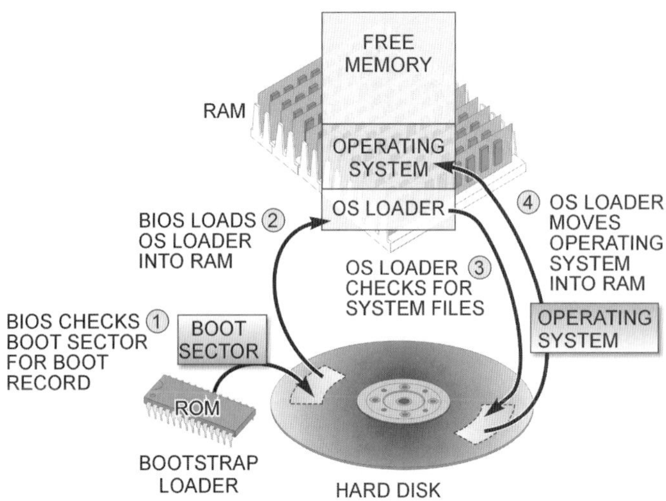

Figure 8-11: The Bootstrap Operation

The very first section on any logical DOS disk is called the **boot sector**. This section contains information about how the disk is organized. It may also contain the small optional master boot record that can access a larger, more powerful bootstrap loader program located in the **root directory**.

In most systems, the master boot record is found at sector-1, head-0, and track-0 of the first logical hard drive. Some texts may refer to the first sector as Sector zero, in keeping with the idea that the first of anything in a digital system is 0. If the disk possesses a master boot record, it can boot up the hardware system to the operating system. The disk is then referred to as a **bootable disk**, or a **system disk**. If not, the disk is simply a **data disk** that can be used for storing information.

boot sector

root directory

bootable disk

system disk

data disk

Supplemental disk

primary bootstrap loader

Non-System Disk or Disk Error

ROM BASIC Interpreter Not Found

The usage of the term "system disk" has changed somewhat over time. In the old days, when MS-DOS came on two disks labeled System disk and **Supplemental disk**, the System disk was the one that contained the files necessary to boot the system. Now, the term is used generally to specify any floppy disk that has a master boot record so that it can boot the system—regardless of the type of operating system it carries.

Traditionally, BIOS programs will search for the master boot record in floppy disk drive A: first. If a bootable disk is in the floppy disk drive, the BIOS will execute the **primary bootstrap loader** routine to move the master boot record into RAM and then begin the process of loading the operating system. In the original IBM PC, the BIOS searched in the floppy disk drive for the boot record. If it was not located there, the BIOS routine turned over control to a BASIC program located in the PC's ROM BIOS IC.

In the PC-XT, the BIOS looked first in the floppy drive, or drives, and then in the hard disk drive. If neither location contained the boot record, the system loaded up the ROM BASIC program. In clone systems, there was no ROM BIOS present to default to when no boot record was found. If the BIOS did not locate the boot record in the floppy or hard drive, it simply displayed a **Non-System Disk or Disk Error**, or **ROM BASIC Interpreter Not Found** message on the screen.

In newer systems, the order in which the BIOS searches drives for the boot record is governed by information stored in the system's CMOS configuration RAM. The order can be set to check the floppy drive first and then the hard drive, or to check the hard drive first, or to check the hard drive only.

In a networked system, a bootstrap loader routine can also be located in the ROM extension of a network card as described earlier. When the system checks the BIOS extensions, the bootstrap routine redirects the bootup process to look for a boot record on the disk drive of another computer. Any boot record on the local drive will be bypassed.

To accomplish the bootup, the BIOS enables the system's Non-Maskable interrupts and causes a single, short tone to be produced by the speaker circuitry. The single beep indicates that the POST portion of the bootup has been successfully completed.

The next BIOS instruction executes an Interrupt19 Disk Drive service routine. This interrupt routine carries out the Primary Bootstrap Loader program, which looks for the master boot record in the first section of the floppy and hard disks. When located, it moves the master boot record into system RAM to be executed.

The master boot record contains the **secondary bootstrap loader**, also called the **operating system loader**. This routine looks for an **operating system boot record**, typically located on the disk. When found, it loads the bigger boot record into RAM and begins executing it. This boot record brings special operating system files into memory so that they can control the operation of the system (i.e., the operating system). In the case of Microsoft DOS, the special files in the OS boot record are the **IO.SYS** and **MSDOS.SYS** files.

secondary bootstrap loader

operating system loader

operating system boot record

IO.SYS

MSDOS.SYS

The operating system loader looks for a command processor file. The command processor can belong to any operating system, such as Microsoft MS-DOS, UNIX, IBM PC-DOS, Novell NetWare, etc. The default command processor for DOS is a system file called **COMMAND.COM**. This file interprets the input entered at the DOS prompt. When the bootstrap program finds the command processor, it moves it into system RAM along with the operating system support files. In DOS systems, the command processor provides the basic user interface, called the **command line**.

COMMAND.COM

command line

In the original PC-DOS from IBM, the files were titled IBMBIO.COM, IBMDOS.COM, and COMMAND.COM. This step marks the end of the BIOS routine. The three system files must be found in the root directory (the starting point for any disk-based operations) in order to successfully boot DOS. The total bootup process is described in Figure 8-12.

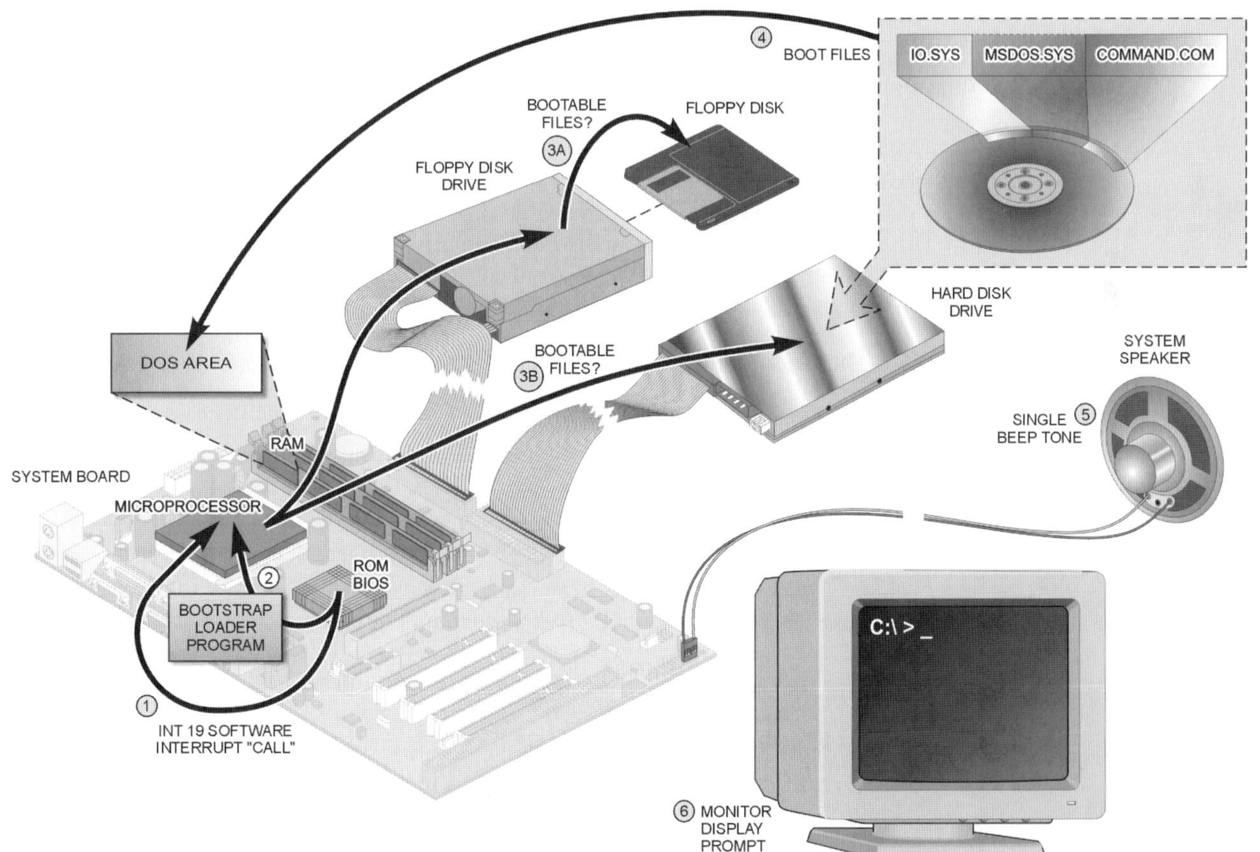

Figure 8-12: The Bootup Process

command line prompt

If the system has performed a standard DOS bootup, without any modifications, it should print Date and Time prompts on the monitor screen, followed by the DOS **command line prompt** (A:\ or C:\). The prompt indicates that DOS is operational and the currently active drive is the A: floppy drive, or the C: hard drive. Now the DOS software will control the movement of data and overall operation of the system.

The following list summarizes the files and their execution order required for bootup in an MS-DOS system:

TEST TIP

Remember the files involved the DOS bootup process and the order of their execution.

- IO.SYS
- MSDOS.SYS
- CONFIG.SYS
- COMMAND.COM
- AUTOEXEC.BAT

In a DOS system, the operation of the system is now in the control of the operator, and whatever software is being used with the system. The system is waiting for the user to do something, such as enter commands and instructions, or run programs from the other two software categories. The user hasn't had anything to do with the operation of the system yet. This is why this type of software is referred to as system software.

DOS Configuration Files

In the MS-DOS operating system, there are two special configuration files, called CONFIG.SYS and AUTOEXEC.BAT, that can be included in the DOS bootup process. These programs are used to optimize the system for operations in particular functions, or with different options.

As the system moves through the bootup procedure, the BIOS checks in the root directory of the boot disk for the presence of the CONFIG.SYS file. Afterward, it searches for the COMMAND.COM interpreter, and finally looks in the root directory for the AUTOEXEC.BAT file. Both the CONFIG.SYS and AUTOEXEC.BAT files play key roles in optimizing the system's memory and disk-drive usage. Their involvement in the bootup process can be summarized as follows:

1. BIOS performs INT19 to search drives for master boot record.
2. Primary Bootstrap Loader moves master boot record into memory.
3. System executes Secondary Bootstrap Loader from master boot record.
4. Secondary Bootstrap Loader moves IO.SYS and MSDOS.SYS into memory.
5. IO.SYS runs the MSDOS.SYS file to load memory and file management functions.
6. IO.SYS checks for CONFIG.SYS file in root directory.
7. If CONFIG.SYS is found, IO.SYS uses it to reconfigure the system in three read sequences (device, install, and shell).
8. IO.SYS loads COMMAND.COM.
9. COMMAND.COM checks for the AUTOEXEC.BAT file in the root directory.
10. If the AUTOEXEC.BAT file is found, COMMAND.COM carries out the commands found in the file.
11. If no AUTOEXEC.BAT file is found, COMMAND.COM displays the DOS Time and Date prompt on the display.

While the system is operating, the BIOS continues to perform several important functions. It contains routines on which the operating system calls to carry out basic services. These services include providing **BIOS interrupt calls** (software interrupt routines) for such operations as printer, video, and disk- drive accesses.

BIOS interrupt calls

BIOS Services

The ROM BIOS services are organized into groups identified by interrupt numbers. Each interrupt may cover several different services. When the microprocessor jumps to a particular interrupt, the software calling the interrupt must have already loaded the service number into the microprocessor to tell it which section of the interrupt handler to access.

The most notable BIOS interrupt calls include the following:

- 10h—Video services (16)
- 13h—Hard and floppy drive services (17 and 11)
- 14h—Serial port services (6)
- 16h—Keyboard services (7)
- 17h—Parallel printer port services (3)
- 18h—ROM BASIC (old systems)/network card services (newer systems)
- 19h—Primary bootstrap loader
- 1Ah—Real time clock services

The numbers in parentheses refer to the number of different services available through the interrupt. For example, 10h—Video services (16) indicates that there are 16 different services available through interrupt call 10.

This list represents only a few of the more notable BIOS interrupts. The most important thing for a technician to remember about BIOS interrupt calls is that they form the backbone of the system's operation. The BIOS and DOS are constantly handing control of the system back and forth as normal system functions are carried out. This relationship is illustrated in Figure 8-13. These BIOS interrupt calls are also responsible for most of the drawbacks of the PC system; that's why so much effort is exerted in the software to work around them. Advanced operating systems implement newer methods of handling system functions in order to avoid handing control over to the BIOS interrupts.

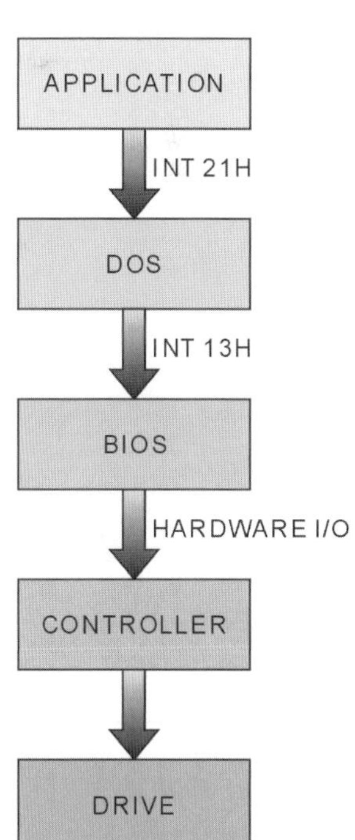

Figure 8-13: DOS/BIOS Relationships

Older PCs have trouble supporting newer hardware because the older BIOS does not support it. To correct this situation, it is usually necessary to load a separate software driver program to support the device. Another possibility is to replace the BIOS with an improved version; however, this operation is not performed often because an upgraded BIOS must be compatible with the older chipset on the system board. Figure 8-14 shows a sample bootup screen featuring the BIOS revision number.

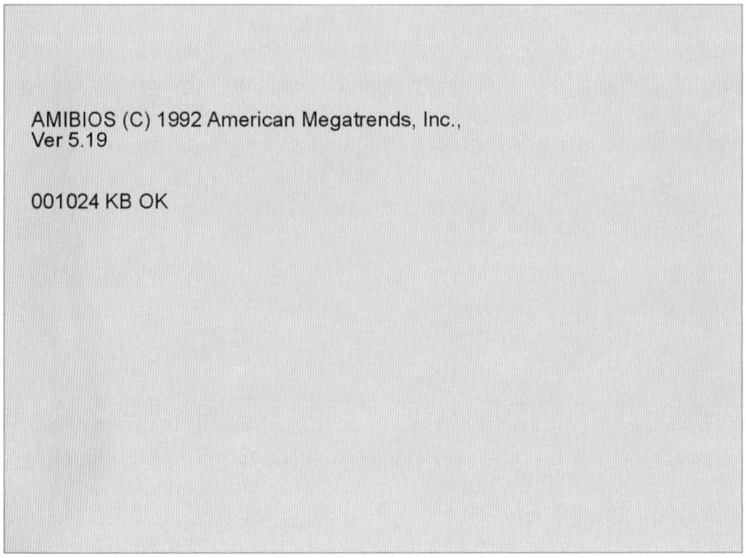

AMIBIOS (C) 1992 American Megatrends, Inc.,
Ver 5.19

001024 KB OK

Figure 8-14: BIOS Version Information

MS-DOS Disk Structure

hidden system files

device drivers

The main portions of MS-DOS are the IO.SYS, MSDOS.SYS, and COMMAND.COM files. IO.SYS and MSDOS.SYS are special **hidden system files** that do not show up in a normal directory listing. The IO.SYS file moves the system's basic I/O functions into memory and then implements the MS-DOS default control programs, referred to as **device drivers**, for various hardware components. These include:

- the boot disk drive
- the console display and keyboard
- the system's time-of-day clock
- the parallel and serial communications port

Conversely, the MSDOS.SYS file provides default support features for software applications. These features include:

- memory management
- character input and output
- real-time clock access
- file and record management
- execution of other programs

There is a little known DOS system requirement that the MSDOS.SYS file must maintain a size in excess of 1 KB.

The COMMAND.COM command interpreter contains the operating system's most frequently used commands. When a DOS command is entered at the DOS prompt, the COMMAND.COM program examines it to see if it is an **internal DOS command**, or an **external DOS command**. Internal commands are understood directly by COMMAND.COM, while external commands are stored in a directory called DOS. If it is one of the internal commands, the COMMAND.COM file can execute it immediately. If not, COMMAND.COM looks in the \DOS directory for the command program.

internal DOS command

external DOS command

Likewise, when DOS runs an application, COMMAND.COM finds the program, loads it into memory, and then gives it control of the system. When the program is shut down, it passes control back to the command interpreter.

The remainder of the operating system is comprised of utility programs to carry out DOS operations such as formatting disks (Format), printing files (Print), and copying files (XCOPY).

DOS Disk Structure

It is also important to understand how operating systems see disks. When a disk is created, its surface is electronically blank. To prepare the disk for use by the system there are three levels of preparation that must take place.

These are, in order:

- the **low-level format** (below DOS)
- the **partition** (DOS - FDISK command)
- the **high-level format** (DOS - Format command)

low-level format

partition

high-level format

In the PC world, floppy disks basically come in four accepted formats—360 kB, 720 kB, 1.2 MB, and 1.44 MB. When they are formatted to one of these standards, the system performs the low- and high-level formats in the same operation. Floppies cannot be partitioned into logical disks, therefore, no partition operation needs to be performed. However, hard disk drives are created in a wide variety of physical specifications and storage capacities and, therefore, need to be partitioned so the operating system knows how they are organized.

A low-level format is very similar to a land developer sectioning off a field for a new housing development. The process begins with surveying the property and placing markers for key structures such as roads, water lines, and electrical service. The low-level format routine is similar in that it marks off the disk into cylinders and sectors, and defines their placement on the disk.

In older **device-level drive types** (such as ST-506 and ESDI drives), the user was required to perform the low-level format. This procedure could be accomplished through the DOS Debug program or through software diagnostic packages that came with a low-level formatting program. System-level drives (such as IDE and SCSI drives) require no additional low-level formatting. This function is furnished by the drive's manufacturer when it is created.

device-level drive types

Disk Preparation

As mentioned in Chapter 1—*Basic PC Hardware*, when a magnetic disk is created it is for all practical purposes blank. In the earliest versions of PC-DOS and MS-DOS, the complete operating system was contained on two uncompressed disks: the system disk and the supplemental disk.

When PCs were floppy drive based, the main portion of the disk operating system was loaded into the system from a system disk during the boot-up process. The most used DOS functions were loaded into RAM during the boot-up process.

Complex operating system functions required that external DOS commands be temporarily loaded into the system from the supplemental disk. Programs and data were stored on data disks, or work disks. Control of the floppy-disk system was built directly in to the system's BIOS.

When the PCs moved to hard drive–based operations, the main DOS files were placed in the root directory on the hard disk as a part of its formatting process. Recall that these files included IO.SYS, MSDOS.SYS, and COMMAND.COM. This function is typically the result of using a /S switch on a FORMAT command. These files can be replaced or upgraded to a new version level through the use of the DOS SYS command. The other DOS files were typically copied into a C:\DOS directory when the unit was set up.

Installing the operating system directly on the hard disk meant that disks did not need to be exchanged for every different function the user wanted to perform. Programs and data were also stored directly on the drive. Who could ever fill up those huge 10 MB drives that came with the PC-XTs?

Installing the operating system on a new hard drive has evolved into the four basic steps outlined in this A+ objective:

1. Partition the drive for use with the operating system.
2. Format the drive with the basic operating system files.
3. Run the appropriate setup utility to install the complete operating system.
4. Load all the drivers necessary to enable the operating system to work with the system's installed hardware devices.

Drive Partitioning

Physical hard disk drives can be divided into multiple logical drives. This operation is referred to as partitioning the drive. With earlier versions of DOS partitioning became necessary because the capacity of hard drives exceeded the ability of the existing DOS structure to track all of the possible sectors.

By creating a second logical drive on the hard disk another complete file tracking structure is created on the drive. The operating system sees this new structure on the hard drive as a completely new disk. Therefore, it must have a new, unique drive letter assigned to it.

Figure 8-15 illustrates the concept of creating multiple logical drives on a single hard drive. This is normally done for purposes of organization and increased access speeds. The partitioning program for MS-DOS, Windows 9x, Unix, and Linux is named **FDISK**. This program creates the disk's boot sector and establishes partition parameters (partition table) for the system's use.

FDISK

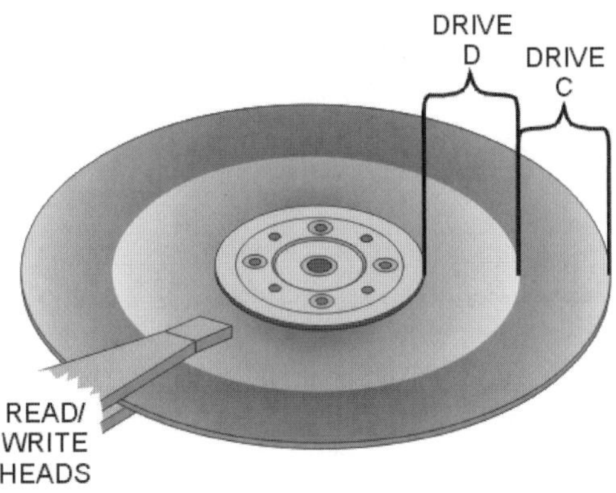

Figure 8-15: HDD Partitions

primary partition

extended partition

Basically, DOS provides for two partitions on an HDD unit. The first, or the **primary partition**, must exist as drive C. After the primary partition has been established and properly configured, an additional partition, referred to as an **extended partition**, is also permitted. However, the extended partition may be subdivided into 23 logical drives. The extended partition cannot be deleted if logical drives have been defined within it. The active partition is the logical drive that the system will boot to. The system files must be located in this partition, and the partition must be set to "Active" for the system to boot up from the drive.

TEST TIP

Be aware of how the primary partition, extended partitions, and the active partition are related.

In local and wide area networks (LANs and WANs), the concept of logical drives is carried a step further. A particular hard disk drive may be a logical drive in a large system of drives along a peer-to-peer network. On the other hand, a very large, centralized drive may be used to create several logical drives for a client/server type of network. This is accomplished by creating a logical **mapping** between the operating system and the desired drive, so that the local system handles the mapped drive as one of its own drives.

mapping

In some applications, partitioning is used to permit multiple operating systems to exist on the same physical drive. Since each partition on the drive contains its own boot sector, FAT, and root directory, each partition can be set up to hold and boot up to a different operating system.

On a partitioned drive, a special table, called the **partition table**, is created in the boot sector at the very beginning of the disk. This table holds information about the location and starting point of each logical drive on the disk, along with the information about which partition has been marked as active and a master boot record.

partition table

The partition table is located at the beginning of the disk because this is the point where the system looks for bootup information. When the system checks the MBR of the physical disk during the boot process, it also checks to see which partition on the disk has been marked as active. It then jumps to that location, reads the information in that partition boot record, and boots to the operating system in that logical drive.

High-Level Formatting

File Allocation Tables (FATs)

Root Directory

The high-level format procedure is performed by the Format command in the MS-DOS program. This command creates two blank **File Allocation Tables (FATs)** and a **Root Directory** on the disk.

These elements tell the system what files are on the disk, and where they can be found. Modifying the format command with a /S after the drive letter designation causes the DOS system files to be moved to the drive.

Never format a disk with an older version of DOS than is currently installed on the disk. The disk can actually be damaged from this action. Before reformatting a disk, use the DOS VER command to determine what version of DOS is currently in use.

Figure 8-16 describes the organization of a DOS disk and illustrates the position of the boot sector, file allocation tables, and the root directory. The remainder of the disk is dedicated to data storage. In the Chapter 1 section on booting up, it was mentioned that the first area on each logical DOS disk, or partition, is the boot sector. While all formatted partitions have this sector, they do not all have the optional master boot record located in the sector. Only those disks created to be bootable disks have this record.

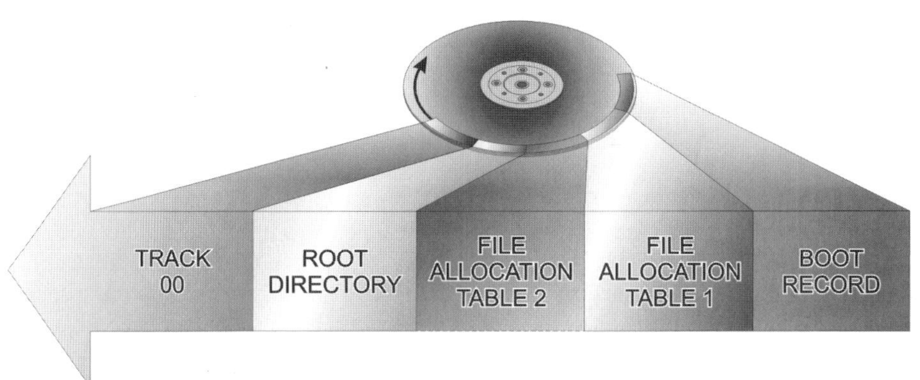

Figure 8-16: DOS Disk Organization

File Allocation Tables

The second section of a DOS disk is occupied by its file allocation tables. This area is a table of information about how the disk is organized. Basically, the system logs the use of the space on the disk in this table.

allocation units

clusters

In older versions of DOS, the amount of space dedicated to tracking the sectors on the disk was 16 bits. Therefore, only 65,536 sectors could be accounted for. This parameter limited the size of a DOS partition to 32 MB (33,554,432 bytes).

TEST TIP

Know what the smallest unit of storage in a disk-based system is.

To more effectively manage the space on the disk, newer versions of DOS divide the disk into groups of logically- related sectors, called **allocation units**, or **clusters**. In a DOS system, the cluster is the smallest piece of manageable information.

The sectors on a DOS disk hold 512 bytes each. On the other hand, files can be any length. Therefore, a single file may occupy several sectors on the disk. The DOS disk routine breaks the file into sector-sized chunks and stores it in a cluster of sectors. In this manner, DOS uses the cluster to track files instead of sectors. Since the file allocation table only has to handle information for a cluster, instead of for each sector, the number of files that can be tracked in a given length table is greatly increased.

TEST TIP

Know the size of sectors in an IBM/PC compatible disk.

The organization of a typical FAT is described in Table 8-1. The first two entries are reserved for DOS information. Each cluster after that holds a value. Each value may represent one of three conditions. A value of 0 indicates that the cluster is available and can be used for storage. Any number besides 0 or FFFh indicates that the cluster contains data, and the number provides the location of the next cluster in a chain of clusters. Finally, a value of FFFh (or FFFFh in a 16-bit entry) indicates the end of a cluster chain.

Table 8-1: File Allocation Table Structure

CLUSTER NUMBER	CONTENTS
Cluster 0	Reserved for DOS
Cluster 1	Reserved for DOS
Cluster 2	3 (contains data go to cluster 3)
Cluster 3	4 (contains data go to cluster 4)
Cluster 4	7 (contains data go to cluster 7)
Cluster 5	0 (free space)
Cluster 6	0 (free space)
Cluster 7	8 (contains data go to cluster 8)
Cluster 8	FFFh (end cluster chain)
Cluster 9	0 (free space)
•	•
Cluster X	0 (free space)
Cluster Y	0 (free space)
Cluster Z	0 (free space)

On floppy disks, common cluster sizes are one or two sectors long. With hard disks, the cluster size may vary from 1 to 16 sectors in length. The FAT keeps track of which clusters are used and which ones are free. It contains a 12- or 16-bit entry for each cluster on the disk. The 12-bit entries are used with floppy disks and hard disks that are smaller than 17 MB. The 16-bit entries are employed with hard disk drives larger than 17 MB. Obviously, the larger entries allow the FAT to manage more clusters.

In free clusters, a value of zero is recorded. In used clusters, the cluster number is stored. In cases where the file requires multiple clusters, the FAT entry for the first cluster holds the cluster number for the next cluster used to store the file. Each subsequent cluster entry has the number of the next cluster used by the file. The final cluster entry contains an end-of-file marker code that tells the system that the end of the file has been reached.

cluster links

cross-linked

These **cluster links** enable the operating system to store and retrieve virtually any size file that will fit on the disk. However, the loss of any link will make it impossible to retrieve the file and use it. If the FAT becomes corrupted, chained files can become **cross-linked** with each other, making them useless. For this reason, two complete copies of the FAT are stored consecutively on the disk under the DOS disk structure. The first copy is the normal working copy while the second FAT is used as a backup measure in case the contents of the first FAT become corrupted.

The Root Directory

The next section following the FAT tables is the disk's root directory. This is a special directory that is present on every DOS disk. It is the main directory of every logical disk, and serves as the starting point for organizing information on the disk.

The location of every directory, subdirectory, and file on the disk is recorded in this table.

TEST TIP

Remember the number of entries that directories in a FAT-based system can hold.

Each directory and subdirectory (including the root directory) can hold up to 512 32-byte entries that describe each of the files in them. The first eight bytes contain the file's name, followed by three bytes for its filename extension.

attributes

The next 11 bytes define the file's **attributes**. Attributes for DOS files include:

- Read Only
- System File
- Volume Label
- Subdirectory Entry
- Archive (backup) status

Two bytes are used to record the time the file was created or last modified. This is followed by two additional bytes that record the date the file was created or last modified.

starting cluster number

byte count number

The final four bytes are divided equally between the value for the **starting cluster number** and a **byte count number** for the file. Unlike the previous information in the directory, the information associated with the last four bytes is not displayed when a directory listing is displayed on the screen.

Since each root directory entry is 32 bytes long, each disk sector can hold 16 entries. Consequently, the number of files or directories that can be listed in the root directory is dependent on how many disk sectors are allocated to it. On a hard disk drive, there are normally 32 sectors set aside for the root directory. Therefore, the root directory for such a disk can accommodate up to 512 entries. A typical 3-1/2" 1.44 MB floppy has 16 sectors reserved for the root directory and can hold up to 224 entries.

On a floppy disk the logical structure normally has a group of files located under the root directory. Directory structures can be created on a floppy, but due to their relatively small capacity, this is not normally done. However, a hard drive is another matter. With hard drives, it is normal to organize the disk into directories and subdirectories as described earlier in the previous chapter.

Technically, every directory on a disk is a subdirectory of the root directory. All additional directories branch out from the root directory in a tree-like fashion. Therefore, a graphical representation of the disk drive's directory organization is called a **directory tree**. Figure 8-17 depicts the directory organization of a typical hard drive.

directory tree

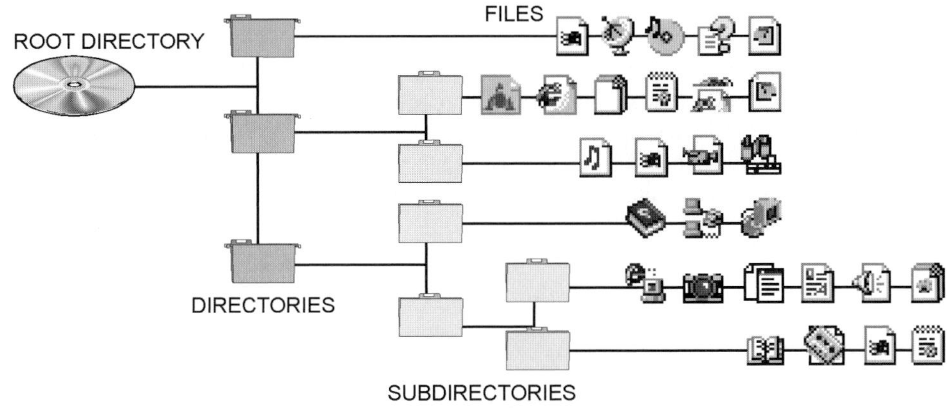

Figure 8-17: The DOS Directory Tree Structure

NAVIGATING IN MS-DOS

It is important to consider that MS-DOS is a disk operating system. Therefore, you must understand how DOS organizes disks. The DOS organizational structure is typically described as being like a common office file cabinet, similar to the one depicted in Figure 8-18. Think of DOS as the filing cabinet structure. Our example has three drawers that can be opened. Think of these as **disk drives** labeled A, B, and C/D. Inside each drawer are hanging folders that can hold different types of items. Think of these as **directories**.

disk drives

directories

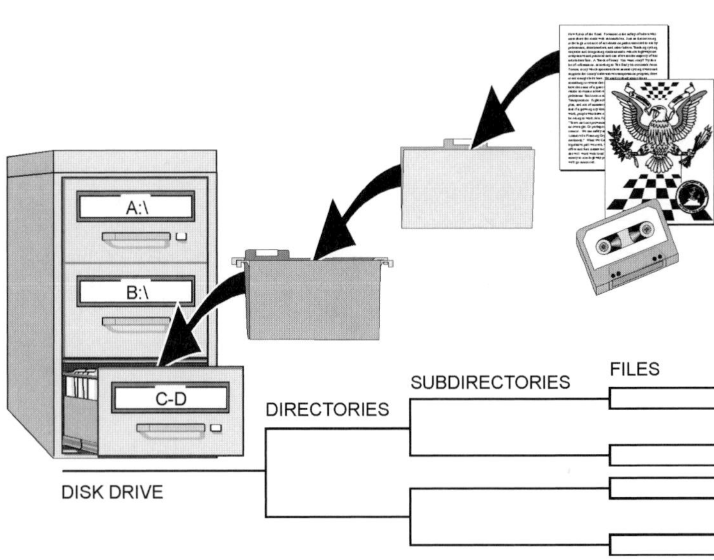

Figure 8-18: DOS Organization

subdirectories

The hanging folders may contain different types of items or other individual folders. Think of these individual folders as **subdirectories**. For organizational purposes, each hanging folder and each individual folder must have a unique label on it.

Inside each hanging folder, or individual folder, are the items being stored. In a real filing cabinet, these items in the folders are usually documents of different types. However, pictures and tapes and other items related to the folders can also be stored in them.

files

Think of the items inside the folders as **files**. Disk-based systems manage data blocks by giving them file names. Recall that a file is simply a block of logically related data, given a single name, and treated as a single unit. Like the contents of the folders, files can be programs, documents, drawings or other illustrations, sound files, etc.

path

In order to find an item in the cabinet, you simply need to know which drawer, hanging folder, and folder it is located in. This concept can be translated directly to the computer system. To locate a particular file, you simply need to know which drive, directory, and subdirectory it is located in. In MS-DOS, the **path** to any file in the system can be written as a direction to the computer so that it will know where the file is that it is being directed toward. This format for specifying a path is as follows:

C:\directory name\subdirectory_name\filename

back slashes (\)

where the C: specifies the C disk drive. The directory, subdirectory, and filenames would naturally be replaced by their real names. The **back slashes** (\) after each item indicate the presence of a directory or subdirectory. The first slash indicates a special directory, called the root directory, which is present on all DOS disks.

filename
extension

If the direction is to a file, the **filename** is always placed at the end of the path. MS-DOS allows for a basic filename of up to eight characters. It also allows for an **extension** of up to three characters. The extension is separated from the main portion of the filename by a period and is normally used to identify what type of file it is (i.e., the file name *file1.ltr* could be used to identify a letter created by a word processor).

.COM
.SYS

NOTE

Filename extensions are not actually required for most files. However, they become helpful in sorting between files in a congested system. You should be aware that the operating system reserves some three-letter combinations, such as **.COM** and .**SYS**, for its own use. More information about filenames and extensions is presented in the subsequent section concerning file-level DOS commands.

The operating system is responsible for providing the system's user interface. The main user interface for DOS is the command line. The command line is the space immediately following the DOS prompt on the screen. All DOS commands are typed in this space. They are executed by pressing the ENTER key on the keyboard.

Command Line Functions

The operating system is responsible for providing the system's user interface. The main user interface for DOS is the command line. The command line is the space immediately following the DOS prompt on the screen. All DOS commands are typed in this space. They are executed by pressing the ENTER key on the keyboard.

The **MS-DOS prompt** for using the C: hard disk drive as the active directory is displayed in Figure 8-19.

MS-DOS prompt

```
Mouse Version 8.00
1988 - 1993

Driver Installed : Mouse Systems Mode
Dynamic Resolution OFF
Mouse setup on COM1:

C:\MOUSE>
```

Figure 8-19: The DOS Prompt

From the DOS prompt, all DOS functions can be entered and executed. DOS application programs are also started from this prompt. These files can be discerned by their filename extensions. Files with .COM, **.EXE**, or **.BAT** extensions can be started directly from the prompt. The .COM and .EXE file extensions are reserved by DOS and can only be generated by programs that can correctly configure them. BAT files are simply ASCII text files that have been generated using DOS functions. Since they contain DOS commands mixed with .COM and .EXE files, DOS can execute .BAT files from the command line.

.EXE

.BAT

TEST TIP

Know which file types can be executed directly from the command line prompt.

Programs with other types of extensions must be **associated** with one of these three file types to be operated. The user can operate application software packages such as graphical user interfaces, word processors, business packages, data communications packages, and user programming languages (i.e., QBASIC and DEBUG). As an example, the core component of a word processor could be a file called WORDPRO.EXE. Document files produced by word processors are normally given filename extensions of .DOC (for document) or .TXT (for text file).

associated

In order to view one of the documents electronically, you would first need to run the executable file and then use its features to load up, format, and display the document. Likewise, a BASIC file normally has an extension of .BAS assigned to it. In order to execute a file with this extension, it is necessary to run a BASIC interpreter, such as QBASIC.EXE, and then use it to load the .BAS file and then run it.

The user can also type DOS commands on the command line to perform DOS functions. These commands can be grouped into drive-level commands, directory-level commands, and file-level commands. The format for using DOS commands is:

COMMAND (*space*) SOURCE location (*space*) DESTINATION location

COMMAND (*space*) location

COMMAND

The first example illustrates how DOS operations that involve a source and a final destination, such as moving a file from one place to another, are entered.

default location

The second example illustrates how single-location DOS operations, such as formatting a diskette in a particular disk drive, are specified. The final example applies to DOS commands that occur in a **default location**, such as obtaining a listing of the files on the current disk drive.

switches

fore-slash (/)

Many DOS commands can be modified by placing one or more software **switches** at the end of the basic command. A switch is added to the command by adding a space, a **fore-slash** (/), and a single letter:

COMMAND (space) option /switch

NOTE

Common DOS command switches include /P for page, /W for wide format, and /S for system. Different switches are used to modify different DOS commands. In each case, the DOS User's Guide should be consulted for switch definitions available with each command.

Drives and Disks

Each disk drive in the system is identified by DOS with a single-letter name (such as A:), and this name must be specified when giving the system commands, so that they are carried out using the proper drive. The format for specifying which drive will perform a DOS operation uses the drive's identifier letter in the command, followed by a colon (i.e., A: or C:).

drive C:

volumes

Figure 8-20 illustrates how the various disk drives are seen by a typical, stand-alone system. DOS reserves the letters A: and B: for the first and second floppy drives. Multiple hard disk drive units can be installed in the system unit, along with the floppy drives. DOS recognizes a single hard disk unit in the system as **drive C:**. DOS utilities can be used to partition a single physical hard disk drive into two or more **volumes** that the system recognizes as logical drives C:, D:, etc.

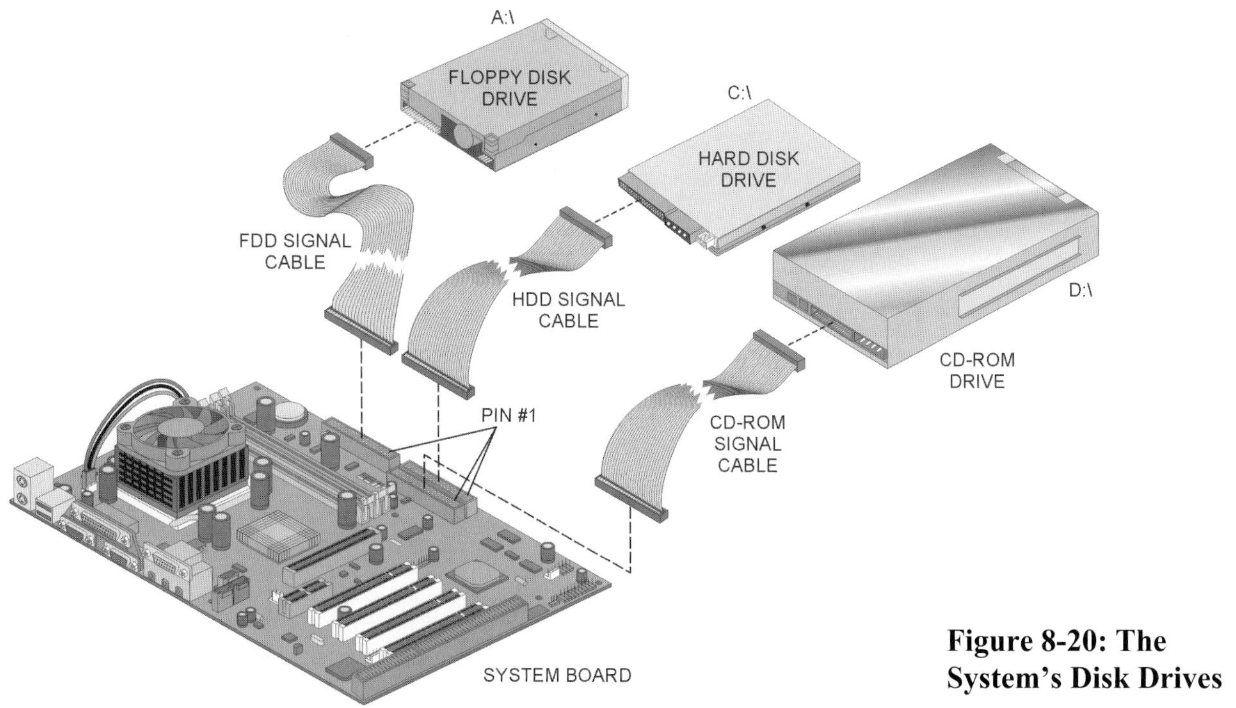

Figure 8-20: The System's Disk Drives

> **NOTE**
>
> The figure shows a CD-ROM drive as drive D: since this is becoming the most common PC configuration. In the case of networked systems, logical drive letters may be extended to define up to Z drives. These drives are actually the hard drives located in remote computers. The operating system in the local machine treats them as additional logical drives (i.e., F:, G:, etc.).

Conversely, a second hard disk drive can be added to the system and set up as logical drive D:. It may also be partitioned into smaller logical drives that the system recognizes as drives E:, F:, and etc.

Some DOS operations are simplified by allowing the system to choose the location for the command to be carried out through the use of **default settings** (special predetermined settings that are automatically used by the system when no specific directions are given to change the setting). These settings are remembered in DOS and used by the system when the operator does not specify a particular location for events to happen. The default setting in your system is the A: drive. In systems with two or more drives, it is imperative that the user specify exactly where the action called for is to occur.

default settings

Drive-Level DOS Operations

The following DOS commands pertain to **drive-level operations**. They must be typed at the DOS prompt, and they carry out the instruction along with any drive modifiers given.

drive-level operations

DISKCOPY

DISKCOPY: This command is used to make a duplicate of a floppy disk. The DISKCOPY operation is normally used to make backup disks and is often followed by a DISKCOMP operation:

```
C:\>DISKCOPY A: B:
```

You should be aware that DISKCOPY operations can only be performed on floppy disks and the disks must be the same capacity.

DISKCOMP

DISKCOMP: This command is used to compare the contents of two disks. It compares the data on the disks not only to see that they are alike, but also to see that the data is located in the same place on both disks. The DISKCOMP operation is normally used to check backup disks, and usually follows a DISKCOPY operation:

```
C:\>DISKCOMP A: B:
```

FORMAT

FORMAT: This command is used to prepare a new disk for use with an operating system. Actual data locations are marked off on the disk for the tracks and sectors, and bad sectors are marked. In addition, the directory is established on the disk. New diskettes must be formatted before they can be used.

C:\>FORMAT A creates the track, sector, and the file system structure on the specified disk (in this case the A: floppy drive).

C:\>FORMAT A:/S causes three system files (boot files—IO.SYS, MSDOS.SYS, and COMMAND.COM) to be copied into the root directory of the disk after it has been formatted. The new diskette will now boot up without a DOS disk.

C:\>FORMAT A:/Q causes the system to perform a quick format operation on the disk. This amounts to removing the FAT and root directory from the disk.

SETVER

SETVER: This command sets the DOS version number that the system reports to an application. Programs designed for previous DOS versions may not operate correctly under newer versions unless the version has been set correctly:

```
C:\>SETVER C:
```

This entry will cause all of the files on the C: drive to be listed in the DOS version table. Note, however, that the SETVER command must be enabled by loading it in the CONFIG.SYS file before it can be used from the command line.

VER

If the current DOS version is not known, typing **VER** at the DOS prompt will display it on the screen. These commands are particularly useful in networking operations where multiple computers are connected together to share information. In these applications, several versions of DOS may exist on different machines attached to the network.

Directories

As mentioned earlier, in hard drive-based systems it is common to organize related programs and data into areas called directories. This makes them easier to find and work with, since modern hard drives are capable of holding large amounts of information. As described earlier, most directories can hold up to 512 directory or file name entries.

It would be difficult to work with directories if you could not know which one you were working in. The DOS prompt can be set up to display which directory is being used. This particular directory is referred to as the **current** or **working directory** (i.e., C:\DOS\forms would indicated that you were working with programs located in a subdirectory of the DOS directory named forms). The first back slash represents the root directory on the C: hard drive. The presence of two dots (..) near the top of a directory listing acts to identify it as a subdirectory. These dots indicate the presence of a **parent directory** above the currently active subdirectory. A single dot (.) is displayed at the top of the listing to represent the current directory.

current directory

working directory

parent directory

The following DOS commands are used for **directory-based operations**. The format for using them is identical to disk-related commands discussed earlier.

directory-based operations

- **DIR**: The Directory command gives a listing of the files on the disk that is in the drive indicated by the drive specifier.

DIR

C:\>DIR or DIR B: (If DIR is used without any drive specifier, the contents of the drive indicated by the prompt will be displayed.) The command may also be used with modifiers to alter the way in which the directory is displayed.

C:\>DIR/W displays the entire directory at one time across the width of the display.

C:\>DIR/P displays the contents of the directory one page at a time. You must press a key to advance to the next display page.

- **MKDIR (MD)**: Will create a new directory in an indicated spot in the directory tree structure.

MKDIR (MD)

C:\>MD C:\DOS\XXX will create a new subdirectory named XXX in the path that includes the ROOT directory (C:\) and the DOS directory.

- **CHDIR (CD)**: Will change the location of the active directory to a position specified with the command.

CHDIR (CD)

C:\>CD C:\DOS will change the working directory from the C: root directory to the C:\>DOS directory.

RMDIR (RD)

- **RMDIR (RD)**: Remove directory will erase the directory specified in the command. You cannot remove a directory until it is empty and you cannot remove the directory if it is currently active.

C:\>RD C:\DOS\forms would remove the DOS subdirectory "forms", provided it were empty.

PROMPT

- **PROMPT**: Changes the appearance of the DOS prompt.

C:\>PROMPT PG will cause the form of the prompt to change from simply C: to C:\ and will cause the complete path from the main directory to the current directory to be displayed at the DOS prompt. (i.e., C:\>DOS).

TREE

- **TREE**: Lists all of the directory and subdirectory names on a specified disk.

C:\>TREE C: will display a graphical representation of the organization of the C hard drive.

DELTREE

- **DELTREE**: Removes a selected directory and all the files and subdirectories below it.

C:\>DELTREE C:\DOS\DRIVER\MOUSE will delete the subdirectory "Mouse" and any subdirectories it may have.

CREATING AND MANAGING FILES

The A+ Operating System Technologies objective 1.2 states that the test taker should be able to identify basic concepts and procedures for creating, viewing, and managing files and directories, including procedures for changing file attributes and the ramifications of those changes (for example, security issues). It also states that the content under this objective may include the following items:

- File attributes - Read Only, Hidden, System, and Archive attributes
- File-naming conventions (most common extensions)
- Command syntax
- Windows 2000 COMPRESS, ENCRYPT

The operating systems of disk-based computers handle information in the form of files. Therefore, the computer technician must be aware of the methods different operating systems use to create and manipulate files.

The following sections of the chapter will begin the discussion of files in a disk-based system. It will describe files and file handling from the MS-DOS perspective. Subsequent chapters will expand these ideas to illustrate how they apply to the Windows 9x and Windows 2000 operating systems.

DOS Files

Disk-based systems store and handle related pieces of information in groups called files. The system recognizes and keeps track of the different files in the system by their **filenames**. Therefore, each file in the system is required to have a filename that is different from that of any other file in the directory.

filenames

If two files having the same name were present within the same directory of the system, the computer would become confused and fail to operate properly. This is because it could not tell which version of the file was supposed to be worked on. Each time a new file of information is created, it will be necessary to give it a unique filename by which DOS can identify and store it.

Files and Filenames

Files are created through programming packages, or by applications. When they are created, they must be assigned a filename. In an MS-DOS environment, there are a few rules that you must remember when creating new filenames. As described earlier in this chapter, the filename consists of two parts: a **name** and an extension. The filename is a combination of alphanumeric characters and is between one and eight characters in length. The extension is an optional addition to the name that begins with a period, and is followed by between one and three characters.

name

Extensions are not required on filenames, but they often prove useful in describing the contents of a file, or in identifying different versions of the same file. If a filename that already exists is used to store another file, the computer will write the information in the new file over that of the old file, assuming that they are both the same. Therefore, only the new file will still exist. The information in the old file will be lost.

Many software packages will automatically generate filename extensions for files they create. The software does this so that other parts of the program, which may work with the same file, will be able to identify where the file came from, or what form it is in.

In any event, you should remember the seven items below when assigning and using filenames:

1. All files must have a filename.
2. All filenames must be different than any other filename in the system, or on the disk presently in use.
3. DOS filenames are up to 8 characters long with an optional 3-character extension (separated from the basic filename by a period).
4. When using a filename in a command, you must also use its extension, if one exists.
5. Some special characters are not allowed in filenames. These are: [,], :, ;, +, =, \, /, >, ? and ,.
6. When telling DOS where to carry out a command, you must tell it on which disk drive the operation is to be performed. The drive must be specified by its letter name followed by a colon (i.e., A:, B:, C:, etc.).
7. The complete and proper way to specify a file calls for the drive specifier, the filename, and the filename extension, in that order (i.e., B:filename.ext).

TEST TIP

Know which characters can legally be used in a DOS filename.

The following DOS commands are used to carry out file-level operations. The format for using them is identical to the disk and directory-related commands discussed earlier. However, the command must include the filename and its extension at the end of the directory path. Depending on the operation the complete path may be required, or a default to the currently active drive will be assumed.

COPY

- **COPY**: The file copy command copies a specified file from one place (disk or directory) to another.

C:\>COPY A:filename.ext B: is used if the file is to have the same name in its new location; the second filename specifier can be omitted.

C:\>COPY A:filename.ext B:filename.ext

In a single-drive system, it will be necessary to switch disks in the middle of the operation. (Notice that the drive B: specifier is used even though only drive A: is present.) Fortunately, the DOS produces a prompt message to tell you when to put the Target diskette in the drive. This is not required in a two-drive system and no prompt is given. The transfer can be specified in any direction desired.

C:\>COPY B:filename.ext A:

The only thing to keep in mind in this situation is to place the Source diskette in drive B: and the Target diskette in drive A: before entering the command.

XCOPY

- **XCOPY**: This command copies all the files in a directory, along with any subdirectories and their files. This command is particularly useful in copying files and directories between disks with different formats (i.e., from a 1.2 MB disk to a 1.44 MB disk:

C:\>XCOPY A: B: /s

This command would copy all of the files and directories from the disk in drive A: (except hidden and system files) to the disk in drive B:. The /s switch instructs the XCOPY command to copy directories and subdirectories.

DEL

ERASE

- **DEL** or **ERASE**: This command allows the user to remove unwanted files from the disk when typed in at the DOS prompt:

C:\>DEL filename.ext

C:\>ERASE B:filename.ext

A great deal of care should be taken when using this command. If a file is erased accidentally, it may not be retrievable.

REN

- **REN**: Enables the user to change the name, or extension of a filename:

C:\>REN A:filename.ext newname.ext

C:\>COPY A:filename.ext B:newname.ext

Using this command does not change the contents of the file, only its name. The original filename (but not the file) is deleted. If you wish to retain the original file and filename, a copy command, using different filenames, can be used.

TYPE

- **TYPE**: Shows the contents of a designated file on the monitor screen.

C:\>TYPE AUTOEXEC.BAT will display the contents of the AUTOEXEC.BAT file

FC

- **FC**: This file-compare command compares two files to see if they are the same. This operation is normally performed after a file copy has been performed to ensure that the file was duplicated and located correctly:

C:\>FC A:filename.ext B:

If the filename was changed during the copy operation, the command would have to be typed as:

C:\>FC A:filename.ext B:newname.ext

ATTRIB

Read-only

Archive

System

Hidden

- **ATTRIB**: Changes file attributes such as **Read-only** (+R or –R), **Archive** (+A or –A), **System** (+S or –S), and **Hidden** (+H or –H). The + and – signs are to add or subtract the attribute from the file.

C:\>ATTRIB +R C:\DOS\memos.doc

This command sets the file MEMOS.DOC as a read-only file. Read-only attributes protect the file from accidentally being overwritten. Similarly, one of the main reasons for giving a file a Hidden attribute is to prevent it from accidentally being erased. The System attribute is reserved for use by the operating system and marks the file as a system file.

TEST TIP

Memorize the different DOS file attributes and be able to use the various attribute switch settings.

A common error message encountered when working with command line operations is the "bad command or file name" error message. This type of error message generally occurs when the path specified to the location of a file is incorrect, or when the file is missing or misspelled.

DOS Shortcuts

command line shortcuts

DOS provides some **command line shortcuts** through the keyboard's function keys. Some of the most notable are the F1 and F3 function keys. The F1 key will bring the previous command back from the command line buffer, one character at a time. Likewise, the F3 key will bring back the entire previous command through a single keystroke.

When using filenames in DOS command line operations, the filename appears at the end of the directory path in the source and destination locations.

wild card

The * notation is called a **wild card** and allows operations to be performed with only partial source or destination information. Using the notation as *.* tells the software to perform the designated command on any file found on the disk using any filename and extension.

TEST TIP

Memorize the DOS wild card characters and be able to use their variations.

A question mark (?) can be used as a wild card to represent a single character in a DOS name or extension. Multiple question marks can be used to represent multiple characters in a filename or extension.

filter commands

More

Find

Sort

pipe symbol (|)

Data from a DOS command can be modified to fit a prescribed output format through the use of **filter commands**. The main filter commands are **More**, **Find**, and **Sort**. The filter command is preceded by a **pipe symbol** (|) on the command line, when output from another DOS command is to be modified. For example, to view the contents of a batch file that is longer than the screen display can present at one time, type **Type C:\xxx.bat|more**. If the information to be modified is derived from another file, the less than (<) symbol is used.

The Find command will search through files, and commands, for specified characters. Likewise, the Sort command will present files in alphabetical order.

MEMORY TYPES

The A+ Operating System Technologies objective 1.1 states that the test taker should be able to identify the operating system's functions, structure, and major system files to navigate the operating system and know how to get needed technical information.

A portion of the objective indicates that the content will deal with Memory Management topics such as:

- Conventional memory
- Extended/upper memory
- High memory
- Expanded memory
- Virtual memory
- HIMEM.SYS
- EMM386.exe

Decisions were made in the original IBM PC design, and thereby in the MS-DOS operating system that ran it, that still affect design of PCs and operating systems. Technicians who work on PC-compatible systems must understand how they allocate memory and how that memory can be manipulated to provide the best system performance.

DOS Memory

The original DOS version was constructed in two sections. The first 640 kB of memory was reserved for use by DOS and its programs. The remaining section was reserved for use by the BIOS and the system's peripherals (i.e., the video card, the hard drive controller card, etc.). This arrangement utilized the entire 1 MB addressing range of the 8088 microprocessor.

As more powerful microprocessors entered the market (80286 microprocessors can access up to 16 MB of memory, while the 80386 and 80486 can handle up to 4 GB of memory), DOS retained the limitations imposed on it by the original version in order to remain compatible with older machines and software.

Special add-on programs called **memory managers** have been created to enable DOS to access and use the additional memory capabilities available with more powerful microprocessors.

memory managers

Basic Memory Organization

Every computer has a memory organization plan called a **memory map**. A simplified memory map, showing RAM, ROM, and I/O address allocations, is shown in Figure 8-21.

memory map

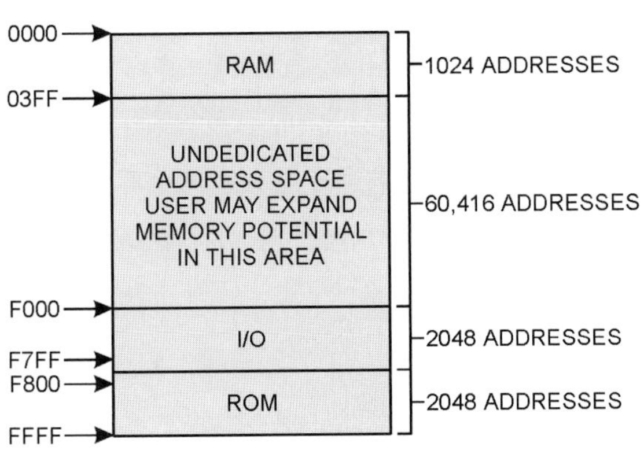

Figure 8-21: A Computer Memory Map

When the original PC was designed, there were certain decisions made in dividing up the 8088's one megabyte of memory address space. These decisions were implemented by the original PC-DOS and MS-DOS operating systems. Due to compatibility issues, these decisions have carried over into the address allocations of all DOS-based PC-compatibles, as described in Figure 8-22.

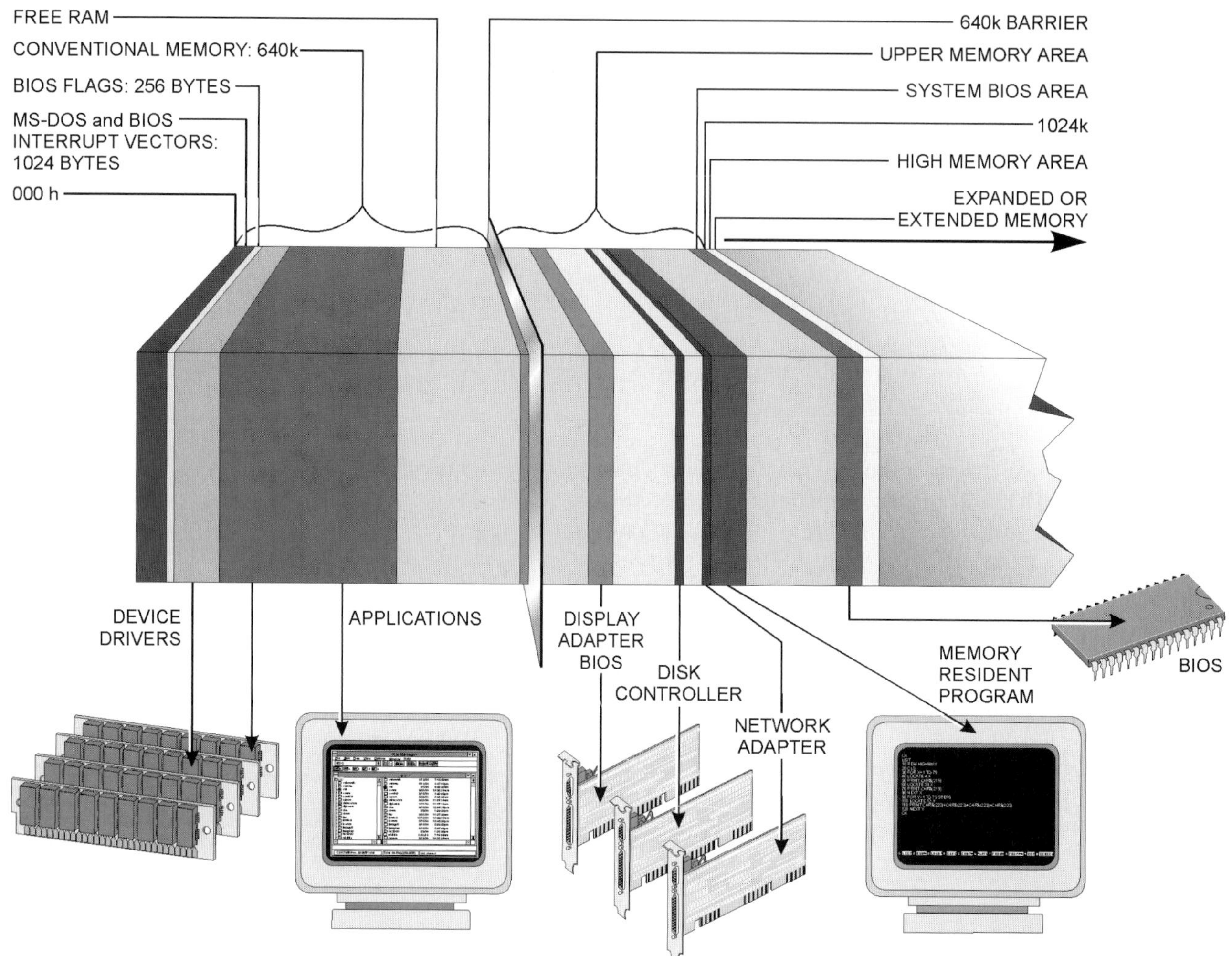

Figure 8-22: PC Memory Allocations

DOS Memory—Basically, DOS can recognize the following classifications of memory: conventional memory, upper memory blocks, high memory area, expanded memory, extended memory, and virtual memory.

The Intel microprocessors have a separate memory map for I/O addresses.

PC Memory Allocations

In the original PC, the 1 MB **memory** range was divided into two sections referred to as **base memory** and **reserved memory**. The base memory area started at address 00000h and extended for 640 kB. It was primarily used for interrupt vectors, data storage, and program execution. The reserved memory area began at address A0000h and occupied the remaining 384 kB of the 1 MB address map. This area was set aside for use as video display memory areas and to hold the system's ROM BIOS as well as any extended hardware adapter BIOS. This organizational structure is illustrated in Figure 8-23.

memory

base memory

reserved memory

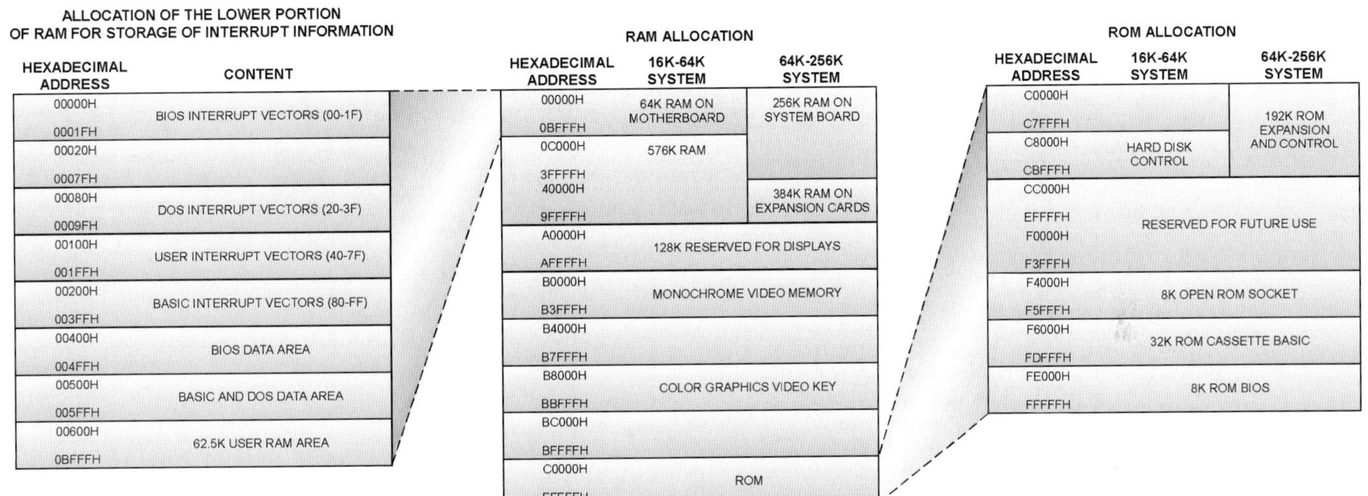

Figure 8-23: Original PC RAM Allocations

As systems became capable of accessing memory in excess of the 8088's 1 MB range, Microsoft, Intel, software companies, and memory board manufacturers began to redefine the PC's memory allocation strategies. Two strategies were put forward to deal with the additional memory available and still service existing DOS-based programs—the **Extended Memory Specification (XMS)** and the **Expanded Memory Specification (EMS)**. Both of these specifications were established as guidelines for hardware and software to use the additional memory capabilities.

Extended Memory Specification (XMS)

Expanded Memory Specification (EMS)

Conventional Memory

In the process of redefining the PC's memory allocations, the base memory area began to be referred to as **conventional memory** and the reserved memory area became the **Upper Memory Area (UMA)**. These sections are illustrated in Figure 8-24. Conventional memory occupies the first 640 kB of addresses while the remaining 384 kB is referred to as **upper memory**.

conventional memory

Upper Memory Area (UMA)

upper memory

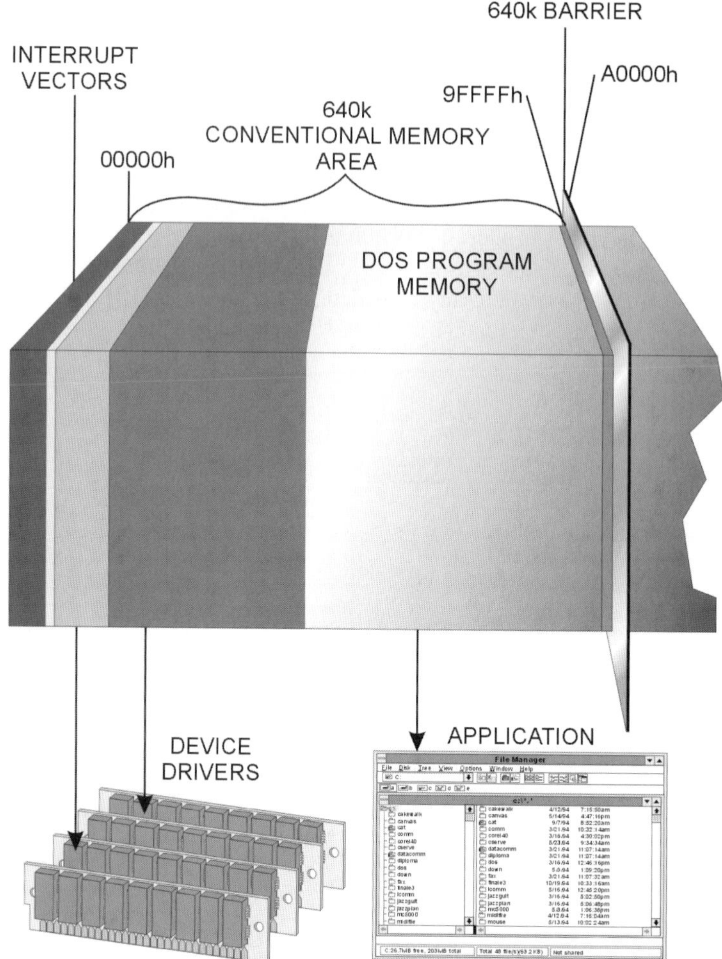

Figure 8-24: Conventional Memory

Conventional memory (locations 00000h through 9FFFFh) is the standard memory area for all PC-compatible systems. It traditionally holds DOS, interrupt vector tables, and relocated ROM BIOS tables. The remaining space in the conventional memory area is referred to as DOS Program Memory. (Programs written to operate under PC-DOS or MS-DOS use this area for program storage and execution).

The Upper Memory Area

The upper memory area occupies the 384 kB portion of the PC's address space from A0000h to FFFFFh. This space is not normally considered as part of the computer's total address space because programs cannot store information in this area. Instead, the area is reserved to run segments of the system's hardware. Address spaces from A0000h through BFFFFh are dedicated addresses set aside for the system's video display memory. The system's ROM BIOS occupies the address space between locations FE000h and FFFFFh.

Between the video memory and system BIOS areas, addresses are reserved to hold BIOS extension programs for add-on hardware adapters. Typical BIOS extensions include those for hard drive adapters, advanced video adapters, and network adapters.

Upper Memory Blocks (UMBs)

After the BIOS extensions are in place, the typical UMA still has many unused memory areas that can have information mapped (copied) into them. This space is segmented into 64 kB sections called **Upper Memory Blocks (UMBs)**, as illustrated in Figure 8-25. The primary use for these blocks is to hold installable device drivers and other memory resident programs moved out of the conventional memory area. By moving these programs out of the conventional memory area, more space is made available there for use by application programs.

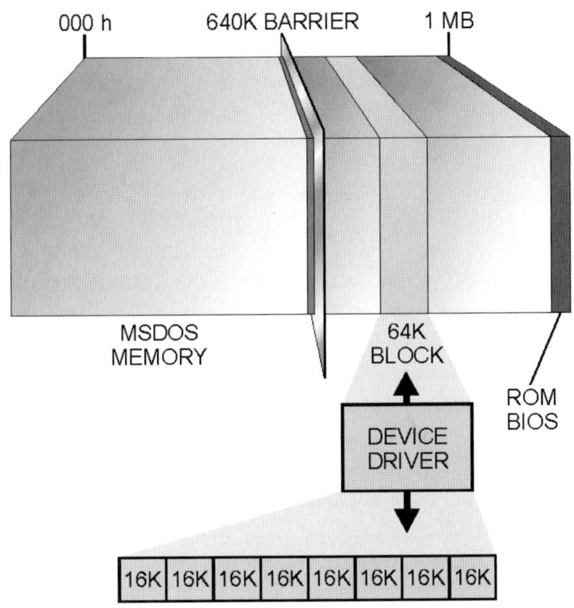

Figure 8-25: Upper Memory Blocks of the UMA

shadow RAM

PCs also use this area to incorporate a memory-usage scheme called **shadow RAM** to improve their overall performance. With this feature, the contents of the system BIOS and/or adapter BIOS are rewritten (shadowed) into faster extended memory RAM locations. The operating system then remaps the ROM addresses to the corresponding RAM locations through unused portions of the UMA.

Shadowing enables the system to operate faster when application software makes use of any of the BIOS' call routines. Instead of accessing an 8-bit IC ROM device, which takes up to 4 Wait States to complete, BIOS calls are redirected by the shadow feature to the same information located in 16-bit, 32-bit, or 64-bit 0-Wait State DRAM devices. Some benchmark tests have shown performance increases between 300% and 400% in systems where the shadow feature is used.

Extended Memory

extended memory

With the advent of the 80286 microprocessor and its protected operating mode, it became possible to access physical memory locations beyond the 1-megabyte limit of the 8088. Memory above this address is generally referred to as **extended memory**.

With the 80286 microprocessor, this could add up to an additional 15 MB of RAM for a total of 16 MB (24-bit address). Extended memory is illustrated in Figure 8-26.

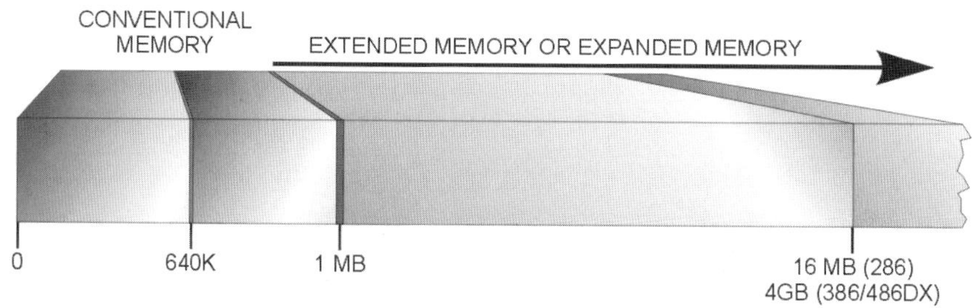

Figure 8-26: Extended Memory

Even though the 80286 could physically access this type of memory using its protected addressing mode, it was impossible for application programs to access it at the time. This was due to the 640 kB DOS limit imposed by earlier architectures. With the 32-bit address bus size of 80386-based and 80486-based computers, extended memory could range up to a total of 4 GB. It was not that software couldn't access memory at these addresses, it was simply a matter of DOS not having the capability to do so.

Application programs can be written to specifically take advantage of these memory locations, but few are. Operating systems, such as Microsoft DOS versions beyond 4.0 and Windows versions beyond 3.0, as well as IBM's OS/2 operating system, can take full advantage of extended memory through the protected addressing modes of the more advanced microprocessors. This ability to manage higher memory allows the system to free up more of the base memory area for use by application programs.

HIMEM.SYS

Extended Memory Specification (XMS)

High Memory Area (HMA)

The DOS versions above 4.0 contain a memory management program called **HIMEM.SYS** that manages extended memory above the 1024 kB level. This utility operates under the Microsoft **Extended Memory Specification** (**XMS**). When the utility is loaded into memory, it shifts most of the operating system functions into the **High Memory Area** (**HMA**) of extended memory. The HMA takes up the first 64 kB of addresses above the 1 MB boundary and is a result of a quirk in the segmented addressing design of the advanced Intel microprocessors.

The HIMEM function is activated by adding a line of instruction to the system's CONFIG.SYS file so that it is executed when the computer is booted. When the HIMEM utility is encountered, the program assumes control of the system's **A20 Interrupt Handler** routine. This function is part of the BIOS program and takes control of the system's A20 address line when activated.

A20 Interrupt Handler

The A20 Interrupt Handler is located at BIOS interrupt 15 (INT15) and is used to transfer data blocks of up to 64 kB in length between the system and extended memory. The INT15 function also supplies entries for the various microprocessor tables that are required for protected virtual addressing mode.

Expanded Memory

Some publications may refer to memory above the 1-megabyte limit as expanded memory (EMS). However, the term **expanded memory** is generally reserved to describe another special memory option. In 1985, three companies (Lotus, Intel, and Microsoft) joined together to define a method of expanding the 8088's memory-usage capabilities by switching banks of memory from outside of the DOS memory area into the usable address ranges of the 8088. This method became known as the **LIM EMS** (for Lotus, Intel, and Microsoft **Expanded Memory Specification**) standard.

expanded memory

LIM EMS

Expanded Memory Specification

bank switching

This idea of **bank switching** was not exactly new; it had been used with older computer systems before the advent of the IBM line. The LIM EMS standard simply defined how this technique should be applied to IBM PCs and their compatibles. The original standard defined specifications for both hardware and software elements of the EMS system. Figure 8-27 illustrates the basic principle behind the EMS standard.

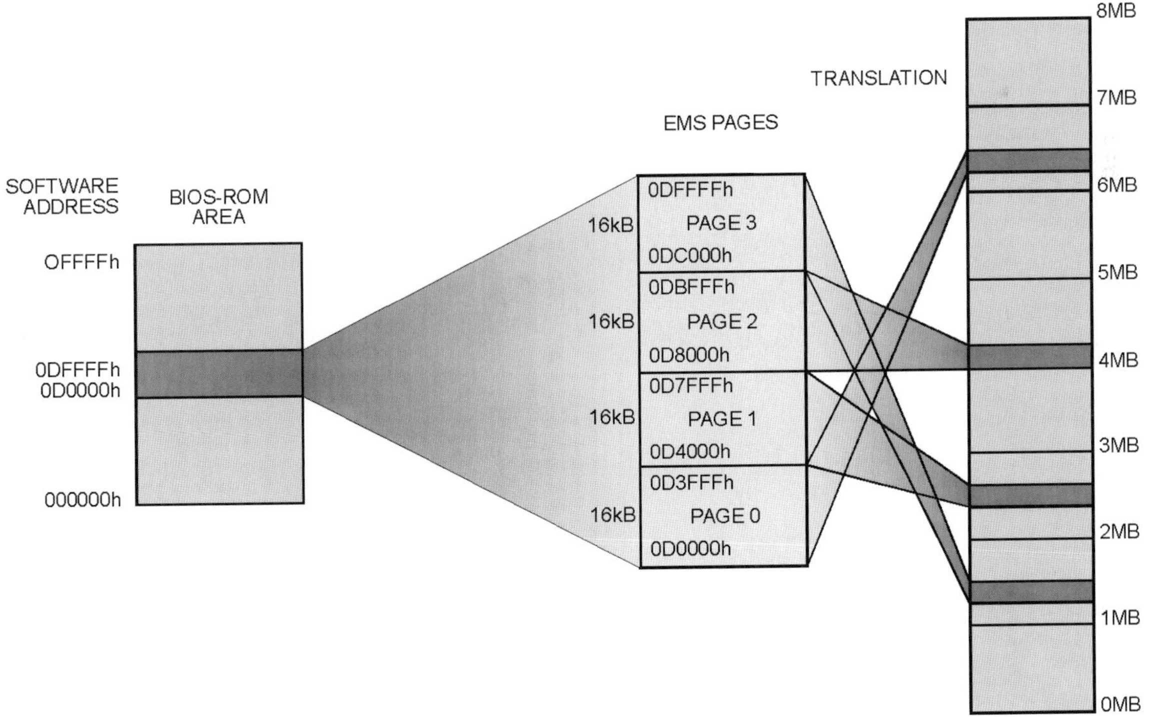

Figure 8-27: Expanded Memory (EMS) Operations

pages

The specification allowed four 16 kB areas of memory between C0000h and EFFFFh, referred to as **pages**, to be used as windows into pre-defined RAM locations above the 1 MB address limit. Originally, these RAM addresses were located on special EMS RAM cards that plugged into one of the system board's expansion slot connectors. Newer system boards, based on the 80486 and Pentium microprocessors, can use their advanced virtual memory paging capabilities to handle the EMS function directly on the board.

Figure 8-27 depicts hex locations D0000h through DFFFFh being used as windows through which the expanded memory addresses are translated. In reality, the four-16 kB windows can be selected from anywhere within the LIM EMS-defined address range, and can be relocated to anywhere within the 32 MB physical address range.

Expanded Memory Manager (EMM)

The EMS software specifications consist of predetermined programs called **Expanded Memory Manager (EMM)** drivers that work with application software to control the bank-switching operations. These drivers contain special function calls that application programs can use to manipulate the expanded memory. Note, however, that the application software must be written to take advantage of the EMS function calls. EMS versions before 4.0 only made provision for the expanded memory to be used as data storage areas. Programs could not actually be executed in these areas. Versions 4.0 and later support much larger bank-switching operations, as well as program execution and multitasking.

Virtual Memory

virtual memory

swapping files

The term **virtual memory** is used to describe memory that isn't what it appears to be. Virtual memory is actually disk drive space that is manipulated to seem like RAM. Software creates virtual memory by **swapping files** between RAM and the disk drive, as illustrated in Figure 8-28. This memory management technique effectively creates more total memory for the system's applications to use. However, since there is a major transfer of information that involves the hard disk drive, an overall reduction in speed is encountered with virtual memory operations.

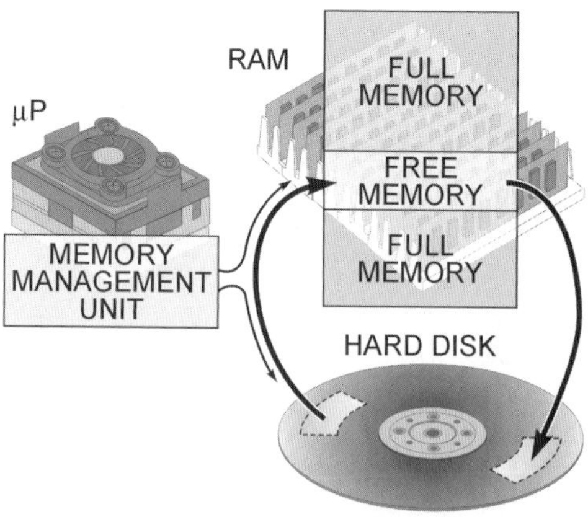

Figure 8-28: Virtual Memory Operations

Most operating systems since Windows 3.x (Windows 9x, Windows NT, Windows 2000, UNIX, and LINUX) feature virtual memory operations. Within these systems, there are three types of swap files used—temporary, permanent, and variable. Some operating systems will permit either a permanent or a temporary swap file to be established on the system's hard drive. A **permanent swap file** is always present and is a constant size. It is composed of contiguous clusters on the drive and cannot be established in fragmented drive space. It also cannot be established on a compressed partition. The following list shows the types of swap files supported by the various Microsoft operating systems:

permanent swap file

- Temporary swap files – Windows 3.x
- Permanent swap files – Windows 3.x, NT, 2000
- Variable swap files – Windows 9x

A compressed partition (or drive) is a special type of logical drive established by a disk-compression utility such as DoubleSpace or DriveSpace. These drives exist as a compressed volume file (CVF) in the root directory of a normal, uncompressed host drive. The advantage of a compressed drive is that it can hold far more data than a non-compressed drive (10 MB of data may be stored in a 5 MB space on the host drive). This reduction is the result of the compression program's data-compacting techniques.

temporary swap file

A **temporary swap file** is created when Windows starts. The size of this type of swap file is variable and can be created in fragmented space.

The permanent swap file option offers more efficient access to data, but it reserves disk space that may not be used. Conversely, the temporary swap file is more flexible and only uses disk space it needs. However, its space can be limited on a crowded drive. Also, its nonstandard location and possibly segmented nature takes more time to find and access.

WIN386.SWP

Windows 95 swap drives do not require contiguous drive space and can be established on compressed drives that use virtual device drivers. The size of the Windows 95 swap file is variable and is dynamically assigned. The Windows 95 swap file is **WIN386.SWP**.

Virtual Memory button

Control of Windows 95 Virtual Memory operations is established through the Control Panel's System\Performance tab. Clicking the **Virtual Memory button** produces the Virtual Memory options screen depicted in Figure 8-29. The default and recommended setting is *Let Windows manage my virtual memory settings*.

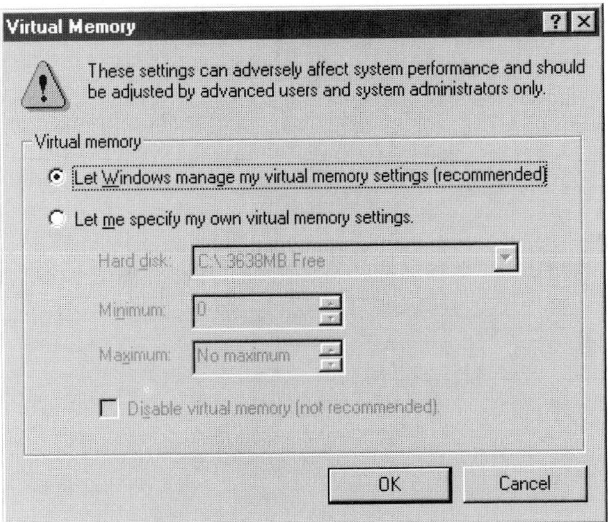

Figure 8-29: The Windows 95 Virtual Memory Dialog Box

Although Windows 9x allows swap files to be used with compressed drives, it does have some limitations. The swap file can only be located on the compressed drive if it has a Protected-mode driver (DRVSPACE.VXD). The driver must mark the file as uncompressed and place the file in an area where it can expand. If the swap file was created with a Real-mode driver and is located on a compressed drive, it should be moved to another drive.

DoubleSpace

If the **DoubleSpace** drive compression utility in Windows 9x will not run properly, check to see whether the swap file is compressed, whether there is a permanent swap drive on the host drive, and that there is enough space on the uncompressed portion of the drive to hold the swap file.

In Windows 2000, the virtual memory functions are located under the Control Panel's System icon. Simply click its Advanced tab followed by the Performance Options button to view the dialog window depicted in Figure 8-30.

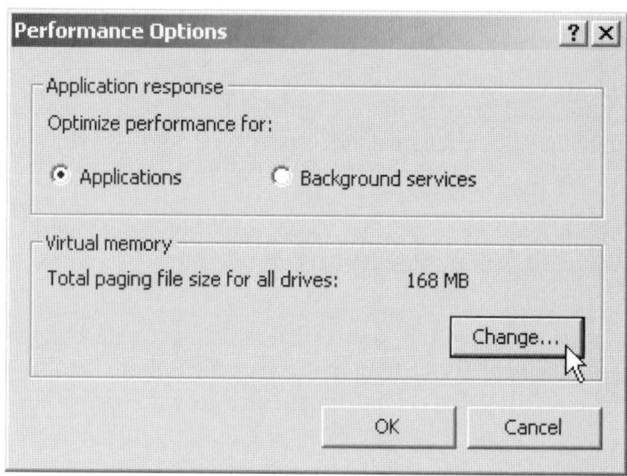

Figure 8-30: The System Performance Options Window

pagefile.sys

Pressing the Change button in the dialog window will produce the Virtual Memory dialog window shown in Figure 8-31. Through this dialog window, you can establish and configure an individual swap file for each drive in the system. By highlighting a drive, you can check its virtual memory capabilities and settings. The values for the highlighted drive can be changed by entering new values in the dialog windows and clicking the Set button.

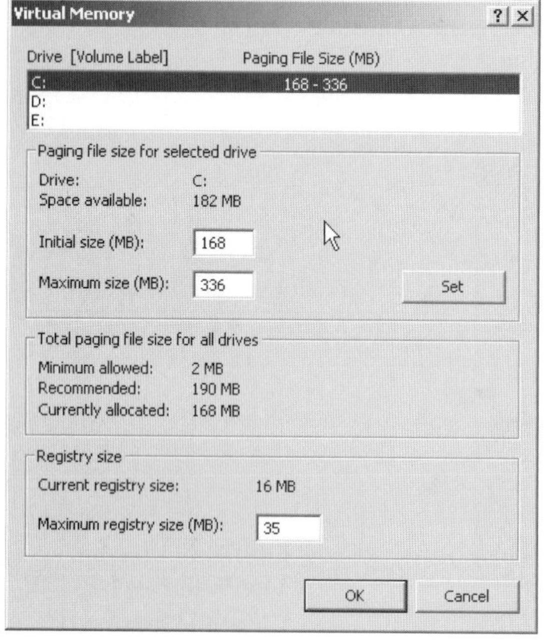

Figure 8-31: The Virtual Memory Dialog Window

The Windows 2000 pagefile (named **pagefile.sys**) is created when the operating system is installed. Its default size is typically set at 1.5 times the amount of RAM installed in the system. It is possible to optimize the system's performance by distributing the swap file space between multiple drives. It can also be helpful to relocate it away from slower or heavily used drives. The swap file should not be placed on mirrored or striped volumes. Also, don't create multiple swap files on logical disks that exist on the same physical drive.

TEST TIP

Memorize the filenames of the virtual memory swap files used in each operating system.

CONFIG.SYS

CONFIG.SYS

During installation, DOS versions from 5.0 forward create a system file called **CONFIG.SYS**. This particular filename is reserved by DOS for use with a special file that contains setup (configuration) instructions for the system. When DOS is loaded into the system, a portion of the bootup program will automatically search in the default drive for a file named CONFIG.SYS. The commands in this file configure the DOS program for use with options devices and application programs in the system.

The CONFIG.SYS program is responsible for:

(1) setting up any memory managers being used,

(2) configuring the DOS program for use with options devices and application programs,

(3) loading up *device-driver software*, and installing *memory-resident programs*.

These activities are illustrated by the sample CONFIG.SYS file:

```
1   Device=C:\DOS\HIMEM.SYS
    Device=C:\DOS\EMM386.EXE 1024 RAM

2   FILES=30
    BUFFERS=15
    STACKS=9,256

3   DEVICE=C:\DOS\SMARTDRV.SYS 1024
    DOS=HIGH,UMB
    DEVICEHIGH=C:\MOUSE\MOUSE.SYS
    DEVICEHIGH=C:\DOS\RAMDRIVE.SYS 4096/a

4   INSTALL=C:/DOS/SHARE.EXE
```

Memory Managers

HIMEM.SYS

In the first section, the system's memory-manager programs are loaded. In this case, the **HIMEM.SYS** command loads the DOS extended memory (XMS) driver.

This driver manages the use of extended memory installed in the system so that no two applications use the same memory locations at the same time. This memory manager should normally be listed in the CONFIG.SYS file before any other memory managers or device drivers.

EMM386.EXE

High Memory Area (HMA)

Upper Memory Area (UMA)

HIMEM.SYS also creates a 64 kB area of memory just above the 1 MB address space called the **High Memory Area (HMA)**. With this, the DOS=HIGH statement is used to shift portions of DOS from conventional memory into the HMA.

The **EMM386.EXE** program provides the system's microprocessor with access to the **Upper Memory Area (UMA)** of RAM. Operating together with the HIMEM.SYS program, this program enables the system to conserve conventional memory by moving device drivers and memory-resident programs into the UMA. This concept is described in Figure 8-32.

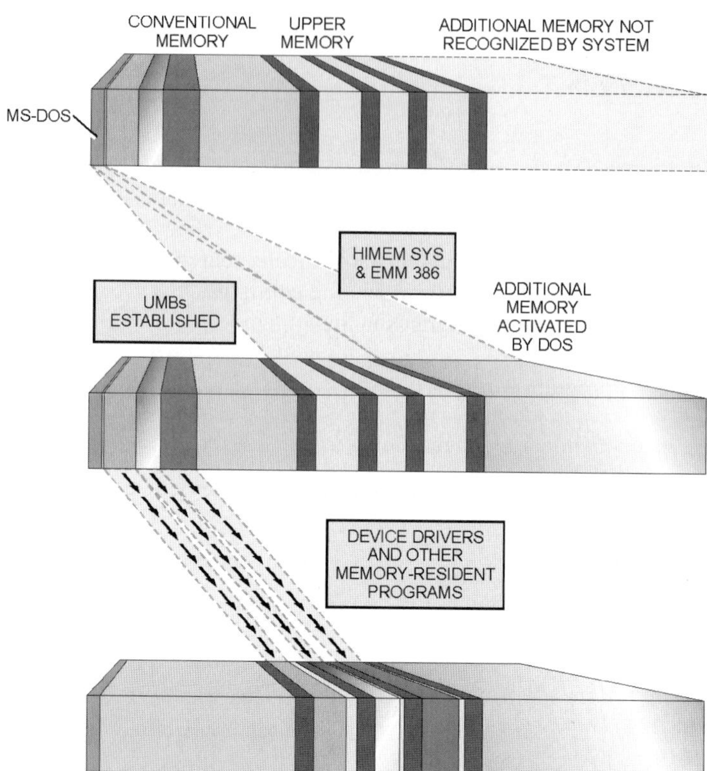

Figure 8-32: Loading Memory Managers

The EMM386.EXE command can also be used to simulate expanded memory mode operations in RAM above the 1 MB mark. In this case, the 1024 RAM switch in the command directs the EMM386 driver to provide upper memory access and establish a 1024-byte area above the 1 MB mark to simulate expanded memory operations.

NOEMS

Another expanded memory manager, named LIM EMS 4.0, could be encountered in a CONFIG.SYS file set up for expanded memory operations. If the CONFIG.SYS file contains commands to load another expanded memory manager, the presence of a **NOEMS** switch in the EMM386.EXE line will prevent it from implemented expanded mode operation when the line is encountered. When this switch is used, the command provides access to the upper memory area, but prevents access to expanded memory. A number of other switches can be used with the EMM386.EXE command. Consult an MS-DOS User's Manual for further information on these switches and their usage. Most computers use additional RAM in Extended mode rather than in Expanded mode.

Files, Buffers, and Stacks

FILES command

BUFFERS command

STACKS command

The second section of the CONFIG.SYS file consists of the commands that define DOS for operation with optional devices and applications. The **FILES command** causes the DOS program to establish the number of files that DOS can handle at any one time at 30. This just happens to be the minimum number required to load Windows for operation. The **BUFFERS command** sets aside 15 blocks of RAM memory space for storing data being transferred to and from disks. Similarly, the **STACKS command** establishes the number and length of some special RAM memory storage operations at 9 memory stacks, with each being 256-bytes long.

Device Drivers

Device drivers are loaded in the third part of the file. Device drivers are programs that tell DOS how to control specific devices. DEVICEHIGH=C:\MOUSE\MOUSE.SYS is a command that loads a third-party device driver supporting the particular mouse being used with the system.

Device drivers

Some device manufacturers include software installation utilities with the device that will automatically install its device drivers into the CONFIG.SYS (or AUTOEXEC.BAT) files during the installation process. With other devices, the device drivers must be installed by manually updating the CONFIG.SYS and AUTOEXEC.BAT files. The device's installation instructions will identify which method must be used to install its drivers.

The order in which device drivers appear in the CONFIG.SYS file is important. The recommended order for listing device drivers is: (1) HIMEM.SYS, (2) the expanded memory manager, if installed, (3) the EMM386.EXE command, and (4) any other device drivers being used.

SMARTDRV.SYS

cache

disk cache

The **SMARTDRV.SYS** driver establishes a disk cache in an area of extended memory as a storage space for information read from the hard disk drive. A **cache** is a special area of memory reserved to hold data and instructions recently accessed from another location. A **disk cache** holds information recently accessed from the hard disk drive. Information stored in RAM is much quicker to access than if it were on the hard drive. When a program or DOS operation requests more data, the SMARTDRV program redirects the request to check in the cache memory area to see if the requested data is there. If SMARTDRV finds the information in the cache, it will operate on it from there. If the requested information is not in the cache, the system will access the hard drive for it.

Using this technique, the overall operating speed of the system is improved. When the system is shut down, SMARTDRV copies the most current information onto the hard drive. Therefore, no data is lost due to it being stored in RAM. The idea behind SMARTDRV operations is described by Figure 8-33.

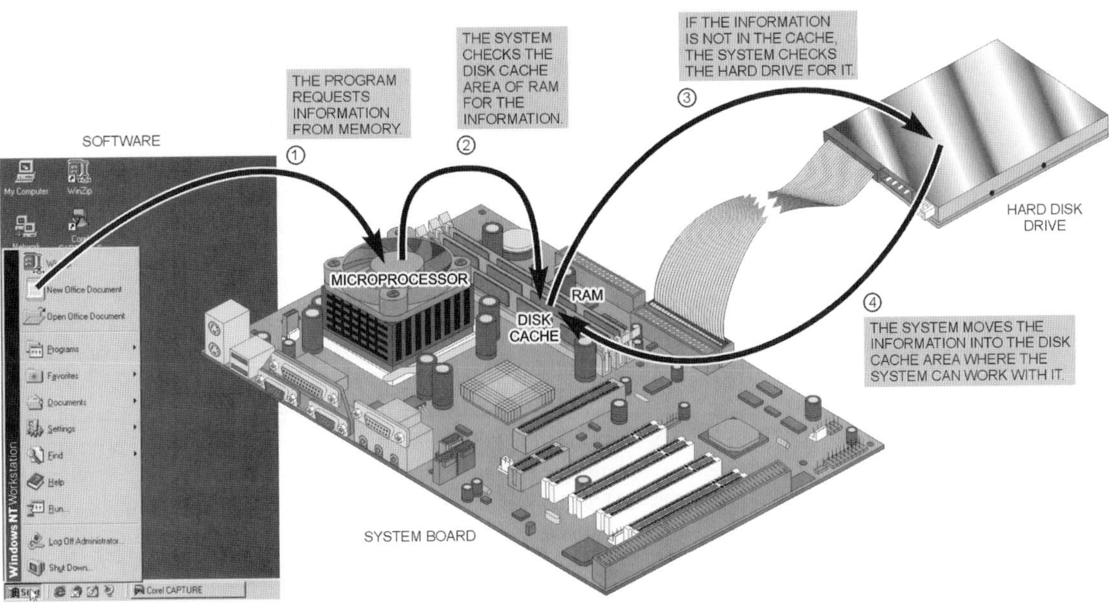

Figure 8-33: How SMARTDRV Works

The 1024 modifier establishes a memory cache size of 1 MB (1024 kB of memory) in extended memory. This is a typical cache size for SMARTDRV; however, 2 MB (2048 kB) is probably the most efficient size for the cache. This is due to the fact that the larger the cache size, the greater the chance that the requested information will be in the cache. So there is no need to go to the hard drive for the information. If the command is modified further by an /a extension, the cache is established under an expanded memory operation instead of extended memory. Extended memory is the default for SMARTDRV operations.

A number of switches can be added to the SMARTDRV statement to modify the operation of the cache. These switches are summarized as follows:

- /C will write all current cache information to the hard disk.
- /F writes cached data before the command prompt returns.
- /L prevents SMARTDRV from loading into upper memory.
- /N won't write cached data until the command prompt returns.
- /Q does not display SMARTDRV status information.
- /R clears the cache and restarts SMARTDRV.
- /S displays additional information about SMARTDRV.
- /U will not load CD-ROM caching.
- /V displays SMARTDRV status messages when loading.
- /X disables write-behind caching for all drives.

Other common SMARTDRV entries include:

- InitCacheSize - Specifies the amount of XMS memory for the cache (in kB).
- WinCacheSize - Specifies the amount of XMS memory for the cache with Windows (in kB).
- /E:ElementSize - Specifies how many bytes of information to move per transfer.
- /B:BufferSize - Establishes the size of the read-ahead buffer.

RAMDRIVE.SYS

virtual disk

DEVICEHIGH=

DEVICE=

DOS=HIGH,UMB

DOS=HIGH

The **RAMDRIVE.SYS** driver simulates the organization of a hard disk drive in RAM memory. This type of drive is called a **virtual disk**. In this case, the **DEVICEHIGH=** command loads the RAMDRV into the upper memory area instead of the base memory area, where a simple **DEVICE=** command would run it. Likewise, the **DOS=HIGH,UMB** command shifts the operation of DOS into the high memory area, and gives the application access to the upper memory area.

The operation of both the SMARTDRV.SYS and RAMDRIVE.SYS device drivers is governed by the HIMEM.SYS memory manager. This is only normal since both programs involve the use of memory beyond the 1 MB conventional memory level. Likewise, the DEVICEHIGH= and **DOS=HIGH** commands that move programs into the upper memory area perform under the guidance of the HIMEM.SYS manager.

The fourth portion of the file sets up the system to use the DOS **INSTALL** command. This command is placed in the CONFIG.SYS file to load memory-resident files into memory when the operating system starts up.

INSTALL

Memory-resident programs, also known as **terminate-and-stay-resident (TSR)** programs, are programs that run in the background of other programs. These files remain in memory as long as the system is on and can typically be reactivated by a predetermined keystroke combination.

terminate-and-stay-resident (TSR)

A common install command is: *INSTALL=C:\DOS\SHARE.EXE*. The **SHARE.EXE** program provides the ability to share files in a networked, or multitasking, environment.

SHARE.EXE

DOS comes with several other standard device driver programs. These drivers can normally be found in the C:\>DOS directory and include the following:

- BREAK sets or clears extended CTRL+C checking.
- COUNTRY enables MS-DOS to use international time, dates, currency, case conversions, and decimal separators.
- DRIVPARM defines parameters for block devices when you start MS-DOS.
- INCLUDE incorporates the contents of one configuration block within another.
- LASTDRIVE specifies the maximum number of drives you can access.
- MENUCOLOR sets the text and background colors for the Startup Menu.
- MENUDEFAULT specifies the default menu item on the Startup Menu and sets a time-out value if desired.
- NUMLOCK specifies whether the NUMLOCK setting on your numeric keypad is set to ON or OFF.
- REM enables you to include comments (remarks) in a batch file or in your CONFIG.SYS file.
- SET displays, sets, or removes MS-DOS environment variables.
- SHELL specifies the name and location of the command interpreter you want MS-DOS to use.
- SUBMENU defines an item on a Startup Menu that, when selected, displays another set of choices.

The definitions and usage of these commands are covered in detail in the MS-DOS User's Guide. The DOS-installable device drivers are also defined in that publication.

DOS comes with several other standard device driver programs. These include:

- KEYBOARD.SYS
- DISPLAY.SYS
- ANSI.SYS
- DRIVER.SYS
- PRINTER.SYS

KEYBOARD.SYS

DISPLAY.SYS

code page

KEYBOARD.SYS is the DOS default keyboard definition file. The **DISPLAY.SYS** driver supports code-page switching for the monitor type in use by the system. A **code page** is the set of 256 characters that DOS can handle at one time, when displaying, printing, and manipulating text.

TEST TIP

Know which driver assigns logical drive letters to the system's floppy drives.

ANSI.SYS supports ANSI escape-code sequences used to modify the function of the system's display, and keyboard. This file is also required to display colors on the monitor in DOS. **DRIVER.SYS** creates the logical drive assignments for the system's floppy drives (that is, A: and B:). Finally, the **PRINTER.SYS** driver supports code-page switching for parallel ports. All these drivers are normally found in the DOS directory.

ANSI.SYS

DRIVER.SYS

PRINTER.SYS

POWER.EXE

Advanced Power Management (APM)

A special power-saving program called **POWER.EXE** is designed for use in notebook computers. When it is loaded in the last line of the CONFIG.SYS file, and the system hardware meets the **Advanced Power Management (APM)** specification, the power savings can be as high as 25%. If you are using battery power, this can be a significant savings. You can realize up to 25% more operation before you need to recharge the battery. The POWER.EXE file must be available in the C:\DOS directory.

TEST TIP

Know which statements and commands are normally located in the CONFIG.SYS file.

Altering CONFIG.SYS Steps

Shift

F5

Starting DOS...

The operation of the CONFIG.SYS file can be altered or bypassed by pressing selected keyboard keys during the bootup process. Holding the **Shift** key, or pressing the **F5** key while the MS-DOS message - "**Starting DOS...**" is on the screen will cause the bootup process to skip all the commands in the CONFIG.SYS file. This action will also bypass all of the steps of the AUTOEXEC.BAT file.

Bad or missing command interpreter

When this option is used, the system will boot up with a complete set of default settings. No installable device drivers will be installed, the current directory will be set to C:\>DOS, and you may receive a "**Bad or missing command interpreter**" message. If this message is received, the system will ask you to manually enter the path to the COMMAND.COM file.

F8

single-step

Similarly, pressing the **F8** function key while the DOS message is on the screen will cause the system to stop between each CONFIG.SYS command and ask for verification before proceeding. This is referred to as a **single-step** startup option and can be very helpful in troubleshooting configuration and bootup problems. This action will also cause the system to ask the user if the AUTOEXEC.BAT file should be run, or skipped. Placing a question mark after a CONFIG.SYS command (before the = sign) will cause the system to automatically seek verification whenever the system is booted up.

The special function keys available during the DOS Startup are summarized as follows:

- F5 (also Left Shift key)– Skips CONFIG.SYS and AUTOEXEC.BAT files
- F8 – Proceeds through the CONFIG.SYS and AUTOEXEC.BAT files one step at a time waiting for Confirmation form the user.

TEST TIP

Know which function keys can be used during the bootup process to alter it.

AUTOEXEC.BAT

After completing the CONFIG.SYS operation, DOS searches for the presence of a file called the AUTOEXEC.BAT file. This file contains a **batch** of DOS commands that will automatically be carried out when DOS is loaded into the system.

batch

This file can also be re-executed from the DOS prompt by simply typing the command "AUTOEXEC". This is not true of the CONFIG.SYS file however: The system must be restarted in order to perform the commands in this file.

Refer to the following sample AUTOEXEC.BAT file:

```
DATE
TIME
PROMPT=$P$G
SET TEMP=C:\TEMP
PATH=C:\;C:\DOS;C:\MOUSE
DOSKEY
SMARTDRV.EXE 2048 1024
CD\
DIR
```

The first two commands cause DOS to prompt you for the date and time (since DOS does not automatically do this when an AUTOEXEC.BAT file is present). The **PROMPT=PG** command causes the active drive and directory path to be displayed on the command line. The SET TEMP= line sets up an area for holding data temporarily in a directory named **TEMP**.

PROMPT=PG

TEMP

The **PATH command** creates a specific set of paths that DOS will use to search for executable (.EXE, .COM, and .BAT) files. In this example, DOS will search for these files first in the root directory (C:\), followed by the DOS directory (C:\DOS), and finally through the Mouse directory (C:\MOUSE).

PATH command

This statement effectively lets a Mouse.com or Mouse.exe driver program—normally located in the Mouse directory—be executed from anywhere in the system.

Upon receiving the mouse command, the operating system looks through all of the directories in the path until it finds the specified filename.

The **syntax** (punctuation and organization) of the PATH command is very important. Each entry must be complete from the root directory and must be separated from the previous entry by a semicolon. There should be no spaces in the PATH command.

syntax

The **DOSKEY** command loads the DOSKEY program into memory. Following this, the **SMARTDRV.EXE 2048 1024** command configures the system for a 2 MB disk cache in DOS, and a 1 MB cache for Windows. After the cache has been established, the CD\ command causes the DOS default directory to change to the root directory. The last line causes a DOS DIR command to be performed automatically at the end of the operation.

DOSKEY

SMARTDRV.EXE 2048 1024

Pause

The execution of the AUTOEXEC.BAT file can be interrupted by pressing the **Pause** key on the keyboard.

The program can be restarted by pressing any key. With DOS version 6.2, the F8 interactive bypass procedure, described for use with the CONFIG.SYS file, was extended to include the AUTOEXEC.BAT file.

You can use the DOS batch file commands to construct elaborate startup procedures. Other programs designed to test ports and peripherals can be constructed using these commands. These test files can be named using the DOS filename conventions. They must be stored with a .BAT extension to be executable from the DOS prompt, but the extension does not need to be entered in order to run the program.

Neither of these two special files are required for normal operation of the computer with DOS. However, they can prove to be very useful in tailoring the operation of the system to your personal use, or to the requirements of different software applications packages. To determine whether either of these files already exists on your DOS disk, simply type the DIR command at the DOS prompt for the designated drive.

TEST TIP

Know which commands are normally located in the AUTOEXEC.BAT file.

Windows Initialization Files

initialization (INI)

When Microsoft added the Windows 3.x operating environment to the DOS structure, it did so by creating several **initialization (INI)** files that established and controlled the parameters of the various Windows components. These files were installed in the \Windows directory with a file extension of .INI. The INI files carried the default, or current, startup settings for various Windows components.

The major Windows 3.x initialization files were as follows:

- WIN.INI
- CONTROL.INI
- WINFILE.INI
- PROGMAN.INI
- SYSTEM.INI

Current versions of Windows 9x and Windows 2000 continue to include these files for compatibility reasons. The \Windows directory may also contain several other INI files. In fact, when a new Windows application is installed, it may very well install its own INI file at that time. These files can be modified to customize, or optimize, the program's execution.

Parameters in INI files are typically modified through normal Windows menus, or through pop-up dialog boxes. Others can only be changed by modifying the INI files directly. The files are broken into sections that contain the individual parameters that can be altered. Changes to the files are automatically updated whenever Windows is exited.

Normal system functions that alter INI settings include changing Control Panel, Desktop, or Windows Explorer entries. However, INI files are basically text files that users can alter with a standard text editor utility such as SysEdit. This utility can also be used to modify the SYSTEM.INI, WIN.INI, CONFIG.SYS, and AUTOEXEC.BAT files. The SysEdit utility can be accessed by simply typing Sysedit in the Windows Start/Run dialog box.

The format of all the INI files is consistent. Each INI file is divided into logical sections. Each section consists of a list of entries in the format of keyname=value. Each section has a name enclosed in brackets. The keyname is just a name that describes the function of the entry and is normally followed by an equals sign. It can be any combination of characters and numbers. The value entry can be any integer or string. Typical enabling entries include On, True, Yes, and 1. Conversely, disabling entries are Off, False, No, and 0.

Flat Memory Models

Unlike MS-DOS, Windows 3.x, or Windows 9x, other operating systems, such as Windows NT, Windows 2000, UNIX, and LINUX, do not employ the address segmentation features of the Intel microprocessors to divide up the computer's memory allocations. Because segments can overlap, memory usage errors can occur when an application attempts to write data into a space being used by the operating system, or by another application.

Using the Flat Memory Model, the memory manager sections map each application's memory space into contiguous pages of physical memory. Using this method, each application is mapped into a truly unique address space that cannot overlap any other address space. The lack of segment overlap reduces the chances of applications interfering with each other and helps to ensure data integrity by providing the operating system and other processes with their own memory spaces.

Figure 8-34 illustrates the Flat Memory Model concept. In this example, the 32-bit address produced by the microprocessor contains three parts dictated by the operating system. The highest 10 bits of the address point to the Page Table Directory. This table sets the address boundaries for each page of memory in the memory. This guarantees that there is only one method of entering the page space—through this table. Therefore, there is no chance for poorly written software to stray into a page it has not been assigned. The lower 22 bits of the address are used to access a particular page within the block of addresses specified in the Page Table Directory (bits 12-21), and then to select a particular physical address within the page (bits 0-11).

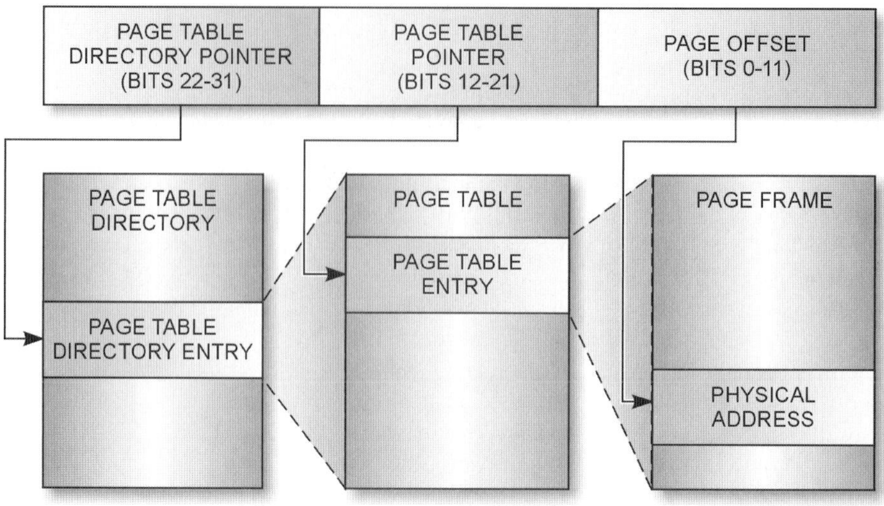

Figure 8-34: Flat Memory Model

Optimizing Memory

MEM command

The real objective in memory management in DOS and Windows 9x is to free up as much conventional memory as possible for use by DOS-based programs. The first step in this process is to use the DOS **MEM command** to determine how much memory is actually in the system and how it is organized. Figure 8-35 shows a typical memory map displayed by the MEM command.

```
C:\>

C:\>mem

Memory Type          Total  =  Used  +  Free
---------------     ------   ------   ------
Conventional          640K      47K     593K
Upper                   0K       0K       0K
Reserved              384K     384K       0K
Extended (XMS)      7,168K   2,112K   5,056K
---------------     ------   ------   ------
Total memory        8,192K   2,559K   5,633K

Total under 1 MB      640K      47K     593K

Largest executable program size       593K  (607,312 bytes)
Largest free upper memory block         0K        (0 bytes)
MS-DOS is resident in the high memory area.
```

Figure 8-35: The MEM Display

When the MEM command is executed without any modifying switches, the system's free and used memory is displayed. Adding a Page (/p) switch to the line causes the output to stop at the end of each screen full of information. In versions of MS-DOS before release 6.0, the /p switch produced a program function that displayed the status of programs currently loaded into memory. Likewise, using a Debug (/d) switch with the MEM command will show the status of currently loaded programs and internal drivers. Another switch, called the Classify (/c) switch, displays the status of programs in conventional memory and the UMA. In addition, it provides each program's size in decimal and hex notation, along with a summary of memory usage and the largest memory blocks available. The MEM command can only be used with one switch at a time.

The Total Memory value is the amount of memory installed in the computer up to 640 KB. Conversely, the Available to MS-DOS entry indicates the amount of conventional memory available to operate the system. The Largest Executable Program Size value describes the size of the largest contiguous section of conventional memory available.

The descriptions of the extended memory are similar to those provided for conventional memory. Total Contiguous Extended Memory applies to the amount of memory installed beyond the 1 MB mark. The Available Extended Memory value applies to extended memory not controlled by memory managers such as HIMEM.SYS, and Available XMS Memory does apply to this type of extended memory. Similar values are displayed when the system is operating with an expanded memory manager such as EMM386.

One of the keys to good memory management is in making the free conventional memory value as large as possible. This is primarily accomplished by moving as many programs into the UMA as possible. Earlier in this chapter, a typical CONFIG.SYS file structure was discussed. Recall that the first line of the file should be the Device=HIMEM.SYS line that loads the DOS extended memory driver from a specified directory.

The second line is typically the Device=EMM386.EXE line that loads the DOS expanded memory driver and establishes the system's upper memory blocks. This line must be loaded after the HIMEM.SYS line. Also, remember that the EMM386 command simulates expanded memory in extended memory if it is not modified by a switch such as /NOEMS (no EMS). This switch cancels the EMS function of the command and provides the maximum amount of available UMA memory to running device drivers and programs.

Conversely, modifying the EMM386 command with a /RAM switch will enable it to run device drivers and programs in upper memory blocks and simulate EMS as well. The amount of memory available for UMBs will be reduced using this switch. However, it will enable Windows to run applications that require EMS.

After the upper memory blocks have been established, several commands can be added to the CONFIG.SYS file to free up conventional memory. The first is the DOS=HIGH command that relocates a major portion of the DOS into the HMA, as illustrated in Figure 8-36. Similarly, the DOS=UMB command enables DOS to access the upper memory blocks established by the EMM386 command. These two lines are typically combined into a single command expressed as DOS=HIGH,UMB.

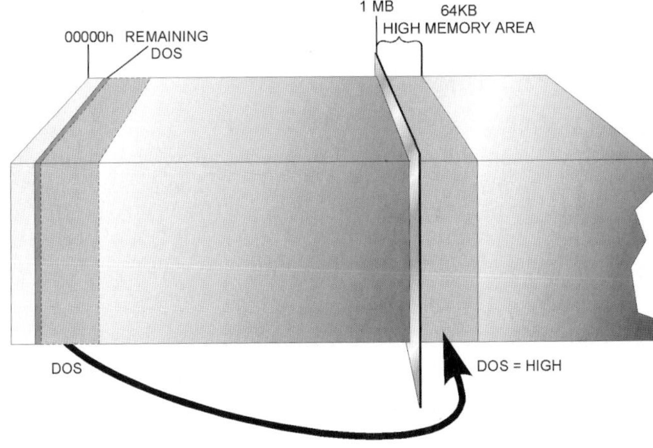

Figure 8-36: The DOS=HIGH Command

After the UMBs have been established and access has been provided to them, two commands can be employed to use them: the DEVICEHIGH= and LOADHIGH commands.

The DEVICEHIGH= command is used to load drivers into the upper memory area instead of loading them into conventional memory as the Device= command does. For example, the command DEVICEHIGH=driverx.sys will attempt to load the device driver driverx into the upper memory area. If the file is too large to fit in the buffer space available in a block of the UMA, the system may lock up. If this happens, the Device= command will load the driver into conventional memory. Run the MEM /d command to determine the hexadecimal size of the file. Finally, modify the CONFIG.SYS file again using a hexadecimal size limit (expressed in bytes) to modify the DEVICEHIGH= line (that is, DEVICEHIGH size=hexsize). This will modify the DEVICEHIGH line to use only the buffer size actually needed.

Similarly, the LOADHIGH (LH) command loads a program into the UMA. The LH command can be used in either the AUTOEXEC.BAT file or it can be executed from the DOS command line. To use it, the DOS=UMB command must have been previously loaded in the CONFIG.SYS file. If the program is too large for the available blocks of the UMA, DOS will load the program into conventional memory instead.

The following Hands-On Activity can be used to optimize the operation of the system at the DOS level:

Hands-On Activity

Optimizing at the DOS Level

1. Use a *DOS=HIGH* or *DOS=HIGH,UMB* command in the CONFIG.SYS file to load DOS into the HMA.
2. Check the CONFIG.SYS and AUTOEXEC.BAT files for lines that load the HIMEM.SYS, EMM386.EXE, SMARTDRV.EXE, and RAMDRIVE.SYS drivers. In each case, make certain that the latest version of the driver is located in the specified directory.
3. Check the order of commands in the CONFIG.SYS file to make certain that the HIMEM.SYS driver is loaded before any other extended memory application or driver. If not, move the command closer to the beginning of the file.
4. Set the memory cache size for the SMARTDRV.EXE command in the AUTOEXEC.BAT file to the largest size possible.
5. Optimize the CONFIG.SYS lines for buffers and files**.** Set files equal to 30 unless a currently installed application requires more handles. This step should also be used if DOS, or Windows 3.x operations return a “Too many files are open” message. The number of buffers should be set to 10 if SMARTDRV is being used and 20 if not. Using more than 10 buffers with SMARTDRV decreases efficiency, and using more than 20 buffers without SMARTDRV uses more of the system’s conventional memory area.
6. Set up the RAMDRIVE to use the TEMP environment. This will improve printing performance and the operation of other applications that use .TMP files.
7. Load EMM386.EXE to allocate upper memory blocks for TSRs and device drivers.

Even using the setup steps just listed, the system's performance will deteriorate over time. Most of this deterioration is due to unnecessary file clutter and segmentation on the system's hard disk drive. The following steps can be used to periodically tune up the performance of the system.

1. Periodically remove unnecessary .TMP and .BAK files from the system.
2. Check for and remove lost file chains and clusters using the DOS CHKDSK and CHKDSK /f commands.
3. Use the DOS DEFRAG utility to realign files on the drive that may have become fragmented after being moved back and forth between the drive and the system.

DOS Versions

Although DOS has remained compatible with its original design, this does not mean that it has not changed significantly since its original version.

In July of 1981, Microsoft purchased the rights to a personal computer DOS from Seattle Computer Products and promptly named it MS-DOS. A month later IBM began shipping a private labeled version of the Microsoft package that it named PC-DOS 1.0.

In May of 1982, Microsoft released MS-DOS version 1.1 to IBM for its units, and released its own brand name DOS product, MS-DOS 1.25, for PC-compatible computers. This version added support for 360 kB double-sided floppy disk drives.

In March of 1983, MS-DOS 2.0 was announced. It added support for 10 MB hard drives, a directory tree structure, and 360 kB floppy drive support to the operating system. A minor revision, titled MS-DOS 2.11, added foreign language and date features to the operating system in March of 1984.

Version 3.0 of MS-DOS was released in August of 1984. It was released along with IBM's AT model and added support for 1.2 MB floppy disk drives and larger hard disk drives. In November of the same year, version 3.1 added support for Microsoft networks. By January of 1986, version 3.2 had entered the market and brought support for 3-1/2 inch, 720 kB floppy disk drives to the operating system.

In August of 1987, version 3.3 delivered a 1.44 MB floppy disk drive and multiple 32 MB partitions for hard drives.

Version 4.0 of MS-DOS was released in June of 1988. This new version introduced a graphical shell for DOS, a mouse interface, and expanded memory drivers. By November, version 4.01 was being shipped to clean up problems with the 4.0 version.

task-swapping

Undelete

Unformat

QBASIC

DoubleSpace

The next version of MS-DOS didn't appear until June of 1991. Version 5.0 brought a full screen editor, **task-swapping** capabilities, **Undelete** and **Unformat** commands, and **QBASIC** to the operating system. In addition, it included support for upper memory blocks, larger hard disk partition sizes (up to 2 GB), support for 2.88 MB floppies, and the ability to load DOS into the HMA, as well as loading device drivers into the UMBs.

Microsoft began shipping the 6.0 version of MS-DOS in March of 1993. This new version included a **DoubleSpace** disk compression utility that allowed users to double the storage capacity of their hard disk drives. Over 1 million copies of this version sold within the first month and a half. An enhanced version, MS-DOS 6.2, was released in November of the same year. By February of 1994, legal problems over the compression utility caused Microsoft to release version 6.21 with the utility removed. However, by June, version 6.22 appeared with the compression software back in the operating system under the name **DriveSpace**.

DriveSpace

PC-DOS 7

In April of 1994, IBM released a new version of PC-DOS. This was version 6.3. In January of 1995, they followed with **PC-DOS 7** that included data compression for hard disk doubling. This marked the last release of a major command line-based DOS operating system. Table 8-2 summarizes the development of DOS products.

Table 8-2: DOS Development Timeline

YEAR	VERSION	FEATURES
1981	V1.0	First operating system for IBM PC.
	V1.25	Double-sided disk support and bug fixes added; widely distributed by OEMs.
1983	V2.0	Hierarchical file support and hard- disk support.
	V2.01	International support added.
	V2.11	V2.01 with bug fixes.
1984	V3.0	Introduced with AT model. Support for 1.2 MB floppy and larger hard disk sizes.
	V3.1	Support for Microsoft networks added.
1986	V3.2	Enhanced support for new media types added.
1987	V3.3	Support for 1.44 MB floppy, support for four serial ports, hard- disk partitions greater than 32 MB, improved national language support.
	V4.0	DOSSHELL, support for TSRs, expanded memory drivers, an install program (select), and the MEM command.
	V4.01	V4.0 with bug fixes.
1992	V5.0	Support for upper memory blocks, larger partition sizes (greater than 2 GB), loading device drivers in UMB, improved DOSSHELL and online help, support for 2.88 MB drives, QBASIC, improved system editor (Edit).
1994	V6.0	DoubleSpace disk compression introduced.
	V6.22	DriveSpace disk compression, replaces DoubleSpace.

CHAPTER SUMMARY

After completing this chapter, you should be able to demonstrate your knowledge of fundamental operating system terminology, components, and principles. In particular, you should be able to describe the basic functions of a typical disk-based operating system.

You should also be able to differentiate between different types of operating systems and state their characteristics. This includes differentiating between single-process and multiple-process systems, between batch-mode and interactive mode processes, and between multiuser, multitasking, and multiprocessor operations.

The chapter has used the MS-DOS operating system as an example of a typical disk-based operating system in terms of its functions and structures. It has also described methods of managing files and running applications in a DOS-based system, as well as navigating through the operating system from a command line, and has presented procedures for accessing and retrieving information. Finally, the chapter has presented procedures for creating and managing files and directories in an MS-DOS system.

At this point, review the objectives listed at the beginning of the chapter to be certain that you understand and can perform each item listed there.

KEY POINTS REVIEW

This chapter has discussed basic attributes associated with operating systems. In particular, it used the MS-DOS operating system as an example of basic operating system functions, structure, operation, and file management. Review the following key points before moving into the Review and Exam Questions sections to make sure you are comfortable with each point. Afterward, answer the Review Questions that follow to verify your knowledge of the information.

- There are literally thousands of different operating systems in use with microcomputers. The complexity of each operating system typically depends on the complexity of the application the microcomputer is designed to fill.

- In multiuser and multitasking operations, the appearance of simultaneous operation is accomplished by switching between different tasks in a predetermined order. The multiuser system switches between different users at multiple locations, while multitasking systems switch between different applications at a single location.

- The POST test is actually a series of tests that are performed each time the system is turned on. The different tests check the operation of the microprocessor, the keyboard, the video display, the floppy and hard disk drive units, as well as both the RAM and ROM memory units.

- If the first 16 kB of RAM successfully passes all five of the bit-pattern tests, the BIOS routine initializes the system's intelligent devices. During this part of the program, startup values stored in the ROM chip are moved into the system's programmable devices to make them functional.

- After the initialization and POST tests are completed, the BIOS checks the area of memory between C0000h and DFFFFh for BIOS extension programs.

7. Which file is the operating system loader looking for during the bootup process?
   a. An OS loader
   b. A primary bootstrap loader
   c. A master boot record
   d. The root directory
8. List the three files that must be located in the root directory in order to successfully boot MS-DOS.
   a. MSDOS.SYS, IO.SYS, and COMMAND.COM
   b. CONFIG.SYS, COMMAND.COM, and AUTOEXEC.BAT
   c. FILES, STACKS, and BUFFERS
   d. HIMEM.SYS, EMM386.EXE, and COMMAND.COM
9. What is the smallest piece of manageable information in a DOS system?
   a. The cluster
   b. The sector
   c. The word
   d. The attribute
10. The value of having virtual memory is that ___________.
    a. it creates more total memory for applications.
    b. it moves applications into the upper memory area.
    c. it shadows applications so they can be recovered if the operating system crashes.
    d. it creates additional extended memory for applications to operate in.

10. What is the primary function of the IO.SYS file?
11. What are the three main files in the DOS structure?
12. What does the System attribute indicate about the file?
13. A _______ is the DOS method of organizing files into directories and subdirectories.
14. How many files or entries can be included in the root directory?
15. What system components are involved in virtual memory operations?

EXAM QUESTIONS

1. Which DOS command prepares a diskette to function as a self-booting disk?
   a. Boot /s
   b. FDISK /s
   c. Format /s
   d. MEM /s
2. In terms of managing processes, what type of operating system is DOS?
   a. A single-process, batch-mode operating system
   b. A multiple-process, interactive-mode operating system
   c. A multiple-process, batch-mode operating system
   d. A single-process, interactive-mode operating system
3. Where would you find the system's memory managers listed?
   a. In the CONFIG.SYS file
   b. In the boot record
   c. In the AUTOEXEC.BAT file
   d. In the COMMAND.COM file
4. Which of the following items is located in the root directory of a hard disk drive?
   a. The drive letter
   b. The file attributes
   c. The member
   d. The IO.SYS file
5. What does HIMEM.SYS do?
   a. It governs the use of shadow RAM.
   b. It governs the use of conventional memory.
   c. It governs the use of extended memory.
   d. It governs the use of base memory.
6. Which memory type do MS-DOS applications run in?
   a. Upper memory
   b. Expanded memory
   c. Conventional memory
   d. Extended memory

- Conventional memory (locations 00000h through 9FFFFh) is the standard memory area for all PC-compatible systems. It traditionally holds DOS, interrupt vector tables, and relocated ROM BIOS tables. The remaining space in the conventional memory area is referred to as DOS Program Memory. (Programs written to operate under PC-DOS or MS-DOS use this area for program storage and execution).

- The upper memory area occupies the 384 kB portion of the PC's address space from A0000h to FFFFFh. This space is not normally considered as part of the computer's total address space because programs cannot store information in this area. Instead, the area is reserved to run segments of the system's hardware. Address spaces from A0000h through BFFFFh are dedicated addresses set aside for the system's video display memory. The system's ROM BIOS occupies the address space between locations FE000h and FFFFFh.

- With the advent of the 80286 microprocessor and its protected operating mode, it became possible to access physical memory locations beyond the 1-megabyte limit of the 8088. Memory above this address is generally referred to as extended memory.

- The term virtual memory is used to describe memory that isn't what it appears to be. Virtual memory is actually disk drive space that is manipulated to seem like RAM. Software creates virtual memory by swapping files between RAM and the disk drive. This memory management technique effectively creates more total memory for the system's applications to use. However, since there is a major transfer of information that involves the hard disk drive, an overall reduction in speed is encountered with virtual memory operations.

- After completing the CONFIG.SYS operation, DOS searches for the presence of a file called the AUTOEXEC.BAT file. This file contains a batch of DOS commands that will automatically be carried out when DOS is loaded into the system.

REVIEW QUESTIONS

The following questions test your knowledge of the material presented in this chapter.

1. Where is the Path statement located?
2. What type of operating system breaks the tasks associated with a process into various threads for execution?
3. Which memory manager should always be listed before any other memory managers or device drivers?
4. What does the "*" character stand for when used in a DOS filename?
5. Write a DOS command that can be inserted in the AUTOEXEC.BAT file to cause the active path and directory to be shown on the DOS command line.
6. What does the BUFFERS= command in the CONFIG.SYS file do?
7. Where is the High Memory Area located?
8. From the system startup point of view, how do a cold and a warm boot differ?
9. List the three distinct sections of a basic operating system.

CHAPTER SUMMARY

After completing this chapter, you should be able to demonstrate your knowledge of fundamental operating system terminology, components, and principles. In particular, you should be able to describe the basic functions of a typical disk-based operating system.

You should also be able to differentiate between different types of operating systems and state their characteristics. This includes differentiating between single-process and multiple-process systems, between batch-mode and interactive mode processes, and between multiuser, multitasking, and multiprocessor operations.

The chapter has used the MS-DOS operating system as an example of a typical disk-based operating system in terms of its functions and structures. It has also described methods of managing files and running applications in a DOS-based system, as well as navigating through the operating system from a command line, and has presented procedures for accessing and retrieving information. Finally, the chapter has presented procedures for creating and managing files and directories in an MS-DOS system.

At this point, review the objectives listed at the beginning of the chapter to be certain that you understand and can perform each item listed there.

KEY POINTS REVIEW

This chapter has discussed basic attributes associated with operating systems. In particular, it used the MS-DOS operating system as an example of basic operating system functions, structure, operation, and file management. Review the following key points before moving into the Review and Exam Questions sections to make sure you are comfortable with each point. Afterward, answer the Review Questions that follow to verify your knowledge of the information.

- There are literally thousands of different operating systems in use with microcomputers. The complexity of each operating system typically depends on the complexity of the application the microcomputer is designed to fill.
- In multiuser and multitasking operations, the appearance of simultaneous operation is accomplished by switching between different tasks in a predetermined order. The multiuser system switches between different users at multiple locations, while multitasking systems switch between different applications at a single location.
- The POST test is actually a series of tests that are performed each time the system is turned on. The different tests check the operation of the microprocessor, the keyboard, the video display, the floppy and hard disk drive units, as well as both the RAM and ROM memory units.
- If the first 16 kB of RAM successfully passes all five of the bit-pattern tests, the BIOS routine initializes the system's intelligent devices. During this part of the program, startup values stored in the ROM chip are moved into the system's programmable devices to make them functional.
- After the initialization and POST tests are completed, the BIOS checks the area of memory between C0000h and DFFFFh for BIOS extension programs.

- If an error or setup mismatch is encountered, the BIOS will issue an error code, either in message form on the display screen, or in beep-coded form through the system's speaker.

- The bootup process starts when the BIOS begins looking through the system for a Master Boot Record (MBR). This record can reside on drive A: or C:, or at any other location.

- While the system is operating, the BIOS continues to perform several important functions. It contains routines on which the operating system calls to carry out basic services. These services include providing BIOS interrupt calls (software interrupt routines) for such operations as printer, video, and disk drive accesses.

- The second section of a DOS disk is occupied by the disk's file allocation tables. This area is a table of information about how the disk is organized. Basically, the system logs the use of the space on the disk in this table.

- The next section following the FAT tables is the disk's root directory. This is a special directory that is present on every DOS disk. It is the main directory of every logical disk, and serves as the starting point for organizing information on the disk.

- The operating system is responsible for providing the system's user interface. The main user interface for DOS is the command line. The command line is the space immediately following the DOS prompt on the screen. All DOS commands are typed in this space. They are executed by pressing the ENTER key on the keyboard.

- Disk-based systems store and handle related pieces of information in groups called files. The system recognizes and keeps track of the different files in the system by their filenames. Therefore, each file in the system is required to have a filename that is different from that of any other file in the directory.

- In any event, you should remember the seven items below when assigning and using filenames:

    1. All files must have a filename.
    2. All filenames must be different than any other filename in the system, or on the disk presently in use.
    3. DOS filenames are up to 8 characters long with an optional 3-character extension (separated from the basic filename by a period).
    4. When using a filename in a command, you must also use its extension, if one exists.
    5. Some special characters are not allowed in filenames. These are: [,], :, ;, +, =, \, /, , ? and ,.
    6. When telling DOS where to carry out a command, you must tell it on which disk drive the operation is to be performed. The drive must be specified by its letter name followed by a colon (i.e., A:, B:, C:, etc.).
    7. The complete and proper way to specify a file calls for the drive specifier, the filename, and the filename extension, in that order (i.e., B:filename.ext).

- The DOS mode command is used to configure the system's I/O devices. These devices include the parallel and serial ports, as well as the monitor display and the keyboard.

- Basically, DOS can recognize the following classifications of memory: conventional memory, upper memory blocks, high memory area, expanded memory, extended memory, and virtual memory.

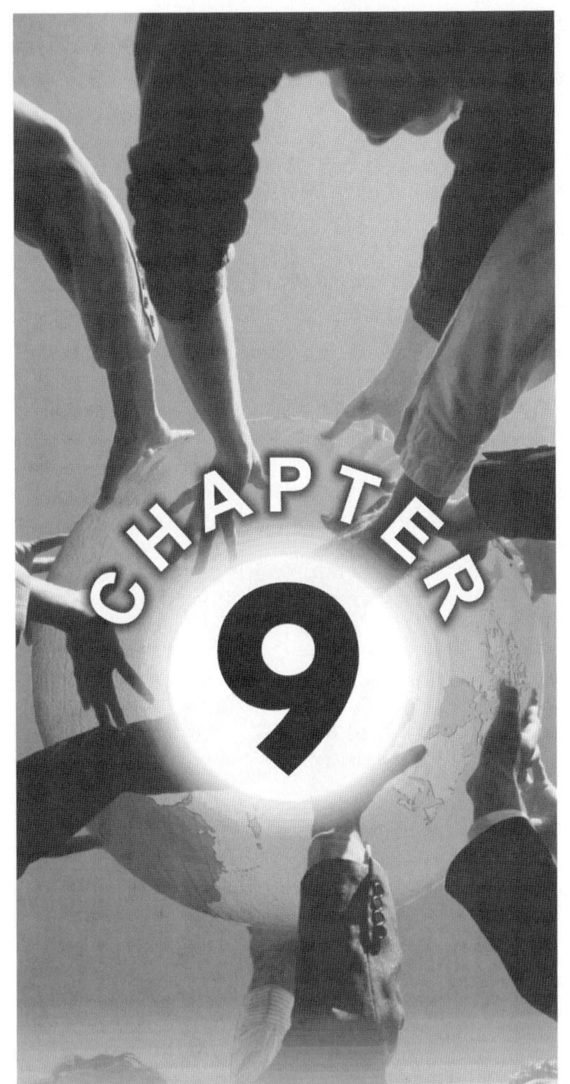

WINDOWS 9X

OBJECTIVES

OBJECTIVES

Upon completion of this chapter and its related lab procedures you will be able to perform the following tasks:

1. Identify the procedures for installing Windows 9x and bringing the software to a basic operational level.
2. Identify the basic Windows 9x boot/startup sequence and alternative ways to boot the system software.
3. Identify the steps to create a Windows 9x Startup Disk with helpful utilities installed.
4. Identify the procedures for loading/adding device drivers and the necessary software for certain devices in a Windows 9x system.
5. Identify procedures for changing options, configuring, and using the Windows 9x printing subsystem.
6. Identify the procedures for installing and launching typical Windows and non-Windows applications in a Windows 9x system.
7. Identify Windows 9x operating system functions, structure, and major system files.
8. Describe the major system files of a Windows 9x system, indicating where they are located and how they are used.
9. Identify ways of navigating through the Windows 9x operating system and how to get to needed technical information.
10. Describe procedures for locating, accessing, and retrieving information in a Windows 9x system.
11. Identify basic concepts and procedures for creating and managing files and folders in a Windows 9x system.
12. Identify the local area networking capabilities of Windows 9x.
13. Describe procedures for connecting to the network from a Windows 9x system.
14. Describe procedures for sharing disk drives, and print and file services in a Windows 9x system.
15. Identify concepts and capabilities relating to the Internet.
16. Describe basic procedures for setting up a Windows 9x system for Internet access.

CHAPTER 9

WINDOWS 9X

INTRODUCTION

This chapter will help you to prepare for the Operating Systems Technology module of the A+ Certification examination by covering the objectives within the Domain 1.0 - Function, Structure, Operation, and File Management section.

The previous chapter explored basic operating systems in some detail. Most of the information covered BIOS operations and the DOS command line structure. Domain 1.0 of the A+ Operating System Technologies exam states that the test taker should be able to demonstrate knowledge of underlying DOS (Command prompt functions) in Windows 9x in terms of its functions and structure, for managing files and directories, and running programs. It also includes navigating through the operating system from command line prompts, as well as using Windows procedures for accessing and retrieving information. Therefore, this chapter continues the exploration of operating system software by examining Microsoft's Windows 9x programs.

It may be natural to think that the Microsoft Windows programs evolved out of the existing DOS program, but this is not the case. Microsoft first introduced Windows in 1984, 10 years before Microsoft introduced its final version of MS-DOS. The pressure for a GUI operating system to work with PCs was actually generated by the popularity of the Apple operating systems.

WINDOWS EVOLUTION

In April 1983, Microsoft demonstrated a **graphical interface manager** that would later become Windows. It gave the appearance of overlapping window panes, with various programs running in each window. In November of the same year, Microsoft formally announced Windows and set a release date of April 1984. Interestingly, IBM passed on the opportunity to market Windows with its units three different times. They were busy developing a GUI called **TopView** for their systems.

graphical interface manager

TopView

Microsoft announced Windows 1.0 in June 1985 and began shipping in November. It found a PC market that was steeped in command-line operations. Many industry analysts predicted it would come and go and "real computer users" would hold on to their DOS disks.

Version 2.0 was announced in April 1987 and actually hit the market in October, along with a version called **Windows/386**. By December of that year, Microsoft had shipped more than 1 million copies of Windows. Two versions of Windows 2.1 shipped in June 1988 under the titles **Windows/286** and /386.

Windows/386

Windows/286

Windows 3.0 did not make it to the market until May 1990. However, it opened with a $3 million, first-day advertising campaign. In March 1992, Microsoft produced its first television advertising campaign for the upcoming Windows 3.1 version. The new version began shipping in April and had reached a level of 1 million copies shipped by June.

Windows for Workgroups (WfW)

The 3.1 version migrated into **Windows for Workgroups (WfW)** in November 1992. This version integrated peer-to-peer networking directly into the operating environment. It was quick and easy to install and set up a workgroup network to share information and resources among different computers. These were terms that were not usually associated with networking computers together. By April 1993 the number of units sold had risen to 25 million licensed copies of Windows sold. By October, Microsoft had begun shipping 3.11, the final 3.x version of Windows.

In September 1994, Microsoft announced the next version of Windows. They called it Windows 95. The first version was released in August 1995 and sold 1 million copies during the first week on the market. Within a month, the sales of Windows 95 climbed to more than 7 million copies, and by March 1996 had topped 30 million copies.

Due to the huge installed base of Windows 3.x and Windows 95 products, every technician needs to be familiar with these operating systems for at least the immediate future (see Table 9-1).

Table 9-1: Windows Development Time Line

YEAR	VERSION	FEATURES
1983		Graphics Interface Manager demonstration
1985	V1.0	First official Windows release
1987	V2.0	Task switching of applications
	Windows/286	Use of all the extended memory for applications
	Windows/386	Cooperative multitasking of applications
1990	V3.0	Preemptive multitasking of applications, enhanced memory support, use of icons, Program Manager interface
1992	V3.1	(Windows for Workgroups) Integrated peer-to-peer networking directly into the operating environment
1993	V3.11	Upgraded 32-bit software and disk capabilities; BIOS calls removed from file accesses
1995	Windows 95	Improved multimedia support, Plug-and-Play hardware support, 32-bit advanced multitasking function, improved email and fax capabilities, WAN usage
1996	Windows 95 OSR2	Incorporated patches and fixes for version 1, along with Internet Explorer 3.0 and Personal Web Server, the FAT32 file system, improved Power Management, MMX multimedia support, Bus mastering, and enhanced PCMCIA functions.
1998	Windows 98	Upgraded Windows 95 and integrated Internet Explorer into the Windows 98 interface
1999	Windows 98SE	The second edition of Windows 98. It was a simple cleanup of the original Windows 98 version
2000	Windows ME Millennium	Extended the Windows 98 interface and features and cleaned up additional Windows 98 bugs

Windows 9x Versions

As you can see from the table, the 9x version of Windows has been produced as five distinct products:

- Windows 95
- Windows 95 OSR2
- Windows 98
- Windows 98SE
- Windows Millennium Edition

The following material describes each of these products and explains some of their key differences.

Windows 95

In 1995, Microsoft released a radically different looking Windows environment called **Windows 95**. This Windows featured many new and improved features over previous versions. Windows 95 offered improved multimedia support for video and sound file applications, Plug-and-Play hardware support, 32-bit advanced multitasking functions, improved **email** and **fax** capabilities through Microsoft Exchange, and the Microsoft Network for easy **Wide Area Network (WAN)** usage.

Windows 95

email

fax

Wide Area Network (WAN)

Even though Windows 95 is optimized for running 32-bit applications, it is still fully compatible with 16-bit Windows 3.x and DOS applications. As a matter of fact, it can be installed over either of these operating system versions as a direct upgrade. The only real concern when installing Windows 95 over either of these operating systems is that the existing system has the hardware resources needed to run Windows 95.

Windows 95 offers full built-in Plug-and-Play capability. When Windows 95 is combined with a hardware system that implements PnP BIOS, expansion slots, and adapter support, and is supported with PnP adapter drivers, fully automated configuration and reconfiguration can take place.

Windows 95 OSR2

Windows 95 OSR2

Windows 95 (b)

FAT32

OSR2

Power Management (APM)

Bus Mastering

MMX

OSR1

Service Pack 1

Windows 95 OSR2, also known as **Windows 95 (b)**, is an upgrade of the original Windows 95 package that includes patches and fixes for version 1, along with Microsoft Internet Explorer 3.0 and Personal Web Server. It also includes an enhanced File Allocation Table system referred to as **FAT32**.

In addition to the FAT32 system, **OSR2** offers improved **Power Management (APM)** functions, **Bus Mastering** support, **MMX** multimedia support, and enhanced PCMCIA functions over version-a (which is referred to as **OSR1**, or **Service Pack 1**).

Also new in OSR2 is HDD/CD-ROM DMA access support. This feature is located in the Control Panel/System/Device Manager/Disk Drives window. At this point, choose the desired drive, select Properties, and click the Settings tab. Check the DMA box and reboot the system. The same procedure should be performed for the CD-ROM drive as well. This box will appear only for IDE drives, and only when using properly installed and configured OSR2 Bus Mastering drivers for the drive.

Windows 98

Microsoft's Windows 98 replaced the Windows 95 operating system. While many of its features remained basically the same as those of Windows 95, Windows 98 did bring certain new items to the system. Most notably, it extended the desktop to the Internet, creating a Web-based desktop environment. This feature was designed to make Internet (or intranet) access as seamless as possible for the user. It also enabled Windows 98 to perform unattended self-upgrades directly from the Microsoft Web site when new items or repairs were released.

Windows 98SE

proxy server

In 1999, Microsoft produces an improved version of Windows 98 that became known as **Windows 98SE** (Second Edition). This edition was basically the original Windows 98 platform with all of the patches incorporated. However, it did transform a relatively unstable operating system into a very stable platform. Along with the patches, Windows 98SE offered additional device drivers and Internet Explorer repair tools. Its only notable new feature was built-in *Internet connection sharing.* This feature enabled a Windows 98 machine to act as a **proxy server** for other nodes in a network. The proxy acted as the connection point to the Internet for all of the computers on the LAN.

Windows Millennium

Millennium Edition (ME)

Windows **Millennium Edition** (**ME**) is the latest variation of the Windows 9x line of consumer operating systems. although it operates in a manner similar to Windows 98, it incorporates more of the look and feel of the Windows 2000 commercial operating system discussed in the next chapter.

Windows ME minimizes the user's access to the command prompt functions. It also includes a number of new self-repairing capabilities that perform some of the technician's repair functions automatically.

Several of the items we will discuss in this chapter and in the Operating System Troubleshooting chapter have been moved to new (Windows 2000-like) locations in Windows ME. The integration of the Windows Internet Explorer is even tighter in Windows ME than it was in the Windows 98 package. All of these additional features and functionality ultimately have produced an operating system whose memory footprint (requirements) is much larger than the Windows 98 operating system that it is replacing. This can be a major consideration when considering whether to upgrade a system with marginal capacity to the new operating system.

INSTALLING WINDOWS 9X

Windows 9x must be installed over an existing operating system, such as MS-DOS, or Windows 3.x. In particular, the Windows 9x installation program must find a recognizable MS-DOS FAT16 partition on the drive. This prevents it from being installed over some other type of operating system, such as Windows NT, or Novell NetWare OS.

TEST TIP

Remember that Windows 9x requires that a FAT 16 partition exist on the drive where it is being installed.

The Windows 95 system must be at least an 80386DX or higher machine, operating with at least 4 MB of RAM (8 MB is recommended). The 80386DX is the listed minimum microprocessor for running Windows 95, and the recommended processor is the 80486DX, but the Pentium processors are actually the preferred microprocessor for running Windows 95. Likewise, 4 MB may be the minimum RAM option, with 8 MB being the recommended option, but 16 MB, 32 MB, or 64 MB are preferred for running Windows 95.

TEST TIP

Memorize the minimum, recommended, and preferred CPU specifications for running Windows 9x.

The system should also possess a mouse and a VGA monitor or better. The system's hard drive should have at least 20 MB of free space available to successfully install Windows 95.

The actual requirements for successfully installing Windows 95 depend on the type of installation being conducted and what level it is being conducted from. As already mentioned, Windows 9x must be installed on a hard drive that already has a FAT16 structure in place, such as MS-DOS, Windows 3.1, and Windows for Workgroups systems.

In addition, the Windows 95 Setup installation routine provides for different types of installations to be established, including Typical, Portable, Compact, and Custom, all of which install different combinations of the possible Windows 95 system. Therefore, they all have different system requirements for proper installation.

TEST TIP

Memorize the minimum and recommended amounts of memory specified to start Windows 95.

To perform a Typical installation in a DOS system requires a minimum of 40 MB of free drive space. Conversely, conducting a Compact installation on the same system would only require 30 MB. When the installation is being conducted from a Windows 3.1 or Windows for Workgroup environment, the free space requirements drop to 30 MB Typical/20 MB Compact for Windows 3.1 and 20 MB Typical /10 MB Compact for Windows for Workgroups. The total required free space can range up to 85 MB when a Custom installation is conducted using all of the Windows 95 options.

Unlike Windows 95, Windows 98 does not need to be installed over an existing operating system. Only the Upgrade version of Windows 98 requires an existing operating system such as MS-DOS, Windows 3.1x, or Windows 95. The distribution CD for the full version of Windows 98 can be used to boot the system and provide options to partition and format the drive. To install Windows 98, the system hardware must be at least an 80486DX/66 or higher machine, operating with at least 16 MB of RAM. The system should also possess a modem, a mouse, and a 16-color VGA monitor or better. The system's hard drive should have between 120 and 355 MB of free space available to successfully install Windows 98. The actual amount of disk space used depends on the type of installation being performed (Typical, Custom, Portable, Compact, New, Upgrade, etc.). Typical installations use between 170 and 225 MB of disk space.

There are several possible circumstances that will determine how Windows 98 should be installed. The primary concern is which operating system it will be replacing. Is the system a new installation, or is it being upgraded from DOS, Windows 3. x, or Windows 95? The second concern is what type of system the installation is being conducted on. Is the system a standalone unit, or is it a networked unit?

If Windows 98 is being installed in a new unit, or to a disk drive that has been reformatted, it will be necessary to boot the system from the Windows distribution CD or run the SETUP.EXE program from the DOS prompt. This method is also employed when Windows 98 is being used to upgrade a system from Windows 95 using new settings.

Using this approach, the Windows 98 Setup program runs a real-mode version of the ScanDisk utility on the drive. This requires that the CD-ROM or network drive's real-mode driver be present and loaded. This ScanDisk version performs FAT, directory, and file checks on the drive and creates a ScanDisk log file. If an error is detected, the program displays an error message indicating that the log file should be checked. The file can be accessed through the ScanDisk screen's View Log selection.

After the ScanDisk inspection has been completed, the Setup program initializes the system and begins copying installation files to the drive. The installation is carried out in the five-step procedure as follows:

Hands-On Activity

1. Preparing to Run Windows 98 Setup

During this part of the procedure, Setup performs the following steps to prepare the Windows 98 Setup Wizard to guide the user through the installation process:

a. Creates a SETUPLOG.TXT file in the drive's root directory.

b. Identifies the source and destination drive locations for the Windows 98 files.

c. Copies a minimal Windows 98 Setup cabinet file, called MINI.CAB, into the Wininst0.400 directory it creates at C:\.

d. Extracts the major Setup files PRECOPY1.CAB and PRECOPY2.CAB into the Wininst0.400 directory.

2. Collecting Information About Your Computer

After the Setup files have been extracted to the hard drive, the Setup Wizard begins operation by presenting the Microsoft Licensing Agreement and asking the user to enter the Product Key number, as illustrated in Figure 9-1. The product key can be found on the software's Certificate of Authenticity, or on the CD's backliner. On stand-alone machines, this number must be entered correctly to continue the installation. Conversely, there will not be any Product Key request when Windows 98 is being installed across a network.

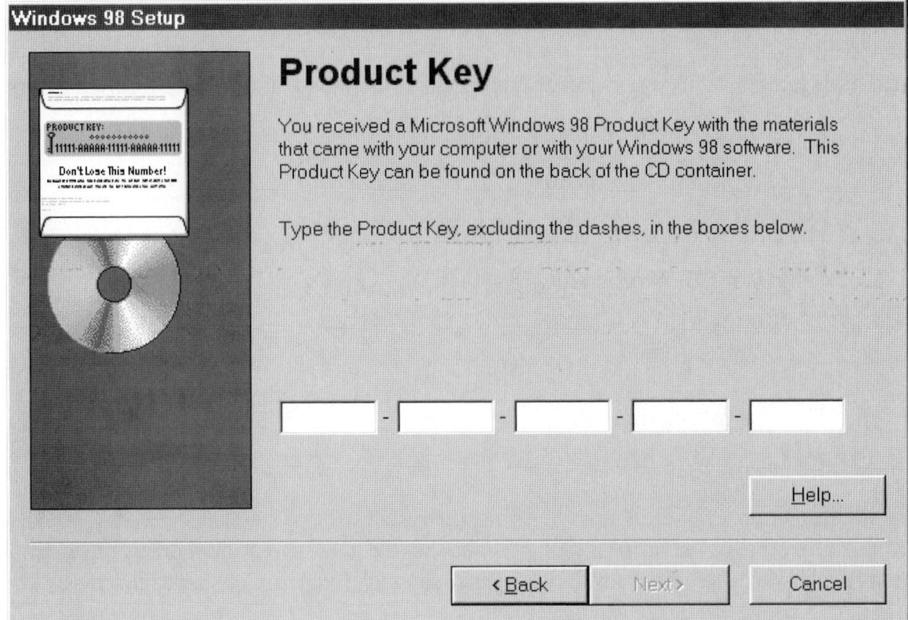

Figure 9-1: Windows 98 Product Key Entry Screen

After the registration information has been gathered, Setup begins to collect information about the system. This information includes:

a. The location of the installation directory into which Windows 98 files should be moved.

b. Verification that the selected drive has enough space to hold the Windows 98 installation.

c. The type of installation desired (that is, Typical, Portable, Compact, and Custom).

d. The user's company and user names.

e. The Windows 98 components that should be installed.

f. The computer's network identification (if installing in a network environment).

g. The Internet location from which the system can receive regional update information.

After gathering this information, the Setup routine stops to prompt the installer to create an Emergency Startup Disk and then begins installing Windows 98 files to the selected drive.

3. Copying Windows 98 Files to Your Computer

This portion of the operation begins when the Start Copying Files dialog box appears on the screen. The complete operation of this phase is automated so that no external input is required. However, any interruption of the Setup operation during this period may prevent the system from starting up again. In this event, it will be necessary to rerun the Setup routine from the beginning.

4. Restarting Your Computer

Once Setup has copied the Windows 98 files into their proper locations, it will present a prompt to restart the system. Doing so allows the newly installed Windows 98 functions to become active. The restart will be conducted automatically if no entry is detected within 15 seconds.

5. Setting Up Hardware and Finalizing Settings

After the system has been restarted, Setup finalizes the installation of the following items:

a. The Control Panel.
b. The contents of the Start Menu.
c. The basic Windows 98 Help functions.
d. Settings for DOS programs.
e. Application Start functions.
f. Time Zone information.
g. The system's configuration information.

Upon completion of these steps, Setup again restarts the system and presents a log-on prompt. After the log-on process, Setup establishes a database of system driver information, updates the system's settings, establishes personalized system options, and presents a "Welcome to Windows 98" page on the screen.

Operating System Upgrading

The A+ Operating System Technologies objective 2.2 states that the test taker should be able to identify steps to perform an operating system upgrade. The reason for this objective is that it is not uncommon for a computer to have its operating system upgraded, possibly several times, during its life span. The following sections of this chapter cover upgrading from DOS, Windows 3.x, or Windows 95 environments to the Windows 95 or Windows 98 operating systems. Upgrading to Windows 2000 is covered in the next chapter.

Upgrading to Windows 95

With the Windows 95 Setup disk or CD-ROM in the drive, the Windows 95 Setup routine can be executed from the DOS command line, from the Windows 3.x Program Manager's Run box, or from the File Manager window. The preferred method is to run the Setup program from Windows 3.x. As already mentioned, with any major system change, all important data should be backed up on some acceptable media before attempting to upgrade the operating system.

To run the Windows 95 Setup program from Windows 3.x:

1. Boot the computer and start Windows.
2. Insert the Windows 95 Start Disk (Disk 1) in the A: drive, or place the Windows 95 CD in the CD-ROM drive.
3. Open the File Manager and select the proper drive.
4. Double-click on the **SETUP.EXE** file entry.

SETUP.EXE

5. Follow the directions from the screen and enter the information requested by the program for the type of installation being performed.

To run the Windows 95 Setup program from DOS:

1. Boot the computer.
2. Insert the Windows 95 Start Disk (Disk 1) in the A: drive, or place the Windows 95 CD in the CD-ROM drive.
3. Move to the drive that contains the Windows 95 Installation files.
4. At the DOS prompt, type **Setup** and press the ENTER key.
5. Follow the directions from the screen and enter the information requested by the program for the type of installation being performed.

The Setup program provides options for performing **Typical (default)**, **Portable**, **Compact**, and **Custom** installations. Figure 9-2 depicts the Windows 95 Setup Wizard's Setup Options screen.

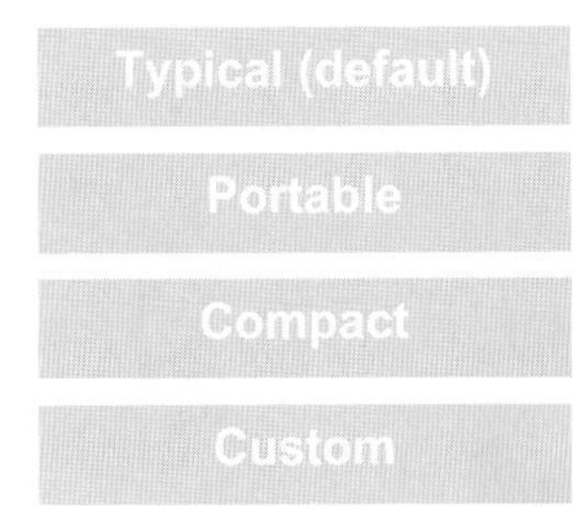

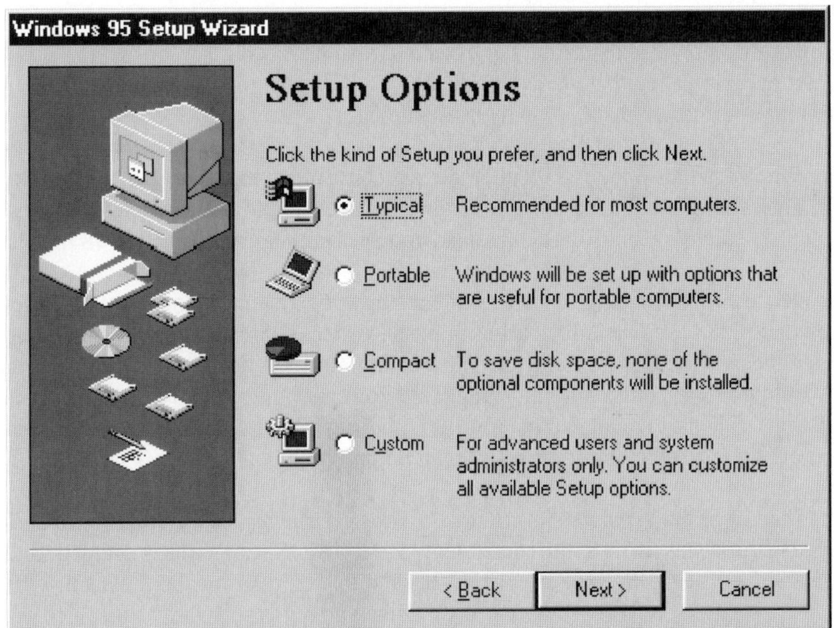

Figure 9-2: The Windows 95 Setup Options Screen

The Typical process normally installs most of the Windows 95 files to the C:\Windows directory without intervention from the user. However, this option does provide the user with the opportunity to install the operating system in another drive or directory. It also prompts the user to provide user and computer identification, as well as allowing the user to decide whether to create an Emergency Start Disk or not. All other aspects of the installation are carried out by the Windows 95 Setup utility.

The Portable option installs those options most closely associated with portable computer systems. The Compact option is a minimal installation for those units with limited disk space available. The Custom option allows the user to make customized selections for most device configurations. This method may be required for installations that are using non-PnP-compliant adapter cards.

If Setup detects the presence of a Windows 3.x operating system, it will ask whether it should install its files in the same directory. If the prompt is answered with "Yes," Windows 95 will act as an upgrade over the existing Windows structure. It will obtain existing configuration information from the SYSTEM.INI, WIN.INI, and PROTOCOL.INI files and move it into the Windows 95 Registry. This will enable these settings to work automatically when Windows 95 is first started.

Windows 95 also migrates the contents of the existing Windows 3.x Group (GRP) files into the Registry during installation. Because Windows 95 rummages around in these files, both the INI and GRP files from the original Windows 3.x setup should be backed up before installing Windows 95.

Upgrading to Windows 98

In order to upgrade to Windows 98 from an existing Windows version, and retain the current system settings, the Setup program should be executed from the Windows 95 user interfaces. Windows 98 Setup will execute the same basic five-step procedure described earlier from either interface. However, the events that occur within each step are dependent on the operating system information that is already available.

While Windows 95 to Windows 98 upgrades are convenient, they can also be unstable afterwards. Therefore, if you do not need to retain any specific settings, you may want to simply back up the system's data, FDISK the disk, and perform a clean Windows 98 installation.

When Windows 98 is installed on a current Windows 95 machine, using the existing settings, the Setup program acquires information about the system's hardware, applications, and utilities from the existing Registry entries. The existing information is simply migrated into the new Windows 98 structure. In this manner, a lot of time is saved since the system does not have to run a full hardware detection routine, or configure the system's hardware. The Setup routine also skips to the option of selecting a Setup type (i.e., Custom, Typical, etc.).

During Phase 1 of the Windows 98 upgrade, the system checks for the presence of anti-virus software in the system. The Setup routine may fail if CMOS Anti-virus is enabled. If this occurs, the SETUPLOG.TXT file should be checked for information about the anti-virus test. In some cases, the Setup program may ask that the anti-virus software be disabled so that it can have access to the Master Boot Record. Setup will also modify the AUTOEXEC.BAT file, causing it to run a file called SUWARN.BAT. This file reboots the system in case of a failure, and presents an explanation of why the Setup failed.

SCANREGW.EXE

In Phase 2 of the upgrade, the real-mode ScanDisk operation is carried out, and Setup runs the **SCANREGW.EXE** file to check the existing Registry for corruption during this phase. The Setup routine also provides a prompt that permits the current DOS or Windows System Files to be saved in case an uninstall operation is required for Windows 98 at some future time.

The Setup routine copies the Windows 98 files to the computer during Phase 3. This segment of the process begins with the appearance of the Start Copying Files dialog box on the screen. The complete operation of this phase is automated and requires no external intervention. However, any interruption of the Setup operation during this period may prevent the system from starting up again. In this event, it will be necessary to repeat the entire Setup routine form the beginning.

In Phase 4, the Restart operation includes a step where the Setup routine modifies the WIN.INI, SYSTEM.INI, and Registry files to include the appropriate Windows 98 entries. Likewise, an existing AUTOEXEC.BAT or CONFIG.SYS file will be examined for device drivers and Terminate and Stay Resident programs that may be incompatible with the upgraded installation. TSR programs can be quite problematic and should be deactivated before conducting any operating system upgrade. The results of this check are logged in a hidden file at *C:\Windows\Inf_folder\Setupc.inf.* The Setup routine disables the questionable entries in these files by using REM statements.

You should be aware that active anti-virus software may prevent Windows 98 from installing to a system. These utilities see the changes to the new operating system's core files as a virus activity and will work to prevent them from occurring. Any anti-virus programs should be disabled prior to running Windows 98 Setup. The program can be re-enabled after the setup process has been completed.

TEST TIP

Be aware that anti-virus utilities can prevent operating system upgrades from occurring.

In cases where it is desirable to install Windows 98 into some directory other than the C:\Windows directory, click on the Other Directory button in the Select Directory dialog box, depicted in Figure 9-3, and select the Next option. This will produce the Change Directory dialog box. Type the new directory name in the dialog box, and click on the Next option. The new directory will be created automatically, if it does not already exist.

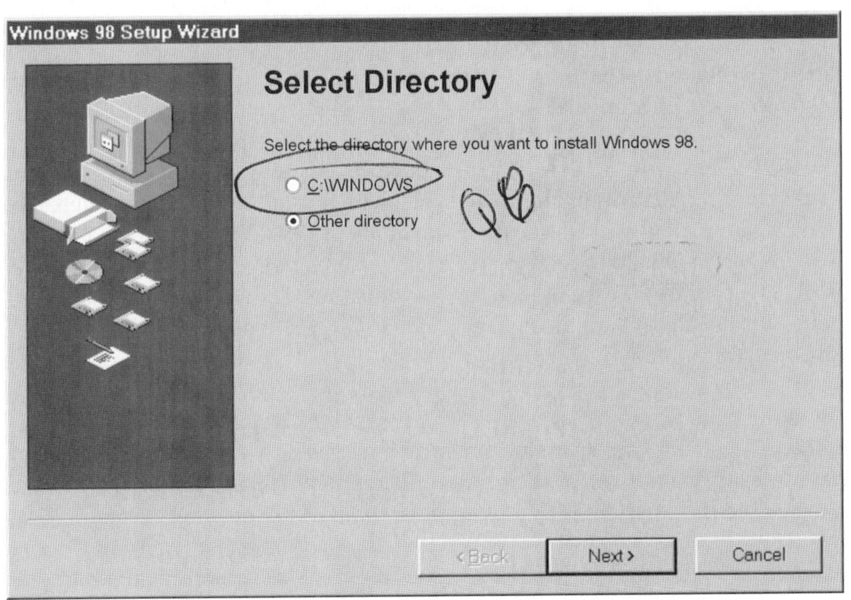

Figure 9-3: The Select Directory Dialog Box

If Windows 98 is installed in a new directory, it will be necessary to reinstall any Windows-based applications in the system. This will be required in order for the applications to function properly. The applications' support DLLs will not be able to automatically access the Windows 98 structure in the new directory. Likewise, existing .GRP and .INI files will not work unless Windows 98 has been installed in the Windows directory.

If Setup detects the presence of a Windows 3.x operating system, it will ask if it should install its files in the same directory. If the prompt is answered with "Yes", then Windows 9x will act as an upgrade over the existing Windows structure. It will obtain existing configuration information from the SYSTEM.INI, WIN.INI, and PROTOCOL.INI files and move it into the Windows 9x **Registry**. This will enable these settings to work automatically when Windows 9x is first started.

Registry

.GRP

Windows 9x also migrates the contents of the existing Windows 3.x Group (**.GRP**) files into the Registry during installation. Since Windows 9x rummages around in these files, both the .INI and .GRP files from the original Windows 3.x Setup should be backed up before installing Windows 9x. However, you should be aware that it is not possible to simply copy the old INI and GRP files to a new installation directory and have Windows use their information. They must be in the existing installation directory when the Windows 9x Setup utility is run, so that it can find them and migrate them into the new Registry structure.

If the answer to the installation directory question is "No", then you will be asked where the Windows 9x files should be installed. By installing Windows 9x in a new directory, it will be possible to preserve and use the old DOS or Windows environment. In order to boot to either operating system it will be necessary to configure the system with dual boot options.

Dual Booting Windows 9x

dual-boot configuration

By establishing a **dual-boot configuration**, it is possible to install Windows 9x, or some other operating system, on an existing system and still retain the original operating system.

As stated above, the first step in establishing a dual boot system is to install the copy of Windows 9x into a new directory.

In order to dual boot with DOS, or DOS/Windows 3.x, the system must have a copy of MS-DOS 5.0 or higher already running. If the Windows 9x installation is a new setup, the dual-boot option can be configured during the installation process. When prompted by the Setup utility to use the C:\Windows directory or specify another directory for the Windows files, choose a new directory for the Windows 9x installation. The Windows 9x Setup program will automatically adjust the existing DOS, CONFIG.SYS, and AUTOEXEC.BAT files for the new operating system.

.DOS extension

The original IO.SYS, MSDOS.SYS, COMMAND.COM, CONFIG.SYS, and AUTOEXEC.BAT files are stored in the root directory using a **.DOS extension**. If Windows 3.x was originally installed on the drive, those files will remain in the C:\Windows directory and can be used if the system is booted to the original DOS operating system.

BootMulti=

Notepad

F4

Previous version of MS-DOS

In addition, the setting for the Windows 9x MSDOS.SYS file's **BootMulti=** entry must be set to a value of 1. This can be done by bringing the file into a text editor, such as **Notepad**, and changing the setting to the desired value. After rebooting the system, it will be possible to boot into the old DOS/Windows 3.x environment by pressing the **F4** function key when the "Starting Windows" message appears during bootup. Pressing the F8 function key will reveal that the **Previous version of MS-DOS** option has been added to the Startup Menu.

If Windows 9x is already installed in the system, it is still possible to set the system up to dual boot with a DOS environment. It will be necessary to copy the IO.SYS, MSDOS.SYS, and COMMAND.COM files from the DOS disk to a bootable floppy. Afterwards, rename these files to **IO.DOS**, **MSDOS.DOS**, and **COMMAND.DOS** and then copy them into the root directory of the boot drive.

IO.DOS

MSDOS.DOS

COMMAND.DOS

ATTRIB command

They will also need to be handled as any other hidden, read-only, system files. Use the **ATTRIB command** to read and copy them (i.e., attrib -h -s -r IO.SYS). It will be necessary to perform the same copy/rename/copy operations to create CONFIG.DOS and AUTOEXEC.DOS files that are appropriate for the version of DOS you are using in the system.

Simply restart the system and perform the necessary steps to start and run the DOS or Windows 9x operating system.

Windows 9x Startup

Basically, the Windows 98 bootup sequence occurs in the same five phases as the Windows 9x bootup did:

- Phase 1 - bootstrap with the BIOS.
- Phase 2 - loading DOS drivers and TSR files.
- Phase 3 - Real-mode initialization of static **Virtual Device Drivers (VxDs)**.
- Phase 4 - Protected-mode switchover.
- Phase 5 - loading of any remaining VxDs.

Virtual Device Drivers (VxDs)

Phase 1: The Bootstrap Process

During the bootstrap process, the Plug-and-Play BIOS checks the system's CMOS RAM to determine which PnP devices should be activated, and where their PnP information should be stored. Each card's DMA, IRQ, and I/O addressing assignments are also collected. After all of the configuration information has been gathered, the BIOS configures the PnP cards and the intelligent system board devices. It then performs the traditional POST and initialization functions for the rest of the system. These functions are illustrated in Figures 9-4, 9-5, and 9-6.

Figure 9-4: Reading PnP Information from CMOS

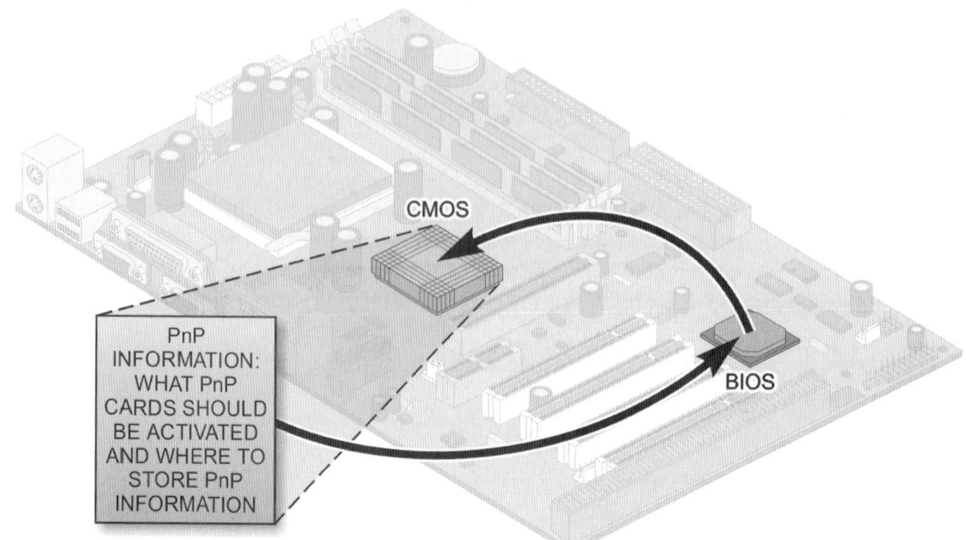

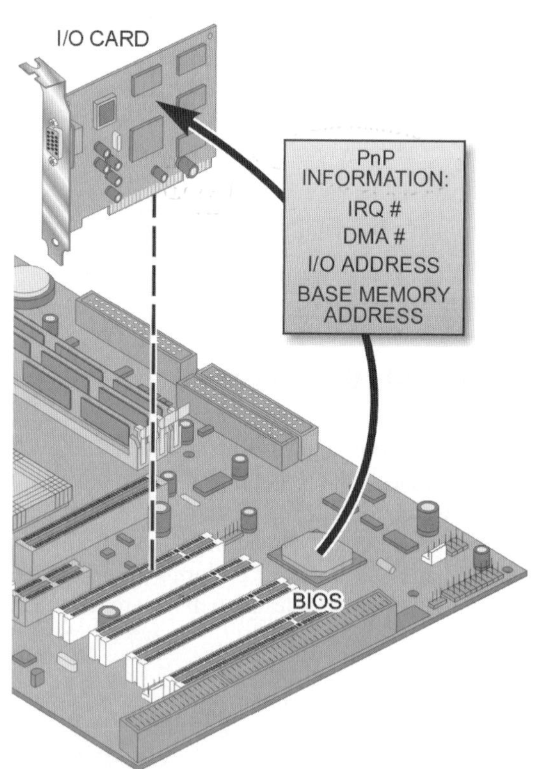

Figure 9-5: Initializing PnP Cards

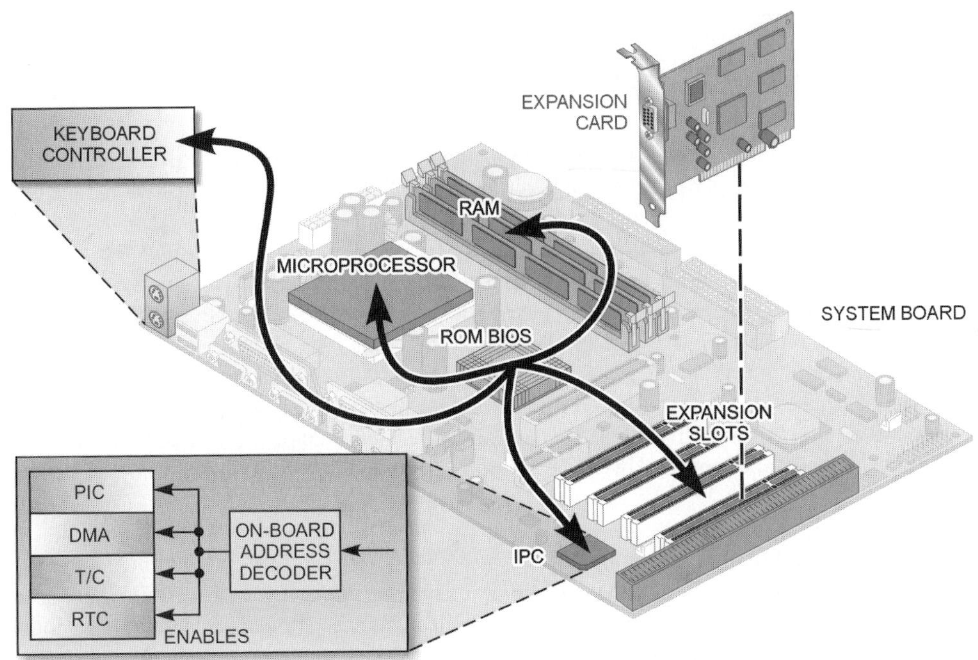

Figure 9-6: Programming the On-Board Devices

The BIOS then moves into the bootup process. The bootstrap loader routine searches for the Master Boot Record as it does with every other operating system. When the MBR is found, the system loads the IO.SYS and MSDOS.SYS files from the disk into memory, and turns over control to the IO.SYS file.

left CTRL key

IO.SYS has the capability to display the Windows 9x Startup Menu, shown in Figure 9-7. The menu can be set up to be displayed each time the system boots by setting the BootMenu=1 option in the MSDOS.SYS file. The same menu can be retrieved by pressing the **left CTRL key** during bootup. The "Starting Windows 9x" message will not appear on the screen using this key. The F8 function key will still perform this function as well.

```
Microsoft Windows 98 Startup Menu

    1. Normal
    2. Logged (\BOOTLOG.TXT)
    3. Safe Mode
    4. Step -by -Step Confirmation
    5. Command prompt only
    6. Safe Mode Command prompt only

Enter a choice: 3

F8 = Safe Mode  Shift + F5 = Command prompt  Shift + F8 = Step -by -Step Confirmation [N]
```

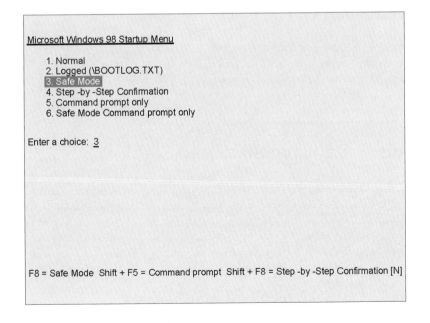

Figure 9-7: Windows 98 Startup Menu

Phase 2: Loading DOS Drivers and TSR Files

After the disk boot operation, IO.SYS checks the system's hardware profile to determine its actual configuration. This profile is a function of the BIOS' detection process during the initialization phase.

IO.SYS begins loading default drivers that were previously taken care of by the CONFIG.SYS file. These files include HIMEM.SYS, IFSHLP.SYS, SETVER.EXE, and DBLSPACE.BIN, as well as files, buffers, stacks, and dos=high settings.

If the F8 option for Step-by-Step startup has been selected, the system begins to generate a BOOTLOG.TXT file. This file, described in greater detail later in this chapter, tracks the Windows 9x components and drivers that successfully load and initialize during the startup process.

At this point, IO.SYS begins looking for a CONFIG.SYS file. If found, the lines of the file are executed, and any values that are different than those loaded by the IO.SYS file are used instead. The CONFIG.SYS values for buffers, files, and stacks must be set to at least equal the default values in the IO.SYS file. The EMM386.EXE function must be initiated from the CONFIG.SYS file for any programs that require this memory manager.

Next, IO.SYS checks the MSDOS.SYS file for paths to find other Windows directories and files. These include such items as the selected location of the Windows 9x directory and startup files, including the Registry. The [Options] section of the file allows selected bootup events to be altered. This section can contain items to automatically display the Boot Menu, and to enable or disable key bootup features.

This is followed by executing the COMMAND.COM file. As with previous Microsoft operating systems, the Windows 9x COMMAND.COM extends the I/O functions of the system, supplies the command interface for the system, and looks for the AUTOEXEC.BAT file. If found, the AUTOEXEC.BAT commands are executed, loading device drivers and TSR programs in Real mode.

In the Windows 9x environment, the CONFIG.SYS and AUTOEXEC.BAT files primarily exist to maintain compatibility with applications written for earlier operating systems and environments. If neither of these files is present, the system will still start and run fine.

Phase 3: Initializing Static VxDs

The system next checks the SYSTEM.DAT file for the first part of the Registry file and processes it. SYSTEM.DAT is a hidden file that contains all of the system's hardware configuration information, including the PnP and application settings. It is always located under the C:\Windows directory. If the Windows 95 system does not find the SYSTEM.DAT file, it will refer to the SYSTEM.DA0 file, created during the previous bootup, as a backup. Likewise, Windows 98 refers to the rb000 Registry backup file located in C:\Windows\Sysbckup.

Afterward, IO.SYS loads the **WIN.COM** file to control the loading and testing of the Windows 9x core components. This is followed by loading the **VMM32.VXD virtual machine manager** and, finally, the SYSTEM.INI file. SYSTEM.INI is loaded so that its information can be used to maintain compatibility with non-dynamic VxDs.

WIN.COM

VMM32.VXD virtual machine manager

The VMM32.VXD file creates the virtual environment and loads the system's VxD files. It contains a list of all the VxD files the system requires. These files are stored in the **Hkey_Local_Machine\System\CurrentControlSet\Services\VxD** branch of the Windows 98 Registry. The virtual machine manager searches this branch of the registry looking for static drivers. If the value in the listing is represented by a StaticVxD= statement, the VMM32.VXD file loads and initializes it in Real mode. It also statically loads any VxDs that have a device=xxxVxD entry. Conversely, the dynamic VxD files in the registry are not loaded by the VMM32.VXD file.

Hkey_Local_ Machine\System\ CurrentControl Set\Services\VxD

VMM32 also checks the [386enh] section of the SYSTEM.INI file for static VxDs (device=xxxVxD). If it finds a VxD in the SYSTEM.INI file, that version will be used instead of any version found in the Registry.

Phase 4: Protected Mode Change Over

After loading all of the static VxDs, the VMM32.VXD file shifts the microprocessor into Protected mode operation and begins loading the Protected-mode components of the system.

The Configuration Manager is loaded and initialized with configuration information from the PnP BIOS' earlier detection efforts. If no PnP information is available, the Configuration Manager develops a PnP tree by loading dynamically loadable drivers. Once the tree is in place, the Configuration Manager reconciles the configuration information for each device, resolves any conflicts, and then reconfigures any necessary devices.

Phase 5: Loading Remaining Components

Following the initialization process, the final Windows 98 components are loaded into the system. During this period:

- The KERNEL32.DLL and KERNEL386.EXE files are executed
- The GDI.EXE and GDI32.EXE files are executed
- The USER.EXE and USER32.EXE files are executed
- All fonts and other associated resources are loaded
- The WIN.INI file values are checked
- The Win 98 shell and machine policies are loaded
- The desktop components are loaded

KERNEL32.DLL

KERNEL386.EXE

GDI files

USER

The **KERNEL32.DLL** contains the Windows 9x core components, while the **KERNEL386.EXE** file loads the Windows 9x device drivers. The **GDI files** provide the base of the graphical device interface, while the **USER** files provide the user interface. The GDI files graphically represent and manage the system hardware devices.

The WIN.INI and SYSTEM.INI files are included in the Windows directory to maintain compatibility functions with older software. These files are retained for use with older 16-bit applications and are not necessary for the operation of Windows 9x applications. However, these files will need to be checked if the Windows 9x system has conflicts with any 16-bit applications.

user name

password

When the shell and desktop components are loaded, the system may display a prompt on the screen for the user to logon. This logon process allows the operating system to configure itself for specific users. Normal logon involves entering a **user name** and **password**. If no logon information is entered, then default values will be loaded into the system. The logon screen only appears if the system is in use with a network, or when there are settings that the user can customize.

If the system is connected to a network, the network logon screen appears, as depicted in Figure 9-8. Logging onto a network is becoming more common every day. Therefore, one of the most common startup actions for Windows 9x users is entering their information into the logon window. After the user logs on, the system's user-specific setup instructions are carried out.

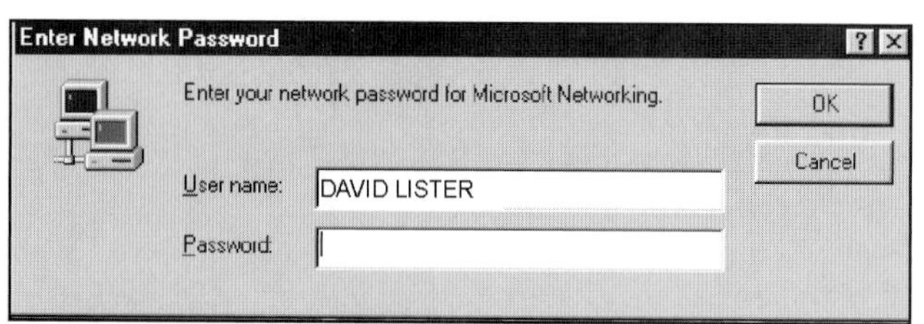

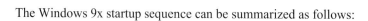

Figure 9-8: Windows 9x Network Logon Screen

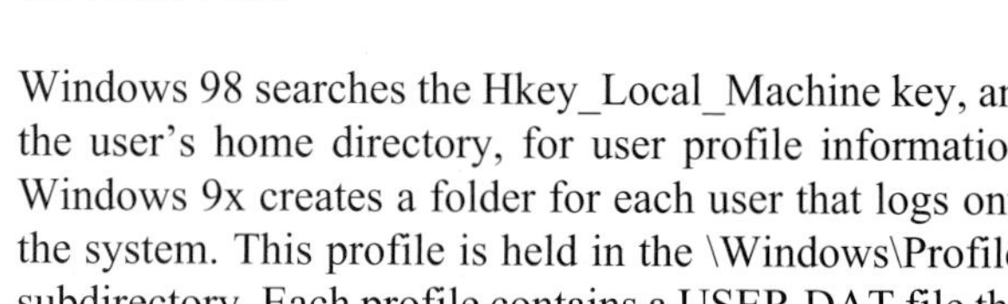

Windows 98 searches the Hkey_Local_Machine key, and the user's home directory, for user profile information. Windows 9x creates a folder for each user that logs onto the system. This profile is held in the \Windows\Profiles subdirectory. Each profile contains a USER.DAT file that holds the registry information for that user. It also contains a number of other files that customize the desktop just for that user.

Earlier in this chapter, we mentioned that the USER.DAT and SYSTEM.DAT files were located in the \Windows folder. The difference between that statement and the one above is that for single-user systems, these files are located in the \Windows folder. However, in multiple user systems, Windows keeps profile information about all of its users and keeps the information in the \Windows\Profiles folder.

The Windows 9x startup sequence can be summarized as follows:

1. POST tests.
2. PnP configuration.
3. Operating system boot up looks for MBR.
4. System loads IO.SYS.
5. IO.SYS loads and executes CONFIG.SYS.
6. IO.SYS loads MSDOS.SYS.
7. IO.SYS loads and executes COMMAND.COM.
8. COMMAND.COM looks for and executes AUTOEXEC.BAT.
9. Windows 9x Core files are loaded.
10. Windows 9x checks the Startup folder.

TEST TIP

Remember the files involved the Windows startup process and the order of their execution.

NAVIGATING WINDOWS 9X

When Windows 95 or Windows 98 is started, it produces the basic **desktop** screen depicted in Figure 9-9. The desktop is the primary graphical user interface for Windows 9x. As with the Windows 3.x Program Manager, it uses icons to quickly locate and run applications. In Windows 9x, however, the **Start button** provides the starting point for most functions. This button provides a menuing system that represents a more intuitive approach to most computer operations than the Program Manager did.

desktop

Start button

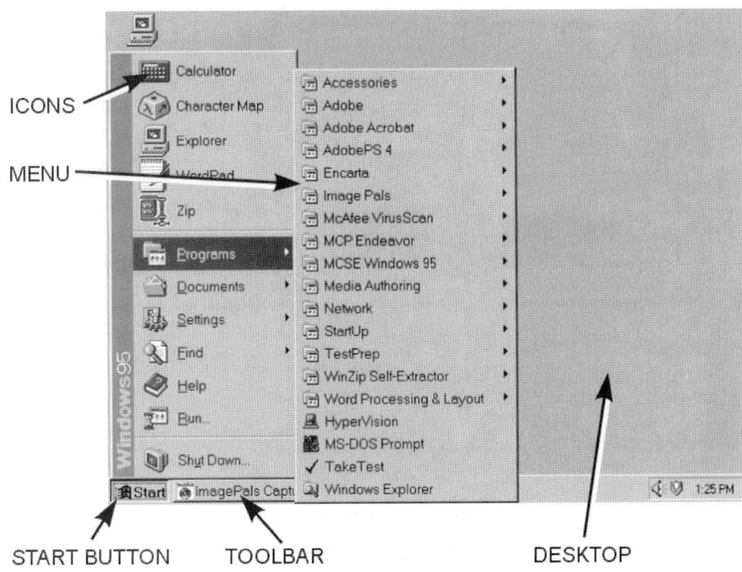

Figure 9-9: The Windows 9x Desktop Screen

The Windows 95 Desktop

The desktop interface provides an easy method for starting tasks and making resource connections. Desktop icons are referred to as **shortcuts** (since the primary method of accessing applications is through the Start menu). Applying a traditional double-click to the icon starts the application, or brings up its window.

shortcuts

In addition to the normal Windows left-click and double-click functions, Windows 95 and Windows 98 both employ the right mouse button for some activities. This is referred to as **right-clicking**, or as **alternate-clicking** for right handers, and is used to pop up a menu of functions on the screen. The right-click menus in Windows 95 are context-sensitive, so the information they contain applies to the item that is being clicked on.

right-clicking

alternate-clicking

Folder

Shortcut

Properties

Alternate-clicking on an item produces a pop-up menu, similar to the left-hand menu in Figure 9-10. These menus enable the user to Open, Cut, or Copy a **Folder** (an icon that represents a directory), Create a **Shortcut**, Delete or Rename a folder , or examine **Properties** of the folder. In the case of clicking on one of the system's hardware devices, the menu will permit you to perform such functions as sharing the device or checking its Properties. These menus may have additional items inserted in their lists by applications that they serve. Alternate-clicking in an open area of the desktop produces a pop-up menu, similar to the one displayed in right-hand side of the figure. This menu enables the user to arrange icons on the desktop, create New folders and Shortcuts, and see the Properties of the system's video display.

TEST TIP

Memorize the common options found in the My Computer Right-click menu.

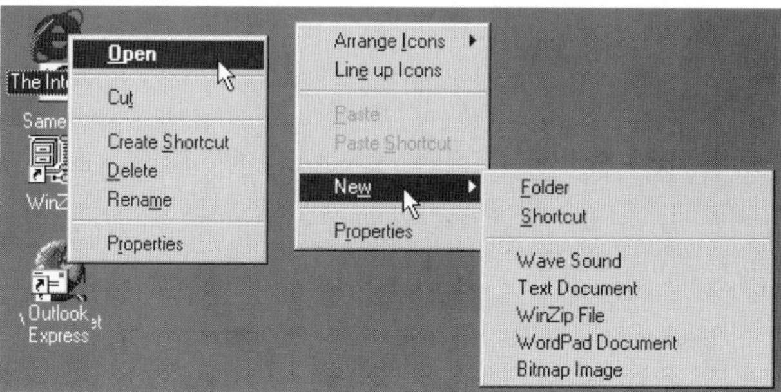

Figure 9-10: Right-Click Menus

The Windows 98 Desktop

In its basic form, the Windows 98 desktop is very similar to the Windows 95 desktop. The basic icons are located along the left border of the screen, the Taskbar runs across the bottom of the screen, and the Start menu pops up from the Start button on the Taskbar. However, some additional features of the new desktop, depicted in Figure 9-11, enable the user to quickly access a wide variety of resources.

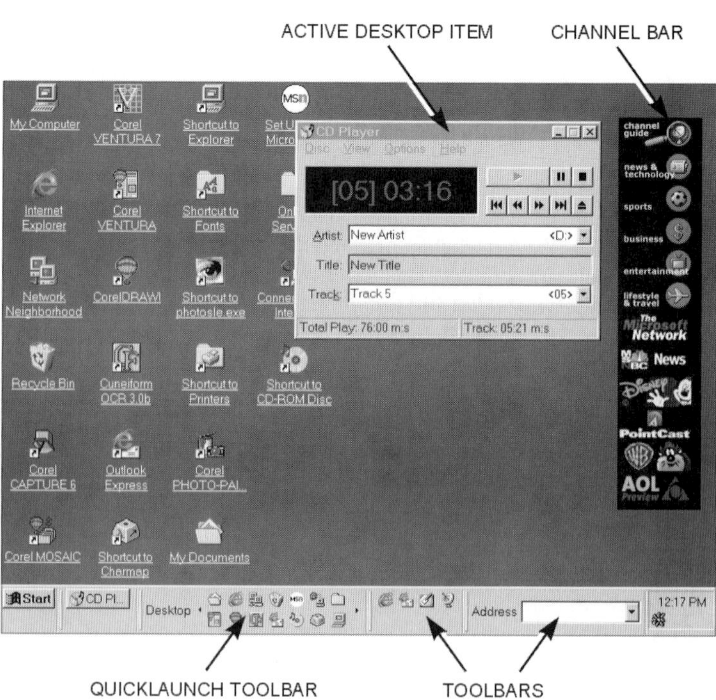

Figure 9-11: Windows 98 Desktop

Since the new desktop integrates the old Windows 95 desktop functions with the Internet Explorer (IE) browser, it can display the icons and windows typically found on the desktop, as well as HTML-based documents. This feature effectively places the desktop on-line, and creates an Active Desktop.

As a matter of fact, Web pages can be loaded into the desktop and automatically updated from the Web. This type of operation is referred to as an Active Channel. On the desktop, the system displays icons representing the Web links to these channels on the Channel Bar. The Web sites listed on the Channel Bar can be located on an intranet or on the Internet (external organization), and are updated automatically from the server. This enables the user to always have access to the most recent information directly from the desktop.

The other items of interest on the Windows 98 desktop include an extended icon system, a QuickLaunch Toolbar, user-defined toolbars, and Active Desktop elements.

Windows 98 allows the user to establish toolbars for easy access to user-specific files. This can be done in any of three ways, as illustrated in Figure 9-12. The user can customize the QuickLaunch toolbar, customize the Windows 98 Taskbar, or create a new toolbar. The new toolbar can be a traditional toolbar that displays on the Taskbar, or it can be a floating toolbar that displays on the Active Desktop.

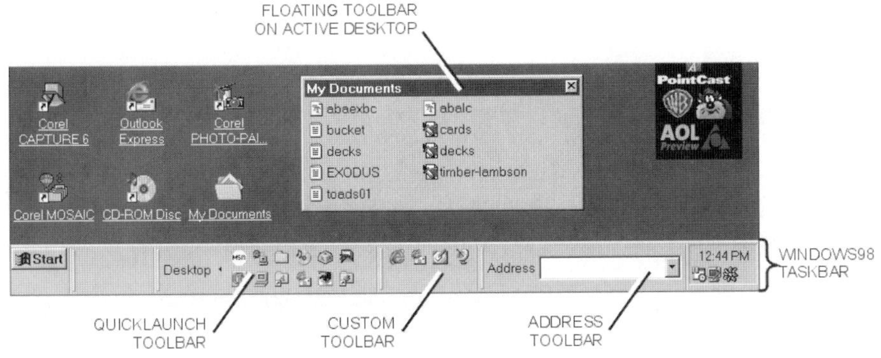

Figure 9-12: Windows 98 Toolbars

Active Desktop elements can be HTML files, JPEG files, GIF files, or an Explorer window. These resources can be used to provide dynamic visual information, such as activity levels of various operations, to the user. Microsoft provides an Active Desktop Gallery Web site at www.microsoft.com/Windows/ie/ie40/gallery/. This Web site provides a variety of free Active Desktop elements that can be downloaded.

Some of the items that appear on the desktop are a function of what the system finds as it looks for user profiles at the end of the bootup process. As mentioned earlier, the \Windows folder holds the system's default USER.DAT file. However, in a multiple user system, the \Windows\Profiles directory contains a folder for each user that logs onto the system. These folders contain the individual user's USER.DAT files, along with a number of their desktop-related folders. These include each user's:

- Internet Explorer Cookies folder
- Desktop folder
- Favorites folder
- History folder
- My Documents folder
- NetHood folder
- Recent folder
- Start Menu folder
- Temporary Internet Files folder

> **NOTE**
> Cookies are collections of information samples from different user's visits to a Web site.

Locating, Accessing, and Retrieving Information in Windows 9x

In its most basic form, the Windows 9x desktop features three standard icons: My Computer, Network Neighborhood, and Recycle Bin.

My Computer

My Computer

The **My Computer** icon is the major user interface for Windows 9x. It enables the user to see the local system's contents and manage its files.

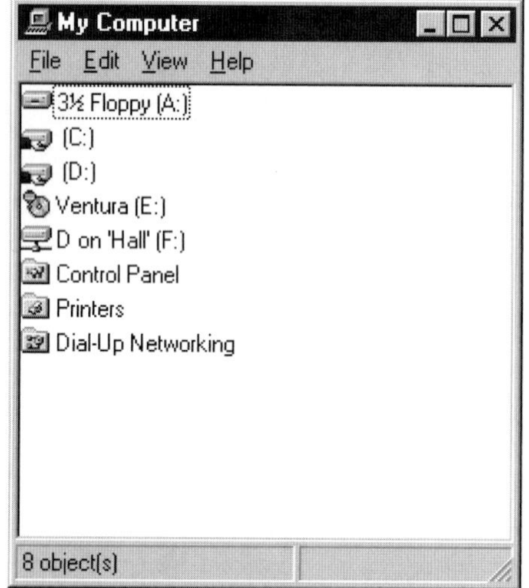

Figure 9-13: My Computer Window

Double-clicking the My Computer icon will produce the My Computer window, depicted in Figure 9-13. This window displays all the system's disk drives as icons, and represents the Control Panel and system Printers as folders.

Double-clicking one of the drive icons produces a display of its contents onscreen. This information can also be displayed in several different formats using the View option. Selecting the Options entry in the View menu produces the Folder Options window displayed in Figure 9-14. This window consists of three tabs (screens): General, View, and File Types.

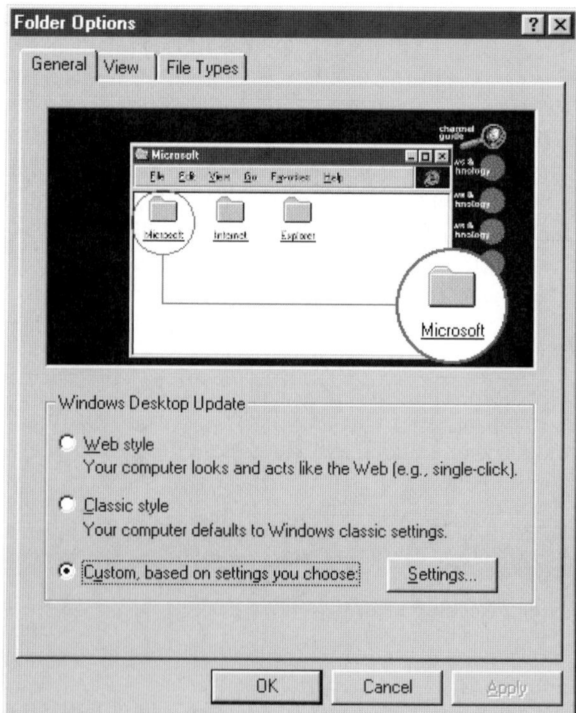

Figure 9-14: The Folder Options Window

General
Show Hidden Files

The **General** tab supplies information about how the desktop will display windows as the user browses through multiple windows. The View window is used to define how the folders and files in the selected window will be displayed onscreen. This screen also determines which types of files will be displayed. To see hidden and system files, select the View tab and click on **Show Hidden Files** button. Files with selected extensions will be hidden. The File Types screen lists the types of files that the system can recognize. New file types can be registered in this window.

> **TEST TIP**
>
> Know how to show hidden files in the Windows 9x system.

Control Panel
Printers

The **Control Panel** and **Printers** folders under My Computer contain information about the system and its printers. The Windows 95 Control Panel is the user interface employed to manage hardware devices attached to the system. The Windows 98 Control Panel is explored in greater detail in a later section of this chapter.

The Printers folder displays the computer's installed printer types. As with other icons in the My Computer window, the printers can be displayed as small icons, large icons, in a simple list, or in a list with details. Details include such items as printer type, number of documents to print, current status, and any comments generated by the print controller.

Minimize
Maximize
Close

The My Computer window is a typical Windows 9x window. Its title bar uses button icons to provide **Minimize**, **Maximize**, and **Close** functions for the window, as described in Figure 9-15. When a program is minimized, its button appears on the Taskbar at the bottom of the screen. The application can be restored by clicking on its button.

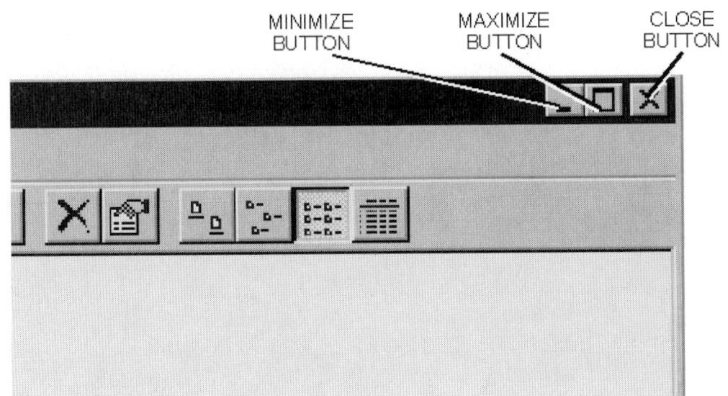

Figure 9-15: Windows 9x Minimize, Restore, and Close Functions

Clicking the X in the Close box will close the window and stop any applications running in it. In Windows 9x, windows can be moved and resized, and items can be moved from one window to another using drag-and-drop techniques.

Windows 9x Pop-Up Menus

menu bars

Most Windows 9x windows have **menu bars** that provide pop-up menus on the screen when they are accessed by clicking on their titles, or by pressing the ALT key and their underlined character (i.e., the ALT/F combination will pop up the File menu). Typical menu bar options include File, Edit, View, and Help. Options that apply to the current window are displayed as dark text. Options that are not applicable to the window are grayed out.

The File option on the My Computer menu bar can be used to perform many disk maintenance procedures. When a disk drive icon is selected, clicking on the File option will produce a menu that includes provisions for formatting the disk, sharing a drive with the network community, backing up the contents of the drive, or displaying its properties.

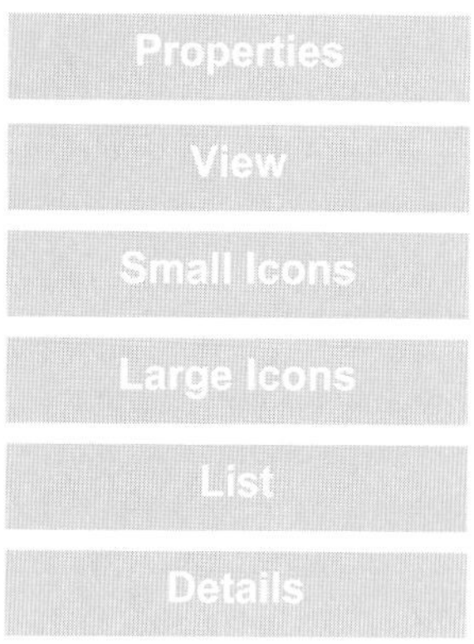

The File menu's **Properties** option displays general information about the drive, such as FAT type, capacity, free space, and used space. This option also provides a notice of how much time has elapsed since the last error-checking, backup, and defragmentation operations were performed on the selected drive.

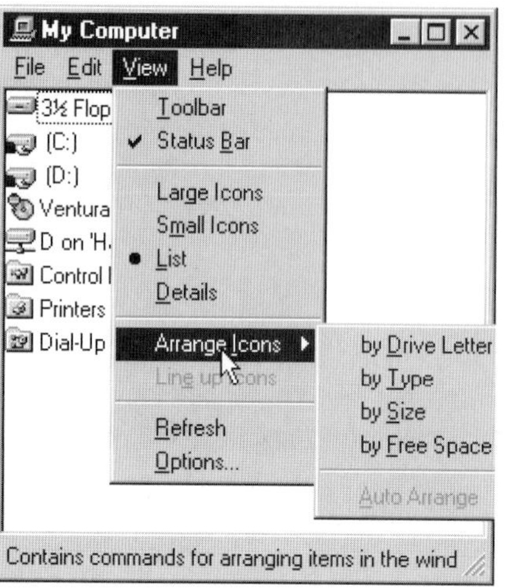

Figure 9-16: The View Menu

The Windows 95 **View** menu option, depicted in Figure 9-16, is one of the most used features of the menu bar. It can be used to alter the manner in which the contents of the window are displayed. The drives and folders in Figure 9-13 are displayed as **Small Icons**. However, they can be reduced to **Large Icons**, displayed as a **List**, or displayed with Name, Type, Size, and Free Space **Details**. Other options in the menu can be used to organize the icons within the window.

Options

Double-clicking one of the drive icons produces a display of its contents on the screen. This information can also be displayed in several different formats using the View option. Selecting the **Options** entry in the View menu produces the Options window displayed in Figure 9-17. This window consists of three tabs (screens)—Folders, View, and File Types.

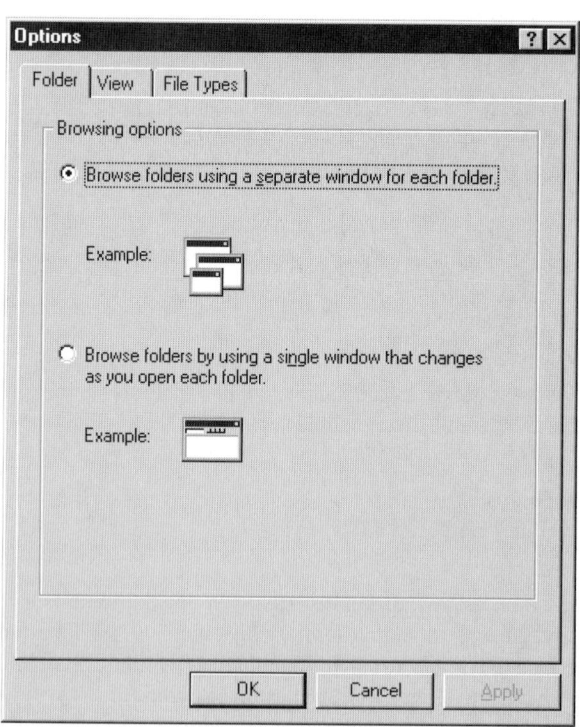

Figure 9-17: The View\Options Window

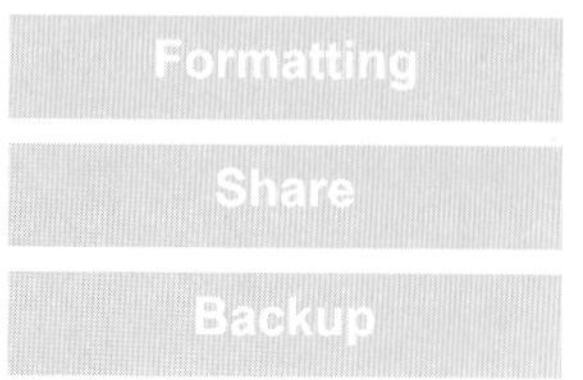

The File option on the My Computer Menu Bar can be used to perform many disk maintenance procedures. When a disk drive icon is selected, clicking on the File option will produce a menu that includes provisions for **Formatting** the disk, **Share** a drive with the network community, **Backup** the contents of the drive, or display its properties.

The Properties option displays general information about the drive, such as FAT type, Capacity, Free Space, and Used Space. This option also provides a notice of how much time has elapsed since the last Error Checking, Backup, and Defragmentation operations were performed on the selected drive.

The Folder window supplies information about how the desktop will display windows as the user browses through multiple windows.

View

Show Hidden Files

File Types

The **View** window is used to define how the folders and files in the selected window will be displayed on the screen. This screen also determines which types of files will be displayed. To see hidden and system files, select the View tab and click on the **Show Hidden Files** radio button. Files with selected extensions will be hidden. The **File Types** screen lists the types of files that the system can recognize. New file types can be registered in this window.

The Control Panel and Printers folders contain information about the system and its printers. The Windows 95 Control Panel is the user interface employed to manage hardware devices attached to the system. The Windows 98 Control Panel is explored in greater detail in a later section of this chapter.

Printers folder

The **Printers folder** displays the computer's installed printer types. As with other icons in the My Computer window, the printers can be displayed as small icons, large icons, in a simple list, or in a list with details. Details include such items as Printer Type, Number of Documents to print, Current Status, and any Comments generated by the print controller.

Right-clicking the My Computer icon produces a menu listing, similar to the one depicted in the left-hand side of Figure 9-10. This menu provides options for Opening the My Computer window, Exploring the system drives and files through the Windows Explorer, working with Network drives, Creating Shortcuts, Renaming the selected folders and files, and accessing the Properties of the system's installed devices.

TEST TIP

Know how to navigate to various parts of Windows 9x through the My Computer icon.

In Windows 98, the My Computer options have been rearranged slightly from those of the Windows 95 My Computer window. In particular, the Options entry under the View menu, has been replaced by Folder Options. The tabs in this window are titled General, View and File Types. As with the Windows 95 version, the View/Folder Options/View window is used to define how folders and files will be displayed and to determines which types of files will be displayed.

The Network Neighborhood

Network Neighborhood

The **Network Neighborhood** icon provides quick information about the world around the system when it's used in a networked environment.

Double-clicking this icon will produce the Network Neighborhood window illustrated in Figure 9-18. Small computer icons represent the various computers attached to the network. They enable the user to browse through the network. Double-clicking on any of the icons will produce a listing of the resources the selected computer offers, such as disk drives and printers.

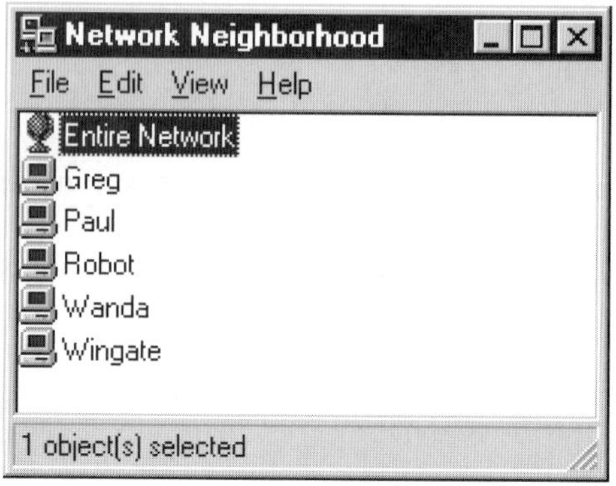

Figure 9-18: Network Neighborhood Window

The Recycle Bin

Recycle Bin

The **Recycle Bin** is a storage area for deleted files that will allow you to retrieve such files if they are deleted by mistake. When you delete a folder or file from the Windows system, it removes the first three letters of its name from the drive's FAT so that it is invisible to the system. However, the system records its presence in the Recycle Bin. The system is free to reuse the space on the drive since it does not know that anything is there. As long as it hasn't been over written with new data, or it hasn't been removed from the Recycle Bin, it can be restored from the information in the Recycle Bin. If it has been thrown out of the bin but has not been overwritten, it can be recovered using a third-party software utility for recovering deleted files.

TEST TIP

Know what happens to files moved into the Recycle Bin.

The Recycle Bin icon should always be present on the desktop. It can only be removed through the Registry. If its icon is missing, there are two alternatives to restoring it: establish a shortcut to the Recycle Bin using a new icon, or just reinstall Windows 9x. This action will always place the Recycle Bin on the desktop.

The Taskbar

The Start button, located at the bottom of the screen, is used to accomplish several different tasks depending on the context of the operation. For example, the Start button is used to start programs, alter system settings, and open documents. Clicking the Start button produces a Start menu onscreen.

Taskbar

Just to the right of the Start button is an area called the **Taskbar**. This area is used to display all the applications currently open. Each time a program is started, or a window is opened, a corresponding button appears on the Taskbar. To switch between applications, just click on the desired program button to make it the active window. The button will disappear from the Taskbar if the program is closed.

Right-clicking on the Taskbar at the bottom of the screen produces a menu that can be used to control the appearance of the Taskbar and open windows onscreen.

The Taskbar can be moved around the display by clicking and dragging it to the left, right or top of the screen. It can be hidden just off screen by clicking its edge and then dragging it toward the edge of the display. If the Taskbar is hidden, it can be retrieved by pressing the CTRL+ESC key combination. This will pop up the Start menu along with the Taskbar. Enter the Start/Settings/Taskbar & Start Menu option to change the Taskbar settings so that it will not be hidden. You can also locate an absent Taskbar by moving the mouse around the edges of the screen until the shape of the cursor changes.

Likewise, pressing the TAB key will cycle control between the Start menu, the Quick launch icons, the Taskbar, and the desktop icons. This key can also be helpful in navigating the system if the mouse fails.

TEST TIP

Know how to move around the desktop, Start menu, and Taskbar using the keyboard.

The Start Menu

All operations begin from the Start button. When you click on the button, a pop-up menu of options appears, as illustrated in Figure 9-19. This menu normally contains the options Programs, Documents, Settings, Find, Help, Run, and Shut Down.

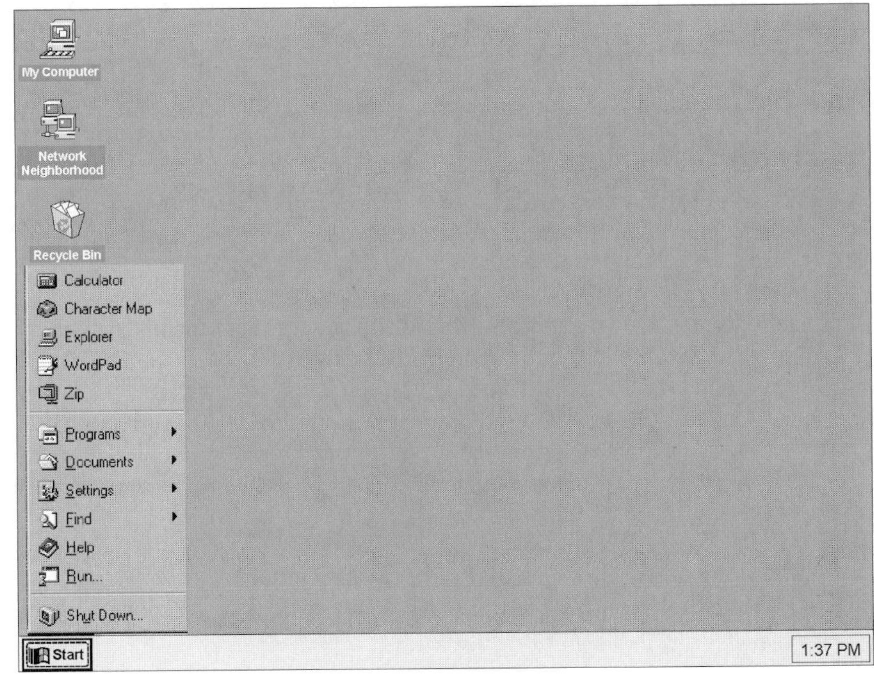

Figure 9-19: The Start Button Menu

Placing the cursor over designated menu items will cause any submenus associated with that option to pop up onscreen. An arrow to the right of the option indicates a submenu is available. To open the selected item, just left-click on it and its window will appear on the desktop.

The Programs submenu, depicted in Figure 9-20, has several options that include Accessories, StartUp, MS-DOS Prompt, and Windows Explorer.

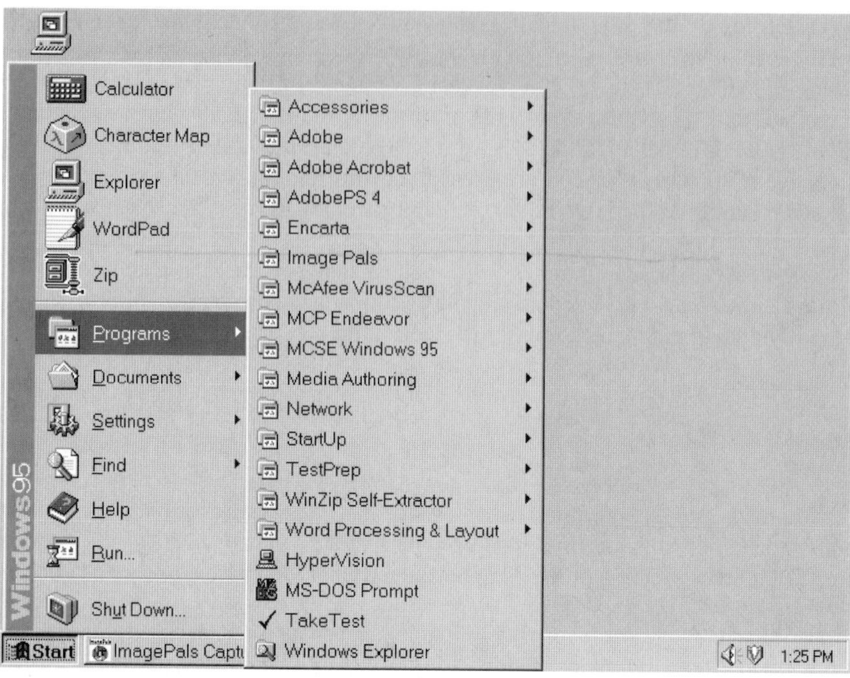

Figure 9-20: The Programs Submenu

The MS-DOS prompt is also accessed through the Programs option. The Start menu's Documents entry displays a list of documents previously opened.

The Settings option displays values for the system's configurable components. It combines previous Windows functions, such as copies of the Control Panel and Print Manager folders, as well as access to the Windows 9x Taskbar.

The Find utility is used to locate folders, files, mail messages, and shared computers. The Find function can be accessed directly from the Start menu, or it can be reached by right-clicking on the My Computer icon. The selection from the Start menu allows files, folders, and computers to be searched for. The My Computer version searches only for files and folders. To locate a file, just type its name in the Named window, tell the system which drive or drive to look in, and click the Find option. Standard DOS wildcards can be included in the search name.

The Help file system provides extensive information about many Windows 9x functions and operations. It also supplies an exhaustive list of guided troubleshooting routines for typical system components and peripherals.

The Run option is used to start programs or open folders from a command-line dialog box. Executable files can be started by typing their filename in the dialog box and clicking the OK button. The Browse button can be used to locate the desired file by looking through the system's file structure.

Start button

The **Start button** is also used to correctly shut down Windows 9x. The Shut Down option from the Start menu shuts down the system, restarts the computer, or logs the user off. It must be used to avoid damaging files and to ensure that your work is properly saved. When it is clicked, the Shut Down Windows dialog box depicted in Figure 9-21 appears. After you select an option from the dialog box, the unit tells you to wait, and then you receive a screen message telling you that it is okay to turn off the system.

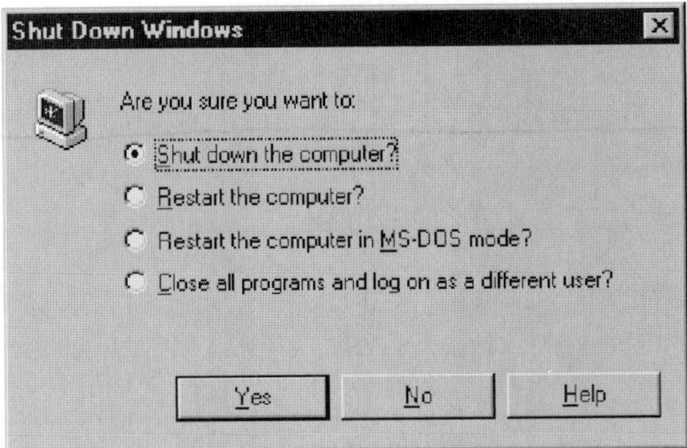

Figure 9-21: The Shut Down Windows Dialog Box

The Windows 98 Start Menu

The Windows 98 Start button remains on the Taskbar at the bottom of the screen. Clicking the button produces the Start menu, similar to the one depicted in Figure 9-22. While most of the entries are carryovers from 95, the Log Off User and Favorites entries are new.

Windows 98 allows individuals in multiuser systems to log onto, and operate in, Windows 98 environments that have been specifically configured to their work needs. The Log Off User option is used to return the system to its natural setup. The Log Off entry may not appear in some installations, such as stand-alone machines that are not connected to a network environment.

The Favorites entry is included to allow the user to store locations of often-used files. These files can be local to the machine, located on a local area network, or remotely located on the Internet. The Internet Explorer checks Web sites specified in the Favorites folder regularly for updated information.

The Shut Down option from the menu has been changed so that there are only three possible methods listed for shutting down the session. They are Shut Down, Restart (warm boot), and Restart in MS-DOS mode. Windows 98 also includes a Standby option in the Shut Down menu. This option enables the user to put the system in a power conservation mode when it will not be active for some time. Standby keeps Windows ready to go when an event happens, but does not keep the system I/O devices awake.

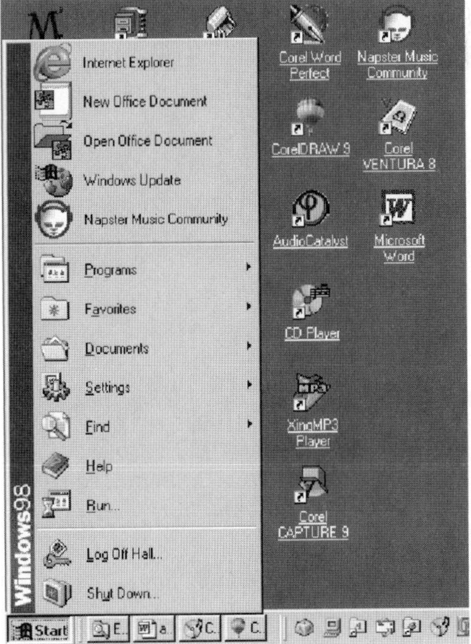

Figure 9-22: Windows 98 Start Menu

Additional items can be added to the Start Menu so that they can be used directly from this menu. In doing so, the normal method of clicking Start, pointing to the Program option, and moving through submenus can be avoided. To move a frequently used item to the top of the Start Menu, simply drag its icon to the Start button on the Taskbar.

TEST TIP

Know how to navigate to various parts of Windows 9x through the Start menus.

In Windows 98 it is also possible to move all of your frequently used programs to the Programs submenu. Frequently used items can be moved to the Windows 98 Taskbar, the QuickLaunch toolbar, or user-created toolbars for easy access.

Windows 95 Control Panel

The Control Panel in Windows 95 can be accessed from multiple locations within the system. One Control Panel folder is located under the My Computer icon while another copy can be found under the *Start\Settings* path. Both folders access the Control Panel window, depicted in Figure 9-23. This window contains icons for every device attached to the system. The Control Panel icon provides access to the configuration information for each of the system's installed devices specific to its type. The icons are visually different from those used in the Windows 3.x Control Panel.

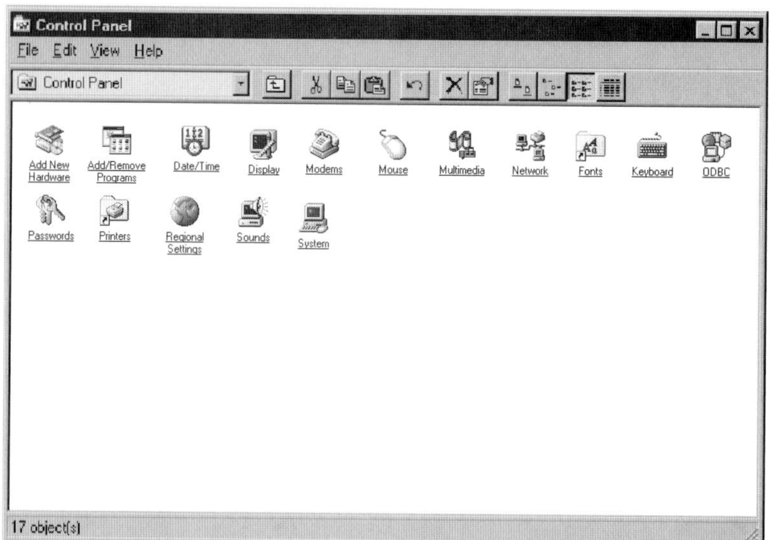

Figure 9-23: The Windows 95 Control Panel

Properties dialog box

Double-clicking on any of the device icons will produce a **Properties dialog box** for that device. Each box is different in that it contains information specific to the selected device. These dialog boxes may have a number of different folder tabs along their tops. Each tab is labeled with the type of information it holds. Clicking on a tab will display additional information for that dialog page.

The most important uses of the Control Panel are:

- adding or removing new hardware or software components to the system
- modifying system device settings
- modifying desktop items

The **Control Panel** is the primary user interface for assigning ports for printers and mice, as well as for specifying how various peripheral devices respond. The **Add New Hardware** and **Add/Remove Programs** icons are used to establish interrupt and port assignments for new hardware devices, and to install device drivers to support the hardware.

Control Panel

Add New Hardware

Add/Remove Programs

Windows 98 Control Panel

The Windows 98 Control Panel remains the user's primary interface for configuring system components. It has been enlarged to control a number of new functions, as illustrated in Figure 9-24. In addition to the Windows 95 configuration icons, Windows 98 adds Infrared device control options, an Internet configuration tool, a Power Management utility, support for scanners/digital cameras, and additional modem and communication control functions in the form of a Telephony utility. The final addition to the Control Panel is the Users icon that provides tools to establish and manage profiles for multiple users on the system.

Figure 9-24: Windows 98 Control Panel Icons

The Control Panel can be accessed through the My Computer icon on the desktop, or through the Settings entry in the Start menu.

Installation Wizards

The Add New Hardware icon brings the Hardware Installation Wizard into action. It will immediately ask the user if Windows should search for the new hardware through a PnP-style detection process. Clicking the Next option will cause Windows to conduct the hardware detection operation. If the device is not PnP, or if it must be installed manually because Windows 9x could not detect it, selecting the No option and clicking Next will produce a hardware component list similar to the one shown in Figure 9-25. The Hardware Wizard will guide the manual installation process from this point, and prompt the user for any necessary configuration information. If Windows 9x does not support the device, click the **Have Disk button** to load drivers supplied by the device's manufacturer.

Have Disk button

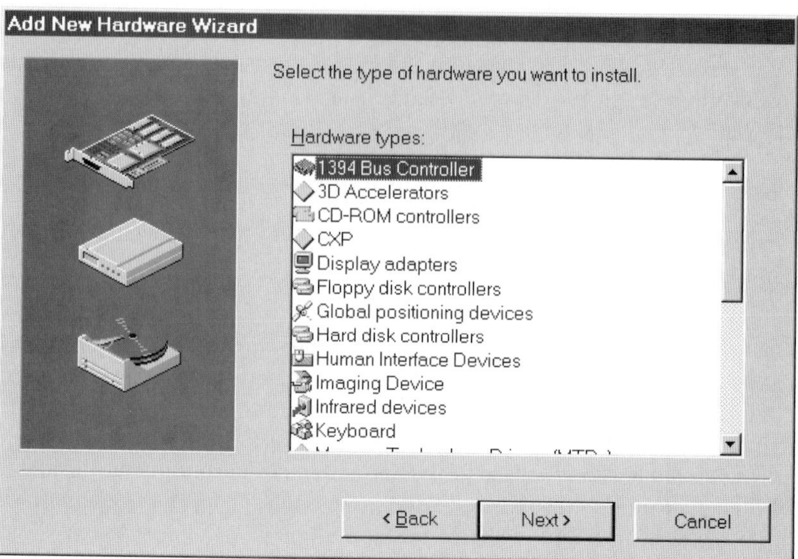

Figure 9-25: The Hardware Wizard's Device Selection Page

The Add/Remove Programs icon leads to the Install/Uninstall screen illustrated in Figure 9-26. This page can be used to install new programs from floppies or CDs by simply clicking the Install button. Conversely, programs listed in the programs window can be removed from the system by highlighting their title and clicking the Add/Remove button.

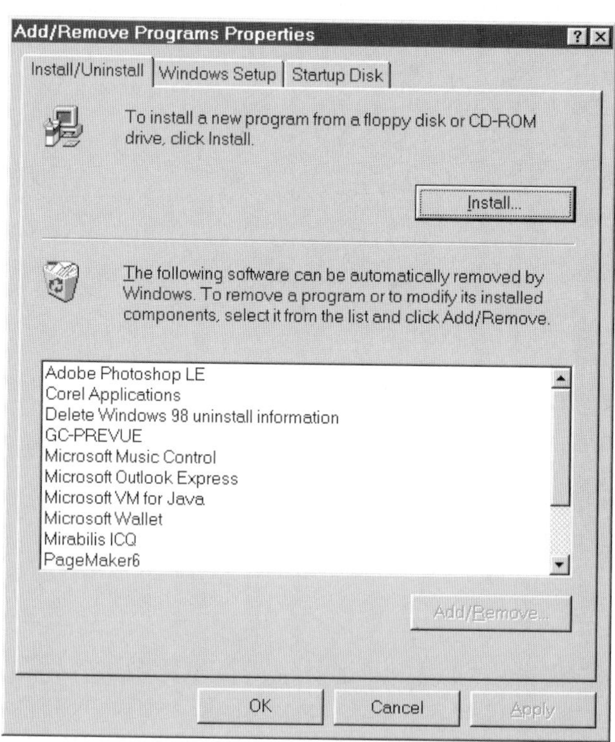

Figure 9-26: The Install/Uninstall Wizard Window

Windows Setup

Startup Disk

The **Windows Setup** tab is used to add or remove selected Windows 9x components, such as communications packages or additional system tools. The Windows **Startup Disk** tab is used to create a clean startup disk for emergency start purposes after a crash. This disk can be used to boot the system to the command prompt (not the Windows desktop) so that you can begin troubleshooting failed startups. The Windows 98 start disk provides CD-ROM support that is not available with the Windows 95 start disk.

> **TEST TIP**
>
> Remember the location of the Control Panel screen that is used to create a Windows Startup Disk.

The System Icon

One of the main Control Panel icons is the **System icon**. Clicking this icon produces the **System Properties** window displayed in Figure 9-27. This window features tabs for General information, the Device Manager, Hardware Profiles, and system Performance.

System icon

System Properties

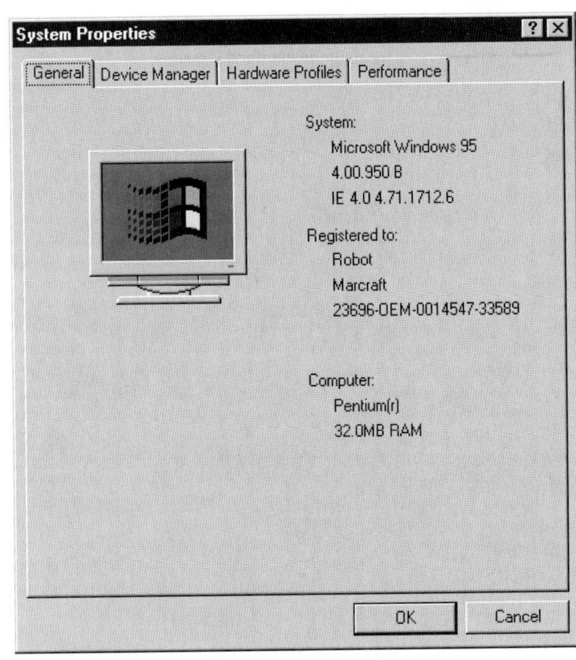

Figure 9-27: The System Properties Window

The **General** tab supplies information about the system's microprocessor type and RAM capacity, as well as its ownership and registration.

General

Device Manager

The **Device Manager** utility, depicted in Figure 9-28, provides a graphical representation of the devices configured in the system. This interface can be used to identify installed ports, update device drivers, and change I/O settings. It can also be used to manually isolate hardware and configuration conflicts. The problem device can be examined to see where the conflict is occurring. In Windows 9x, the Device Manager can be accessed through the *Start/Settings/Control Panel/System* path.

Device Manager

TEST TIP

Memorize the pathway to the Device Manager's Properties screens.

The Device Manager will display an exclamation point (!) inside a yellow circle whenever a device is experiencing a direct hardware conflict with another device. Similarly, when a red "X" appears at the device's icon, the device has been disabled due to a User Selection Conflict.

User Selection Conflict

If a conflict is suspected, click on the offending device in the listing, make sure that the selected device is the current device, and then click on the **User Selection Conflict** tab to examine its **Conflicting devices** list. Make sure that the device has not been installed twice.

Conflicting devices

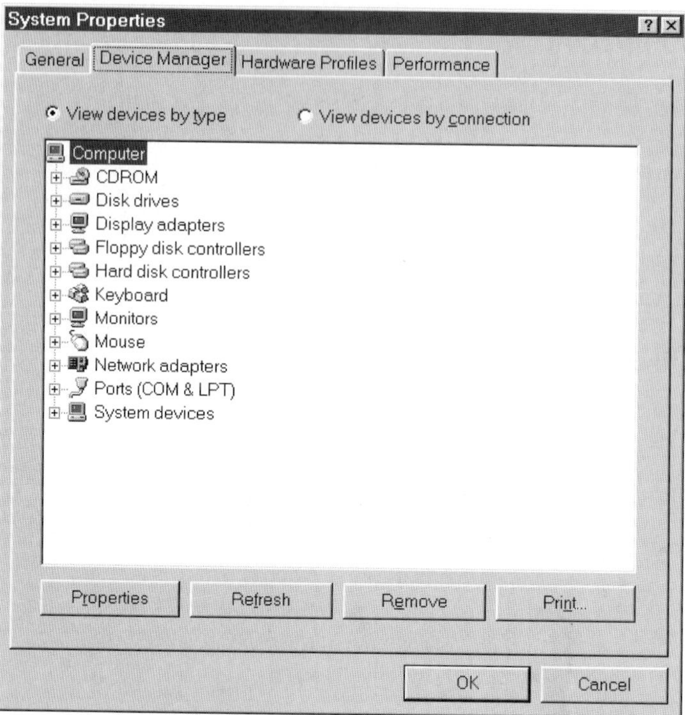

Figure 9-28: The Windows 9x Device Manager

The Device Manager page contains a set of buttons that permit its various functions to be accessed. These buttons include: Properties, Refresh, Remove, and Print.

Typical Device Manager Properties pages provide tabs that can be used to access General information, device Settings, device Drivers information, and device Resources requirements and usage. Each device may have some or all of these tabs available depending on what type of device it is and what its requirements are.

The information under the tabs can be used to change the properties associated with the selected device. This often becomes necessary when resource conflicts occur in a system that has legacy devices installed. The Device Manager can be used to identify possible causes of these IRQ, DMA, I/O, and memory settings conflicts.

Hardware Profiles

Hardware Profiles

Performance

The System icon's **Hardware Profiles** tab provides a window that can be used to establish different hardware configuration profiles to be implemented at startup. Most systems do not require any additional profiles. The System icon's **Performance** tab displays information about the system's installed RAM, system resource usage, virtual memory settings, and disk FAT type.

wallpaper

screen savers

The final major Control Panel function is to enable users to customize the Windows 95 desktop. This customization includes such things as setting screen colors, changing the Windows **wallpaper**, and selecting **screen savers**.

Wallpaper is the pattern that shows behind the various application windows. Screen savers are screen displays that remain in motion while the system is setting idle. This utility prevents a single display from remaining on the screen for a prolonged time. This keeps the image from being "burned into" the screen. When this happens, the image becomes a permanent ghost on the screen and the monitor is ruined.

Windows 9x Files

The Windows 9x file system does away with the 8+3 character filename system implemented under DOS. In Windows 9x, **long filenames** of up to 255 characters can be used, so that they can be more descriptive in nature. When these filenames are displayed in non-Windows 9x systems, they are **truncated** (shortened) to fit the 8.3 DOS character format and identified by a tilde character (~) followed by a single-digit number.

long filenames

truncated

The tilde character is placed in the seventh character position of the filename to show that the filename is being displayed in a shortened manner as an alias for the full-length filename. The number following the mark will have a value of 1 assigned to it, unless another file has already been assigned the alias with a 1 value. Customers with older operating systems may overlook files because they are saved in this manner. Consider the following examples:

- oldlongfile.txt = oldlon~1.txt
- oldlongtable.txt = oldlon~2.txt
- oldlonggraphic.txt = oldlo~63.txt

TEST TIP

Know how Windows 9x handles similar long file names in a DOS format.

The tilde character is inserted into the seventh character space for up to 9 iterations of similar filenames. After that, Windows will replace the sixth character for iterations up to 99. Windows 95 applies this same convention to the naming of directories as well. To change a log directory name from the command line requires that quote marks be placed around the name.

Additional characters are allowed to be used in the Windows 9x long filenames. These characters include: + , : = [and]. Blank spaces can also be used in long filenames.

Windows Explorer

The **File Management** functions in Windows 9x and NT/2000 is performed through the **Windows Explorer** interface. This manager is located under the *Start/Programs* path from the desktop.

File Management

Windows Explorer

By clicking on the Windows Explorer entry, the system's directory structure will appear, as shown in Figure 9-29. The Windows Explorer can also be accessed by right-clicking on the Start button or the My Computer icon and then selecting the Explore option.

The Windows Explorer enables the user to copy, move, and erase files on any of the system's drives. Its screen is divided into two parts. The left side displays the system's directory tree, showing all of the directories and subdirectories of its available drives.

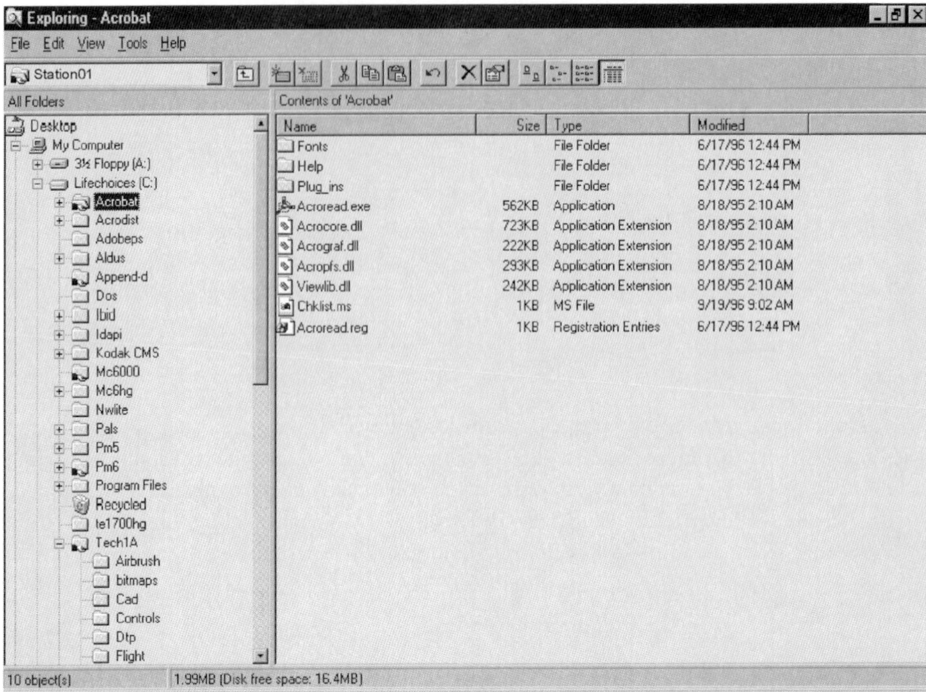

Figure 9-29: The Windows 9x Explorer Screen

subfolders

In Windows 9x, directories and subdirectories are referred to, and depicted as, folders (and **subfolders**). Any drive or directory can be selected by clicking on its icon or folder. The contents of the folder can be expanded by clicking on the (+) sign beside the folder. Conversely, the same folder can be contracted by clicking on the minus (-) sign in the same box.

Windows 9x is not limited to simply showing the directories, subdirectories, and files on local drives. It will also display drives and folders from throughout the network environment. The contents of the local drives are displayed at the top of the directory tree. If the system is connected to a network, the additional resources available through the network are displayed below those of the local system, as a continuation of its tree structure. One noticeable difference exists between the Windows 9x and Windows 2000 main tree structures in Windows Explorer – the Printers folder has been removed from the main tree and placed as a sub-branch of the Control Panel folder.

Status bar

The right side of the Windows Explorer screen displays the files of the selected directory. Applications can be started from this window by double-clicking their executable file. Double-clicking on a file produced by an associated application will cause Windows to open the application and load the selected file. The **Status bar** at the bottom of the screen provides information about the number and size of the files in the selected directory. The View menu on the Explorer Menu Bar can be used to set the display for large or small icons, as well as simple or detailed lists. The Explorer's View functions are the same as those described for the My Computer Menu Bar in Figure 9-16.

drag-and-drop

It is possible to display multiple directories on the Explorer screen. This feature makes it easy to perform file operations by simply opening another window. Windows 9x provides drag-and-drop file copies and moves for single and multiple files, as well as **drag-and-drop** printing capabilities.

The Windows Explorer is also used to perform DOS-like functions, such as formatting and copying diskettes. Alternate-clicking on a folder icon will produce a menu that includes a **Send To** option, as shown in Figure 9-30. Moving the mouse to this entry will produce a submenu that can be used to send a selected folder or file to a floppy drive, or to the desktop. Several files or folders can be selected for copying using the Shift key.

Send To

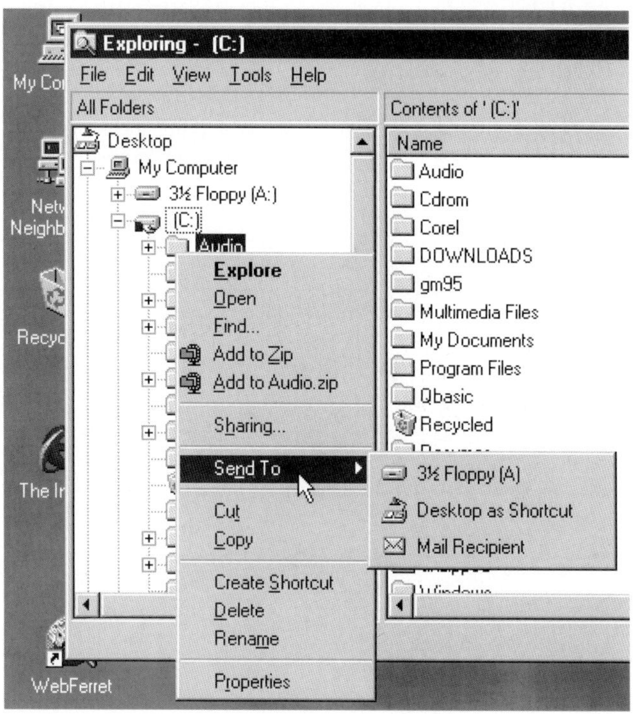

Figure 9-30: The Send To Option

The contents of the alternate-click menu change in the Explorer, depending on the item that is selected. Since the right-click function is context-sensitive, the menu produced for a folder will be different than the one displayed for a document file. Each menu will have options that apply to the selected item.

Right-clicking on a document file will produce options that enable the user to Copy, Cut, Rename, Open, or Print the document from the Windows Explorer. This menu also provides options to Create a Shortcut for the document, or to Change its Attributes. By default, Windows Explorer does not show SYS, INI, or DAT files. To change file attributes from the Explorer, right-click on the desired file, select the Properties option from the pop-up list, move to the General page, and click on the desired attribute boxes. To see hidden and system files in Windows Explorer, click the View menu option, select the Folder Options entry, click the View tab, and check the **Show All Files** box. If you experience difficulty with this operation from the Windows environment, you can always access the file from the command prompt and change its attributes with the ATTRIB command.

Show All Files

If Windows cannot identify the application associated with the selected file, the operator will need to start the application and then manually open the file. However, the user can also register the file's extension type under the View/Folders option from the Menu Bar. This will produce the Registered file types dialog box depicted in Figure 9-31.

TEST TIP

Know how to navigate to various parts of Windows 9x through the Windows Explorer.

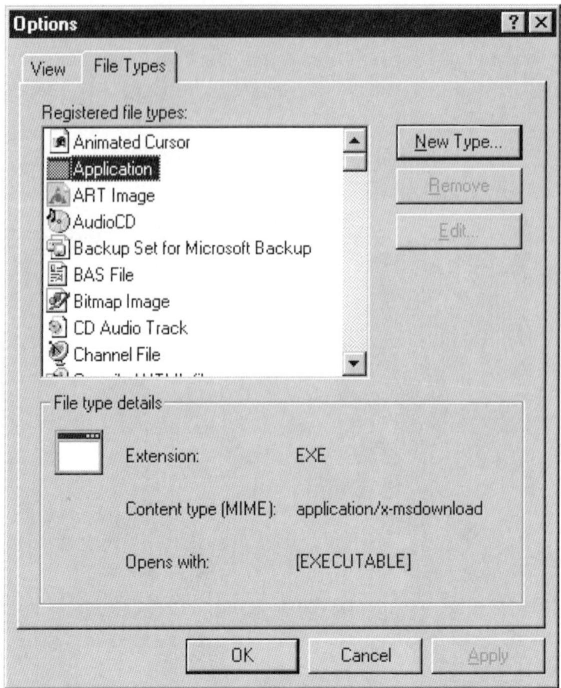

Figure 9-31: The Registered File Types Window

The Windows 9x File Menu

File menu

The Windows 9x drop-down **File menu** performs basic file management-related functions for files and folders. These functions include the typical Open, Close, and Save activities that users constantly employ with files. In addition, the menu provides options that enable the user to rename the file or folder, create a shortcut for it, or establish properties for it. The File menu also includes an entry at the top of the menu titled New. Clicking on this option produces the New options submenu depicted in Figure 9-32. This menu is used to create new folders, shortcuts, and files.

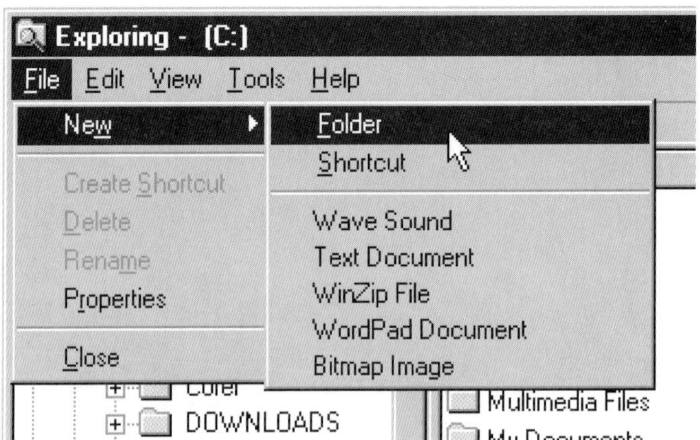

Figure 9-32: The New Options

To create a new folder in Explorer, select a parent directory by highlighting it in the left window. Then click the File menu button, move the cursor to the New entry, slide across to the Folder option, and click on it. A new unnamed folder icon will appear in the right Explorer window.

The same process is used to create new files. A file icon can be produced for any of the file types registered. Alternate-clicking on the new icon will produce the menu with options for renaming the icon, creating a shortcut for it, and establishing its properties (including its attributes).

Shortcut icons are identified by a small arrow in the lower left corner of the icon. When a shortcut is created, Windows does not place a copy of the file or application in every location that references it. Instead, it creates an icon in each location and defines it with a link to the actual location of the program in the system. This reduces the amount of disk space required to reference the file from multiple locations.

Shortcut icons

WINDOWS 9X STRUCTURE

When Windows 9x starts, several major files are loaded into the system. These include:

- the KERNEL32.DLL and KERNEL386.EXE files
- the **GDI.EXE** and **GDI32.EXE** files
- the **USER.EXE** and **USER32.EXE** files
- all fonts and other associated resources
- the WIN.INI file
- the Windows 9x shell and desktop files

GDI.EXE

GDI32.EXE

USER.EXE

USER32.EXE

The KERNEL32.DLL and KERNEL386.EXE files are the basis of the Windows 9x core and load its device drivers. The GDI files provide the base of the graphical device interface, while the USER files provide the user interface. The GDI files graphically represent and manage the system hardware devices.

Any WIN.INI, SYSTEM.INI, and WINFILE.INI files that previously existed are included in the Windows directory to maintain compatibility functions with older software. These files are retained for use with older 16-bit applications and are not necessary for the operation of Windows 9x applications. However, these files will need to be checked if the Windows 9x system has conflicts with any 16-bit applications.

The Windows 9x shell program is normally the desktop.

If the operating system has been configured to employ passwords for users, when the shell and desktop components are loaded. it will display a prompt on screen for the user to logon. Similar to the logon process associated with networked systems, the Windows 9x logon enables the operating system to configure itself for specific users. Normal logon involves entering a username and password. If no logon information is entered, default values will be loaded into the system. The logon screen appears only if the system has been configured to use a password, or when there are settings that the user can customize.

It is possible for the system to require two password logons, one for the system and the second for the network. However, most administrators simply combine these two elements into the network logon, as depicted in Figure 9-33.

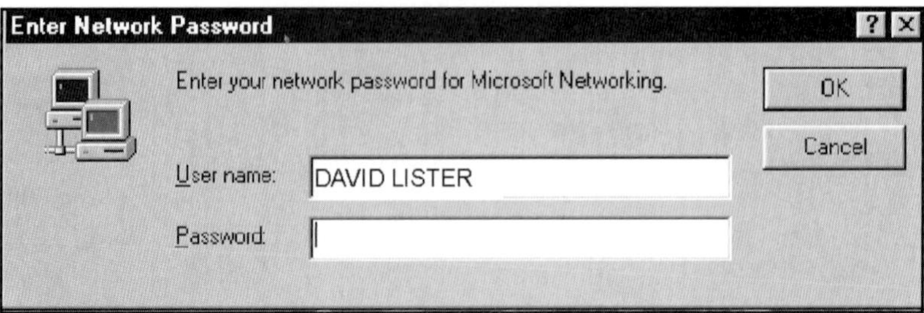

Figure 9-33: The Windows 9x Logon Dialog Box

Windows 9x possesses system bootup files that replace the DOS bootup files. The Windows 9x version of IO.SYS is a real-mode operating system that replaces the DOS version. It also takes over many of the functions associated with the CONFIG.SYS file. An MSDOS.SYS file is created to retain compatibility with older applications. However, the Windows 95 VMM32 and VxD files take over control of the system from the IO.SYS file during the startup process. Windows 9x supplies its own version of COMMAND.COM as well.

No CONFIG.SYS or AUTOEXEC.BAT files are created when Windows 9x is installed in a new system. These files are also not required by Windows 9x to start up or to run. Even so, both files will be retained from the previous operating system in upgraded systems in order to maintain compatibility with older applications. However, entries in the CONFIG.SYS file override the values in the Windows 9x IO.SYS file.

The Windows 9x IO.SYS file also handles some of the AUTOEXEC.BAT commands. In both cases, the system uses REM statements to deactivate those CONFIG.SYS and AUTOEXEC.BAT functions that are implemented in the IO.SYS file. Similarly, the functions of the SYSTEM.INI and WIN.INI files have been moved to the Windows 9x Registry.

.DOS extensions

The Windows 9x Setup routine stores existing MS-DOS files under **.DOS extensions** when it is installed as an upgrade over a previous operating system. In particular, the AUTOEXEC.BAT, COMMAND.COM, CONFIG.SYS, IO.SYS, and MSDOS.SYS files are stored with this extension. This enables an option known as dual booting to be established. In a dual-booting system, Windows 9x establishes a Startup Menu that can be used to boot up the system into different operating systems. To accomplish this, Windows swaps versions of the bootup files back and forth between their standard names and a designated set of backup names. Depending on which OS option the user selects at the start of bootup, Windows will retrieve the correct set of files, change their names, and then use them to boot the system.

.W40 extensions

If the system is started with the other operating system, the Windows 95 versions of AUTOEXEC.BAT, COMMAND.COM, CONFIG.SYS, IO.SYS, and MSDOS.SYS are stored under **.W40 extensions** and the renamed DOS versions of the files are returned to their normal extensions.

System Editor (SysEdit)

As with Windows 3.x, the SYSTEM.INI, WIN.INI, PROTOCOL.INI, CONFIG.SYS, and AUTOEXEC.BAT files can be modified through the **System Editor**(**SysEdit**) in Windows 95. The SysEdit utility can be accessed by selecting the SysEdit option in the Start/Run dialog box.

Startup

Windows 9x allows programs to be started automatically whenever Windows starts by adding them to the system's **Startup** folder. This is accomplished by accessing the Start Menu Programs tab and selecting Add. Browse until the desired program is found and then double-click on it. Finish the addition by clicking Next and then double-clicking on the Startup folder. These programs can be bypassed for troubleshooting purposes by pressing the left Shift key during startup.

TEST TIP

Remember how to prevent the items in the Windows 9x Startup folder from running at startup.

Installable File System (IFS) manager

32-bit Shell

User Interface tools

When fully installed, the Windows 9x structure is as depicted in Figure 9-34. The new Registry, Configuration Manager, and Virtual Machine Manager have already been introduced. However, they have been joined by an **Installable File System (IFS) manager** to function between the Windows 95 core and the device drivers that service the system's hardware. On the other side of the Windows 95 core, applications running on the system are accessed through the new **32-bit Shell** and **User Interface tools**.

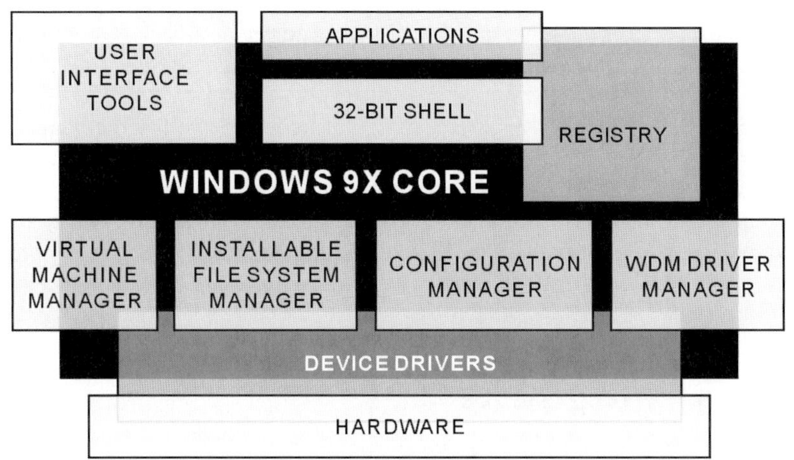

Figure 9-34: The Windows 9x Organizational Structure

The 32-bit Windows 98 structure basically built on the earlier Windows 95 structure. However, Windows 98 did add enhanced video display support, power management functions, and additional hardware support to the operating system. It also featured built-in Internet Explorer functions.

The other major feature that Windows 98 added to the operating system was support for a new driver model that permitted devices to operate under Windows 98 and future versions of Windows NT. This feature is referred to as the Win32 Driver Model (WDM) and exists in the Windows structure on the same level as the Virtual Machine, IFS, and Configuration Managers.

Windows 9x Core Components

kernel

GDI

USER

The Windows 9x Core consists of three components: the **kernel**, the **GDI**, and the **USER** files, as illustrated in Figure 9-35. Each component contains two .DLL files, one 16-bit version and one 32-bit version, that facilitate applications run on the system. Their functions remain basically the same in both Windows 95 and Windows 98 architectures.

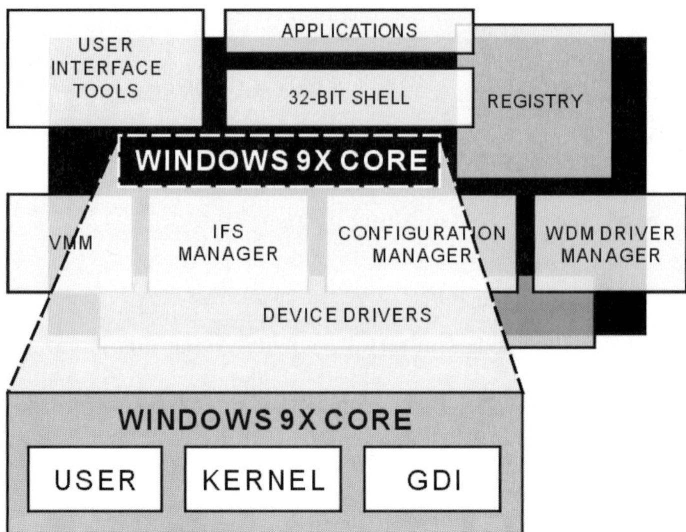

Figure 9-35: Windows 9x Core Components

The kernel is the foundation of the system, and handles basic memory and I/O management, task scheduling, error (exception) handling, and program execution functions. The USER files manage input from hardware devices, and output to the user interface components (i.e., the icons and screen structures). The GDI component controls what appears on the display. It includes two main subsystems: the Graphics subsystem and the Printing subsystem.

Windows 9x Registries

In Windows 9x, the system's configuration information is held a large hierarchical database called the Registry. This includes the local hardware configuration, the network environment, file associations, and user configurations. Many of Windows 3.1's SYSTEM.INI, CONTROL.INI, PROGRAM.INI, and WIN.INI management functions have been relocated to the Registry.

USER.DAT

SYSTEM.DAT

The contents of the Registry are located in two files located in the Windows directory. These are the **USER.DAT** and **SYSTEM.DAT** files. The USER.DAT file contains user-specific information, while the SYSTEM.DAT file holds hardware- and computer-specific profiles and setting information.

When applications were removed from the system in earlier Windows versions, the configuration information distributed between the various .INI files remained, unless the user, or a special Windows Uninstall program, looked them up and removed them individually. With Windows 9x, their headings and the associated configuration information are all removed from the Registry, unlike the old .INI method of tracking this information.

TEST TIP

Know where the Windows 9x Registry files are stored and what they are called.

Each time Windows 95 boots up successfully, these files are backed up with a **.DA0 extension**. The contents of the Registry can be viewed and altered through the **Registry Editor (Regedit.exe)** utility, as depicted in Figure 9-36. If the system experiences a Registry corruption problem, the USER.DA0 and SYSTEM.DA0 files can be renamed to .dat files and used to restore the Registry to its previous working configuration.

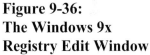

.DA0 extension

Registry Editor (Regedit.exe)

TEST TIP

Know which two files make up the Windows 9x Registry and where they are located in the system.

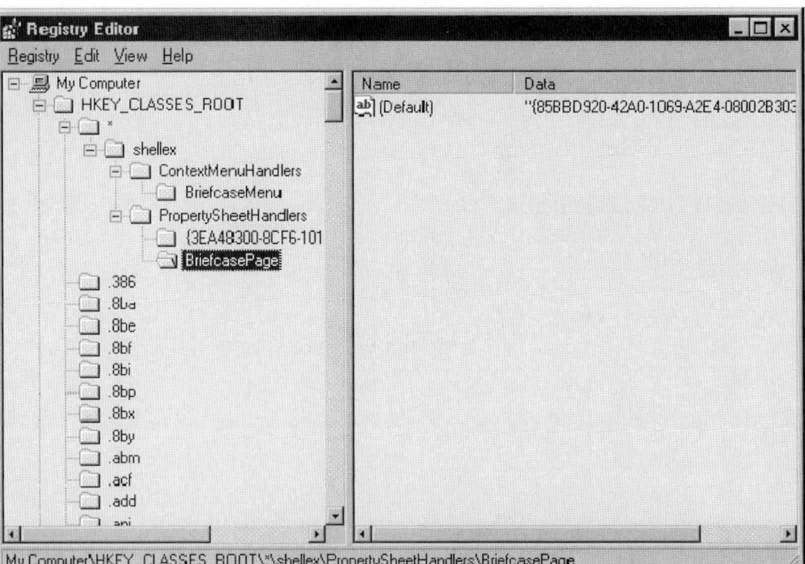

Figure 9-36: The Windows 9x Registry Edit Window

The contents of the Registry are not backed up in the same way under Windows 98 that they were in Windows 95. The Windows 98 system makes up to five backup copies of the Registry structure each time it successfully starts Windows. The backed-up contents of the Registry are stored in the \Windows\Sysbckup directory in the form of **cabinet (.CAB) files** (not as .da0 files). These files contain the following Registry-related files:

cabinet (.CAB) files

- System.dat
- User.dat
- System.ini
- Win.ini

The Sysbckup folder is a hidden folder. To examine its contents, you must remove the hidden attribute from it. Inside the folder, the backup files are stored under an **RB0XX.CAB** format, where XX is a sequential backup number given to the file when it is created. Running the Scanreg /restore command will also produce a listing of the available backup files to select from for troubleshooting purposes.

RB0XX.CAB

The Registry uses English-language descriptions and a hierarchical organization strategy. The hierarchy is divided into **Headkeys**, **Keys**, **Subkeys**, and **Values**. Keys are descriptive section headers that appear at the left side of the RegEdit window. Values, on the other hand, are definitions of topics organized under the keys. This organization can be thought of in the same terms as the organization of any book; the head keys are similar to chapter titles, the keys and subkeys are equivalent to the major and minor headings of the chapters, while values are equal to the sentences that convey information.

Headkeys

Keys

Subkeys

Values

RegEdit

TEST TIP

Know what type of database Windows uses for its Registry.

DWORDS

strings

Values can contain a wide variety of information types. They can contain interrupt and port address information for a peripheral system, or simply information about an installed application program. The information can be encoded into binary, **DWORDS**, or **strings**. Values are always located at the right side of the RegEdit window.

If you examine the My Computer heading using the RegEdit option, you will find six categories listed. The head keys all start with an HKEY_ notation.

Under My Computer the categories are:

- HKEY_CLASSES_ROOT
- HKEY_CURRENT_USER
- HKEY_USERS
- HKEY_LOCAL_MACHINE
- HKEY_DYN_DATA
- HKEY_CURRENT_CONFIG

Classes_Root

Most of the HKEY titles should appear very descriptive of their contents. The **Classes_Root** key divides the system's files into two groups by file extension type and by association. This key also holds data about icons associated with the file.

Current_User

The **Current_User** key holds the data about the user-specific configuration settings of the system, including color, keyboard, desktop, and start settings. The values in the Current_User key reflect those established by the user that is currently logged into the system. If a different user logs in, then the contents of the Users key are moved into the Current_User key.

Users

The **Users** key contains the information about the various users that have been defined to log into the system. The information from the Current_User key is copied into this section whenever a user logs off the system, or when the system is shut down.

Local_Machine

The **Local_Machine** key contains information about the system's hardware. All of the hardware drivers and configuration information is contained in this key. The system will not be able to use peripheral devices that are not properly documented in the Local_Machine key.

Dyn_Data

Current_Config

The **Dyn_Data** key and **Current_Config** keys work with the Local_Machine key. The Dyn_Data key works with the branch of the Local_Machine key that holds PnP dynamic status information for various system devices including current status and problems. The Current_Config key works with the Local_Machine branch containing current information about hardware devices.

The Windows 9x Registry structure is primarily used to hold information about system hardware that has been identified by the enumeration or detection processes of the Plug-and-Play system. When a device is installed in the system, Windows 9x detects it, either directly or through the system's bus managers, and searches the Registry and installed media sources for an appropriate driver. When the driver is found, it is recorded in the Registry along with its selected settings.

Some devices, such as PCMCIA devices can be inserted and removed under hot conditions (while power is on). The system will detect the removal or insertion of the device, and adjust its registry configuration on the fly. Legacy, or PnP ISA, devices must be installed in the system before startup, and go through the PnP process.

The Registry also holds information that enables the system to serve and track multiple users. It does this by retaining user- and configuration-specific information that can be used to customize the system to different users, or to different configuration situations.

Remote Procedure Call (RPC)

Windows 98 offers remote access to Win32-based Registry APIs through a procedure called a **Remote Procedure Call** (**RPC**). This enables system management tools to be used on remote units across a network.

Windows 9x System Policies

System Policies

Since Windows 9x provides multiuser operations, operational system policies are necessary to govern the rights and privileges of different users. Windows 9x **System Policies** establish guidelines to restrict user access to the options in the Control Panel and Desktop. They also allow an administrator to customize the desktop and configure network settings.

When a user logs on to the system, Windows 9x checks that user's configuration information. When found, the policy information associated with that user is moved into the Registry and replaces theexisting settings. This information is held in the CONFIG.POL file. Policies can be established for individual users, for defined groups of users, for a specific computer, for a network environment, or for default settings.

System Policy Editor (PolEdit)

The system policies that govern these functions are established and modified using an editor similar to the Registry Editor, called the **System Policy Editor** (**PolEdit**). The Policy Editor is another tool that can be used to access the information in the Registry. Unlike the RegEdit utility, the Policy Editor can access only subsets of keys. The Registry Editor can access the entire Registry.

Admin

Normally, the use of the PolEdit tool is restricted to the Network administrator. Therefore, it is not normally installed on users' com-puters. The utility is located on the Windows 9x CD under the **Admin** folder so that only the keeper of the CD can adjust the sys-tem's policies. The path to access the Policy Editor on the CD is Admin\Apptools\Poledit. Once located, it can be executed by enter-ing **PolEdit** in the Run box. This causes the Policy Editor screen to display, as depicted in Figure 9-37.

With any multiuser system, it may be necessary to establish various working environments for different users. Some users are entrusted with access to more of the system than other users. As described earlier, this is the purpose of logon procedures. The Windows 9x policy file tracks policies for different users in a file named CONFIG.POL. The contents of this file are moved into the USER.DAT and SYSTEM.DAT files when a user logs on.

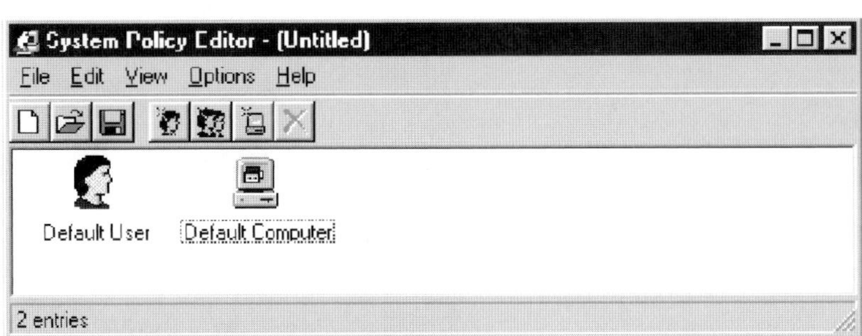

Figure 9-37: The Windows 9x Policy Editor

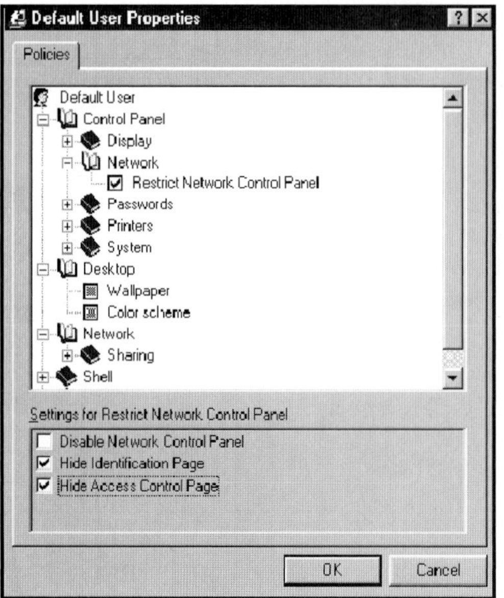

Figure 9-38: Inside the Policy Editor

The editor allows system administrators to configure the Windows desktop differently for different users. For some users, it may not be necessary for them to have access to certain system options, such as printers or Registry editing tools. Through the Policy Editor, access to these options can be removed from the desktop for a given user.

The window in the figure contains an icon for a default user and a default computer. When the user logs onto the system, Windows searches for a user profile that matches the user logging in. If none is found, the default policies are copied into the new user's profile and used until modified by a system administrator. The editing screen used to modify the Default User's policies is depicted in Figure 9-38.

Like the Registry Editor, the branches of the Policy Editor can be expanded or contracted by clicking on the plus (+) and minus (–) signs in the nodes of the tree. Three options can be selected for each setting: checked, cleared, or dimmed (grayed out). When a policy is checked, it is being implemented. If it is cleared (open), the policy is not implemented. When the policy is grayed out, the policy has not been changed since the last time the user logged on and Windows will not make any related changes to the system configuration and users can make changes to the setting.

As an example of the effects of these settings, consider the system's Wallpaper setting in the Control Panel. If the setting is checked, the designated wallpaper will be displayed. If the setting is cleared, no wallpaper will be displayed. Finally, if the setting is grayed out, Windows will not enforce the policy and the user can select his or her own wallpaper pattern through the Control Panel.

Windows 9x Managers

The Windows managers sit between the Windows 9x Core/Registry and the system's device drivers. These components gather information about the system and store it in the Registry. Both Windows 95 and Windows 98 versions of the operating system provide basic services for classes of devices, so that the device's driver software need only contain device-specific information.

Configuration Manager

Configuration Manager

The **Configuration Manager** oversees the complete Plug-and-Play configuration process for Windows 9x. Its primary purpose is to ensure that each device in the system can access an interrupt request channel without conflict and that it has a unique I/O Port address.

The I/O Port address is a location where the system communicates with an intelligent programmable device. It constantly tracks the number and location of devices in the system and reconfigures them when required.

The Configuration Manager charts a hardware tree for the system similar to the one illustrated in Figure 9-39. The tree represents all of the buses and intelligent devices in the system. Information about the buses and devices is collected by the Configuration Manager's **bus enumerators**. The information can be obtained from the BIOS interrupt services used by the devices, device drivers installed for the devices, and directly from the hardware.

bus enumerators

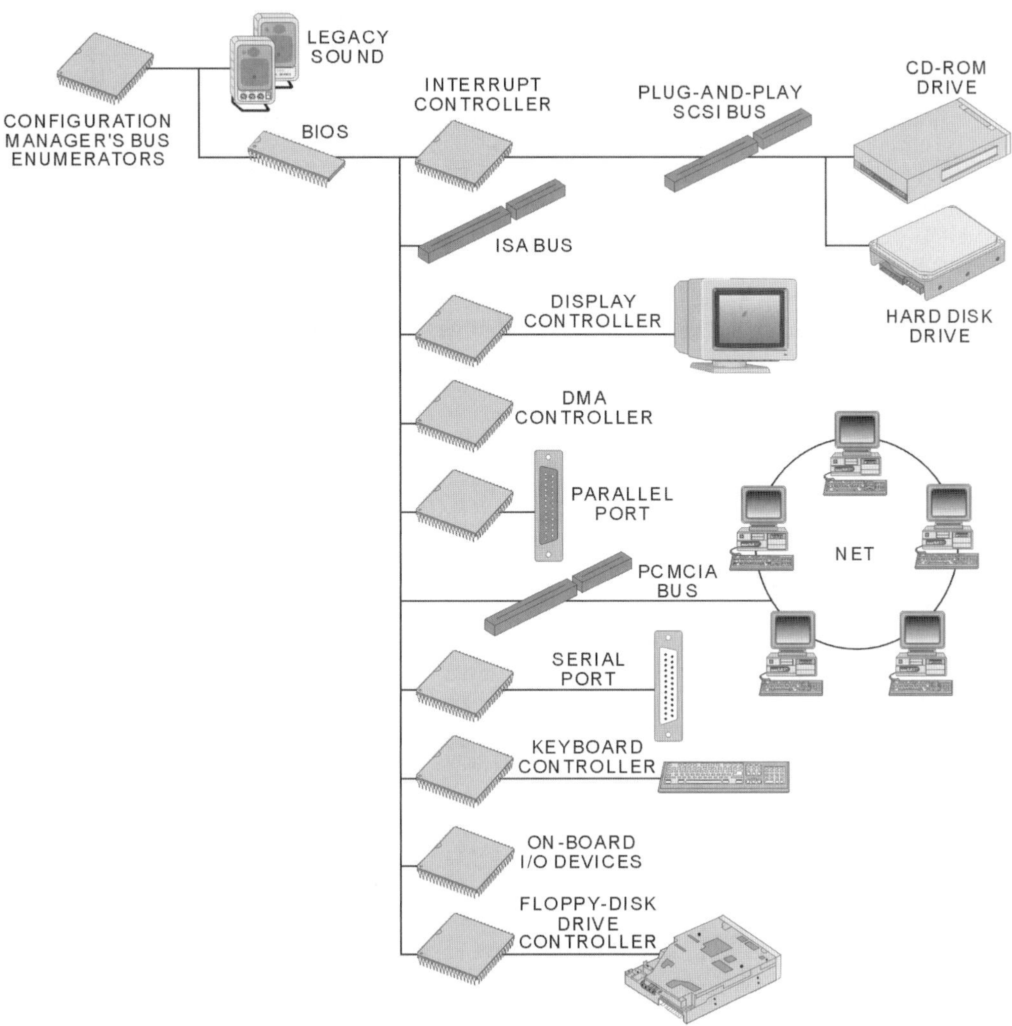

Figure 9-39: The Configuration Manager's Tree Structure

The Configuration Manager recognizes, configures, and allocates the system's resources to its installed devices. It uses **resource arbitrator** routines to provide interrupts, DMA channels, I/O addressing, and memory allocations for all of the system's devices. The arbitrator resolves any conflicts between the devices and then informs each device driver about its particular resource allocations.

resource arbitrator

Virtual Machine Manager

task switching

Windows brought multitasking to the personal computer with Windows 3.0. The system would work its way around all of the open applications allowing them to run for a period of time before resetting and moving to the next application. One of the simplest forms of multitasking is **task switching**. In a task switching operation, several applications can be running at the same time. When you have multiple applications open in Windows, the window that is currently being accessed is called the active window and appears in the foreground (on top of the other windows). The activity of the other open windows is suspended, as denoted by their gray color, and they run in the background.

Special key combinations allow the user to move between tasks easily. By pressing the ALT and TAB keys together, you can move quickly through the open applications. The ALT/ESC key combination allows the user to cycle through open application windows.

386 Enhanced mode

cooperative multitasking

In **386 Enhanced mode** Windows 3.x operated under a **cooperative multitasking** system. In these operations, some applications gained control of the system and used the resources until they were finished. Some Windows 3.x applications took up more than their share of the system's resources. When an application crashed under this type of multitasking, a General Purpose Fault was created and Windows would lock up or become too unstable to use.

preemptive multitasking

When Microsoft designed Windows 95, they designed it for **preemptive multitasking** operation, so that the operating system only allowed an application to run for a predetermined amount of time, based on how critical its task is in the overall scheme of the system. More time was allotted to high-priority tasks than to low-priority tasks. However, the operating system remained the controlling force. When the application's time was up, the operating system simply cut it off.

Under cooperative multitasking, the system is tied up with a single application whenever Windows is displaying an hourglass on the screen. With preemptive multitasking, a new task can be opened, or switched to, while the hourglass is being displayed on the screen. Work can be performed under that task window while the other task is being worked on by the system. More importantly, if the system locks up while working on a specific task in Windows 9x, you can simply end the task instead of restarting the machine.

Virtual Machine Manager (VMM)

The components of the Windows 9x **Virtual Machine Manager (VMM)** are depicted in Figure 9-40. It consists of a Process Scheduler, a Memory Pager, and an MS-DOS protected mode interface.

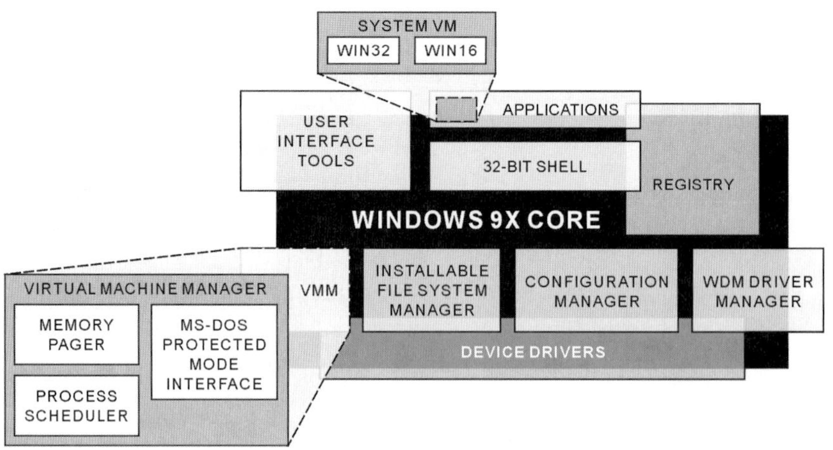

Figure 9-40: Windows 9x VMM Manager

Both Windows 95 and Windows 98 are primarily designed for preemptive multitasking operations. They conduct preemptive multitasking with Win32-based applications, but revert to cooperative multitasking with Win16-based applications in order to maintain compatibility with older operating systems. The **Process Scheduler** manages the system's multitasking operations for both types of applications. It also provides a separate virtual machine environment for each DOS-based application running in the system.

Process Scheduler

The VMM's **Memory Pager** allocates to each application a virtual memory space of 4 GB. The first 2 GB is private to the application, while the next 2 GB is shared. The entire linear address range is divided into equal-size blocks, referred to as **pages**. These pages are moved between memory and disk as demanded by the application. Consecutive pages may, or may not reside in a linear fashion in memory. The Pager tracks the location of all the pages in use.

Memory Pager

pagers

Most MS-DOS-based application will run smoothly in Windows 9x. However, Some MS-DOS-based applications require exclusive access to the system's resources. For these applications that won't run normally under Windows 9x, these operating systems provide the **MS-DOS Mode interface** that establishes a special MS-DOS environment when called for. In MS-DOS mode, the application retains complete control of the system resources, and no other applications can compete for them. Before running this type of application, Windows 9x ends all of its active tasks, calls up a real mode version of MS-DOS and executes special versions of CONFIG.SYS and AUTOEXEC.BAT to support the application. When the MS-DOS application is finished, the system reloads the Windows operating system and returns to normal service. Microsoft included this mode just to handle MS-DOS applications that do not work under Windows.

MS-DOS Mode interface

Installable File System Manager

When a file or disk access request is received by Windows 98, a subsection of the interface known as the **Installable File System** (**IFS**) manager processes the request by passing it to the proper **File System Driver** (**FSD**). Figure 9-41 depicts the Windows 9x IFS system. The FSDs communicate with the IFS manager and the drivers that work directly with the hardware device controllers. These device-specific drivers work within the **I/O Supervisor** (**IOS**) layer. The IOS layer handles I/O systems that transmit and receive data in multiple-byte transfers. Devices in this category include hard disk drives, CD-ROM drives, tape drives, and network controllers.

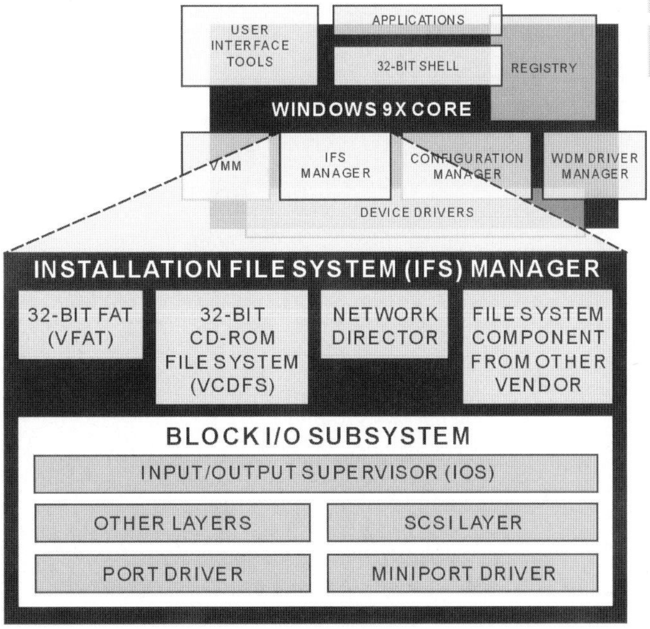

Installable File System (IFS)

File System Driver (FSD)

I/O Supervisor (IOS)

Figure 9-41: IFS Manager

VFAT

CD-ROM File System (CDFS)

Universal Disk Format (UDF)

Optical Storage Technology Association (OSTA)

The major file system drivers supported by the Windows 9x IFS are the 32-bit **VFAT** driver, a 32-bit protected-mode **CD-ROM File System** (**CDFS**) driver, a 32-bit **Universal Disk Format** (**UDF**) driver, and a 32-bit network redirector. The Windows 9x VFAT works with the 32-bit VCACHE protected-mode cache driver. Unlike the SMARTDRV utility, the size of the cache under VCACHE is dynamic and depends on the needs of the system. Likewise, the 32-bit protected-mode CDFS driver provides a dynamic cache for CD-ROM operations. The UDF file system is implemented in Windows 98 to satisfy the **Optical Storage Technology Association** (**OSTA**) specification for devices such as DVD discs. Disk caching under UDF is a function of VCACHE and is dynamic.

Win32 Driver Model Manager

Win32 Driver Model (WDM) Manager

The **Win32 Driver Model** (**WDM**) **Manager** was introduced in the Windows 98 version of Windows 9x. Its main function is to support WDM drivers. This model permits hardware manufacturers to develop device drivers that will work on both Windows 98 and future Windows NT machines. The WDM manager does this by simulating the Windows NT kernel in a new layer of the VxD driver architecture.

The WDM layered architecture is depicted in Figure 9-42. This layered arrangement allows the same device drivers to be used in multiple types of operating systems.

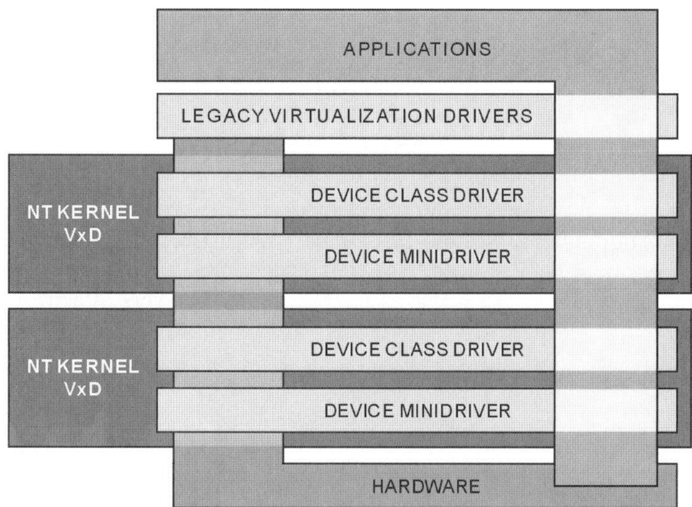

Figure 9-42: Win32 Driver Model Layers

FAT32

FAT16

FAT12

Earlier versions of DOS and Windows supported what is now termed as **FAT16** (or **FAT12**). The OSR2 version of Windows 9x introduced the FAT32 File Allocation Table. As described earlier, the size of the operating system's FAT determines the size of the clusters for a given size disk partition. Of course, smaller cluster sizes are better due to the fact that even a single byte stored in a cluster will remove the entire cluster from the available storage space on the drive. This can add up to a lot of wasted storage space on larger drives. Table 9-2 describes the relationships between clusters and maximum partition sizes for various FAT entry sizes.

Table 9-2: FAT Relationships

FAT TYPE	PARTITION SIZE	CLUSTER SIZE (IN BYTES)
FAT12	16 MB	4096
FAT16	32 MB	2048
FAT16	128 MB	2048
FAT16	256 MB	4096
FAT16	512 MB	8192
FAT16	1 GB	16384
FAT16	2 GB	32768
FAT32	<260 MB	512
FAT32	8 GB	4096
FAT32	16 GB	8192
FAT32	32 GB	16384
FAT32	>32 GB	32768

In order to use the FAT32 system, the hard drive must be formatted using the FDISK/FORMAT functions in OSR2. This makes FAT32 incompatible with older versions of Windows (even Windows 95(a) and Windows NT) and with disk utilities and troubleshooting packages designed for FAT12/16 systems.

FAT32 FDISK

Large Disk Support

To use the **FAT32 FDISK** function in OSR2, it is necessary to enable the **Large Disk Support** option. After completing the FDISK function and exiting, it is necessary to manually reboot the system. After this, it is usually a simple matter of performing a FORMAT operation using the OSR2 CD, or Start Disk, to install the FAT32 drive. Failure to reboot between the FDISK and FORMAT operations will produce an error.

To verify that the hard drive is formatted with FAT32, select the My Computer option from the desktop and right-click on the C: drive icon. This will produce the [C:] Properties window displayed in Figure 9-43. The Type entry should read Local Disk [FAT 32]. The hard drive usage pie chart will not work correctly with drives larger than 2 GB. It will show the drive as empty until at least 2 GB of space is used.

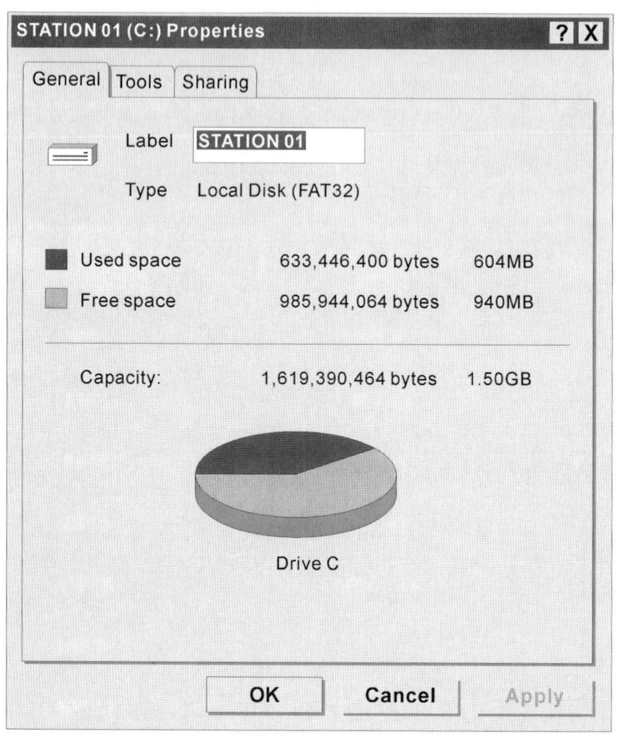

Figure 9-43: Showing FAT32 in the HDD Properties Window

OSR2 does not require that FAT32 be used. It will operate just as well, if not better using the FAT16 format. Depending on the application of the system, it may run slower with FAT32. Remember that FAT32 is designed to optimize storage space, not performance. The simple fact that FAT32 offers the potential for more clusters makes it slower than a drive with fewer clusters. With this in mind, the decision to use FAT32 or FAT16, or to use different cluster sizes in FAT32, usually depends on the balance the user establishes between performance and storage. The default cluster size set by Microsoft for FAT32 is 4 kB.

TEST TIP

Know how to convert FAT16 partitions to FAT32 partitions.

In Windows 9x, it is possible to convert partitions created on a FAT16 drive into a FAT32 file system using the CVT.EXE utility. The main drawback to doing this is that there is some possibility of data corruption and loss. Not surprisingly, there is no utility for converting FAT32 partitions to FAT16.

Virtual File Allocation Table

Protected Mode FAT File System

Virtual File Allocation Table (VFAT)

Windows 9x streamlines the 32-bit file and disk access operations by removing both the DOS and the BIOS from the access equation, as illustrated in Figure 9-44. This allows Windows 9x to always run in Protected Memory mode, so that no mode switching need occur.

Microsoft refers to this portion of the system as the **Protected Mode FAT File System**. It is also called the **Virtual File Allocation Table** or **VFAT**. As its full name implies, the VFAT provides a Protected mode method of interacting with the file system on the disk drive. VFAT operates in 32-bit mode; however, the actual FAT structure of the disk remains as 12-bit or 16-bit allocations.

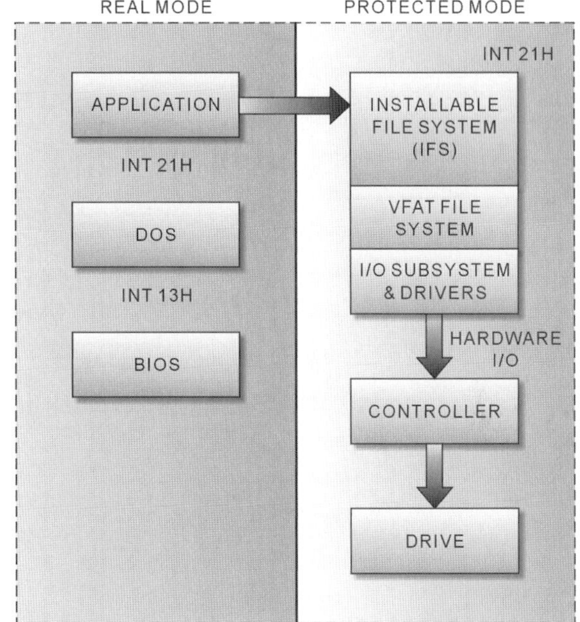

Figure 9-44: 32-bit Access in Windows 9x

Since the system does not normally have to exit and reenter protected mode, performance is increased considerably. The logical blocks of the VFAT are described in Figure 9-45.

VCACHE

The VFAT system replaces the SMARTDRV disk caching utility with a protected-mode driver named **VCACHE**. Under VCACHE, the size of the cache data pool is based on the amount of free memory in the system instead of a fixed amount. The program automatically allocates blocks of free memory to caching operations as needed. Under Windows 9x, the VCACHE driver controls the cache for the system's CD-ROM drive, as well as for hard disk and file operations.

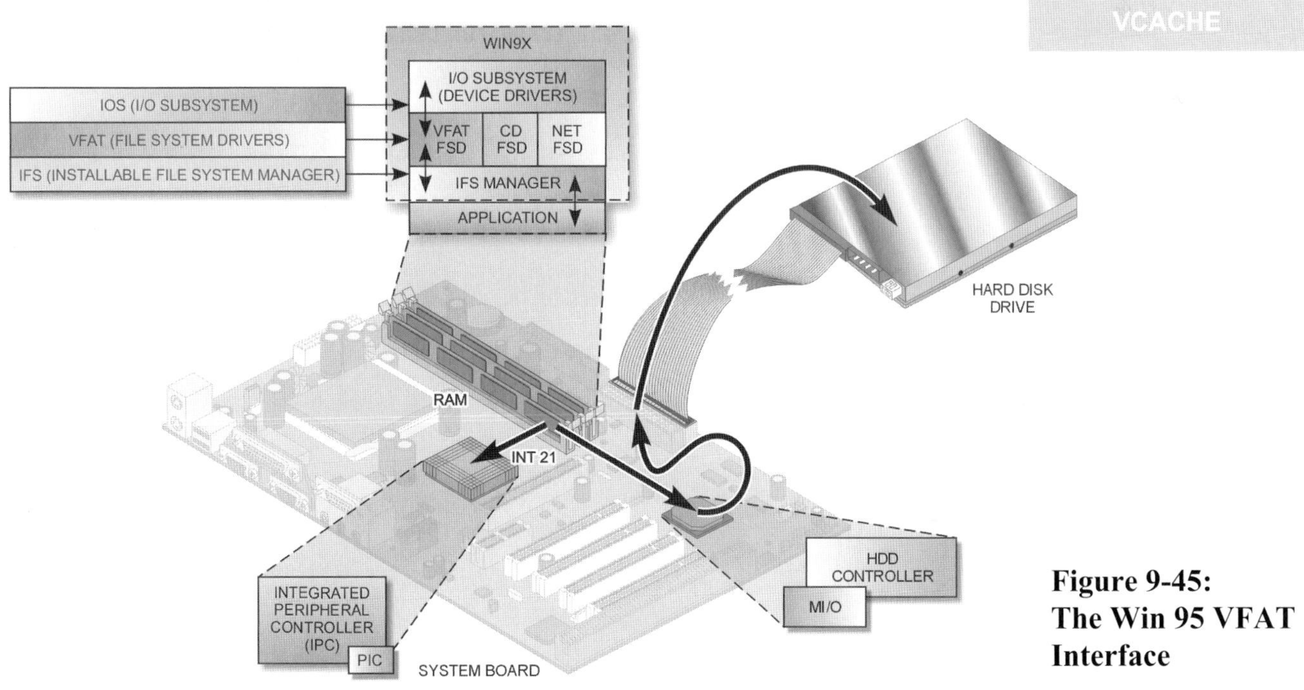

Figure 9-45: The Win 95 VFAT Interface

Installable File System (IFS)

File System Driver (FSD)

I/O Supervisor Layer (IOS)

When a file or disk access request is received by Windows 9x, a subsection of the interface known as the **Installable File System** (**IFS**) processes the request by passing it to the proper **File System Driver** (**FSD**).

The FSDs communicate with the IFS manager and the drivers that work directly with the hardware device controllers. These device-specific drivers work within the **I/O Supervisor Layer** (**IOS**). The IOS layer handles I/O systems that transmit and receive data in multiple-byte transfers. Devices in this category include hard disk drives, CD-ROM drives, tape drives, and network controllers.

LOADING AND ADDING DEVICE DRIVERS

The portion of the A+ Operating System Technologies objective 2.4 states that the test taker should be able to identify procedures for loading/adding device drivers and the necessary software for certain devices.

One of the reasons for the success of the PC-compatible system is its open architecture and its versatility. This versatility is the result of an architecture that allows all types of devices to be added to it. In the PC world, this is accomplished through the use of software device drivers that interface diverse equipment to the basic system. Although the process for installing equipment and their drivers in a PC has become increasingly easy, the technician must still be able to install whatever drivers are necessary. Therefore, the following sections of this chapter are dedicated to device-driver installations.

Add New Hardware Wizard

The PnP-compliant design of Windows 9x makes installing most new hardware nearly automatic (as long as the new device is also PnP compatible). The PnP function will automatically detect new PnP-compliant hardware when it is started. If the device is not PnP compliant, or the system just can't detect it for some reason, it will be necessary to use the Windows 9x **Add New Hardware Wizard**.

Add New Hardware

Setting Up New Hardware—Windows 9x is designed to assist the user in setting up any new hardware components that may be added to the system. The **Add New Hardware** icon can be found under the Control Panel option of the Settings menu.

Double-clicking on this icon will activate the Windows 9x Hardware Wizard, depicted in Figure 9-46. The Wizard program is designed to guide you through hardware setup steps. The new card or device should already be installed in the system before running this procedure.

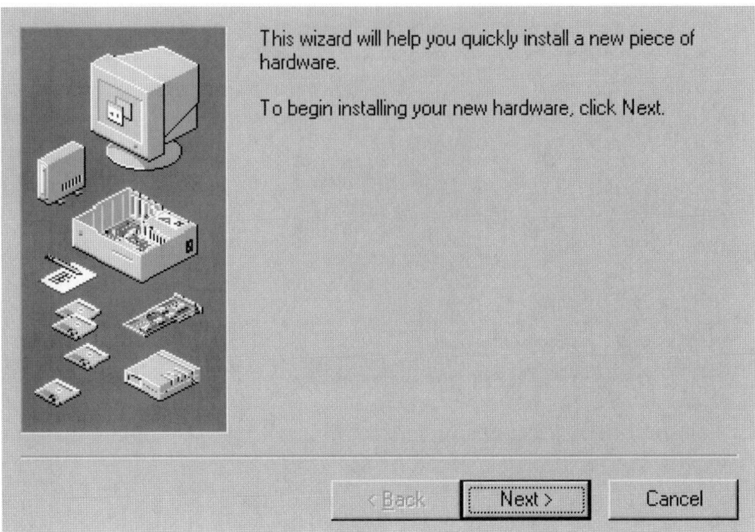

Figure 9-46: The Windows 95 Hardware Wizard

The Hardware wizard is a series of screens that will guide the installation process for the new device. The first user-selectable option is to use the AutoDetect function, described in Figure 9-47. The progress indicator bar at the bottom of the page displays the progress of the detection operation in bar-chart format. When it has filled the opening, Windows will indicate what hardware it has found that can be installed. Clicking the Details button will show which hardware it found.

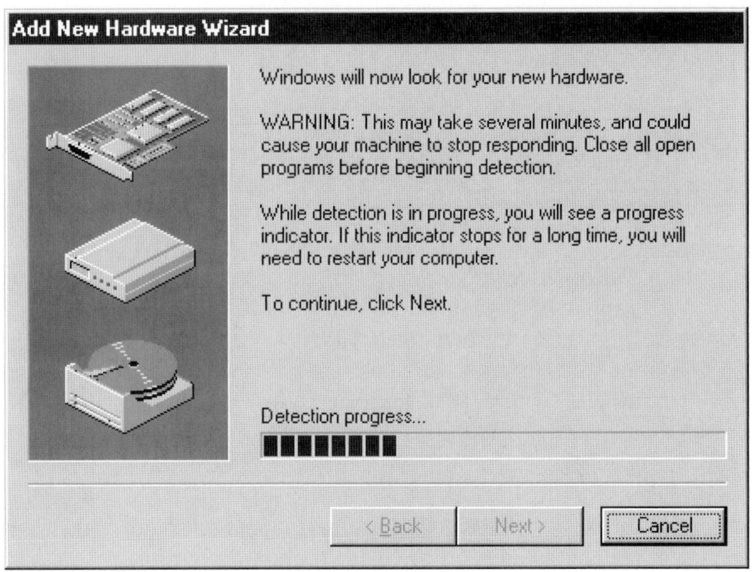

Figure 9-47: Windows 95 Detecting New Hardware

If the wizard does not detect the hardware, the user can attempt to locate the device in the wizard's list of supported devices, as shown in Figure 9-48. The only other option for installing hardware devices is to obtain an OEM disk or CD for the device that has Windows 95 drivers. If the driver disk does not have an AutoStart function, it will be necessary to click the Have Disk button and supply the file's location to complete the installation process.

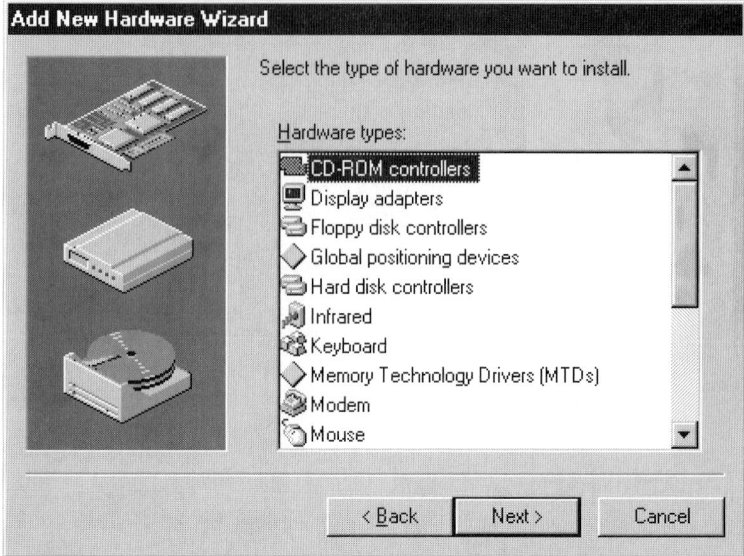

Figure 9-48: Windows 95 Supported Hardware Listing

Finish

The installation process can be concluded by clicking the **Finish** button. This will cause Windows to install the drivers for the new hardware in the system. It may also request configuration information from the user before finishing. Afterward, the system will need to be rebooted for the configuration changes to take effect.

WINDOWS 9X APPLICATIONS

A portion of the A+ Operating System Technologies objective 2.4 states that the test taker should be able to identify the procedures for installing and launching typical Windows and non-Windows applications.

The other factor that makes PC-compatible systems so widely accepted is the fact that there are so many software applications available for them. Because these applications are, at least for the most part, not installed by the computer maker, the technician must be able to successfully install application software and configure it according to the customer's specifications. The following sections deal with application installations under Windows 9x.

Add/Remove Programs

Like the Hardware Wizard, Windows 9x offers the user assistance in installing new programs. The Add/Remove New Programs icon under the Control Panel is used to install new programs automatically. The **Add/Remove Programs** screen is depicted in Figure 9-49.

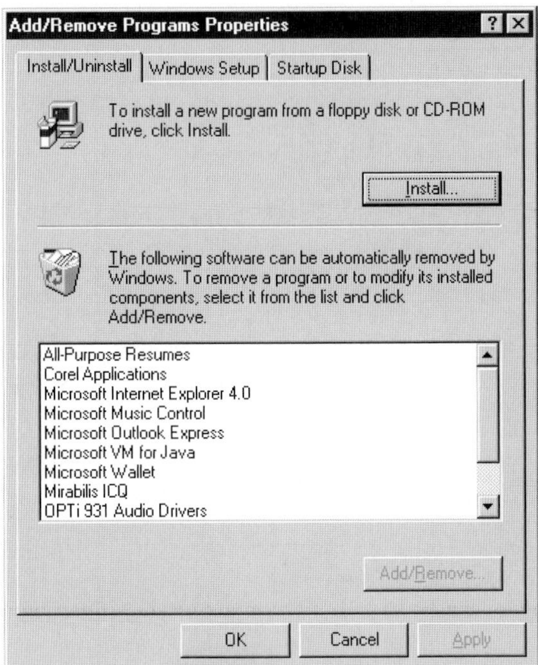

Figure 9-49: The Windows 95 Add/Remove Programs Window

In DOS, adding a program to the system was normally a simple process of copying it to the hard drive. Removing the program was also simple—just delete its directory and files. However, in Windows 3.x removing a program would normally leave several .INI and .DLL files scattered around the hard drive. Not only did these files take up disk space, they could also become a source of conflict with new software added to the system.

Install

The main page of the Add/Remove window is the Install/Uninstall page used to add and remove the desired software package. The upper half of the page contains the **Install** button that is clicked to start the software installation process.

The lower half of the page lists the Windows 9x software packages that are already installed in the system. However, non-Windows 9x-compliant software packages will not appear in the list. Only those programs that the Windows 9x Install/Uninstall utility can uninstall appear here.

Some Windows 9x applications may share support files with other applications. In these instances, the Uninstall utility will produce a dialog box asking about deleting the shared files. The best response is to keep the file to avoid disabling the other application. If the files are to be deleted, then a backup should be made before running the uninstall utility so that the files can be replaced if needed.

Launching Applications

In the DOS environment, starting or launching an application was a simple matter of typing the name of its executable file at the DOS prompt of the directory that it was installed in. Special startup batch files could also be used. However, in the Windows 3.x environment starting an application became as simple as double-clicking on its icon.

In Windows 9x, there are several acceptable methods of launching an application. These include:

- From the Start menu, select the Applications entry, click the folder where the desired application is, and double-click its filename.
- From the Start menu, select the Run entry, and then enter the full path and filename for the desired executable file.
- Double-click the application's filename in Windows Explorer or in My Computer.
- Click the File menu option from the Menu Bar in My Computer or Windows Explorer, and select the Open option. (You can also alternate-click on the application and choose Open.)
- Create a shortcut icon on the desktop for the application, so that it can be started directly from the desktop by simply double-clicking its icon.

TEST TIP

Be aware of the various methods of launching an application in the Windows environment.

In Windows, an application can be set up to run by association. Using this method, the application will be called into action any time that an associated file (such as a document and its related word processor) is double-clicked. This is accomplished by defining the file's type in the Registry.

Since the Registry is a delicate place to operate, you can also associate an application program with a given file using the following steps:

Hands-On Activity

1. Click the Folder Options entry in the My Computer (or Windows Explorer) View menu
2. Click the File Types tab
3. Select the file type you want to change from the list
4. Click the Edit button
5. In the Actions dialog window, click the Open option
6. Click the Edit button
7. In the Application used to perform action dialog window, enter the name of the program you want to use to open files that have the designated extension
8. Click the OK button to complete the association process. The settings for selected file types are shown in File type details.

In Windows NT/2000, this is accomplished by defining the file's type in the Open With dialog box. The first time you attempt to open an application, the Open With dialog box, depicted in Figure 9-50, will appear. The Open With dialog box can also be accessed by alternate-clicking the file's Properties/General tab and then selecting the Change option.

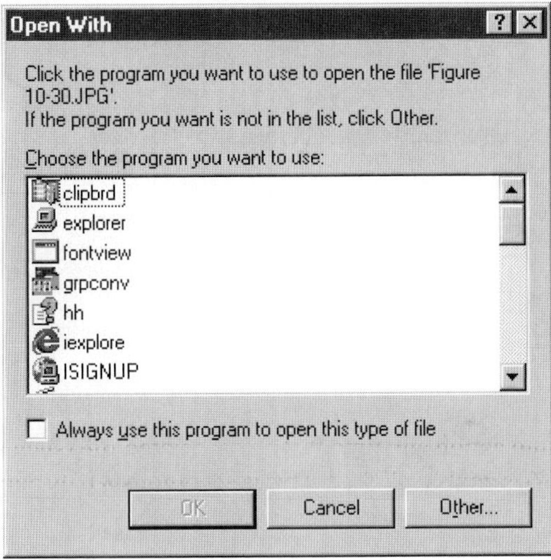

Figure 9-50: The Windows NT Open With Dialog Box

Non-Windows Applications

Even though Windows provides mechanisms for simulating a MS-DOS command-line environment, in many instances, it is desirable to run a DOS application from within the Windows environment.

Prior to the Windows 3.1 operating system, a simple request for a hard disk access while running in protected mode would result in Windows, DOS and the BIOS handing the request back and forth a number of times (that is, application-to-Windows-to-DOS-to-Windows-to-BIOS-to -Windows-to-DOS-to-Windows-to-application). Figure 9-51 depicts this operation.

Windows 3.x introduced 32-bit access to the Windows package. Contrary to the sound of its name, 32-bit access had nothing to do with moving data in 32-bit blocks. Instead, it was a method of reducing the need to move back-and-forth between real and protected memory modes when an access request was made.

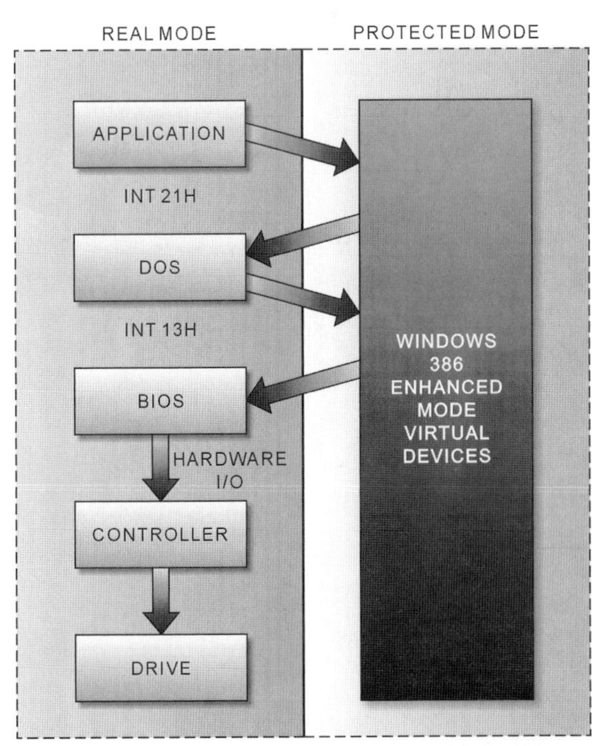

Figure 9-51: The Windows/DOS/BIOS Relationship

The new access method reduced the work associated with disk and file operations by removing the BIOS completely from the loop. A protected-mode device driver called FastDisk emulated the BIOS routines in Windows. The upgraded software capabilities sped up the operation of the system by eliminating the changes between real and protected modes that occurred each time Windows had to hand over control to the DOS or BIOS. Figure 9-52 demonstrates the advanced access process using FastDisk.

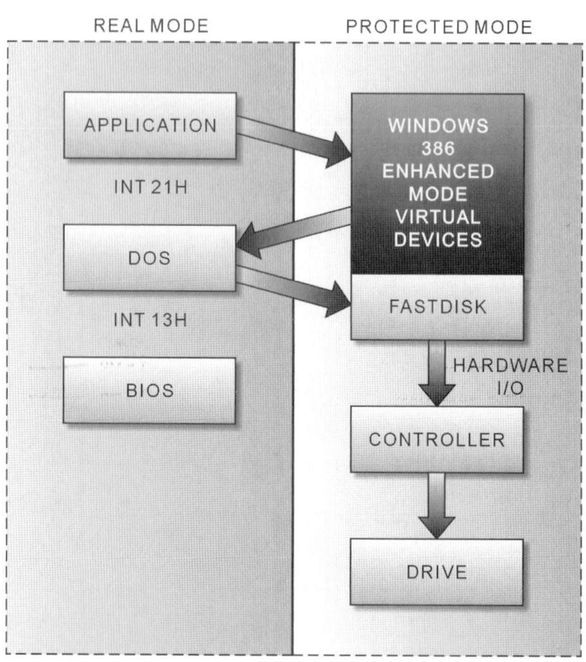

Figure 9-52: 32-bit Access with FastDisk

Windows 3.x also added 32-bit capabilities to file accesses as well as disk accesses. This further increased the system's overall operating speed by removing BIOS calls from file accesses as well.

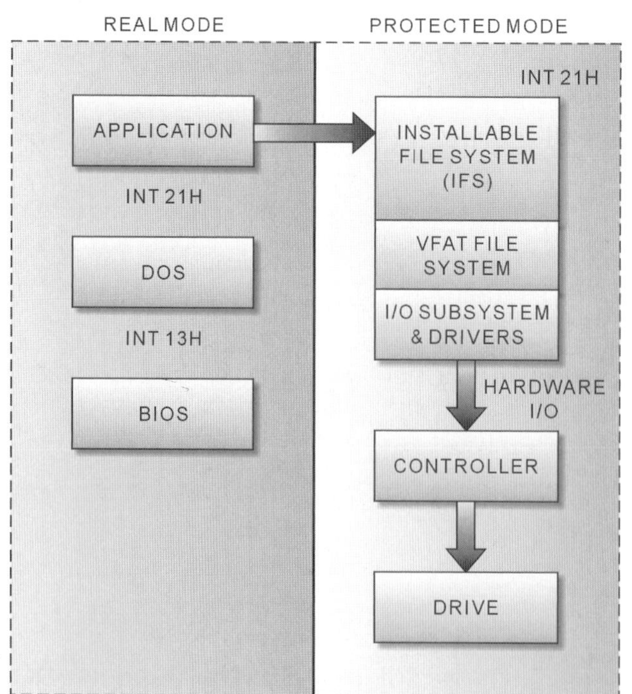

Figure 9-53: 32-bit Access in Windows 9x

Windows 9x streamlined the 32-bit file and disk-access operations further by removing both the DOS and the BIOS from the access equation, as illustrated in Figure 9-53. The Windows 9x VFAT module enables the operating system to always remain in protected memory mode so that no mode switching needs to occur.

From this discussion of how Windows, DOS and the BIOS interact, it should be apparent that running a DOS program from within Windows can be a difficult undertaking.

Windows Setup

The Windows 9x Setup tab, depicted in Figure 9-54, is also located under the Control Panel's Add/Remove Programs icon. This utility allows different Windows 9x components to be added to or removed from the system. Windows Configuration settings can be changed through its dialog boxes. The window in the center of the Setup page provides a list of the standard Windows 9x groups, along with their total sizes.

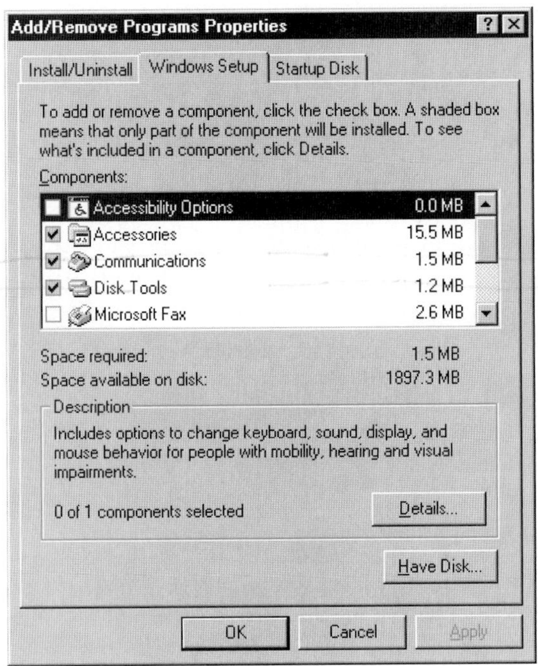

Figure 9-54: The Windows 95 Setup Page

An empty box beside the option indicates that it has not been installed. Conversely, a checkmark inside the box indicates that the complete group has been installed in the system. Finally, a gray checkmark indicates that some of the files in the group have been installed.

> **TEST TIP**
>
> Know where to go to set up an application that does not feature automated installation utilities.

Highlighting a group title with the cursor, and then clicking the Details button will cause a listing of the group's files to appear. Items in this list may be added to the system by checking on the box next to them. Once the options to be added have been checked, the system will need to be restarted in order for the new options to become active.

Most software manufacturers include a proprietary setup program for their Windows 9x applications. These programs normally run directly from the CD-ROM when they are inserted into the drive for the first time (unless the AutoPlay function is disabled). For applications that don't feature the automatic installation function, or if the AutoPlay function is disabled, the software will need to be installed manually. This is accomplished through the Have Disk button. Clicking this button will produce a dialog box asking for the name and location of the application's installation file. Most software suppliers will provide a Setup.exe or Install.exe file to handle the actual installation and configuration process for their software.

Accessibility

One of the optional groups that you may typically leave out is the **Accessibility** option. This group contains programs that modify the operations of the Windows keyboard, audio and video output for use by those who have physical conditions that inhibit their use of the computer. If you require visual warning messages for hearing disabilities or special color controls for visual difficulties, install this component and select the options that you need access to.

> **TEST TIP**
>
> Know where to access options that can be used to enable users with physical challenges to use the computer.

When the Accessibility option is installed, its icon appears in the Control Panel and when it's removed, it disappears. This option uses 4.6 MB of space when it is installed.

DOS and Windows 9x

APPS.INF

DOS-based applications are installed in Windows 9x by simply running their executable file from the Run dialog box, or from the Windows 9x Explorer. If the file has never been run under Windows 9x, the operating system creates a default entry in its **APPS.INF** file for that program. A copy of the new entry is also used to create a Program Information File (PIF) for the application. A PIF file is a file created to serve as a bridge between a DOS-based application and the Windows environment in older versions of Windows. These files contain information about how much memory the application requires and which system resources it needs.

After the APPS.INF entry has been created, it can be accessed and modified through the Properties window for that application. These Properties windows replace the PIF editor used in previous versions of Windows. The Properties window contains the following six tabs that enable the operation of the application to be modified:

- General
- Program
- Font
- Memory
- Screen
- Misc

Program

The **Program** tab allows the user to define where the DOS program is located, what it is called, and how it should be displayed. The tab's Run entry is used to establish the initial window size setting for the application. Options for this setting include Normal Window, Maximized Window, and Minimized Window.

MS-DOS mode

Nearly every DOS-based program should run successfully in Windows 9x. Even DOS programs that require access to all of the system's resources can run successfully in the Windows 9x **MS-DOS mode**. In this mode, basically all but a small portion of Windows exits from memory. When the application is terminated, Windows restarts and returns to the desktop screen.

Advanced Program Settings

MS-DOS mode is established for the application by configuring its properties in the **Advanced Program Settings** dialog box under the My Computer/Application_name/Properties/Program tab, as illustrated in Figure 9-55. Simply right-click on the application's executable filename in the My Computer window choose Properties, Program tab and select the MS-DOS mode setting in the Advanced screen.

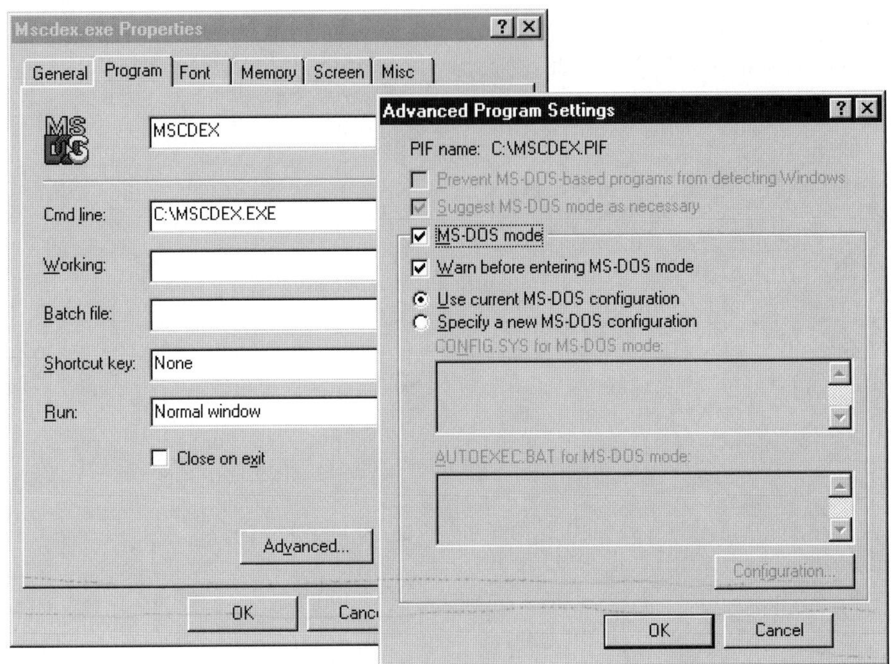

Figure 9-55: Establishing MS-DOS Mode in Windows 95

It is also possible to adjust the memory allocated to the program through the My Computer/Properties/Memory tab. This function is accessed by right-clicking its executable file name, moving to the Memory window, and increasing or decreasing the memory available, as illustrated in Figure 9-56.

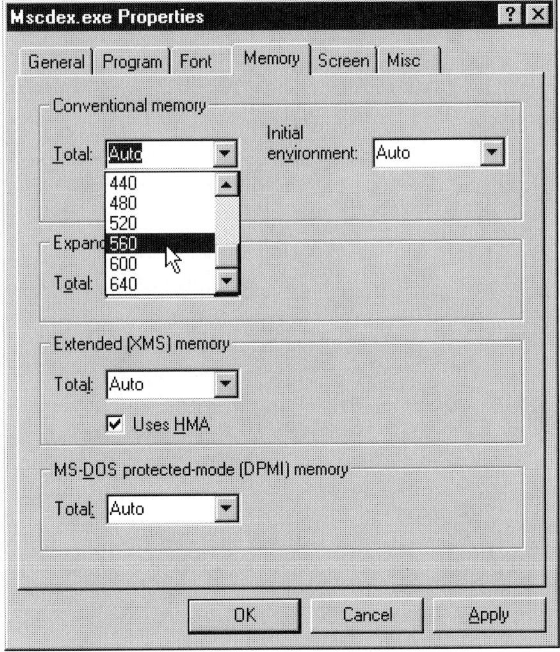

Figure 9-56: Adjusting DOS Mode Memory

The Memory tab allows the user to establish memory allocation properties for the application. Values can be selected for Conventional, Extended, and Expanded memory usage, as well as for configuring HMA and UMB operations. These settings are still dependent on the information that may exist in the CONFIG.SYS file. In particular, check the CONFIG.SYS file for the NOEMS parameter in the EMM386.EXE statement. If present, replace it with an appropriate **RAM** or **x=mmmm-nnnn** parameter.

Screen

The **Screen** tab provides several options for how the application will be presented on the screen. It is possible to set the window size that the application will run in. These options include Full Screen, a user-definable window size, and a default window size based on the graphic mode the application is using.

This tab also allows the Windows 9x toolbar to be displayed on the bottom of the screen. This feature can be valuable if the application becomes unstable or has trouble running in Windows.

Dynamic Memory Allocation

Finally, the Screen tab allows the application to use the Windows 9x Fast ROM emulation and **Dynamic Memory Allocation** features. These functions are selected to speed up video output operations.

Tool Bar

If a DOS application takes up the entire screen in Windows 9x, it will be necessary to press the ALT/ENTER key combination to switch the application into a window. The ALT/TAB key combination switches the screen to another application. Some applications may grab the entire screen and cover the **Tool Bar** and Start menu button when maximized. When this occurs, it will be necessary to resize the application's window through the screen tab to access the Tool Bar. The Start menu can be accessed simply by pressing the CTRL/ESC key combination.

Printing in Windows 9x

print spooler

Printing is significantly improved in Windows 9x. The Print Manager function and its support components have been integrated into a single print-processing architecture, referred to as the **print spooler**. This integration provides smooth printing in a background mode and quick return-to-application time. The key to this operation is in how the print spooler sends data to the printer. Data is only moved to the printer when it is ready. Therefore, the system is never waiting for the printer to digest data that has been sent to it.

Figure 9-57: Printer Right-Click Pop-Up Menu

To print an open file in Windows 9x, just move to the application's File menu as normal and click on the Print option. If the file is not open, it is still possible to print files in Windows 9x. Under the My Computer icon, right-clicking on a selected file will produce a Print option in a pop-up menu. From the Windows Explorer screen, files can be printed by following the same right-click menu method. The document can also be dragged-and-dropped onto a printer icon in the Printers folder, in the Network Neighborhood listing, or on the desktop. Obviously, this option can be performed with both local and remote networked printers.

The settings for any printer can be changed through the My Computer icon on the desktop or through the Printers option under the Start menu's Settings entry. The process is the same for both routes, just double-click on the Printer folder, right-click on the desired printer, and select its Properties entry from the menu as illustrated in Figure 9-57.

To view documents waiting to be printed from the print spooler, double-click on the desired printer's icon in the Printer folder. This will display the existing print queue, as illustrated in Figure 9-58. Unlike earlier Windows Print Managers, closing the Print window does not interrupt the print queue in Windows 9x. The fact that the print spooler runs in its own 32-bit virtual environment means that printer hang-ups will not lock up the system. The print jobs in the queue will be completed unless they are deleted from the list.

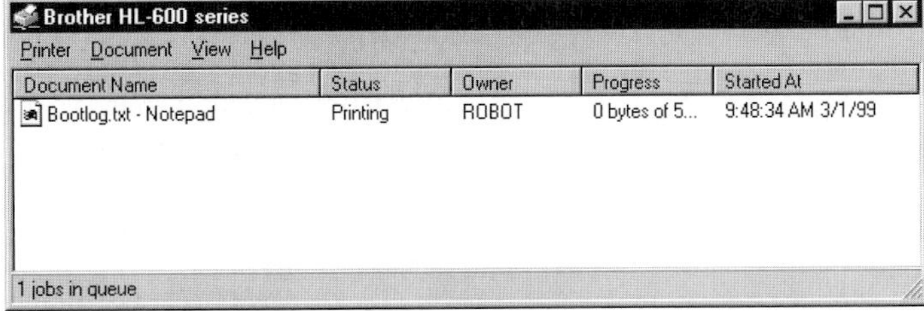

Figure 9-58: Windows 9x Print Queue Display

The Print Spooler window's menu bar items permit printing to be paused and resumed. They can also be used to delete print jobs form the queue. Right-clicking on a printer icon will produce a pop-up menu that can also be used to control printing operations being performed by that printer. Both options offer a Properties option that can be used to access the printer's configuration and connection information. One of the most important Printer Properties tabs is the Details page depicted in Figure 9-59.

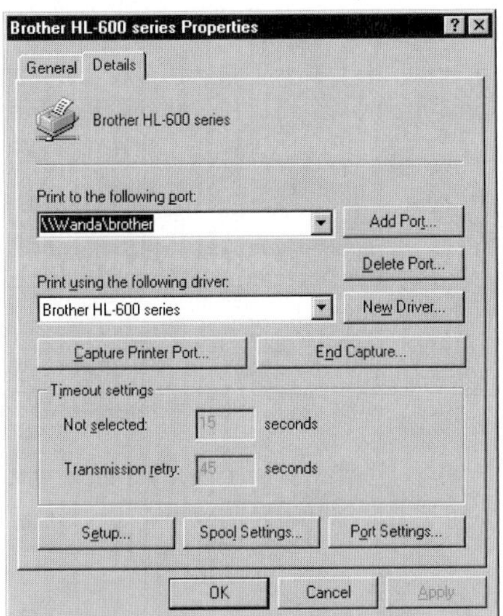

Figure 9-59: Typical Printer Properties/Details Page in Windows 9x

Installing Printers in Windows 9x

Add Printer Wizard

Windows 9x automatically adopts any printers that have been established prior to its installation. If no printers are already installed, the Setup program will run the new **Add Printer Wizard** to allow a printer to be installed. Each printer in the system has its own print window and icon to work from. The wizard can be accessed at any time through the Windows 9x My Computer icon or Start menu. In the Start menu, move to the Settings entry and click on Printers. Likewise, through the My Computer icon, or the Control Panel window, double-click on the Printers folder or icon.

To install a printer, open the Printers folder and double-click the Add Printers icon. From this point, the Printer Wizard guides the installation process. Because Windows 9x has built-in networking support, the printer can be a local unit (connected to the computer) or a remote unit located somewhere on the network. If the physical printer is connected to a remote computer, referred to as a print server, the remote unit must supply the printer drivers and settings to control the printer. Likewise, the print server must be set up to share the printer with the other users on the network.

To install the network printer, access the Network Neighborhood icon on the desktop, select the remote computer's network name, the remote unit's printer name, and right-click on the Install option, as illustrated in Figure 9-60. After the remote printer has been installed, the local computer can access it through the Network Neighborhood icon.

TEST TIP

Memorize the procedure for installing a network printer in Windows 9x.

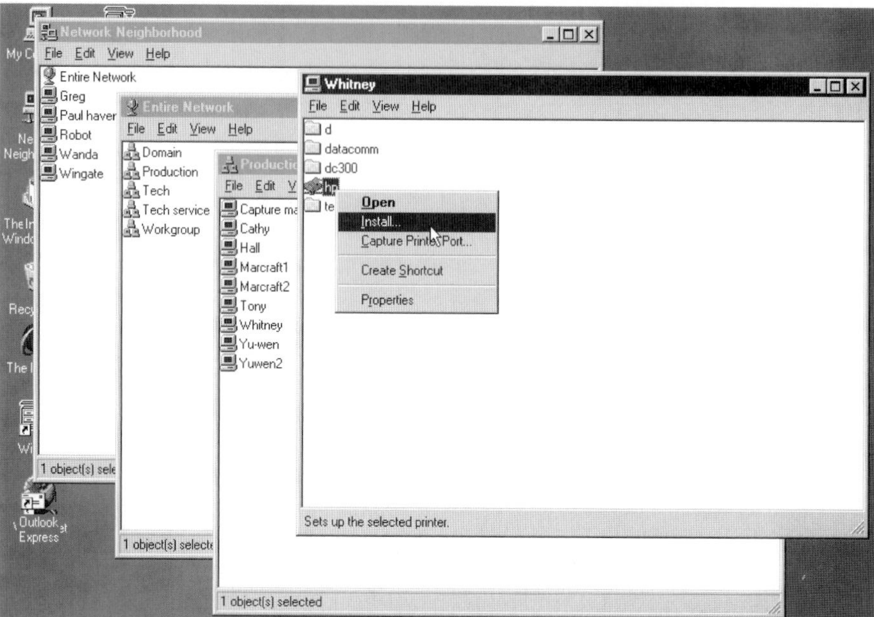

Figure 9-60: Installing a Network Printer in Windows 9x

TEST TIP

Know how to install Printer drivers in Windows 9x if the particular device is not listed in the standard Windows driver listings.

If the printer is not recognized as a model supported by the Windows 9x driver list, OEM drivers can be installed from a disk containing the OEMSETUP.INF file.

OPTIMIZING WINDOWS 9X

In a purely 32-bit Windows 9x environment, very little memory management is needed. In these systems, new 32-bit virtual device drivers (VxDs) are automatically loaded into extended memory during the boot-up process. This eliminates the need for DEVICE= and LOADHIGH commands for devices that have VxDs and Windows 9x application programs. When 16-bit device drivers or DOS applications are being used, however, Windows 9x must create a Real-mode DOS environment for them. For this reason, Windows 9x will execute a CONFIG.SYS and/or AUTOEXEC.BAT file it encounters during boot up.

If no DOS-based drivers or applications are in the system, the CONFIG.SYS and AUTOEXEC.BAT files are not necessary. However, the Windows 9x version of the IO.SYS file will automatically load the Windows 9x version of the HIMEM.SYS file during boot up. This file must be present for Windows 9x to boot up. Even though Windows loads a version of HIMEM.SYS, a DEVICE=HIMEM.SYS line must be present in a CONFIG.SYS file if a DEVICE=EMM386 line, or a 16-bit device driver is required. There are likely to be multiple versions of the HIMEM.SYS file in a Windows 9x system (there could be three or more versions). Booting up Windows 9x and VxDs are examined in greater detail in the following chapter.

If a Windows 9x system has a CONFIG.SYS and AUTOEXEC.BAT file that has been held over from previous operating systems, you should be aware that any unneeded commands in these files have the potential to reduce system performance. In particular, the SMARTDRV function from older operating systems will inhibit dynamic **VCACHE** operation and slow the system down.

VCACHE

If the system runs slowly, check the CONFIG.SYS and AUTOEXEC.BAT files for SMARTDRV and any other disk cache software, settings. Remove these commands from both files to improve performance. Also, remove any SHARE commands from the AUTOEXEC.BAT file.

TEST TIP

Be aware of the affect that active commands in a CONFIG.SYS, AUTOEXEC.BAT, or INI file can have on the operation of an advanced Windows operating system.

The most obvious cure for most Windows 9x memory errors is to install extra RAM for extended memory. RAM has become very inexpensive to add to most systems and the Windows 9x memory-management system is very stable. If the system has troublesome DLL and/or TSR programs installed, remove them and reinstall them one by one until the offending files have been identified. Check with the application manufacturer for updated versions of these files.

Hands-On Activity

Setting Up Supplemental Cache

The overall operation of the Windows 9x system can be enhanced by establishing a supplemental cache for the CD-ROM drive. This cache enables data to be paged between the CD and the system (or hard disk). The supplemental cache is established through the Control Panel's System icon:

1. Under the System icon, click the Performance tab and select File System button.
2. Set the Supplemental Cache Size slider to the desired cache size.
3. Set the Optimize Access Pattern for setting to the Quad-speed or higher option (unless you have an old single- or double-speed drive). This will establish a 1238 KB supplemental cache (provided the system's RAM size is larger than 12 MB).
4. Click the OK button and restart the system to create the cache.

TEST TIP

Know how to optimize the operation of a CD-ROM drive.

NETWORKING WITH WINDOWS 9X

The A+ Operating System Technologies objective 4.1 states that the test taker should be able to identify the networking capabilities of DOS and Windows including procedures for connecting to the network.

The prevalence of local area networks (LANs) in businesses requires that PC technicians know how to install and maintain LAN equipment and software. This is evident by the increased weight of the "Networking" domain in the new A+ exams. The following sections of this chapter deal with the software side of local area networking. LAN hardware installation and troubleshooting were discussed in Chapter 5—*Data Communications*. Taken together, these two chapters provide a comprehensive study of desktop networking.

Network Hardware

Networking PCs begins with the network type and card. Although the hardware side of networking was covered in Chapter 5—*Data Communications*, some information about the network type and the network card must be obtained before the software side of the network can be addressed. The type of network determines which transfer protocol you need to load, and the network card determines which adapter driver you can install. You can find the network card's information in its user manual or installation guide. You also can find the network type information that the network adapter can support in these guides.

You should configure network interface cards (NICs) to communicate with the system software before installing them in the system. On older network cards, you accomplish this by setting hardware jumpers to a specified pattern on the card. With software-configured ISA and PCI cards, you accomplish this through configuration software that downloads information to a configuration EEPROM on the card. The typical parameters that must be established for the NIC include the following:

IRQ-5

300h

D0000h

- IRQ level (**IRQ-5**/10/11/15)
- Base I/O port address (**300h**/210h/220h)
- Base memory address (**D0000h**/C800h)

Typical values used for these parameters in a PC are presented in parentheses, with the typical default values in bold. The address values presented in literature may drop the last zero. You also might have to find alternative settings for one or more of the parameters if those default values are already being used in the system. Record the hardware setting so that there is less chance for mix-ups when setting the corresponding software parameters.

Some network cards do not provide a user-definable base memory address because they do not use system RAM to exchange information between the local and remote units. For those cards that do use a base memory address, it should be apparent that the addresses given falls within the Upper Memory Blocks used by the EMM386 line of the CONFIG.SYS file. To avoid Upper Memory Block conflicts in a networked system, use the X= switch to modify the EMM386 line so that it excludes the UMB used by the network adapter. (For instance, DEVICE=EMM386.EXE X=C800–CEFFh will exclude addresses between C8000h and CEFF0h from being used for anything except the network adapter.)

Resource Sharing

The concept of sharing directories, files, and hardware resources is central to the design of any **network operating system (NOS)**. The overriding features that distinguish a NOS system from a DOS system are the sharing and security features of the NOS. These features are typically manifested in passwords, permission levels, and access rights for the system's users.

network operating system (NOS)

Initially, MS-DOS made no provision for sharing resources across LANs. The only computer-to-computer communications practiced in the early days of the PC were point-to-point communications between two units. This could be performed through a direct, null-modem connection between the serial ports of the two systems, or through a pair of modems.

> **TEST TIP**
> Know what the DOS SHARE command does.

In later versions of DOS, however, Microsoft added the **SHARE.EXE** command to provide file-sharing and -locking capabilities for files on a local hard disk drive. These capabilities enabled multiple users to access the same file at the same time in a networked or multitasking environment. The SHARE command had to be loaded in the CONFIG.SYS file using an INSTALL= statement (that is, INSTALL=SHARE /F:4096 /l:25).

SHARE.EXE

With version 3.11, the Windows operating system added built-in, peer-to-peer networking capabilities to the operating environment and titled it **Windows for Workgroups (WfW)**.

Windows for Workgroups (WfW)

In a network environment, only shared directories and resources can be accessed across the network. The sharing function is instituted at the remote computer. In Windows, the presence of a hand under the folder or device icon notifies other potential users that this resource or directory has been shared and can be accessed.

To access a shared remote resource, the local operating system must first connect to it. When the connection is established with a remote drive or folder, the local operating system creates a new logical drive on the local machine to handle the shared directory. Normally, the local file management system assigns the directory the next available drive letter in the local system.

The path to the shared resource contains a little more information than the path to a local directory. The remote path must include the remote computer's name and shared resource name (directory or printer). It also must be expressed using the **universal naming convention (UNC)** Format. This format begins with a pair of back slashes followed by the computer name and the resource name. Each name in the path is separated by a single backslash. Therefore, the format of a shared path is *\\computer_name\directory_name*.

universal naming convention (UNC)

Valid computer names in Windows 9x can be up to 15 characters in length and cannot contain any blank spaces. In Windows 2000 using the TCP/IP protocol, computer names can range up to 63 characters in length and should be made up of the letters A through Z, numbers 0 through 9, and hyphens.

> **TEST TIP**
> Know the specifications for setting up computer names in a given operating system.

Network Neighborhood

Network Neighborhood

In Windows 9x, the peer-to-peer local area networking function is an integral part of the system. The heart of the Windows 9x networking system is contained in the desktop's **Network Neighborhood** icon and the Control Panel's Network icon.

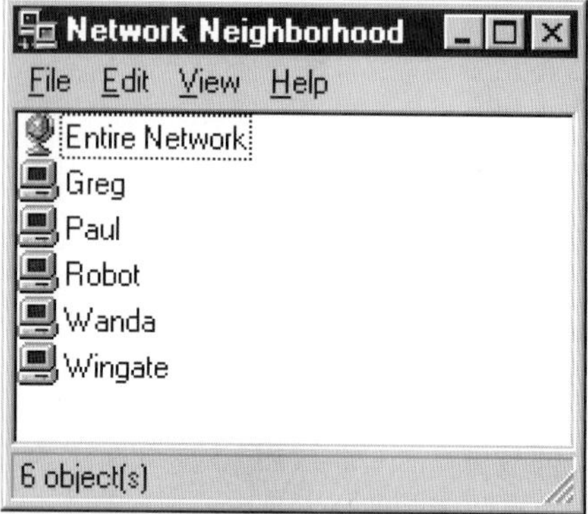

Figure 9-61: The Network Neighborhood Window

The Network Neighborhood display, depicted in Figure 9-61, is the primary network user interface for Windows 9x. This screen is used to browse and access shared resources on the LAN in a method similar to that used with the Windows Explorer for a local hard drive. As a matter of fact, most directory and file-level activities, such as opening and saving files, can be performed through the Network Neighborhood screen.

Microsoft networks group logically related computers together in **workgroups** for convenient browsing of resources. The local computer is a part of a workgroup. Double-clicking the Network Neighborhood icon displays the printers and folders available in the workgroup in either a list or an icon format. As with the Windows Explorer, you can change the format through the View menu options.

If the desired computer does not display, double-click the **Entire Network** icon. This action produces any other workgroups in the system and displays additional printers and folders that are available.

workgroups

Entire Network

If the Network Neighborhood window is empty, or if its icon is missing, networking connections have not been established. If this is the case, you must correctly configure networking on the local unit to connect to any other computers on the network. This is done through the Control Panel's Network icon. After you have located the desired computer, double-click its icon (or entry), to view its resources.

The Network Neighborhood also provides an easy way to connect to and use other network resources. If the local computer is connected to the network, double-click any remote computer in the list to connect to it. This action displays its contents in the neighborhood. In this condition, it is possible to copy files between the local and remote computers.

Mapping a Drive

mapping the drive

It is possible for the local system to assign a logical drive letter to the remote unit, or folder. This is referred to as **mapping the drive** letter to the resource. This mapping allows non-Windows 9x applications running on the local computer to use the resource across the network.

map

Map Network Drive

To **map** (assign) a drive letter to a remote network computer, or folder, open the Windows Explorer. From the Tools menu, select the **Map Network Drive** option. The Map Network Drive dialog box displays (see Figure 9-62).

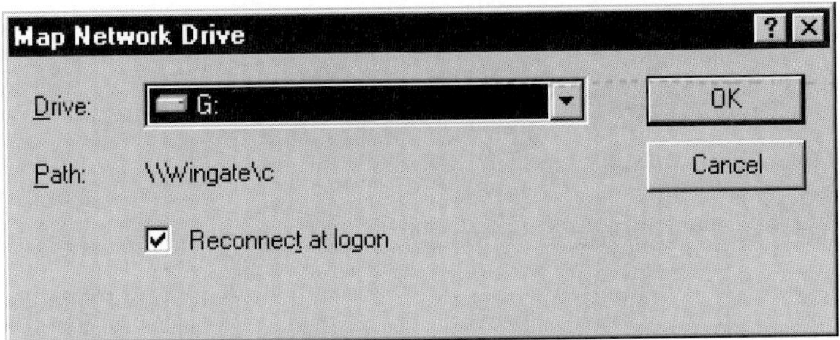

Figure 9-62: Map Network Drive Dialog Box

Windows 9x attempts to assign the next available drive letter to the computer or folder indicated in the Path dialog box. Establishing the map to the resource is a simple matter of entering the required path and share name in the dialog box using the **Universal Naming Convention (UNC)** format (i.e., *\\Path\Remote_name\folder_name*).

Universal Naming Convention (UNC)

Windows produces a prompt for a password if the remote unit requires one. You can map a computer or a folder that has been used recently by clicking the down arrow beside the Path window and then choosing the desired resource from the pop-up list.

> **TEST TIP**
>
> Know what will cause a mapped drive to disappear from a system when it is shut down and restarted.

The Reconnect at Logon option must be selected in the Map Network Drive page for the drive mapping to become a permanent part of the system. If the option is not selected when the user logs off, the mapped drive information disappears and needs to be remapped for any further use. If a red X appears on the icon of a properly mapped drive, this indicates that the drive is no longer available. Its host computer may be turned off, the drive may have been removed, or it may no longer be on the same path. If the drive was mapped to a particular folder and the folder name has been changes, the red X will also appear.

Network components

Primary Network Logon

The Network Icon in Control Panel

The Control Panel's Network screen, shown in Figure 9-63, provides configuration and properties information about the system's networks. The system's installed **Network components** are listed under the Network Configuration tab.

Double-clicking an installed adapter's driver, or clicking the Properties button when the driver is highlighted, produces its Configuration information page. The Add and Remove buttons on this page are used to install and remove network drivers from the system.

The **Primary Network Logon** window is used to establish which type of network Windows 9x will enter when it starts up. This proves particularly helpful on systems that may be working in multiple network environments (i.e., such as a computer that may need to access Microsoft network resources in some situations, and Novell network resources at other times).

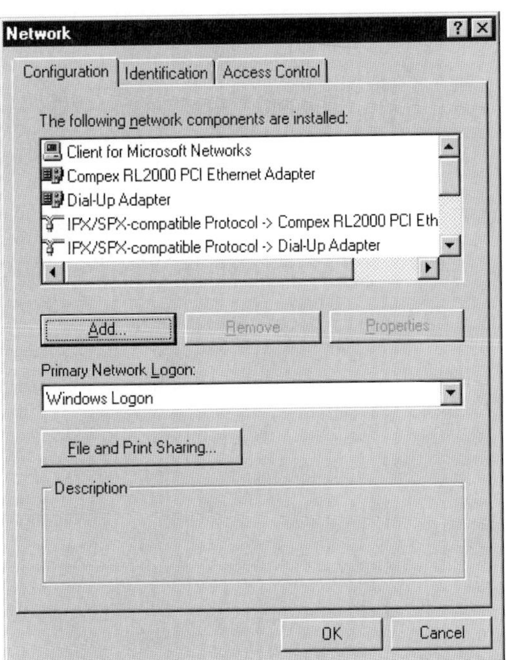

Figure 9-63: The Network Control Panel Screen

File and Print Sharing

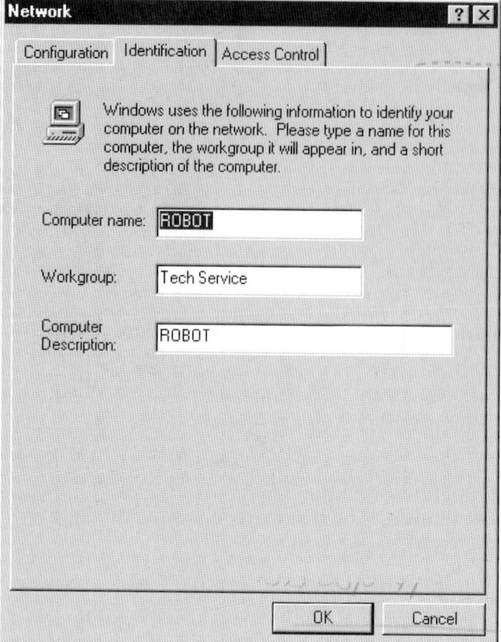

Figure 9-64: Network Identification Page

The **File and Print Sharing** button is used to select the first level of resource sharing for the local unit. Sharing can be individually enabled/disabled for file and printer accesses from remote computers.

Identification

The page's **Identification** tab is used to establish a network identity for the local computer, as illustrated in Figure 9-64. This page establishes the local computer's share name and workgroup association.

Access Control

Similarly, the **Access Control** tab enables the local user to set the level of access control that is applied to remote accesses. The possible options include: assign a password requirement for each access, or grant access to selected groups or users.

Resources

As mentioned earlier, double-clicking a driver in the Configuration tab opens a series of pages describing its properties. The **Resources** section of an NE-2000-compatible network adapter's configuration (common in Ethernet installations) is depicted in Figure 9-65.

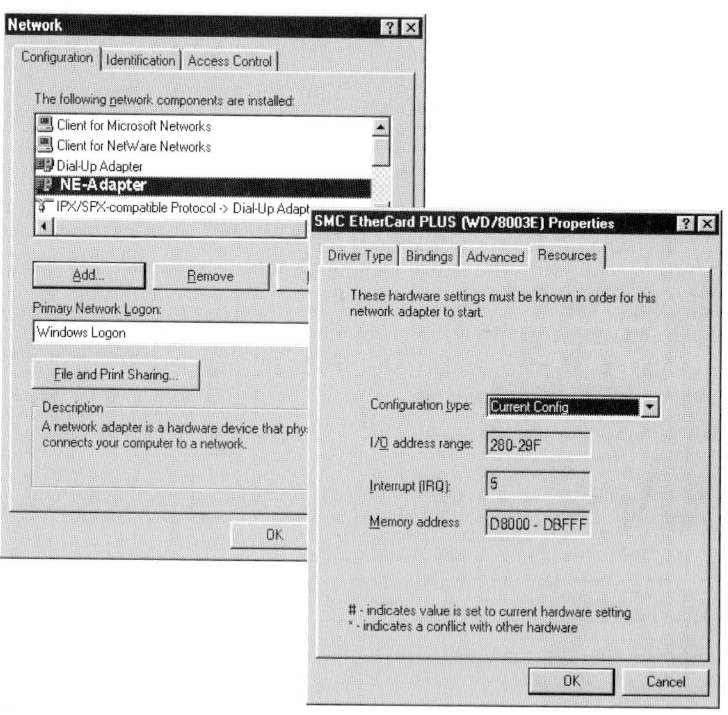

Figure 9-65: NE-2000 Compatible Resources Screen

This page shows the adapter's current system resource allocations (using IRQ5, I/O addresses 280h–29Fh, and memory addresses D8000h–DBFFFh).

Installing Network Components

After the network adapter card has been configured and installed, the next step in setting up the computer on the network is to load its drivers, protocols, and services. In most Windows 9x installations, the majority of these steps are accomplished simply by rebooting the computer and allowing Windows to detect the network adapter.

Microsoft Client protocol

Novell NetWare Client protocol

Select Network Component Type

The Windows 9x networking utilities should produce an adapter driver, a **Microsoft Client protocol**, and a **Novell NetWare Client protocol** in the Network Configuration window in a typical installation. A default set of file and print services also are loaded.

The only items that must be installed manually are the protocols for the particular type of network in which the computer is being used. Clicking the Add button in the Network Configuration page brings up the **Select Network Component Type** screen depicted in Figure 9-66.

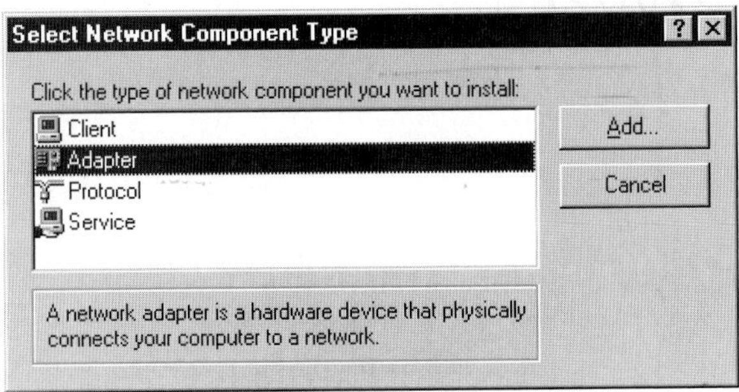

Figure 9-66: The Select Network Component Type Screen

The types of networking components include four categories:

- **Client**. Software that enables the system to use files and printers shared on other computers
- **Adapter**. Drivers that control the physical hardware connected to the network
- **Protocol**. Rules that the computers use to govern the exchange of information across the network
- **Service**. Utilities that enable resources and provide support services, such as automated backup, remote registry, and network monitoring facilities

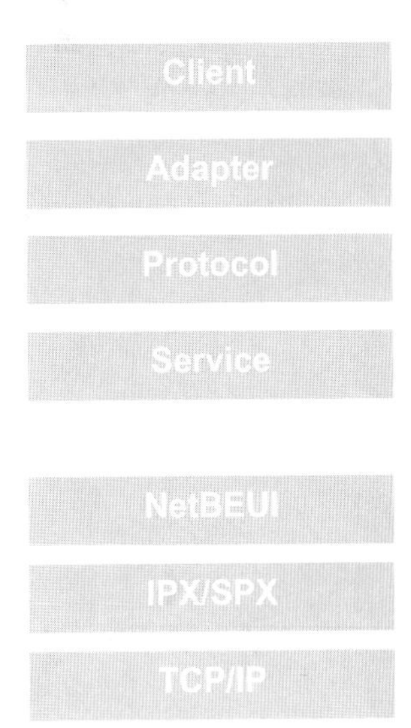

Each entry contains a list of primary and alternative drivers, protocols, and configuration settings that can be viewed by clicking the title in the window. These alternatives are included because there are many non-Microsoft networks in use, and Windows 9x attempts to support the most common ones.

If a particular network type is not supported in the standard listings, the Components page features a Have Disk button that permit the system to upload Windows-compatible drivers and protocols.

Because the boot-up detection process loads the adapter driver, two types of clients to choose from, and a set of sharing parameters, most installation procedures require only that the appropriate protocols be loaded for the network type. In a Microsoft network applications, these usually include the **NetBEUI** and **IPX/SPX** protocols for the LAN. An additional **TCP/IP** protocol may be added for Internet support.

TEST TIP

Know where TCP/IP Properties are established in Windows.

NetBIOS Extended User Interface (NetBEUI)

In a Windows network, the set of rules that govern the exchange of data between computers is the **NetBIOS Extended User Interface (NetBEUI)** protocol. This protocol works in most purely Windows networks, so another protocol is rarely called for. If an additional protocol is required, choose the Add Protocol option in the Network Components dialog box to add another protocol. Network adapters can typically handle up to four different protocols. The key to protocol selection is that the devices on the network must use the same protocol to be able to talk with each other.

> **TEST TIP**
>
> Remember the meaning of the term NetBEUI and know what type of network operating system it belongs to.

> **TEST TIP**
>
> Be aware that NetBEUI is required to navigate a dial-up connection to a local area network.

Although NetBEUI is easy to implement, it is a non-routable protocol. Because NetBEUI uses broadcast techniques to find other nodes on the network, it has no inherent capabilities to access nodes outside the immediate physical network segment. Therefore, it is not used in wide area networking applications. However, NetBEUI is required to support dial-up **Remote Access Services** (**RAS**) through a modem. The RAS service uses the NetBEUI protocol to navigate through a network after you have dialed into it. Both the calling client and the receiving server in the LAN must be running NetBEUI. If either computer does not have this protocol active, the client will be able to connect with the LAN, but will not be able to navigate through it.

Remote Access Services (RAS)

IPX/SPX is a Novell network protocol for LANs, and TCP/IP is the Internet protocol supported by Windows 9x and Windows NT/2000.

Network Printing with Windows 9x

Network printing in Windows 9x is a matter of creating and linking an icon on the local computer with a shared physical device attached to a remote computer.

Printers folder

The standard method of installing a printer in Windows 9x is to activate the Add Printer wizard through the **Printers folder**. This folder provides a central location for adding and managing printer operations. The Printers folder can be accessed from:

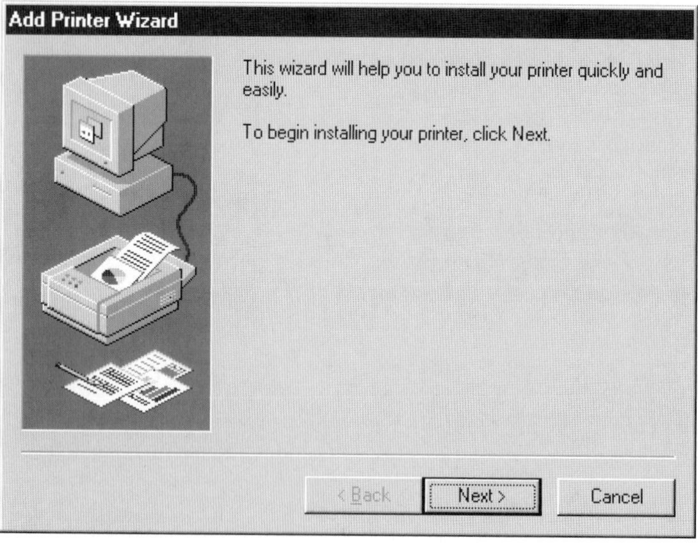

Figure 9-67: The Add Printer Wizard

- *Start/Settings/Printers*
- *My Computer/Printers*
- *Control Panel/Printers*

To install a network printer on the local computer, access the local Printers folder and double-click the Add Printer option. This action starts the Windows 9x Add Printer Wizard depicted in Figure 9-67. This wizard asks a number of questions about how the printer will be used. Since you are installing a remote, network printer, you will need to supply the complete path to the printer, or browse for the network to find its location.

You can also use the Network Neighborhood icon to browse the network until you locate the desired computer. Then double-click it so that its designated printer displays. A hand under the icon indicates a shared printer.

You can also install the desired remote printer by clicking and dragging its icon to the local Printers window and then dropping it anywhere inside the window.

The Add Printer Wizard performs three basic tasks in setting up the local unit to use the remote printer. First it establishes the printing path for DOS-based applications. Because these programs do not handle UNC-based paths, a logical **port name**, such as LPT2, must be established for them.

port name

If the Yes option is selected, Windows captures a local port for those applications to use. Clicking the Capture Printer Port button produces the **Capture Printer Port** dialog box depicted in Figure 9-68. This is a logical port designation and does not need to actually be installed in the system. As a matter of fact, any actual port in the local unit that has been assigned that handle will be disabled.

Capture Printer Port

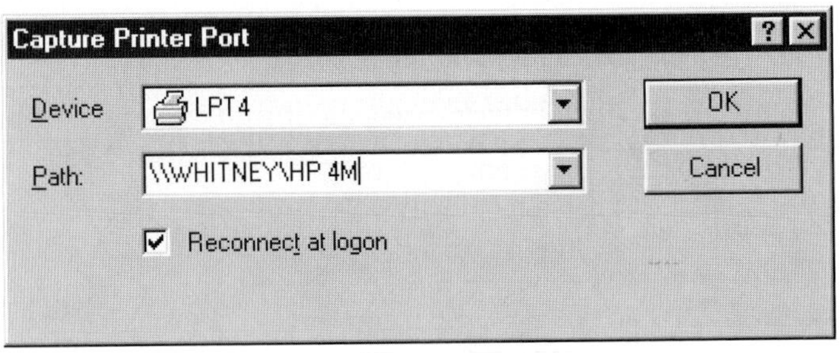

Figure 9-68: The Capture Printer Port Dialog Box

The next step in setting up the remote printer is to assign it a unique printer name. In a network environment, this name should have some relevance to what type of printer it is, or what relationship it has to the local unit.

The final step in setting up the printer is to configure its icon properties as if it were a local printer. Right-click the printer icon and select Properties. Enter all the information required to bring the printer to operation.

WIDE AREA NETWORKING WITH WINDOWS 9X

The Internet is the most famous example of wide area networking. The primary way to connect to the Internet with Windows 9x is through a **dial-up networking** connection (using a modem). The dial-up communications system in Windows 9x offers many improvements over previous operating systems. Under Windows 9x, applications can cooperatively share the dial-up connections through its **Telephony Application Programming Interface (TAPI)**. This interface provides a universal set of drivers for modems and COM ports to control and arbitrate telephony operations for data, faxes, and voice.

dial-up networking

Telephony Application Programming Interface (TAPI)

TEST TIP

Know what the Telephony Application Programming Interface (TAPI) is and what it does.

The Windows 9x Internet Connection

To establish dial-up Internet connection using the Windows 9x operating systems, follow the steps in the following Hands-On Activity:

Hands-On Activity

1. Configure the Windows 9x Dial-up Networking feature
2. Establish the Windows 9x modem configuration
3. Set up the ISP dial-up connection information
4. Establish the server address for the connection (if required by the ISP)
5. Set up the Internet Explorer (or other browser)
6. Connect to the Internet

The following sections discuss each of these steps in more detail.

Configuring the Dial-Up Networking Feature

To set up dial-up networking to connect to the Internet, turn on the computer, double-click the My Computer icon on the Desktop and click the Dial-Up Networking icon. You can also reach this icon through the Start button. Choose the Programs option from the Start menu, point at the Accessories entry, and click the Dial-Up Networking entry.

Welcome to Dial-Up Networking

Make New Connection

Internet Service Provider (ISP)

If this option has never been set up before, a Welcome to Dial-Up Networking message comes up. Press the Next button to advance into the **Make New Connection** screen, illustrated in Figure 9-69. At this point, enter the name of the **Internet Service Provider** (**ISP**) in the Type window.

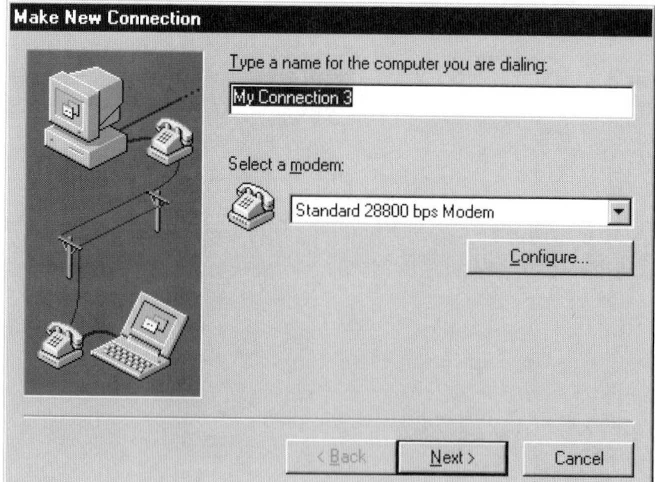

Figure 9-69: The Make New Connection Window

Establishing the Windows 9x Modem Configuration

Configure

Connection preferences

Click the **Configure** button and set the maximum speed value to its fastest available setting, to allow compression and smoother connection. Next, click the Connection tab to see the modem **Connection preferences** information, as illustrated in Figure 9-70.

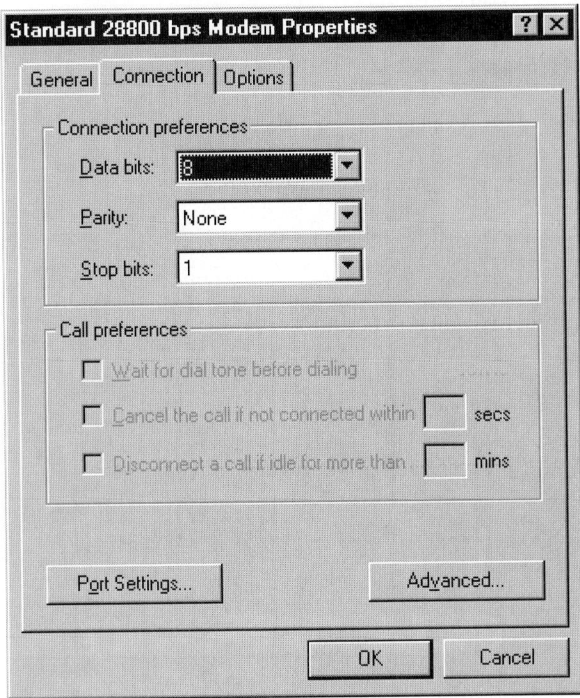

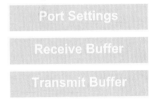

Figure 9-70: The Connection Preferences Window

Port Settings

Receive Buffer

Transmit Buffer

Click the **Port Settings** button and set the **Receive Buffer** speed setting to 75%. Also, set the **Transmit Buffer** speed setting to 100%. You must set the Receive buffer speed below the Transmit buffer speed, otherwise the modem will try to receive as fast as it sends and will end up filling the buffer, slowing the operation of the connection.

Click the OK button to return to the Connection Preference window. Select the Advanced button and add any extra settings desired for the installed modem. For example, an M0 setting should turn the volume on your modem off so that it is quiet when connecting to the Internet. Click the OK button to return to the Modem Preferences window.

Setting Up the ISP Dial-Up Connection Information

From the Modem Preferences window, click the OK button to move into the Make New Connection entry. Click the Next button to advance to the phone number entry page described in Figure 9-71.

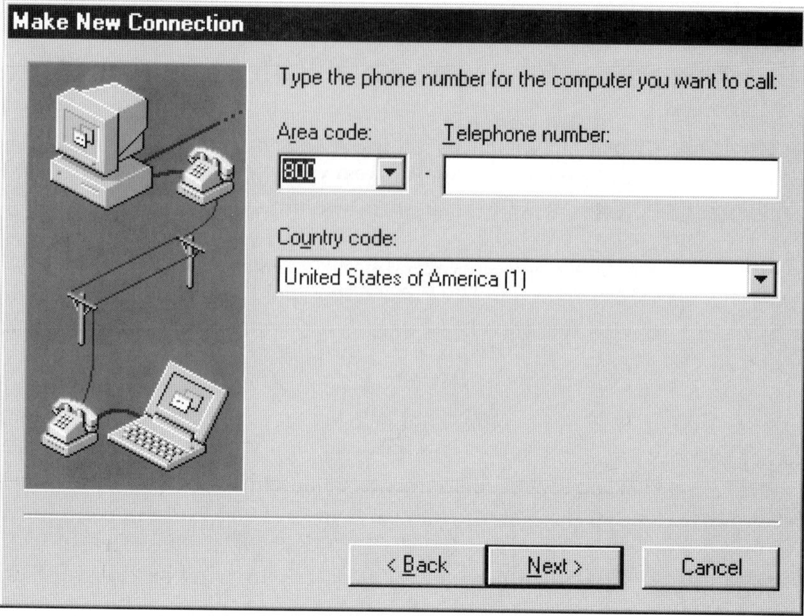

Figure 9-71: ISP Connection Window

Type in the dial-in phone number of your ISP—area code and local number. If a dialing prefix is required, such as 9, set this up as well. If the number is a long-distance number, Windows detects this during dialing and automatically enters the appropriate long-distance prefix (i.e., a 1 in the United States). Click the Next button to record the information and click Finish. Then an icon displays in the Dial-Up Networking window, similar to the one depicted in Figure 9-72.

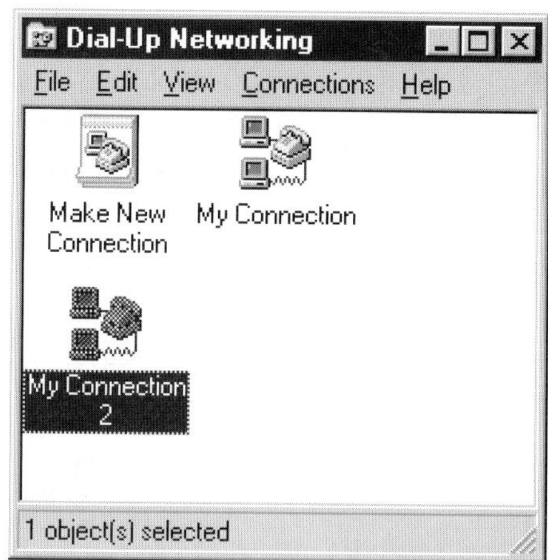

Figure 9-72: The Dial-Up Networking Window

> **NOTE**
>
> When using the dial-up networking functions outside the U.S. there are several configuration settings that must be changed. Most international telephone systems do not feature the same dial tone/ ring characteristics used in the U.S. If your modem fails to detect a dial tone in a foreign country, you will need to disable the modem's dial tone detection feature. This is accomplished by accessing the Connections tab under the *Control Panel/Modems* path and then clearing the check box beside the "Wait for dial tone before dialing" option. You may also need to increase the cancel call waiting period if connections take a relatively long time where you are calling from. This is accomplished by increasing the number of seconds in the "Cancel the Call If Not Connected" setting under the Connection tab.

Establishing the IP and Server Addresses

As described in Chapter 5—*Data Communications*, most ISPs use dynamic IP address assignments for their customers. The **Dynamic Host Configuration Protocol** (**DHCP**) service makes this possible by dynamically assigning IP addresses to the server's clients. This service is available in both Windows 9x and Windows NT/2000 and must be located on both the server and the client computers. In Windows 9x, the path to the TCP/IP Properties window is *Start/Settings/Control_Panel/Network/TCP/IP_Properties*. In Windows 2000, the path is *Start/Settings/Network_and_Dial-Up_Connections/desired_connection/Properties/TCP/IP_Properties*.

Dynamic Host Configuration Protocol (DHCP)

The ISP will also have one, or more, **name server** computers to route traffic onto and off of the Internet, and to reconcile IP addresses to domain names. These are the computers that users dial into to establish and conduct their Internet communications. Each name server has a DNS number/name, just as every other Internet computer does. Like IP addresses, the domain **server address** can be static, or dynamic. If the ISP has several servers, the ISP may allow traffic to be routed to the servers with the lightest workload instead of waiting for a particular server to become free.

name server

server address

With some ISPs, it may be necessary to manually enter server addresses and IP information that they supply. Some users require that their IP address not be changed. Therefore, they purchase an IP address from the ISP that is always assigned to them. Of course, this removes an assignable address from the ISP's bank of addresses, but the customer normally pays a great deal more for the constant address. In these situations, it may be necessary to enter the IP address information into the Internet connection's TCP/IP configuration.

Server Types

Dial-Up Server type

TCP/IP Settings

Likewise, some ISPs may assign static server addresses that must be entered manually, while others assign their server addresses dynamically and, therefore, do not require that this information be entered into the TCP/IP configuration.

In both cases, Windows 9x allows for the local unit to assign values to IP and server addresses, or for the server to assign those values after the connection has been made. In dial-up situations, the ISP typically determines which option is used.

In those situations in which the ISP requires a server and/or IP address to be supplied, just move into the Dial-Up Networking window and right-click the Internet Connection icon. Select the Properties option from the list and move into the **Server Types** page, depicted in Figure 9-73. From this page, verify the **Dial-Up Server type**—usually PPP for Windows 9x, Windows NT ,and Windows 2000—and click the **TCP/IP Settings** button. Set the TCP/IP settings as directed by the ISP's instructions. If a specific set of values are entered into this page, the ISP connects the system to the Internet through a specific server address.

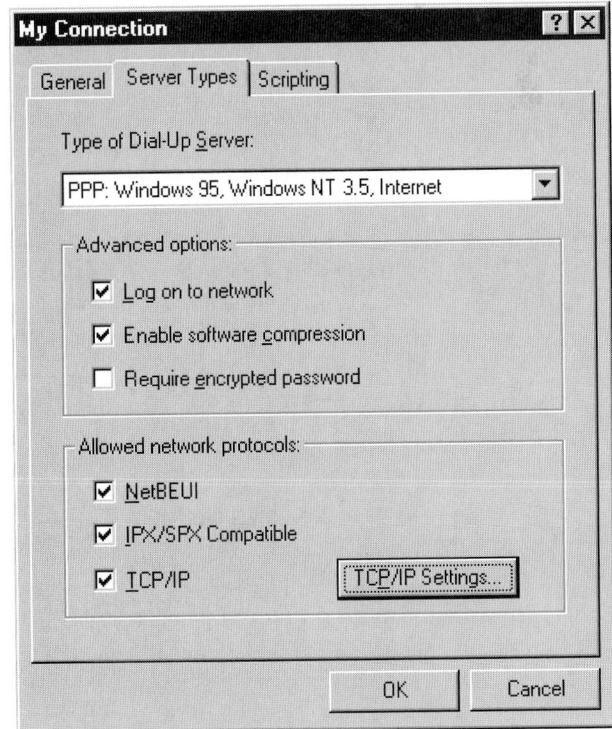

Figure 9-73: The Server Types Page

Specify name server addresses

Primary DNS

Secondary DNS

Click the **Specify name server addresses** radio button and enter the **Primary DNS** and **Secondary DNS** addresses provided to you by the ISP. The screen should be similar to the one depicted in Figure 9-74. Return to the Dial-Up Networking window.

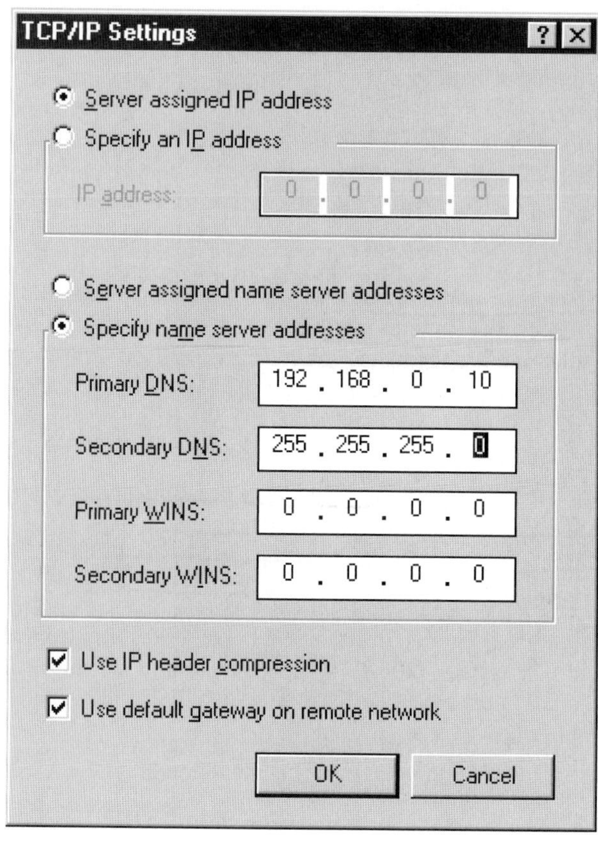

Figure 9-74: TCP/IP Settings Numbers

NOTE: The TCP/IP information (IP address and subnet mask) can also be accessed through the Control Panel/Network/desired TCP-IP Protocol/Properties/IP Address path.

Windows Internet Naming Service (WINS)

Although DNS is the naming service used by the Internet, it is not the only name-resolution service used with PCs. In the case of Windows LANs, the Microsoft preferred naming system is the **Windows Internet Naming Service (WINS)**. This service can be used to translate IP addresses to NetBIOS names within a Windows LAN environment. The LAN must include a Windows name server running the WINS server software that maintains the IP address/NetBIOS name database for the LAN.

TEST TIP

Know what DNS and WINS are, what they do, and how they are different.

WINS Configuration

Each client in the WINS LAN must contain the WINS client software and be WINS enabled. In Windows 9x, you can establish the WINS client service through the Control Panel's Network icon. On the Network page, select the TCP/IP LAN adapter from the list and click the Properties button. Select the **WINS Configuration** tab to obtain the page shown in Figure 9-75, and enable the WINS resolution function. Then, enter the IP address of the WINS server.

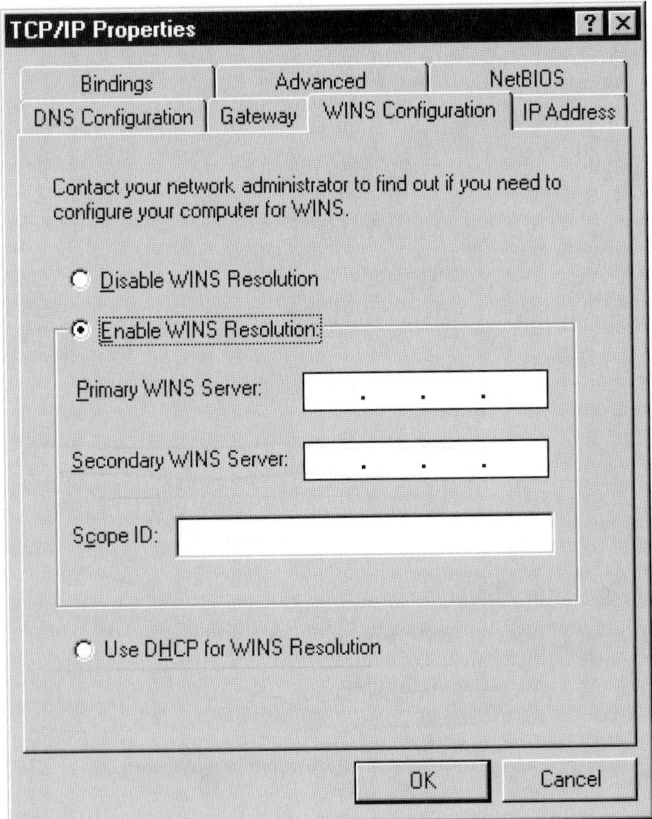

Figure 9-75: WINS Enabling

Setting Up the Internet Explorer Browser

As mentioned previously in this chapter, Internet browsers make the Internet much easier to navigate. Nearly every Internet connection is made through a browser of some type. Windows 9x includes a default browser called **Internet Explorer (IE)**. Unless a different browser is installed, Windows 9x places the IE icon on the desktop and automatically refers to this browser for Internet access.

Internet Explorer (IE)

In order to browse the Internet using the IE, it will be necessary to configure it for use. You can do so in three different ways:

- From the IE View menu select the Internet Options entry
- Right-click the desktop Internet icon and click the Properties tab
- Click the Internet icon under the *Start/Settings/Control_Panel* path

Internet Options

Internet Properties

Get Connected

Selecting one of these options leads to an **Internet Options** page or **Internet Properties** page. From either page, choose the Connection tab and click the Connect button to bring up the Windows Internet Connection Wizard and feature the **Get Connected** page. Pressing the Next button provides three possible options for setting up the Internet connection and the browser:

- I want to choose an Internet service provider and set up an Internet account. (MSN is the default).
- I want a new connection on this computer to my existing Internet account using my phone line or local area network (LAN).
- I already have an Internet connection set up on this computer and I do not want to change it.

If you choose the first option, the Internet Wizard asks for the first three digits of the local phone number and tries to dial the MSN Web page. It is suggesting that the Microsoft Network be selected using the Microsoft Internet Explorer.

Internet Connection Wizard

Unless the default is acceptable, select the "I want a new connection on this computer to my existing Internet account using my phone line or local area network (LAN)" statement. The **Internet Connection Wizard** window page, similar to the one in Figure 9-76, should appear.

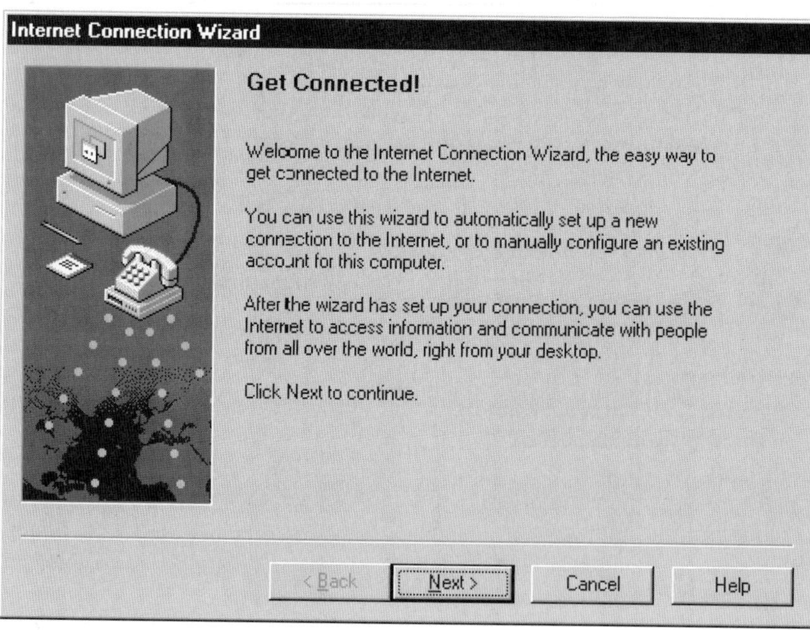

Figure 9-76: The Internet Connection Wizard

The first page of the wizard asks whether the connection will be made through a phone line or a local area network. Most home-use and small-business connections are of the dial-up modem type. Small, medium, and large businesses typically use LAN-based connections.

In a dial-up situation, click the **Connect Using My Phone Line** option and advance to the next page. The Dial-Up Connection page displays, as depicted in Figure 9-77.

Connect Using My Phone Line

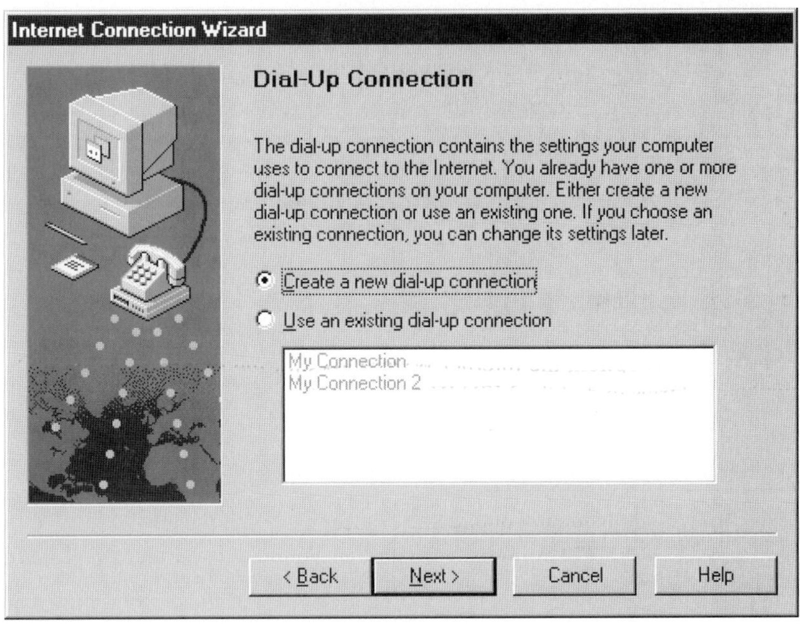

Figure 9-77: The Windows 9x Dial-Up Connection Screen

If the dial-up connection scheme has already been entered, a connection will already exist in the dialog box. Highlight the desired connection in the window, select the **Use an existing dial-up connection** option, and click the Next button to establish this connection for use.

Use an existing dial-up connection

If the desired connection is not present in the list, or if a new connection is being established, select the **Create a new dial-up connection** option and click Next. A guided setup sequence for the new connection displays.

Create a new dial-up connection

Choosing the **I already have a connection to the Internet**... option and clicking the Next button brings up the installed browser.

I already have a connection to the Internet

Installing Other Browsers

Although Windows 9x includes the Microsoft Internet Explorer, there are other browsers that the public may prefer to use. To use another browser in the system, it will be necessary to install it in the system. This is typically a function of the browser's Windows 95 Install Wizard.

If the install process detects an existing Dial-Up Networking configuration in Windows, it normally imports those values into its structure. If not, the Windows 9x Dial-Up Connection Wizard runs as a part of the third-party installation process. The User Manual for the browser normally provides exact instructions for installing its software in a Windows 9x system.

Connecting to the Internet

Connect

Double-click the icon of the new connection. Enter the username and password supplied by your ISP. Click the **Connect** option. You should hear the modem dialing at this point (unless the M0 parameter was specified in the Modem Properties - Extra Settings dialog windows to silence the modem's volume). A Connecting To window should appear on the screen, displaying the status of the modem. When it comes up, the Connected To window should minimize to the Taskbar. The system is now connected to the Internet.

Setting Up Internet Email

Outlook Express

Windows systems that run Microsoft Internet Explorer 4.0 or newer have a built-in email manager called **Outlook Express** the resides on the desktop task bar. To set up an email account, open Outlook Express and click on the drop down Tools menu. From the menu, choose the Account option, click the Add button, and select the Mail entry.

On successive screens you will need to enter:

- your display name (the name that will be displayed to those receiving emails from you)
- email address
- **Internet Mail Server** information (POP3 and SMTP server names) for incoming and outgoing mail
- the ISP-supplied Mail Account name and password

Internet Mail Server

At the end of the setup process you simply click the Finish button to complete the email setup.

All email managers require these pieces of information. If you are using a different email manager (i.e., Eudora, Netscape Mail, etc.) you will need to enter this information in the appropriate spaces provided by the particular manager.

Accessing the Internet Explorer

After the hardware has been installed and the Internet connection has been arranged, click the desktop Internet icon to access the Internet. In the **Connect To** window, click the Connect button. You should hear the modem communications sounds again. The Internet Explorer main screen displays, as depicted in Figure 9-78.

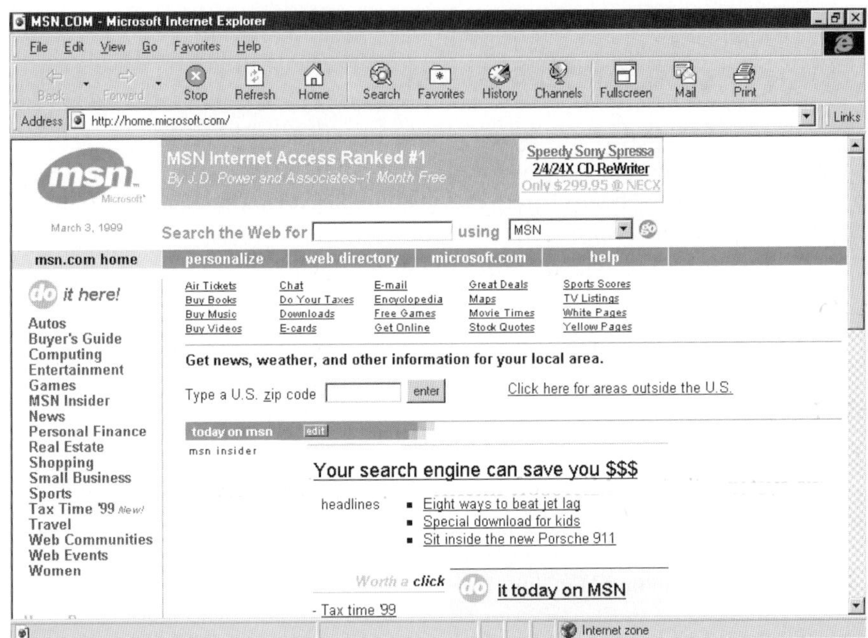

Figure 9-78: Internet Explorer Main Screen

CHAPTER SUMMARY

This chapter has presented an extensive discussion covering the Microsoft Windows 9x operating systems. The chapter started by discussing the installation and configuration of the Windows 9x operating systems and the steps required for bringing them to a basic operational level. After completing this material, you should be able to identify the basic Windows 9x boot/startup sequence and alternative ways to boot the system software.

As with other operating systems, there are normally three elements involved in bringing the system to a fully functional status. These include employing procedures for loading/adding device drivers and the necessary software for devices, changing options, configuring and using the Windows 9x printing subsystem, and installing and launching typical Windows and non-Windows applications in a Windows 9x system.

The second portion of the chapter covered the Windows 9x operating systems in terms of their function and structure, as well as methods of managing files and running applications. This section included procedures for navigating through the operating system from the Windows 9x desktop, as well as methods of accessing and retrieving information.

The next section of the chapter dealt with networking Windows 9x systems. This discussion began by describing topics associated with Local Area Networking with Windows 9x operating systems.

The final sections of the chapter covered the Internet, including its capabilities, as well as basic concepts related to Internet access. You should be able to identify concepts and capabilities relating to the Internet and describe basic procedures for setting up a system for Internet access with Windows 9x.

At this point, review the objectives listed at the beginning of the chapter to be certain that you understand and can perform each item listed there.

KEY POINTS REVIEW

This chapter has provided an extensive exploration of the Windows 9x operating systems. Review the following key points before moving into the Review and Exam Questions sections to make sure you are comfortable with each point. Afterward, answer the Review Questions that follow to verify your knowledge of the information.

- Windows 9x must be installed over an existing operating system, such as MS-DOS, or Windows 3.x. In particular, the Windows 9x installation program must find a recognizable MS-DOS FAT16 partition on the drive. This prevents it from being installed over some other type of operating system, such as Windows NT/2000, or Novell NetWare OS. The system must be at least an 80386DX or higher machine, operating with at least 4 MB of RAM (8 MB is recommended). The 80386DX is the listed minimum microprocessor for running Windows 9x, and the recommended processor is the 80486DX, but the Pentium processors are actually the preferred microprocessor for running Windows 9x. Likewise, 4 MB may be the minimum RAM option, with 8 MB being the recommended option, but 16 MB, 32 MB, or 64 MB are preferred for running Windows 9x.
- By establishing a dual-boot configuration, it is possible to install Windows 9x, or some other operating system, on an existing system and still retain the original operating system.
- The My Computer icon is the major user interface for Windows 9x. It enables the user to see the local system's contents and manage its files.
- The Network Neighborhood icon provides quick information about the world around the system when it's used in a networked environment.
- One of the main Control Panel icons is the System icon. Clicking this icon produces the System Properties window. This window features tabs for General information, the Device Manager, Hardware Profiles, and system Performance.
- The Device Manager utility provides a graphical representation of the devices configured in the system. This interface can be used to identify installed ports, update device drivers, and change I/O settings. It can also be used to manually isolate hardware and configuration conflicts. The problem device can be examined to see where the conflict is occurring.
- The Windows 9x file system does away with the 8+3 character filename system implemented under DOS. In Windows 9x, long filenames of up to 255 characters can be used, so that they can be more descriptive in nature. When these filenames are displayed in non-Windows 9x systems, they are truncated (shortened) to fit the 8.3 DOS character format and identified by a tilde character (~) followed by a single-digit number.
- The File management functions in Windows 9x and NT/2000 are performed through the Windows Explorer interface. This manager is located under the *Start\Programs* path from the desktop.
- In Windows 9x, the system's configuration information is held in an area known as the Registry. This includes the local hardware configuration, the network environment, file associations, and user configurations. Many of Windows 3.1's SYSTEM.INI, CONTROL.INI, PROGRAM.INI, and WIN.INI management functions have been relocated to the Registry.

- The contents of the Registry are located in two files located in the Windows directory. These are the USER.DAT and SYSTEM.DAT files. The USER.DAT file contains user-specific information, while the SYSTEM.DAT file holds hardware- and computer-specific profiles and setting information.

- The Configuration Manager oversees the complete Plug-and-Play configuration process for Windows 9x. Its primary purpose is to ensure that each device in the system can access an interrupt request channel without conflict and that it has a unique I/O Port address.

- Microsoft refers to this portion of the system as the Protected Mode FAT File System. It is also called the Virtual File Allocation Table or VFAT. As its full name implies, the VFAT provides a Protected mode method of interacting with the file system on the disk drive. VFAT operates in 32-bit mode; however, the actual FAT structure of the disk remains as 12-bit or 16-bit allocations.

- The Plug-and-Play-compliant design of Windows 9x makes installing most new hardware nearly automatic (as long as the new device is also PnP compatible). The PnP function will automatically detect new PnP-compliant hardware when it is started. If the device is not PnP compliant, or the system just can't detect it for some reason, it will be necessary to use the Windows 9x Add New Hardware Wizard.

- Windows 9x is designed to assist the user in setting up any new hardware components that may be added to the system. The Add New Hardware icon can be found under the Control Panel option of the Settings menu.

- Like the Hardware Wizard, Windows 9x offers the user assistance in installing new programs. The Add/Remove New Programs icon under the Control Panel is used to install new programs automatically.

- DOS-based applications are installed in Windows 9x by simply running their executable file from the Run dialog box, or from the Windows 95 Explorer. If the file has never been run under Windows 9x, the operating system creates a default entry in its APPS.INF file for that program. A copy of the new entry is also used to create a .PIF file for the application.

- In later versions of DOS, Microsoft added the SHARE.EXE command to provide file sharing and locking capabilities for files on a local hard disk drive. These capabilities enabled multiple users to access the same file at the same time in a networked or multitasking environment. The Share command should be loaded in the CONFIG.SYS file using an Install= statement (i.e., Install=Share /f:4096 /l:25).

- In Windows 9x, the peer-to-peer local area networking function is an integral part of the system. The heart of the Windows 9x networking system is contained in the desktop's Network Neighborhood icon and the Control Panel's Network icon.

- It is possible for the local system to assign a logical drive letter to the remote unit, or folder. This is referred to as mapping the drive letter to the resource. This will enable non-Windows 9x applications running on the local computer to use the resource across the network.

- After the network adapter card has been configured and installed, the next step in setting up the computer on the network is to load its drivers, protocols, and services. In most Windows 95 installations, the majority of these steps are accomplished simply by rebooting the computer and allowing Windows to detect the network adapter.

REVIEW QUESTIONS

The following questions test your knowledge of the material presented in this chapter.

1. Describe the steps required to change a file's attributes in Windows 9x Explorer?
2. What action must be taken to see hidden files in Windows 9x?
3. Why are drives mapped in Windows 9x?
4. What type of File Allocation Table must be located on the partition that Windows 9x will be installed in?
5. If a DOS application is running in Windows 9x but it is taking up the entire screen, and you wish to switch to another application, what action should be taken?
6. What action should be taken if an older application covers the tool bar and the Start Menu button in a Windows 9x system?
7. In Windows 9x, a filename can be up to _____ characters long.
8. Which command allows the simultaneous editing of the SYSTEM.INI, WIN.INI, AUTOEXEC.BAT, CONFIG.SYS, and PROTOCOL.INI?
9. Which Control Panel is used to check protocols installed in the system?
10. If a properly mapped drive disappears when the system is rebooted, what could be wrong?
11. If a user cannot connect to a remote system over the network in Windows 9x, what might be the problem?
12. When Windows 95 boots up successfully, the Registry files are backed up with the ______ extension.
13. Describe the procedure used to view information about the network's connections using the Network Neighborhood icon.
14. What is the minimum microprocessor type that can be used to run Windows 98?
15. Which disk utility does Windows 98 run on the system during the installation process? What items does it check?

EXAM QUESTIONS

1. What is the purpose of NetBEUI?
   a. Novell LAN protocol
   b. Windows Internet protocol
   c. Novell Internet protocol
   d. Windows LAN protocol
2. What is IPX/SPX and what is its function?
   a. Novell LAN protocol
   b. Windows Internet protocol
   c. Novell Internet protocol
   d. Windows LAN protocol
3. Which of the following recognize, configure, and allocate system resources in Windows 9x?
   a. The Registry
   b. Plug-and-Play
   c. The Windows Explorer
   d. The Control Panel
4. Which of the following best describes the boot sequence for Windows 9x?
   a. IO.SYS, MSDOS.SYS, COMMAND.COM, WIN.COM, SYSTEM.DAT, USER.DAT
   b. IO.SYS, SYSTEM.DAT, USER.DAT, MSDOS.SYS, COMMAND.COM, CONFIG.SYS, AUTOEXEC.BAT
   c. IO.SYS, MSDOS.SYS, COMMAND.COM, SYSTEM.DAT, USER.DAT, CONFIG.SYS, WIN.COM
   d. IO.SYS, MSDOS.SYS, COMMAND.COM, WIN.COM
5. Which of the following is a legitimate Windows 9x installation file type?
   a. XXXX.DLL
   b. XXXX.BAT
   c. XXXX.EXE
   d. XXXX.CAB
6. To sort out a Windows 9x Startup problem that occurs during the detection phase of the bootup, use _________.
   a. the F5 key
   b. the F8 key
   c. the F3 key
   d. the F4 key
7. If you save the file MYDOCUMENT.TXT in Windows 9x, how will it look in a DOS directory?
   a. MYDOCUME.NTT
   b. MYDOCU~T.TXT
   c. MYDOCU~1.TXT
   d. MYDOCUME.~XT

8. A customer complains that Windows 9x will not detect hardware in the system that it has been installed on. Possible causes for this include:
   a. The hardware detection mechanism is disabled in CMOS.
   b. The BIOS is not PnP-compatible.
   c. The detection drivers have not been loaded for the hardware.
   d. Windows 9x does not support automatic hardware detection.

9. In Windows 9x, the ______ networking component provides the rules that the computer will use to govern the exchange of information across the network.
   a. Client
   b. Adapter
   c. Protocol
   d. Service

10. Which of the following is a format for providing a common telephony control system for Windows 9x communications products?
    a. ATAPI
    b. SCSI
    c. TAPI
    d. WINS

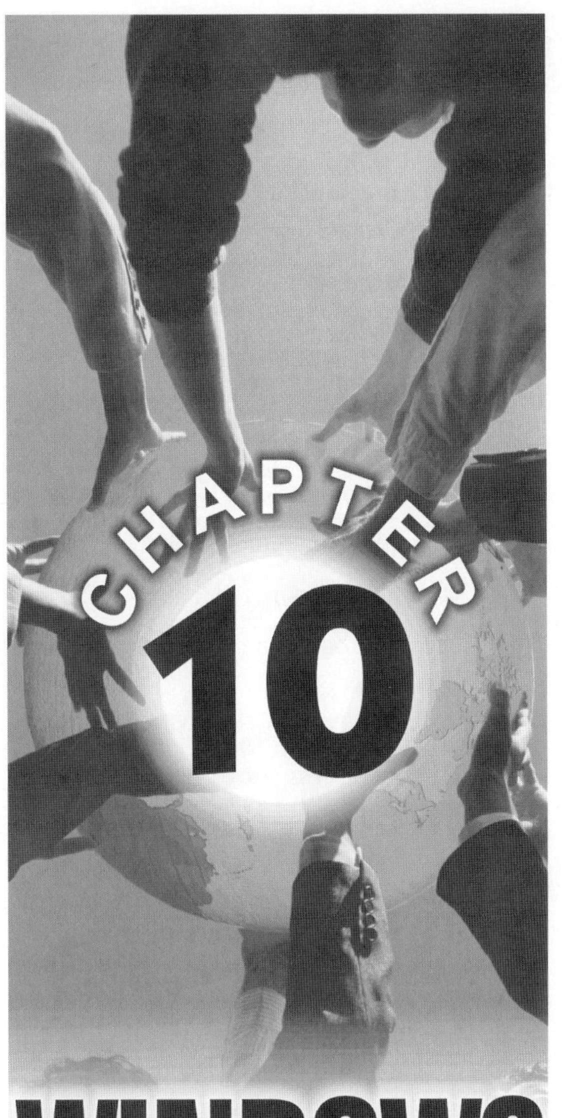

WINDOWS NT/2000

OBJECTIVES

OBJECTIVES

This chapter focuses on the Windows NT and Windows 2000 operating systems. After completing this chapter and its associated lab procedures, you will be able to:

1. Install Windows NT 4.0 and Windows 2000 to new systems.
2. Upgrade systems from Windows 9x or Windows NT 4.0 to Windows 2000.
3. Describe the bootup sequence employed by Windows NT/2000.
4. Navigate through the Windows NT/2000 system, including the Internet Explorer.
5. Explain the structure of Windows NT/2000.
6. List the core files in the Windows NT and Windows 2000 structures.
7. Identify the components of the Windows NT/2000 Registry structure.
8. Install and access printers in Windows NT 4.0 and 2000.
9. Install and access software applications in Windows NT and 2000.
10. Install and configure hardware devices and drivers in Windows NT and 2000.
11. Install and configure Local Area Networking functions in Windows NT and 2000.
12. Install and configure Wide Area Networking and Internet functions in Windows NT 4.0 and 2000.

CHAPTER 10

WINDOWS NT/2000

INTRODUCTION

While Microsoft developed and improved the Windows 3.x and Windows 9x products for desktop use by the general population, it also developed a more robust and complicated operating system for corporate client/server networking installations. This new windowed operating system was introduced as **Windows New Technology**, or **Windows NT**.

Windows New Technology

Windows NT

From the beginning, the Windows NT design departed from the mainstream Windows development path.

> It was built around a new operating system kernel that focused on enhanced reliability, scalability, and security elements required for corporate applications, while retaining the strengths of the Windows operating system.

Instead of being designed to operate on a single type of computer, the Windows NT operating system was designed to be portable between systems using different microprocessor architectures. By exchanging a single component, the Windows NT kernel can be used to exploit advances in PC hardware including 32-bit microprocessors, **Reduced Instruction Set Computer (RISC) architectures**, and multiprocessor (parallel processing) systems, as well as high-capacity RAM and disk storage for the purposes of creating advanced line-of-business platforms.

Reduced Instruction Set Computer (RISC) architectures

The Windows NT operating system actually exists as three distinct products:

- A Workstation operating system
- A Server operating system
- An Extended Server operating system to manage large enterprise networks

While all three Windows NT product types are referenced in this chapter, the scope of the A+ examination deals with the Workstation versions of the software. Therefore, the discussions in this chapter will primarily be aimed at these portions of the Windows NT platform. When aspects of the Server side of the package must be mentioned, this will be pointed out.

Although there have been several versions of the Windows NT operating system, the A+ examination has limited its involvement to the two most recent versions. These are **Windows NT 4.0** and the newest version of NT, called **Windows 2000.** Throughout most of this chapter, these two versions will be referenced as a single topic. Differences between the two versions will be pointed out as necessary.

Windows NT 4.0

Windows 2000

WINDOWS NT

NT Workstation

NT Server

Windows 2000 Professional

In the spring of 1992, Microsoft introduced the Windows NT operating system, designed for corporate business networking environments. Unlike the mainstream Windows 3.x and 9x packages that include a peer-to-peer networking function, Windows NT was designed from the beginning to perform in a client/server networking environment. Consequently, the Windows NT package was originally developed in two parts — the **NT Workstation** and the **NT Server** operating systems. The server software has simply been known as NT Server. With the advent of Windows 2000, Microsoft changed the name of the workstation software to **Windows 2000 Professional**.

clients

server

domain

Recall that a client/server network is one in which standalone computers, called **clients**, are connected to, and administered by, a master computer called a **server**. Collectively, the members of the group make up a body called a **domain**. Figure 10-1 depicts a typical Domain-based Network arrangement. The members of the domain share a common directory database and are organized in levels. Every domain is identified by a unique name and is administered as a single unit having common rules and procedures.

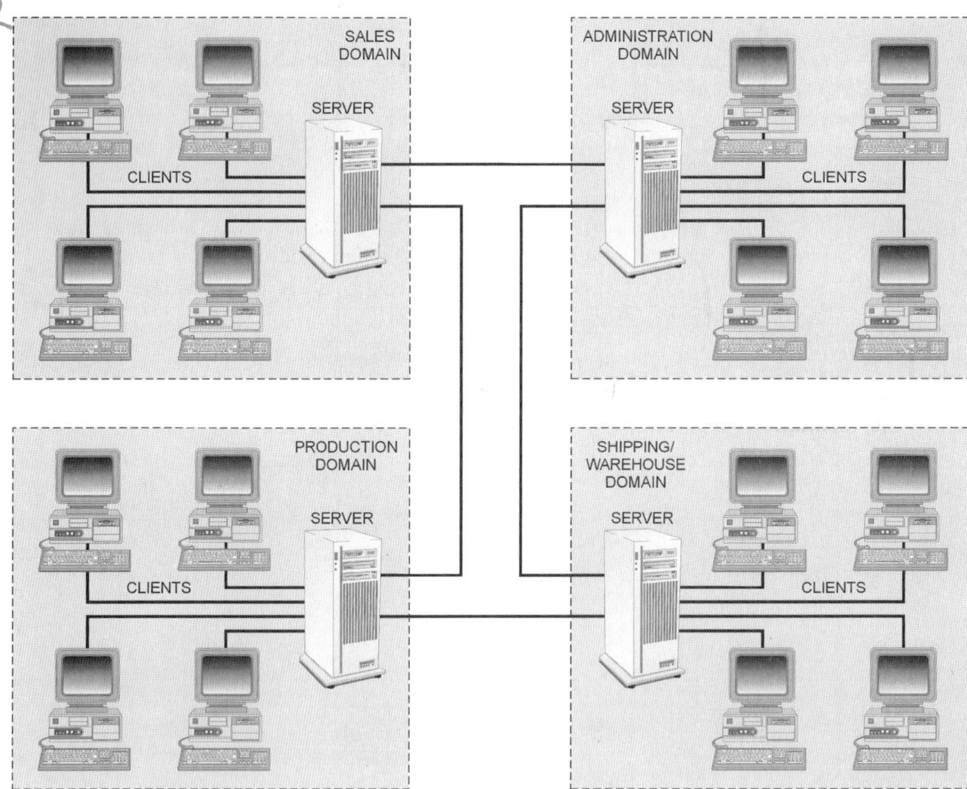

Figure 10-1: A (Client/Server or Domain-based) Network

Although earlier Windows operating systems attempted to retain compatibility with the original MS-DOS platform, Windows NT made no such attempts. Instead, Windows NT offers a fairly specific set of software and hardware requirements that must be met for proper operation. Fortunately, more Windows NT compatible hardware and software systems have become available over time. With Windows 2000, Microsoft opened an even wider range of compatible hardware and software options for the Windows NT platform. Even so, Windows 2000 still does not support nearly as many hardware and software options as Windows 95/98.

Windows NT Workstation

The Windows NT Workstation operating system can be employed as a client workstation in a client/server network, or it can be used as an operating system for a standalone computer that's not connected to anything. However, Windows NT was designed to work in a strong network environment. As such, many of the features that make Windows 9x packages easier to use are not located in Windows NT workstation.

Windows NT 4.0 Workstation supports advanced multitasking and multiprocessor operations. It can maintain different hardware profiles for multiple configurations within the same system. The Windows NT memory management system does a much better job of protecting applications from violating each other's space than the Windows 9x products do. Finally, Windows NT workstation provides a much higher level of file, folder, and resource security than the 9x versions do. Windows NT can control access to these resources through passwords and logins on the desktop, or through a the central network controller called a server in a client/server relationship.

Windows NT Server

The Windows NT 4.0 Server package provides the same features and functions found in the Windows NT Workstation. However, the Server package also provides the tools necessary to administer and control a network from its central location.

domain controller

Recall that in a peer-to-peer workgroup setting, all of the nodes may act as servers for some processes and clients for others. In a domain-based network, the network is controlled from a centralized server (**domain controller**). In a Windows NT network, this concept is embodied by the location where the Administration and Security databases are kept. In the workgroup, each machine maintains its own security and administration databases. In a domain environment, the server is responsible for keeping the centralized user account and security databases.

With some network operating systems, servers cannot function as active workstations in the network. With the Windows NT operating system, however, both the Workstation and Server versions can be used as nodes in peer-to-peer (workgroup) networks, and as workstations in domain-based, client/server networks. While Windows NT server can operate as a workstation, doing so would be a very expensive waste of its abilities. There are actually three types of workstation operating systems supported in a Windows NT domain. These include Windows 9x, Windows NT Workstation, and Windows NT Server — set up for standalone use. However, servers are not normally used as workstations, so that network operations are not slowed down or interrupted by local tasks.

Primary Domain Controllers (PDC)

Backup Domain Controllers (BDC)

User Accounts

Group Accounts

Computer Accounts

Security Accounts Manager (SAM)

Authentication

In the Windows NT Client/Server environment, two types of domain controllers exist — **Primary Domain Controllers (PDC)** and **Backup Domain Controllers (BDC)**. The PDC contains the directory database for the network. This database contains information about **User Accounts**, **Group Accounts**, and **Computer Accounts**. You may also find this database referred to as the **Security Accounts Manager (SAM)**. BDCs are servers within the network that are used to hold read-only backup copies of the directory database. As illustrated in Figure 10-2, a network may contain one or more BDCs. These servers are used to authenticate user logons. **Authentication** is the process of identifying an individual as who they claim to be. This process is normally based on user names and passwords.

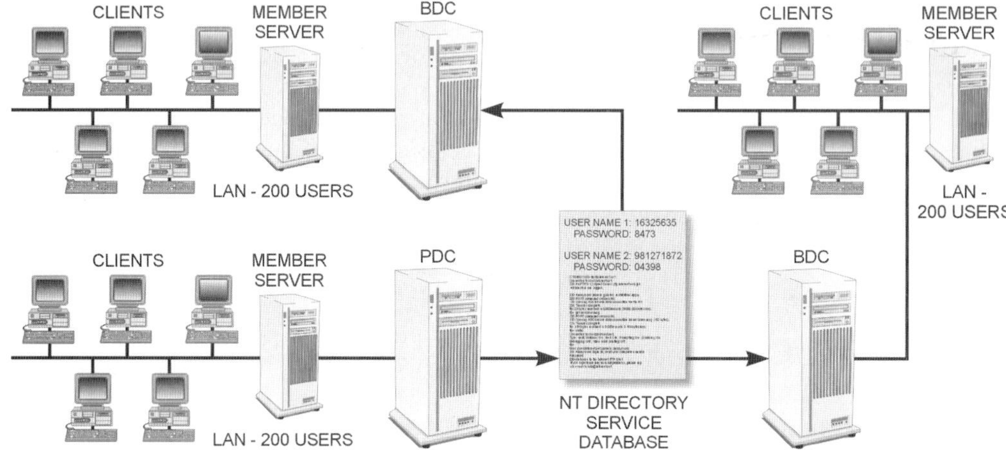

Figure 10-2: A PDC/BDC Arrangement in a Network

Enterprise Server

Enterprise networks

As mentioned in the introduction, Windows NT 4.0 is sold in two different versions, a Standard NT Server version and an extended **Enterprise Server** package.

Enterprise networks are those networks designed to facilitate business-to-business, or business-to-customer operations. Because monetary transactions and customers' personal information travel across the network in these environments, enterprise networks feature facilities for additional, highly protective security functions.

trusted domains

An enterprise network consists of multiple domains (called **trusted domains**) where the domains are linked together, but managed independently.

Intranets

intranets

Most enterprise networks are actually **intranets**.

An intranet is a network built on the TCP/IP protocol that belongs to a single organization. It is in essence a private Internet. Like the Internet, intranets are designed to share information and are accessible only to the organization's members, with authorization.

A **firewall** blocks unauthorized outside users from accessing the intranet site. A relatively new term, extranet, is being used to describe intranets that grant limited access to authorized outside users such as corporate business partners.

firewall

Microsoft continues to improve its Windows NT packages with intentions of being a major force in the Internet/Corporate Intranet markets that are currently dominated by the **UNIX** and **Novell NetWare** operating systems. This is the major reason for the extended Enterprise Server version of the Windows NT package.

UNIX

Novell NetWare

WINDOWS 2000

Windows 2000 is the successor of the Windows NT 4.0 operating system. As a matter of fact, it was originally titled Windows NT 5. This operating system brings together the stability and security of Windows NT 4.0 and the Plug-and-Play capabilities of Windows 9x.

Windows 2000 also includes built-in support for many new technologies including DVD drives, USB devices, Accelerated Graphics Ports, multifunction adapter cards, and a full line of PC Cards. Finally, Windows 2000 provides a new, distributed directory service for managing resources across an enterprise, FAT 32 support, and the Internet Explorer 5 web browser.

Like previous NT versions, Windows 2000 comes in two basic variations: the corporate workstation version, titled Windows 2000 Professional, and the network server version, called Windows 2000 Server. The server product is also available in two extended enterprise versions — **Windows 2000 Advanced Server** and **Windows 2000 Datacenter Server**.

Windows 2000 Advanced Server

Windows 2000 Datacenter Server

Windows 2000 Professional

The workstation side of Windows 2000 has been named **Windows 2000 Professional**. This operating system is designed to be the reliable, powerful desktop for the corporate computing world. It has been designed to be easier to set up and configure than previous Windows NT platforms. Windows 2000 Professional employs several wizards, such as the New Hardware wizard and the Network Connection wizard, to make installation and configuration processes easier for users.

Windows 2000 Professional

Windows 2000 Professional extends and improves the Windows 95/98 user interface. It also brings Plug-and-Play to the NT workstation. The hardware supported by Windows 2000 Professional has been upgraded to include those items commonly found in newer systems.

While it offers many improvements over previous Windows NT versions, Windows 2000 Professional may still be too complex for general consumer usage. For this reason, Microsoft has decided to continue with at least one additional upgrade version of the Windows 9x product for the general consumer market with its release of Windows ME.

Windows 2000 Server

Windows 2000 Server

On the server side, Windows 2000 offers a more scalable and flexible server platform than its Windows NT predecessors. **Windows 2000 Server** actually comes in three versions that correspond to the size and complexity of the network environment they are used in. These versions include the standard Server edition, the Advanced Server edition, and the Windows 2000 Datacenter Server edition.

The Standard Server edition offers a more scalable and flexible file server platform. It also functions as an application server that handles large data sets. It can be used to implement a standards-based, secured Internet/intranet* server.

Symmetrical Microprocessing (SMP)

The standard Windows 2000 Server package can manage up to 4 GB of RAM and is capable of distributing work between two microprocessors at a time. This type of operation is referred to as **Symmetrical Microprocessing** (**SMP**). If Windows 2000 Server has been installed as an upgrade to an existing Windows NT 4.0 Server, it can support up to four different microprocessors simultaneously.

NOTE

Recall that an intranet is simply a private, web-based network, typically established by an organization for the purpose of running an exclusive web site not open to the public (i.e., company web sites for internal company use only). Intranets can be based on local or wide area networks, or constructed as combinations of the two.

The Advanced Server edition can support up to 8 symmetrical processors and up to 8 GB of memory. These features enable it to function well in medium size networks running between 100 and 500 concurrent users.

In other respects, the Advanced Server product is the same as the standard Server version. However, some enterprise versions of applications will run only on the Enterprise version of the operating system.

The Windows 2000 Datacenter Server edition can handle up to 64 GB of RAM and 32 processors. This will enable it to support up to 1000 simultaneous users with heavy processing demands.

Network Load Balancing (NLB)

Microsoft Cluster Server (MSCS)

Both the Advanced and Datacenter Server editions employ a pair of high-availability features that allow them to effectively handle the traffic levels found on medium and large web sites. These features are **Network Load Balancing** (**NLB**) and **Microsoft Cluster Server** (**MSCS**). The load balancing feature enables the operating system to distribute IP requests to the most available web server in a cluster of up to 32 web servers.

With the Cluster Service feature, when one server in a cluster is taken down (crashes or goes off line), another server takes over its processing duties. This is referred to as fail-over and is described in Figure 10-3. In the Advanced version, the **fail-over** function is performed by one other processor, while the Datacenter version supports four-server fail-over clusters. This feature also allows servers in the system to be swapped out without interrupting service on the network.

fail-over

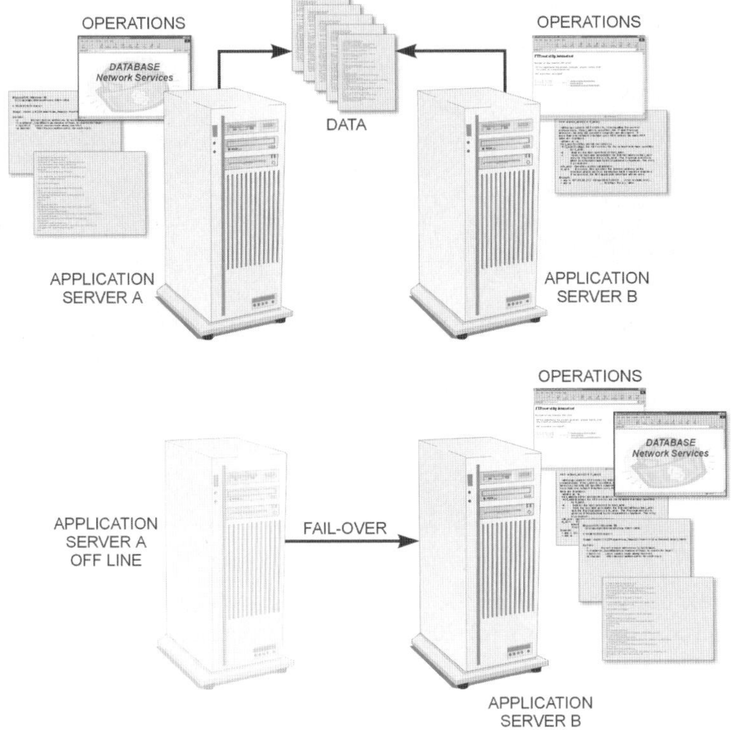

Figure 10-3: Fail-Over Operations

NAVIGATING WINDOWS NT/2000

Many of the Windows NT/2000 structures and navigation methods should appear very familiar after reading the Windows 9x material in Chapter 9—*Windows 9x*. With Windows NT Version 4.0, Microsoft introduced a Windows 9x-like user interface to the Windows NT operating system. This includes the desktop with its icons, the pop-up Start menu, and the Taskbar.

Windows NT/2000 Desktops

The Windows NT/2000 desktop includes most of the same features found in their Windows 9x counterpart. The standard desktop icons are the same as those mentioned for Windows 9x (i.e., My Computer, My Network Places, Inbox, and the Recycle Bin). If the operating system is installed on a stand-alone unit that does not have a network card installed, the Network Neighborhood icon will not be presented on the desktop. The functions of these icons are identical to those described for the Windows 9x versions.

Figure 10-4 depicts the Windows 2000 desktop with the Start Menu expanded. Notice that the standard desktop icons for Windows 2000 include My Computer, My Network Places and the Recycle Bin).

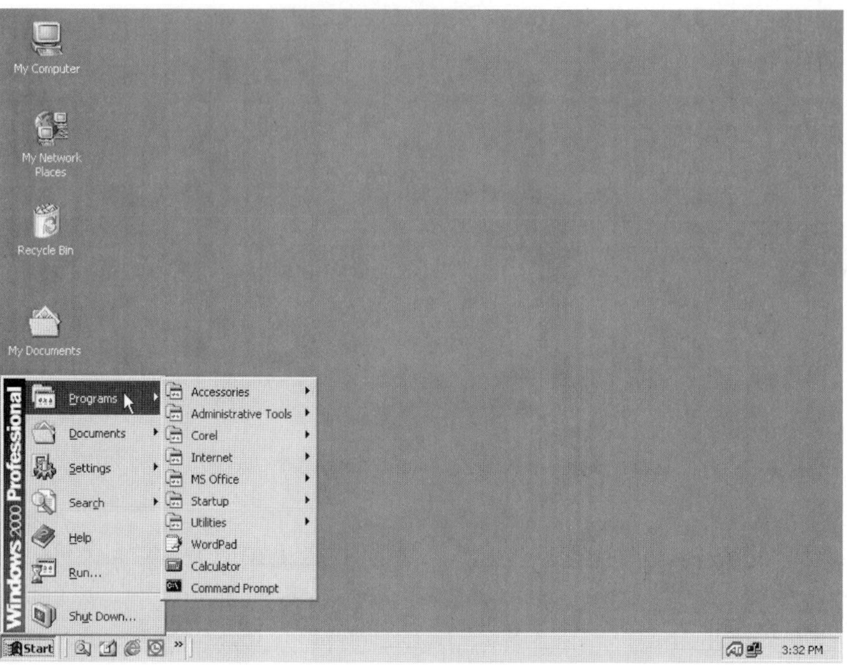

Figure 10-4: Windows 2000 Desktop

Windows 2000 operations typically begin from the Start menu that pops up when the Start button is clicked. The Windows NT/2000 Start menu contains Programs, Documents, Settings, Find, Help, Run, and Shut Down options. Selecting one of these options from the menu will cause a pop-up submenu or dialog box to be displayed. As with the desktop icons, the operations of the Windows NT/2000 Start menu options are identical to the descriptions of their Windows 9x counterparts.

Windows 2000 Taskbar

The **Windows 2000 Taskbar** is located at the bottom of the display by default. The Taskbar displays icons that represent programs running in the system. Even though the Taskbar is normally located at the bottom of the screen, it can be moved to either side of the screen, or to the top of the display. When moved to the top of the screen, the Start menu will drop down from above instead of pop up from the bottom.

Windows 2000 features an intelligent, personalized Programs menu. It monitors the user's program usage, and after the first six accesses, arranges the menu options according to those most frequently used. The menu options displayed change based on their usage. Less frequently used programs are not displayed in the list, but can be accessed by clicking on the double arrow at the bottom of the list. The hidden portion of the list will appear after a short delay. When this occurs, the six most frequently used applications are highlighted. This reduces screen clutter and makes it easier for users to access their most used items.

Start menu items can easily be renamed in Windows 2000. This is accomplished by right-clicking on the menu item and choosing the Rename option from the context-sensitive pop-up menu. Then, the user types the new name in the text entry box. This is all accomplished without opening the Start menu.

The contents of the Windows 2000 Control Panel can be cascaded as a submenu of the Start button for quick access. The My Documents menu can also be cascaded off the Start menu for fast access to documents.

The My Documents concept has been expanded to include a My Pictures folder that acts as the default location to hold graphic files. The Windows 2000 dialog boxes include an image preview function that allows the user to locate graphic files efficiently. The dialog box View menu option enables the user to toggle between Large and Small Icons, Details, and Thumbnail views. The dialog boxes can be resized to accommodate as many Thumbnail images as desired.

The **My Network Places** folder replaces the Network Neighborhood folder employed in previous Windows NT and 9x versions. This utility enables the user to create shortcut icons to network shares on the desktop.

My Network Places

A **network share** is an existing shared resource (i.e., printer, drive, modem, or folder) located on a remote system.

network share

The new icon acts as an **alias** to link the system to the share point on the remote unit.

alias

Locating, Accessing, and Retrieving Information in Windows 2000

Locating, accessing and retrieving information in Windows NT is virtually the same as with the Windows 9x operating systems.

The major Windows 2000 user interfaces are:

- My Computer
- Start menu
- Windows Explorer
- Internet Explorer
- My Network Places
- Windows 2000 dialog boxes (windows)

These interfaces provide user access to all of the major areas of the system. The My Computer window enables users to access every hardware device in the system. The Start menu provides the user with access to the system regardless of what else is occurring in the system. In doing so, it provides access to the system's installed applications, a search engine for finding data in the system, and the operating system's Help file structure. The Windows 2000 Windows Explorer graphically displays the entire computer system in a hierarchical tree structure. This enables the user to manipulate all of the system's software and hardware. Similarly, the Network Neighborhood window extends the Windows Explorer structure to include network and domain structures. The Internet Explorer supplies the system with a tightly linked Web connection.

From Windows NT 4.0 forward, the Windows NT operating system has been able to handle long filenames. Filenames in Windows 2000 can be up to 256 characters long. Windows NT uses a proprietary method for reducing long filenames to MS-DOS-compatible 8.3 filenames.

Instead of simply truncating the filename, inserting a tilde, and then assigning a number to the end of the filename, Windows NT performs a mathematical operation on the long name to generate a truly unique MS-DOS compatible filename.

Basically, the Windows NT algorithm employed to produce DOS-compatible filenames removes any characters that are illegal under DOS, removes any extra periods from the filename, truncates the filename to six characters, inserts a tilde, and adds an ID number to the end of the name.

However, when five or more names are generated that would result in duplicate short names, Windows NT changes its truncation method. Beginning with the sixth filename, the first two characters of the name are retained, the next four characters are generated through the mathematical algorithm, and, finally, a tilde with an ID number is attached to the end of the name.

Windows NT file system (NTFS)

This method is used to create DOS-compliant short filenames for MS-DOS, Windows 3.x, and Windows 9x-compliant FAT systems, as well as the proprietary **Windows NT file system (NTFS)**.

Alternate-clicking, (right-clicking) is also employed in the Windows NT platform to access context-sensitive options through pop-up menus on the screen. Alternate-clicking on an item produces a pop-up menu, similar to the one depicted in Figure 10-5. As with Windows 9x operating systems, these Windows 2000 menus enable the user to Copy a File, Create a Shortcut, Close a Folder, or examine properties of the system's installed devices. Right-click menus may also contain additional items that have been inserted by applications that they serve.

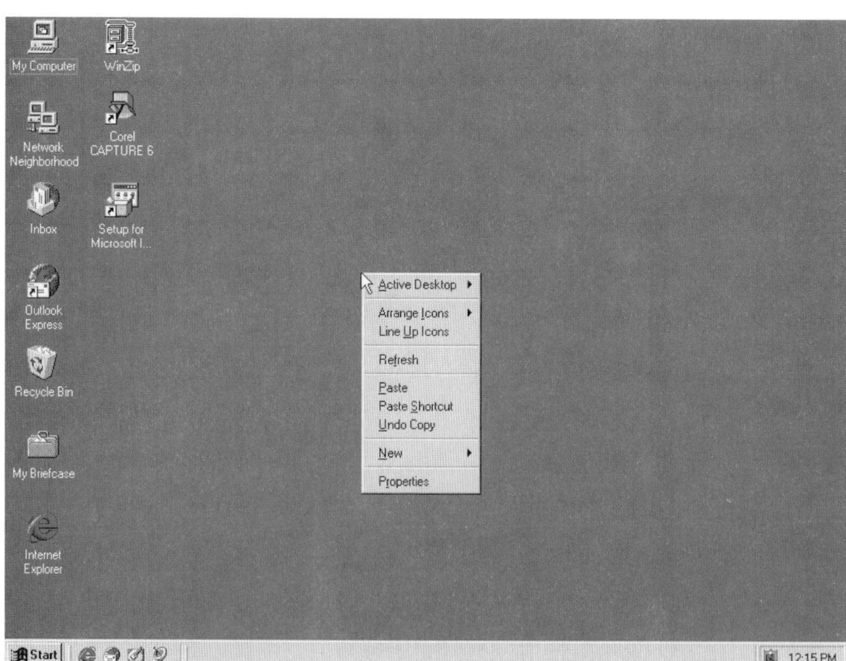

Figure 10-5: Windows NT Right-Click Menus

Alternate-clicking over an open area of the desktop produces a pop-up menu that enables the user to arrange icons on the desktop, create new folders and shortcuts, and see the properties of the system's video display.

Windows 2000 offers extended common dialog boxes for File/Open, File/Print, and File/Save options. These dialog boxes provide easy organization and navigation of the system's hard drives, as well as providing navigation columns that grant quick access to frequently used folders, such as the My Documents and My Pictures folders.

Figure 10-6 depicts the File/Open, File/Save_As, and File/Print common dialog boxes. The navigation column also provides easy access to the My Network Places folder.

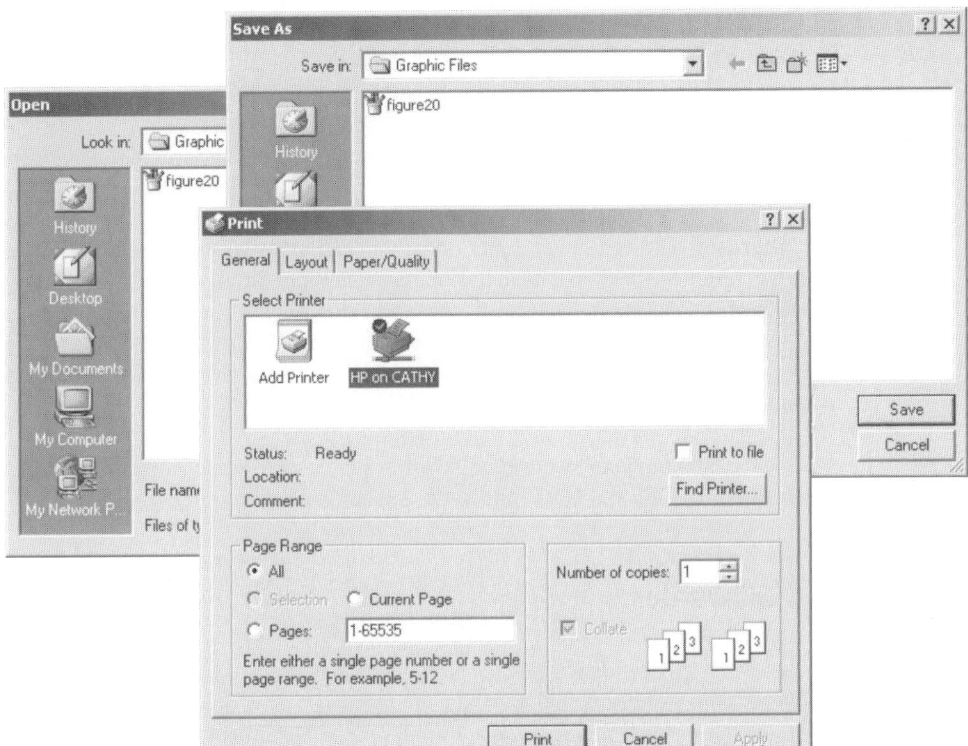

Figure 10-6: Windows 2000 Common Dialog Boxes

Windows 2000 folders include a customizable toolbar with Windows 98-like navigation buttons. The Explorer Toolbar, depicted in Figure 10-7, comes with a collection of about 20 add-on buttons that can be used to customize its available options. The Toolbar can be modified by alternate-clicking on the toolbar, and then selecting the Customize option from the pop-up menu. Additional buttons include Move To, Copy To, Search, Map Drive, Favorites, and Full Screen. The **Full Screen** option is new and can be used to toggle between maximized and normal window sizes.

Full Screen

Figure 10-7: Windows 2000 Explorer Toolbar

Search function

Windows 2000 also includes powerful new search capabilities for searching the local hard drive and the web. The new HTML-like **Search function** in Windows 2000 replaces the Start menu's Find option from previous Windows desktops. The Search feature provides three distinct search options:

1. For Files and Folders
2. On the Internet
3. For People

For Files and Folders

The **For Files and Folders** option opens a dual-page version of the Windows 98/NT 4 Find Files and Folders dialog window. This window provides all of the old Windows search functions and adds powerful new ones, such as case-sensitive searches. These options are available through the Advanced button.

On the Internet

Selecting the **On the Internet** option brings up a search bar that establishes a link to a predetermined Internet search engine such as Yahoo or AOL.

Search for People

Lightweight Directory Access Protocol (LDAP)

The **Search for People** option opens a **Lightweight Directory Access Protocol (LDAP)** dialog window that resembles the one in Windows 98 or Internet Explorer 4.0.

Microsoft Index Server

Indexing Service

Index Service Management

Enabling the **Microsoft Index Server** function produces particularly fast searches. The **Indexing Service** runs in the background to provide content indexing on the local hard drive. Windows 2000 Professional includes a local version of the indexing service that operates with the local hard drive. In a network environment that uses Windows 2000 Servers, the content indexing service can be performed by the server. The **Index Service Management** tools are located in the *Start/Programs/Administrative_Tools* path.

Searching with the context index feature enabled allows the user to write Boolean logic expressions (such as AND, OR, and NOT) for finding specific content quickly.

Windows 2000 Files

From Windows NT 4.0 forward, the Windows NT operating systems have been able to handle long filenames. Filenames in Windows 2000 can be up to 215 characters long including spaces. Windows 2000 uses a proprietary method for reducing long filenames to MS-DOS-compatible 8.3 filenames. Instead of simply truncating the filename, inserting a tilde, and then assigning a number to the end of the filename, Windows 2000 performs a mathematical operation on the long name to generate a truly unique MS-DOS-compatible filename. Windows 2000 filenames cannot contain the following characters: /\:*?"<> | .

TEST TIP

Know which characters can legally be used in a Windows 2000 filename.

Basically, the Windows 2000 algorithm employed to produce DOS-compatible filenames removes any characters that are illegal under DOS, removes any extra periods from the filename, truncates the filename to six characters, inserts a tilde, and adds an ID number to the end of the name. However, when five or more names are generated that would result in duplicate short names, Windows NT changes its truncation method. Beginning with the sixth filename, the first two characters of the name are retained, the next four characters are generated through the mathematical algorithm, and, finally, a tilde with an ID number is attached to the end of the name. This method is used to create DOS-compliant short filenames for MS-DOS, Windows 3.x, and Windows 9x-compliant FAT systems, as well as the proprietary Windows NT file system.

Windows 2000 creates properties sheets for each file and folder in the system. These sheets contain information about the file (or folder) such as its size, location, and creation date. When you view the file's properties, you can also see its attributes, file type, the program that is designed to open it, and when the file was last opened or modified.

The NTFS file system employed in Windows 2000 provides two new file types that technicians must deal with. These are **encrypted files** and **compressed files**. The Windows 2000 NTFS system provides an **Encrypted File System (EFS)** utility that is the basis of storing encrypted files on NTFS volumes. Once a file or folder has been encrypted, only the user who encrypted it can access it. The original user can work with the file or folder just as they would a regular file. However, other users cannot open or share the file (although they can delete it).

encrypted files

compressed files

Encrypted File System (EFS)

decrypted

For other users to be able to access the file or folder, it must first be **decrypted**. The encryption protection disappears when the file or folder is moved to a non-NTFS partition. Only files on NTFS volumes can be encrypted. Conversely, system files and compressed files cannot be encrypted.

cipher

Files and folders can be encrypted from the command line using the **cipher** command. Information about the cipher command and its many switches can be obtained by typing cipher /? at the command prompt. Files can also be encrypted through the Windows Explorer. Encryption is treated as a file attribute in Windows 2000. Therefore, to encrypt a file you simply need to access its properties page by right-clicking on it and selecting its Properties option from the pop-up menu. Move to the Advanced screen under the General tab and click the Encrypt contents to secure data check box, as illustrated in Figure 10-8. Decrypting a file is a simple matter of clearing the check box.

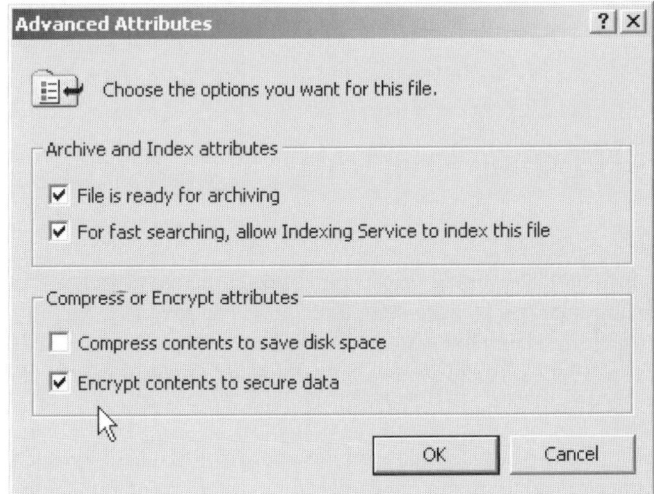

Figure 10-8: Encrypting a File

The Windows Explorer can also be used to compress files and folders on NTFS volumes. Like encryption, Windows 2000 treats NTFS compression as a file attribute. To compress a particular file or folder, right-click on it in the Windows Explorer, and then select the Properties option, followed by the Advanced button to access its advanced properties screen, as illustrated in Figure 10-9. Click in the Compress contents to save disk space check box to compress the file or folder.

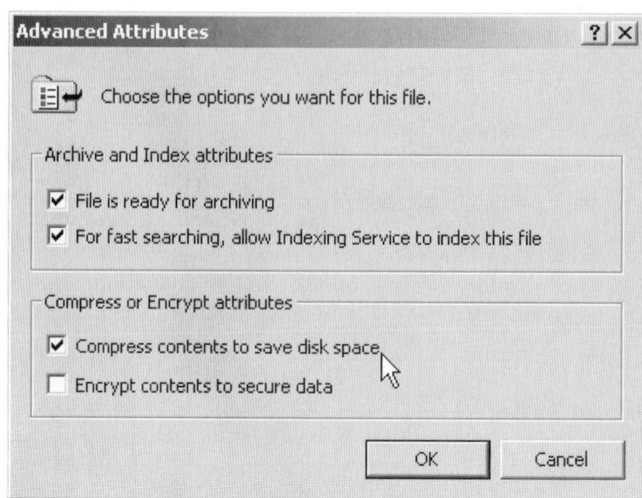

Figure 10-9: Compressing a File

Likewise, an entire drive can be compressed through the My Computer icon. From the File menu, select the Properties option, and click in the Compress drive to save disk space check box.

As with the encryption function, Windows 2000 files and folders can only be compressed on NTFS volumes. If you move a file into a compressed folder, the file will be compressed automatically. These files cannot be encrypted while they are compressed. Compressed files can be marked so that they are displayed in a second color for easy identification. This is accomplished through the Folder Options setting in the Control Panel. From this page, select the View tab and click in the Display compressed files and folder with alternate color check box. The only other indication that you will have concerning a compressed or encrypted file or folder is an attribute listing when the view setting is configured to display in web style.

Windows NT/2000 Structure

Kernel Mode

User Mode

When fully installed, the Windows NT logical structure exists as depicted in Figure 10-10. It is a modular operating system that allows for advances in computing technology to be integrated into the system. The operating system exists in two basic layers referred to as Modes. These two levels are the **Kernel Mode** and the **User Mode**.

Supervisor Mode

Protected Mode

The Kernel Mode may also be referred to as the **Supervisor Mode** or **Protected Mode**. This two-level structure is used to separate the operating system from applications packages.

Basically, the operating system runs in the Kernel Mode while applications run in User Mode. The User Mode is a more restrictive operating mode where there is no direct access of hardware permitted.

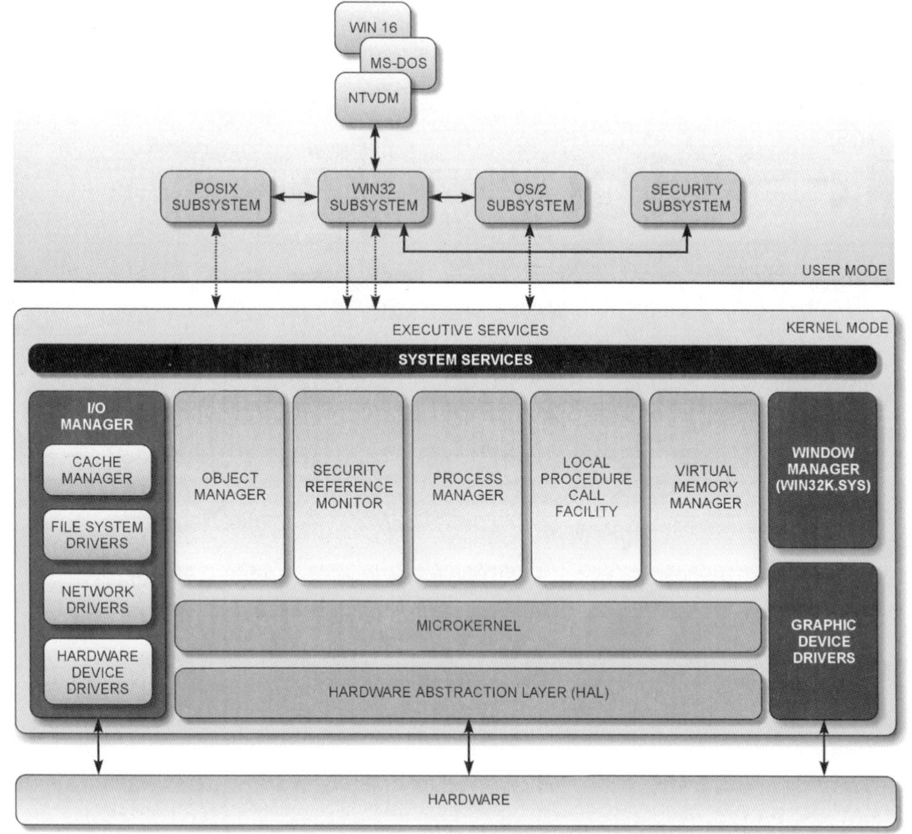

Figure 10-10: The Windows NT Organizational Structure

Only system code can run in the most-privileged Executive Services section of the Kernel Mode. To switch between User Mode and Kernel Mode, applications must use highly defined **Application Programming Interfaces (APIs)** to pass threads between the two modes.

Application Programming Interfaces (APIs)

APIs are routines, protocols, and tools built into the operating system that provide application designers with consistent building blocks to design their applications with. For the user, these building blocks lead to consistent interfaces being designed for all applications.

The design of the APIs in the Windows NT Kernel/User arrangement guarantees that no process can dominate the system to interfere with the operating system, or with another process. This protects the operating system from software bugs and unauthorized accesses by preventing a failing application from interfering with the operating system.

It should be apparent that the organizational structure of Windows 2000, depicted in Figure 10-11, is very similar to the Windows NT structure depicted in Figure 10-10. However, Windows 2000 adds two additional managers to the Executive section. These are the Plug-and-Play Manager and the Power Manager.

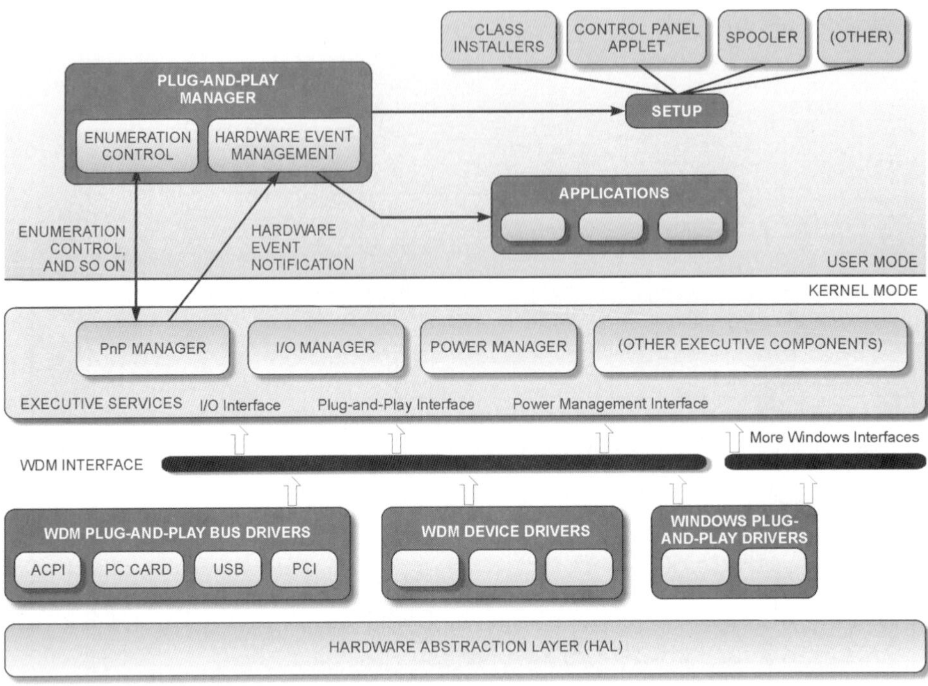

Figure 10-11: Windows 2000 Organizational Structure

The PnP manager employs the enumeration process to discover PnP devices installed in the system. Afterwards, it loads appropriate drivers and creates Registry entries for those devices. These drivers and entries are based on Information (INF) scripts developed by Microsoft and the hardware vendors for the device being configured. The PnP manager then allocates the system's resources (IRQ settings, DMA channels, and I/O addresses) between the devices that require them.

The Power Manager interacts with key system components to conserve energy (especially useful for portable computers) and reduce wear on system devices. Both managers depend on PnP-compliant system components as well as the APM and ACPI power management standards described in Chapter 7—*Portable Systems*.

Kernel Mode

> The Kernel Mode is the operating mode where the program has unlimited access to all memory, including those of system hardware, the User Mode applications, and other processes (such as I/O operations).

Win32k Executive Service

Hardware Abstraction Layer (HAL)

Microkernel

As mentioned earlier, no application can directly access hardware or memory in the Windows NT Kernel Mode. Even though the operating system is highly protected, it is the responsibility of the microprocessor to enforce the protection strategy.

The Kernel Mode consists of three major blocks, the **Win32k Executive Service** module, the **Hardware Abstraction Layer (HAL)**, and the **Microkernel**. Together, these blocks make up the Windows NT Executive.

Kernel

Windows NT Executive

In the Windows NT environment, Kernel Mode should not be confused with the term **Kernel**, or Microkernel. In this environment, Kernel Mode is a highly privileged processing mode, while the term Kernel refers to the complete **Windows NT Executive**, and Microkernel pertains to a functional block of the Windows NT Executive.

The Hardware Abstraction Layer

The Windows NT HAL is a library of hardware drivers that operate between the actual hardware and the rest of the system. These software routines act to make every architecture look the same to the operating system.

The HAL occupies the logical space directly between the system's hardware and the rest of the operating system's Executive Services. In Windows NT 4.0, the HAL enables the operating system to work with different types of microprocessors. The Windows NT 4.0 Installation disk actually contains three different HALs for use on Intel and RISC processors. A different HAL exists for each type of microprocessor architecture the operating system might be used with. Although Windows 2000 originally included support for RISC alpha processors in its beta copies, the first full production version only provides a HAL to work with Intel x86 processors.

The HAL accomplishes its tasks by providing a standard access port for all system hardware operations. In this manner, the rest of the operating system never "sees," or deals with the hardware, only the HAL. Its device driver routines are accessed by the other components of the Windows NT Executive, as well as by higher-level device drivers.

The Windows NT Microkernel

The Microkernel works closely with the HAL to keep the system's microprocessor as busy as possible. It does this by scheduling threads for introduction to the microprocessor on a priority basis.

This includes preempting lower-priority threads for those with higher priorities. NT code is written to be reentrant. This means that it can be interrupted and restarted efficiently.

The Microkernel also synchronizes the activities of the Executive Services blocks, such as the I/O and Process Managers. The Windows NT design employs preemptive multitasking to schedule processes. It also uses an asynchronous input/output system to control data flow between the system hardware and the operating system. These two elements put the user and the operating system in control of the system instead of the applications.

The operating system automatically assigns applications running in the foreground high priority, as well as giving priority to processes receiving input or completing I/O operations. Windows NT makes it impossible for a single application to lock up the keyboard or mouse even when the application is loading. Therefore, the system is always available to the user.

The preemptive task scheduler can also support tasks, such as communications packages, that require constant processing availability. The scheduler allocates processing time to threads based on priority, and can preempt any thread at any time. It allows very high priority tasks to run and maintain control until an equal or higher-priority task takes over.

Symmetric Multiprocessing

The Microkernel's task scheduling capabilities extend to controlling multiple microprocessors. In the case of hardware with multiple microprocessors, the Windows NT Microkernel provides synchronization between the different processors.

The Microkernel's Symmetric Multiprocessing function enables threads of any process to be applied to any available processor in the system. The SMP function also enables microprocessors within a system to share memory space and assign threads to the next available microprocessor.

Windows 2000 Professional supports dual (2x) processor operations while Windows 2000 Server can support up to 4 (4x) simultaneous processors. The Advanced and Datacenter versions of the Server package support 8x and 16x SMP respectively (or 32 processors using a special OEM version of Windows 2000 Datacenter). With versions of the Server running more than 4 processors, the hardware manufacturer must supply a special, proprietary version of the Windows 2000 HAL.DLL file for their machines.

Windows NT Managers

The Win32k Executive Services block provides all the basic operating system functions for the NT environment.

It is made up of a number of managers that include:

- I/O Manager
- Object Manager
- Security Reference Manager
- Process Manager
- Virtual Memory Manager
- Window Manager
- Graphic Device Interface
- Graphic Device Drivers

These managers support the activities of the User Mode's protected subsystems, depicted in Figure 10-12. Together, these subsystems implement functions such as basic operating system services, application environments, and APIs for the various types of applications that the Windows NT system can handle. The Executive Services block consists of a set of common API services available to all the operating system's components.

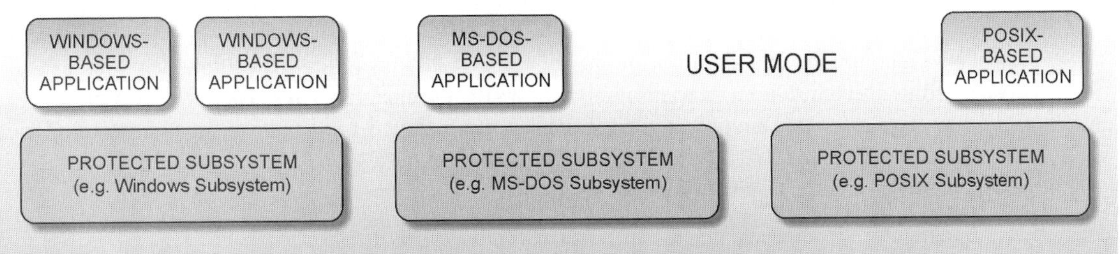

Figure 10-12: The Protected Subsystems

I/O Manager

As its name indicates, the Windows NT **I/O Manager** manages all input and output functions for the operating system. Its major function involves controlling communications between file system drivers, hardware device drivers, and network drivers and the system.

I/O Request Packets (IRPs)

These drivers communicate with each other through data structures called **I/O Request Packets (IRPs)**. The I/O manager passes these packets from higher-level drivers to device drivers that actually access the physical device for the manager. This translation feature is responsible for Windows NT's ability to have multiple file systems and devices active at the same time.

Object Manager

The **Object Manager** provides specifications for naming, retaining, and setting security levels for objects. In Windows NT, objects are defined as software components made up of a data type, attributes, and a set of operations that the object performs. Each object in Windows NT is given an object handle that provides access control and a pointer to the object that processes can use to manipulate them. Windows NT 4.0 objects include:

- Directory Objects
- File Objects
- Port Objects
- Process and Thread Objects
- Symbolic Link Objects
- Event Objects
- and Others

Process Manager

The Windows NT **Process Manager** creates and deletes processes and tracks both process and thread objects. A process is a modular part of an application that the operating system sees as a set of objects and threads. The process object is a specification that describes the virtual memory space mapping for the threads that make up the object. A thread, as you may recall from Chapter 8—*Operating System Fundamentals*, is the smallest schedulable block in the system. Each thread in a process is assigned its own set of registers in the microprocessor, its own kernel stack, an environment section, and its own user stack in its associated process's address space.

Window Manager

The **Window Manager** is the functional block responsible for creating and tracking the user interface GUI. The User Window Manager and Graphics Device Interface (GDI) functions are combined in a single component in the Win32k.sys file. In previous versions of Windows NT, the GDI was a part of the Win32 subsystem and ran in User Mode. In Windows NT 4.0, the GDI was moved to the Executive and runs in Kernel Mode to speed up graphics and memory communications for the system.

The Window Manager notifies applications when a user interacts with the graphical interface (such as clicking the mouse on an icon or moving a window). The GDI interprets requests from applications for graphic output to a display or printer and sends them to the appropriate driver. The driver then administers the request on the hardware.

Windows NT/2000 Memory Management

flat memory model

Virtual Memory Manager (VMM)

The Windows NT memory management scheme employs a full 32-bit architecture with a **flat memory model**. In the Windows NT model, the **Virtual Memory Manager (VMM)** section of the Executive Services block assigns unique memory spaces to every active 32-bit and 16-bit DOS/Windows 3.x application. The VMM works with the environmental subsystems of the User Mode to establish special environments for the 16-bit applications to run in. These environments are discussed in greater detail under the *User Mode* and *DOS and Windows NT* headings later in this chapter.

Unlike MS-DOS, Windows 3.x, or Windows 9x, Windows NT does not employ the address segmentation features of the Intel microprocessors. Because segments can overlap, memory usage errors can occur when an application attempts to write data into a space being used by the operating system, or by another application.

pages

In Windows NT, the VMM section maps each application's memory space into contiguous 4 kB **pages** of physical memory. Using this method, each application is mapped into a truly unique address space that cannot overlap any other address space. The lack of segment overlap reduces the chances of applications interfering with each other and helps to ensure data integrity by providing the operating system and other processes with their own memory spaces.

Because the flat memory model employs consecutive, unique addresses, the 32-bit addressing model enables the VMM to directly access up to 4 GB of memory. As Figure 10-13 illustrates, the VMM allocates this memory in virtual memory pages so that each process appears to have its own 2 GB storage area, with an additional 2 GB reserved for use by the system. The VMM hides the actual organization of physical and disk memory from the system processes.

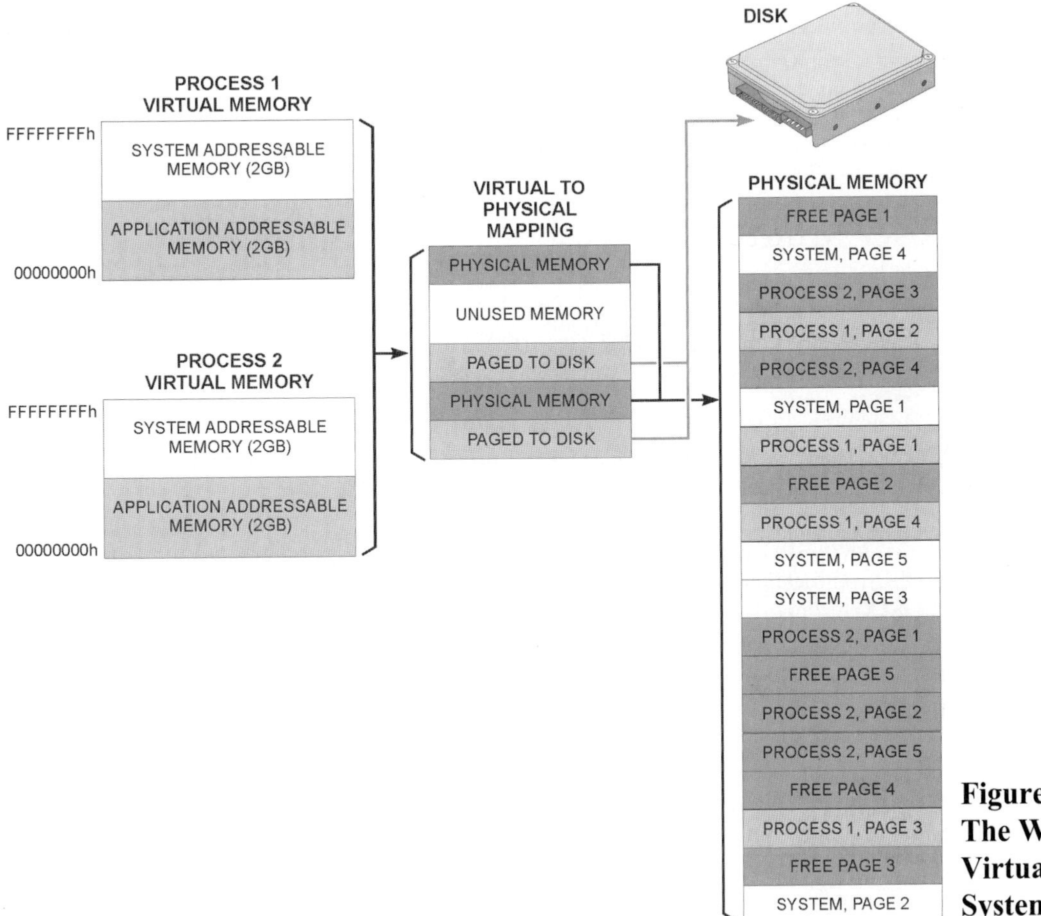

Figure 10-13: The Windows NT Virtual Memory System

Windows NT Virtual Memory

When the VMM has exhausted the physical RAM locations available, it maps memory pages into virtual memory addresses, as described in Figure 10-14. Windows NT establishes virtual memory by creating a **PAGEFILE.SYS** file on the disk. The VMM shifts data between RAM memory and the disk in 4 kB pages. This theoretically provides the operating system with a total memory space that equals the sum of the system's physical RAM and the capacity of the hard disk drive.

PAGEFILE.SYS

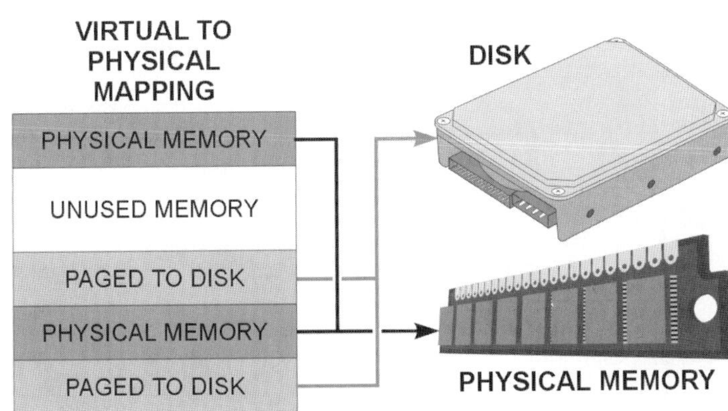

Figure 10-14: Virtual Memory in Windows NT

To take advantage of high RAM capacity, Windows NT automatically tunes itself to take advantage of any available RAM. The VMM dynamically balances RAM between paged memory and the virtual memory disk cache.

User Mode

The other basic Windows NT layer is referred to as the User Mode. This mode is a collection of subsystems that interact with users and applications.

As mentioned earlier, User Mode is a less privileged mode that has no direct access to the system's hardware.

Portable Operating System Interface for Unix (POSIX)

OS/2

The Windows NT package supports programs based on 16- and 32-bit Windows, MS-DOS, POSIX, and character-based OS/2 structures through protected subsystems in this layer. **POSIX**, or **Portable Operating System Interface for Unix**, is a set of standards that Unix programmers go by to ensure that their applications can be ported to operating systems, such as UNIX and Windows NT, that feature POSIX compatibility. **OS/2** is the GUI-based Operating System 2 that IBM developed in conjunction with Microsoft for its PS/2 line of personal computers. While the PS/2 line was not a very successful group of products, the operating system remains in fairly wide usage with IBM products.

Running applications in User Mode protects the operating system by forcing the applications to run in their own address spaces. This is accomplished through the User Mode subsystem structure depicted in Figure 10-15. Each subsystem employs well defined APIs that enable the application to request services from the system. The APIs are responsible for the interaction with the applications and users.

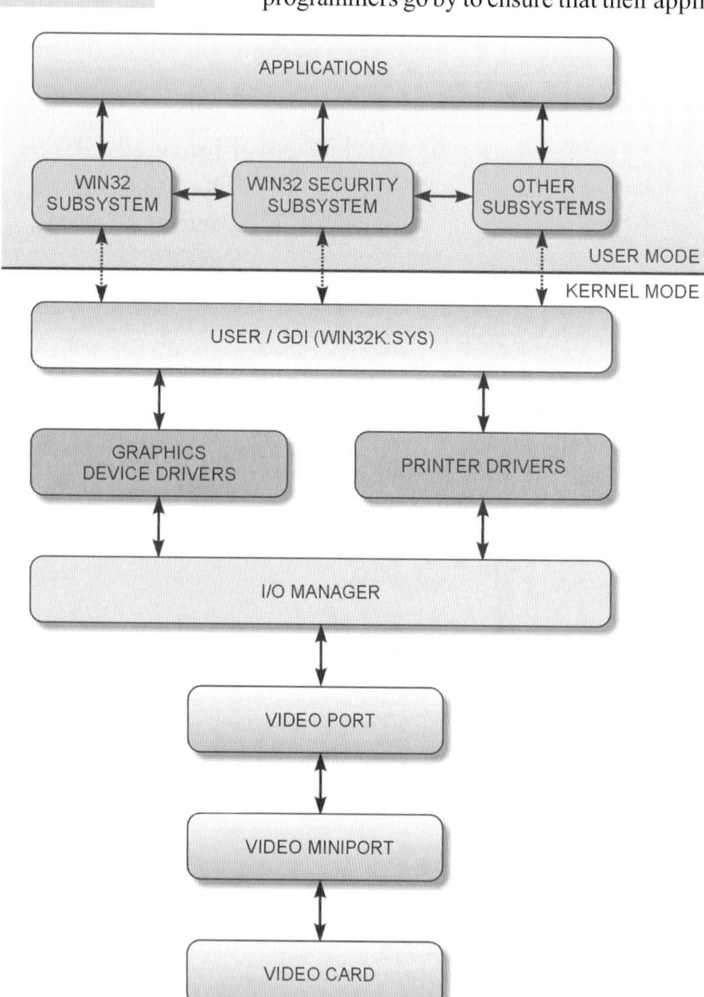

Figure 10-15: The User Mode Subsystems

Win32 Subsystem

Environmental Subsystems

The **Win32 Subsystem** is the most noteworthy of the subsystems because it manages all 32-bit, protected-mode applications, as well as supplying the Windows user interfaces. The Security subsystem provides the system's basic security functions such as logon and user privileges. Other subsystems include those **Environmental Subsystems** designed to work with MS-DOS, Win 16, OS/2, and POSIX applications that may, or may not, be running at any given time. These subsystems are designed to emulate other operating systems so that their applications can run successfully in the Windows NT environment. They are loaded when their services are required by an application.

In the Windows NT environment, applications are not allowed to directly access physical memory. It is the responsibility of the Environmental Subsystems in the User Mode to deliver addresses to the applications in the Windows NT memory management strategy. Notice in the figure that each environment is under the control of the Win32 Subsystem. All communications between the Kernel Mode and the different types of applications must pass through this subsystem.

NT Virtual DOS Machine (NTVDM)

While 32-bit applications run in protected mode and can contact the Win32 Subsystem directly, 16-bit DOS and Win16 applications must be housed in a protective memory management scheme called an **NT Virtual DOS Machine (NTVDM)** environment. This environment protects the other parts of the system from the applications. These applications can only contact the Win32 Subsystem through a single thread. In the case of 32-bit applications, multithread communications can be conducted directly between the application and the Win32 Subsystem.

NTIO.SYS

NTDOS.SYS

If a 16-bit DOS application is executed, the User Mode must create an isolated NTVDM environment for it to run in. The NTVDM provides an emulation of the IO.SYS/MSDOS.SYS/COMMAND.COM environment of MS-DOS. The Windows NT emulation files are named **NTIO.SYS** and **NTDOS.SYS**. Each DOS application runs all by itself in the system with full access to all of the system's resources through the APIs in the Win32 Subsystem. However, the application is also shut off from the rest of the system, so that it cannot exchange data with applications outside the NTVDM. This prevents the 16-bit application from interfering with other applications running in the system.

WOW

In the case of 16-bit Windows 3.x applications, a special environment called Win16-on-Win32 (**WOW**) can be established to allow multiple Win16 applications to run in the same NTVDM. This environment emulates the Windows 3.x KRNL386, GDI, and USER kernel for these applications. In this scenario, the VMM relies on the applications to manage their own memory usage within the WOW environment.

The applications have the ability to exchange information within the WOW. As with the DOS environment, the applications within the WOW cannot exchange data with applications outside the immediate NTVDM. Conversely, if these applications were each loaded into separate NTVDMs, they would have full access to all system resources, but they would not be able to exchange information with each other. Figure 10-16 shows the relationship of NTVDMs and WOWs and the WIN32 sub-system.

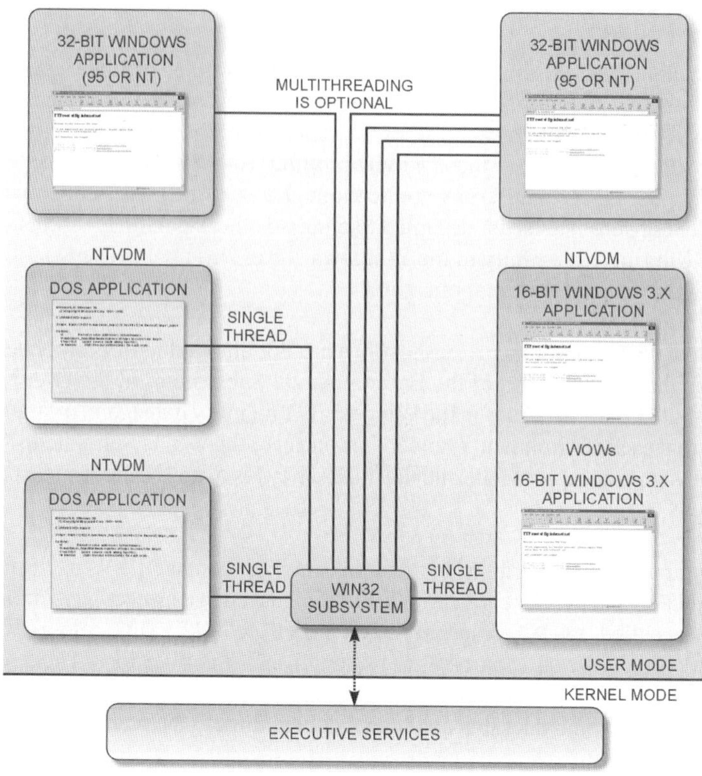

Figure 10-16: The NTVDMs and WOWs

Figure 10-17 illustrates a typical interaction between an application and the video display, as it applies to the Windows NT structure. This particular discussion concerns the movement of information from the application to the hardware. From the double-headed arrows in the drawing, it should be apparent that data can also move in the reverse direction.

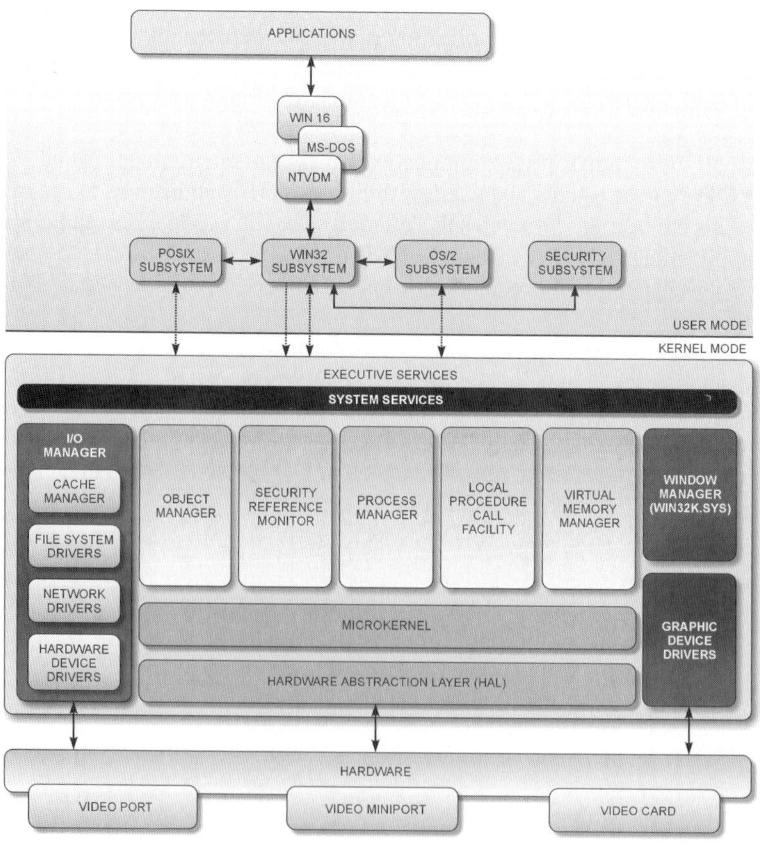

Figure 10-17: Movement of Information in Windows NT

The application communicates with the Windows NT system through the User Mode's Win32 Subsystem. In turn, the Win32 Subsystem communicates with the Kernel Mode's Win32K.sys Window Manager. In the case of the video information, it is processed and passed through the high-level Graphics device driver and is presented to the I/O Manager. Finally, the I/O Manager processes the data through a **miniport** and applies it to the video card through the video port. The term miniport refers to hardware manipulating drivers supplied by the device manufacturer.

miniport

Windows 2000 Registry

Like Windows 9x, Windows NT and Windows 2000 use a multipart database, called the Registry, to hold system and user configuration information.

> However, the Windows NT Registry is not compatible with the Windows 9x Registries.

The Windows NT Registry is depicted in Figure 10-18. As with the Windows 9x Registry discussed in the previous chapter, the Windows NT Registry is organized into Headkeys, Subkeys, and Values. Comparing Figure 10-18 to Figure 9-33, you should notice that both Registries contain the same HKEYs, except that no HKEY_DYN_DATA key is present in the Windows NT Registry.

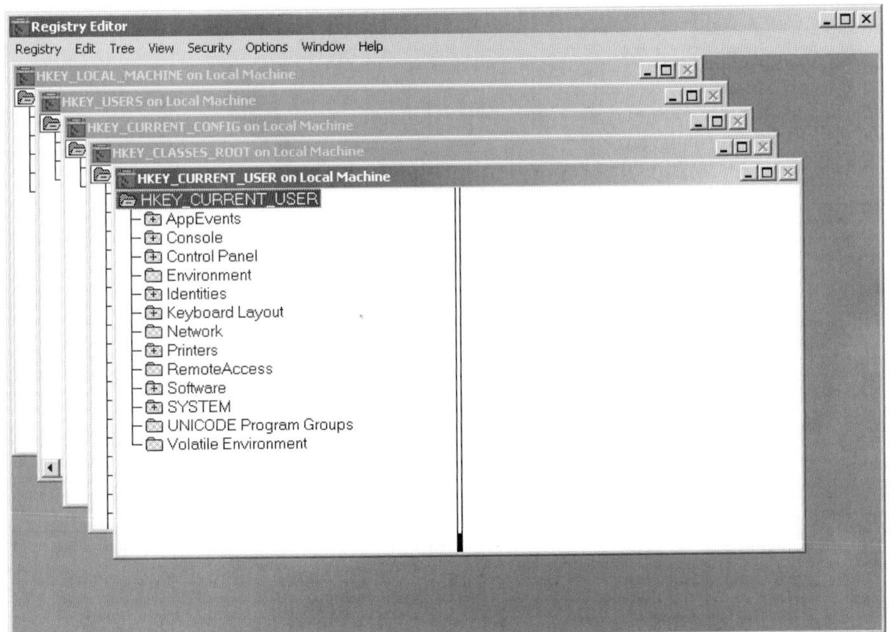

Figure 10-18: The Windows NT/2000 Registry

In the Windows NT world, the HKEYs are also referred to as **Subtrees,** while the Registry itself is referred to as the **Tree**. Under each Subtree are one or more Subkeys, which, in turn, will have one or more **Values** assigned to them.

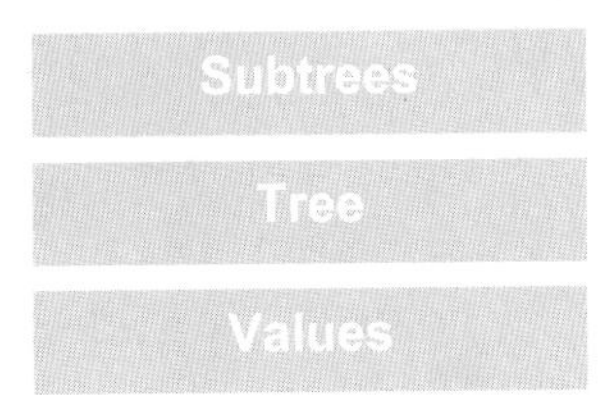

Hives

The contents of the Registry are physically stored in five files referred to as **Hives**. Hives represent the major divisions of all the Registry's keys, subkeys, subtrees, and values.

SAM hive

Security hive

Software hive

System hive

Default hive

The hives of the Windows NT Registry are:

- The **SAM hive**
- The **Security hive**
- The **Software hive**
- The **System hive**
- The **Default hive**

These files are stored in the *\Winnt\System32\Config* directory along with a backup copy and log file for each hive.

Ntuser.dat

Configuration information about every user who has logged into the system is maintained in a named subfolder of the \Winnt\Profiles directory. The actual user configuration file is named **Ntuser.dat** (i.e., \Winnt\Profiles\Charles\Ntuser.dat). In Windows 2000, the Ntuser.dat file is stored in \Documents_and_Settings\username.

The major Windows NT hives and their files are described in Table 10-1.

Table 10-1: Major Windows NT Hives and Their Files

SUBTREE/KEY	FILE	LOG FILE
HKEY_LOCAL_MACHINE\SOFTWARE	SOFTWARE	SOFTWARE.LOG
HKEY_LOCAL_MACHINE\SECURITY	SECURITY	SECURITY.LOG
HKEY_LOCAL_MACHINE\SYSTEM	SYSTEM	SYSTEM.LOG
HKEY_LOCAL_MACHINE\SAM	SAM	SAM.LOG
HKEY_CURRENT_USER	USERxxx	USERxxx.LOG
	ADMINxxx	ADMINxxx.LOG
HKEY_USERS\DEFAULT	DEFAULT	DEFAULT.LOG

The HKEY_LOCAL_MACHINE subtree is the Registry's major branch. It contains five major keys. The SAM and SECURITY keys hold information such as user rights, user and group information for domain or workgroup organization, and password information. The HARDWARE key is a database built by device drivers and applications during bootup. The database is updated each time the system is rebooted. The SYSTEM key contains basic information about startup including the device drivers loaded and which services are in use. The **Last Known Good configuration** settings are stored here. Finally, the SOFTWARE key holds information about locally loaded software, including file associations, OLE information, and configuration data.

Last Known Good configuration

The second most important subtree is HKEY_USERS. It contains a subkey for each local user that accesses the system. These subkeys hold Desktop settings and User profiles. When a server logs in across a domain, the subkey is stored on the Domain Controller.

The HKEY_CURRENT_USER and HKEY_CLASSES_ROOT keys contain partial copies of the HKEY_USERS and HKEY_LOCAL_MACHINE keys.

Regedt32.exe

The contents of the Registry can be edited directly using the Windows NT/2000 RegEdit utility — **Regedt32.exe**. This file is located in the \Winnt\System32 folder. As with the Windows 9x packages, most changes to the Registry should be accomplished through the Wizards in the Windows NT/2000 Control Panels.

Rdisk.exe

The Control Panel Wizards are designed to correctly make changes to the Registry in a manner that the operating system can understand. Editing the Registry directly opens the possibility of changing an entry in a manner that Windows NT cannot accept, and thereby, crashing the system. In either event, it is a good practice to back up the contents of the Registry before installing new hardware or software, or modifying the Registry directly. The **Rdisk.exe** utility, located in the \Winnt\System32 folder can be used to create a backup copy of the Registry in the \Winnt\Repair folder.

TEST TIP

Know how to make a backup copy of the Registry in Windows NT 4.0.

Windows 2000 relies on the same Registry structure used in previous Windows NT versions. For this reason, it is not compatible with Windows 9x Registries. As with Windows NT 4.0, the user settings portion of the Registry is stored in the NTUSER.DAT file located in the \Documents_and_Settings\userxxx folder. The System portions of the Registry are stored in the SOFTWARE, SYSTEM, SECURITY, and SAM hives. These files are stored in the \Winnt\System32\Config folder.

TEST TIP

Be aware of the utility used to directly edit Registry entries of the various operating systems.

Although there is a RegEdit tool in Windows 2000, this tool was designed to work with Windows 9x clients. The editor used to manage the Windows 2000 Registry is Regedt32. However, in some instances, such as Registry searches, the RegEdit utility offers superior operation, even in Windows 2000.

Active Directory

Active Directory (AD)

The central feature of the Windows 2000 architecture is the **Active Directory (AD)** structure. Active Directory is a distributed database of user and resource information that describes the makeup of the network (i.e., users and application settings).

It is also a method of implementing a distributed authentication process. The Active Directory replaces the domain structure used in Windows NT 4.0. This feature helps to centralize system and user configurations, as well as data backups on the server in the Windows 2000 network.

Windows 2000 remains a domain-dependent operating system. It uses domains as boundaries for administration, security, and replication purposes. Each domain must be represented by at least one domain controller. Recall that a domain controller is a server set up to track the names of all of the objects and requests for resources within a domain.

In Windows 2000, the Primary and Backup Domain Controller structure from Windows NT has been replaced by a peer model where individual servers can be converted to Active Directory domain controllers without shutting down the system to reinstall the operating system.

Lightweight Directory Access Protocol (LDAP)

Domain Name Service (DNS)

The Active Directory structure employs two common Internet standards — the **Lightweight Directory Access Protocol (LDAP)** and **Domain Name Service (DNS)**. The LDAP protocol is used to define how directory information is accessed and exchanged. DNS is the Internet standard for resolving domain names to actual IP addresses. It is also the standard for exchanging directory information with clients and other directories.

The Active Directory arranges domains in a hierarchy and establishes trust relationships among all of the domains in a tree-like structure, as illustrated in Figure 10-19.

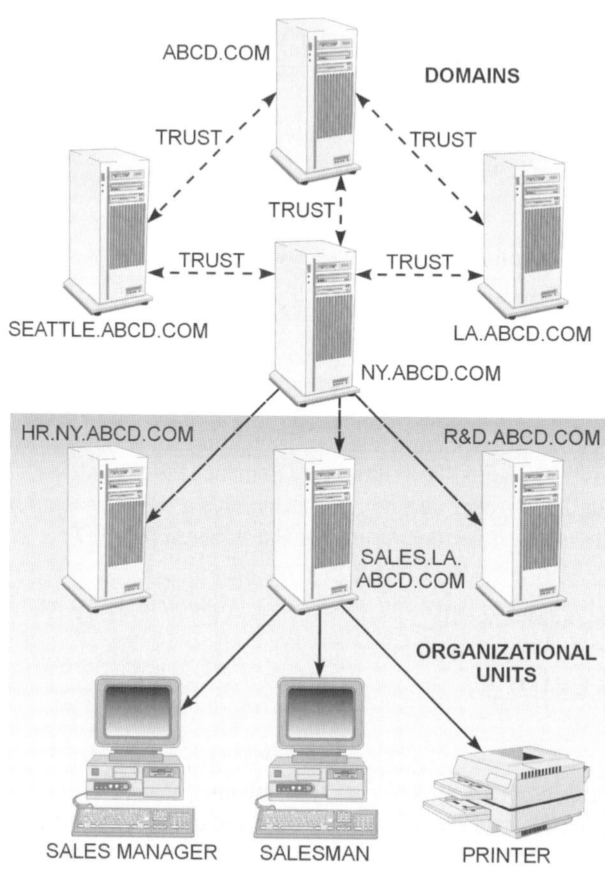

Figure 10-19: Basic Active Directory Structure

tree

leaf objects

A **tree** is a collection of objects that share the same DNS name. Active Directory can subdivide domains into organizational units (i.e., sales, admin, etc.) that contain other units, or **leaf objects**, such as printers, users, etc.

forest

Conversely, Windows 2000 can create an organizational structure containing more than one tree. This structure is referred to as a **forest**. Figure 10-20 expands the AD structure to demonstrate these relationships.

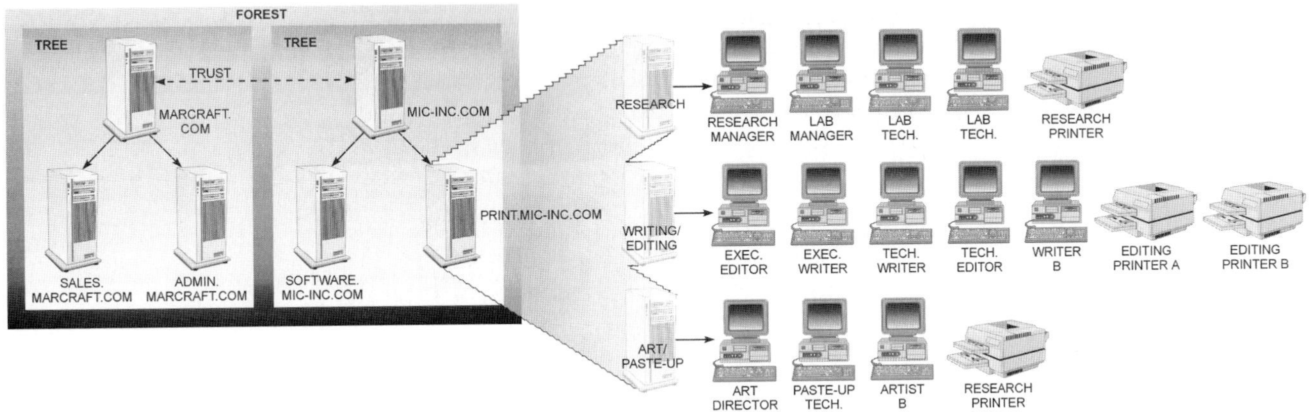

Figure 10-20: Active Directory Relationships

Windows 2000 automatically joins all of the domains within a tree through two-way trusts.

> **Trusts** are relationships that enable users to move between domains and perform prescribed types of operations.

Trusts

If a trust relationship is established between the sales and marketing domains in the example and a similar trust exists between the sales and admin domains, then a trust relationship also exists between the marketing and admin domains.

Trusts allow administrators to provide user and group rights to objects.

> **Rights** are the permission settings that control a user's (or groups of users') authority to access objects and perform operations (such as reading or writing a file). **Administrative Rights** provide authority to users down to the Organizational Unit level.

Rights

Administrative Rights

However, they do not cross boundaries established at the domain level but can be inherited by other OUs having subordinate positions within the same tree. On the other hand, **User Rights** must be established for individual users or for members of groups. Using groups allows common rights to be assigned to multiple users with a single administrative action (as opposed to setting up and maintaining rights for each individual in, say, a 150-person accounting staff).

User Rights

In a network supported by Windows 2000 servers, the network administrator can assign applications to users so that they appear on their Start menus. When the application is selected for the first time, it is installed on the local machine. The administrator can also place optional applications on the Add/Remove Programs dialog box in the Control Panel. The user can install these applications from this location at any time.

The network administrator can also cause the contents of the local My Documents folder to reside on the server instead of the local desktop. This option provides safe, centralized storage for user files. The server security and backup functions safeguard the data.

In Windows 2000, application software can be installed remotely across the network. This enables the network administrator to control user application software across the network and keep it uniform throughout an enterprise.

Active Directory Users and Computers

Organizational Units (OUs)

The primary tool for working with the Active Directory is the **Active Directory Users and Computers**, depicted in Figure 10-21. The organizational units of a domain contain users, groups, and resources. The Active Directory Manager tool is used to add users, groups, and **Organizational Units** (**OUs**) to the directory.

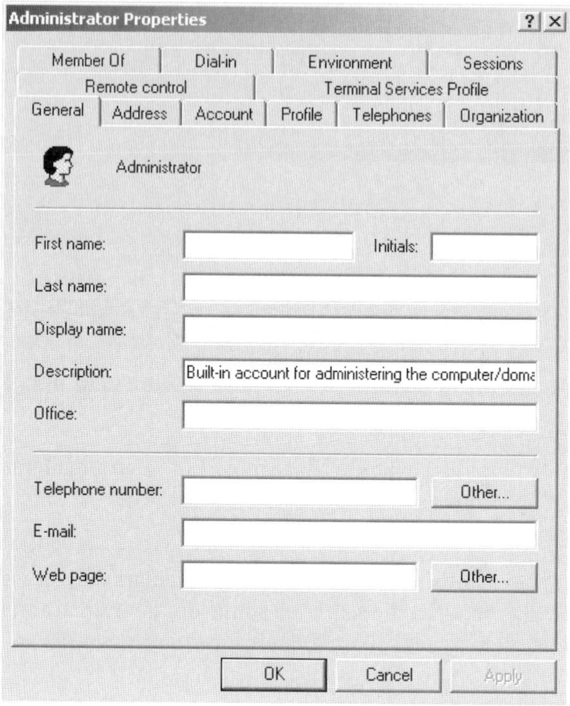

Figure 10-21: Active Directory Users and Computers

While the Active Directory structure is designed primarily to help manage a network, it can also be a valuable desktop tool. The Active Directory Service running on a Windows 2000 Server enables Windows 2000 Professional installations to locate printers, disk drives, and other network devices across the network.

Administering Windows 2000

Windows NT and 2000 are designed to be used in an administrated LAN environment. As such, it must provide network administrators with the tools necessary to control users and data within the network. To empower the network administrator, Windows 2000 furnishes five powerful administrative tools:

- System Policies
- User Profiles
- Groups
- Network Shares
- NTFS Rights

Each of these tools is designed to enable administrators to limit, or grant, users' access to files, folders, services, and administrator-level services.

Computer Management Consoles

Windows 2000 concentrates many of the system's administration tools in a single location, under the Control Panel's Administrative Tools icon. The tools are combined in the Windows 2000 **Computer Management Console**, depicted in Figure 10-22. The Management Console can be accessed by alternate-clicking the My Computer icon and selecting the Manage option from the pop-up menu. As the figure illustrates, the console includes three primary **Microsoft Management Consoles (MMCs)**:

Computer Management Console

Microsoft Management Consoles (MMCs)

- System Tools
- Storage
- Services and Applications

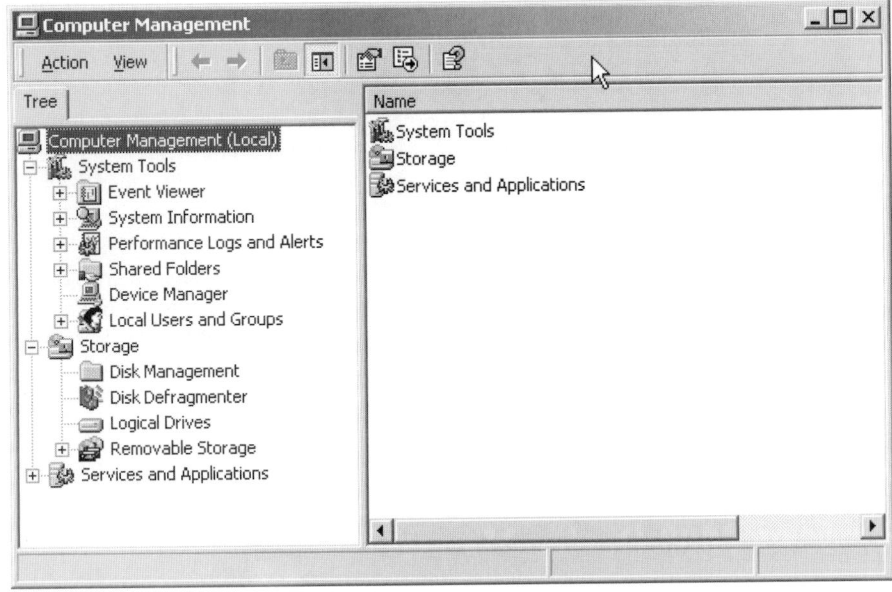

Figure 10-22: The Windows 2000 Computer Management

The **System Tools** console provides a collection of tools that can be used to view and manage system objects. They can also be used to track and configure all of the system's hardware and software. They can also be used to configure network options and view system events.

System Tools

Likewise, the Storage console provides a standard set of tools for maintaining the system's disk drives. These tools include the **Disk Management** tool, the Disk Defragmenter utility, and a **Logical Drives** utility. The Disk Management tool enables the user to create and manage disk partitions and volumes. The Disk Defragmenter is used to optimize file operations on disks by rearranging their data into the most effective storage pattern for reading and writing. Finally, the Logical Drives tool shows a listing of all the logical drives in the system, including remote drives that have been mapped to the local system.

Disk Management

Logical Drives

The final entry, Services and Applications, includes an advanced set of system management tools. These tools include the **Windows Management Instrumentation (WMI)** tools, a listing of all the system's available services, and access to the Windows 2000 Indexing functions. The WMI tools are used to establish administrative controls with another computer, provide logging services, view user security settings, and enable the Windows 2000 advanced scripting services.

Windows Management Instrumentation (WMI)

Some of the Windows 2000 management consoles are not loaded when the operating system is installed. However they are available for installation from the Windows 2000 CD. These consoles are referred to as snap-ins. In addition to the Control Panel path, all of the installed MMCs can be accessed under the *Start/Programs/Administrative_Tools* path. Extended discussions of these tools are presented throughout the remainder of the text as they apply to managing and troubleshooting the operating system.

Thin and Fat Clients

thin client

fat client

In most Windows 2000 installations, the administrative architecture is set up to store some information, such as user configurations and backup data, on the server, while leaving applications and some data on the client. However, Windows 2000 networks can be configured to operate within a range between two administration levels known as **thin client** and **fat client**.

The term thin client describes installation strategies that place a limited amount of information on the workstation and most of the applications on the server. The local workstation has very little control over its own operation. This enables the network administrator to exercise a very high level of control over what users do and have access to.

Conversely, a fat client installation strategy places much of the operating system and applications on the client and the processing is done locally — not on the server. Fat clients are more likely to be able to operate in a stand-alone manner. Currently, they also represent the more widely used strategy. Bear in mind, however, that the thin/fat client arrangement is a Server feature rather than a Windows 2000 Professional feature.

Windows 2000 Device Manager

Windows NT Diagnostic

Windows 2000 employs the Windows 9x-like Device Manager illustrated in Figure 10-23. The Device Manager replaces the **Windows NT Diagnostic** utility found in Windows NT 4.0. As with Windows 9x, the Windows 2000 Device Manager plays a major role in modifying hardware configurations and for troubleshooting hardware problems encountered in Windows 2000.

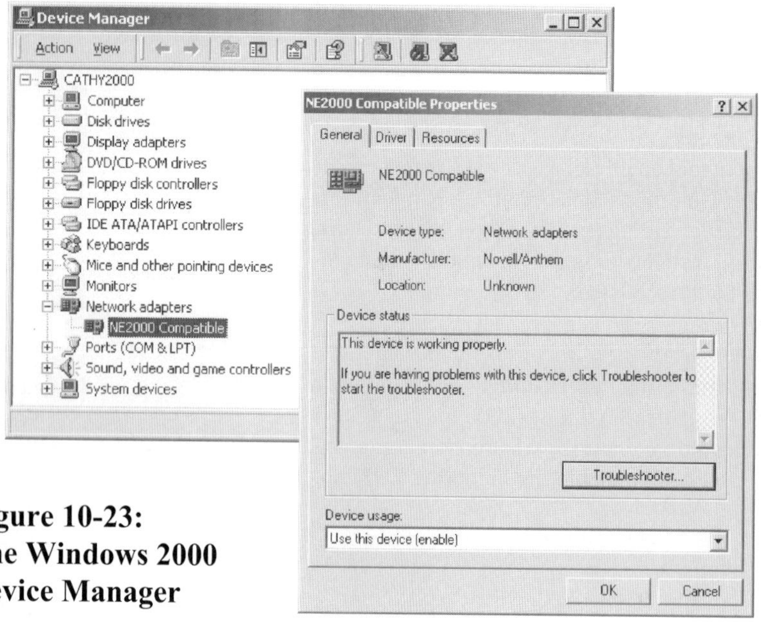

Figure 10-23: The Windows 2000 Device Manager

The Windows 2000 Device Manager utility can be accessed by clicking its button located under the Hardware tab of the Control Panel's System properties page. However, in Windows 2000, the Device Manager is usually accessed through the Computer Management Console. Operation of the Device Manager is very similar to its Windows 9x counterparts. It can be used to identify installed ports, update device drivers, and change I/O settings for hardware installed in the system.

Even though entries in the Registry can be altered through the **RegEdt32** and **RegEdit** utilities, the safest method of changing hardware settings is to change their values through the Device Manager. Steps for using the Device Manager are covered in some detail in Chapter 12—*Operating System Troubleshooting*.

RegEdt32

RegEdit

Windows NT/2000 Group Policies

As with other Windows versions, the overall operation of Windows 2000 is governed by System Policies. Basically, policies give administrators control over users. Using System Policies, the network administrator can give or limit users' access to local resources, such as drives and network connections. Administrators can establish policies that force certain users to log in during specified times and lock them out of the system at all other times. System policies also allow the administrator to send updates and configure desktops for network clients. Fundamentally, any item found in the Control Panel can be regulated through System Policies.

Each Windows NT user is assigned a profile directory under their username the first time they log into a given Windows NT/2000 system. This profile contains system information and settings that become particular to the user and is stored under the Documents and Settings directory. Inside the directory, the system creates the Ntuser.dat file, along with various other data files. As discussed previously, this file contains the User portion of the Windows NT Registry. This file contains the user-specific settings that have been established for this user. When the user logs onto the system, the User and System hive portions of the Registry are used to construct the user-specific environment in the system.

The first time a user logs onto a system, the Default User profile directory is copied into the directory established under the user's name. When the user makes changes to the desktop, Start menu, My Documents, etc., the data is stored in the appropriate files under the username. Both Windows NT and Windows 2000 provide methods of storing user profiles on the server in a networked environment. This prevents the user's profile directories from being recreated at each machine the user logs into. Instead, these operating systems provide roaming profiles that are downloaded from the server to the client when the user logs in. Changes made during sessions are uploaded to the server when the user logs out.

As with previous versions of Windows NT, Windows 2000 uses **profiles** to provide customized operating environments for its users. These profiles are stored in different locations, hold more information, and are more customizable than previous Windows NT versions, but they perform the same functions. However, Windows 2000 policies work very differently under the Active Directory structure than they did in the Windows NT Domain structure.

profiles

Group Policy Editor (GPE)

In Windows 2000, Policies are established through the **Group Policy Editor (GPE)** depicted in Figure 10-24. Administrators use this editor to establish which applications different users have access to, as well as to control applications on the user's desktop.

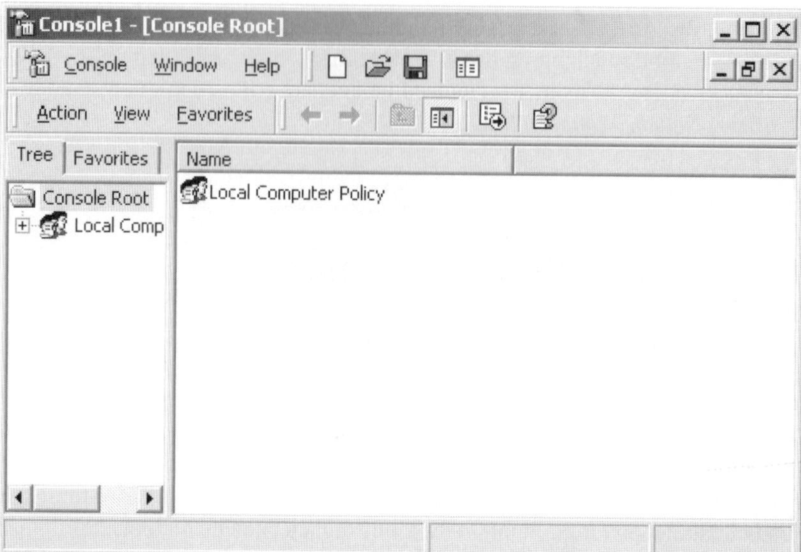

Figure 10-24: The Windows 2000 Group Policy Editor

Group Policy Objects (GPOs)

Many of the Windows NT administration features have been moved to the Control Panel in Windows 2000. While Windows NT used system policies, the Windows 2000 environment functions on **Group Policy Objects (GPOs)**. Group Policies are the Windows 2000 tool for implementing changes for computers and users throughout an enterprise. The Windows 2000 Group Policies can be applied to individual users, domains, organizational units, and sites. In addition, the Windows 2000 policies are highly secure.

With Group Policies, administrators can institute a large number of detailed settings for users throughout an enterprise, without establishing each setting manually.

GPOs can be used to apply a large number of changes to machines and users through the Active Directory. These changes appear in the GPE under three headings:

- Software Installation Settings
- Windows Settings
- Administrative Templates

Each heading appears in two places — the first version is listed under Computer Configuration while the second copy is found under User Configuration. Values will normally differ between the versions of the headings since the user and computer settings will be different.

Software Installation Settings

Microsoft Installer (MSI)

The **Software Installation Settings** heading can be used to install, update, repair, and remove applications. The *Designed for Windows 2000* logo program requires that all applications designed for Windows 2000 use the **Microsoft Installer (MSI)** technology. This program replaces the traditional Setup.exe program used for installing applications in previous Windows versions. The MSI is created by the software application developer and contains all of the information that the system needs to interact with it.

The MSI is aware of the files the application requires to operate properly, where they should be installed, their sizes, and their version numbers. The administrator has the ability to customize this information to fit the needs of the installation. Examples of customized settings might include language support selections and logical drive locations. The customized information is referred to as a **transform** and is used by the installer to ensure that the appropriate files are installed and configured properly.

transform

The MSI technology also provides the operating system with the ability to self-repair applications. If one or more of a complaint application's core files are damaged or removed, the icon used to start the application checks with the MSI to see that no critical data is missing. If any material is missing, the MSI copies the data to the correct locations and starts the application. This same technology can be used to auto-install applications on machines that attempt to open files with MSI-recognized extensions. The MSI can also be employed to automatically deploy applications when a user logs on, or accesses the Active Directory looking for the application.

The **Windows Settings** portion of the GPO contains startup and shutdown scripts as well as security settings. The Security Setting portion of this heading covers such topics as Account policies, Password policies, and User Right Assignments, to name a few. User Rights are special abilities granted to accounts or operating systems to perform tasks such as determining whether an account can add workstations to a domain or manipulate devices at a lower level.

Windows Settings

The **Administrative Templates** portion of the GPO stores changes to the Registry settings that pertain to the HKEY_LOCAL_MACHINE. Figure 10-25 depicts the hierarchy of items in the Computer Administrative Templates window of the Group Policy Editor.

Administrative Templates

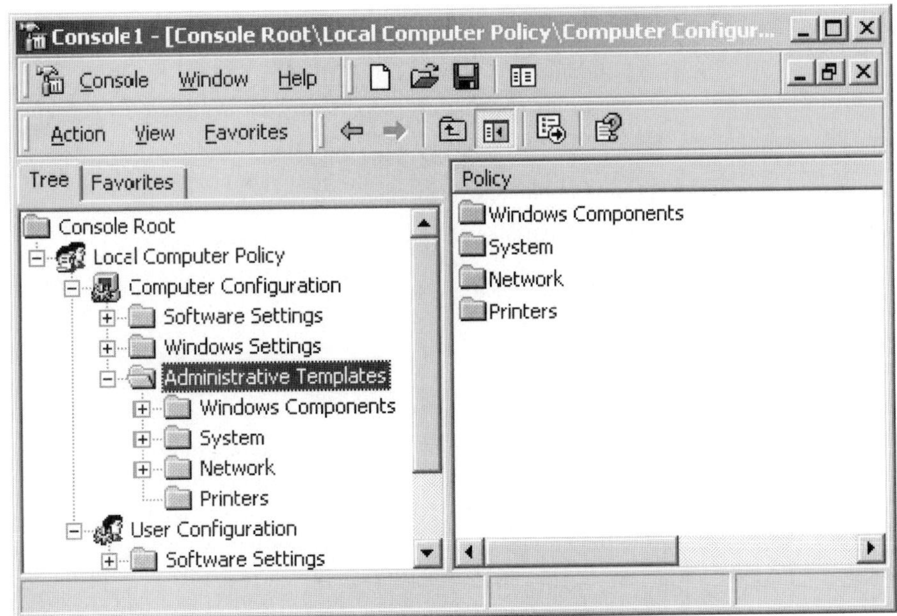

Figure 10-25: Computer Administrative Templates

Windows NT File System

Windows NT can function in two very different disk organizational structures. Like MS-DOS, Windows 3.x, and Windows 9x, it can employ the MS-DOS FAT system.

Windows NT File System (NTFS)

In addition, Windows NT offers its own proprietary **Windows NT File System (NTFS)**. The NTFS structure is designed to provide better data security and to operate more efficiently with larger hard drives than FAT systems do.

Master File Table (MFT)

The NTFS structure uses 64-bit entries to keep track of storage on the disk (as opposed to the 16- and 32-bit entries used in FAT and FAT32 systems). The core component of the NTFS system is the **Master File Table (MFT)**. This table replaces the FAT in a MS-DOS compatible system and contains information about each file being stored on the disk. In order of occurrence, this information includes:

- Header information
- Standard information
- Filename
- Security information
- Data

When a volume is formatted in an NTFS system, several system files and the MFT are created on the disk. These files contain the information required to implement the file system structure on the disk. The system files produced during the NTFS formatting process include:

0/1. A pair of MFT files (the real one and a shorter backup version).

2. A Log file to maintain transaction steps for recovery purposes.
3. A Volume file that includes the volume name, NTFS version, and other key volume information.
4. An Attribute definition table file.
5. A Root Filename file that serves as the drive's root folder.
6. A Cluster Bitmap that represents the volume and shows which clusters are in use.
7. The partition boot sector file.
8. A Bad Cluster file containing the locations of all bad sectors identified on the disk.
9. A Quota Table for tracking allowable storage space on the disk for each user.
10. An Upper Case Table for converting lowercase characters to Unicode uppercase character.

Unicode

Unicode is a 16-bit character code standard, similar to 8-bit ASCII, used to represent characters as integer numbers. The 16-bit format allows it to represent over 65,000 different characters. This is particularly useful for languages that have very large character sets.

Figure 10-26 illustrates the organization of an NTFS disk volume. The first information in the NTFS volume is the 16-sector **Partition Boot Sector**. The sector starts at physical sector-0 and is made up of two segments — the **BIOS Parameter Block** and the **Code section**. The BIOS Parameter Block holds information about the structures of the volume and disk file system. The Code section describes the method to be used to locate and load the startup files for the specified operating system. This code loads the Windows NT bootstrap loader file **NTLDR** in Intel-based computers running Windows NT.

Partition Boot Sector

BIOS Parameter Block

Code section

NTLDR

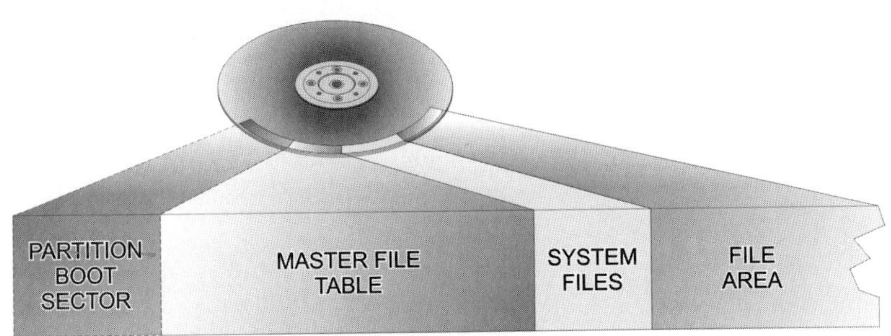

Figure 10-26: The Organization of an NTFS Disk Volume

The MFT contains information about each folder and file on the volume. The NTFS system relates to folders and files as a collection of attributes. All the folder's, or file's, elements (i.e., filename, security information, and data) are considered to be attributes. The system allocates space in the MFT for each file or folder based on the cluster size being used on the disk.

Standard Information

Security Descriptor

Figure 10-27 shows a typical MFT record. The first section of the record contains **Standard Information** about the file or folder, such as its date and time stamp and number of links. The second section contains the file's or folder's name. The next section contains the file's or folder's **Security Descriptor** (which holds information about who can access it, who owns it, and what they may do with it).

The next section of the MFT record is the Data (or Index) area. The information for smaller files and folders is stored in the MFT itself. The data area is 2 kB long on smaller drives, but can be bigger on larger drives. When the data fits within the MFT record, the various portions of the file are referred to as **resident attributes**.

Figure 10-27: Basic NTFS Master File Table Record

For larger files and folders that cannot be stored in a single MFT, the NTFS may resort to two other methods of using the MFT. For medium-size folders and files, the system stores standard information about the folder or file, such as its name and time information, in the MFT and then establishes Index links to external cluster locations to store the rest of the data. The external clusters are referred to as **data runs** and are identified by 64-bit **Virtual Cluster Numbers (VCNs)** assigned to them. The attributes stored outside the MFT are referred to as **non-resident attributes**. An **Attribute List** attribute that contains the locations of all the file or folder's non-resident attributes is created in the data area of the MFT record. This arrangement is depicted in Figure 10-28.

resident attributes

data runs

Virtual Cluster Numbers (VCNs)

non-resident attributes

Attribute List

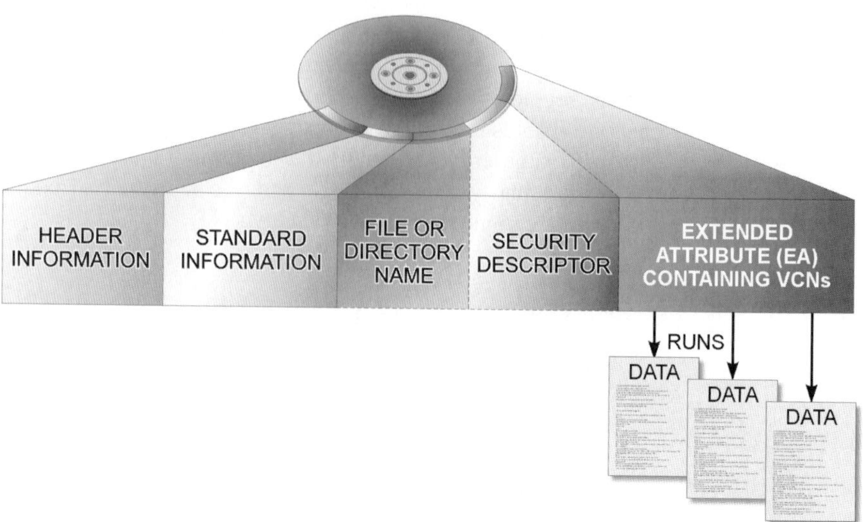

Figure 10-28: Extended MFT Record Organization

For extremely large files that cannot be identified by a single MFT record, multiple MFT records are employed. The first record contains a pointer to additional MFT records. The original MFT record contains the file's or folder's standard information, followed by index links to other MFT records that, in turn, have index links to the actual data runs. In these cases, the data is stored outside the table and can theoretically range up to 16 **EB (exabytes** – 2^{60}).

EB (exabytes)

All entries in the MFT are stored in alphabetical order by filename. Like FAT systems, NTFS systems use the cluster as the basic unit of disk storage. In Windows 4.0, NTFS clusters can range between 512 bytes and 64 kB, depending on the size of the drive and how the disk was prepared. Clusters can range up to 64 kB when established using the FORMAT command from the command prompt. However, cluster sizes are limited to a maximum of 4 kB when using the **Windows NT Disk Manager** to handle the disk organization. Clusters are numbered sequentially on the disk from start to end. These numbers are referred to as **Logical Cluster Numbers (LCNs)**. The default cluster size is determined by the volume size and can be specified in the Disk Administrator utility. Table 10-2 lists the default cluster sizes for NTFS systems in Windows 4.0 environments.

Windows NT Disk Manager

Logical Cluster Numbers (LCNs)

Table 10-2: NTFS Cluster Sizes

PARTITION SIZE	SECTORS/CLUSTER	CLUSTER SIZE
<512 MB	1	512 bytes
512 MB-1 GB	2	1 kB
GB-2 GB	4	2 kB
2 GB-4 GB	8	4 kB
4 GB-8 GB	16	8 kB
8 GB-16 GB	32	16 kB
16 GB-32 GB	64	32 kB
>32 GB	128	64 kB

The smaller cluster size of the NTFS format makes it more efficient than FAT formats for storing smaller files. It also supports larger drives (over 1 GB) much more efficiently than FAT16 or FAT32 structures. The NTFS system is more complex than the FAT systems and, therefore, is not as efficient for smaller drives.

The NTFS structure provides recoverable file system capabilities including a **hot-fix function** and a full recovery system to quickly restore file integrity. The NTFS system maintains a copy of the critical file system information. If the file system fails, the NTFS system will automatically recover the system from the backup information as soon as the disk is accessed again. In addition, NTFS maintains a transaction log to ensure the integrity of the disk structure even if the system fails unexpectedly.

hot-fix function

Security is a very big issue in large business networks.

The Windows NT file system provides security for each file in the system, as well as supplying complete file access auditing information to the system administrator. NTFS files and folders can have permissions assigned to them whether they are shared or not.

Data security is also improved by Windows NT's ability to support mirrored drives. You should recall from the RAID discussions in Chapter 4—*Mass Storage Systems*, that mirroring is a technique of storing separate copies of data on two different drives. This protects the data from loss due to hard drive failures. This is a very important consideration when dealing with server applications. Additional fault tolerance capabilities such as disk mirroring, drive duplexing, striping, RAID, and support for UPS are provided with the Windows NT LAN Manager.

NTFS Permissions

The NTFS system includes security features that enable **permission levels** to be assigned to files and folders on the disk. These permissions set parameters for activities that users can conduct with the designated file or folder.

permission levels

Standard NTFS permissions include:

- **Read (R)**. This permission enables the file or folder to be displayed along with its attributes and permissions.
- **Write (W)**. This permission enables the user to add files or folders, change file and folder attributes, add data to an existing file, and change display attributes.
- **Execute (X)**. The Execute permission enables users to make changes to subfolders, display attributes and permissions, as well as to run executable file types.
- **Delete (D)**. The Delete permission makes it possible for users to remove files and folders.
- **Change Permission (P)**. This permission enables users to change permission assignments of files and folders.
- **Take Ownership (O)**. Ownership permission enables the user to take ownership of the file or folder.

Read

Write

Execute

Delete

Change Permission

Take Ownership

Some of these permission settings apply only to file-level objects, while others apply to both files and folders. Some combinations of the permissions are woven together in Standard NTFS file and folder permissions. These include:

- **No Access (none)**. File and Folder level
- **Read (RX)**. File and Folder level
- **Change (RWXD)**. File and Folder level
- **Add (WX)**. Folder level only

- **Add & Read** (**RWX**). Folder level (RX) File level
- **List** (**RX**). Folder level only
- **Full Control** (**RWXDPO**). File and Folder level

While the NTFS system provides permission-level security for files and folders, other operating systems under Windows NT do not. For example, when a file is moved from an NTFS partition to a FAT partition, the NTFS-specific attributes are discarded. However, NTFS permissions do apply over a network connection.

Permissions can be assigned directly by the administrator, or they can be inherited through group settings. If a user only has Read permissions to a particular file, but is assigned to a group that has wider permissions, then that individual would gain those additional rights through the group. In a server environment, the default permission setting for files is No Access.

Windows NT Disk Partitions

Windows NT can be used to partition a hard drive so that different operating systems can be used in each partition (and in extended partitions). The NTFS format lacks compatibility with other operating systems. Therefore, it will not allow other operating systems to access files on the NTFS drive. This can be a problem on partitioned drives that support multiple operating systems.

System Partition

Boot Partition

Windows NT employs very difficult terminology when referring to types of disk partitions. The disk partition where the BIOS looks for the master boot record is called the **System Partition**, while the partition containing the Windows NT operating system is called the **Boot Partition**. Either, or both, types of partitions can be formatted as FAT or NTFS file systems. In practice, both partition types can be assigned to a single partition, or they can exist as separate partitions. Figure 10-29 depicts the Windows NT partitioning scheme applied to a two-partition disk.

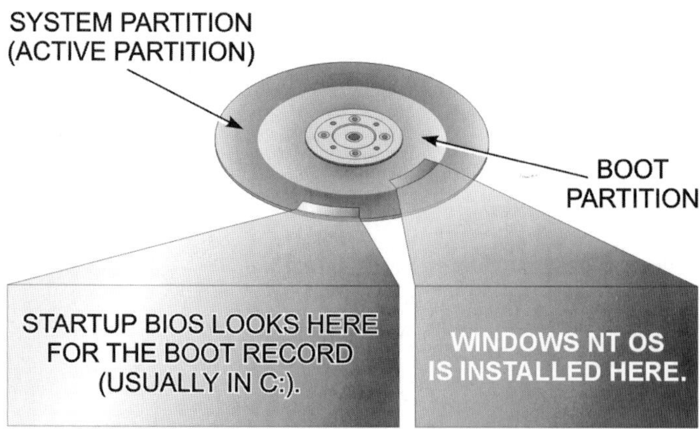

Figure 10-29: Windows NT Partitions

Windows 2000 NTFS

NTFS5

Windows 2000 features an improved NTFS referred to as **NTFS5**. This version enables administrators to establish user hard disk quotas limiting the amount of hard drive space users can have access to. The new NTFS system also offers enhanced system security. Windows 2000 NTFS provides an encrypted file system and secure network protocol and authentication standards.

Windows NT 4 provides directory-level access and use controls. User rights to an individual file cannot be manipulated in Windows NT 4. However, in Windows 2000, the administrator can limit what the user can do to any given file or directory.

Hierarchical Storage Management (HSM)

Windows 2000 includes a **Hierarchical Storage Management** (**HSM**) system that enables the system to shift seldom-used data to selected backup media. When a user requests a file from a server, the server checks to see if the file is still in residence, or if it has been off-loaded to a storage device. If the file has been off-loaded, the server brings it back to the server and delivers it to the requestor, as illustrated in Figure 10-30. The Windows 2000 HSM system provides drivers for DAT and DLT devices to perform this function.

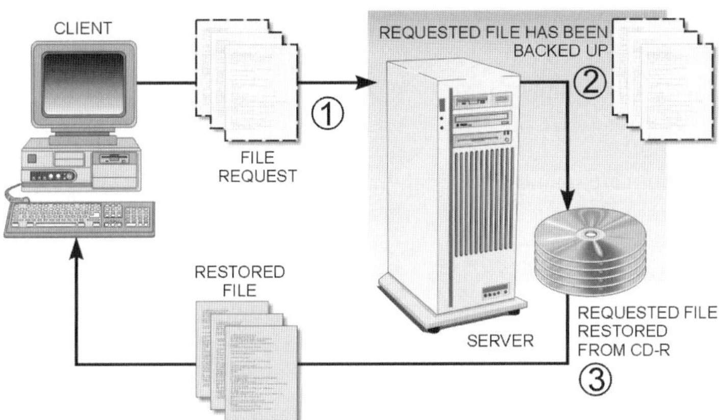

Figure 10-30: Windows 2000 Hierarchical Storage Management

Windows 2000 is based on NTFS Version 5.0. This version of NTFS enables the user to establish disk space quotas for users and locate files by owner.

Access Control List (ACL)

The new NTFS system provides the tools for the administrator to manage user access and usage rights to individual files and directories. File-level control was not possible in earlier NT versions. The **Access Control List** (**ACL**) is used to view which files a user can have access to. This feature is new to the NT world, but it has been available in the Novell NetWare products for a long time.

Dynamic Volume Management

The Windows 2000 Disk Management utility contains a **Dynamic Volume Management** feature that permits the capacity of an existing volume to be extended without rebooting or reformatting. The Disk Management utility also features a new user interface that enables administrators to configure drives and volumes located in remote computers.

Basic disks

Dynamic disks

dynamic volumes

Disk Management is a graphical tool that handles two distinctive types of disks – **Basic disks** and **Dynamic disks**. This tool enables it to handle **dynamic volumes**, created on **dynamic disks**.

A basic disk is a physical disk that contains partitions, drives or volumes created With Windows NT 4.0 or earlier operating systems. Dynamic disks are physical disks created through the Windows 2000 Disk Management utility. These disks can only hold dynamic volumes (not partitions, volumes, or logical drives). However, with dynamic disks the four volume limit inherent with other Microsoft operating systems has been removed.

There are five different types of dynamic volumes:

- Simple
- Spanned
- Mirrored
- Striped
- RAID 5

Only systems running Windows 2000 can access dynamic volumes. Therefore, basic volumes should be established on drives that Windows 9x or Windows NT 4.0 systems need to access. To install Windows 2000 on a dynamic volume, it must be either a simple or a mirrored volume and it must be a volume that has been upgraded from a basic volume. Installing Windows 2000 on the volume requires that it has a partition table, which dynamic volumes do not have unless they have been upgraded from a basic volume. Basic volumes are upgraded by upgrading a basic disk to a dynamic disk. Windows 2000 will not support dynamic volumes on Portable computers. Mirrored and RAID-5 volumes are only supported on Windows 2000 Servers.

Administrators group

Dynamic volumes are managed through the Windows 2000 Disk Management snap in tool, depicted in Figure 10-31, located under the Computer Management console. To access the Disk Manager, follow the *Start/Settings/Control Panel/Administrative_Tools* path. Double-click the Computer Management icon and click on the Disk Management entry. Since working with dynamic volumes is a major administrative task, you must be logged in as an administrator or as a member of Windows 2000's **Administrators group** in order to carry out the procedure. Also, system and boot volumes cannot be formatted as dynamic volumes.

TEST TIP

Know what is required to install Windows 2000 in a dynamic volume.

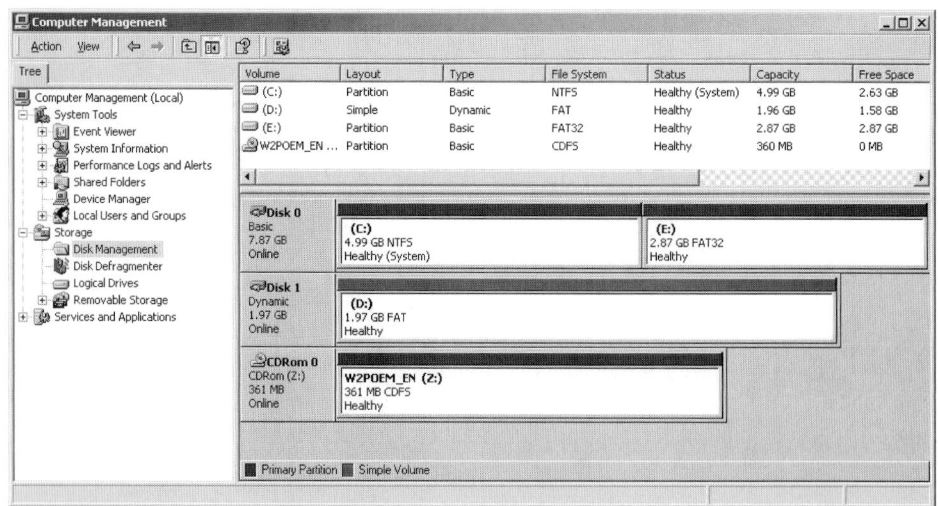

Figure 10-31: Windows 2000 Disk Management Snap In

NTFS Advantages

In most situations, the NTFS system offers better performance and features than a FAT16 or FAT32 system. The exceptions to this occur when smaller drives are being used, other file systems are being used on the same drive, or the operating system crashes.

In most other situations, the NTFS system offers:

- More efficient drive management due to its smaller cluster size capabilities
- Support for very large drives made possible by its 64-bit clustering arrangement
- Increased folder and file security capabilities
- Recoverable file system capabilities
- Built-in RAID support

High Performance File System

IBM followed their successful PC-AT system with a line of personal computers called PS/2 (Personal System 2). The line was advertised around a proprietary 32-bit bus, called Micro Channel Architecture (MCA), and a new GUI-based operating system called OS/2 (Operating System 2). The PS/2 line has long since faded into the background of PC hardware, but the OS/2 software continues in some circles.

At the heart of the OS/2 operating system is the **High Performance File System** (**HPFS**). It provided a very robust file system for its time. The HPFS structure retained the FAT directory structure, but featured long file names (up to 254 characters) and volume sizes up to 8 GB. Under HPFS, the unit of management was changed to physical sectors rather than clusters.

High Performance File System (HPFS)

Its other attributes include good performance when directories contain several files, built-in fault tolerance, fragmentation resistance, and good effectiveness when working with large partitions.

HPFS employs banding to organize the disk efficiently. Using this arrangement, HPFS segments the drive into 8 MB bands with 2 KB allocation bitmaps between each band. The bitmaps are used to record which sectors have been used within a band. Whenever possible, the operating system tries to retain files within a single band. In doing so, the drive's R/W head does not have to return to track-0 for reference.

The HPFS file system is only accessible under the OS/2 and Windows NT 3.51 operating systems.

INSTALLING WINDOWS NT/2000

The installation process for Windows NT versions, including Windows NT/2000, can be a little more difficult than that of the Windows 9x versions. In particular, the lack of extensive hardware and software compatibilities requires some advanced planning before installing, or upgrading to Windows NT/2000.

Hardware Compatibility List (HCL)

The first issue to deal with is the hardware compatibility issue. Windows NT/2000 makes no claim to maintaining compatibility with a wide variety of hardware devices. Is the hardware being used supported by the intended version of Windows 2000? If the current hardware does not appear in the Microsoft **Hardware Compatibility List** (**HCL**) of the new version, you are on your own for technical support.

The second factor to sort out is which file management system should be used. Windows NT/2000 can be configured to use either a typical FAT-based file system, or its own proprietary NTFS file system. Review the NTFS advantages section from earlier in this chapter to determine which file system is better suited to the particular situation.

Installing Windows 2000 Professional

The minimum hardware requirements for installing Windows 2000 Professional on a PC-compatible system are:

- Microprocessor – 133 MHz Pentium (P5 equivalent or better)
- RAM – 64 MB (4 GB maximum)
- HDD Space – 650 MB or more free on a 2 GB drive
- VGA Monitor

For installation from a CD-ROM, a 12x drive is required. If the CD-ROM drive is not bootable, a high-density 3.5-inch floppy drive is also required.

checkupgradeonly

upgrade.txt

Before installing Windows 2000 Professional from the CD, it is recommended that the file **checkupgradeonly** be run. This file is located on the installation CD under \i386\winnt32 and checks the system for possible hardware compatibility problems. The program generates a text file report named **upgrade.txt** that can be found under the \Windows folder. It contains Windows 2000 compatibility information about the system along with a list of potential complications.

If your system has hardware devices that are not on the Windows 2000 Hardware Compatibility List, you should contact the manufacturer of the device to determine whether they have new, updated Windows 2000 drivers for their device. Many peripheral makers have become very proactive in supplying updated drivers for their devices. Often, posting their latest drivers and product compatibility information on their Internet Web sites, where they can be downloaded by customers. This is a good place to begin looking for needed drivers. The second alternative is to try the device with Windows NT or Windows 9x drivers to see if it will work. The final option is to get a device that is listed on the Windows 2000 HCL.

TEST TIP

Know what to do if you encounter hardware devices not listed on the Windows 2000 HCL.

> If Windows Professional is to be installed across a network, a Windows 2000 Professional-compatible NIC is required.

HCL.TXT

A list of Microsoft verified network cards can be read from the **HCL.TXT** file on the Windows 2000 Professional distribution CD. The system must also have access to the network share that contains the Setup files.

If several machines in a given organization are being upgraded to the same status, the Windows 2000 Scripting capabilities can be put to good use. This feature can be used to create installation routines that require no user interaction. Microsoft has also added increased support for third-party disk copy and imaging utilities that perform multiple installs within a networked system.

To conduct a New Windows 2000 Professional installation, you will need the Windows 2000 Professional distribution CD. If the installation is being performed on a system that cannot boot to the CD-ROM drive, you will also need Windows 2000 Professional Setup disks.

Hands-On Activity

1. To initiate the installation from a floppy disk, turn the system off, place the Windows 2000 professional Startup Disk #1 in the floppy drive, and turn the system on.

   When the Setup program starts, it brings the Windows 2000 Setup Wizard, depicted in Figure 10-32, to the screen. The Setup Wizard collects information, including Names, Passwords, and Regional Settings, and writes the information to files on the hard drive. Afterwards, the Wizard checks the system's hardware and properly configures the installation.

2. The first step in the Setup process is to choose whether the installation is a Clean Install or an Upgrade. If a new installation is being performed, the Setup program will install the Windows 2000 files in the \WINNT folder.

Figure 10-32: Windows 2000 Setup Wizard

3. Follow the instructions the Wizard places on the screen, entering any information required. The choice made concerning the type of setup being performed and user-provided input determines the exact path the installation process will take.

Hands-On Activity

1. For a CD-ROM install, boot the system to the existing operating system and then insert the Windows 2000 Professional distribution CD in the CD-ROM drive.
2. If the system detects the CD in the drive, simply click the Install Windows 2000 option. If not, start Setup through the Run command. In Windows 9x and NT 4.0, click Start and then Run. In Windows 3.x and NT 3.51 click File and the Run.
3. At the prompt, enter the location on the Windows 2000 start file (Winnt.exe or Winnt32.exe) on the distribution CD (i.e., d:\i386\Winnt32.exe). In the case of Windows 3.x, the Winnt.exe option should be used.
4. Choose whether the installation is a New Install or an Upgrade.
5. Follow the instructions the Wizard places on the screen, entering any information required.

To install Windows 2000 Professional across a network, it will be necessary to establish a shared connection between the local unit and the system containing the Windows 2000 Professional Setup files.

Hands-On Activity

1. Boot the local unit to the existing operating system and establish a connection with the remote unit.
2. At the command prompt, enter the path to the remote Winnt32.exe file (use the Winnt.exe file if an older 16-bit operating system is being used on the local unit).
3. Choose whether the installation is a Clean Install or an Upgrade.
4. Follow the instructions the Setup Wizard places on the screen, entering any information required.

The Windows 2000 Setup Wizard collects information about the system and the user during the installation process. The most important information that must be provided includes the type of file management system that will be used (FAT or NTFS), Computer Name and Administrator Password, Network Settings, and Workgroup or Domain operations.

Upgrading to Windows 2000

Systems can be upgraded to Windows 2000 Professional from Windows 3.x and 9x, as well as Windows NT 3.5 and 4.0 workstations. This includes older NTFS, FAT16, and FAT32 installations. When you install Windows 2000, it can recognize all three of these file system types.

The process of upgrading to Windows 2000 can be performed in incremental steps. This enables network administrators to bring network machines up to Windows 2000 status over time. During the system upgrade process the Windows NT 4.0 units can interact with the Windows 2000 units because they see them as NT 4 systems.

Upgrading Windows 2000 from a Windows NT 4.0 or Windows 9x base is quicker than performing a new installation.

When a system is upgraded to Windows 2000 Professional, the Setup utility replaces any existing Windows files with Windows 2000 Professional versions. However, existing settings and applications will be preserved in the new environment.

As with previous Windows NT products, Windows 2000 does not attempt to remain compatible with older hardware and software. Therefore, some applications may not be compatible with Windows 2000 and may run poorly, or fail completely after an upgrade.

Upgrading to Windows 2000 is suggested for those using an existing Windows operating system that is compatible with Windows 2000 and who wish to maintain their existing data and preference settings.

Hands-On Activity

1. To upgrade a system to Windows 2000 from a previous operating system using a CD-ROM install, boot the system to the existing operating system and then insert the Windows 2000 Professional distribution CD in the CD-ROM drive.
2. If the system detects the CD in the drive, simply click the Install Windows 2000 option. If not, start Setup through the Run command. In Windows 9x and NT 4.0, click Start and then Run. In Windows 3.x and NT 3.51, click File and then Run.
3. At the prompt, enter the location on the Windows 2000 start file (Winnt.exe or Winnt32.exe) on the distribution CD (i.e., *d:\i386\Winnt32.exe*). In the case of Windows 3.x, the Winnt.exe option should be used.
4. Choose whether the installation is a Clean Install or an Upgrade.
5. Follow the instructions the Wizard places on the screen, entering any information required.

To upgrade Windows 2000 Professional from a previous operating system across a network, it will be necessary to establish a shared connection between the local unit and the system containing the Windows 2000 Professional Setup files.

1. Boot the local unit to the existing operating system and establish a connection with the remote unit.
2. At the command prompt, enter the path to the remote Winnt32.exe file (use the Winnt.exe file if an 16-bit older operating system is being used on the local unit). The Winnt command is used with 16-bit operating systems such as DOS or Windows 3x. The Winnt32 version is used with 32-bit operating systems including Windows 95, 98, NT3.5, NT4.0
3. Choose the "Upgrade your computer to Windows 2000" option.
4. Follow the instructions the Setup Wizard places on the screen, entering any information required.

Windows 2000 Setup Wizard

During the installation process, the **Windows 2000 Setup Wizard** collects information about users and the system. Most of this information is collected automatically. However, some information must be provided by the user/technician.

The most important information required during the setup process is the file management system to be used, the computer name and administrator password, network settings, and Workgroup/Domain selection.

DUAL BOOTING

Windows NT can be set up to dual-boot with DOS or Windows 9x operating systems. This provides the option for the system to boot up into a Windows NT environment, or into a DOS/Windows 9x environment. In such cases, a startup menu appears on the display that asks which operating system should be used. Establishing either of these dual-boot conditions with Windows NT require that the DOS or Windows 9x operating systems must be installed first.

The major drawback of dual booting with Windows NT is that neither operating system is capable of using applications installed in the other operating system's partition. Therefore, software to be used by both operating systems must be installed in the system twice. Once for each operating system's partition.

Care must also be taken when formatting a logical drive in a Windows NT dual-boot system. The file management formats of Windows NT and the other operating systems are not compatible. If the disk is formatted with NTFS, the DOS, or Windows 9x operating systems will not be able to read the files in the NTFS partition. However, Windows NT can operate with the FAT file systems used by DOS and Windows 3.x/9x. As a matter of fact, Windows 2000 can be installed on FAT16, FAT32, or NTFS partitions. Windows 2000 also supports the CDFS file system used with CD-ROM drives in PCs. Therefore, it is recommended that logical drives in a dual-boot system be formatted with the FAT system.

WINDOWS NT STARTUP MODES

Unlike the Windows 9x products, Windows NT 4.0 provides very few options when it starts up. The user is normally offered two options. The NTLDR file causes the system to display a selection menu of which operating system to boot from, along with an option to start the system in *VGA mode*. The menu listing is based on what NTLDR find in the Boot.ini file. If the VGA option is selected, the system will startup as normal, with the exception that it will only load the standard VGA driver to drive the display.

The second option presented is the **Last Known Good Hardware Configuration mode** option. Selecting this option will cause the system to start up using the configuration information that it recorded the last time a user successfully logged onto the system. The option appears on the screen for a few seconds after the operating system selection has been made. You must press the SPACEBAR while the option is displayed on the screen to select this startup mode. If no selection is made, the system continues on with a normal startup as previously outlined, using the existing hardware configuration information.

Last Known Good Hardware Configuration mode

WINDOWS NT STARTUP

The sequence of steps in the Windows NT bootup and startup processes is similar to that presented in the previous chapters for DOS and Windows 9x systems. The main differences lay in terminology and the names of the files that Windows NT employs.

Like any other PC system, the Windows NT-based PC starts up by running a series of POST tests, performing an initialization of its intelligent system devices, and performing a system boot process. It is in the boot process that the descriptions of the two operating systems diverge.

When the BIOS executes the Master Boot Record on the hard drive, the MBR examines the disk's partition table to locate the active partition. The boot process then moves to the boot sector of that partition (referred to as the **partition boot sector**) located in the first sector of the active partition. Here the MBR finds the code to begin loading the secondary bootstrap loader from the root directory of the boot drive.

partition boot sector

In the case of a Windows NT partition, the bootstrap loader is the **NT Loader** file named **NTLDR**. This file is the Windows NT equivalent of the DOS IO.SYS file and is responsible for loading the NT operating system into memory. Afterwards, NTLDR passes control of the system over to the Windows NT operating system.

NT Loader

NTLDR

When Windows NT gains control of the system, its first action is to initialize the video hardware and switch the microprocessor into protected mode. In the Windows NT system, the microprocessor is switched into the 32-bit flat memory mode described earlier in this chapter.

Next, a temporary miniature file system that can read both FAT and NTFS file structures is loaded to aid NTLDR in reading the rest of the system. Recall that Windows NT has the capability to work in either FAT or proprietary NTFS partitions. However, at this stage of the boot process, the operating system is still uncertain as to which system it will be using.

BOOT.INI

Boot Loader Menu

With the minifile system in place, the NTLDR can locate and read a special hidden boot loader menu file named **BOOT.INI**. NTLDR uses this text file to generate the **Boot Loader Menu** that is displayed on the screen. If no selection is made after a given time delay, the default value is selected.

NTDETECT.COM

If Windows NT is the designated operating system to be used, the NTLDR program executes a hardware detection file called **NTDETECT.COM**. This file is responsible for collecting information about the system's installed hardware devices and passing it to the NTLDR program. This information is later used to upgrade the Windows NT Registry files.

BOOTSECT.DOS

If a different operating system is to be loaded, as directed by the Boot Loader Menu entry, the NTLDR program loads a file called **BOOTSECT.DOS** from the root directory of the system partition and passes control to it. From this point, the BOOTSECT file is responsible for loading the desired operating system.

NTOSKRNL.EXE

HAL.DLL

Finally, the NTLDR program examines the partition for a pair of files named **NTOSKRNL.EXE** and **HAL.DLL**. NTOSKRNL.EXE is the Windows NT kernel file that contains the Windows NT core and loads its device drivers. HAL.DLL is the Hardware Abstraction Layer driver that holds the information specific to the CPU that the system is being used with.

Even though NTLDR reads the NTOSKRNL and HAL files at this time, it does not load or execute them. Instead, it uses a file named NTDETECT.COM to gather information about the hardware devices present and passes it to the NTLDR. Note: this should not be confused with the PnP enumeration process that occurs later in the Windows 2000 bootup process. The information gathered by NTDETECT is stored to be used later for updating the Hardware Registry hive.

In particular, the NTDETECT program checks for information concerning:

- Machine ID
- Bus Types
- Keyboard
- Mouse
- Video Type
- Floppy Drives
- Parallel Ports
- COMM Ports

Once the information has been passed back to NTLDR, it opens the System Hive portion of the Registry to find the Current Control Set. At this point, the system displays the Starting Windows NT logo on the display along with a sliding progress bar that shows the degree of progress being made in loading the drivers. After the drivers have been loaded, the NTLDR program passes control to the NTOSKRNL file to complete the bootup sequence.

BOOTVID.DLL

Session Manager

SMSS.EXE

AUTOCHK

PAGEFILE.SYS

When NTOSKRNL gains control of the system, it initializes the HAL.DLL file along with the **BOOTVID.DLL** file and shifts the video display to graphics mode. It then initializes the drivers prepared by NTLDR and uses the NTDETECT information to create a temporary Hardware Hive in memory. Finally, NTOSKRNL executes a **Session Manager** file titled **SMSS.EXE** to carry out pre-start functions such as running a boot-time version of CHKDSK called **AUTOCHK**. It also establishes parameters concerning the Windows NT paging file (**PAGEFILE.SYS**) to hold RAM memory swap pages.

After these tasks have been performed, the Session Manager loads the console logon service file (**WINLOGON.EXE**) to begin the authentication verification process. WINLOGON starts the **Local Security Authority Subsystem** (**LSASS.EXE**) and the print spooler (**SPOOLS.EXE**) along with their supporting files. Finally, WINLOGON loads the **Service Controller** (**SCREG.EXE**) that completes the loading process by bringing in the remaining devices and services.

WINLOGON.EXE

Local Security Authority Subsystem (LSASS.EXE)

SPOOLS.EXE

Service Controller (SCREG.EXE)

Windows 2000 Startup

The Windows 2000 boot process is almost identical to the Windows NT boot up. The major events in the Windows 2000 startup include:

1. NTLDR looks into memory and OS loader V5.0 message appears on screen.
2. NTLDR switches processor to 32-bit flat memory mode.
3. NTLDR starts mini-file system (FAT or NTFS) to read disk files.
4. NTLDR reads Boot.ini file and displays the Advanced Boot Options menu on screen.
5. NTLDR runs Ntdetect.com to gather system hardware information. Ntdetect checks for the following hardware items:
   - Machine ID
   - Video Type
   - Keyboard
   - Parallel Ports
   - SCSI adapters
   - Bus Types
   - Floppy Drives
   - Pointing devices
   - COMM Ports
   - Math coprocessor
6. NTLDR loads Ntoskrnl and hal files into memory and passes the hardware information to it.
7. NTLDR reads the SYSTEM Registry key, places it in memory, and implements the hardware profile (configuration and control set) from the proper Registry.
8. NTLDR loads startup device drivers into memory.
9. NTLDR passes control to the Ntoskrnl file.
10. Ntoskrnl creates the Registry's HARDWARE key from the information gathered earlier by Ntdetect.
11. Ntoskrnl executes additional device drivers.
12. Ntoskrnl starts the SMSS.EXE session file.
13. The Win32 subsection runs the WINLOGON.EXE and LSASS.EXE programs, the CTRL+ALT+DEL window is presented on the display, and the logon screen is displayed.
14. The SCREG.EXE service controller program starts and loads all remaining services specified in the Registry, including the Windows 2000 shell and desktop.

TEST TIP

Remember the files involved the Windows 2000 startup process and the order of their execution.

As with Windows 9x, the Windows 2000 shell program is the Windows desktop. When the shell and desktop components are loaded, the system displays a prompt on the screen for the user to log in, as depicted in Figure 10-33.

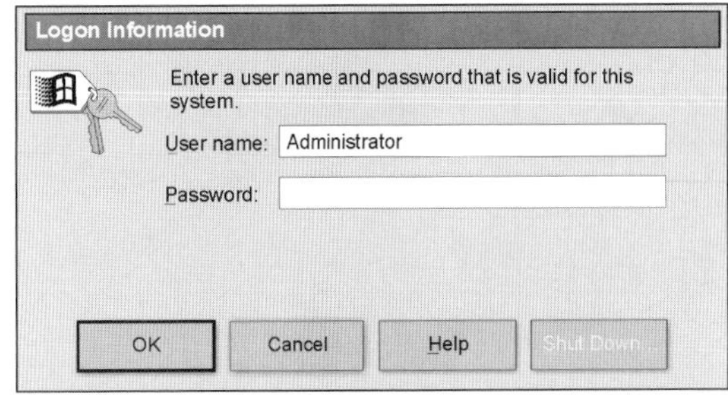

Figure 10-33: The Windows NT Logon Dialog Box

The Windows NT/2000 logon allows the operating system to configure itself for specific users. Normal logon involves entering a user name and password. If no logon information is entered, then default values will be loaded into the system.

In Windows 2000, the login screen always appears even if the system is not being used with a network.

WINDOWS NT/2000 DEVICE DRIVERS

As mentioned earlier in the chapter, Windows NT/2000 does not support as many hardware devices as the Windows 9x platforms do. However, Windows NT still offers support for a fairly wide range of disk drive types, VGA video cards, network interface cards, tape drives, and printers. To determine what components Windows NT supports, it is necessary to consult the Hardware Compatibility List for the version of Windows NT/2000 being used*.

NOTE

*This information can be obtained from the Microsoft web site (www.microsoft.com/st/hcl), depicted in Figure 10-34.

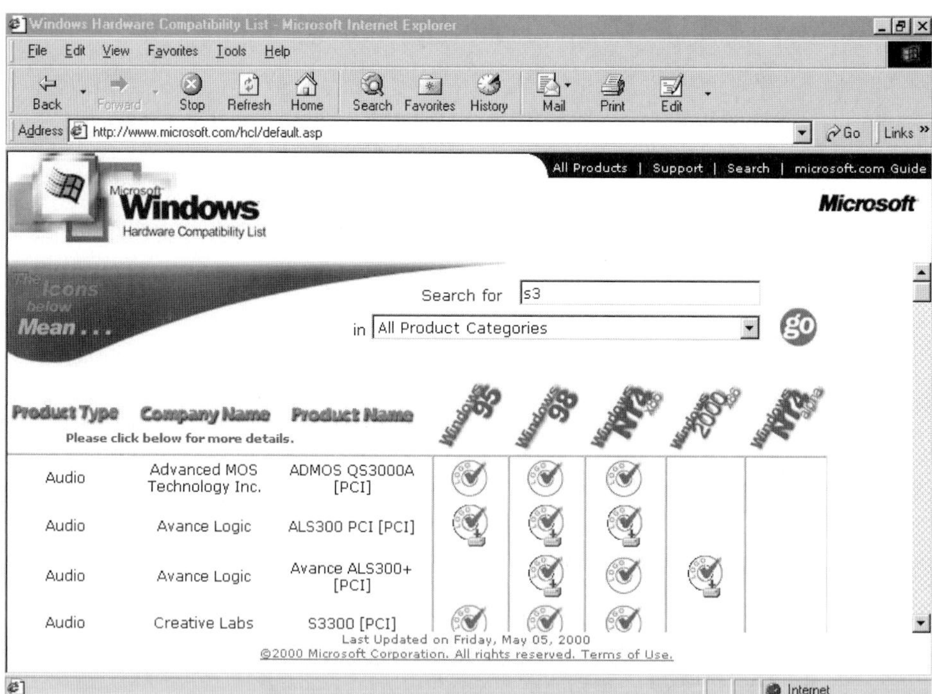

Figure 10-34: Microsoft 2000 Drivers Page

Windows 2000 supports a wide array of newer hardware devices. These devices include DVD, USB, and IEEE 1394 devices. Microsoft works with hardware vendors to certify their drivers. These drivers are digitally signed so that they can be loaded automatically by the system.

Windows 2000 brings Plug-and-Play capabilities to the Windows NT environment. The Windows NT PnP manager can assign and reallocate system resources as needed.

If drivers for the device being installed are not listed at this location, there is a good chance the device will not operate, or will not operate well in the Windows NT environment. If this is the case, the only recourse is to contact the device's manufacturer for Windows NT drivers.

Adding new devices to Windows 2000 is accomplished through the Add /Remove Hardware icon located in the Control Panel. Figure 10-35 depicts the Windows 2000 Control Panel icons. As with Windows 9x systems, the Windows 2000 Control Panel is used to add or remove new hardware and software components to the system, modify device settings, and to modify desktop items.

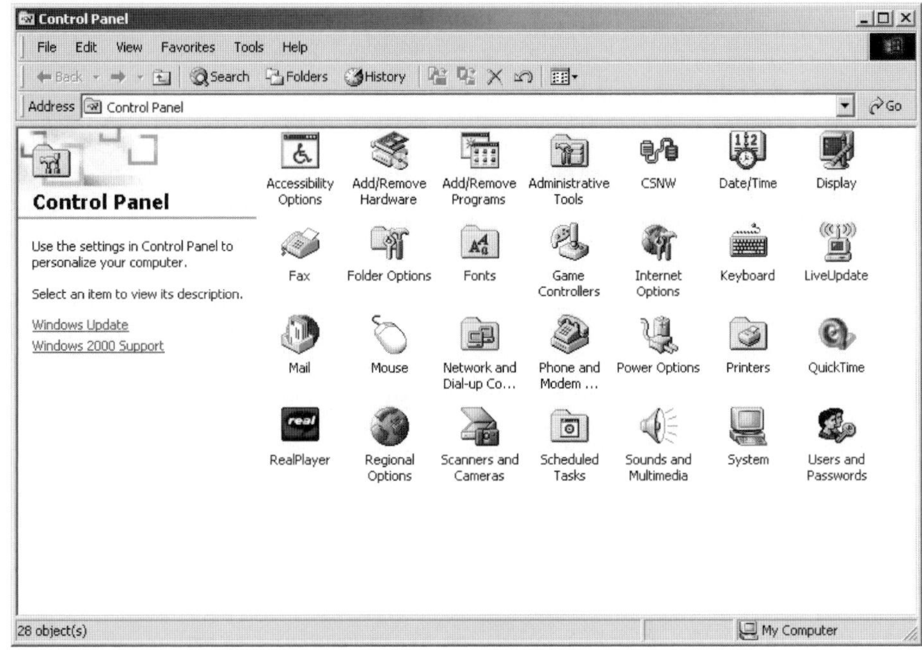

Figure 10-35: Windows 2000 Control Panel Icons

Double-clicking on a device icon in the Control Panel will produce a Properties dialog box for that device. The dialog box holds configuration information specific to that device. The tabs located along the tops of the dialog boxes can be used to review and change settings and drivers for the device.

Windows NT 4.0 does not possess Plug-and-Play although it does feature some autodetection capabilities. It also provided no Add New Hardware wizard. Devices had to be installed manually under Windows NT 4.0 through the icons in the Control Panel, or through installation routines provided by the equipment manufacturer.

Printing in Windows 2000

Windows 2000 employs a print spooler processing architecture similar to that found in Windows 9x. This structure provides smooth printing in a background mode and quick return-to-application time.

The key to this operation is in how the print spooler sends data to the printer. Data is moved to the printer only when it is ready to receive more. Therefore, the system is never waiting for the printer to digest data that has been sent to it.

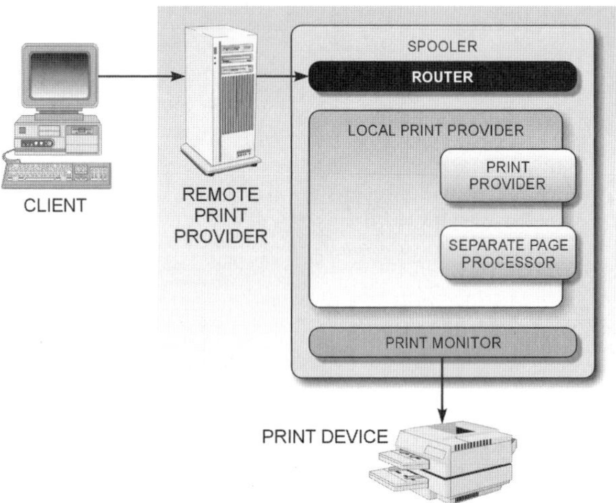

Figure 10-36: The Windows 2000 Print Spooler

The Windows 2000 print spooler, depicted in Figure 10-36, is actually a series of 32-bit virtual device drivers and DLLs. In the figure, the spooler consists of the logical blocks between the client computer and the print device. These blocks process threads in the background and pass them to the printer when it is ready. In essence, the application prints to the Windows printer driver, the driver controls the operation of the spooler, and the driver prints to the printer from the spooler.

In a network printing operation, the print spooler must run on both the local server and the remote client systems. The user can start and stop the local print spooler process through the Control Panel's Services icon. Once the spooler service has been stopped by the user, it will be necessary to restart it before printing can occur again, unless the printer driver has been configured to bypass the spooler. Also, the local user is not capable of controlling the print operation to a server. The server print function is managed independently.

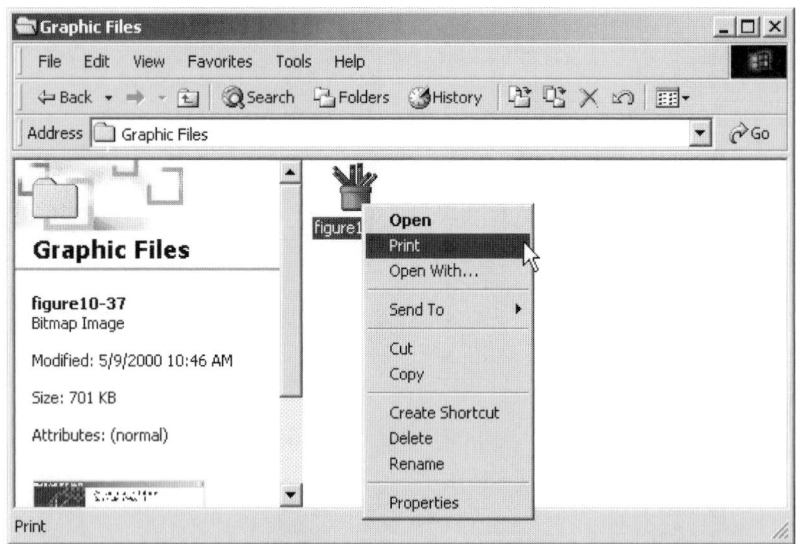

Figure 10-37: Printing from My Computer Pop-up Menu

To print an open file in Windows 2000, simply move to the application's File menu as normal and click on the Print option. If the file is not open, it is still possible to print files in Windows 2000. Under the My Computer icon, clicking the right mouse button on a selected file will produce a print option in a pop-up menu like the one in Figure 10-37. Files can be printed from the Windows Explorer screen by employing the same right-click menu method. The document can also be dragged-and-dropped onto a printer icon in the Printers folder, in the My Network Places listing, or on the desktop. Obviously, this option can be performed with both local and remote networked printers.

The settings for any printer can be changed through the My Computer icon on the desktop or through the Printers option under the Start menu's Settings entry. The process is the same for both routes: Simply double-click on the Printer folder, alternate-click on the desired printer, and select its Properties entry from the menu.

To view documents waiting to be printed from the print spooler, double-click on the desired printer's icon in the Printer folder. This will display the existing print queue, as illustrated in Figure 10-38. Closing the print window does not interrupt the print queue in Windows 2000.

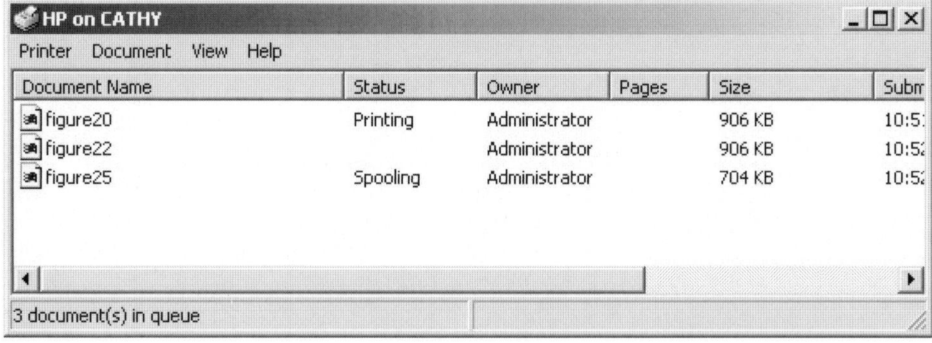

Figure 10-38: Windows 2000 Print Queue

The fact that the print spooler runs in its own 32-bit virtual environment means that printer stalls will not lock up the system. The print jobs in the queue will be completed unless they are deleted from the list.

The print spooler window's menu bar contains the same basic tool set as the one described for the Windows 9x Print Spooler. The menu items allow printing to be paused and resumed. They can also be used to delete print jobs from the queue. Right-clicking a printer icon will produce a pop-up menu that can also be used to control printing operations being performed by that printer. Both options offer a "Properties" option that can be used to access the printer's configuration and connection information.

Internet Printing Protocol (IPP)

The Windows 2000 Printers dialog box enables users to sort between different printers based on their attributes. Windows 2000 Professional possesses the capability of printing across the Internet using the new standards-based **Internet Printing Protocol** (**IPP**). Using this protocol Windows 2000 Professional can print to a URL, view the print queue status using an Internet browser, and install print drivers across the Internet.

OpenType

Windows 2000 Professional also supports a new universal font format called **Open-Type**. This font type combines the best features of TrueType and Type 1 fonts. Open-Type is supported by subsetting and compression technology that makes it efficient for transmission over the Internet.

Establishing Printers in Windows 2000

Add Printer Wizard

Like Windows 9x, Windows 2000 will automatically adopt any printers that have been established prior to its installation in the system. If no printers have been installed, the Setup routine will run the new **Add Printer Wizard**, depicted in Figure 10-39, to allow a printer to be installed. Each printer in the system possesses its own print window and icon to work from. The wizard can be accessed at any time through the Start menu.

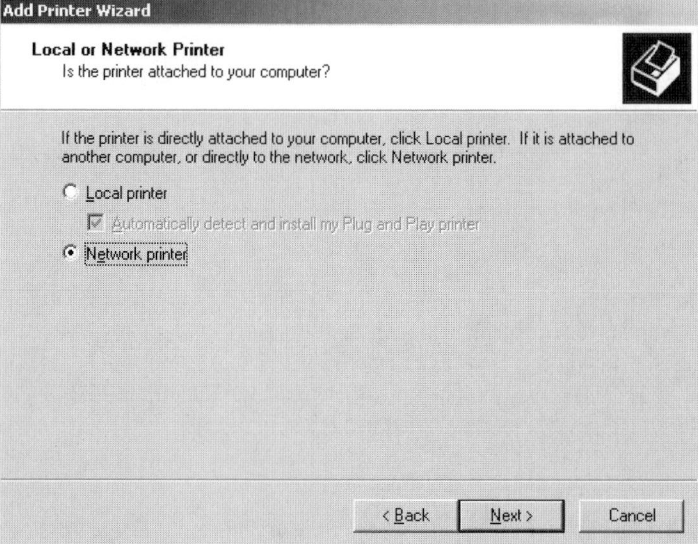

Figure 10-39: The Windows 2000 Add Printer Wizard

Add Printer icon

To use the Start menu, move to the Settings entry and click on Printers. To install a printer, open the Printers folder and double-click the **Add Printer icon**. From this point, the Printer Wizard guides the installation process. Since Windows 2000 has built-in networking support, the printer can be a local unit (connected to the computer), or a remote unit located somewhere on the network.

To install local printers, choose the Local Printer option and click the Next button. Normally, the LPT1 options should be selected from the list of port options. Next, the Add Printer Wizard will produce a list of manufacturers and models to choose from. This list will be similar to the one depicted in Figure 10-40. Simply select the correct manufacturer and then the desired model from the list and inform the wizard about the location of the \I386 directory to fetch the driver from. If the \I386 directory has been copied to the hard drive, it will be faster to access the driver there. If not, the Windows 2000 distribution CD will be required.

If the printer is not recognized as a model supported by the Windows 2000 driver list, OEM drivers can be installed from a disk containing the OEMSETUP.INF file. Select the Have Disk option from the Add Printer Wizard screen.

After loading the driver, the wizard will request a name for the printer to identify it to the network system. Enter a unique name or choose to use the default name supplied by Windows and continue.

> **TEST TIP**
>
> Know how to install device drivers in Windows 2000 if the particular device is not listed in the standard Windows driver listings.

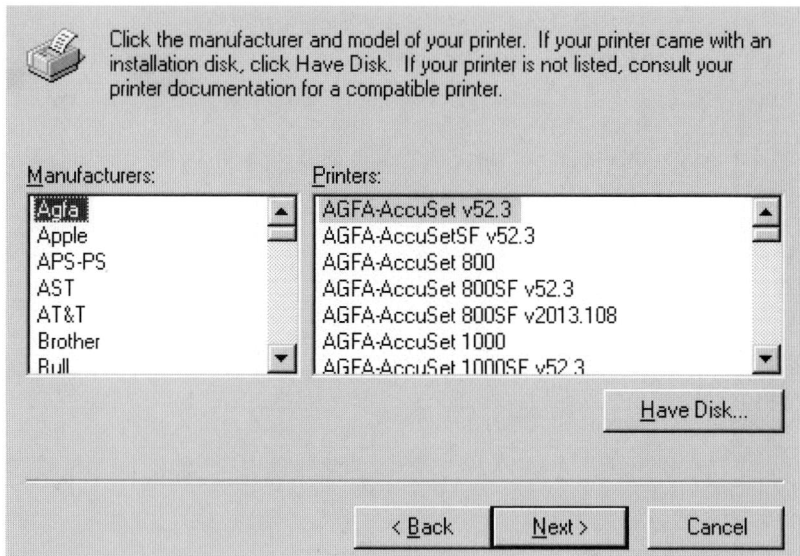

Figure 10-40: A List of Printer Manufacturers and Models

Finally, the Add Printer Wizard will ask whether the printer is to be shared with other units on the network. If so, the printer must have a unique name to identify it to others on the network and must be set as Shared. The shared printer must also be set up for the different types of operating systems that may want to use it. The wizard will display a list of OS types on the network. Any, or all, of the OS types may be selected. The installation process is completed when the Finish button is clicked.

The Add Printer Wizard can also be accessed through the My Computer icon, the Control Panel, or by double-clicking on the Printers folder or icon.

Printer Properties

Printer Properties are all of the defining features about a selected printer and include information that ranges from which port it uses to what security features have been implemented with it.

To examine or change the properties of a printer in Windows 2000, select the Printers option from the Start button menu. Inside the printer window, click the desired printer to select it. From the File menu option, select the Properties entry to display the printer's properties sheet, as depicted in Figure 10-41.

The General tab provides general information about the printer. This includes such information as its description, physical location, and installed driver name. The Ports tab lists the system's physical ports while the Scheduling tab displays the printer's availability, priority level, and spooling options. The Sharing tab shows the printer's share status and share name.

The Security tab provides access to three major components. These are the Permissions button, the Auditing button, and the Ownership button. The Permissions button enables the system administrator to establish the level of access for different users in the system. The Auditing button provides user and event tracking capabilities for the administrator. Finally, the Ownership button displays the name of the printer's owner.

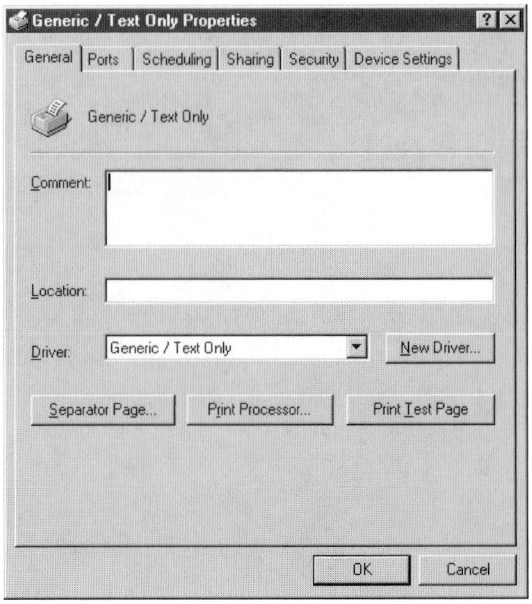

Figure 10-41: Printer Properties Sheet

The Device Settings tab provides a wide array of information about the printer, including such items as paper tray sizes and its font substitution tables. This feature is used to import downloadable font sets, install font cartridges, and increase the printer's virtual memory settings. The Device Settings tab, depicted in Figure 10-42, is one of the most important tabs in the Printer Properties page.

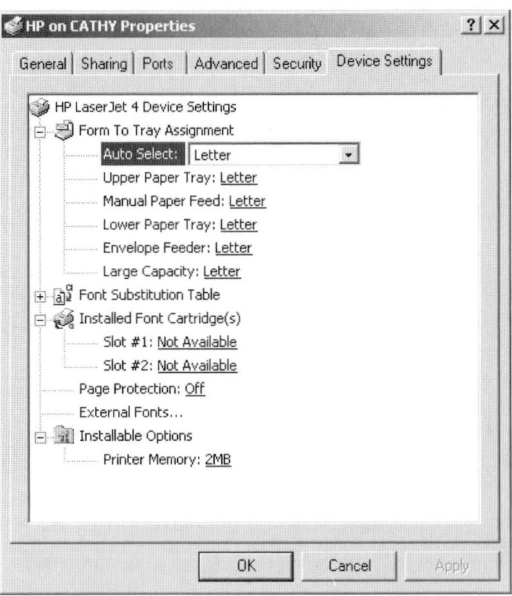

Figure 10-42: Windows 2000 Printer Properties/Device Settings Tab

Windows Applications

The Windows 2000 environment employs an Add/Remove Programs wizard to assist users in installing new applications. The Windows 2000 Add/Remove Programs icon is located in the main Control Panel, as illustrated in Figure 10-43. As you can see, it is very similar to the Windows 9x Control Panel.

Figure 10-43: Windows 2000 Add/Remove Programs Icon

Double-clicking on the Add/Remove Programs icon produces the Add/Remove Programs dialog box. Any application that employs a Setup.exe or Install.exe installation routine can be installed through this window. Clicking the Install button will cause the system to request the location of the installation program.

TEST TIP

Know the consequences of running DOS utilities from a Windows environment and how to solve problems associated with DOS applications running in the Windows environment.

In addition to third-party applications, the Add/Remove Programs wizard can be used to install or remove optional components of the Windows 2000 operating system. Clicking on the Windows 2000 Setup tab under the Properties box produces a list of 2000 components that can be selected for inclusion or removal from the Windows 2000 system.

Windows 2000 Application Installer

Windows 2000 Application Installer

As we've already mentioned, Windows 2000 features a new, more versatile MSI applications installer called the **Windows 2000 Application Installer.** This program is designed to better handle DLL files in the Windows 2000 environment. In previous versions of Windows, applications would copy similar versions of shared DLL files, and other support files, into the \Windows folder. When a new application overwrites a particular DLL file that another application needs to operate properly, a problem is likely to occur with the original software package.

The Windows 2000 Application Installer enables applications to check the system before introducing new DLLs to the system. Software designers who want their products to carry the Windows 2000 logo must write code that does not place proprietary support files in the Windows directory — including DLL files. Instead, the DLL files are located in the application's folder.

Windows Installer-compatible applications can repair themselves if they become corrupted. When the application is started, the operating system checks the properties of its key files. If a key file is missing, or appears to be damaged, it will invoke the Installer and prompt the user to insert the application distribution CD. When the CD has been inserted, the Installer automatically reinstalls the file in question.

Install on Demand

This Installer enables applications to be installed on demand, or in a partial manner. Most major applications packages contain features that many users will never need. To avoid installing unnecessary functions and options, the Windows 2000 Installer allows a service called "**Install on Demand**". If the application is written to take advantage of this feature, the program's installable modules will appear on the toolbar. The Installer will automatically load the option the first time the application calls for it. Likewise, the partial application installation can be updated as desired.

The Hierarchical Storage Management System

Remote Storage Service

Hierarchical Storage Management (HSM)

In a network environment, the **Remote Storage Service** function of the Windows 2000 Server's **Hierarchical Storage Management (HSM)** system moves infrequently used programs and data to slower storage devices, such as tape or CD-R, while still maintaining the appearance of the data being present. The operation of the HSM system is illustrated in Figure 10-44. When the server receives a request from a user for a file that has been off-loaded, it retrieves the data from the storage device and ships it to the user. This frees up space on the server without creating an inconvenience when users need to access these files.

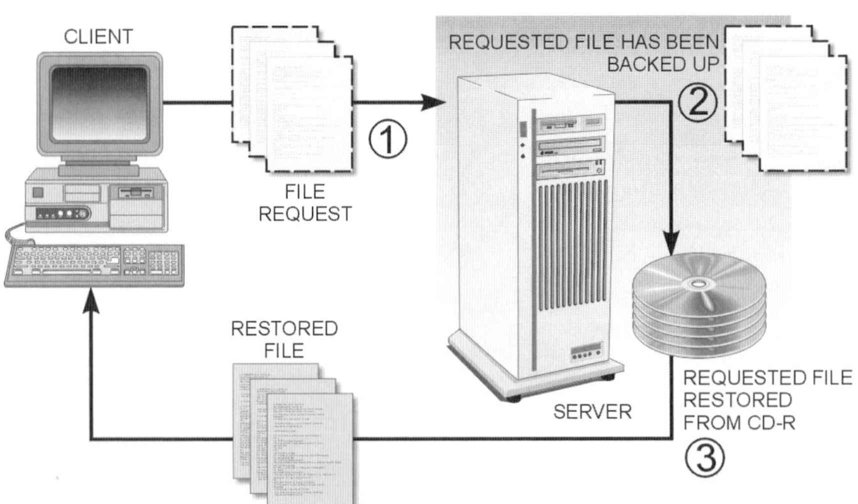

Figure 10-44: The Microsoft Hierarchical Storage Management System

Windows 2000 includes a Hierarchical Storage Management system that enables the system to shift seldom-used data to selected backup media. When a user requests a file from a server, the server checks to see if the file is still in residence, or if it has been off-loaded to a storage device. If the file has been off-loaded, the server brings it back to the server and delivers it to the requester. The Windows 2000 HSM system provides drivers for DAT and DLT devices to perform this function.

The RSS function is an MMC snap-in that is only available with the Windows 2000 Server packages, not the Professional version. As with the other Windows 2000 Microsoft Management Consoles, the RSS console is accessed through the Start/Programs/Administrative Tools option.

Windows 2000 includes an improved RAID controller utility. This built-in backup utility provides control of Levels 0 through 5 RAID structures and provides changes between levels without needing to rebuild the array.

IntelliMirror

Another Windows 2000 manageability feature is referred to as **IntelliMirror**. This set of functions automatically backs up applications, documents, and settings to the server for recovery purposes. If the system crashes, the client's entire structure can be recovered quickly from the server.

IntelliMirror

This feature also provides consistent working environments for individuals that work from multiple locations. In a network using Windows 2000 servers, users can move between workstations on the network and maintain individual settings, such as desktop icons, favorites, and drive and printer mappings. When the user logs in at a given location, the IntelliMirror function can move their personal backup information to the new unit. The **Settings Management** function enables the administrator to copy the contents of the remote Registry to the server as well. At logon, the server loads the workstation with the user's personal settings.

Settings Management

In cases where files are sent to workstations that do not have a copy of the associated application installed, the Installer will attempt to locate the application's installation files on the server. If they are available through the Active Directory, Windows 2000 will install them automatically.

IntelliMirror can even be set up to automatically load any missing pieces from the server. This feature creates a self-healing environment for applications. When a key support file is missing, the system automatically locates it and installs it where it is needed.

Launching Applications in Windows 2000

In Windows 2000 there are several acceptable methods of launching an application. These include:

- Select the application from the extended Start menu, click the folder containing the application, and double-click its filename.
- Select the Run entry from the Start menu, and then enter the full path and filename for the desired executable file.
- Double-click the application's filename in the Windows Explorer or in My Computer.

- Click the File menu option from the My Computer Menu Bar, or through the Windows Explorer, and select the Open option. (You can also alternate-click on the application and choose Open).

- Create a shortcut icon on the desktop for the application, so that it may be started by simply double-clicking on its icon.

In Windows NT, an application can also be set up to run by association. Using this method, the application will be started whenever an associated file is double-clicked.

Open With

This is accomplished by defining the file's type in the **Open With** dialog box. The first time you attempt to open a non-associated application, the Open With dialog box, depicted in Figure 10-45, will appear. The Open with option can also be accessed by holding the left SHIFT key and alternate-clicking the file's icon.

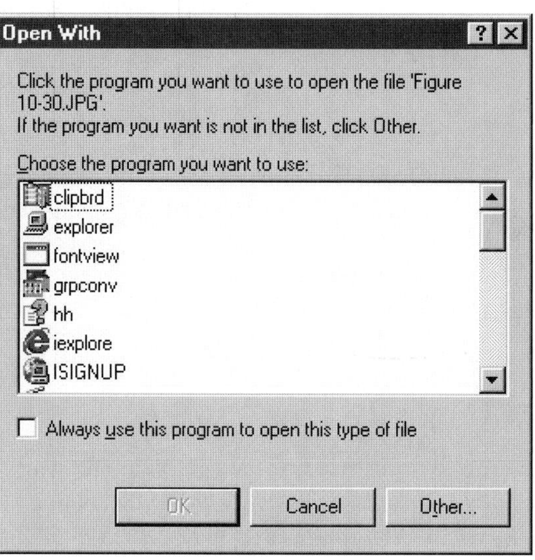

Figure 10-45: The Windows 2000 Open With Dialog Box

Windows 9x and Windows NT

Microsoft did not intend for the Windows NT and Windows 9x systems to be compatible with each other. There is no direct pathway between the two and no direct upgrade path from Windows 9x to Windows NT. Because both rely on Registry structures and because those structures are incompatible with each other, there is no way to bring them together.

Virtual Device Drivers (VxDs)

Hardware support is another difference that prevents the two Windows operating systems from working with each other. While some Windows 9x device drivers require direct access to system hardware, the Windows NT HAL cannot tolerate such operations. Therefore, the Windows 9x drivers simply will not work in Windows NT and neither will the devices they support. Windows NT also lacks support for the **Virtual Device Drivers** (**VxDs**) employed by Windows 9x.

For these reasons, Microsoft does not recommend or support dual booting operation of the two operating systems. However, the Windows 2000 design does allow for upgrading from Windows 9x platforms.

DOS and Windows NT

Command Prompt window

CMD

Like Windows 9x, Windows NT provides a **Command Prompt window**. However, unlike Windows 9x, when this feature is engaged in Windows NT, no separate DOS version is being accessed. Windows NT simply provides a DOS-like interface that enables users to perform some DOS functions. There is no MS-DOS icon in the Windows NT system. To access the DOS emulator, select the Run option from the Start menu and type the command **CMD** into the dialog box.

As mentioned earlier in this chapter, under Windows NT, 16-bit DOS applications run in special NTVDM environments. Likewise, Win16 applications run in special Win16-on-Win32 NTVDMs. These environments prevent the 16-bit applications from interacting with any other applications while providing full access to all of the system's resources through the APIs in the Win32 Subsystem.

After placing a 16-bit application on the system's hard drive, the next step in establishing a NTVDM environment for it is to create a shortcut for the program on the desktop. This is accomplished through the Windows NT Explorer utility. Start the Explorer and then click-and-drag the application's executable filename to the desktop to create the shortcut icon. Click on the shortcut text box to edit its name.

Windows NT PIF Settings

The Properties of the shortcut must be edited through the shortcut icon. Alternate-click on the icon, select Properties from the floating menu, click on the Program tab, and click on the Windows NT button. This should produce the **Windows NT PIF Settings** dialog box depicted in Figure 10-46.

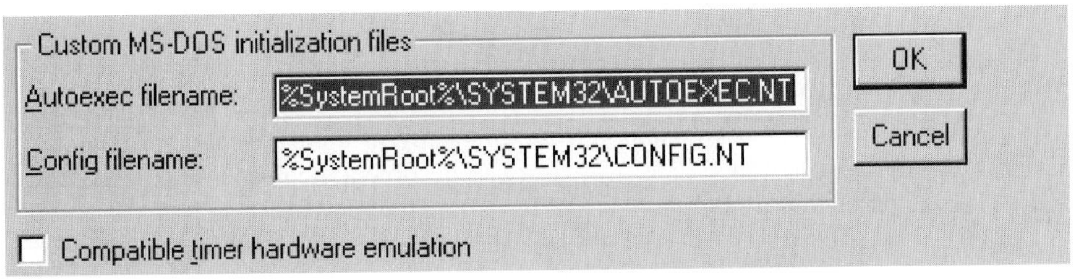

Figure 10-46: Windows NT PIF Settings Dialog Box

AUTOEXEC.NT

CONFIG.NT

Notice that **AUTOEXEC.NT** and **CONFIG.NT** initialization files exist to support DOS applications. These files mimic the functions of the AUTOEXEC.BAT and CONFIG.SYS files found in MS-DOS and Windows 3.x environments. While it's possible to establish separate initialization files for each DOS application, normally all such applications use the default files. The DOS commands inside the files are executed by the NTVDM when it is first loaded.

The next step in setting up DOS applications to run in Windows NT is to configure memory for it. This is accomplished by clicking on the Memory tab in the DOS Properties page. This should produce the Memory Usage screen depicted in Figure 10-47. The Auto mode settings are normally selected so that Windows NT retains control over memory usage.

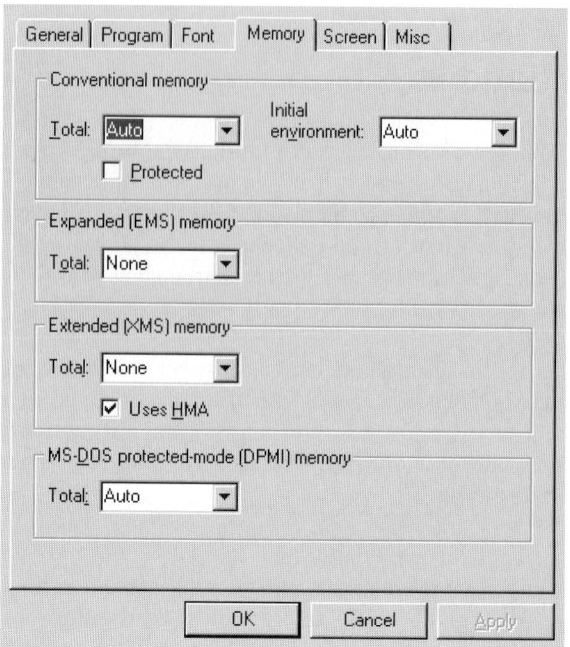

Figure 10-47: Windows NT Memory Usage Screen

In the case of 16-bit Windows applications, select the Shortcut tab from the Shortcut Properties window. To run the application in its own NTVDM, click on the Run option and select the Run in Separate Memory Space box.

Networking with Windows 2000

During the Windows 2000 setup process, the system must be configured to function as a workgroup node, or as part of a domain. A workgroup is a collection of networked computers assigned the same workgroup name. Any user can become a member of a workgroup by specifying the particular workgroup's name during the setup process.

Conversely, a domain is a collection of networked computers established and controlled by a network administrator. As mentioned earlier in this chapter, domains are established for security and administration purposes.

The Setup routine requires that a computer account be established before a computer can be included in the domain. This account is not the same as the user accounts that the system uses to identify individual users.

If the system has been upgraded from an existing Windows NT version, Windows 2000 adopts the current computer account information. If the installation is new, the Setup utility requests that a new computer account be established. This account is normally assigned by the network administrator prior to running Setup. Joining the domain during setup requires a username and password.

My Network Places

My Network Places

Add Network Place

In the Windows 2000 system, the Network Neighborhood folder has been replaced with a more powerful **My Network Places** folder, depicted in Figure 10-48. The new folder includes new Recently Visited Places and Computers Near Me views. The **Add Network Place** options enable you to more easily establish connections to other servers on the network. The user can establish shortcuts to virtually every server on the network.

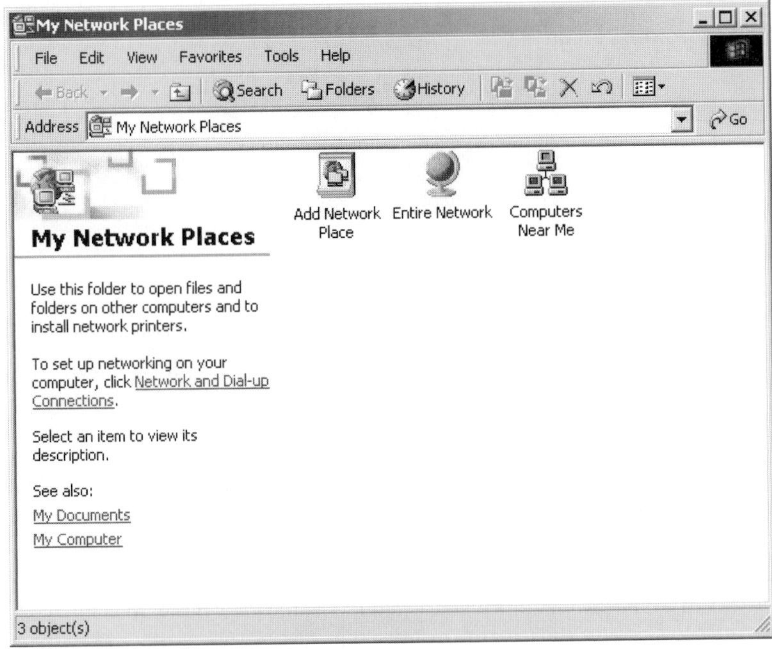

Figure 10-48: My Network Places

If the system has been upgraded from an existing Windows NT version, Windows 2000 will adopt the current computer account information. If the installation is new, the setup utility will request that a New Computer Account be established. This account is normally assigned by the network administrator prior to running Setup. Joining the domain during Setup requires a user name and password.

In Windows 2000 using the TCP/IP protocol, computer names can range up to 63 characters in length and should be made up of the letters A through Z, numbers 0 through 9, and hyphens.

> **TEST TIP**
>
> Know the specifications for setting up computer names in a given operating system.

Mapping a Drive

Network File Service (NFS)

As illustrated in the previous chapter, a drive map is a very important tool in a network environment. It allows a single computer to act as though it possesses all the hard drives that reside in the network. The **Network File Service (NFS)** portion of the operating system coordinates the systems so that drives located on other physical machines show up as logical drives on the local machine. This shows up in the Windows Explorer and My Computer screens, as illustrated in Figure 10-49. It also makes the additional drives available through the command line prompt.

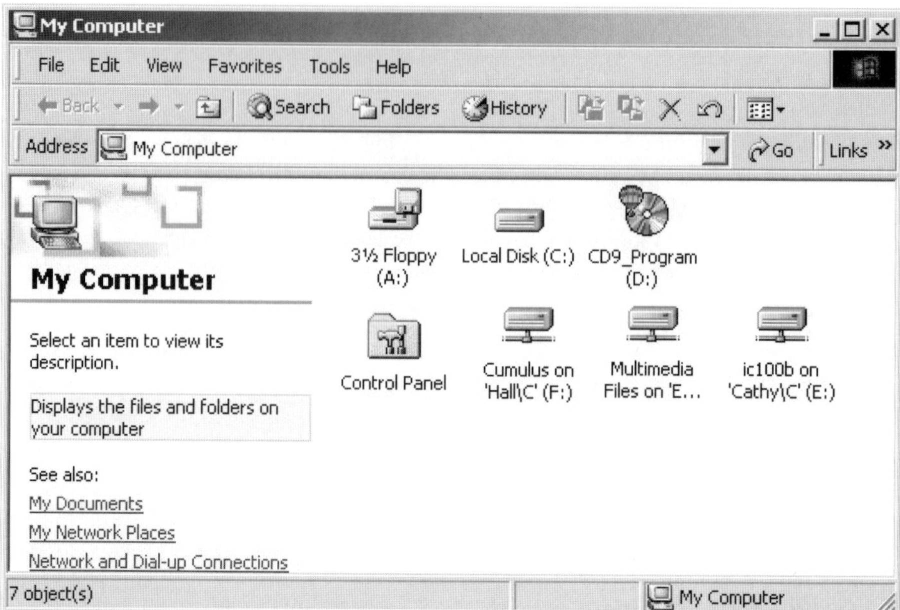

Figure 10-49: A Mapped Drive Display

The primary reason to map a drive in a network environment is because some applications cannot recognize volume names. They can see only drive letters. In Windows, the number of recognizable drive letters is 26 (A–Z).

Some network operating systems can recognize an extended number of drive letters (i.e., A-Z and AA-ZZ). However, by using unique volume names to identify drives, the system is capable of recognizing a vast number of network drives.

For a local system to access a remote resource, the resource must be shared, and the local user must have a valid network user ID and password. The user's assigned rights and permissions are tied to his or her password throughout the network, either through individual settings or through group settings.

The Network Icon in Control Panel

The Network icon under the Windows 2000 Control Panel has been changed to the Network and Dial-Up Connections folder. It provides access to the Network and Dial-Up Connections window depicted in Figure 10-50. This window provides several key functions associated with local and wide area networking. It is used to install new network adapter cards and change their settings, change network component settings, and to install TCP/IP.

Windows 2000 includes a printing feature called **Autopublish** (or point and print). This feature enables the user to install a printer driver on a client PC from any application. The Active Directory also enables the user to browse the network for a specific printer type or location.

Autopublish

Windows 2000 features Internet printing capabilities. This function enables the user to print to a remotely located printer using the Internet as the network. Microsoft designed this feature to compete with document faxing. Instead of faxing a document to a remote fax machine, just print it out on a printer at that location. Any standard printer can be used for this operation, as long as it is being hosted by a Windows 2000 Server.

The File/Print window, depicted in Figure 10-53, includes a Find Printer button that you can use to search for printers locally, connected to the LAN, or connected across the Internet. After a printer has been located, Windows 2000 automatically installs the driver for that printer on the client PC.

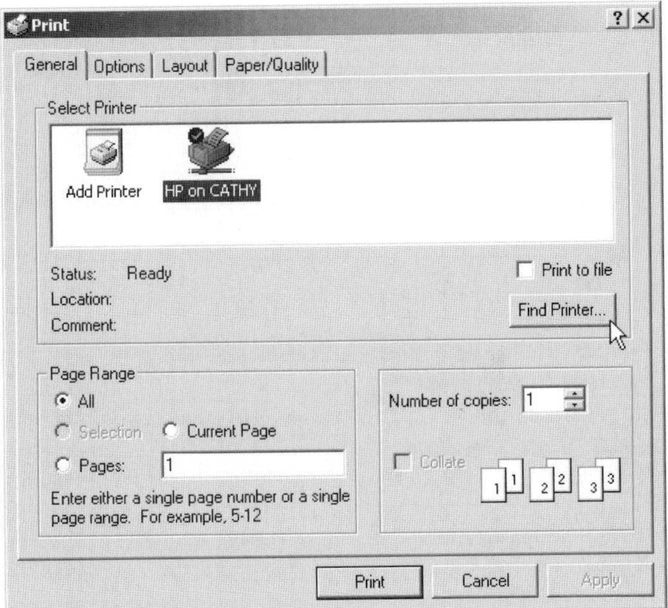

Figure 10-53: The Windows 2000 File/Print Window

Windows 2000 includes a library of more than 2500 printer drivers. If the local unit is not set up for the type of printer selected, it is possible to add these files and initiate the print job without leaving the Print dialog box.

Sharing Printers in Windows 2000

Shared printers, also referred to as networked printers, receive data from computers throughout the network and direct it to a local printer. As in other networks, these printers must be selected as shared printers in the Windows 2000 environment in order for remote computers to be able to access them.

To share a printer under Windows 2000, select the Printers option from the *Start/Settings* path. Alternate-click the printer to be shared and select the Sharing option. This action produces the Sharing tab depicted in Figure 10-54. From this page, click the Shared As option, enter a share name for the printer, and click the OK button to complete the sharing process. Unlike the Windows 9x systems, you must have administrative rights to make these changes in Windows 2000.

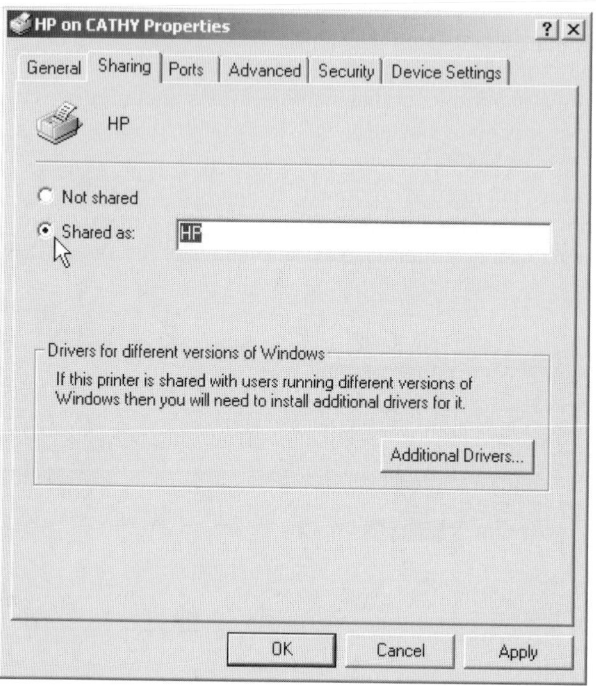

Figure 10-54: Sharing a Printer in Windows 2000

TEST TIP

Know how to correctly write a UNC path to a shared directory located on a remote computer.

To connect to a printer on the network, select the Printers option from the *Start/Settings* path and double-click the Add Printer icon. The Welcome to the Add Printer Wizard page displays. Click the Next button to move forward in the connection process. In the Local or Network Printer page, select the Network Printer option, click the Next button, and then enter the network printer name. Use the UNC format to specify the path to the printer being connected to (that is, *\\computer_name\share_name*). If the printer's name is not known, click the Type the Printer Name option or click the Next to Browse for a Printer option.

To link up with a printer over the Internet (or the company intranet), select the Connect to Printer on the Internet or on Your Intranet option and enter the URL address of the printer. The URL must be expressed in standard HTTP addressing format (that is, *http://servername/printer/*). The connection wizard guides the connection from this point.

WIDE AREA NETWORKING WITH WINDOWS 2000

Remote Access Services (RAS)

Dial-Up Networking

Older versions of Windows NT refer to all aspects of the dial-up networking function as **Remote Access Services** (**RAS**). With Windows NT 4.0, however, Microsoft changed the nomenclature to **Dial-Up Networking** on its client side elements. Microsoft did so to maintain compatibility with Windows 9x descriptions. The server side elements are still referred to as RAS. This same convention continues in the Windows 2000 product.

Windows NT Workstation provides all the software tools required to establish an Internet connection. These include a TCP/IP network protocol and the Windows NT Workstation Dial-Up Networking component. The Dial-Up Networking component is used to establish a link with the ISP over the public telephone system. This link also can be established over an ISDN line. Windows NT versions from 4.0 forward feature the built-in Microsoft Internet Explorer Web browser and a personal Web Server.

The Windows 2000 Internet Infrastructure

Windows 2000 replaces the Network Settings item from the Windows NT 4.0 Control Panel with a New Network Connections folder, located in the My Computer window.

To create a dial-up connection in Windows 2000, click the Make New Connection icon in the My Computer Network Connections folder. This action opens the Windows 2000 Network Connection Wizard that guides the connection process. The wizard requires information about the type of connection, modem type, and the phone number to be dialed. The connection types offered by the wizard include private networks, virtual private networks, and other computers.

The Network Connection Wizard enables users to employ the same device to access multiple networks that may be configured differently. This is accomplished by enabling users to create connection types based on who they are connecting to, rather than how they are making the connection.

Establishing the Windows 2000 Modem Configuration

Under Windows 2000, the operating system should detect, or offer to detect, the modem through its Plug-and-Play facilities. It may also enable you to select the modem drivers manually from a list in the Control Panel.

After the modem has been detected, or selected, it appears in the Windows 2000 Modem list. The settings for the modem can be examined or reconfigured by selecting it from the list and clicking its Properties tab. In most cases, the device's default configuration settings should be used.

Configuring the modem to operate properly with an ISP is much easier in Windows 2000 than it was in Windows NT 4.0. The Connection Settings tab from the Windows NT 4.0 Modem Properties dialog window has been replaced by the Advanced tab with space to enter the initialization string received from the ISP.

Establishing Dialing Rules

For Windows 2000 to connect to a network or dial-up connection, it must know what rules to follow in establishing the communication link. These rules are known as the dialing rules. In Windows 2000, the Dialing Rules are configured through the *Start/Settings/Control Panel/Phone and Modem Options* path. If the connection is new, a Location Information dialog window displays, enabling you to supply the area code and telephone system information.

To create a new location, click the New button and move through the General, Area Code Rules, and Calling Card tabs, depicted in Figure 10-38, to add information as required. The default rules for dialing local, long-distance, and international calls are established under the General tab. These rules are based on the country or region identified on this page. Ways to reach an outside line (such as dialing 8 or 9 to get an outside line in a hotel or office building) are established here. Similarly, the Area Code Rules information modifies the default information located under the General tab. As its name implies, the information under the Calling Cards tab pertains to numbers dialed using a specific calling card or long-distance company.

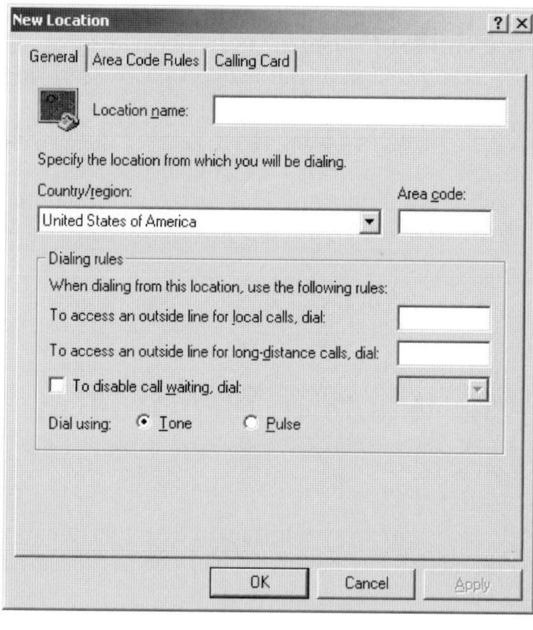

Figure 10-55: The Windows 2000 Phone and Modem Options/New Dialog Window

Establishing Dial-Up Internet Connections

Internet Connection Wizard

The Windows 2000 **Internet Connection Wizard**, depicted in Figure 10-56, provides an efficient way to establish Internet connectivity. You can use the Internet Connection Wizard to set up the Web browser, the Internet email account, and the newsgroup reader. To create the Internet connection to an existing account with an ISP, you need to know the following:

- The ISP's name
- The user name and password
- The ISP's dial-in access number

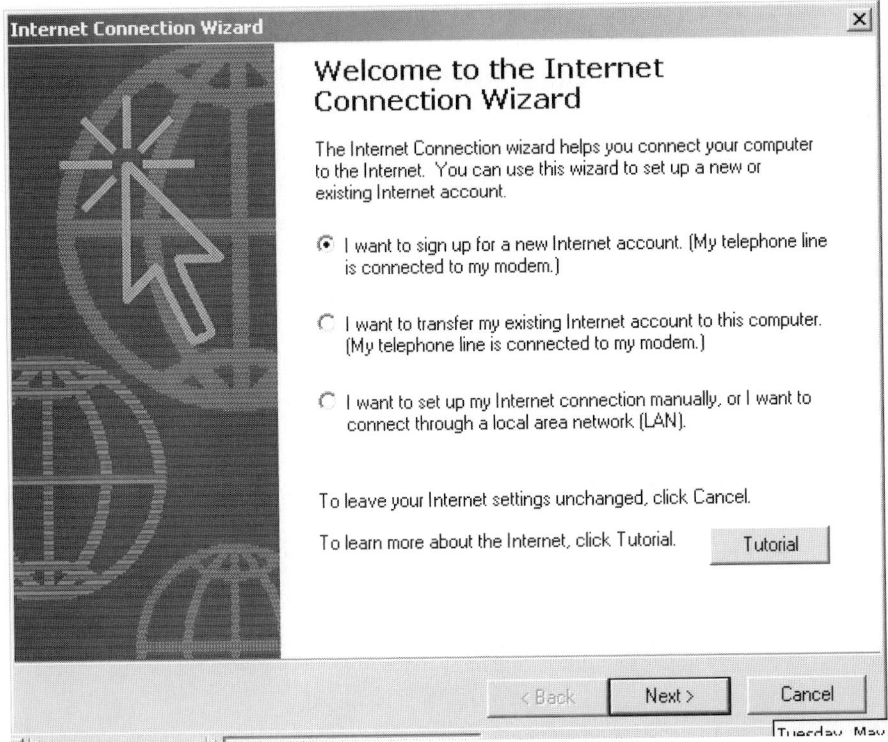

Figure 10-56: The Internet Connection Wizard

If the system is equipped with a **cable modem** or an **Asymmetrical Digital Subscriber Line (ADSL)**, the ISP will need to furnish any additional connection instructions. The cable modem is a device that transmits and receives data through cable television connections. Conversely, ADSL is a special, high-speed modem technology that transmits data over existing telephone lines. The Internet Connection Wizard collects this information and then creates the Internet connection.

cable modem

Asymmetrical Digital Subscriber Line (ADSL)

To connect to the Internet, select the Internet Connection Wizard option from the *Start/Programs/Accessories/Communications* path. If the connection is new, the Location Information dialog boxes, depicted in Figure 10-57, along with the Dialing Rules defined in the preceding section of this chapter will appear. You also need to click the "I want to sign up for a new Internet account" option, click the Next button, and follow the wizard's instructions.

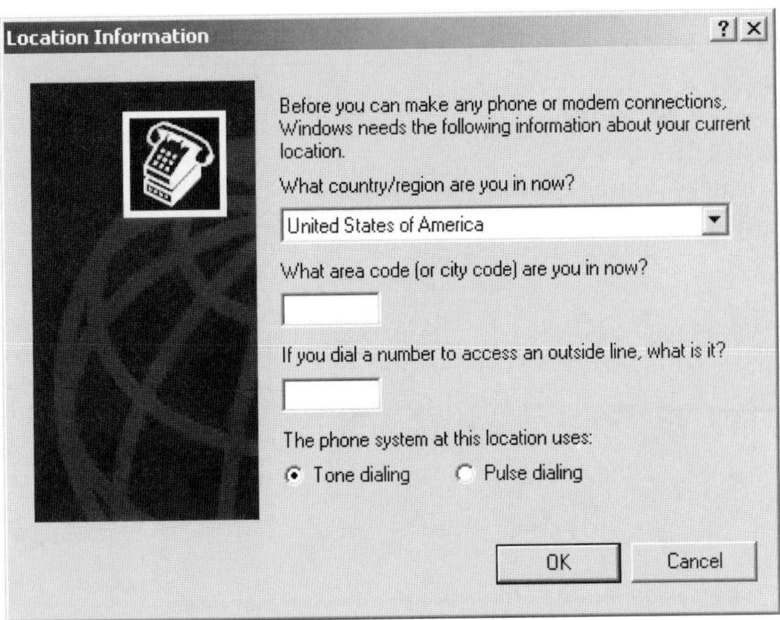

Figure 10-57: The Location Information Dialog Box

Establishing Internet Connection Sharing

Windows 2000 makes it possible to share resources such as printers, folders, and Internet connections across a network.

Sharing an Internet connection allows several computers to be connected to the Internet through a single dial-up connection. These connections can be made individually, or simultaneously, with each user maintaining the ability to use the same services it did when it was connected directly to the Internet.

Internet Connection sharing

To establish **Internet connection sharing**, you must log on to the computer using an account that has Administrator rights. Afterward, click Start/Settings and select the Network and Dial-Up Connections option. Alternate-click the connection to be shared and select the Properties option. The Internet Connection Sharing screen displays, as depicted in Figure 10-58.

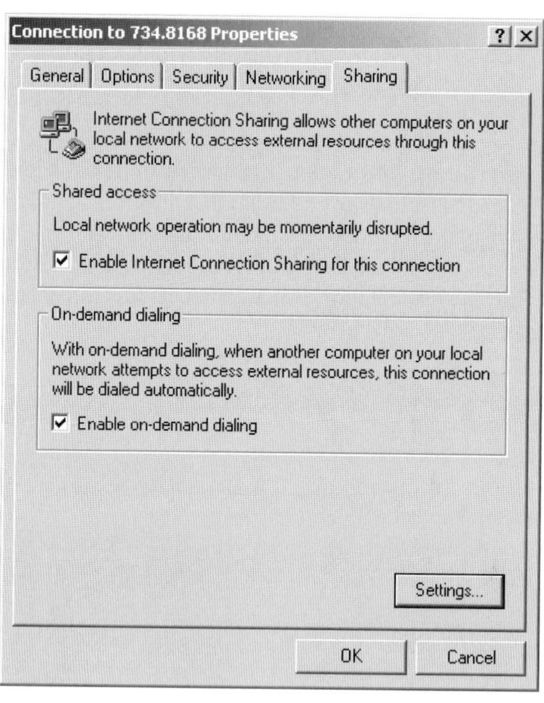

Figure 10-58: The Internet Connection Sharing Screen

Under the Internet Connection-Sharing tab, select the Enable Internet Connection Sharing for This Connection check box. If the connecting computer is supposed to dial in to the Internet automatically, click the Enable on Demand Dialing check box. Clicking the OK button causes protocols, services, interfaces, and routes to be configured automatically.

SECURITY

security

Since its creation, one of the main features of the Windows 2000 operating system has been its **security** capabilities. As an operating system designed to work in business networks, data security is one of its most important functions.

Windows 2000 provides security in four forms:

User Logon

Passwords

- User security in the form of **User Logon** and **Passwords** required to access the system
- User security between users of the same computer to control access to local data
- Identification of attempted security breaches through audit trails
- Memory usage protection between applications running on the same hardware

User Account

In a Windows NT system, a user must have a **User Account** on a particular computer to gain access to its operation. In a workgroup setting, this account must be set up on each computer. However, in a domain environment, the account can be established on the domain server.

Administrator Account

When Windows 2000 is first installed, a master **Administrator Account** is established.

The administrator has rights and permissions to all of the system's hardware and software resources. The administrator in turn grants rights and permissions to other users as necessary.

Groups

The administrator can deal with users on an individual basis, or may gather users into **Groups** that can be administered uniformly. In doing so, the administrator can assign permissions or restrictions on an individual or an entire group. The value of using groups lies in the time saved by being able to apply common rights to several users instead of applying them one by one.

Profile

Each user and group in the NT environment has a **Profile** that describes the resources and desktop configurations created for them. Settings in the profile can be used to limit the actions users can perform, such as installing, removing, configuring, adjusting, or copying resources. When users log into the system, it checks their profile and adjusts the system according to their information. In Windows NT 4.0, this information is stored in the \WINNT*login_name*\NTUSER.DAT file. In Windows 2000 this file has been moved to \Documents and Settings*login_name*\NTuser.dat.

The Windows 2000 Server operating system can be used to establish profiles for the entire network from a central location. Its administration package can also be used to establish Roaming Profiles that enable users to log into any workstation on the network and work under their own profile settings.

User Manager

The Windows NT 4.0 **User Manager** utility can be accessed through the Start button's *Start\Programs\Administrative_Tools* path. Clicking on the User Manager entry should produce the User Manager window. To create a new user, select the New User option from the User pull-down menu to produce the New User window displayed in Figure 10-59. Enter the necessary user information in the New User dialog box. The user's Username and Password will need to be supplied to them at least the first time they log in. If the User Must Change Password… option is selected, the user will be able to change the password to something more personal as soon as they log in.

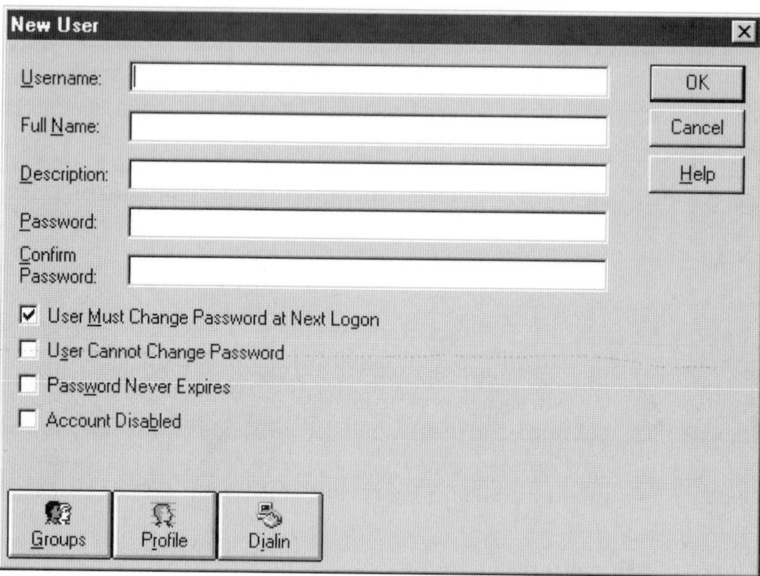

Figure 10-59: The New User Window

Selecting the Groups icon at the bottom of the screen brings up the Group Memberships dialog box depicted in Figure 10-60. Groups that the designated user is a part of are listed in the left window. Groups that the user is not a part of are listed in the right-hand window. To add the user to a group, simply highlight the desired group in the right-hand window and click on the Add button.

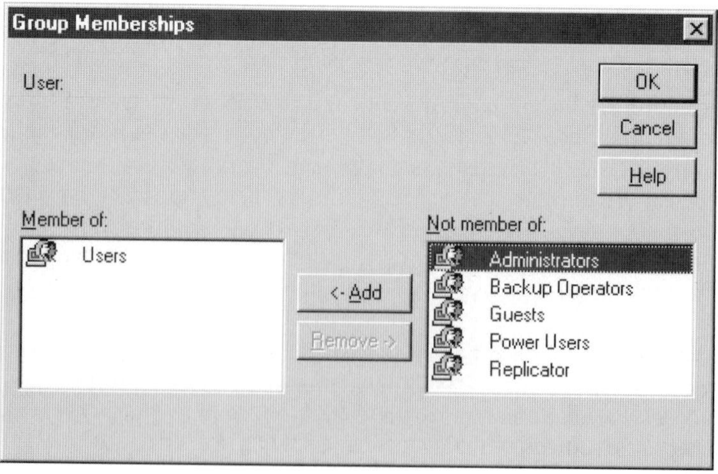

Figure 10-60: The Group Memberships Dialog Box

Windows 2000 Security

Windows 2000 offers a much improved security structure over previous Windows versions. The new security features apply to both LAN and wide area communications. The main security improvement is the adoption of the **Kerberos** authentication protocol.

Kerberos

> **Authentication** is a process that determines that users on the network are who they say they are.

Authentication

The Kerberos protocol is used to enable users to authenticate without sending a password over the network. Instead, the user acquires a unique key from the network's central security authority at login. The security authority is provided by the domain controller referred to as the **Key Distribution Center (KDC)**.

Key Distribution Center (KDC)

When a client makes a request to access a network resource or program, it authenticates itself with the KDC as described in Figure 10-61. The KDC responds by returning a session ticket to the client that is used to establish a connection to the requested resource. The ticket can only be used to authenticate the client's access to services and resources for a limited amount of time. During that time, the client presents the ticket to the application server that verifies the user and provides access to the requested program.

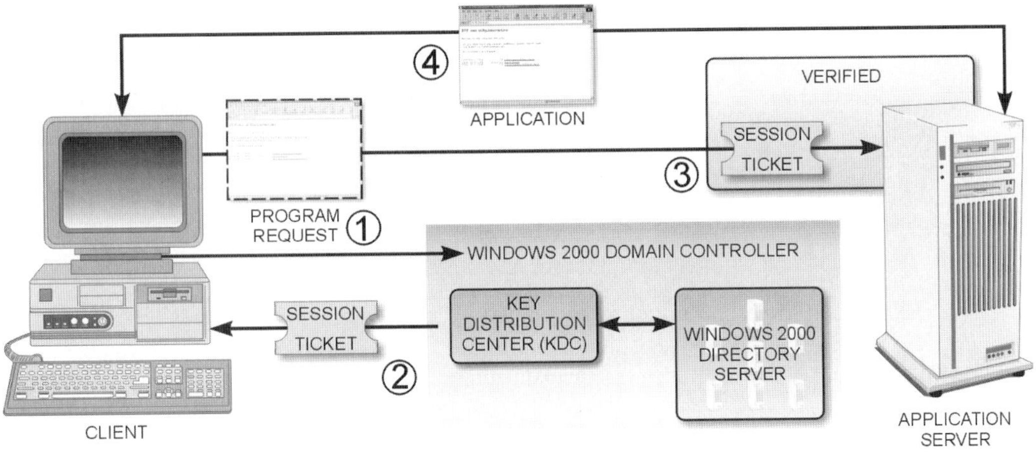

Figure 10-61: Kerberos Protocol Operations

The key is cached on the local machine so that the user can reuse the key at a later time to access the resource. Keys are typically good for about eight hours so there is no need for repeated interaction between the user and the KDC. This reduces the number of interactions that must be made across the network and, thereby, reduces the traffic load on the network in general. In addition, no passwords are circulated during the process so there is no chance of compromising them.

Digital certificates are another major security feature in Windows 2000.

Digital certificates

> Digital certificates are password-protected, encrypted data files that include data that identifies the transmitting system and can be used to authenticate external users to the network through **Virtual Private Networks (VPNs)**.

Virtual Private Networks (VPNs)

VPNs use message encryption and other security techniques to ensure that only authorized users can intercept and access the message as it passes through public transmission media. In particular, VPNs provide secure Internet communications by establishing encrypted data tunnels across the WAN that cannot be penetrated by others.

IP Security Protocol (IPSec)

When the certificates are combined with security standards such as the **IP Security Protocol (IPSec)** secure, encrypted TCP/IP data can be passed across public networks, such as the Internet. IPSec is a secure, encrypted version of the IP protocol. IPSec client software connects remote users to a VPN server by creating an encrypted tunnel across the Internet to the remote user as illustrated in Figure 10-62.

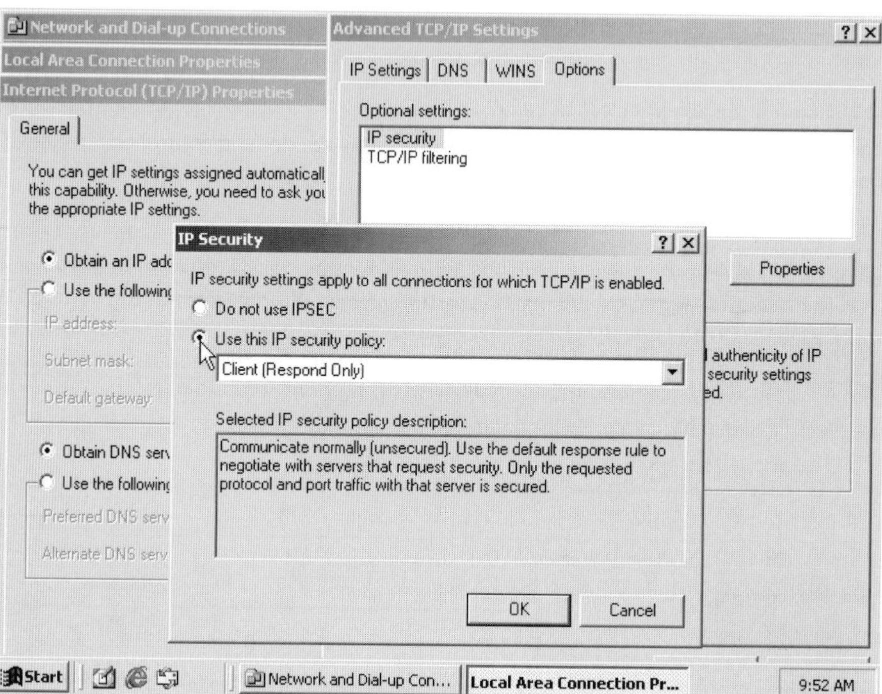

Figure 10-62: IP Security Protocol Operations

Point-to-Point Tunneling Protocol

Layer 2 Tunneling Protocol (L2TP)

Network Address Translation

Encrypted File System (EFS)

In addition to IPSec, Windows 2000 continues to offer **Point-to-Point Tunneling Protocol (PPTP)** and **Layer 2 Tunneling Protocol (L2TP)** as alternative security technologies for VPNs. L2TP can be used in conjunction with IPSec to pass the IPSec packets through routers that perform **Network Address Translation.**

In addition to the outstanding network security features, Windows 2000 provides effective local hard drive security through its **Encrypted File System (EFS)** feature. EFS enables the user to encrypt files stored on the drive using keys only the designated user (or an authorized recovery agent) can decode. This prevents theft of data by those who do not have the password or a decoding tool. EFS is simple to use since it is actually an attribute that can be established for files or folders.

Portable Design

The Windows 2000 operating system brings many new features for portable computers to the Windows NT line. In addition to furnishing the power management and plug-and-play features discussed earlier, Windows 2000 provides increased data security functions and greater administrator control over mobile PCs.

Portable computer users in the business world typically spend some time connected to a company network and other times traveling away from the network connection. The Windows 2000 Synchronization Manager enables the user to select network files and folders and to travel without an active connection to a server.

When the client wishes to take files the files are moved from the server to the portable and the Synchronization Manager synchronizes the time and date version information concerning the files. While the portable client is off-line, the user can continue to use the files under their network names. When the user returns to the network environment, the client resynchronizes the files with the server versions and the newer copy overwrites the older version. The synchronization process is described in Figure 10-63.

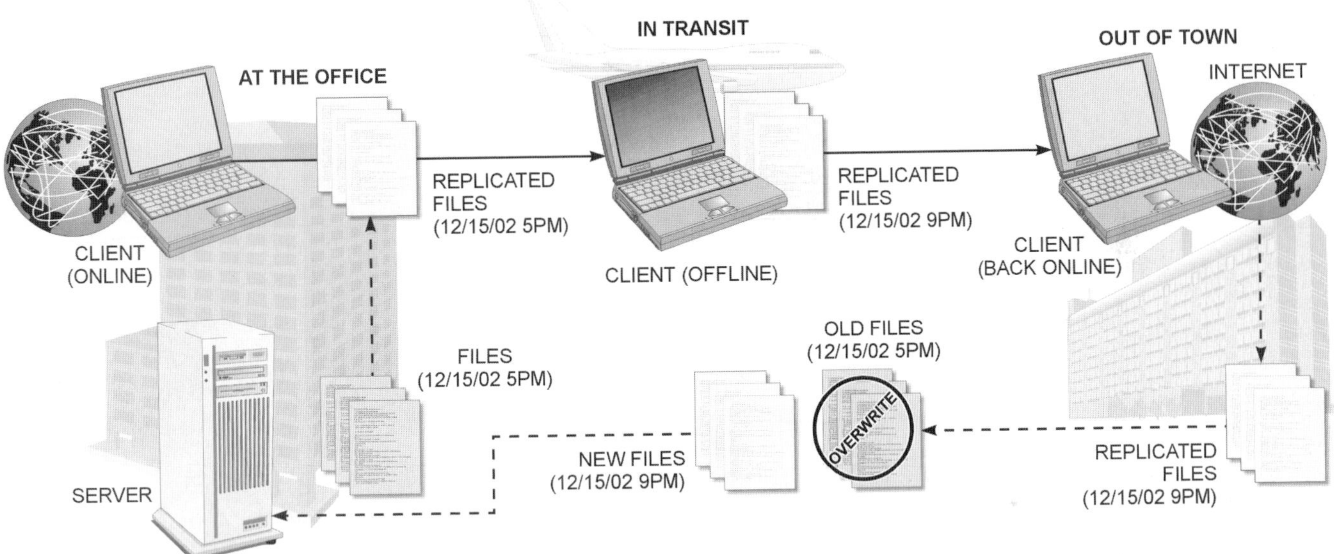

Figure 10-63: Windows 2000 Synchronization Manager

The Windows 2000 EFS feature further enhances the security of files on portable computers by enabling users to designate files and folders so that they can only be accessed using the proper **encryption key**. Public key encryption techniques employ two keys to ensure the security of the encrypted data — a **public key** and a **private key**. The public key (known to everyone) is used to encrypt the data, while the private or secret key (known only to the specified recipient) is used to decrypt it. The public and private keys are related in such a way that the private key cannot be decoded simply by possessing the public key.

encryption key

public key

private key

Roaming Profiles

Windows 2000 portability features are not limited to mobile computers. Many organizations have mobile employees that work at different computers within a given location. To accommodate this type of mobility, Windows 2000 uses **Roaming Profiles** that store each user's desktop, Start menu setup, and My Document folder on the server and redirects them to the local client where the user logs in. Windows 2000 can also install applications the user requires on the local client when they logon.

CHAPTER SUMMARY

This chapter has presented an extensive, technical exploration of the Windows NT and Windows 2000 operating systems. It has explored both operating systems in terms of their functions and structures. In many instances, the material in this chapter has built on, or contrasted with, the Windows 9x material from the previous chapter.

Having completed the chapter, you should able to describe the processes for installing or upgrading systems with Windows NT 4.0 and Windows 2000. You should also be able to describe the bootup sequence employed by Windows NT/2000.

Secondly, you should be able to describe the structure of Windows NT and Windows 2000, including their core files and Registry components. In addition, you should be able to describe accepted methods for navigating through either system, including the Internet Explorer.

Finally, you should be able to successfully install, configure, and access software applications and peripheral systems such as printers, and Local Area Networking functions, as well as Wide Area Networking and Internet functions in Windows NT 4.0 and 2000.

At this point, review the objectives listed at the beginning of the chapter to be certain that you understand and can perform each item listed there.

KEY POINTS REVIEW

This chapter has investigated the structure and operation of the Windows NT and Windows 2000 operating systems. Review the following key points before moving into the Review and Exam Questions sections to make sure you are comfortable with each point. Afterward, answer the Review Questions that follow to verify your knowledge of the information.

- While Microsoft improved the Windows 3.x and Windows 9x products for use by the general population, it also developed a more robust and complicated Windows New Technology, or Windows NT, operating system for corporate client/server networking installations.
- It was built around a new operating system kernel that focused on enhanced reliability, scalability, and security elements required for corporate applications, while retaining the strengths of the Windows operating system.
- The Windows NT Server package provides the same features and functions found in the Workstation, except the Server package also provides the tools necessary to administer and control a network from a central location.
- Enterprise networks are designed to facilitate business-to-business, or business-to-customer operations. Because monetary transactions and personal information travels across the network in these environments, enterprise networks feature facilities for additional, highly protective security functions.
- An intranet is a network built on the TCP/IP protocol that belongs to a single organization — in essence a private Internet. Like the Internet, intranets are designed to share information and are only accessible to the organization's members, with authorization.

- Windows 2000 is the successor of the Windows NT 4.0 operating system. It brings together the stability and security of Windows NT 4.0 and the Plug-and-Play capabilities of Windows 9x.

- The Windows 2000 Server product is also available in two extended enterprise versions — Windows 2000 Advanced Server and Windows 2000 Datacenter Server.

- The standard server package supports four-way Symmetrical Microprocessor operations (i.e., it can distribute work between four different microprocessors at a time) and can manage up to 4 GB of RAM.

- The Advanced Server edition can support up to 8 symmetrical processors and up to 8 GB of memory. These features enable it to function well in medium-size networks running between 100 and 500 concurrent users.

- The Windows 2000 Datacenter Server edition can handle up to 64 GB of RAM and 32 processors. This will enable it to support up to 1000 simultaneous users with heavy processing demands.

- The Windows NT desktop includes most of the same features found in its Windows 9x counterpart (i.e., My Computer, Network Neighborhood, Inbox, and the Recycle Bin).

- The Windows NT Start Menu contains Programs, Documents, Settings, Find, Help, Run, and Shut Down options.

- Locating, accessing, and retrieving information in Windows NT is virtually the same as with the Windows 9x operating systems.

- Instead of simply truncating the filename, inserting a tilde, and then assigning a number to the end of the filename, Windows NT performs a mathematical operation on the long name to generate a truly unique MS-DOS compatible filename.

- When five or more names are generated that would result in duplicate short names, Windows NT changes its truncation method. Beginning with the sixth filename, the first two characters of the name are retained, the next four characters are generated through the mathematical algorithm, and, finally, a tilde with an ID number is attached to the end of the name.

- Windows 2000 features an intelligent, personalized Programs menu. It monitors the user's program usage, and after the first six accesses, arranges the menu options according to those most frequently used.

- A network share is an existing shared resource (i.e., printer, drive, modem, or folder) located on a remote system.

- Windows 2000 offers extended common dialog boxes for File/Open, File/Print, and File/Save options. These dialog boxes provide easy organization and navigation of the system's hard drives, as well as providing navigation columns that grant quick access to frequently used folders.

- The Windows NT logical structure is a modular system that allows for advances in computing technology to be integrated into the system. It exists in two basic layers referred to as Modes — the Kernel Mode and the User Mode.

- Basically, the operating system runs in the Kernel Mode while applications run in User Mode. User Mode is a more restrictive operating mode where no direct access of hardware is permitted.

- APIs are routines, protocols, and tools built into the operating system that provide application designers with consistent building blocks to design their applications with. For the user, these building blocks lead to consistent interfaces being designed for all applications.

- The Kernel Mode is an operating mode where the program has unlimited access to all memory, including those of system hardware, the user mode applications, and other processes (such as I/O operations).

- The Windows NT HAL is a library of hardware drivers that operate between the actual hardware and the rest of the system. These software routines act to make every architecture look the same to the operating system.

- The Microkernel works closely with the HAL to keep the system's microprocessor as busy as possible. It does this by scheduling threads for introduction to the microprocessor on a priority basis.

- The Win32k Executive Services block provides all the basic operating system functions for the NT system.

- The Windows NT I/O Manager manages all input and output functions for the operating system. Its major function involves controlling communications between file system drivers, hardware device drivers, and network drivers and the system.

- Windows NT User Mode is a collection of subsystems that interact with users and applications.

- The Windows NT Registry is not compatible with the Windows 9x Registries.

- The contents of the Registry are physically stored in five files referred to as Hives. Hives represent the major divisions of all the Registry's keys, subkeys, subtrees, and values.

- The NT Registry hive files are stored in the \Winnt\System32\Config directory along with a backup copy and log file for each hive.

- The contents of the Registry can be edited directly using Regedt32.exe. This file is located in the \Winnt\System32 folder. As with the Windows 9x packages, most changes to the Registry should be accomplished through the Wizards in the Windows NT Control Panel.

- The Rdisk.exe utility, located in the \Winnt\System32 folder can be used to create a backup copy of the Registry in the \Winnt\Repair folder.

- The overall operation of Windows NT 4.0 is governed by System Policies that give administrators control over users. Using System Policies, the network administrator can give or limit users' access to local resources, such as drives and network connections.

- The Windows 2000 structure adds two additional managers to the Executive section — the Plug-and-Play Manager and the Power Manager.

- The central feature of the Windows 2000 architecture is the Active Directory structure. Active Directory is a distributed database of user and resource information that describes the makeup of the network (i.e., users and application settings).

- In Windows 2000, Policies are established through the Group Policy Editor. Administrators use this editor to establish which applications different users have access to, as well as to control applications on the user's desktop.

- With Group Policies, administrators can institute a large number of detailed settings for users throughout an enterprise, without establishing each setting manually.

- Windows NT offers its own proprietary NTFS file system that is designed to provide better data security and to operate more efficiently with larger hard drives than FAT systems do.

- The Windows NT file system provides security for each file in the system, as well as supplying complete file access auditing information to the system administrator. NTFS files and folders can have permissions assigned to them whether they are shared or not.

- The NTFS system includes security features that allow permission levels to be assigned to files and folders on the disk. These permissions set parameters for activities that users can conduct with the designated file or folder.

- Windows 2000 includes a Hierarchical Storage Management system that enables the system to shift seldom-used data to selected backup media. When a user requests a file from a server, the server checks to see if the file is still in residence.

- A member server is most often referred to as a standalone server. As such, the member server maintains a local domain database that only it uses. These servers are most commonly used as application and file servers.

- The Primary Domain Controller server is the first domain controller installed in a Windows NT domain and maintains the working security and account databases for the domain.

- The Backup Domain Controller server maintains backup copies of the PDC's security and account databases. These copies are used to assist in authenticating user account logins.

- The minimum hardware requirements for installing Windows 2000 Professional on a PC-compatible system are:

    - Microprocessor – 133 MHz Pentium (P5 equivalent or better)
    - RAM – 64 MB (4 GB maximum)
    - HDD Space – 650 MB or more free on a 2 GB drive
    - VGA Monitor

- For installation from a CD-ROM, a 12x drive is required. If the CD-ROM drive is not bootable, a high-density 3.5-inch floppy drive is also required. If Windows Professional is to be installed across a network, a Windows 2000 Professional-compatible NIC is required.

- If Windows NT is placed on an under powered system, it will very likely run slower than the same machine running Windows 9x operating systems.

- Systems can be upgraded to Windows 2000 Professional from Windows 3.x and 9x, as well as Windows NT 3.5 and 4.0 workstations. This includes older NTFS, FAT16, and FAT32 installations. When you install Windows 2000, it can recognize all three of these file system types.

- As with previous Windows NT products, Windows 2000 does not attempt to remain compatible with older hardware and software. Therefore, some applications may not be compatible with Windows 2000 and may run poorly, or fail completely after an upgrade.

- Windows NT can be set up to dual-boot with DOS or Windows 9x operating systems.

- The best recovery method is to boot the system to a floppy, run FDISK to repartition the drive, format the drive, and run the Windows NT Setup utility — provided your data was backed up beforehand.

- The Windows NT logon allows the operating system to configure itself for specific users. Normal logon involves entering a user name and password. If no logon information is entered, then default values will be loaded into the system.

- Windows 2000 supports a wide array of newer hardware devices. These devices include DVD, USB, and IEEE 1394 devices. Microsoft works with hardware vendors to certify their drivers. These drivers are digitally signed so that they can be loaded automatically by the system.

- Windows NT employs a print spooler processing architecture similar to that found in Windows 9x. This structure provides smooth printing in a background mode and quick return-to-application time.

- Windows 2000 Professional also supports a new universal font format called OpenType. This font type combines the best features of TrueType and Type 1 fonts and is supported by subsetting and compression technology that makes it efficient for transmission over the Internet.

- Printer Properties are all of the defining features about a selected printer and include information that ranges from which port it should use, to what security features have been implemented with it.

- Active Directory arranges domains in a hierarchy and establishes trust relationships among all of the domains in a tree-like structure.

- In AD, a tree is a collection of objects that share the same DNS name. Active directory can subdivide domains into organizational units that contain other units, or leaf objects, such as printers, users, etc.

- Windows 2000 can create an organizational structure containing more than one tree. This structure is referred to as a forest.

- Trusts are relationships that enable users to move between domains and perform prescribed types of operations.

- Rights are the permission settings that control a user's (or groups of users') authority to access objects and perform operations (such as reading or writing a file). Administrative Rights provide authority to users down to the Organizational Unit level.

- In the Windows 2000 system, the Network Neighborhood folder has been replaced with a more powerful My Network Places folder. The new folder includes new Recently Visited Places and Computers Near Me views.

- The primary reason for mapping a drive in a network environment is that some applications cannot recognize volume names. They can only see drive letters. In Windows NT, the number of recognizable drive letters is 26 (A-Z).

- Windows 2000 includes a printing feature called Autopublish (or point and print). This feature enables the user to install a printer driver on a client PC from any application. The Active Directory also enables the user to browse the network for a specific printer type, or location.

- Windows 2000 replaces the Network Settings item from the Windows NT 4.0 Control Panel with a New Network Connections folder, located in the My Computer window.

- Windows 2000 makes it possible to share resources such as printers, folders, and Internet connections across a network. Sharing the connection allows several computers to access the Internet through a single dial-up connection. These connections can be made individually, or simultaneously, with each user maintaining the ability to use the same services it did when it was connected directly to the Internet.

- Since its creation, one of the main features of the Windows NT operating system has been its security capabilities. As an operating system designed to work in business networks, data security is one of its most important functions.

- The administrator has rights and permissions to all of the system's hardware and software resources. The administrator in turn grants rights and permissions to other users as necessary.
- Authentication is a process that determines that users on the network are who they say they are.
- Digital certificates are password-protected, encrypted data files that include data that identifies the transmitting system and can be used to authenticate external users to the network through Virtual Private Networks.

REVIEW QUESTIONS

The following questions test your knowledge of the material presented in this chapter.

1. The presence of what type of device indicates a domain structure?
2. List the two types of domain controllers employed in Windows NT networks.
3. Describe four types of security found in the Windows 2000 environment.
4. What is the core component of the NTFS system, and what is its counterpart in a FAT system?
5. Describe the sequence of events required to upgrade a Windows 95 Registry HKEY to a Windows NT HKEY.
6. How much memory is required to install Windows 2000 Professional?
7. Where are the Windows NT Hive files stored?
8. Which file contains the user-related configuration information for Windows NT?
9. Where should changes to Registry items be made from?
10. Where does the Windows 2000 setup utility install the Windows 2000 OS files in a typical installation?
11. What is the function of the BOOT.INI file in a Windows NT system?
12. Name two factors that must be taken into account when considering upgrading a system to a Windows NT or Windows 2000 operating system.
13. ________ are the Windows 2000 tool for implementing changes for computers and users throughout an enterprise.
14. Name three advantages of the Windows NT file system over FAT16 and FAT32 file management structures.
15. Which Windows 2000 utility can be used to create a backup copy of the Registry? Where is the utility located and where will the backup copy be stored?

EXAM QUESTIONS

1. Which Windows NT file is responsible for guiding the Windows NT bootup process?
   a. NTLDR
   b. NTDETECT.COM
   c. NTOSKRNL.EXE
   d. BOOT.INI
2. Which types of applications can communicate directly with the Win32 Services block?
   a. 16-bit DOS applications
   b. 16-bit Windows 3.x applications
   c. 32-bit Windows 9x applications
   d. 64-bit POSIX applications
3. What is the basic unit of storage in an NTFS system?
   a. The file
   b. The cluster
   c. The MFT
   d. The organizational unit
4. In the Windows NT environment, ______ is a collection of objects that share the same domain name.
   a. a leaf
   b. an organizational unit
   c. a tree
   d. a forest
5. _____ are relationships that enable users to move between domains and perform certain types of operations.
   a. Trusts
   b. Permissions
   c. Rights
   d. Privileges
6. The portion of the Windows NT structure that communicates directly with the system hardware is ________.
   a. the Win32 Executive
   b. the User Mode
   c. the HAL
   d. the Hardware Subsystem
7. How many drives can be mapped in a Windows 2000 system?
   a. 10
   b. 26
   c. 4
   d. 16
8. What is the maximum length of a Windows 2000 filename?
   a. 8 characters
   b. 16 characters
   c. 256 characters
   d. 1024 characters

9. Where will the Windows NT Setup utility install the Windows NT files in a typical installation?
   a. The \Winnt directory
   b. The \I386 folder
   c. The \Windows\system folder
   d. The \Windows directory
10. The members of a _______ share a common directory database and are organized in levels.
   a. workgroup
   b. tree
   c. group
   d. domain

BASIC SYSTEM TROUBLESHOOTING

OBJECTIVES

OBJECTIVES

Upon completion of this chapter and its related lab procedures, you should be able to perform these tasks:

1. Describe the characteristics of a good work space.
2. Outline steps for using a digital multimeter to perform voltage, resistance, and current checks on a system, as well as identify common DMM tests associated with personal computers.
3. List preliminary steps for diagnosing computer problems.
4. Perform visual inspections of a system.
5. Describe the three general categories of problems into which symptoms can be grouped, and differentiate between them.
6. Differentiate between software- and hardware-based troubleshooting techniques.
7. Use disk-based diagnostic tools to isolate system problems.
8. Describe the function of a POST card.
9. Describe quick checks that can be used to determine the nature of system hardware problems.
10. Describe FRU-level troubleshooting.
11. Describe the steps for isolating power supply problems.
12. Outline checks to isolate problems that produce a dead system.
13. Discuss methods of dealing with symptoms that are not defined well enough to point to a particular component.

CHAPTER 11

BASIC SYSTEM TROUBLESHOOTING

INTRODUCTION

Effective troubleshooting of electronic equipment is a matter of combining good knowledge of the equipment and its operation with good testing techniques and deductive reasoning skills.

In general, the process of troubleshooting microprocessor-based equipment begins at the outside of the system and moves inward. The first step always involves trying the system to see what symptoms are produced. Second, you must isolate the problem as either a software- or hardware-related issue. After this, the problem can be isolated to a particular section of the hardware or software. Finally, the problem must be isolated to the offending component.

The information in this chapter instructs you in the theory behind using successful troubleshooting tools and methods you will need to effectively troubleshoot microprocessor-based equipment.

BASIC TROUBLESHOOTING TECHNIQUES

The A+ Core Hardware objective 2.2 states that the test taker should be able to identify basic troubleshooting procedures and good practices for eliciting problem symptoms from customers.

- Troubleshooting/isolation/problem determination
- Determine whether a problem is a hardware or software problem

Gather information from user regarding:

- Customer environment
- Symptoms/Error codes
- Situation when the problem occurred

One of the most important aspects of troubleshooting anything is the gathering of information about the problem at hand and the symptoms it is showing. One of the best sources for this type of information is the computer user. As this A+ objective states, the computer technician should be able to effectively acquire information from the customer (user) concerning the nature of a problem and then be able to practice basic troubleshooting methods to isolate and repair the problem. To this end, the following sections of the chapter address these topics. A place to start this discussion is with your tools and work space.

Work Space

The first order of business when working on any type of electronic equipment is to prepare a proper work area.

flat work space

You need a clear, **flat work space** on which to rest the device. Make sure that your work space is large enough to accommodate the work piece. Confirm that you have an adequate number of power receptacles to handle all of the equipment you may need. Try to locate your work space in a low-traffic area.

Good lighting

Good lighting is a prerequisite for the work area since the technician must be able to see small details, such as part numbers, cracked circuit foils, and solder splashes. An adjustable lamp with a shade is preferable. Fluorescent lighting is particularly desirable. In addition, a magnifying glass helps to read small part numbers.

Organizational Aids

organizational aids

Since some troubleshooting problems may require more than one session, it is a good idea to have some organizational aids in hand before you begin to disassemble any piece of equipment. The following list identifies some of the **organizational aids** you need:

- A parts organizer to keep track of small parts such as screws and connectors you may remove from the device. This organizer need not be extravagant. A handful of paper cups or clear plastic sandwich bags will do nicely.
- A roll of athletic or masking tape. You can use the tape to make tags and labels to help identify parts, where they go, and how they are connected in the circuit. Take the time to write notes and stick them on your parts organizers, circuit boards, and cables you remove from the system, and so forth.
- A small note pad or notebook to keep track of your assembly/troubleshooting steps.

Diagnostic and Repair Tools

Obviously, anyone who wants to work on any type of equipment must have the proper tools for the task. Let's discuss the tools and equipment associated with the testing and repair of digital systems.

Hand Tools

The well-prepared technician's tool kit should contain a wide range of both **flat-blade** and **Phillips-head screwdriver** sizes. At a minimum it should have a small jeweler's and a medium-sized flat-blade screwdriver, along with a medium-size Phillips screwdriver. In addition, you may want to include a small set of miniature nut drivers, a set of **Torx drivers**, and a special nonconductive screwdriver-like device called an **alignment tool**.

flat-blade

Phillips-head screwdriver

Torx drivers

alignment tool

You also need a couple of pairs of **needle-nose pliers**. These pliers are available in a number of sizes. You need at least one pair with a sturdy, blunt nose and one pair with a longer, more tapered nose. You also might wish to get a pair that has a cutting edge built into its jaws. You may perform this same function with a different type of pliers called **diagonals**, or cross-cuts. Many technicians carry a pair of surgical forceps in addition to their other pliers.

needle-nose pliers

diagonals

Another common set of tools associated with computer repair are **IC pullers**, or **IC extractors**. These tools come in various styles, as illustrated in Figure 11-1, and are used to remove ICs from sockets. Socket-mounted ICs are not as common on modern PC boards as they were in the past. Potential failures associated with the mechanical connections between sockets and chips, coupled with the industry's reliance on surface-mount soldering techniques, have led to far fewer socket-mounted chips. However, on some occasions, such as upgrading a ROM BIOS chip, the IC puller comes in handy.

IC pullers

IC extractors

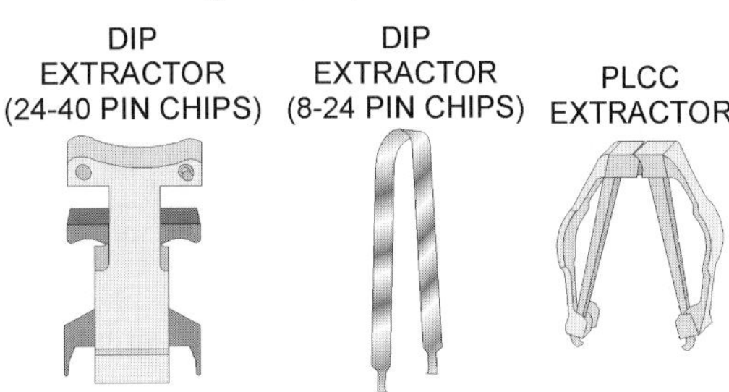

Figure 11-1: IC Pullers

Figure 11-2 depicts **hand tools** commonly associated with microcomputer repair.

hand tools

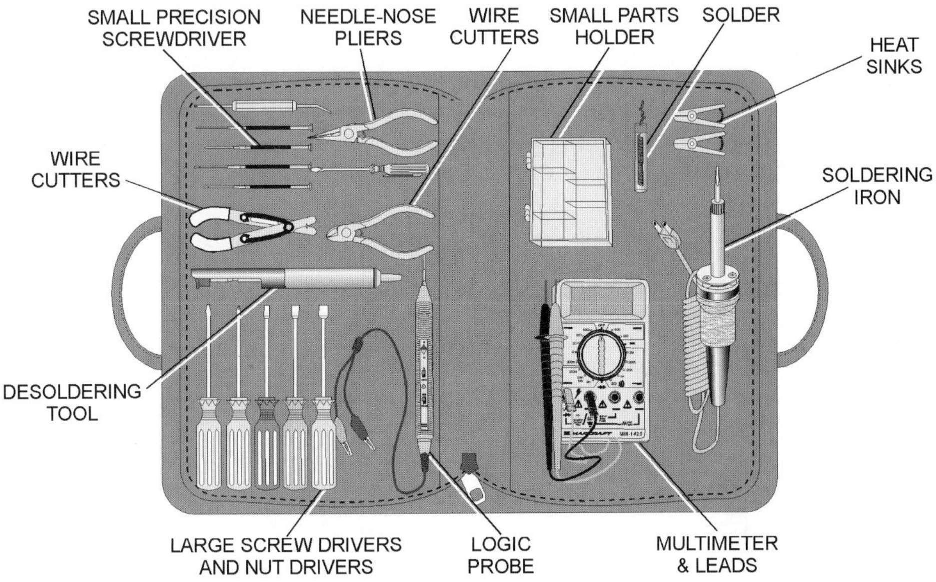

SMALL PRECISION SCREWDRIVER
NEEDLE-NOSE PLIERS
WIRE CUTTERS
SMALL PARTS HOLDER
SOLDER
HEAT SINKS
WIRE CUTTERS
SOLDERING IRON
DESOLDERING TOOL
LARGE SCREW DRIVERS AND NUT DRIVERS
LOGIC PROBE
MULTIMETER & LEADS

Figure 11-2: Hand Tools

multimeter

voltage

current

resistance

VOMs (Volt-Ohm-Milliammeters)

DMMs (Digital MultiMeters)

Using a Multimeter

There are a number of test instruments that can help you to isolate problems. One of the most basic pieces of electronic troubleshooting equipment is the **multimeter**. These test instruments are available in both analog and digital read-out form and can be used to directly measure values of **voltage** (V), **current** in milliamperes (mA) or amperes (A), and **resistance** in ohms (Ω). Therefore, these devices are referred to as **VOMs (Volt-Ohm- Milliammeters)** for analog types, or **DMMs** (**Digital MultiMeters**) for digital types. Figure 11-3 depicts a digital multimeter.

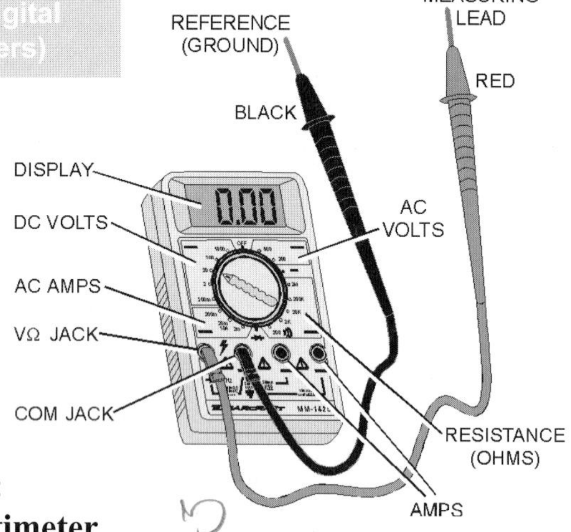

Figure 11-3: Digital Multimeter

With a little finesse, you can use this device to check diodes, transistors, capacitors, motor windings, relays, and coils. This particular DMM contains facilities built into the meter to test transistors and diodes. These facilities are in addition to its standard functions of current, voltage, and resistance measurement.

The first step in using the multimeter to perform tests is to select the proper function. For the most part, you never a need to use the current functions of the multimeter when working with computer systems. However, the voltage and resistance functions can be very valuable tools.

dc voltage function

In computer and peripheral troubleshooting, fully 99% of the tests made are dc voltage readings. These measurements most often involve checking the dc side of the power supply unit. You can make these readings between ground and one of the expansion slot pins, or at the P8/P9 power supply connectors. It is also common to check the voltage level across a system-board capacitor to verify that the system is receiving power. The voltage across most of the capacitors on the system board is 5 Vdc. The dc voltages that can normally be expected in a PC-compatible system are +12V, +5V, -5V, and -12V. The actual values for these reading may vary by 5% in either direction.

WARNING

Setting the meter—It is normal practice to *first set the meter to its highest voltage range* to make certain that the voltage level being measured does not damage the meter.

The **dc voltage function** is used to take measurements in live dc circuits. It should be connected in parallel with the device being checked. This could mean connecting the reference lead (black lead) to a ground point and the measuring lead (red lead) to a test point to take a measurement, as illustrated in Figure 11-4.

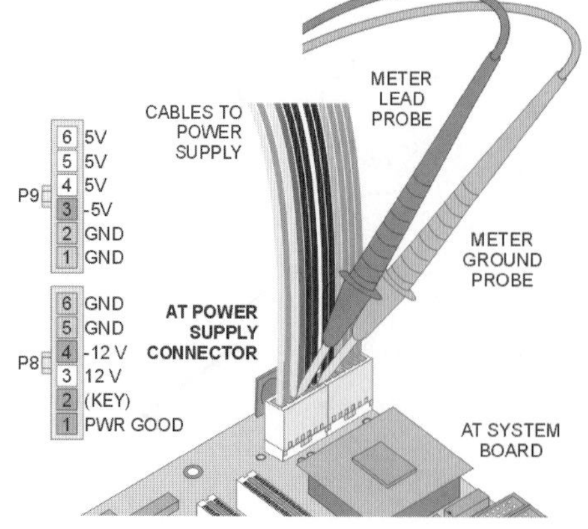

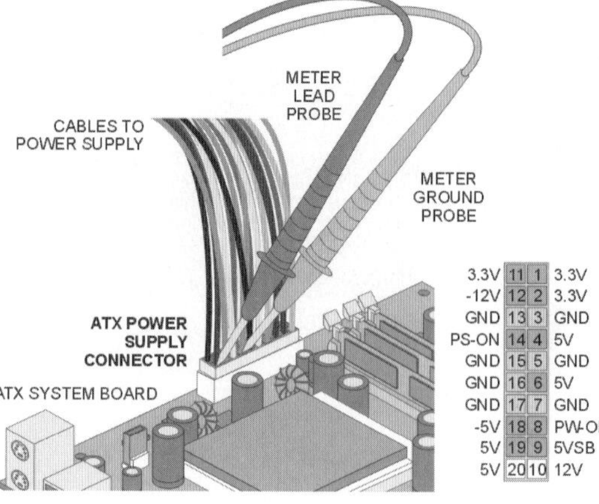

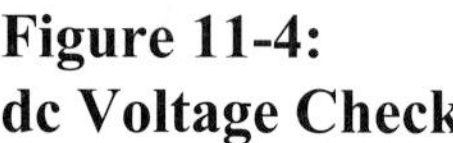

Figure 11-4: dc Voltage Check

As an approximate value is detected, you can decrease the range setting to achieve a more accurate reading. Most meters allow for over-voltage protection. However, it is still a good safety practice to decrease the range of the meter after you have achieved an initial value.

The second most popular test is the resistance, or **continuity test**.

continuity test

> **WARNING**
>
> **Power off**—Unlike the voltage check, resistance checks are always made with power removed from the system.

Failure to turn off the power when making resistance checks can cause serious damage to the meter and can pose a potential risk to the user. Resistance checks also require that you electrically isolate the component being tested from the system. For most circuit components, this means desoldering at least one end from the board.

The resistance check is very useful in isolating some types of problems in the system. One of the main uses of the resistance function is to test fuses. You must disconnect at least one end of the fuse from the system. You should set the meter on the 1k ohm resistance setting. If the fuse is good, the meter should read near 0 ohms. If it is bad, the meter reads infinite. The resistance function also is useful in checking for cables and connectors. By removing the cable from the system and connecting a meter lead to each end, you can check the cable's continuity conductor by conductor to verify its integrity. You also use the resistance function to test the system's speaker. To check the speaker, just disconnect the speaker from the system and connect a meter lead to each end. If the speaker is good, the meter should read near 8 ohms. If the speaker is defective, the resistance reading should be 0 or infinite.

ac voltage function

dc

Only a couple of situations involve using the **ac voltage function** for checking microcomputer systems. The primary use of this function is to check the commercial power being applied to the power supply unit. As with any measurement, it is important to select the correct measurement range. However, the lethal voltage levels associated with the supply power call for additional caution when making such measurements. The second application for the ac voltage function is to measure ripple voltage from the **dc** output side of the power supply unit. This particular operation is very rarely performed in field service situations.

> **TEST TIP**
>
> Know what readings to expect from a multimeter when testing fuses, speakers, and typical power-supply voltages in a PC.

Information Gathering

> **Careful observation**—The most important thing to do when checking a malfunctioning device is to be observant. Begin by talking to the person who reported the problem. You can obtain many clues from this person. Careful listening also is a good way to eliminate the user as a possible cause of the problems. Part of the technician's job is to determine whether the user could be the source of the problem—either trying to do things with the system that it cannot do, or not understanding how some part of it is supposed to work.

> **TEST TIP**
>
> Be well aware that the user is one of the most common sources of PC problems. In most situations, your first troubleshooting step should be to talk to the user.

Situations

From the user, gather information regarding the environment the system is being used in, any symptoms or error codes produced by the system, and the situations that existed when the failure occurred. Ask the user to list the procedures that led to the malfunction. This communication can help you narrow a problem down to a particular section of the computer. It does no good to check the video display when the user is having trouble using the disk drive.

Finally, observe the symptoms of a malfunction to verify the problem for yourself. After you have identified a problem, try to associate the malfunction with a section of the system responsible for that operation.

Environment

Take note of the environment that the equipment is being used in and how heavy its usage is. If the system is located in a particularly dirty area, or an area given to other environmental extremes, it may need to be cleaned and serviced more frequently than if it were in a clean office environment. The same proves true for systems subjected to heavy or continuous use. In an industrial environment, check with the management to see whether any office or industry maintenance standards for servicing apply.

Finally, use simple observation of the wear and tear on the equipment to gauge the need for additional or spot maintenance steps. Look for signs of extended use (such as frayed cords, missing slot covers, keyboards with letters worn off, and so on) to spot potential problems resulting from age or usage.

Symptoms/Error Codes

Most PCs have reasonably good built-in self-tests that are run each time the computer is powered up. These tests can prove very beneficial in detecting hardware-oriented problems within the system.

beep codes

Error message formats—Whenever a self-test failure or setup mismatch is encountered, the BIOS may indicate the error through a blank screen, or a visual error message on the video display, or an audio response (**beep codes**) produced by the system's speaker.

Some PCs issue numerically coded error messages on the display when errors occur. Conversely, other PCs display a written description of the error. Figure 11-5 defines the error messages and beep codes produced by a particular BIOS version from American Megatrends. The error messages and codes will vary among different BIOS manufacturers and from version to version.

BEEP CODE MESSAGES

1 beep - DRAM refresh failure
2 beeps - RAM failure (base 640 kB)
3 beeps - System Timer failure
5 beeps - Microprocessor failure
6 beeps - Keyboard Controller failure
7 beeps - Virtual Mode Exception failure
9 beeps - ROM BIOS checksum failure
1 long, 2 short beeps - Video controller failure
1 long, 3 short beeps - Conventional and extended test failure
1 long, 8 short beeps - Display test failure

VISUAL DISPLAY ERROR MESSAGES

SYSTEM HALTED ERRORS

CMOS INOPERATIONAL - Failure of CMOS shutdown register test
8042 GATE A20 ERROR - Error getting into protected mode
INVALID SWITCH MEMORY FAILURE - Real/Protected mode change over error.
DMA ERROR - DMA controller failed page register test
DMA #1 ERROR - DMA device # 1 failure
DMA #2 ERROR - DMA device # 2 failure

NON-FATAL ERRORS - WITH SETUP OPTION

CMOS BATTERY LOW - Failure of CMOS battery or CMOS checksum test
CMOS SYSTEM OPTION NOT SET - Failure of CMOS battery or CMOS checksum test
CMOS CHECKSUM FAILURE - CMS battery low or CMOS checksum test failure
CMOS DISPLAY MISMATCH - Failure of display type verification
CMOS MEMORY SIZE MISMATCH - System Configuration and Setup failure
CMOS TIMER AND DATE NOT SET - System Configuration and Setup failure in timer circuitry

NON-FATAL ERRORS - WITHOUT SETUP OPTION

CH-X TIMER ERROR - Channel X (2, 1, or 0) TIMER failure
KEYBOARD ERROR - Keyboard test failure
KB/INTERFACE ERROR - Keyboard test failure
DISPLAY SWITCH SETTING NOT PROPER - Failure to verify display type
KEYBOARD IS LOCKED - Unlock it
FDD CONTROLLER ERROR - Failure to verify floppy disk setup by System Configuration file
HDD CONTROLLER FAILURE - Failure to verify hard disk setup by System Configuration file
C:DRIVE ERROR - Hard disk setup failure
D:DRIVE ERROR - Hard disk setup failure

Figure 11-5: Error Messages and Beep Codes

Initial Troubleshooting Steps

As a general rule, you can reduce the majority of all equipment problems to the simplest things you can think of. The problem is, most people don't think of them. Successful troubleshooting results from careful observation, deductive reasoning, and an organized approach to solving problems. These techniques apply to the repair of any type of defective equipment.

Effective troubleshooting of electronic equipment is a matter of combining good knowledge of the equipment and its operation with good testing techniques and deductive reasoning skills. In general, the process of troubleshooting microprocessor-based equipment begins at the outside of the system and moves inward. First, always try the system to see what symptoms you produce. Second, you must isolate the problem to either software- or hardware-related problems. Finally, you should isolate the problem to a section of the hardware or software.

Perform a Visual Inspection

If no prior knowledge of the type of malfunction exists, you should proceed by performing a careful visual inspection of the system. Check the outside of the system first. Look for loose or disconnected cables. Consult all the external front-panel lights. If no lights display, check the power outlet, the plugs and power cords, as well as any power switches that may affect the operation of the system. You also might want to check the commercial power distribution system's fuses or circuit breakers to confirm their functionality.

localize the problem

If part of the system is active, try to **localize the problem** by systematically removing peripheral devices from the system. Try swapping suspected devices with known good parts from another computer of the same type. Try to revive the system, or its defective portion, by restarting it several times. As a matter of fact, you should try to restart the system after performing each correctional step.

Check the outside—Check all externally accessible switch settings.

modems

For example, check all system jumper settings to see that they are set correctly for the actual configuration of the system. In Pentium-based systems, check the BIOS advanced CMOS configuration screens for enabling settings that may not be correct. Also, make certain that any peripheral devices in the system, such as printers or **modems**, are set up correctly.

user's manual

Consult any additional user's or operations manuals liberally. Indeed, many of the computers and peripheral systems on the market, such as printers, have some level of self-diagnostics built into them. Generally, these diagnostics programs produce coded error messages. The key to recognizing and using these error messages is usually found in the device's **user's manual**. In addition, the user's manual may contain probable causes and suggested remedy information, and/or specialized tests to isolate specific problems.

Documenting things—Take time to **document the problem**, including all of the tests you perform and their outcomes. Your memory is never as good as you think it is, especially in stressful situations such as with a **down** computer. This recorded information can prevent you from making repetitive steps that waste time and may cause confusion. This information also proves very helpful when you move on to more detailed tests or measurements. Also, label all cables and connectors prior to removing them. This will assist you in reconnecting things as you progress through the troubleshooting process.

document the problem

down

Observe the Bootup Procedure

Observing bootup—Carefully **observing the steps of a bootup** procedure can reveal a great deal about the nature of problems in a system. Faulty areas can be included or excluded from possible causes of errors during the bootup process.

observing the steps of a bootup

The observable actions of a working system's cold-boot procedure are listed as follows, in their order of occurrence:

1. When power is applied, the power supply fan activates.
2. The keyboard lights flash as the rest of the system components are being reset.
3. A BIOS message displays on the monitor.
4. A memory test flickers on the monitor.
5. The floppy disk drive access light comes on briefly (if enabled in the CMOS bootup sequence.)
6. The hard disk drive access light comes on briefly.
7. The system beeps, indicating that it has completed it power on self tests and initialization process.
8. The floppy disk drive access light comes on briefly before switching to the hard drive. At this point in the process, the BIOS is looking for additional instructions (boot information), first from the floppy drive and then from the hard drive (assuming that the CMOS setup is configured for this sequence).
9. For Windows machines, the "Starting Windows message" appears on the screen.

TEST TIP

Memorize the order of the series of observable events that occur during the normal (DOS) boot up.

If a section of the computer is defective, you will observe just some (or possibly none) of these events. By knowing the sections of the computer involved in each step, you can suspect a particular section of causing the problem if the system does not advance past that step. For instance, it is illogical to replace the floppy disk drive (step 5) when a memory test (step 4) has not been displayed on the monitor.

When a failure occurs, you can eliminate components as a possible cause by observing the number of steps that the system completes in the preceding list. You can eliminate those subsystems associated with steps successfully completed. Focus your efforts only on those sections responsible for the symptom. When that symptom is cleared, the computer should progress to another step. However, another unrelated symptom may appear further down the list. You should deal with this symptom in the same manner. Always focus on diagnosing the present symptom and eventually all the symptoms will disappear.

Determining Hardware/Software/Configuration Problems

It should be obvious that a functional computer system is composed of two major parts: the system's hardware and the software that controls it. These two elements are so closely related that it is often difficult to determine which part might be the cause of a given problem. Therefore, one of the earliest steps in troubleshooting a computer problem (or any other programmable system problem) is to determine whether the problem is due to a hardware failure or to faulty programming.

In PCs, you can use a significant event that occurs during the boot-up process as a key to begin separating hardware problems from software problems the single beep that most PCs produce between the end of the POST and the beginning of the boot-up process (step 7 in the preceding list).

Errors that occur, or are displayed, before this beep indicate that a hardware problem of some type exists. This conclusion should be easy to understand because up to this time, only the BIOS and the basic system hardware have been active. The operating system side of the system does not come into play until after the beep occurs.

If the system produces an error message (such as The System Has Detected Unstable RAM at Location x) or a beep code before the beep, for example, the system has found a problem with the RAM hardware. In this case, a bad memory device is indicated.

You can still group errors that occur before the beep into two distinct categories:

Configuration errors

Hardware failures

- **Configuration errors**
- **Hardware failures**

Configuration problems—You can trace the majority of all problems that occur in computer systems back to configuration settings.

configuration problems

setup problems

This category of problems tends to occur whenever a new hardware option is added to the system, or when the system is used for the very first time. These problems are called **configuration problems**, or **setup problems**, and result from mismatches between the system's programmed configuration, held in CMOS memory, and the actual equipment installed in the system.

This mismatch also can exist between the system's CMOS configuration settings and the option's hardware jumper or switch settings.

It is usually necessary to run the system's CMOS setup utility in the following three situations:

1. The first situation occurs when the system is first constructed.
2. The second occurrence happens if it becomes necessary to replace the CMOS backup battery on the system board.
3. Whenever a new or different option is added to the system (such as a hard drive, floppy drive, or video display), it may be necessary to run the Setup utility (although see the note "CMOS Setup Utility and Plug-and-Play").

CMOS Setup Utility and Plug-and-Play—In most newer systems, the BIOS and operating system use Plug-and-Play (PnP) techniques to detect new hardware that has been installed in the system. These components work together with the device to allocate system resources for the device. In some situations, the PnP logic will not be able to resolve all the system's resource needs and a configuration error will occur. In these cases, the user must manually resolve the configuration problem.

Configuration problems occur with some software packages when first installed. The user must enter certain parameters into the program to match its capabilities to the actual configuration of the system. These configuration settings are established through the startup software in the ROM BIOS. If these configuration parameters are set incorrectly, the software cannot direct the system's hardware properly and an error occurs.

When you are installing new hardware or software options, be aware of the possibility of this type of error. If you encounter configuration (or setup) errors, refer to the installation instructions found in the new component's User Manual. Table 11-1 lists typical configuration error codes and messages produced when various types of configuration mismatches are incurred.

Table 11-1: Common Configuration Error Codes

CONFIGURATION ERROR MESSAGE	MEANING
CMOS System Option Not Set	Failure of CMOS battery or CMOS Checksum test
CMOS Display Mismatch	Failure of display type verification
CMOS Memory Size Mismatch	System configuration and setup failure
Press F1 to Continue	Invalid configuration information

If you cannot confirm a configuration problem, the problem most likely is a defective component. The most widely used repair method involves substituting known good components for suspected bad components. Other alternatives for isolating and correcting a hardware failure that appears before the boot up depend on how much of the system is operable.

TEST TIP

Know the situations that cause a Press F1 to Continue error message to display.

These alternatives include running a diagnostic program to test the system's components, and using a POST card to determine what problems a system may have. Several diagnostic software packages enable you to test system components. However, these diagnostic tools require that certain major blocks of the system be operational. The POST card is a device that plugs into the system's expansion slots and reads the information moving through the system's buses. It is used when not enough of the system is running to support any other type of diagnostic tool. Both of these options are discussed in greater detail later in this chapter.

After the beep, the system begins looking for and loading the operating system. Errors that occur between the beep and the presentation of the operating system's user interface (command prompt or GUI) generally have three possible sources:

- Hardware failure (physical problem with the boot drive)
- Corrupted or missing boot files
- Corrupted or missing operating system files

You can read more about the process of sorting out these potential problems in Chapter 12—*Operating System Troubleshooting*. In these cases, checking the drive hardware is generally the last step of the troubleshooting process. Unless some specific symptom indicates otherwise, the missing or corrupted boot files and operating system files are checked first.

Software Diagnostics

Many companies produce disk-based diagnostic routines that check the system by running predetermined tests on different areas of its hardware. The diagnostic package evaluates the response from each test and attempts to produce a status report for all of the system's major components. Like the computer's self-test, these packages produce visual and beep-coded error messages. Figure 11-6 shows the Main menu of a typical self-booting software diagnostic.

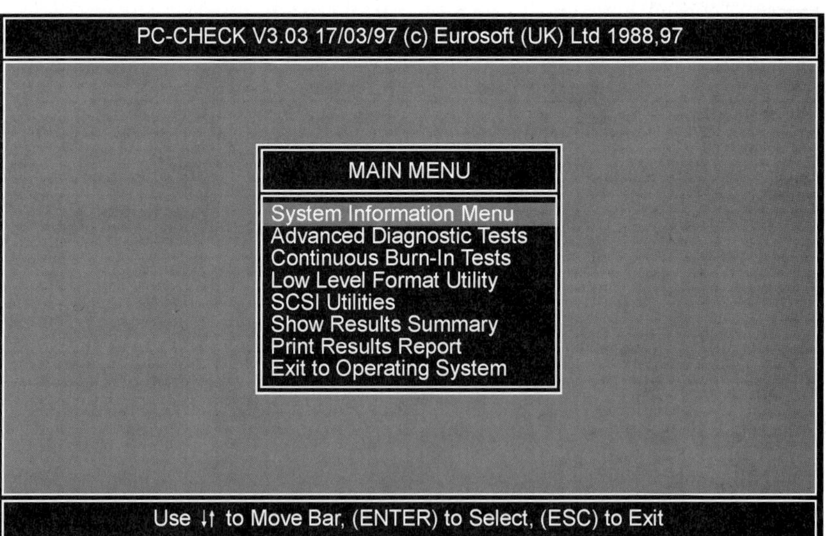

Figure 11-6: The Main Menu

This menu is the gateway to information about the system's makeup and configuration, as well as the entryway to the program's Advanced Diagnostic Test functions. You can find utilities for performing low-level formats on older hard drive types and for managing SCSI interface devices through this menu. Additionally, options to print or show test results are available here, as is the exit point from the program.

System Information Menu

IRQ Information

I/O Port Information

Device Drivers

The most common software-troubleshooting packages test the system's memory, microprocessor, keyboard, display monitor, and the disk drive's speed. If at least the system's CPU, disk drive, and clock circuits are working, you may be able to use one of these special software-troubleshooting packages to help localize system failures. They can prove especially helpful when trying to track down non-heat-related intermittent problems.

The first option in the sample diagnostic package is the **System Information Menu**. As described in Figure 11-7, this option provides access to the system's main functional blocks. The menu's **IRQ Information**, **I/O Port Information**, and **Device Drivers** options are valuable aids in locating configuration conflicts.

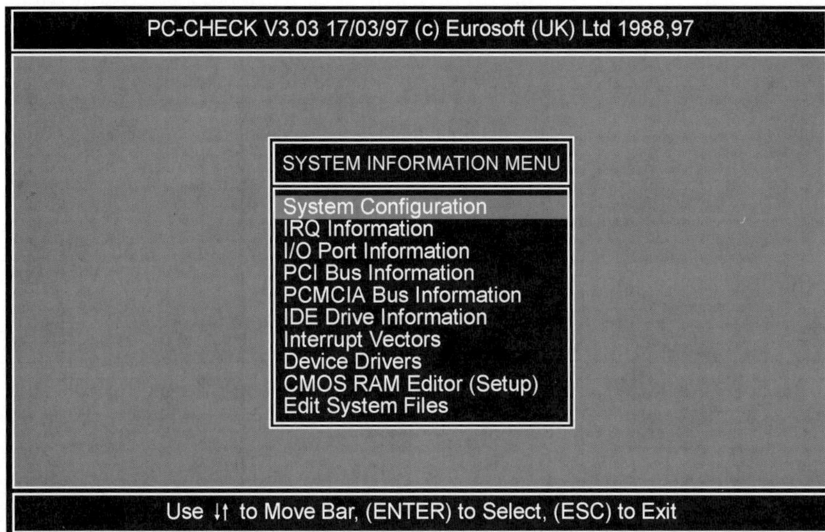

Figure 11-7: The System Information Menu

Advanced Diagnostics

overlay boxes

The **Advanced Diagnostics** Tests selection from the main menu performs extended tests in 13 system areas. These tests, listed in Figure 11-8, contain several lower-level tests that you can select from submenus. Error notices and diagnostic comments appear on the display in the form of **overlay boxes**. In addition to these fundamental software tests, this diagnostic includes tests for multimedia-related devices such as CD-ROMs. The CD-ROM tests cover both access time and transfer performance. Both of these values have an effect on the multimedia performance of the system. The multimedia tests also check the system's speaker and sound card capabilities.

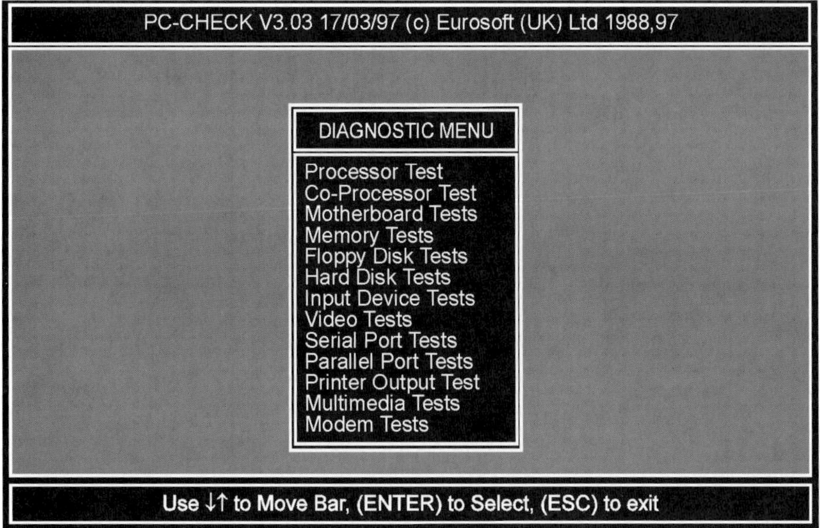

Figure 11-8: The Advanced Diagnostics Tests

If a diagnostic program indicates that multiple items should be replaced, replace the units one at a time until the unit starts up. Then, replace any units removed prior to the one that caused the system to start. This process ensures that there were not multiple bad parts. If you have replaced all the parts, and the unit still does not function properly, the diagnostic software is suspect.

burn-in

For enterprises that repair computers, or build computers from parts, diagnostic programs that perform continuous burn-in tests are a valuable tool. After the system has been built or repaired, this program runs continuous tests on the system for an extended **burn-in** period, without intervention from a technician or operator.

The tests performed are similar to the selection from the main menu. However, these tests are normally used for reliability testing instead of general troubleshooting. Different parts of the system can be selected for the burn-in tests. Since the burn-in tests are meant to be run unattended, the user must be careful to select only tests that apply to hardware that actually exists. The diagnostic keeps track of how many times each test has been run, and how often it failed during the designated burn-in period. This information is displayed on the monitor, as depicted in Figure 11-9.

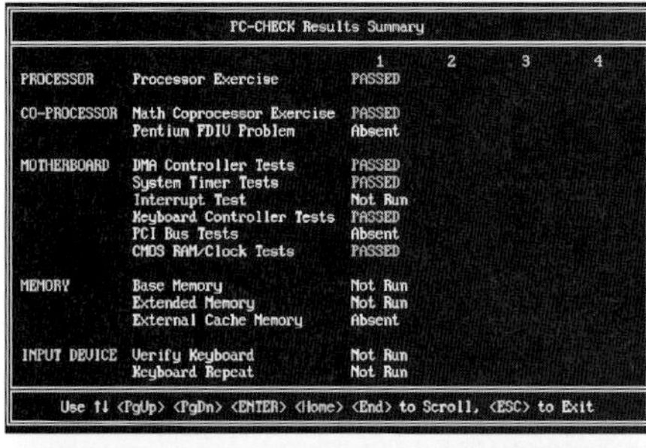

PC-CHECK Results Summary

		1	2	3	4
PROCESSOR	Processor Exercise	PASSED			
CO-PROCESSOR	Math Coprocessor Exercise	PASSED			
	Pentium FDIV Problem	Absent			
MOTHERBOARD	DMA Controller Tests	PASSED			
	System Timer Tests	PASSED			
	Interrupt Test	Not Run			
	Keyboard Controller Tests	PASSED			
	PCI Bus Tests	Absent			
	CMOS RAM/Clock Tests	PASSED			
MEMORY	Base Memory	Not Run			
	Extended Memory	Not Run			
	External Cache Memory	Absent			
INPUT DEVICE	Verify Keyboard	Not Run			
	Keyboard Repeat	Not Run			

Use ↑↓ <PgUp> <PgDn> <ENTER> <Home> <End> to Scroll, <ESC> to Exit

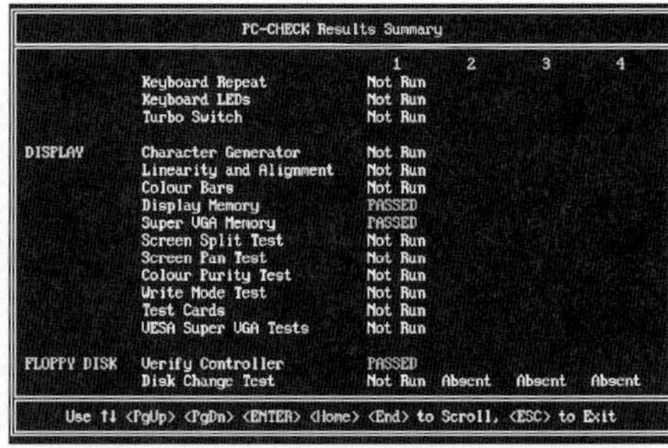

PC-CHECK Results Summary

		1	2	3	4
	Keyboard Repeat	Not Run			
	Keyboard LEDs	Not Run			
	Turbo Switch	Not Run			
DISPLAY	Character Generator	Not Run			
	Linearity and Alignment	Not Run			
	Colour Bars	Not Run			
	Display Memory	PASSED			
	Super VGA Memory	PASSED			
	Screen Split Test	Not Run			
	Screen Pan Test	Not Run			
	Colour Purity Test	Not Run			
	Write Mode Test	Not Run			
	Test Cards	Not Run			
	VESA Super VGA Tests	Not Run			
FLOPPY DISK	Verify Controller	PASSED			
	Disk Change Test	Not Run	Absent	Absent	Absent

Use ↑↓ <PgUp> <PgDn> <ENTER> <Home> <End> to Scroll, <ESC> to Exit

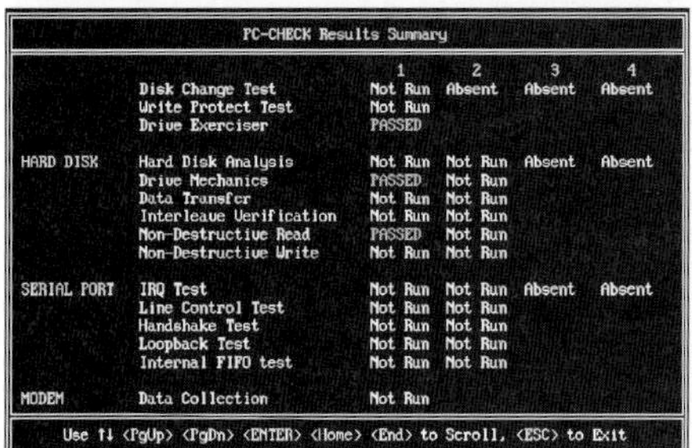

PC-CHECK Results Summary

		1	2	3	4
	Disk Change Test	Not Run	Absent	Absent	Absent
	Write Protect Test	Not Run			
	Drive Exerciser	PASSED			
HARD DISK	Hard Disk Analysis	Not Run	Not Run	Absent	Absent
	Drive Mechanics	PASSED	Not Run		
	Data Transfer	Not Run	Not Run		
	Interleave Verification	Not Run	Not Run		
	Non-Destructive Read	PASSED	Not Run		
	Non-Destructive Write	Not Run	Not Run		
SERIAL PORT	IRQ Test	Not Run	Not Run	Absent	Absent
	Line Control Test	Not Run	Not Run		
	Handshake Test	Not Run	Not Run		
	Loopback Test	Not Run	Not Run		
	Internal FIFO test	Not Run	Not Run		
MODEM	Data Collection	Not Run			

Use ↑↓ <PgUp> <PgDn> <ENTER> <Home> <End> to Scroll, <ESC> to Exit

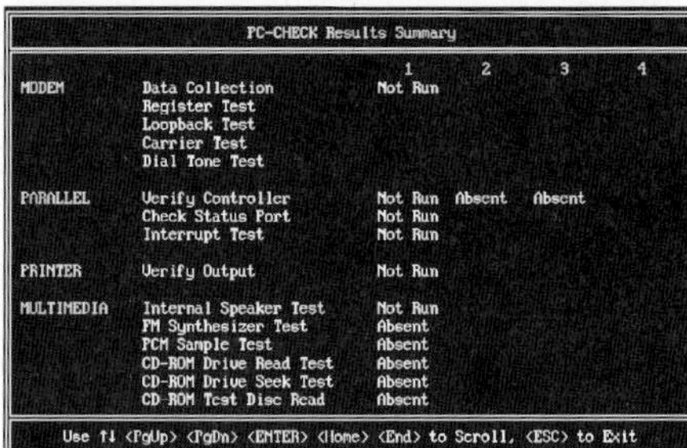

PC-CHECK Results Summary

		1	2	3	4
MODEM	Data Collection	Not Run			
	Register Test				
	Loopback Test				
	Carrier Test				
	Dial Tone Test				
PARALLEL	Verify Controller	Not Run	Absent	Absent	
	Check Status Port	Not Run			
	Interrupt Test	Not Run			
PRINTER	Verify Output	Not Run			
MULTIMEDIA	Internal Speaker Test	Not Run			
	FM Synthesizer Test	Absent			
	PCM Sample Test	Absent			
	CD-ROM Drive Read Test	Absent			
	CD-ROM Drive Seek Test	Absent			
	CD-ROM Test Disc Read	Absent			

Use ↑↓ <PgUp> <PgDn> <ENTER> <Home> <End> to Scroll, <ESC> to Exit

Figure 11-9: The Burn-In Test Report

Using POST Cards

POST cards

Most BIOS program chips do not have an extensive set of on-board diagnostics built into them. Therefore, several companies produce **POST cards** and diagnostic software to aid in hardware troubleshooting. A POST card is a diagnostic device that plugs into the system's expansion slot and tests the operation of the system as it boots up. These cards can be as simple as interrupt and DMA channel monitors, or as complex as full-fledged ROM BIOS diagnostic packages that carry out extensive tests on the system.

POST cards are normally used when the system appears to be dead, or when the system cannot read from a floppy or hard drive. The firmware tests on the card replace the normal BIOS functions and send the system into a set of tests. The value of the card lies in the fact that the tests can be carried out without the system resorting to software diagnostics located on the hard disk or in a floppy drive.

The POST tests located in most BIOS chips will report two types of errors: fatal and nonfatal. If the POST encounters a fatal error, it stops the system. The error code posted on the indicator corresponds to the defective operation. If the POST card encounters a nonfatal error, however, it notes the error and continues through the initialization routine to activate as many additional system resources as possible. When these types of errors are encountered, the POST card must be observed carefully, because the error code on its indicator must be coordinated with the timing of the error message or beep code produced by the BIOS routines.

Simple POST cards come with a set of light-emitting diodes (LEDs) on them that produce coded error signals when a problem is encountered. Other cards produce beep codes and seven-segment LED readouts of the error code. Figure 11-10. depicts a typical XT/AT-compatible POST card.

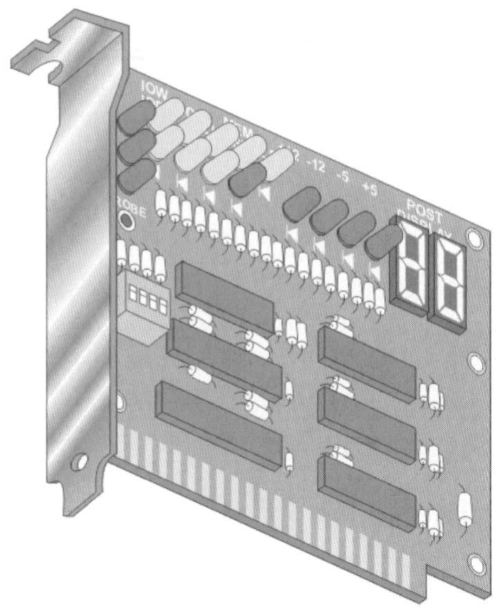

Figure 11-10: A Typical POST Card

Hardware Troubleshooting

Unfortunately, most software diagnostics packages do not lead to specific components that have failed. Indeed, you might not even be able to use a software package to isolate faults if major components of the system are inoperative. If you have eliminated software and configuration problems, you need to pull out the test equipment and check the system's internal hardware for proper operation under controlled conditions.

Turn off the power and remove any peripheral devices from the system one at a time. Make sure to restore the power and retry the system after you remove each peripheral. If you have removed all the peripherals and the problem persists, you must troubleshoot the basic components of the system. This troubleshooting usually involves checking the components inside the system unit.

Performing Quick Tests

visual inspection

After you have removed the cover of the system unit, perform a careful **visual inspection** of its interior. Look for signs of overheating, such as charred components or wires. When electronic components overheat, they produce a noticeable odor, so you may be able to do some troubleshooting with your nose. If you do find an overheated component, especially a resistor, don't assume that you can clear up the problem by just replacing the burnt component. Many times when a component fails, it causes another component to fail.

You can make a very quick check of the system's integrated circuits (ICs) by just touching the tops of the chips with your finger to see whether they are hot.

Metal Oxide Semiconductor (MOS)

Ground yourself—Because there may be **Metal Oxide Semiconductor** (**MOS**) devices on the board, you want to ground yourself before performing this test. You can do so by touching an exposed portion of the unit's chassis, such as the top of the power supply.

If the system has power applied to it, all the ICs should be warm. Some will be warmer than others by nature; if a chip burns your finger, however, it is probably bad and needs to be replaced. Just replacing the chip might not clear up your problem, however. Instead, you may end up with two dead chips (the original and the replacement). The original chip may have been wiped out by some other problem in the system. For this reason, you should use this quick test only to localize problems.

Other items to check include components and internal connections that may have come loose. Check for foreign objects that may have fallen through the device's air vents. Remove any dust buildup that might have accumulated, and then retry the system.

Field-Replaceable Unit Troubleshooting

Field-Replaceable Units (FRUs)

Field-Replaceable Units (**FRU**s) are the portions of the system that you can conveniently replace in the field.

Typical microcomputer FRUs are depicted in Figure 11-11. FRU troubleshooting involves isolating a problem within one section of the system. A section consists of one device such as a keyboard, video display, video adapter card, I/O adapter card, system board, disk drive, printer, and so on. These are typically components that can simply be exchanged for a replacement on site and require no actual repair work.

TEST TIP

Know which devices in a typical PC system are FRU devices.

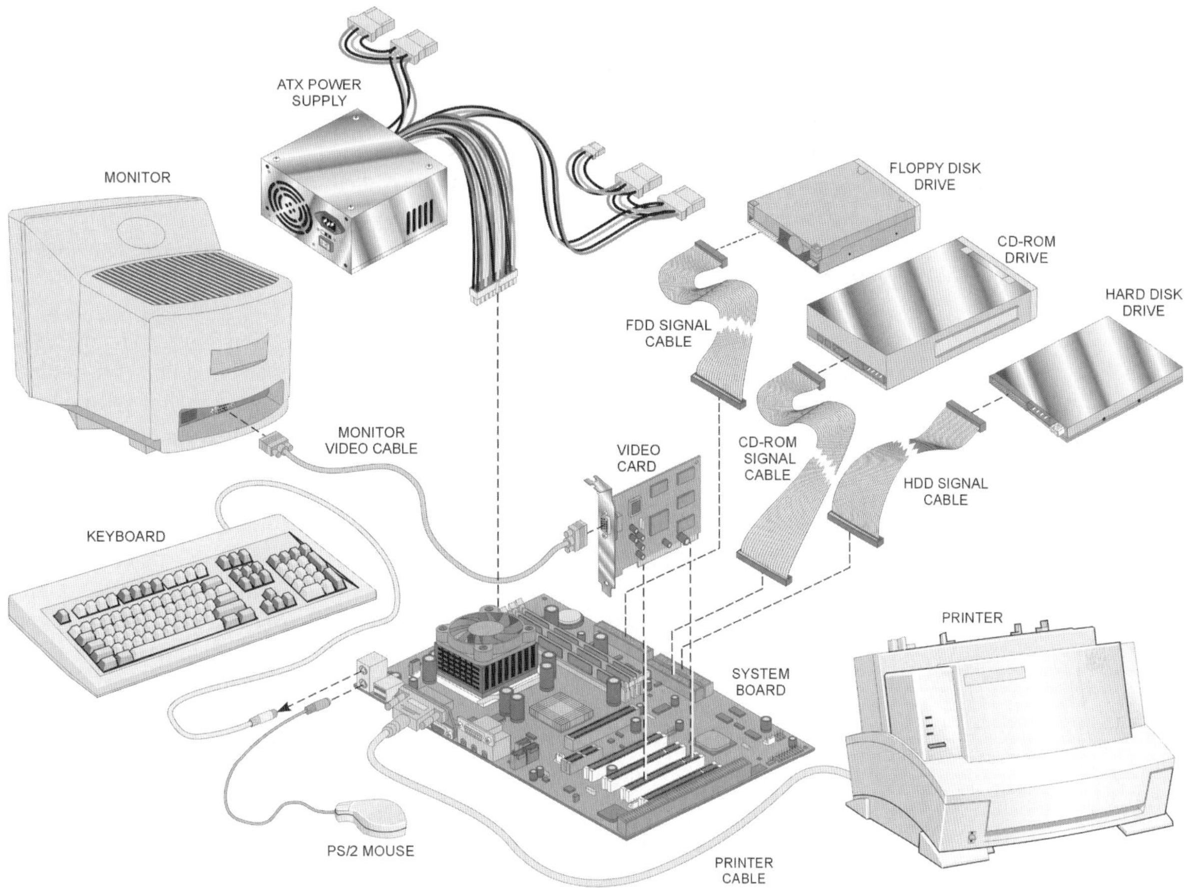

Figure 11-11: The Typical FRUs of a Microcomputer System

This is the level of troubleshooting most often performed on PCs. Due to the relative low cost of computer components, it is normally not practical to troubleshoot failed components to the IC level. The cost of using a technician to diagnose the problem further, and repair it, can quickly exceed the cost of the new replacement unit.

Exchanging FRU components—Once a hardware error has been indicated, start troubleshooting the problem by exchanging components (cards, drives, etc.) with **known good ones**.

known good ones

When exchanging system components, be sure to replace the device being removed with one of exactly the same type. Just because two components have the same function does not mean that they can be substituted for each other. (For example, an EGA video adapter card cannot just be used to replace a monochrome adapter card without making other modifications to the system.) Interchanging similar parts is possible in some cases and not in others. Whether two components can be exchanged depends on the particular modules.

Assume that only a single component has failed. The odds against more than one component failing at the same time are extremely high. At the point where the system's operation is restored, it can reasonably be assumed that at least the last component removed was defective.

If a diagnostic tool indicates that multiple components have failed, use the one-at-time exchange method, starting with the first component indicated, to isolate the original source of the problem. Test the system between each component exchange and work backward through the exchanged components after the system has started to function again.

If it is necessary to disconnect cables or connectors from boards, take the time to mark the cables *and* their connection points so that they are easy to identify later. The simplest way to mark cables is to place identification marks on tape (masking or athletic) and then attach the tape to the cables and connection points.

Match the markings on the cable with the markings at its connection point. At many connection points, the color of the wire connected to a certain pin may be important. When placing the identifying marks on the tape, you may want to note the color arrangement of the wires being disconnected so that you can be sure to get them back in their proper places after you have swapped the component.

Always check cabling connections after plugging them in. Look for missed connections, bent pins, and so on. Also, check the routing of cables. Try to establish connections that do not place unnecessary strain on the cable. Route cables away from ICs as much as possible. Some ICs, such as microprocessors, can become quite hot, so hot that they and may eventually damage cables. Avoid routing cables near cooling fans as well since they produce high levels of EMI that can be introduced into the signal cables as electrical noise.

re-seat connections

Corrosion

It is often helpful to simply **re-seat** (remove and reinstall) **connections** and adapter cards in the expansion slots when a problem occurs. **Corrosion** may build up on the computer's connection points and cause a poor electrical contact to occur. By re-seating the connection, the contact problem often disappears.

Write it down—Make certain to take the time to document the symptoms associated with the problem, including all of the tests you make, and any changes that occur during the tests. This information can keep you from making repetitive steps.

Work backwards—Once you have isolated the problem, and the computer boots up and runs correctly, work backwards through the troubleshooting routines, reinstalling any original boards and other components removed during the troubleshooting process.

Working backwards, one component at a time, through any components that have been removed from the system, enables you to make certain that only one failure occurred in the machine. If the system fails after installing a new card, check the card's default configuration settings against those of the devices already installed in the system.

Isolating Undefined Problems

Effective troubleshooting is a process of observing symptoms and applying logic to isolate and repair the cause as quickly and efficiently as possible. If the FRU troubleshooting system were taken to its most extreme, it would be logical to expect that anyone could repair a computer by simply exchanging all of the parts one at a time until the system started working.

Although this is technically possible, it is also highly unlikely to occur. In addition, such a scenario would not be efficient or cost effective to carry out. Therefore, technicians use symptoms and tools to provide effective troubleshooting.

However, there may be problems that simply refuse to be classified under a particular symptom. If a multiple-component failure occurs, or if one failure causes a second failure to occur, the symptoms produced by the computer may not point to any particular cause. Secondary problems may also hide the symptoms of the real failure. These types of failures that do not point to a clear-cut component in the system, are referred to as **undefined problems**.

undefined problems

Even in these cases, the technician should use the symptoms presented to isolate the problem to an *area* of the system for checking. Normally, symptoms can be divided into three sections. These include configuration problems, bootup problems, and operational problems.

The system's configuration settings are normally checked first. It is important to observe the system's symptoms to determine in which part of the system's operation the fault occurs. Error messages typically associated with configuration problems include the following:

- CMOS Display Type Mismatch
- CMOS Memory Size Mismatch
- CMOS Battery State Low
- CMOS Checksum Failure
- CMOS System Options Not Set
- CMOS Time and Date Not Set

These errors occur and are reported before the single beep tone is produced at the end of the POST routines.

After the beep tone has been produced in the startup sequence, the system shifts over to the process of booting up. Typical error messages associated with boot-up problems include the following:

- General Failure Error Reading Drive x
- Bad or Missing Command Interpreter
- Non-System Disk or Disk Error
- Bad File Allocation Table

Both configuration and bootup problems can be caused by a hardware problem. If no configuration settings are incorrect but the symptoms are present, then a hardware problem is indicated as the cause of the problem. Procedures for diagnosing and troubleshooting problems associated with typical PC hardware components are presented throughout the Symptoms and Troubleshooting section in this chapter.

Conversely, bootup problems are typically associated with the operating system. Steps for isolating and correcting operating system problems are presented in Chapter 12—*Operating System Troubleshooting.*

The Shotgun Approach

logical starting point

There are those rare times when it is best to simply begin with some **logical starting point** and work through the entire system until you cure the problem. One such method, referred to as the shotgun method, divides the system into logical sections to quickly isolate the cause of the problem to an area.

The system may be made up of the basic computer, monitor, and keyboard, or it may be a highly developed combination of equipment, involving the basic computer and a group of peripherals. For troubleshooting purposes, you should divide the system into logically related subsections.

basic system

other devices

The first division naturally falls between the components that make up the **basic system** and **other devices**. The basic system consists of the system unit, the keyboard, and the video display monitor. Other devices consist of components that are *optional* as far as the system's operation is concerned. You can remove these items from the system without changing its basic operation. They include such things as printers, mouse devices, digitizing tablets, hard disk drives, tape drives, scanners, and so on.

When a problem occurs, you should first remove the optional items from the system. By doing so, you divide the system in half and can determine whether the problem exists in one of the computer's main components or in one of its options.

internal and external options

The second logical division falls between the **internal and external options**. When you have no idea what the problem is, you should test all external devices before removing the outer cover to check internal devices.

Inside the system unit, the next dividing point exists between the system board and all the internal options. The first items to be removed from the system are the options adapters, except for the disk drive and video controller cards. You should check these cards only if the system still won't work properly with the other options adapters removed.

The next components to exchange are the floppy drives and the power supply unit, in that order. The system board is the most difficult component to exchange. Therefore, it should be the last component in the system to be exchanged.

SYMPTOMS AND TROUBLESHOOTING

The A+ Core Hardware objective 2.1 states that the test taker should be able to identify common symptoms and problems associated with each module and how to troubleshoot and isolate the problems. Contents may include:

- Processor/Memory symptoms
- Mouse
- Floppy drive failures
- Parallel ports
- Hard drives
- Power supply
- Sound card/audio
- POST audible/visual error codes
- Large LBA, LBA
- Troubleshooting tools (for example, multimeter)
- Motherboards
- Modems
- BIOS
- USB
- CMOS
- Monitor/Video
- Slot covers

One of the primary responsibilities of every PC technician is to diagnose and troubleshoot computer problems. As this A+ objective points out, the technician should be able to identify common symptoms associated with computer components, and to use those symptoms to effectively troubleshoot and repair the problem. Numerous sources of problems and symptoms are discussed below, beginning with those that relate to the power supply.

Isolating Power Supply Problems

Typical symptoms associated with power-supply failures include:

- No indicator lights visible, with no disk drive action, and no display on the screen. Nothing works, and the system is dead.
- The ON/OFF indicator lights are visible, but there is no disk drive action and no display on the monitor screen. The system fan may or may not run.
- The system produces a continuous beep tone.

The power supply unit is one of the few components in the system that is connected to virtually every other component in the system. Therefore, it has the ability to affect all of the other components if it fails. Figure 11-12 illustrates the interconnections of the power supply unit with the other components in the system.

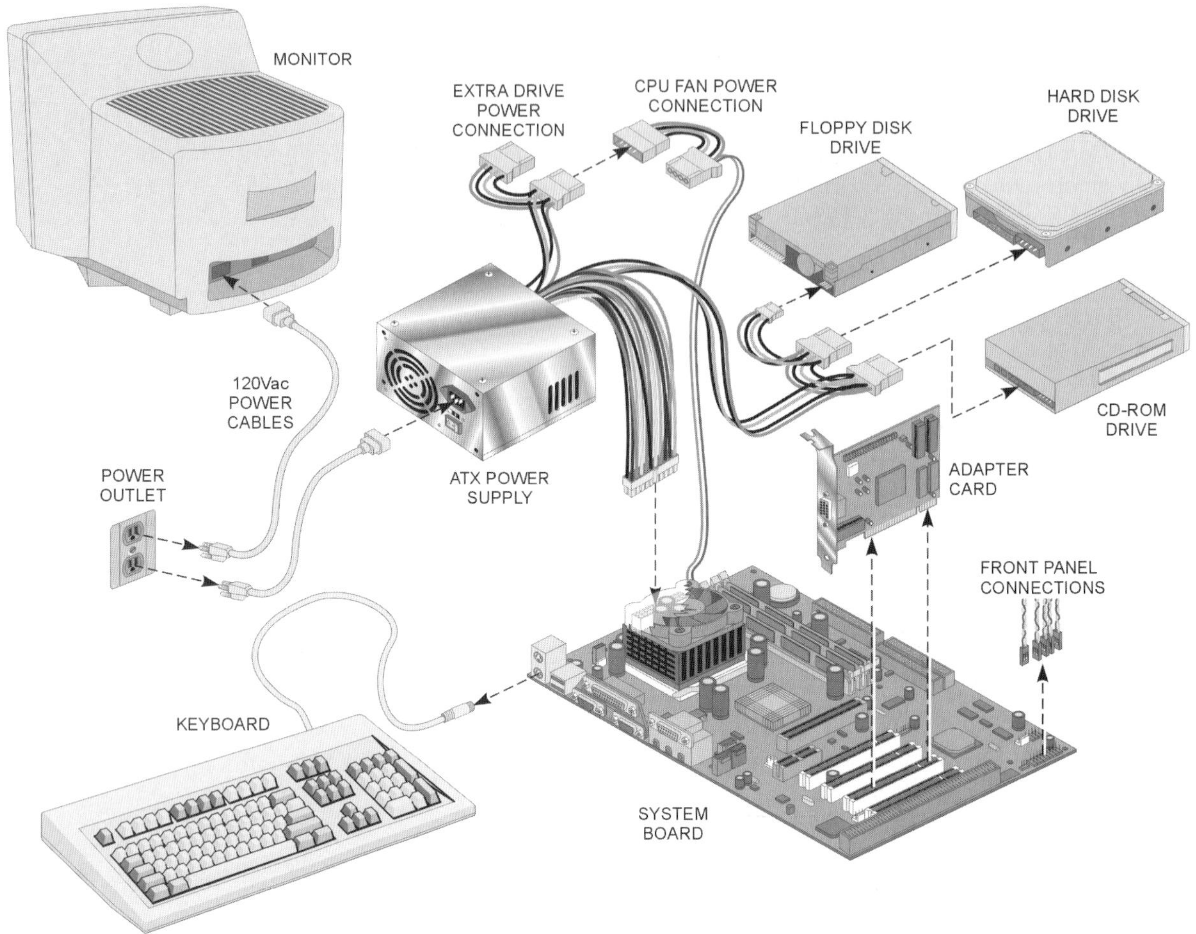

Figure 11-12: Power Supply Interconnections

When tracking down power supply problems, remember that in addition to the obvious power connections shown in the diagram, the power supply also delivers power to other components through the system board. These include: (1) all of the options adapter cards (through the expansion-slot connectors) and (2) the keyboard (through the keyboard connector). Power supply problems can cause symptoms to occur in all of these areas, and problems in any of these areas can affect the operation of the power supply.

Checking a Dead System

Special consideration must be taken when a system is inoperable. In a totally inoperable system, there are no symptoms to give clues where to begin the isolation process. In addition, it is impossible to use troubleshooting software or other system aids to help isolate the problem.

The following discussion is a standard method of troubleshooting dead microprocessor-based equipment. The first step in troubleshooting any dead system is to visually inspect the system. Check for unseated cards, loose cables, or foreign objects within the system unit.

When the system exhibits no signs of life—including the absence of lights—*the best place to start looking for the problem is at the power supply*. The operation of this unit affects virtually every part of the system. Also, the absence of any lights working usually indicates that no power is being supplied to the system by the power supply.

external connections

1. Begin by checking the **external connections** of the power supply. This is the first step in checking any electrical equipment that shows no signs of life.
2. Confirm that the power supply cord is plugged into a functioning outlet.
3. Check the position of the ON/OFF switch.
4. Examine the power cord for good connection at the rear of the unit.
5. Check the setting of the 110/220 switch setting on the outside of the power supply. The normal setting for equipment used in the United States is 110.
6. Check the power at the commercial receptacle using a voltmeter, or by plugging in a lamp (or other 110 volt device) into the outlet.

TEST TIP

Remember the first step of checking out electrical equipment that appears dead.

If power is reaching the power supply and nothing is happening, the next step in isolating the cause of the problem is to determine which component is causing the problem. The most likely cause of the problems in a totally dead system is the power supply itself. However, be aware that in an ATX system, if the cable that connects the system board to power switch has become loose, the power supply will appear dead. Use a voltmeter to check for the proper voltages at one of the system's option's power connectors. (All system voltages should be present at these connectors.) If any voltage is missing, check the power supply by substitution.

If the power supply is not the reason the system is dead, one of the other components must be overloading the power supply. Under such conditions, it is normal for the system to trip the breaker or to blow the fuse in the commercial power system. You must sort out which component is affecting the power supply. Remove the peripheral devices so that only the basic system needs to be checked. Divide the system into **basic and optional sections** for testing. Remove all external options from the system and restart the system. If the system begins to work, troubleshoot the optional portions of the system.

basic and optional sections

Finally, divide the basic system into **optional and basic components**. Remove all optional adapter cards from their expansion slots and restart the system. If the system begins to work, troubleshoot the various options adapters by reinstalling them one at a time until the system fails again.

optional and basic components

WARNING

Turn It Off First!—Before changing any board or connection, always turn the system off first. In an ATX-style system, you should also disconnect the power cable from the power supply. This is necessary because even with the power switch off, there are still some levels of voltages applied to the system board in these units.

Other Power Supply Problems

If the front panel lights are on and the power-supply fan is running, but no other system action is occurring, you should consider the power supply as one of the most likely sources of such a problem.

The presence of the lights and the fan operation indicate that power is reaching the system and that at least some portion of the power supply is functional. This type of symptom results from the following two likely possibilities:

1. A portion of the power supply has failed, or is being overloaded. One or more of the basic voltages supplied by the power supply is missing while the others are still present.
2. A key component on the system board has failed, preventing it from processing, even though the system has power. A defective capacitor across the power input of the system board can completely prevent it from operating.

Check the power supply by substitution. If the power supply is not the cause of the dead system, one of the other components must be overloading that portion of the power supply. You must sort out which component is causing the problem.

Adding and Removing Power Supplies

Figure 11-13 illustrates the steps involved in removing the power supply from a PC. To exchange the power supply, all of its connections to the system must be removed.

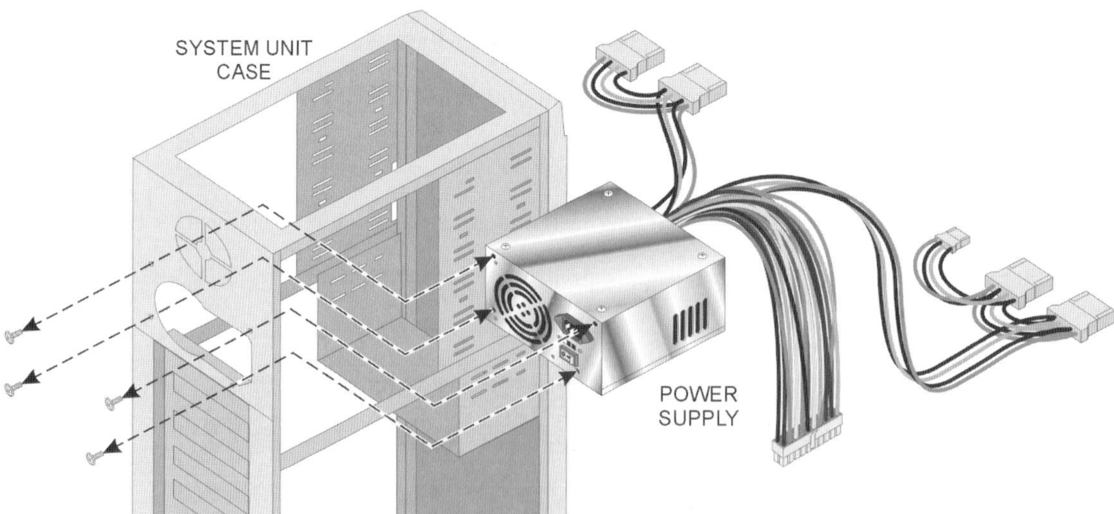

Figure 11-13: Power Supply Connections

Hands-On Activity

Typical steps for removing a power supply:

1. Disconnect the exterior power connections from the system unit
   a. Unplug the power cable from the commercial receptacle
   b. Disconnect the monitor's power cable from the power supply
2. Disconnect the interior power connections
   a. Disconnect the power supply connections from the system board
   b. Disconnect the power supply connector from the floppy disk drive
   c. Disconnect the power supply connector from the hard disk drive
   d. Disconnect the power supply connector from the CD-ROM drive (if present)
   e. Disconnect the power supply connector to the front panel switch (if used in your case style)
3. Remove the power supply unit from the system
   a. Remove the 4 retaining screws that secure the power supply unit to the rear of the system unit (Note: in some AT style cases, an additional pair of screws are used along the front edge of the power supply to secure it to the metal bracket it is mounted on)
   b. Store the screws properly
   c. Remove the power supply from the system unit by lifting it out of the unit

These steps would be reversed for the installation of a power supply.

Troubleshooting the System Board

Troubleshooting problems related to the system board can be difficult to solve because of the system board's relative complexity. So many system functions at least partially rely on the system board that certain symptoms can be masked by other symptoms.

As with any troubleshooting procedure, begin by observing the symptoms produced by bootup and operation. Observe the steps that lead to the failure and determine under what conditions the system failed. Were any unusual operations in progress? Note any error messages or beep codes.

Try any obvious steps, such as adjusting brightness controls on a dim monitor or checking for loose connections on peripheral equipment. Retry the system several times to observe the symptoms clearly. Take time to document the problem—write it down.

Refer to the User Manuals for the system board and peripheral units to check for configuration problems. Examine the CMOS setup entries for configuration problems. In Pentium systems, also check the advanced CMOS setup parameters to make certain that all the appropriate system board–enabling settings have been made.

If possible, run a software diagnostics package to narrow the possible causes. Remember that the microprocessor, RAM modules, ROM BIOS, CMOS battery, and possibly cache ICs are typically replaceable units on the system board. If enough of the system is running to perform tests on these units, you can replace them. If symptoms suggest that one or more of these devices may be defective, you can exchange them with a known good unit of the same type.

If the diagnostics program indicates a number of possible bad components, replace them one at a time until isolate the bad unit. Then insert any possible good units back into the system and check them. You also should consider the possibility of bad software when multiple FRU problems are indicated.

System Board Symptoms

So much of the system's operation is based on the system board that it can have several different types of symptoms. Typical symptoms associated with system board hardware failures include:

- The On/Off indicator lights are visible, the display is visible on the monitor screen, but there is no disk drive action and no bootup.
- The On/Off indicator lights are visible, the hard drive spins up, but the system appears dead and there is no bootup.
- The system locks up during normal operation.
- The system produces a beep code with 1, 2, 3, 5, 7, or 9 beeps is produced.
- The system produces a beep code of 1 long and 3 short beeps is produced.
- The system will not hold date and time.
- An "8042 Gate A20 Error" message displays—Error getting into Protected mode.
- An "Invalid Switch Memory Failure" message displays.
- A "DMA Error" message displays—DMA Controller failed page register test.
- A "CMOS Battery Low" message displays, indicating failure of CMOS battery or CMOS checksum test.
- A "CMOS System Option Not Set" message displays, indicating failure of CMOS battery or CMOS checksum test.
- A "CMOS Checksum Failure" message displays, indicating CMOS battery low or CMOS checksum test failure.
- A 201 error code displays, indicating a RAM failure.
- A parity check error message displays, indicating a RAM error.

TEST TIP

Memorize standard IBM error code numbers.

Typical symptoms associated with system board setup failures include:

- A "CMOS Inoperational" message displays, indicating failure of CMOS shutdown register.
- A "Display Switch Setting Not Proper" message displays—Failure to verify display type.
- A "CMOS Display Mismatch" message displays—Failure of display type verification.
- A "CMOS Memory Size Mismatch" message displays—System Configuration and Setup failure.
- A "CMOS Time & Date Not Set" message displays—System Configuration and Setup failure.
- An IBM-compatible error code displays, indicating that a configuration problem has occurred.

Typical symptoms associated with system board I/O failures include the following:

- Speaker doesn't work during operation. The rest of the system works, but no sounds are produced through the speaker.
- Keyboard does not function after being replaced with a known good unit.

Most of the hardware problems that occur with computers, outside of those already described, involve the system board. Because the system board is the center of virtually all the computer's operations, it is only natural that you must check it at some point in most troubleshooting efforts. The system board normally marks the end of any of the various troubleshooting schemes given for different system components. It occupies this position for two reasons. First, the system board supports most of the other system components, either directly or indirectly. Second, it is the system component that requires the most effort to replace and test.

Other System Board Problems

In addition to containing the circuitry that directs all the system's operations, the system board contains a number of other circuits on which the rest of the system's components depend. These include the system's DRAM memory (which all software programs use) and the system's data, address, and signal buses. The part of the buses you are most familiar with are the expansion slots.

Problems with key system board components produce symptoms similar to those described for a bad power supply. Both the microprocessor and the ROM BIOS can be sources of such problems. You should check both by substitution when dead system symptoms are encountered but the power supply is good.

Because all the system's options adapter cards connect to the buses through the expansion slots, failure of any component attached to one of the slots can prevent information movement between other components along the bus. In this case, you must remove the offending component from the bus before any operation can proceed.

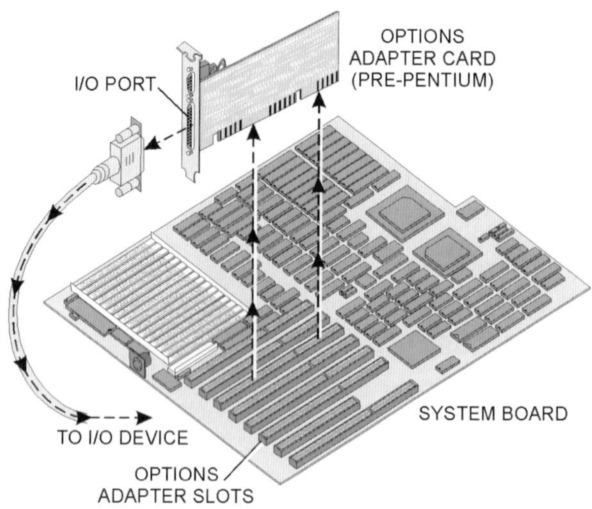

Figure 11-14: Moving Information to an I/O Port

You can add a number of other optional devices to the system just by installing an appropriate adapter card in one of the system board's expansion slots and then connecting the option to it. Figure 11-14 illustrates the flow of information between the system board and a typical connection port (a parallel printer port) located on an option's adapter card.

An often overlooked output device is the system's speaker. Unlike other I/O devices, all the circuitry that controls the speaker is contained on the system board. Therefore, the speaker should fail for only a few reasons, including - the speaker itself is defective, the speaker circuitry on the system board is defective, the speaker is unplugged from the system board, or the software is failing to drive the speaker circuits.

The easiest time to detect a speaker problem is during the boot-up process. The system may use the speaker to produce different sounds at various points in this process. However, the most direct method of checking a speaker is to check across its leads using the resistance function of a digital multimeter. The DMM should read approximately 8 ohms for most speakers used with PCs. Figure 11-15 depicts a system's typical speaker-related components.

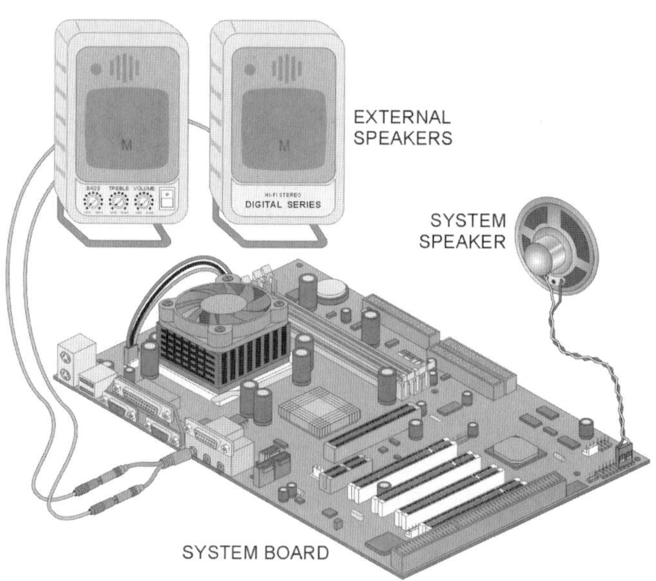

Figure 11-15: Speaker-Related Components

The keyboard is another I/O device supported directly from the system board. When examining keyboard problems, there are only three items to check: the keyboard, the system board, and the keyboard driver software. The most basic way to determine keyboard problems is to watch the keyboard's NumLock and ScrollLock lights during the boot-up process. These lights should flash when the system attempts to initialize the keyboard.

Configuration Checks

Observe the bootup RAM count to see that it is correct for the amount of physical RAM actually installed in the system. If not, swap RAM devices around to see if the count changes. Use logical rotation of the RAM devices to locate the defective part.

Normally, the only time a configuration problem occurs is when the system is being set up for the first time, or when a new option is installed. The other condition that causes a configuration problem involves the system board's CMOS backup battery. If the battery fails, or has been changed, the contents of the CMOS setup will be lost. After replacing the battery, it is always necessary to run the CMOS setup utility to reconfigure the system.

The values stored in CMOS must accurately reflect the configuration of the system; otherwise, an error occurs. You can access these values for change by pressing a predetermined key combination during the boot-up procedure.

> In Pentium-based systems, check the advanced CMOS configuration and enabling settings in the BIOS and Chipset Features screens. These settings, illustrated in Figure 11-16, usually include the disk drives, keyboard, and video options, as well as on-board serial and parallel ports.

In addition, the user can turn on or off certain sections of the system's RAM for shadowing purposes and establish parity or nonparity memory operations.

Incorrectly set BIOS-enabling parameters cause the corresponding hardware to fail. Therefore, check the enabling functions of the advanced CMOS settings as a part of every hardware configuration troubleshooting procedure.

The complexity of modern system boards has created a huge number of configuration options for the CMOS, as reflected in the complexity of their advanced CMOS configuration screens. It is very easy to place the system in a condition where it cannot respond. Because the problem is at the BIOS level, it may be difficult to get back into the CMOS to correct the problem. Therefore, system designers have included a couple of options to safeguard the system from this condition.

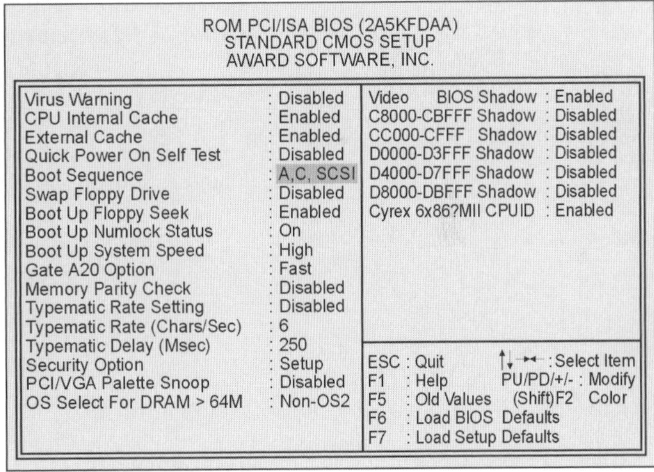

Figure 11-16: BIOS Enabling Settings

In some BIOS, holding down the DEL key throughout the startup erases the CMOS contents and starts from scratch. The system board may have a jumper that can be shorted to reset the contents of CMOS to its default values. This jumper may also be used to clear a forgotten CMOS password. In either case, you must rebuild any advanced features in the CMOS configuration afterward.

Auto Configure with Power-On Defaults

Auto Configure with BIOS Defaults

Newer system boards have an autoconfiguration mode that takes over most of the setup decisions. This option works well in the majority of applications. Its settings produce an efficient, basic level of operation for standard devices in the system. However, they do not optimize the performance of the system. To do that, you must turn off the autoconfiguration feature and insert desired parameters into the configuration table. There are typically two options for the autoconfiguration function: **Auto Configure with Power-On Defaults** and **Auto Configure with BIOS Defaults**.

Using power-on defaults for autoconfiguration loads the most conservative options possible into the system from the BIOS. This is the most effective way to detect BIOS-related system problems. These settings replace any user-entered configuration information in the CMOS setup registers. Any turbo-speed mode is disabled, all memory caching is turned off, and all wait states are set to maximum. This allows the most basic part of the system to start up. If these default values fail to get the system to boot up, it is an indication of hardware problems (such as incorrect jumper settings or bad hardware components).

Using autoconfiguration with BIOS defaults provides a little more flexibility than the power-on option. If you have entered an improper configuration setting and cannot determine which setting is causing the problem, this option is suggested. Like the power-on option, this selection replaces the entered configuration settings with a new set of parameters from the BIOS. Choosing this option will likely get you back into the CMOS setup screen so that you can track down the problem. It also is the recommended starting point for optimizing the system's operation.

The many configuration options available in a modern BIOS requires the user to have a good deal of knowledge about the particular function being configured. Therefore, an extended discussion of the advanced CMOS setup options cannot be conducted at this point. However, such information is covered along with the system component it relates to as the book moves through various system components.

CMOS setup utilities may also offer a wide array of exit options. One common mistake in working with CMOS configuration settings is that of not saving the new settings before exiting. When this happens, the new settings are not stored, and so the old settings are still in place when the system reboots.

Typically, if the boot-up process reaches the point where the system's CMOS configuration information displays onscreen, you can safely assume that no hardware configuration conflicts exist in the system's basic components. After this point in the boot-up process, the system begins loading drivers for optional devices and additional memory. If the error occurs after the CMOS screen displays and before the boot-up tone, you must clean boot the system and single-step through the remainder of the boot-up sequence.

Software Checks

Boot up the system and start the selected diagnostic program if possible. Try to use a diagnostic program that deals with the system board components. It should include memory, microprocessor, interrupt, and DMA tests.

System Board Tests

Run the program's **System Board Tests** function and perform the equivalent of the ALL tests function. These types of tests are particularly good for detecting memory errors, as well as interrupt and DMA conflicts. Note all of the errors indicated by the tests. If a single type of error is indicated, you might be able to take some corrective actions, such as replacing a memory module or reconfiguring interrupt/DMA settings, without replacing the system board. However, if more complex system board problems are indicated, exit the diagnostic program and use the following Hardware Checks and Installation/Removal procedure to troubleshoot and replace the system board.

You can use the DOS **MEM command** (**MEM.EXE**) to view the system's memory-utilization scheme. It displays both the programs currently loaded into memory, and the system's free memory areas. You can use the **/C** switch with the MEM command as a valuable tool to sort out TSR conflicts in upper memory. Likewise, you can add a **/D** switch to the MEM command to view detailed information about memory usage. This switch gives very detailed information about all items stored in memory.

MEM command (MEM.EXE)

/C

/D

Hardware Checks

If the system's CMOS configuration setup appears to be correct and a system board hardware problem is suspected, you probably need to exchange the system board for a working unit. Because most of the system must be dismantled to exchange it, however, a few items are worth checking before doing so.

Check the system board for signs of physical problems, such as loose cables and devices. If nothing is apparently wrong, check the power-supply voltage levels on the system board. Check for +5V and +12V (DC) on the system board, as illustrated in Figure 11-17. If these voltages are missing, turn off the system, disconnect power to all disk drives, and swap the power-supply unit with a known good one.

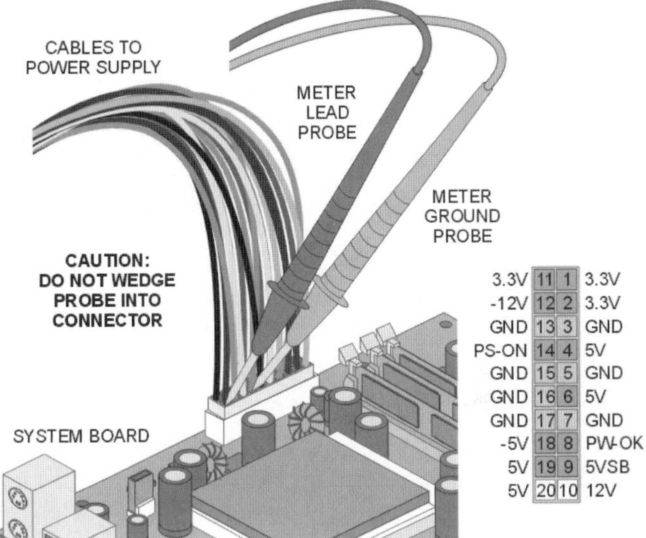

Figure 11-17: The System Board Voltage Check Location

Onboard FRU Devices

Finally, consider checking the FRU devices present on the board. There are normally a few serviceable items on the system board that might be checked by substitution before doing so. These include the RAM modules, the microprocessor (and its cooling fan), the ROM BIOS chip(s), and the system battery.

RAM

The system board's memory is a very serviceable part of the system. RAM failures basically fall into two major categories and create two different types of failures. The first category of memory errors, called **soft-memory errors**, are caused by infrequent and random glitches in the operation of applications and the system. You can clear these events just by restarting the system. However, the other category of RAM failures are referred to as **hard-memory errors**. These are permanent physical failures that generate NMI errors in the system and require that the memory units be checked by substitution.

soft-memory errors

hard-memory errors

You can swap the RAM modules out one at a time, to isolate defective modules. These modules are also swapped out when a system upgrade is being performed. The burn-in tests in most diagnostic packages can prove helpful in locating borderline RAM modules.

TEST TIP

Know what type of failures hard- and soft-memory errors are and how they affect the system.

Take care when swapping RAM into a system for troubleshooting purposes to make sure that the new RAM is the correct type of RAM for the system and that it meets the system's bus speed rating. Also, make sure that the replacement RAM is consistent with the installed RAM. Mixing RAM types and speeds can cause the system to lock up and produce hard memory errors.

Microprocessor

In the case of the microprocessor, the system may issue a slow, single beep, with no display or other I/O operation. This indicates that an internal error has disabled a portion of the processor's internal circuitry (usually the internal cache). Internal problems also may allow the microprocessor to begin processing, but then fail as it attempts operations. Such a problem results in the system continuously counting RAM during the boot up process. It also may lock up while counting RAM. In either case, the only way to remedy the problem is to replace the microprocessor.

If the system consistently locks up after being on for a few minutes, this is a good indication that the microprocessor's fan is not running or that some other heat buildup problem is occurring. You also should check the microprocessor if its fan has not been running, but the power is on. This situation may indicate that the microprocessor has been without adequate ventilation and has overheated. When this happens, you must replace the fan unit and the microprocessor. Check to make certain that the new fan works correctly; otherwise, a second microprocessor will be damaged.

TEST TIP

Know the effects on the system of heat buildup and microprocessor fan failures.

You can easily exchange the microprocessor on most system boards. Only the 80386SX is a soldered-in device, so it presents more of a challenge to exchange (and is not likely worth the expense involved). However, the fact that most microprocessors, as well as the BIOS chips, are mounted in sockets brings up another point. These items should be pulled and reseated in their sockets if they seem to be a possible cause of problems. Sockets are convenient for repair and upgrade purposes, but they also can attract corrosion between the pins of the device, and those of the socket. Over time, the corrosion may become so bad that the electrical connection becomes too poor for the device to operate properly.

ROM

Like the microprocessor, a bad or damaged ROM BIOS typically stops the system dead. When you encounter a dead system board, examine the BIOS chip(s) for physical damage. If these devices overheat, it is typical for them to crack or blow a large piece out of the top of the IC package. Another symptom of a damaged BIOS is indicated by the boot up moving into the CMOS configuration, but never returning to the boot-up sequence. In any case, you must replace the defective BIOS with a version that matches the chipset used by the system.

Battery

Corrosion also can affect the system clock over time. If a system refuses to maintain time and date information after the backup battery has been replaced, check the contacts of the holder for corrosion. Two types of batteries are commonly used for CMOS backup: **Nickel-Cadmium (Ni-Cad)** and **lithium** batteries. Of the two, Ni-Cads have historically been the most favored. Conversely, lithium batteries are gaining respect due to their long-life capabilities when installed in systems designed to recharge lithium batteries. However, lithium battery life is noticeably short when they are installed in systems designed for the higher current drain Ni-Cads. Therefore, you should always use the correct type of battery to replace a system board battery.

Nickel-Cadmium (Ni-Cad)

lithium

Exchanging the System Board

If there is any uncertainty about the system board being the source of the problem, use the isolation step presented in the Isolating Undefined Problems section earlier in this chapter to isolate the fault down to the system board.

Reduce the system to its basic components. If it still refuses to boot up, remove the basic adapter cards one by one and restart the system.

If possible, back up the contents of the system's hard drive to some other media before removing the system board. Also, record the CMOS configuration settings, along with the settings of all jumpers and switches, before exchanging the system board.

If the system still won't boot up, remove any adapter card from the system board's expansion slots. Disconnect the system board from the power-supply unit and the system board/front-panel connections. Take care to mark any connection removed from the system board, and its connection point, to ensure proper reconnection. Exchange the system board with a known good one. Reconnect all of the power-supply and front-panel connections to the system board. Reinstall the video and disk-drive controller cards in the expansion slots and try to reboot the system.

Reconfigure the system board to operate with the installed peripherals. Reseat the video and disk-drive controller cards in the system unit. Reset the CMOS setup to match the installed peripherals, and turn on the system.

When the system boots up, reinstall any options removed from the system and replace the system unit's outer cover. Return the system to full service and service the defective system board. If the system still does not boot up, retest all the system components one at a time until you find a cause. Check the small things such as cable connections and key switches carefully.

Troubleshooting Keyboard Problems

Most of the circuitry associated with the computer's keyboard is contained in the keyboard itself. However, some keyboard interface circuitry is located on the system board. Therefore, the steps required to isolate keyboard problems are usually confined to the keyboard, its connecting cable, and the system board.

This arrangement makes isolating keyboard problems relatively easy. Just check the keyboard and the system board. Figure 11-18 depicts the components associated with the keyboard.

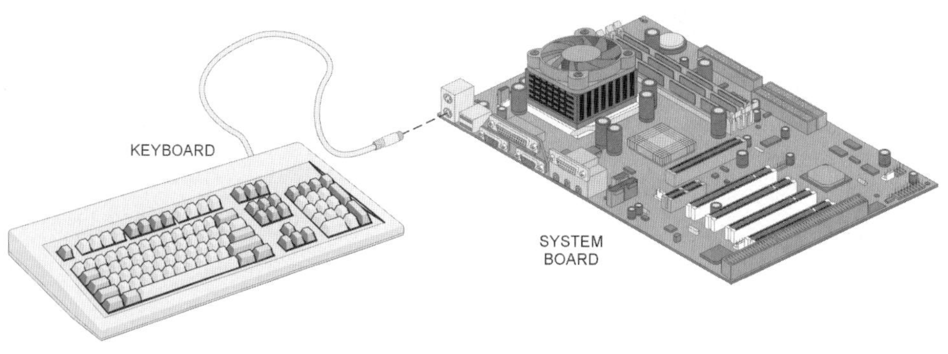

Figure 11-18: Keyboard-Related Components

Keyboard Symptoms

Typical symptoms associated with keyboard failures include the following:

- No characters appear onscreen when entered from the keyboard.
- Some keys work, whereas others do not work.
- A "Keyboard Is Locked—Unlock It" error displays.
- A "Keyboard Error—Keyboard Test Failure" error displays.
- A "KB/Interface Error—Keyboard Test Failure" error displays.
- An error code of 6 short beeps is produced during bootup.
- Wrong characters display.
- An IBM-compatible 301 error code displays.

TEST TIP

Memorize the IBM-compatible error codes.

Configuration Checks

Keyboard information is stored in the CMOS setup memory, and must accurately reflect the configuration of the system; otherwise, an error occurs. In most CMOS screens, the setup information includes keyboard enabling, NumLock key condition at startup, typematic rate, and typematic delay. The typematic information applies to the keyboard's capability to repeat characters when the key is held down. The typematic rate determines how quickly characters are repeated, and the delay time defines the amount of time the key can be held before typematic action occurs. A typical typematic rate setting is 6 characters per second; the delay is normally set at 250 milliseconds.

As with other components, the only time a configuration problem is likely to occur is when the system is being set up for the first time or when a new option is installed. The other condition that causes a configuration problem involves the system board's CMOS backup battery. If the battery fails, or has been changed, the contents of the CMOS setup will be lost. After replacing the battery, you must always run the setup utility to reconfigure the system.

Software Checks

Turn on the system and observe the BIOS screens as the system boots up. Note the Keyboard Type listed in the BIOS summary table. If possible, run a selected diagnostic program to test the keyboard. Run the program's Keyboard Tests function, and perform the equivalent of the All Tests function if available. These tests are normally very good at testing the keyboard for general operation and sticking keys.

The keys of the keyboard can wear out over time. This may result in keys that don't make good contact (no character is produced when the key is pushed) or one that remains in contact (sticks) even when pressure is removed. The stuck key will produce an error message when the system detects it. However, it has no way of detecting an open key. If you detect a stuck key, or keys, you can desolder and replace the individual key switches with a good key from a manufacturer or a similar keyboard. However, the amount of time spent repairing a keyboard quickly drives the cost of the repair beyond the cost of a new unit.

TEST TIP

Know the most common conditions that will produce a keyboard error message.

If the keyboard produces odd characters on the display, check the Windows keyboard settings in the Control Panel's Device Manager. If the keyboard is not installed, or is incorrect, install the correct keyboard type. Also, make certain that you have the correct language setting specified under the Control Panel's keyboard icon.

Keyboard Hardware Checks

If you suspect hardware problem, you must first isolate the keyboard as the definite source of the problem (a fairly easy task). Because the keyboard is external to the system unit, detachable, and inexpensive, begin by exchanging the keyboard with a known good keyboard.

If the new keyboard works correctly, return the system to full service and service the defective keyboard appropriately. Remove the back cover from the keyboard and check for the presence of a fuse in the +5V (DC) supply and check it for continuity. Disconnecting or plugging in a keyboard with this type of fuse while power is on can cause it to fail. If the fuse is present, just replace it with a fuse of the same type and rating.

TEST TIP

Be aware that standard 5-pin DIN and PS/2 mini-DIN keyboards cannot be hot swapped and that doing so can cause damage to the keyboard and system board.

If the system still won't boot up, recheck the CMOS setup to make sure that the keyboard is enabled. Check the keyboard cabling for continuity. And, finally, check the video display system (monitor and adapter card) to make sure that it is functional.

If replacing the keyboard does not correct the problem, and no configuration or software reason is apparent, the next step is to troubleshoot the keyboard receiver section of the system board. On most modern system boards, this ultimately involves replacing the system board with another one. Refer to the system board removal and installation instructions in Chapter 2—*Advanced System Boards*, to carry out this task.

After you have removed the system unit's cover, examine the keyboard connector on the system board. Also, look for auxiliary BERG connectors for the keyboard. Make certain that no item is shorting the pins of this connector together. Check for enable/disable jumpers for the keyboard on the system board.

Troubleshooting Mouse Problems

The levels of mouse troubleshooting move from configuration problems to software problems—including command line, Windows, and applications—to hardware problems.

TEST TIP

Be aware of the condition that causes the cursor to jump and freeze on the display.

Maintenance of the mouse is fairly simple. Most of the problems with mice involve the trackball. As the mouse is moved across the table, the trackball picks up dirt or lint, which can hinder the movement of the trackball, typically evident by the cursor periodically freezing and jumping onscreen. On most mice, you can remove the trackball from the mouse by a latching mechanism on its bottom. Twisting the latch counterclockwise enables you to remove the trackball. Then you can clean dirt out of the mouse.

Mouse Configuration Checks

When the mouse does not work in a Windows system, restart it and move into Safe Mode by pressing the F5 function key when the "Starting Windows" message is displayed. This will start the operating system with the most basic mouse driver available.

If the mouse will not operate in Safe Mode, restart the system and check the CMOS Setup screen during bootup for the presence of the serial port that the mouse is connected to.

If the mouse works in Safe Mode, click the Mouse icon in the Control Panel to check its configuration and settings. Follow this by checking the port configuration in Windows Control Panel. Consult the Device Manager entry under the Control Panel's System icon. Select the Ports option, click the COM x properties option in the menu, and click Resources. Make certain that the selected IRQ and address range match that of the port.

Click on the Mouse entry in the Device Manager and double-click its driver to obtain the Mouse Properties page depicted in Figure 11-19. Move to the Resources tab as illustrated and check the IRQ and base address settings for the mouse in Windows. Compare these settings to the actual configuration settings of the hardware. If they differ, change the IRQ or base address setting in Windows to match those of the installed hardware.

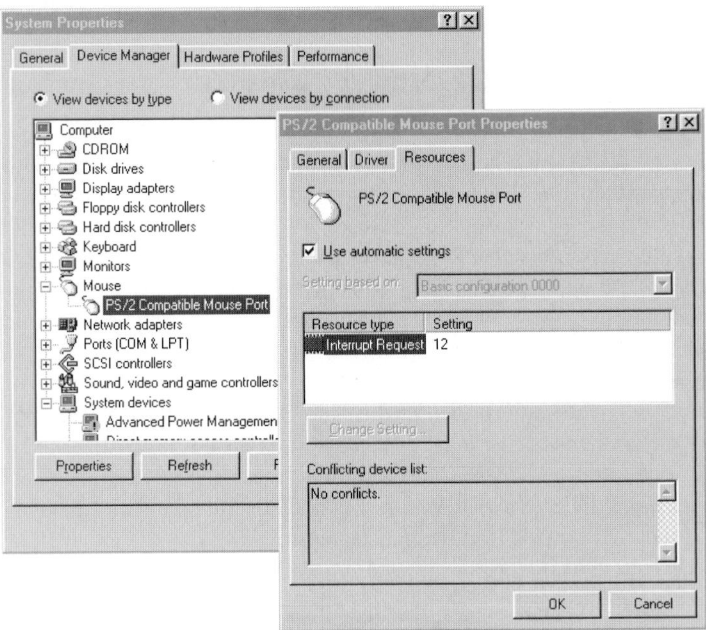

Figure 11-19: Mouse Properties

If the correct driver is not available in the Windows list, place the manufacturer's driver disk in the floppy drive and load it using the Other Mouse (requires disk from OEM) option. If the OEM driver fails to operate the mouse in Windows, contact the mouse manufacturer for an updated Windows driver. Windows normally supports mice only on COM1 and COM2. If several serial devices are being used in the system, you might have to establish alternative IRQ settings for COM3 and COM4.

In older systems, check the directory structure of the system for a Mouse directory. Also, check for AUTOEXEC.BAT and CONFIG.SYS files that may contain conflicting device drivers. Two common driver files may be present: the MOUSE.COM file called for in the AUTOEXEC.BAT file; and the MOUSE.SYS file referenced in the CONFIG.SYS file. If these files are present and have mouse lines that do not begin with a REM statement, they could be over riding the settings in the operating system. In particular, look for a DEVICE= command associated with the mouse.

Mouse Hardware Checks

If the 2/3 button switch and driver setup is correct, you must divide the port circuitry in half. For most systems, this involves isolating the mouse from the serial port. Just replace the mouse to test its electronics.

If the replacement mouse works, the original mouse is probably defective. If the electronics are not working properly, few options are available for servicing the mouse. It may need a cleaning, or a new trackball. However, the low cost of a typical mouse generally makes it a throwaway item if simple cleaning does not fix it.

If the new mouse does not work either, chances are very high that the mouse's electronics are working properly. In this case, the driver software, or port hardware, must be the cause of the problem. If the driver is correct for the mouse, the port hardware and CMOS configuration must be checked. In most newer systems, the system board contains all of the port hardware and must be replaced to restore the port/mouse operation.

Troubleshooting Joystick Problems

As with other input devices, there are three levels of possible problems with a joystick: configuration, software, and hardware.

Attempt to run the joystick with a DOS-based program. If the joystick does not work at the DOS level, check the game port's hardware configuration settings. Compare the hardware settings to that of any software using the game port. Try to swap the suspect joystick for a known good one.

Windows 9x contains a joystick icon in the Start/Settings/Control Panel window. Figure 11-20 shows the contents of the Windows 9x Joystick Properties dialog box. The Joystick icon is not loaded into the Control Panel window if the system does not detect a game port during installation. If the port is detected during boot up, but no joystick device is found, the window says that the joystick is not connected correctly.

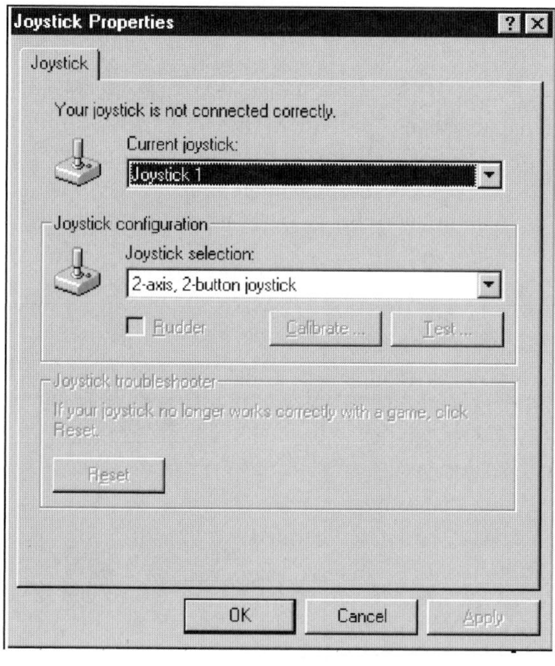

Figure 11-20: The Joystick Properties Dialog Box

yoke assemblies

The Joystick Properties dialog box is used to select different numbers of joysticks (1–16) that can be used. It shows the currently selected joystick type, and allows other devices to be selected. The default joystick setting is a two-axis, two-button device. You also can select None, or Custom, joystick types. Other selections include two-axis, four-button joysticks, and two-button game pads, as well as specialized flight **yoke assemblies** and flight stick assemblies.

The Joystick Properties dialog box also contains a button to calibrate the joystick's position. This button allows the zero-position of the stick to be set for the center of the screen. The Test button allows the movement of the stick and its button operation to be checked, as directed by the test program. Windows 95 also allows for a rudder device to be added to the system. The Joystick Troubleshooter section contains a Reset button to reinitialize the game port. This function is normally used if the stick stops responding to the program.

Troubleshooting Video

Figure 11-21 depicts the components associated with the video display. It may be most practical to think of the video information as starting out on the system board. In reality, the keyboard, one of the disk drives, or some other I/O device, may be the actual originating point for the information. In any case, information intended for the video display monitor moves from the system board to the video adapter card by way of the system board's expansion slots. The adapter card also obtains power for its operation from these expansion slots. Finally, the information is applied to the monitor through the video signal cable.

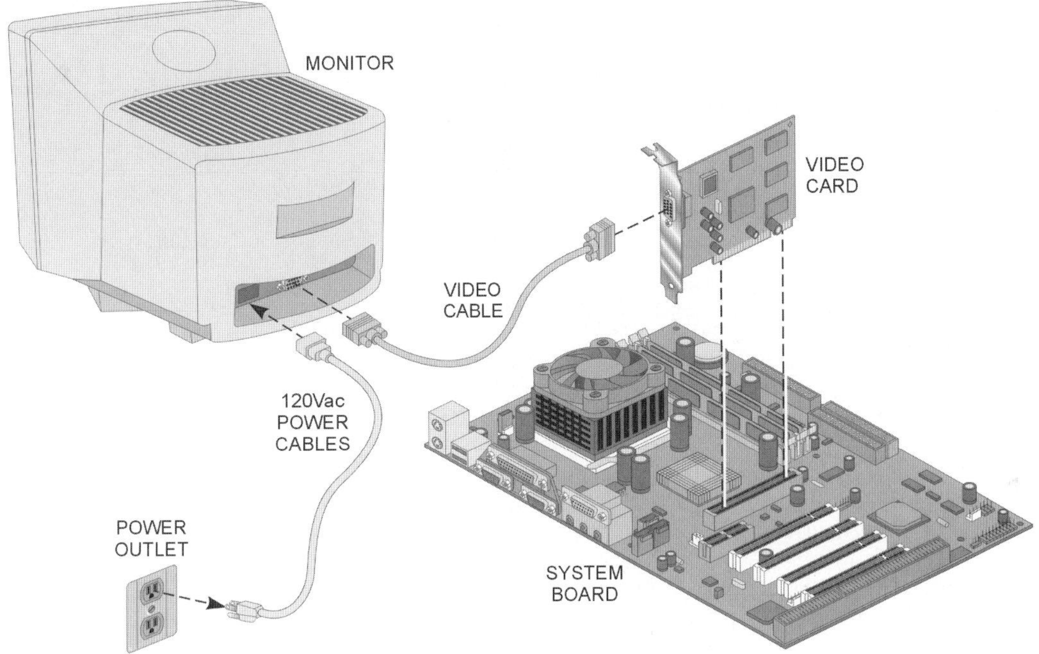

Figure 11-21: Video-Related Components

Basically, three levels of troubleshooting apply to video problems: the DOS level, the Windows level, and the hardware level. At the DOS level, you have two considerations: configuration problems and hardware problems.

In the case of hardware problems, the components associated with video problems include the video adapter card and the monitor. To a lesser degree, the system board and optional adapter cards, such as sound and scanner cards, can cause video problems. Figure 11-22 illustrates some of the typical symptoms produced by video display failures.

Figure 11-22: Video Failures

Other common symptoms associated with display problems include the following:

- No display.
- Wrong characters displayed onscreen.
- Diagonal lines onscreen (no horizontal control).
- Display scrolls (no vertical control).
- An error code of 1 long and 6 short beeps is produced by the system.
- A "Display Switch Setting Not Proper—Failure to verify display type" error displays.
- A "CMOS Display Mismatch—Failure to verify display type" error displays.
- An error code of 1 long and 2 short beeps indicates a display adapter problem.

The following sections cover the digital portion of the video system. Troubleshooting the actual monitor is discussed immediately following the video adapter troubleshooting sections. Only experienced technicians should participate in troubleshooting internal monitor problems because of the very high voltages present there.

Configuration Checks

While booting up the system to the DOS prompt, observe the BIOS video type information displayed on the monitor. The values stored in this CMOS memory must accurately reflect the type of monitor installed in the system; otherwise, an error occurs. You can access these values for change by pressing the CTRL and DEL keys (or some other key combination) simultaneously during the bootup procedure.

Basic Checks

Reboot the system and run a diagnostic software program, if possible. Try to use a diagnostic program that conducts a bank of tests on the video components. Run the program's Video Tests function and perform the equivalent of the All Tests function.

Note all the errors indicated by the tests. If a single type of error is indicated, you might be able to take some corrective actions. If more complex system board problems are indicated, however, exit the diagnostic program and use the troubleshooting information in the "Hardware Checks" section of this chapter to locate and repair the video problem.

Windows Checks

You can gain access to the Windows video information by double-clicking the Control Panel's Display icon. From the Display page, there are a series of file folder tabs at the top of the screen. Of particular interest is the Settings tab. Under this tab, the Change Display Type button provides access to both the adapter type and monitor type settings.

In the Adapter type window, information about the adapter's manufacturer, version number, and current driver files is given. Pressing the Change button beside this window brings a listing of available drivers to select from. You also can use the Have Disk button with an OEM disk to install video drivers not included in the list. You also can alter the manner in which the list displays by choosing the Show Compatible Devices or the Show All Devices options.

In the Monitor type window, there is an option list for both manufacturers and models. You also can use this function with the Have Disk button to establish OEM settings for the monitor.

You can access additional Windows video information under the Control Panel's System icon. Inside the System Properties page, click the Device Manager and select the Display Adapters option from the list. Double-click the monitor icon that appears as a branch.

The adapter's Properties page pops up onscreen. From this page, the Driver tab reveals the driver file in use. Selecting the Resources tab displays the video adapter's register address ranges and the video memory address range, as described in Figure 11-23. You can manipulate these settings manually by clicking the Set Configuration Manually button. You also can obtain information about the monitor through the System icon.

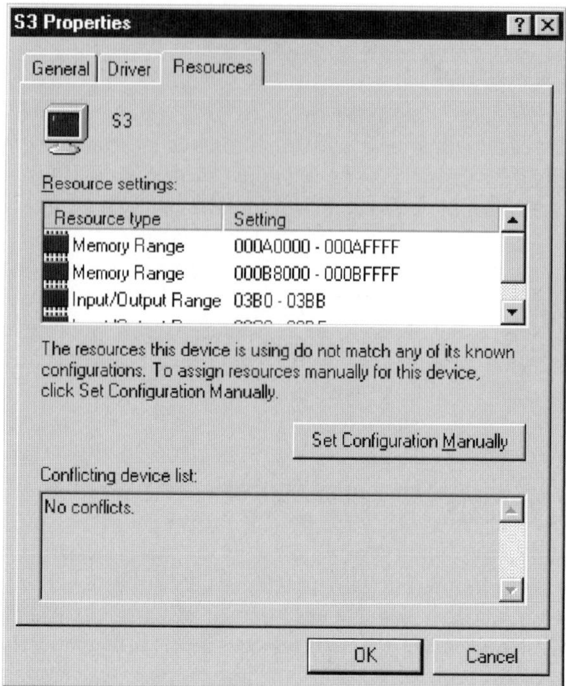

Figure 11-23: Video Adapters Resources

The first step when isolating Windows video problems involves checking the video drivers. Check for the drivers in the locations specified in the previous paragraphs. If the video driver from the list is not correct, reload the correct driver. If the problem persists, reinstall Windows.

If the Windows video problem prevents you from seeing the driver, restart the system, press the F8 function key when the Starting Windows message appears, and select Safe Mode. This should load Windows with the standard 640 x 480 x 16–color VGA driver (the most fundamental driver available for VGA monitors), and should furnish a starting point for installing the correct driver for the monitor being used.

Microsoft Download Service (MSDL)

If the problem reappears when a higher resolution driver is selected, refer to the Color Palette box under the Control Panel's Display option/Settings tab, and try minimum color settings. If the problem goes away, contact the **Microsoft Download Service** (**MSDL**) or the adapter card maker for a new, compatible video driver. If the problem remains, reinstall the driver from the Windows 9x distribution disk or CD. If the video is distorted or rolling, try an alternative video driver from the list.

Hardware Checks

If you suspect a video display hardware problem, the first task is to check the monitor's On/Off switch to see that it is in the On position. Also, check the monitor's power cord to see that it is either plugged into the power supply's monitor outlet, or into an active 120V (AC) commercial outlet. Also check the monitor's intensity and contrast controls to make certain that they are not turned down.

The next step is to determine which of the video-related components is involved. On most monitors, you can do this by just removing the video signal cable from the adapter card. If a raster appears onscreen with the signal cable removed, the problem is probably a system problem, and the monitor is good. If the monitor is an EPA-certified Energy Star–compliant monitor, this test may not work. Monitors that possess this power-saving feature, revert to a low-power mode when they do not receive a signal change for a given period of time.

With the system off, remove any multimedia-related cards such as VGA-to-TV converter cards and video capture cards. Try to reboot the system.

If the system boots up, and the display is correct with these options removed, you can safely assume that one of them is the cause of the problem. To verify which device is causing the problem, reinstall them, one at a time, until the problem reappears. The last device reinstalled before the problem reappears is defective.

Replace this item and continue reinstalling options, one at a time, until all options have been reinstalled.

If the display is still wrong or missing, check the components associated with the video display monitor. Start by disconnecting the monitor's signal cable from the video controller card at the rear of the system unit, and its power cord from the power supply connector, or the 120V (AC) outlet. Then, exchange the monitor for a known good one of the same type (that is, VGA for VGA). If the system boots up and the video display is correct, return the system to full service and service the defective monitor as indicated.

If the display is still not correct, exchange the video controller card with a known good one of the same type. Remove the system unit's outer cover. Disconnect the monitor's signal cable from the video controller card. Swap the video controller card with a known good one of the same type. Reconnect the monitor's signal cable to the new video controller card and reboot the system.

Other symptoms that point to the video adapter card include a shaky video display and a high-pitched squeal from the monitor or system unit.

If the system boots up and the video display is correct, replace the system unit's outer cover, return the system to full service, and service the defective video controller appropriately. If the system still does not perform properly, the source of the problem may be in the system board.

Troubleshooting Monitors

All the circuitry discussed so far is part of the computer or its video adapter unit. The circuitry inside the monitor is responsible for accepting, amplifying, and routing the video and synchronizing information to the CRT's electron guns and the deflection coils.

Figure 11-24 shows the components located inside a typical CRT color monitor. Of particular interest is the high-voltage anode that connects the tube to the high-voltage sections of the signal-processing board. This is a very dangerous connection that is not to be touched.

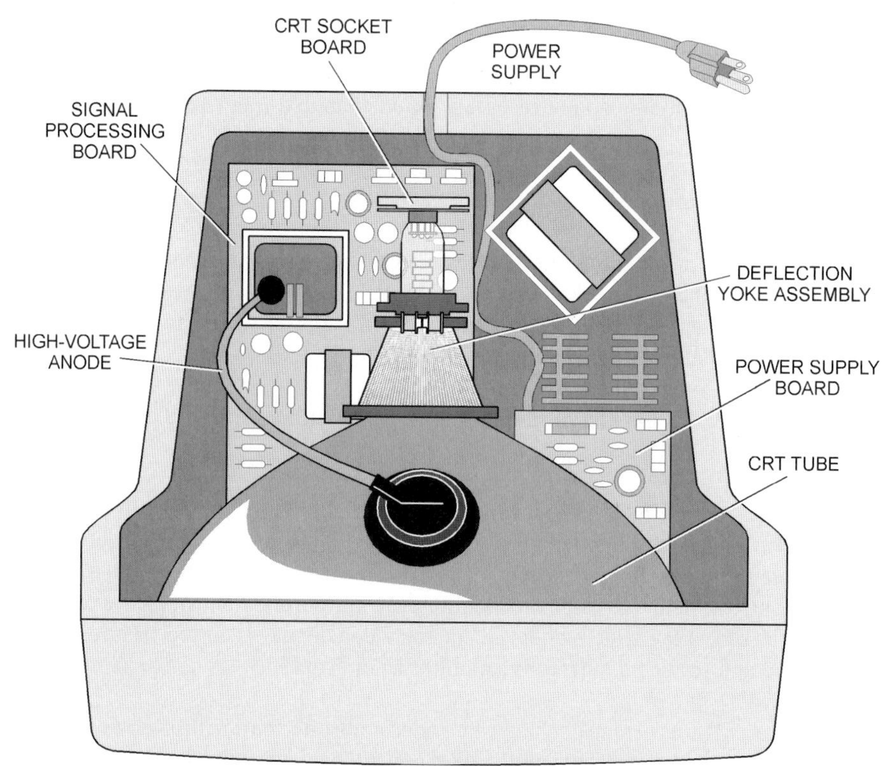

Figure 11-24: The Circuitry Inside a Typical CRT

WARNING

Lethal voltage levels—You must exercise great caution when opening or working inside the monitor. The voltage levels present during operation are lethal. Electrical potentials as high as 25,000V are present inside the unit when it is operating.

TEST TIP

Memorize the values of lethal voltage associated with the inside of the CRT video monitor. The values given on tests may not be exactly the same as those stated in the textbook, but they will be in the same high range.

Operation of a monitor with the cover removed poses a shock hazard from the power supply. Therefore, anyone unfamiliar with the safety precautions associated with high-voltage equipment should not attempt servicing.

The high voltage levels do not necessarily disappear because the power to the monitor is turned off. Like television sets, monitors have circuitry capable of storing high-voltage potentials long after power has been removed. Always discharge the anode of the picture tube to the receiver chassis before handling the CRT tube. Due to the high voltage levels, you should never wear antistatic grounding straps when working inside the monitor.

An additional hazard associated with handling CRTs is that the tube is fragile. Take extra care to prevent the neck of the tube from striking any surface. Never lift the tube by the neck—especially when removing or replacing a CRT tube in the chassis. If the picture tube's envelope is cracked or ruptured, the inrush of air will cause a high-velocity **implosion**, and the glass will fly in all directions. Therefore, you should always wear protective goggles when handling picture tubes.

implosion

Color monitors produce a relatively high level of **X-rays**. The CRT tube is designed to limit X-rays at its specified operating voltage. If a replacement CRT tube is being installed, make certain to replace it with one of the same type, and with suffix numbers that are the same. You can obtain this information from the chassis schematic diagram inside the monitor's housing.

X-rays

Troubleshooting FDDs

Typical symptoms associated with floppy disk drive (FDD) failures during boot up include the following:

- FDD errors are encountered during bootup.
- The front-panel indicator lights are visible, and the display is present on the monitor screen, but there is no disk drive action and no boot up.
- An IBM-compatible 6xx (that is, 601) error code displays.
- An FDD Controller Error message displays, indicating a failure to verify the FDD setup by the System Configuration file.
- The FDD activity light stays on constantly, indicating that the FDD signal cable is reversed.

Additional FDD error messages commonly encountered during normal system operation include:

- Disk Drive Read Error messages.
- Disk Drive Write Error messages.
- Disk Drive Seek Error messages.
- No Boot Record Found message, indicating that the system files in the disk's boot sector are missing or have become corrupt.
- The system stops working while reading a disk, indicating that the contents of the disk have become contaminated.
- The drive displays the same directory listing for every disk inserted in the drive, indicating that the FDD's disk-change detector or signal line is not functional.

TEST TIP

Memorize the IBM error codes for different types of hardware devices.

Causes of floppy disk problems—A number of things can cause improper floppy disk drive operation or disk drive failure. These items include the use of unformatted disks, incorrectly inserted disks, damaged disks, erased disks, loose cables, drive failure, adapter failure, system board failure, or a bad or loose power connector.

Figure 11-25 depicts the components associated with the operation of the floppy disk drive.

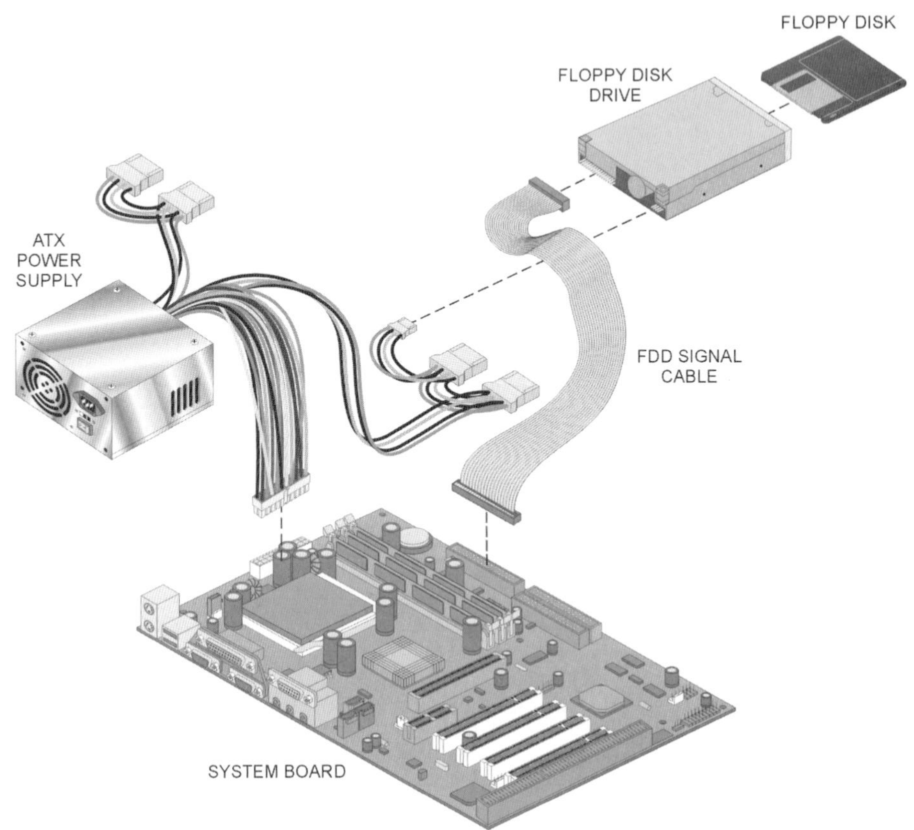

Figure 11-25: FDD-Related Components

Information is written to, and read from, the floppy disks by the floppy disk drive unit. This unit moves information and control signals back and forth between the disk-drive controller and the surface of the disks. The information moves between the controller and the drive through a flat, ribbon cable. The small printed circuit board, located on the drive unit, is called the analog control board. It is responsible for turning the digital information received from the adapter card into magnetic information that can be stored on the surface of the disk, and vice versa.

configuration

software level

hardware level

Levels of troubleshooting—Basically three levels of troubleshooting apply to FDD problems: **configuration**, the **software level**, and the **hardware level**. No Windows-level troubleshooting applies to floppy disk drives.

FDD Configuration Checks

The other condition that causes a configuration problem involves the system board's CMOS backup battery. If the battery fails, or has been changed, the contents of the CMOS setup will be lost. After replacing the battery, you must always run the CMOS setup utility to reconfigure the system.

While booting up the system to the DOS prompt, observe the BIOS FDD type information displayed on the monitor. Note the types of FDDs that the BIOS believes are installed in the system. With newer BIOS, you must examine the advanced CMOS setup to check the boot-up order. In these BIOS, you can set the boot order so that the FDD is never examined during startup.

The values stored in this CMOS memory must accurately reflect the type, and number, of FDDs installed in the system; otherwise, an error occurs. You can access these values for change during the boot-up procedure.

Basic Checks

If the FDD configuration information is correct, and a floppy disk drive problem is suspected, the first task is to make certain that the system won't boot up from the floppy disk drive if a disk with a known good boot file is in the drive. Try the boot disk in a different computer to see if it works on that machine. If not, there is a problem with the files on the disk. If the disk boots up the other computer, you must troubleshoot the floppy disk drive system.

FDD tests

ALL tests

If possible, run a diagnostic software program from the hard drive or a B: floppy disk drive. Try to use a diagnostic program that conducts a bank of tests on the FDD's components. Run the program's **FDD tests**, and perform the equivalent of the **All tests** function.

COPY CON:FDDTEST.BAT

DIR

F6

From the command-prompt level, it is also very easy to test the operation of the drive using a simple batch program. At the command prompt, type **COPY CON:FDDTEST.BAT**, and press the Enter key. On the first line, type the DOS **DIR** command. On the second line, type FDDTEST. Finally, press the **F6** function key to exit, and save the program to the hard disk drive.

You can execute this test program from the command prompt just by typing its name. When invoked, it exercises the drive's R/W head-positioning motors, and read channel-signal processing circuitry. At the same time, the signal cable and the FDC circuitry are tested.

FDD Hardware Checks

If you do not find any configuration or enabling problems, you must troubleshoot the hardware components associated with the floppy disk drives. These components consist of the drives, the signal cable, and the FDC controller. The controller may be located on an adapter card or integrated into the system board. Begin the process by exchanging the suspect floppy disk drive with another one of the same type.

If the system has a second floppy disk drive, turn off the computer and exchange its connection to the floppy disk drive's signal cable so that it becomes the A: drive. Try to reboot the system using this other floppy disk drive as the A: drive.

Also, check the floppy disk drive's signal cable for proper connection at both ends. In many systems, the pin-1 designation is difficult to see. Reversing the signal cable causes the FDD activity light to stay on continuously. The reversed signal cable will also erase the master boot record from the disk, making it non-bootable. Because this is a real possibility, you should always use an expendable backup copy of the boot disk for troubleshooting FDD problems.

Insert the bootable disk in the new A: drive and turn on the system. If the system boots up, reinstall any options removed and replace the system unit's outer cover. Return the system to full service and repair the defective floppy disk drive accordingly.

If the system still refuses to boot up, turn it off, and exchange the disk drive controller card (if present) with a known good one. Disconnect the disk drive's signal cable from the controller card and swap the controller card with a known good one of the same type. Make certain to mark the cable and its connection point to ensure proper reconnection after the exchange. Reconnect the signal cable to the FDD controller. Try to reboot the system with the new disk drive controller card installed. If the controller is built into the system board, it may be easier to test the drive and signal cable in another machine, than to remove the system board. If the system boots up, reinstall any options removed, and replace the system unit's outer cover. Return the system to full service and return the defective controller card.

Try to reboot the system with the new disk drive controller card installed. If the controller is built in to the system board, it may be easier to test the drive and signal cable in another machine than to remove the system board. If the system boots up, reinstall any options removed and replace the system unit's outer cover. Return the system to full service and return the defective controller card.

If the system still will not boot up, or perform FDD operations correctly, check the disk drive cables for proper connection at both ends. If necessary, exchange the signal cable with a known good one. Finally, exchange the system board with a known good one.

Troubleshooting HDDs

Typical symptoms associated with hard disk drive failures include:

- The computer does not boot up when turned on.
- The computer boots up to a system disk in the A: drive, but not to the hard drive, indicating that the system files on the HDD are missing or have become corrupt.
- No motor sounds are produced by the HDD while the computer is running. (In desktop units, the HDD should always run when power is applied to the system—this also applies to portables because of their advanced power-saving features.)
- An IBM-compatible 17xx error code is produced on the monitor screen.
- In HDD Controller Failure message displays, indicating a failure to verify hard disk setup by system configuration file error.

- A C: or D: Fixed Disk Drive Error message displays, indicating a hard disk CMOS setup failure.

- An Invalid Media Type message displays, indicating the controller cannot find a recognizable track/sector pattern on the drive.

- A No Boot Record Found, a Non-System Disk or Disk Error, or an Invalid System Disk message displays, indicating that the system boot files are not located in the root directory of the drive.

- The video display is active, but the HDD's activity light remains on and no boot up occurs, indicating that the HDD's CMOS configuration information is incorrect.

- An Out of Disk Space message displays, indicating that the amount of space on the disk is insufficient to carry out the desired operation.

- A Missing Operating System, a Hard Drive Boot Failure, or an Invalid Drive or Drive Specification message displays, indicating that the disk's master boot record is missing or has become corrupt.

- A No ROM BASICS—System Halted, or ROM BASIC Interpreter Not Found message displays, followed by the system stopping, indicating that no master boot record was found in the system. This message is produced only by PCs, XTs, and some clones.

- A Current Drive No Longer Valid message displays, indicating that the HDD's CMOS configuration information is incorrect or has become corrupt.

Figure 11-26 depicts the relationship between the hard disk drive and the rest of the system. It also illustrates the control and signal paths through the system.

TEST TIP

Be able to describe the conditions indicated by Invalid Drive or Drive Specification, Missing Operating System, and the Hard Drive Boot Failure error messages.

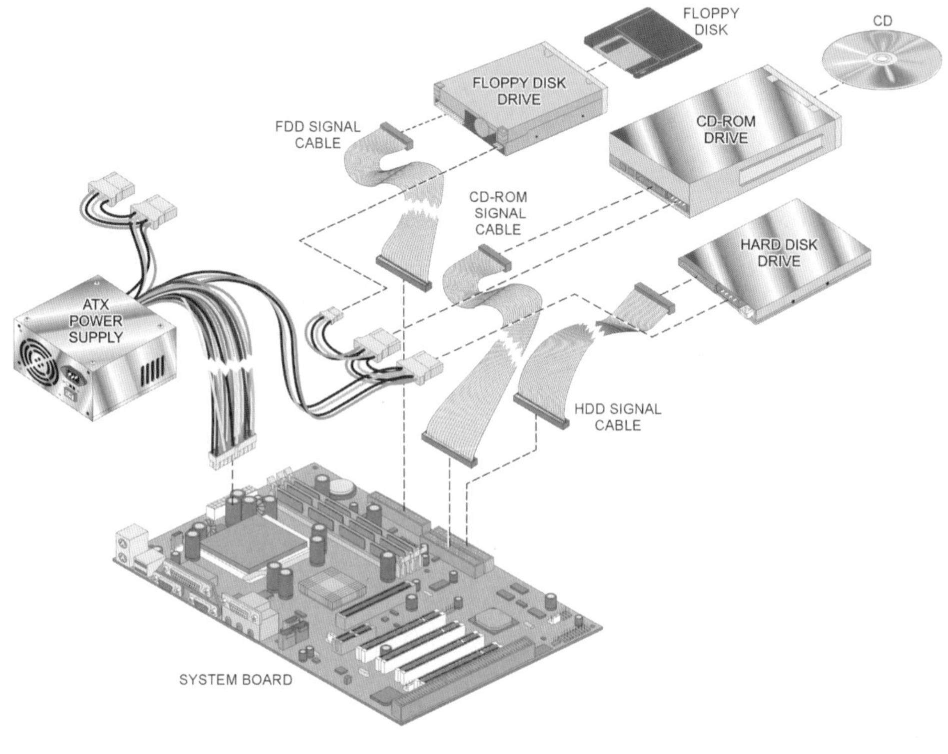

Figure 11-26: Hard Disk Drive-Related Components

controller

power cable

drive unit

Hard Drive Systems—Hard drive systems are very much like floppy drive systems in structure—they have a **controller**, one or more signal cables, a **power cable**, and a **drive unit**. The troubleshooting procedure typically moves from setup and configuration, to formatting, and, finally, into the hardware component isolation process.

The system board is a logical extension of the components that make up the HDD system. However, unless the HDD controller is integrated into it, the system board is typically the least likely cause of HDD problems.

Notice that unlike a floppy drive, there is no Windows component to check with a hard disk drive. Windows relies on the system's DOS/BIOS structure to handle HDD operations.

HDD Configuration Checks

Drive Mismatch Error

Invalid Media Type

HDD enabling jumper

terminated

While booting up the system, *observe the BIOS's HDD type information* displayed on the monitor. Note the type of HDD(s) that the BIOS believes is installed in the system. The values stored in this CMOS memory must accurately reflect the actual HDD(s) format installed in the system; otherwise, an error occurs. Possible error messages associated with HDD configuration problems include the **Drive Mismatch Error** message and the **Invalid Media Type** message. You can access these values for change by pressing the CTRL and DEL keys (or some other key combination) simultaneously, during the boot-up procedure.

If the HDD is used with a system board–mounted controller, check for the presence of an **HDD-enabling jumper** on the system board. Make certain that it is set to enable the drive, if present. Check the drive to make sure that it is properly **terminated**. Every drive type requires a termination block somewhere in the interface. On system-level drives, check the Master/Slave jumper setting to make sure that it is set properly for the drive's logical position in the system.

TEST TIP

Know that there can only be one master drive selection on each IDE channel.

If you have more than one device attached to a single interface cable, make sure that they are of the same type (i.e., all are EIDE devices or all are ATA100 devices). Mixing device types will create a situation where the system cannot provide the different types of control information each device needs. The drives are incompatible and you may not be able to access either device.

TEST TIP

Be aware that mixing drive types on a single signal cable can disable both devices.

If the drive is a SCSI drive, check to see that it's ID has been set correctly and that the SCSI chain has been terminated correctly. Either of these errors will result in the system not being able to see the drive. Also, check the CMOS Setup utility to make sure that SCSI support has been enabled, along with large SCSI drive support.

TEST TIP

Know that in newer systems, SCSI drive support and large drive support are both enabled in the BIOS.

Basic Checks

If the HDD configuration information is correct and you suspect a hard disk drive problem, the first task is to determine how extensive the HDD problem is. Place a clean boot disk in the A: drive and try to **boot the system**. Then, **execute a DOS DIR command** to access the C: drive. If the system can see the contents of the drive, the boot files have been lost or corrupted, but the architecture of the disk is intact.

boot the system

execute a DOS DIR command

Modify the DOS DIR command with an /AH or /AS switch (that is, DIR C: /AH or DIR C: /AS) to look in the root directory for the system files and the COMMAND.COM file. It is common to receive a **Disk Boot Failure** message onscreen if this type of situation occurs. The *No (or Missing) ROM BASIC Interpreter* message may also be produced by this condition.

Disk Boot Failure

If the clean boot disk has a copy of the FDISK program on it, attempt to restore the drive's master boot record (including its partition information) by typing the following at the A: prompt:

FDISK /MBR

FDISK /MBR

Provided that the hard disk can be accessed with the DIR command, type and enter the following command at the DOS prompt (with the **Clean Boot Disk** still in the A: drive):

Clean Boot Disk

SYS C:

SYS C:

This command copies the IO.SYS, MSDOS.SYS, and COMMAND.COM system files from the DOS disk to the hard disk drive. Turn off the system, remove the DOS disk from the A: drive, and try to reboot the system from the hard drive.

If the system boots up properly, check to see that the operating system commands are functioning properly. Also, check to see that all installed software programs function properly. Re-check the installation instructions of any program that does not function properly. Reinstall the software program if necessary.

TEST TIP

Know how and when to use the **FDISK /MBR** and **SYS C:** commands.

Three conditions will produce a Bad or Missing COMMAND.COM error message. These conditions include the following:

1. The first condition occurs when the COMMAND.COM file cannot be found on the hard drive (because it has become corrupted), and no bootable disk is present in drive A:.
2. The COMMAND.COM file is not located in the hard drive's root directory. This message is likely when installing a brand new hard drive, or a new DOS version.
3. The message also occurs if the user inadvertently erases the COMMAND.COM file from the root directory of the hard drive.

If the system cannot see the drive after booting to the floppy disk drive, an "Invalid Drive" message or an "Invalid Drive Specification" message should be returned in response to any attempt to access the drive. Under these conditions, you must examine the complete HDD system. Use the FDISK utility to partition the drive. Next, use the FORMAT /S command to make the disk bootable. Any data that was on the drive will be lost in the formatting process, but it was already gone because the system could not see the drive.

HDD tests

Attempt to run a diagnostic software program, if possible. Try to use a diagnostic program that conducts a bank of tests on the HDD's components. Run the program's **HDD tests**, and perform the equivalent of the ALL tests function.

HDD Hardware Checks

If you cannot access the hard disk drive, and its configuration settings are correct, you must troubleshoot the hardware components associated with the hard disk drive. As previously indicated, these components include the drive, its signal cable, and the HDC. Like the FDC from the floppy disk drive, the HDC can be mounted on an adapter card, or it can be integrated into the system board. Normally, you must remove the outer cover from the computer to troubleshoot these components.

Exchange the controller card

In a pre-Pentium system, the easiest component to check is the controller card that holds the HDD interface circuitry. **Exchange the controller card** with a known good one of the same type. Make certain to mark all of the card's control/signal cables before disconnecting them. Also, identify their connection points and direction. Your markings help to ensure their proper reinstallation. Reconnect the disk drive signal cables to the new controller card.

Try to reboot the system from the hard drive. If the system boots up properly, check to see that all of the DOS commands (DIR, COPY, etc.) are working properly. Also, check the operation of all the hard disk's software programs to make sure they are still functioning correctly. Reinstall any program that does not function properly.

If the system still won't boot up, recheck the system configuration setup to see that it matches the actual configuration of the HDD. Record the HDD values from the setup so that they are available if a replacement drive needs to be installed.

The next logical step may seem to be to replace the hard drive unit. However, it is quite possible that the hard drive may not have any real damage. It may just have lost track of where it was, and now it cannot find its starting point. In this case, the most attractive option is to reformat the hard disk. This action gives the hard drive a new starting point to work from. Unfortunately, it also destroys anything that you had on the disk before. At the very least, attempting to reformat the drive before you replace it may save the expense of buying a new hard disk drive that is not needed. Make certain to use the /S modifier, or repeat the SYS C: operation with the FORMAT command to restore the system files to the hard drive.

Cable Select

CSEL

Check the HDD signal cable for proper connection at both ends. Exchange the signal cable(s) for a known good one. Check the HDD Drive Select jumper and Master/Slave/Single jumper settings to make sure they are set correctly, as illustrated in Figure 11-27. Check to see whether the system might be using the **Cable Select** option also depicted in the figure. This setting requires a special **CSEL** signal cable designed to determine the master/slave arrangements for multiple IDE drives. Exchange the HDD power connector with another one from the power supply, to make certain that it is not a source of problems.

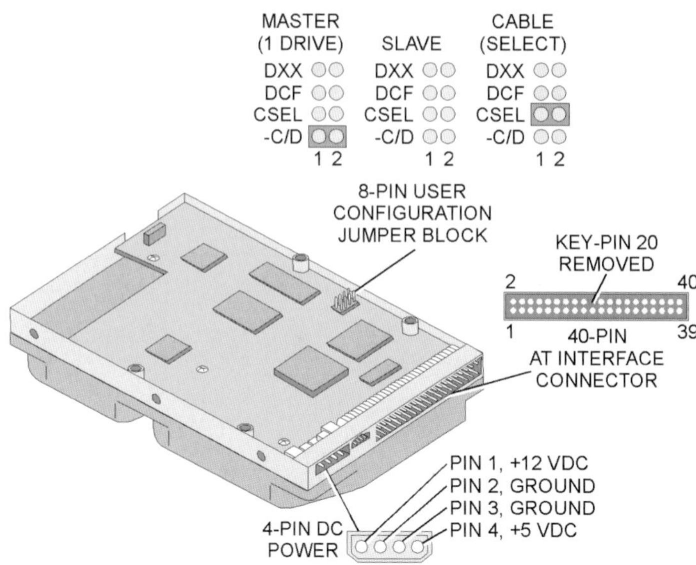

Figure 11-27: IDE Master/Slave Settings

If the reformatting procedure is not successful, or the system still won't boot from the hard drive, you must replace the hard disk drive unit with a working one. Disconnect the signal, control, and power cords from the HDD unit, and exchange it with a known good one of the same type. Reconnect the signal, control, and power cords to the replacement HDD unit.

If a similar computer is being used as a source of test parts, take great care in removing the HDD from its original computer and reinstalling it in the defective computer. With pre-system-level interfaces (IDE/SCSI), such as an MFM drive, it is advisable, and common practice, to swap both the disk drive and the controller card together.

Try to reboot the system from the new hard drive. If no bootup occurs, reformat the new drive. Make sure that any information on the replacement drive has been backed up on floppy disks, or tape, before removing it from its original system.

If the system still won't boot up with a different HDD, swap the hard disk drive's signal/control cables with known good ones. Make certain to mark the cables for identification purposes so that they will be reinstalled properly. Also, use a different power connector from the power supply unit to make certain that the current connector is not a source of the problems.

Check the system's Configuration Setup to see that it matches the actual configuration of the new HDD. Check to see that all installed software programs function properly.

If the system reboots from the replacement drive without reformatting, replace the drive (either with the one you have just installed or with a new one). Also, try reinstalling the original disk drive controller card to see whether it works with the new drive.

If the system still boots up and operates properly, reinstall any options removed from the system. Replace the system unit's outer cover, and return the system to full service. Reboot the system and reinstall all software programs to the new hard disk drive. (See the installation guide from the software manufacturer.) Return the system to full service, and return the defective controller card appropriately.

Troubleshooting CD-ROM Drives

configuration level

Windows level

The troubleshooting steps for a CD-ROM drive are almost identical to those of an HDD system. The connections and data paths are very similar. Basically, four levels of troubleshooting apply to CD-ROM problems. These are the **configuration level**, the DOS level, the **Windows level**, and the hardware level. Figure 11-28 shows the parts, and drivers, associated with CD-ROMs.

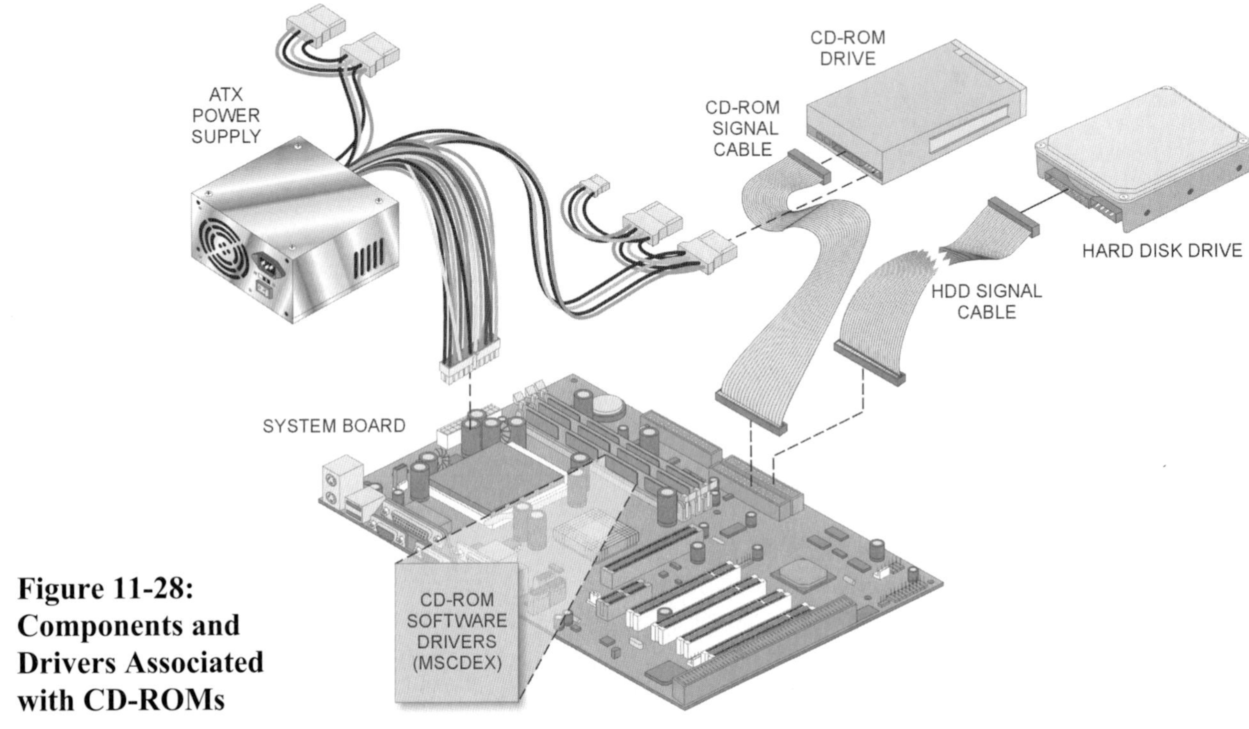

Figure 11-28: Components and Drivers Associated with CD-ROMs

Basic Checks

Since the CD-ROM does not appear in the CMOS configuration information, reboot the system and observe the bootup information that scrolls up the screen. In particular, look for error messages associated with the CD-ROM drive (such as an *MSCDEX.EXE xxxx* error).

Microsoft CD-ROM Extensions (MSCDEX)

The simplest point to test the operation of the CD-ROM drive is in the DOS environment. For the CD-ROM drive to work at this level, its drivers must be referenced in the CONFIG.SYS and AUTOEXEC.BAT files. The Microsoft driver for CD-ROMs is the **Microsoft CD-ROM Extensions (MSCDEX)** file.

Check the CONFIG.SYS file for a CD-ROM "Device=" line similar to the following:

DEVICE=C:\CDROM\ATAPI.SYS /D:MSCD001

This statement loads the ATAPI Enhanced IDE interface to support an IDE CD-ROM device that the system will know as MSCD001.

Then, check the AUTOEXEC.BAT for a statement that looks like the following:

C:\DOS\MSDCEX /D:MSCD001 /L:E /M:12

This line loads the Microsoft CD-ROM driver into the system and defines its operating parameters. In this case, the switch modifiers set up the drive for drive E: as the upper possibility for CD-ROM drive letters, EMS memory mode enabled, and 12-sector buffers. The /D:MSCD001 designation identifies the drive as the MSCS001 drive defined in the CONFIG.SYS file.

These statements define the CD-ROM drive for the system and make it usable under DOS. Most CD-ROMs come with installation programs that automatically write these lines into your AUTOEXEC.BAT and CONFIG.SYS files correctly. If you have any question about their validity, run the drive's installation program and allow it to reinstall these statements.

If the MSCDEX XXX error appears in the DOS environment, check for the MSCDEX statement in the AUTOEXEC.BAT file.

Many of the software diagnostic packages available include test functions for CD-ROM drives. Try to choose a diagnostic package that includes a good variety of CD-ROM test functions. Run the program's CD-ROM function from the Multimedia selection menu. Select the equivalent of the program's Run All Tests option.

Use a diagnostic program to check the IRQ and I/O address settings for possible conflicts with other devices. If the settings are different than those established by the hardware jumpers on the controller, change the settings so that they both match each other, and so that they do not conflict with other devices.

Settings

Windows 9x Checks

In Windows 9x, you can access the CD-ROM through the CD icon in the desktop's My Computer icon. The CD-ROM drive's information is contained in the Control Panel's System icon. The properties of the installed drive are located under the **Settings** tab. Figure 11-29 shows a typical set of CD-ROM specifications in Windows 9x.

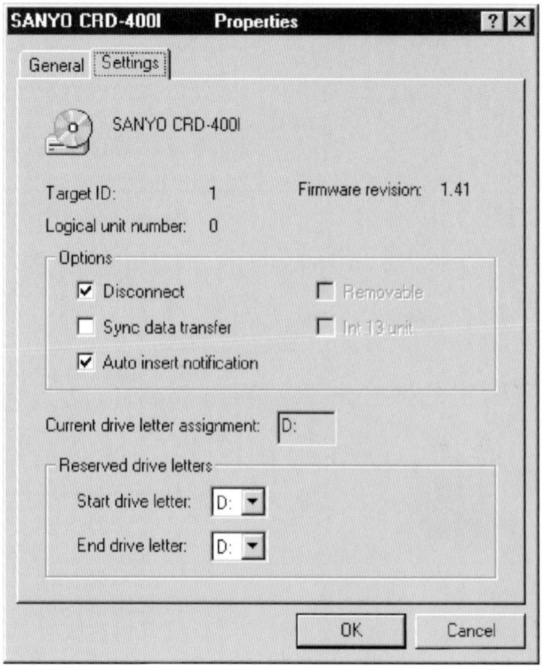

Figure 11-29: Control Panel/ System/Device Manager/Settings

WordPad

REM C:\XXX\MSCDEX

REM Device=C:\XXX\XXX /D:MSCDXXX

Check the system for AUTOEXEC.BAT and CONFIG.SYS files that could contain updated information. To do this, open the **WordPad** program from the Windows Accessories listing, check the AUTOEXEC.BAT file for the following line:

REM C:\XXX\MSCDEX

Then check the CONFIG.SYS file for this line:

REM Device=C:\XXX\XXX /D:MSCDXXX

If the correct drivers are not installed, load the correct driver, or contact the CD-ROM manufacturer for the correct Windows driver.

CD-ROM Hardware Checks

If the configuration and software checks do not remedy the CD-ROM problem, you must troubleshoot the CD-ROM-related hardware. Basically, the hardware consists of the CD-ROM drive, the signal cable, the power cord, and the controller. The controller may be mounted on a host adapter card or, in a Pentium system, on the system board. For external drives, you also need to check the plug-in power adapter.

In most systems, the CD-ROM drive shares a controller or host adapter with the hard disk drive. Therefore, if the hard drive is working and the CD-ROM drive is not, the likelihood that the problem is in the CD-ROM drive is very high.

Before entering the system unit, check for simple user problems. Is there a CD in the drive? Is the label side of the disk facing upward? Is the disk a CD-ROM or some other type of CD? If the CD-ROM drive is inoperable and there is a CD locked inside, you should insert a straightened paper clip into the tray-release access hole that's usually locate beside the ejection button. This will release the spring-loaded tray and pop out the disc.

TEST TIP

Know how to retrieve a CD from a disabled CD-ROM drive.

If no simple reasons for the problem are apparent, begin by exchanging the CD-ROM drive with a known good one of the same type. For external units, just disconnect the drive from the power and signal cords, and then substitute the new drive for it. With internal units, you must remove the system unit's outer cover and disconnect the signal and power cords from the drive. Remove the screws that secure the drive in the drive bay. Install the replacement unit and attempt to access it.

If the new drive does not work, check the CD-ROM drive's signal cable for proper connection at both ends. Exchange the signal cable for a known good one.

If the drive still refuses to operate, turn off the system and exchange the controller card (if present) with a known good one. In Pentium systems, the controller is mounted on the system board. In other systems, the controller is normally mounted on an MI/O card. Disconnect the disk drive's signal cable from the controller card and swap the card with a known good one of the same type. If the controller is built in to the system board, it may be easier to test the drive and signal cable in another machine than to remove the system board. Make certain to mark the cable and its connection points to ensure proper reconnection after the exchange.

If the controller is built into the system board and becomes defective, it is still possible to install an IDE host adapter card in an expansion slot and use it without replacing the system board. This action can also be taken to upgrade older IDE systems to EIDE systems so they can use additional IDE devices. The onboard IDE controller may need to be disabled before the system will address the new host adapter version.

TEST TIP

Remember that card-mounted IDE host adapters can be used to repair system boards with defective on-board IDE controllers and to upgrade older IDE systems.

Reconnect the signal cable to the controller and try to reboot the system with the new controller card installed. If the system boots up, reinstall any options removed and replace the system unit's outer cover. Return the system to full service and service the defective controller card as appropriate.

If the drive still refuses to work, check to see whether the CD-ROM drive has been properly terminated. Exchange the CD-ROM's power connector with another one to make sure that it is not a cause of problems. Finally, exchange the system board with a known good one.

Troubleshooting Port Problems

There are basically three levels of testing that apply to troubleshooting port problems. These are the DOS level, the Windows level, and the hardware level.

Before concentrating on any of these levels, troubleshooting should begin by observing the symptoms produced by operation of the port. Observe the steps that lead to the failure. Determine under what conditions the port failed. Was a new peripheral device installed in the system? Were any unusual operations in progress? Note any error messages or beep codes. Use the troubleshooting hints that follow to isolate the parallel-, serial-, or game-port circuitry as the source of the problem. Retry the system several times to observe the symptoms clearly. Take the time to document the problem.

Figure 11-30 illustrates the components involved in the operation of the serial, parallel, and game ports. Failures in these devices tend to end with poor or no operation of the peripheral. Generally, there are only four possible causes for a problem with a device connected to an I/O port:

- The port is defective.
- The software is not configured properly for the port.
- The connecting signal cable is bad.
- The attached device is not functional.

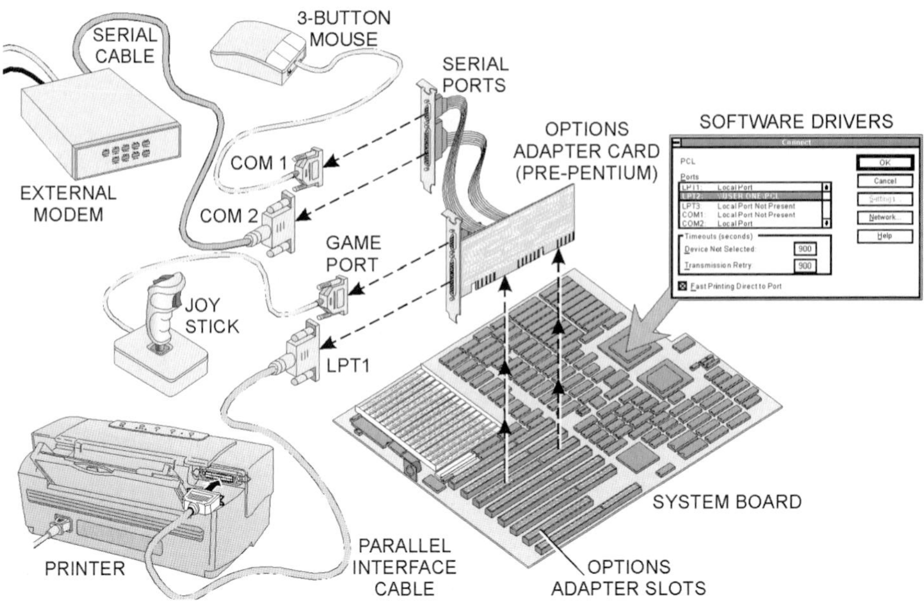

Figure 11-30: Components Associated with I/O Ports

Port Problem Symptoms

Typical symptoms associated with serial, parallel, or game port failures include:

- A 199, 432, or 90x IBM-compatible error code displays on the monitor (Printer Port).
- The on-line light is on but no characters are printed by the printer.
- An 110x IBM-compatible error code displays on the monitor (Serial Port).
- Device not found error message displays, or you have an unreliable connection.
- Input device does not work on the game port.

As you can see from the symptoms list, I/O ports do not tend to generate many error messages onscreen.

Port Hardware Checks

In the area of hardware, only a few items pertain to the system's ports. The port connector, signal cabling between the port circuitry and the connector in some units, the port circuitry itself, and finally the system board. As mentioned earlier, you can find the port circuitry on video cards in some older units, on specialized I/O cards in other units, and on the system board in newer units. In any of these situations, some configuration settings must be correct.

Check the board containing the I/O port circuitry and its User Guide for configuration information, which normally involves LPT, COM, and IRQ settings. Occasionally, you must set up hexadecimal addressing for the port addresses; however, this is becoming rare.

Checking ports on newer Pentium-based systems—With newer Pentium systems, you must check the advanced CMOS setup to determine whether the port in question has been enabled, and, if so, whether it has been enabled correctly.

For example, a modern parallel port must be enabled and set to the proper protocol type in order to operate advanced peripherals.

For typical printer operations, the setting can normally be set to Standard Parallel Port (SPP) mode. However, devices that use the port in a bidirectional manner need to be set to EPP or ECP mode for proper operation. In both cases, the protocol must be set properly for both the port and the device to carry out communications.

Figure 11-31 illustrates the movement of data to the parallel port mounted on an AT system board. On an ATX-style board, the standard I/O port connectors are mounted directly on the system board and extend from the rear of the system unit. No connecting cables are needed.

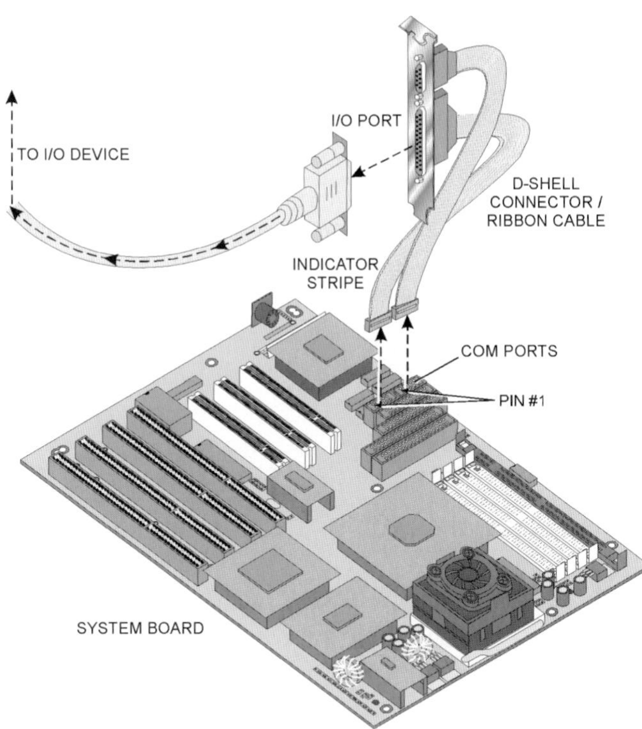

Figure 11-31: Moving Information Through an AT Port

It is helpful to single-step through the bootup in order to read the port assignments in the bootup window. If serial or parallel port problems are occurring, the CMOS configuration window is the first place to look. If the system does not detect the presence of the port hardware at this stage, then none of the more advanced levels will find it either. If values for any of the physical ports installed in the system do not appear in this window, check for improper port configuration jumpers or switches.

Since the unit has not loaded DOS at the time the configuration window appears, DOS and Windows cannot be sources of port problems at this time. If all jumpers and configuration settings for the ports appear correct, assume that a hardware problem exists. Diagnose the hardware port problem to a section of the system (in this case, the board containing the port).

Basic Checks

If possible, run a software diagnostic package to narrow the possible problem causes. This is not normally a problem since port failures do not generally affect the main components of the system. Try to use a diagnostic program that deals with the system board components. It should include parallel- and serial-port tests, as well as a game-port test if possible.

Port Tests function

Run the program's **Port Tests function** and perform the equivalent of the All Tests function. Note all the errors indicated by the tests. If a hardware error is indicated, such as those already mentioned, you might be able to take some corrective actions, such as resetting or reconfiguring LPT, COM, or IRQ settings, without replacing the unit containing the port hardware. If more complex port problems are indicated, however, exit the diagnostic program and replace the port hardware.

Parallel Ports

Loopback Test Plug

loopback plugs

Software diagnostic packages normally ask you to place a **Loopback Test Plug** in the parallel port connector in order to run tests on the port. The **loopback plugs** simulate a printer device by redirecting output signals from the port into port input pins. Figure 11-32 describes the signal-rerouting scheme used in a parallel port loopback plug.

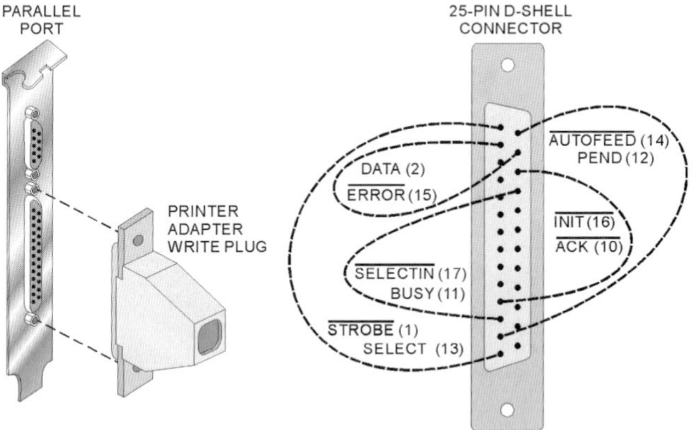

Figure 11-32: Parallel Port Loopback Connections

You can use a live printer with the port for testing purposes, but this action elevates the possibility that problems can be injected into the troubleshooting process by the printer.

COPY AUTO-EXEC.BAT LPT1:

If the software diagnostic program does not provide enough information to solve the problem, attempt to print to the first parallel port from the DOS level. To do this, type **COPY AUTOEXEC.BAT LPT1:** at the DOS prompt, and press the ENTER key.

If the file is not successfully printed, at the C:\> DOS prompt, type **EDIT AUTOEXEC.BAT**. Check the file for a "SET TEMP = " command. If the command is not present, add a SET TEMP statement to the AUTOEXEC.BAT file. At the C:\> DOS prompt, type EDIT AUTOEXEC.BAT. Create a blank line in the file and type **SET TEMP=C:\WINDOWS\TEMP** into it. Save the updated file to disk and reboot the system. Make sure to check the SET TEMP= line for blank spaces at the end of the line.

EDIT AUTOEXEC.BAT

SET TEMP=C:\ WINDOWS\TEMP

Is there a printer switch box between the computer and the printer? If so, remove the print-sharing equipment, connect the computer directly to the printer, and try to print from the command-prompt level as previously described.

Check the free space on the HDD. Remove any unnecessary files to clear space on the HDD and defragment the drive.

TEST TIP

Be aware that print-sharing equipment (such as switch boxes) can be responsible for parallel port/printer problems and should be removed as part of port testing.

Serial Ports

As with parallel ports, diagnostic packages typically ask you to place a loopback test plug in the serial port connector to run tests on the port. Use the diagnostic program to determine whether any IRQ or addressing conflicts exist between the serial port and other installed options. The serial loopback plug is physically connected differently from a parallel loopback plug so that it can simulate the operation of a serial device. Figure 11-33 describes the signal-rerouting scheme used in a serial port loopback plug.

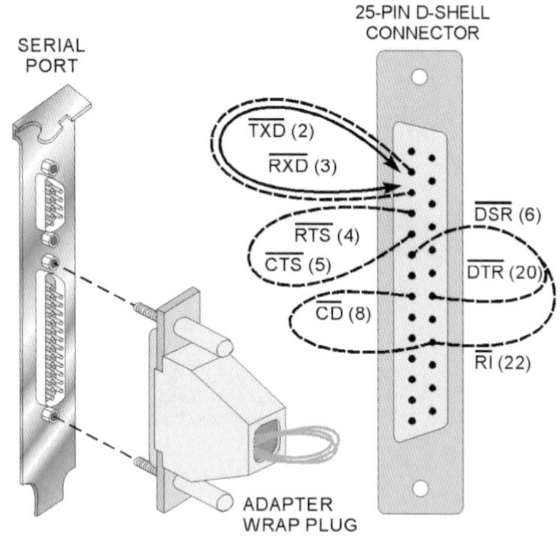

Figure 11-33: Serial Port Loopback Connections

You can use a live serial device with the port for testing purposes but, as with the printer, this elevates the possibility that nonport problems can be injected into the troubleshooting process.

If the software diagnostic program does not provide enough information to solve the problem, attempt to print to the serial port from the DOS level. To do this, type **DIR COMx** at the DOS prompt. The value of x is equal to the COM port being printed to.

DIR. COMx

Windows 9x Checks

You can reach the I/O port functions in Windows 9x through two avenues. You can access port information through the desktop's Start/Settings buttons. You also can reach this information through the My Computer icon on the desktop. Printer port information can be viewed through the Printers icon; serial port information is accessed through the System/Device Manager entries under the Control Panel icon.

Windows 9x Parallel Ports

Isolate the problem to the Windows 9x program by attempting to print from a non-Windows environment. Restart the computer in MS-DOS mode, and attempt to print a batch file from the command prompt.

Add Printer Wizard

If the system prints from DOS, but not from Windows 9x, check to see whether the Print option from the application's File menu is *unavailable* (gray). If so, check the My Computer/Printers window for correct parallel port settings. Make certain that the correct printer driver is selected for the printer being used. If no printer (or the wrong printer type) is selected, use the **Add Printer Wizard** to install and set up the desired printer.

The system's printer configuration information is also available through the Device Manager tab under the System icon in the Control Panel. Check this location for printer port setting information. Also, check the definition of the printer under the Control Panel's Printer icon.

Print Troubleshooter

F1

Windows 9x comes with an online tool, called **Print Troubleshooter**, to help solve printing problems. To use the Print Troubleshooter, click the Troubleshooting entry in the Windows 9x Help system, as illustrated in Figure 11-34. Press **F1** to enter the Help system. The Troubleshooter asks a series of questions about the printing setup. After you have answered all of its questions, the Troubleshooter returns a list of recommendations for fixing the problem.

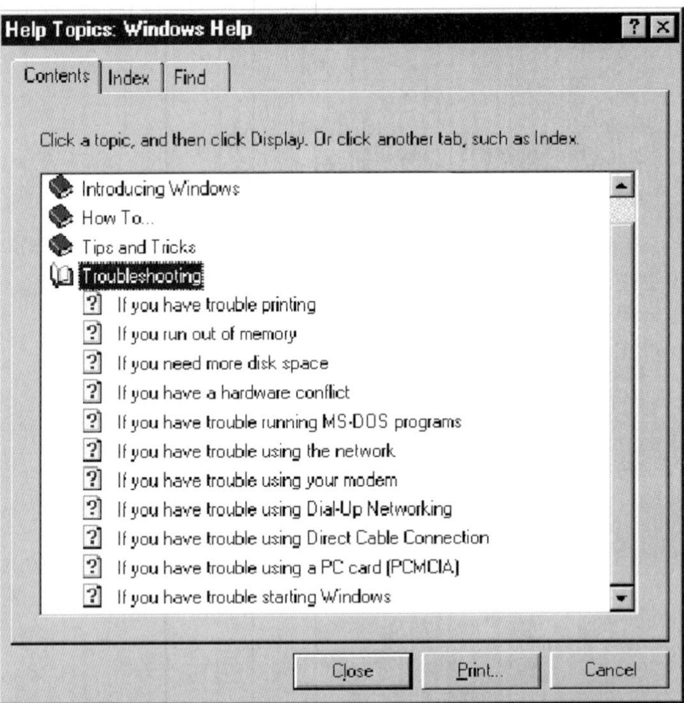

Figure 11-34: Accessing Windows 95 Troubleshooting Help

If the conclusions of the troubleshooter do not clear up the problem, try printing a document to a file. This enables you to separate the printing software from the port hardware. If the document successfully prints to a file, use the DOS COPY command to copy the file to the printer port. The format for doing this is as follows:

Copy /b filename.prn lpt1:

Copy /b filename.prn lpt1:

If the document prints to the file, but does not print out on the printer, the hardware setup and circuitry are causing the problem.

Continue troubleshooting the port by checking the printer driver to ensure that it is the correct driver and version number. Click the Printer icon and select the Properties entry from the menu. Click the Details tab to view the driver's name. Click the **About** entry under the **Device Options** tab to verify the driver's version number.

About

Device Options

Click the printer port in question (under the Printer icon) to open the Print Manager screen. Check the Print Manager for errors that have occurred and that might be holding up the printing of jobs that follow it. If an error is hanging up the print function, highlight the offending job and remove it from the print spool by clicking the Delete Document entry of the Document menu.

Windows 9x Serial Ports

Information on the system's serial ports is contained in three areas under the **Device Manager**. These are the **Resources** entry, the **Driver** entry, and the Port Settings entry. The Resources entry displays port address ranges and IRQ assignments. The Driver entry displays the names of the installed device drivers and their locations. The Port Settings entry, depicted in Figure 11-35, contains speed and character frame information for the serial ports. The Advanced button under Port Settings enables you to adjust the transmit and receive buffer speeds for better operation.

Device Manager

Resources

Driver

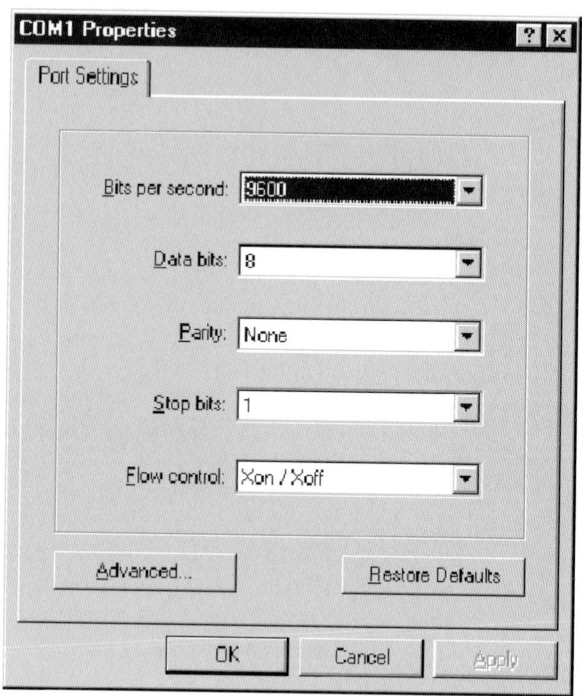

Figure 11-35: Port Settings Entry

Check under the Windows 9x Control Panel/System/Device Manager window for correct serial port settings.

Hands-On Activity

Xon-Xoff

1. Click the Port Settings option to see the setup for the ports. Most serial printers use settings of 9600 Baud, No Parity, 8 Bits, 1 Stop Bit, and Hardware Handshaking (**Xon-Xoff**).
2. Click the Resources button to determine the IRQ Setup for the port.
3. Check the user's manual to document the correct settings for the device using the port in question.

USB Port Checks

Because nearly any type of peripheral device can be added to the PC through the USB port, the range of symptoms associated with USB device can include all the symptoms listed for peripheral devices in this chapter. Therefore, problems associated with USB ports can be addressed in three general areas:

- The USB hardware device
- The USB controller
- The USB drivers

Human Interface Devices

The first step in troubleshooting USB problems is to check the CMOS setup screens to make sure that the USB function is enabled there. If the USB function is enabled in BIOS, check in the Windows Control Panel/System/Device Manager to make certain that the USB controller appears there. In Windows 2000, the USB controller should be listed under the Universal Serial Bus Controllers entry, or in the **Human Interface Devices** entry (using the default Devices by Type setting).

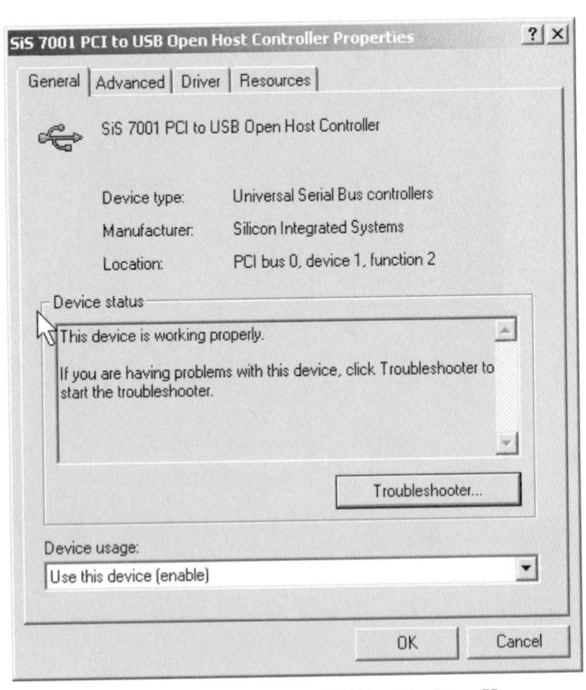

Figure 11-36: The USB Controller Properties Page

If the controller does not appear in Device Manager, or a yellow warning icon appears next to the controller, the system's BIOS may be outdated. Contact the BIOS manufacturer for an updated copy of the BIOS.

If the controller is present in the Device Manager, right-click the USB controller entry and click the Properties tab. If there are any problems, a message appears in the Device Status window, depicted in Figure 11-36, describing any problems and suggesting what action to take.

If the BIOS and controller settings appear to be correct, the next items to check are the USB port drivers. These ports have a separate entry in the Device Manager that you can access by clicking the Universal Serial Bus Controllers option, right-clicking the USB Root Hub entry, and then clicking the Properties tab.

If a USB device does not install itself automatically, you may have conflicting drivers loaded for that device and you may need to remove them.

Authority Needed—To use the Windows 2000 Device Manager utility to troubleshoot USB problems, you must be logged on as an administrator, or as a member of the Administrators group.

Hands-On Activity

Removing Potentially Conflicting USB Drivers

1. Disconnect any USB devices connected to the system and start the system in Safe mode.
2. Under Windows 2000, you are asked about which operating system to use. Use the up- and down-arrow keys to highlight Windows 2000 Professional or Windows 2000 Server, and then press ENTER.

If alert messages appear, read each alert and then click the OK button to close it.

3. Open the Device Manager, click the USB device, and then click the Remove option.

Your particular USB device may be listed under the Universal Serial Bus Controller, Other Devices, Unknown Devices, or a particular device category (such as the Modem entry if the device is a USB modem).

4. Click the Start menu, select the Shut Down option followed by the Restart entry, and then click the OK button.
5. Connect the USB device directly to the USB port on your computer. If the system does not autodetect the device, you must install the drivers manually. You may need drivers from the device manufacturer to perform this installation.

Troubleshooting Scanners

The driver software that comes with the scanner must be configured to match the settings on its adapter card. The adapter card settings are normally established through hardware jumpers. Check the scanner software's setup screen to confirm the settings.

Most **scanners** have three important configuration parameters to consider. These are: the **I/O address**, the **IRQ setting**, and the **DMA channel setting**.

scanners

I/O address

IRQ setting

DMA channel setting

Typical I/O address settings for the scanner adapter are 150h to 151h (default), 170h to 171h, 350h to 351h, or 370h to 371h. Typical IRQ settings are: 10 (default) 3, 5, and 11. Likewise, typical DMA channel settings are: channel 5 (default), 1, 3, or 7. Figure 11-37 shows the components associated with scanners.

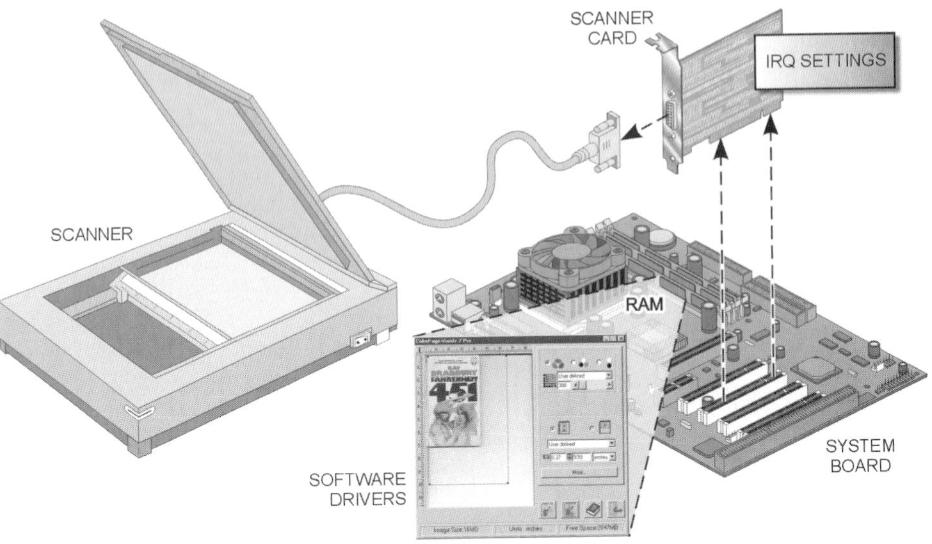

Figure 11-37: Scanner-Related Components

IRQ conflicts

Traditionally, **IRQ conflicts** with network and sound cards tend to be the biggest problem associated with scanners. Typical symptoms associated with IRQ conflicts include:

- The image on the screen appears misaligned.
- The scanning function appears to be activated and the scanner light comes on, but no image is produced onscreen.

In these cases, a good software diagnostic package can be quite helpful in spotting and correcting the conflicts.

The scanning function appears to be activated and the scanner light comes on symptom also can apply to the DMA channel of the interface card conflicting with the DMA setting of another card. Select another DMA channel for the card and software.

If the scanner light does not come on when trying to scan, there are two possible causes of the problem. First, the system may not meet minimum system requirements for the particular scanner being used. If this is the case, research the minimum system requirements of the scanner to make sure that it can be used with the system. If the system requirements are not met, either return the scanner to the supplier, or upgrade the system to meet the minimum specifications for the scanner. The second possible cause of the problem is that the I/O address setting conflicts with another card in the computer. Try other address settings on the adapter card, and in the software.

If the problem seems to be a hardware problem, make the checks described in the Performing Quick Checks section earlier in this chapter. Make sure the power to the scanner is plugged in, and turned on. Exchange the signal cable for a new one, if available. Refer to the User Guide for troubleshooting hints.

Troubleshooting Tape Drives

Because the fundamentals of recording on tape are so similar to those used with magnetic disks, the troubleshooting process is also very similar.

The basic components associated with the tape drive include: the tape drive, the signal cable, the power connection, the controller, and the tape drive's operating software.

The tape itself can be a source of several problems. Common points to check with the tape include:

- Is the tape formatted correctly for use with the drive in question?
- Is the tape inserted securely in the drive?
- Is the tape write-protected?
- Is the tape broken or off the reel in the cartridge?

As cartridge tapes are pulled back and forth, their mylar base can become stretched over time. This action can cause the tape's format to fail before the tape actually wears out. To remedy this, you should retention the tape periodically using the software's retention utility. Cartridge tapes are typically good for about 150 hours of operation. If the number of tape errors begins to increase dramatically before this time, try reformatting the tape to restore its integrity. After the 150-hour point, just replace the tape.

If the tape is physically okay and properly formatted, the next easiest thing to check is the tape software. Check the software setup and configuration settings to make sure they are correct for any hardware settings. Refer to the tape drive's user guide for a list of system requirements, and check the system to make sure they are being met.

If any configuration jumpers or switches are present on the controller, verify that they are set correctly for the installation. Also, run a diagnostic program to check for resource conflicts that may be preventing the drive from operating (such as IRQ and base memory addressing).

The software provided with most tape drives includes some error-messaging capabilities. Observe the system and note any tape-related error messages it produces. Consult the User Manual for error-message definitions and corrective suggestions. Check for error logs that the software may keep. You can view these logs to determine what errors have been occurring in the system.

Since many tape drives are used in networked and multiuser environments, another problem occurs when you are not properly logged in, or enabled to work with files being backed up or restored. In these situations, the operating system may not allow the tape drive to access secured files, or any files, because the correct clearances have not been met. Consult the network administrator for proper password and security clearances.

Reinstall the drive's software and reconfigure it. Go through the installation process carefully, paying close attention to any user-selected variables and configuration information requested by the program.

If you suspect hardware problems, begin by cleaning the drive's R/W heads. Consult the user's guide for cleaning instructions, or use the process described in Core Section 3.1 for manual cleaning of floppy drive R/W heads. The R/W heads should be cleaned after about 20 backups or restores. Also, try to use a different tape to see whether it works. Make certain that it is properly formatted for operation. It should also be a clean tape, if possible, to avoid exposing any critical information to potential corruption.

If cleaning does not restore the drive to proper operation, continue by checking the power and signal cables for good connection and proper orientation.

Since matching tape drives are not common at a single location, checking the drive by substitution should be considered as a last step. Check the user's guide for any additional testing information and call the drive manufacturer's technical service number for assistance before replacing the drive.

Troubleshooting Modems

A section on troubleshooting modems has to be subdivided into two segments:

- external modems
- internal modems

An internal modem is checked out in the same basic sequence as any other I/O card. First, check the modem's hardware and software configuration, check the system for conflicts, and check for correct drivers. Improper software setup is the most common cause of modems not working when they are first installed. Inspect any cabling connections to see that they are made correctly and functioning properly, and test the modem's hardware by substitution. If an external modem is being checked, it must be treated as an external peripheral, with the serial port being treated as a separate I/O port. Figure 11-38 shows the components associated with internal and external modems.

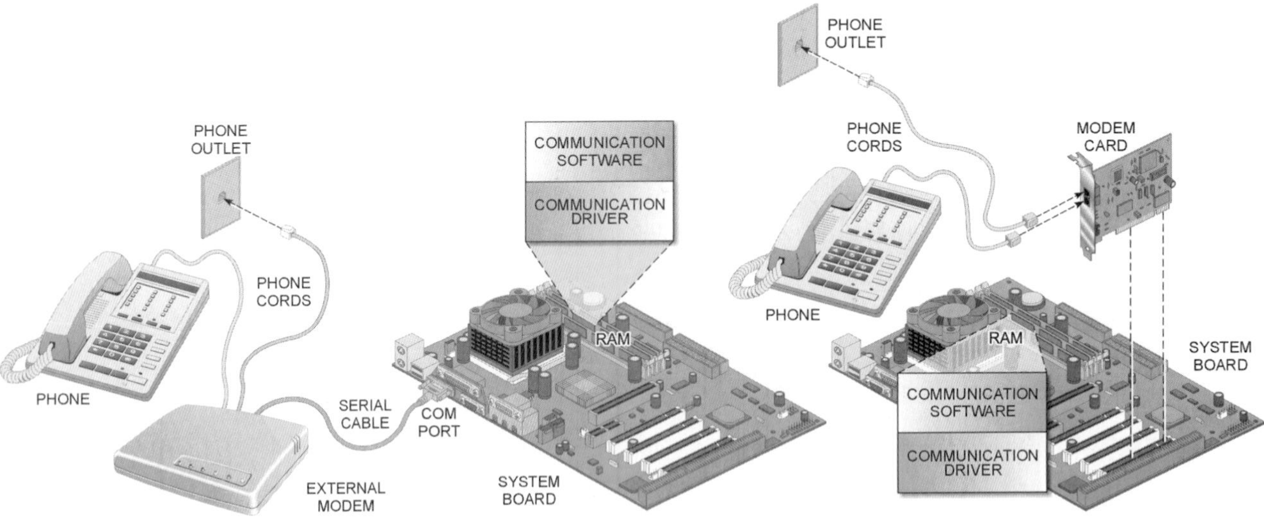

Figure 11-38: Internal and External Modem Components

Modem Problem Symptoms

Typical symptoms associated with modem failures include:

- No response from the modem.
- Modem does not dial out.
- Modem does not connect after number has been dialed.
- Modem does not transmit after making connection with remote unit.
- Cannot get modem installed properly for operation.
- Garbled messages are transmitted.
- Cannot terminate a communication session.
- Cannot transfer files.

COM Port Conflicts

As stated earlier, every COM port on a PC requires an IRQ line in order to signal the processor for attention. In most PC systems, two COM ports share the same IRQ line. The IRQ4 line works for COM1 and COM3, and the IRQ3 line works for COM2 and COM4. This is common in PC compatibles. The technician must make sure that two devices are not set up to use the same IRQ channel.

If more than one device is connected to the same IRQ line, a conflict occurs, because it is not likely that the interrupt handler software can service both devices.

If a mouse is set for COM1 and a modem is set for COM3, for example, neither device can communicate effectively with the system, because COM1 and COM3 both use IRQ4. Both the mouse and the modem may be interrupting the microprocessor at the same time. The same is true if two devices are connected to IRQ3, because COM2 and COM4 use this IRQ. Therefore, the first step to take when installing a modem is to check the system to see how its interrupts and COM ports are allocated. You can alleviate this particular interrupt conflict by using a bus mouse rather than a serial mouse, thus freeing up a COM port.

To install a non-PnP device on a specific COM port (i.e., COM2), you must first disable that port in the system's CMOS settings in order to avoid a device conflict. If not, the system may try to allocate that resource to some other device, since it has no way of knowing that the non-PNP device requires it.

TEST TIP

Be aware that the system may conflict with non-PNP devices for resources if it is not informed they are have been reserved.

Use a software diagnostic package to obtain information about the serial port's **Base I/O Port Address**. A typical value for this setting is 02E8h. Also, obtain the modem's IRQ setting. This setting is typically IRQ=3. Other common modem settings are:

Base I/O Port Address

- COM1 with IRQ=4, 5, or 7
- COM2 with IRQ=3, 5, or 7
- COM3 with IRQ=4, 5, or 7
- COM4 with IRQ=3, 5, or 7

Take care when using IRQ5 or IRQ7 with the modem. These interrupt channels are typically reserved for LPT1 (IRQ7) and LPT2 (IRQ5). The arrangements in the previous list assume that IRQ3 and IRQ4 are already taken. It also assumes that at least one of the LPT interrupts is not being used by a printer.

Modem Software Checks

Run All Tests

ATZ

Many of the software diagnostic packages available include a utility for testing modems. If such a program is available, run the equivalent of its **Run All Tests** entry to test the modem. If all of the configuration settings are correct, attempt to run the modem's DOS-based communications package to test the modem's operation. At the command line, type **ATZ** to reset the modem and enter the Command mode using the Hayes-compatible command set. You should receive a 0, or OK response, if the command was processed.

OK code

If no result code is returned to the screen, check the modem's configuration and setup again for conflicts. Also, check the speed setting of the communication software to make sure it is compatible with that of the modem. On the other hand, a returned **OK code** indicates that the modem and the computer are communicating properly.

ATL2

AT&Dn

Other AT-compatible commands can be used to check the modem at the DOS level. The **ATL2** command sets the modem's output volume to medium, to make sure that it is not set too low to be heard. If the modem dials, but cannot connect to a remote station, check the modem's speed and DTR settings. Change the DTR setting by entering **AT&Dn**. When:

n = 0 the modem ignores the DTR line

n = 1 the modem goes to async command state when DTR goes off

n = 2 DTR off; switches modem to off-hook and back to Command mode

n = 3 DTR switching off initializes modem

The complete AT Command Set should be located in the modem's user's guide.

If the modem connects, but cannot communicate, check the character framing parameter of the receiving modem, and set the local modem to match. Also, match the terminal emulation of the local unit to that of the remote unit. ANSI terminal emulation is the most common. Finally, match the file transfer protocol to the other modem.

There are a number of things that can occur to prevent the modem from going into the on-line state. An intelligent modem will wait a specified length of time, after pick-up, before it starts dialing. This allows the phone system time to apply a dial tone to the line. After the number has been dialed, the modem waits for the ring back from the telephone company (this is what you hear when you are making a call).

When the ringing stops, indicating that the call has gone through, the modem will wait a specified length of time for an answer tone (carrier) from the receiving modem. If the carrier is not detected within the allotted time, the originating modem will begin automatic disconnect procedures. If a busy signal is detected, the originating modem will also hang up, or refer to a second number.

During the data transfer, both modems monitor the signal level of the carrier to prevent the transfer of false data due to signal deterioration. If the carrier signal strength drops below some predetermined **threshold level**, or is lost for a given length of time, one or both modems will initiate automatic disconnect procedures.

threshold level

ATDT*70

Use the **ATDT*70** command to disable call waiting if the transmission is frequently garbled. The +++ command should interrupt any activity the modem is engaged in, and bring it to the Command mode.

In Windows 9x, the modem configuration information is found in the Control Panel under the Modems icon. Under the icon are two tabs: the General tab, and the Diagnostics tab. The Properties button, in the General window, provides Port and Maximum-speed settings. The Connection tab provides character framing information, as illustrated in Figure 11-39. The Connection tab's Advanced button provides error and flow-control settings, as well as modulation type.

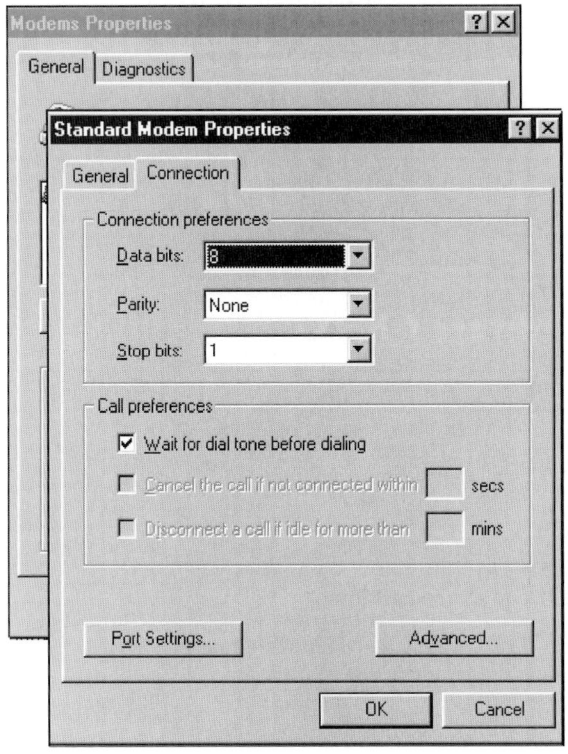

Figure 11-39: The Connection Tab of the Standard Modem Properties Dialog Box

The Diagnostics tab's dialog box, depicted in Figure 11-40, provides access to the modem's driver, and additional information. The Plug-and-Play feature reads the modem card, and returns its information to the screen, as demonstrated in the depiction.

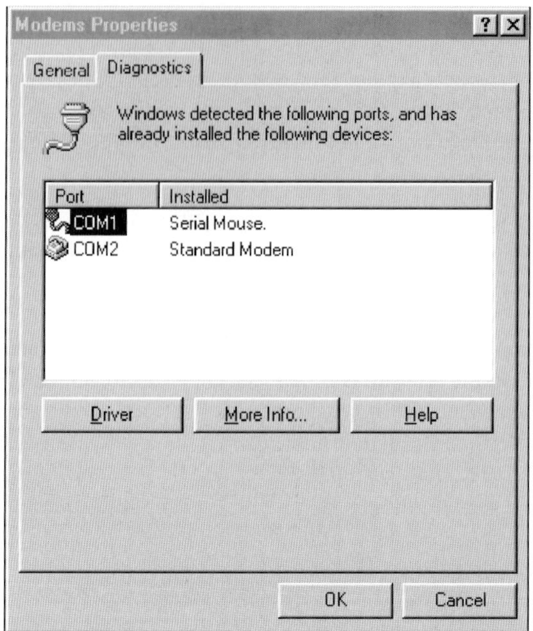

Figure 11-40: The Diagnostics Tab of the Modem Properties Dialog Box

Windows 9x provides fundamental troubleshooting information for wide area networking through its system of Help screens. Simply select Help from the Control Panel's toolbar, and click on the topic that you are troubleshooting.

Modem Hardware Checks

Most serial ports and modems can perform self tests on their circuitry.

Modems have the capability to perform three different kinds of self-diagnostic tests:

- The local digital loopback test
- The local analog loopback test
- The remote digital loopback test

local digital loopback test

loopback plug

wrap-plug

local analog loopback test

remote digital loopback test

In a **local digital loopback test**, data is looped through the registers of the port's UART. When testing the RS-232 port itself, a device called a **loopback plug** (or **wrap-plug**) channels the output data directly back into the received data input, and only the port is tested.

Many modems can extend this test by looping the data through the local modem, and back to the computer (the **local analog loopback test**). Some modems even possess the ability to loopback data to a remote computer through its modem (**remote digital loopback test**). In this manner, the entire transmit and receive path can be validated, including the communication line (i.e., the telephone line). One of the most overlooked causes of transmission problems is the telephone line itself. A noisy line can easily cause garbled data to be output from the modem. Figure 11-41 illustrates adapter, analog, and digital loopback tests.

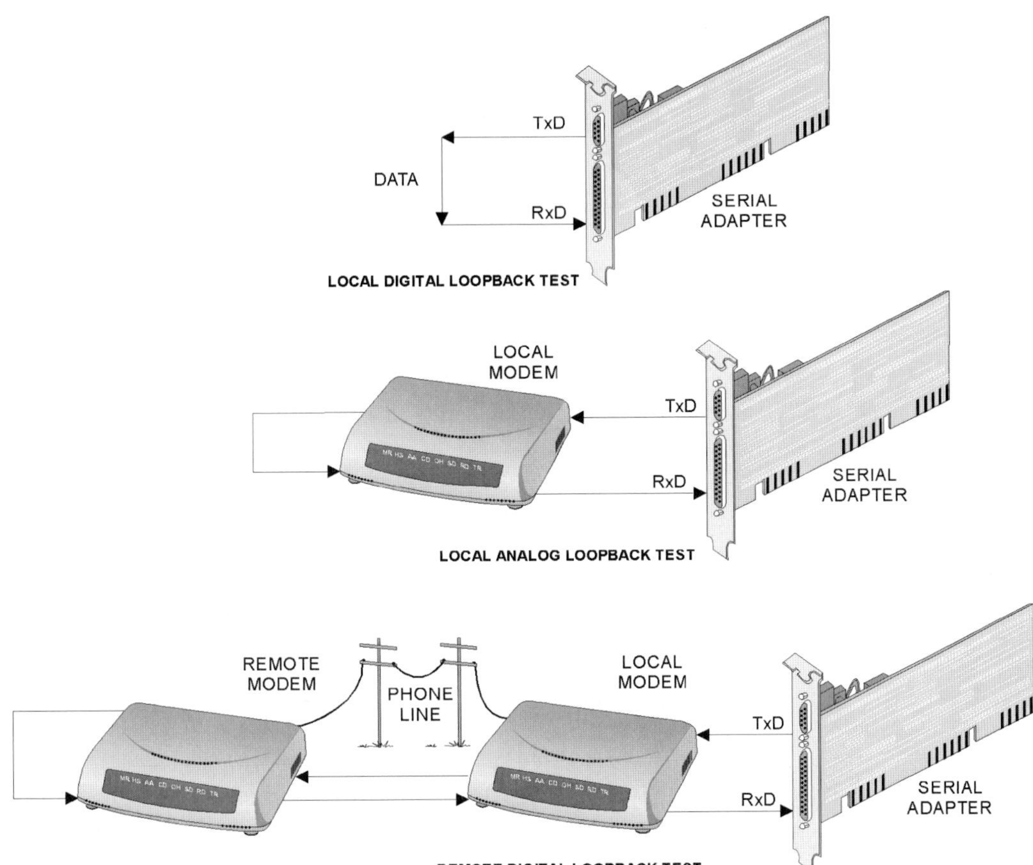

Figure 11-41: Loopback Tests

If transmission errors occur frequently, you should use the various loopback tests to locate the source of the problem. Begin by running the remote digital loopback test. If the test runs successfully, the problem is likely to be located in the remote computer.

If the test fails, run the **Local Digital Loopback Test with Self Tests**. If the test results are positive, the problem may be located in the local computer. On the other hand, you should run the local analog loopback test if the local digital test fails.

Local Digital Loopback Test with Self Tests

If the local analog test fails, the problem is located in the local modem. If the local analog test is successful, and problems are occurring, you should run the local analog test on the remote computer. The outcome of this test should pinpoint the problem to the remote computer or the remote modem.

If the modem is an internal unit, you can test its hardware by exchanging it with a known good unit. If the telephone line operates correctly with a normal handset, only the modem, its configuration, or the **communications software** can be causes of problems. If the modem's software and configuration settings appear correct and problems are occurring, the modem hardware is experiencing a problem and it will be necessary to exchange the modem card for a known good one.

communications software

With an external modem, you can use the front-panel lights as diagnostic tools to monitor its operation. You can monitor the progress of a call, and its handling, along with any errors that may occur.

Figure 11-42 depicts the front panel lights of a typical external modem.

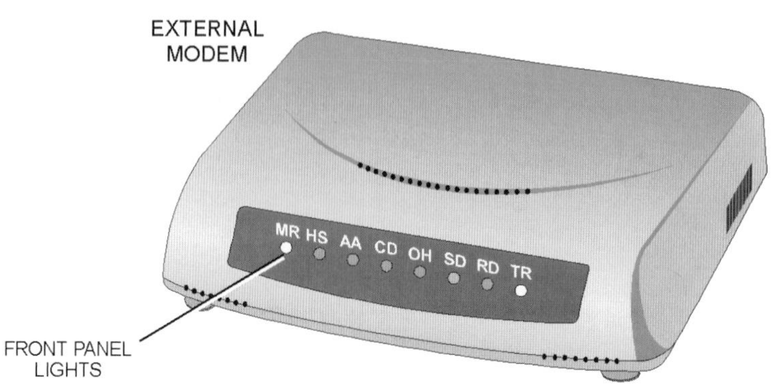

Figure 11-42: Modem Front Panel Indicators

Modem Ready (MR)

Terminal Ready (TR)

Auto Answer (AA)

The **Modem Ready (MR)**, **Terminal Ready (TR)**, and **Auto Answer (AA)** lights are preparatory lights that indicate that the modem is plugged in, powered on, ready to run, and prepared to answer an incoming call. The MR light becomes active when power is applied to the modem and the modem is ready to operate. The TR light becomes active when the host computer's communication software and the modem contact each other. The AA light just indicates that the Auto Answer function has been turned on.

Off-Hook (OH)

Ring Indicator (RI)

Carrier Detect (CD)

ring signal

The **Off-Hook (OH)**, **Ring Indicator (RI)**, and **Carrier Detect (CD)** lights indicate the modem's on-line condition. The OH light indicates that the modem has connected to the phone line. This action can occur when the modem is receiving a call, or when it is commanded to place a call. The RI light becomes active when the modem detects an incoming **ring signal**. The CD light activates when the modem detects a carrier signal from a remote modem. As long as this light is on, the modem can send and receive data from the remote unit. If the CD light will not activate with a known good modem, a problem with the data communication equipment exists.

Send Data (SD)

Received Data

High Speed (HS)

The final three lights indicate the status of a call in progress. The **Send Data (SD)** light flickers when the modem transmits data to the remote unit, while the **Received Data** light flickers when the modem receives data from the remote unit. The **High Speed (HS)** light becomes active when the modem is conducting transfers at its highest possible rate. If an external modem will not operate at its highest rated potential, check the specification for the UART on the adapter card to make certain that it is capable of operating at that speed.

Troubleshooting Sound Cards

sound card

speakers

audio-related software

host computer system

play

record

Some very basic components are involved in the audio output of most computer systems: a **sound card**, some **speakers**, the **audio-related software**, and the **host computer system**. Several software diagnostic packages enable you to test sound card operation.

Most sound cards perform two separate functions. The first is to **play** sound files; the second is to **record** them. You might need to troubleshoot problems for either function.

Sound Card Configuration Checks

If sound problems are occurring in the multimedia system, two of the first things to check are the hardware and audio software configuration settings. Refer to the sound card manufacturer's documentation for proper hardware settings. These items usually include checking the card's jumper settings for IRQ and I/O address settings. However, with more plug-and-play cards in the market, software configuration of IRQ and I/O addressing is becoming more common.

In the past, sound cards have been notorious for interrupt conflict problems with other devices. Because these conflicts typically exist between peripheral devices, they may not appear during boot up. If the sound card operates correctly except when a printing operation is in progress, for example, an IRQ conflict probably exists between the sound card and the printer port. Similar symptoms would be produced for tape backup operations if the tape drive and the sound card were configured to use the same IRQ channel. Use a software diagnostic program to check the system for interrupt conflicts.

Checking the system for resource conflicts in Windows is relatively easy. Access the Control Panel and select the System icon. From this point, click the Device Manager and select the Sound, video, and game controller option. If the system detects any conflicts, it places an exclamation point within a circle on the selected option.

From the Device Manager, choose the proper sound card driver from the list and move into its Resource window. The page's main window displays all the resources the driver is using for the card. The Conflicting devices list window provides information about any conflicting resource that the system has detected in conjunction with the sound card.

If the Windows PnP function is operating properly, you should be able to remove the driver from the system, reboot the computer, and allow the operating system to re-detect the sound card and assign new resources to it.

Sound Card Software Checks

Many diagnostic packages offer testing features for sound cards and other multimedia-related components. Sound card problems should not prevent the system from loading a software diagnostic, so run the All Tests equivalent in the multimedia section of the diagnostic package. Also, run checks to see whether addressing (IRQ or DMA) conflicts are causing a problem. If they are, reconfigure the system's components to remove the conflicts.

Is the software application running a DOS version? If so, it may not be able to output audio under Windows.

You can use the Windows Sound Recorder to check the operation of WAV files under Windows. WAV is a Microsoft specification for audio files and is one of the most popular file formats for use with audio files. The Sound Recorder utility can be accessed through the *Start/Programs/Accessories* menu path under the Multimedia entry in Windows 95 or the Entertainment entry in Windows 98. If an audio file will not play from the Sound Recorder, make sure the Sound Recorder is working by attempting to play audio files that have played on the system before. If the files play from the Sound Recorder, examine the other application that was attempting to play the file for proper installation and setup.

If the Sound Recorder will not play an audio file through the sound card, check to see that the multimedia icon is installed in the Control Panel, and available through the *Start/Programs/Accessories* path. Also check the Control Panel's Device Manager to see that the correct audio driver is installed, and that its settings match those called for by the sound card manufacturer. If the drivers are missing, or wrong, add them to the system through the Control Panels' Add/Remove Hardware wizard.

If the driver is not installed, or is incorrect, add the correct driver from the available drivers list. If the correct driver is not available, reinstall it from the card's OEM disk, or obtain it from the card's manufacturer.

MIDI

Professional music users like to work with a special file and equipment standard for music known as **MIDI**. Windows is capable of handling and playing MIDI files through its MIDI Player utility located under the *Start/Programs/Accessories* menu path. Like the Sound Recorder utility, the MIDI Player is located under the Multimedia entry in Windows 95, or the Entertainment entry in Windows 98. If the Windows Media Player will not play MIDI files, look in the System/Device Manager section of the Control Panel to see that the MIDI driver is set up properly. Check to see whether more than one MIDI device is connected. If so, disconnect the other MIDI devices.

REFERENCE SHELF

For more in-depth technical information about multimedia systems and the MIDI sound standard, refer to the *Multimedia* section of the Electronic Reference Shelf located on the CD that accompanies this book.

Sound Card Hardware Checks

Figure 11-43 depicts the system's sound card–related components. Provided that the sound card's configuration is properly set, and the software configuration matches it, the sound card and speakers will need to be checked out if problems exist. Most of these checks are very simple. They include checking to see that the speakers are plugged into the speaker port. It is not uncommon for the speakers to be mistakenly plugged into the card's MIC (microphone) port. Likewise, if the sound card will not record sound, make certain that the microphone is installed in the proper jack (not the speaker jack), and that it is turned on. Check the amount of disk space on the drive, to ensure that there is enough to hold the file being produced.

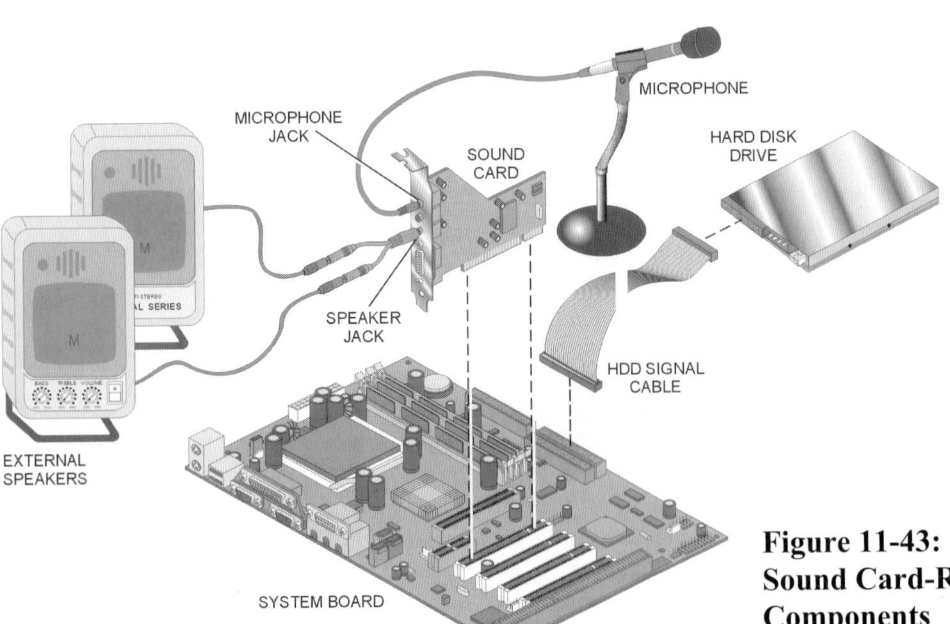

Figure 11-43: Sound Card-Related Components

In the case of stereo speaker systems, it is possible to place the speakers on the wrong sides. This will produce a problem when you try to adjust the balance between them. Increasing the volume on the right speaker will instead increase the output of the left speaker. The obvious cure for this problem is to physically switch the positions of the speakers.

TEST TIP

Know how to correct a balance problem that occurs with add on stereo speakers.

If the system will not produce sound, troubleshoot the audio output portion of the system. Do the speakers require an external power supply? If so, is it connected, and are the speakers turned on? If the speakers use batteries for their power source, check them to see that they are installed and good. Check the speakers' volume setting to make certain they are not turned down.

Troubleshooting General Multimedia Problems

Typical symptoms associated with multimedia failures include the following:

- Sound not working.
- The system will not capture video.
- Software cannot access the CD-ROM.
- The system will not play video.

Figure 11-44 depicts various multimedia support systems. These systems include a sound card, a CD-ROM drive, external speakers, and a video capture card. Most or all of these devices are included in any particular multimedia system. These types of equipment typically push the performance of the system, and therefore they require the most services from technicians (especially during setup and configuration).

One of the major points to be aware of when building or upgrading a multimedia PC is the interrupt channel usage of the system. It is important that all the devices have access to unique, acceptable interrupt request lines. To ensure this, the technician should map out the system's IRQ capabilities with the number and level of interrupts needed by the different devices being installed. In some instances, it also is necessary to map the DMA capabilities of the system to the number of available DMA channels. IRQ and DMA availability and utilization is covered in detail in Chapter 2—*Advanced System Boards*.

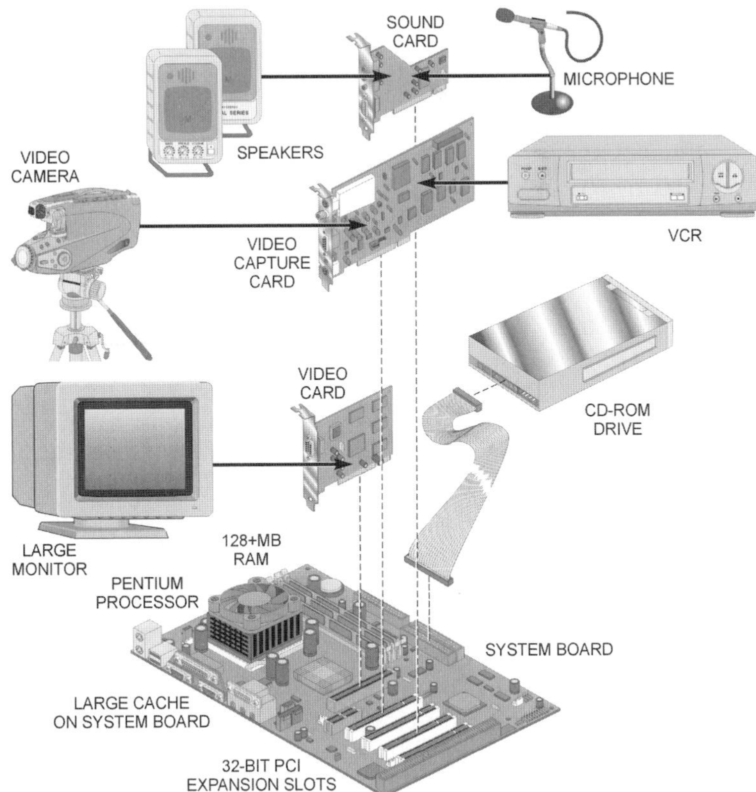

Figure 11-44: Multimedia Components

The wide variety of I/O systems that come together to create a true multimedia machine can quickly use up all the available I/O slots on most system boards, especially in Pentium systems (where the expansion slots are often a mix of ISA and PCI buses). This lack of available slots sometimes leads to problems getting I/O cards with the correct mix of bus connectors.

REFERENCE SHELF

For more in-depth technical information about multimedia systems, refer to the *Multimedia* section of the Electronic Reference Shelf located on the CD that accompanies this book.

NETWORK REPAIR

A portion of the A+ Core Hardware objective 6.1 states that the test taker should be able to identify the ramifications of repairs on the network. Examples include:

- Reduced bandwidth
- Loss of data
- Network slowdown

Begin troubleshooting a general network problem by determining what has changed since it was running last. If the installation is new, it will need to be inspected as a setup problem.

Check to see if any new hardware, or new software, has been added. Has any of the cabling been changed? Have any new protocols been added? Has a network adapter been replaced or moved? If any of these events has occurred, begin by checking them specifically.

Network Troubleshooting Basics

If the system has not been changed, and has operated correctly in the past, the next step is to make certain that it functions properly as a stand-alone unit. Begin by disconnecting the unit from the network and testing its operation. Run diagnostics on the system to see if there are any problems that show up. If a hardware problem is encountered at the stand-alone level, troubleshoot the indicated portion of the system using the procedures already discussed.

network drop cabling

If the problem does not appear in, or is not related to, the stand-alone operation of the unit, it will be necessary to check the portions of the system that are specific to the network. These elements include the network adapter card, the network-specific portions of the operating system, and the **network drop cabling**. Figure 11-45 depicts the network-specific portions of a computer system.

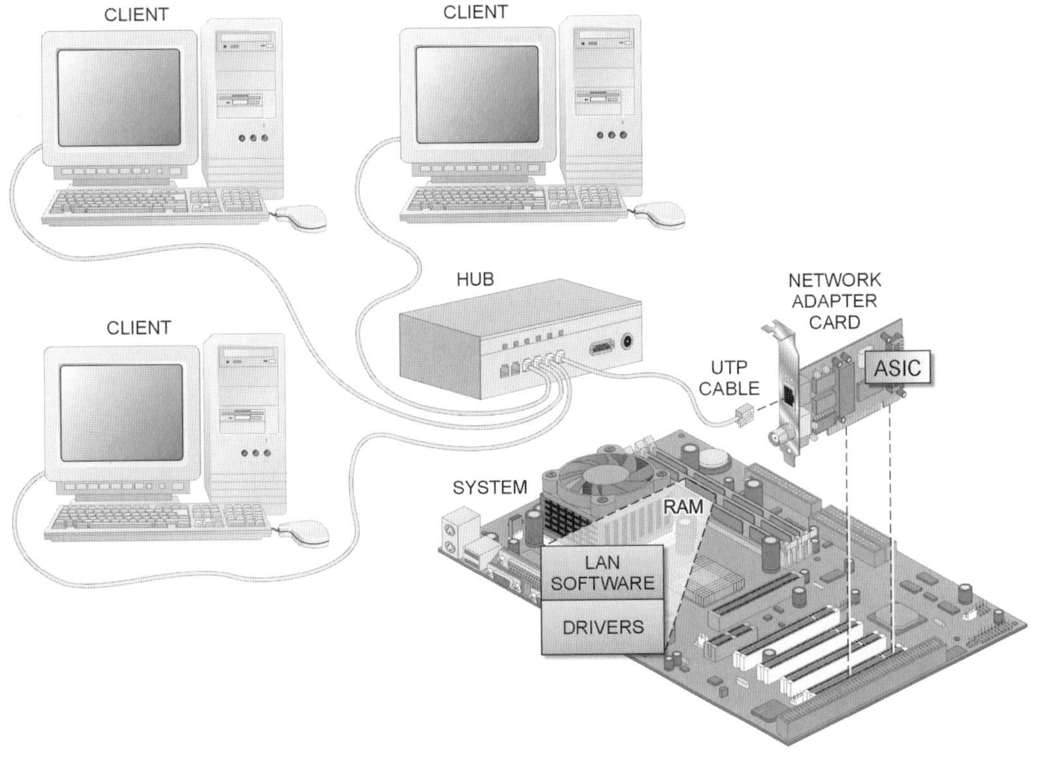

Figure 11-45: Network-Related Components

Be aware that in a network environment, no unit really functions alone. Unlike working on a stand-alone unit, the steps performed on a network computer may affect the operation of other units on the network.

For example, disconnecting a unit from a network that uses coaxial cable creates an unterminated condition in the network. This condition can cause several different types of problems:

- Data moving through the network can be lost.
- A general slowdown of data movement across the network can occur due to reduced bandwidth.
- Nodes may not be able to "see," or connect to, each other.

TEST TIP

Be aware of the affects of a missing terminator or bad cable/connector can have on an Ethernet network.

If a unit must be removed from the network, it is a good practice to place a terminator in the empty connector where the unit was attached. This should allow the other units to function without the problems associated with an open connection. Care must be taken to ensure that the proper value of terminating resistor is used. Substituting a terminator from an obsolete ArcNet network into an Ethernet system may create as many problems as the open connection would have and they may be harder to track down. Systems that use concentrators have fewer connection problems when a unit needs to be removed for servicing.

Even if the unit does not need to be removed from the network, diagnostic efforts and tests run across the network can use a lot of the network's bandwidth. This reduced bandwidth causes the operation of all the units on the network to slow down. This is due simply to the added usage of the network.

TEST TIP

Be aware of the effects that running applications across the network can have on its performance.

Because performing work on the network can affect so many users, it is good practice to involve the network administrator in any such work being performed. This person can run interference for any work that must be performed that could disable the network or cause users to lose data.

LAN Configuration Checks

TEST TIP

Be aware that many ISA NIC cards are not PnP configurable, so they must be configured manually.

As with any peripheral device, the LAN card's configuration must be correct for the software that is driving the peripheral, and for the adapter card it is communicating through. An improperly configured network adapter card can prevent the system from gaining access to the network. Many newer network cards possess plug-and-play capabilities. With other non-PnP network cards, such as most ISA NIC cards, it is necessary to configure the card through hardware jumpers, or through logical configuration switches in BIOS Extension EPROM.

Check the adapter card's hardware settings to see if they are set according to the manufacturer's default settings, or if they have been changed to some new setting. If they have been changed, refer to the system information from the software diagnostic tool to see if there is some good explanation for the change. If not, record the settings as they are and reset them to their default values.

Also, check the software's configuration settings, and change them to match as necessary. If a defective card is being replaced with an identical unit, simply transfer the configuration settings to the new card.

Use a software diagnostic package to check the system's interrupt request allocations. Try to use a package that has the capabilities to check the system's I/O port addresses, and shadow RAM and ROM allocations. Finally, check the physical IRQ settings of any other adapter cards in the system.

LAN Software Checks

Windows NT/2000

It is at the LAN system software level that troubleshooting activities diverge. The differences between Novell NetWare, Microsoft's **Windows NT/2000**, Windows for Workgroups (Windows 3.11), and Windows 9x are significant enough that there are nationally recognized certifications just for NetWare and NT. Novell NetWare and Windows 2000 are client/server types of network management software, while Windows 3.11 and Windows 9x are peer-to-peer networking environments.

data security

One of the major concerns in most network environments is **data security**. Since all of the data around the network is potentially available to anyone else attached to the net, all LAN administration software employs different levels of security. Passwords are typically used at all software levels to lock people out of hardware systems, as well as out of programs and data files.

Security Access Problems

Log-on passwords

scripts

Log-on passwords and **scripts** are designed to keep unauthorized personnel from accessing the system, or its contents. Additional passwording may be used to provide access to some parts of the system, and not others (i.e., lower-level accounting personnel may be allowed access to accounts receivable and payable sections of the business management software package, but not allowed into the payroll section). A series of passwords may be used to deny access to this area.

access and privileges

network administrator

access rights

In other LAN management packages, **access and privileges** to programs and data can be established by the **network administrator** through the software's security system. These settings can be established to completely deny access to certain information, or to allow limited **access rights** to it. An example of limited rights would be the ability to read data from a file, but not to manipulate it (write, delete, print, or move it) in any way.

The reason for discussing security at this point is because established security settings can prevent the technician from using any, or all, of the system's resources. In addition, having limited access to programs can give them the appearance of being defective. Because of this, the service technician must work with the network administrator when checking a networked machine. The administrator can provide the access, and the security relief, needed to repair the system. The administrator can also keep you away from data that may not be any of your business.

Refer to Chapter 12—*Operating System Troubleshooting*, which covers the Operating System Technologies module for in-depth network software troubleshooting information.

LAN Hardware Checks

No Network Node is an Island—In a network, no node is an island, and every unit has an impact on the operation of the network when it is on line. Changes made in one part of a network can cause problems, and data loss, in other parts of the network. You should be aware that changing hardware and software configuration settings for the adapter can have adverse effects when the system is returned to the network. In addition, changing hard drives in a network node can have a negative impact on the network when the unit is brought back on line.

Some LAN adapters come with software diagnostic programs that can be used to isolate problems with the adapter. If this type of software is included, use it to test the card. The diagnostic software can also be used to change the adapter's configuration, if necessary.

If the card fails any of the diagnostic tests, check it by exchanging it with a known good one of the same type. Set the replacement card's station address so that it is unique (usually the same as the card being removed). Depending on the type of system being tested, the file server may need to be cycled off, and then back on, to detect the presence of the new LAN card.

Check the activity light on the back plate of the LAN card (if available) to see if it is being recognized by the network. If the lights are active, the connection is alive. If not, check the adapter in another node. Check the cabling to make sure that it is the correct type, and that the connector is properly attached. A LAN cable tester is an excellent device to have in this situation.

If the operation of the local computer unit appears normal, it will be necessary to troubleshoot the network from the node out. As mentioned earlier, always consult the network administrator before performing any work on a network, beyond a stand-alone unit.

concentrators

routers

bridges

Check the system for **concentrators**, **routers**, and **bridges** that may not be functioning properly. Check the protocol's frame settings to make sure that they are compatible from device to device, or that they are represented on the file server. The operation of these devices will have to be verified as separate units.

Testing Cable

Time Domain Reflectometry (TDR)

As we mentioned earlier in this chapter, the most frequent hardware-related cause of network problems involve bad cabling and connectors. There are several specialized, hand-held devices designed for testing the various types of data communication cabling. These devices range from inexpensive continuity testers, to moderately priced Data Cabling testers, to somewhat expensive **Time Domain Reflectometry** (**TDR**) devices.

The inexpensive continuity testers can be used to check for broken cables. This function can also be performed by the simple DMM described in Chapter 2. Data Cabling testers are designed to perform a number of different types of tests on twisted pair and coaxial cables. These wiring testers normally consist of two units – a master test unit and a separate load unit, as illustrated in Figure 11-46

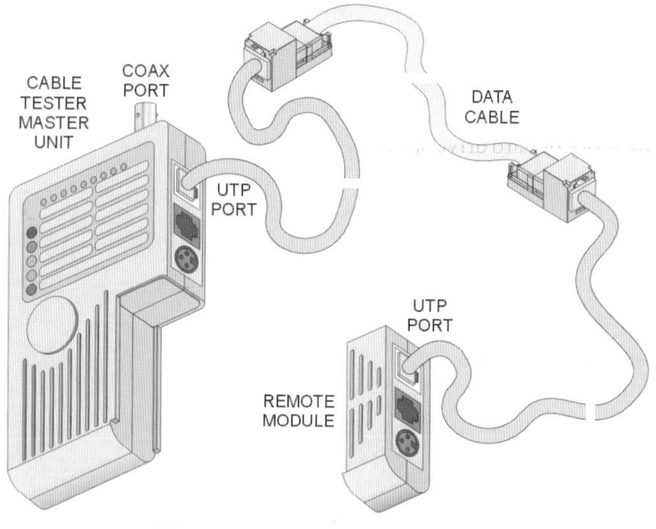

Figure 11-46: Cable Tester

The master unit is attached to one end of the cable and the load unit is attached at the other. The master unit sends patterns of test signal through the cable and reads them back from the load unit. Many of these testers feature both RJ-45 and BNC connectors for testing different types of cabling. When testing twisted pair cabling these devices can normally detect such problems as broken wires, crossed over wiring, shorted connections, and improperly paired connections.

TDRs are sophisticated testers that can be used to pinpoint the distance to a break in a cable. These devices send signals along the cable and wait for them to be reflected. The time between sending the signal and receiving it back is converted into a distance measurement. The TDR function is normally packaged along with the other cable testing functions just described. TDRs used to test fiber optic cables are known as **Optical Time Domain Reflectometers** (**OTDRs**).

Optical Time Domain Reflectometers (OTDRs)

Network Printing Problems

Transferring data from the system to the printer over a parallel port and cable is largely a matter of connecting the cable and installing the proper printer driver for the selected printer. The protocol for sending data consists largely of a simple hardware handshake routine. Even in a serial printer, the protocol is only slightly more complex. However, when a network is involved, the complexity becomes that much greater again, due to the addition of the network drivers.

The first step in troubleshooting network printer problems is to verify that the local computer and the remote printer are set up for remote printing. Check the operating system to see that the printer is configured to be a **shared resource** for other computers on the network. If the local computer cannot see files and printers at the remote print server station, file and print sharing may not be enabled there. Chapter 12—*Operating System Troubleshooting*, which covers the Operating System Technologies module, provides additional solutions to Windows-related network printing problems.

shared resource

The next step is to verify the operation of the printer. Run a self-test on the printer to make certain that it is working correctly. Turn the printer off and allow a few seconds for its buffer memory to clear. Try to run a test page to verify the operation of the printer's hardware.

If the test page does not print, there is obviously a problem with the printer. Troubleshoot the printer using the information from Chapter 6 until the self-test works correctly. With the printer working, attempt to print across the network again.

The third step is to determine whether the **print server** (computer actually connected to the network printer) can print to the printer. Try to open a document on the print server and print it. If the local printing operation is unsuccessful, move to the command prompt, create a small batch file, and copy it to the local LPT port.

print server

If the file prints, there are a few possible causes of printing problems. The first possibility is that a problem exists with the printer configuration at the print server. Check the print server's drivers.

Another common problem is that there may not be enough memory or hard drive space available in the print server. Use Windows utility programs to determine the amount of hard drive and memory space available in the system and to optimize the system for further use. The Windows utility programs are covered in detail in Chapter 12—*Operating System Troubleshooting.*

The fourth step is to verify the operation of the network. This can be accomplished by trying other network functions, such as transferring a file from the remote unit to the print server. If the other network functions work, examine the printer driver configuration of the remote unit.

If the print drivers appear to be correct, install a generic or text only printer driver and try to print to the print server. Also, move to the command prompt in the remote unit and create a batch text file. Attempt to copy this file to the network printer. If the generic driver or the batch file works, reinstall the printer driver, or install new drivers for the designated printer.

In the event that other network functions are operational, the final step is to verify the printer operation of the local computer. If possible, connect a printer directly to the local unit and set its print driver up to print to the local printer port. If the file prints to the local printer, a network/printer driver problem still exists. Reload the printer driver and check the network print path. Check the network cabling for good connections.

stalls

crashes

If the printer operation **stalls**, or **crashes**, during the printing process, a different type of problem is indicated. In this case, the remote printer was functioning, the print server was operational, and the network was transferring data. Some critical condition must have been reached to stop the printing process. Check the Print Spooler or Print Manager in the print server to see if an error has occurred. Also, check the hard disk space and memory usage in the print server. Figure 11-47 illustrates the process of isolating network printing problems.

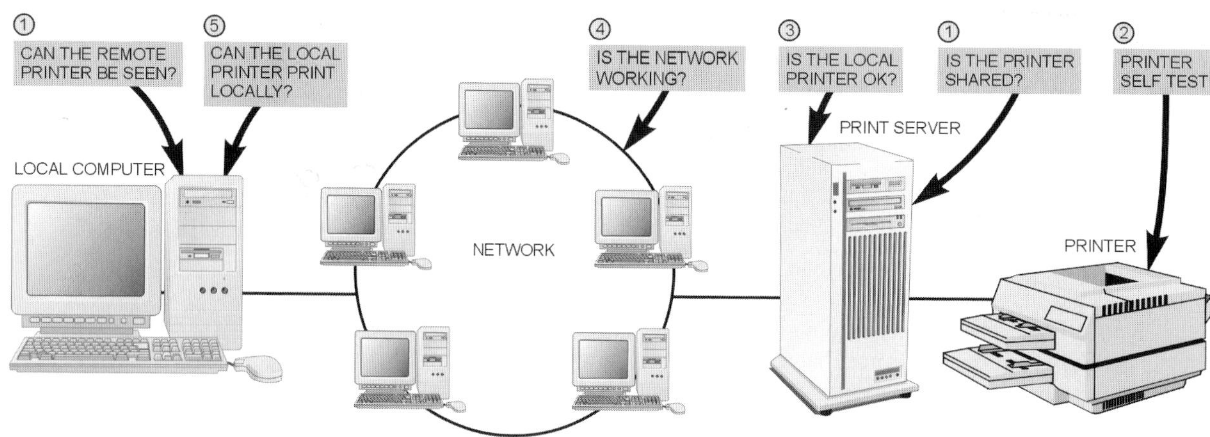

Figure 11-47: Isolating Network Printing Problems

CHAPTER SUMMARY

This chapter has covered fundamental troubleshooting tools and techniques. The first half of the chapter presented the basic tools and investigative techniques used to troubleshoot computer systems. It dealt with the early steps of computer problem solving, including differentiating hardware versus software problems and identifying configuration problems. The final portion of this section focused on software diagnostic packages and their use. Upon completion of this material, you should be able to identify basic troubleshooting procedures and good practices for eliciting problem symptoms from customers.

The second half of the chapter presented typical symptoms and standard troubleshooting procedures for various system components. It included FRU troubleshooting procedures that included software, configuration, and hardware segments for each device. The procedures for most of the devices included related troubleshooting information associated with command prompt and Windows problems. After completing the chapter, you should be able to identify common symptoms and problems associated with each module and know how to troubleshoot and isolate the problems.

At this point, review the objectives listed at the beginning of the chapter to be certain that you understand and can perform each item listed there.

KEY POINTS REVIEW

This chapter has discussed basic troubleshooting and diagnostic methods associated with the system hardware. Review the following key points before moving into the Review and Exam Questions sections to make sure you are comfortable with each point. Afterward, answer the Review Questions that follow to verify your knowledge of the information.

- It is normal practice to first set the meter to its highest voltage range to make certain that the voltage level being measured does not damage the meter.
- Unlike the voltage check, resistance checks are always made with power removed from the system.
- The most important thing to do when checking a malfunctioning device is to be observant. Begin by talking to the person who reported the problem. Many clues can be obtained from this person. Careful listening is also a good way to eliminate the user as a possible cause of the problems occurring. Part of the technician's job is to determine whether the user could be the source of the problem—either trying to do things with the system that it cannot do, or not understanding how some part of it is supposed to work.
- Whenever a self-test failure or setup mismatch is encountered, the BIOS may indicate the error through a blank screen, or a visual error message on the video display, or through an audio response (beep codes) produced by the system's speaker.
- Check all externally accessible switch settings.
- Take the time to document the problem, including all of the tests you perform and their outcomes. Your memory is never as good as you think it is, especially in stressful situations such as with a down computer. This recorded information can prevent you from making repetitive steps that waste time and may cause confusion. This information will also be very helpful when you move on to more detailed tests or measurements.
- Carefully observing the steps of a bootup procedure can reveal a great deal about the nature of problems in a system. Faulty areas can be included or excluded from possible causes of errors during the bootup process.
- The majority of all problems that occur in computer systems are in the area of configuration settings.
- In most newer systems, the BIOS and operating system use Plug-and-Play techniques to detect new hardware that has been installed in the system. These components work together with the device to allocate system resources for the device. In some occasions, the PnP logic will not be able to resolve all of the system's resource needs and a configuration error will occur. In these cases, the user will be required to manually resolve the configuration problem.
- Since there may be MOS (Metal Oxide Semiconductor) devices on the board, you'll want to ground yourself before performing this test. This may be done by touching an exposed portion of the unit's chassis, such as the top of the power supply.
- Field Replaceable Units (FRUs) are the portions of the system that can be conveniently replaced in the field.
- Once a hardware error has been indicated, start troubleshooting the problem by exchanging components (cards, drives, etc.) with known good ones.

- Make certain to take the time to document the symptoms associated with the problem, including all of the tests you make, and any changes that occur during the tests. This information can keep you from making repetitive steps.

- Once you have isolated the problem, and the computer boots up and runs correctly, work backwards through the troubleshooting routines, reinstalling any original boards and other components removed during the troubleshooting process.

- Special consideration must be taken when a system is inoperable. In a totally inoperable system, there are no symptoms to give clues where to begin the isolation process. In addition, it is impossible to use troubleshooting software or other system aids to help isolate the problem.

- In Pentium-based systems, check the Advanced CMOS configuration and enabling settings in the BIOS and Chipset Features screens. These settings usually include the disk drives, keyboard, and video options, as well as on-board serial and parallel ports.

- Typically, if the bootup process reaches the point where the system's CMOS configuration information is displayed on the screen, it can be assumed that no hardware configuration conflicts exist in the system's basic components. After this point in the bootup process, the system begins loading drivers for optional devices and additional memory. If the error occurs after the CMOS screen is displayed and before the bootup tone, it will be necessary to clean boot the system and single-step through the remainder of the bootup sequence.

- A number of things can cause improper floppy disk drive operation or disk drive failure. These items include the use of unformatted diskettes, incorrectly inserted diskettes, damaged disks, erased disks, loose cables, drive failure, adapter failure, system board failure, or a bad or loose power connector.

- There are basically three levels of troubleshooting that apply to FDD problems: configuration, the DOS level, and the hardware level. There is no Windows-level troubleshooting that applies to floppy drives.

- Hard drive systems are very much like floppy drive systems in structure—they have a controller, one or more signal cables a power cable, and a drive unit. The troubleshooting procedure typically moves from setup and configuration, to formatting, and, finally, into the hardware component isolation process.

- The troubleshooting steps for a CD-ROM drive are almost identical to those of an HDD system. The connections and data paths are very similar. There are basically four levels of troubleshooting that apply to CD-ROM problems. These are the configuration level, the DOS level, the Windows level, and the hardware level.

- There are basically three levels of testing that apply to troubleshooting port problems. These are the DOS level, the Windows level, and the hardware level.

- With newer Pentium systems, it will be necessary to check the Advanced CMOS Setup to determine whether the port in question has been enabled, and, if so, whether it has been enabled correctly.

- Most scanners have three important configuration parameters to consider. These are the I/O address, the IRQ setting, and the DMA channel setting.

- The basic components associated with the tape drive include the tape drive, the signal cable, the power connection, the controller, and the tape drive's operating software.

- Every COM port on a PC requires an IRQ line in order to signal the processor for attention. In most PC systems, two COM ports share the same IRQ line. The IRQ4 line works for COM1 and COM3, and the IRQ3 line works for COM2 and COM4. This is common in PC-compatibles. The technician must make sure that two devices are not set up to use the same IRQ channel.

- During the data transfer, both modems monitor the signal level of the carrier to prevent the transfer of false data due to signal deterioration. If the carrier signal strength drops below some predetermined threshold level, or is lost for a given length of time, one or both modems will initiate automatic disconnect procedures.
- Modems have the capability to perform three different kinds of self-diagnostic tests.
- With an external modem, the front panel lights can be used as diagnostic tools to monitor its operation. The progress of a call, and its handling, can be monitored along with any errors that may occur.
- The components involved in the audio output of most computer systems are very simple. There is a sound card, some speakers, the audio-related software, and the host computer system. Several software diagnostic packages are available with the capability of testing sound card operation.
- Be aware that in a network environment, no unit really functions alone. Unlike working on a stand-alone unit, the steps performed on a network computer may affect the operation of other units on the network.
- One of the major concerns in most network environments is data security. Since all of the data around the network is potentially available to anyone else attached to the net, all LAN administration software employs different levels of security. Passwords are typically used at all software levels to lock people out of hardware systems, as well as out of programs and data files.
- No Network Node is an Island—In a network, no node is an island, and every unit has an impact on the operation of the network when it is on line. Changes made in one part of a network can cause problems, and data loss, in other parts of the network. You should be aware that changing hardware and software configuration settings for the adapter can have adverse effects when the system is returned to the network. In addition, changing hard drives in a network node can have a negative impact on the network when the unit is brought back on line.

REVIEW QUESTIONS

The following questions test your knowledge of the material presented in this chapter.

1. If the system issues a single beep and the C:\> prompt appears on the screen, what condition is indicated?
2. List the FDD-related hardware components that should be checked when floppy disk problems are suspected.
3. List three situations that would normally require that the CMOS Setup routines be run.
4. What type of problem is indicated by a "Strike F1 to continue" message during bootup?
5. What is the recommended method of using a digital multimeter to check voltage in a computer system.
6. If you are replacing components one at a time and the system suddenly begins working properly, what can be assumed?

7. List three items commonly tested using the resistance function of a multimeter.
8. What resistance reading would normally be expected from a fuse if it is functional?
9. If you are measuring across a capacitor on the system board with a DMM, what voltage reading would you normally expect to see from a DMM?
10. Which non-computer possibility should be eliminated early in the troubleshooting process?
11. What range should the voltage function of a DMM be set to for an initial measurement?
12. Logon passwords and scripts are designed to ________.
13. In a LAN environment, access and privileges to programs and data can be established by the _______.
14. What is the first step in checking a networked computer?
15. Describe two actions that should be taken if a networked printer stalls during a remote printing operation.

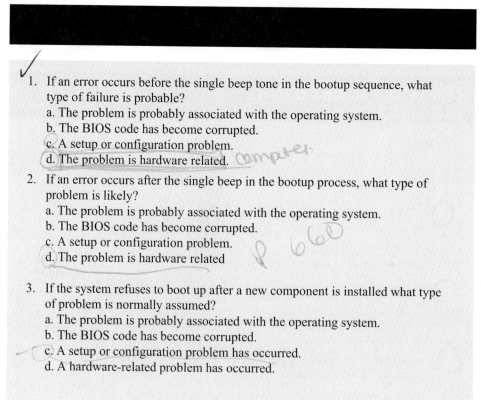

1. If an error occurs before the single beep tone in the bootup sequence, what type of failure is probable?
   a. The problem is probably associated with the operating system.
   b. The BIOS code has become corrupted.
   c. A setup or configuration problem.
   d. The problem is hardware related.
2. If an error occurs after the single beep in the bootup process, what type of problem is likely?
   a. The problem is probably associated with the operating system.
   b. The BIOS code has become corrupted.
   c. A setup or configuration problem.
   d. The problem is hardware related
3. If the system refuses to boot up after a new component is installed what type of problem is normally assumed?
   a. The problem is probably associated with the operating system.
   b. The BIOS code has become corrupted.
   c. A setup or configuration problem has occurred.
   d. A hardware-related problem has occurred.

4. What component has the ability to affect the operation of all the other sections of the computer system?
   a. The power supply
   b. The ROM BIOS
   c. The microprocessor
   d. The system board
5. What function and reading would be appropriate for checking a system's speaker?
   a. Infinity
   b. Near zero ohms
   c. 4 ohms
   d. 8 ohms
6. What type of problem is indicated by a continuous beep tone from the system?
   a. A power supply failure
   b. An undefined problem
   c. A configuration problem
   d. A bootup problem
7. If a system appears to be completely dead, what item should logically be checked first?
   a. The system board
   b. The microprocessor
   c. The hard disk drive
   d. The power supply
8. The error message "Bad File Allocation Table" indicates _____ problem.
   a. an operating system
   b. a Run Time
   c. a configuration
   d. a bootup
9. If a "CMOS" Display Type Mismatch" message appears on the screen, what type of error is indicated?
   a. An operating system problem
   b. A Run Time error
   c. A setup or configuration problem
   d. A bootup failure
10. Which of the following is not normally considered an FRU?
    a. A system board
    b. A floppy disk drive
    c. A power supply
    d. A video controller IC

OPERATING SYSTEM TROUBLESHOOTING

OBJECTIVES

OBJECTIVES

Upon completion of this chapter and its related lab procedures, you should be able to perform the following tasks:

1. Identify and solve Windows 9x Setup problems.
2. Locate and solve Windows 9x startup problems.
3. Locate and solve Windows 9x operational problems.
4. Identify and solve Windows 2000 Setup problems.
5. Locate and solve Windows 2000 startup problems.
6. Locate and solve Windows 2000 operational problems.
7. Describe Windows 2000 system tools.
8. Use the Policy Editor to change Windows NT/2000 policy settings.
9. Use various Safe Mode startup scenarios.
10. Use log files to determine the location of Windows 2000 operating system problems.
11. Employ Microsoft On-line Help utilities in Windows 9x and 2000.

OPERATING SYSTEM TROUBLESHOOTING

INTRODUCTION

As you have seen in previous chapters, operating systems are tremendous collections of complex programming code brought together to control every operation of the computer hardware and link it to the software applications that users want to employ. As with anything so complex, operating systems fail from time to time—some more than others—and although potentially millions of things can go wrong with complex software systems, you should be happy to know that you can group operating system problems into three basic areas:

- Setup problems (those that occur during installation or upgrading)
- Startup problems (those that occur when the system is booting up)
- Operational problems (those that occur during the normal course of operations)

By isolating a particular software problem to one of these areas, the troubleshooting process becomes less complex.

Setup problems typically involve failure to complete an OS install or upgrade operation. In some cases, this can leave the system stranded between an older OS version and a newer OS version, making the system unusable.

Startup problems usually produce conditions that prevent the system hardware and software from coming up and running correctly. These problems fall into two major groups:

- Hardware configuration problems
- OS boot-up problems

Operational problems are problems that occur after the system has booted up and started running. These problems fall into three main categories:

- When performing normal application and file operations
- When printing
- When performing network functions

TROUBLESHOOTING SETUP PROBLEMS

Setup problems are those errors that occur during the process of installing the operating system on the hard disk drive. With early DOS versions, installation was a simple matter of making a \DOS directory on the hard drive and copying the contents of the DOS disks into it. For operating system versions from MS-DOS 5.0 forward, however, the installation procedure became an automated process requiring an Install or Setup program to be run.

One of the most common OS setup problems involves situations in which the system's hard drive does not have enough free space to carry out the installation process. When this occurs, you must remove files from the disk until you have cleared enough room to perform the installation. Unless you can remove enough obsolete files from the drive to make room for the new operating system, it is recommended that the files be backed up to some other media before erasing them from the drive.

Setup problems also occur when the system's hardware will not support the operating system that is being installed. These errors can include the following:

- Memory speed mismatches
- Insufficient memory problems
- Incompatible device drivers

Protection Error

The memory speed mismatch or mixed RAM-type problem produces a Windows **Protection Error** message during the installation process. This error indicates that the operating system is having timing problems that originate from the RAM memory used in the system. Correcting this problem involves swapping the system's RAM for devices that meet the system's timing requirements.

It is not uncommon for mouse or video drivers to fail during the installation of an operating system. If the video driver fails, you must normally turn off the system and attempt to reinstall the operating system from scratch. Conversely, if the mouse driver fails during the install, it is possible to continue the process using the keyboard. This problem is normally self-correcting after the system reboots. A similar problem occurs when the operating system is looking for a PS/2 mouse and the system is using a serial mouse. It will not detect the serial mouse, and you will need to complete the installation process using the keyboard. Afterward, you can check the CMOS Port Settings for the serial port the mouse is connected to and install the correct driver for the serial mouse if necessary.

The best way to avoid hardware-compatibility problems is to consult Microsoft's Web site to see that the hardware you are using is compatible with the operating system version you are installing.

Most error messages produced during an operating system installation stop the system. However, some errors offer to continue the process. It is our experience that continuing the installation rarely works out. Instead, just shut down the system, attempt to clear the problem, and then reinstall the operating system.

Windows 9x Setup Problems

Windows 9x draws from the existing FAT structure when it is being installed. Therefore, an interruption, or a crash during the installation process may leave the system with no workable operating system in place. If this occurs, you must boot the system from a bootable floppy disk and reinstall Windows 9x from that point. If the FAT version that Setup detects on the hard drive is older than MS-DOS 3.1, it presents an Incorrect MS-DOS Version message onscreen. If so, you must reformat the hard drive with a more current version of DOS.

If the system crashes during the hardware detection phase of a Windows 9x install, Microsoft recommends that you simply reboot the system until the installation process is successful. The Windows Setup wizard will mark startup steps that have failed and will bypass that step the next time you attempt to install the operating system. The failed steps are recorded in the Setuplog text file, described later in this chapter. This process is known as **Safe Recovery**.

Safe Recovery

The Windows 9x installation files are stored on the installation disk in a compressed **Cabinet (CAB)** file format. Therefore, they cannot just be copied over to the hard drive to repair files damaged in an aborted installation. The best recovery method for this situation is to boot the system to a floppy disk, run **FDISK** to repartition the drive, format the drive, and run the Windows 9x Setup utility (provided your data was backed up beforehand).

Cabinet (CAB)

FDISK

If some programs or hardware options fail to run properly after a system has been upgraded to a Windows 9x operating system, you must determine whether they require specific real-mode drivers to be retained in the CONFIG.SYS and AUTOEXEC.BAT files. Recall that during the Restart phase of the installation process, Windows 9x deactivates files that it perceives as incompatible, or unnecessary by placing a **Remark (REM)** statement at the beginning of the line. This may cause different applications or hardware to fail if they require these specific entries for operation.

Remark (REM)

This condition can be detected by removing the REM comment and retrying the program or hardware. Be aware that restoring the driver can cause other problems within Windows 9x. The best choice is always to contact the software or hardware manufacturer for a Windows 9x driver.

Blue Screen of Death (BSOD)

Windows NT/2000 Setup Problems

When an attempt to install Windows NT or Windows 2000 fails, a Stop screen error will normally result. Stop errors occur when Windows NT or Windows 2000 detects a condition from which it cannot recover. The system stops responding, and a screen of information with a blue or black background displays, as illustrated in Figure 12-1. Stop errors are also known as Blue Screen errors, or the "**Blue Screen of Death (BSOD)**." Troubleshooting these types of errors is discussed in more detail later in the chapter.

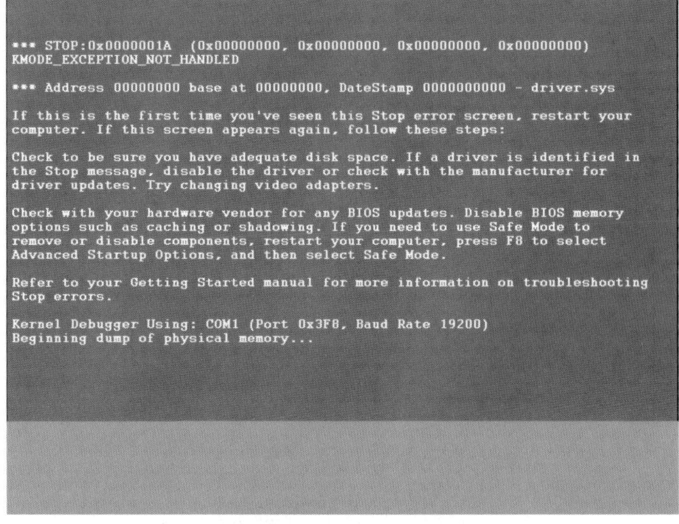

Figure 12-1: Stop Error or Blue Screen Error

Some other problems can typically occur during the Windows 2000 installation process. These problems include items such as the following:

- Noncompliant hardware failures.
- Insufficient resources.
- File system type choices.
- The installation process starts over after rebooting.
- WINNT32.EXE will not run from the command-line errors.

Ways to correct these particular installation-related problems include the following:

Verify Hardware Compatibility - The hardware-compatibility requirements of Windows NT and Windows 2000 are more stringent than those of the Windows 9x platform are. When either of these operating systems encounters hardware that is not compatible during the setup phase, they fail. In some cases, the system incorrectly detects the hardware, whereas in other cases the system produces a **blue screen** error.

blue screen

Make certain to check the Hardware Compatibility List to ensure that your hardware is compatible with Windows 2000. If the hardware is not listed, contact the hardware vendor to determine whether they support Windows 2000 before starting the installation.

TEST TIP

Be aware that you should check hardware manufacturer's web sites for updated device drivers before installing Windows 2000.

Verify Minimum System Resource Requirements - Also, make certain that your hardware meets the minimum hardware requirements, including the memory, free disk space, and video requirements. When the Windows NT or Windows 2000 Setup routines detect insufficient resources (that is, processor, memory, or disk space), it either informs you that an error has occurred and halts or it just hangs up and refuses to continue the install.

Establish the File System Type - During the installation process, you must decide which file system you are going to use. If you are going to dual-boot to Windows 98, and have a drive that is larger than 2 GB, you must choose FAT32. Choosing NTFS for a dual boot system renders the NTFS partition unavailable when you boot to Windows 98. FAT16 does not support drives larger than 2 GB. You can upgrade from FAT16 to FAT32 or from FAT32 to NTFS; however, you can never revert to the older file system after you have converted it. You should also be aware that Windows NT does not support FAT32 partitions. Therefore, Windows NT 4.0 or earlier cannot be used on a Windows 9x drive. Consider using the lowest common file system during installation and upgrade later.

Installation process reboots - If you discover after the initial installation of Windows 2000, and the subsequent rebooting of the system to finish the installation, that the installation program seems to start over again, check the CD-ROM drive for the installation disc. Leaving the bootable CD-ROM in the CD player normally causes this condition because the BIOS settings instruct the computer to check for a bootable CD-ROM before looking on the hard drive for an operating system. To correct this problem, remove the Windows 2000 CD from the player, or change the System Setup configuration to not check the CD player during boot up.

WINNT32 will not run from the command prompt - The WINNT32.EXE program is designed to run under a 32-bit operating system and will not run from the command line. It is used to initiate upgrades from Windows 9x or Windows NT to Windows 2000. From a 16-bit operating system, such as DOS or Windows 95a, you must run the WINNT.EXE program from the command line to initiate the installation of Windows 2000.

In most cases, a failure during the Windows 2000 setup process produces an unusable system. When this occurs, you usually must reformat the disc and reinstall the system files from the Windows 2000 Setup (boot) disks.

Upgrade Problems

You will encounter many of the same problems performing an operating system upgrade that you do when performing a clean install. To review, these problems are normally related to the following:

- Insufficient hard drive or partition sizes
- Memory speed mismatches
- Insufficient memory problems
- Incompatible device drivers

In addition to these basic installation problems, upgrade operations can encounter problems created by version incompatibilities. New versions of operating systems are typically produced in two styles: full versions and upgrade versions. In some cases, you cannot use a full version of the operating system to upgrade an existing operating system. Doing so will produce an Incompatible Version error message telling you that you cannot use this version to upgrade. You must either obtain an upgrade version of the operating system, or partition the drive and perform a new installation (losing your existing data).

You also must have the appropriate version of the upgrade for the existing operating system. (That is, Windows 98SE comes in two versions—one upgrades both Windows 95 and Windows 98, whereas the other version upgrades only Windows 98.)

TEST TIP

Know how to display the current version of Windows information for a system.

In order to determine the current version of a Windows operating system running on a computer, alternate-click on the My Computer icon, select the properties option from the pop-up menu and select the General tab of the System Properties window.

TROUBLESHOOTING STARTUP PROBLEMS

Fortunately, only a few problems can occur during the startup process of a disk-based computer. These problems include the following:

- hardware problems
- configuration problems
- bootup (or OS-startup) problems

All three of these problem types can result in startup failures. Some prevent any activity from appearing in the system, others produce symptoms that can be tracked to a cause, and yet others produce error messages that can be tracked to a source.

As indicated in Chapter 11, an interesting troubleshooting point occurs at the single beep in the boot-up process of most computers. If the system produces an error message, or a beep-coded error signal before the beep, the problem is hardware related.

On the other hand, if the error message or beep code is produced after the single beep occurs, the problem is likely to be associated with starting up the operating system. At this point, the problem becomes an operating system startup problem.

When dealing with a disk operating system, the following four things can prove very useful to help you isolate the cause of startup problems:

- Error messages and beep codes
- Clean boot disks (Emergency Start Disks)
- Single-step startup procedures
- System log files

The following Hands-On Activity identifies the preliminary ways to troubleshoot startup problems.

Hands-On Activity

Troubleshooting Startup Problems

1. Try to reboot the system.
2. Check system log files if available to determine where the process was interrupted.
3. Perform a clean boot with minimal configuration settings to remove nonessential elements from the process.
4. Perform a single-step boot up to isolate any driver problems that are preventing boot up from taking place.

Error Codes and Startup Messages

Error messages that occur during the boot-up process indicate that a problem exists that must be sorted out before the system can boot up and operate correctly.

Emergency Start disk

If the system will not boot up correctly, you need to boot the system to a minimum configuration and establish a point to begin troubleshooting the problem. This startup method enables you to bypass any unnecessary configuration and normally involves using a clean boot disk or the **Emergency Start disk** to start the system.

If the system boots up from the minimal condition, the problem exists in the bypassed files. Restart the system and select a startup mode that single-steps through the configuration and startup file sequence.

The **single-step startup procedure** enables you to isolate the problem command. If the system crashes while trying to execute a particular command, restart the boot-up process and skip the offending command. Repeat the process until the system reaches boot up. Track all offending commands so that you can correct them individually. Check the syntax (spelling, punctuation, and usage) of any offending lines.

single-step startup procedure

When the system will boot to the clean boot disk, but will not boot up to the hard drive, and has no configuration or startup file errors, a problem exists in the operating system's boot files. These errors typically return some type of Bad or Missing Command Interpreter message, or a **Disk Boot Failure** message. Basically, three conditions produce these types of error messages:

Disk Boot Failure

- The Master Boot Record or Command interpreter file cannot be found on the hard drive, and no bootable disk is present in the A: drive.
- The Master Boot Record or operating system's Command interpreter file is not located in the partition's root directory. This message is likely when installing a new hard drive or a new operating system version.
- The user has inadvertently erased the Master Boot Record or operating system Command interpreter file from the hard drive, possibly during the process of establishing a dual-boot disk or when setting up a multiple operating system environment.

You can repair a Missing Command Interpreter error by restoring the boot record and operating system files to the hard disk. To do so, you normally copy or extract the files from the clean boot disk to the hard drive. Similarly, if the boot disk contains a copy of the FDISK command, you can use the FDISK /MBR command to restore the hard drive's Master Boot Record, along with its partition information.

Windows 9x Startup Problems

Windows 9x offers many improved features over previous operating systems. However, it can suffer many of the same problems as any other operating system. To overcome some of the typical system problems, Windows 9x includes several built-in troubleshooting tools. These tools include several **Safe-Mode startup options**, a trio of **system log files**, and an extensive **interactive troubleshooting Help file** system.

Safe-Mode startup options

system log files

interactive troubleshooting Help file

As with previous operating systems, you can use three important tools when a Windows 9x system is having startup problems: the Emergency Start (clean boot) disk, Safe modes, and the step-by-step startup sequence. With Windows 9x, the clean boot disk is referred to as an Emergency Start disk. To access the Safe modes and the single-step with confirmation startup process, press the Shift and F8 function keys simultaneously when the Starting Windows 9x message appears onscreen.

The special function keys available during the Windows 9x startup are:

TEST TIP

Memorize the shortcut keys used to skip startup sections and to single-step through the boot-up process.

- F5 – Safe Mode
- F6 – Safe mode with Network Support
- F8 – Step-by-Step Confirmation mode
- Shift+F5 – Safe mode Command Prompt Only

Typical Windows 9x startup error messages include the following:

- HIMEM.SYS not loaded.
- Unable to initialize display adapter.
- Device referenced in WIN.INI could not be found.
- Bad or missing COMMAND.COM.
- Swap file corrupt.
- Damaged or missing core files.
- Device referenced in SYSTEM.INI could not be found.

These and other Windows 9x-related startup messages indicate the presence of problems that must be corrected before the system can boot up and run correctly.

The generic process for isolating the cause of a Windows 9x startup problem is as follows:

1. Use the Emergency Start disk to gain access to the system and the hard drive.
2. If necessary, repair the system files and command interpreter files as described earlier in this chapter.
3. Attempt to boot up into Safe mode to see if the problem is driver-related.
4. Reboot the system into the step-by-step confirmation startup mode to isolate configuration and driver problems. Continue single stepping through the startup process until all offending steps have been identified and corrected.
5. Review the Windows 9x log files for problem steps.

Be aware that the MSDOS.SYS file in Windows 9x is used to provide startup options, load some drivers, and to establish paths for certain system files. You should check these entries if Windows 9x does not start properly.

In the case of the HIMEM.SYS error, use the System Editor to check the syntax and correctness of the entry in the CONFIG.SYS file if present. With Windows 9x, the HIMEM.SYS statement must be present and correct for the operating system to run. Also check the HIMEM.SYS file to make sure it is the correct version and in the correct location. In the case of a Windows 9x upgrade, as many as three versions of HIMEM.SYS may be present in the system.

The "Unable to Initialize Display Adapter" error message is indicative of errors that occur during the hardware-detection phase of the Windows 9x PnP boot-up routine. These errors normally occur either because the Windows 9x PnP function cannot detect the hardware component, or because it cannot reconcile the adapter's needs to the available system resources. However, do not assume that PnP is in effect and running just because Windows 9x is running. The system's BIOS and the peripheral device also must be PnP compliant for the autodetection function to work.

You should be able to sort-out problems that occur during the detection phase by starting the system in step-by-step confirmation mode (pressing F8 during the boot up) and then single-step through the driver loading process to sort out the display driver/hardware problem. You must use the Control Panel's Add New Hardware Wizard to install device drivers when the PnP detection function does not work.

Key Windows 9x files prevent the system from starting up if they become corrupted. These files include those associated with the Master Boot Record, the boot sector, the FATs, and the Windows Core files. Errors that occur between the single beep that marks the end of the POST and the appearance of the Starting Windows 9x message on the screen, are associated with the boot sector. Problems that show up between the Starting Windows message and the appearance of the Desktop involve the Windows core files. In any event, if disk corruption is detected, you must rebuild the corrupted file structures.

When IO.SYS is corrupted in Windows 9x, the system hangs up before the Starting Windows message appears and produces a System Disk Invalid error message onscreen. If the MSDOS.SYS file is missing or corrupted, Windows displays a blue screen with an Invalid VxD Dynamic Link message and fails to start up.

Other MSDOS.SYS-related problems relate to the Registry, the **Extended Memory Manager (XMS)**, and the **Installable File System Manager (IFSMGR)**. These problems produce errors that appear during startup and are caused by syntax errors in the [Paths] section of the file.

Extended Memory Manager (XMS)

Installable File System Manager (IFSMGR)

Likewise, the COMMAND.COM problem produces an error message onscreen and fails to start up Windows. You can repair the missing COMMAND.COM error by using the DOS *COPY* and *SYS* commands, as described in Chapter 11. These commands copy the COMMAND.COM and system files from the clean boot disk to the hard drive. Similarly, if the boot disk contains a copy of the FDISK command, you can use the FDISK/MBR command to restore the hard drive's Master Boot Record, along with its partition information.

As mentioned in Chapter 11, the following conditions produce a Bad or Missing COMMAND.COM error message:

- The COMMAND.COM file cannot be found on the hard drive, and no bootable disk is present in the A: drive.

- The COMMAND.COM file is not located in the hard drive's root directory. This message is likely when installing a new hard drive or a new DOS version.

- The user inadvertently erases the COMMAND.COM file from the hard drive.

Attribute command

To correct these problems, start the system using the emergency start disk. At the command prompt, type **SYS C:** to copy the IO.SYS, MSDOS.SYS, and COMMAND.COM files onto the hard disk. You can use the DOS **Attribute command** to verify that the hidden system files have been successfully copied to the disk (that is, Attrib -r -s -h c:\IO.SYS and Attrib –r –s –h C:\MSDOS.SYS to make them visible and to remove their read-only and system status).To locate and correct the "Missing Core file..." problem cited earlier, check for corrupted files on the disk drive. To accomplish this, start the system in Safe mode using the Command Prompt Only option. When the command prompt appears, move to the Windows Command directory and run the ScanDisk utility. If ScanDisk detects corrupted files it will be necessary to replace them. The ScanDisk utility can locate and fix several types of problems on the hard drive. These problems include corrupted FATs, long filenames, lost clusters and cross-linked files, tree structure problems, and bad sectors on the drive.

The COMMAND.COM file can also be restored from the command line, or through the Windows Explorer. To restore the COMMAND.COM file from the command line, start the system from the startup disk and use the *Copy* command to transfer the file manually.

The COMMAND.COM file can also be dragged from the startup disk to the root directory of the hard drive using the Windows 9x My Computer or Windows Explorer functions. As with the manual copy procedure, the COMMAND.COM file's read-only, system, and hidden attributes must be removed so that it can be manipulated within the system.

To locate and correct the "Missing Core File" problem cited earlier, check for corrupted files on the disk drive. To accomplish this, start the system in safe mode using the Command Prompt Only option. When the command prompt appears, move to the Windows Command directory and run the *ScanDisk* utility. If ScanDisk detects corrupted files, you must replace them. The ScanDisk utility can locate and fix several types of problems on the hard drive. These problems include corrupted FATs, long filenames, lost clusters, cross-linked files, tree structure problems, and bad sectors on the drive.

Check the Versions—The ScanDisk version used with a Windows 9x system must be the one specifically designed for that operating system (i.e., A Windows 95 ScanDisk version should not be used on a Windows 98 system). Using other versions may not work correctly and could result in data loss. When using ScanDisk to isolate startup problems, the Windows 9x version used should be the version that is located on the particular computer's Emergency Start disk and it should be the version that runs from the command prompt.

You can use the Windows 9x Setup function to verify or repair damaged Windows operating system files. To accomplish this, run the Setup utility and select the Verify option when presented by the Setup procedure. You then can repair damaged system files without running a complete reinstall operation.

Cabinet (CAB)

It is also possible to extract Windows 9x components from the installation disk using the Extract command. Windows 9x stores its files in a compressed **Cabinet** (**CAB**) format on the distribution CD. If corrupted Windows 9x files are found in the system, it is not possible to just copy new ones onto the drive from the CD. Instead, you must run Setup using the distribution CD and the Validate/Restore option.

EXTRACT.EXE

You also can run the **EXTRACT.EXE** command from the Windows Command directory to extract selected compressed files from the CD. The preferable method is the Setup option. In most cases, however, it is simpler to reinstall Windows than to search for individual files and structures.

The Windows 9x swap file is controlled through the System icon in the Control Panel. From this point, enter the Performance page and click its Virtual Memory button. Typically, the *Let Windows Manage Virtual Memory* option should be selected. If the system locks up and does not start, the swap file may have become corrupted, or the Virtual Memory setting may have been changed to Disabled. In either case, you must reinstall Windows 9x to correct the problem.

TEST TIP

Know the effects of checking the Disable Virtual Memory setting in Windows 9x.

The device or driver files referenced in the *missing INI files* error messages should be checked to make certain that they have been properly identified, and that their location and path are correct. If they are not, use the System Editor to make the necessary changes by installing the specified device driver in the designated INI file. If the path and syntax is correct for the indicated files, you should reload them from the Emergency Startup disk to correct the offending lines.

If a DOS-based application is causing the system to stall during Windows 9x startup, you should reboot the computer. When the Starting Windows 9x message appears onscreen, press the F8 key to bring up the Startup menu. Select the Restart in MS-DOS mode option from the list. From this point, you must edit the AUTOEXEC.BAT and CONFIG.SYS files to disable selected lines. In the AUTOEXEC.BAT file, place Remark (Rem) statements at the beginning of the following lines:

- \Windows\command
- \call c:\windows\command***
- \windows\win.com/wx

Also REM the dos=single line in the CONFIG.SYS file.

After making these corrections, shut the system down and restart it. The system should boot up and run correctly with these lines removed.

Errors in the CONFIG.SYS and AUTOEXEC.BAT files will produce the *Error in CONFIG.SYS Line XX* or *Error in AUTOEXEC.BAT Line XX* messages described in the A+ objectives. The line specified by the XX in the error message contains a syntax (spelling, punctuation, or usage) error that prevents it from running. Syntax errors can also produce an *Unrecognized command in CONFIG.SYS* message. These errors can also be caused by missing, or corrupted files specified in the CONFIG.SYS or AUTOEXEC.BAT files. To correct these errors, correct the line in the file, reload the indicated file and restart the computer.

password

One of the final problems that could affect startup in Windows 9x is the **password**. Normally, when a user forgets his local Windows logon password, he can click the Cancel option and gain access to most of the local resources. However, the user will not be able to see any network resources, or access resources restricted through the System Policy setting. The system declares network resources "Unavailable" to the user.

The most direct way to get around a local logon password is to access the local machine and delete the *username.PWL* file in the C:\Windows directory. You could also create a new user account in Windows 9x to establish another password.

To get around a forgotten network password, remove the Client for Microsoft Networks protocol from the Network Components window and then reinstall it. When you restart the system, it asks you to establish a new user who will have a new password.

Creating a Windows 95 Emergency Start Disk

Because Windows 95 does not startup through DOS, it will be very difficult to gain access to the system if Windows becomes disabled. Therefore, it is helpful to have an emergency start disk to troubleshoot Windows 95–related problems. In the event that the Windows program becomes nonfunctional, it will be necessary to use the start disk to gain access to the system so that you can restore it to proper operation.

The Windows 95 Startup disk will only boot the system up to the command prompt. From this point you will need to be familiar with command line operations so that you can employ tools and utilities that will get the system up and running again.

During the Windows setup operation, the software provides an option for creating an emergency startup disk. This option should be used for every Windows 95 installation. Setup copies the operating system files to the disk along with utilities for troubleshooting startup problems. The disk can then be used to boot up the system in safe mode and display a DOS command-line prompt. The emergency start disk can also be used to replace lost or damaged system files on the hard disk.

TEST TIP

Be aware of the two methods of creating Emergency Start disks in Windows 9x and know when these disks should be employed.

An Emergency Start disk can also be created through the Control Panel's Add/Remove Programs icon. This option is normally used to create a new startup disk after new hardware has been installed, or when configuration information has been changed.

In addition to creating a startup floppy disk, Windows 95 transfers a number of diagnostic files to the disk, including the following:

TEST TIP

Know which files should be present on a Windows Emergency Start disk.

- IO.SYS
- MSDOS.SYS
- COMMAND.COM
- SYS.COM
- FDISK.EXE
- FORMAT.COM
- EDIT.COM
- REGEDIT.EXE
- ATTRIB.EXE
- SCANDISK.EXE AND .INI

These utilities are particularly helpful in getting a Windows 95 machine operational again. This disk provides one of the few tools for the technician to service a down machine with this operating system. The steps involved in creating the boot disk are as follows:

Hands-On Activity

Create the Emergency Startup disk

1. Click the Start button
2. Move to Settings option in the Start menu
3. Select the Control Panel from the list
4. Double-click on the Add/Remove Programs icon
5. Select the Startup Disk tab
6. Click the Create Disk button
7. Place the Windows 95 CD in the CD-ROM drive when prompted
8. Follow the menu items as directed
9. Place a blank diskette in drive A: when prompted
10. Remove the Windows 95 CD from the drive when the operation is complete

Next, you can examine the startup disk by following these steps.

Examining the Startup disk

1. Close the Control Panel window
2. Select the Windows Explorer option from the Start/Programs menu
3. Click the 3.5" Floppy A: option from the list in the All Folders window.
   Since many of these files are special system files, you will need to remove their hidden attributes to see them.
4. Label the disk as an Emergency Startup Disk

If you want to examine the CONFIG.SYS file, do the following:

Examining the new CONFIG.SYS file on the boot disk

1. Select the Notepad utility in the Start/Programs/Accessories menu
2. Click the File and Open options in the Notepad window
3. Select the 3.5" Floppy (A:) option in the Look in window
4. Select the All Files (*.*) option from the Files of Type window
5. Double-click on the CONFIG.SYS entry in the window

Several files can also come in handy when on the startup disk. Do the following steps to add them:

Adding helpful files to the Start disk

1. Close the Notepad utility
2. Select the Windows Explorer option from the Start/Programs menu
3. Click the File and Open options in the Notepad window
4. Select the 3.5" Floppy (A:) option in the Look in window
5. Select the Folder option from the File/New menu
6. Type your three initials in the box for the new subdirectory
7. Select the (C:) option in the Look in window
8. Locate the AUTOEXEC.BAT file in the "Contents of C:\" window
9. Click, hold, and drag the file to the 3.5" Floppy (A:) option on the Look in window and release
10. Repeat Step 9 for the SYSTEM.DAT, CONFIG.SYS, WIN.INI, and SYSTEM.INI files
11. Exit the Windows Explorer

If you want to examine the AUTOEXEC.BAT file, do the following:

Examining the New AUTOEXEC.BAT File on the boot disk

1. Select the Notepad utility in the Start/Programs/Accessories menu
2. Click the File and Open options in the Notepad window
3. Select the 3-1/2" Floppy (A:) option in the Look in window
4. Select the All Files (*.*) option from the Files of Type window
5. Double-click on the AUTOEXEC.BAT entry in the window

Because the system settings are basically contained in the two Registry files SYSTEM.DAT and USER.DAT, it is not uncommon to back them up on the Emergency Start disk. This operation is performed with the RegEdit utility's Export function. The Export function can be used to save a selected branch or the entire Registry as a REG text file.

The steps for exporting the Registry are as follows:

Hands-On Activity

Exporting the Registry

1. Start the RegEdit function.
2. Select the Run option from the Start menu.
3. Type **REGEDIT** in the Filename dialog box and click OK.
4. From the RegEdit toolbar, select the Registry menu.
5. Choose the Export Registry file option from the drop-down menu.
6. In the Export window, click the All button.
7. Type the filename **REGBACK** in the Filename window.
8. Select the 3.5 Floppy (A:) entry from the Save In window.
9. Click the Save button
10. Check the contents of the A: drive to make certain that the REGBACK.REG file is there

The Registry backup file can be used to restore the Registry to the system after a crash. Once again, this involves using the RegEdit Import function to restore the Registry for use. The RegEdit Import function can be performed using the Windows-based version, or it can be conducted from the command line using the real-mode version located on the emergency start disk. For the purposes of this text, this discussion focuses on the version needed in a troubleshooting-and-repair scenario.

To restore the Registry, follow these steps:

Using the Start Disk to Restore the Registry

1. Restart the system.
2. Place the emergency start disk in the A: drive.
3. Turn the computer on.
4. Import the original Registry into Windows 95 to return it to its original condition.
5. Place the disk containing the REGBACK.REG file in the floppy drive.
6. From the RegEdit toolbar, select the Registry menu.
7. At the A:\> prompt, type **REGEDIT /C REGBACK**.
8. Wait for the file to be imported.
9. Remove the floppy disk from the A: drive.
10. Turn the system off and then back on again.

The system should be restored to the same operating parameters that it had when the Registry backup file was created.

Registry Restoration Caveat—The REGEDIT /C command should not be used except for cases where the Registry is heavily corrupted. It must have a complete image of the Registry to be used in this manner. Also realize that Windows 9x backs up the Registry files each time it is started. There should be several iterations of the Registry files that could be renamed and copied over the existing Registry files to repair them.

The Windows 95 Emergency Start disk should be stored in a convenient place and clearly labeled so that it is easy to find when you need it.

The Windows 98 Emergency Start Disk

Emergency Start Disk

As with any other operating system, one of the most important tools to have on hand is the **Emergency Start Disk**. In the event that the system software becomes corrupt, or that an option hangs Windows up and doesn't let it restart, the Windows 98 Emergency Start disk will provide access to the system, and allow repair steps to be taken.

The Emergency Start disk is basically a DOS disk, with key utilities included, to assist in restarting the system when Windows 98 doesn't boot. This disk can be created during the installation process, or by accessing the Startup disk tab in the Control Panel's Add/Remove Programs window. From this point, creating the emergency disk is simply a matter of inserting a blank disk in the floppy drive and clicking on the Create Disk button. As always, store the Start disk in an obvious, but safe location.

TEST TIP

Know where to make Emergency Start Disks in Windows 9x.

In addition to the necessary system files required to start the system in a minimal, real-mode condition, the Windows 98 Startup disk provides a number of diagnostic programs, and a pair of real-mode CD-ROM drivers, to allow the CD-ROM drive to operate from Safe Mode. One driver is a generic ATAPI driver called OAKCDROM.SYS. Of course this driver is incompatible with SCSI drives. However, the Startup disk does include real-mode SCSI CD-ROM support. Along with these drivers, the disk provides a RAMDrive and a new Extract command (EXTRACT.EXE). The Extract command is used to pull necessary files from the cabinet (.CAB) files on the Windows 98 CD-ROM.

If the CD-ROM drive uses a sound card for its interface, it will be necessary to include a copy of the correct real-mode driver on the startup disk. It will also be necessary to edit the Startup disk's CONFIG.SYS file to load the driver from the disk.

TEST TIP

Know which files should be present on an Emergency Start disk.

You should be aware that Windows 98 will not run if the system is started with an Emergency Start disk from another Windows version. The machine can be started on the older versions of the Start disk, and some repair operations can be carried out, but the new version will not be able to be started, and some items could become corrupted with the older operating system.

Windows 9x Startup Modes

The Windows 9x Startup menu (not to be confused with the desktop's Start menu), depicted in Figure 12-2, can be obtained on a nonstarting system by holding down the F8 function key when the Starting Windows 9x is displaying onscreen. The menu offers several startup options including Normal, Logged, Safe, Step-by-Step Confirmation, and DOS Modes. These startup modes play an important role in getting the Windows 9x operating system up and running when to fails to start.

TEST TIP

Be aware that the BOOTLOG.TXT file is not normally created during startup. It has to be initiated with the logged mode.

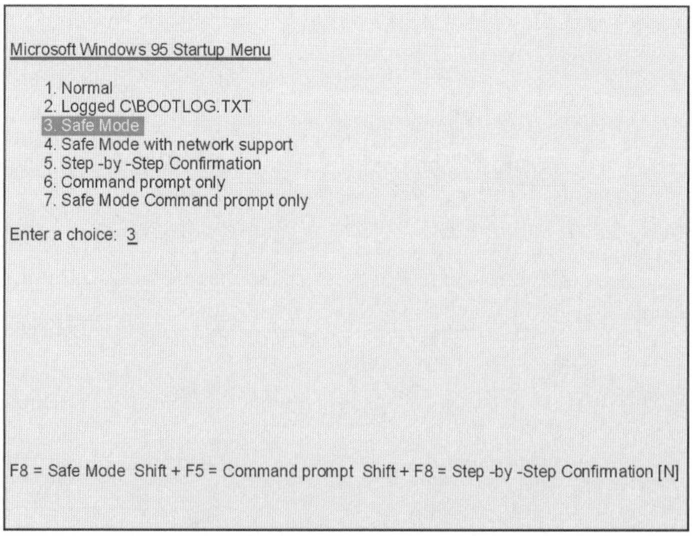

Figure 12-2: The Windows 9x Startup Menu

Logged mode

In Normal mode, the system just tries to restart as it normally would, loading all of its normal startup and Registry files. The **Logged mode** option also attempts to start the system in Normal mode, but keeps an error log file that contains the steps performed and outcome. You can read this text file (BOOTLOG.TXT) with any text editor, or you can print it out on a working system.

Safe Mode

If Windows determines that a problem prevents the system from starting has occurred, or if it senses that the Registry is corrupt, it automatically attempts to restart the system in **Safe Mode**. This mode bypasses several startup files to provide access to the system's configuration settings. In particular, any existing CONFIG.SYS and AUTOEXEC.BAT files are bypassed, along with the Windows 9x Registry and the [Boot] and [386enh] sections of the SYSTEM.INI file. The contents of these files are employed to retain compatibility with older hardware and applications.

Safe Mode

> **What's active in Safe Mode?**—In Safe Mode, the minimal device drivers (keyboard, mouse, and standard-mode VGA drivers) are active to start the system. However, the CD-ROM drive will not be active in Safe mode.

> **TEST TIP**
>
> Know what files are loaded into the system when it is started in Safe mode.

You also can access Safe Mode by pressing the F5 function key while the Starting Windows 9x message is displaying onscreen. Windows 9x also reverts to this mode if an application requests it.

Unless modified, the Safe Mode screen appears as depicted in Figure 12-3. Active functions appear onscreen along with the "Safe-mode" notice in each corner. However, there is no Taskbar in Safe Mode.

Windows 9x has four Safe Mode startup options: Safe Mode, Safe Mode with Network Support, Safe Mode Command Prompt Only, and Safe Mode Without Compression. Each option is customized for specific situations and disables selected portions of the system to prevent them from interfering with the startup process.

> **NOTE**
>
> Windows 98 does not officially support Safe Mode with Network Support. However, it can be accessed by pressing the F6 function key during bootup.

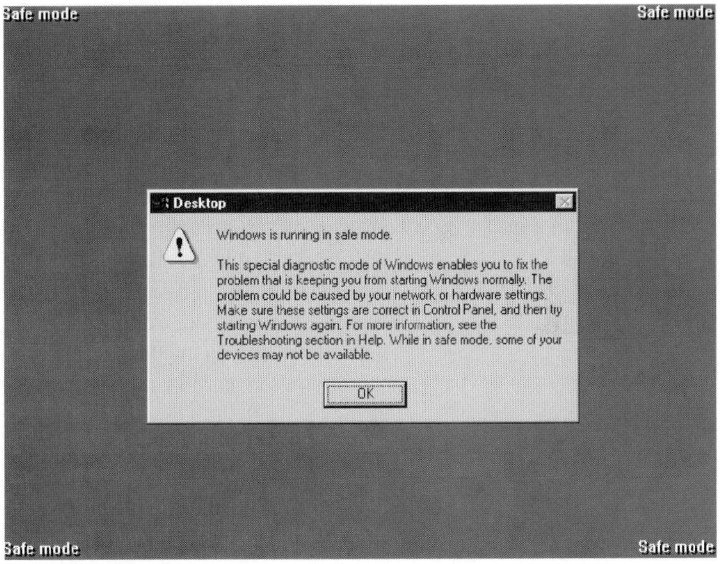

Figure 12-3: The Safe Mode Startup Screen

The standard Safe Mode startup is used when the system:

- Will not start after the Starting Windows9x message appears onscreen
- Stalls repeatedly or for long periods of time
- Cannot print to a local printer after a complete troubleshooting sequence
- Has video display problems
- Slows down noticeably, or does not work correctly

In standard Safe Mode startup, Windows bypasses certain startup and configuration files and loads a standard set of device drivers to start the system. The bypassed files include the following:

- The Registry
- The CONFIG.SYS and AUTOEXEC.BAT files
- The [boot] and [386enh] sections of the SYSTEM.INI file

The only device drivers loaded in Safe Mode are the mouse driver, the standard keyboard driver, and the standard VGA driver. This should enable enough of the Windows structure to operate so that the offending portions can be isolated and repaired using step-by-step checking procedures.

Step-by-Step Confirmation

The **Step-by-Step Confirmation** option enables you to check each line of the startup procedure individually. In doing so, the Step-by-Step option enables you to verify which drivers are being loaded, temporarily disable any offending drivers, and check other startup errors that may be indicated through error messages. You should use this option when the system

This option is obtained by pressing the F8 function key at the Startup Menu and should be employed when the system:

- Fails while loading the startup files
- Needs to load real-mode drivers
- Displays a Registry Failure error message

As the startup process moves forward, the system asks whether each line is correct. Press the ENTER key to confirm the line, or press the Esc key to skip a line. Keep track of any skipped lines so that you can check them individually. If the system crashes after a line has been confirmed, mark it as a problem and restart the system using the Step-by-Step option. Bypass the offending line on the next attempt to reach boot up. Record all lines that prevent the boot-up process and troubleshoot them one by one.

The sequence of the Step-by-Step prompts is as follows:

Hands-On Activity

1. Load the DoubleSpace/DriveSpace driver (if present).
2. Process the Registry.
3. Create a Startup log file.
4. Process the CONFIG.SYS file.
5. Process the AUTOEXEC.BAT file.
6. Run WIN.COM to start Windows 9x.
7. Load all Windows drivers.

As the list illustrates, the Step-by-Step option provides an opportunity to create a startup log file called BOOTLOG.TXT. This file help you isolate startup problems—such as real-mode, 16-bit adapter drivers that refuse to load and prevent the system from booting. You can check the contents of the log file for offending entries that stop the system. More information is provided concerning the BOOTLOG.TXT file later in this chapter.

Responses for the CONFIG.SYS and AUTOEXEC.BAT prompts are Y and N for individual lines. You can use the Tab key to accept the entire file. An N answer to the Load All Windows Drivers prompt results in Windows operating in Safe Mode. Otherwise, answering Y to all the prompts starts Windows 9x as normal, with the exception that the Windows logo does not appear at startup.

Safe Mode with Network Support

The **Safe Mode with Network Support** option typically bypasses the CONFIG.SYS and AUTOEXEC.BAT files and loads the COMMAND.COM processor. It then loads HIMEM.SYS and IFSHLP.SYS, followed by any drive-compression drivers, the Windows 9x files Core and Registry files, and the basic network driver files.

This mode is used in networked environments when the system:

- Stops responding when a remote network is accessed
- Cannot print to a remote printer
- Stalls during startup and cannot be started using a normal Safe Mode startup

Because this mode loads the Windows Registry, it cannot be used if the Registry has been corrupted. If the system will load Windows in standard Safe Mode, but not with the Network Support option, check the network configuration settings.

Also be aware that Windows 9x uses the MSDOS.SYS file to establish paths for some options. In the case of real-mode networking, the [Paths] entry, WINDIR=, must be defined for the NETSTART.BAT file used to start the network. If this file does not run, Windows will fail to load.

DOS Modes

Other startup options may also be available from the menu depending on the configuration of the system. Some options start the system and bring it to a DOS command-line prompt.

Command Prompt Only mode

Selecting the **Command Prompt Only mode** causes the system to boot up to the command line, using the startup files and the Registry. If this option will not start the system, reboot the computer and select the Safe Mode Command Prompt Only option from the Startup menu. This option performs the same function as pressing the SHIFT and F5 keys simultaneously (SHIFT+F5) during the boot-up process. The system will start in safe mode with minimal drivers (while not executing any of the startup files) and will produce the DOS command-line prompt.

Safe Mode Command Prompt Only

The **Safe Mode Command Prompt Only** option loads just two items — the command interpreter (COMMAND.COM in Windows 9x and CMD.EXE in Windows NT/2000) and if present, the disk-compression utility files (DriveSpace or DoubleSpace). It does not load any of the Windows 9x files, HIMEM.SYS, or IFSHLP.SYS. This option should be chosen when the system fails to start in safe mode. You can enter this mode directly during the startup process by pressing the SHIFT and F5 keys simultaneously (SHIFT+F5) when the Starting Windows9x message is onscreen. You also can use it to:

- Employ command line switches, such as WIN d/x
- Employ command line tools, such as DOS editors
- Avoid loading HIMEM.SYS or IFSHLP.SYS

Safe Mode without Compression

The **Safe Mode without Compression** option only appears in systems that are using compressed drives. In operation, it is similar to the Command Prompt Only option with the exception that no compression drivers are loaded. The following list provides reasons for selecting this option.

- The system stops responding when a compressed drive is accessed.
- A Corrupt CVF (Compressed Volume File) error displays during startup.
- When Safe Mode and Safe Mode Command Prompt Only options fail to start the system.

If the BootMulti= option was set to 1 during the Windows 9x setup, the menu will contain an option to Start Using the Previous Version of MS-DOS. As its name indicates, this option starts the system with the version of DOS that was on the hard drive before Windows 9x was installed. Dual-booting must be enabled in the MSDOS.SYS file for this option to function.

WIN Switches

When Windows 9x refuses to start up, a number of options are available for starting it from the command line. Starting Windows using a /D switch is often helpful in isolating possible areas of the operating system as problem sources (that is, WIN /D). You can modify the /D switch to start Windows in a number of different configurations:

- Using an /D:F switch disables 32-bit disk access.
- The /D:M and /D:N switches start Windows in Safe Mode, or Safe with Networking Mode.
- An /D:S switch inhibits Windows from using address space between F0000h and FFFFFh.
- The /D:V switch prevents Windows from controlling disk transfers. Instead, HDD interrupt requests are handled by the BIOS.
- The /D:X switch prevents Windows from using the area of memory between A000h and FFFFh.

Other switches can be used with the WIN command. The WIN /B switch causes Windows to start in logged mode and to produce a BOOTLOG.TXT file during startup. This option enables you to determine whether specific device drivers are stalling the system. Logged mode can also be selected by pressing the F8 key while the Starting Windows 9x message is onscreen. After selecting the Logged option, restart the system using the Safe Mode Command Prompt Only option. Then, use a text editor to examine the contents of the BOOTLOG.TXT file and determine which driver has failed to load.

Using a question mark as a switch with the WIN command (that is, WIN /?) shows a listing of all the switches associated with the command. You can use these switches to start Windows with various portions of the operating system disabled. If the system runs with a particular section disabled, at least some portion of the problem can be linked to that area.

Windows 9x Log Files

Windows 9x maintains four log files: BOOTLOG.TXT, SETUPLOG.TXT, DETLOG.TXT, and DETCRASH.LOG. These files maintain a log of different system operations and enable you to see what events occurred leading up to a failure. The TXT files can be read with Notepad, DOS Editor, or any other text editor.

Their filenames are indicative of the types of information they log. As described earlier, the BOOTUPLOG.TXT file tracks the events of the startup procedure. Likewise, SETUPLOG.TXT tracks the events of the setup process. The DETLOG.TXT file monitors the presence of detected hardware devices and identifies the parameters for them. This file just happens to be a very good description of the system's PnP operations.

TEST TIP

Know which log file is not generated during the Windows installation process.

BOOTLOG.TXT

BOOTLOG.TXT

The **BOOTLOG.TXT** file contains the sequence of events conducted during the startup of the system. The original BOOTLOG.TXT file is created during the Windows 9x setup process. You can update the file by pressing the F8 key during Startup, or by starting Windows 9x with a WIN /b switch. It is not updated automatically each time the system is started. The log information is recorded in five basic sections.

The log information is recorded in five basic sections.

1. Loading real-mode drivers

This section records a two-part loading report during the bootup process. In the example section that follows, the system successfully loads the HIMEM.SYS and EMM386.EXE memory managers. Afterward, other Real Mode Drivers are loaded. In the case of an unsuccessful load operation, the report returns a LoadFailed= entry.

```
[000E3FDC] Loading Device = C:\WINDOWS\HIMEM.SYS
[000E3FE0] LoadSuccess    = C:\WINDOWS\HIMEM.SYS
[000E3FE0] Loading Device = C:\WINDOWS\EMM386.EXE
[000E3FEC] LoadSuccess    = C:\WINDOWS\EMM386.EXE
*
*
```

2. Loading VxDs

In the second section, the system loads the VxD drivers. The following list includes a sample of various VxDs that have been loaded. The asterisks in the sample listing are included to indicate sections of omitted lines. This is done to shorten the length of the file for illustration purposes.

```
*
[000E41F3] Loading Vxd = int13
[000E41F3] LoadSuccess = int13
[000E41F3] Loading Vxd = vmouse|
[000E41F4] LoadSuccess = vmouse
[000E41F6] Loading Vxd = msmouse.vxd
[000E41F9] LoadSuccess = msmouse.vxd
[000E41F9] Loading Vxd = vshare
[000E41F9] LoadFailed  = vshare
*
```

3. Initialization of Critical VxDs

Check this section to verify that system-critical VxDs have been initialized.

```
[000E420A] SYSCRITINIT  = VMM
[000E420A] SYSCRITINITSUCCESS  = VMM
[000E420A] SYSCRITINIT  = VCACHE
[000E420A] SYSCRITINITSUCCESS  = VCACHE
*
*
```

4. Device Initialization of VxDs

This section of the log shows the VxDs that have been successfully initialized. In each cycle, the system attempts to initialize a VxD and then reports its success or failure.

```
[000E420D] DEVICEINIT  = VMM
[000E420D] DEVICEINITSUCCESS  = VMM
*
[000E421F] Dynamic load device  isapnp.vxd
[000E4225] Dynamic init device  ISAPNP
[000E4226] Dynamic init success ISAPNP
[000E4226] Dynamic load success isapnp.vxd
*
*
```

The information in the above listing points out the dynamic loading and initialization of the PnP driver for the ISA bus.

5. Successful Initialization of VxDs

The entries in this section verify the successful completion of the initialization of the system's VxDs. A partial listing of these activities follows:

```
[000E4430] INITCOMPLETE = VMM
[000E4430] INITCOMPLETESUCCESS = VMM
[000E4430] INITCOMPLETE = VCACHE
[000E4430] INITCOMPLETESUCCESS = VCACHE
*
*
```

SETUPLOG.TXT

SETUPLOG.TXT

The **SETUPLOG.TXT** file holds setup information that was established during the installation process. The file is stored on the system's root directory and is used in Safe Recovery situations.

The log file exists in seven basic sections, as described in the following sample sections. Entries are added to the file as they occur in the setup process. Therefore, the file can be read to determine what action was being taken when a setup failure occurred.

```
[OptionalComponents]
"Accessories"=1
"Communications"=1
*
"Monitor"="(Unknown Monitor)"
"Mouse"="Standard Serial Mouse"
"Power"="No_APM"
"Locale"="L0409"
*
[Setup]
InstallType=1
Customise=0
Express=0
ChangeDir=1
Network=1
*
CleanBoot=0
Win31FileSystem=-8531
CopyFiles=1
*
[Started]
version=262144,950
OldLogFile
*
Display_InitDevice:Checking display driver. No PNP registry found.
Mouse_InitDevice:Checking mouse driver. No PNP registry found.
```

The text in the above sample section shows the system's response to not finding a PnP Registry entry for different devices.

```
[FileQueue]
CacheFile() C:\WINDOWS\win.ini returns=0
CacheFile() C:\WINDOWS\exchng32.ini returns=0
CacheFile() C:\WINDOWS\control.ini returns=0
CacheFile() C:\WINDOWS\qtw.ini returns=0
CacheFile() C:\WINDOWS\system.cb returns=0
SrcLdid:(11)skyeagle.cpl
CacheFile() C:\WINDOWS\msoffice.ini returns=0
*
[FileCopy]
VcpClose:About to close
VcpClose:Delete 1514
VcpClose:Rename 4
VcpClose:Copy 827
CAB-No volume name for LDID 2, local copy - path C:\WININST0.400
*
diskdrv.inf=17,,7915,20032
drvspace.bin=13,,7915,20032|
*
[Restart]
*
Resolve Conflict:C:\DBLSPACE.BIN ConflictType: 240
drvspace.bin=31,DBLSPACE.BIN,7915,20032
Resolve Conflict:C:\drvspace.bin ConflictType: 240
drvspace.bin=31,,7915,20032
drvspace.sys=13,dblspace.sys,7915,20032
*
*
```

The bold lines in the example demonstrate the capability of the PnP system to resolve conflicts between programs and devices. In this case, a conflict exists between a driver named DBLSPACE and another named DRVSPACE.

DETCRASH.LOG

DETLOG.TXT

This Detect Crash log file is created when the system crashes during the hardware detection portion of the startup procedure. It contains information about the detection module that was running when the crash occurred. This file is a binary file and cannot be read directly. However, a text version of the file, named **DETLOG.TXT**, is available under the root directory of the drive.

DETLOG.TXT

DETCRASH.LOG

The DETLOG.TXT file holds the text equivalent of the information in the **DETCRASH.LOG** file. This file can be read with a text editor to determine which hardware components have been detected by the system and what its parameters are. This printout is really a detailed explanation of the hardware-detection phase of the system's PnP operation.

The following section of a sample DETLOG.TXT file demonstrates the type of information logged in this file:

```
[System Detection: 11/07/97 - 12:05:11]
Parameters "", InfParams "", Flags=01004233
SDMVer=0400.950, WinVer=0700030a, Build=00.00.0, WinFlags=00000419
LogCrash: crash log not found or invalid
SetVar: CDROM_Any=
Checking for: Programmable Interrupt Controller
QueryIOMem: Caller=DETECTPIC, rcQuery=0
   IO=20-21,a0-a1
Detected: *PNP0000\0000 = [1] Programmable interrupt controller
   IO=20-21,a0-a1
   IRQ=2
Checking for: Direct Memory Access Controller
QueryIOMem: Caller=DETECTDMA, rcQuery=0
   IO=0-f,81-83,87-87,89-8b,8f-8f,c0-df
Detected: *PNP0200\0000 = [2] Direct memory access controller
   IO=0-f,81-83,87-87,89-8b,8f-8f,c0-df
   DMA=4
*
Checking for: Standard Floppy Controller
QueryIOMem: Caller=DETECTFLOPPY, rcQuery=0
   IO=3f2-3f5
QueryIOMem: Caller=DETECTFLOPPY, rcQuery=0
   IO=372-375
Detected: *PNP0700\0000 = [11] Standard Floppy Disk Controller
   IO=3f2-3f5
   IRQ=6
   DMA=2
Checking for: Serial Communication Port
QueryIOMem: Caller=DETECTCOM, rcQuery=0
   IO=3f8-3ff
GetCOMIRQ: IIR=1
Detected: *PNP0500\0000 = [12] Communications Port
   IO=3f8-3ff
   IRQ=4
SetVar: COMIRQ3f8=4,0
SetVar: COMIRQ2f8=3,0
Checking for: Serial Mouse
QueryIOMem: Caller=DETECTSERIALMOUSE, rcQuery=2
   IO=3f8-3ff
Serial mouse ID: M (004d)
Detected: *PNP0F0C\0000 = [14] Standard Serial Mouse
SetVar: COMIRQ3f8=4,0
*
```

Referring to the information in the sample file, it should be easy to see the type of information that is logged about the system. The detection routine cycles through a three-part process; first it identifies the activity it is about to perform (that is, Checking for: Serial Mouse), and then it queries the system at addresses normally allocated to that type of device (IO=3f8-3ff), and finally verifies that it was detected (or not). Some entries also include a listing of the IRQ and DMA resources allocated to the device. The sample list includes information about many of the system and I/O devices found in a typical PC system.

In each case, the PnP system inquires about particular system devices and logs the parameters of the device it detects. The sample also shows that, at least in this case, no crash log has been created. To use the file for crash-detection purposes, just check the last entry created in the log. To determine exactly where a problem has occurred, it may be necessary to compare this information to the listing in a file named DETLOG.OLD. This file is the old version of the DETLOG file that was renamed before the latest detection phase began.

Using the Windows 98 Startup Disk

If the system will not make it to the Startup menu, you must boot the system with the Startup disk and begin checking the operating system on the boot drive. When the system is booted from a Windows 98 Startup disk, a menu such as the following displays:

1. Start the computer with CD-ROM support.
2. Start the computer without CD-ROM support.
3. View the Help file.

If the CD-ROM support option is selected, the system will execute the portion of the CONFIG.SYS file that loads the CD-ROM driver, and will set up a 2 MB RAMdrive.

Use the Startup disk to boot the system and gain access to the operating system's files. After gaining access to the system, you can use the built-in troubleshooting aids on the Windows 9x Startup disk to isolate the cause of the problem.

Using Windows 98 System Tools on Startup Problems

In addition to the clean-boot, Safe mode, and log file functions previously described, the Windows 98 contains a wealth of other troubleshooting tools that you can use to isolate and correct problems.

MSCONFIG.EXE

If a startup problem disappears when the system is started using any of the safe modes, use the System Configuration utility (**MSCONFIG.EXE**) to isolate the conflicting items. Of course, you may need to enter this command from the command line.

Select the Diagnostic Startup option to interactively load device drivers and software options from the General tab screen. When the Startup menu appears, select the Step-by-Step option. Begin by starting the system with only the CONFIG.SYS and AUTOEXEC.BAT files disabled. If the system starts, move into those tabs and step through those files, one line at a time, using the Selective Startup option. The step-by-step process is used to systematically enable or disable items until all the problem items are identified. If an entry is marked with a Microsoft Windows logo, it is used when the Selective Startup option is disabled.

If the problem does not go away, you can use the Advanced button from the General tab to inspect lower level configuration settings, such as real-mode disk accesses, and VGA standard video settings. You also can start the *Device Manager* from the MSCONFIG View option. This will allow the protected-mode device drivers to be inspected. The MSINFO-Problem Devices section also should be examined to check for possible problem-causing devices. Other items to check include missing or corrupted system files (using the System File Checker utility), corrupted Registry entries (using the Registry Checker), viruses (using a virus checker program), and hardware conflicts using the CMOS Configuration screens.

When a potential problem setting has been identified in the CONFIG.SYS, AUTOEXEC.BAT, or Registry, use the **Automatic Skip Driver** utility to automatically isolate and disable the suspect line. Just select the ASD option from the System Information's Tools menu. Select the operation that has failed by marking it in the Hardware Troubleshooting Agent dialog box, and then select the Details option. This action should cause the Enumerating a Device dialog box to provide recommendations for correcting any problems. This normally involves replacing the driver disabled by the ASD utility. This series of automated tests basically replaces the manual isolation method performed with the Step-by-Step Startup option.

Automatic Skip Driver

The system may contain up to five backup copies of the Registry structure. If the system fails to start up after installing some new software or hardware component, run the Registry Checker utility using the /Restore option (**ScanReg /Restore**) to return the Registry to its previous condition. Just type "ScanReg /Restore" at the MS-DOS prompt to view a list of available backup copies. Generally, the most recent version should be selected for use. These tools are discussed in greater detail later in this chapter.

ScanReg /Restore

WINDOWS 2000 STARTUP PROBLEMS

For Windows 2000, you can build on the operating system troubleshooting methodology previously discussed. If Windows 2000 fails to boot, the first troubleshooting step is to determine whether the computer is failing before or after the operating system takes control.

If the startup process makes it to the beep that indicates the end of the POST, but you do not see the operating system *Boot Selection menu*, the problem is probably one of the following:

- System partition
- Master Boot Record
- Partition boot sector

These types of problems are usually the result of hard disk media failure, or a virus, and must be repaired before the operating system can function. Typical symptoms associated with these failures include the following:

- Blue screen or Stop message appears.
- Bootup stops after the POST.
- The Boot Selection menu is never reached.
- An error message is produced.

Windows 2000 displays a number of error messages related to these problems, including the following:

- Missing Operating System
- Disk Read Error
- Invalid Partition Table
- Hard Disk Error (or Absent/Failed)
- Insert System Disk
- Error Loading Operating System

The BOOT.INI file allows Windows 2000 to boot to separate operating systems. If this file is missing or corrupt you will not be able to boot to the Previous version of Windows. The computer will only boot to Windows 2000. To correct this condition copy the BOOT.INI file from a backup, or from another machine running the same setup and using the same installation directories.

The NTDETECT.COM or NTLDR files could also be missing or have become corrupt. If you receive the message "NTLDR is missing" or "NTDETECT failed", the partition boot sector is okay, but the NTLDR or NTDETECT.COM file is missing or corrupt. To correct these errors, you must reinstall Windows 2000 or boot to the Recovery Console and copy the missing or corrupt file from a backup.

The Missing Operating System and Invalid Partition Table errors indicate a problem with the Master Boot Record. Use the FIXMBR command in the Recovery Console to replace the Master Boot Record. Although this works well on a stand-alone drive, it does not work with disks that contain partitions or logical drives that are part of striped or volume sets.

If the startup problem occurs at some point after the screen clears and the operating system selection menu appears, or after selecting Windows 2000 from the boot menu, the issue is probably with the operating system. Most likely, necessary files are missing or corrupt.

Windows 2000 provides a wealth of tools for recovering from a startup problem, including the following:

- Windows 2000 Safe-mode options
- Windows 2000 Recovery console
- Windows 2000 Emergency Repair Disk

The following sections describe these tools and their use in detail.

Windows NT Startup Modes

VGA mode

Unlike the Windows 9x products, Windows NT 4.0 provides very few options when it starts up. The user is normally offered two options. The NTLDR file causes the system to display a selection menu of which operating system to boot from, along with an option to start the system in **VGA mode**. The menu listing is based on what NTLDR find in the BOOT.INI file. If the VGA option is selected, the system will startup as normal, with the exception that it will only load the standard VGA driver to drive the display.

Last Known Good Hardware Configuration mode

The second option presented is the **Last Known Good Hardware Configuration mode** option. Selecting this option will cause the system to start up using the configuration information that it recorded the last time a user successfully logged onto the system. The option appears on the screen for a few seconds after the operating system selection has been made. You must press the SPACEBAR while the option is displayed on the screen to select this startup mode. If no selection is made, the system continues on with a normal startup as previously outlined, using the existing hardware configuration information.

Windows 2000 Startup Modes

The Windows 2000 operating system incorporates a number of Windows 9x-like startup options that can be engaged to get the system up and running in a given state to provide a starting point for troubleshooting operations.

Advanced Options Menu

The **Advanced Options Menu**, depicted in Figure 12-4, contains several options that can be of assistance when troubleshooting startup failures. To display this menu, press F8 at the beginning of the Windows 2000 startup process.

```
Windows 2000 Advanced Options Menu
Please select an option:

    Safe Mode
    Safe Mode with Networking
    Safe Mode with Command Prompt

    Enable Boot Logging
    Enable VGA Mode
    Last Known Good Configuration
    Directory Services Restore Mode (Windows 2000 domain controllers only)
    Debugging Mode

    Boot Normally
    Return to OS Choices Menu

Use ↑ and ↓ to move the highlight to your choice.
Press Enter to choose.
```

Figure 12-4: The Advanced Options Menu

Safe Mode

Safe Mode with Networking

Safe Mode with Command Prompt

The Windows 2000 Startup Menu basically provides the same Safe Mode options as the Windows 9x operating systems – i.e., Boot Normally, **Safe Mode**, **Safe Mode with Networking**, and **Safe Mode with Command Prompt**.

However, the Windows 2000 menu also provides a number of Windows NT-like options:

Enable Boot Logging

NTBTLOG.TXT

- **Enable Boot Logging** - which creates a log file called **NTBTLOG.TXT** in the root folder. This log is very similar to the BOOTLOG.TXT file described earlier in that it contains a listing of all the drivers and services that the system attempts to load during startup and can be useful when trying to determine what service or driver is causing the system to fail.

Enable VGA Mode

- **Enable VGA Mode** - when selected, this option boots the system normally, but uses only the standard VGA driver. If you have configured the display incorrectly and are unable to see the Desktop, booting into VGA Mode will enable you to reconfigure those settings.

Last Known Good Configuration

- **Last Known Good Configuration** - This option will start Windows 2000 using the settings that existed the last time a successful user logon occurred. All system setting changes made since the last successful startup are lost. This is a particularly useful option if you have added or reconfigured a device driver that is causing the system to fail.

Debugging Mode

- **Debugging Mode** - will start Windows 2000 in a kernel debug mode that will enable special debugger utilities to access the kernel for troubleshooting and analysis.

Windows 2000 Recovery Console

Recovery Console

The **Recovery Console** is a command-line interface that provides you with access to the hard disks and many command-line utilities when the operating system will not boot. The Recovery Console can access all volumes on the drive, regardless of their file system type. However, if you have not added the Recovery Console option prior to a failure, you will not be able to employ it and will need to use the Windows 2000 Setup disks instead. You can use the Recovery Console to perform tasks such as the following:

- Copy files from a floppy disk, CD, or another hard disk to the hard disk used for bootup, enabling you to replace or remove files that may be affecting the boot process. Because of the security features in Windows 2000, you are only granted limited access to certain files on the hard drive. You cannot copy files from the hard drive to a floppy or other storage device under these conditions.
- Control the startup state of services, enabling you to disable a service that could potentially be causing the operating system to crash.
- Add, remove, and format volumes on the hard disk.
- Repair the MBR or boot sector of a hard disk or volume.
- Restore the registry.

The Recovery Console can be permanently installed on a system and be made accessible from the Advanced Options menu. It also can be started at any time by booting from the Windows 2000 Setup disks or CD, choosing to repair an installation, and selecting Recovery Console from the repair options.

Hands-On Activity

To install the Recovery Console onto a computer, follow these steps:

1. Put the Windows 2000 distribution CD in the CD drive, or connect to an installation share on the network.
2. Run the **winnt32 /cmdcons** command. Windows 2000 Setup will startup, as illustrated in Figure 12-5, and install the Recovery Console.
3. The Recovery Console will automatically be added to the Advanced Options menu.

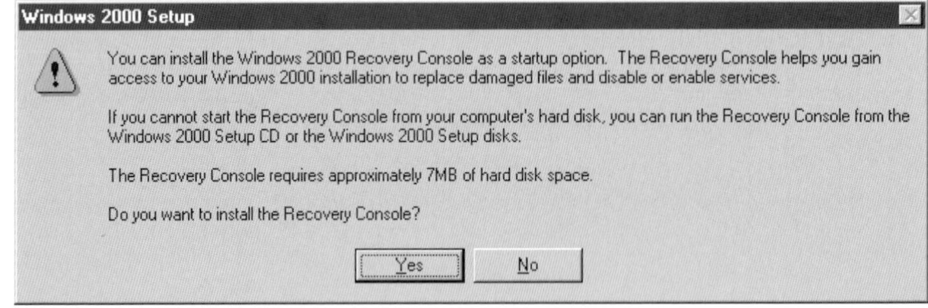

Figure 12-5: Installing the Recovery Console Using winnt32 /cmdcons

Calling for Help—When you start the Recovery Console, you are prompted to choose the folder that contains the Windows 2000 installation that you are trying to repair, and then to log on as Administrator. When logged on, type **HELP** to get a list of available commands.

One of the primary uses of the Recovery Console is to restore the Registry. Every time you back up the **system state data** with the Windows 2000 Backup utility, a copy of the Registry is placed in the *\Repair\RegBack* folder. If you copy the entire contents of this folder or only particular files to *\System32\Config* (which is the folder where the working copy of the Registry is stored), you can restore the Registry to the same condition as last time you performed a system state data backup. It is recommended that you create a copy of the files in *\System32\Config* prior to restoring the other files from backup so that you can restore the Registry to the original condition if necessary.

system state data

TROUBLESHOOTING STOP ERRORS

Stop errors occur most frequently when new hardware, or their device drivers have been installed, or when the system is running low on disk space. Also, stop errors can occur on a system that has been running without a problem for months, but for whatever reason experiences a hardware error of some sort that causes the system to crash. You need to be aware that they can happen for a variety of other reasons and can be very difficult to troubleshoot.

There is no set procedure for resolving Stop errors, but you can do many things to potentially eliminate the error, or to gain additional information about what caused the error.

Hands-On Activity

Use the following steps to troubleshoot stop errors:

1. Restart the system to see whether the error will repeat itself. In many cases, an odd series of circumstances within the system can cause the error, and simply restarting it will correct the condition. However, if the Stop Error appears again, you will need to take additional action.
2. If you have recently installed new hardware in the system, verify that it has been installed correctly and that you are using the most current version of its device drivers.
3. Check the HCL to verify that any newly installed hardware and device drivers are compatible with Windows 2000.
4. Remove any newly installed hardware to see whether that relieves the Stop error. If Windows 2000 starts, immediately use the **Event Viewer** to view any additional error messages that were generated before the Stop Error occurred. These messages will provide further information as to why the hardware caused the system to crash.

Event Viewer

5. Try to start Windows 2000 in Safe Mode. If you can start the system in Safe Mode, then you can remove any newly installed software that could be causing the Stop Error. You can also remove or update device drivers that could be causing the Stop Error.
6. Attempt to start the system using the Last Known Good configuration. This resets the system configuration to whatever the hardware configuration was the last time you were able to successfully boot the system, and gives you the opportunity to try to install or configure a new hardware device again.
7. Verify that the system has the latest Windows 2000 Service Pack installed.
8. Use TechNet or visit the Microsoft Support Center Web site and search for the particular Stop error number to see whether you can get any additional information. The Stop error number is noted in the upper-left corner of the Stop screen. In Figure 12-1 the Stop error number is 0x0000001A.
9. Disable memory caching or shadowing options in the system CMOS Setup.
10. If possible, run diagnostic software on the system to check for memory errors.
11. Use a virus utility to check for viruses and eliminate any viruses if found.
12. Verify that the system's BIOS is the latest revision. If not, contact the manufacturer of your system to determine how to update the BIOS.

One of these steps should enable you to resolve the error, or pinpoint it to a particular component that you can eliminate from the system to clear up the symptom.

Windows NT/2000 Emergency Repair Disks

In the Windows NT/2000 arena, there are two different types of troubleshooting-related disks that the technician should have on hand.

These are:

- The Setup Disks
- The Emergency Repair Disk

Setup disks are the equivalent of the Windows 9x Startup Disk. Windows 2000 creates a four-disk set. Unlike the Windows 9x Start Disk, the Setup disks do not bring the system to a command prompt. Instead, they initiate the Windows Setup process.

Emergency Repair Disk (ERD)

Both Windows NT 4.0 and Windows 2000 provide for an **Emergency Repair Disk (ERD)** to be produced. The ERD is different than the Setup disks in that it is intended for use with an operational system when it crashes. It is not a bootable disk and must be used with the Setup disks, or the distribution CD. While the Setup disks are uniform for a given version of Windows NT, the ERD is specific to the machine it is created from. It contains a copy of the Registry in Windows 2000. When dealing with the Windows 2000 ERD, it is necessary to manually copy the Registry files to the disk.

Windows NT Setup Disks

The Windows Setup disks basically perform three functions. They load a miniature file system into the system, initialize its drives, and start the installation process. All Windows NT Setup disks are the same for all machines running that version of Windows NT.

Under Windows NT 4.0, you must install the NT distribution CD in the system and type **WINNT /ox** at the command prompt.

MAKEBT32.EXE

BOOTDISK

Under Windows 2000, you must place the distribution CD in the drive and launch the MakeBootDisk utility to create the four disk images for its Windows 2000 Setup disks. You can also create Setup disk from the command prompt using the **MAKEBT32.EXE** file for Windows 2000. These disks can also be made from the *Start/Run/Browse/CD-ROM* path. From the CD, select the **BOOTDISK** option followed by the MAKEBT32.EXE command.

Windows NT 4.0 ERD

RDISK.EXE

During the installation process, Windows NT Setup asks whether you want to create an Emergency Repair Disk. You can also create an ERD later using the Repair Disk program (**RDISK.EXE**). To do so, select the Run option from the Start menu, enter the *cmd* command in the Run box, and then type **rdisk** at the command prompt.

When Windows NT is installed, the Setup routine stores Registry information in the %systemroot%\system32\config folder and creates a %systemroot%\repair folder to hold key files.

Windows 2000 ERD

The Windows 2000 Setup routine prompts you to create an ERD during the Installation process. The ERD can also be created using the Windows 2000 Backup utility located under the *Programs/Accessories/System_Tools* path. Choosing this option will activate the Windows 2000 ERD Creation Wizard, depicted in Figure 12-6. The Windows 2000 ERD disk contains configuration information that is specific to the computer that will be required during the emergency repair process.

TEST TIP

Know where ERDs are created in Windows NT 4.0 and in Windows 2000.

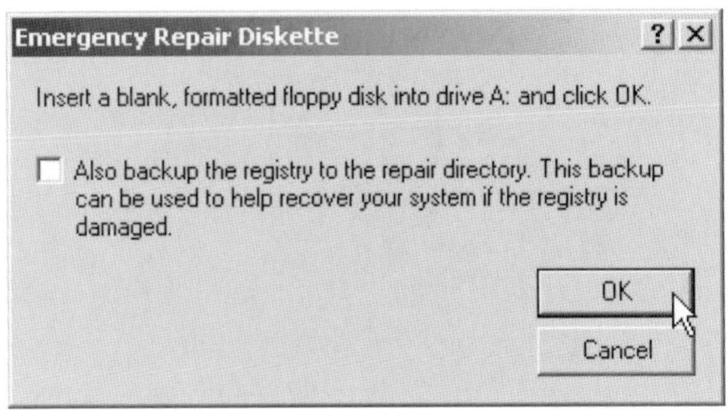

Figure 12-6: The ERD Creation Screen

Performing an Emergency Repair

The Emergency Repair Disk provides another option if Safe Mode and the Recovery Console do not enable you to repair the system. If you have already created an ERD, you can start the system with the Windows 2000 Setup CD or the Setup floppy disks, and then use the ERD to restore core system files.

The emergency repair process enables you to do the following:

- Repair the boot sector
- Replace the system files
- Repair the startup files

> **Limited to OS Repair**—The emergency repair process is designed to repair the operating system only, and cannot be of assistance in repairing application or data problems.

Hands-On Activity

To perform an emergency repair, follow these steps:

MAKEBOOT.EXE

1. Boot the system from the Window 2000 CD. If the system will not boot from CD, you must boot with the Setup Boot Disk, which is the first of four Setup floppy disks that are required. You create the Setup floppy disks with **MAKEBOOT.EXE**, which is in the *\BOOTDISK* folder in the Windows 2000 CD root directory.
2. When the text-mode portion of setup begins, follow the initial prompts. When you reach the Welcome to Setup screen, as shown in Figure 12-7.
3. When prompted, choose the Emergency Repair Process by pressing R.
4. When prompted, press F for fast repair.
5. Follow the instructions, and insert the Emergency Repair Disk into the floppy disk drive when prompted.

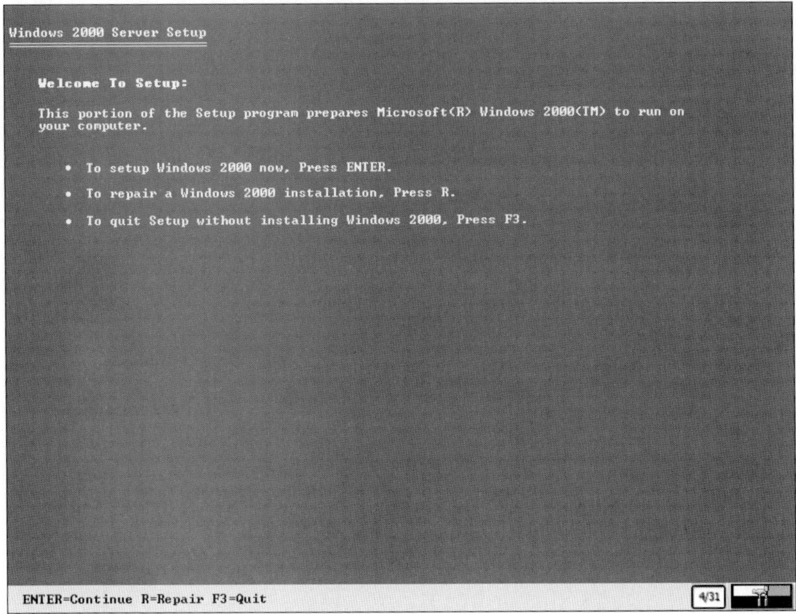

Figure 12-7: The Welcome to Setup Screen

Logon Problems

One last problem that can occur during startup (even though it is not actually a startup problem) is a logon problem. Basically, users cannot log on to systems when they have the proper authorization to do so. These problems tend to be very common in secure environments such as those that use Windows 2000.

The most common logon problem is a forgotten or invalid username and password. Invalid usernames and passwords typically result from poor typing, or from having the Caps Lock function turned on.

Users also can be prevented from logging on due to station or time restrictions imposed. Check with the network administrator to see whether the user's rights to the system have been restricted.

COMMON OS OPERATIONAL PROBLEMS

The technician should be able to recognize common problems and determine how to resolve them. Once the operating system has been started up and is functional, there are particular types of problems that come into play. Many of these problems are documented in this A+ objective. It indicates that the technician must be able to identify and correct operational problems associated the operating system. To this end, the following sections deal specifically with OS operational symptoms and problems, including the following:

- Memory usage
- Application
- Printing
- Networking

Memory Usage Problems

general protection faults (GPF)

Memory usage problems occur when the operating system, or one of its applications, attempts to access an unallocated memory location. When these memory conflicts occur, the data in the violated memory locations is corrupted and may crash the system. In Windows 3.x, these types of problems were labeled **general protection faults** (**GPF**) and were generally the product of data protection errors induced by poorly written programs. These programs typically use stray pointers or illegal instructions that access areas of memory that have been protected.

Although the Windows 9x structure provides a much better multitasking environment than its predecessor did, applications can still attempt to access unallocated memory locations, or attempt to use another application's space. When these memory conflicts occur, the system can either return an error message or just stop processing. Due to the severity of the GPF problems in Windows 3.x, Microsoft chose to provide memory usage error messages in Windows 9x that say "This Operation Has Performed an Illegal Operation and Is About to Be Shut Down".

dynamic link library (DLL)

Some memory usage errors are nonfatal and provide an option to ignore the fault and continue working, or to just close the application. These errors are generally caused by Windows applications and can sometimes be tracked to **dynamic link library** (**DLL**) files associated with a particular application. Although the application may continue to operate, it is generally not stable enough to continue working on an extended basis. It is recommended that the application be used only long enough to save any existing work.

On the other hand, some memory usage errors affect the Windows Core files (KRNL*XXX*.EXE, GDI.EXE, or USER.EXE). If a kernel file is damaged, you need to restart the Windows program. Any work that was not saved prior to the error will be lost. If the error is in the GDI or User files, it may be linked to a display driver, or to an I/O device driver.

Windows NT and Windows 2000 employ a flat memory management scheme that does not use the segmented memory mapping features associated with the Intel microprocessors. Therefore, these operating systems have very few memory usage problems.

General Protection Faults

A **GPF** occurs when Windows 3.x, or one of its applications, attempts to access an unallocated memory location. When these memory conflicts occur, the data in the violated memory locations is corrupted and may crash the system. GPFs are generally the product of data protection errors induced by poorly written programs that use stray pointers or illegal instructions that access areas of memory that have been protected.

Application Error

CORELDRW caused a General Protection Fault in module OLE2.DLL at 0003:069B.

Close

Figure 12-8: A Typical GPF Message

In Windows 3.0, a GPF usually required that Windows be exited and the system be rebooted. Version 3.1 provided improved control of GPFs. In this version, the error notice, depicted in Figure 12-8, includes information about where the error occurred and which application caused the error. In addition, Windows 3.1 remains stable enough after a GPF to allow the work in progress to be saved before exiting the program.

Typical causes of GPFs include the following:

- Running applications written specifically for a different Windows version.
- Selecting an incorrect machine or network during the installation process.
- The CONFIG.SYS or AUTOEXEC.BAT files contain incompatible or unsupported TSR programs or network drivers.
- An incorrect version of DOS is being used in the system.

Windows 9x and GPFs—The Windows 9x structure provides a much improved multitasking environment over its predecessor (Windows 3.x). Applications can still attempt to access unallocated memory locations, however, or attempt to use another application's space. When these memory conflicts occur, the system can either return an error message or just stop processing.

Hands-On Activity

If the GPF error occurs in random locations, follow these steps:

1. Check the DOS version to see that it is correct for the system.
2. Check the HIMEM.SYS version to see that it is 3.01 or higher.
3. Check the device drivers in the CONFIG.SYS file.
4. Perform a CHKDSK /F operation from the DOS prompt to check for cross-linked files.
5. Start Windows using the WIN /D:XSV switch.

   If the GPF continues, you must reinstall the operating system.

   If the GPF disappears, reduce the switch to WIN /D:XS.

   If the GP fault does not return, reduce the switch to WIN /D:X.

Windows 9x Operating Problems

Aside from the application, printing and networking problem categories listed earlier, if the Windows 9x operating system starts up properly, only a limited number things can go wrong afterward. The disk drive can run out of space, files can become corrupt, or the system can lock up due to software exception errors. When these problems occur, the system can either return an error message or just stop processing.

The System Information utility in the *\Programs\Accessories\System_Tools* path can be used to view the disk drive's space parameters. You also can check the drive's used/available space information by performing a *CheckDisk* operation on it.

If the system produces an Out of Memory error in Windows 9x, it is very unlikely that the system is running out of RAM, unless you are running DOS-based applications. In Windows 9x, this error indicates that the system is running out of memory space altogether – RAM and virtual.

Run the Windows System Monitor utility described later in this chapter to observe system memory usage and determine the nature of the error. If you are running DOS-based applications, you can optimize the system's use of conventional memory by running the old DOS MEMMAKER utility from the \Tools\Oldmsdos directory on the Windows distribution CD.

You can view the drive's swap file settings through the Control Panel's System/Performance/Virtual Memory option or through the System Tool's System Information utility. As always, any lost clusters taking up space on the drive can be identified and eliminated using the ScanDisk utility. A heavily used, heavily fragmented hard drive can affect the system's virtual memory and produce memory shortages as well. Run the Defrag utility to optimize the storage patterns on the drive.

If the system is running a FAT16 drive, you can free up additional space by converting it to a FAT32 drive. The command line utility for this is CVT1.EXE. The smaller sector clustering available through FAT32 frees up wasted space on the drive. The drawbacks of performing this upgrade are that you run some risk of losing data if a failure occurs in the conversion process, and that larger files will have slightly slower read/write times than they did under FAT16.

TEST TIP

Be aware of the part that the disk drive plays in Windows 9x memory management and how to optimize its use.

If these corrective actions do not clear the memory error, you will need to remove unnecessary files from the drive, or install a larger drive.

If the system begins to run out of hard disk space, remember that there may be up to five backup copies of the Registry on the drive. This is a function of using the SCANREGW utility to check out the Registry structure for corruption. Each backup can be up to 2 MB in size and can be removed to free up additional disk drive space.

The Windows 9x structure provides a much better multitasking environment than its predecessors. However, applications can still attempt to access unallocated memory areas, or attempt to access another application's designated memory areas. These actions create a software exception error in the system. Windows 9x typically responds to these errors by placing a *This Program Has Committed an Illegal Operation and Is About To Be Shut Down* message onscreen. When this happens, Windows may take care of the error and allow you to continue operating by just pressing a specific key.

If the system locks up, or an application stalls, it is often possible to regain access to the Close Program Dialog box by pressing the CTRL+ALT+DEL key combination. Once the Close Program dialog box is onscreen, you can close the offending application and continue operating the system without rebooting.

TEST TIP

Know how to clear a stalled application in the Windows environment.

If the application repeatedly locks the system up, it will be necessary to reinstall the application and check its configuration settings. The Dr. Watson utility is also very useful in detecting application faults. When activated, Dr. Watson intercepts the software actions, detects the failure, identifies the application, and provides a detailed description of the failure. The information is automatically transferred to the disk drive, and stored in the \Windows\Drwatson*.wlg file. The information stored in the file can be viewed and printed from a word processor.

As an example, in Windows 9x the Windows Explorer shell (EXPLORER.EXE) may crash and leave the system without a Start Button or Taskbar. To recover from this condition, use the CTRL+ALT+DEL combination to access the Close Programs dialog box and shut the system down in a proper manner. The ALT+F4 key combination can also be used to close active windows. Pressing this key combination in an application stops the application and moves to the next active application in the task list. If the ALT+F4 combination is pressed when no applications are active, the Windows Shut Down menu will appear on the display. This will enable you to conduct an orderly shut down or restart of the system.

If the application repeatedly locks the system up, you must reinstall the application and check its configuration settings. The Dr. Watson utility also proves very useful in detecting application faults. When activated, Dr. Watson intercepts the software actions, detects the failure, identifies the application, and provides a detailed description of the failure. The information is automatically transferred to the disk drive and stored in the \Windows\Drwatson*.WLG file. You can view and print the information stored in the file from a word processor.

If a DOS-based program is running and the system locks up, you must restore Windows 9x. To accomplish this, attempt to restart the system from a cold boot. If the system starts in Windows 9x, check the properties of the DOS application. This information can be obtained by locating the program through My Computer or through the Windows Explorer interfaces, right-clicking on its filename, and selecting the properties option from the pop-up menu. From the Properties window, select the Programs tab and then click the Advanced button to view the file's settings, as depicted in Figure 12-9. If the application is not already set for MS-DOS-mode operation, click the box to select it. Also select the Prevent MS-DOS-based programs from detecting Windows option. Return to the failing application to see whether it will run correctly in this environment.

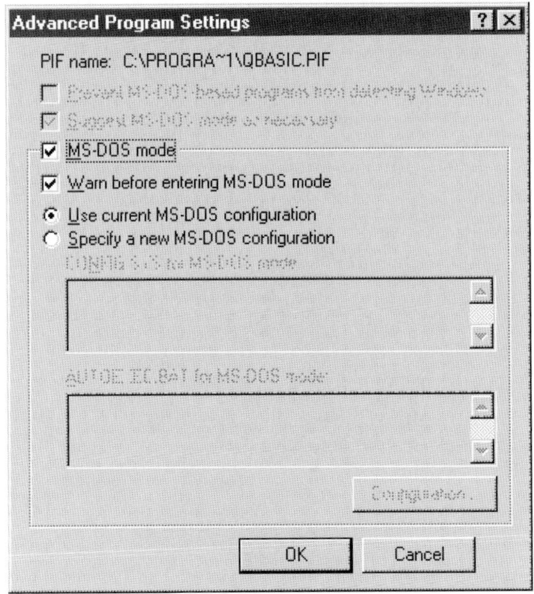

Figure 12-9: DOS Program Properties

Windows 98 occasionally produces an error message that says you are running out of resources. This message indicates that the operating system believes that it has exhausted all the system's real and virtual memory. Although the message tells you to correct the problem by shutting down applications, and it provides an endless series of application shutdown dialog windows, this process almost never works. Even shutting the applications down through the Close Program dialog box will not restore the system. Therefore, you should shut down the system and restart it. This action normally clears the problem.

Windows 2000 Operating Problems

You should be aware of some typical symptoms that can pop up during the normal operation of the Windows 2000 operating system, including the following:

- User cannot log on.
- You cannot recover an item that was deleted by another user.
- You cannot recover any items deleted.
- The video adapter supports higher resolution than the monitor does.
- Personalized menus are not working.

The first time you log on to the Windows 2000 system, the only usable account is the Administrator account; the Guest account is disabled. If a user cannot log on, check the user's password. The password is case sensitive, so verify that the Caps Lock key is not an issue. If you have forgotten the Administrator password and you have not created any other accounts with Administrator privileges, you must reinstall Windows 2000. Some third-party utilities may be able to help you recover the Administrator password, but you will usually find it easier to just reinstall the operating system at this point.

You cannot recover an item that was deleted by another user because the Recycle Bin is maintained on a user-by-user basis. If one user deletes something, only that user can recover it. You must log on as the user who deleted the items.

Files and folders deleted from a floppy disk or network drive are permanently deleted and cannot be recovered. Once the Recycle Bin fills to capacity, any newly deleted file or folder added causes older deleted items to be automatically deleted for the Recycle Bin.

Many video cards can display very high resolution at high refresh rates. However, some monitors do not have the same capabilities. When you configure the video card with settings that the monitor cannot display, symptoms may range from a simple blank screen, to several ghost images being displayed onscreen. To correct this problem, start Windows 2000 in Safe mode. This action causes Windows 2000 to load a basic VGA video driver, enabling you to then change the display properties of the video card.

If the personalized menus are not working, the Personalized Menu feature may be turned off. To turn this feature on, click Start, point to Settings, click Taskbar & Start Menu, and then select Use Personalized Menus on the General tab.

Hide File Extensions for Known Files

By default, Windows 2000 hides known filename extensions. If you cannot see filename extensions, open the Windows Explorer, click Tools, click Folder Options, click the View tab, locate and deselect the **Hide File Extensions for Known Files** option.

Likewise, Windows 2000 by default does not display hidden or system files in Explorer. To see hidden or system files, open the Windows Explorer, click Tools, click Folder Options, click the View tab, locate and select the Show Hidden Files and Folders option.

Troubleshooting Application Problems

One of the other major operational problems that affect operating systems involves the application programs running in the system. In the Microsoft world, if the application is a BAT, EXE, or COM file, it should start when its name is properly entered on the command line. If such an application will not start in a command-line environment, you have a few basic possibilities to consider: It has been improperly identified; it is not located where it is supposed to be; or the application program is corrupted.

Check the spelling of the filename and reenter it at the command prompt. Also, verify that the path to the program has been presented correctly and thoroughly. If the path and filename are correct, the application may be corrupted. Reinstall it and try to start it again.

Other possible reasons for application programs not starting in a command-line environment include low conventional memory or disk space, and file attributes that will not let the program start. In client/server networks, permission settings may not permit a user to access a particular file or folder.

Windows 9x Application Problems

If an application will not start in Windows 9x, you have four basic possibilities to consider: The application is missing; part or all of the application is corrupted; the application's executable file is incorrectly identified; or its attributes are locked.

As with other GUI-based environments, Windows 9x applications hide behind icons. The properties of each icon must correctly identify the filename and path of the application's executable file; otherwise, Windows will not be able to start it. Likewise, when a folder or file, accessed by the icon or by the shortcut from the Windows 9x Start menu, is moved, renamed, or removed, Windows will again not be able to find it when asked to start the application. Check the application's properties to verify that the filename, path, and syntax are correct.

Some applications require Registry entries to run. If these entries are missing or corrupt, the application will not start. In addition, Windows 9x retains the DLL structure of its Windows 3.x predecessor under the \Windows\System directory. Corrupted or conflicting DLL files prevent applications from starting. To recover from these types of errors, you must reinstall the application.

Windows 2000 Application Problems

Windows 2000 may suffer the same types of application problems described for the Windows 9x versions:

- Incorrect application properties (filename, path, and syntax)
- Missing or corrupt Registry entries
- Conflicting DLL files

Because Windows NT and Windows 2000 are typically used in client/server networks, however, some typical administrative problems are associated with files, folders, and printers and can pop up during their normal operations. These problems include such things as the following:

- Users cannot gain access to folders.
- Users send a print job to the printer, but cannot locate the documents.
- Users have Read permissions to a folder, but they can still make changes to files inside the folder.
- Users complain that they can see files in a folder, but cannot access any of the files.
- Users complain that they cannot set any NTFS permissions.

The following paragraphs identify ways that you can correct these particular administrative problems.

A user's inability to gain access to folders can come from many places. Check the effective permissions; remember that permissions combine, giving the user the highest level permission, except when the Deny permission is set. Also remember that lesser and included permissions will be denied.

Print Pooling

If the print job is not still in the local spooler or the print server, but **Print Pooling** is enabled, check all the printers in the pool. You cannot dictate which printer receives the print job. If the print job is visible in the spooler but does not print, this can be caused by the printer availability hours being set for times other than when you submitted the print job.

For users who have Read permission for a folder, but can still make changes to files inside the folder, their file permissions must be set to Full Control, Write, or Modify. These permissions are set directly to the file and override the folder permissions of Read. You can correct this by changing the permissions on the individual files or at the folder level and allow the permissions to propagate to files within the folder.

TEST TIP

Know what items to look for when applications will not start.

When users complain that they can see files in a folder but cannot access any of the files, they have most likely been assigned the List permission at the folder level. The List permission allows users to view the contents of the folder only, denying them all other permissions, including Read and Execute.

With users who complain that they cannot set any NTFS permissions, the first item to check is that the file or folder is on an NTFS partition. FAT16 and FAT32 have no security options that can be assigned. If the partition is NTFS the user must have Full Control permission to set any security permissions to a file or folder.

Task Manager

Windows 2000 Task Manager

In Windows NT and Windows 2000, the Close Program dialog window is referred to as the **Task Manager**. This utility can be used to determine which applications in the system are running or stopped, as well as which resources are being used. You can also determine general microprocessor and memory usage levels are.

When an application hangs up in these operating systems, you can access the Task Manager window depicted in Figure 12-10 and remove it from the list of tasks. The Task Manager can be accessed by pressing CTRL+ALT+DEL or by pressing CTRL+SHIFT+ESC.

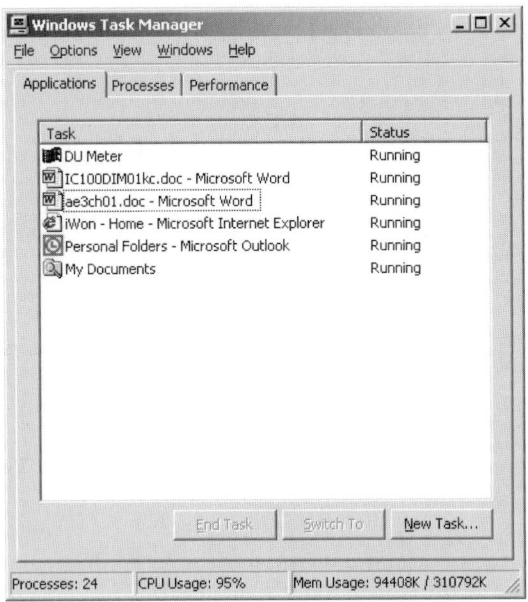

Figure 12-10: Task Manager

To use the Task Manager, select the application from the Applications tab and press the End Task button. If prompted, press the End Task button again to confirm the selection. The Performance tab provides a graphical summary of the system's CPU and memory usage. The Process tab provides information that can be helpful in tracking down problems associated with slow system operation.

Troubleshooting Printing Problems

In operating systems, there are two lines of thought when it comes to applications printing information to a printer: Let the application control the printer; or have the application communicate with the operating system's printer mechanisms. Older operating systems tended to turn over control of printing operations to the application. However, most newer operating system reserve the right to control printing operations themselves.

In a Windows-based system, the Windows environment controls the printing function through its drivers. When an application presents a particular font type for printing, Windows must locate or create the font codes. If the code is a TrueType code, it just creates the bitmaps required and sends them to the printer. If the printer code is some other font style, however, Windows must attempt to locate that font in the system.

If the requested font is not available or is not supported by the selected printer, Windows must substitute a font for it. In these cases, the Windows Font Map is used to decide the most appropriate font to use. Windows bases this choice on several factors including the character set, family, typeface, height, and width of the possible substitute font.

When Windows is forced to substitute fonts other than the one called for by the application, printing problems can occur. The printer can lock up or just produce print that is not correct or that is out of place. (That is, the substituted font may be the wrong size or may have undesired attributes that shove the text onto a following page or wrap it around a frame within the page.)

If font-related printing problems are suspected, check to see that TrueType fonts are selected. Some font converters do not work properly with Windows. Therefore, their output is corrupted and will not drive the printer correctly. This should produce a GPF message.

Other factors that can cause font problems include low system RAM and third-party video or printer drivers. Check the video driver setting in the Windows Setup window to determine which video driver is being used. Substitute the standard VGA driver and try to print a document. Check the printer driver using the Control Panel's Print icon to make certain that the correct driver is installed.

Some types of drivers are known to conflict with the Windows TrueType fonts. These include the Adobe Type Manager, Bitstream FaceLift, and Hewlett Packard's Intellifont. If any of these font managers are present, they should be disabled and/or removed from the system for troubleshooting purposes.

If printer problems continue, try printing a sample file from a non-Windows environment. The easiest check of this type involves trying to use the Print Screen key on the keyboard to print from a DOS environment. Another good example of this type of test is to copy the AUTOEXEC.BAT or CONFIG.SYS files to the LPT1 port. If this does not work from the DOS level, a hardware or configuration problem is indicated.

Is there a printer switch box between the computer and the printer? If so, remove the print sharing equipment, connect the computer directly to the printer, and try to print from the DOS level as previously described.

Determine whether the Print option from the application's File menu is unavailable (gray). If so, check the Windows Control Panel/Printers window for correct parallel port settings. Make certain that the correct printer driver is selected for the printer being used.

If no printer type, or the wrong printer type is selected, just set the desired printer as the default printer.

Windows Printing Problems

If a printer is not producing anything in a Windows 9x/NT/2000 environment, even though print jobs have been sent to it, check the Print Spooler to see whether any particular type of error has occurred. To view documents waiting to be printed, double-click the desired printer's icon. Return to the Printer folder, right-click the printer's icon, click Properties, and then select Details. From this point, select Spool Settings and select the Print Directly to the Printer option. If the print job goes through, there is a spooler problem. If not, the hardware and printer driver are suspect.

> **TEST TIP**
> Remember how to test the operation of the Windows Print Spooler when the printer will not print.

To check spooler problems, examine the system for adequate hard disk space and memory. If the Enhanced Metafile (EMF) Spooling option is selected, disable it, clear the spooler, and try to print. To check the printer driver, right-click the printer's icon, select Properties, and click the Details option. Reload or upgrade the driver if necessary.

If a Windows printer operation stalls, or crashes, during the printing process, some critical condition must have been reached to stop the printing process. The system was running but stopped. Restart the system in Safe Mode and try to print again. If the system still will not print, check the print driver, the video driver, and the amount of space on the hard disk drive. Delete backed up spool files (SPL and TMP) in the System/Spool/Printers directory.

DOS-based applications should have no trouble printing in the different Windows environments. Windows has enhanced DOS printing capabilities that can take part in the new spooling function and usually result in quicker printing of DOS documents. If a particular DOS application has trouble printing, check other DOS applications to see whether they share the problem. If so, use the normal Windows 9x troubleshooting steps previously outlined to locate and correct the problem. If the second DOS application prints correctly, check the print settings of the original malfunctioning application.

Troubleshooting Local Area Networks

Figure 12-11 depicts the system components associated with LAN troubleshooting. Generally, the order of isolating LAN problems is as follows:

1. Check the local networking software
2. Check the cabling and connectors
3. Check the NIC adapter

The order of checking is based on convenience and speed of isolating problems. The configuration checks performed on the operating system do not require that any hardware be disassembled. Likewise, cables and connectors are easier and faster to check than internal hardware.

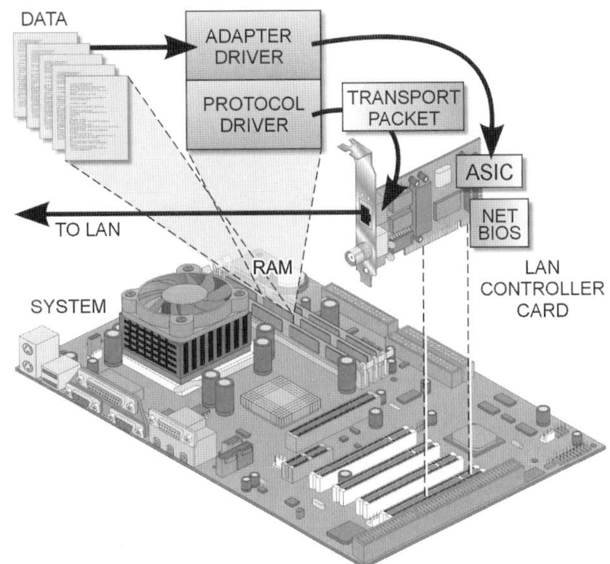

Figure 12-11: LAN Components

Most network adapter cards come from the manufacturer with a disk, or CD-ROM, of drivers and diagnostic utilities for that particular card. You can run these diagnostic utilities to verify that the LAN hardware is functioning properly. However, it may be easier to run the Windows PING utility from the command prompt and attempt to connect to the network. In a LAN environment, you will need to know the IP address, or the name of a computer in the network that you can direct the PING to.

line tester

Cabling is one of the biggest problems encountered in a network installation. Is it connected? Are all the connections good? Is the cable type correct? Has there been any termination, and if so, has it been done correctly? The most efficient way to test network cable is to use a **line tester** to check its functionality.

With UTP cabling, just unplug the cable from the adapter card and plug it into the tester. If coaxial cable is used, you must unplug both ends of the cable from the network, install a terminating resistor at one end of the cable, and plug the other end into the tester. The tester performs the tests required to analyze the cable and connection.

Windows 9x Networking Problems

There are several possible reasons why users cannot log on to a network in Windows 9x. Some of these reasons are hardware related. Running the Add New Hardware Wizard and allowing it to detect the network hardware should point out these types of problems. However, also click the Network icon in the Control Panel to review the NIC settings. Use the Advanced tab under the Properties window to confirm that the Transceiver Type value is correct for the type of physical network being used. Also, check under the Resources tab to confirm the adapter card's settings. Use the Detected Config option, illustrated in Figure 12-12, if the NIC settings are not known.

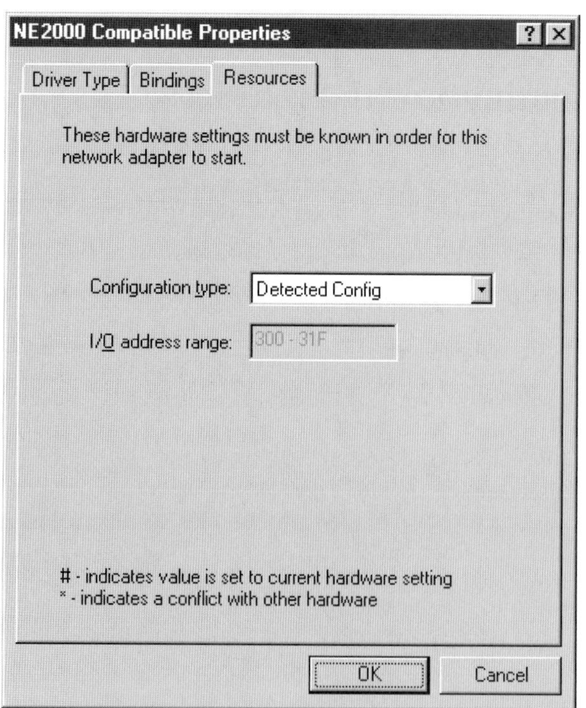

Figure 12-12: The Detected Config Option

If the network adapter card is installed in the system and the cabling is connected correctly, the operating system's network support must be checked. The most obvious items to check are those found in the Properties pages of the Network Neighborhood window. Possible reasons for not being able to log on to the network include the following:

- Incorrect Services Settings (Configuration page)
- Incorrect Protocol Settings (Configuration page)
- Incorrect Adapter Settings (Configuration page)
- Incorrect Primary Network Logon Settings (Configuration page)
- Missing Computer Name (Identification page)
- Missing Workgroup Name (Identification page)

Right-click the Network Neighborhood icon and select the Properties option from the pop-up list. The information that could prevent network logon is found under the Configuration and Identification tabs. Review each setting for correctness and reload if necessary.

In Windows 9x, begin by checking the system for resource conflicts that might involve the network adapter card. You can obtain this information by accessing the Control Panel's Device Manager. If a conflict exists, an exclamation point (!) should appear beside the network adapter card in the listing. If Windows thinks the card is working properly, the Device Manager displays a normal listing.

If a conflict is detected, move into the network adapter's Properties page, depicted in Figure 12-13, and check the adapter's resources against those indicated by the card's diagnostic utility. The conflict must be resolved between the network adapter and whatever device is using its resources.

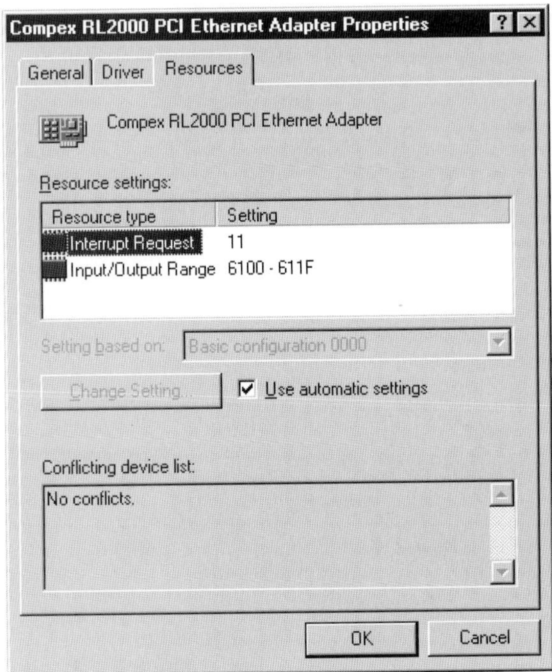

Figure 12-13: Network Adapter Properties Page

If the adapter resources are okay, the next step depends on the type of symptom being encountered:

- Can any units be seen on the network?
- Can other units be seen but not used?

If the network cannot be seen in the Network Neighborhood, or the network cannot be browsed from this utility, the network protocols and drivers should be checked.

Network adapters and protocols are checked through the Control Panel's Network icon. Check the protocols listed in the Configuration tab's Installed Components window. Compare these to those listed on working units in the workgroup. Each machine must have all the clients and protocols other machines are using; otherwise it will not be possible to browse the network. The local computer and the Entire Network icon should be present, but the other units will not be visible.

Other reasons for not being able to browse the network include the Primary Network Logon setting is incorrect for the type of network being used, and the local computer is not listed in the correct workgroup under the Identification tab.

If you can browse the network but cannot use certain resources in other locations, sharing is not turned on in the remote unit, or the local unit does not have proper access rights to that resource.

To use the remote resource across the network, the system's File and Print functions must be turned on, and its Share function must be enabled. Turning on the file and print functions place the local resources in the network's Browse listing. However, this does not enable the Share function. The Share function is established by supplying the system with a valid Share Name. In addition, the computer must be running Client for Microsoft Networks for File and Print to be available on a Microsoft network. If this client service is not installed, the File and Print functions will be unavailable for use (grayed out). The Client for Microsoft Networks services component must be installed in the Select Network Component Type screen.

Windows 2000 Networking Problems

login prompt

In most respects, the process for troubleshooting Windows 2000 LAN problems are the same as those described for the Windows 9x system. In a client/server system such as a Windows 2000 system, however, the computer professional's main responsibility is to get the local station to boot up to the network's **login prompt**. At this point, the network administrator, or network engineer, becomes responsible for directing the troubleshooting process.

Some typical networking problems can occur during normal Windows 2000 operations, including such things as the following:

- The user cannot see any other computers on the local network.
- The user cannot see other computers on different networks.
- The clients cannot see the DHCP server, but do have an IP address.

- The clients cannot obtain an IP address from a DHCP server that is on the other side of a router.

If a client cannot see any other computers on the network, improper IP addressing may be occurring. This is one of the most common problems associated with TCP/IP. Users must have a valid IP address and subnet to communicate with other computers. If the IP address is incorrect, invalid, or conflicting with another computer in the network, you will be able to see your local computer, but will not be able to see others on the network.

One reason for an incorrect IP address problem would be that the local system in a TCP/IP network is looking for a DHCP Server that is present. In some LANs, a special server called a DHCP Server is used to dynamically assign IP addresses to its clients in the network. In large networks, each segment of the network would require its own DHCP Server to assign IP addresses for that segment. If the DHCP Server were missing, or not functioning, none of the clients in that segment would be able to see the network.

Likewise, if a DHCP client computer were installed in a network segment that did not use DHCP, it would need to be reconfigured manually with a static IP address. The DHCP settings are administered through the TCP/IP Properties window. This window is located under the Start/Settings/Networking and Dialup Connections option. From this point, open the desired Local Area or Dial-Up Connection and click the Properties button. DHCP operations are covered in more detail later in this chapter.

Begin the troubleshooting process for this type of problem by checking the TCP/IP Properties under the Network icon. Next, check the current TCP/IP settings using the command line IPCONFIG/ALL (or the WINIPCFG) utility. They will display the current IP settings and offer a starting point for troubleshooting. Afterward, use the PING utility to send test packets to other local computers you find. The results of this action indicate whether the network is working.

As mentioned earlier, another area that can cause connectivity problems is the physical layer. Check to see that the computer is physically connected to the network and that the status light is glowing (normally green). The presence of the light indicates whether the NIC sees any network traffic.

NET VIEW

If users can see other local computers in a TCP/IP network, but cannot see remote systems on other networks, the problem may be routing. Check to see that the address for the default gateway listed in the TCP/IP properties is valid. Use the **NET VIEW** command to see whether the remote computer is available. If the user is relying on the My Network Places feature to see other computers, a delay in updating the Browse list may cause remote systems to not be listed. The NET VIEW command directly communicates with the remote systems and displays available shares.

If the clients have an IP address of 169.254.xxx.xxx, it is because they cannot communicate with the DHCP server. Windows 2000 automatically assigns the computer an IP address in the 169.254 range if it cannot be assigned one from a DHCP server. Check the previously discussed procedures to determine what the problem may be.

Many routers do not pass the broadcast traffic generated by DHCP clients. If clients cannot obtain an IP address from a DHCP server that is on the other side of a router, the network administrator must enable the forwarding of DHCP packets, or place a DHCP server on each side of a router.

Troubleshooting Network Printing Problems

The complexity of conducting printer operations over a network is much greater because the addition of the network drivers and protocols. Many of the problems encountered when printing over the network involve components of the operating system. Therefore, its networking and printing functions must both be checked.

When printing cannot be carried out across the network, verify that the local computer and the network printer are set up for remote printing. In the Windows operating systems, this involves sharing the printer with the network users. The local computer that the printer is connected to, referred to as the print server, should appear in the Windows 9x Network Neighborhood window of the remote computer. If the local computer cannot see files and printers at the print server station, file and print sharing may not be enabled there.

In Windows 9x, file and printer sharing can be accomplished at the print server in a number of ways. First, double-click the printer's icon in the My Computer window, or the Windows Explorer screen. Select the Printer/Properties/Sharing option and then choose the desired configuration. The second method uses a right-click on the printer's icon, followed by selecting Share in the Context menu, and choosing the desired configuration. The final method is similar except that you right-click the printer's icon and click Properties, Sharing, and then choose the configuration.

Run a printer's self-test to verify that its hardware is working correctly. If it will not print a test page, there is obviously a problem with the printer hardware. Next, troubleshoot the printer hardware. When the operation of the hardware is working, attempt to print across the network again.

Next, determine whether the print server can print directly to the printer. Open a document on the print server and attempt to print it. If the local printing operation is unsuccessful, move to the MS-DOS prompt, create a small batch file, and copy it to the local LPT port. If the file prints, there is a possibility that a problem exists with the printer's configuration at the print server. Check the print server's printer drivers.

The print server may not have enough memory or hard drive space available. In Windows 9x, check the spool settings, shown in Figure 12-14, under the Details entry of the *Control Panel/Printers/Properties* path. If the spooler is set to EMF, set it to RAW spooling. If the print spool is set to RAW, turn the spool off and click the 2 button. If the unit prints the test page, use the ScanDisk utility to check the disk space. Clear the contents of the \Temp directory.

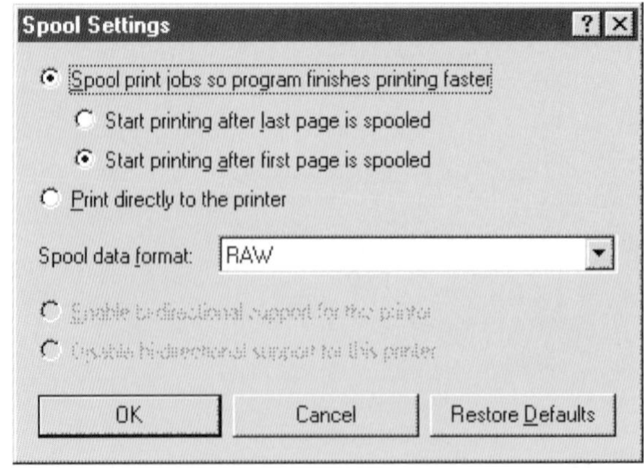

Figure 12-14: Windows 95 Spool Settings

If the file will not print directly to the local printer, there is a problem in the local hardware. Troubleshoot the problem as a local, standalone printing problem.

Next, verify the operation of the network by attempting to perform other network functions, such as transferring a file from the remote unit to the print server. If other network functions work, examine the printer driver configuration of the remote computer. In Windows 9x, open the Control Panel's Printer folder and select the Properties entry in the drop-down File menu. Check the information under the Details and Sharing tabs.

If the print drivers appear to be correct, install a generic or text-only printer driver and try to print to the print server. Next, move to the command prompt in the remote computer and create a batch text file. Attempt to copy this file to the network printer. If the generic driver or the DOS file works, reinstall the printer driver or install new drivers for the designated printer.

In the event that other network functions are operational, verify the printer operation of the local computer. If possible, connect a printer directly to the local unit and set its print driver up to print to the local printer port. If the file prints to the local printer, a network/printer driver problem still exists. Reload the printer driver and check the network print path, as depicted in Figure 12-15. The correct format for the UNC network path name is *\\computer_name\shared device_name*.

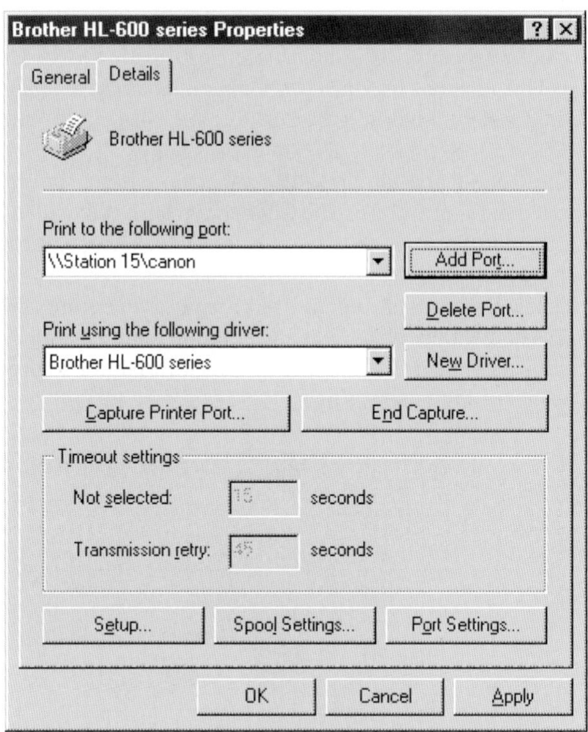

Figure 12-15: Checking the Printer Path

If the printer operation stalls, or crashes, during the printing process, a different type of problem is indicated. In this case, the remote printer was functioning, the print server was operational, and the network was transferring data. Some critical condition must have been reached to stop the printing process. Check the print spooler in the print server to see whether an error has occurred. Also, check the hard disk space and memory usage in the print server.

TEST TIP

Know how to create a UNC path from a local computer to a remote printer, or a directory located on a remote computer.

Troubleshooting WAN Problems

Unless you work for an Internet service provider, most of the work at an Internet site involves the components, and software, of the local computer. In most single-user situations, this is confined to the system, a modem, and the dial-up communications software. In some business settings, the range of components is increased to include network cards, concentrators, routers, and LAN servers. The information that follows pertains to typical dial-up Internet access applications.

The quickest items to check in a WAN application are the dial-up network software settings. Check the spelling of Fully Qualified Domain Name to make sure they are spelled exactly as they should be. If the spelling is wrong, no communications will take place. The major difference in checking WAN problems occurs in checking the Internet-specific software, such as the browser.

Most of the WAN troubleshooting steps from the local computer level involve the modem. The modem hardware should be examined as described in Chapter 11. If the hardware is functional, the operating system's driver and resource configuration settings must be checked.

In Windows 9x, you can find the modem configuration information in the Control Panel under the Modems icon. This icon has two tabs: the General tab and the Diagnostics tab. The Properties button in the General window provides Port and Maximum Speed settings.

The Connection tab provides character-framing information, as illustrated in Figure 12-16. The Connection tab's Advanced button provides Error and Flow Control settings, as well as Modulation Type.

The Diagnostics tab's dialog box, depicted in Figure 12-17, provides access to the modem's driver and additional information. The PnP feature reads the modem card and returns its information to the screen, as demonstrated in the depiction.

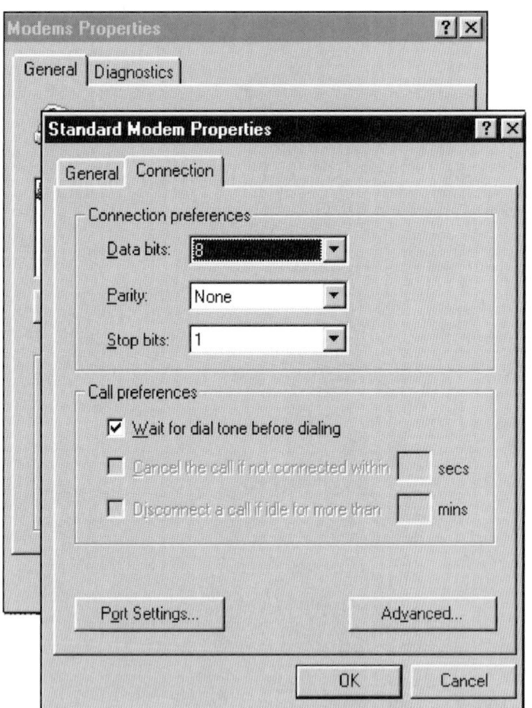

Figure 12-16: The Connection Dialog Box

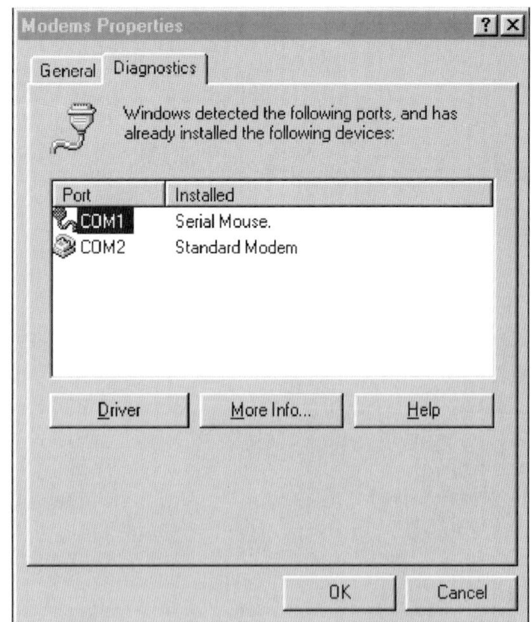

Figure 12-17: The Diagnostics Dialog Box

Each user should have received a packet of information from his or her ISP when the service was purchased. These documents normally contain all the ISP-specific configuration information needed to set up the user's site. This information should be consulted when installing, and configuring, any Internet-related software.

The ISP establishes an Internet access account for each user. These accounts are based on the user's account name and password that are asked for each time the user logs onto the account. Forgetting, or misspelling either item will result in the ISP rejecting access to the Internet. Most accounts are paid for on a monthly schedule. If the account isn't paid up, the ISP may cancel the account and deny access to the user. In either of these situations, if the user attempts to log onto the account they will repeatedly be asked to enter their account name and password until a predetermined number of failed attempts has been reached.

TEST TIP

Be aware of reasons that ISP accounts become invalid and what the consequences of this situation are.

Checking the modem, or network card, is the major hardware-related activity normally involved with Internet sites. However, you may be required to work with the customer's local Internet service provider to solve some types of problems.

The most common communication error is the Disconnected message. This message occurs for a number of reasons, including a noisy phone line or random transmission errors. You can normally overcome this type of error by just retrying the connection. Other typical error messages include the following:

- **No Dial Tone**. This error indicates a bad or improper phone-line connection, such as the phone line plugged into the modem's line jack rather than the phone jack.
- **Port In Use**. This error indicates a busy signal or an improper configuration parameter.
- **Can't Find Modem**. This error indicates that the PnP process did not detect the modem, or that it has not been correctly configured to communicate with the system.

If the system cannot find the modem, the first step is to reboot the system and allow Windows 9x to redetect the modem. If rebooting does not detect the modem, run any diagnostics available for the modem. In particular, use the utility disk, or CD-ROM, that comes with the modem to run tests on the hardware. Check any hardware configuration settings for the modem and compare them to the settings in the Control Panel's Device Manager. These values can be checked through the Control Panel's Modems/Properties page, but the Device Manager must be used to make changes.

If the modem is present, move into the Device Manager and check the modem for resource conflicts. If there is a conflict with the modem, an exclamation point (!) should appear beside the modem listing.

If you detect a conflict, move into the Modems Properties page and check the modem's resources. Also, record the Connection Preferences from the Connection page and make certain the character-framing configuration is correct. The conflict must be resolved between the modem and whatever device is using its resources.

If no conflict is indicated, move into the Diagnostics page and highlight the installed device. Click the More Info button. This action causes Windows to communicate with the modem hardware. If no problems are detected by this test, Windows 9x displays the modem's port information, along with a listing of the AT commands that it used to test the hardware, as illustrated in Figure 12-18. If an error is detected during the Windows testing, an error message displays onscreen. These messages are similar to those previously listed.

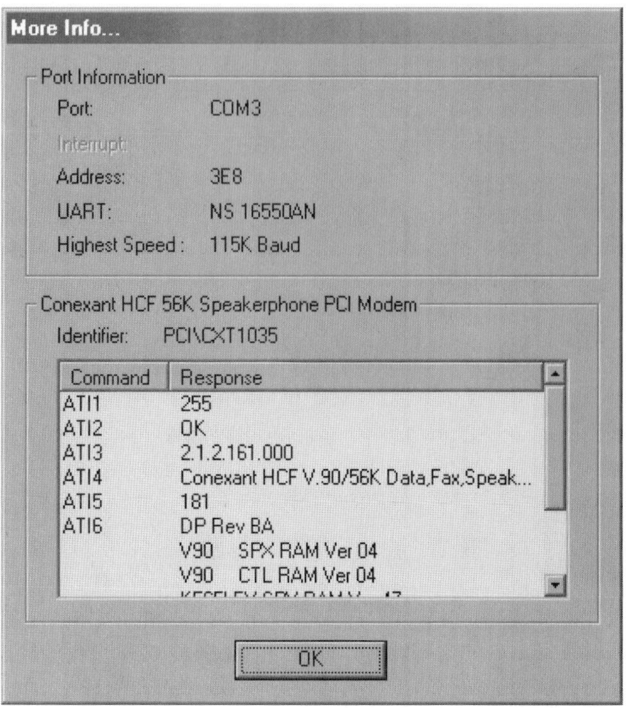

Figure 12-18: Modem Properties More Info Response

If the modem tests are okay, check the User Name and Password settings. This can be accomplished through the *My Computer/Dial-Up Networking* path, or through the *Start/Programs/Accessories/Communications/Dial-Up Networking* path in Windows 98. In the Dialup Networking window, right-click the desired connection icon and select the Properties option from the list. Check the phone number and modem type on the General page. Next move into the Server Types page and check Type of Dial-Up Server installed. For Windows Internet dial-up service, this is typically a "PPP, Internet, Windows NT, Windows 98" connection. Also, disable the NetBEUI and IPX/SPX settings from the page and make certain that the TCP/IP setting is enabled.

Click on the TCP/IP Settings button to examine these settings. Most ISPs use DHCP to assign IP, DNS and Gateway addresses to clients for dialup accounts. Therefore, in a dialup situation, the Server Assigns IP Address option and the Server Assigns Name Server Address option are normally enabled. Check the ISP-supplied package to make sure that these settings do not need to be set manually. If they are, set up the page to match the ISP-specified settings. In the case of intranets with "in-house" clients, the network administrator determines how the values are assigned—statically or via DHCP.

Network Troubleshooting Tools

Windows provides fundamental troubleshooting information for wide area networking through its system of Help screens. Just select Help from the Control Panel's toolbar and click the topics related to the problem. Also use a word processing package to read the Windows 9x SETUPLOG.TXT and BOOTLOG.TXT files. These files record where setup and booting errors occur. Use the F8 function key during boot up, to examine each driver being loaded.

When TCP/IP is installed in Windows 9x or Windows 2000, a number of TCP/IP troubleshooting tools are automatically installed with it. All TCP/IP utilities are controlled by commands entered and run from the command prompt. These TCP/IP tools include the following:

TEST TIP

Know where TCP/IP utilities are run from.

- **Address Resolution Protocol (ARP)** command. This utility enables you to modify IP-to-Ethernet address-translation tables.
- **FTP**. This utility enables you to transfer files to and from FTP servers.
- **PING**. This utility enables you to verify connections to remote hosts.
- **NETSTAT**. This utility enables you to displays the current TCP/IP network connections and protocol statistics. A similar command, called NBTSTAT, performs the same function using NetBIOS over the TCP/IP connection.
- **Trace Route (TRACERT)**. This utility enables you to displays the route, and a hop count, taken to a given destination. The route taken to a particular address can be set manually using the ROUTE command.
- **IPCONFIG**. This command-line utility enables you to determine the current TCP/IP configuration (MAC address, IP address, and subnet mask) of the local computer. It also may be used to request a new TCP/IP address from a DHCP server. IPCONFIG is available in both Windows 98 and Windows 2000. Windows 95 did not support IPCONFIG.

  The IPCONFIG utility can be started with two important option switches - /renew and /release. These switches are used to release and update IP settings received from a DHCP server. The /all switch to view the TCP/IP settings for all the adapter cards that the local station is connected to.

TEST TIP

Know which TCP/IP utilities can be used to release and renew IP address information from a DHCP server.

- **WINIPCFG**. This is a GUI version of the IPCONFIG command available only in Windows 95. The various command-line switches available with the IPCONFIG command are implemented in graphical buttons. Like IPCONFIG, WINIPCFG can be used to release and renew IP addresses leased from a DHCP server.

TEST TIP

Know which TCP/IP utilities show the host IP address.

Although all of these utilities are useful in isolating different TCP/IP problems, the most widely used commands are PING and TRACERT.

The PING utility sends Internet Control Message Packets (ICMP) to a remote location and then waits for echoed response packets to be returned. The command waits for up to one second for each packet sent and then displays the number of transmitted and received packets. You can use the command to test both the name and IP address of the remote unit. A number of switches can be used to set parameters for the PING operation. Figure 12-19 depicts the information displayed by a typical PING operation.

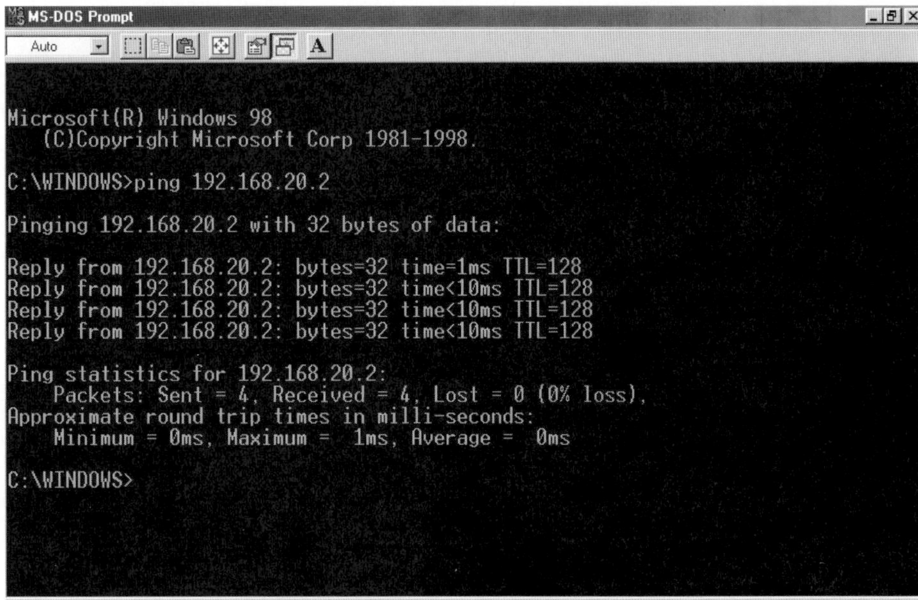

Figure 12-19: A PING Operation

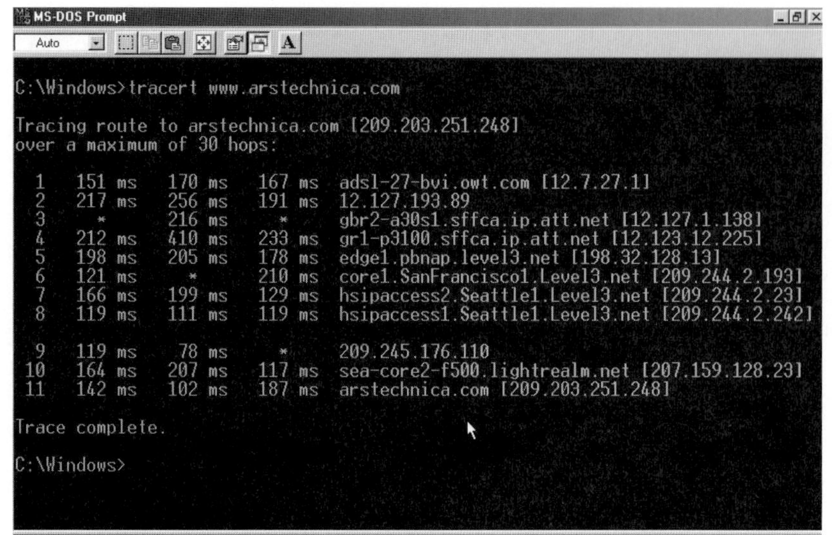
MS-DOS Prompt
Auto
C:\Windows>tracert www.arstechnica.com
Tracing route to arstechnica.com [209.203.251.248]
over a maximum of 30 hops:
1 151 ms 170 ms 167 ms adsl-27-bvi.owt.com [12.7.27.1]
2 217 ms 256 ms 191 ms 12.127.193.89
3 * 216 ms * gbr2-a30s1.sffca.ip.att.net [12.127.1.138]
4 212 ms 410 ms 233 ms gr1-p3100.sffca.ip.att.net [12.123.12.225]
5 198 ms 205 ms 178 ms edge1.pbnap.level3.net [198.32.128.13]
6 121 ms * 210 ms core1.SanFrancisco1.Level3.net [209.244.2.193]
7 166 ms 199 ms 129 ms hsipaccess2.Seattle1.Level3.net [209.244.2.23]
8 119 ms 111 ms 119 ms hsipaccess1.Seattle1.Level3.net [209.244.2.242]
9 119 ms 78 ms * 209.245.176.110
10 164 ms 207 ms 117 ms sea-core2-f500.lightrealm.net [207.159.128.23]
11 142 ms 102 ms 187 ms arstechnica.com [209.203.251.248]
Trace complete.
C:\Windows>

Figure 12-20: TRACERT Operation

Most Internet servers do not respond to ICMP requests created by pinging. However, you can use the PING utility to access. By doing so, you can get a reply that will verify that TCP/IP, DNS and gateway are working.

The TRACERT utility traces the route taken by ICMP packets sent across the net, as described in Figure 12-20. Routers along the path return information to the inquiring system and the utility displays the host name, IP address, and round trip time for each hop in the path.

Since the TRACERT report shows how much time is spent at each router along the path, it can be used to help determine where network slow-downs are occurring.

TEST TIP

Know which Windows tools to use to check out network-related problems.

Operating System Utilities

Successful troubleshooting of operating systems requires tools. In addition to the startup tools already described (clean boot disks and single-step boot-up utilities), a number of other utilities are available through the Windows operating systems to isolate and correct operating system problems.

Many of these utilities can be added directly to the startup disk so that they will be readily available in emergency situations. Some of the utilities that should be added to the startup disk include the following:

- **SCANDISK.EXE**. Checks the disk for lost clusters and cross-linked files and can examine disks and their contents for errors.
- **DEFRAG.EXE**. Realigns the file structure on the disk to optimize its operation.
- **MEM.EXE**. Used to view system memory organization.
- **SYSEDIT.EXE/REGEDIT.EXE**. These utilities can be used to edit Windows 9x system structures such as CONFIG.SYS, AUTOEXEC.BAT, and INI files, as well as the Windows 9x Registry structure.
- **FDISK.EXE**. Used to create, view, and manage partitions on a hard disk.
- **ATTRIB.EXE**. Can be employed to change the attribute of files (such as hidden, read-only, and system files) so that they can be seen and manipulated for troubleshooting purposes.
- **FORMAT.COM**. Used to establish the high-level format on disk drives.
- **SYS.COM**. Used to copy key system files to a disk so that it will be self-booting.

In the case of Windows 9x, the *Create Startup Disk* option under the Add/Remove Programs tab includes most of these utilities on the emergency start disk when it is created. Other utilities that can be very helpful in troubleshooting operating system problems include the Microsoft Diagnostic program and the Windows 9x Device Manager.

Windows 98 Troubleshooting Tools

The Windows operating system has become quite complex, both in structure and operation. The Windows 98 Resource Kit, from Microsoft Press, is nearly 1,800 pages and growing. This is considerably larger than the combined MS-DOS and Windows 3.1x manuals that supported DOS and Windows 3.1x. To help contend with these complexities, Microsoft has included an extensive set of troubleshooting system tools in Windows 98. It has also expanded the built-in Troubleshooting menu located in the Windows 98 Help functions. Both of these items are included to assist in the location and correction of many problems.

The System Tools

The following list identifies the Windows 98 troubleshooting tools:

- Microsoft System Information
- Windows Report Tool
- MS-DOS Report Tool
- Dr. Watson
- System File Checker
- Registry Checker
- System Configuration Utility
- Automatic Skip Driver Agent
- Version Conflict Manager
- Scheduling Tasks
- Maintenance Wizard
- Microsoft Backup
- Microsoft System Recovery
- Digital Signal Check
- Signature Verification Tool
- Windows Update

The **Microsoft System Information** tool (**MSINFO32.EXE**) is located at Program Files\Common Files\Microsoft Shared\MSINFO. You can use this utility to view system hardware resources, installed devices, and drivers. It can also be used to view reports generated by Web-based Windows and MS-DOS Report Tools. This enables remote service providers to inspect MSINFO information from local units across a LAN or WAN.

Microsoft System Information

MSINFO32.EXE

MSINFO is typically started by clicking the System Information option in the *Programs\Accessories\System_Tools* path from the Start menu. If Windows 98 does not run, the program can be executed by typing **MSINFO32** at the DOS command prompt. When the utility starts, the System Information screen depicted in Figure 12-21 appears.

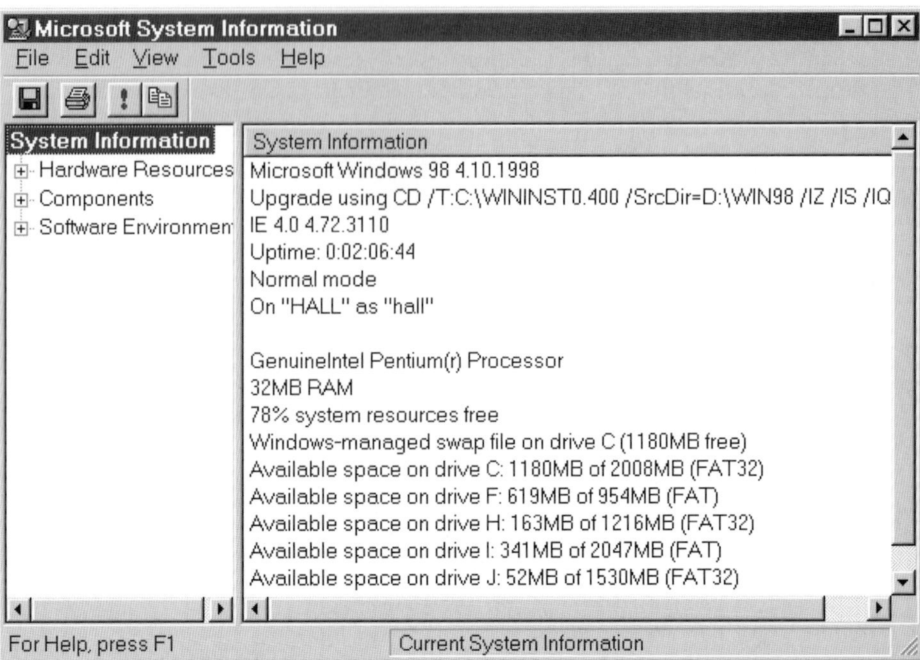

Figure 12-21: System Information Screen

The information is divided into a four-part arrangement. The main System Information screen displays general system information. The Hardware Resources entry provides information about system hardware settings, including IRQ, DMA, I/O, and memory addresses. The Components entry shows information about multimedia-related software, networking software, and device drivers. The final entry, Software Environment, lists the software loaded into the system's memory.

Windows Report Tool (WINREP.EXE)

MS-DOS Report Tool (DOSREP.EXE)

The **Windows Report Tool** (**WINREP.EXE**) is located in the Windows directory and provides a copy of the MSINFO information in HTML format. The **MS-DOS Report Tool** (**DOSREP.EXE**), also located in the Windows directory, provides a snapshot of the system files and can upload it to an FTP site when Windows is not working.

Dr. Watson

The **Dr. Watson** function from Windows 3.1x is alive and well in the Windows 98 version. As before, it is used to trace problems that appear under certain conditions, such as starting, or using a certain application. When Dr. Watson is started, it runs in the background with only an icon appearing on the Taskbar to signify that it is present. When a system error occurs, Dr. Watson logs the events that were going on up to the time of the failure. In many cases, the program will describe the nature of the error, and possibly suggest a fix. However, Dr. Watson is less than perfect. In some cases, the utility will completely miss the failing event.

The Dr. Watson utility is not located in any of the Windows 98 menus. To use the utility, it is necessary to execute the program from the Start menu's Run option. Just type the name **drwatson** in the dialog box, and click OK to start the log file. The Dr. Watson icon should appear on the Taskbar. Dr. Watson also can be started through the Tools menu in the System Information screen. This option is located in the *Programs\Accessories\System_Tools* path.

To see the resulting log file, alternate-click the icon. This action produces the Dr. Watson main screen, depicted in Figure 12-22. From this screen, select the System tab. This information also can be viewed from the System Information section of the System Tools menu.

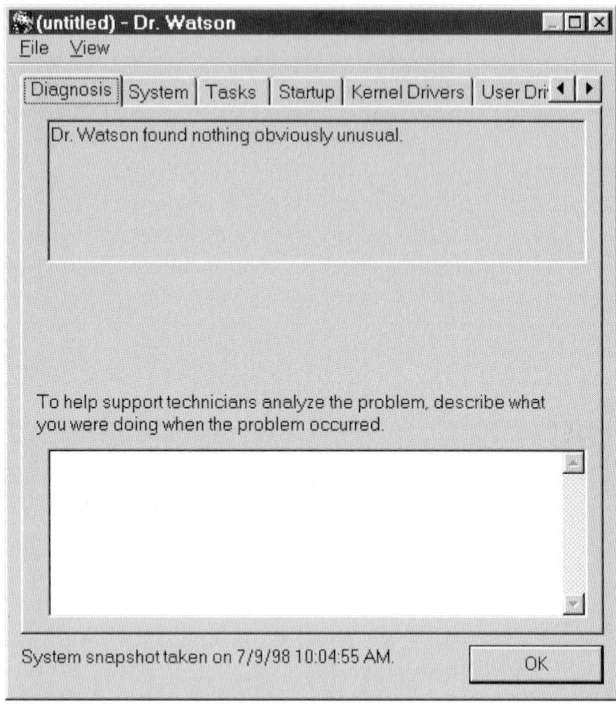

Figure 12-22: Dr. Watson's Main Screen

The **System File Checker utility** (**SFC.EXE**) checks the system files for changed, deleted, or possibly corrupt files. If it finds such files, it attempts to extract the original version of the file from Windows files. This file can be found at Windows\System.

System File Checker utility (SFC.EXE)

The System File Checker is activated by clicking the System File Checker entry in the System Information Tools menu. When it is activated, the utility's main screen, depicted in Figure 12-23, appears. This provides two options: scanning for altered system files, or extracting a file from the Windows 98 distribution CD.

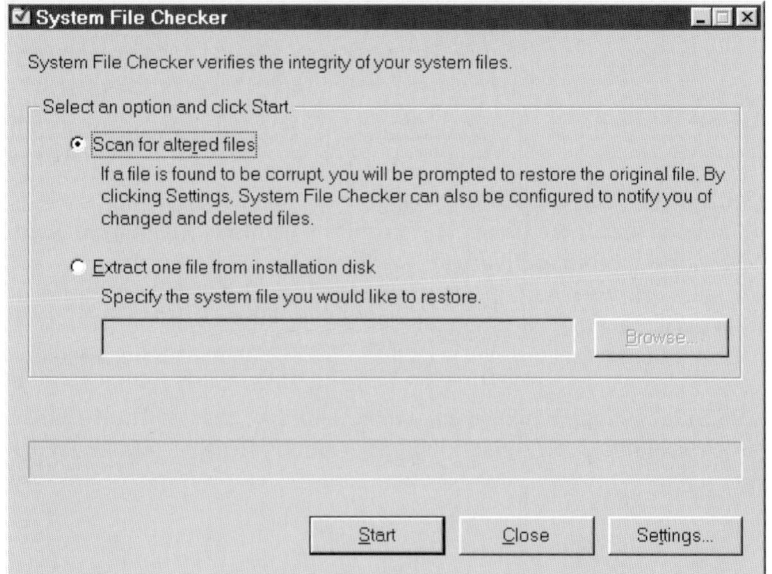

Figure 12-23: System File Checker's Main Menu

SCANREG

SCANREGW

System Configuration Utility (MSCONFIG.EXE)

Automatic Skip Driver Agent (ASD.EXE)

Version Conflict Manager (VCMUI.EXE)

System Configuration Utility

Windows 98 also includes a pair of Registry checker utilities (SCANREG.EXE and SCANREGW.EXE) to scan, fix, back up, and restore Registry files. The **SCANREG** file is a DOS-based program, whereas **SCANREGW** is a Windows-based version. The DOS version is located in the Windows\Command directory, whereas the Windows version is just in the Windows directory.

Windows 98 has a collection of configuration-related troubleshooting tools. These utilities include the **System Configuration Utility** (**MSCONFIG.EXE**), the **Automatic Skip Driver Agent** (**ASD.EXE**), and the **Version Conflict Manager** (**VCMUI.EXE**).

The **System Configuration Utility** enables you to examine the system's configuration through a check-box system. By turning different configuration settings on and off, problem settings can be isolated, and corrected, by a process of elimination. You can access this utility through the System Information screen. From the Tools menu, select the System Configuration Utility. This action brings up the System Configuration Utility's main screen, depicted in Figure 12-24.

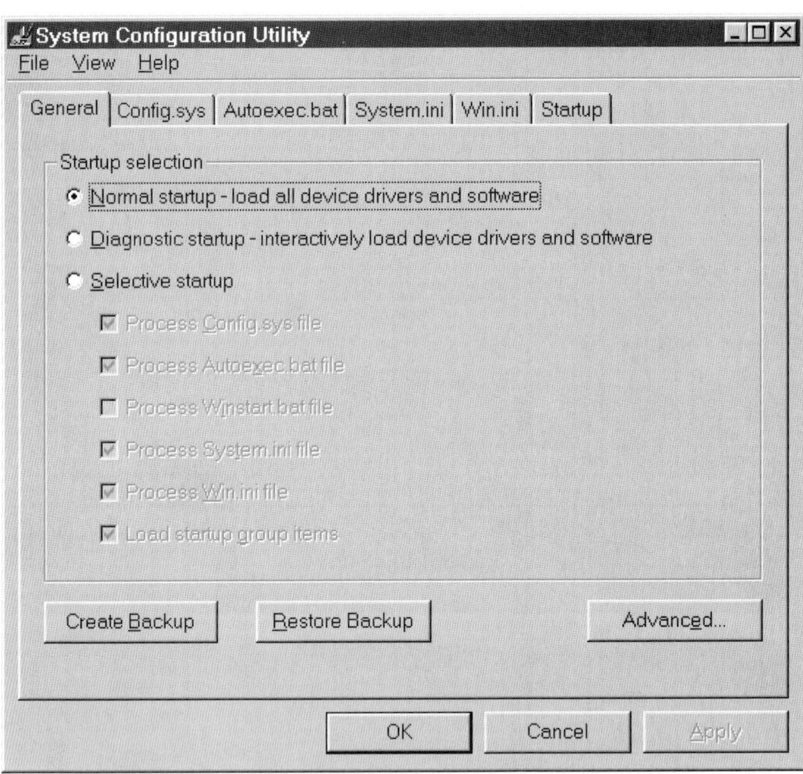

Figure 12-24: System Configuration Utility's Main Screen

The screen is divided into six tabs that correspond to the files that run during the startup process. The information under the General tab enables you to select the type of startup. For most troubleshooting efforts, the Diagnostic Startup is selected first to provide a clean environment. When the Selective Startup option is chosen, complete sections of the boot-up sequence can be disabled. Once an offending section has been isolated, you can use the individual tabs to enter that section and selectively disable individual lines within the file.

Automatic Skip Driver Agent

In cases in which the configuration problem is more severe, you can use the **Automatic Skip Driver Agent**. This utility senses, and skips, configuration steps that prevent Windows 98 from starting.

Finally, the Version Conflict Manager automatically installs Windows 98 drivers over other drivers that it finds, even if these drivers are newer. The System Configuration Manager is located in the *Windows\System* directory, whereas the other two utilities are found under the Windows directory.

Scheduling Tasks (MSTASK.EXE)

Windows 98 Maintenance Wizard (TUNEUP.EXE)

Windows 98 offers two utilities that you can use to automate the operation of important preventive maintenance utilities such as Backup, ScanDisk, Defrag, and so on. The **Scheduling Tasks (MSTASK.EXE)** program allows these utilities to be run at preset time intervals, such as every 24 hours, or each week. On the other hand, the **Windows 98 Maintenance Wizard (TUNEUP.EXE)** allows the operation of the housekeeping utilities to be independently scheduled. The Schedule Tasks utility is located in the *Windows\System* directory, whereas the Maintenance Wizard can be found under the \Windows directory.

The Windows 98 Backup and Recovery utilities (MSBACKUP.EXE and PCRESTOR.BAT) are invaluable tools for protecting against application and data loss due to hardware crashes. The Recovery utility has been updated to operate completely in protected mode. It is located on the Windows 98 CD, and provides a step-by-step process for recovering MSBACKUP files. The Backup utility is located in the *Program Files\Accessories\System_Tools\Backup* directory.

The Windows 98 Backup screen is depicted in Figure 12-25. As with previous Microsoft Backup utilities, the process of backing up is fairly straightforward. Start the Backup utility, select the type of backup to perform, what items to back up, where to back them up to, select any desired backup options, and then click Start.

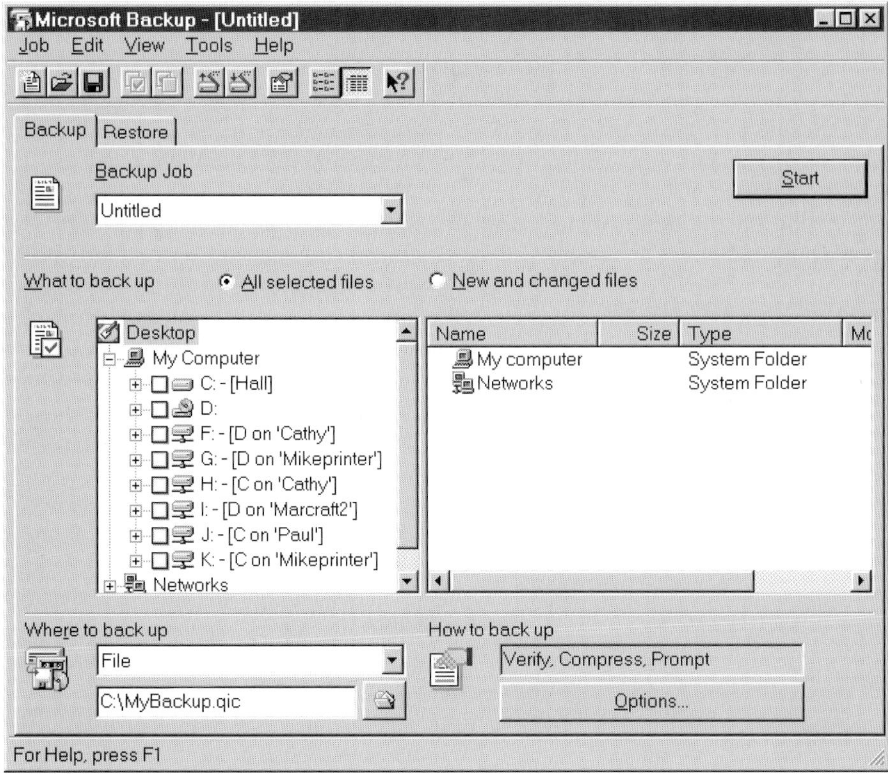

Figure 12-25: Backup Main Menu

Windows 98 Backup supports a variety of backup media. These include removable media (such as floppy disks, JAZ, and SyQuest cartridges, as well as tape drives—including QIC-80, 3010, 3020, and DC-6000 formats). This version of Backup is compatible with Windows 95 backup files, but not with DOS or Windows 3.x backups.

Both Backup and Restore can be run with or without the help of their wizards. The Wizards provide step-by-step guidance through each procedure. Without the Wizards, the processes are roughly equal to older Microsoft Backup and Restore operations.

The Backup utility is not installed as a default item when Windows 98 is installed. It must be set up using the Add/Remove Programs icon in the Control Panel. From the Add/Remove Programs screen, select the Windows Setup tab and double-click the System Tools entry. Check the box next to the Backup entry, click OK, select the Apply box, and click OK. These actions copy the Backup utility files into the System Tools menu in the Start menu's *Programs\Accessories* path.

Driver Signing

Signature Verification Tool

TEST TIP

Be aware of driver signing and know why it is implemented.

The final tools covered here deal with Microsoft-approved drivers and files. Microsoft works with hardware suppliers and signs (certifies) their drivers for Windows 98 compatibility by adding special digital codes to them. The Digital Signal Check function is enabled through the Windows 98 Policy Editor in the Hkey_Local_Machine\Software\Microsoft Registry subkey. This check verifies that driver files have been signed by Microsoft. This **Driver Signing** tool is valuable to administrators who do not want users to introduce questionable devices and drivers into the system.

The **Signature Verification Tool** (SIGVERIF.EXE) checks files to determine whether Microsoft has signed them. It also determines whether the files have been modified since they were signed.

Finally, the Windows Update utility (WUPDMGR.EXE) is a Windows 98 extension located on the Microsoft Web site (www.microsoft.com/windowsupdate). It enables you to update the system's files and drivers with new or improved versions over the Web.

System Monitor

System Resource Meter

Two other valuable utilities in Windows 9x are the **System Monitor** and the **System Resource Meter** programs. The System Monitor can be used to track the performance of key system resources for both evaluation and troubleshooting purposes. If system performance is suspect but there is no clear indication of what might be slowing it down, the System Monitor can be used to determine which resource is operating at capacity, thereby, limiting the performance of the system.

Typical resources that the System Monitor is capable of tracking include those associated with Processor usage and memory management. Results can be displayed in real-time using Statistical mode, Line Chart mode, or Bar Chart mode. Figure 12-26 illustrates the monitor operating in Line Chart mode. The System Monitor can be set up to run on top of other applications so that it can be used to see what effect they are having on the system.

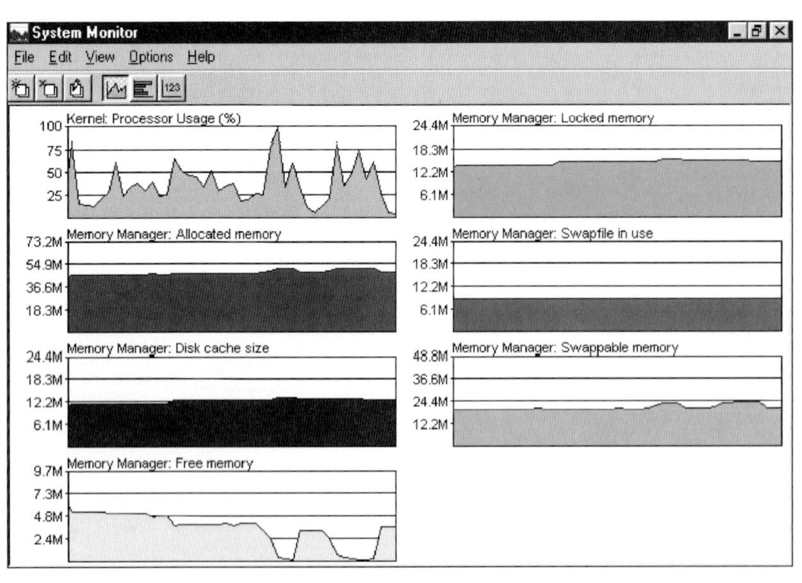

Figure 12-26: Using the System Monitor

The Resource Meter depicted in Figure 12-27 is a simple bar chart display that shows the percent usage of the system resources, user resources, and GDI resources. When activated, the meter normally resides as an icon on the extreme right side of the Taskbar, at the bottom of the desktop. Double-clicking the icon brings the bar chart display to the desktop. As with the System Monitor, the Resource Meter can be used to evaluate hardware and software performance.

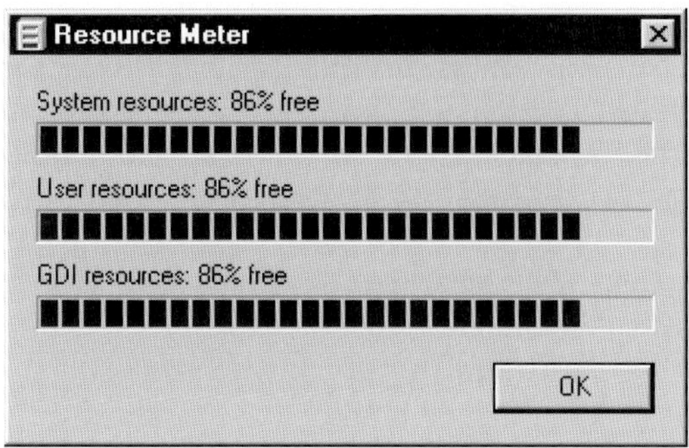

Figure 12-27: Using the Resource Meter

Both the System Monitor and the Resource Meter are installed through the Setup tab under the Control Panel's Add/Remove Programs applet. From the Setup tab, highlight the System Tools entry and click on the Details button. Select the utilities and click the Apply button.

Windows 2000 System Tools

As mentioned earlier, Windows 2000 clusters a number of administrative, diagnostic, and troubleshooting tools under the Control Panel's Microsoft Management Console.

Event Viewer

Event Viewer

In Windows 2000, significant events (such as system events, application events, and security events) are routinely monitored and stored. These events can be viewed through the **Event Viewer** utility depicted in Figure 12-28. As described earlier, this tool is located under the *Control Panel/Administrative Tools/Computer Management* path.

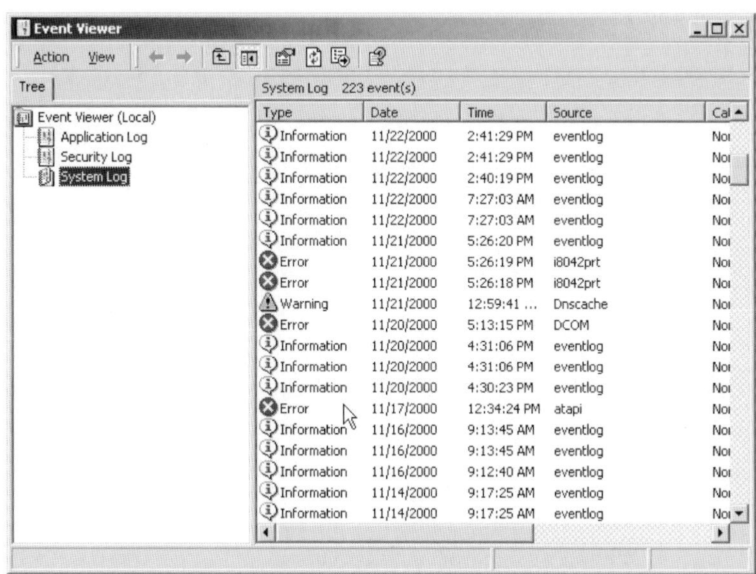

Figure 12-28: Windows 2000 Event Viewer

System events include items such as successful and failed Windows component startups, as well as successful loading of device drivers. Likewise, application events include information about how the system's applications are performing. Not all Windows applications generate events that the Event Viewer will log. Finally, security events are produced by user actions such as logons and logoffs, file and folder accesses, and creation of new Active Directory accounts.

Three default event logs track and record the events just mentioned. The system log records events generated by the operating system and its components. The application log tracks events generated by high-end applications. Likewise, the security log contains information generated by audit policies that have been enacted in the operating system. If no audit policies are configured, the security log will remain empty.

In addition to the default logs, some special systems such as domain controllers and DNS systems will have specialized logs to track events specifically related to the function of the system.

The Event Viewer produces three categories of system and application events:

- **Information events**—Events that indicate an application, service, or driver has loaded successfully. These events require no intervention.
- **Warning events**—Events that have no immediate impact, but that could have future significance. These events should be investigated.
- **Error events**—Events that indicate an application, service, or driver has failed to load successfully. These events require immediate intervention.

Figure 12-29 depicts the Windows 2000 Event Viewer displaying these types of events. Notice that the information events are denoted by a small "i" in a cloud, whereas the warning and error events are identified by an exclamation mark (!) and an X respectively.

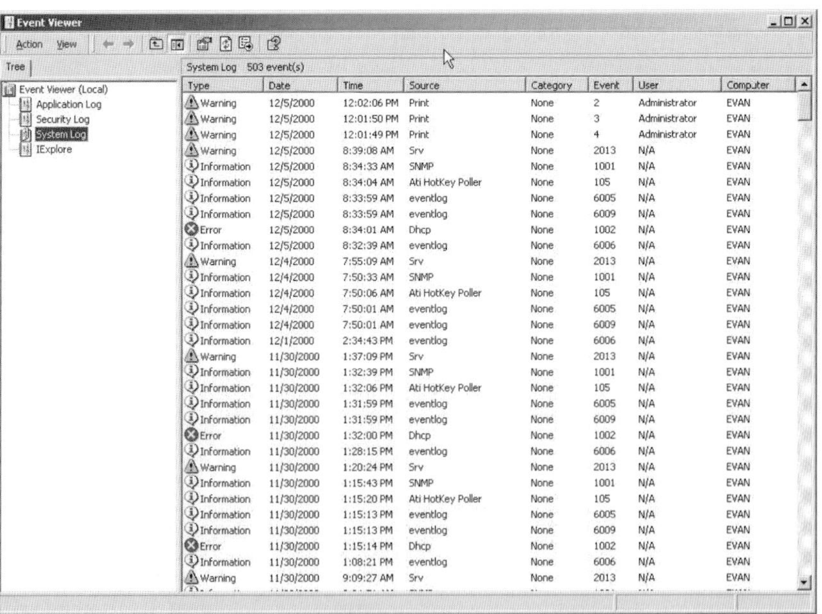

Figure 12-29: Viewing Event Types

System Information

The Windows 2000 System Information utility, depicted in Figure 12-30, provides five subfolders of information about the system. These folders include a System Summary, a list of Hardware Resources being used, a list of I/O Components in the system, a description of the system's current Software Environment, and a description of the Windows Internet Explorer.

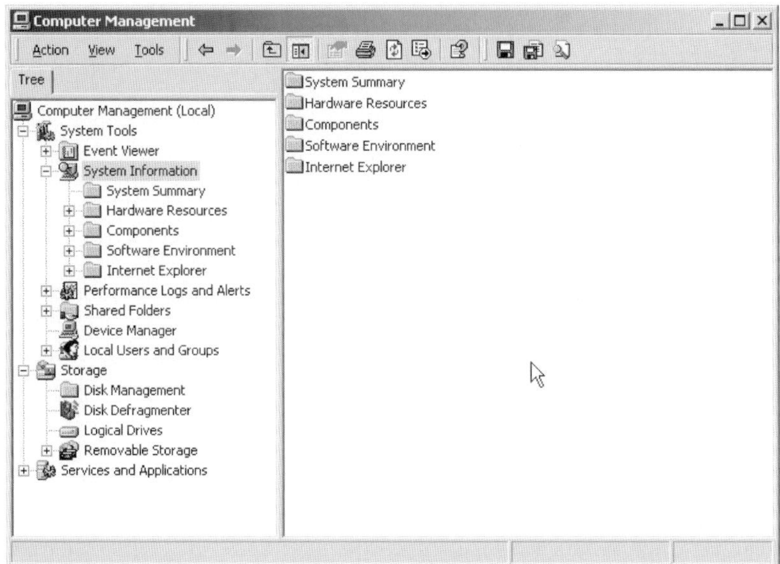

Figure 12-30: The System Information Utility

As with the Windows 98 System Information tool, the Windows 2000 version can be used to enable remote service providers to inspect the system's information across a LAN environment.

To save system information to a file, right-click the System Information entry and select the Save As option from the resulting menu. Saving this information enables you to document events and conditions when errors occur. You can use the results of different system information files to compare situations and perhaps determine what changes may have occurred to cause the problem.

Using Device Manager

Hardware and configuration conflicts also can be isolated manually using the Windows 9x **Device Manager** from the Control Panel's System icon. This utility is basically an easy-to-use interface for the Windows 9x and Windows 2000 Registries.

Device Manager

You can use the Device Manager, depicted in Figure 12-31, to identify installed ports, update device drivers, and change I/O settings. From this window, the problem device can be examined to see where the conflict is occurring.

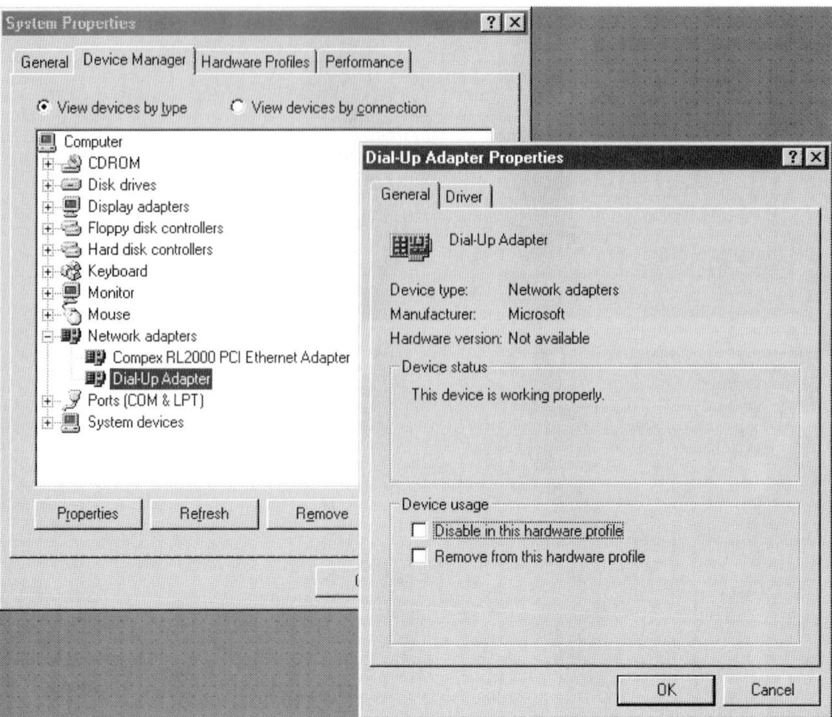

Figure 12-31: The Device Manager's Display

Two radio buttons on the Device Manager page can be used to alter the way it displays the devices installed in the system. Clicking the left button (the page's default setting), displays the system's devices alphabetically by device type. The rightmost radio button shows the devices by their connection to the system. As with the Registry and Policy Editors, the presence of plus (+) and (ms) signs in the nodes of the devices indicates expandable and collapsible information branches at those nodes.

> **TEST TIP**
>
> Memorize symbols used by the Windows Device Manager.

The Device Manager will display an exclamation point (!) inside a yellow circle whenever a device is experiencing a direct hardware conflict with another device. The nature of the problem is described in the device's Properties dialog box. Similarly, when a red X appears at the device's icon, the device has been disabled due to a user-selection conflict.

This situation can occur when a user wishes to disable a selected device without removing it. For example, a user that travels and uses a notebook computer may want to temporarily disable device drivers for options that aren't used in travel. This can accomplished through the Device Manager's "Disable in this hardware profile" option. This will keep the driver from loading up until it is re-activated.

Clicking the Properties button at the bottom of the Device Manager screen produces the selected device's Properties sheet. The three tabs at the top of the page provide access to the device's general information, Driver specifications, and system resource assignments.

When a device conflict is suspected, just click the offending device in the listing, make sure that the selected device is the current device, and then click the Resources tab to examine the conflicting device's list, as depicted in Figure 12-32.

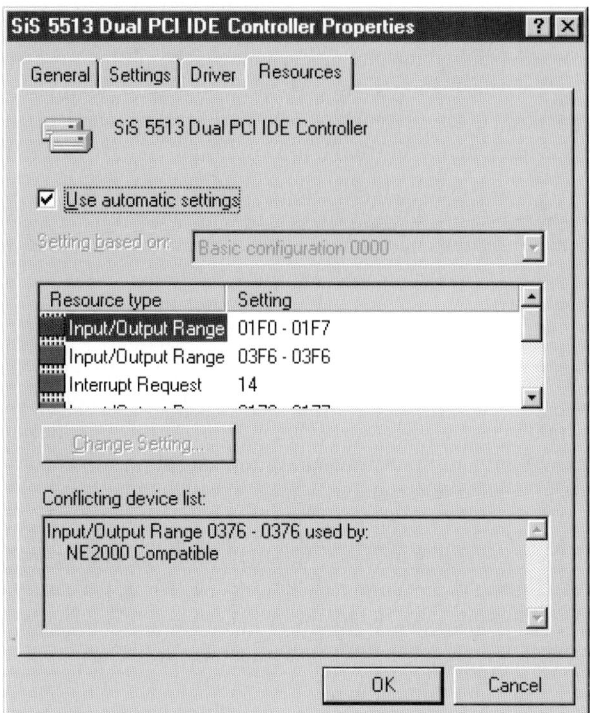

Figure 12-32: The Device Manager Resources Page

To change the resources allocated to a device, click the resource to be changed, remove the check mark from the Use Automatic Settings box, click the Change Setting button, and scroll through the resource options. Take care when changing resource settings. The Resource Settings window displays all the available resources in the system, even those that are already spoken for by another device. You must know which resources are acceptable for a given type of device and which ones are already in use.

> **TEST TIP**
>
> Know how to find conflicts using the Windows Device Manager.

To determine what resources the system already has in use, click the Computer icon at the top of the Device Manager display. The Computer Properties page, depicted in Figure 12-33, provides ways to view and reserve system resources.

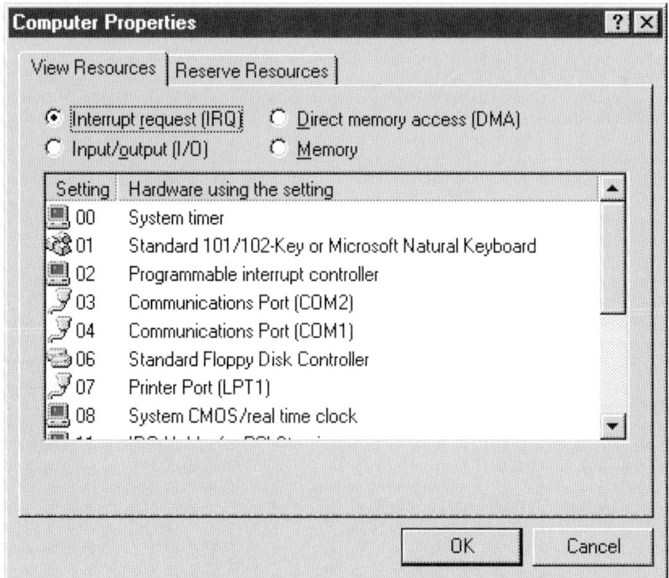

Figure 12-33: The Device Manager Computer Properties Page

Through this page, you can click radio buttons to display the system's usage of four key resources: IRQ channels, DMA channels, I/O addresses, and memory addresses. The Reserve Resources page is used to set aside key resources to avoid conflicts with the PnP configuration operations. If a resource is reserved and Windows detects it as already in use, a warning dialog box displays onscreen and asks for a confirmation.

Normal causes for conflict include devices sharing IRQ settings, I/O address settings, DMA channels, or base memory settings. The most common conflicts are those dealing with the IRQ channels. Nonessential peripherals, such as sound and network adapters, are most likely to produce this type of conflict.

When a device conflict is reported through the Resource tab's Conflicting Device list, record the current settings for each device, refer to the documentation for each device to determine what other settings might be used, and change the settings for the most flexible device. If either device continues to exhibit problems, reset the configurations to their original positions and change the settings for the other device.

Make sure that the device has not been installed twice. When this occurs, it is normally impossible to determine which driver is correct. Therefore, it will be necessary to remove both drivers and allow the PnP process to redetect the device. If multiple drivers are present for a given device, remove the drivers that are not specific to the particular device installed in the system.

System Editors

The Windows operating systems contain three important editors: the System Editor (**SysEdit**), the **Registry Editor** (**RegEdit** and **RegEdt32**), and the **Policy Editor** (**PolEdit**). Windows 2000 also includes a very powerful **Group Policy Editor** (**GPE**).

Later versions of DOS contain a small text editor program (EDIT.COM) that enables users to easily modify text files. This package is started by typing EDIT, and the filename, at the DOS prompt. The DOS Editor's working screen is depicted in Figure 12-34.

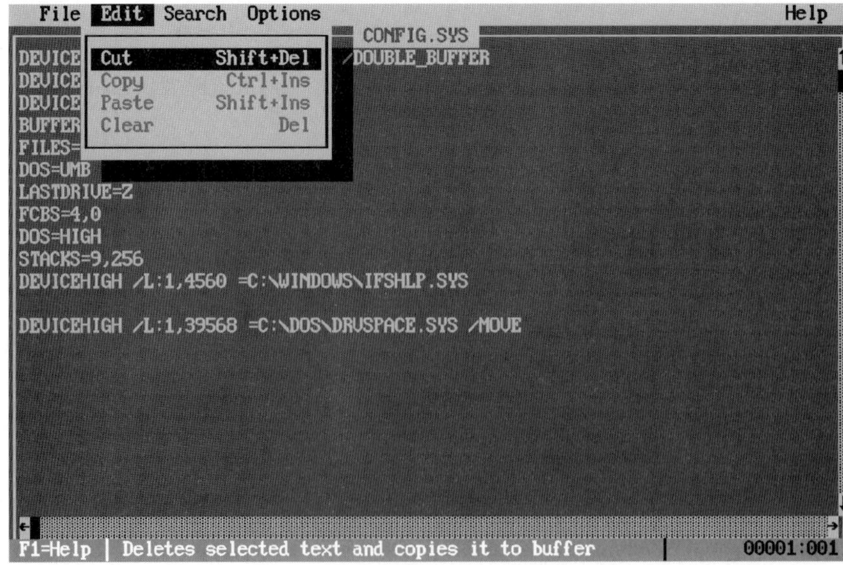

Figure 12-34: The DOS Editor Screen

The editor is particularly useful in modifying the CONFIG.SYS and AUTOEXEC.BAT files. The DOS Editor is an unformatted text file editor. It does not introduce formatting codes, such as underlining and italic, into the text in the manner that more powerful word processors do. This is an important consideration when dealing with DOS utility files. Formatting codes can introduce errors in these files, because DOS cannot recognize them.

In Windows, this editor is the System Editor (SYSEDIT.EXE), depicted in Figure 12-35.

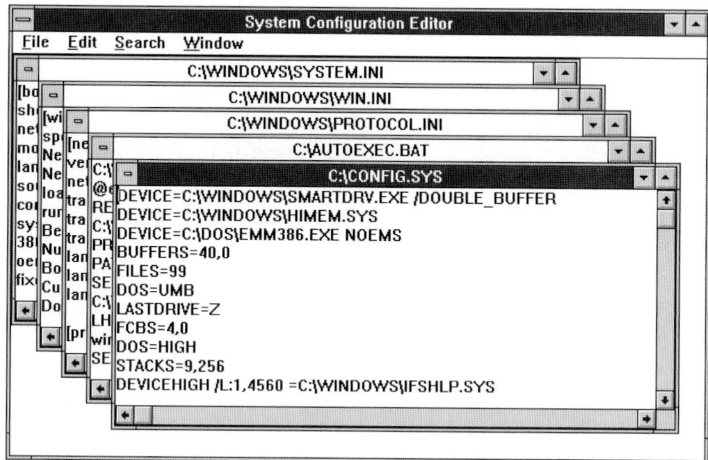

Figure 12-35: The Windows 3.x System Editor Screen

To start the SysEdit function, select the Run option from the Start menu. Type **SYSEDIT** in the Run dialog box and click the OK button. The SysEdit commands are similar to those of other Windows-based text editing programs, such as Notepad or Write.

Windows 9x contains three important editors: the System Editor (SysEdit), the Registry Editor (RegEdit), and the Policy Editor (PolEdit). The Windows 9x SysEdit function is used to modify text files, such as any INI files in the system, as well as the CONFIG.SYS and AUTOEXEC.BAT files.

Windows 2000 includes two Registry editors: RegEdit and RegEdt32. Both utilities enable you to add, edit, and remove Registry entries and to perform other basic functions. However, specific functions can be performed only in one editor or the other.

RegEdt32 is the Registry editor that has historically been used with Windows NT. It presents each subtree as an individual entity in a separate window. RegEdit is the Registry editor that was introduced with Windows 95, and also was included with Windows NT 4.0. The subtrees are presented as being part of the same entity in a single window, as illustrated in Figure 12-36.

The Registry has a permissions system that is similar to NTFS permissions, which enables you to control access to the keys and assigned values. RegEdt32 enables you to view and set permissions through the Security menu. RegEdit does not allow you to access the permissions system.

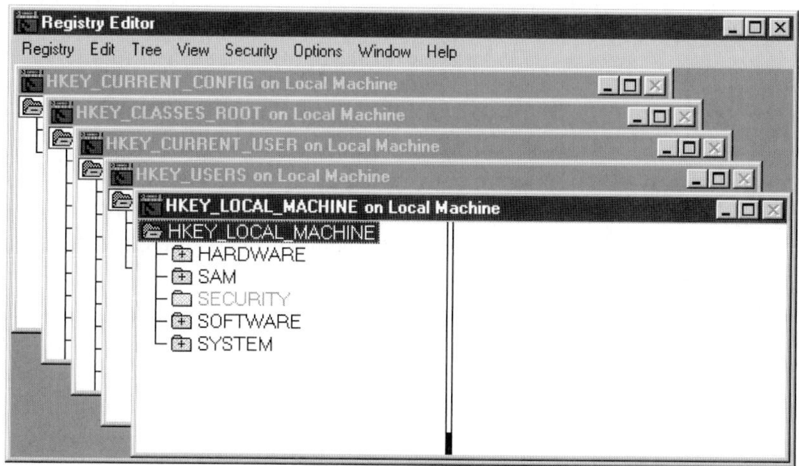

Figure 12-36: RegEdt32 Registry Editor

The Find capabilities of RegEdt32 are accessed from the View menu, and are very limited. You can search only for keys, not assigned values or their corresponding data. This is the equivalent of being able to search for folders in the file system, but not for files. Also, you can initiate a search in only one subtree at a time. The Find capabilities of RegEdit are accessed through the Edit menu, and are very strong. You have the option to search for keys and assigned values, and you can search all subtrees at once.

RegEdit also enables you to save frequently accessed Registry locations as favorites to enable quicker access.

WARNING

Editing the Registry with RegEdit or RegEdt32 should be done only when you have no other alternative. These editors bypass all the safeguards provided by the standard utilities, and allow you to enter values that are invalid or that conflict with other settings. Incorrect editing of the Registry can cause Windows 2000 to stop functioning correctly, prompting a significant amount of troubleshooting or a reinstall of the operating system.

Using Dr. Watson

In an earlier section of this chapter, you learned what GPFs are and how they occur. They are memory-usage faults that occur when one application tries to use memory that has been set aside for another application. The main tool for isolating and correcting GPFs is the Dr. Watson utility provided in all Windows versions.

If the GPF cannot be directly attributed to the Windows operating software, an application program may be the source of the problem. This information is typically part of the GPF error message onscreen. In these cases, the Dr. Watson utility should be set up to run in the background as the system operates.

As the system operates, the Dr. Watson utility monitors its operation and logs its key events in the DRWATSON.LOG file. This log provides a detailed listing of the events that led up to a failure, such as a GPF. The information is automatically stored in the log file.

If a GPF error occurs in the same program each time it is run, the application probably contains defective code that requires repair before it can run under Windows. Programmers and application developers can use the Dr. Watson logs to debug their software and provide patches (software fixes) to their users. They should ask for a copy of the Dr. Watson log file if they are not already aware of the problem.

Using Windows HDD Utilities

Even with normal usage, every system's performance deteriorates over time. Most of the deterioration is due to unnecessary file clutter and segmentation on the system's hard disk drive. Each disk operating system possesses a set of disk utilities that you can use to perform housekeeping functions on the system's disk drives. In Windows 9x and Windows 2000, the most important disk utilities are still CheckDisk/ScanDisk and Defrag.

In Windows 9x, they are located in several areas of the system. The icons for ScanDisk and Defrag are located in the *Start/Programs/Accessories/System_Tools* navigation path. The executable file for ScanDisk can be found in the C:\Windows\Command directory, whereas the Defrag icon is just under C:\Windows.

You should use these HDD utilities periodically to tune-up the performance of the system. To do so, follow these steps:

1. Periodically remove unnecessary TMP and BAK files from the system.
2. Check for and remove lost file chains and clusters using the CheckDisk or ScanDisk utilities.
3. Use the Defrag utility to realign files on the drive that may have become fragmented after being moved back and forth between the drive and the system.

CHKDSK

The DOS CHKDSK (Check Disk) command is a command line utility that has remained in use with Windows 3.x, 9x, NT and 2000 and is used to recover **lost allocation units** from the hard drive. These lost units occur when an application terminates unexpectedly.

lost allocation units

Over a period of time, lost units can pile up and occupy large amounts of disk space. To remove these lost units from the drive, an /F modifier is added to the command so that the lost units will be converted into files that can be investigated, and removed if necessary. In some cases, the converted file is a usable data file that can be rebuilt for use with an application. The CHKDSK /F command is often used before running a drive defragmentation program.

The CheckDisk and ScanDisk utilities are used to search the system's drives for lost allocation units and corrupted files that may have been cross-linked in the FAT. The **CheckDisk (CHKDSK)** utility was used with early MS-DOS systems; the ScanDisk version is associated with the MS-DOS 6.x and Windows 9x operating systems. Both programs are used to optimize disk storage by locating and removing files that have been corrupted. Figure 12-37 depicts a typical CHKDSK display. CHKDSK just locates lost clusters and, when used with an /F switch, converts them into files that can be viewed with a text editor.

CheckDisk (CHKDSK)

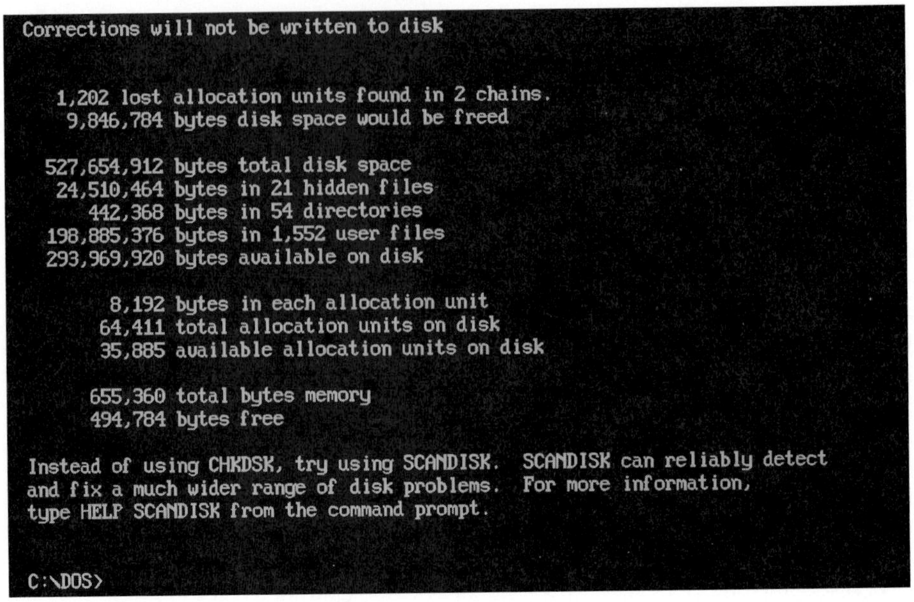

```
Corrections will not be written to disk

   1,202 lost allocation units found in 2 chains.
     9,846,784 bytes disk space would be freed

   527,654,912 bytes total disk space
    24,510,464 bytes in 21 hidden files
       442,368 bytes in 54 directories
   198,885,376 bytes in 1,552 user files
   293,969,920 bytes available on disk

         8,192 bytes in each allocation unit
        64,411 total allocation units on disk
        35,885 available allocation units on disk

       655,360 total bytes memory
       494,784 bytes free

Instead of using CHKDSK, try using SCANDISK.  SCANDISK can reliably detect
and fix a much wider range of disk problems.  For more information,
type HELP SCANDISK from the command prompt.

C:\DOS>
```

Figure 12-37: A CheckDisk Display

ScanDisk

A similar program, called ScanDisk, is available in DOS 6.x and Windows 9x. ScanDisk searches the disk drive for disconnected file clusters and converts them into a form that can be checked and manipulated. This enables the user to determine whether there is any information in the lost clusters that can be restored. ScanDisk also detects, and deletes if necessary, cross-linked files. Cross-linked files occur when information from two or more files is mistakenly stored in the same sector of a disk.

The standard ScanDisk operation examines the system's directory and file structure. However, a Thorough option can be selected to examine the physical disk surface as well as its files and directories. If potential defects exist on the surface, ScanDisk can be used to recover data stored in these areas.

ScanDisk

In addition to locating and converting lost clusters on the disk drive, the **ScanDisk** utility can detect and delete cross-linked files from the drive. It also can make corrections to file and disk errors that it detects. ScanDisk can be run from the DOS command line or as a Windows utility program. As with other disk utilities, only a Windows version of ScanDisk should be used on a Windows system. Using a command-line-based version of ScanDisk may cause data loss rather than optimization, because the command-line version does not lock out the system when the file structure is being modified. By default, the command line version of ScanDisk runs automatically during startup whenever the operating system detects that the system has not been shut down correctly.

TEST TIP

Be aware of what events will cause ScanDisk to run automatically.

Windows 9x actually provides two ScanDisk utilities: an MS-DOS-based version that remains on the Windows 9x Startup disk, and a Windows-compatible graphics-based version (ScanDskw) that can be run from the Windows 9x environment. The MS-DOS version (ScanDisk) is designed to be run from the Startup disk's command line in emergency recovery operations.

The Windows version of ScanDisk is located in the *Start/Programs/Accessories/System Tools* directory. It can be run from the System Tools location, or it can be started through the Start/Run dialog box by typing **ScanDisk**. The Windows version repairs long filenames and is the recommended version for repairing disks. Figure 12-38 shows a typical Windows ScanDisk main page.

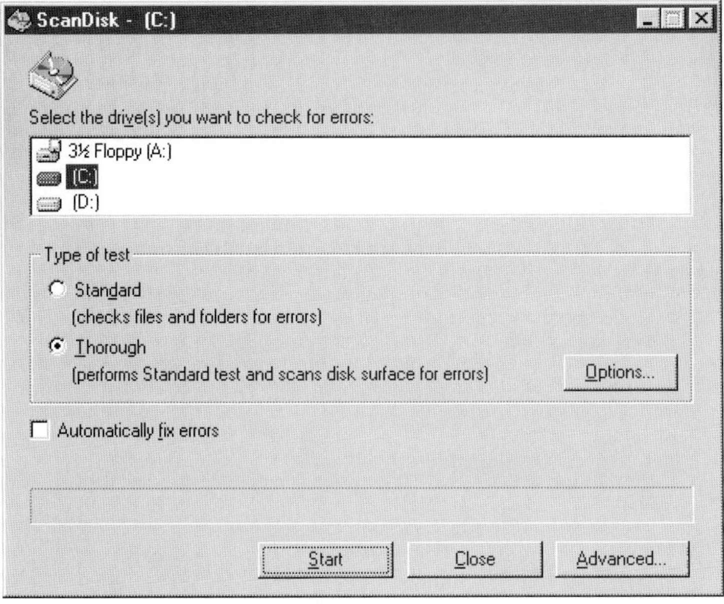

Figure 12-38: A ScanDisk Display

In the ScanDisk main window, select the drive to be examined, choose the type of test to be performed (Standard or Thorough), and set ScanDisk so that it will automatically attempt to fix errors it finds. The Standard test checks the folders and files on the drive for errors; the Thorough test also examines the disk's physical surface for problems.

Selecting the Thorough option will pop up the Surface Scan Options page depicted in Figure 12-39. This page is used to control the scope of the surface scan, and therefore the time involved in checking it. The entire disk may be checked, or the test can be limited to only the data or system areas of the disk.

TEST TIP

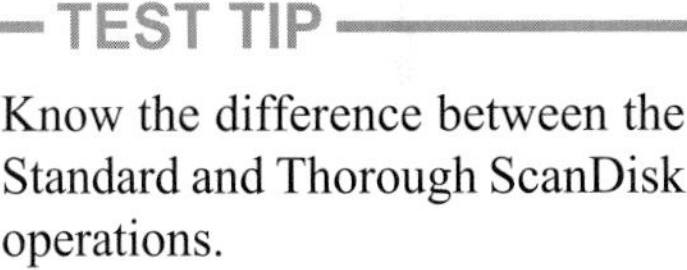
Know the difference between the Standard and Thorough ScanDisk operations.

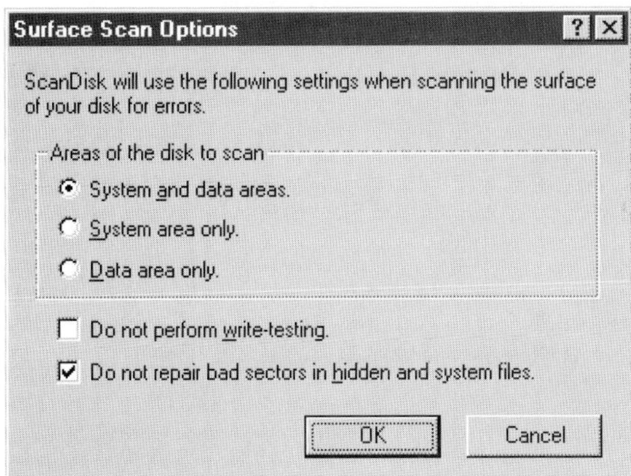

Figure 12-39: Surface ScanDisk Options

Clicking the Advanced button on the ScanDisk main page produces another options page, shown in Figure 12-40. The Advanced Options page is used to determine how ScanDisk will deal with errors it finds. Its options include what to do with lost and cross-linked clusters, how to handle the log file, and how to display its results.

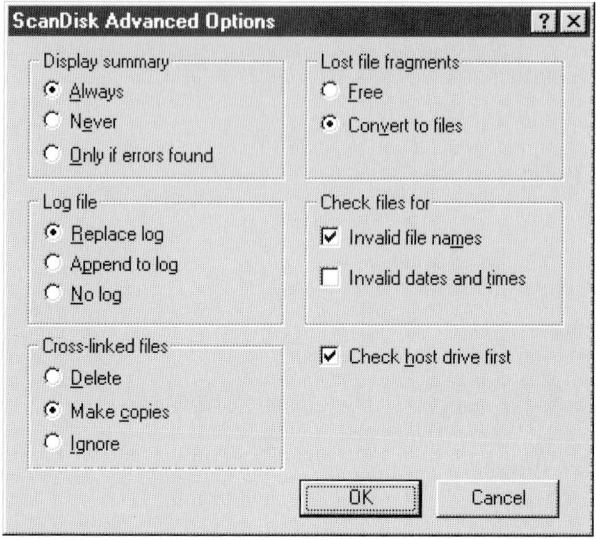

Figure 12-40: ScanDisk Advanced Options Page

HDD Defragmentation

In the normal use of the hard disk drive, files become fragmented on the drive, as illustrated in Figure 12-41. This file fragmentation creates conditions that cause the drive to operate more slowly. Fragmentation occurs when files are stored in non-continuous locations on the drive. This happens when files are stored, retrieved, modified, and rewritten due to differences in the sizes of the before and after files.

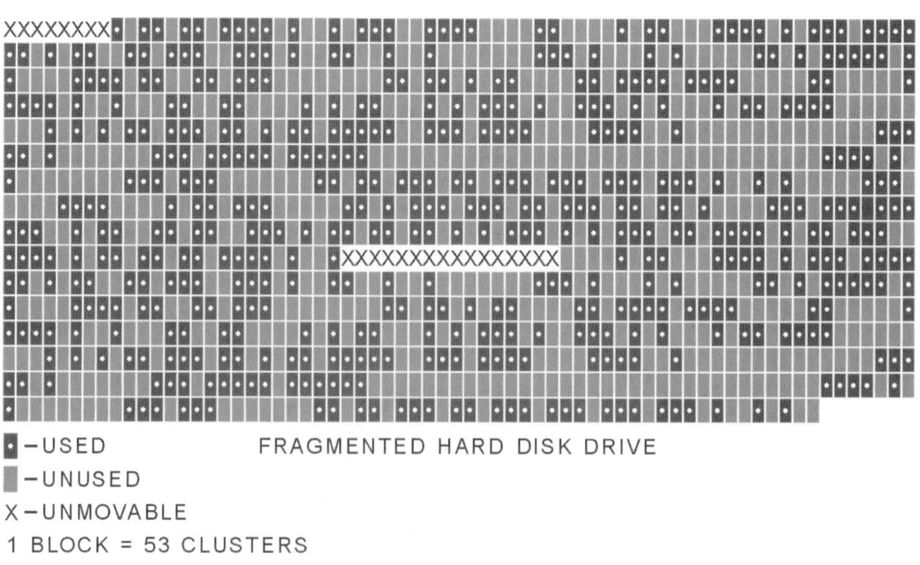

Figure 12-41: Data Sectors

Because the fragmented files do not allow efficient reading by the drive, it takes longer to complete multisector read operations. The defragmentation program realigns the positioning of related file clusters, to speed up the operation of the drive.

Some portions of files may become lost on the drive when a program is unexpectedly interrupted (such as when software crashes, for example, or during a power failure). These lost allocation units (chains) will also cause the drive to operate slowly. Therefore, it is customary to use the DOS CHKDSK command to find these chains and remove them before performing a defrag operation.

It may also be necessary to remove some data from the drive to defragment it. If the system is producing "Out of Disk Space" error messages, the defragmentation utility will not have enough room on the drive to realign clusters. When this happens, some of the contents of the drive will need to be transferred to a backup media (or discarded) to free up some disk space for the realignment process to occur.

The Defrag utility also is used to optimize the operation of the system's disk drives. It does this by reorganizing data on the disk into logically contiguous blocks. With data arranged in this manner, the system does not need to reposition the drive's read/write heads as many times to read a given piece of data.

Although the operation of the Windows 9x version of Defrag is identical, its usage is not. To start the Windows 9x version, click the Start button on the desktop, select the Run option, and enter **Defrag** in the Run dialog box. Specify the drive to be defragmented in the Select Drive dialog box, and click the OK button.

The Defrag utility has been available since the later versions of MS-DOS (with the exception of Windows NT). In Windows 9x and Windows 2000, the Defragmenter utility is located under the *Start/Program/Accessories/System_Tools* path.

In Windows 2000, the Defragmenter can be accessed through the *Start/Settings/Control Panel/Administrative Tools/Computer Management* path. To use the Defrag tool from this point:

1. Click the Disk Defragmenter option
2. Click the desired drive to highlight it
3. Click the Defragment button to begin the operation

The DEFRAG main screen should appear, similar to that shown in Figure 12-42.

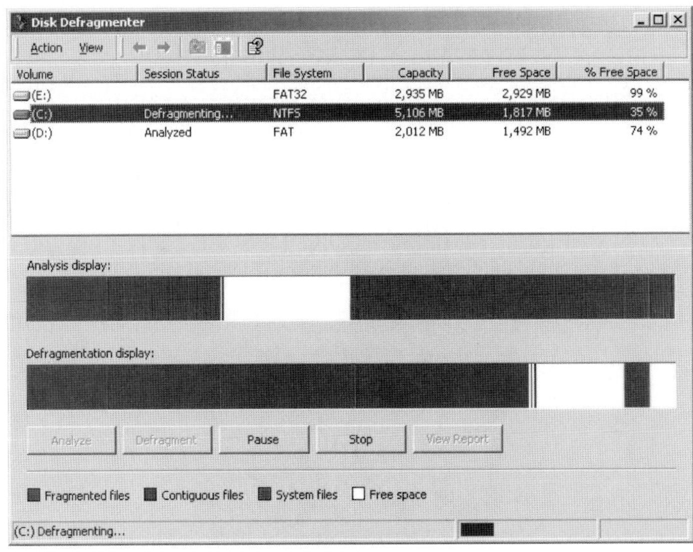

Figure 12-42: The DEFRAG Main Screen

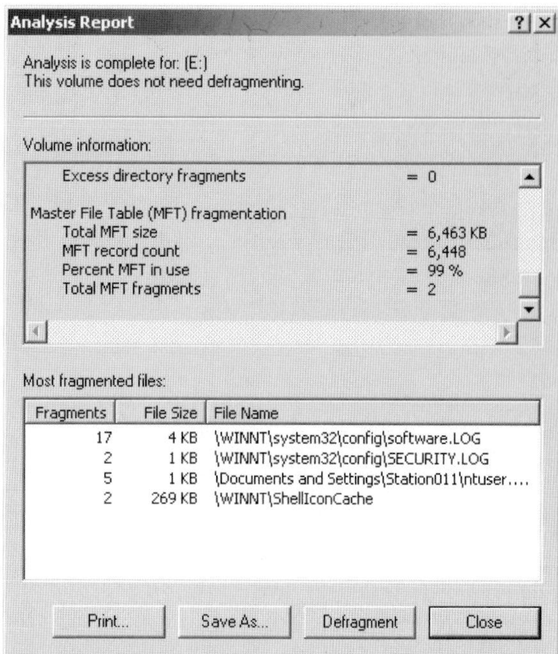

Figure 12-43: The Defrag Analysis Report

The Defragmenter utility contains a disk analysis tool that reports the current status of the volume's key parameters. Figure 12-43 shows a sample analysis report.

Viewing the defragmentation operation is possible through the My Computer window. Just right-click the drive icon and select the Properties option. From this point, click the Tools option and select Defrag. However, viewing the operation of the defragmentation process makes the operation longer. It is better to run this utility in a minimized condition.

The Defrag utility has been available since the later versions of MS-DOS (with the exception of Windows NT). In Windows 9x and Windows 2000, the Defragmenter utility is located under the *Start/Program/Accessories/System_Tools* path.

Backup

Backup utilities enable the user to quickly create extended copies of files, groups of files, or an entire disk drive. This operation is normally performed to create backup copies of important information, for use if the drive crashes or the disk becomes corrupt.

The Backup and Restore commands can be used to back up and retrieve one or more files to another disk.

Because a backup of related files is typically much larger than a single floppy disk, serious backup programs allow information to be backed up to a series of disks; they also provide file compression techniques to reduce the size of the files stored on the disk. Of course, it is impossible to read or use the compressed backup files in this format. To be usable, the files must be decompressed (expanded) and restored to the DOS file format.

This disk management utility is found in both Windows 9x and Windows 2000. This utility is not automatically installed when Windows is set up. If the user decides to install this feature, the actual Backup file (BACKUP.EXE) is placed in the *C:\Program_Files\Accessories* directory. Windows also creates a shortcut icon for the Backup utility in the *C:\Windows\Start_Menu\Programs\Accessories\System_Tools* directory.

Backup Types

Most backup utilities allow backups to be performed in a number of ways. Typically, backups fall into four categories:

- Full or Total
- Incremental
- Selective
- Differential (or modified only)

full backup

total backup

In a **full**, or **total backup**, the entire contents of the designated disk is backed up. This includes directory and subdirectory listings and their contents. This backup method requires the most time each day to backup, but also requires the least time to restore the system after a failure. Only the most recent backup copy is required to restore the system.

Incremental backups

selective backups

differential backups

Three partial backup techniques are used to store data, but yet conserve space on the storage media: **Incremental backups**, **selective backups**, and **differential backups**.

In an incremental backup operation, the system backs up those files that have been created or changed since the last backup. Restoring the system from an incremental backup requires the use of the last full backup and each incremental backup taken since then. However, this method requires the least amount of time to backup the system but the most amount of time to restore it.

To conduct a selective backup the operator moves through the tree structure of the disk marking, or tagging, directories and files to be backed up. After all the desired directories/files have been marked, they are backed up in a single operation.

Specifying a differential backup causes the backup utility to examine each file to determine whether it has changed sine the last full backup was performed. If not, it is bypassed. If the file has been altered, however, it will be backed up. This option is a valuable time-saving feature in a periodic backup strategy. To restore the system, you need a copy of the last full backup and the last differential backup.

TEST TIP

Know which backup type requires the least amount of time to perform and the least amount of effort to restore the system.

In DOS, the basic backup command can be modified through command switches. An /S switch causes all files and subdirectories to be backed up. The /M switch modifies the command so that only those files that have changed are backed up. The /D and /T switches examine the date and time stamps of each file and back up only those files modified after a specified date or time. Other switches can be used to format the backup media and to maintain a backup log on the disk.

Data Backup

Use the CHKDSK/F command to clean up lost file clusters. Instruct the program to convert any lost chains into files that can be checked later. The operation of the Microsoft Windows 98 backup utility is described in the following paragraphs.

Start the backup program. Click Start, point to Programs, Accessories, and then System Tools. If you do not see the Backup entry in the Accessories menu it has not been installed.

Add the Backup utility to the System Tools menu through the Windows Setup tab. Click the Start button, point to Settings, click Control Panel, and double-click the Add/Remove Programs icon. This will open the Add/Remove Programs Properties screen. Click the Windows Setup tab to access the list of available utilities. If you used a compact disc to install Windows, you will be prompted to insert it into your computer.

Select the Backup option from the System Tools menu to start the Backup program and display the Backup Welcome screen, depicted in Figure 12-44. If you select the Create a new backup job option, the Windows Backup wizard will appear to guide you through the Backup setup process. The wizard will ask you questions about which items to backup (entire computer or selected folder and files), What to backup (selected files or only new/changed files), and where to backup to. It will also ask you to supply a name for the backup job.

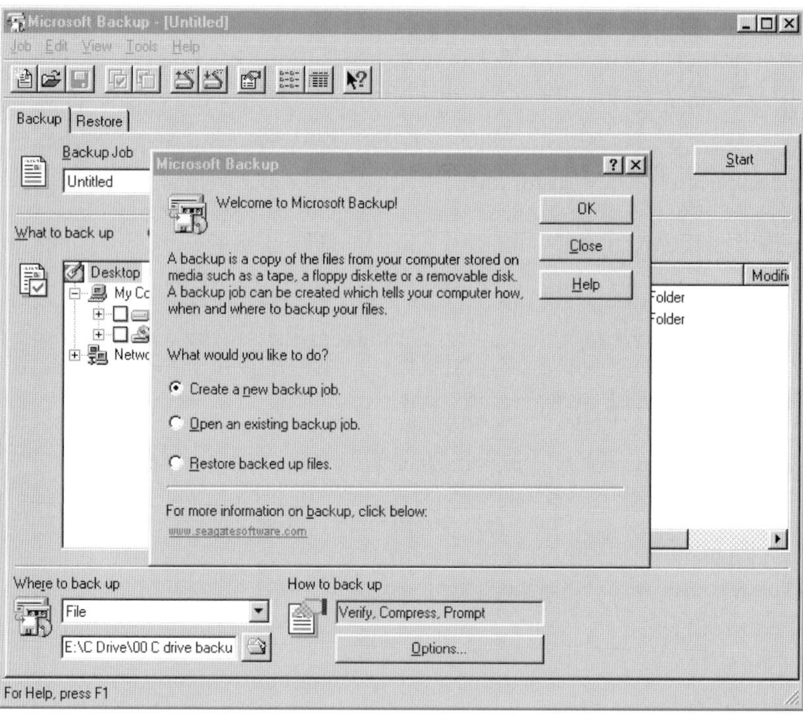

Figure 12-44: Welcome to Backup

If you select the Open an existing Backup job option you will be asked to select the name of the existing backup job from a pop-up dialog box. Select a job and the Backup screen, similar to that shown in Figure 12-45, should appear. Under this option, you can accept the parameters of the existing job, or change them to new values.

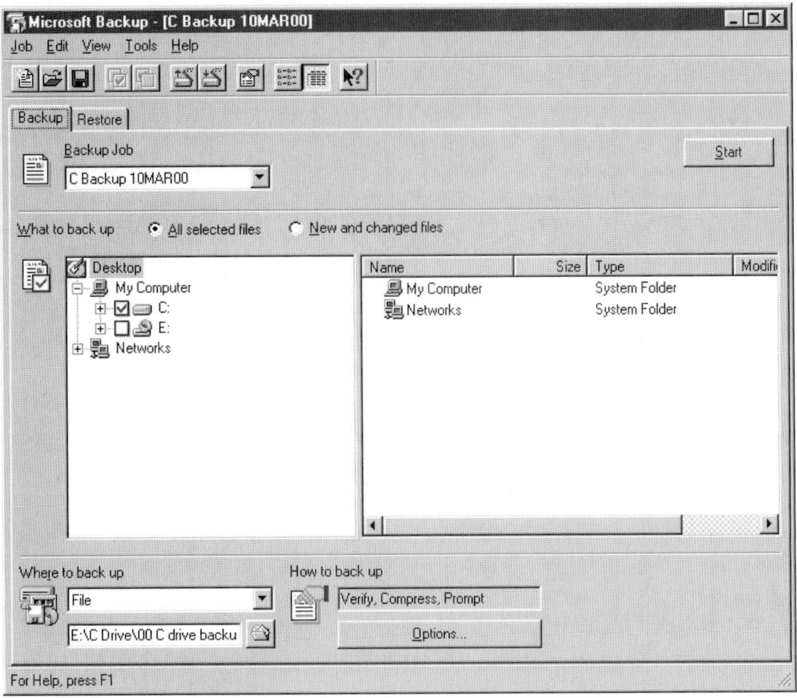

Figure 12-45: The Windows Backup Screen

To set new backup parameters:

Hands-On Activity

1. Click the desired radio button in the What to Backup area (i.e., All Selected Files or New and Changed Files)
2. Select the desired drive in the left pane by clicking on its icon. Expand or contract the branches of the directory tree to gain access to any particular folders or files that you wish to backup. Checking an object will mark all of its sub-folders and files. To unmark any selected files of folders you must click the check box next to it.
3. Identify where to backup by specifying that the backup will be a file and the path to the location where it should be stored. Select the backup options by clicking on the Options button. This will provide access to the Backup Job Options screen depicted in Figure 12-46. Select the desired backup options from the window by clicking on the radio button next to each option. Under the Type tab, verify the All selected files or New and changed files only option. Click the OK button to accept the new options.
4. Click the Job option on the Menu bar and select the appropriate Save As... or Save option. If you select the Save As option, you will be required to supply a new name for the job. If you select Save, the job, along with any new parameters will be saved under its existing name.
5. Click the Start button to begin the Backup operation.

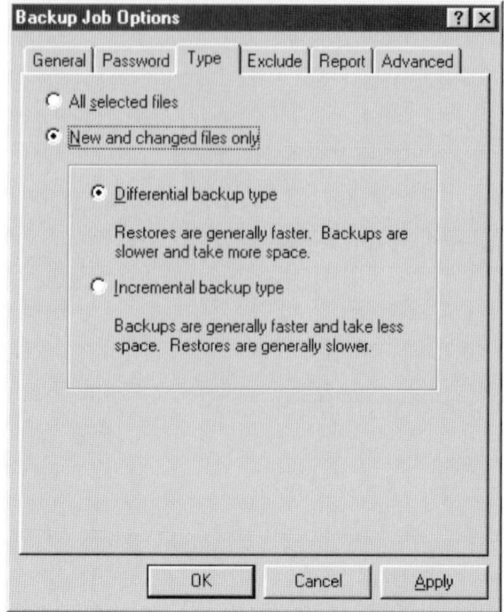

Figure 12-46: The Backup Options Screen

Restoring Data

To restore data in Windows 98, start the BACKUP utility by selecting it from the System Tools sub menu.

Hands-On Activity

1. From the Backup Welcome screen, select the Restore option by checking its radio button and then clicking the OK button.
2. The Backup wizard will appear, as shown in Figure 12-47. Supply the file and path of where the restore should come from in the dialog boxes. Click the Next button to continue with the Restore operation.

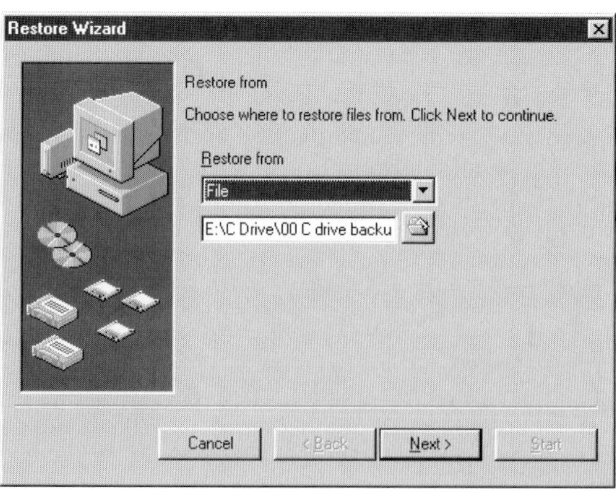

Figure 12-47: The Restore Wizard

3. Check the parameters of the Backup job. Make any changes to the job by manually checking on any items that you do not want to Restore.

4. In the Where to Restore dialog box, you can select to use the Original location for the restore, or you can select an Alternate location option for the restored folders and files. If you select this option, you will need to specify the new location in the drop down dialog window.

5. Under the How to Restore option, click the Options button to access the Restore Options screen depicted in Figure 12-48. Select the restore options from the window by checking the box next to each option. Click the OK button to return to the Restore screen.

6. Click the Start button to restore the specified directories and files from the backup location.

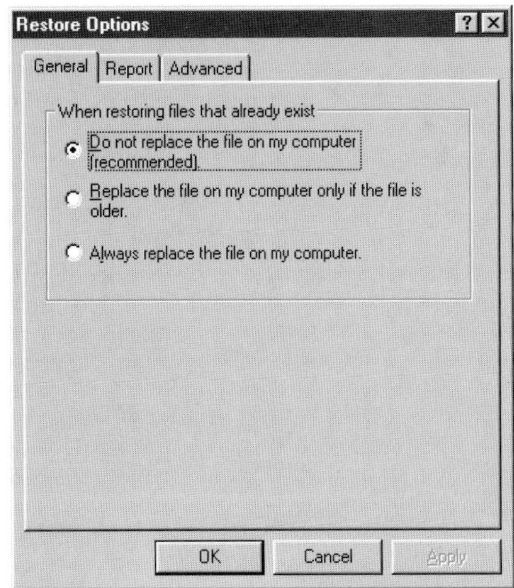

Figure 12-48: The Restore Screen

Other Backup Methods

In a network environment, the **Remote Storage Service** function of the Windows 2000 Server's **Hierarchical Storage Management (HSM)** system can be set up to move infrequently used programs and data to slower storage devices, such as tape or CD-R, while still maintaining the appearance of the data being present. The operation of the HSM system is illustrated in Figure 12-49. When the server receives a request from a user for a file that has been off-loaded, it retrieves the data from the storage device and ships it to the user. This frees up space on the server without creating an inconvenience when users need to access these files.

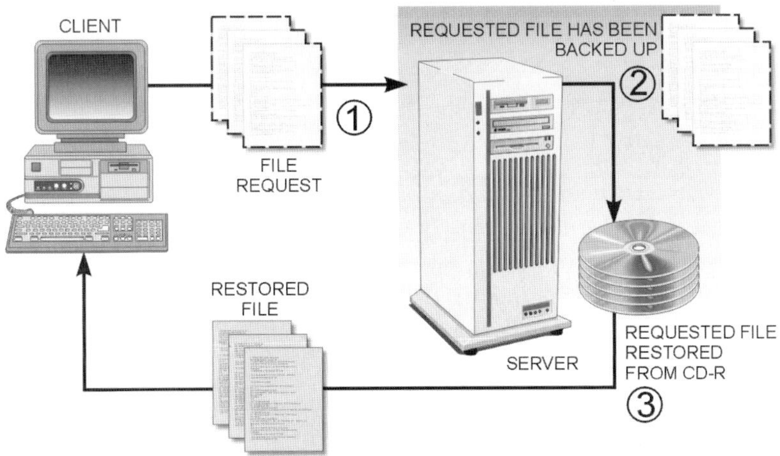

Figure 12-49: The Microsoft Hierarchical Storage Management System

The RSS function is an MMC snap-in that is only available with the Windows 2000 Server packages, not the Professional version. As with the other Windows 2000 Microsoft Management Consoles, the RSS console is accessed through the Start/Programs/Administrative Tools option.

Windows 2000 includes an improved RAID controller utility. This built-in backup utility provides control of Levels 0 through 5 RAID structures and provides changes between levels without needing to rebuild the array.

Windows Help Files

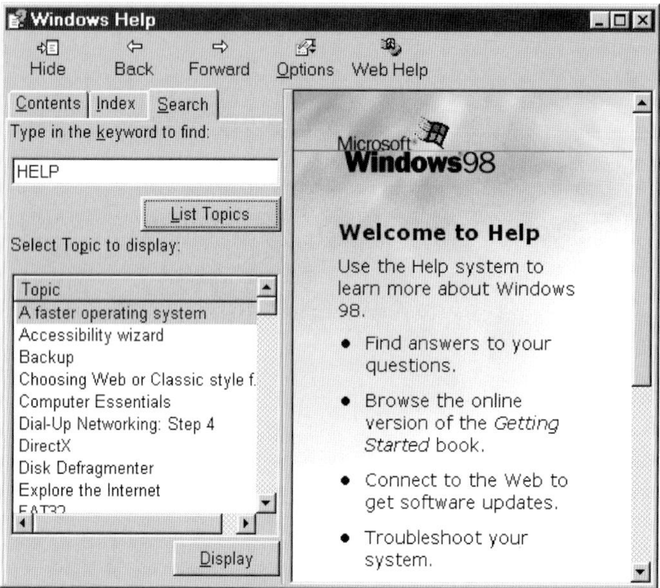

Figure 12-50: The Windows 9x Help Topics Window

Windows 9x, NT 4.0, and 2000 come with built-in troubleshooting Help file systems. This feature includes troubleshooting assistance for a number of different Windows problems. The Windows 9x and Windows 2000 troubleshooters are much more expansive than the Windows NT troubleshooters.

In all three systems, the troubleshooter utilities can be accessed from the Start menu, or from the Help menu entry on the Taskbar. In either case, the Help Topics window appears, as shown in Figure 12-50.

Double-clicking the Troubleshooting entry accesses the Troubleshooting Help section. This section contains a list of several entries with information about common Windows problems and situations. Clicking a topic produces a Help window with information about the troubleshooting process associated with that particular problem (for instance, Hardware Conflict Troubleshooting). This window is depicted in Figure 12-51. The interactive text contains a step-by-step procedure for isolating the problem listed.

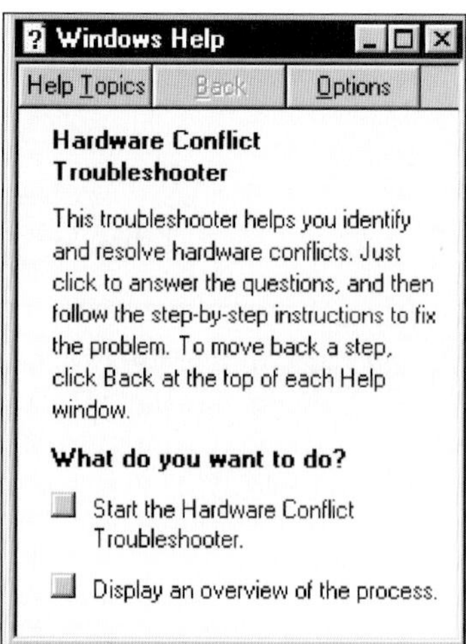

Figure 12-51: Hardware Conflict Troubleshooting Window

Windows Troubleshooting Help Files

Along with the additional troubleshooting tools, the Windows 98 Help file system has been upgraded to provide extended troubleshooting topics. The new Windows 98 Help function includes both the local help, such as that supplied by Windows 95, as well as online help through a built-in Web browser. The online help allows the system to access Microsoft's significant online help resources. The updated Windows 98 Help file system can be accessed through the Start menu.

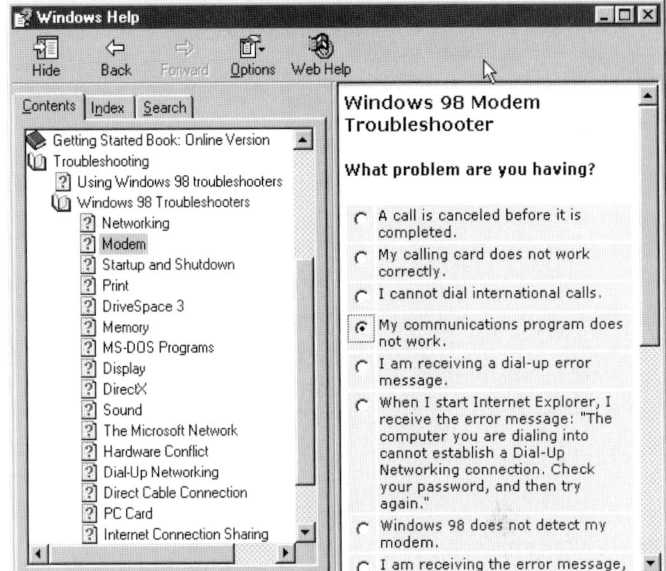

Figure 12-52: Windows 98 Help Window

Selecting the Help entry from the Start menu produces the main Help window, depicted in Figure 12-52. The local Help screens are manipulated by making a selection from the electronic Contents list. In the Troubleshooting entry, just follow the questions and suggestion schemes provided.

The Windows troubleshooters are a special type of help that is available in Windows 9x and 2000. These utilities enable you to pinpoint problems and identify solutions to those problems. Troubleshooters ask a series of questions and then provide you with detailed troubleshooting information based on your responses to those questions.

There are troubleshooters to help you diagnose and solve problems in the following areas, to name a few:

- Sound/Multimedia/Games
- Internet connections
- Active Directory and Group Policy
- Startup and Shutdown
- Hardware
- Display
- Modems
- Printing
- DNS
- WINS
- CSNW
- Stop errors

You can access the troubleshooters in many ways, including through context-sensitive Help, through the Help option on the Start menu, and through the Device Manager.

Other Information and Troubleshooting Resources

You can turn to many resources outside of the operating system for information and troubleshooting assistance, such as **Windows Resource Kits**, the Internet, and **Microsoft TechNet**. The following sections discuss these additional resources.

Windows Resource Kits

Microsoft TechNet

Windows 2000 Resource Kits

Resource Kits

The Windows 95, 98, NT 4.0, and 2000 **Resource Kits** provide thousands of pages of in-depth technical information on these Windows operating systems, as well as hundreds of additional utilities that you can use to enhance deployment, maintenance, and troubleshooting of your Windows network. The Resource Kit is an excellent printed reference for Windows 2000, and also comes with searchable electronic versions.

There are two different versions of the Resource Kit for each NT operating system: one for Windows NT Workstation, and one for Windows NT Server (as well as one for Windows 2000 Professional, and one for Windows 2000 Server). The Resource Kits are published by Microsoft Press and are available from major book retailers.

Internet Help

The Windows 98 and Windows 2000 online Help functions are activated by selecting a topic from the menu and then clicking the Web Help button. This must be followed by clicking the Support On-line at the lower right of the Help window. This action brings up the Internet Sign-In dialog box, if the system is not already logged on to the Internet. After signing in, the Microsoft technical support page appears, as shown in Figure 12-53.

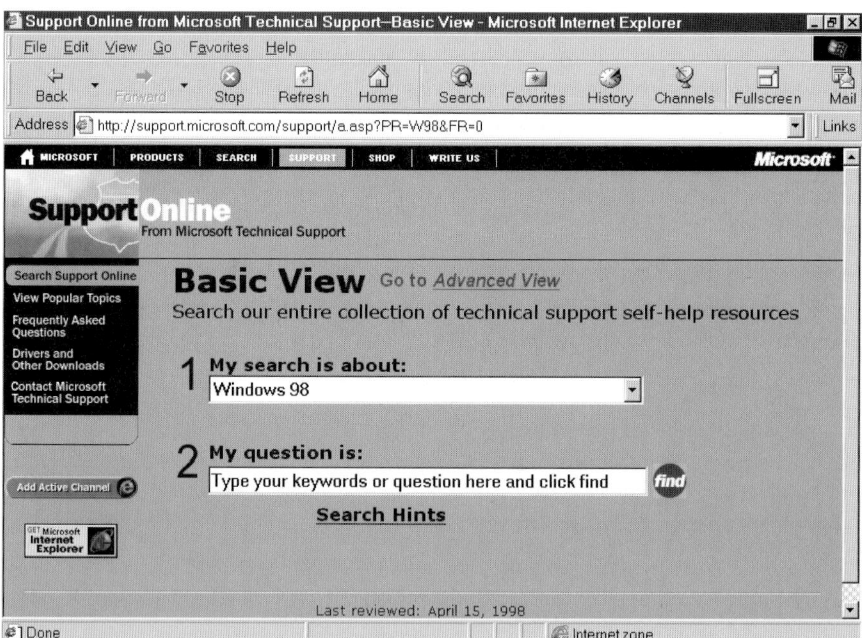

Figure 12-53: Microsoft On-line Help Window

Microsoft's online Product Support Services can provide a wealth of information about Microsoft products, including their operating systems. The URL for Product Support Services is www.Microsoft.com/support. Features of Microsoft Product Support include the following:

- *Microsoft Knowledge Base*, which is a searchable database of information and self-help tools. The Knowledge Base is used by Microsoft Technical Support to support their customers and is made available to you free of charge.
- *Download Center,* which enables you to search all available downloads for any Microsoft product, including service packs, patches, and updates.
- *Facts by Product*, which enables you to browse for information by product, and includes a list of most frequently asked questions about each product.
- Listing of support phone numbers (in case you want to speak to a "real" person). A charge applies for phone support.
- *Online Support Requests*, which enable you to submit questions to Microsoft support personnel. A charge applies for online support.

Microsoft TechNet

Microsoft's TechNet Web site is designed to support IT professionals. The URL for this site is www.Microsoft.com/technet. This is an excellent site for getting the latest information about Windows 2000 (and all other Microsoft products and technologies).

TechNet features include the following:

- Search capabilities for the Technical Information database and the Knowledge Base.
- What's New section that highlights new issues every month.
- Access to the Product Support Services Web site.
- Information categorized by product to help you troubleshoot, maintain, and deploy software.
- Chats, user groups, and Feedback Central for communicating with your peers and with Microsoft.

Microsoft also provides a TechNet subscription service. For an annual fee, the Technical Information database, Knowledge Base, service packs, patches, fixes, software utilities, product enhancements, Resource Kits, beta versions of future Microsoft products, training information, and many other useful items will be shipped to you each month in CD format. A TechNet subscription can be purchased at the TechNet Web site.

CHAPTER SUMMARY

This chapter has focused on diagnosing and troubleshooting operating system problems. The first section of the chapter examined Installation and Startup problems associated with Windows 9x and Windows 2000 systems. Typical startup error messages were related to probable causes for each type of system. Full discussions of Safe Mode startups and Windows log files were also presented in this section.

The second section of the chapter contained materials that pertain to operational problems associated with Microsoft operating systems. This topic explored memory usage problems, application problems, printing problems, and networking problems. Once again, Windows 9x and Windows 2000 systems were discussed, and typical error messages and symptoms were related to probable causes for each type of problem, along with procedures for correcting them.

The final section of the chapter provided an extended discussion of Windows file and disk management utilities, including methods and occasions of using them.

At this point, review the objectives listed at the start of the chapter to be certain that you understand each point and can perform each task listed there.

KEY POINTS REVIEW

This chapter has discussed troubleshooting and diagnostic methods associated with the Windows operating systems. Review the following key points before moving into the Review and Exam Questions sections to make sure you are comfortable with each point. Afterward, answer the Review Questions that follow to verify your knowledge of the information.

- During the bootup process, an interesting troubleshooting point occurs at the single beep in the bootup process of most computers. If the system produces an error message, such as "The system has detected unstable RAM at location XXXX", or a beep coded error signal before the beep, the problem is hardware related.
- On the other hand, if the error message, or beep code is produced after the single beep occurs, the problem is likely to be associated with starting up the operating system. At this point, the problem becomes an operating system startup problem.
- Windows 9x offers many improved features over previous operating systems. However, it can suffer many of the same problems as any other operating system. To overcome some of the typical system problems, Windows 9x includes several built-in troubleshooting tools. These tools include several Safe Mode startup options, a trio of system log files, and an extensive interactive troubleshooting help file system.
- Since Windows 9x does not start up through DOS, it will be very difficult to gain access to the system if Windows becomes disabled. Therefore, it is helpful to have an Emergency Start disk to troubleshoot Windows 9x-related problems. In the event that the Windows program becomes non-functional, it will be necessary to use the Start disk to restore the system to proper operation.
- When Windows 9x fails to start up properly, there is no separate underlying DOS platform that can be accessed to separate bootup/configuration problems from operating environment problems. However, Windows 9x provides the Safe Mode startup utility that can be employed to isolate and repair startup problems.

- When Windows 9x refuses to start up, a number of options are available for starting it from the command line. Starting Windows using a /D switch is often helpful in isolating possible areas of the operating system as problem sources (that is, WIN /D). You can modify the /D switch to start Windows in a number of different configurations:

    1. Using an /D:F switch disables 32-bit disk access.
    2. The /D:M and /D:N switches start Windows in Safe Mode, or Safe with Networking Mode.
    3. An /D:S switch inhibits Windows from using address space between F0000h and FFFFFh.
    4. The /D:V switch prevents Windows from controlling disk transfers. Instead, HDD interrupt requests are handled by the BIOS.
    5. The /D:X switch prevents Windows from using the area of memory between A000h and FFFFh.

- Windows 9x maintains four log files named BOOTLOG.TXT, SETUPLOG.TXT, DETLOG.TXT, and DETCRASH.LOG. These files maintain a log of different system operations and can be used to see what events occurred leading up to a failure.

- The BOOTLOG.TXT file contains the sequence of events conducted during the Startup of the system. The original BOOTLOG.TXT file is created during the Windows 9x Setup process. The file can be updated by pressing the F8 key during Startup, or by starting Windows 9x with a WIN /B switch. It is not updated automatically each time the system is started. The log information is recorded in five basic sections.

- The SETUPLOG.TXT file holds setup information that was established during the installation process. The file is stored on the system's root directory and is used in Safe Recovery situations.

- The DETLOG.TXT file holds the text equivalent of the information in the DETCRASH.LOG file. This file can be read with a text editor to determine which hardware components have been detected by the system and what its parameters are.

- The Windows 9x structure provides a much improved multitasking environment over Windows 3.x. However, applications can still attempt to access unallocated memory locations, or attempt to use another application's space. When these memory conflicts occur, the system can either return an error message, or simply stop processing.

- Windows 9x produces a "This program has performed an illegal operation and is about to shut down" message when a memory conflict occurs. When this happens, Windows may take care of the error and allow you to continue operating by simply pressing a key.

- If nothing is being produced by the printer, even though print jobs have been sent to it, check the Print Spooler to see if any particular type of error has occurred. To view documents waiting to be printed, double-click on the desired printer's icon. Return to the Printer folder, right-click on the printer's icon, click Properties, and then select Details. From this point, select Spool Settings and select the Print Directly to the Printer option. If the print job goes through, there is a spooler problem. If not, the hardware and printer driver are suspect.

- The complexity of conducting printer operations over a network becomes much greater due to the addition of the network drivers and protocols. Many of the problems encountered when printing over the network involve components of the operating system. Therefore, its networking and printing functions must both be checked.

- In a client/server system such as a Novell NetWare or Windows NT system, the computer professional's main responsibility is to get the local station to boot up to the network's Login Prompt. At this point, the network administrator, or network engineer, becomes responsible for directing the troubleshooting process.

- During the data transfer, both modems monitor the signal level of the carrier to prevent the transfer of false data due to signal deterioration. If the carrier signal strength drops below some predetermined threshold level, or is lost for a given length of time, one or both modems will initiate automatic disconnect procedures.

- Checking the modem or network card is the major hardware-related activity normally involved with Internet sites. However, you may be required to work with the customer's local Internet service provider to solve some types of problems.

- Windows 9x comes with a built-in Troubleshooting Help file system. This feature includes troubleshooting assistance for a number of different Windows 9x problems.

- Hardware and configuration conflicts can also be isolated manually using the Windows 9x Device Manager from the Control Panel's System icon. This utility is basically an easy-to-use interface for the Windows 9x Registry.

REVIEW QUESTIONS

The following questions test your knowledge of the material presented in this chapter.

1. If a Windows 9x system locks up while running a DOS application, what item should be checked first?
2. List the four preliminary steps used to troubleshoot operating system startup problems.
3. If an application will not start in a Windows 9x environment, list four possible causes.
4. What type of error is indicated by a "This Program Has Performed an Illegal Operation..." message?
5. Why are defragmentation programs run on computers?
6. What is the purpose of running a CHKDSK operation before performing a backup or defrag operation on the hard drive?
7. Which Windows utility can be used to examine and change ASCII text files such as the CONFIG.SYS and Windows INI files?
8. If an application will not start in Windows 9x when its icon is clicked, what action should be taken?
9. How can the Print Spooler be isolated as a cause of printing problems in Windows 9x?
10. Name two important tools for solving startup problems in Windows 9x.

11. Which devices are loaded in Safe Mode startup?
12. What prevents printer hangups in Windows from locking up the system?
13. Why would a Step-by-Step Confirmation mode startup be performed?
14. What Windows 9x tool is used to determine the configuration settings of a network card?
15. Name three items that can typically go wrong after Windows 98 has successfully booted up.

EXAM QUESTIONS

1. What action occurs if the HIMEM.SYS file is missing in Windows 9x?
   a. Windows will not start.
   b. Windows will start in DOS mode.
   c. Windows will start in Standard mode.
   d. Windows will start in Safe mode.
2. Which utility can be used to detect and repair corrupted files in a Windows 9x system?
   a. ScanDisk
   b. Chkdsk
   c. System Monitor
   d. Defrag
3. What Windows 9x utility can be used to change Registry entry values?
   a. SysEdit
   b. Polyedit
   c. Device Manager
   d. Resourcedit
4. If an exclamation point inside a yellow circle is displayed by an entry in the Windows 9x Device Manager, what is indicated?
   a. The device has been disabled by a user selection conflict.
   b. The device is experiencing a direct hardware conflict with another device.
   c. The device's real-mode driver is not being loaded.
   d. The device's virtual-mode driver is not being loaded.
5. If an "X" is displayed by an entry in the Windows 9x Device Manager, what is indicated?
   a. The device has been disabled by a user selection conflict.
   b. The device is experiencing a direct hardware conflict with another device.
   c. The device's real-mode driver is not being loaded.
   d. The device's virtual-mode driver is not being loaded.

6. What function does the BOOTUPLOG.TXT file serve?
   a. It tracks the events of the Startup procedure.
   b. It carries out the steps of the Startup procedure.
   c. It tracks the events of the Shut Down procedure.
   d. It tracks the events of the POST sequence.
7. If one computer cannot see another computer on the network, what might the most logical problem be?
   a. The Device Manager does not recognize the adapter.
   b. A matching protocol is not installed.
   c. The Network Control Panel has not been enabled.
   d. The Networking Services have not been installed.
8. If Plug-and-Play is not working in a Windows 9x system, where can a device driver be installed from?
   a. The Start Menu
   b. The Device Manager
   c. The Add/Remove Programs wizard
   d. The Add New Hardware wizard
9. If a modem listed in the Device Manager indicates a resource conflict, what action should be taken to clear up the situation?
   a. Run MSD.EXE.
   b. Run MEM.EXE.
   c. Click the Resources tab and check for conflicts.
   d. Change the IRQ setting for the device.
10. Starting the Windows 98 system in _____ mode will bypass real-mode drivers, and load a Protected-Mode version of Windows 98.
    a. Normal
    b. Logged
    c. Safe
    d. Step-by-Step Confirmation

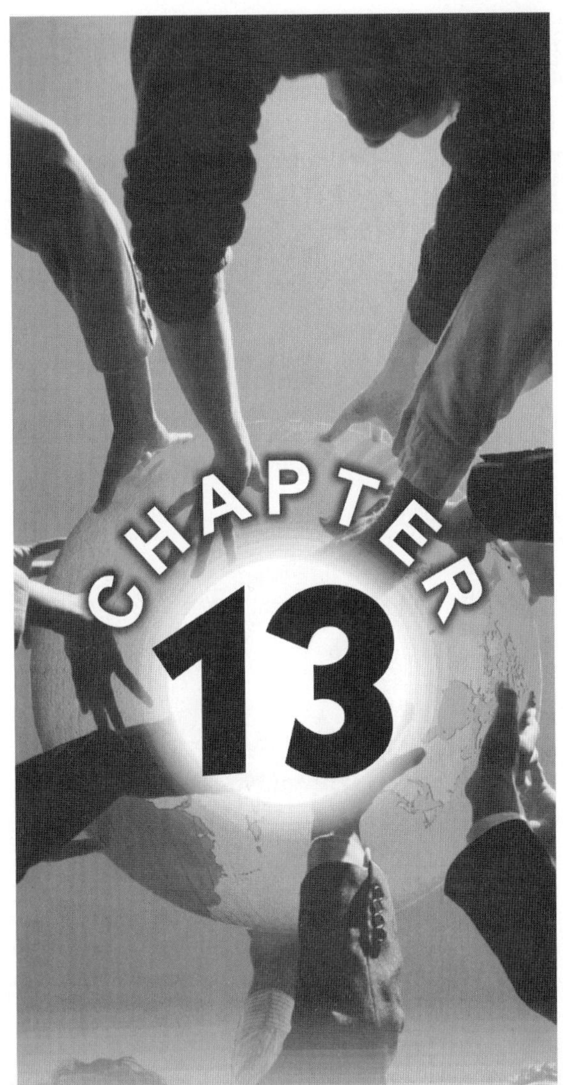

PREVENTIVE MAINTENANCE

OBJECTIVES

OBJECTIVES

Upon completion of this chapter and its related lab procedures, you should be able to perform the following tasks:

1. Demonstrate proper cleaning procedures for various system components.
2. Describe electrostatic discharge hazards and methods of preventing ESD.
3. List the steps for proper IC handling.
4. Define the term ground.
5. Describe the two types of uninterruptible power supplies (UPS) and state their qualities.
6. State typical precautions that should be observed when working on computer equipment.
7. Perform generic preventive maintenance routines as required (for example, remove excess toner, replace printer ribbons, defragment hard drives, and create back-up copies).
8. Detail routine preventive maintenance procedures as they apply to hard and floppy disks.
9. Perform basic disk-management functions on a hard drive, including using ScanDisk, CHKDSK, and Defrag utilities.
10. Use backup software to create backups of important data.
11. Differentiate between the Total, Selective, and Differential backup methods.
12. Use software utilities to identify and remove viruses from computer systems.
13. List precautionary steps that should be taken when handling floppy disks.
14. List steps to clean a dot-matrix, ink-jet, or laser printer.
15. Establish and maintain preventive maintenance schedules for users.
16. Differentiate between various UPS specifications and state how they apply to a given situation.
17. State potential hazards that are present when working with laser printers, monitors, and other equipment.

CHAPTER 13

PREVENTIVE MAINTENANCE

INTRODUCTION

This domain requires the test taker to show knowledge of safety and preventive maintenance. With regard to safety, it includes the potential hazards to personnel and equipment when working with lasers, high-voltage equipment, ESD, and items that require special disposal procedures that comply with environmental guidelines. With regard to preventive maintenance, this includes knowledge of preventive maintenance products, procedures, environmental hazards, and precautions when working on microcomputer systems.

PREVENTIVE MAINTENANCE

The A+ Core objective 3.1 states that the test taker should be able to identify the purpose of various types of preventive maintenance products and procedures, and when to use/perform them. Content may include the following:

- Liquid cleaning compounds
- Types of materials to clean contacts and connections
- Vacuum out systems, power supplies, fans

It has long been known that one of the best ways to fix problems with complex systems is to prevent them before they happen. This is the concept behind preventive maintenance procedures. Breakdowns never occur at convenient times. By planning for a few minutes of non-productive activities, hours of repair and recovery work can be avoided.

Cleaning

Cleaning is a major part of keeping a computer system healthy. Therefore, the technician's tool kit should also contain a collection of cleaning supplies. Along with hand tools, it will need a lint-free, soft cloth (**chamois**) for cleaning the plastic outer surfaces of the system.

Cleaning

chamois

> **TEST TIP**
>
> Know the common methods of cleaning various computer components.

Outer surface cleaning can be accomplished with a simple soap and water solution, followed by a clear water rinse. Care should be taken to make sure that none of the liquid splashes, or drips, into the inner parts of the system. A damp cloth is easily the best general-purpose cleaning tool for use with computer equipment.

antistatic spray

antistatic solution

The cleaning should be followed by the application of an **antistatic spray** or **antistatic solution** to prevent the build-up of static charges on the components of the system. A solution composed of 10 parts water and one part common household fabric softener makes an effective and economical antistatic solution. To remove dust from the inside of cabinets, a small paint brush is handy.

> **TEST TIP**
>
> Know what types of materials/techniques can be used to clean different areas of the computer system.

oxidation build-up

Another common problem is the build-up of **oxidation**, or corrosion, at electrical contact points. These build-ups occur on electrical connectors and contacts, and can reduce the flow of electricity through the connection. Some simple steps can be used to keep corrosion from becoming a problem. The easiest step in preventing corrosion is observing the correct handling procedures for printed circuit boards and cables, as shown in Figure 13-1. Never touch the electrical contact points with your skin, since the moisture on your body can start corrosive action.

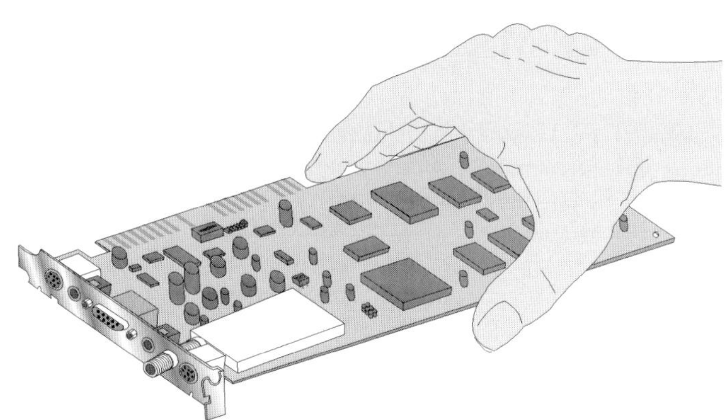

Figure 13-1: How to Handle a PC Board

electrical contact cleaner

Even with proper handling, some corrosion may occur over time. This oxidation can be removed in a number of ways. The oxide build-up can be sanded off with emery cloth, rubbed off with a common pencil eraser or special solvent-wipe, or dissolved with an **electrical contact cleaner** spray. Socketed devices should be reseated (removed and reinstalled to establish a new electrical connection) as a part of an anti-corrosion cleaning. However, they should be handled according to the MOS Handling guidelines in this chapter to make certain that no static discharge damage occurs.

If you use the emery cloth, or rubber eraser, to clean your contacts, always rub towards the outer edge of the board, or connector, to prevent damage to the contacts. Rubbing the edge may lift the foil from the PC board. Printed-circuit board connectors are typically very thin. Therefore, rub hard enough to remove only the oxide layer. Also, take time to clean up any dust or rubber contamination generated by the cleaning effort.

Cleaning other internal components, such as disk drive Read/Write heads, can be performed using lint-free foam swabs, and isopropyl alcohol or methanol. It's most important that the cleaning solution be one that dries without leaving a residue. The following list includes the tools and equipment recommended for a well-prepared computer repair toolbox:

- Assorted flat-blade screwdrivers
- Assorted Phillips screwdrivers
- Assorted small nut drivers
- Assorted small torx bit drivers
- Needle-nose pliers
- Diagonal pliers
- Contact cleaner
- Foam swabs
- Tweezers
- Cleaning supplies
- Magnifying glass
- Clip leads
- IC extractors

PM (Preventive Maintenance) Procedures

The environment around a computer system, and the manner in which the computer is used, determines greatly how many problems it will have. Occasionally dedicating a few moments of care to the computer can extend its **Mean Time Between Failures (MTBF)** period considerably. This activity, involving maintenance not normally associated with a breakdown, is called **Preventive Maintenance (PM)**.

Mean Time Between Failures (MTBF)

Preventive Maintenance (PM)

The following sections of this chapter describe PM measures for the various areas of the system.

TEST TIP

Know what environmental conditions, or activities, are most likely to lead to equipment failures.

As with any electronic device, computers are susceptible to failures caused by dust build-up, rough handling, and extremes in temperature.

Over time, dust builds up on everything it can gain access to. Many computer components generate static electrical charges that attract dust particles. In the case of electronic equipment, dust forms an insulating blanket that traps heat next to active devices and can cause them to overheat. Excessive heat can cause premature aging and failure. The best dust protection is a dust-tight enclosure. However, computer components tend to have less than dust-tight seals. Power supply and microprocessor fans pull air from outside through the system unit.

Another access point for dust is uncovered expansion slot openings. Missing expansion slot covers adversely affect the system in two ways. First, the missing cover permits dust to accumulate in the system, forming the insulating blanket described above, which causes component overheating. Second, the heat problem is complicated further by the fact that the missing slot cover interrupts the designed airflow patterns inside the case, causing components to overheat due to missing or inadequate airflow.

TEST TIP

Be aware of the effect that missing expansion slot covers have on the operation of the system unit.

Smoke

Smoke is a more dangerous cousin of dust. Like dust particles, smoke collects on all exposed surfaces. The residue of smoke particles is sticky and clings to the surface. In addition to contributing to the heat build-up problem, smoke residue is particularly destructive to moving parts such as floppy disks, fan motors, and so forth.

static-free vacuum

Dust build-up inside system components can be taken care of with a soft brush. A **static-free vacuum** can also be used to remove dust from inside cases and keyboards. Be sure to use a static-free vacuum, since normal vacuums are by their nature static generators. The static-free vacuum has special grounding to remove the static buildup it generates. Dust covers are also helpful in holding down dust problems. These covers are simply placed over the equipment when not in use and removed when the device is needed.

TEST TIP

Know that computer vacuums have special grounding to dissipate static buildup that can damage computer devices.

Rough handling is a either a matter of neglect, or a lack of knowledge about how equipment should be handled. Therefore, overcoming rough handling problems requires that technicians be aware of proper handling techniques for sensitive devices, such as hard disk drives and monitors, and that they adjust their component handling practices to compensate.

Identifying and controlling heat build-up problems can require some effort and planning. Microcomputers are designed to run at normal room temperatures. If the ambient temperature rises above about 85 degrees F, heat build-up can become a problem. High humidity can also lead to heat-related problems.

To combat heat problems, make sure that the area around the system is uncluttered so that free air flow around the system can be maintained. Make sure the power supply's fan is operational. If it is not, replace the power supply unit. Likewise, be sure that the microprocessor fan is plugged in and operational. It is very easy for a high-speed microprocessor to fry if its fan fails. A good rule of thumb is to install a fan on any microprocessor running above 33 MHz.

If heat build-up still exists, check to make sure that the outer cover is secured firmly to the machine and that all of the expansion clot covers are in place. These items can disrupt the designed air-flow characteristics of the case. Finally, add an additional case fan to draw more air through the system unit.

Protecting Monitors

periodic cleaning

dusting

common-sense practices

The PM associated with video display monitors basically consists of **periodic cleaning**, **dusting**, and good, **common-sense practices** around the monitor. The monitor's screen and cabinet should be dusted frequently, and cleaned periodically. Dust and smoke particles can build up very quickly around the monitor's screen, due to the presence of static charges on its face. When cleaning the screen, some caution should be used to avoid scratching its surface, and in the case of antiglare screens, preserve its glare-reduction features.

Aerosol sprays, solvents, and commercial cleaners should be avoided, because they can damage the screen and cabinet. The simple cleaning solution, described earlier, is also fine for cleaning the monitor. Make sure that the monitor's power cord is disconnected from any power source before washing. The monitor's screen should be dried with a soft cloth after rinsing.

The monitor should not be left on for extended periods with the same image displayed on the screen. Over a period of time, the image will become permanently "burnt" into the screen. If it is necessary to display the same information on the screen for a long period of time, turn the intensity level of the monitor down, or install a **screen saver** program to alter the screen image periodically.

screen saver

Inside the monitor's housing are very dangerous voltage levels (in excess of 25,000 volts, more than enough to kill or badly injure someone). Therefore, you should only remove the monitor's outer cabinet if you are fully qualified to work on CRT-based units. Even if the monitor has been turned off and unplugged for a year, it may still hold enough electrical potential to be deadly. Figure 13-2 shows the areas of the monitor that should be avoided, if you must work inside its housing.

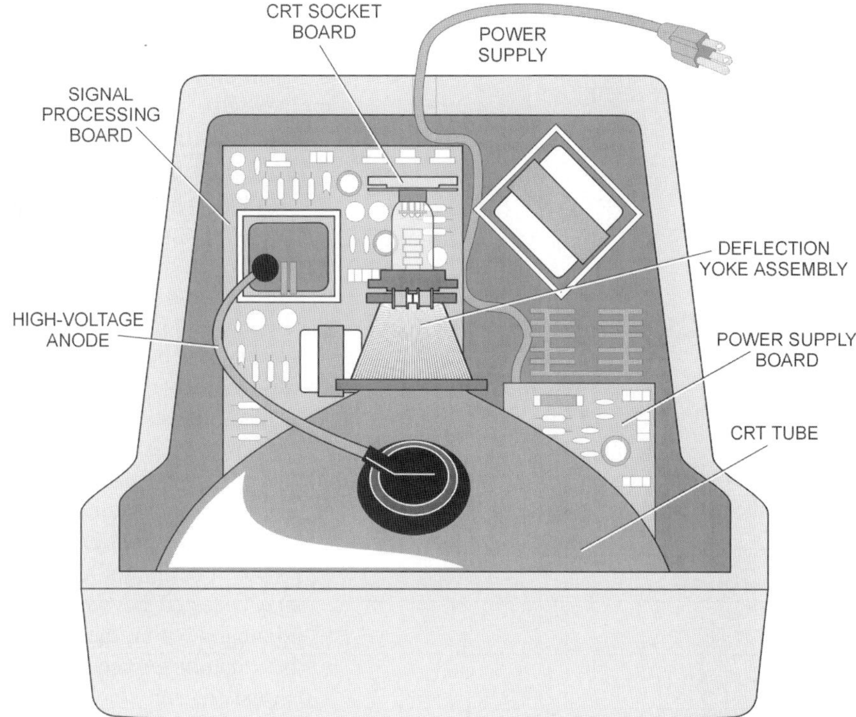

Figure 13-2: Caution Areas Inside the Monitor

Video display monitors often include a tilt/swivel base that allows the users to position it at whatever angle is most comfortable. This offers additional relief from eyestrain by preventing the users from viewing the display at an angle. Viewing the screen at an angle causes the eyes to focus separately, which places strain on the eye muscles.

Protecting Hard Disk Drives

Hard disk drives don't require much preventive maintenance, since the Read/Write (R/W) heads and disks are enclosed in sealed, dust-tight compartments. However, there are some things that can be done to optimize the performance, and life span, of hard disk systems. Rough handling is responsible for more hard disk drive damage than any other factor.

box-within-a-box

clean room

The drive should never be moved while you can still hear its disks spinning. The disk is most vulnerable during startup and shutdown, when the heads are not fully flying. Even a small jolt during these times can cause a great deal of damage to both the platters and the R/W heads. If the drive must be moved, a waiting period of one full minute should be allotted after turning the system off.

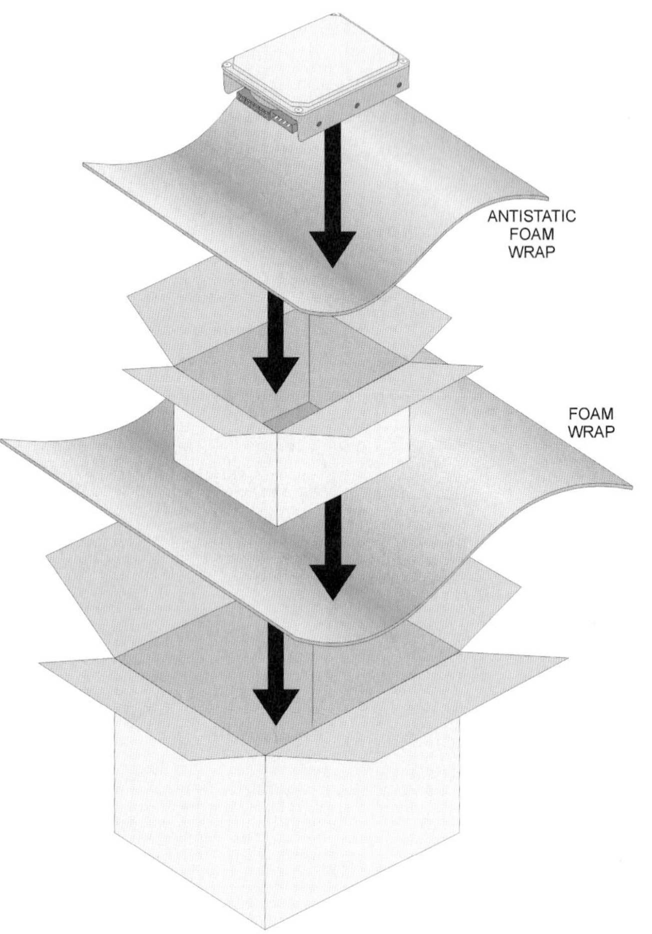

Figure 13-3: Proper Packing of a Hard Drive for Shipment

If the drive is to be transported, or shipped, make sure to pack it properly. The forces exerted on the drive during shipment may be great enough to cause the R/W heads to slap against the disk surfaces, causing damage to both. Pack the drive unit in an oversized box, with antistatic foam all around the drive. You may also pack the drive in a **box-within-a-box** configuration, once again using foam as a cushion. This concept is illustrated in Figure 13-3.

At no time should the hard drive's housing, which protects the platters, be removed in open air. The drive's disks and R/W heads are sealed in the airtight housing under a vacuum. The contaminants floating in normal air will virtually ruin the drive. If the drive malfunctions, the electronic circuitry and connections may be tested, but when it comes to repairs within the disk chamber, factory service, or a professional service facility with a proper **clean room** is a must!

software backup

In order to recover quickly from hardware failures, operator mistakes, and acts of nature, some form of **software backup** is essential with a hard disk system. The most common backup for larger systems is high-speed, streaming-tape cartridges, which can automatically back up the contents of the entire disk drive on magnetic tape. In the event of data loss on the disk, a full reinstall from the tape is possible in a matter of a few minutes.

optical drives

removable hard drives

Backups may also be kept on diskettes. However, the volume of data stored on modern hard disks would require a tremendous number of floppies to back up. The floppies would also need to be stored. Other high-volume disk-based devices, such as **optical drives** and **removable hard drives**, have become attractive methods for backing up the contents of large hard drives. CD-R and CD-RW drives provide an attractive option for storing limited amounts (680 MB) of critical data. Their high capacities allow large amounts of information to be written on a single disc. The major drawback of using a CD-R disc is that after the disc has been written to, it cannot be erased or reused. Various backup methods are depicted in Figure 13-4. In any case, failure to maintain backups will eventually result in a great deal of grief when the system goes down due to a hardware or software failure.

Copies of the system backup should be stored in a convenient, but secure place. In the case of secure system backups, such as client/server networks, the backup copies should be stored where the network administrators can have access to them, but not the general public (i.e., a locked file cabinet). Left unsecured, these copies could be used by someone without authority to gain access to the system, or to its data. Even Emergency Repair Disks associated with Windows NT and Windows 2000 should be stored in a secure location. These disks can also be used by people other than administrators to gain access to information in client/server networks. Many companies maintain a copy of their backup away from the main site. This is done for protection in case of disasters such as fire.

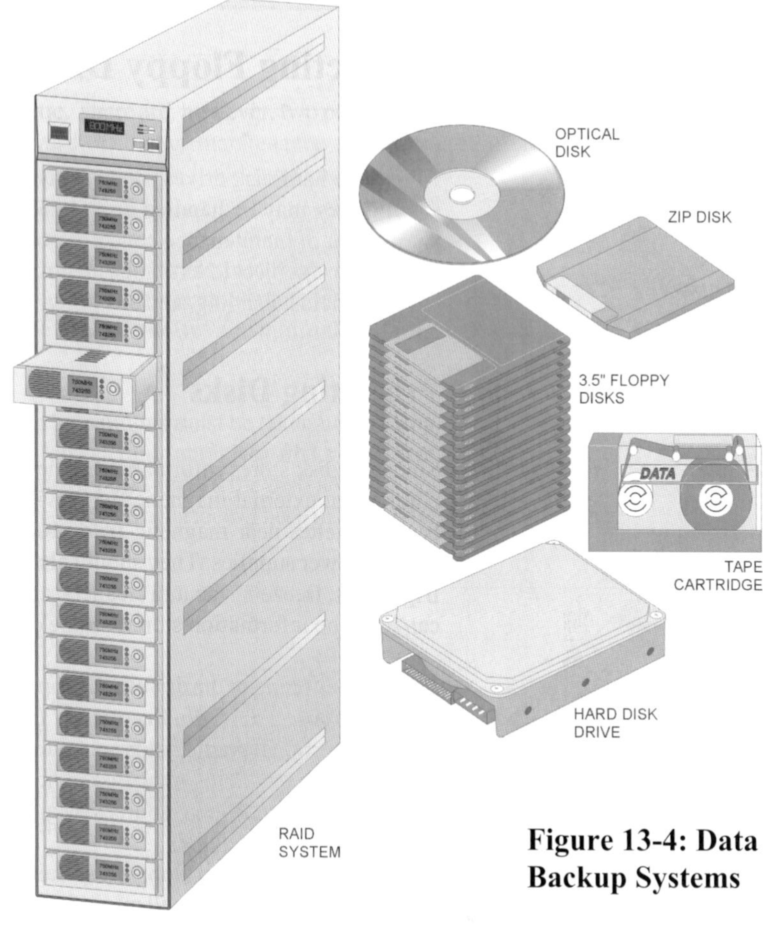

Figure 13-4: Data Backup Systems

The operation of hard drives can slow down with general use. Files stored on the drive may be erased and moved, causing parts of them to be scattered around the drive. This is referred to as **file fragmentation** and causes the drive to reposition the R/W heads more often during read and write operations, thereby requiring more time to complete the process.

There are a number of hard disk drive software utilities designed to optimize and maintain the operation of the hard disk drive. They should be used as part of a regular preventive maintenance program. The primary HDD utilities are the CHKDSK, **ScanDisk**, **Defrag**, **Backup**, and **Antivirus** utilities that have been available with different version of DOS and Windows since early MS-DOS versions.

TEST TIP

Be aware of the precautions that should be employed with storing system backups.

In Windows 9x, these functions are located in several areas of the system. The icons for backup, ScanDisk, and Defrag are located in the *Programs\Accessories\System_Tools* path. The executable file for ScanDisk can be found in *C:\Windows\Command*; the Defrag icon is just under C:\Windows. The backup file is located in *C:\Program_Files\Accessories*. The built-in antivirus function is missing from Windows 9x. An add-on program from a second party should be used. The MSAV and MWAV programs from DOS and Windows 3.x, respectively, can be found in the C:\DOS directory if Windows 9x was installed as an upgrade.

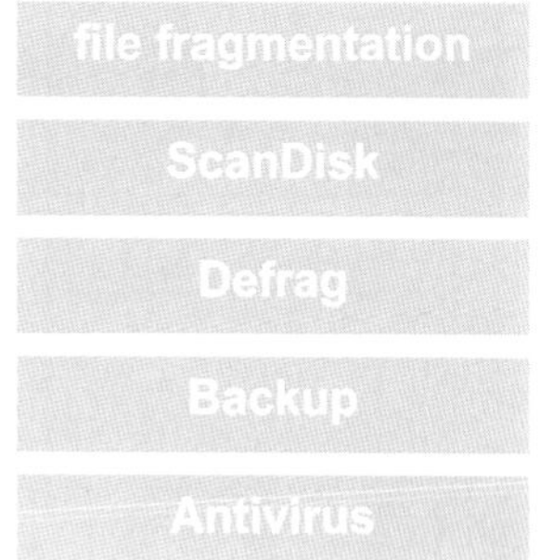

TEST TIP

Remember where the HDD utility programs are located in the Windows 9x environments.

isopropyl alcohol

methanol

cellular foam swabs

lint-free cloths

The cleaning solution can be **isopropyl alcohol**, **methanol**, or some other solvent that does not leave a residue when it dries. Common cotton swabs are not recommended for use in manual cleaning, because they tend to shed fibers. These fibers can contaminate the drive and, in certain circumstances, damage the R/W heads. Instead, **cellular foam swabs**, or **lint-free cloths**, are recommended for manual head cleaning. Using either cleaning method, the interval of time between head cleanings is dependent on several factors, such as the relative cleanliness of your computer area, and how often you use your disk drive. A good practice is to clean the heads after 40 hours of disk-drive operation. If read/write errors begin to appear before this time elapses, more frequent cleaning, or the use of higher-quality diskettes, may be required.

Protecting Input Devices

dusting

Input peripherals generally require very little in the way of preventive maintenance. An occasional **dusting** and cleaning should be all that's really required.

There are, however, a few common-sense items to keep in mind when using input devices that should prevent damage to the device, and ensure its longevity.

soft brush

lint-free swab

The keyboard's electronic circuitry is open to the atmosphere and should be vacuumed, as described in Figure 13-7, when you are cleaning around your computer area. Dust build-up on the keyboard circuitry can cause its ICs to fail due to over heating. To remove dirt and dust particles from inside the keyboard, disassemble the keyboard, and carefully brush particles away from the board with a **soft brush**. A **lint-free swab** can be used to clean between the keys. Take care not to snag any exposed parts with the brush, or swab. To minimize dust collection in the keyboard, cover your keyboard when not in use.

TEST TIP

Remember that dust can settle into the keyboard through the cracks between the keys.

Figure 13-7: Cleaning the Keyboard

Never set keyboards, or pointing devices, on top of the monitor, or near the edge of the desk, where they may fall off. To prevent excessive wear on special keys, avoid applications and game programs that use keys in a repetitive manner. For these applications, use an appropriate pointing device, such as a mouse or joystick, for input.

Maintaining the Floppy Drive

So far, each preventive action has involved the diskette. There are, however, two procedures which the users can perform on the disk drive to ward off bigger maintenance problems. These are **routine cleaning** of the R/W heads (to remove oxide build-ups) and periodic **disk-drive speed tests and adjustments**, when necessary.

routine cleaning

disk-drive speed tests and adjustments

Cleaning R/W heads removes residue and oxide build-ups from the face of the head to ensure accurate transfer of data from the head to the disk. There are two accepted methods that may be used to clean the heads. These are special **head-cleaning diskettes** and **manual cleaning** of the heads.

head-cleaning diskettes

manual cleaning

Head-cleaning disks are convenient to use, but some precautions must be taken when using them. There are, basically, two types of cleaning disks: **dry** (abrasive) **disks**, and **wet** (chemical) **disks**. Abrasive head-cleaning disks remove build-ups as the disk spins in the drive. This is similar to using sandpaper to remove paint from a surface. These disks can be damaging to the head if used for too long a time.

dry disks

wet disks

The dry disk must be left in the drive just long enough to remove the build up on the head, but not long enough to scratch the head surface. Due to the difficulties of timing this operation, manufacturers have developed non-abrasive, cloth-covered disks, which are used with a solvent solution. Depending on the type of kit you purchase, the diskette may be pre-moistened, or come with a separate solvent solution that must be applied to the diskette before cleaning, as illustrated in Figure 13-5.

The opportunity for abrasion of the head still exists with this type of cleaning disk. However, it is not as great as with the dry disks. The instructions that come with the cleaning kit should be consulted for proper usage and cleaning-time duration.

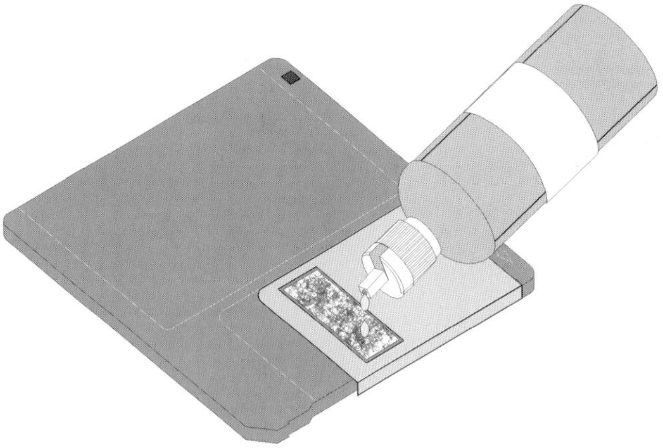

Figure 13-5: FDD Cleaning Disks

A somewhat more complicated method of cleaning R/W heads is to clean them manually, as depicted in Figure 13-6. This operation involves removing the cover of the drive, gaining access to the R/W heads, and cleaning them manually with a swab that has been dipped in **alcohol**. While this may appear to be a lot of work compared to the cleaning disk, manual cleaning is much safer for the drive. This is particularly true when combined with other cleaning, oiling, and inspection work. Together, these steps provide an excellent preventive maintenance program that should ensure effective, long-term operation of the drive.

alcohol

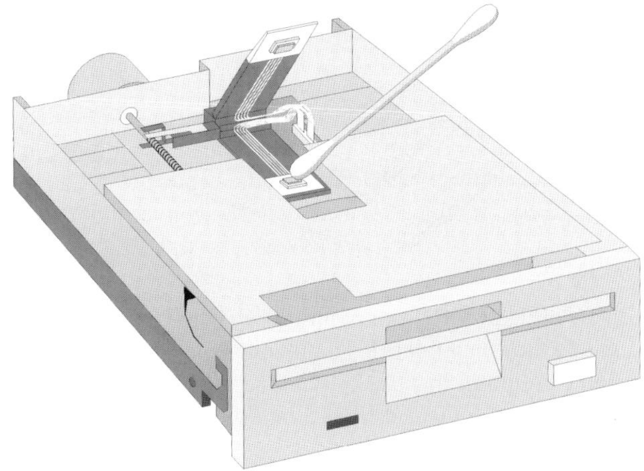

Figure 13-6: Cleaning the R/W Heads

isopropyl alcohol

methanol

cellular foam swabs

lint-free cloths

The cleaning solution can be **isopropyl alcohol**, **methanol**, or some other solvent that does not leave a residue when it dries. Common cotton swabs are not recommended for use in manual cleaning, because they tend to shed fibers. These fibers can contaminate the drive and, in certain circumstances, damage the R/W heads. Instead, **cellular foam swabs**, or **lint-free cloths**, are recommended for manual head cleaning. Using either cleaning method, the interval of time between head cleanings is dependent on several factors, such as the relative cleanliness of your computer area, and how often you use your disk drive. A good practice is to clean the heads after 40 hours of disk-drive operation. If read/write errors begin to appear before this time elapses, more frequent cleaning, or the use of higher-quality diskettes, may be required.

Protecting Input Devices

dusting

Input peripherals generally require very little in the way of preventive maintenance. An occasional **dusting** and cleaning should be all that's really required.

There are, however, a few common-sense items to keep in mind when using input devices that should prevent damage to the device, and ensure its longevity.

soft brush

lint-free swab

The keyboard's electronic circuitry is open to the atmosphere and should be vacuumed, as described in Figure 13-7, when you are cleaning around your computer area. Dust build-up on the keyboard circuitry can cause its ICs to fail due to over heating. To remove dirt and dust particles from inside the keyboard, disassemble the keyboard, and carefully brush particles away from the board with a **soft brush**. A **lint-free swab** can be used to clean between the keys. Take care not to snag any exposed parts with the brush, or swab. To minimize dust collection in the keyboard, cover your keyboard when not in use.

TEST TIP

Remember that dust can settle into the keyboard through the cracks between the keys.

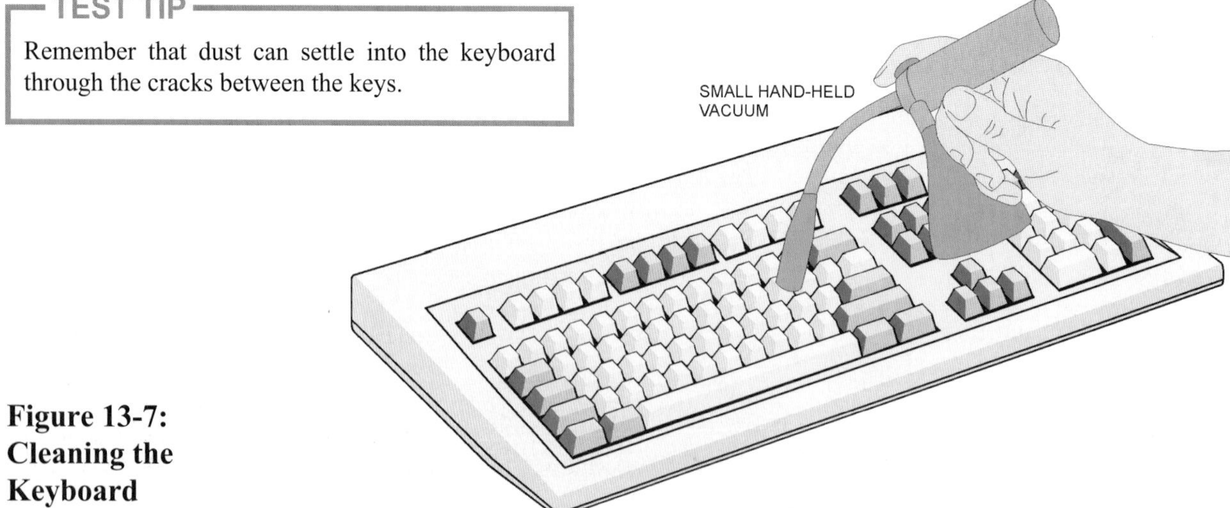

Figure 13-7: Cleaning the Keyboard

Never set keyboards, or pointing devices, on top of the monitor, or near the edge of the desk, where they may fall off. To prevent excessive wear on special keys, avoid applications and game programs that use keys in a repetitive manner. For these applications, use an appropriate pointing device, such as a mouse or joystick, for input.

Copies of the system backup should be stored in a convenient, but secure place. In the case of secure system backups, such as client/server networks, the backup copies should be stored where the network administrators can have access to them, but not the general public (i.e., a locked file cabinet). Left unsecured, these copies could be used by someone without authority to gain access to the system, or to its data. Even Emergency Repair Disks associated with Windows NT and Windows 2000 should be stored in a secure location. These disks can also be used by people other than administrators to gain access to information in client/server networks. Many companies maintain a copy of their backup away from the main site. This is done for protection in case of disasters such as fire.

Figure 13-4: Data Backup Systems

The operation of hard drives can slow down with general use. Files stored on the drive may be erased and moved, causing parts of them to be scattered around the drive. This is referred to as **file fragmentation** and causes the drive to reposition the R/W heads more often during read and write operations, thereby requiring more time to complete the process.

There are a number of hard disk drive software utilities designed to optimize and maintain the operation of the hard disk drive. They should be used as part of a regular preventive maintenance program. The primary HDD utilities are the CHKDSK, **ScanDisk**, **Defrag**, **Backup**, and **Antivirus** utilities that have been available with different version of DOS and Windows since early MS-DOS versions.

> **TEST TIP**
>
> Be aware of the precautions that should be employed with storing system backups.

In Windows 9x, these functions are located in several areas of the system. The icons for backup, ScanDisk, and Defrag are located in the *Programs\Accessories\System_Tools* path. The executable file for ScanDisk can be found in *C:\Windows\Command*; the Defrag icon is just under C:\Windows. The backup file is located in *C:\Program_Files\Accessories*. The built-in antivirus function is missing from Windows 9x. An add-on program from a second party should be used. The MSAV and MWAV programs from DOS and Windows 3.x, respectively, can be found in the C:\DOS directory if Windows 9x was installed as an upgrade.

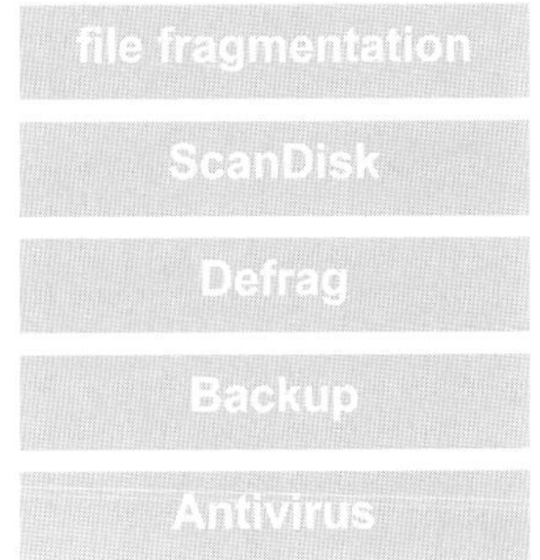

> **TEST TIP**
>
> Remember where the HDD utility programs are located in the Windows 9x environments.

Protecting Floppy Disk Drives

Unlike hard disk drives, floppy drives are at least partially open to the atmosphere, and they may be handled on a regular basis. This opens the floppy disk drive to a number of maintenance concerns not found in hard disk drives. Also, the removable disks are subject to extremes in temperature, exposure to magnetic and electromagnetic fields, bending, and airborne particles that can lead to information loss.

Protecting Disks

Since the disk stores information in the form of magnetized spots on its surface, it is only natural that external magnetic fields will have an adverse effect on the stored data. Never bring diskettes near magnetic-field-producing devices, such as CRT monitors, television sets, or power supplies. They should also never be placed on, or near, appliances such as refrigerators, freezers, vacuum cleaners, and other equipment containing motors. Any of these can alter the information stored on the diskette.

Radio Frequency Interference (RFI)

Proper positioning of the drive, and proper connection of peripheral interface cables, helps to minimize noise and **Radio Frequency Interference** (**RFI**). RFI can cause the drive to operate improperly. Magnetic fields generated by power supplies and monitors can interfere with the magnetic recording on the disk. The drive and signal cables should be positioned away from these magnetic-field sources. Magnets should never be brought near the drive unit.

surface contamination

Another major cause of floppy disk failures is **surface contamination**. There are several preventive measures that will minimize disk contamination and lengthen the life expectancy of your disks. Even though the disk is enclosed in a protective case, or envelope, whose liner sweeps contaminants from its surface, enough dust particles may collect to overpower the liner over time. Care should be taken to never touch the exposed surfaces of the disk. Store disks in their protective envelopes, and keep your computer area as clean and free from dust as possible.

There should be no smoking around the computer. Residues from tobacco smoke are a problem for floppy disk drives because they tend to build up on the exposed surfaces of both the diskettes and the drive. These deposits are detrimental to both the drive and the disk, because they gum up the close-tolerance mechanics of the drive, and cause scratching to occur on the disk surface and the faces of the Read/Write heads. This makes the heads less effective in reading and writing information to and from the disk, and eventually, leads to failure of the disk and the drive.

Floppy disks wear out. R/W heads ride directly on the floppy disk surface, and so produce a certain amount of contamination, and wear, on the disk and heads. During Read and Write operations, the abrasion between the heads and disk causes some of the oxide coating on the disk to be transferred to the head. This makes the head less effective in reading and writing operations, and eventually leads to the failure of the disk.

Additional measures to protect your diskettes include storing them in a cool, dry, clean environment, out of direct sunlight. Excessive temperature will cause the disk and its jacket to warp. Take care when inserting the disk into the drive so as not to damage its jacket or the drive's internal mechanisms.

When using a mouse, keep its workspace clear, dry, and free from dust. The trackball should be removed and cleaned periodically. Use a lint-free swab to clean the X and Y trackball rollers inside the mouse, as described in Figure 13-8.

TEST TIP

Know how to clean a trackball mouse.

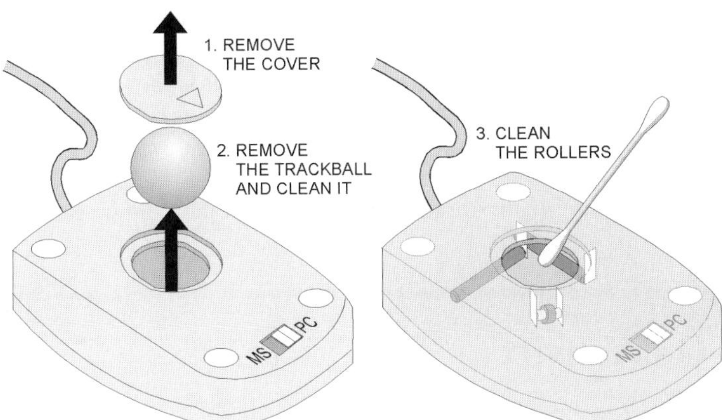

Figure 13-8: Cleaning the Rollers in a Mouse

As with detachable keyboards, keep the connecting cables of all pointing devices out of harm's way.

PRINTER PM AND SAFETY ISSUES

Because printers tend to be much more mechanical than other types of computer peripherals, they require more effort to maintain. Printers generate pollutants, such as paper dust and ink droplets, in everyday operation. These pollutants can build up on mechanical parts and cause them to wear. As the parts wear, the performance of the printer diminishes. Therefore, printers require periodic cleaning and adjustments to maintain good performance.

Dot-Matrix Printers

Adjust the printhead spacing, as described in Chapter 10. If the printhead is too far away from the platen, the print should appear washed-out. The tension on the printhead positioning belt should be checked periodically. If the belt is loose, the printer's dot-positioning will become erratic. The belt should be reset for proper tension.

Clean the printer's roller surfaces. Use a damp, soft cloth to clean the surface of the platen. Rotate the platen through several revolutions. Do not use detergents, or solvents, on the rollers.

WARNING

Cleaning the printer and its mechanisms periodically adds to its productivity by removing contaminants that cause wear. Vacuum the inside of the unit, after applying antistatic solution to the vacuum's hose tip. Wipe the outside with a damp cloth, also using antistatic solution. Brush any contaminant build-up from the printer's mechanical components, using a soft-bristled brush. ***Never lubricate the platen assembly of the printer.***

Use a non-fibrous swab, dipped in alcohol, to clean the face of the dot-matrix printhead. This should loosen up paper fibers, and ink, that may cause the print wires to stick. Apply a small amount of oil to the face of the printhead.

Clean the paper-handling motor's gear train. Use a swab to remove build-up from the teeth of the gear train. If the gear train has been lubricated before, apply a light oil to the gears, using a swab. Turn the platen to make sure the oil gets distributed throughout the gear train. Apply a light coating of oil to the rails that the head-positioning carriage rides on. Move the carriage assembly across the rails several times to spread the lubricant evenly.

The steps to cleaning a dot-matrix printer are described in the following steps:

Hands-On Activity

Cleaning an Dot-Matrix Printer

1. Adjust the printhead spacing.
2. Check the tension on the printhead positioning belt.
3. Clean the printer and its mechanisms.
4. Clean the printer's roller surfaces.
5. Clean the surface of the platen.
6. Clean the surface of the dot-matrix printhead.
7. Clean the paper-handling motor's gear train.
8. Apply light oil to the gears using a swab.
9. Turn the platen to distribute the oil.
10. Apply a light coating of oil to the rails.
11. Move the carriage assembly to distribute the oil.

Ink-Jet Printers

The printheads in some ink-jet printers require cleaning and adjustment similar to those described for dot-matrix printers.

Clean the paper-handling motor's gear train. Use a swab to remove build-up from the teeth of the gear train. If the gear train has been lubricated before, apply a light oil to the gears using a swab. Turn the platen to make sure the oil gets distributed throughout the gear train. Apply a light coating of oil to the rails that the printhead-positioning carriage rides on. Move the carriage assembly across the rails several times to spread the lubricant evenly.

The steps to cleaning an ink-jet printer are provided by the following steps:

Hands-On Activity

Cleaning an Ink-Jet Printer

1. Adjust the printhead spacing.
2. Check the tension on the printhead positioning belt.
3. Clean the printer and its mechanisms.
4. Clean the printer's roller surfaces.
5. Clean the surface of the platen.
6. Clean the surface of the ink-jet printhead.
7. Clean the paper-handling motor's gear train.
8. Apply light oil to the gears using a swab.
9. Turn the platen to distribute the oil.
10. Apply a light coating of oil to the rails.
11. Move the carriage assembly to distribute the oil.

Laser Printers

Use a vacuum cleaner to remove dust build-up, and excess toner, from the interior of the laser printer. Care should be taken to remove all excess toner from the unit. Vacuum the printer's ozone filter. Since water can mix with the toner particles in the printer, using wet sponges or towels to clean up toner inside the laser printer can create a bigger mess than the original one you were cleaning up. Remove the toner cartridge before vacuuming.

Clean the laser printer's rollers using a damp cloth, or **denatured alcohol**. Also, clean the paper-handling motor's gear train. Use a swab to remove build-up from the teeth of the gear train. If the gear train has been lubricated before, apply a light oil to the gears using a swab. Make sure the oil gets distributed throughout the gear train.

denatured alcohol

Clean the writing mechanism thoroughly. Use **compressed air** to blow out dust and paper particles that may collect on the lenses and shutters. If possible, wipe the laser lens with lint-free wipes to remove stains and fingerprints.

compressed air

monofilament wires

If accessible, use a swab, dipped in alcohol, to clean the corona wires. Rub the swab across the entire length of the wires. Take extra care to not break the strands that wrap around the corona. If these wires are broken, the printer will be rendered useless until new **monofilament wires** can be reinstalled.

TEST TIP

Remember acceptable methods for cleaning laser printers.

Steps to cleaning a laser printer are described in the following hands-on activity:

Hands-On Activity

Cleaning an Laser Printer

1. Remove dust build-up, and excess toner, from the interior.
2. Clean the laser printer's rollers.
3. Clean the paper-handling motor's gear train.
4. Apply light oil to the gears, using a swab.
5. Distribute the oil throughout the gear train.
6. Clean the corona wires.

third-party refill cartridges

In some laser printer models, the toner cartridges are designed so that they can be refilled. At this time, the **third-party refill cartridges** are not typically as good as those from the manufacturer. However, they tend to be much cheaper than original equipment cartridges. If the output from the printer does not have to be very high-quality, then refilled toner cartridges might be an interesting possibility to consider. To date, there are no regulations governing the disposal of laser printer cartridges.

Preventive Maintenance Scheduling

There is no perfect preventive maintenance (PM) schedule; however, the following is a reasonable schedule that can be used to effectively maintain most computer equipment. The schedule is written from the point of view of a personal computer. From an outside maintenance perspective, some of the steps will need to be shared with the daily users. As a matter of fact, most of the daily and weekly PM activities are carried out by the users.

Daily Activities

Back up important data from the unit. This can be done to floppy disks, backup tape, another network drive, or some other backup media. Check computer ventilation to make sure that papers and other desk clutter are not cutting off air flow to the unit. Check for other sources of heat buildup around the computer and its peripherals. These sources include:

- Direct sunlight from an outside window
- Locations of portable heaters in the winter
- Papers/books piled up around the equipment

Weekly Activities

Clean the outside of the computer, and its peripheral equipment. Wipe the outsides of the equipment with a damp cloth. The cloth can be slightly soapy. Wipe dry with an antistatic cloth. Clean the display screen using a damp cloth with the antistatic solution described earlier in this chapter. An antistatic spray can also be used for static build-up prevention.

CHKDSK/f

Run **CHKDSK/f** on all hard drives to locate and remove any lost clusters from the drives. This utility is available in all of the Microsoft operating systems including Windows 9x, Windows NT, and Windows 2000. The CHKDSK command must be run from the command prompt in all versions. Run a current virus-check program to check for hard drive infection. Back up any revised data files on the hard drive. Inspect the peripherals (mice, keyboard, and so on), and clean them if needed.

Monthly Activities

Clean the inside of the system. Use a long-nozzle vacuum cleaner attachment to remove dust from the inside of the unit. Wipe the nozzle with antistatic solution before vacuuming. A soft brush can also be used to remove dust from the system unit.

Clean the inside of the printer using the same equipment and techniques as those used with the system unit. Check system connections for corrosion, pitting, or discoloration. Wipe the surface of any peripheral card's edge connectors with a lubricating oil to protect it from atmospheric contamination.

Vacuum the keyboard out. Clean the X and Y rollers in the trackball mouse (illustrated in Figure 13-8) using a lint-free swab, and a non-coating cleaning solution.

.TMP

Defragment the system's hard drive using the Defrag utility. Remove unnecessary temporary (**.TMP**) files from the hard drive. Check software and hardware manufacturers for product updates that can remove problems and improve system operation. Back up the entire hard disk drive.

Six Months' Activities

Every six months, perform an extensive PM check. Apply an antistatic wash to the entire computer/peripheral work area. Wipe down books, the desk top, and other work area surfaces with antistatic solution. Disconnect power and signal cables from the system's devices, and reseat them. Clean the inside of the printer. Run the printer's self-tests.

Use a software diagnostic package to check each section of the system. Run all system tests available, looking for any hint of pending problems.

Annual Activities

Reformat the hard drive by backing up its contents, and performing a high-level format. If the drive is an MFM, RLL, or ESDI drive, a low-level format should also be performed annually. Reinstall all the applications software from original media, and reinstall all user files from the backup system. Check all floppy disks in the work area with a current antivirus program.

Clean the R/W heads in the floppy drive, using a lint-free swab. Cotton swabs have fibers that can hang up in the ceramic insert of the head and damage it. Perform the steps outlined in the monthly and semiannual sections.

While this is a good model PM schedule, it is not the definitive schedule. Before establishing a firm schedule there are several other points to take into consideration. These points include any manufacturer's guidelines for maintaining the equipment. Read the user's guides of the various system components and work their suggested maintenance steps into the model.

Over time, adjust the steps and frequency of the plan to effectively cope with any environmental or usage variations. After all, the objective isn't to complete the schedule on time, it's to keep the equipment running and profitable.

SYSTEM PROTECTION

The A+ Core objective 3.2 states that the test taker should be able to identify procedures and devices for protecting against environmental hazards.

- UPS (uninterruptible power supply), suppressers, noise filters, and plug strips
- Determining the signs of power issues
- Proper methods of component storage for future use

As this A+ objective indicates, computer technicians should be aware of potential environmental hazards and know how to prevent them from becoming a problem. A good place to start checking for environmental hazards is with the incoming power source. The following sections of the chapter deal with power line issues and solutions.

Power Line Protection

power variations

Avoid power variations—Digital systems tend to be sensitive to power variations and losses. Even a very short loss of electrical power can shut a digital computer down, resulting in a loss of any current information that has not been saved to a mass storage device.

Typical power supply variations fall into two categories:

Transients

spikes

surges

Sags

voltage sags

brownouts

- **Transients**—an over-voltage condition, while sags are an under-voltage condition. Over-voltage conditions can be classified as **spikes** (measured in nanoseconds), or as **surges** (measured in milliseconds).

- **Sags**—can include **voltage sags** and **brownouts**. A voltage sag typically lasts only a few milliseconds, while a brownout can last for a protracted period of time.

The effects of these power supply variations are often hard to identify as power issues. Brownouts and power failures are easy to spot because of their duration. However, faster-acting disturbances can cause symptoms that are not easily traced to the power source. Spikes can be quite damaging to electronic equipment, damaging devices such as hard drives and modems. Other occurrences will simply cause data loss. Sags may cause the system to suddenly reboot because it thinks the power has been turned off. These disturbances are relatively easy to detect since they typically cause any lights in the room to flicker.

TEST TIP

Be aware of how under-voltage and over-voltage situations are categorized (i.e., time lengths).

In general, if several components go bad in a short period of time, or if components go bad more often than usual at a given location, these are good indicators of power-related issues. Likewise, machines that crash randomly and often could be experiencing power issues. If "dirty" power problems are suspected, a voltage-monitoring device should be placed in the power circuit and left for an extended period of time. These devices observe the incoming power over time and will produce a problem indicator if significant variations occur.

Surge Suppressers

power line filters

surge suppressers

Inexpensive **power line filters**, called **surge suppressers**, are good for cleaning up dirty commercial power. These units passively filter the incoming power signal to smooth out variations. There are two factors to consider when choosing a surge suppresser:

- Clamping speed
- Clamping voltage

TEST TIP

Know what type of devices will protect systems from minor power sags and power surges.

These units will protect the system from damage, up to a specified point. However, large variations, such as surges created when power is restored after an outage, can still cause considerable data loss and damage. In the case of startup surges, making sure that the system is turned off, or even disconnected from the power source, until after the power is restored is one option. In the case of a complete shutdown, or a significant sag, the best protection from losing programs and data is an **Uninterruptible Power Supply (UPS).**

TEST TIP

Know what type of device prevents power interruptions that can corrupt data.

Uninterruptible Power Supply (UPS)

Uninterruptible Power Supplies

Uninterruptible power supplies are battery-based systems that monitor the incoming power and kick in when unacceptable variations occur in the power source. The term **UPS** is frequently used to describe two different types of power backup systems.

UPS

standby power system

uninterruptible power system

The first is a **standby power system**, and the second is a truly **uninterruptible power system**. A typical UPS system is depicted in Figure 13-9.

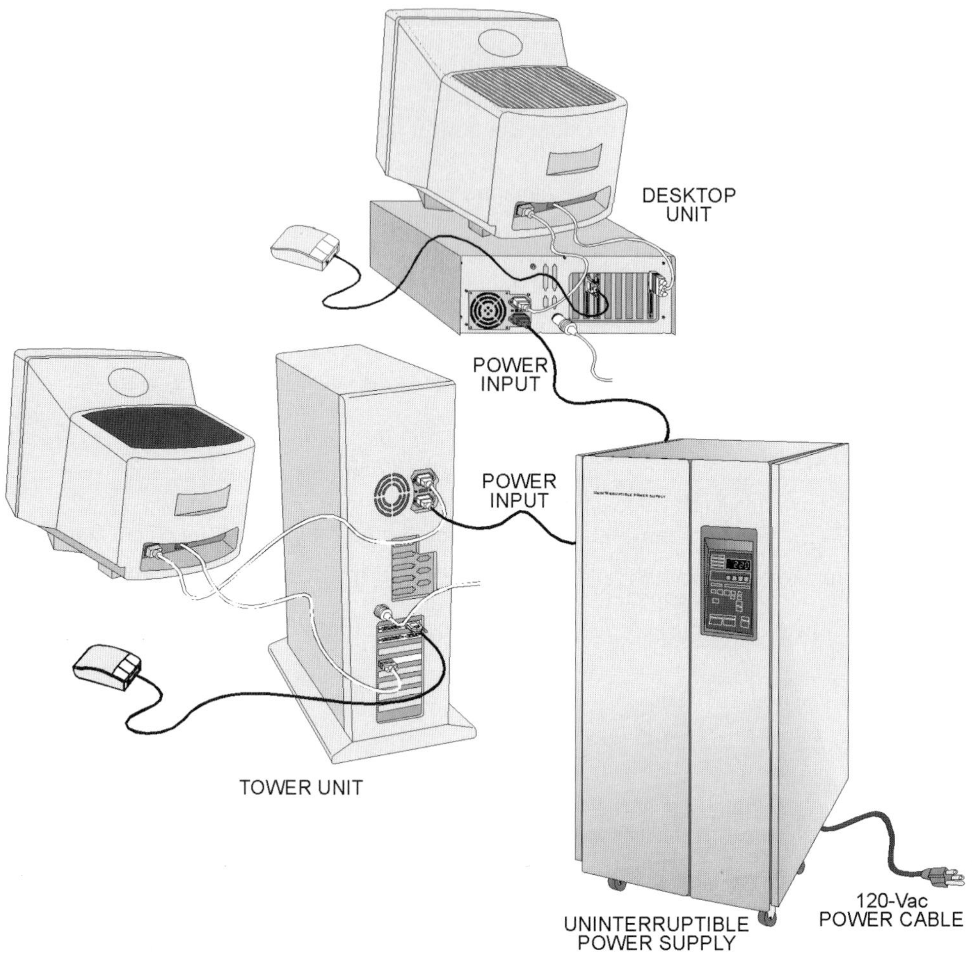

Figure 13-9: UPS System

The standby system monitors the power input line, and waits for a significant variation to occur. The batteries in this unit are held out of the power loop, and only draw enough current from the AC source to stay recharged. When an interruption occurs, the UPS senses it and switches the output of the batteries into an inverter circuit that converts the DC output of the batteries into an AC current and voltage that resemble the commercial power supply. This power signal is typically applied to the computer within 10 milliseconds.

The uninterruptible systems do not keep the batteries off-line. Instead, the batteries and converters are always actively attached to the output of UPS. When an interruption in the supply occurs, no switching of the output is required. The battery/inverter section simply continues under its own power. Figure 13-10 shows how a UPS connects into a system.

Standby systems don't generally provide a high level of protection from sags and spikes. However, they do include additional circuitry to minimize such variations. Conversely, an uninterruptible system is an extremely good power-conditioning system. Since it always sits between the commercial power and the computer, it can supply a constant power supply to the system.

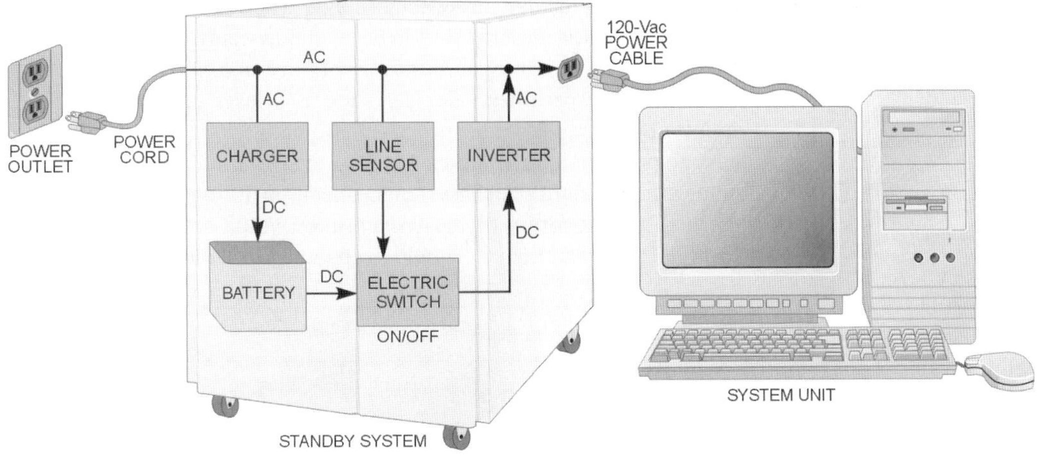

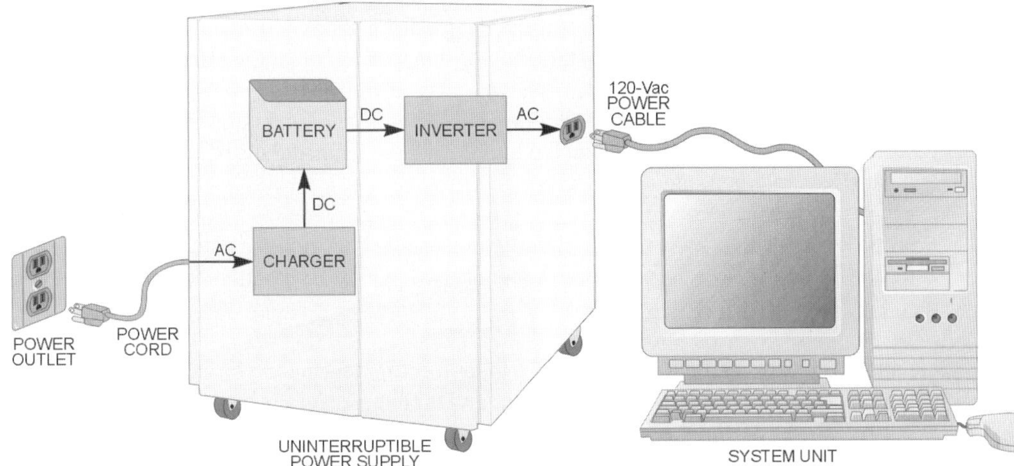

Figure 13-10: Connecting the UPS in the System

When dealing with either type of UPS system, the most important rating to be aware of is its **Volt-Ampere (VA) rating**. The VA rating indicates the ability of the UPS system to deliver both voltage (V) and current (A) to the computer, simultaneously. This rating is different than the device's **wattage rating**, and the two should not be used interchangeably.

Volt-Ampere (VA) rating

wattage rating

The wattage power rating is a factor of multiplying the voltage and current use, at any particular time, to arrive at a power consumption value. The VA rating is used in AC systems because peak voltage and current elements do not occur at the same instant. This condition is referred to as being **out-of-phase**, and makes it slightly more difficult to calculate power requirements. In general, always make sure that the UPS system has a higher wattage capability than the computer requires, and likewise that the VA rating of the UPS is higher than that required by the computer.

out-of-phase

High-power-consumption peripheral devices, such as laser printers, should not be connected directly to the UPS. These devices can overload the UPS and cause data loss.

The other significant specification for UPS systems is the length of time they can supply power. Since the UPS is a battery-powered device, it uses an **ampere-hour rating**. This is the same time notation system used for automobile batteries and other battery-powered systems. The rating is obtained by multiplying a given current drain from the battery, by a given amount of time (i.e., a battery capable of sustaining 1.5 amps of output current for 1 hour would be rated at 1.5 amp-hours).

ampere-hour rating

The primary mission of the UPS is to keep the system running when a power failure occurs (usually, long enough to conduct an orderly shutdown of the system). Because it's battery-based, it cannot keep the system running infinitely. For this reason, you should not connect non-essential, power-hungry peripheral devices such as a laser printer to the UPS supply. If the power goes out, it is highly unlikely that you will really have to print something before shutting the system down. If the UPS is being used to keep a critical system in operation during the power outage, the high current drain of the laser printer would severely reduce the length of time that the UPS could keep the system running.

TEST TIP

Remember that non-essential peripheral devices should not be connected to UPS supplies.

Protection during Storage

The best storage option for most computer equipment is the original manufacturer's box. These boxes are designed specifically to store and transport the device safely. They include form-fitting protective foam to protect the device from shock hazards. The device is normally wrapped in a protective antistatic bag or wrapper to defeat the affects of ESD.

Printed circuit boards are normally shipped on a thin piece of antistatic foam. The board is typically placed solder-side down on the foam. Both the foam and the board are placed in an antistatic bag and then into a storage box.

Hard disk drives are usually placed directly into a static bag and then placed in a thick foam box. The foam box is then inserted into a storage carton. FDDs typically receive less padding than HDD units do.

Monitors, printers, scanners, and other peripheral equipment should be stored in their original boxes, using their original packing foam and protective storage bag. The contours in the packing foam of these devices are not generally compatible from model to model, or device to device. If the original boxes and packing materials are not available, make sure to use sturdy cartons and cushion the equipment well on all sides before shipping.

TEST TIP

Know that the best device for transporting computer equipment is the original manufacturer's packaging, including the anti-static foam and bags used to pack it.

All electronic devices should be stored in dry cool areas away from heat sources and direct sunlight. Low-traffic areas are also preferable for storage since there is less chance of incidental damage from people and/or equipment passing by.

HAZARDS AND SAFETY PROCEDURES

The A+ Core objective 3.3 states that the test taker should be able to identify the potential hazards and proper safety procedures relating to lasers and high-voltage equipment.

- Lasers can cause blindness.
- High-voltage equipment (such as the power supply and CRT) can cause electrocution.

Avoiding High-Voltage Hazards

In most IBM compatibles, there are only two potentially dangerous areas. One of these is inside the **CRT display**, and the other is inside the power supply unit. Both of these areas contain electrical voltage levels that are lethal. However, both of these areas reside in self-contained units, and you will normally not be required to open either unit.

CRT display

As a matter of fact, you should never enter the interior of a CRT cabinet unless you have been trained specifically to work with this type of equipment. The tube itself is dangerous if accidentally cracked. In addition, extremely **high voltage levels** (in excess of 25,000 volts) may be present inside the CRT housing, even up to a year after electrical power has been removed from the unit.

TEST TIP

Be aware of the voltage levels that are present inside a CRT cabinet.

high voltage levels

Never open the power supply unit either. Some portions of the circuitry inside the power supply carry extremely high voltage levels and have very high current capabilities.

Generally, there are no open shock hazards present inside the system unit. However, you should not reach inside the computer while power is applied to the unit. Jewelry and other metallic objects do pose an electrical threat, even with the relatively low voltage present in the system unit.

Never have liquids around energized electrical equipment. It's a good idea to keep food and drinks away from all computer equipment at all times. When cleaning around the computer with liquids, make certain to unplug all power connections to the system, and its peripherals, beforehand. When cleaning external computer cabinets with liquid cleaners, take care to prevent any of the solution from dripping or spilling into the equipment.

Do not defeat the safety feature of three-prong power plugs by using two-prong adapters. The equipment ground of a power cable should never be defeated or removed. This plug connects the computer chassis to earth ground through the power system. This provides a reference point for all of the system's devices to operate from, as well as supplying protection for personnel from electrical shock. In defeating the ground plug, a very important level of protection is removed from the equipment.

Periodically examine the power cords of the computer, and peripherals, for cracked or damaged insulation. Replace worn or damaged power cords promptly. Never allow anything to rest on a power cord. Run power cords and connecting cables safely out of the way, so that they don't become **trip** or **catch** hazards. Remove all power cords associated with the computer, and its peripherals, from the power outlet during thunder or lightning storms.

trip hazard

catch hazard

Don't apply liquid or aerosol cleaners directly to computer equipment. Spray cleaners on a cloth, and then apply the cloth to the equipment. Freon-propelled sprays should not be used on computer equipment, since they can produce destructive electrostatic charges.

Check equipment vents to see that they are clear and have ample free-air space to allow heat to escape from the cabinet. Never block these vents, and never insert or drop objects into them.

Avoiding Laser and Burn Hazards

Laser printers contain many hazardous areas. The laser light can be very damaging to the human eye. In addition, there are multiple high-voltage areas in the typical laser printer and a high-temperature area to contend with as well.

The technician is normally protected from these areas by interlock switches built into the unit. However, it is often necessary to bypass these interlocks to isolate problems. When doing so, proper precautions must be observed, such as avoiding the laser light, being aware of the high temperatures in the fuser area, and taking proper precautions with the high-voltage areas of the unit. The laser light is a hazard to eyesight, the fuser area is a burn hazard, and the power supplies are shock hazards. More information about these areas of laser printers is presented in Chapter 6—*Printers*.

TEST TIP

Know the areas of the computer system that are dangerous for personnel and how to prevent injury from these areas.

Another potential burn hazard is the printhead mechanism of a dot-matrix printer. During normal operation it can become hot enough to be a burn hazard if touched.

first-aid kit

Class-C fire extinguisher

Since computers do have the potential to produce these kinds of injuries, it is good practice to have a well-stocked **first-aid kit** in the work area. In addition, a **Class-C fire extinguisher** should be on hand. Class-C extinguishers are the type specified for use around electrical equipment. You can probably imagine the consequences of applying a water-based fire extinguisher to a fire with live electrical equipment around. The class, or classes, that the fire extinguisher is rated for are typically marked on its side.

TEST TIP

Remember the type of fire extinguisher that must be used with electrical systems, such as a PC.

You may think that there's not much chance for a fire to occur with computer equipment, but this is not so. Just let a capacitor from a system board blow up and have a small piece land in a pile of packing materials in the work area. It becomes a fire.

This covers the major safety precautions, and considerations, that you need to be aware of while working on computer equipment. Most of all, use common sense and sound safety practices around all electronic equipment.

DISPOSAL PROCEDURES

The A+ Core objective 3.4 states that the test taker should be able to identify items that require special disposal procedures that comply with environmental guidelines. Examples include:

- Batteries
- CRTs
- Chemical solvents and cans
- Toner kits/cartridges
- MSDS (Material Safety Data Sheet)

As with any mechanical device, a computer eventually becomes obsolete in the application that it was originally intended for. Newer machines, with improved features, arise to replace earlier models. And, slowly, but surely, components fail and get replaced. Then comes the question: What do we do with the old stuff? Can it simply be placed in the garbage bin so that it is hauled to the land fill and buried?

In today's world of environmental consciousness, you might not think so. Computers and peripherals contain some environmentally unfriendly materials.

Most computer components contain some level of **hazardous substances**. Printed circuit boards consist of plastics, precious metals, fiberglass, arsenic, silicon, gallium, and lead. CRTs contain glass, metal, plastics, lead, barium, and rare earth metals. Batteries from portable systems can contain lead, cadmium, lithium, alkaline manganese, and mercury.

hazardous substances

While all of these materials can be classified as hazardous materials, so far there are no wide-spread regulations when it comes to placing them in the land fill. Conversely, **local regulations** concerning acceptable disposal methods for computer-related components should always be checked before disposing of any electronic equipment.

local regulations

Laser printer toner cartridges can be refilled and recycled. However, this should only be done in draft mode operations where very good resolution is not required. Ink cartridges from ink-jet printers can also be refilled and reused. Like laser cartridges, they can be very messy to refill and often do not function as well as new cartridges do. In many cases, the manufacturer of the product will have a policy of accepting spent cartridges.

TEST TIP

Remember that toner cartridges from a laser printer should be recycled.

For both batteries and cartridges, the desired method of disposal is **recycling**. It should not be too difficult to find a **drop site** that will handle recycling these products. On the other hand, even **non-hazardous, sub-title D dump sites** can handle the hardware components if need be. Sub-title D dump sites are non-hazardous, solid waste dump sites that have been designed to meet EPA standards set for this classification. Sub-title C dump sites are those designed to hold hazardous materials safely.

TEST TIP

Remember that the proper disposal method for batteries is to recycle them.

recycling

drop site

non-hazardous, sub-title D dump sites

Fortunately, there seem to be several charitable organizations around the country that take in old computer systems and refurbish them for various applications. Contact your local **Chamber of Commerce** for information about such organizations. The Internet also has several computer disposal organizations that will take old units and redistribute them. In addition, there are a few companies that will dispose of your old computer components in an "environmentally friendly" manner—for a fee.

Chamber of Commerce

cleaning substances

free liquids

Material Safety Data Sheets (MSDS)

In addition to the computer parts that provide hazardous materials, many of the **cleaning substances** used on computer equipment can be classified as hazardous materials. When it comes to the chemical solvents used to clean computers, as well as the containers they come in, it will normally be necessary to clear these items with the local waste management agencies before disposing of them. Many dump sites will not handle **free liquids**. Free liquids are those substances that can pass through a standard paint filter. If the liquid will pass through the filter, it is a free liquid and cannot be disposed of in the landfill. Therefore, solvents and other liquid cleaning materials must be properly categorized and disposed of at an appropriate type of disposal center.

All hazardous materials are required to have **Material Safety Data Sheets** (**MSDS**) that accompany them when they change hands. They are also required to be on hand in areas where hazardous materials are stored and commonly used. The MSDS contains information about:

- What the material is
- Its hazardous ingredients
- Its physical properties
- Fire and explosion data
- Reactivity data
- Spill or leak procedures
- Health hazard information
- Any special protection information
- Any special precaution information

This information sheet must be provided by the supplier of the hazardous material. If you supply this material to a third party, you must also supply the MSDS for the material. The real reason for the sheets is to inform workers and management about hazards associated with the products and how to handle them safely. It also provides instructions about what to do if an accident occurs involving the material. For this reason, employees should know where the MSDS are stored in their work area.

ELECTROSTATIC DISCHARGE

The A+ Core objective 3.5 states that the test taker should be able to identify ESD (Electrostatic Discharge) precautions and procedures, including the use of ESD protection devices.

- What ESD can do, how it may be apparent, or hidden
- Common ESD protection devices
- Situations that could present a danger or hazard

The first step in avoiding ESD (Electrostatic Discharge) is being able to identify when and why it occurs.

Identifying and Avoiding Electrostatic Discharge

What is ESD— Electrostatic Discharges (ESD) are the most severe form of **Electromagnet Interference (EMI)**. The human body can build up static charges that range up to **25,000 volts**. These build-ups can discharge very rapidly into a electrically grounded body, or device. Placing a 25,000-volt surge through any electronic device is potentially damaging to it.

Electrostatic Discharges (ESD)

Electromagnet Interference (EMI)

25,000 volts

Static can easily discharge through digital computer equipment. The electronic devices that are used to construct digital equipment are particularly susceptible to damage from ESD. As a matter of fact, ESD is the most damaging form of electrical interference associated with digital equipment.

TEST TIP

Remember what the acronym ESD stands for.

The most common causes of ESD are:

- Moving people
- Improper grounding
- Unshielded cables
- Poor connections
- Moving machines
- Low humidity (hot and dry conditions)

TEST TIP

Memorize the conditions that make ESD more likely to occur.

Elementary school teachers demonstrate the principles of static to their students by rubbing different materials together. When people move, the clothes they are wearing rub together, and can produce large amounts of electrostatic charge on their bodies. Walking across carpeting can create charges in excess of 1,000 volts. Motors in electrical devices, such as vacuum cleaners and refrigerators, generate high levels of ESD.

TEST TIP

Be aware that compressed air can be used to blow dust out of components and that it does not create ESD.

low humidity

ESD is most likely to occur during periods of **low humidity**. If the relative humidity is below 50%, static charges can accumulate easily. ESD generally does not occur when the humidity is above 50%. Anytime the charge reaches around 10,000 volts, it is likely to discharge to grounded metal parts.

TEST TIP

Memorize conditions and actions that produce electrostatic discharge.

While ESD won't hurt humans, it will destroy certain electronic devices. The high-voltage pulse can burn out the inputs of many IC devices. This damage may not appear instantly. It can build up over time, and cause the device to fail. Electronic logic devices, constructed from **Metal Oxide Semiconductor (MOS)** materials, are particularly susceptible to ESD. The following section describes the special handling techniques that should be observed when working with equipment containing MOS devices.

Metal Oxide Semiconductor (MOS)

You may be a little confused by the fact that we warn you about the lethal 25,000 volts present inside the monitor and then say that the 10,000 to 25,000 volts of ESD is not harmful to humans. The reason for this is the difference in current-delivering capabilities created by the voltage. For example, the circuitry in the monitor and the power supply is capable of delivering amps of current, while the current-producing capability of the electrostatic charge is less than a thousandth of that. Therefore, the 120 Vac, 1 amp current produced by the power supply unit is lethal, while the 25,000 Vdc, microamp current produced by ESD is not.

TEST TIP

Remember that the current capabilities of electrical devices establish the potential danger levels associated with working around them.

MOS Handling Techniques

Complementary-Symmetry Metal Oxide Semiconductor (CMOS)

In general, MOS devices are sensitive to voltage spikes and static electricity discharges. This can cause many problems when you have to replace MOS devices, especially **Complementary-Symmetry Metal Oxide Semiconductor (CMOS)** devices. The level of static electricity present on your body is high enough to destroy the inputs of a CMOS device if you touch its pins with your fingers.

conductive-plastic tubes

antistatic foam

antistatic bags

In order to minimize the chances of damaging MOS devices during handling, special procedures have been developed to protect them from static shock. ICs are generally shipped and stored in special **conductive-plastic tubes** or trays. You may want to store MOS devices in these tubes, or you may simply ensure their safety by inserting the IC's leads into aluminum foil or **antistatic** (conductive) **foam**—not styrofoam. PC boards containing static-sensitive devices are normally shipped in special **antistatic bags**. These bags are good for storing ICs, and other computer components, that may be damaged by ESD. They are also the best method of transporting PC boards with static-sensitive components.

grounding straps

Professional service technicians employ a number of precautionary steps when they are working on systems, that may contain MOS devices. These technicians normally use **grounding straps**, like the one depicted in Figure 13-11. These antistatic devices may be placed around the wrists or ankle to ground the technician to the system being worked on. These straps release any static present on the technician's body, and pass it harmlessly to ground potential.

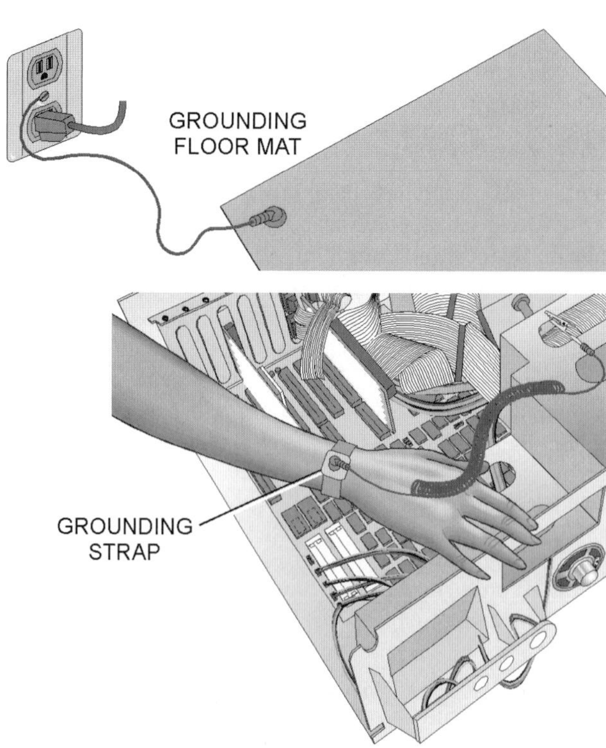

Figure 13-11: Typical Antistatic Devices

Antistatic straps should never be worn while working on higher-voltage components, such as monitors and power supply units. Some technicians wrap a copper wire around their wrist or ankle, and connect it to the ground side of an outlet. This is not a safe practice, since the resistive feature of a true wrist strap is missing. As an alternative, most technician's work areas include **antistatic mats** made out of rubber or other antistatic materials that they stand on while working on the equipment. This is particularly helpful in carpeted work areas, since carpeting can be a major source of ESD build-up. Some antistatic mats have ground connections that should be connected to the safety ground of an AC power outlet.

antistatic mats

TEST TIP

Know when not to wear an antistatic wrist strap.

To avoid damaging static-sensitive devices, the following procedures will help to minimize the chances of destructive static discharges:

- Since computers and peripheral systems may contain a number of static-sensitive devices, before touching any components inside the system, touch an exposed part of the chassis or the power supply housing with your finger, as illustrated in Figure 13-12. Grounding yourself in this manner will ensure that any static charge present on your body is removed. This technique should be used before handling a circuit board, or component. Of course, you should be aware that this technique will only work safely if the power cord is attached to a grounded power outlet. The ground plug on a standard power cable is the best tool for overcoming ESD problems.

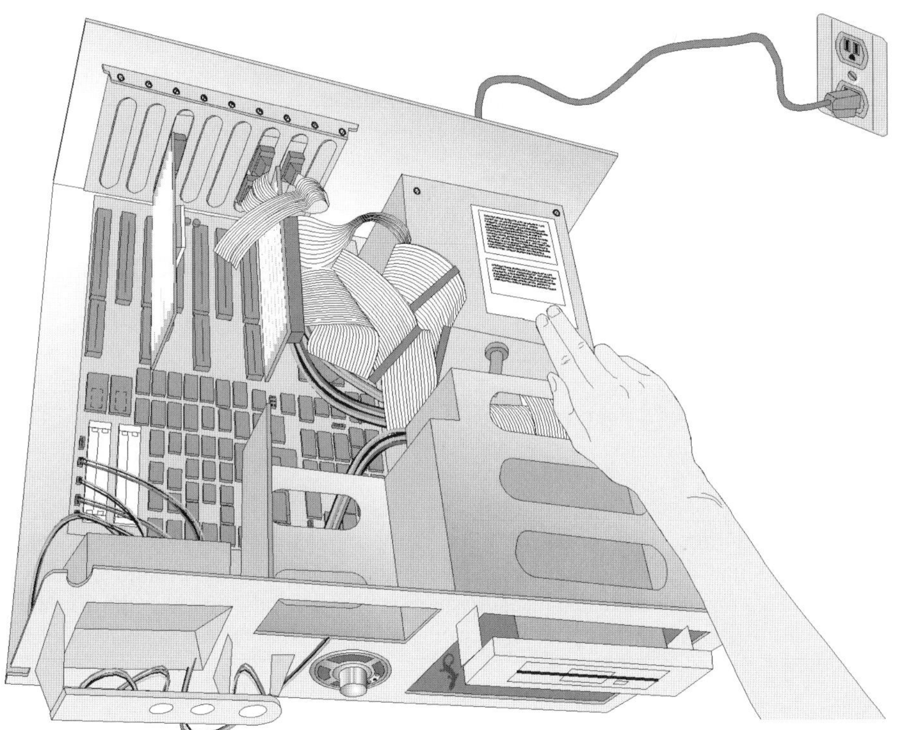

Figure 13-12: Discharging Through the Power Supply Unit

- Do not remove ICs from their protective tubes (or foam packages) until you are ready to use them. If you remove a circuit board, or component, containing static-sensitive devices from the system, place it on a conductive surface, such as a sheet of aluminum foil.

- If you must replace a defective IC, use a soldering iron with a grounded tip to extract the defective IC, and while soldering the new IC in place. Some of the ICs in computers and peripherals are not soldered to the printed circuit board. Instead, an IC socket is soldered to the board, and the IC is simply inserted into the socket. This allows for easy replacement of these ICs.

temperature cycling

chip creep

- In the event that you have to replace a hard-soldered IC, you may want to install an IC socket along with the chip. Be aware that normal operating vibrations and **temperature cycling** can degrade the electrical connections between ICs and sockets over time. This gradual deterioration of electrical contact between chips and sockets is referred to as **chip creep**. It is a good practice to reseat any socket-mounted devices when handling a printed circuit board. Before removing the IC from its protective container, touch the container to the power supply of the unit in which it is to be inserted.

TEST TIP

Be aware of the effects that temperature cycling can have on socket-mounted devices.

solder-sucker

- Some devices used to remove solder from circuit boards and chips can cause high static discharges that may damage the good devices on the board. The device in question is referred to as a **solder-sucker**, and is available in antistatic versions for use with MOS devices.

- Use antistatic sprays or solutions on floors, carpets, desks, and computer equipment. An antistatic spray or solution, applied with a soft cloth, is an effective deterrent to static.

static-free carpeting

- Install **static-free carpeting** in the work area. You can also install an antistatic floor mat as well. Install a conductive tabletop to carry away static from the work area. Use antistatic table mats.

- Use a room humidifier to keep the humidity level above 50% in the work area. Figure 13-13 summarizes proper IC handling procedures.

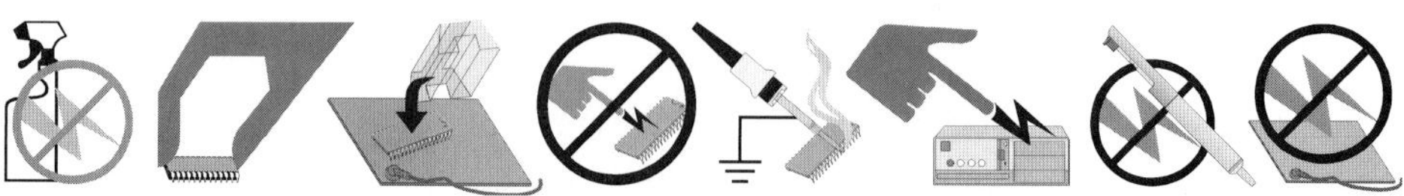

Figure 13-13: Antistatic Precautions

Checking the Grounds

ground

earth ground

What are grounds—The term **ground** is often a source of confusion for the novice, because it actually encompasses a collection of terms. Generically, ground is simply any point from which electrical measurements are referenced. However, the original definition of ground actually referred to the ground. This ground is called **earth ground**.

The movement of the electrical current along a conductor requires a path for the current to return to its source. In early telegraph systems and even modern power transmission systems, the earth provides a return path and, hypothetically, produces an electrical reference point of absolute zero. This type of ground is shown in Figure 13-14.

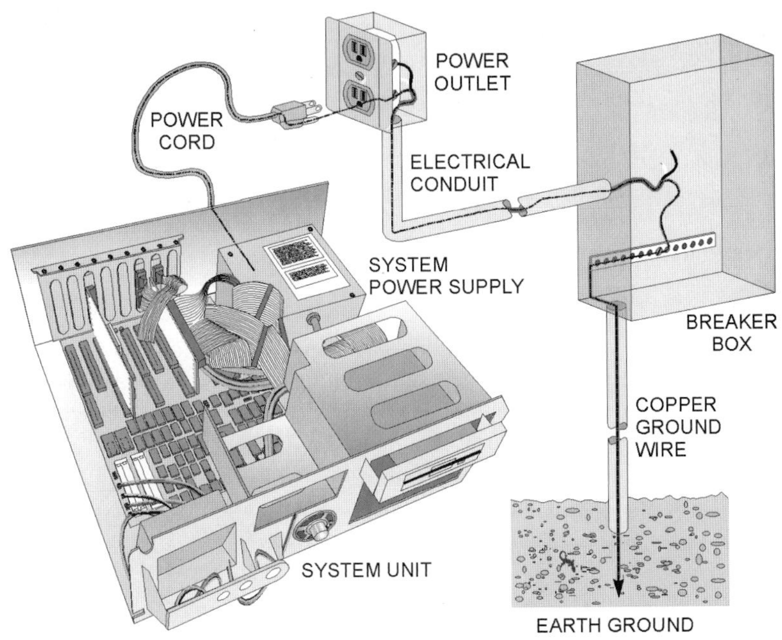

Figure 13-14: Power Transmission System

Many electronic circuits use an actual conductor as a return path. This type of ground is referred to as a **signal ground**. Electronic devices may also contain a third form of ground called **chassis ground**, or **protective ground**. In any event, ground still remains the reference point from which most electrical signals are measured. In the case of troubleshooting computer components, measurements referenced to ground may be made from the system unit's chassis.

signal ground

chassis ground

protective ground

The other measurement reference is the signal ground point on the printed circuit board, where the test is being performed. This point isn't too difficult to find in a circuit board full of ICs, because most DIP-style chips use the highest-numbered pin for the positive supply voltage, and the last pin on the pin-1 side of the chip as the ground pin. This type of ground is illustrated in Figure 13-15. Some caution should be used with this assumption, since not all ICs use this pin for ground. However, if you examine a number of ICs and connectors on the board, you should be able to trace the ground foil and use it as a reference.

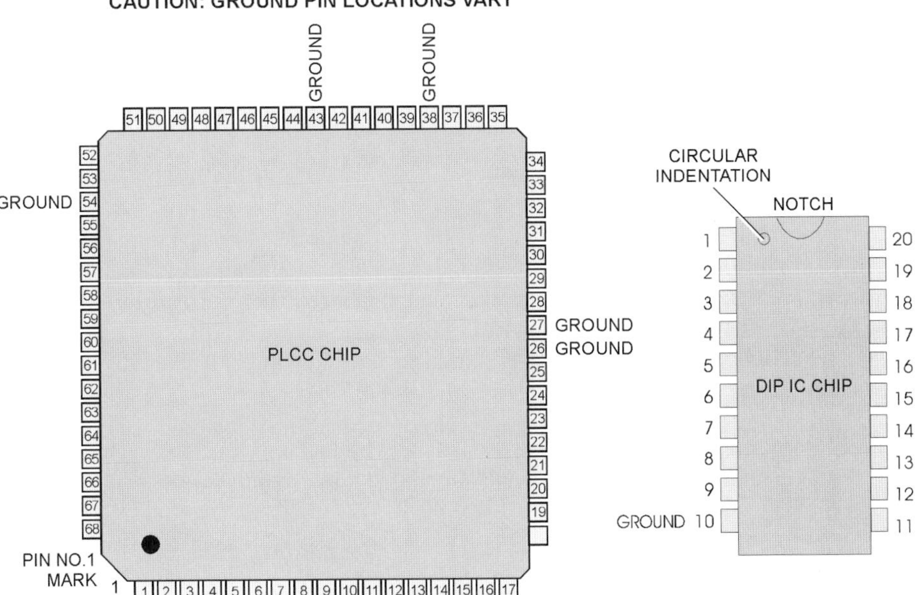

Figure 13-15: Grounds on IC Chips

Grounding is an important aspect of limiting EMI in computer systems. Left unchecked, EMI can distort images on the video display, interfere with commercial communication equipment (such as radios and televisions), and corrupt data on floppy disks. In addition, EMI can cause signal deterioration and loss from improper cable routing. If a signal cable is bundled with a power cable, radiation from the power cable may be induced into the signal cable, affecting the signals that pass through it. Good grounding routes the induced EMI signals away from logic circuitry and toward ground potential, preventing them from disrupting normal operations. Unlike ESD, which is destructive, the effects of EMI can be corrected without damage.

TEST TIP

Remember that ESD is destructive and EMI is not.

Because the computer system is connected to an actual earth ground, it should always be turned off and disconnected from the wall outlet during electrical storms. This includes the computer and all of its peripherals. The electrical pathway through the computer equipment can be very inviting to lightning on its way to earth ground. The extremely high electrical potential of a lightning strike is more than any computer can withstand.

TEST TIP

Know the best protection for a computer system during an electrical storm.

VIRUSES

The A+ Operating Systems Technology objective 4.4 states that the test taker should be able to identify concepts relating to viruses and virus types—their danger, their symptoms, sources of viruses, how they infect, how to protect against them, and how to identify/remove them. Topics include:

- What they are
- Sources
- How to determine their presence

Computer viruses

Computer viruses are destructive software programs designed to replicate, and spread, on their own. Viruses are created to sneak into personal computers. Sometimes these programs take control of a machine to leave a humorous message, and sometimes they destroy data. Once they infiltrate one machine, they can spread into other computers through infected diskettes that friends and co-workers pass around, or through local and wide area network connections.

National Computer Security Association

Researchers at the **National Computer Security Association** estimated that between 200 and 300 new viruses are being introduced into the computer community every month. However, the top 10 viruses in the United States account for about 80 percent of virus infections.

There are basically three types of viruses, based on how they infect a computer system:

boot-sector virus

- A **boot-sector virus**. This type of virus copies itself onto the boot sector of floppy and hard disks. The virus replaces the disk's original boot-sector code with its own code. This allows it to be loaded into memory before anything else is loaded. Once in memory, the virus can spread to other disks.

file infectors

- A **file infector**. File infectors are viruses that add their virus code to executable files. After the file with the virus is executed, it spreads to other executable files.

A similar type of virus, called a **macro virus**, hides in the macro programs of word processing document files. These files can be designed to load when the document is opened or when a certain key combination is entered. In addition, these types of viruses can be designed to stay resident in memory after the host program has been exited (similar to a TSR program), or may just stop working when the infected file is terminated.

macro virus

- A **Trojan horse**. This type of virus appears to be a legitimate program that may be found on any system. Trojan horse viruses are more likely to do damage by destroying files, and can cause physical damage to disks.

Trojan horse

A number of different viruses have been created from these three virus types. They have several different names, but they all inflict basically the same damage. After a virus file has become active in the computer, it basically resides in memory when the system is running. From this point, it may perform a number of different types of operations that can be as complex and damaging as the author designs them to be.

As an example, a strain of boot-sector virus, known as **CMOS virus**, infects the hard drive's master boot record and becomes memory resident. When activated, the virus writes over the system's configuration information in the CMOS area. Part of what gets overwritten is the HDD and FDD information. Therefore, the system will not be able to boot up properly. The initial infection comes from booting from an infected floppy disk. The virus overwrites the CMOS once in every 60 bootups.

CMOS virus

A similar boot-sector virus, referred to as the **FAT virus**, becomes memory resident in the area of system memory where the IO.SYS and MSDOS.SYS files are located. This allows it to spread to any non-write protected disks inserted into the computer. In addition, the virus moves the system pointers for the disk's executable files to an unused cluster and rewrites the pointers in the FAT to point to the sector where the virus is located. The result is improper disk copies, inability to back up files, large numbers of lost clusters, and all executable files being cross-linked with each other.

FAT virus

FAT table virus

TEST TIP

Know how the different types of viruses attack the system.

In another example, a file infector virus strain, called the **FAT table virus**, infects .EXE files but does not become memory resident. When the infected file is executed, the virus rewrites another .EXE file.

Virus Symptoms

Because virus programs tend to operate in the background, it is sometimes difficult to realize that the computer has been infected. Typical virus symptoms include the following:

- Hard disk controller failures.
- Disks continue to be full even when files have been deleted.
- System cannot read write-protected disks.
- The hard disk stops booting and files are corrupted.
- The system will boot to floppy disk, but will not access the HDD. An Invalid Drive Specification message usually displays when attempting to access the C: drive.
- CMOS settings continually revert to default even though the system board battery is good.

- Files change size for no apparent reason.
- System operation slows down noticeably.
- Blank screen when booting (flashing cursor).
- Windows crashes.
- The hard drive is set to DOS compatibility and 32-bit file access suddenly stops working.
- Network data transfers and print jobs slow down dramatically.

There are a few practices that increase the odds of a machine being infected by a virus. These include use of **shareware software**, **software of unknown origin**, or **bulletin board software**. One of the most effective ways to reduce these avenues of infection is to buy shrink-wrapped products from a reputable source.

Another means of virus protection involves installing a virus-scanning program that checks disks and files before using them in the computer. MS-DOS provided a minimal antivirus scanner called **VSafe** that could be installed as a TSR program to continuously monitor the system for viruses. DOS also included an **MSAV** utility that could be run from the DOS prompt to scan for and remove viruses.

TEST TIP

Know how viruses are spread.

Several other companies offer third-party virus-protection software that can be configured to operate in various ways. If the computer is a stand-alone unit, it may be nonproductive to have the antivirus software run each time the system is booted up. It would be much more practical to have the program check floppy disks only, because this is the only possible entryway into the computer.

A networked or online computer has more opportunity to contract viruses than a stand-alone unit, however, because viruses may enter the unit over the network or through the modem. In these cases, setting the software to run at each boot up is more desirable. Most modern antivirus software includes utilities to check files downloaded to the computer through dial-up connections, such as from the Internet.

Antivirus Programs

Antivirus programs

msav.exe

Later versions of MS-DOS included an antivirus utility called MSAV. To run the MSDOS Antivirus program, type **msav.exe** at the DOS command line. This should produce the antivirus program's main screen as depicted in Figure 13-16. Windows 3.x included an updated version known as MWAV. With Windows 95, Microsoft abandoned integrated antivirus protection. Therefore, you must use third-party antivirus programs with Windows 9x and Windows 2000.

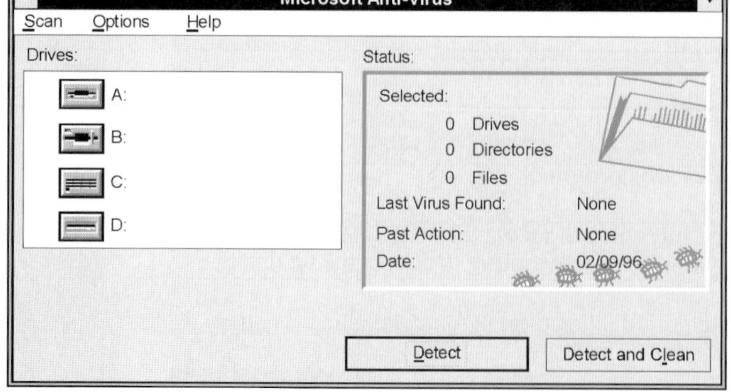

Figure 13-16: The Antivirus Screen

Complete the following steps:

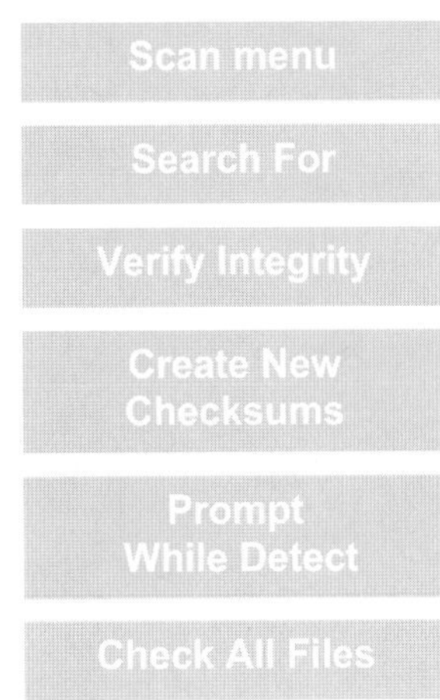

Hands-On Activity

1. Select the Virus List from the **Scan menu** to produce the virus list window. In this window, you can read the information about the viruses recognized by the current version of the program. Since the list of viruses is long, you may search for virus names by typing the first few letters of the virus in the **Search For** box.
2. Configure the Antivirus program. Select Options to see the menu. Verify that an X appears in the box for **Verify Integrity**, **Create New Checksums**, **Prompt While Detect**, and **Check All Files**, as depicted in Figure 13-17.

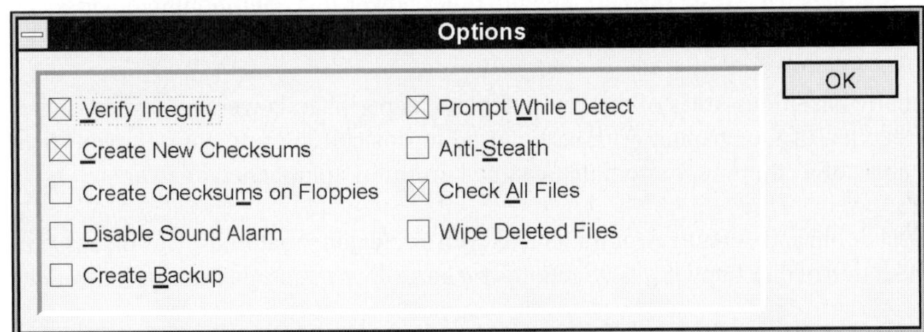

Figure 13-17: The Antivirus Options Dialog Box

3. Select the **Anti-Stealth** and **Wipe Deleted Files** entries to activate them. An **X** should appear in the boxes beside them. Click the C: in the Drives: box. A small window will show that the program is reading the directories for drive C:. The Status: window will show the number of drives, directories, and files it found on the system.
4. Run the Antivirus program. Activate the **DETECT** button to search for viruses. The program will first scan RAM memory for any viruses. If any are found in memory, they will be cleaned from the system memory. The program will then search the files on the hard drive. Select the Update option if the program tells you that a file has been changed.
5. When the program is finished scanning the drive, a **Statistics** window will appear. Exit the Statistics window, and select the Scan option to see the menu.
6. Alter the AUTOEXEC.BAT file to automatically start the antivirus program when the computer is booted up. Type **C:\DOS\VSAFE.COM** into the AUTOEXEC.BAT file, so that the program will check for viruses when you **Start a Program**, **Copy a File**, or **Save a File** to disk. VSafe will notify you if any viruses infect your computer.

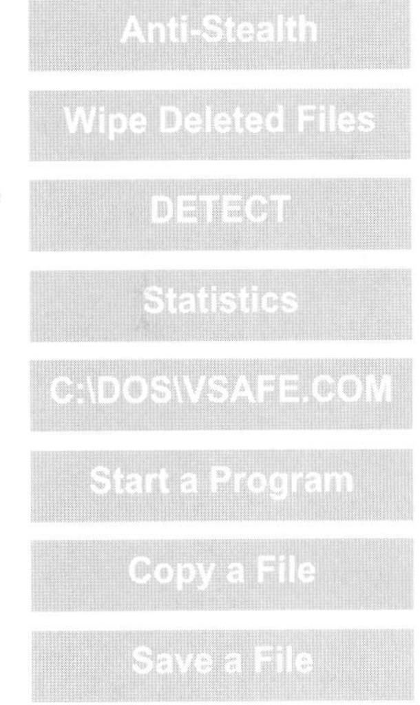

CHAPTER SUMMARY

The focus of this chapter has been to present important points for inclusion in preventive maintenance programs associated with personal computer systems. The first section of the chapter dealt with typical cleaning chores. It also featured preventive maintenance procedures for the system's different components. A suggested PM schedule was also presented. this is time-proven information and should always be shared freely with customers.

The second major section of the chapter focused on environmental hazards that affect the operation of computer equipment. The majority of this section dealt with problems that revolve around fluctuations in the computer's incoming power line. Different types of Universal Power Supplies were discussed, along with other power line conditioning devices. The remainder of the section discussed proper storage methods for computer components.

Potentially hazardous areas of the computer and its peripherals were presented in the third major section of the chapter. Although not an intrinsically unsafe environment, there are some areas of a computer system that can be harmful if approached unawares.

Disposal of old and defective equipment, as well as cleaning materials, was discussed in the fourth section of the chapter. MSDS records for hazardous materials were also introduced.

The final section of the chapter described the danger and causes of electrostatic discharges, as well as providing information about how to eliminate them.

At this point, review the objectives listed at the beginning of the chapter to be certain that you understand and can perform each item listed there.

KEY POINTS REVIEW

The focus of this chapter has been to present important points for inclusion in the preventive maintenance programs associated with personal computer systems. Review the following key points before moving into the Review and Exam Questions sections to make sure you are comfortable with each point. Afterward, answer the Review Questions that follow to verify your knowledge of the information.

- Cleaning is a major part of keeping a computer system healthy. Therefore, the technician's tool kit should also contain a collection of cleaning supplies. Along with hand tools, it will need a lint-free, soft cloth (chamois) for cleaning the plastic outer surfaces of the system.

- The environment around a computer system, and the manner in which the computer is used, determines greatly how many problems it will have. Occasionally dedicating a few moments of care to the computer can extend its Mean Time Between Failures (MTBF) period considerably. This activity, involving maintenance not normally associated with a breakdown, is called Preventive Maintenance (PM).

- Unlike hard disk drives, floppy drives are at least partially open to the atmosphere, and they may be handled on a regular basis. This opens the floppy disk drive to a number of maintenance concerns not found in hard disk drives. Also, the removable disks are subject to extremes in temperature, exposure to magnetic and electromagnetic fields, bending, and airborne particles that can lead to information loss.

- Input peripherals generally require very little in the way of preventive maintenance. An occasional dusting and cleaning should be all that's really required.

- Because printers tend to be much more mechanical than other types of computer peripherals, they require more effort to maintain. Printers generate pollutants, such as paper dust and ink droplets, in everyday operation. These pollutants can build up on mechanical parts and cause them to wear. As the parts wear, the performance of the printer diminishes. Therefore, printers require periodic cleaning and adjustments to maintain good performance.

- Digital systems tend to be sensitive to power variations and losses. Even a very short loss of electrical power can shut a digital computer down, resulting in a loss of any current information that has not been saved to a mass storage device.

- Uninterruptible power supplies are battery-based systems that monitor the incoming power and kick in when unacceptable variations occur in the power source. The term UPS is frequently used to describe two different types of power backup systems.

- In most IBM compatibles, there are only two potentially dangerous areas. One of these is inside the CRT display, and the other is inside the power supply unit. Both of these areas contain electrical voltage levels that are lethal. However, both of these areas reside in self-contained units, and you will normally not be required to open either unit.

- Laser printers contain many hazardous areas. The laser light can be very damaging to the human eye. In addition, there are multiple high-voltage areas in the typical laser printer and a high-temperature area to contend with as well.

- Most computer components contain some level of hazardous substances. Printed circuit boards consist of plastics, precious metals, fiberglass, arsenic, silicon, gallium, and lead. CRTs contain glass, metal, plastics, lead, barium, and rare earth metals. Batteries from portable systems can contain lead, cadmium, lithium, alkaline manganese, and mercury.

- Electrostatic Discharges (ESD) are the most severe form of Electromagnet Interference (EMI). The human body can build up static charges that range up to 25,000 volts. These build-ups can discharge very rapidly into a electrically grounded body, or device. Placing a 25,000-volt surge through any electronic device is potentially damaging to it.

- In general, MOS devices are sensitive to voltage spikes and static electricity discharges. This can cause many problems when you have to replace MOS devices, especially Complementary-Symmetry Metal Oxide Semiconductor (CMOS) devices. The level of static electricity present on your body is high enough to destroy the inputs of a CMOS device if you touch its pins with your fingers.

- The term ground is often a source of confusion for the novice, because it actually encompasses a collection of terms. Generically, ground is simply any point from which electrical measurements are referenced. However, the original definition of ground actually referred to the ground. This ground is called earth ground.

- Computer viruses are destructive software programs designed to replicate, and spread, on their own. Viruses are created to sneak into personal computers. Sometimes these programs take control of a machine to leave a humorous message, and sometimes they destroy data. Once they infiltrate one machine, they can spread into other computers through infected diskettes that friends and co-workers pass around, or through local and wide area network connections.

REVIEW QUESTIONS

The following questions test your knowledge of the material presented in this chapter.

1. List the two most dangerous areas of a typical microcomputer system, and describe why they are so dangerous.
2. Name three devices used to minimize ESD in the repair area.
3. The best general-purpose cleaning tool for computer equipment is _______.
4. List at least three environmental conditions that can adversely affect microcomputer equipment.
5. A short under-voltage condition, lasting milliseconds, is called ________.
6. Are there any restrictions on disposing of a spent toner cartridge?
7. Which type of IC device is most likely to be damaged by ESD?
8. Can an effective ESD strap be constructed by simply wrapping a grounded bare wire around your wrist?
9. What is the most effective method of dealing with EMI problems?
10. The best method of protecting computer equipment from a thunderstorm is to _______.
11. The best method for transporting electronic devices is _________.
12. List computer-related PM items that should be performed annually.
13. Name two characteristics that should be checked carefully before purchasing a UPS for a given computer system.
14. Describe the normal duration of a voltage spike.
15. Once a virus has infected a computer, where does it normally reside?

EXAM QUESTIONS

1. Do viruses normally attack the system's CMOS settings?
   a. Yes, this is how a virus attacks most computers.
   b. No, viruses do not normally attack CMOS settings.
   c. Yes, this is how viruses attack all computers.
   d. No, viruses never attack CMOS settings.
2. How are most computer viruses spread from computer to computer?
   a. By downloading programs from networks
   b. By passing infected diskettes between individuals
   c. By not formatting disks before use
   d. By transferring files over modems
3. What is the most common cause of ESD in microcomputer systems?
   a. Moving people
   b. High humidity
   c. Rubber mats
   d. Grounded power supply cables
4. Where would it be inappropriate to use an ESD wrist strap?
   a. While working on hard disk drives
   b. While working on system boards
   c. While working on CRT video monitors
   d. While working on printers
5. What is the best substance for cleaning the plastic surfaces of a computer system?
   a. A water and fabric softener solution
   b. A water and ammonia solution
   c. A water and bleach solution
   d. A hydrogen tetrachloride solution
6. A short over-voltage occurrence (nanoseconds) is called _________.
   a. a spike
   b. a surge
   c. a brownout
   d. a sag
7. ESD is most likely to occur during periods of _________.
   a. low humidity
   b. high humidity
   c. medium humidity
   d. rain
8. The best protection against power-failure data loss is _______.
   a. a tape backup
   b. a surge suppresser
   c. a UPS
   d. a line filter

9. Define a voltage sag.
   a. An over-voltage condition that lasts for a few milliseconds
   b. An under-voltage condition that lasts for an extended period
   c. An over-voltage condition that lasts for an extended period
   d. An under-voltage condition that lasts for a few milliseconds
10. The most effective grounding system for a microcomputer is ________.
   a. an ESD wrist or ankle strap
   b. the safety ground plug at a commercial ac receptacle
   c. the ground plane of the system board
   d. the chassis ground provided by brass standoffs

APPENDIX A

A+ OBJECTIVE MAP

CompTIA requires the successful completion of two exams in order to qualify for A+ Certification. The A+ Core Hardware Service Technician exam focuses on hardware and systems integration. The A+ Operating System Technologies exam focuses on software and operating system competencies.

The CompTIA organization has established the following objectives for the A+ Certification exams.

A+ CORE HARDWARE SERVICE TECHNICIAN EXAMINATION (220-201)

The Core Hardware examination measures essential competencies for a microcomputer hardware service technician with six months of on-the-job experience. The student must demonstrate basic knowledge of installing, configuring, upgrading, troubleshooting, and repairing microcomputer systems at the standard defined by this test specification.

Domain 1.0 Installation, Configuration, and Upgrading

The topics covered by this domain are included in approximately 30% of the questions in the A+ Core Hardware exam. This domain requires the knowledge and skills to identify, install, configure, and upgrade microcomputer components and peripherals. The student must be able to follow the established basic procedures for system assembly and disassembly of field replaceable units.

1.1 Identify basic terms, concepts, and functions of system modules, including how each module should work during normal operation and during the boot process.

Examples of concepts and modules are:

- System board - Chapter 2, Lab Procedure 1
- Power supply - Chapter 1, Lab Procedure 8
- Processor /CPU - Chapter 2, Lab Procedure 9
- Memory - Chapter 2, Lab Procedure 6

- Storage devices - Chapter 4, Lab Procedure 7
- Monitor - Chapter 3
- Modem - Chapter 5, Lab Procedure 18
- Firmware - Chapter 2, Lab Procedure 3
- Boot process - Chapter 8, Lab Procedure 2
- BIOS - Chapter 1, Lab Procedure 3
- CMOS - Chapter 2, Lab Procedure 3
- LCD (portable systems) - Chapter 7
- Ports - Chapter 3, Lab Procedure 6
- PDA (Personal Digital Assistant) - Chapter 7

1.2 Identify basic procedures for adding and removing field replaceable modules for both desktop and portable systems.

Examples of modules:

- System board - Chapter 11, Lab Procedure 8
- Storage device - Chapter 11, Lab Procedure 7
- Power supply - Chapter 11, Lab Procedure 8
- Processor/CPU - Chapter 11, Lab Procedure 9
- Memory - Chapter 11, Lab Procedure 8
- Input devices - Chapter 11, Lab Procedure 8
- Hard drive - Chapter 11, Lab Procedure 7
- Keyboard - Chapter 11, Lab Procedure 8
- Video card - Chapter 11, Lab Procedure 10
- Mouse - Chapter 11, Lab Procedure 8
- Network Interface Card (NIC) - Chapter 5, Lab Procedure 19

Portable system components:

- AC adapters - Chapter 7
- DC controllers - Chapter 7
- LCD panel - Chapter 7
- PC Card - Chapter 7
- Pointing devices - Chapter 7

1.3 Identify available IRQs, DMAs, I/O addresses, and procedures for device installation and configuration.

Content may include the following:

- Standard IRQ settings - Chapter 7
- Modems - Chapter 5, Lab Procedure 18
- Floppy drive controllers - Chapter 4
- Hard drive controllers - Chapter 4, Lab Procedure 4
- USB port - Chapter 3
- Infrared port - Chapter 5
- Hexadecimal/Addresses - Chapter 3

1.4 Identify common peripheral ports, associated cabling, and their connectors.

Content may include the following:

- Cable types - Chapter 3
- Cable orientation - Chapter 3
- Serial versus parallel - Chapter 3
- Pin connections - Chapter 3

Examples of types of connectors:

- DB-9 - Chapter 3
- DB-25 - Chapter 3
- RJ-11 - Chapter 5
- RJ-45 - Chapter 5
- BNC - Chapter 5
- PS2/MINI-DIN - Chapter 3
- USB - Chapter 3
- IEEE-1394 - Chapter 3

1.5 Identify proper procedures for installing and configuring IDE/EIDE devices.

Content may include the following:

- Master/slave - Chapter 4, Lab Procedure 7
- Devices per channel - Chapter 4
- Primary/Secondary - Chapter 4

1.6 Identify proper procedures for installing and configuring SCSI devices.

Content may include the following:

- Address/Termination conflicts - Chapter 4
- Cabling - Chapter 4
- Types (example: regular, wide, ultra-wide) - Chapter 4
- Internal versus external - Chapter 4
- External slots, EISA, ISA, PCI - Chapter 2
- Jumper block settings (binary equivalents) - Chapter 4

1.7 Identify proper procedures for installing and configuring peripheral devices.

Content may include the following:

- Monitor/Video card - Chapter 3
- Modem - Chapter 5
- USB peripherals and hubs - Chapter 3
- IEEE-1284 - Chapter 3
- IEEE-1394 - Chapter 3
- External storage - Chapter 4

Portables:

- Docking stations - Chapter 7
- PC Cards - Chapter 7
- Port replicator - Chapter 7
- Infrared devices - Chapter 5

1.8 Identify hardware methods of upgrading system performance, procedures for replacing basic subsystem components, unique components, and when to use them.

Content may include the following:

- Memory - Chapter 11
- Hard drives - Chapter 11, Lab Procedure 7
- CPU - Chapter 2, Lab Procedure 9
- Methods for upgrading BIOS - Chapter 11
- When to upgrade BIOS - Chapter 11
- Portable Systems:
- Battery - Chapter 7
- Hard drive - Chapter 7
- Types I, II, III cards - Chapter 7
- Memory - Chapter 7

Domain 2.0 Diagnosing and Troubleshooting

The topics covered by this domain are included in approximately 30% of the questions in the A+ Core Hardware exam. This domain requires the ability to apply knowledge relating to diagnosing and troubleshooting common component problems and system malfunctions. This includes symptoms and causes related to common problems.

2.1. Identify common symptoms and problems associated with each module and how to troubleshoot and isolate the problems.

Content may include the following:

- Processor/Memory symptoms - Chapter 11, Lab Procedure 8
- Mouse - Chapter 11
- Floppy drive failures - Chapter 11
- Parallel ports - Chapter 11
- Hard drives - Chapter 11, Lab Procedure 4
- CD-ROM - Chapter 11, Lab Procedure 7
- DVD - Chapter 11
- Sound card/audio - Chapter 11

- Monitor/Video - Chapter 11
- Motherboards - Chapter 11
- Modems - Chapter 11
- BIOS - Chapter 11
- USB - Chapter 3
- NIC - Chapter 11
- CMOS - Chapter 11
- Power supply - Chapter 11
- Slot covers - Chapter 1
- POST audible/visual error codes - Chapter 11
- Troubleshooting tools (e.g., multimeter) - Chapter 1
- Large LBA, LBA - Chapter 4
- Cables - Chapter 11
- Keyboard - Chapter 11
- Peripherals - Chapter 11

2.2. Identify basic troubleshooting procedures and how to elicit problem symptoms from customers.

Content may include the following:

- Troubleshooting/isolation/problem determination procedures - Chapter 11
- Determining whether problem is hardware- or software-related - Chapter 11
- Gathering information from user, such as the following:
    - Customer environment - Chapter 11
    - Symptoms/Error codes - Chapter 11
    - Situation when the problem occurred - Chapter 11

Domain 3.0 Preventive Maintenance

The topics covered by this domain are included in approximately 5% of the questions in the A+ Core Hardware exam. This domain requires knowledge of safety and preventive maintenance. Safety includes the potential hazards to personnel and equipment when working with lasers, high-voltage equipment, ESD, and items that require special disposal procedures that comply with environmental guidelines. Preventive maintenance includes knowledge of products, procedures, environmental hazards, and required precautions when working on microcomputer systems.

3.1. Identify the purpose of various types of preventative maintenance products and procedures and when to use them.

Content may include the following:

- Liquid cleaning compounds - Chapter 13
- Types of materials to clean contacts and connections - Chapter 13
- Non-static vacuums (chassis, power supplies, and fans) - Chapter 13

3.2. Identify issues, procedures, and devices for protection within the computing environment, including people, hardware, and the surrounding workspace.

Content may include the following:

- UPSs (Uninterruptible Power Supplies) and suppressors - Chapter 13
- Determining the signs of power issues - Chapter 13
- Proper methods of storage of components for future use - Chapter 13

Potential hazards and proper safety procedures relating to lasers:

- High-voltage equipment - Chapter 13
- Power supply - Chapter 13
- CRTs - Chapter 13

Special disposal procedures that comply with environmental guidelines:

- Batteries - Chapter 13
- CRTs - Chapter 13
- Toner kits/cartridges - Chapter 13

- Chemical solvents and cans - Chapter 13
- MSDS (Material Safety Data Sheet) - Chapter 13

ESD (electrostatic discharge) precautions and procedures:

- What ESD can do; how it may be apparent, or hidden - Chapter 13
- Common ESD protection devices - Chapter 13
- Situations that could present a danger or hazard - Chapter 13

Domain 4.0 Motherboard/Processors/Memory

The topics covered by this domain are included in approximately 15% of the questions in the A+ Core Hardware exam. This domain requires knowledge of specific terminology, facts, ways and means of dealing with classifications, categories and principles of motherboards, processors, and memory in microcomputer systems.

4.1 Distinguish between the popular CPU chips in terms of their basic characteristics.

Content may include the following:

- Popular CPU chips (Pentium class and higher) - Chapter 2, Lab Procedure 9
- CPU Characteristics:
    - Physical size - Chapter 2, Lab Procedure 9
    - Voltage - Chapter 2, Lab Procedure 9
    - Speeds - Chapter 2, Lab Procedure 9
    - Onboard cache or not - Chapter 2, Lab Procedure 9
    - Sockets - Chapter 2, Lab Procedure 9
    - SEC (Single Edge Contact) - Chapter 2, Lab Procedure 9

4.2 Identify the categories of RAM (Random Access Memory), their locations, and physical characteristics.

Content may include the following:

- EDO RAM (Extended Data Output RAM) - Chapter 2
- DRAM (Dynamic RAM) - Chapter 2
- SRAM (Static RAM) - Chapter 2
- RIMM (Rambus Inline Memory Module (184 pins)) - Chapter 2

- VRAM (Video RAM) - Chapter 2
- SDRAM (Synchronous Dynamic RAM) - Chapter 2
- WRAM (Windows accelerator card RAM) - Chapter 2
- Memory bank - Chapter 2
- Memory chips (8-bit, 16-bit, and 32-bit) - Chapter 2
- SIMMs (single in-line memory module) - Chapter 2
- DIMMs (dual in-line memory module) - Chapter 2
- Parity chips versus non-parity chips - Chapter 2

4.3 Identify the most popular type of motherboards, their components, and their architecture (bus structures and power supplies).

Content may include the following:

- Types of motherboards:
    - AT (full and baby) - Chapter 2
    - ATX - Chapter 2
- Motherboard components:
    - Communication ports - Chapter 3
    - SIMM and DIMM - Chapter 2
    - Processor sockets - Chapter 2
    - External cache memory (Level 2) - Chapter 2
    - Bus architecture:
        - ISA - Chapter 2
        - PCI - Chapter 2
        - AGP - Chapter 2
        - USB (Universal Serial Bus) - Chapter 3
        - VESA local bus (VL-BUS) - Chapter 2
        - Basic compatibility guidelines - Chapter 2
        - IDE (ATA, ATAPI, ULTRA-DMA, EIDE) - Chapter 4
        - SCSI (Wide, Fast, Ultra, LVD (Low Voltage Differential) - Chapter 4

4.4 Identify the purpose of CMOS (Complementary Metal-Oxide Semiconductor), what it contains, and how to change its basic parameters.

Example basic CMOS settings:

- Printer parallel port: unidirectional, bi-directional, disable/enable, ECP, EPP - Chapter 2
- COM/serial port: memory address, interrupt request, disable - Chapter 2, Lab Procedure 3
- Hard drive: size and drive type - Chapter 2, Lab Procedure 4
- Floppy drive: enable/disable drive or boot, speed, density - Chapter 2, Lab Procedure 4
- Boot sequence - Chapter 2, Lab Procedure 2
- Memory: parity, non-parity - Chapter 2, Lab Procedure 3
- Date/Time - Chapter 2, Lab Procedure 3
- Passwords - Chapter 2, Lab Procedure 3
- Plug-and-Play BIOS - Chapter 2, Lab Procedure 3

Domain 5.0 Printers

The topics covered by this domain are included in approximately 10% of the questions in the A+ Core Hardware exam. This domain requires knowledge of basic types of printers, basic concepts, printer components, how they work, how they print onto a page, paper path, care and service techniques, and common problems.

5.1 Identify basic concepts, printer operations, and printer components.

Content may include the following:

Paper-feeder mechanisms - Chapter 6

- Types of printers
    - Laser - Chapter 6, Lab Procedures 20 & 21
    - Ink-jet - Chapter 6, Lab Procedures 20 & 21
    - Dot-matrix - Chapter 6, Lab Procedures 20 & 21

- Types of printer connections and configurations
    - Parallel - Chapter 6, Lab Procedures 20 & 21
    - Network - Chapter 6, Lab Procedures 20 & 21
    - USB - Chapter 6, Lab Procedures 20 & 21
    - Infrared - Chapter 6
    - Serial - Chapter 6, Lab Procedures 20 & 21

5.2 Identify care and service techniques and common problems with primary printer types.

Content may include the following:

- Feed and output - Chapter 6
- Errors (printed or displayed) - Chapter 6
- Paper jam - Chapter 6
- Print quality - Chapter 6
- Safety precautions - Chapter 13
- Preventive maintenance - Chapter 13

Domain 6.0 Basic Networking

The topics covered by this domain are included in approximately 10% of the questions in the A+ Core Hardware exam. This domain requires knowledge of basic network concepts and terminology, ability to determine whether a computer is networked, knowledge of procedures for swapping and configuring network interface cards, and knowledge of the ramifications of repairs when a computer is networked. The scope of this topic is specific to hardware issues on the desktop and connecting it to a network.

6.1 Identify basic networking concepts, including how a network works and the ramification of repairs on the network.

Content may include the following:

- Installing and configuring network cards - Chapter 5, Lab Procedures 18 & 19
- Network access - Chapter 5, Lab Procedure 32
- Full-duplex, half-duplex - Chapter 5
- Cabling:Twisted pair, coaxial, fiber-optic, RS-232 - Chapter 5

- Ways to network a PC - Chapter 5
- Physical network topologies - Chapter 5
- Increasing bandwidth - Chapter 5
- Loss of data - Chapter 12
- Network slowdown - Chapter 12, Lab Procedure 33
- Infrared - Chapter 5
- Hardware protocols - Chapter 5

OPERATING SYSTEM TECHNOLOGIES EXAMINATION (220-202)

The OS Technologies examination measures essential operating system competencies for microcomputer hardware service technicians with six months of on-the-job experience. The student must demonstrate basic knowledge of command line prompt, Windows 9x, and Windows NT/2000 for installing, configuring, upgrading, troubleshooting, and repairing microcomputer systems.

Domain 1.0 Operating System Fundamentals

The topics covered by this domain are included in approximately 30% of the questions in the A+ OS Technologies exam. This domain requires knowledge of the underlying DOS (command prompt functions) in Windows 9x and Windows NT/2000 operating systems in terms of its functions and structure for managing files and directories and running programs. It also includes navigating through the operating system from command line prompts and Windows procedures for accessing and retrieving information.

1.1 Identify the operating system's functions, structure, and major system files to navigate the operating system and know how to get to needed technical information.

Content may include the following:

- Major operating system functions
    - Create folders - Chapter 8, Lab Procedure 11
    - Checking OS Version - Chapter 8, Lab Procedure 22

- Major operating system components
    - Explorer - Chapter 8, Lab Procedure 11
    - My Computer - Chapter 8, Lab Procedure 11
    - Control Panel - Chapter 8, Lab Procedure 11
- Contrasts between Windows 9x and Windows 2000
- Major system files: what they are, where they are located, how they are used, and what they contain:
    - System, configuration, and user interface files
        - IO.SYS - Chapter 8
        - BOOT.INI - Chapter 8
        - WIN.COM - Chapter 8
        - MSDOS.SYS - Chapter 8
        - AUTOEXEC.BAT - Chapter 8
        - CONFIG.SYS - Chapter 8
        - Command line prompt - Chapter 8, Lab Procedure 12
    - Memory management
        - Conventional - Chapter 8
        - Extended/Upper memory - Chapter 8
        - High memory - Chapter 8
        - Virtual memory - Chapter 8, Lab Procedure 14
        - HIMEM.SYS - Chapter 8
        - EMM386.exe - Chapter 8
    - Windows 9x
        - IO.SYS - Chapter 9
        - WIN.INI - Chapter 9
        - USER.DAT - Chapter 9, Lab Procedure 13
        - SYSEDIT - Chapter 9
        - SYSTEM.INI - Chapter 9
        - SETVER.EXE - Chapter 9
        - SMARTDRV.EXE - Chapter 9
        - MSCONFIG (98) - Chapter 9
        - COMMAND.COM - Chapter 9
        - DOSSTART.BAT - Chapter 9

- REGEDIT.EXE - Chapter 9, Lab Procedure 13
- SYSTEM.DAT - Chapter 9, Lab Procedure 13
- RUN command - Chapter 9
- DriveSpace - Chapter 9

- Windows 2000
    - Computer Management - Chapter 10, Lab Procedure 17
    - BOOT.INI - Chapter 10
    - REGEDT32 - Chapter 10, Lab Procedure 26
    - REGEDIT - Chapter 10
    - RUN CMD - Chapter 10
    - NTLDR - Chapter 10
    - NTDETECT.COM - Chapter 10
    - NTBOOTDD.SYS - Chapter 10
- Command prompt procedures (command syntax)
    - DIR - Chapter 8
    - ATTRIB - Chapter 8
    - VER - Chapter 8
    - MEM - Chapter 8
    - ScanDisk - Chapter 12, Lab Procedure 23
    - DEFRAG - Chapter 12, Lab Procedure 23
    - EDIT - Chapter 8
    - XCOPY - Chapter 8
    - COPY - Chapter 8
    - FORMAT - Chapter 8
    - FDISK - Chapter 8
    - MSCDEX - Chapter 8
    - SETVER - Chapter 8
    - SCANREG - Chapter 12, Lab Procedure 22

1.2 Identify basic concepts and procedures for creating, viewing, and managing files, directories, and disks. This includes procedures for changing file attributes and the ramifications of those changes (for example, security issues).

Content may include the following:

- File attributes - Read Only, Hidden, System, and Archive attributes - Chapter 8
- File-naming conventions (most common extensions) - Chapter 8
- Windows 2000 COMPRESS, ENCRYPT - Chapter 10
- IDE/SCSI - Chapter 4
- Internal/External - Chapter 4
- Backup/Restore - Chapter 12
- Partitioning/Formatting/File system
    - FAT - Chapter 9
    - FAT16 - Chapter 9
    - FAT32 - Chapter 9
    - NTFS4 - Chapter 10
    - NTFS5 - Chapter 10
    - HPFS - Chapter 8
- Windows-based utilities:
    - ScanDisk - Chapter 12
    - Device Manager - Chapter 12
    - System Manager - Chapter 12
    - Computer Manager - Chapter 10
    - MSCONFIG.EXE - Chapter 9
    - REGEDIT.EXE (View information/Back up Registry) - Chapter 9
    - REGEDT32.EXE - Chapter 10
    - ATTRIB.EXE - Chapter 8
    - EXTRACT.EXE - Chapter 9
    - DEFRAG.EXE - Chapter 12
    - EDIT.COM - Chapter 8
    - FDISK.EXE - Chapter 8
    - SYSEDIT.EXE - Chapter 9
    - SCANREG - Chapter 9

- WSCRIPT.EXE - Chapter 9
- HWINFO.EXE - Chapter 10
- ASD.EXE (Automatic Skip Driver) - Chapter 12
- CVT1.EXE (Drive Converter FAT16 to FAT32) - Chapter 9

Domain 2.0 Installation, Configuration, and Upgrading

The topics covered by this domain are included in approximately 15% of the questions in the A+ OS Technologies exam. This domain requires knowledge of installing, configuring, and upgrading Windows 9x and Windows NT/2000. This includes knowledge of system boot sequences and minimum hardware requirements.

2.1 Identify the procedures for installing Windows 9x and Windows 2000 and bringing the software to a basic operational level.

Content may include the following:

- Start up - Chapter 9
- Partition - Chapter 9
- Format drive - Chapter 9
- Loading drivers - Chapter 9, Lab Procedure 10
- Run appropriate setup utility - Chapter 9

2.2 Identify steps to perform an operating system upgrade.

Content may include the following:

- Upgrading Windows 95 to Windows 98 - Chapter 9
- Upgrading from Windows NT Workstation 4.0 to Windows 2000 - Chapter 10
- Replacing Windows 9x with Windows 2000 - Chapter 10
- Dual boot Windows 9x/Windows NT 4.0/2000 - Chapter 9

2.3 Identify the basic system boot sequences and boot methods, including steps to create an emergency boot disk with utilities installed for Windows 9x, Windows NT, and Windows 2000.

Content may include the following:

- Startup disk - Chapter 12
- Safe Mode - Chapter 12, Lab Procedure 27
- MS-DOS mode - Chapter 12
- NTLDR (NT Loader), BOOT.INI - Chapter 12
- Files required to boot - Chapter 12
- Creating an Emergency Repair Disk (ERD) - Chapter 12

2.4 Identify procedures for loading/adding and configuring application device drivers, and the necessary software for certain devices.

Content may include the following:

- Windows 9x Plug-and-Play and Windows 2000 - Chapter 9, Lab Procedure 18
- Identify the procedures for installing and launching typical Windows and non-Windows applications (Note: There is no content related to Windows 3.1) - Chapter 8, Lab Procedure 11
- Procedures for setup and configuration of the Windows printing subsystem
    - Setting Default printer - Chapter 6, Lab Procedure 20
    - Installing/Spool setting - Chapter 6
    - Network printing (with help of LAN admin) - Chapter 6, Lab Procedure 21

Domain 3.0 Diagnosing and Troubleshooting

The topics covered by this domain are included in approximately 40% of the questions in the A+ OS Technologies exam. This domain requires the ability to apply knowledge to diagnose and troubleshoot common problems relating to Windows 9x and Windows 2000. This includes understanding normal operation and symptoms relating to common problems.

3.1 Recognize and interpret the meaning of common error codes and startup messages from the boot sequence, and identify steps to correct the problem.

Content may include the following:

- Safe Mode - Chapter 12, Lab Procedure 27
- No operating system found - Chapter 12, Lab Procedure 43
- Error in CONFIG.SYS line XX - Chapter 12, Lab Procedure 43
- Bad or missing COMMAND.COM - Chapter 12, Lab Procedure 43
- HIMEM.SYS not loaded - Chapter 12, Lab Procedure 43
- Missing or corrupt HIMEM.SYS - Chapter 12, Lab Procedure 43
- SCSI - Chapter 11
- Swap file - Chapter 18
- NT boot issues - Chapter 12, Lab Procedure 44
- Dr. Watson - Chapter 12, Lab Procedure 43
- Failure to start GUI - Chapter 12, Lab Procedure 43
- Windows protection error - Chapter 12, Lab Procedure 43
- Event Viewer; event log is full - Chapter 12, Lab Procedure 29
- A device referenced in SYSTEM.INI, WIN.INI, or Registry that is not found - Chapter 12, Lab Procedure 43

3.2 Recognize common problems and determine how to resolve them.

Content may include the following:

- Eliciting problem symptoms from customers - Chapter 11
- Have customer reproduce error as part of diagnostic process - Chapter 11
- Identify recent changes to the computer environment from the user - Chapter 11
- Identify Windows-specific printing problems and the procedures for correcting them
    - Print spool is stalled - Chapter 6
    - Incorrect/incompatible driver for print - Chapter 6
    - Incorrect parameter - Chapter 6
- Other common problems
    - General protection faults - Chapter 12

- Illegal operation - Chapter 12
- Invalid working directory - Chapter 12
- System lockup - Chapter 12
- Option (sound card, modem, input device) will not function - Chapter 11
- Application will not start or load - Chapter 12
- Cannot log on to network (option - NIC not functioning) - Chapter 11
- TSR (Terminate and Stay Resident) programs and virus - Chapter 12
- Applications don't install - Chapter 12
- Network connection - Chapter 5

- Viruses and virus types
    - What they are - Chapter 13
    - Sources (floppy, email, etc.) - Chapter 13
    - How to determine their presence - Chapter 13, Lab Procedure 30

Domain 4.0 Networks

The topics covered by this domain are included in approximately 15% of the questions in the A+ OS Technologies exam. This domain requires knowledge of network capabilities of Windows and how to connect to networks on the client side, including what the Internet is about, its capabilities, basic concepts relating to Internet access, and generic procedures for system setup. The scope of this topic is only what is needed on the desktop side to connect to a network.

4.1 Identify the networking capabilities of Windows, including procedures for connecting to the network.

Content may include the following:

- Protocols - Chapter 5, Lab Procedure 32
- IPCONFIG.EXE - Chapter 5, Lab Procedure 33
- WINIPCFG.EXE - Chapter 5, Lab Procedure 33
- Sharing disk drives - Chapter 5, Lab Procedure 34
- Sharing print and file services - Chapter 5, Lab Procedure 34
- Network type and network card - Chapter 5
- Installing and configuring browsers - Chapter 5, Lab Procedure 38
- Configure OS for network connection - Chapter 5, Lab Procedure 31

4.2 Identify concepts and capabilities relating to the Internet and basic procedures for setting up a system for Internet access.

Content may include the following:

- Concepts and terminology
    - ISP - Chapter 5
    - TCP/IP - Chapter 5
    - IPX/SPX - Chapter 5
    - NetBEUI - Chapter 5
    - E-mail - Chapter 5, Lab Procedure 38
    - PING.EXE - Chapter 5, Lab Procedure 33
    - HTML - Chapter 5
    - HTTP:// - Chapter 5, Lab Procedure 38
    - FTP - Chapter 5, Lab Procedure 39
    - Domain names (web sites) - Chapter 5
    - Dial-up networking - Chapter 5, Lab Procedure 31
    - TRACERT.EXE - Chapter 5, Lab Procedure 33
    - NSLOOKUP.EXE

GLOSSARY

An Extended Glossary can be found in the electronic Reference Shelf located on the CD that accompanies this book.

A

Accelerated Graphics Port (AGP) A newer 32-bit video interface specification based on the PCI bus design. Rather than using the PCI bus for video data, the AGP system provides a dedicated point-to-point path between the video graphics controller and system memory. The AGP bus was designed specifically to handle the high data transfer demands associated with 3-D graphic operations.

ACK (ACKnowledge) A data communications code used by the receiver to tell the transmitter it is ready to accept data. During a data transfer this signal is continually used to indicate successful receipt of the last data character or block and to request more.

Active Directory Active Directory (AD) is the central feature of the Windows 2000 architecture. It is a distributed database of user and resource information that describes the makeup of the network (i.e., users and application settings). It is also a method of implementing a distributed authentication process. The Active Directory replaces the domain structure used in Windows NT 4.0. This feature helps to centralize system and user configurations, as well as data backups on the server in the Windows 2000 network.

active partition The disk partition that possesses the system files required to boot the system. This is the logical drive that the system reads at bootup.

adapter A device which permits one system to work with and connect to another. Many I/O device adapters interface with the microcomputer by plugging into the expansion slots on the system board. These specialized circuit boards are often called adapter cards.

Add New Hardware Wizard Windows 9x/2000 applet designed to guide the installation process for non-PnP hardware. When installing Plug-and-Play devices, the Add New Hardware wizard should not be used. Instead, the Windows PnP function should be allowed to detect the new hardware. The new hardware must be installed in the computer before running the wizard.

Add/Remove Programs Wizard Windows 9x/2000 applet designed to guide the installation or removal of application programs. This utility can also be used to install or remove optional Windows components, such as Accessibility options, or to create a Windows Start disk.

Add/Remove Windows components Windows 9x/2000 utilities that can be used to change optional hardware (Add New Hardware) and software (Add/Remove Programs) components installed in the system. These utilities are located in the Windows Control Panel.

Address The unique location number of a particular memory storage area, such as a byte of primary memory, a sector of disk memory, or a peripheral device itself.

address bus A unidirectional pathway that carries address data generated by the microprocessor to the various memory and I/O elements of the computer. The size of this bus determines the amount of memory a particular computer can use and, therefore, is a direct indication of the computer's power.

A: drive The commonly understood term designating the first floppy disk drive in Microsoft's DOS microcomputer operating system.

ASCII (American Standard Code for Information Interchange) The 7-bit binary data code used in all personal computers, many minicomputers, and also in communications services. Of the 128 possible character combinations, the first 32 are used for printing and transmission control. Because of the 8-bit byte used in digital computers, the extra bit can be used either for parity checking, or for the extended ASCII set of characters, which includes foreign language characters and line-draw graphic symbols.

ASIC (Application Specific Integrated Circuit) A very large-scale integration device designed to replace a large block of standardized PC circuitry. Once the parameters of the device have achieved a pseudo standard usage status, IC manufacturers tend to combine all of the circuitry for that function into a large IC custom designed to carry out that function. Examples include integrated VGA controllers, integrated MI/O controllers, and integrated peripheral controllers.

asynchronous transmission A method of serial data transmission in which the receiving system is not synchronized by a common clock signal with the transmitting system.

AT Attachment (ATA) Also known also as IDE. A system-level interface specification that integrates the disk drive controller on the drive itself. The original ATA specification supports one or two hard drives through a 16-bit interface using Programmed IO (PIO) modes. The ATA-2 specification, also known as EIDE or Fast ATA, supports faster PIO and DMA transfer modes, as well as logical block addressing (LBA) strategies.

AT bus Also referred to as the ISA (Industry Standard Architecture) bus. The 16-bit data bus introduced in the AT class personal computer that became the industry standard for 16-bit system.

ATTRIB The DOS command used to change attributes assigned to files (i.e., system, read-only, and hidden status).

Attribute Properties of DOS files. Special file attributes include system, read-only, and hidden status. These conditions can be altered using the external DOS command ATTRIB.

ATX form factor A newer system board form factor that improves on the previous Baby AT form factor standard by reorienting the system board by 90 degrees. This makes for a more efficient design, placing the IDE connectors nearer to the system unit's drive bays and positioning the microprocessor in line with the output of the power supply's cooling fan.

AUTOEXEC.BAT An optional DOS program that the system's command interpreter uses to carry out customized startup commands at bootup.

B

backup An operation normally performed to create backup copies of important information in case the drive crashes, or the disk becomes corrupt. Backup utilities allow the user to quickly create extended copies of files, groups of files, or an entire disk drive.

Backup Wizard An automated software routine in Windows 2000 designed to lead users through a step-by-step process of configuring and scheduling a backup job.

Backup Domain Controller (BDC) Backup Domain Controllers are servers within the network that are used to hold read-only backup copies of the directory database. A network may contain one or more BCDs. These servers are used to authenticate user logons.

BAT file (batch file) A filename extension used to identify a batch file in Microsoft DOS versions. A batch file, created by a word processor, contains a list of DOS commands that are executed as if each were typed and entered one at a time.

baud rate The number of electrical state changes per second on a data communication line. At lower speeds, the baud rate and the bits-per-second rate are identical. At higher speeds, the baud rate is some fraction of the bits-per-second rate.

binary This means base two. In digital computers, all data is processed only after being converted into binary numbers consisting of the two digits 0 and 1.

BIOS (Basic Input Output System) See *ROM BIOS*.

bit (binary digit) One digit of a binary number (0 or 1). Groups of bits are manipulated together by a computer into various storage units called nibbles, bytes, words, or characters.

bit map A term used in computer graphics to describe a memory area containing a video image. One bit in the map represents one pixel on a monochrome screen, while in color or gray scale monitors, several bits in the map may represent one pixel.

Blue Screen A kernel-mode stop that indicates a failure of a core operating system function. Also known as the Blue Screen of Death because the system stops processing and produces a blue screen, rather than risking catastrophic memory and file corruption.

boot To start the computer. It refers to the word bootstrap, since just as the straps help in pulling boots on, the bootable disk helps the computer to get its first instructions.

bootable disk A disk that starts the operating system. Normally refers to a floppy disk containing the computer operating system.

Boot Menu The Startup options screen menu displayed during the Windows 2000 bootup process. This menu is produced when the F8 function key is depressed while the "Starting Windows" message is on the screen.This menu is generated by the Boot.ini Boot Loader Menu file. Options in this menu include the variety of operating systems installed on the computer. If no selection is made from this menu after a given time, the default value is selected.

boot partition The disk partition that possesses the system files required to load the operating system into memory. Also referred to as the *active partition*.

boot sector The first sector on a disk (or partition). On bootable disks or partitions, this sector holds the code (called the boot record) that causes the system to move the operating system files into memory and begin executing them.

Boot.ini Boot.ini is a special, hidden boot-loader menu file used by the NTLDR during the bootup process to generate the Boot Loader Menu that is displayed on the screen. If no selection is made from this menu after a given time, the default value is selected.

Bootsect.dos A Windows NT file used to load operating systems other than Windows NT. If an entry from the Boot Loader Menu indicates an operating system other than Windows NT is to be loaded, the NTLDR program loads the BOOTSECT.DOS file from the root directory of the system partition and passes control to it. From this point, the BOOTSECT file is responsible for loading the desired operating system.

bootstrap loader A term used to refer to two different software routines involved in starting a system and loading the operating system. The primary bootstrap loader is a firmware routine that locates the boot record required to load the operating system into memory. The OS loader takes over from the primary bootstrap loader and moves the operating system into memory (known as booting the OS).

bps (bits per second) A term used to measure the speed of data being transferred in a communications system.

bus A parallel collection of conductors that carry data or control signals from one unit to another.

bus master Any class of intelligent devices having the ability to take control of the system buses of a computer.

byte The most common word size used by digital computers. It is an 8-bit pattern consisting of both a high- and a low-order nibble. Computers of any size are frequently described in terms of how many bytes of data can be manipulated in one operation or cycle.

C

cache An area of high-speed memory reserved for improving system performance. Blocks of often-used data are copied into the cache area to permit faster access times. A disk cache memory is an area of RAM used to hold data from a disk drive that the system may logically want to access, thereby speeding up access.

cache controller A highly automated memory controller assigned the specific task of managing a sophisticated cache memory system.

carriage The part in a printer or typewriter that handles the feeding of the paper forms.

cartridge A removable data storage module, containing disks, magnetic tape, or memory chips, and inserted into the slots of disk drives, printers, or computers.

C: drive This is the commonly understood term designating the system or first hard disk drive in the DOS and OS/2 microcomputer operating systems.

Centronics interface The 36-pin standard for interfacing parallel printers, and other devices, to a computer. The plug, socket, and signals are defined.

certificate A security service used to authenticate the origin of a public key to a user possessing a matching private key.

character printer Any printer that prints one character at a time, such as a dot-matrix printer of a daisy wheel.

chip The common name for an integrated circuit (IC). Preceded by the development of the transistor, ICs can contain from several dozen to several million electronic components (resistors, diodes, transistors, etc.) on a square of silicon approximately 1/16th to 1/2 inch wide and around 1/30th of an inch in thickness. The IC can be packaged in many different styles depending on the specific use for which it is intended.

chipset A group of specifically engineered ICs designed to perform a function interactively.

Chkdsk DOS disk maintenance utility used to recover lost allocation units from a hard drive. These lost units occur when an application terminates unexpectedly. Over a period of time, lost units can pile up and occupy large amounts of disk space.

clients Workstations that operate in conjunction with a master server computer that controls the operation of the network.

client/server network Workstations or clients operate in conjunction with a master server computer to control the network.

clock An internal timing device. Several varieties of clocks are used in computer systems. Among them are the CPU clock, the real-time clock, a timesharing clock, and a communications clock.

cluster Clusters are organizational units used with disk drives to represent one or more sectors of data. These structures constitute the smallest unit of storage space on the disk.

CMOS (Complementary Metal Oxide Semiconductor) A MOS technology used to fabricate IC devices. It is traditionally slower than other IC technologies, but it possesses higher circuit-packing density than other technologies. CMOS ICs are very sensitive to voltage spikes and static discharges and must be protected from static shock.

CMOS setup A software setup program used to provide the system with information about what options are installed. The configuration information is stored in special CMOS registers that are read each time the system boots up. Battery backup prevents the information from being lost when power to the system is removed.

cold boot Booting a computer by turning the power on.

color monitor Also known as an RGB monitor, this display type allows the user to run text and/or color-based applications such as graphics drawing and CAD programs. There are two basic RGB-type monitors: digital (TTL) and analog. Analog RGB monitors allow the use of many more colors than digital RGB monitors.

color printer Any printer capable of printing in color, using thermal-transfer, dot-matrix, electro-photographic, electrostatic, ink-jet, or laser printing techniques.

COM1 The label used in Microsoft DOS versions assigned to serial port #1.

COMMAND.COM COMMAND.COM is the DOS command interpreter that is loaded at the end of the bootup process. It accepts commands issued through the keyboard, or other input devices, and carries them out according to the command's definition. These definitions can be altered by adding switches to the command.

command prompt A screen symbol that indicates to the user that the system is ready for a command. It usually consists of the current drive letter, followed by a colon and a blinking cursor.

compatible A reference to any piece of computer equipment that works like, or looks like a more widely known standard or model. A PC-compatible, or clone, is a PC that, although physically differing somewhat from the IBM-PC, runs software developed for the IBM-PC and accepts its hardware options.

Computer Management Console A Windows 2000 Management Console, that enables the user to track and configure all of the system's hardware and software. It can also be used to configure network options and view system events.

computer name A name created for a computer by a network administrator. This name identifies the computer to other members of the network. It is generally recommended that computer names be 15 characters or less. However, if the computer has the TCP/IP networking protocol installed, its name can range up to 63 characters long but should only contain the numbers 0-9, the letters A-Z and a-z, and hyphens. It is possible to use other characters, but doing so may prevent other users from finding your computer on the network.

CONFIG.SYS A Microsoft operating system configuration file that, upon startup, is used to customize the system's hardware environment. The required peripheral device drivers (with SYS file extensions) are initialized.

configuration A customized computer system or communications network composed of a particular number and type of interrelated components. The configuration varies from system to system, requiring that some means be established to inform the system software about what options are currently installed.

Configuration Manager A component of the Windows Plug-and-Play system that coordinates the configuration process for all devices in the system.

continuous forms Paper sheets that are joined together along perforated edges and used in printers that move them through the printing area with motorized sprockets. Sprockets may fit into holes on both sides of the paper.

control bus A pathway between the microprocessor and the various memory, programmable, and I/O elements of the system. Control bus signals are not necessarily related to each other and can be unidirectional or bi-directional.

control character A special type of character that causes some event to occur on a printer, display, or communications path such as a line feed, a carriage return, or an escape.

Control Panel The Windows component used to customize the operation and appearance of Windows functions. In Windows 9x and Windows NT/2000 the Control Panel can be accessed through the Start button/Settings route, or under the My Computer icon on the desktop.

control protocols Protocols that configure the communication interface to the networking protocols employed by the system. Each network transport supported under Windows 2000 has a corresponding control protocol.

CPU (Central Processing Unit) The part of the computer that does the thinking. It consists of the control unit and the Arithmetic Logic Unit. In personal computers, the CPU is contained on a single chip, while on a minicomputer it occupies one or several printed circuit boards. On mainframes, a CPU is contained on many printed circuit boards. Its power comes from the fact that it can execute many millions of instructions in a fraction of a second.

CRC (Cyclic Redundancy Check) The error-checking technique that ensures communications channel integrity by utilizing division to determine a remainder. If the transmitter and receiver do not agree on what the remainder should be, an error is detected.

CRT (Cathode Ray Tube) The vacuum tube that is used as the display screen for both TVs and computer terminals. Sometimes the term is used to mean the terminal itself.

CTS (Clear To Send) An RS-232 handshaking signal sent from the receiver to the transmitter indicating readiness to accept data.

cursor The movable display screen symbol that indicates to the user where the action is taking place. The text cursor is usually a blinking underline or rectangle, while the graphics cursor can change into any predetermined shape at different parts of the screen.

cursor keys Special keyboard keys that can be used to move the cursor around the display screen. Enhanced keyboards have two clusters of cursor keys so that the numeric keypad portion of the keyboard can be used separately.

cylinder The combination of all tracks, normally on multiple-platter disk drives, that reside at the same track number location on each surface.

D

data Information assembled in small units of raw facts and figures.

data bus A bi-directional pathway linking the microprocessor to memory and I/O devices, the size of which usually corresponds to the word size of the computer.

data compression Most compression algorithms use complex mathematical formulas to remove redundant bits, such as successive 0s or 1s, from the data stream. When the modified word is played back through the decompression circuitry the formula reinserts the missing bits to return the data stream to its original state.

Data Encryption Standard (DES) A U.S. standard method of encrypting data into a secret code. Down-level clients employ the DES standard to encrypt user passwords.

DCE (Data Communications Equipment) A communications device, usually a modem, that establishes, maintains, and terminates a data transfer session. It also serves as a data converter when interfacing different transmission media.

default The normal action taken, or setting used, by the hardware or software when the user does not otherwise specify.

defragmentation Disk maintenance operation performed to optimize the use of disk space by moving scattered file fragments into continuous chains to speed up data retrieval from the drive.

demodulator A device that removes the data from the carrier frequency and converts it to its originally unmodulated form.

DEVICE= CONFIG.SYS commands used to load specified device drivers into memory at bootup (i.e., the statement DEVICE=C:\MOUSE\MOUSE.SYS loads a mouse driver from the MOUSE directory. Used as "DEVICEHIGH=", the command will load the specified device driver into the Upper Memory Blocks, thereby freeing up conventional memory space.

device driver Special memory-resident program that tells the operating system how to communicate with a particular type of I/O device, such as a printer or a mouse.

Device Manager A Windows 95/98/2000 Control Panel utility that provides a graphical representation of devices in the system. It can be used to view resource allocations and set hardware configurations properties for these devices. This utility can also be used to identify and resolve resource conflicts between system devices. The Device Manager is located under the Control Panel's System icon.

diagnostics Software programs specifically designed to test the operational capability of the computer memory, disk drives, and other peripherals. The routines are available on disks or on ROM chips. Errors may be indicated by beep codes or visual reports. They can normally point to a board-level problem, but not down to a particular component, unless the routine has been written for a particular board being used in the system under test. A complete system failure would require a ROM-based diagnostic program as opposed to a disk-based routine.

dial-up networking Methods of accessing the public telephone system to carry on data networking operations. These methods include modem, ISDN, and DSL accesses.

DIMMs Dual in-line memory modules. DIMMs are 168-pin plug-in memory modules similar to SIMMs.

direct I/O An I/O addressing method that uses no address allocations but requires extra control lines.

directory A hierarchical collection of disk files organized under one heading and simulating the concept of a drawer in a file cabinet. In the structure of a disk drive system, the directory is the organizational table that holds information about all files stored under its location. This information includes the file's name, size, time, date of when it was last changed, and its beginning location on the disk.

disk arrays A collection of multiple disk drives operating under the direction of a single controller for the purpose of providing fault tolerance and performance. Data files are written on the disks in ways that improve the performance and reliability of the disk drive subsystem, as well as to provide detection and corrective actions for damaged files. Redundant Array of Inexpensive Disks (RAID) 5 in Windows 2000 is an example.

disk drive The peripheral storage device that reads and writes data to spinning magnetic or optical disks. The drive can either hold removable disks or contain permanent platters.

diskette A term usually applied to a removable, floppy-disk memory storage device.

DMA (Direct Memory Access) The ability of certain intelligent, high-speed I/O devices to perform data transfers themselves, with the help of a special IC device called a DMA controller.

docking station Special platforms designed to work with portable computers to provide additional I/O capacity. The docking station is designed so that the portable computer inserted into it can have access to the docking station's expansion slots, additional storage devices, and other peripheral devices, such as full-size keyboards and monitors. No standards exist for docking stations, so they must be purchased for specific types of portable computers.

domain Collectively, a domain is a group of members that share a common directory database and are organized in levels. Every domain is identified by a unique name and is administered as a single unit having common rules and procedures.

domain name A unique name that identifies a host computer site on the Internet.

Domain Name Service (DNS) A database organizational structure whereby higher-level Internet servers keep track of assigned domain names and their corresponding IP addresses for systems on levels under them. The IP addresses of all the computers attached to the Internet are tracked with this listing system. DNS evolved as a method of organizing the members of the Internet into a hierarchical management structure that consists of various levels of computer groups called domains. Each computer on the Internet is assigned a domain name, which corresponds to an additional domain level.

DOS (Disk Operating System) Can be a generic term, but in most cases it refers to the Microsoft family of computer operating systems (PC-DOS for IBM equipment or MS-DOS for compatibles).

dot-matrix printer A type of printer that forms its images out of one or more columns of dot hammers. Higher resolutions require a greater number of dot hammers to be used.

dot pitch A measurement of the resolution of a dot-matrix. The width of an individual dot in millimeters describes a display's resolution, with the smaller number representing the higher resolution. The number of dots per linear inch describes a printer's resolution, with the higher number representing the higher resolution.

DRAM (Dynamic Random Access Memory) A type of RAM that will lose its data, regardless of power considerations, unless it is refreshed at least once every 2 milliseconds.

drive: (1) An electromechanical device that moves disks, discs, or tapes at high speeds so that data can be recorded on the media, or read back from it. (2) In the organizational structure of a DOS system, a drive can be thought of as the equivalent of a file drawer that holds folders and documents. (3) In electronic terms, it is a signal output of a device used to activate the input of another device.

DSR (Data Set Ready) An RS-232 handshaking signal sent from the modem to its own computer indicating its ability to accept data.

DTR (Data Terminal Ready) An RS-232 handshaking signal that is sent to a modem by its own computer to indicate a readiness to accept data.

dual booting A condition that can be established on a hard disk drive that holds two or more operating systems. A pre-boot option is created that enables the system to be booted from one of the designated operating systems (i.e., Windows 98 or Windows 2000 Professional).

Dynamic Host Configuration Protocol (DHCP) Software protocol that dynamically assigns IP addresses to a server's clients. This software is available in both Windows 9x and Windows NT/2000 and must be *located* on both the server and the client computers (installed on servers and activated on clients). This enables ISPs to provide dynamic IP address assignments for their customers.

Dynamic Link Library (DLL) files Windows library files that contain small pieces of executable code that can be shared between Windows programs. These files are used to minimize redundant programming common to certain types of Windows applications.

E

edge connector The often double-sided row of etched lines on the edge of an adapter card that plugs into one of the computer's expansion slots.

EEPROM (Electrically Erasable Programmable Read Only Memory) A type of nonvolatile semiconductor memory device that allows erasure and reprogramming from within a computer using special circuitry. These devices allow specific memory cells to be manipulated, rather than requiring a complete reprogramming procedure as in the case of EPROM's.

EIA (Electronics Industries Association) An organization, founded in 1924, made up of electronic parts and systems manufacturers. It sets electrical and electronic interface standards such as the RS-232C.

EISA (Extended Industry Standard Architecture) A PC bus standard that extends the AT bus architecture to 32 bits and allows older PC and AT boards to plug into its slot. It was announced in 1988 as an alternative to the IBM Micro Channel.

electron gun The device by which the fine beam of electrons is created that sweeps across the phosphor screen in a CRT.

Electrostatic Discharge (ESD) As it applies to computer systems, a rapid discharge of static electricity from a human to the computer, due to a difference of electrical potential between the two. Such discharges usually involve thousands of volts of energy and can damage the IC circuits used to construct computer and communications equipment.

Emergency Repair Disk A disk created to repair the Windows NT/2000 system when its boot disk fails. The Emergency Repair Disk (ERD) provides another option if Safe Mode and the Recovery Console do not provide a successful solution to a system crash. If you have already created an ERD, you can start the system with the Windows NT/2000 Setup CD, or the Setup floppy disks, and then use the ERD to restore core system files.

EMI (ElectroMagnetic Interference) A system-disrupting electronic radiation created by some other electronic device. The FCC sets allowable limits for EMI in Part 5 of its Rules and Regulations. Part A systems are designed for office and plant environments, and Part B systems are designed for home use.

EMM (Expanded Memory Manager) Any software driver that permits and manages the use of expanded memory in 80386 and higher machines.

EMS (Expanded Memory Specification) A method of using memory above one megabyte on computers using DOS. Co-developed by Lotus, Intel, and Microsoft, each upgrade has allowed for more memory to be used. EMS is dictated by the specific application using it. In 286 machines, EMS is installed on an adapter card and managed by an EMS driver. See *EMM*.

Enhanced Cylinder Head Sector (ECHS) format BIOS translation mode used to configure large hard drives (over 504 MB) for operation. This mode is an extended CHS mode and is identical to Large and LBA modes. However, reconfiguring drives to other configration settings risks the prospects of losing data.

Enhanced IDE (EIDE) An improved version of the Integrated Drive Electronics interface standard. The new standard supports data transfer rates up to four times that of the original IDE standard. It also makes provisions for supporting storage devices of up to 8.4 GB in size, as opposed to the old standard's limit of 528 MB. The new standard is sometimes referred to as Fast ATA or Fast IDE.

enterprise networks Enterprise networks are those networks designed to facilitate business-to-business, or business-to-customer operations. Because monetary transactions and customers' personal information travels across the network in these environments, enterprise networks feature facilities for additional highly protective security functions.

EPROM (Erasable Programmable Read Only Memory) A type of nonvolatile semiconductor memory device that can be programmed more than once. Selected cells are charged using a comparatively high voltage. EPROMs can be erased by exposure to a source of strong ultraviolet light, at which point they must be completely reprogrammed.

ergonomics The study of people-to-machine relationships. A device is considered to be ergonomic when it blends smoothly with a person's body actions.

error checking The act of testing the data transfer in a computer system or network for accuracy.

ESC key (Escape key) This keyboard key is used to cancel an application operation or to exit some routine.

Ethernet A popular network topology that uses Carrier Sense Multiple Access with Collision Detection (CSMA/CD) for collision detection and avoidance. Ethernet can be physically implemented as either a bus, or a star network organization.

Expanded Memory (EMS) A memory management strategy for handling memory beyond the 1 MB of conventional memory. Using this strategy, the additional memory is accessed in 16K pages through a window established in the upper memory area.

expansion slot The receptacle mounted on the system board into which adapter cards are plugged to achieve system expansion. The receptacle interfaces with the I/O channel and system bus, and so the number of slots available determines the expansion potential of the system.

extended memory The memory above one megabyte in Intel 286 and higher computers, and used for RAM disks, disk caching routines, and for locating the operating system files in recent versions of Microsoft DOS.

Extended Memory (XMS) A memory management strategy for handling memory beyond the 1 MB of conventional memory. Using this strategy, Windows and Windows-based programs directly access memory above the 1 MB marker. Extended memory requires that the HIMEM.SYS memory manager be loaded in the DOS CONFIG.SYS.

extended partition Secondary partitions that can be created after the drive's primary partition has been established. It is the only other partition allowed on a disk once the primary partition has been made using FDISK. However, an extended partition can be subdivided into up to 23 logical drives.

Extended System Configuration Data (ESCD) portion of CMOS memory that holds PnP configuration information.

F

FAT (File Allocation Table) The part of the DOS file system that keeps track of where specific data is stored on the disk.

FDISK command The disk utility program that permits the partitioning of the hard disk into several independent disks.

file Any program, record, table, or document that is stored under its own filename.

File Allocation Table (FAT) A special table located on a formatted DOS disk that tracks where each file is located on the disk.

File menu A drop-down menu attached to Windows graphical interfaces whose options enable users to Open, Move, Copy, and Delete selected folders, files, or applications.

file systems File management systems. The organizational structures that operating systems employ to organize and track files. Windows 2000 employs the NTFS5 file system to perform these functions. It is a hierarchical directory system that employs directories to organize files into a tree-like structure.

filenames Names assigned to files in a disk-based system. These systems store and handle related pieces of information in groups called files. The system recognizes and keeps track of the different files in the system through their names. Therefore, each file in the system is required to have a filename that is different from that of any other file in the directory.

Firewire Also known as IEEE-1394, Firewire is a very fast I/O bus standard designed to support the high bandwidth requirements of real time audio/visual equipment. The IEEE-1394 standard employs streaming data transfer techniques to support data transfer rates up to 400 Mbps. A single Firewire connection can be used to connect up 63 external devices.

firmware A term used to describe the situation in which programs (software) are stored in ROM ICs (hardware) on a permanent basis.

floppy disk Also called a diskette, a removable secondary storage medium for computers, composed of flexible magnetic material and contained in a square envelope or cartridge. A floppy disk can be recorded and erased hundreds of times.

flow control A method of controlling the flow of data between computers. The receiving system signals the sending PC when it can and cannot receive data. Flow control can be implemented through hardware or software protocols. Using the software method, the receiving PC sends special code characters to the sending system to stop or start data flow. Xon/Xoff is an example of a software flow control protocol.

folders Icons that represent directories. In Windows 9X/NT/2000, directories and subdirectories are referred to and depicted as folders.

Folder Options Options that enable the user to change the appearance of their desktops and folder content, and to specify how their folders will open. Users can select whether they want a single window to open, as opposed to cascading windows, and they can designate whether folders will open with a single-click or double-click. This option can also be used to turn on the Active Desktop, change the application used to open certain types of files, or make files available when they're not on-line with the network. Changes made in Folder Options apply to the appearance of the contents of Windows Explorer (including My Computer, My Network Places, My Documents, and Control Panel) windows.

font One set of alphanumeric characters possessing matching design characteristics such as typeface, orientation, spacing, pitch, point size, style, and stroke weight.

forests A group of one or more Active Directory domain trees that trust each other. Unlike directory trees, forests do not share a contiguous namespace. This permits multiple namespaces to be supported within a single forest. In the forest, all domains share a common schema, configuration, and global catalog.

form feed The moving of the next paper form into the proper printing position, accomplished either by pressing the form feed (FF) button on the printer or by sending the printer the ASCII form feed character.

FORMAT command An MS-DOS utility that prepares a disk for use by the system. Track and sector information is placed on the disk while bad areas are marked so that no data will be recorded on them.

formatting The act of preparing a hard or floppy disk for use with an operating system. This operation places operating system-specific data tracking tables on the media and tests its storage locations (sectors or blocks) to make certain they are reliable for holding data.

FQDN Fully Qualified Domain Name. A name that consists of the host name and the domain name, including the top-level domain name (i.e., www.mic-inc.com where www is the host name, mic-inc is the second-level domain name, and .com is the top-level domain name).

fragmentation A condition that exists on hard disk drives after files have been deleted, or moved, and areas of free disk space are scattered around the disk. These areas of disk space cause slower performance because the drive's read/write heads have to be moved more often to find the pieces of a single file.

frame (1) A memory widow that applications and the operating system exchange data through, such as the EMS frame in Upper Memory that Expanded Memory managers use to move data between conventional memory and additional memory beyond the 1 MB mark. (2) The construction of a complete package of data with all overhead (headers) for transferring it to another location (i.e., an Ethernet frame). (3) One screen of computer graphics data, or the amount of memory required to store it.

FRU (Field-Replaceable Unit) The components of the system that can be conveniently replaced in the field.

FTP (File Transfer Protocol) An application layer protocol that copies files from one FTP host site to another.

full-duplex A method of data transmission that allows data flow in both directions simultaneously.

function keys A special set of keyboard keys used to give the computer special commands. They are frequently used in combination with other keys, and can have different uses depending on the software application being run.

G

GDI.EXE A Windows core component that is responsible for managing the operating system's/environment's graphical user interface.

General Protection Fault (GPF) A Windows memory usage error that typically occurs when a program attempts to access memory currently in use by another program.

GHz (gigahertz) One billion hertz or cycles per second.

graphics The creation and management of pictures using a computer.

ground (1) Any point from which electrical measurements are referenced. (2) *Earth* ground is considered to be an electrical reference point of absolute zero, and is used as the electrical return path for modern power transmission systems. This ground, often incorporated by electronic devices to guard against fatal shock, is called *chassis* or *protective* ground. (3) An actual conductor in an electronic circuit being used as a return path, alternately called a *signal* ground.

group policies Administrators use these tools to institute large numbers of detailed settings for users throughout an enterprise, without establishing each setting manually.

Group Policy Editor Utility employed to establish policies in Windows 2000. Administrators use this editor to establish which applications different users have access to, as well as to control applications on the user's desktop.

groups The administrative gathering of users that can be administered uniformly. In establishing groups, the administrator can assign permissions or restrictions to the entire body. The value of using groups lies in the time saved by being able to apply common rights to several users instead of applying them one by one.

GUI (Graphical User Interface) A form of operating environment that uses a graphical display to represent procedures and programs that can be executed by the computer.

H

HAL.DLL HAL.DLL is the Hardware Abstraction Layer driver that holds the information specific to the CPU that the system is being used with.

half-duplex communication Communications that occur in both directions, but can only occur in one direction at a time. Most older networking strategies were based on half-duplex operations.

handshaking A system of signal exchanges conducted between the computer system and a peripheral device during the data transfer process. The purpose of these signals is to produce as orderly a flow of data as possible.

hard disk A metal disk for external storage purposes, coated with ferromagnetic coating and available in both fixed and removable format.

hardware Any aspect of the computer operation that can be physically touched. This includes IC chips, circuit boards, cables, connectors, and peripherals.

Hardware Abstraction Layer (HAL) The Windows NT HAL is a library of hardware drivers that operate between the actual hardware and the rest of the system. These software routines act to make every architecture look the same to the operating system. The HAL occupies the logical space directly between the system's hardware and the rest of the operating system's Executive Services. In Windows NT 4.0, the HAL enables the operating system to work with different types of microprocessors.

Hardware Compatibility List (HCL) The list of Microsoft-certified compatible hardware devices associated with Windows 2000 Professional and Windows 2000 Server products.

HIMEM.SYS The DOS memory manager that enables Expanded and Extended Memory strategies for memory operations above the 1 MB conventional memory range.

hives The five files that hold the contents of the Windows NT Registry. Hives represent the major divisions of all the Registry's keys, subkeys, subtrees, and values. The hives of the Windows NT Registry are the SAM hive, the Security hive, the Software hive, the System hive, and the Default hive. These files are stored in the \Winnt\System32\Config directory along with a backup copy and log file for each hive.

host Any device that communicates over the network using TCP/IP. The term refers to a device that has an assigned (dedicated) IP address.

I

IC (Integrated Circuit) The technical name for a chip. See *chip*.

icons Graphical symbols that are used to represent commands. These symbols are used to start and manipulate a program without the user having to know where that program is, or how it is configured.

IDE (Integrated Drive Electronics) A method of disk drive manufacturing that locates all the required controller circuitry on the drive itself, rather than on a separate adapter card. Also known as the AT Attachment interface.

impact printer Any printer that produces a character image by hammering onto a combination of embossed character, ribbon, and paper.

Infrared Data Association (IrDA) A data transmission standard for using infrared light. IrDA ports provide wireless data transfers between devices. These ports support data transfer rates roughly equivalent to those of traditional parallel ports. The only down side to using IrDA ports for data communications is that the two devices must be within one or two meters of each other and have a clear line of sight between them.

INI files Windows initialization text files that hold configuration settings that are used to initialize the system for Windows operation. Originally these files formed the basis of the Windows 3.x operating environments. They were mostly replaced in Windows 9x and NT/2000 by the Registry structure. However, some parts of the INI files still exist in these products.

initialization The process of supplying startup information to an intelligent device or peripheral (i.e., the system board's DMA controller, or a modem), or to a software application, or applet.

ink-jet printer A high-resolution printer that produces its image by spraying a specially treated ink onto the paper.

input device Any computer input-generating peripheral device such as keyboard, mouse, light pen, scanner, or digitizer.

instruction word A class of binary coded data word that tells the computer what operation to perform and where to find any data needed to perform the operation.

intelligent controller Usually an IC, or series of ICs, with built-in microprocessor capabilities dedicated to the controlling of some peripheral unit or process. Single-chip controllers are sometimes referred to as *smart chips*.

interface The joining of dissimilar devices so that they function in a compatible and complementary manner.

interlaced The method of rewriting the monitor screen repeatedly, by alternately scanning every other line and then scanning the previously unscanned lines.

Internet This most famous wide area network is actually a network of networks working together. The main communication path is a series of networks established by the U.S. government that has expanded around the world and offers access to computers in every part of the globe.

Internet Printing Protocol (IPP) A protocol included with Windows 2000 that enables users to sort between different printers based on their attributes. This standards-based Internet protocol provides Windows users with the capability of printing across the Internet. With IPP, the user can print to a URL, view the print queue status using an Internet browser, and install print drivers across the Internet.

Internet Protocol (IP) Address A 32-bit network address consisting of four dotted-decimal numbers separated by periods that uniquely identifies a device on the network. Each IP address consists of two parts—the network address and the host address. The network address identifies the entire network, while the host address identifies an intelligent member within the network (router, a server, or a workstation).

interrupt A signal sent to the microprocessor from the interrupt controller, or generated by a software instruction, which is capable of interrupting the microprocessor during program execution. An interrupt is usually generated when an input or output operation is required.

interrupt controller A special programmable IC responsible for coordinating and prioritizing interrupt requests from I/O devices, and sending the microprocessor the starting addresses of the interrupt service routines so that the microprocessor can service the interrupting device and then continue executing the active program.

intranet An intranet is a network built on the TCP/IP protocol that belongs to a single organization. It is in essence a private Internet. Like the Internet, intranets are designed to share information and are accessible only to the organization's members, with authorization.

I/O (Input/Output) A type of data transfer occurring between a microprocessor and a peripheral device. Whenever any data transfer occurs, output from one device becomes an input to another.

I/O port The external window or connector on a computer, used to create an interface with a peripheral device. The I/O port may appear as either parallel data connections or serial data connections.

IO.SYS A special hidden, read-only bootup file that the bootstrap loader finds and moves into RAM to manage the bootup process. After the bootup has been completed, this file manages the basic input/output routines of the system. This includes communication between the system and I/O devices such as hard disks, printers, floppy disk drives, etc.

IP (Internet Protocol) The Network layer protocol where logical addresses are assigned. IP is one of the protocols that make up the TCP/IP stack.

IPCONFIG A TCP/IP networking utility that can be used to determine the IP address of a local machine.

IPX/SPX Internetwork Packet Exchange/Sequential Packet Exchange protocol. A proprietary transport protocol developed by Novell for the NetWare operating system. The IPX portion of the protocol is a connectionless, Network layer protocol, which is responsible for routing. The SPX portion of the protocol is a connection-oriented, Transport layer protocol that manages error checking. These protocols are primarily found on local area networks that include NetWare servers.

IRQ (Interrupt Request) Hardware interrupt request lines in a PC-compatible system. System hardware devices use these lines to request service from the microprocessor as required. The microprocessor responds to the IRQ by stopping what it is doing, storing its environment, jumping to a service routine, servicing the device, and then returning to its original task.

ISA (Industry Standard Architecture) A term that refers to the bus structures used in the IBM PC series of personal computers. The PC and XT use an 8-bit bus, while the AT uses a 16-bit bus.

ISDN (Integrated Services Digital Network) A digital communications standard that can carry digital data over special telephone lines, at speeds much higher than those possible with regular analog phone lines.

ISPs (Internet Service Providers) Companies that provide the technical gateway to the Internet. An ISP connects all of the users and individual networks together.

J

joystick A computer input device that offers quick, multi-directional movement of the cursor for CAD systems and video games.

jumper Normally, a 2- or 4-pin BERG connector, located on the system board or an adapter card, which permits the attachment of a wired, hardware switch or the placement of a shorting bar to implement a particular hardware function or setting.

K

kernel The Windows 3.x and 95 core files that are responsible for managing Windows resources and running applications.

Kernel Mode The Kernel Mode is the operating mode in which the program has unlimited access to all memory, including those of system hardware, the user mode applications, and other processes (such as I/O operations). The Kernel Mode consists of three major blocks, the Win32k Executive Service module, the Hardware Abstraction Layer, and the Microkernel.

keyboard The most familiar computer input device, incorporating a standard typewriter layout with the addition of other specialized control and function keys.

L

LAN (Local Area Network) A collection of local computers and devices that can share information. A LAN is normally thought of as encompassing a campus setting, room, or collection of buildings.

laser printer Any printer that utilizes the electro-photographic method of image transfer. Light dots are transferred to a photosensitive rotating drum, which picks up electrostatically charged toner before transferring it to the paper.

LCD (Liquid Crystal Display) The type of output display created by placing liquid crystal material between two sheets of glass. A set of electrodes is attached to each sheet of glass. Horizontal (row) electrodes are attached to one glass plate, while vertical (column) electrodes are fitted to the other plate. These electrodes are transparent and let light pass through. A pixel is created in the liquid crystal material at each spot where a row and a column electrode intersect. When the pixel is energized, the liquid crystal material bends and prevents light from passing through the display.

LED (Light Emitting Diode) A particular type of diode that emits light when conducting. It is used in computers and disk drives as active circuit indicator.

legacy devices Adapter cards and devices that do not include plug-and-play capabilities. These are typically older ISA expansion cards that are still being used for some reason.

letter quality Refers to a print quality as good or better than that provided by an electric typewriter.

Logical Block Addressing (LBA) A hard disk drive organizational strategy that permits the operating system to access larger drive sizes than older BIOS/DOS FAT-management schemes could support.

logon The process of identifying oneself to the network. Normally accomplished by entering a valid user name and password that the system recognizes.

loopback A modem test procedure that allows a transmitted signal to be returned to its source for comparison with the original data.

lost allocation units Also referred to as lost clusters. File segments that do not currently belong to any file in the file allocation table. The DOS command CHKDSK/F can be used to locate and free these segments for future use.

LPT1 The label used in Microsoft DOS versions assigned to parallel port #1, usually reserved for printer operation.

M

magnetic disk The most popular form of secondary data storage for computers. Shaped like a platter and coated with an electromagnetic material, magnetic disks provide direct access to large amounts of stored data, and can be erased and rerecorded many times.

magnetic tape Traditionally, one of the most popular forms of secondary data storage backup for computers. However, Windows 2000 offers a number of other backup capabilities that may render tape an undesirable backup media in the future. Since access to data is sequential in nature, magnetic tape is primarily used to restore a system that has suffered a catastrophic loss of data from its hard disk drive.

mapped drives A technique employed to enable a local system to assign a logical drive letter to the remote disk drive, or folder. This is referred to as *mapping the drive letter* to the resource. This will enable applications running on the local computer to use the resource across the network.

Master Boot Record (MBR) Also referred to as the Master Partition Boot Sector. This file is located at the first sector of the disk. It contains a Master Partition Table that describes how the hard disk is organized. This table includes information about the disk's size, as well as the number and locations of all partitions on the disk. The MBR also contains the Master Boot Code that loads the operating system from the disk's active partition.

Master File Table (MFT) The core component of the NTFS system, this table replaces the FAT in an MS-DOS compatible system and contains information about each file being stored on the disk.

MEM.EXE The DOS command that can be used to examine the total and used memory of the system.

memory Computer components that store information for future use. In a PC, memory can be divided into two categories: primary and secondary (i.e., semiconductor RAM and ROM and other devices). Primary memory can be divided into ROM, RAM, and cache groups. Likewise, secondary memory contains many types of storage devices—floppy drives, hard disk drives, CD-ROM drives, DVD drives, tape drives , etc.)

memory management Methodology used in handling a computer's memory resources, including bank switching, memory protection, and virtual memory.

memory map A layout of the memory and/or I/O device addressing scheme used by a particular computer system.

memory-mapped I/O An I/O addressing method where I/O devices are granted a portion of the available address allocations, thus requiring no additional control lines to implement.

menu A screen display of available program options or commands that can be selected through keyboard or mouse action.

MHz (megahertz) One million hertz, or cycles per second.

microcomputer The same thing as a personal computer, or a computer using an microprocessor as its CPU.

Microsoft Management Console (MMC) A collection of manageability features that accompany Windows 2000. These features exist as "Snap-in" applets that can be added to the operating system through the MMC.

mirroring A RAID fault tolerance method in which an exact copy of all data is written to two separate disks at the same time.

MMX (Multimedia Extensions) technology An advanced Pentium microprocessor that includes specialized circuitry designed to manage multimedia operations. Its additional multimedia instructions speed up high-volume input/output needed for graphics, motion video, animation, and sound.

modem (modulator-demodulator) Also called a DCE device, it is used to interface a computer or terminal to the telephone system for the purpose of conducting data communications between computers often located at great distances from each other.

monitor (1) A name for a CRT computer display. (2) Any hardware device, or software program, such as the Windows 95 System Resource Monitor, that checks, reports about, or automatically oversees a running program or system.

MOS (Metal Oxide Semiconductor) A category of logic and memory chip design that derives its name from the use of metal, oxide, and semiconductor layers. Among the various families of MOS devices are PMOS (P-Type semiconductor material), NMOS (N-Type semiconductor material), and CMOS (Complimentary/Symmetry MOS material). The first letter of each family denotes the type of construction used to fabricate the chip's circuits. MOS families do not require a highly regulated +5V dc power supply like TTL devices.

mouse A popular computer I/O device used to point or draw on the video monitor by rolling it along a desktop as the cursor moves on the screen in a corresponding manner.

MSD (Microsoft Diagnostics) Microsoft diagnostic program that can be used from the command prompt to examine different aspects of a system's hardware and software configuration. The MSD utility has been included with MS-DOS 6.x, Windows 3.x, and Windows 9x.

MSDOS.SYS One of the hidden, read-only system files required to boot the system. It is loaded by the IO.SYS file during the bootup process. It handles program and file management functions for MS-DOS systems. In Windows 95, its function is changed to that of providing pathways to other Windows files and supporting selected startup options.

multimedia A term applied to a range of applications that bring together text, graphics, video, audio, and animation to provide interactivity between the computer and its human operator.

multitasking The ability of a computer system to run two or more programs simultaneously.

N

NAK (Negative Acknowledge) A data communications code used by a receiver to tell the transmitter that its last message was not properly received.

NetBEUI (NetBIOS Extended User Interface) The Microsoft networking protocol used with Windows-based systems.

NetBIOS An emulation of IBM's *NETwork Basic Input/Output System*. NetBIOS represents the basic interface between the operating system and the LAN hardware. This function is implemented through ROM ICs located on the network card.

NetWare The Novell client/server network operating system.

Network Connection Wizard Automated setup routine in Windows 2000 that can be invoked to guide the user through the process of creating a network connection.

Network Neighborhood The Windows 95 utility used to browse and connect multiple networks, and to access shared resources on a server without having to map a network drive.

nibble A 4-bit binary pattern, which can easily be converted into a single hexadecimal digit.

NLQ (Near-Letter Quality) A quality of printing nearly as good as that of an electric typewriter. The very best dot-matrix printers can produce NLQ.

NMI (Non-Maskable Interrupt) A type of interrupt that cannot be ignored by the microprocessor during program execution. Three things can cause a non-maskable interrupt to occur: (1) A numeric coprocessor installation error. (2) A RAM parity check error. (3) An I/O channel check error.

non-impact printer Any printer that does not form its characters by using a hammer device to impact the paper, ribbon, or embossed character.

nonvolatile memory Memory that is not lost after the power is turned off, such as ROM.

NT File System (NTFS) The proprietary Windows NT file system. The NTFS structure is designed to provide better data security and to operate more efficiently with larger hard drives than FAT systems do. Its structure employs 64-bit entries to keep track of storage on the disk (as opposed to the 16 and 32-bit entries used in FAT and FAT32 systems).

NTDETECT NTDETECT.COM is the Windows NT hardware detection file. This file is responsible for collecting information about the system's installed hardware devices and passing it to the NTLDR program. This information is later used to upgrade the Windows NT Registry files.

NTLDR NT Loader is the Windows NT bootstrap loader for Intel-based computers running Windows NT. It is the Windows NT equivalent of the DOS IO.SYS file and is responsible for loading the NT operating system into memory. Afterwards, NTLDR passes control of the system over to the Windows NT operating system.

NTOSKRNL NTOSKRNL.EXE is the Windows NT kernel file that contains the Windows NT core and loads its device drivers.

NTSC (National Television Standards Committee) This organization created the television standards in the United States, and is administered by the FCC.

NTUSER.DAT The Windows NT/200 file that contains the User portion of the Windows NT Registry. This file contains the user-specific settings that have been established for this user. When a user logs onto the system, the User file and System hive portions of the Registry are used to construct the user-specific environment in the system.

null modem cable A cable meeting the RS-232C specification, used to cross-connect two computers through their serial ports by transposing the transmit and receive lines. They must be physically located very close to one another, eliminating the need for a modem.

O

odd parity The form of parity checking in which the parity bit is used in order to make the total number of 1's contained in the character an odd number.

off-hook A condition existing on a telephone line that is now capable of initiating an outgoing call, but unable to receive an incoming call.

off-line Any computer system or peripheral device that is not ready to operate, not connected, not turned on, or not properly configured.

on-hook A condition that exists on any telephone line that is capable of receiving an incoming call.

on-line Any computer system or peripheral device that is not only powered up, but is also ready to operate.

operating system A special software program, first loaded into a computer at power up, and responsible for running it. The operating system also serves as the interface between the machine and other software applications.

optical mouse A mouse that emits an infrared light stream to detect motion as it is moved around a special x-y matrix pad.

output device Any peripheral device, such as a monitor, modem, or printer, that accepts computer output.

P

paging files Also known as the swap file. The hidden file located on the hard disk that makes up half of the Windows 2000 virtual memory system. This file holds the programs and data that the operating system's virtual memory manager moves out of RAM memory and stores on to the disk as virtual memory.

parallel interface The multi-line channel through which the simultaneous transfer of one or more bytes occurs.

parallel mode The mode of data transfer in which an entire word is transferred at once, from one location to another, by a set of parallel conductors.

parallel port The external connector on a computer that is used to create an interface between the computer and a parallel peripheral such as a printer.

parity bit Used for error checking during the sending and receiving of data within a system and from one system to another. The parity bit's value depends on how many 1 bits are contained in the byte it accompanies.

parity checking A method to check for data transmission errors by using a ninth bit to ensure that each character sent has an even (even parity) or odd (odd parity) number of logic 1's before transfer. The parity bit is checked for each byte sent.

parity error This error occurs when a data transfer cannot be verified for integrity. At least one data bit or the parity bit has been corrupted during the transfer process.

partition A logical section of a hard disk. Partitioning allows a single physical disk to be divided into multiple logical drives that can each hold a different operating system. Most disks contain a single partition that holds a single operating system.

partition boot sector The boot sector of that partition located in the first sector of the active partition. Here the MBR finds the code to begin loading the secondary bootstrap loader from the root directory of the boot drive.

partitioning Partitioning establishes the logical structure of the hard disk in a format that conforms to the operating system being used on the computer. It is a function of the operating system being used. In the case of Microsoft operating systems, the FDISK utility is used to establish and manipulate partitions.

partition table The table present at the start of every hard disk that describes the layout of the disk, including the number and location of all partitions on the disk.

passwords Unique code patterns associated with a user's logon account that are used to access the resources of a network.

path The location of the file on the disk in reference to the drive's root directory. The file's full path is specified by a logical drive letter and a listing of all directories between the root directory and the file.

PC bus Refers to the bus architectures used in the first IBM PCs, the original 8-bit bus, and the 16-bit bus extension used with the AT.

PCI (Peripheral Component Interconnect) bus A low-cost, high-performance 32-/64-bit local bus developed jointly by IBM, Intel, DEC, NCR, and Compaq.

PCMCIA (Personal Computer Memory Card International Association) card A credit-card-sized adapter card designed for use with portable computers. These cards slide into a PCMCIA slot and are used to implement modems, networks, and CD-ROM drives.

peer-to-peer network A network that does not have a centralized point of management and in which each computer is equal to all the others. In this scenario, all of the members can function as both clients and servers.

peripherals Also called I/O devices, these units include secondary memory devices such as hard disk drives, floppy disk drives, magnetic tape drives, modems, monitors, mice, joysticks, light pens, scanners, and even speakers.

permissions A feature that enables security levels to be assigned to files and folders on the disk. These settings provide parameters for activities that users can conduct with the designated file or folder.

Personal Digital Assistant (PDA) Handheld computing devices that typically include telephone, fax, and networking functions. A typical PDA can function as a cell phone, a fax, and a personal organizer. Most are pen-based devices that use a wand for input rather than a keyboard or mouse. PDAs are a member of the palmtop class of computers.

PIFs (Program Information Files) Windows 3.x information files used to identify resources required for DOS-based applications.

pin feed A method of moving continuous forms through the print area of a printer by using mounting pins on each side of a motorized platen to engage the holes on the right and left sides of the paper.

PING Network troubleshooting utility command that is used to verify connections to remote hosts. The PING command sends Internet Control Message Packets to a remote location and then waits for echoed response packets to be returned. The command will wait for up to one second for each packet sent and then display the number of transmitted and received packets. The command can be used to test both the name and IP address of the remote unit. A number of switches can be used to set parameters for the ping operation.

pixel Also called a PEL, or picture element, it is the smallest unit (one dot for monochrome) into which a display image can be divided.

Plug-and-Play (PnP) A specification that requires the BIOS, operating system, and adapter cards to be designed so that the system automatically configures new hardware devices to eliminate system resource conflicts.

pointing device Any input device used for the specific purpose of moving the screen cursor or drawing an image.

Point-to-Point Protocol (PPP) A connection protocol that controls the transmission of data over the wide-area network. PPP is the default protocol for the Microsoft Dial-Up adapter. In a dial-up situation, Internet software communicates with the service provider by embedding the TCP/IP information in a PPP shell for transmission through the modem in analog format. The communications equipment, at the ISP site, converts the signal back to the digital TCP/IP format. PPP has become the standard for remote access.

Point-to-Point Tunneling Protocol (PPTP) The de facto industry standard tunneling protocol first supported in Windows NT 4.0. PPTP is an extension of the Point-to-Point Protocol (PPP) and takes advantage of the authentication, compression, and encryption mechanisms of PPP. PPTP is installed with the Routing and Remote Access service. By default, PPTP is configured for five PPTP ports that can be enabled for inbound remote access and demand-dial routing connections through the Windows 2000 Routing and Remote Access wizard. PPTP and Microsoft Point-to-Point Encryption (MPPE) provide the primary security technology to implement Virtual Private Network services of encapsulation and encryption of private data.

polarizer An optical device that will either block or allow the passage of light through it depending on the polarity of an electrical charge applied to it.

policies Network administrative settings that govern the rights and privileges of different users in multi-user operations.

POLEDIT The system policy editor that is used to establish or modify system policies that govern user rights and privileges. The Policy Editor is another tool that can be used to access the information in the Registry. However, unlike the RegEdit utility, Poledit can only access subsets of keys. The Registry editor can access the entire Registry.

polling A system of initiating data transfer between a computer system and a peripheral in which the status of all the peripherals is examined periodically under software program control by having the microprocessor check the READY line. When it is activated by one of the peripherals, the processor will begin the data transfer using the corresponding I/O port.

POST (Power-On Self-Tests) A group of ROM BIOS-based diagnostic tests that are performed on the system each time it is powered up. These tests check the PC's standard hardware devices including the microprocessor, memory, interrupts, DMA, and video.

power supply The component in the system that converts the AC voltage from the wall outlet to the DC voltages required by the computer circuitry.

preventive maintenance Any regularly scheduled checking and testing of hardware and software with the goal of avoiding future failure or breakdown.

Primary Domain Controller (PDC) Primary Domain Controllers contain the Directory Databases for the network. These databases contain information about User Accounts, Group Accounts, and Computer Accounts. PDCs also are also referred to as Security Accounts Managers.

primary partitions Bootable partitions created from unallocated disk space. Under Windows 2000, up to four primary partitions can be created on a basic disk. The disk can also contain three primary partitions and an extended partition. The primary partition becomes the system's boot volume by being marked as "Active". The free space in the extended partition can be subdivided into up to 23 logical drives.

printer A peripheral device for the printing of computer text or graphics output.

printer font A prescribed character set properly formatted for use by the printer.

profiles Information about each user and group defined in the system that describes the resources and desktop configurations created for them. Settings in the profiles can be used to limit the actions users can perform, such as installing, removing, configuring, adjusting, or copying resources. When users log into the system, it checks their profile and adjusts the system according to their information. This information is stored in the \WINNT*login_name*\NTUSER.DAT file.

program Any group of instructions designed to command a computer system through the performance of a specific task. Also called *software*.

programmed I/O A system of initiating data transfer between a computer system and a peripheral in which the microprocessor alerts the specific device by using an address call. The I/O device can signal its readiness to accept the data transfer by using its Busy line. If Busy is active, the microprocessor can perform other tasks until the Busy line is deactivated, at which time the transfer can begin.

prompt A software-supplied message to the user, requiring some specific action or providing some important information. It can also be a very simple symbol, indicating that the program is successfully loaded and waiting for a command from the user.

protected mode An operational state that allows an 80286 or higher computer to address all of its memory, including that memory beyond the 1 MB MS-DOS limit.

protocol A set of rules that govern the transmitting and receiving of data communications.

Q

queue A special and temporary storage (RAM or registers) area for data in printing or internal program execution operations.

quotas Windows 2000 security settings that enable administrators to limit the amount of hard drive space users can have access to.

QWERTY keyboard A keyboard layout that was originally designed to prevent typists from jamming old-style mechanical typewriters, it is still the standard English language keyboard. The name spells out the first six leftmost letters in the first alphabetic row of keys.

R

RAID (Redundant Array of Inexpensive Disks) A set of specifications for configuring multiple hard drives to store data to increase storage capacity and improve performance. Some variations configure the drives in a manner to improve performance, while others concentrate on data security.

RAM (Random Access Memory) A type of semiconductor memory device that holds data on a temporary or volatile basis. Any address location in the RAM memory section can be accessed as fast as any other location.

RAM disk An area of memory that has been set aside and assigned a drive letter to simulate the organization of a hard disk drive in RAM memory. Also referred to as a virtual disk.

raster graphics A graphics representation method that uses a dot-matrix to compose the image.

raster scan The display of a video image, line by line, by an electron beam deflection system.

read only (1) A file parameter setting that prevents a file from being altered. (2) Refers to data that is permanently stored on the media or to such a medium itself.

read/write head Usually abbreviated "R/W head," the device by which a disk or tape drive senses and records digital data on the magnetic medium.

real mode A mode of operation in 80286 and higher machines in which the computer functions under the same command and addressing restrictions as an 8086 or 8088.

reboot To restart the computer or to reload the operating system.

refresh A required method of re-energizing a memory cell or display pixel in order for its data to continually be held.

RegEdit The editing utility used to directly edit the contents of the Registry (Regedit.exe and Regedit32.exe). This file is located in the \Winnt\System32 folder.

Registry A multi-part, hierarchical database established to hold system and user configuration information in Windows 9x, NT, and 2000.

Registry keys The Registries in Windows 9X, NT and 2000 are organized into Headkeys, Subkeys, and Values.

RESET A control bus signal, activated by either a soft or a hard switch, which sets the system microprocessor and all programmable system devices to their startup, or initialization, values. This allows the computer to begin operation following the application of the RESET input signal.

resolution A measurement of the sharpness of an image or character, either of a printer or a display monitor. For a monitor, resolution consists of the number of dots per scan line times the number of scans per picture. For a printer, resolution consists of the number of dots present per linear inch of print space.

ROM (Read Only Memory) A type of semiconductor memory device that holds data on a permanent or nonvolatile basis.

ROM BIOS A collection of special programs (native intelligence) permanently stored in one or two ROM ICs installed on the system board. These programs are available to the system as soon as it is powered up, providing for initialization of smart chips, POST tests, and data transfer control.

root directory The main directory of every logical disk. It follows the FAT tables and serves as the starting point for organizing information on the disk. The location of every directory, subdirectory, and file on the disk is recorded in this directory.

RS-232C The most widely used serial interface standard, it calls for a 25-pin D-type connector. Specific pins are designated for data transmission and receiving, as well as a number of handshaking and control lines. Logic voltage levels are also established for the data and the control signals on the pins of the connector.

RS-422 An enhancement to the original RS-232C interface standard and adopted by the EIA, it uses twisted-pair transmission lines and differential line voltage signals, resulting in higher immunity for the transmitted data.

RS-423 Another enhancement to the original RS-232C interface standard and adopted by the EIA, it uses coaxial cable to provide extended transmission distances and higher data transfer rates.

S

Safe Mode A special Windows 95, 98, 2000 startup mode that starts the system by loading minimum configuration drivers. This mode is used to allow the correction of system errors when the system will not boot up normally. Safe Mode is entered by pressing F5 or F8 when "Starting Windows 9x" message is displayed during bootup.

scan rate The total number of times per second that a video raster is horizontally scanned by the CRT's electron beam.

SCSI (Small Computer System Interface) bus A system-level interface standard used to connect different types of peripheral equipment to the system. The standard actually exists as a group of specifications (SCSI, SCSI-2, and SCSI-3) featuring several cabling connector schemes. Even within these three specifications there can exist major variations—Wide SCSI, Fast SCSI, and Fast/Wide SCSI. Apple was the first personal computer maker to select the SCSI interface as the bus standard for peripheral equipment that can provide high-speed data transfer control for up to seven devices, while occupying only one expansion slot. The standard is gaining more widespread support in the PC market, particularly in the area of portable PCs. See *system-level interface*.

sector One of many individual data-holding areas into which each track of a disk is divided during the format process.

serial interface A channel through which serial digital data transfer occurs. Although multiple lines may be used, only one of these will actually carry the data. The most popular serial interface standard is the EIA RS-232C.

serial mode The mode of data transfer in which the word bits are transferred one bit at a time along a single conductor.

serial mouse A type of mouse that plugs into a serial port rather than an adapter card.

serial port The external connector on a computer that is used to create an interface between the computer and a serial device such as a modem. A typical serial port uses a DB-25 or a DB-9 connector.

servers Powerful network computers (or devices) that contain the network operating system and manage network resources for other computers (clients). Some servers take on special management functions for the network. Some of these functions include print servers, web servers, file servers, database servers, etc.

setup disks Disks created to get a failed Windows NT/2000 system restarted. These disks are created by the Windows 2000 Backup utility and contain information about the system's current Windows configuration settings.

shadow RAM An area of RAM used for copying the system's BIOS routines from ROM. Making BIOS calls from the RAM area improves the operating speed of the system. Video ROM routines are often stored in shadow RAM also.

shared resource A system resource (device or directory) that has been identified as being available for use by multiple individuals throughout the network environment.

shares Resources, such as printers and folders, which have been made available for use by other network users.

SIMM (Single In-line Memory Module) A circuit board module containing eight (without parity) or nine (with parity) memory chips, and designed to plug into special sockets.

simplex communications Communications that occur in only one direction. An public address system is an example of simplex communications.

SLIP (Serial Line Internet Protocol) Older units running *UNIX* employ this Internet connection protocol for dial-up services. The protocol wraps the TCP/IP packet in a shell for transmission through the modem in analog format. The communications equipment, at the service provider's site, converts the signal back to the digital TCP/IP format.

SMARTDRV.EXE (SmartDrive) A DOS driver program that establishes a disk cache in an area of extended memory as a storage space for information read from the hard disk drive. When a program requests more data, the SMARTDRV program redirects the request to check in the cache memory area to see if the requested data is there.

software Any aspect of the computer operation that cannot be physically touched. This includes bits, bytes, words, and programs.

speaker The computer system's audio output device. Measuring 2-1/4 inches in diameter, and rated at 8 ohms, 1/2 watts, the speaker is usually used as a system prompt and as an error indicator. It is also capable of producing arcade sounds, speech, and music.

SRAM (Static Random Access Memory) A type of RAM that can store its data indefinitely as long as power to it is not interrupted.

start bit In asynchronous serial data transmission, this bit denotes the beginning of a character and is always a logic low pulse, or space.

static electricity This is often a serious problem in environments of low humidity. It is a stationary charge of electricity normally caused by friction, and potentially very damaging to sensitive electronic components.

stop bit The bit, sent after each character in an asynchronous data communications transmission, that signals the end of a character.

stop errors Errors that occur when Windows 2000 detects a condition that it cannot recover from. The system stops responding, and a screen of information with a blue, or black, background is displayed. Stop errors are also known as blue screen errors, or the "blue screen of death (BSOD)".

subnet mask The decimal number 255 is used to hide, or mask, the network portion of the IP address while still showing the host portions of the address. The default subnet mask for Class A IP addresses is 255.0.0.0. Class B is 255.255.0.0, and Class C is 255.255.255.0.

swap file A special file established on the hard drive to provide virtual memory capabilities for the operating system. Windows 3.x can work with temporary or permanent swap files. Windows 95 uses a dynamically assigned, variable-length swap file.

synchronous transmission A method of serial data transmission in which both the transmitter and the receiver are synchronized by a common clock signal.

SYSEDIT.EXE A special Windows text editor utility that can be used to alter ASCII text files such as CONFIG.SYS, AUTOEXEC.BAT, WIN.INI, and SYSTEM.INI files.

system board The large printed circuit board (mother board) into which peripheral adapter boards (daughter boards) may plug into, depending on the number of devices working with the system. The system board is populated with 100 or more IC chips, depending on how much onboard memory is installed. Besides RAM chips, the system board contains the microprocessor, BIOS ROM, several programmable controllers, system clock circuitry, switches, and various jumpers. Also, most system boards come with an empty socket into which the user may plug a compatible co-processor chip to give the computer some high-level number crunching capabilities.

system files Files that possess the system attribute. These are normally hidden files used to boot the operating system.

system-level interface An interface that allows the system to directly access the I/O device through an expansion slot without an intermediate interface circuit. The system is isolated from the peripheral device and only sees its logical configuration.

system partitions Normally the same as the boot partition. More precisely, the disk partition that contains the hardware-specific files (Ntldr, Osloader, Boot.ini, and Ntdetect) required to load and start Windows 2000.

system software A class of software dedicated to the control and operation of a computer system and its various peripherals.

system unit The main computer cabinet housing containing the primary components of the system. This includes the main logic board (system or mother board), disk drive(s), switching power supply, and the interconnecting wires and cables.

T

tape drive The unit that reads, writes, and holds the tape being used for backup purposes.

task switching The changing of one program or application to another either manually by the user, or under the direction of a multitasking operating system environment.

telephony In the computer world, this term refers to hardware and software devices that perform functions typically performed by telephone equipment. Microsoft offers the TAPI interface for both clients and servers. See *Telephony API.*

Telephony API (TAPI) Telephony Application Programming Interface. This software interface provides a universal set of drivers that enable modems and COM ports to control and arbitrate telephony operations for data, faxes, and voice. Through this interface, applications can cooperatively share the dial-up connection functions of the system.

TCP/IP (Transfer Control Protocol/Internet Protocol) A collection of protocols developed by the U. S. Department of Defense in the early days of the network that became the Internet. It is the standard transport protocol used by many operating systems and the Internet.

toner A form of powdered ink that accepts an electrical charge in laser printers and photocopying machines. It adheres to a rotating drum containing an image that has been given an opposite charge. The image is transferred to the paper during the printing process.

TRACERT A network troubleshooting utility that displays the route, and a hop count, taken to a given destination. The route taken to a particular address can be set manually using the ROUTE command. The TRACERT utility traces the route taken by ICMP packets sent across the net. Routers along the path return information to the inquiring system and the utility displays the host name, IP address, and round trip time for each hop in the path.

track A single disk or tape data storage channel, upon which the R/W head places the digital data in a series of flux reversals. On disks, the track is a concentric data circle, while on tapes it is a parallel data line.

track ball (1) A pointing device that allows the user to control the position of the cursor on the video display screen by rotating a sphere (track ball). (2) The sphere inside certain types of mice that the mouse rides on. As the mouse moves across a surface, the trackball rolls, creating X-Y movement data.

tractor feed A paper-feeding mechanism for printers that use continuous forms. The left and right edges of the forms contain holes through which the tractor pins pull the paper through the print area.

transmit Although this term usually means to send data between a transmitter and receiver over a specific communications line, it can also describe the transfer of data within the internal buses of a computer or between the computer and its peripheral devices.

Transport Control Protocol (TCP) TCP is a Transport layer protocol used to establish reliable connections between clients and servers.

trees In Active Directory, a collection of objects that share the same DNS name. All of the domains in a tree share a common security context and global catalog.

Troubleshooters A special type of Help utilities available in Windows 9x and 2000. These utilities enable the user to pinpoint problems and identify solutions to those problems by asking a series of questions and then providing detailed troubleshooting information based on the user's responses.

U

UART (Universal Asynchronous Receiver Transmitter) A serial interface IC used to provide for the parallel-to-serial and serial-to-parallel conversions required for asynchronous serial data transmission. It also handles the parallel interface to the computer's bus, as well as the control functions associated with the transmission.

Ultra DMA A burst mode DMA data transfer protocol, used with Ultra ATA IDE devices, to support data transfer rates of 33.3 MBps. While the official name of the protocol is Ultra DMA/33, it is also referred to as UDMA, UDMA/33, and DMA mode 33.

Ultra SCSI A series of advanced SCSI specifications that include: (1) Ultra SCSI, which employs an 8-bit bus and supports data rates of 20 MBps; (2) SCSI-3 (also referred to as Ultra Wide SCSI) that widens the bus to 16-bits and supports data rates of 40 MBps; (3) Ultra2 SCSI that uses an 8-bit bus and supports data rates of 40 MBps; and (4) Wide Ultra2 SCSI that supports data rates of 80 MBps across a 16-bit bus.

Uninterruptible Power Supply (UPS) A special power supply unit that includes a battery to maintain power to key equipment in the event of a power failure. A typical UPS is designed to keep a computer operational after a power failure long enough for the user to save their current work and properly shut down the system. Many UPSs include software that provides automatic backup and shut down procedures when the UPS senses a power problem.

Universal Naming Convention (UNC) A standardized method of specifying a path to a network computer or a device (i.e., \\computername\sharename).

Universal Serial Bus (USB) A specification for a high-speed, serial communication bus that can be used to link various peripheral devices to the system. The standard permits up to 127 USB-compliant devices to be connected to the system in a daisy-chained, or tiered-star configuration.

Upgrading The process of replacing an older piece of hardware or software with a newer version of that hardware or software. Upgrading also serves as an interim solution for bugs discovered in software.

Upper Memory Area (UMA) The area in the DOS memory map between 640 kB and 1 MB. This memory area was referred to as the Reserved Memory Area in older PC and PC-XT systems. It typically contains the EMS Page Frame, as well as any ROM extensions and video display circuitry.

Upper Memory Blocks (UMBs) Special 16 kB blocks of memory established in the upper memory area between the 640 kB and 1 MB marks.

URL (Universal Resource Locator) A unique address on the World Wide Web used to access a web site.

USART (Universal Synchronous Asynchronous Receiver Transmitter) A serial interface IC used to provide for the parallel-to-serial and serial-to-parallel conversions required for both asynchronous and synchronous serial data transmission. It also handles the parallel interface to the computer's bus, as well as the control functions associated with the transmission.

user profiles User profiles are records that permit each user that logs on to a computer to have a unique set of properties associated with them, such as particular desktop or Start menu configurations. In Windows 2000, user profiles are stored in C:\Documents and Settings by default. User profiles are local, meaning that they reside only on that computer. Therefore, users may have different profiles created and stored for them on each computer they logon to.

user name The public portion of the user login name that identifies permissions and rights to network resources.

utility program A term used to describe a program designed to help the user in the operation of the computer.

V

VESA (Video Electronics Standards Association) bus A 64-bit local bus standard developed to provide a local bus connection to a video adapter. Its operation has been defined for use by other adapter types, such as drive controllers, network interfaces, and other hardware.

VGA (Video Graphics Array) Another video standard, developed by IBM, providing medium and high text and graphics resolution. It was originally designed for IBM's high-end PS/2 line, but other vendors have created matching boards for PC and AT machines also, making it the preferred standard at this time. Requiring an analog monitor, it originally provided 16 colors at 640x480 resolution. Third-party vendors have boosted that capability to 256 colors, while adding an even greater 800x600 resolution, calling it Super VGA.

video adapter Sometimes referred to as a display adapter, graphics adapter, or graphics card, it is a plug-in peripheral unit for computers, fitting in one of the system board option slots, and providing the interface between the computer and the display. The adapter usually must match the type of display (digital or analog) it is used with.

View menu A Windows 2000 dialog box drop-down menu that enables the user to toggle screen displays between Large and Small Icons, Details, and Thumbnail views. The dialog boxes can be resized to accommodate as many Thumbnail images as desired.

virtual disk A method of using RAM as if it were a disk.

virtual memory A memory technique that allows several programs to run simultaneously, even though the system does not have enough actual memory installed to do this. The extra memory is simulated using disk space.

Virtual Memory Manager (VMM) The section of the Windows 9x, NT, and 2000 structure that assigns unique memory spaces to every active 32-bit and 16-bit DOS/Windows 3.x application. The VMM works with the environmental subsystems of the User mode to establish special environments for the 16-bit applications to run in.

Virtual Private Network (VPN) Virtual Private Networks use message encryption and other security techniques to ensure that only authorized users can intercept and access the message as it passes through public transmission media. In particular, VPNs provide secure Internet communications by establishing encrypted data tunnels across the WAN that cannot be penetrated by others.

virus A destructive program designed to replicate itself on any machine that it comes into contact with. Viruses are spread from machine to machine by attaching themselves to (infecting) other files.

VLSI (Very Large-Scale Integration) IC devices containing a very large number of electronic components (from 100,000 to 1,000,000 approximately).

volatile memory Memory (RAM) that loses its contents as soon as power is discontinued.

volumes Portions of disks signified by single drive designators. In the Microsoft environment, a volume corresponds to a partition.

VOM (Volt Ohm Milliammeter) A basic piece of electronic troubleshooting equipment that provides for circuit measurements of voltage, current, and resistance in logarithmic analog readout form.

W

warm boot Booting a computer that has already been powered up. This can be accomplished by pressing the Reset switch on the front of most computers, or by selecting one of the Restart options from the Windows Exit options dialog box.

web site A location on the World Wide Web. Web sites typically contain a home page that is displayed first when the site is accessed. They usually contain other pages and programs that can be accessed through the home page.

wild cards Characters, such as * or ?, used to represent letters or words. Such characters are typically used to perform operations with multiple files.

Windows A graphical user interface from Microsoft. It uses a graphical display to represent procedures and programs that can be executed by the computer. Multiple programs can run at the same time.

Windows Explorer The Windows 95, Windows 98, and Windows NT/2000 utility that graphically displays the system as drives, folders, and files in a hierarchical tree structure. This enables the user to manipulate all of the system's software using a mouse.

WINNT32 WINNT32.EXE or WINNT.EXE are the programs that can be run to initiate the installation of Windows 2000. The WINNT32.EXE program is designed to run under a 32-bit operating system and will not run from the command line. The WINNT.EXE program is designed to run under a 16-bit operating system and will not run from within a 32-bit operating system such as Windows NT.

WINS A Microsoft-specific naming service that can be used to assign IP addresses to computer domain names within a LAN environment. The LAN must include a Windows NT name server running the WINS server software that maintains the IP address/domain name database for the LAN. Each client in the LAN must contain the WINS client software and be WINS enabled.

wizards Special Windows routines designed to lead users through installation or setup operations using a menu style of selecting options. The wizards carry out these tasks in the proper sequence, requesting information from the user at key points in the process.

word The amount of data that can be held in a computer's registers during a process. It is considered to be the computer's basic storage unit.

workgroups A network control scenario in which all of the nodes may act as servers for some processes and clients for others. In a workgroup environment, each machine maintains its own security and administration databases.

X

x-axis (1) In a two-dimensional matrix, the horizontal row/rows, such as on an oscilloscope screen. (2) The dimension of width in a graphics representation.

Xmodem A very early, and simple, asynchronous data communications protocol developed for personal computers, and capable of detecting some transfer errors, but not all.

Xon-Xoff An asynchronous data communications protocol that provides for synchronization between the receiver and transmitter, requiring the receiver to indicate its ability to accept data by sending either an Xon (transmit on-buffer ready) or Xoff (transmit off-buffer full) signal to the transmitter.

x-y matrix Any two-dimensional form or image, where *x* represents width and *y* represents height.

Y

y-axis (1) In a two-dimensional matrix, the vertical column/columns, such as on an oscilloscope screen. (2) The dimension of height in a graphics representation.

Ymodem An improvement of the Xmodem protocol that increases the data block size from 128 bytes to 1024 bytes. An off-shoot known as Ymodem Batch includes filenames in the transmission so that multiple files can be sent in a single transmission. Another variation, labeled Ymodem G, modified the normal Ymodem flow control method to speed up transmissions

Z

Zmodem This dial-up protocol can be used to transmit both text and binary files (such as .EXE files) across telephone lines (not the Internet though). It employs advanced error checking/correcting schemes and provides Autofile Restart crash recovery techniques.

INDEX

B

C

D

E

F

G

H

I

M

N

O

P

Q

R

S

T

U

V

W

X

Y

Z

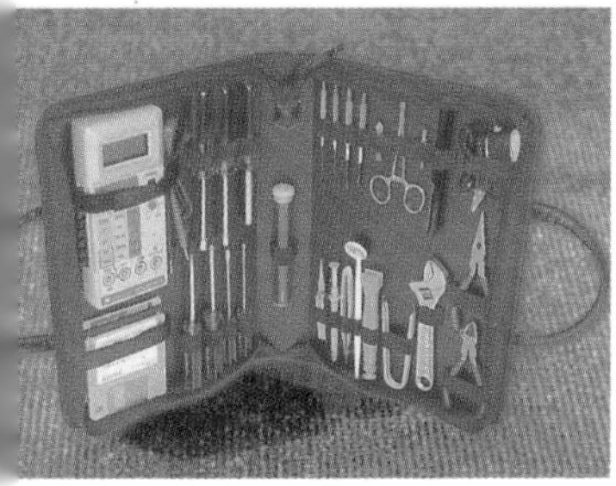

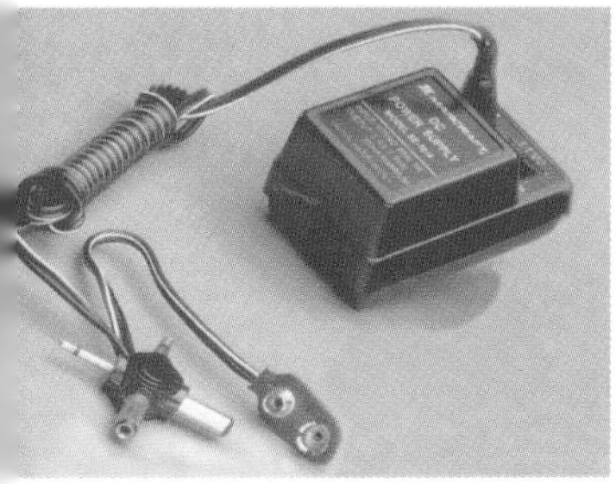

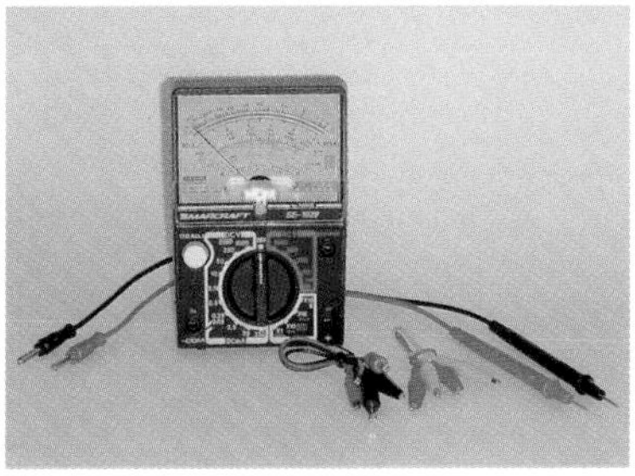

Linux+ Certification

The Linux+ certification measures vendor-neutral Linux knowledge and skills for an individual with at least 6 months practical experience. Linux+ Potential Job Roles: Entry Level Helpdesk, Technical Sales/Marketing, Entry Level Service Technician, Technical Writers, Resellers, Application Developers, Application Customer Service Reps.

Linux+ Exam Objectives Outline: User administration, Connecting to the network, Package Management, Security Concept, Shell Scripting, Networking, Apache web server application, Drivers (installation, updating, removing), Kernel (what it does, why to rebuild), Basic printing, Basic troubleshooting.

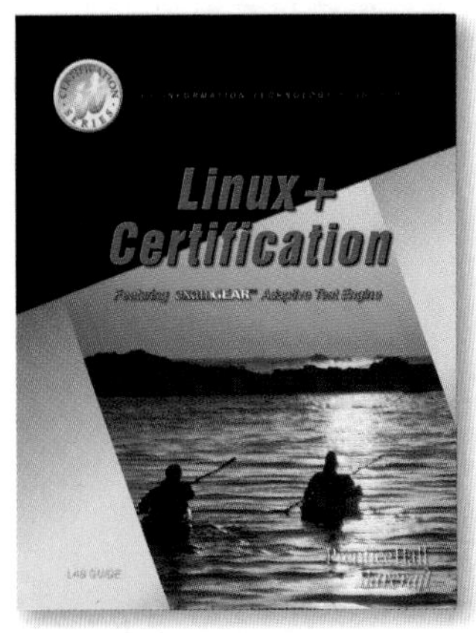

Server+ Certification

Server+ certification deals with advanced hardware issues such as RAID, SCSI, multiple CPUs, SANs and more. This is vendor-neutral with a broad range of support, including core support by 3Com, Adaptec, Compaq, Hewlett-Packard, IBM, Intel, EDS Innovations Canada, Innovative Productivity, and Marcraft.

This book focuses on complex activities and solving complex problems to ensure servers are functional and applications are available. It provides an in-depth understanding of the planning, installing, configuring, and maintaining servers, including knowledge of server-level hardware implementations, data storage subsystems, data recovery, and I/O subsystems.

Data Cabling Installer Certification

The Data Cabling Installer Certification provides the IT industry with an introductory, vendor-neutral certification for skilled personnel that install Category 5 copper data cabling.

The Marcraft *Enhanced Data Cabling Installer Certification Training Guide* provides students with the knowledge and skills required to pass the Data Cabling Installer Certification exam and become a certified cable installer. The DCIC is recognized nationwide and is the hiring criterion used by major communication companies. Therefore, becoming a certified data cable installer will enhance your job opportunities and career advancement potential.

Fiber Optic Cabling Certification

There is a growing demand for qualified cable installers who understand and can implement fiber optic technologies. These technologies cover terminology, techniques, tools and other products in the fiber optic industry. This text/lab book covers basics of fiber optic design discipline, installations, pulling and prepping cables, terminations, testing and safety considerations. Labs will cover ST-compatible and SC connector types, both multimedia and single mode cables and connectors. Learn about insertion loss, optical time domain reflectometry, and reflectance. Cover mechanical and fusion splices and troubleshooting cable systems. This Text/Lab covers the theory and hands-on skills needed to prepare you for fiber optic entry-level certification.

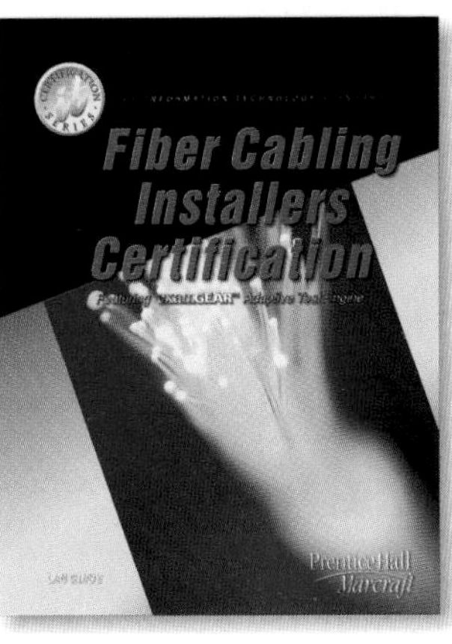

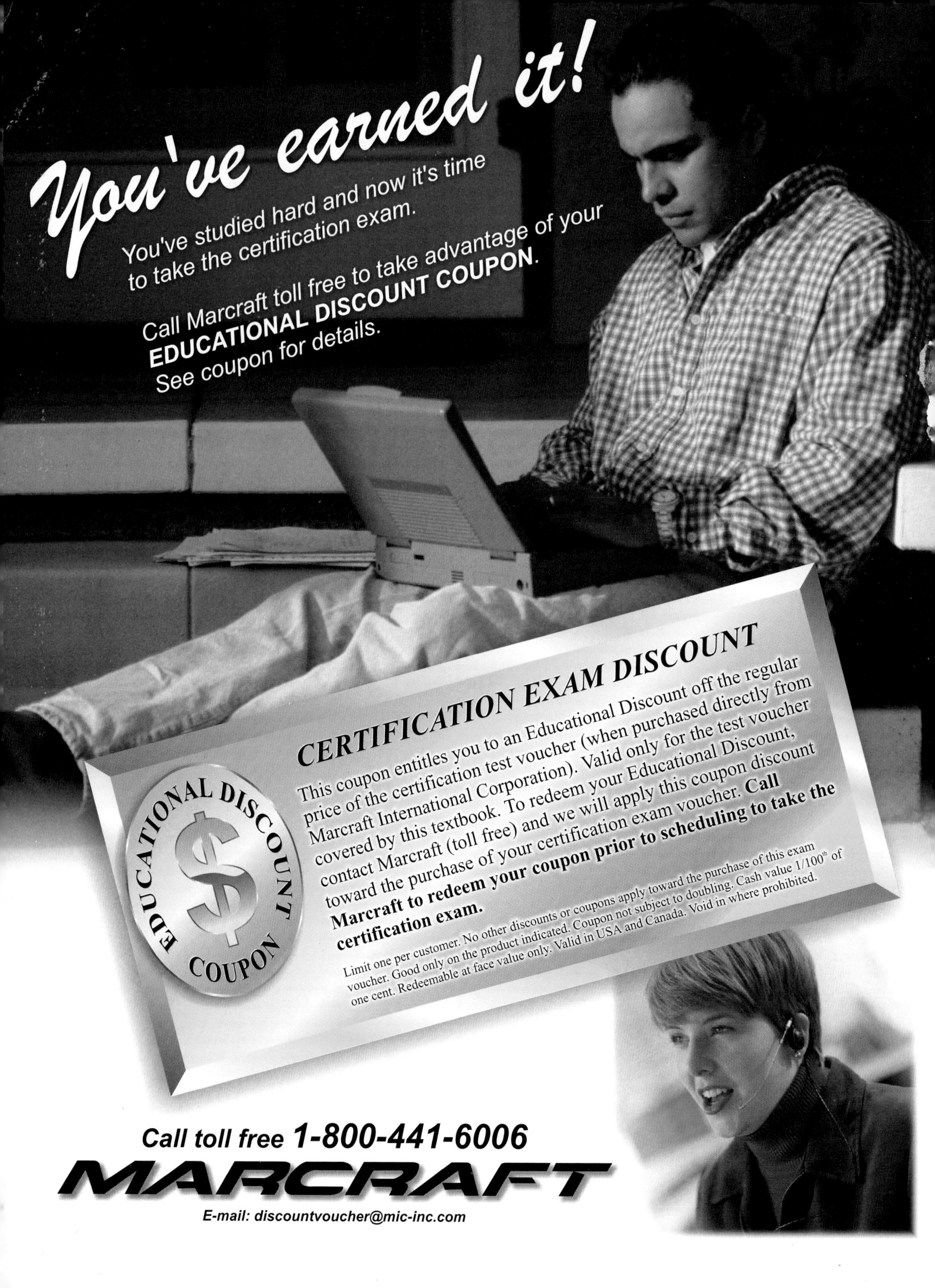

You've earned it!
You've studied hard and now it's time to take the certification exam.
Call Marcraft toll free to take advantage of your EDUCATIONAL DISCOUNT COUPON.
See coupon for details.
CERTIFICATION EXAM DISCOUNT
EDUCATIONAL DISCOUNT COUPON
This coupon entitles you to an Educational Discount off the regular price of the certification test voucher (when purchased directly from Marcraft International Corporation). Valid only for the test voucher covered by this textbook. To redeem your Educational Discount, contact Marcraft (toll free) and we will apply this coupon discount toward the purchase of your certification exam voucher. Call Marcraft to redeem your coupon prior to scheduling to take the certification exam.
Limit one per customer. No other discounts or coupons apply toward the purchase of this exam voucher. Good only on the product indicated. Coupon not subject to doubling. Cash value 1/100th of one cent. Redeemable at face value only. Valid in USA and Canada. Void in where prohibited.
Call toll free 1-800-441-6006
MARCRAFT
E-mail: discountvoucher@mic-inc.com